Just What You Need to Know and Do NOW!

CengageNOW is an online teaching and learning resource that provides you more control in less time and delivers better student outcomes—NOW!

What instructors are saying...

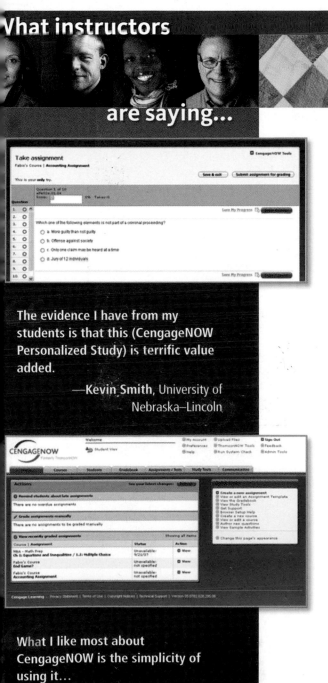

The evidence I have from my students is that this (CengageNOW Personalized Study) is terrific value added.

—**Kevin Smith**, University of Nebraska–Lincoln

What I like most about CengageNOW is the simplicity of using it...

—**Mina Yavari**, Hancock College

CENGAGENOW IS AN ONLINE TEACHING AND LEARNING RESOURCE.

CengageNOW offers all of your teaching and learning resources in one intuitive program organized around the essential activities you perform for class - lecturing, creating assignments, grading, quizzing, and tracking student progress and performance. CengageNOW's intuitive "tabbed" design allows you to navigate to all key functions with a single click and a unique homepage tell you just what needs to be done and when. CengageNOW, in most cases, provides students access to an integrated eBook, interactive tutorials, videos, animations, games, and other multimedia tools to help them get the most out of your course.

CENGAGENOW PROVIDES MORE CONTROL IN LESS TIME

CengageNOW's flexible assignment and grade book options provides you more control while saving you valuable time in planning and managing your course assignments. With CengageNOW, you can automatically grade all assignments, weigh grades, choose points or percentages and set the number of attempts and due dates per problem to best suit your overall course plan.

CENGAGENOW DELIVERS BETTER STUDENT OUTCOMES

CengageNOW Personalized Study; a diagnostic tool (featuring a chapter specific Pre-test, Study Plan, and Post-test) empowers students to master concepts, prepare for exams, and be more involved in class. It's easy to assign and if you want, results will automatically post to your grade book. Results to Personalize Study provide immediate and ongoing feedback regarding what students are mastering and why they're not - to both you and the student. In most cases, Personalized Study links to an integrated eBook so students can easily review topics.

academic.cengage.com/now

CengageNOW MAKES IT EASIER TO DO WHAT YOU ALREADY DO.

Designed by instructors for instructors, CengageNOW mirrors your natural workflow and provides time-saving, performance-enhancing tools for you and your students—all in one program!

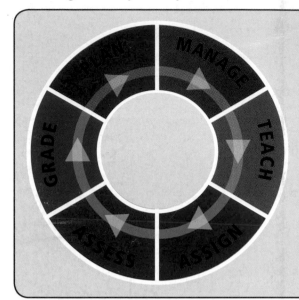

YOU CAN USE CENGAGENOW TO...

- ▶ **Plan** your curriculum;
- ▶ **Manage** your course and communicate with students;
- ▶ **Teach** with more freedom;
- ▶ **Assign** practice or homework to reinforce key concepts;
- ▶ **Assess** student performance outcomes;
- ▶ **Grade** with efficiency and control to get the results you want.

STUDENTS CAN USE CENGAGENOW TO...

- ▶ **Manage** their time;
- ▶ **Prepare** for class;
- ▶ **Practice & Reinforce** key concepts learned in class;
- ▶ **Study** for exams more effectively;
- ▶ **Get the Grade** they want.

The flexibility of CengageNOW allows you to use a single aspect of the program, or for maximum power and effectiveness, to use all of the teaching and learning resources to create and customize your own material to match your course objectives.

CENGAGENOW SEAMLESSLY INTEGRATES WITH POPULAR COURSE MANAGEMENT PROGRAMS

CengageNOW on Blackboard, WebCT, and eCollege provides students with seamless single sign-on access to CengageNOW through the school's course management system (CMS). After entering a simple access code just once at the beginning of the term, students get seamless access to both their CMS and CengageNOW textbook specific assignments and activities, with results flowing to your Blackboard, WebCT, or eCollege gradebook. Rich content, seamless integration with CengageNOW functionality, and only one gradebook to manage.

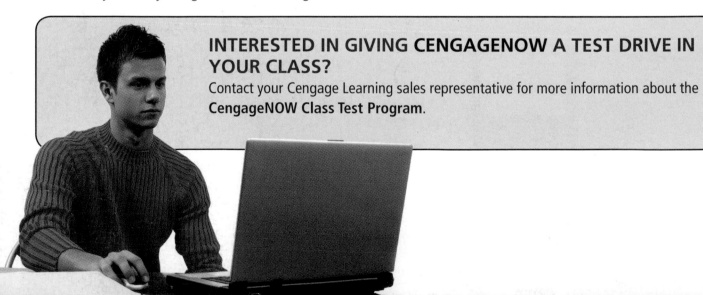

INTERESTED IN GIVING CENGAGENOW A TEST DRIVE IN YOUR CLASS?

Contact your Cengage Learning sales representative for more information about the **CengageNOW Class Test Program**.

academic.cengage.com/now

Childhood AND Adolescence

Voyages in Development

FIRST CANADIAN EDITION

Spencer A. Rathus
New York University

Christina M. Rinaldi
University of Alberta

NELSON / EDUCATION

NELSON / EDUCATION

Childhood and Adolescence: Voyages in Development, First Canadian Edition

by Spencer A. Rathus and Christina M. Rinaldi

Associate Vice President, Editorial Director:
Evelyn Veitch

Editor-in-Chief, Higher Education:
Anne Williams

Executive Editor:
Cara Yarzab

Executive Marketing Manager:
Lenore Taylor-Atkins

Managing Developmental Editor:
Alwynn Pinard

Permissions Coordinator:
Sandra Mark

Content Production Manager:
Christine Gilbert

Production Service:
GEX Publishing Services

Copy Editor:
Cathy Witlox

Proofreader:
GEX Publishing Services

Indexer:
GEX Publishing Services

Manufacturing Coordinator:
Loretta Lee

Design Director:
Ken Phipps

Managing Designer:
Katherine Strain

Interior Design:
GEX Publishing Services

Cover Design:
Peter Papayanakis

Cover Image:
Diverse group of children:
© iStockphoto.com/Daniela Andreea Spyropoulos

Kids in classroom: © 2007 Jupiterimages Corporation

Twin babies: © Beth Yarzab
Toddler: © Lenore Taylor-Atkins

Compositor:
GEX Publishing Services

Printer:
Courier

FIRST CANADIAN EDITION COPYRIGHT © 2009, by Nelson Education Ltd.

Adapted from *Childhood and Adolescence: Voyages in Development*, Second Edition, by Spencer A. Rathus, published by Thomson Wadsworth. Copyright ©2006 by Thomson Wadsworth.

Printed and bound in Canada.
1 2 3 4 09 08 07 06

For more information contact Nelson Education Ltd., 1120 Birchmount Road, Toronto, Ontario, M1K 5G4. Or you can visit our Internet site at http://www.nelson.com

Statistics Canada information is used with the permission of Statistics Canada. Users are forbidden to copy this material and/or redisseminate the data, in an original or modified form, for commercial purposes, without the expressed permissions of Statistics Canada. Information on the availability of the wide range of data from Statistics Canada can be obtained from Statistics Canada's Regional Offices, its World Wide Web site at <http://www.statcan.ca>, and its toll-free access number 1-800-263-1136.

Library and Archives Canada Cataloguing in Publication

Rathus, Spencer A
   Childhood and adolescence: voyages in development / Spencer A. Rathus, Christina M. Rinaldi. — 1st Canadian ed.

First published under the title: Voyages.
Includes bibliographical references and indexes.
ISBN 978-0-17-610435-1

1. Child development—Textbooks.
2. Adolescence—Textbooks.
I. Rinaldi, Christina M.
II. Rathus, Spencer A. Voyages.
III. Title.

HQ767.9.R347 2008   305.231
C2007-907300-X

Brief CONTENTS

—For Kate and Michele, the miracle workers
S.A.R.

—This book is dedicated to the memory of my father,
whose love and support was unparalleled.
C.M.R.

About the Authors

Spencer Rathus at various
stages of development

Numerous personal experiences enter into Spencer Rathus's textbooks. For example, he was the first member of his family to go to college. He found college textbooks to be cold and intimidating, and when his opportunity came to write college textbooks, he wanted them to be different—warm and encouraging, especially to students who were also the first generation in their families to be entering college.

Rathus's first professional experience was in teaching high school English. Part of the task of the high school teacher is to motivate students and make learning fun. Through this experience he learned the importance of humour and personal stories, which later became part of his textbook approach. Rathus wrote poetry and novels while he was an English teacher—and some of the poetry was published in poetry journals. The novels never saw the light of day (which is just as well, Rathus admits).

Rathus earned his Ph.D. in psychology and he entered clinical practice and teaching. He went on to publish more than twenty research articles in journals such as *Adolescence, Behavior Therapy, Journal of Clinical Psychology, Behaviour Research and Therapy, Journal of Behavior Therapy and Experimental Psychiatry*, and *Criminology*. His research interests lie in the areas of human growth and development, psychological disorders, methods of therapy, and psychological assessment.

Foremost among his research publications is the Rathus Assertiveness Schedule, which remains widely used in research and clinical practice. Rathus has since poured his energies into his textbooks, while teaching at Northeastern University, St. John's University, and currently at New York University. His introductory psychology textbook, *Psychology: Concepts and Connections*, is in its ninth edition.

Rathus is proud of his family. His wife, Lois, is a successful author and chairs her art department. His twenty-two-year-old daughter, Allyn, graduated from New York University's Tisch School of the Arts as a musical theatre major, and his twenty-year-old daughter, Jordan, is at the NYU Tisch School of the Arts as a film/video production major. The youngest daughter, Taylor, an eighth-grader, can dance the pants off of both of them. Rathus's eldest daughter, Jill, has become a psychologist and teaches at C. W. Post College of Long Island University.

Christina Rinaldi is an associate professor at the University of Alberta in Edmonton and a registered psychologist in both Alberta and Quebec. She researches and works with children, adolescents, and families. Since earning her Ph.D. in school psychology at McGill University, she has published research articles in journals such as *Child Development, Emotional and Behavioural Difficulties, Infant and Child Development Merrill-Palmer Quarterly, Social Development, and Youth* and *Adolescence*. Broadly defined, her research interests and activities centre on children's primary relationships (i.e., family and peer) and their links to the development and maintenance of social competence in early and middle childhood and adolescence. Through funding from the Social Sciences and Research Council of Canada (SSHRC) and the Alberta Centre for Child, Family and Community Research, she is currently investigating (1) how parent, child, and bidirectional mutuality influence children's emotional regulation strategies and social competence with peers; (2) the influence of context on (a) parent–child mutuality and (b) child–peer interactions; and (3) the association between emotion-regulation strategies and social competence with peers. Rinaldi is also the co-editor of the *Exceptionality Education Canada* journal, along with colleague and Canada Research chair in special education Judy Lupart. Finally, Rinaldi takes most pleasure in spending time with her family and friends. She especially enjoys playing and sharing quality time with her children.

Christina Rinaldi at various
stages of development

Prenatal Development 82

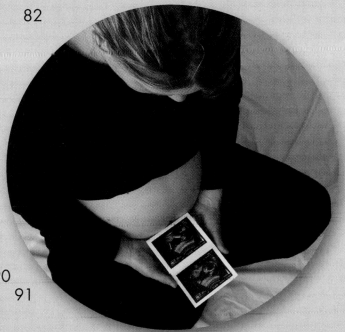

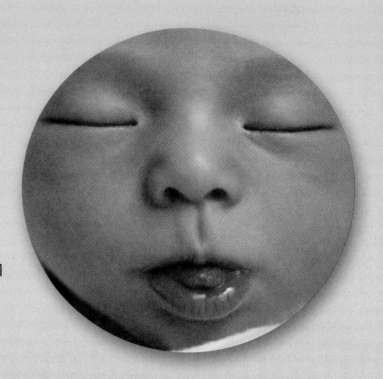

4 Birth and the Newborn Baby: In the New World 116

Part 3 | *Infancy*

Infancy: Physical Development 158

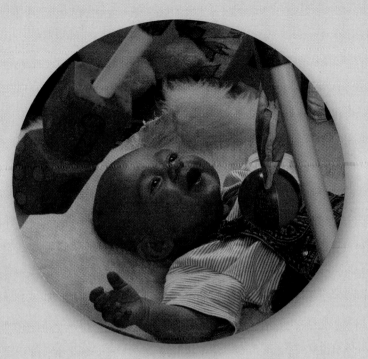

6 Infancy: Cognitive Development 198

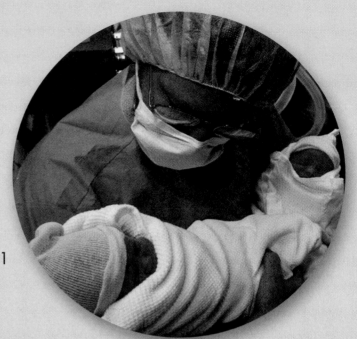

CONTENTS

Part 1 | *What Is Child Development?*

Part 2 | *Beginnings*

Heredity and Conception   50

7 Infancy: Social and Emotional Development   234

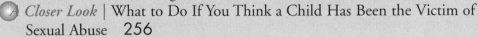

Part 4 | *Early Childhood*

Early Childhood: Physical Development   280

10 Early Childhood: Social and Emotional Development   356

Part 5 | *Middle Childhood*

Middle Childhood: Physical Development   402

12 Middle Childhood: Cognitive Development 432

13   Middle Childhood: Social and Emotional Development 478

Part 6 | *Adolescence*

Adolescence: Physical Development 520

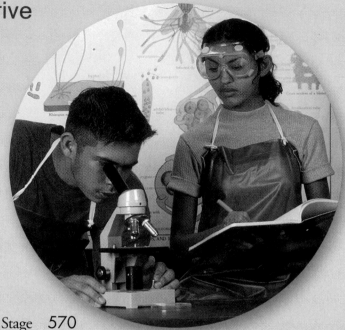

Adolescence: Cognitive Development 564

16 Adolescence: Social and Emotional Development 594

Preface

These are our children.
These are our selves.

I n children, we have the making of ourselves. In children, parents have the most impetuous, comical, ingratiating, delightful, and—at times—frustrating versions of themselves. Will the little babies we hold in our hands at birth someday be larger and stronger, more talented, and more insightful than us?

Portraying the Fascination of Children: Personal and Scientific

Our goal in writing this book has been to capture the wonder of child and adolescent development, while portraying the field of development as the rigorous science it is. Our approach is designed to help motivate students by showing them the joy of observing children and adolescents. How can one hope to convey a true sense of development if one is unaware of its marvels?

Childhood and Adolescence: Voyages in Development, First Canadian Edition, evolved from our scientific interests and research in human growth and development and also from our own personal and professional experiences. While our intention is to keep the tone of this text engaging and accessible, this book is rigorous in its reporting of research methods and science. On the other hand, the book is also "hands on"; it contains many applications, ranging from preventing protein-energy malnutrition (PEM) and keeping up with immunization schedules to helping children overcome enuresis and handling bullying in school.

What's New in This Edition

In many ways, the first Canadian edition of *Childhood and Adolescence: Voyages in Development* is a completely new book. It has:

- up-to-date Canadian material (research, references, statistics, examples, pictures);
- a multicultural approach to child development with sensitivity to the limitation of generalizing universal child development theories; and
- new photos, charts, tables, and figures pertinent to Canadians.

Let us have a look at the Canadian content additions, updates, and improvements.

Inclusion of Canadian Material

This is an exciting time to be studying child and adolescent development in Canada: every day new research and new insights help us to better understand the mysteries and marvels of many aspects of development. Included in this text are numerous references to Canadian statistics and research studies, such as the 2007 edition of the Canada's Food Guide and recent Canadian recommendations for the National Immunization Program of the Centers for Disease Control and Prevention.

In addition to containing new research data where applicable, every chapter has undergone major changes to reflect the Canadian context in child and adolescent development, topics, and pedagogy. Following is a sampling of what is new in each chapter:

Chapter 1—History, Theories, and Methods

- New Canadian historical information, such as background on the first Canadian female to attend university
- *Canadian Code of Ethics for Psychologists* conducting research with children and adolescents
- Highlights of the importance of understanding child and adolescent development in context of social and cultural variables
- Table on Canadian immigration statistics
- Canadian web links throughout

Chapter 2—Heredity and Conception

- New and current Canadian statistics related to prenatal development (e.g., number of twins in Canada)
- Information from the Canadian Down Syndrome Society
- New table with information on risks of giving birth to an infant with a chromosomal variation based on a report from Toronto's Mount Sinai Hospital
- Canadian gene therapy information
- New tables on Canadian birth rates and international adoption rates
- Web link to the J. P. Das Developmental Disabilities Centre at the University of Alberta
- Canadian Cystic Fibrosis Association information
- The Canadian connection to the Human Genome Project (HGP)
- Updated definitions of autism and autism spectrum disorders
- Information from the Canadian *Assisted Human Reproduction Act* (Bill C-13)

Chapter 3—Prenatal Development

- Public Health Agency of Canada guidelines to a healthy pregnancy, along with Canadian web links
- Health Canada's (2007) Guide to a Healthy Pregnancy
- New Fetal Alcohol Spectrum Disorder (FASD) feature box
- Vitamin recommendations for pregnant women in Canada
- Additional information on methamphetamine
- Research on the Canadian ice storm of 1998

Chapter 4—Birth and the Newborn Baby: In the New World

- Canadian statistics reflecting the increase of C-sections, as well as reference to several Canadian websites that provide up-to-date information on C-sections
- Guidelines and recommendations from the Society of Obstetricians and Gynaecologists of Canada
- New table on longitudinal preterm birth rates
- Information on maternal and infant mortality rates
- Postpartum depression information for Canadian women
- New Canadian SIDS rates, along with a public service announcement put forth by the Public Health Agency of Canada, the Canadian Foundation for the Study of Infant Deaths, and the Canadian Paediatric Society

Chapter 5—Infancy: Physical Development

- Current CDC growth charts (also in Chapters 8 and 11)
- Canadian Pediatric Society guidelines for infant nutrition
- A reference and web link to Canada's Public Health Agency report on "Attachment Across Cultures"
- New table offering practical tips for supporting physical development in infancy

Chapter 6—Infancy: Cognitive Development

- Updated information on the new Bayley-III scales
- Expanded definition and explanation of "canalization"

Chapter 7—Infancy: Social and Emotional Development

- Canadian research study on feeding disorders
- An "Attachment Across Cultures" diagram depicting various factors influencing parent–child attachment
- The reciprocal-relationship phase of attachment
- Elaboration of Erik Erikson's psychosocial development theory
- Information on reactive attachment disorder (RAD)
- Canadian incidence rates on child abuse and neglect and highlights from the 2003 Canadian Incidence Study of Reported Child Abuse and Neglect
- Canadian public service flyer dealing with spanking
- "A Closer Look" feature dealing with child abuse that includes Canadian guidelines for "what to do"
- Guide for professionals who work with children, with current Canadian web links and resources
- New tables outlining the development of emotional and behavioural control in infants and toddlers
- New table about emotion regulation milestones for infants and toddlers and the role of adults
- Canadian daycare information and Canada's Universal Child Care Plan
- New Centre of Excellence for Early Childhood paper by Martha Friendly
- Specific child care links by province and updated information on how to find quality child care

Chapter 8—Early Childhood: Physical Development

- New information relevant to Canadian children as put forth in Safe Kids Canada (2005)
- Physical activity guidelines put forth by Health Canada
- Reference to both *Eating Well with Canada's Food Guide* (2007) and *Canada's Food Guide to Healthy Eating: Focus on Preschoolers, 2002*, and the addition of a table with examples of one child-size serving
- Updated Canadian information on immunizations and reference to the Canadian Coalition for Immunization Awareness & Promotion
- Table depicting publicly funded immunization programs by province/territory
- Canadian Dental Association recommendations for oral health and hygiene
- New Canadian immunization schedule from the Canadian Immunization Guide (6th Edition, 2002)
- New ten leading causes of death in Canadian preschoolers

Chapter 9—Early Childhood: Cognitive Development

- Canadian research studies in the area of pretend play
- New table comparing and contrasting the behaviourist, cognitive constructivist (Piaget), and social constructionist (Vygotsky) theories of development
- "A Closer Look" feature dealing with Canada's multilingualism
- New table with French immersion rates across Canada
- Information on Canadian and Aboriginal Head Start programs

Chapter 10—Early Childhood: Social and Emotional Development

- New table on the development of emotional and behavioural control in infants and toddlers
- Revised table depicting Diana Baumrind's Patterns of Parenting
- New references to Canadian research in the area of family studies
- New diagram demonstrating the compliance process
- The important and distinctive role fathers play in parenting
- Additional information on Vygotsky's theory, especially a section titled "Learning through Play: A Vygotskian Perspective"
- Information on how adults can support the development of prosocial behaviours
- New Canadian media viewing guidelines put forth by the Canadian Paediatric Society

Chapter 11—Middle Childhood: Physical Development

- Information from In Canada, the Canadian Broadcasting Corporation (CBC), and the National Film Board of Canada (NFB)
- Table indicating the prevalence of obesity by age group in Canada
- Canadian web links and resources such as Health Canada's *Physical Activity Guide* and *Gotta Move!* magazine for children
- New figure illustrating one province's policy statement on physical health and children: Alberta Education's Daily Physical Activity (DPA) Policy Statement
- Table depicting province or territory promotion of physical activity
- Canadian media consumption rates
- "A Closer Look" feature dealing with Canadian community approaches to fitness
- Canadian statistics related to AD/HD
- Learning Disability Association of Canada's official *learning disability* definition
- Canadian information on inclusion and special education programming with complete provincial web links

Chapter 12—Middle Childhood: Cognitive Development

- New example for application of Piaget's theory
- Update of Sternberg's Triarchic Theory of Intelligence
- New WISC-IV (2003) description and sample items
- Culture-fair practices in conducting psychoeducational assessments
- Updated terminology to reflect more inclusive language terms
- List of Canadian-based resources on topics of intellectual disabilities
- Example of special education coding criteria used by the Government of Alberta
- Implications of using standardized intelligence tests with minority populations such as Aboriginal children and youth
- New table of graduation rates across Canada
- Discussion of Canadian Council on Learning (2007) report titled *Lessons in Learning*

Chapter 13—Middle Childhood: Social and Emotional Development

- Information from Canadian resource site Egale Canada
  (http://www.egale.ca/index.asp)
- Canadian divorce statistics
- New information on families in transition
- Canadian maternal employment statistics
- Canadian research on child-rearing practices and children with
  depressive symptoms
- Table showing Canadian kindergarten programming by province
- Current bullying prevention research by leading Canadian researchers
- Canadian anti-bullying resources and web links
- Prevalence rates of emotional and behavioural difficulties among Canadian students
- Information from the 2006 Report Card on Child and Family Poverty in Canada

Chapter 14—Adolescence: Physical Development

- CDC growth charts
- Canadian web links on adolescent sexuality
- Health Canada's (2003) *Canadian Guidelines for Sexual Health Education*
- Canadian statistics on sexual health from SIECAN (2005)
- Report on Trends in the Health of Canadian Youth
- Canadian youth tobacco statistics
- Information on methamphetamine also known as speed, meth, chalk, ice, crystal,
  and crystal meth
- Drinking statistics for Canadian youth

Chapter 15—Adolescence: Cognitive Development

- New research on sex differences in math and spatial abilities
- Cultural critique of Kohlberg's theory of moral development
- Two new figures documenting Canadian dropout rates
- Canadian Youth in Transition surveys data
- Updates to vocational counselling of Canadian youth
- Coverage of the Canadian SCIberMENTOR program
- Coverage of Canadian youth working statistics
- New table outlining female and male students' daily activity breakdown

Chapter 16—Adolescence: Social and Emotional Development

- Expanded coverage of Erikson's Identity versus Identity Confusion stage
- Expanded coverage of Brown and Gilligan's research
- Susan Harter's work on self-concept
- Expanded multi-ethnic research studies on self-esteem
- Canadian sexual health statistics
- Information on oral sex activity among youth
- Expanded coverage of cyberbullying and Canadian resources
- New Canadian teen pregnancy statistics and First Nations data
- "Talk to Me Sexuality Education for Parents" by the Public Health Agency
  of Canada
- New Canadian youth crime statistics and 2003's *Youth Criminal Justice Act (YCJA)*
- Canadian suicide rates and a new table with suicide death rates in First Nations youth

Lessons in Observation Boxes

One of the themes of this text is how children learn by observation. College and university students and other adults also learn by observation. One of the best ways to learn about child development is to observe the behaviour of children. Unfortunately, many students do not have everyday access to children and therefore cannot observe for themselves how the many concepts and theories discussed in this textbook evidence themselves in the everyday lives of children.

Fortunately, all users of the first Canadian edition of *Childhood and Adolescence: Voyages in Development* will find a free series of observational videos called Observing Children and Adolescents on four CD-ROMs. Integrated into every chapter, these observational videos illustrate a wide range of topics, such as:

- Chapter 2: Prenatal Assessment
- Chapter 8: Gross and Fine Motor Skills
- Chapter 9: Piaget's Preoperational Stages
- Chapter 10: Gender
- Chapter 12: Piaget's Concrete-Operational Stage

Each video is discussed in an interactive format in the text. Each new Lessons in Observation box includes Learning Objectives, Applied Lessons, and Critical Thinking questions. This format makes the observation experience more meaningful and encourages higher-order thinking. An online version of Lessons in Observation with accompanying videos allows students to e-mail their responses, making this feature easily assignable.

Concept Reviews

Concept Reviews are more than simple summaries. They take complex developmental concepts, such as theories of intelligence, and present them in dynamic layouts that readily communicate the key concepts and the relationships among concepts. Many of them have photographs and figures as well as text. Here is a sampling of the Concept Reviews found in *Childhood and Adolescence: Voyages in Development:*

- Concept Review 1.3: Perspectives on Child Development
- Concept Review 5.1: Sequences of Physical Development
- Concept Review 7.1: Theories of Attachment
- Concept Review 10.1: Theories of the Development of Sex Differences
- Concept Review 12.2: Theories of Intelligence

"Developing in a World of Diversity" Boxes

This textbook is inclusive. We address the most challenging issues as to how children and adolescents are influenced by their ethnic backgrounds and gender roles in areas ranging from intellectual development to substance abuse. In many cases, cultural and ethnic factors affect the very survival of the child. This coverage helps students understand why parents of different backgrounds and sexes rear their children and adolescents in certain ways, why children and adolescents from various backgrounds behave and think in different ways, and how the study of child and adolescent development is enriched by addressing similarities as well as differences.

Examples of "Developing in a World of Diversity" topics include:

- Chapter 1: Influence of the Macrosystem on the Development of Independence
- Chapter 4: Maternal and Infant Mortality around the World (including Canadian statistics)

- Chapter 5: Alleviating Protein-Energy Malnutrition (PEM)
- Chapter 8: Cross-Cultural Differences in Sleeping Arrangements
- Chapter 16: Ethnicity, Gender Roles, and Self-Esteem (expanded to include Francophone youth)

"A Closer Look" Boxes

The "A Closer Look" features in this edition allow expanded treatment of a number of topics that serve a strong pedagogical purpose, present issues of high currency or interest, and allow readers to "take this book home with them"—that is, to apply what they are learning with children and adults in their own lives.

The following are examples of "A Closer Look" features that explain how researchers carry out their work:

- Chapter 4: Studying Visual Acuity in Neonates: How Well Can They See?
- Chapter 6: Counting in the Crib? Findings from a "Mickey-Mouse Experiment"

The following features allow readers to apply what they are learning with their own children, in their own lives:

- Chapter 7: Finding Child Care You (and Your Child) Can Live With (for Canadian parents)
- Chapter 8: Ten Things You Need to Know about Immunizations (based on Canadian resources and current information)
- Chapter 9: Helping Children Use Television Wisely (including teaching children not to imitate the violence they observe in the media)
- Chapter 10: Helping Children Cope with Fears

The following features share developmental information especially related to those studying to be child educators:

- Chapter 6: Teaching Sign Language to Infants
- Chapter 7: What to Do if You Think a Child Has Been the Victim of Sexual Abuse
- Chapter 10: Helping Children Cope with Fears
- Chapter 13: Bullying—An Epidemic of Misbehaviour and Fear
- Chapter 15: Beyond the Classroom: How Parents Can Help Teenagers Improve Their Academic Performance

An Enhanced Pedagogical Package: PQ4R

PQ4R discourages students from believing that they are sponges who will automatically soak up the subject matter in the same way that sponges soak up water. The PQ4R method stimulates students to *actively* engage in the subject matter. Students are encouraged to become *proactive* rather than *reactive*.

PQ4R is the acronym for Preview, Question, Read, Reflect, Review, and Recite, a method that is related to the work of educational psychologist Francis P. Robinson. PQ4R is more than the standard built-in study guide. It goes well beyond a few pages of questions and exercises that are found at the ends of the chapters of many textbooks. It is an integral part of every chapter. It flows throughout every chapter. It begins and ends every chapter, and it accompanies the student page by page.

The PQ4R method has been enhanced in this edition of *Childhood and Adolescence: Voyages in Development* to include *Truth or Fiction?* sections in the preview material and "Reflect and Relate" items in each *Active Review*. Moreover, as we see above, there are new *Concept Reviews* throughout the text.

Chapter Previews

Previewing the material helps shape students' expectations. It enables them to create mental templates or "advance organizers" into which they categorize the subject matter. Each chapter of *Childhood and Adolescence: Voyages in Development* previews the subject matter with a *Truth or Fiction?* section and a chapter *Preview*. The *Truth or Fiction?* items stimulate students to delve into the subject matter by challenging folklore and common sense (which is often common *non*sense). Then the *Preview* outlines the material in the chapter, creating mental categories that guide students' reading.

Following is a sampling of challenging *Truth or Fiction?* items from various chapters:

(T)(F) You can carry the genes for a deadly illness and not become sick yourself.

(T)(F) More children die from sudden infant death syndrome (SIDS) than from cancer, heart disease, pneumonia, child abuse, AIDS, cystic fibrosis, and muscular dystrophy combined.

(T)(F) Infants need to have experience crawling before they develop fear of heights.

(T)(F) It is dangerous to awaken a sleepwalker.

(T)(F) Three-year-olds usually say "Daddy goed away" instead of "Daddy went away" because they do understand rules of grammar.

(T)(F) Children who watch two to four hours of TV a day will see 8000 murders and another 100 000 acts of violence by the time they have finished elementary school.

Question

Devising questions about the subject matter, before reading it in detail, is another feature of the PQ4R method. Writing questions gives students goals: They attend class or read the text *in order to answer the questions*. Questions are placed in all primary sections of the text to help students use the PQ4R method most effectively. They are printed in *blue*. When students see a question, they can read the following material in order to answer that question. If they wish, they can also write the questions and answers in their notebooks, as recommended by Robinson.

Read

Reading is the first *R* in the PQ4R method. Although students will have to read for themselves, they are not alone. The text helps by providing:

- *Previews* of the chapter that help students organize the material;
- *Truth or Fiction?* sections that stimulate students by challenging common knowledge and folklore;
- presentation of the subject matter in clear, stimulating prose;
- a running glossary that defines key terms in the margin of the text, near where the terms appear in the text; and
- development of concepts in an orderly fashion so that new concepts build on previously presented concepts.

We have chosen a writing style that is "personal." It speaks directly to the student and employs humour and personal anecdotes designed to motivate and stimulate students.

Review

The second *R* in PQ4R stands for Review. Regular reviews of the subject matter help students learn. Therefore, reviews are incorporated into *Active Review* sections that follow all major sections in the text.

Active Reviews contain two types of items that foster active learning, retention, and critical thinking. "Fill in the blanks" are the first type of item. The fill-in-the-blank format challenges students to *produce*, not simply *recognize*, the answer. Items are numbered, and answers are found at the end of the book. For example, an *Active Review* from the chapter on "Heredity and Conception" has the following fill-in-the-blank items:

13. The sets of traits that we inherit are referred to as our (genotypes or phenotypes?).
14. The actual traits that we display at any point in time are the product of genetic and environmental influences and are called our (genotypes or phenotypes?).
15. Parents and children have a(n) _____ percent overlap in their genetic endowments.
16. _____ (MZ) twins share 100 percent of their genes.
17. _____ (DZ) twins have a 50 percent overlap, as do other siblings.

Because reviewing the subject matter is so important, and because of the value of visual cues in learning, *Concept Reviews* are also found throughout the text (see page xxx of this Preface).

Reflect & Relate

Students learn more effectively when they reflect on (the third *R* in PQ4R is for Reflect), or *relate* to, the subject matter. Psychologists who study learning and memory refer to reflection on subject matter as *elaborative rehearsal*. One way of reflecting on a subject is to *relate* it to things already known about, whether it be academic material or events in one's own life (Willoughby et al., 1994).[1] Reflecting on, or relating to, the material makes it meaningful and easier to remember (Woloshyn et al., 1994).[2] It also makes it more likely that students will be able to apply the information to their own lives (Kintsch, 1994).[3] Through effective reflection, students can embed material firmly in their memory so that rote repetition is unnecessary.

Because reflecting on the material is intertwined with relating to it, the second kind of item in each *Active Review* section is termed *Reflect & Relate*. Here is the *Reflect & Relate* item from Chapter 12's *Active Review* following the section on moral development in middle childhood:

> *Reflect & Relate:* Ariel becomes angry that one of her best friends, Azarah, has told other friends a secret she confided in her. Ariel is hurt, and in retaliation spreads malicious rumours about Azarah at school. Shannon makes a mistake at the nuclear energy plant where she works, causing a nuclear accident in which a great deal of radiation is released, killing 300 people within a week and shortening the lives of more than 1 million people because of cancer. Which person has done something naughtier—Ariel or Shannon? Explain your viewpoint.

Recite

The PQ4R method recommends that students recite the answers to the questions aloud. Reciting answers aloud helps students remember them by means of repetition, by stimulating students to produce concepts and ideas they have learned, and by associating them with spoken words and gestures (Dodson & Schacter, 2001).[4]

Recite sections are found at the end of each chapter. They help students summarize the material, but they are active summaries. For this reason, the sections are termed *Recite: An Active Summary*. They are written in question-and-answer format. To provide a sense of closure, the active summaries repeat the questions found within the chapters. The answers are concise but include most of the key terms found in the text.

The *Recite: An Active Summary* sections are designed in two columns so that students can cover the second column (the answers) as they read the questions. Students can recite the answers as they remember or reconstruct them, and then check what they have recited against the answers they had covered. Students should not feel that they are incorrect if they have not produced the answer exactly as written in the second column; their individual approach might be slightly different, even more inclusive. The answers provided in the second column are intended to be a guide, to provide a check on students' learning. They are not carved in stone.

What Carries through to the Canadian Edition

The first Canadian edition of *Childhood and Adolescence: Voyages in Development* continues to present cutting-edge topic coverage, emphasizing the latest findings and research in key areas. The text is organized chronologically, beginning with introductory theoretical material followed by the developmental sequences.

Themes

Childhood and Adolescence: Voyages in Development, First Canadian Edition, also continues its emphasis on a number of themes:

- Human Diversity in Development and the Importance of the Cultural Context
- Biology: Neuroscience, Evolution, Genes, Hormones, and Behaviour
- Applications

Coverage of these themes is summarized in the following Theme Indexes.

Human Diversity in Development and the Importance of the Cultural Context

- Economic circumstances that affect development (pp. 24–26)
- Differences in being schooled in a monolingual or bilingual environment (p. 26)
- Influence of the macrosystem on the development of independence (p. 27)
- The sociocultural perspective and human diversity (p. 28)
- Naturalistic observations in children of different cultures (p. 37)
- Ethnic differences in incidence of bearing fraternal twins (p. 54)
- Ethnic differences in chromosomal and genetic disorders (p. 62)
- Maternal malnutrition around the world (p. 97)
- Cross-cultural differences when using a doula during delivery (p. 125)
- Maternal and infant mortality around the world (p. 132)
- Ethnic differences in habituation (p. 146)
- Socioeconomic status and nutrition (p. 166)
- Differences in preference for breastfeeding (p. 167)
- Ethnic differences in infant capacity to walk (p. 178)
- Differences in babbling across cultures (p. 218)
- Two-word sentence development across different languages (p. 223)
- Cultural differences in talking to infants (p. 225)
- Cross-cultural patterns of attachment (pp. 238–239)
- Low-income families and levels of child attachment (p. 240)
- Attachment of Ugandan and Scottish infants (pp. 242–243)
- Social deprivation in a Guatemalan tribe (p. 251)

- Stranger anxiety across cultures (pp. 260–261)
- Sex differences in personality (pp. 268–270)
- Cultural differences in rough-and-tumble play (p. 287)
- Sex differences in motor activity (p. 288)
- Cultural differences in the perception of handedness (p. 289)
- Differences in accidental death rate (p. 301)
- Cross-cultural differences in sleeping arrangements (p. 306)
- Development of concepts of ethnicity and race (p. 323)
- Cultural variations in the home environment (p. 345)
- Cross-cultural differences in effects of parental styles (p. 360)
- Cultural and gender differences in authoritarian parenting and the results on children (p. 363)
- Individualism, collectivism, and patterns of child rearing (pp. 366–367)
- Differences in the presence of a father (p. 371)
- Sex differences in play (pp. 375–376)
- Cultural differences in empathy (p. 377)
- Aggressiveness in sons of criminal and noncriminal fathers (p. 379)
- Sex differences in effects of TV violence (pp. 381–383)
- Development of gender roles and sex differences (pp. 387–388)
- Possible sex differences in organization of the brain (pp. 389–390)
- Cross-cultural differences in gender identity, stability, and constancy (p. 394)
- Psychological androgyny (pp. 395–396)
- Sex differences and motor skills (p. 413)
- Education of children with disabilities (p. 426)
- Discrimination in standardized testing (pp. 459–460)
- Testing bias and culture-free tests (p. 460)
- Cognitive delays and giftedness (pp. 462–464)
- Understanding socioeconomic and ethnic differences in IQ (p. 465)
- Sex differences in self-esteem (p. 484)
- Sex differences in self-concept (p. 483)
- Sex differences in learned helplessness (p. 485)
- Sex differences in development of friendships (pp. 495–496)
- Effects of divorce across cultures (p. 489)
- Sex differences in coping with divorce (p. 489)
- Differences in preparedness for school (p. 502)
- Sexism in the classroom (pp. 504–505)
- Gender differences in social impact of acne (pp. 527–528)
- Cultural impact of menarche (p. 531)
- Sex differences in anorexia nervosa (p. 545)
- Sex, education, and substance abuse (p. 536–544; 551–558)
- Differences in formal-operational thought (p. 570)
- Sex differences in verbal ability (p. 572)
- Sex differences in visual-spatial ability (pp. 572–573)
- Sex differences in mathematical ability (p. 574)
- Cross-cultural differences in moral development and limitations of certain developmental theories (p. 577)
- Sex differences in moral development (p. 578)
- Differences in postconventional thought (pp. 576–577)
- Sex differences in career development (p. 587)
- Ethnicity and development of identity (p. 599)
- Gender roles and development of identity (p. 600)
- Ethnicity, gender roles, and self-esteem (p. 602)

- Ways of reversing infertility (pp. 73–74)
- Choosing the sex of one's child (pp. 75–76)
- Maternal nutrition during pregnancy (pp. 96–97)
- Effects of maternal health problems on the embryo and fetus (p. 98)
- Effects of environmental hazards on the embryo and the fetus (pp. 106–107)
- Using the Lamaze method to decrease fear and pain during delivery (p. 124)
- Using C-section to avoid disease transmission from mother to infant (pp. 125–126)
- How interaction, talking, and stimulation can help preterm infants develop (p. 134)
- Support available for women with postpartum depression (pp. 135–136)
- Understanding visual accommodation (p. 142)
- How to soothe an infant and ease crying (p. 151)
- How to introduce infants to new food (pp. 166–167)
- Where women can go to learn more about breast feeding (p. 170)
- Teaching sign language to infants (p. 220)
- "Motherese" (p. 228)
- Establishing attachment (p. 239–240)
- Hormones and attachment (p. 245)
- How child abuse may lead to psychological disorders in adulthood (p. 256)
- What to do if you think a child has been the victim of sexual abuse (p. 256)
- Finding daycare you and your child can live with (p. 273)
- Brain development and visual skills (pp. 283–284)
- Right brain/left brain (p. 284)
- Plasticity of the brain (pp. 284–285)
- Teaching a child to enjoy healthy food (p. 293)
- Ten things you need to know about immunizations (p. 296)
- Watching how children show (or don't show) conservation (p. 321)
- Memory strategies (p. 341)
- Techniques for restricting children's behaviour (p. 360)
- Techniques parents can use to help control their children's behaviour (p. 363)
- Helping children cope with fears (p. 386)
- Piaget's theory applied to education (p. 438)
- Vygotsky's theory applied to education (p. 343)
- Tips for adults wishing to help foster prosocial skills in young children (p. 376)
- How parents can model effective emotion-regulation skills (p. 386)
- Rehearsal strategies for memory (p. 449)
- How to ask children questions that elicit truthful answers (p. 450)
- How teachers can help motivate students (p. 504)
- How to help children with conduct disorders (p. 507)
- How parents and teachers can help children with mild depression (p. 510)
- How parents and teachers can help children with school phobia (p. 513)
- Prevention of sexually transmitted infections (p. 541)
- Preventing HIV/AIDS and other STIs (p. 542)
- Treatment and prevention of eating disorders (p. 549)
- Treatment and prevention of substance abuse (p. 557)
- How parents can help teenagers improve their academic performance (p. 584)
- How to get help if someone is being cyberbullied (p. 503)
- How to talk to your child about sexual health (p. 540–541)
- What to do about online solicitation of sex (p. 614)

The Package

Childhood and Adolescence: Voyages in Development, First Canadian Edition, is accompanied by a wide array of supplements prepared for both the instructor and student.

For the Instructor

Instructor's Manual by Karen Davis of Mohawk College. This comprehensive manual offers learning objectives, chapter outlines, lecture topics, student exercises (such as Internet activities), film and videotape suggestions, activities for the "Observing Children and Adolescents" video series, and the Resource Integration Guide. It also includes a complete instructor's guide to the "Observing Children and Adolescents Workbook and CD-ROM."

Test Bank by Susannah Cole of Sir Sandford Fleming College. For each chapter of the text, the Test Bank includes 100–120 multiple-choice, 10–20 matching, 10–20 true/false, and 5–10 short-answer questions with model answers.

ExamView Computerized Testing (available on the Instructor's Resource CD-ROM). Create, deliver, and customize tests and study guides (both print and online) in minutes with this easy-to-use assessment and tutorial system. ExamView offers both a Quick Test Wizard and an Online Test Wizard that guide you step by step through the process of creating tests. Its "what you see is what you get" interface allows you to see the test you are creating on the screen exactly as it will print or display online. You can build tests of up to 250 questions using up to 12 question types. Using ExamView's complete word-processing capabilities, you can enter an unlimited number of new questions or edit existing questions.

Classroom Presentation Tools for the Instructor

Instructor's Resource CD-ROM. This one-stop lecture and class preparation tool makes it easy for you to assemble, edit, publish, and present custom lectures for your course using Microsoft PowerPoint. The Multimedia Manager lets you bring together text-specific lecture outlines and art, along with video and animations from the web or your own materials—culminating in a powerful, personalized, media-enhanced presentation. The CD-ROM also contains a full Instructor's Manual, Computerized Test Bank, and other instructor resources.

For the Student

CengageNOW! ™. CengageNOW is an **online learning and homework assessment program** created by Susan McBride of Langara College in concert with the text to present a seamless, integrated learning tool.

With CengageNOW, instructors can dramatically affect student success. Assigning text-specific tutorials requires no instructor setup. In addition, faculty can use the same system to create tailored homework assignments, quizzes, and tests that autograde and flow directly into the instructor's grade book! This means instructors can actually assign marks to homework assignments, motivating students to study the material and come to class prepared.

Students can improve their grades and save study time with CengageNOW. It isn't just reading—it provides a **customized study plan** that lets students **master what they need to know without spending time on what they already know**! The study plan provides a road map to interactive exercises, videos, e-books, and other resources that help students master the subject. Pretests and posttests allow students to monitor their progress. Focused studying via CengageNOW will minimize student efforts and yet maximize results.

Student Companion Website at http://www.voyages1CE.nelson.com. Students will find a variety of online resources directly linked to this book. The website includes interactive exercises and Power Visuals for mastering and reviewing key concepts as well as quizzing, chapter outlines, and much more.

Observing Children and Adolescents Workbook and CD-ROM by Michie Swartwood, State University of New York, and Kathy H. Trotter. This CD-ROM, with approximately 200 minutes of video segments that feature highlights of infant, child, and adolescent development, comes free with this text. The corresponding student workbook features concept overviews, key terms and definitions, and a variety of critical thinking applications, many of which ask the student to approach the same video segment from more than one theoretical perspective.

Study Guide by Patricia Boechler, University of Alberta. For each chapter of the text, this comprehensive student guide includes a chapter summary, quiz, critical thinking exercises, exercises related to the "Observing Children and Adolescents" video series, and an Internet activity.

Observation Worksheets by Debra Schwiesow of Creighton University. Perfect for homework or small group assignments, these Observational Worksheets encourage students to directly apply their knowledge and experience to their work as parents, counsellors, caretakers, and teachers. The easy-to-complete, hands-on activities guide students through the process of observing, recording, and analyzing the behaviour of children and adolescents they encounter in the real world. For each chapter of the text there is one individual activity and one small group activity. These observation worksheets are free when ordered with the text—check with your Nelson Education representative for more information.

Acknowledgments

The first Canadian edition could not have been possible without the help of many individuals who assisted with small and large tasks from start to finish. This book is the product of teamwork.

First, I must thank our professional academic colleagues—the people who teach about child and adolescent development and make the book come alive for students, as well as the people who conduct the research. They know better than anyone what's going on "out there"—out there in the world of children and adolescents, out there in the classroom. The book you hold in your hands would not be what it is without their valuable insights and suggestions. Thank you, in particular, to the reviewers of this Canadian edition:

Sherrill Brown, Grant MacEwan College

David Lockwood, Humber College

Mary Knight, Durham College

Susannah Cole, Sir Sandford Fleming College

Janice Quade, Loyalist College

Monica Monahan, George Brown College

Karen Davis, Mohawk College

Dhanna Mistri, Sheridan College

Susan McBride, Langara College

Nancy Thomas, Grant MacEwan College

My special thanks also go to my colleagues Anna Kirova and Gretchen Hess at the University of Alberta, who provided me with invaluable feedback and support as I adapted this text to make it uniquely beneficial to Canadian students.

It has been a pleasure to work with the professional team at Nelson Education Ltd. They are responsible for all the behind-the-scenes magic that goes into editing and producing a textbook. First and foremost, I want to thank Alwynn Pinard (Managing Developmental Editor), whose work ethic and genuine commitment to the Canadian Edition project has been unparalleled since day one. Thank you also to my Executive Editor, Cara Yarzab, and Executive Marketing Manager, Lenore Taylor-Atkins, as well as to Evelyn Veitch, Associate Vice-President, Editorial Director, who was there from the day we launched this project to make sure I was in good hands. I am also very grateful to Cathy Witlox, whose thorough copy editing is second to none. I would like to thank Christine Gilbert, Content Product Manager, for her hard work, advice, and enthusiasm during the later stages of the project. In addition, I would like to acknowledge Marisa Taylor, Project Manager at GEX, for all of her behind-the-scenes effort involved in bringing such a text to life.

Finally, I would like to thank my family for providing me with the encouragement and support to take on this project and see it through to the end.

Notes

[1] Willoughby, T., Wood, E., & Khan, M. (1994). Isolating variables that impact on or detract from the effectiveness of elaboration strategies. *Journal of Educational Research*, 86, 279–289.

[2] Woloshyn, V. E., Paivio, A., & Pressley, M. (1994). Use of elaborative interrogation to help students acquire information consistent with prior knowledge and information inconsistent with prior knowledge. *Journal of Educational Psychology*, 86, 79–89.

[3] Kintsch, W. (1994). *Text comprehension, memory, and learning*. American Psychologist, 49, 294–303.

[4] Dodson, C. S., & Schacter, D. L. (2001). "If I had said it I would have remembered it": Reducing false memories with a distinctiveness heuristic. *Psychonomic Bulletin & Review*, 8(1), 155–161.

1

History, Theories, and Methods

PREVIEW

TRUTH OR FICTION

● ● ● ● ● ● ● ● ● ● ● ●

T F During the Middle Ages, children were often treated as miniature adults.

T F Children come into the world as "blank tablets"—without inborn differences in intelligence and talents.

T F Nail biting and smoking cigarettes are signs of conflict experienced during early childhood.

T F Some theorists contend that children actively strive to understand and take charge of their worlds, whereas other theorists argue that children respond passively to environmental stimulation.

T F Research with monkeys has helped psychologists understand the formation of attachment in humans.

T F To learn how a person develops over a lifetime, researchers have tracked some individuals for more than 50 years.

Go to w w w
www.voyages1ce.nelson.com
for an interactive version of this "Truth or Fiction" feature.

© Getty Images

T his book has a story to tell. An important story. A remarkable story. It is your story. It is about the remarkable journey you have already taken through childhood. It is about the unfolding of your adult life. Billions have made this journey before. You have much in common with them. Yet you are unique, and things will happen to you—and because of you—that have never happened before.

The development of children, from a Canadian context, is what this book is about. In a very real sense, we cannot hope to understand ourselves as adults—we cannot catch a glimpse of the remarkable journeys we have taken—without understanding children.

In this chapter we explore some of the reasons for studying child development. We then take a brief tour of the history of child development. It may surprise you that until relatively recent times, people were not particularly sensitive to the ways in which children differ from adults. Next, we examine some controversies in child development research, such as whether there are distinct stages of development. We see how theories help illuminate our observations and how theories help point the way toward new observations. Then we consider methods for the study of child development. Scientists have devised sophisticated methods for studying children, and ethics helps us determine the types of research that are deemed proper and improper. But first, let us embark on our search for ourselves by considering a basic question: *Question: What is child development?*

Motor Development
This infant has just mastered the ability to pull herself up to a standing position. Soon she will be able to stand alone, and then she will begin to walk.

© Digital Vision/Getty Images

child A person undergoing the period of development from infancy through puberty.

infancy The period of very early childhood characterized by lack of complex speech; the first two years after birth.

conception The process of becoming pregnant; the process by which a sperm cell joins with an ovum to begin a new life.

prenatal period The period of development from conception to birth (from roots meaning "prior to birth").

What Is Child Development? Coming to Terms with Terms

You have heard the word *child* all your life, so why bother to define it? We do so because words in common usage are frequently used inexactly. A **child** is a person undergoing the period of development from *infancy* to *puberty*—two more familiar words that are frequently used inexactly. Derived from Latin roots meaning "not speaking," the term **infancy** is usually defined as the first two years of life, or the period of life before the development of *complex* speech. We stress the word *complex* because many children have a large vocabulary and use simple sentences well before their second birthday.

Western researchers commonly speak of two other periods of development that lie between infancy and adolescence: early childhood and middle childhood. Early childhood encompasses the ages from two to five years. Middle childhood generally is defined as the years from ages six to twelve. In Canadian society, the beginning of this period is usually marked by the child's entry into first grade. This book takes a Western approach to understanding child development by presenting studies and statistics relevant to Canadian children and youth, and using developmental definitions based in Western education, health, and psychological traditions. To quote the opening line in Barbara Rogoff's (2003) recent book, "human development is a cultural process" (p. 3). Because there is great cultural diversity in Canada, it is important to question the generalizability of the research presented (i.e., who were the participants in the studies, and can the results be extended to include other populations within Canada). To study development, we must also look further back to the origin of sperm and ova (egg cells), the process of **conception,** and the **prenatal period.** Yet this is not far enough to satisfy scientists. We also describe the mechanisms of heredity that give rise to traits in both humans and other animals.

Development is the orderly appearance, over time, of physical structures, psychological traits, behaviours, and ways of adapting to the demands of life. The changes brought on by development are both *qualitative* and *quantitative*. Qualitative changes are changes in type or kind. Consider **motor development**. As we develop, we gain the abilities to lift our heads, sit up, crawl, stand, and walk. These changes are qualitative. However, within each of these qualitative changes are quantitative developments, or changes in *amount*. After babies begin to lift their heads, they lift them higher and higher. Soon after children walk, they begin to run. Then they gain the capacity to run faster.

Development occurs across many dimensions—physiological, cognitive, social, emotional, and behavioural. Development is spurred by internal factors, such as genetics, and it is shaped by external factors, such as nutrition and culture.

The terms *growth* and *development* are not synonymous, although many people use them interchangeably. **Growth** is usually used to refer to changes in size or quantity, whereas *development* also refers to changes in quality. During the early days after conception, the fertilized egg cell develops rapidly. It divides repeatedly, and cells begin to take on specialized forms. However, it does not "grow" in that there is no gain in mass. Why? It has not yet become implanted in the uterus and therefore is without any external source of nourishment. Language development refers to the process by which the child's use of language becomes progressively more sophisticated and complex during the first few years of life. Vocabulary growth, by contrast, refers to the simple accumulation of new words and their meanings.

Child development, then, is a field of inquiry that attempts to understand the processes that govern the appearance and growth of children's physical structures, psychological traits, behaviour patterns, understanding, and ways of adapting to the demands of life.

Professionals from many fields are interested in child development. They include psychologists, educators, anthropologists, sociologists, nurses, and medical researchers. Each brings his or her own brand of expertise to the quest for knowledge. Intellectual cross-fertilization enhances the skills of developmentalists and enriches the lives of children.

development The processes by which organisms unfold features and traits, grow, and become more complex and specialized in structure and function.

motor development The development of the capacity for movement, particularly that made possible by changes in the nervous system and the muscles.

growth The processes by which organisms increase in size, weight, strength, and other traits as they develop.

Why Do We Study Child Development?

Question: Why do researchers study child development? An important motive for studying child development is curiosity—the desire to learn about children. Curiosity may be driven by the desire to answer questions about development that remain unresolved. It may also be driven by the desire to have fun. (Yes, children and the study of children can be fun.) There are other motives:

To Gain Insight into Human Nature

For centuries, philosophers, scientists, and educators have argued over whether children are aggressive or loving, whether children are conscious and self-aware, whether they have a natural curiosity that demands to unravel the mysteries of the universe, or whether they merely react mechanically to environmental stimulation. The quest for answers has an impact on the lives of children, parents, educators, and others who interact with children.

To Gain Insight into the Origins of Adult Behaviour

How do we explain the origins of empathy in adults? Of antisocial behaviour? How do we explain the assumption of "feminine" and "masculine" behaviour patterns? The origins of special talents in writing, music, athletics, and math?

gender roles Complex clusters of behaviour that are considered stereotypical of females and males.

To Gain Insight into the Origins of Sex Differences and Gender Roles, and the Effects of Culture on Development

How do **gender roles**—culturally induced expectations for stereotypical feminine and masculine behaviour—develop? Are there sex differences in cognition and behaviour? If so, how do they develop? How are other aspects of development influenced by children's ethnic backgrounds—their race, their religion, their language, and their country of origin?

To Gain Insight into the Origins, Prevention, and Treatment of Developmental Problems

PKU Phenylketonuria. A genetic abnormality in which a child cannot metabolize phenylalanine, an amino acid, which consequently builds up in the body and causes mental retardation. If treated with a special diet, retardation is prevented.

Fetal alcohol syndrome, **PKU, SIDS,** Down syndrome, autism, hyperactivity, dyslexia, child abuse—these are but a handful of the buzzwords that stir fear in parents and parents-to-be. A major focus in child development research is the search for the causes of such problems so that they can be prevented and, when possible, treated.

To Optimize Conditions of Development

SIDS Sudden infant death syndrome (discussed in Chapter 5).

Most parents want to provide the best in nutrition and medical care so that their children will develop strong and healthy bodies. Parents want their infants to feel secure with them. They want to ensure that major transitions, such as the transition from the home to the school, will be as stress-free as possible. Developmentalists therefore undertake research to learn about issues such as,

- the effects of various foods and chemicals on the development of the embryo;
- the effects of parent-infant interaction immediately following birth on bonds of attachment;
- the effects of bottle feeding versus breast feeding on mother-infant attachment and the baby's health;
- the effects of daycare programs on parent-child bonds of attachment and on children's social and intellectual development; and
- the effects of various patterns of child rearing on development of independence, competence, and social adjustment.

The Development of Child Development

Child development as a field of scientific inquiry has existed for little more than a century. *Question: What views of children do we find throughout history?*

In ancient times and in the Middle Ages, children often were viewed as innately evil, and discipline was harsh. Legally, medieval children were treated as property and servants. They enjoyed no civil rights. They could be sent to the monastery, married without consultation, or convicted of crimes. Children were nurtured until they were seven years old, which was considered the "age of reason." Then they were expected to work alongside adults in the home and in the field. They ate, drank, and dressed as miniature adults. *Truth or Fiction Revisited:* Children were treated as miniature adults throughout most of the Middle Ages. (For much of the Middle Ages, artists depicted children as small adults.) However, this means that more was expected of them, not that they were given more privileges.

The transition to the study of development in modern times is marked by the thinking of philosophers such as John Locke and Jean-Jacques Rousseau. *Truth or Fiction Revisited:* The Englishman John Locke (1632-1704) believed that the child came into the world as a *tabula rasa*—a "blank tablet" or clean slate—that was written upon by experience. Locke did not believe that inborn predispositions toward good

A View of Children as Perceived in the 1600s
Centuries ago, children were viewed as miniature adults. In this 17th-century painting, notice how the body proportions of the young princess (in the middle) are similar to those of her adult attendants.

or evil played an important role in the conduct of the child. Instead, he focused on the role of the environment or of experience. Locke believed that social approval and disapproval are powerful shapers of behaviour. Jean-Jacques Rousseau (1712–1778), a Swiss-French philosopher, reversed Locke's stance. Rousseau argued that children are inherently good and that, if allowed to express their natural impulses, they will develop into generous and moral individuals.

During the Industrial Revolution, family life came to be defined in terms of the nuclear unit of mother, father, and children, rather than the extended family. Children became more visible, fostering awareness of childhood as a special time of life. Still, children often laboured in factories from dawn to dusk through the early years of the twentieth century.

In the twentieth century, laws were passed to protect children from strenuous labour, to require that they attend school until a certain age, and to prevent them from getting married or being sexually exploited. Whereas children were once considered the property of parents to do with as they wished, laws now protect children from the abuse and neglect of parents and other caretakers. Juvenile courts see that children who break the law receive fair and appropriate treatment in the criminal justice system.

A Young Child Labourer
Children often worked long days in factories up through the early years of the 20th century. A number of cultures in the world today still use child labour.

Pioneers in the Study of Child Development

Various thoughts about child development coalesced into a field of scientific study in the nineteenth and early twentieth centuries. Many individuals, including Charles Darwin, G. Stanley Hall, and Alfred Binet, contributed to the emerging field.

Charles Darwin (1809–1882) is perhaps best known as the originator of the theory of evolution. But he was also one of the first observers to keep a *baby biography*, in which he described his infant son's behaviours in great detail. G. Stanley Hall (1844–1924) is credited with founding child development as an academic discipline. He adapted the questionnaire method for use with large groups of children so that he could study the "contents of children's minds." The Frenchman Alfred Binet (1857–1911), along with Theodore Simon, developed the first standardized intelligence test near the turn of the twentieth century. Binet's purpose was to identify public school children who were at risk of falling behind their peers in academic achievement. By the beginning of the twentieth century, child development had emerged as a scientific field of study. Within a short time, major theoretical views of the developing child had begun to emerge, proposed by such developmentalists as Arnold Gesell, Sigmund Freud, John B. Watson, and Jean Piaget. We describe their theories of child development, and those of others, next.

Active Review

1. A child is a person undergoing the period of development from *infancy* to _____.

2. _____ is the orderly appearance, over time, of structures, traits, and behaviours.

3. The word *growth* is usually used to refer to changes in size or quantity, whereas the term _____ also refers to changes in quality.

Reflect & Relate: Do you believe that children are "wild"? That children must be "tamed"? Do you see dangers (to children) in answering yes to either question? Explain.

Go to
W W W www.voyages1ce.nelson.com
for an interactive version of this review.

Theories of Child Development

"Give me a dozen healthy infants, well-formed, and my own specified world to bring them up in, and I'll guarantee to train them to become any type of specialist I might suggest—doctor, lawyer, merchant, chief, and, yes, even beggar and thief, regardless of their talents, penchants, tendencies, abilities, vocations, and the race of their ancestors" (Watson, 1924, p. 82).

behaviourism John B. Watson's view that a science or theory of development must study observable behaviour only and investigate relationships between stimuli and responses.

John B. Watson, the founder of American **behaviourism,** viewed development in terms of learning. He generally agreed with Locke's idea that children come into the world as a tabula rasa—that their ideas, preferences, and skills are shaped by experience. There has been a long-standing nature-nurture debate in the study of children. In his theoretical approach to understanding children, Watson came down on the side of nurture, the importance of the physical and social environments, as found, for example, in parental training and approval.

Watson's view turned upside down the history of approaches to understanding children. Nature, or the inherited, genetic characteristics of the child, had long been the more popular explanation of how children get to be what they are. Just 4 years after Watson sounded his clarion call for the behavioural view, Arnold Gesell expressed the opposing idea that biological **maturation** was the main principle of development: "All things considered, the inevitability and surety of maturation are the most impressive characteristics of early development. It is the hereditary ballast which conserves and stabilizes growth of each individual infant" (Gesell, 1928, p. 378).

maturation The unfolding of genetically determined traits, structures, and functions.

Watson was talking largely about the behaviour patterns that children develop, whereas Gesell was focusing mainly on physical aspects of growth and development. Still, the behavioural and maturational perspectives lie at opposite ends of the continuum of theories of development. Many scientists fall into the trap of overemphasizing the importance of either nature or nurture at the risk of overlooking the ways in which nature and nurture interact. Just as a child's environments and experiences influence the development of his or her biological endowment, children often place themselves in environments that are harmonious with their personal characteristics.

Children, for example, are influenced by teachers and other students. Nevertheless, because of the traits they bring to school with them, some children may prefer to socialize with other children, and others with teachers. Still other children may prefer solitude.

What Are Theories of Child Development? Why Do We Have Them?

Child development is a scientific enterprise. Like other scientists, developmentalists seek to describe, explain, predict, and influence the events they study. They attempt to describe and explain behaviour in terms of concepts such as heredity, perception, language, learning, cognition, emotion, socialization, and gender roles. For example, we may describe learning as a process in which behaviour changes as a result of experience. We can be more specific and describe instances of learning in which children memorize the alphabet through repetition or acquire gymnastic skills through practice. We may explain how learning occurs in terms of rules or principles that govern learning. Thus, we might explain the trainer's use of words such as "fine" and "good" as *reinforcers* that provide the gymnast with positive feedback.

Questions: What are theories? Why do we have them? **Theories** are related sets of statements about events. When possible, descriptive terms and concepts are interwoven into theories. Theories are based on certain assumptions about behaviour, such as Watson's assumption that training outweighs talents and abilities or Gesell's assumption that the unfolding of maturational tendencies holds sway. Theories allow us to derive explanations and predictions. Many developmental theories combine statements about psychological concepts (such as learning and motivation), behaviour (such as reading or problem solving), and anatomical structures or biological processes (such as maturation of the nervous system). For instance, children's ability to learn to read is influenced by their motivation, attention span, perceptual development—and also by biological processes in the brain.

A satisfactory theory allows us to make predictions. A theory concerning the development of gender roles, for example, should allow us to predict the circumstances under which children will acquire stereotypical feminine or masculine gender-typed behaviour patterns. A broadly satisfying, comprehensive theory should have a wide range of applicability. A broad theory of the development of gender roles might apply to children from different cultural and racial backgrounds and, perhaps, to children with a homosexual orientation, as well as to those with a heterosexual orientation. If observations cannot be explained by or predicted from a theory, we may need to revise or replace the theory.

Useful theories enable researchers to influence events. This does not mean that developmentalists seek to make children do their bidding—as if they were puppets on strings. Instead, it means that useful theories help developmental professionals consult with parents, teachers, nurses, and children themselves to promote the welfare of children. Psychologists may summarize and interpret theory and research on the effects of daycare to help daycare workers provide an optimal child-care environment. Teachers may use learning theory to help children learn to read and write. In each case, the professional is influencing children, but with the benefit of the children in mind and also, ultimately, with the understanding and approval of parents. Let us consider various theoretical approaches to child development.

theory A formulation of relationships underlying observed events. A theory involves assumptions and logically derived explanations and predictions.

The Psychoanalytic Perspective

According to the psychoanalytic perspective, much—much!—goes on beneath the surface. A number of theories fall within the psychoanalytic perspective. Each one owes its origin to Sigmund Freud and views children—and adults—as caught in conflict. Early in development, the conflict is between the child and the world outside. The expression of basic drives, such as sex and aggression, conflict with parental expectations, social rules, moral codes, even laws. However, the external limits—parental demands and social rules—are brought inside. That is, they are *internalized.* Once this happens, the conflict actually takes place between opposing *inner* forces. The child's observable behaviour and inmost thoughts and emotions all reflect the outcomes of these hidden battles.

In this section, we explore Freud's theory of psychosexual development and Erik Erikson's theory of psychosocial development. Each is a **stage theory.** That is, each theory sees children as developing through distinct periods of life. Each suggests that the child's experiences during early stages affect the child's emotional balance and social adjustment.

Question: What is Freud's psychoanalytic theory of child development?

stage theory A theory of development characterized by hypothesizing the existence of distinct periods of life. Stages follow one another in an orderly sequence.

Sigmund Freud's Theory of Psychosexual Development

Sigmund Freud (1856–1939) was a mass of contradictions. He has been lauded as the greatest thinker of the twentieth century, the most profound of psychologists. He has been criticized as overrated, even called a "false and faithless prophet." He preached liberal views on sexuality but was himself a model of sexual restraint. He invented a popular form of psychotherapy but experienced lifelong psychological problems such as migraine headaches, fainting under stress, hatred of the telephone, and an addiction to cigars. He smoked twenty cigars a day and could not or would not break the habit, even after he developed cancer of the jaw. Yet few people have shaped our thinking about human nature as deeply.

Freud formulated the psychoanalytic theory of development and the form of psychotherapy called *psychoanalysis.* He focused on the emotional and social development of children and on the origins of psychological traits such as dependence, obsessive neatness, and vanity. Let us dive into Freud's theory. (*Diving* is a good metaphor because Freud believed that most of the human mind lies beneath consciousness.)

Freud labelled those parts that lie beneath the surface of conscious awareness the preconscious and unconscious parts of the mind. The **preconscious** mind is near the surface. It contains ideas and feelings that are presently beyond awareness, but children and adults can become aware or conscious of them simply by focusing attention on them. An example might be a teacher's name. The **unconscious** mind contains genetic instincts and urges such as hunger, thirst, sexuality, and aggression that we only partly perceive because of the depth of their fury.

The parts of the human personality are intense and often at war with one another; these parts—the *id,* the *ego,* and the *superego*—all try to prevail. We cannot see the id, ego, and superego, which Freud called *psychic structures* rather than *physical structures.* But Freud inferred their presence from the behaviour of the adults he saw in therapy. The only psychic structure present at birth is the id. The id is unconscious and demands instant gratification of biological drives. The ego begins to develop when children learn to obtain gratification for themselves, without screaming or crying. The ego curbs the appetites of the id and makes plans that are in keeping with social conventions so that a person can find gratification yet avoid the disapproval of others. The superego develops throughout infancy and early childhood. It brings inward the wishes and morals of the child's caregivers and other members of the community. Throughout the remainder of the child's life, the superego will monitor the intentions and behaviour of the ego and hand down judgments of right and wrong. If the child misbehaves, the superego will flood him or her with guilt and shame.

According to Freud, childhood is dominated by four distinct stages. If a child receives too little or too much gratification during a stage, the child can become *fixated* in that

© Bettmann / CORBIS

Sigmund Freud
Freud is the originator of psychoanalytic theory. He proposed five stages of psychosexual development and emphasized the importance of biological factors in the development of personality.

preconscious In psychoanalytic theory, that which is not in awareness but is capable of being brought into awareness by focusing of attention.

unconscious In psychoanalytic theory, that which is not available to awareness by simple focusing of attention.

stage. For example, during the first year of life, which Freud termed the *oral stage*, "oral" activities such as sucking and biting bring pleasure and gratification. If the child is weaned early or breast-fed too long, the child may become fixated on oral activities such as nail biting or smoking, or may even show a "biting wit."

Truth or Fiction Revisited: Actually, however, there is no research evidence that nail biting and smoking cigarettes are signs of conflict experienced during early childhood, even though these beliefs are consistent with Freudian theory.

In the second stage, called the *anal stage*, gratification is obtained through control and elimination of waste products. Excessively strict or permissive toilet training can lead to the development of anal-retentive traits, such as perfectionism and neatness, or anal-expulsive traits such as sloppiness and carelessness. In the third stage, the *phallic stage*, parent-child conflict may develop over masturbation, which many parents treat with punishment and threats. It is normal for children to develop strong sexual attachments to the parent of the other sex during the phallic stage and to begin to view the parent of the same sex as a rival. Girls in this stage may express the wish to marry their fathers when they grow up. Boys are likely to have similar designs on their mothers.

By age five or six, Freud believed, children enter a *latency stage* during which sexual feelings remain unconscious, children turn to schoolwork and typically prefer playmates of their own sex. The final stage of psychosexual development, the *genital stage*, begins with the biological changes that usher in adolescence. Adolescents generally desire sexual gratification through intercourse with a member of the other sex. Freud believed that oral or anal stimulation, masturbation, and male-male or female-female sexual activity are immature forms of sexual conduct that reflect fixations at early stages of development.

Evaluation Freud's theory has had tremendous appeal and was a major contribution to twentieth-century thought. It is one of the richest theories of development, explaining the childhood origins of many behaviours and traits, and stimulating research on attachment, development of gender roles, moral development, and identification. Freud's views about the anal stage have influenced child-care workers to recommend that toilet training not be started too early or handled punitively. His emphasis on the emotional needs of children has influenced educators to be more sensitive to the possible emotional reasons behind a child's misbehaviour.

Yet Freud's work has been criticized on many grounds. For one thing, Freud developed his theory on the basis of contacts with patients (mostly women) who were experiencing emotional problems (Hergenhahn, 2005). He also concluded that most of his patients' problems originated in childhood conflicts. It is possible that he might have found less evidence of childhood conflict if his sample had consisted of less troubled individuals. He was also dealing with recollections of his patients' pasts, rather than observing children directly. Such recollections are subject to errors in memory. Freud may also have inadvertently guided patients into expressing ideas that confirmed his views.

Some of Freud's own disciples, including Erik Erikson and Karen Horney, believe that Freud placed too much emphasis on basic instincts and unconscious motives. They argue that people are motivated not only by drives such as sex and aggression but also by learning, social relationships, and conscious desires to achieve, have esthetic experiences, and help others.

Nor has Freud's theory of **psychosexual development** escaped criticism. Children may begin to masturbate as early as the first year of life, rather than in the phallic stage. As parents can testify from observing their children play doctor, sexuality in the "latency stage" is not as latent as Freud believed. Freud's view of female development and gender-role behaviour reflects the ignorance and male-centred prejudice of his times.

psychosexual development
In psychoanalytic theory, the process by which libidinal energy is expressed through different erogenous zones during different stages of development.

Renate Horney

Karen Horney
Horney, a follower of Freud, argued that Freud placed too much emphasis on sexual and biological determinants of behaviour while neglecting the importance of social factors.

Harvard University Archives

Erik Erikson

There has been a historical prejudice against self-assertive, competent women (Worell & Johnson, 2001). Freud's views thus reflected the cultural belief of his times that motherhood and family life were the proper venues of fulfillment for women.

Once we have catalogued our criticisms of Freud's views, what is left? A number of things. Freud pointed out that behaviour is determined and not arbitrary. He pointed out that childhood experiences can have far-reaching effects. He noted that we have defensive ways of looking at the world, that our cognitive processes can be distorted by our efforts to defend ourselves against anxiety and guilt. If these ideas no longer impress us as unique or innovative, it is largely because they have been so widely accepted since Freud gave voice to them.

Erik Erikson's Theory of Psychosocial Development

Question: How does Erikson's theory differ from Freud's? Erik Erikson (1902–1994) modified and expanded Freud's theory. Erikson's psychoanalytic theory, like Freud's, focuses on the development of the emotional life and psychological traits—on social adjustment. But Erikson also focuses on the development of self-identity. Out of the

Concept Review 1.1 — Comparison of Freud's and Erikson's Stages of Development

Age	Freud's Stages of Psychosexual Development	Erikson's Stages of Psychosocial Development
Birth to 1 year	**Oral Stage.** Gratification derives from oral activities, such as sucking. Fixation leads to development of oral traits such as dependence, depression, gullibility.	**Trust versus Mistrust.** The developmental task is to come to trust the key caregivers, primarily the mother, and the environment. It is desirable for infants to connect their environment with inner feelings of satisfaction and contentment.
About 1 to 3 years	**Anal Stage.** Gratification derives from anal activities involving elimination. Fixation leads to development of anal-retentive traits (e.g., excessive neatness) or anal-expulsive traits (e.g., sloppiness).	**Autonomy versus Shame and Doubt.** The developmental task is to develop the desire to make choices and the self-control to regulate one's behaviour so that choices can be actualized.
About 3 to 6 years	**Phallic Stage.** Gratification derives from stimulation of the genital region. Oedipal and Electra complexes emerge and are resolved. Fixation leads to development of phallic traits, such as vanity.	**Initiative versus Guilt.** The developmental task is to add initiative—planning and attacking—to choice. The preschooler is on the move and becomes proactive.
About 6 to 12 years	**Latency Stage.** Sexual impulses are suppressed, allowing the child to focus on development of social and technological skills.	**Industry versus Inferiority.** The developmental task is to become absorbed in the development and implementation of skills, to master the basics of technology, to become productive.

chaos of his own identity problems, Erikson forged a personally meaningful life pattern, and his theory of development differs dramatically from that of his intellectual forebear, Sigmund Freud. To Erikson, development is not the outcome of environmental forces and intrapsychic conflict. Erikson's social relationships had been more crucial determinants of his development than sexual or aggressive instinct were. Therefore, Erikson speaks of **psychosocial development** rather than of *psychosexual development*. Furthermore, it seemed to Erikson that he had developed his own personality through a series of conscious and purposeful acts. Consequently, he places greater emphasis on the ego and on one's ability to actively deal with life's conflicts than Freud did.

Erikson (1963) extended Freud's five developmental stages to eight to include changing concerns throughout adulthood. Rather than label his stages after parts of the body, Erikson labelled his stages after the **life crises** that the child (and later, the adult) might encounter during that stage. Erikson's stages are compared with Freud's in Concept Review 1.1.

psychosocial development Erikson's theory, which emphasizes the importance of social relationships and conscious choice throughout the eight stages of development.

life crisis An internal conflict that attends each stage of psychosocial development. Positive resolution of early life crises sets the stage for positive resolution of subsequent life crises.

Age	Freud's Stages of Psychosexual Development	Erikson's Stages of Psychosocial Development
Adolescence	**Genital Stage.** Reappearance of sexual impulses, with gratification sought through sexual relations with an adult of the other sex.	**Identity versus Role Diffusion.** The developmental task is to associate one's skills and social roles with the development of career goals. More broadly, the development of identity refers to a sense of who one is and what one believes in.
Young adulthood		**Intimacy versus Isolation.** The developmental task is to commit oneself to another person, to engage in a mature sexual love.
Middle adulthood		**Generativity versus Stagnation.** The developmental task is to appreciate the opportunity to "give back." Not only are generative people creative, but they also give encouragement and guidance to the younger generation, which may include their own children.
Late adulthood		**Ego Integrity versus Despair.** The developmental task is to achieve wisdom and dignity in the face of declining physical abilities. Ego integrity also means accepting the time and place of one's own life cycle.

Erikson proposed that our social relationships and our levels of physical maturation give each stage its character. For example, the parent-child relationship and the infant's utter dependence and helplessness are responsible for the nature of the earliest stages of development. The six-year-old's capacity to profit from the school setting reflects the cognitive capacities to learn to read and to understand the rudiments of mathematics and the physical and perceptual capacities to sit relatively still and focus on schoolwork.

According to Erikson, early experiences exert a continued influence on future development. With proper parental support during the early years, most children resolve early life crises productively. Successful resolution of each crisis bolsters their sense of identity—of who they are and what they stand for—and their expectation of future success.

Stages of Psychosocial Development Each stage in Erikson's theory of psychosocial development carries a specific developmental task. Successful completion of this task depends heavily on the nature of the child's social relationships at each stage. The stages are described in Concept Review 1.1.

Erikson's views, like Freud's, have influenced child rearing, early childhood education, and therapy with children. For example, Erikson's views about an adolescent identity crisis have entered the popular culture and have affected the way many parents and teachers deal with teenagers. Some schools help students master the crisis by means of life-adjustment courses and study units on self-understanding in social studies and literature classes.

Evaluation Erikson's views have received much praise and much criticism. They are appealing in that they emphasize the importance of human consciousness and choice and minimize the role—and the threat—of dark, poorly perceived urges. They are also appealing in that they paint us as prosocial and giving, whereas Freud portrayed us as selfish and needing to be forced into adherence to social norms. Erikson has been praised as well for presenting a unified view of development throughout the life span.

There is also some empirical support for the Eriksonian view that positive outcomes of early life crises help put children on the path to positive development. For example, infants who come to trust in their parents are more likely to achieve autonomy and ego identity later on (Hoegh & Bourgeois, 2002).

The Learning Perspective: Behavioural and Social Cognitive Theories

During the 1930s, psychologists derived an ingenious method for helping five- and six-year-old children overcome bed-wetting from the behavioural perspective. Most children at this age wake up and go to the bathroom when their bladders are full. But bed wetters sleep through bladder tension and reflexively urinate in bed. The psychologists' objective was to teach sleeping children with full bladders to wake up rather than wet their beds.

The psychologists placed a special pad beneath the sleeping child. When the pad was wet, an electrical circuit was closed, causing a bell to ring and the sleeping child to waken. After several repetitions, most children learned to wake up before they wet the pad. How? Through a technique called *classical conditioning*, which is explained in this section.

The so-called bell-and-pad method for bed-wetting is an exotic example of the application of learning theory in child development. However, most applications of learning theory to development are found in everyday events. For example, children

identity crisis According to Erikson, a period of inner conflict during which one examines one's values and makes decisions about one's life roles.

behaviour modification The systematic application of principles of learning to change problem behaviours or encourage desired behaviours.

classical conditioning A simple form of learning in which one stimulus comes to bring forth the response usually brought forth by a second stimulus by being paired repeatedly with the second stimulus.

stimulus A change in the environment that leads to a change in behaviour.

elicit (i-LI-sut) To bring forth; evoke.

are not born knowing what the letters *A* and *B* sound like or how to tie their shoes. They learn these things. They are not born knowing how to do gymnastics. Nor are they born understanding the meanings of abstract concepts such as "big," "blue," "decency," and "justice." All these skills and knowledge are learned.

In this section, we discuss learning theories and how they are involved in child development. We will see that children are capable of mechanical learning by association (as in the bell-and-pad method), but we will also see that children are capable of intentional learning. Children purposefully engage in rote learning and trial-and-error learning. They purposefully observe and imitate the behaviour of other people. We will also see how the principles of learning have been used in **behaviour modification** to help children overcome behaviour disorders or cope with adjustment problems. Let us begin with John B. Watson's theory of behaviourism.

Behaviourism

Question: What is the theory of behaviourism? John B. Watson argued that scientists must address observable behaviour only. A scientific approach to development must focus on the observable behaviour of humans and not on thoughts, fantasies, and other mental images.

Let us see how two types of learning—classical conditioning and operant conditioning—have contributed to behaviourism and the understanding of development. Then we will consider a more recently developed theory of learning that deals with children's cognitive processes and their overt behaviour—social cognitive theory.

Classical conditioning is a simple form of learning in which an originally neutral **stimulus** comes to bring forth, or **elicit,** the response usually brought forth by a second stimulus as a result of being paired repeatedly with the second stimulus. Like many other important scientific discoveries, classical conditioning was discovered by accident. Russian physiologist Ivan Pavlov (1849–1936) was researching salivation in dogs when he discovered that reflexes can be learned, or conditioned, through association. Pavlov's dogs began salivating in response to clinking food trays, because clinking had been paired repeatedly with the arrival of food. Pavlov then carried out experiments in which he conditioned his dogs to salivate to the sound of a bell, which had been paired with food.

In the bell-and-pad method for bed-wetting, psychologists repeatedly pair tension in the children's bladders with a stimulus that wakes them up (the bell). The children learn to respond to the bladder tension as if it were a bell—that is, they wake up (see Figure 1.1).

The bell is an unlearned or **unconditioned stimulus** (UCS). Waking up in response to the bell is an unlearned or **unconditioned response** (UCR). Bladder tension is at first a meaningless, or neutral, stimulus (see Figure 1.1). Then,

unconditioned stimulus (UCS) A stimulus that elicits a response from an organism without learning.

unconditioned response (UCR) An unlearned response; a response to an unconditioned stimulus.

Ferdinand Hamburger Jr. Archives of Johns Hopkins University

John B. Watson

Watson is shown here testing the grasping reflex of an infant. As a behaviourist, Watson believed that the environment is all-important in shaping development.

Figure 1.1

Schematic Representation of Classical Conditioning

Before conditioning, the bell elicits waking up. Bladder tension, a neutral stimulus, does not elicit waking up. During conditioning, bladder tension always precedes urination, which in turn causes the bell to ring. After conditioning, bladder tension has become a conditioned stimulus (CS) that elicits waking up, which is the conditioned response (CR).

POWER VISUAL! See your student companion website for an interactive version of Figure 1.1.

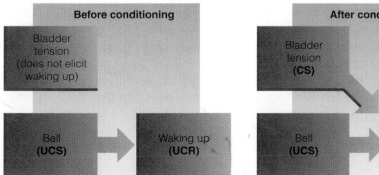

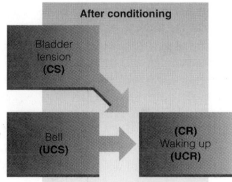

conditioned stimulus (CS)
A previously neutral stimulus that elicits a response because it has been paired repeatedly with a stimulus that already elicited that response.

conditioned response (CR)
A learned response to a previously neutral stimulus.

B. F. Skinner
Skinner, a behaviourist, developed principles of operant conditioning and focused on the role of reinforcement of behaviour.

operant conditioning   A simple form of learning in which an organism learns to engage in behaviour that is reinforced.

through repeated association with the bell, bladder tension becomes a learned or **conditioned stimulus** (CS) for waking up. Waking up in response to bladder tension (the CS) is a learned or **conditioned response** (CR). Behaviourists argue that a good deal of emotional learning is acquired through classical conditioning. For example, touching a hot stove is painful, and one or two incidents may elicit a fear response when a child looks at a stove or considers touching it again.

In classical conditioning, children learn to associate stimuli so that a response made to one is then made to the other. But in **operant conditioning** (a different kind of conditioning), children learn to "operate on," or manipulate, the environment—that is, to engage in certain behaviour—because of the effects of that behaviour. B. F. Skinner introduced one of the central concepts of operant conditioning—the concept of **reinforcement.** Reinforcers are stimuli that increase the frequency of the behaviour they follow. Most children learn to adjust their behaviour to conform to social codes and rules to earn reinforcers such as the attention and approval of their parents and teachers. Other children, ironically, may learn to misbehave, since misbehaviour also draws attention.

In operant conditioning, it matters little how the first desired response is earned. The child can happen on it by chance, as in random behaviour, or the child can be physically or verbally guided. An adult may place his or her hand over a two-year-old child's to show the child how to turn the crank on a music box to play a tune. The child is reinforced by the sound of music, and after training he or she will be able to turn the crank alone. Various behaviours—such as vocalizing, smiling, and looking at objects—have been conditioned in infants (Gewirtz & Pelaez-Nogueras, 1992).

How do we know whether a stimulus is a reinforcer? Any stimulus that increases the frequency of the responses preceding it serves as a reinforcer. Most of the time, food, social approval, and attention serve as reinforcers.

Skinner distinguished between positive and negative reinforcers. **Positive reinforcers** increase the frequency of behaviours when they are *applied*. Food and approval usually serve as positive reinforcers. **Negative reinforcers** increase the frequency of behaviours when they are *removed*. Fear acts as a negative reinforcer in that its removal increases the frequency of the behaviours preceding it. For example, fear of failure is removed when students study for a quiz. Figure 1.2 compares positive and negative reinforcers.

Extinction results from repeated performance of operant behaviour without reinforcement. After a number of trials, the operant behaviour is no longer shown. In many cases, children's temper tantrums and crying at bedtime can be extinguished within a few days by parents' simply staying out of the bedroom after the children have been put to bed. Previously, parental attention and companionship

Figure 1.2
Positive versus Negative Reinforcers

All reinforcers *increase* the frequency of behaviour. In these examples, teacher approval functions as a positive reinforcer when students study harder because of it. Teacher *disapproval* functions as a negative reinforcer when its *removal* increases the frequency of studying.

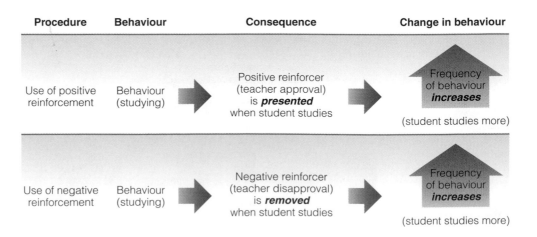

Procedure	Behaviour	Consequence	Change in behaviour
Use of positive reinforcement	Behaviour (studying)	Positive reinforcer (teacher approval) **is presented** when student studies	Frequency of behaviour *increases* (student studies more)
Use of negative reinforcement	Behaviour (studying)	Negative reinforcer (teacher disapproval) **is removed** when student studies	Frequency of behaviour *increases* (student studies more)

had reinforced the tantrums and crying. When the reinforcement of the problem behaviour was removed, the behaviour was eliminated.

Punishments are aversive events that suppress or *decrease* the frequency of the behaviour they follow. (Figure 1.3 compares negative reinforcers with punishments.) Punishing events can be physical (e.g., spanking) or verbal (e.g., scolding or criticizing) or may involve removal of privileges. Punishments, like rewards, can influence the probability of the behaviour. Punishments can rapidly suppress undesirable behaviour and may be warranted in emergencies, such as when a child tries to run out into the street. But many learning theorists agree that punishment is usually undesirable, especially in rearing children, for reasons that include the following:

- Punishment does not in itself suggest an alternative, acceptable form of behaviour.
- Punishment tends to suppress undesirable behaviour only when its delivery is guaranteed. It does not take children long to learn that they can "get away with murder" with one parent or one teacher but not with another.
- Punished children may withdraw from the situation. Severely punished children may run away, cut class, or drop out of school.
- Punishment can create anger and hostility. After being spanked by their parents, children may hit smaller siblings or destroy objects in the home.
- Punishment may generalize too far. The child who is punished severely for bad table manners may stop eating altogether. Overgeneralization is more likely to occur when children do not know exactly why they are being punished and when they have not been shown acceptable alternative behaviours.
- Punishment may be imitated as a way of solving problems or coping with stress. Children learn by observing others. Even though children may not immediately perform the behaviour they observe, they may do so later on, even as adults, when their circumstances are similar to those of the person they observed. For example, many child abusers and abusers of intimate partners were harshly punished by their own parents (Ertem, Leventhal, & Dobbs, 2000; Swinford, DeMaris, Cernkovich, & Giordano, 2000).

It is usually preferable to reward children for desirable behaviours than to punish them for unwanted behaviour. By ignoring their misbehaviour or by giving a **time-out** from positive reinforcement, we can consistently avoid reinforcing children's misbehaviour.

We can teach children complex behaviours by **shaping,** or at first reinforcing small steps toward the behavioural goals. In teaching a two-year-old child to put on her own coat, it helps to praise her for first trying to stick her arm into a sleeve on a couple of occasions, then to praise her for actually getting her arm into the sleeve, and so on.

reinforcement The process of providing stimuli following a response, which has the effect of increasing the frequency of the response.

positive reinforcer A reinforcer that, when applied, increases the frequency of a response.

negative reinforcer A reinforcer that, when removed, increases the frequency of a response.

extinction The cessation of a response that is performed in the absence of reinforcement.

punishment An unpleasant stimulus that suppresses behaviour.

time-out A behaviour-modification technique in which a child who misbehaves is temporarily placed in a drab, restrictive environment in which reinforcement is unavailable.

shaping A procedure for teaching complex behaviour patterns by means of reinforcing small steps toward the target behaviour.

Procedure	Behaviour	Consequence	Change in behaviour
Use of negative reinforcement	Behaviour (studying)	Negative reinforcer (teacher disapproval) is ***removed*** when student studies	Frequency of behaviour ***increases*** (student studies more)
Use of punishment	Behaviour (talking in class)	Punishment (detention) is ***presented*** when student talks in class	Frequency of behaviour ***decreases*** (student talks less in class)

Figure 1.3
Negative Reinforcers versus Punishments

Both negative reinforcers and punishments tend to be aversive stimuli. However, reinforcers *increase* the frequency of behaviour. Punishments *decrease* the frequency of behaviour. Negative reinforcers increase the frequency of behaviour when they are *removed*.

 **POWER VISUALS!**
See your student companion website for an interactive version of Figures 1.2 and 1.3.

socialization A process through which children are encouraged to adopt socially desirable behaviour patterns through a system of guidance, rewards, and punishments.

Operant conditioning is used every day in the **socialization** of young children. For example, as we will see in Chapter 10, parents and peers influence children to acquire gender-appropriate behaviours through the elaborate use of rewards and punishments. Thus, boys may ignore other boys when they play with dolls and housekeeping toys but play with boys when they use transportation toys.

Many studies have found that when teachers praise and attend to appropriate behaviour and ignore misbehaviour, study behaviour and classroom performance improve while disruptive and aggressive behaviours decrease (McIlvane & Dube, 2003; Takahashi & Sugiyama, 2003). Teachers frequently use time-out from positive reinforcement, placing children in drab, restrictive environments for a specified time period, usually about ten minutes, when they behave disruptively. When isolated, they cannot earn the attention of peers or teachers, and no reinforcing activities are present.

It may strike you that these techniques are not new. Perhaps we all know parents who have ignored their children's misbehaviour and have heard of teachers making children sit facing the corner. What is novel is the focus on (1) avoiding punishment and (2) being consistent so that undesirable behaviour is not reinforced.

Social Cognitive Theory

Behaviourists tend to limit their discussions of human learning to the classical and operant conditioning of observable behaviours. They theorize that complex behaviour can be explained as the additive results of numerous associations of stimuli (classical conditioning) or reinforcements (operant conditioning).

Question: How does social cognitive theory differ from behaviourism? Adherents to **social cognitive theory**,[1] such as Canadian-born Albert Bandura (1986, 2002; Bandura & Locke, 2003; Bandura, Barbaranelli, Vittorio Caprara, & Pastorelli, 2001), have shown that much of children's learning occurs by observing parents, teachers, other children, and even characters on TV. Children may need some practice to refine their skills, but they can acquire basic know-how through observation. Children can also let these skills *lie latent*. For example, children (and adults) are not likely to imitate aggressive behaviour unless they are provoked and believe that they are more likely to be rewarded than punished for aggressive behaviour.

social cognitive theory A cognitively oriented learning theory that emphasizes observational learning in the determining of behaviour.

In the view of behaviourists, learning occurs by mechanical conditioning. There is no reference to thought processes. In social cognitive theory, by contrast, cognition plays a central role. Social cognitive theorists believe that learning alters children's **mental representation** of the environment and influences their belief in their ability to change the environment. In social cognitive theory, children choose whether or not to show the behaviours they have learned, and they acquire behaviours without necessarily being directly reinforced. Their values and expectations of reinforcement also affect whether they will imitate the behaviour they observe.

mental representations The mental forms that a real object or event can take, which may differ from one another. (Successful problem solving is aided by accurate mental representation of the elements of the problem.)

Social cognitive theorists see children as active, believing that they intentionally seek out or create environments in which reinforcers are available. As an example of how children's behaviour and characteristics create a reinforcing environment, consider children who have artistic ability. They may develop their skill by taking art lessons and by modelling the behaviours of art teachers. In doing so, they create an environment of social reinforcement in the form of praise from others. This reinforcement, in turn, influences the children's view of themselves as good artists.

observational learning The acquisition of expectations and skills by means of observing others.

[1] The name of this theory remains somewhat in flux. It was originally termed social-learning theory. More recently, it has been referred to as social cognitive theory and sometimes as cognitive social theory. Because a major proponent of this view, Albert Bandura, refers to it as social cognitive theory in recent writings, we have chosen to use this terminology.

Observational learning may account for most of human learning. It occurs when children observe how parents cook, clean, or repair a broken appliance. It takes place when children watch teachers solve problems on the blackboard or hear them speak a foreign language. Observational learning does not occur because of direct reinforcement. Children can learn without engaging in overt responses at all. Learning will occur so long as children pay attention to the behaviour of others. Once children are a few years old, observational learning becomes intentional. Children appear to imitate those who show certain positive characteristics. In social cognitive theory, the people after whom children choose to pattern their own behaviour are termed *models*.

Truth or Fiction Revisited: Yes, some theorists, including social cognitive theorists, contend that children actively strive to understand and take charge of their worlds. Other theorists, including behaviourists, argue that children respond passively to environmental stimulation. We will see that cognitive-developmental theorists side with social cognitive theorists on this matter.

Evaluation of Learning Theories

Learning theories have done a fine job of allowing us to describe, explain, predict, and influence several aspects of children's behaviours. Psychologists and educators have developed many innovative applications of conditioning and social cognitive theory. The use of the bell-and-pad method for bed-wetting is an example of behaviour modification that probably would not have been derived from any other theoretical approach. Behaviour modification has been used in innovative ways to deal with autistic children, self-injurious children, and children displaying temper tantrums and conduct disorders. Many of the teaching approaches used in educational TV shows are based on learning theory.

Despite the demonstrated effectiveness of behaviour modification, learning-theory approaches to child development have been criticized in several ways. First, there is the theoretical question of whether the conditioning process in children is mechanical or whether it changes the ways that children mentally represent, or perceive, the environment. In addition, learning theorists may have exaggerated the role of learning in development by underestimating the role of biological and maturational factors (Hergenhahn, 2005). Social cognitive theorists seem to be working on these issues. For example, they place more value on cognition and view children as being active, not as merely reacting mechanically to stimuli. Now let us turn to theories that place cognition at the heart of development.

The Cognitive Perspective

Psychologists with a cognitive perspective focus on children's mental processes. They investigate the ways in which children perceive and interpret the world, how they develop thought and logic, how they develop the ability to solve problems. Cognitive psychologists, in short, attempt to study all those things we refer to as the *mind*. The cognitive perspective has many faces. One is the **cognitive-developmental theory** advanced by the Swiss biologist Jean Piaget (1896–1980). Another is the information-processing theory.

Jean Piaget's Cognitive-Developmental Theory

During adolescence, Piaget studied philosophy, logic, and mathematics, but years later he completed his Ph.D. in biology. In 1920, he obtained a job at the Binet Institute in Paris, where research on intelligence tests was being conducted. Piaget tried out items on children in various age groups. The task was becoming boring until Piaget became intrigued by the children's *incorrect* answers. Another investigator might have shrugged them off and forgotten them, but young Piaget realized that there were methods to his

Albert Bandura
Bandura and other social cognitive theorists have shown that one way children learn is by observing others. Whereas behaviourists like John Watson and B. F. Skinner portrayed children as reactive to environmental stimuli, social cognitive theorists depict children as active learners who are capable of fashioning new environments.

Jean Piaget
Piaget's cognitive-developmental theory is a stage theory that focuses on the ways children adapt to the environment by mentally representing, or perceiving, the world and solving problems. Piaget's early training as a biologist led him to view children as mentally assimilating and accommodating of aspects of their environment.

cognitive-developmental theory The stage theory that holds that the child's abilities to mentally represent the world and solve problems unfold as a result of the interaction of experience and the maturation of neurological structures.

children's madness. The wrong answers seemed to reflect consistent, if illogical, cognitive processes. Piaget investigated these "wrong" answers by probing for the underlying patterns of thought that had led to them. He began to publish a series of articles on children's thought processes.

Piaget wrote dozens of books and scores of articles, but his work was almost unknown in English-speaking countries until the mid-1950s. For one thing, Piaget's writing is difficult to understand, even to native speakers of French. (One of Piaget's favourite jokes was that he had the advantage of *not* having to read Piaget.) For another, it took him years to formulate his ideas. Piaget's views were also quite different from those of other developmentalists. Psychology in England and the United States was dominated by behaviourism and psychoanalysis, and Piaget's writings had a biological-cognitive favour. They didn't fit the mould. Today the world of child development has been turned topsy-turvy, with many English-speaking developmentalists trying to fit their views to Piaget's.

Theorists have attempted to explain different types of events and have had different views of the basic nature of children. Behaviourists, such as John B. Watson, focus on the acquisition of overt behaviour. They see children as blank slates that are written upon by experience—as *reactors* to environmental stimulation, not as actors. Freud's psychoanalytic theory focuses on personality and emotional development. It portrays children as largely irrational and at the mercy of instinctive impulses—as driven creatures caught between sexual and aggressive urges and the stifling codes of parents and society.

Question: What are Jean Piaget's views on development? Piaget was concerned with how children form ideas, or mental representations of the world, and how they manipulate their concepts to plan changes in the external world. But Piaget, like the behaviourists, recognized that thoughts cannot be measured directly, and so he tried to link his views on children's mental processes to observable behaviour.

Piaget regarded maturing children as natural physicists who actively intend to learn about and take intellectual charge of their worlds. In the Piagetian view, children who squish their food and laugh enthusiastically are often acting as budding scientists. In addition to enjoying a response from parents, they are studying the texture and consistency of their food. (Parents, of course, often prefer that their children practise these experiments in the laboratory, not the dining room.)

Piaget's Basic Concepts Researchers tie concepts together in theoretical packages. Psychoanalysts integrate concepts such as *ego* and *anal traits* into principles that govern personality development. Behaviourists tie concepts such as *stimulus* and *reinforcement* into principles that govern processes of learning. Piaget tied together such concepts as *schemes, adaptation, assimilation, accommodation,* and *equilibration* to describe and explain cognitive development.

scheme According to Piaget, an action pattern or mental structure that is involved in the acquisition and organization of knowledge.

Piaget defines the **scheme** as a pattern of action or a mental structure that is involved in acquiring or organizing knowledge. According to Piaget, acting on the environment and acquiring knowledge occur simultaneously. As action patterns, schemes tend to be repeated and to occur in certain types of situations.

Among older children and adults, a scheme may be the inclusion of an object in a class. For example, the mammal class, or concept, includes a group of animals that are warm-blooded and nurse their young. The inclusion of cats, apes, buffalo, whales, and people in the mammal class involves a series of schemes that expand the child's knowledge of the natural world.

But schemes need not involve words. Babies, for example, are said to have sucking schemes, grasping schemes, and looking schemes. Newborn babies tend to suck things that are placed in their mouths, to grasp objects placed in their hands, and to visually track moving objects. Piaget would say that infants' schemes give meaning to the objects around them. Even in the first months of life, infants are responding to objects as "things I can suck" versus "things I can't suck," and as "things I can grasp" versus "things I can't grasp."

Adaptation refers to the interaction between the organism and the environment. This term reflects Piaget's early interest in biology. According to Piaget, all organisms adapt to their environment; it is a biological tendency. Adaptation consists of two complementary processes, *assimilation* and *accommodation,* that occur throughout life.

The concept of **assimilation** also has its roots in biology. In biology, assimilation is the process by which food is digested and converted into the tissues that compose an animal. Cognitive assimilation refers to the process by which someone responds to new objects or events according to existing schemes or ways of organizing knowledge. Infants, for example, usually try to place new objects in their mouths to suck, feel, or explore them. Piaget would say that the child is assimilating (fitting) a new toy or object into the sucking-an-object activity or scheme. Similarly, two-year-olds who refer to sheep and cows as "doggies" or "bowwows" can be said to be assimilating these new animals into the doggy (or bowwow) scheme. As they develop, children adapt by acquiring more precise schemes for assimilating these animals.

Sometimes, a novel object or event cannot be made to fit (i.e., it cannot be assimilated into an existing scheme). In that case, the scheme may be changed or a new scheme may be created to incorporate the new item. This process is called **accommodation.** Accommodation is also a biological term, meaning a change in structure that permits an organism to adjust or adapt to a novel object or event, to a new source of stimulation. Consider the sucking reflex. Within the first month of life, infants modify sucking behaviour as a result of experience sucking various objects. The nipple on the bottle is sucked one way, the thumb in a different way. Infants accommodate further by rejecting objects that are too large, that taste bad, or that are of the wrong texture or temperature. They learn that certain things are not to be sucked and may experiment with new ways to relate to them.

Piaget theorized that when children can assimilate new events to existing schemes, they are in a state of cognitive harmony, or equilibrium. When something that does not fit happens along, their state of equilibrium is disturbed and they may try to accommodate to it. The process of restoring equilibrium is termed **equilibration.** Piaget believed that the attempt to restore equilibrium is the source of intellectual motivation and lies at the heart of the natural curiosity of the child.

Piaget's Stages of Cognitive Development

Piaget (1963) hypothesized that children's cognitive processes develop in an orderly sequence, or series, of stages. As with motor development, some children may be more advanced than others at particular ages, but the developmental sequence remains the same. Piaget identified four major stages of cognitive development: *sensorimotor, preoperational, concrete operational,* and *formal operational.* These stages are described in Concept Review 1.2 and are discussed in subsequent chapters.

Piaget believed that the cognitive developments of each stage, and of the substages within them, are universal. One reason for this is that cognitive development largely depends on the maturation of the brain, and, assuming minimal nourishment, the course of brain maturation is similar from one child to the next. Second, cognitive developments are based on children's interactions with their environments. Although no two children share exactly the same environment, the broad realities are compelling enough that practically all children must learn to cope with them. For example, gravity affects us all, so all children have the opportunity to learn that dropped objects move downward. Children from different cultures may reach for

adaptation According to Piaget, the interaction between the organism and the environment. It consists of two processes: assimilation and accommodation.

assimilation According to Piaget, the incorporation of new events or knowledge into existing schemes.

accommodation According to Piaget, the modification of existing schemes to permit the incorporation of new events or knowledge.

equilibration The creation of an equilibrium, or balance, between assimilation and accommodation as a way of incorporating new events or knowledge.

different objects, but all normally learn that reaching for things enables them to touch or grasp them.

Because Piaget's theory focuses on cognitive development, its applications are primarily in educational settings. Teachers following Piaget's views would engage the child actively in solving problems. They would gear instruction to the child's developmental level and offer activities that challenge the child to advance to the next level. For example, five-year-olds learn primarily through play and direct sensory contact with the environment. Early formal instruction using workbooks and paper may be less effective in this age group (Crain, 2000).

Evaluation Many researchers, using a variety of methods, have found that Piaget may have underestimated the ages when children are capable of doing certain things. It also appears that cognitive skills may develop more gradually than Piaget thought and not in distinct stages. Here, let it suffice to note that Piaget presented us with a view of children that is different from the psychoanalytic and behaviourist views, and he provided a strong theoretical foundation for researchers concerned with sequences in children's cognitive development.

Concept Review 1.2 Jean Piaget's Stages of Cognitive Development

Stage	Approximate Age	Comments	
Sensorimotor	Birth–2 years	At first, the child lacks language and does not use symbols or mental representations of objects. In time, reflexive responding ends, and intentional behaviour—as in making interesting stimulation last—begins. The child develops the object concept and acquires the basics of language.	
Preoperational	2–7 years	The child begins to represent the world mentally, but thought is egocentric. The child does not focus on two aspects of a situation at once and therefore lacks conservation. The child shows animism, artificialism, and objective responsibility for wrongdoing.	
Concrete operational	7–12 years	Logical mental actions—called operations—begin. The child develops conservation concepts, can adopt the viewpoints of others, can classify objects in series, and shows comprehension of basic relational concepts (such as one object being larger or heavier than another).	
Formal operational	12 years and older	Mature, adult thought emerges. Thinking is characterized by deductive logic, consideration of various possibilities (mental trial and error), abstract thought, and the formation and testing of hypotheses.	

Information-Processing Theory

Another face of the cognitive perspective is information processing (Flavell, Miller, & Miller, 2002; Siegler & Alibali, 2005). ***Question: What is information-processing theory?*** Psychological thought has long been influenced by the status of the physical sciences of the day. For example, Freud's psychoanalytic theory was related to the development of thermodynamics in the nineteenth century. Many of today's cognitive psychologists are influenced by concepts of computer science. Computers process information to solve problems. Information is encoded so that it can be accepted as input and then fed ("inputted") into the computer. Then it is placed in working memory (RAM) while it is manipulated. The information can be stored more permanently on a storage device, such as a hard drive or a CD. Many psychologists speak of people as having working or short-term memory (corresponding to RAM) and a more permanent long-term memory (corresponding to storage). If information has been placed in long-term memory, it must be retrieved before we can work on it again. To retrieve information from computer storage, we must know the code or name for the data file and the rules for retrieving data files. Similarly, note psychologists, we must have appropriate cues to retrieve information from our own long-term memories, or the information is lost to us.

Thus, many cognitive psychologists focus on information processing in people—the processes by which information is encoded (input), stored (in long-term memory), retrieved (placed in short-term memory), and manipulated to solve problems (output). Our strategies for solving problems are sometimes referred to as our "mental programs" or "software." In this computer metaphor, our brains are the "hardware" that runs our mental programs. Our brains—consisting of billions of neurons that can be combined in multiple ways—become the most "personal" computers.

When psychologists who study information processing contemplate the cognitive development of children, they are likely to talk in terms of the size of the child's short-term memory at a given age and of the number of programs a child can run simultaneously. Research suggests that these are indeed useful ways of talking about children (see Chapter 12).

The most obvious applications of information processing occur in teaching. For example, information-processing models alert teachers to the sequence of steps by which children acquire information, commit it to memory, and retrieve it to solve problems. By understanding this sequence, teachers can provide experiences that give students practice with each stage. The information-processing model is also a useful guide in diagnosing and treating children's learning difficulties. Each "component" in the information-processing "system" can be assessed when the trouble spot has been identified, and methods for correcting the problem can be applied.

Now that we have established that the brain can be thought of as a biological computer, let us see what other aspects of biology can be theoretically connected with child development.

The Biological Perspective

The biological perspective pertains to aspects of physical development. ***Question: What is the scope of the biological perspective?*** The biological perspective refers to gains in height and weight, development of the nervous system, developments that are connected with hormones, and heredity. The key role of the biological perspective threads its way through this book, from the discussion of heredity to the ways in which sperm and ova are formed, the dramatic multiplication of cells during the embryonic stage of prenatal development, and ways in which hormones stoke the changes of puberty. But psychological and social developments are also rooted in biological structures and processes. Here we consider one biologically oriented theory of development: *ethology.*

Ethology: "Doing What Comes Naturally"

ethology The study of behaviours that are specific to a species.

Ethology is another biologically oriented theory, and it points to the evolution of humans within the animal kingdom. It was heavily influenced by the nineteenth-century work of Charles Darwin and by the work of twentieth-century European ethologists Konrad Lorenz and Niko Tinbergen.

Question: What is ethology? The core of ethology involves instinctive, or inborn, behaviour patterns. There is no question that physical traits are inborn, but the notion of "inheriting" behaviour has been more controversial. Yet it would appear that animals tend to be neurally "prewired"—that is, born with preprogrammed tendencies— to respond to specific situations in specific ways. For example, birds that are reared in isolation from other birds will build nests during the mating season—even if they have never seen another bird building a nest or, for that matter, a nest itself. Similarly, male Siamese fighting fish that are reared in isolation will assume stereotypical threatening stances and attack other males that are introduced into their tanks. These behaviours could not have been learned. They are "built in," or instinctive. They are also referred to as inborn **fixed action patterns (FAPs).**

fixed action pattern (FAP) A stereotyped pattern of behaviour that is evoked by a "releasing stimulus"; an instinct.

Why are male Siamese fighting fish more aggressive than females? It is known that during prenatal development, genes and sex hormones are responsible for the physical development of female and male sex organs. Most theorists also believe that in many species, including humans, sex hormones can "masculinize" or "feminize" the embryonic brain by creating tendencies to behave in stereotypical masculine or feminine ways (Bailey, 2003). Testosterone, the male sex hormone, seems to be connected with feelings of self-confidence, high activity levels, and—the negative side—aggressiveness (Pope, Kouri, & Hudson, 2000; A. Sullivan, 2000).

Evaluation Most theorists with an ethological perspective do not maintain that human behaviours are as mechanical as those of lower animals. Moreover, they tend to assume that instinctive behaviours can be modified through learning. Research into the ethological perspective suggests, however, that instinct continues to play a role in human behaviour. The questions that research seeks to answer include What areas of behaviour and development involve instinct? How vital a role does instinct play? What are the ways in which instinct manifests itself among humans?

The Ecological Perspective

ecology The branch of biology that deals with the relationships between living organisms and their environment.

Ecology is the branch of biology that deals with the relationships between living organisms and their environment. *Question: What is the ecological systems theory of child development?* The **ecological systems theory** of child development addresses aspects of psychological, social, and emotional development as well as aspects of biological development. Ecological systems theorists explain child development in terms of the interaction between children and the settings in which they live (Bronfenbrenner, 1989, 2002; Bronfenbrenner & Evans, 2000; Evans, 2004).

ecological systems theory The view that explains child development in terms of the reciprocal influences between children and the settings that make up their environment.

According to Urie Bronfenbrenner, the first proposition of the ecological systems theory is that the traditional, unidirectional approach to understanding child-environment relationships is insufficient. The ecological systems approach argues that the developmental process cannot be completely understood unless we focus on the *reciprocal interactions* between the child and the parents, not just maturational forces (nature) or parental child-rearing approaches (nurture).

Consider the example of the ways in which parents interact with infants. Some parents may choose to feed newborns on demand, whereas others may decide to adhere to a schedule in which feedings occur four hours apart. Certainly, parental feeding plans will affect the child. But the basic (apparently inborn) temperaments of children differ, as we will see in Chapter 7. The point is this: Parents are part of the child's environment, and although parents have a major influence on the child, that influence is not a one-way street.

Bronfenbrenner (1979, 1989) suggested that we can view the setting or contexts of human development as consisting of five systems. Each of these systems is embedded within the next larger context. From narrowest to widest, these systems consist of the microsystem, the mesosystem, the exosystem, the macrosystem, and the chronosystem (see Figure 1.4).

The Microsystem
The **microsystem** involves the interactions of the child and other people in the immediate setting, such as the home, the school, or the peer group. Initially, the microsystem is small, involving care-giving interactions with the parents or others, usually at home. As children get older, they do more, with more people, in more places.

The Mesosystem
The **mesosystem** involves the interactions of the various settings within the microsystem. For instance, the home and the school interact during parent-teacher conferences. The school and the larger community interact when children are taken on field trips. The ecological systems approach addresses the joint effect of two or more settings on the child.

microsystem The immediate settings with which the child interacts, such as the home, the school, and one's peers (from the Greek *mikros*, meaning "small").

mesosystem The interlocking settings that influence the child, such as the interaction of the school and the larger community when children are taken on field trips (from the Greek *mesos*, meaning "middle").

Figure 1.4
The Contexts of Human Development

According to the ecological systems theory, the systems within which children develop are embedded within larger systems. Children and these systems reciprocally influence each other.

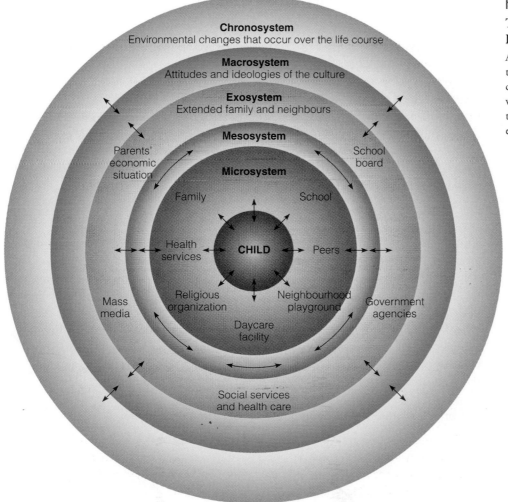

exosystem Community institutions and settings that indirectly influence the child, such as the school board and the parents' workplaces (from the Greek *exo*, meaning "outside").

The Exosystem

The **exosystem** involves the institutions in which the child does not directly participate but which exert an indirect influence on the child. For example, the school board is part of the child's exosystem because board members construct curricula for the child's education, determine what books will be in the school library, and so forth. In similar fashion, the parents' workplaces and economic situations determine the hours during which they will be available to the child, what mood they will be in when they interact with the child, and so on. For example, poverty and unemployment cause psychological distress in parents, which in turn decreases their capacity for supportive, consistent, and involved parenting (Corcoran, 2001; Stockhammer, Salzinger, Feldman, Mojica, & Primavera, 2001). As a result, their children may experience adjustment problems both at home and in school (Evans, 2004). Studies that address the effects of housing, health care, TV programs, spirituality, government agencies, or even the presence or absence of a telephone on children all examine the interactions of the exosystem and the child.

macrosystem The basic institutions and ideologies that influence the child, such as the American ideals of freedom of expression and equality under the law (from the Greek *makros*, meaning "long" or "enlarged").

The Macrosystem

The **macrosystem** involves the interaction of children with the beliefs, values, expectations, and lifestyles of their cultural settings. Cross-cultural studies examine children's interactions with their macrosystem in different cultures. Various macrosystems exist within a single culture as well. For example, in Canada, the two-wage-earner family, the low-income single-parent household, and the family with father as sole breadwinner constitute three different macrosystems. Each exhibits its own characteristic lifestyle, set of values, and expectations (Bronfenbrenner, 2002).

chronosystem The environmental changes that occur over time and have an impact on the child (from the Greek *chronos*, meaning "time").

The Chronosystem

The **chronosystem** considers the environmental changes that occur over time and have an effect on the child. For example, as we will see in Chapter 13, the effects of divorce peak about a year after the event, and then children begin to recover. The breakup has more of an effect on boys than on girls and tends to contribute to conduct disorders and academic problems in boys.

The ecological ("multisystemic") approach broadens the strategies for intervention in problems such as teenage pregnancy (Corcoran, 2000, 2001), child abuse (Stockhammer et al., 2001), and juvenile offending, including substance abuse (Brunswick, 1999).

Evaluation

The ecological systems theory may be most valuable in helping researchers become aware of the systems that children interact with. Much research on the mesosystem focuses on the shifts in setting that children encounter as they develop. For example, the health of the child requires interlocking relationships between parents and the health system, just as the education of the child requires the interaction of parents and school personnel as discussed in McCain and Mustard's (1999) Early Years Report (see Chapter 9). At the level of the exosystem, researchers look into the effects of parents' work lives, welfare agencies, transportation systems, shopping facilities, and so on. At the level of the macrosystem, we may compare child-rearing practices in Canada, and North America overall, with those in other countries. We will learn more about the role of culture in our discussion of the sociocultural perspective.

Developing in a World of Diversity

Influence of the Macrosystem on the Development of Independence

Cross-cultural studies provide interesting insights into the way children interact with their macrosystems. Consider the development of independence. Among the !Kung people of Namibia, babies are kept in close contact with their mothers during the first year (Konner, 1977). !Kung infants are frequently carried in slings across their mothers' hips that allow the mothers to nurse at will—literally all day long. The !Kung seem to follow the commandment "The infant shall not go hungry"—not even for five seconds. In every way,

!Kung mothers try to respond at once to their babies' cries and whims. By Western standards, !Kung babies are "spoiled." However, overindulgence does not appear to make !Kung babies overly dependent on their mothers. By the time they are capable of walking, they do. They do not cling to their mothers. In comparison to Western children of the same age, !Kung children spend less time with their mothers and more time with their peers.

Also compare Urie Bronfenbrenner's (1973) observations of child rearing in

the United States and Russia. Russian babies, as a group, are more likely than U.S. babies to be cuddled, kissed, and hugged. Russian mothers are not quite so solicitous as their !Kung counterparts, but they are highly protective compared with U.S. mothers. However, Russian children are taught to take care of themselves at younger ages than U.S. children. By 18 months of age, Russian children are usually learning to dress themselves and are largely toilet trained.

The Sociocultural Perspective

According to the sociocultural perspective, children (and adults) are social beings who are greatly influenced by the cultures in which they live. Yes, we all have a certain genetic heritage. There is no question that we are affected by biochemical forces such as neurotransmitters and hormones. We may be biologically "prewired" to form attachments and engage in other behaviours. Perhaps there are psychological tendencies to learn in certain ways, or maybe there are ways that the psychological past affects the present. But, as noted within the ecological perspective, we are also affected by the customs, traditions, languages, and heritages of the societies in which we live. *Question: What is meant by the sociocultural perspective?* The sociocultural perspective has many overlaps with other perspectives on child development; however, developmentalists are likely to use the term *sociocultural* in a couple of different ways. One way refers quite specifically to the *sociocultural theory* of the Russian psychologist Lev Semonovich Vygotsky (1896–1934). The other way broadly addresses the effect on children of human diversity, including such factors as ethnicity and gender.

Lev Semonovich Vygotsky
Vygotsky is known for showing how social speech becomes inner speech and how "scaffolding" by others assists children in developing the cognitive skills to succeed.

zone of proximal development (ZPD)
Vygotsky's term for the situation in which a child carries out tasks with the help of someone who is more skilled, frequently an adult who represents the culture in which the child develops.

scaffolding Vygotsky's term for temporary cognitive structures or methods of solving problems that help the child as he or she learns to function independently.

Vygotsky's Sociocultural Theory

Whereas genetics is concerned with the biological transmission of traits from generation to generation, Vygotsky's (1978) theory is vitally concerned with the transmission of information and cognitive skills from generation to generation. The transmission of skills involves teaching and learning, but Vygotsky is no behaviourist. He does not view learning as a mechanical process that can be described in terms of the conditioning of units of behaviour. Rather, he focuses more generally on how the child's social interaction with more knowledgeable peers or adults, largely in the home, organizes a child's learning experiences in such a way that the child can obtain cognitive skills—such as computation or reading skills—and use them to acquire information. Like Piaget, Vygotsky sees the child's functioning as adaptive (Piaget & Smith, 2000), and the child adapts to his or her social and cultural interactions.

Question: What are the key concepts of Vygotsky's sociocultural theory? Key concepts in Vygotsky's theory include the zone of proximal development and scaffolding. The word proximal means "nearby" or "close," as in the words approximate and proximity. The **zone of proximal development (ZPD)** refers to a range of tasks that a child can carry out with the help of someone who is more skilled (Haenen, 2001). It is similar to the context of an apprenticeship. Many developmentalists find that observing how a child learns when working with others provides more information about that child's cognitive abilities than does a simple inventory of knowledge (Meijer & Elshout, 2001). When learning with other people, the child tends to internalize—or bring inward—the conversations and explanations that help him or her gain the necessary skills (Prior & Welling, 2001; Vygotsky, 1962; Yang, 2000). In other words, children not only learn the meanings of words from teachers but also learn ways of talking to themselves (inner speech) about solving problems within a cultural context (DeVries, 2000). Outer speech becomes inner speech. What was the teacher's becomes the child's. What was a social and cultural context becomes embedded within the child (Moro & Rodriguez, 2000).

A *scaffold* is a temporary skeletal structure that enables workers to fabricate a building, bridge, or other more permanent structure. In Vygotsky's theory, teachers and parents provide children with problem-solving methods that serve as cognitive **scaffolding** while the child gains the ability to function independently. For example, a child's instructors may offer advice on sounding out letters and words that provide a temporary support until reading "clicks" and the child no longer needs the device. Children may be offered scaffolding that enables them to use their fingers or their toes to do simple calculations. Eventually, the scaffolding is removed and the cognitive structures stand alone. A Puerto Rican study found that students also use scaffolding when they are explaining to one another how they can improve school projects, such as essay assignments (De Guerrero & Villamil, 2000). Children at first even view the value of education in terms of their parents' verbalizations about school success (Bigelow, 2001). Vygotsky's theory points out that children's attitudes toward schooling are embedded within the parent-child relationship.

The Sociocultural Perspective and Human Diversity

The field of child development focuses mainly on individuals and is committed to the dignity of the individual child. *Question: What is the connection between the sociocultural perspective and human diversity?* The sociocultural perspective recognizes that we cannot understand individual children without an awareness of the richness of their diversity (Basic Behavioral Science Task Force, 1996). For example, children diverge or differ in their ethnicity, gender, and socioeconomic status.

Until recently, much of the research on child development was confined to middle-class European American children. But we live in a world of diverse cultures, and psychology—of which developmental psychology is a part that has become more global. There is a growing recognition among developmentalists that the cultural context in which the child grows up must be taken into account to better understand children's development and behaviour. One kind of cultural diversity involves children's **ethnic groups,** which tend to unite them according to features such as their cultural heritage, their race, their language, and their common history. One reason for studying ethnic diversity is the multicultural makeup of Canada. According to a recent Statistics Canada research report on the ethnocultural diversity in Canada, our ethnic and cultural makeup is undergoing rapid change (see Figure 1.5).

ethnic groups Groups of people distinguished by cultural heritage, race, language, and common history.

Studying diversity is also important so that children have appropriate educational experiences. Educators need to understand children's family values and cultural expectations in order to teach them and guide their learning. Many professionals—psychologists, teachers, social workers, psychiatrists, and others—are called on to help children and families who are having problems in school or in the community. In many cases, these are individual problems, and professionals may be sensitive to their nature and know how to intervene. But in many cases, individual problems are intertwined with cultural issues, such as prejudice and discrimination. Professionals are then handicapped in their efforts to help unless they are familiar with the ethnic group's history of interaction with the dominant culture. Professionals may need special training to identify the problems of children and families from ethnic minority groups and to treat them in culturally sensitive ways (Dana, 2002; Kim & Omizo, 2003; Olson, 2003).

Throughout the text, we consider many issues that affect children from various ethnic groups. A handful of them include bilingualism, ethnic differences in intelligence test scores, the prevalence of suicide among members of different ethnic minority groups, and patterns of child rearing among parents of various cultural backgrounds.

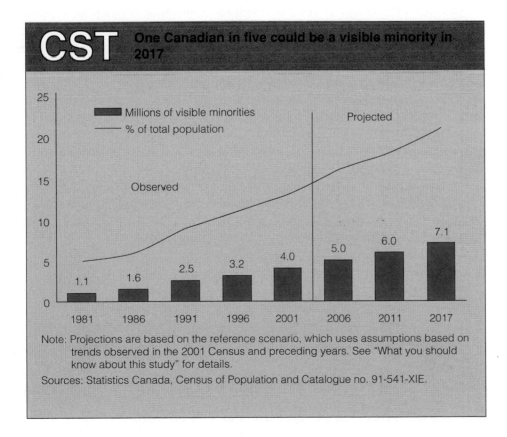

Figure 1.5

Future Trends of Ethnocultural Diversity in Canada

gender   The psychological state of being female or being male, as influenced by cultural concepts of gender-appropriate behaviour. Compare and contrast the concept of gender with *anatomic sex*, which is based on the physical differences between females and males.

Gender is another aspect of human diversity. Gender is the psychological state of being male or being female, as influenced by cultural concepts of gender-appropriate behaviour. The French have a saying, *Vive la différence* ("Long live the difference!"), which celebrates the difference between females and males. The French expression exudes the excitement people may feel when they are interacting with individuals of the other sex, but, unfortunately, it also alludes to the problem that females and males are often polarized by cultural expectations. That is, the differences may be exaggerated, as in the case of intellectual abilities. Put it this way: Males may very well differ from females in some respects, but history has created more burdens for women than men as a result. Gender-role expectations affect children's self-esteem and limit their hopes and dreams for the future.

Historically, girls have been traditionally discouraged from careers in the sciences, politics, and business. Not until recent times have there even been large numbers of women in the arts. Women today are making inroads into academic and vocational spheres—such as medicine, law, engineering, and the military—that were traditionally male preserves. Today the number of women in medical and law schools has risen to equal or surpass the number of men entering these professions (Glater, 2001). But in other professional fields, particularly math, science, and engineering, the gap has not narrowed as much. Still, it is no longer widely expected—at least not in Canada and other developed nations—that girls will have to remain in the domestic arena.

Today most university and college students in Canada are female, but it is worth noting that females were not considered qualified for education until relatively recent times. How many gifted and talented girls and women have been lost to history because of prejudice? How many have lived lives of quiet frustration? Who, for example, is Lucinda Foote? She was a brilliant young woman who is known to us only because of her rejection letter from Yale University in 1792, which confirmed that she was qualified for Yale in every way—*except* for her sex (Lerner, 1993). It may surprise you to learn that women were not admitted to college in the United States until 1833, the year that Oberlin College opened its doors to women. In 1880 the medical school at Queen's University in Kingston, Ontario, was the first to admit females to its undergraduate courses. However, as recounted by Cataudella (1999), Queen's was also one of the first Canadian universities to subsequently exclude women. Eventually, it accepted females again, becoming the last to readmit them to their programs. Yet there remain many—many!—parts of the world in which women are not permitted to obtain an education.

Opportunities for women are crucial to the development of girls. Children learn early about gender roles and gender-role stereotypes. Cultural opportunities for and limitations on adults give children their own sense of what is possible for them and what is not. Just as many children from ethnic minority groups wonder whether they can experience the rewards and opportunities they see in the dominant culture, so do girls wonder whether the career and social roles they admire are available to them. Many females question the representativeness of females in parliament and whether there will be another female prime minister in the near future. The effects of cultural expectations on girls' self-concepts, motivation, and behaviour are clear and compelling.

In this book, the focus on human diversity extends beyond ethnicity and gender to include children with various sexual orientations and a number of disabilities. This approach broadens our understanding of all children as they experience the developmental changes brought about by quite different influences of heredity and experience. Yes, the presentation of human diversity complicates matters, but that is only because the matters are complex. If we simplify, we fail reality.

Concept Review 1.3 summarizes some of the important similarities and differences among the various perspectives on child development.

Concept Review 1.3 Perspectives on Child Development

Perspective or Theory	Core Concepts	Is Nature or Nurture More Important?	Is Development Viewed as Being Continuous or Discontinuous?	Is the Child Viewed as Being Active or Passive?
The Psychoanalytic Perspective				
Theory of psychosexual development (Sigmund Freud)	Instinctive impulses are channelled via social codes, but conflict develops as a result. Much of the mind is unconscious.	Interaction of nature and nurture: Biological maturation sets the stage for reaction to social influences.	Discontinuous: There are five stages of development, each of which involves the expression of sexual impulses.	Passive: The child is largely at the mercy of older people and cultural modes of conduct.
Theory of psychosocial development (Erik Erikson)	Child (and adult) experiences life crises that are largely based on social relationships, opportunities, and expectations.	Interaction of nature and nurture: Biological maturation sets the stage for reaction to social influences and opportunities.	Discontinuous: There are eight stages of development, each of which involves a particular kind of life crisis.	Active: The child (and adult) makes conscious decisions about formation of his or her own personality and behaviour.
The Learning Perspective: Behavioural and Social Cognitive Theories				
Behaviourism (John B. Watson, Ivan Pavlov, B. F. Skinner)	Behaviour is learned by association; two key types of learning are classical conditioning and operant conditioning.	Nurture: Children are seen almost as blank tablets.	Continuous: Behaviour reflects the summation of conditioned responses.	Passive: Responses are learned by association, and behaviour is maintained due to its effects.
Social cognitive theory (Albert Bandura and others)	Conditioning occurs, but children also learn purposefully by observing others, and they choose whether to display learned responses.	Emphasizes nurture but allows for expression of natural tendencies.	Continuous.	Active: Principle of reciprocal determinism states that children influence the environment even as the environment influences them.
The Cognitive Perspective				
Cognitive-developmental theory (Jean Piaget)	Children adapt to the environment via processes of assimilation to existing mental structures (schemes) or by changing these structures (accommodation).	Emphasizes nature but allows for influences of experience.	Discontinuous: Cognitive development follows an invariant sequence of four stages.	Active: Children are budding scientists who seek to understand and manipulate their worlds.

(continued)

Perspective or Theory	Core Concepts	Is Nature or Nurture More Important?	Is Development Viewed as Being Continuous or Discontinuous?	Is the Child Viewed as Being Active or Passive?
Information-processing theory (numerous theorists)	Children's cognitive functioning is compared to that of computers, involving the inputting, manipulation, storage, and output of information.	Interaction of nature and nurture.	Continuous: Development facilitates the child's storage capacity and ability to run multiple "programs" simultaneously; cognitive skills are cumulative.	Active: Children seek to obtain and manipulate information.

The Biological Perspective

Ethology (Charles Darwin, Konrad Lorenz, Niko Tinbergen)	Organisms are biologically "prewired" to show inborn fixed action patterns (FAPs) in response to species-specific releasing stimuli.	Emphasizes nature but experience is also critical; for example, imprinting occurs at a given point in development, but *what* an organism is imprinted on is determined by experience.	Discontinuous: Certain kinds of learning, for example, are said to occur during *critical periods*, which are biologically determined.	Not indicated, although organisms are depicted as responding automatically (passively) to FAPs.

The Ecological Perspective

Ecological systems theory (Urie Bronfenbrenner)	Children's development occurs within interlocking systems. Development is enhanced by intervening at the levels of various systems.	Interaction of nature and nurture: Children's personalities and skills contribute to their development.	Not specifically indicated.	Active: Influences are bidirectional: Systems influence the child, and vice versa.

The Sociocultural Perspective

Sociocultural theory (Lev Vygotsky)	Addresses the ways in which children internalize sociocultural dialogues as ways of guiding their own behaviour and developing problem-solving skills.	Interaction of nature and nurture; nurture is discussed in social and cultural terms.	Continuous: Learning in the presence of experienced members of a culture enables the child to accumulate knowledge and skills.	Both: Children seek to develop problem-solving abilities by internalizing cultural dialogues, but the dialogues originate within society, not within the individual.
Sociocultural perspective and human diversity (numerous theorists)	Focuses on the influences of sociocultural factors, such as ethnic background and sex, on development.	Nurture.	Not specifically indicated.	Not indicated.

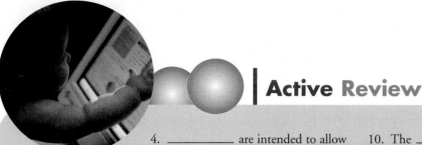

Active Review

4. _____ are intended to allow us to explain, predict, and control events.

5. _____ hypothesized five stages of psychosexual development.

6. Erikson extended Freud's five stages of development to _____.

7. Behaviourism sees children's learning as mechanical and relies on classical and _____ conditioning.

8. According to _____, children assimilate new events to existing schemes or accommodate schemes to incorporate novel events.

9. Information-_____ theory focuses on the processes by which information is encoded, stored, retrieved, and manipulated.

10. The _____ systems theory explains child development in terms of the interaction between children and the settings in which they live.

11. Vygotsky's _____ theory is concerned with the transmission of information and cognitive skills from generation to generation.

Reflect & Relate: How have your ethnic background and your gender influenced your development? Consider factors such as race, country of origin, language, nutrition, values, and the dominant culture's reaction to people of your background.

 Go to

W W W www.voyages1ce.nelson.com
for an interactive version of this review.

Controversies in Child Development

The discussion of theories of development reveals that developmentalists can see things in very different ways. Let us consider how they react to three of the most important debates in the field.

The Nature-Nurture Controversy

Question: Which exerts the greater influence on children: nature or nurture? Think about your friends for a moment. Some may be tall and lanky, others short and stocky. Some are outgoing and sociable; others are more reserved and quiet. One may be a good athlete; another, a fine musician. What made them this way? How much does inheritance have to do with it, and how much does the environment play a role?

Researchers are continually trying to sort out the extent to which human behaviour is the result of **nature** (heredity) and of **nurture** (environmental influences). What aspects of behaviours originate in our **genes** and are biologically programmed to unfold in the child as time goes on, so long as minimal nutrition and social experience are provided? What aspects of behaviour can be traced largely to such environmental influences as nutrition and learning?

Scientists seek the natural causes of development in children's genetic heritage, the functioning of the nervous system, and in the process of maturation. Scientists seek the environmental causes of development in children's nutrition, cultural and family backgrounds, and opportunities to learn about the world, including cognitive stimulation during early childhood and formal education.

Some theorists lean heavily toward natural explanations of development (e.g., cognitive-developmental and biological theorists), whereas others lean more heavily toward environmental explanations (e.g., learning theorists). But today nearly all

nature The processes within an organism that guide that organism to develop according to its genetic code.

nurture The processes external to an organism that nourish it as it develops according to its genetic code or that cause it to swerve from its genetically programmed course. Environmental factors that influence development.

genes The basic building blocks of heredity.

Stages of Physical Development
Certain aspects of physical development seem to occur in stages. However, girls usually spurt in growth before boys.

researchers would agree that, broadly speaking, both nature and nurture play important roles in virtually every area of child development. Consider the development of language. Language is based in structures found in certain areas of the brain. Thus, biology (nature) plays an indispensable role in language development. But children also come to speak the languages spoken by their caretakers. Parent-child similarities in accent and vocabulary provide additional evidence for an indispensable role for learning (nurture) in language development.

The Continuity-Discontinuity Controversy

Question: Is development continuous or discontinuous? Do developmental changes occur gradually (continuously), the way a seedling becomes a tree? Or do changes occur in major qualitative leaps (discontinuously) that dramatically alter our bodies and behaviour, the way a caterpillar turns into a butterfly?

Some developmentalists have viewed human development as a continuous process in which the effects of learning mount gradually, with no major sudden qualitative changes. In contrast, other theorists believe that a number of rapid qualitative changes usher in new stages of development. Maturational theorists point out that the environment, even when enriched, profits us little until we are ready, or mature enough, to develop in a certain direction. For example, newborn babies will not imitate their parents' speech, even when parents speak clearly and deliberately. Nor does aided practice in "walking" during the first few months after birth significantly accelerate the emergence of independent walking.

Stage theorists such as Sigmund Freud and Jean Piaget saw development as being discontinuous. Both theorists saw biological changes as providing the potential for psychological changes. Freud focused on the ways in which biological developments might provide the basis for personality development. Piaget emphasized the ways in which maturation of the nervous system permitted cognitive advances. Stage theorists see the sequences of development as being the same, although they allow for individual differences in timing.

Certain aspects of physical development do appear to occur in stages. For example, from the age of two years to the onset of puberty, children gradually grow larger. Then the adolescent growth spurt occurs, ushered in by hormones and characterized by rapid biological changes in structure and function (as in the development of the sex organs) and in size. A new stage of life begins. Psychologists disagree more strongly on whether aspects of development such as cognition, attachment, and assumption of gender roles occur in stages.

The Active-Passive Controversy

In the broad sense, all living organisms are active. However, in the field of child development, the question has a more specific meaning. *Question: Are children active (prewired to act on the world) or passive (shaped by experience)?*

Historical views of children as wilful and unruly suggest that people have generally seen children as active—even if mischievous (at best) or evil (at worst). John Locke introduced a view of children as passive beings (blank tablets) upon whom external experience writes features of personality and moral virtue.

At one extreme, educators who view children as passive may assume that instructors must motivate them to learn. Such educators are likely to provide a traditional curriculum with rigorous exercises in spelling, music, and math to promote absorption of the subject matter. They are also likely to apply a powerful system of rewards and punishments to keep children on the straight and narrow.

At the other extreme, educators who view children as active may assume that they have a natural love of learning. Such educators are likely to espouse open education and encourage children to explore an environment rich with learning materials. Rather than attempting to coerce children into specific academic activities, such educators are likely to listen to the children to learn about their unique likes and talents and then support children as they pursue their inclinations.

These are extremes. Most educators would probably agree that children show major individual differences and that some children require more guidance and external motivation than others. In addition, children can be active in some subjects and passive in others. Whether children who do not actively seek to master certain subjects are coerced tends to depend on how important the subject is to functioning in today's society, the age of the child, the attitudes of the parents, and many other factors.

Urie Bronfenbrenner (1977) argued that we miss the point when we assume that children are either entirely active or passive. Children are influenced by the environment, but children also influence the environment. The challenge is to observe the many ways in which children interact with their settings. Social cognitive theorist Albert Bandura agrees. He refers to the mutual influences of people and the environment as *reciprocal determinism.*

These debates are theoretical. Scientists value theory for its ability to tie together observations and suggest new areas of investigation, but they also follow an **empirical** approach. That is, they engage in research methods, such as those described in the following section, to find evidence for or against various theoretical positions.

empirical   Based on observation and experimentation.

Active Review

12. Researchers in child development try to sort out the effects of _____ (heredity) and nurture (environmental influences).

13. Learning theorists tend to see development as continuous, whereas stage theorists see development as _____ .

Reflect & Relate: Consider the active-passive controversy. Do you see yourself as being active or passive? Explain.

Go to
www.voyages1ce.nelson.com
for an interactive version of this review.

How Do We Study Child Development?

What is the relationship between intelligence and achievement? What are the effects of aspirin and alcohol on the fetus? How can you rear children to become competent and independent? What are the effects of divorce on children?

Many of us have expressed opinions on questions such as these at one time or another. But scientists insist that such questions be answered by research. Strong arguments, reference to authority figures, even tightly knit theories are not considered adequate as scientific evidence. Scientific evidence is obtained by the scientific method.

The Scientific Method

Question: What is the scientific method? The scientific method is a way of formulating and answering research questions that makes (some) scientists more qualified to study children than parents and grandparents. The scientific method allows scientists to test the theories discussed in the previous section. It consists of five basic steps.

Step 1: Formulating a Research Question

Our daily experiences, developmental theory, and even folklore help generate questions for research. Daily experience in using daycare centres may motivate us to conduct research to find out whether daycare influences children's intellectual or social development or the bonds of attachment between children and their parents. Social cognitive principles of observational learning may prompt research into the effects of TV violence.

Step 2: Developing a Hypothesis

hypothesis
(high-PAH-thuh-sis) A Greek word meaning "groundwork" or "foundation" that has come to mean a specific statement about behaviour that is tested by research.

The second step is the development of a hypothesis. A **hypothesis** is a specific statement about behaviour that is tested through research.

One hypothesis about daycare might be that preschool children placed in daycare will acquire greater social skills in relating to peers than will preschool children who are cared for in the home. A hypothesis about TV violence might be that elementary schoolchildren who watch more violent TV shows tend to behave more aggressively toward their peers.

The Scientific Method
What is the cause of this boy's aggression? Would he behave differently if the other child reacted to him with anger instead of fear? How does the scientific method help us answer these types of questions?

© Mary Kate Denny / PhotoEdit

Step 3: Testing the Hypothesis

The third step is testing the hypothesis. Psychologists test the hypothesis through carefully controlled information-gathering techniques and research methods, such as **naturalistic observation,** the case study, correlation, and the experiment.

For example, we could introduce daycare and non-daycare children to a new child in a college child-research centre and observe how each group acts toward the new acquaintance. Concerning the effects of TV violence, we could have parents help us tally which TV shows their children watch and rate the shows for violent content. Each child could receive a total score for exposure to TV violence. Teachers could report on how aggressively the children act toward their peers. Then we could determine whether more aggressive children also watch more violence on TV. We describe research methods such as these later in the chapter.

Step 4: Drawing Conclusions about the Hypothesis

The fourth step is drawing conclusions. Psychologists draw conclusions about the accuracy of their hypothesis on the basis of the results of their research findings. When research does not bear out their hypotheses, the researchers may modify the theories from which the hypotheses were derived. Research findings often suggest new hypotheses and new studies.

In our research on the effects of daycare, we would probably find that daycare children show somewhat greater social skills than children cared for in the home (see Chapter 7). We would probably also find that more aggressive children spend more time watching TV violence, as we shall see in Chapter 10. But we will also see in the following pages that it might be wrong to conclude from this kind of evidence that TV violence *causes* aggressive behaviour.

Step 5: Publishing Findings

Scientists publish their research findings in professional journals and make their data available to scientists and the public at large for scrutiny. Thus, they grant their peers the opportunity to review their data and conclusions to help determine their accuracy.

Now let us consider the information-gathering techniques and the research methods used by developmentalists. Then we will discuss ethical issues concerning research in child development.

Gathering Information

Developmentalists use various methods to gather information. For example, they may ask children to keep diaries of their behaviour, ask teachers or parents to report on the behaviour of their children, or use interviews or questionnaires with children themselves. They also directly observe children in the laboratory or in the natural setting. Let us discuss two ways of gathering information: the naturalistic-observation method and the case-study method.

Naturalistic Observation

Question: What is naturalistic observation? Naturalistic-observation studies of children are conducted in "the field"—that is, in the natural, or real-life, settings in which they happen. In field studies, investigators observe the natural behaviour of children in such settings as homes, playgrounds, and classrooms and try not to interfere with it. Interference could influence or bias the results so that researchers would be observing child-investigator interactions and not genuine behaviour. Thus, researchers may try to blend into the woodwork by sitting quietly in the back of a classroom or by observing the class through a one-way mirror.

naturalistic observation A method of scientific observation in which children (and others) are observed in their natural environments.

Naturalistic observation is frequently the first type of study carried out in new areas of investigation. Through careful observation, scientists gather an initial impression of what happens in certain situations. In their interpretation of the data, they may use the mathematical correlational method, described later in this chapter, to refine their observations of how strongly different **variables** are related. For example, they may explore whether the rate of vocabulary growth is related to sex or to cultural background. Afterward, they may attempt to investigate cause and effect through experimental research.

A number of important naturalistic-observation studies have been done with children of different cultures. For example, researchers have observed the motor behaviour of Native American Hopi children who are strapped to cradle boards during the first year. They have observed language development in Canada, the United States, Mexico, Turkey, Kenya, and China—seeking universals that might suggest a major role for maturation in the acquisition of language skills. They have also observed the ways in which children are socialized in Russia, Israel, Japan, and other nations in an effort to determine what patterns of child rearing are associated with development of behaviours such as attachment and independence.

variables Quantities that can vary from child to child or from occasion to occasion, such as height, weight, intelligence, and attention span.

The Case Study

Another way of gathering information about children is the case-study method. *Question: What is the case study?* The **case study** is a carefully drawn account of the behaviour of an individual. Parents who keep diaries of their children's activities are involved in informal case studies. Case studies themselves often use a number of different kinds of information about children. In addition to direct observation, case studies may include questionnaires, **standardized tests,** and interviews with the child and his or her parents, teachers, and friends. Information gleaned from school and other records may be included. Scientists who use the case-study method take great pains to record all the relevant factors in a child's behaviour, and they are cautious in drawing conclusions about what leads to what.

case study A carefully drawn biography of an individual.

standardized test A test of some ability or trait in which an individual's score is compared to the scores of a group of similar individuals.

Jean Piaget used the case-study method in carefully observing and recording the behaviour of children, including his own (see Chapter 6). Sigmund Freud developed his psychoanalytic theory largely on the basis of case studies. Freud studied his patients in great depth and followed some of them for many years.

In many instances, case studies, like naturalistic observation, form the basis for sophisticated experimental studies that follow. The early case studies of Freud and Piaget have led to countless experiments that have attempted to find evidence to support or disconfirm their theories.

Correlation: Putting Things Together

Question: What does it mean to correlate information? Correlation is a mathematical method that researchers use to determine whether one behaviour or trait being studied is related to, or correlated with, another. Consider, for example, the variables of intelligence and achievement. These variables are assigned numbers such as intelligence test scores and academic grade averages. Then the numbers or scores are mathematically related and expressed as a correlation coefficient. A **correlation coefficient** is a number that varies between +1.00 and −1.00.

correlation coefficient A number ranging from +1.00 to −1.00 that expresses the direction (positive or negative) and strength of the relationship between two variables.

Numerous studies report **positive correlations** between intelligence and achievement. In general, the higher children score on intelligence tests, the better their academic performance is likely to be. The scores attained on intelligence tests are positively correlated (about 10.60 to 10.70) with overall academic achievement.[2]

positive correlation A relationship between two variables in which one variable increases as the other variable increases.

---

[2] Of course 10.60 is the same as 1.60. We insert the zeroes to help prevent the decimal points from getting lost.

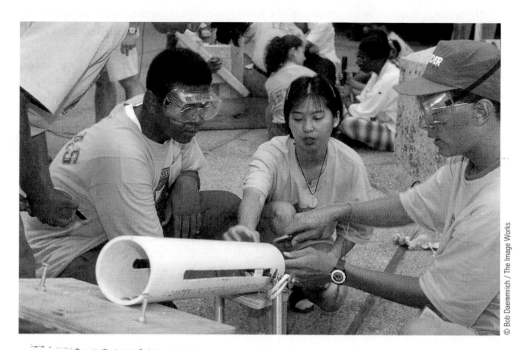

What Is the Relationship Between Intelligence and Achievement?
These high school students spend their summer at an engineering camp where they are working together to build a catapult. With what kinds of skills does engineering ability correlate? Does the correlational method allow us to say that intelligence causes or is responsible for academic achievement?

© Bob Daemmrich / The Image Works

There is a **negative correlation** between children's school grades and their commission of delinquent acts. The higher a child's grades in school, the less likely the child is to engage in criminal behaviour. Figure 1.6 illustrates positive and negative correlations.

negative correlation A relationship between two variables in which one variable increases as the other variable decreases.

Limitations of Correlational Information

Correlational information can reveal relationships between variables, but they do not show cause and effect. For example, children who watch TV shows with a lot of violence are more likely to show aggressive behaviour at home and in school. It may seem logical to assume that exposure to TV violence makes children more aggressive. But it may be that children who are more aggressive to begin with prefer violent TV shows. The relationship between viewing violence and behaving aggressively may not be so clear-cut.

Similarly, it has been reported in certain studies that children (especially boys) in divorced families sometimes show more problems than do children in intact families (Amato, 2001; Chao, Wang, & He, 2001). However, these studies do not show that divorce causes these adjustment problems. It could be that the factors that led to divorce (such as parental disorganization or conflict) also led to adjustment problems among the children (Clarke-Stewart, Vandell, McCartney, Owen, & Booth, 2000). Or having a child with problems might put a strain on the parents' marriage and ultimately be a factor contributing to divorce.

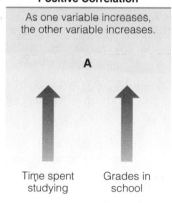

Positive Correlation

As one variable increases, the other variable increases.

A

Time spent studying — Grades in school

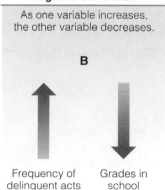

Negative Correlation

As one variable increases, the other variable decreases.

B

Frequency of delinquent acts — Grades in school

Figure 1.6

Examples of Positive and Negative Correlations

When two variables are correlated *positively,* one increases as the other increases. There is a positive correlation between the amount of time spent studying and grades, as shown in Part A. When two variables are correlated *negatively,* one increases as the other decreases. There is a negative correlation between the frequency of a child's delinquent acts and his or her grades, as shown in Part B. As one's delinquent behaviour increases, grades tend to decline.

In the studies on patterns of child rearing, we must also ask why parents choose to raise their children in certain ways. It is possible that the same factors that lead them to make these choices also influence the behaviour of their children. Thus, correlational research does not allow us to place clear "cause" and "effect" labels on variables. To investigate cause and effect, researchers turn to the experimental method. Nonetheless, there are benefits of correlation research. The most common is that finding correlational relationships helps point us in the right direction when designing experimental studies aiming to draw conclusions about the cause of these relationships.

The Experiment: Trying Things Out

The experiment is the preferred method for investigating questions of cause and effect. *Question: What is an experiment?* An **experiment** is a research method in which a group of participants receives a **treatment** and another group does not. The participants are then observed to determine whether the treatment makes a difference in their behaviour.

Experiments are used whenever possible, because they allow researchers to directly control the experiences of children and other participants to determine the outcomes of a treatment. Experiments, like other research methods, are usually undertaken to test a hypothesis. For example, a social cognitive theorist might hypothesize that TV violence will cause aggressive behaviour in children because of principles of observational learning. To test this hypothesis, he or she might devise an experiment in which some children are purposely exposed to TV violence and others are not. Remember that it is not enough to demonstrate that children who choose to watch more violent shows behave more aggressively; such evidence is only correlational. We review this research—correlational and experimental—in Chapter 10.

Independent and Dependent Variables

In an experiment to determine whether TV violence causes aggressive behaviour, participants in the experimental group would be shown a TV program containing violence, and its effects on behaviour would be measured. TV violence would be considered an **independent variable,** a variable whose presence is manipulated by the experimenters so that its effects can be determined. The measured result—in this case, the child's behaviour—is called a **dependent variable.** Its presence or level presumably depends on the independent variables.

Experimental and Control Groups

Experiments use experimental and control groups. Participants in the **experimental group** receive the treatment, whereas participants in the **control group** do not. Every effort is made to ensure that all other conditions are held constant for both groups of participants. By doing so, we can have confidence that experimental outcomes reflect the treatments and not chance factors. In a study on the effects of TV violence on children's behaviour, children in the experimental group would be shown TV programs containing violence, and children in the control group would be shown programs that do not contain violence.

Random Assignment

Subjects should be assigned to experimental or control groups on a chance or random basis. We could not conclude much from an experiment on the effects of TV violence if the children were allowed to choose whether they would be in a group that watched

---

experiment A method of scientific investigation that seeks to discover cause-and-effect relationships by introducing independent variables and observing their effects on dependent variables.

treatment In an experiment, a condition received by participants so that its effects may be observed.

independent variable A condition in a scientific study that is manipulated (changed) so that its effects can be observed.

dependent variable A measure of an assumed effect of an independent variable.

experimental group A group made up of participants who receive a treatment in an experiment.

control group A group made up of participants in an experiment who do not receive the treatment but for whom all other conditions are comparable to those of participants in the experimental group.

violent TV shows or in a group that watched nonviolent TV shows. This is because children who choose to watch TV violence might have more aggressive tendencies to begin with. Therefore, if children who watched violent TV programs wound up showing more aggression, we could not attribute this difference to the TV viewing itself. It might, instead, reflect the children's greater initial aggressiveness.

In an experiment on the effects of TV violence, we would therefore have to assign children randomly to view TV shows with or without violence, regardless of their personal preferences. As you can imagine, this would be difficult, if not impossible, to do in the child's own home. But such studies can be performed in laboratory settings, as we will see in Chapter 10.

Ethical and practical considerations also prevent researchers from doing experiments on the effects of many significant life circumstances, such as divorce or different patterns of child rearing. We cannot randomly assign some families to divorce or conflict and assign other families to perpetual harmony. Nor can we randomly assign parents with an authoritarian bent to raising their children in a permissive manner, or vice versa. In some areas of investigation, we must be relatively satisfied with correlational evidence.

When experiments cannot ethically be performed on humans, researchers sometimes carry out experiments with animals and then generalize the findings to humans. For example, no researcher would separate human infants from their parents to study the effects of isolation on development. But experimenters have deprived monkeys of early social experience. Such research has helped psychologists investigate the formation of parent-child bonds of attachment (see Chapter 7). ***Truth or Fiction Revisited:*** Although it is true that research with monkeys has helped psychologists understand the formation of attachment in humans, ethics would prevent investigators from carrying out this type of research with humans.

Longitudinal Research: Studying Development over Time

The processes of development occur over time, and researchers have devised different strategies for comparing children of one age to children (or adults) of other ages. *Question: How do researchers study development over time?* In **longitudinal research,** the same children are observed repeatedly over time, and changes in development, such as gains in height or changes in approach to problem solving, are recorded. In **cross-sectional research,** children of different ages are observed and compared. It is assumed that when a large number of children are chosen at random, the differences found in the older age groups are a reflection of how the younger children will develop, given time. Concept Review 1.4 summarizes the major features of cross-sectional and longitudinal research.

Longitudinal Studies

Some ambitious longitudinal studies have followed the development of children and adults for more than half a century. One, the Fels Longitudinal Study, began in 1929. Children were observed twice a year in their homes and twice a year in the Fels Institute nursery school. From time to time, younger investigators dipped into the Fels pool of subjects, further testing, interviewing, and observing these individuals as they grew into adults. In this way, researchers have been able to observe, for example, the development of intelligence and of patterns of independence and dependence.

The Terman Studies of Genius, also begun in the 1920s, tracked children with high IQ scores for more than half a century. ***Truth or Fiction Revisited:*** It is true that researchers have followed some subjects in developmental research for more than 50 years. Male subjects, but not female subjects, went on to high achievements

longitudinal research The study of developmental processes by taking repeated measures of the same group of children at various stages of development.

cross-sectional research The study of developmental processes by taking measures of children of different age groups at the same time.

in the professional world (see Chapter 12). Why? Contemporary studies of women show that those with high intelligence generally match the achievements of men and suggest that women of the earlier era were held back by traditional gender-role expectations.

Most longitudinal studies span months or a few years, not decades. In Chapter 13, for example, we will see that briefer longitudinal studies have found that the children of divorced parents undergo the most severe adjustment problems within a few months of the divorce. By two or three years afterward, many children have regained their equilibrium, as indicated by improved academic performance, social behaviour, and other measures (Hetherington & Clingempeel, 1992).

Longitudinal studies have drawbacks. For example, it can be difficult to enlist volunteers to participate in a study that will last a lifetime. Many subjects fall out of touch as the years pass; others die. Also, those who remain in the study tend to be more motivated than those who drop out. The researchers must be patient. To compare three-year-olds with six-year-olds, they must wait three years. In the early stages of such a study, the idea of comparing three-year-olds with twenty-one-year-olds remains a distant dream. When the researchers themselves are middle-aged or older, they must hope that the candle of yearning for knowledge will be kept lit by a new generation of researchers.

Cross-Sectional Studies

Because of the drawbacks of longitudinal studies, most research that compares children of different ages is cross-sectional. In other words, most investigators gather data on what the "typical" six-month-old is doing by finding children who are six months old today. When they expand their research to the behaviour of typical twelve-month-olds, they seek another group of children, and so on.

© Mehmet Dilsiz/Shutterstock, Inc.

Does Text Messaging or Using Facebook Illustrate the Cohort Effect?
Children and adults of different ages experience cultural and other events unique to their age group. This is known as the cohort effect. For example, today's children—unlike their parents—are growing up taking video games, the Internet, and rap stars for granted.

Concept Review 1.4 Comparison of Cross-Sectional and Longitudinal Research

	Cross-Sectional Research	Longitudinal Research
Description	• Studies children of different ages at the same point in time	• Studies the same children repeatedly over time
Advantages	• Can be completed in short period of time • No dropout or practice effects	• Allows researchers to follow development over time • Studies the relationships between behaviour at earlier and later ages
Disadvantages	• Does not study development across time • Cannot study relationship between behaviour displayed at earlier and later ages • Is prey to cohort effect (subjects from different age groups may not be comparable)	• Expensive • Takes a long time to complete • Subjects drop out • Subjects who drop out may differ systematically from those who remain in study • Practice effects may occur

A major drawback to cross-sectional research is the **cohort effect.** A cohort is a group of people born at about the same time. As a result, they experience cultural and other events unique to their age group. In other words, children and adults of different ages are not likely to have shared similar cultural backgrounds. People who are seventy years old today, for example, grew up without TV. (It could happen.) People who are fifty years old today grew up before the era of space travel. When they were children, no explorers had yet left Earth. Today's forty-year-olds did not spend their earliest years with *Sesame Street,* a TV program that has greatly influenced millions of children and young adults of a somewhat younger cohort. And today's children are growing up taking video games and the Internet for granted. In fact, for today's children, Britney Spears is an older woman.

Children of past generations also grew up with different expectations about gender roles and appropriate social behaviour. Women in the Terman Studies of Genius generally chose motherhood over careers. Today's girls are growing up with female role models who are astronauts, government officials, and athletes. Moreover, today the great majority of mothers are in the workforce, and their attitudes about women's roles have changed.

In other words, today's seventy-five-year-olds are not today's five-year-olds as seen seventy years later. The times change, and their influence on children changes also. In longitudinal studies, we know that we have the same individuals as they have developed over five, twenty-five, even fifty years or more. In cross-sectional research, we can only hope that they will be comparable.

cohort effect Similarities in behaviour among a group of peers that stem from the fact that group members are approximately of the same age. (A possible source of misleading information in cross-sectional research.)

Cross-Sequential Research

Cross-sequential research combines the longitudinal, cross-sectional, and time-lag methods so that many of their individual drawbacks are overcome. In the cross-sequential study, the full span of the ideal longitudinal study is broken up into convenient segments (see Figure 1.7). Assume that we wish to follow the attitudes of children toward gender roles from the age of four through the age of twelve. The typical longitudinal study would take eight years. However, we can divide this eight-year span in half by attaining two samples of children (a cross-section) instead of one: four-year-olds and eight-year-olds. We would then interview, test, and observe each group at the beginning of the study (2008) and again four years later (2012). By the time of the second observation period, the four-year-olds would have become eight years old, and the eight-year-olds would have become twelve.

cross-sequential research An approach that combines the longitudinal and cross-sectional methods by following individuals of different ages for abbreviated periods of time.

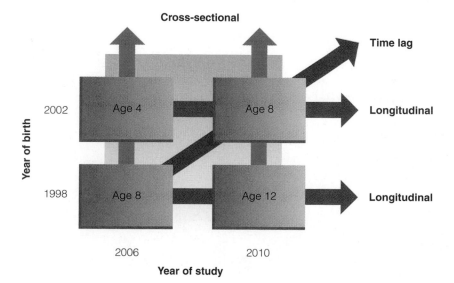

Figure 1.7

Example of Cross-Sequential Research

Cross-sequential research combines three methods: cross-sectional, longitudinal, and time lag. The child's age at the time of testing appears in the boxes. Vertical columns represent cross-sectional comparisons. Horizontal rows represent longitudinal comparisons. Diagonals represent time-lag comparisons.

time lag The study of developmental processes by taking measures of children of the same age group at different times.

An obvious advantage to this collapsed method is that the study is completed in four years rather than eight. Still, the testing and retesting of samples provides some of the continuity of the longitudinal study. By observing both samples at the age of eight (this is called a **time-lag** comparison), we can also determine whether they are, in fact, comparable or whether the four-year difference in their birthdates is associated with a cohort effect—that is, cultural and other environmental changes that lead to different attitudes.

Ethical Considerations

Psychologists adhere to a number of ethical standards that are intended to promote the dignity of the individual, foster human welfare, and maintain scientific integrity. These standards also ensure that psychologists do not undertake research methods or treatments that are harmful to research participants (Canadian Psychological Association, 2000; American Psychological Association, 1992). *Question: What ethical guidelines are involved in research in child development?*

Various professional groups—such as the Canadian Psychological Association, the American Psychological Association, and the Society for Research in Child Development—and government review boards have proposed guidelines for research with children. The overriding purpose of these guidelines is to protect children from harm. These guidelines include the following:

- Researchers are not to use methods that may do physical or psychological harm.
- Children and their parents must be informed of the purposes of the research and about the research methods.
- Children and their parents must provide voluntary consent to participate in the study.
- Children and their parents may withdraw from the study at any time, for any reason, and without penalty.
- Children and their parents should be offered information about the results of the study.
- The identities of the children participating in a study are to remain confidential.
- Researchers should present their research plans to a committee of their colleagues and gain the committee's approval before proceeding.

These guidelines present researchers with a number of hurdles to overcome before proceeding with and while conducting research. But because they protect the welfare of children, the guidelines are valuable.

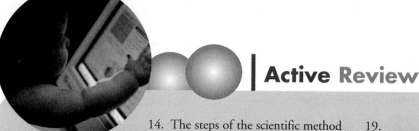

Active Review

14. The steps of the scientific method include formulating a research question, developing a _____, testing the hypothesis, drawing conclusions, and publishing results.

15. _____ observation studies are conducted in the real-life setting.

16. The _____ study is a carefully drawn account or biography of an individual child.

17. A correlational study describes relationships but does not reveal _____ and effect.

18. In an experiment, members of an experimental group receive a treatment, whereas members of a _____ group do not.

19. _____ research observes the same children repeatedly over time.

20. In cross-_____ research, children of different ages are observed and compared.

Reflect & Relate: How do you gather information about the behaviour and mental processes of other people? Which of the methods described in this section come closest to your own? Are your methods adequately scientific? Explain.

Go to
W W W www.voyages1ce.nelson.com
for an interactive version of this review.

Recite: *An Active Summary*™

1. What is child development?

The field of child development attempts to advance knowledge of the processes that govern the development of children's physical structures, traits, behaviours, and cognitions. *Growth* usually refers to changes in size or quantity, whereas *development* refers also to changes in quality.

2. Why do researchers study child development?

Researchers study child development to gain insight into human nature, the origins of adult behaviour, the origins of developmental problems, ways of optimizing development, the origins of sex differences and gender roles, and the effects of culture on development.

3. What views of children do we find throughout history?

Locke focused on the role of the environment or experience in development. Rousseau argued that children are good by nature, and if allowed to express their natural impulses, they would develop into moral and giving people. Darwin originated the modern theory of evolution and was one of the first observers to keep a baby biography. Hall founded child development as an academic discipline. Binet developed the first modern standardized intelligence test.

4. What are theories? Why do we have them?

Theories are related sets of statements about events. Theories of development help us describe, explain, and predict, and they influence development.

5. What is Freud's psychoanalytic theory of child development?

Freud viewed children as caught in conflict. He believed that people undergo *oral, anal, phallic, latency,* and *genital* stages of psychosexual development. Too little or too much gratification in a stage can lead to fixation.

6. How does Erikson's theory differ from Freud's?

Erikson's psychosocial theory sees social relationships as more important than sexual or aggressive impulses. Erikson extended Freud's five developmental stages to eight (to include adulthood) and labelled stages after life crises.

7. What is the theory of behaviourism?

Watson argued that scientists must address observable behaviour only, not mental activity. Behaviourism relies on two types of learning: classical conditioning and operant conditioning. In classical conditioning, one stimulus comes to signal another by being paired repeatedly with it. In operant conditioning, children learn to engage in or to discontinue behaviour because of its effects (reinforcement or lack of reinforcement).

8. How does social cognitive theory differ from behaviourism?

Social cognitive theorists, such as Bandura, argue that much learning occurs by observing models and that children choose whether or not to engage in behaviours they have learned.

9. What are Jean Piaget's views on development?

Piaget saw children as actors on the environment, not reactors. He studied how children form mental representations of the world and manipulate them. Piaget's theory uses the concepts of *schemes, adaptation, assimilation, accommodation,* and *equilibration.* He hypothesized that children's cognitive processes develop in an invariant series of stages: *sensorimotor, preoperational, concrete operational,* and *formal operational.*

10. What is information-processing theory?

Information-processing theory deals with the ways in which children encode information, transfer it to working memory (short-term memory), manipulate it, place information in storage (long-term memory), and retrieve it from storage.

11. What is the scope of the biological perspective?

The biological perspective refers to heredity and to developments such as formation of sperm and ova, gains in height and weight, maturation of the nervous system, and the way hormones spur the changes of puberty.

12. What is ethology?

Ethology involves instinctive, or inborn, behaviour patterns, termed *fixed action patterns (FAPs).* Many FAPs, such as those involved in attachment, occur during a *critical period* of life.

13. What is the ecological systems theory of child development?

Bronfenbrenner's ecological theory explains development in terms of the *reciprocal interaction* between children and the settings in which development occurs. These settings are the *microsystem, mesosystem, exosystem, macrosystem,* and *chronosystem.*

14. What is meant by the sociocultural perspective?

The sociocultural perspective emphasizes that children are social beings who are influenced by their cultural backgrounds.

15. What are the key concepts of Vygotsky's sociocultural theory?

Vygotsky's key concepts are the *zone of proximal development* (*ZPD*) and *scaffolding.* Children internalize conversations and explanations that help them gain skills. Children learn ways of solving problems within a cultural context.

16. What is the connection between the sociocultural perspective and human diversity?

The sociocultural perspective addresses the richness of children's diversity, as in their ethnicity and sex. Understanding the cultural heritages and historical problems of children from various ethnic groups is necessary for education and psychological intervention.

17. Which exerts the greater influence on children: nature or nurture?

Development would appear to reflect the interaction of nature (genetics) and nurture (nutrition, cultural and family backgrounds, and opportunities to learn about the world).

18. Is development continuous or discontinuous?

Maturational, psychoanalytic, and cognitive-developmental theorists see development as discontinuous (occurring in stages). Aspects of physical development, such as the adolescent growth spurt, do occur in stages. Learning theorists tend to see development as more continuous.

19. Are children active ("prewired" to act on the world) or are they passive (shaped by experience)?

Bronfenbrenner and Bandura do not see children as entirely active or entirely passive. They believe that children are influenced by the environment but that the influence is reciprocal.

20. What is the scientific method?

The scientific method is a systematic way of formulating and answering research questions that includes formulating a research question, developing a hypothesis, testing the hypothesis, drawing conclusions, and publishing results.

21. What is naturalistic observation?

Naturalistic observation is conducted in "the field"—in the real-life settings in which children develop.

22. What is the case study?

The case study is a carefully drawn account or biography of the behaviour of a child. Information may be derived from diaries, observation, questionnaires, standardized tests, interviews, and public records.

23. What does it mean to correlate information?

Correlation enables researchers to determine whether one behaviour or trait is related to another. A correlation coefficient can vary between +1.00 and −1.00. Correlational studies reveal relationships but not cause and effect.

24. What is an experiment?

In an experiment, an experimental group receives a treatment (independent variable), whereas another group (a control group) does not. Participants are observed to determine whether the treatment has an effect.

25. How do researchers study development over time?

Longitudinal research studies the same children repeatedly over time. Cross-sectional research observes and compares children of different ages. A drawback to cross-sectional research is the cohort effect. Cross-sequential research combines the longitudinal and cross-sectional methods by breaking down the full span of the ideal longitudinal study into convenient segments.

26. What ethical guidelines are involved in research in child development?

Ethical standards promote the dignity of the individual, foster human welfare, and maintain scientific integrity. Researchers are not to use treatments that may do harm. Subjects must participate voluntarily.

W W W **Go to**
www.voyages1ce.nelson.com
for an interactive version of this summary review.

Key Terms

child *(page 4)*
infancy *(page 4)*
conception *(page 4)*
prenatal period *(page 4)*
development *(page 5)*
motor development *(page 5)*
growth *(page 5)*
gender roles *(page 6)*
PKU *(page 6)*
SIDS *(page 6)*
behaviourism *(page 8)*
maturation *(page 8)*
theory *(page 9)*
stage theory *(page 10)*
preconscious *(page 10)*
unconscious *(page 10)*
psychosexual development *(page 11)*
psychosocial development *(page 13)*
life crisis *(page 13)*
identity crisis *(page 14)*
behaviour modification *(page 14)*
classical conditioning *(page 14)*
stimulus *(page 14)*
elicit *(page 14)*
unconditioned stimulus *(page 15)*
unconditioned response *(page 15)*
conditioned stimulus *(page 16)*
conditioned response *(page 16)*

operant conditioning *(page 16)*
reinforcement *(page 17)*
positive reinforcer *(page 17)*
negative reinforcer *(page 17)*
extinction *(page 17)*
punishment *(page 17)*
time-out *(page 17)*
shaping *(page 17)*
socialization *(page 18)*
social cognitive theory *(page 18)*
mental representations *(page 18)*
observational learning *(page 18)*
cognitive-developmental theory *(page 20)*
scheme *(page 20)*
adaptation *(page 21)*
assimilation *(page 21)*
accommodation *(page 21)*
equilibration *(page 21)*
ethology *(page 24)*
fixed action pattern (FAP) *(page 24)*
ecology *(page 24)*
ecological systems theory *(page 24)*
microsystem *(page 25)*
mesosystem *(page 25)*
exosystem *(page 26)*
macrosystem *(page 26)*
chronosystem *(page 26)*

zone of proximal development (ZPD) *(page 28)*
scaffolding *(page 28)*
ethnic groups *(page 29)*
gender *(page 30)*
nature *(page 33)*
nurture *(page 33)*
genes *(page 33)*
empirical *(page 35)*
hypothesis *(page 36)*
naturalistic observation *(page 37)*
variables *(page 38)*
case study *(page 38)*
standardized test *(page 38)*
correlation coefficient *(page 38)*
positive correlation *(page 38)*
negative correlation *(page 39)*
experiment *(page 40)*
treatment *(page 40)*
independent variable *(page 40)*
dependent variable *(page 40)*
experimental group *(page 40)*
control group *(page 40)*
longitudinal research *(page 41)*
cross-sectional research *(page 41)*
cohort effect *(page 43)*
cross-sequential research *(page 43)*
time lag *(page 44)*

Active Learning Resources

Observing Children and Adolescents CD-ROM

Check out your Observing Children and Adolescents CD-ROM. Observational videos cover child development from infancy to adolescence. This package will allow you to experience and learn critical concepts in the field of child development.

Visit Your Companion Website for This Book
http://www.voyages1CE.nelson.com

Check out this companion website, where you will find online resources directly linked to your book. The website includes interactive exercises related to PQ4R and Power Visuals for mastering and reviewing key concepts as well as quizzing, chapter outlines, and much more!

CengageNOW!™
http://hed.nelson.com

Go to this site for the link to CengageNOW™, your one-stop study shop. Take a Pretest for this chapter, and CengageNOW™ will generate a personalized Study Plan based on your test results! The Study Plan will identify the topics you need to review and direct you to online resources to help you master those topics. You can then take a Posttest to help you determine the concepts you have mastered and those you still need to work on.

Heredity and Conception

PREVIEW

TRUTH OR FICTION?

● ● ● ● ● ● ● ● ● ● ●

(T)(F) Your father determined whether you are female or male.

(T)(F) Brown eyes are dominant over blue eyes.

(T)(F) You can carry the genes for a deadly illness and not become sick yourself.

(T)(F) One hundred and twenty to 150 boys are conceived for every 100 girls.

(T)(F) Sperm travel about at random inside the woman's reproductive tract, so that reaching the ovum is a matter of luck.

(T)(F) Extensive athletic activity may contribute to infertility in the male.

(T)(F) "Test-tube" babies are grown in a laboratory dish throughout their nine-month gestation period.

(T)(F) You can select the sex of your child.

Go to

http://www.voyages1CE.nelson.com
for an interactive version of this "Truth or Fiction" feature.

S he went for the girl. Kathy des Jardins (2001) had three boys—a pair of ten-year-old twins and a five-year-old—and decided, "Enough is enough." How delightful it would be to have a little girl. Although she was in her early forties and had some fertility problems, she would try. But was she going to leave the sex of her baby to chance? You might think that after having three boys, the odds were now in her favour. But that's not the way it works.

The more boys you have already, the more likely it is that you will have another boy if you try again (because there may be something systematic—even if unknown—about the way the couple determines the sex of their child).

So Kathy placed her (sex-selection) fate in the hands of a company that touted a 90 percent success rate in helping couples have girls rather than boys (and a lower success rate in selecting boys). How does the company do it? By sorting sperm according to whether they bear Y sex chromosomes (which combine with ova to develop into boys) or X sex chromosomes (which make girls). Kathy and her husband spent thousands of dollars, chemically induced her reluctant **ovaries** to produce **ova,** and underwent artificial insemination to maximize the chances of conception, but—as it turns out—she didn't get pregnant.

Yet each year, millions upon millions of other women do. In this chapter, we explore heredity and conception. We could say that development begins long before conception. Development involves the origins of the genetic structures that determine that human embryos will grow arms rather than wings, lungs rather than gills, and hair rather than scales. Our discussion thus begins with an examination of the building blocks of heredity: genes and chromosomes. Then, we describe the process of conception and find that the odds against any one sperm uniting with an ovum are, as Kathy found, quite literally astronomical.

The Influence of Heredity on Development: The Nature of Nature

Consider some of the facts of life:

- People cannot breathe underwater (without special equipment).
- People cannot fly (without special equipment).
- Fish cannot learn to speak French or dance an Irish jig, even if you raise them in enriched environments and send them to finishing school.

We cannot breathe underwater or fly because we have not inherited gills or wings. Fish are similarly limited by their heredity. *Question: What is meant by heredity?* **Heredity** defines one's nature—which is based on the biological transmission of traits and characteristics from one generation to another. Because of their heredity, fish cannot speak French or do a jig.

Heredity plays a momentous role in the determination of human traits. The structures we inherit both make our behaviours possible and place limits on them. The field within the science of biology that studies heredity is called **genetics.**

Genetic (inherited) influences are fundamental in the transmission of physical traits, such as height, hair texture, and eye colour. Genetics also appears to be a factor in intelligence and in the origins of personality traits such as activity level, sociability, shyness, fearfulness, **neuroticism,** empathy, effectiveness as a parent, happiness, even interest in arts and crafts (Bouchard & Loehlin, 2001; Carey & DiLalla, 1994; Lykken & Csikszentmihalyi, 2001). Genetic influences are also implicated in psychological problems and disorders, such as schizophrenia; anxiety and depression; dependence on nicotine, alcohol, and other substances; and criminal behaviour (Kendler et al., 2000a; Kendler, Myers, & Neale, 2000b; Nurnberger et al., 2001;

ovary A female reproductive organ, located in the abdomen, that produces female reproductive cells (ova).

ovum (pl. ova) A female reproductive cell.

heredity The transmission of traits and characteristics from parent to child by means of genes.

genetics The branch of biology that studies heredity.

neuroticism A personality trait characterized by anxiety and emotional instability.

Plomin & McGuffin, 2003; Sullivan, Neale, & Kendler, 2000). Even so, most behaviour patterns also reflect life experiences and, once people come to understand their situations and their own abilities, personal choice (Sullivan et al., 2000).

Chromosomes and Genes

Heredity is made possible by microscopic structures called chromosomes and genes. *Question: What are chromosomes and genes?* **Chromosomes** are rod-shaped structures found in cells. A normal human cell contains forty-six chromosomes organized into twenty-three pairs. Each chromosome contains thousands of segments called genes. **Genes** are the biochemical materials that regulate the development of traits. Some traits, such as blood type, appear to be transmitted by a single pair of genes—one of which is derived from each parent. Other traits, referred to as **polygenic,** are determined by combinations of pairs of genes. Most human behaviours are believed to be effected by combinations of genes (McGuffin, Riley, & Plomin, 2001).

We have 30 000 to 40 000 genes in every cell of our bodies (International Human Genome Sequencing Consortium, 2001). Genes are segments of large strands of **deoxyribonucleic acid (DNA).** The form of DNA was first demonstrated in the 1950s by James Watson and Francis Crick (1958). DNA takes the form of a double spiral, or helix, similar in appearance to a twisting ladder (see Figure 2.1). In all living things, from one-celled animals to fish to people, the sides of the "ladder" consist of alternating segments of phosphate (P) and simple sugar (S). The "rungs" of the ladder are attached to the sugars and consist of one of two pairs of bases, either adenine with thymine (A with T) or cytosine with guanine (C with G). The sequence of the rungs is the genetic code that will cause the developing organism to grow arms or wings, skin or scales.

Mitosis and Meiosis

We begin life as a single cell, or **zygote,** that divides again and again. *Question: What happens during cell division?* There are two types of cell division: *mitosis* and *meiosis.* **Mitosis** is the cell-division process by which growth occurs and tissues are replaced.

chromosomes   Rod-shaped structures composed of genes that are found within the nuclei of cells.

gene   The basic unit of heredity. Genes are composed of deoxyribonucleic acid (DNA).

polygenic   Resulting from many genes.

deoxyribonucleic acid (DNA)   Genetic material that takes the form of a double helix composed of phosphates, sugars, and bases.

zygote   A new cell formed from the union of a sperm and an ovum (egg cell); a fertilized egg.

mitosis   The form of cell division in which each chromosome splits lengthwise to double in number. Half of each chromosome combines with chemicals to retake its original form and then moves to the new cell.

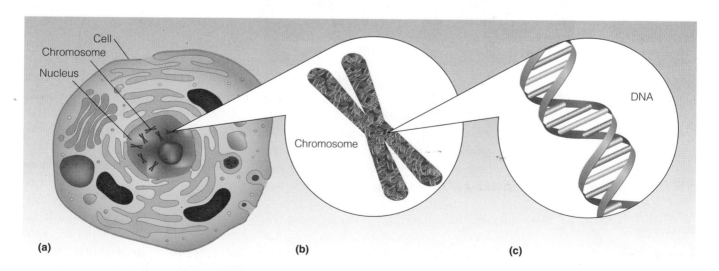

Figure 2.1

Cells, Chromosomes, and DNA

(a) The nuclei of cells contain chromosomes. (b) Chromosomes are made up of DNA. (c) DNA takes the form of a double spiral, or helix.

POWER VISUAL!
See your student companion website for an interactive version of Figure 2.1.

mutation A sudden variation in a heritable characteristic, as by an accident that affects the composition of genes.

meiosis The form of cell division in which each pair of chromosomes splits so that one member of each pair moves to the new cell. As a result, each new cell has 23 chromosomes.

autosome Either member of a pair of chromosomes (with the exception of sex chromosomes).

sex chromosome A chromosome in the shape of a Y (male) or X (female) that determines the sex of the child.

Through mitosis, our genetic code is carried into new cells in our bodies. In mitosis, strands of DNA break apart, or "unzip" (see Figure 2.2). The double helix is then rebuilt in a process of duplication. Each incomplete rung combines with the appropriate "partner" element (i.e., G combines with C, A with T, and so on) to form a new complete ladder. The two resulting identical copies of the DNA strand move apart when the cell divides, each becoming a member of one of the newly formed cells. As a consequence, the genetic code is identical in new cells unless **mutations** occur through radiation or other environmental influences. Mutations are also believed to occur by chance, but not often.

Sperm and ova are produced through **meiosis,** or *reduction division.* In meiosis, the forty-six chromosomes within the cell nucleus first line up into twenty-three pairs. The DNA ladders then unzip, leaving unpaired chromosome halves. When the cell divides, one member of each pair goes to each newly formed cell. As a consequence, each new cell nucleus contains only twenty-three chromosomes, not forty-six. Thus, a cell that results from meiosis has half the genetic material of a cell that results from mitosis.

When a sperm cell fertilizes an ovum, we receive twenty-three chromosomes from our father's sperm cell and twenty-three from our mother's ovum; the combined chromosomes form twenty-three pairs (Figure 2.3). Twenty-two of the pairs are **autosomes**—that is, pairs that look alike and possess genetic information concerning the same set of traits. The twenty-third pair consists of the **sex chromosomes,** which look different and determine our sex. We all receive an X sex chromosome (so called because of its X shape) from our mothers. *Truth or Fiction Revisited:* It is true that your father determined whether you are female or male, either by supplying a Y or an X sex chromosome. If we receive an X sex chromosome from our fathers, we develop into females. If we receive a Y sex chromosome (named after its Y shape) from our fathers, we develop into males.

Identical and Fraternal Twins

Question: How are twins formed? Now and then, a zygote divides into two cells that separate so that each subsequently develops into an individual with the same genetic makeup. These individuals are known as identical twins, or **monozygotic (MZ) twins.** If a woman produces two ova in the same month, and they are each fertilized by a different sperm cell, they develop into fraternal twins, or **dizygotic (DZ) twins.**

More than 4000 sets of twins are born in Canada each year (Multiple Births Canada, 2007). MZ twins, though rarer than DZ twins (National Center for Health Statistics, 2003), occur with equal frequency in all ethnic groups (about three per 1000 pregnancies), but the incidence of DZ twins varies with age and race (Tong, Caddy, & Short, 1997).

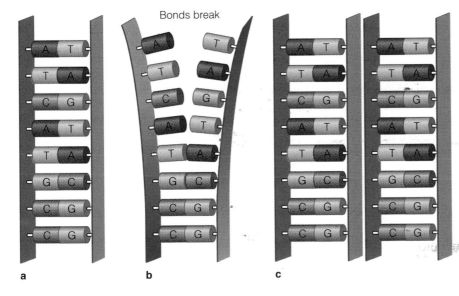

Bonds break

a   b   c

■ Adenine
■ Thymine
■ Cytosine
■ Guanine

Figure 2.2
Mitosis

(a) A segment of a strand of DNA before mitosis. (b) During mitosis, chromosomal strands of DNA "unzip." (c) The double helix is rebuilt in the cell as each incomplete "rung" combines with appropriate molecules. The resulting identical copies of the DNA strand move apart when the cell divides, each joining one of the new cells.

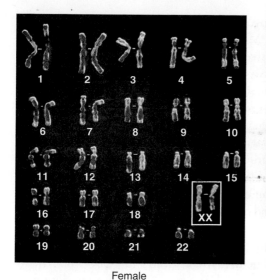

Female

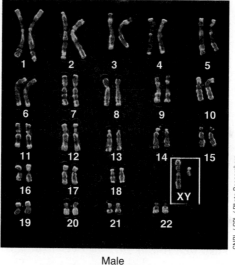

Male

CNRL / SPL / Photo Researchers

Figure 2.3
23 Pairs of Human Chromosomes
People normally have 23 pairs of chromosomes. Females have two X chromosomes, whereas males have an X and a Y sex chromosome.

DZ twins run in families. If a woman is a twin, if her mother was a twin, or if she has previously borne twins, the chances rise that she will bear twins (National Center for Health Statistics, 2003). Similarly, women who have borne several children have an increased likelihood of twins in subsequent pregnancies.

As women reach the end of their childbearing years, **ovulation** becomes less regular, resulting in a number of months when more than one ovum is released. Thus, the chances of twins increase with parental age (Raschka, 2000). Fertility drugs also enhance the chances of multiple births by causing more than one ovum to ripen and be released during any particular cycle (Division of Reproductive Health et al., 2000).

Dominant and Recessive Traits

Question: How do genes determine traits? Traits are determined by pairs of genes. Each member of a pair of genes is referred to as an **allele.** When both of the alleles for a trait, such as hair color, are the same, the person is said to be **homozygous** for that trait. (*Homo,* in this usage, derives from the Greek root meaning "same," not the Latin root meaning "man.") When the alleles for a trait differ, the person is **heterozygous** for that trait.

Gregor Mendel (1822-1884), an Austrian monk, established a number of laws of heredity through his work with pea plants. Mendel realized that some traits result from an "averaging" of the genetic instructions carried by the parents. When the effects of both alleles are shown, there is said to be incomplete dominance or codominance.

Mendel also discovered the "law of dominance." When a *dominant* allele is paired with a *recessive* allele, the trait determined by the dominant allele appears in the offspring. For example, the offspring from the crossing of purebred tall peas and purebred dwarf peas were tall, suggesting that tallness is dominant over dwarfism. We now know that many genes determine **dominant traits** or **recessive traits.**

Truth or Fiction Revisited: Brown eyes, for instance, are dominant over blue eyes. If one parent carried genes for only brown eyes and the other parent carried genes for only blue eyes, the children would invariably have brown eyes. But brown-eyed parents can also carry recessive genes for blue eyes, as shown in Figure 2.4. Similarly, the offspring of Mendel's crossing of purebred tall and purebred dwarf peas were not pure. They carried recessive genes for dwarfism.

If the recessive gene from one parent combines with the recessive gene from the other parent, the recessive trait will be shown. As suggested by Figure 2.4,

monozygotic (MZ) twins
Twins that derive from a single zygote that has split into two; identical twins. Each MZ twin carries the same genetic code.

dizygotic (DZ) twins Twins that derive from two zygotes; fraternal twins.

ovulation The releasing of an ovum from an ovary.

allele A member of a pair of genes.

homozygous Having two identical alleles.

heterozygous Having two different alleles.

dominant trait A trait that is expressed.

recessive trait A trait that is not expressed when the gene or genes involved have been paired with dominant genes. Recessive traits are transmitted to future generations and expressed if they are paired with other recessive genes.

approximately 25 percent of the offspring of brown-eyed parents who carry recessive blue eye colour will have blue eyes. Mendel found that 25 percent of the offspring of parent peas that carried recessive dwarfism would be dwarfs. Table 2.1 shows a number of dominant and recessive traits in humans.

Our discussion of eye colour has been simplified. The percentages are not always perfect, because other genes can alter the expression of the genes for brown and blue eyes, producing hazel, or greenish, eyes. Some genes also switch other genes "on" or "off" at various times during development. For example, we normally reach reproductive capacity in the teens and not earlier, and men who go bald usually do so during adulthood. Similarly, the heart and the limbs develop at different times in the embryo, again because of the switching on or off of certain genes by other genes.

carrier A person who carries and transmits characteristics but does not exhibit them.

People who bear one dominant gene and one recessive gene for a trait are said to be carriers of the recessive gene. In the cases of recessive genes that give rise to serious illnesses, carriers of those genes are fortunate to have dominant genes that cancel their effects. ***Truth or Fiction Revisited:*** It is true that you can carry the genes for a deadly illness and not become sick yourself. This occurs when genes are recessive and dominant genes cancel their effects.

Chromosomal or genetic abnormalities can cause health problems. Some chromosomal disorders reflect abnormalities in the twenty-two pairs of autosomes (such as Down syndrome); others reflect abnormalities in the twenty-third pair—the sex chromosomes (e.g., XYY syndrome). Some genetic abnormalities, such as cystic fibrosis, are caused by a single pair of genes; others are caused by combinations of genes. Diabetes mellitus, epilepsy, and peptic ulcers are **multifactorial problems;** that is, they reflect both a genetic predisposition *and* environmental contributors. Chromosomal and genetic abnormalities are discussed in the following sections and are summarized in Concept Review 2.1.

multifactorial problems Problems that stem from the interaction of heredity and environmental factors.

Figure 2.4

Transmission of Dominant and Recessive Traits

Two brown-eyed parents each carry a gene for blue eyes. Their children have an equal opportunity of receiving genes for brown eyes and blue eyes.

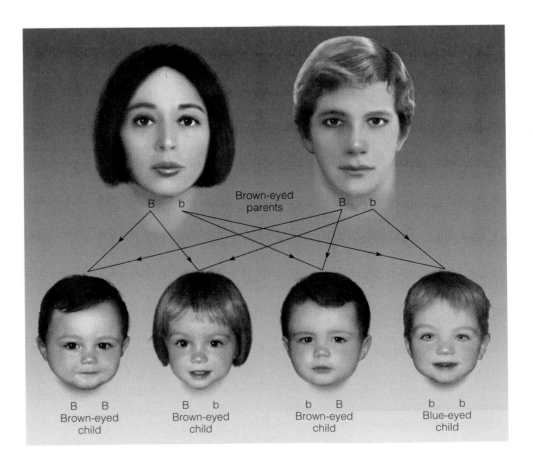

Examples of Dominant and Recessive Traits	
Dominant Trait	**Recessive Trait**
Dark hair	Blond hair
Dark hair	Red hair
Curly hair	Straight hair
Normal colour vision	Red-green colour blindness
Normal vision	Myopia (nearsightedness)
Farsightedness	Normal vision
Normal pigmentation	Deficiency of pigmentation in skin, hair, and retina (albinism)
Normal sensitivity to touch	Extremely fragile skin
Normal hearing	Some forms of deafness
Dimples	Lack of dimpling
Type A blood	Type O blood
Type B blood	Type O blood
Tolerance of lactose	Lactose intolerance

Chromosomal Abnormalities

People normally have forty-six chromosomes. Children with more or fewer chromosomes usually experience health problems or behavioural abnormalities. The risk of chromosomal abnormalities rises with the age of the parents (American Infertility Association, 2002; Centers for Disease Control and Prevention, 2002b). *Questions: What kinds of disorders are caused by chromosomal abnormalities?*

Down Syndrome

Down syndrome is usually caused by an extra chromosome on the twenty-first pair, resulting in forty-seven chromosomes. The probability of having a child with Down syndrome varies positively with the age of the parents: Older parents are more likely to bear children with the syndrome (see Table 2.2). The Canadian Down Syndrome Society (http://www.cdss.ca) describes Down syndrome as a naturally occurring chromosomal arrangement that occurs in approximately one in 800 births in Canada.

Down syndrome A chromosomal abnormality characterized by mental retardation and caused by an extra chromosome in the twenty-first pair.

	Risk of Giving Birth to an Infant with Chromosomal Abnormality According to Age of the Mother	
Maternal Age at Delivery	**Risk of Down Syndrome**	**Risk of all Chromosomal Abnormalities**
25	1/1380	1/480
30	1/966	1/390
35	1/428	1/180
40	1/129	1/65
45	1/28	1/19

Source: Prenatal Diagnosis and Medical Genetics Program, Mount Sinai Hospital (2001).

Concept Review 2.1 Chromosomal and Genetic Variations

Health Problem	Incidence	Comments	Treatment
Chromosomal Variations			
Down syndrome http://www.cdss.ca http://www.ndss.org	1 birth in 700-800 overall; risk increases with parental age	A condition characterized by a third chromosome on the twenty-first pair. A child with Down syndrome has a characteristic fold of skin over the eye and mental retardation.	No treatment, but educational programs are effective; usually fatal as a result of complications by middle age.
Klinefelter syndrome http://www .klinefeltersyndrome .org	1 male in 500-900	A disorder affecting males that is characterized by an extra X sex chromosome and that is connected with underdeveloped male secondary sex characteristics, gynecomastia, and mild mental retardation, particularly in language skills.	Hormone (testosterone) replacement therapy; special education.
Turner syndrome http://www .turnersyndrome.ca http://www.turner-syndrome-us.org	1 girl in 2500	A disorder that affects females, characterized by single X-sex-chromosomal structure and associated with infertility, poorly developed ovaries, underdevelopment of female secondary sex characteristics, and problems in visual-spatial skills and mathematics.	Hormone (estrogen) replacement therapy; special education.
XXX syndrome http://www.triplo-x .org	1 girl in 1000	A sex-chromosomal disorder that affects females and is connected with mild mental retardation.	Special education.
XYY syndrome http://www.aaa.dk/ turner/engelsk/index .htm	1 male in 700-1000	A sex-chromosomal disorder that affects males—sometimes referred to as "supermale syndrome"—and is connected with heavy beards, tallness, and mild mental retardation, particularly in language development.	None.
Genetic Disorders			
Cystic fibrosis http://www .cysticfibrosis.ca http://www.cff.org	1 birth in 3600 in Canada	A genetic disease caused by a recessive gene in which the pancreas and lungs become clogged with mucus, impairing the processes of respiration and digestion.	Physical therapy to loosen mucus and prompt bronchial drainage; antibiotics for infections of respiratory tract; management of diet.
Duchenne muscular dystrophy http://www.mdausa .org	1 male in 3000-5000	A fatal sex-linked degenerative muscle disease caused by a recessive gene, usually found in males and characterized by loss of ability to walk during middle childhood or early adolescence.	None; usually fatal by adolescence because of respiratory infection or cardiovascular damage.

Health Problem	Incidence	Comments	Treatment
Hemophilia **http://www .hemophilia.org http://www .hemophilia.ca**	1 male in 4000-10 000	A sex-linked disorder in which blood does not clot properly.	Transfusion of blood to introduce clotting factors; proactive avoidance of injury.
Huntington's disease **http://www.hdsa.org http://www.hsc-ca .org**	1 birth in 10 000 In Canada	A fatal neurological disorder caused by a dominant gene; onset occurs in middle adulthood.	None; usually fatal within 20 years of onset of symptoms.
Neural tube defects **http://ibis- birthdefects.org/ start/ntdfact.htm**	1 birth in 1000	Disorders of the brain or spine, such as *anencephaly,* in which part of the brain is missing, and *spina bifida,* in which part of the spine is exposed or missing. Some individuals with spina bifida survive for years, albeit with handicaps.	None for anencephaly, which is fatal; surgery to close spinal canal in spina bifida.
Phenylketonuria (PKU) **http://www .pkunetwork.org**	1 birth in 8000-10 000	A disorder caused by a recessive gene in which children cannot metabolize the amino acid phenylalanine, which builds up in the form of phenylpyruvic acid and causes mental retardation. PKU is diagnosable at birth.	Controlled by special diet, which can prevent mental retardation.
Sickle-cell anemia **http://www.ascaa.org**	Most common in Western and Central Africa, where as many as 25% have sickle cell traits and 1-2% of all babies are born with a form of the disease	A blood disorder caused by a recessive gene that mainly afflicts people whose families come from Africa, the Caribbean, the Eastern Mediterranean, the Middle East and Asia; deformed blood cells obstruct small blood vessels, decreasing their capacity to carry oxygen and heightening the risk of occasionally fatal infections.	Transfusions to treat anemia and prevent strokes; antibiotics for infections; anesthetics; fatal before adulthood to about half of those with disorder.
Tay-Sachs disease **http://www.ntsad.org**	1 in 3000-3600 Jews of Eastern European origin	A fatal neurological disorder caused by a recessive gene. High risk populations include: Ashkenazi Jews, French Canadians, Louisiana Cajun,and Pennsylvania Dutch.	None; usually fatal by age 3-4.
Thalassemia (Cooley's anemia) **http://www .thalassemia.org**	1 birth in 400-500 among children of Mediterranean descent	A disorder caused by a recessive gene that primarily afflicts people of Mediterranean origin and causes weakness and susceptibility to infections.	Frequent blood transfusions; usually fatal by adolescence or young adulthood.

Figure 2.5

Down Syndrome

The development and adjustment of children with Down syndrome are related to their acceptance by their families. Children with Down syndrome who are reared at home develop more rapidly and achieve higher levels of functioning than those who are reared in institutions.

Children with Down syndrome have characteristic facial features that include a rounded face, a protruding tongue, a broad, flat nose, and a sloping fold of skin over the inner corners of the eyes (Figure 2.5). More than 40 percent of children with Down syndrome have a congenital heart malformation (Canadian Down Syndrome Society, 2007). Often persons with Down syndrome die from cardiovascular problems by middle age, although modern medicine has extended life appreciably. The children show deficits in cognitive development, including language development (Bates, 2004; Nichols et al., 2004), and in motor development (Berglund, Eriksson, & Johansson, 2001; Capone, 2001). They encounter frequent disorders of the ear, nose, and throat, which also contribute to academic problems (Shott, 2000).

As you can imagine, children with Down syndrome may face adjustment problems in school and in the community at large (King, Scollon, Ramsey, & Williams, 2000). Other children are not always sensitive to their needs and feelings and may poke fun at them. Children with Down syndrome also tend to need more attention from their parents. Parental response is variable; some parents are overwhelmed, and a few are abusive, but many parents report that the special needs of their children have contributed to their own self-esteem and self-worth (King et al., 2000). We can make the generalization that parents who *want* their children usually do a better job of parenting, and this same principle applies when their children have special needs.

Some individuals with Down syndrome attend postsecondary schools, work, and get married. When people with Down syndrome are given the opportunity to be fully contributing members of society, it can be a very positive experience for all. A two-minute video on the website of the J. P. Das Developmental Disabilities Centre at the University of Alberta (http://www.ualberta.ca/~jpdasddc/inclusion/index.html) depicts the friendship between two students in an inclusive high school.

Sex-Linked Chromosomal Abnormalities

A number of disorders stem from an abnormal number of sex chromosomes and are therefore said to be **sex-linked chromosomal abnormalities.** Most individuals with an abnormal number of sex chromosomes are infertile. Beyond that common finding, there are many differences, some of them associated with "maleness" or "femaleness."

sex-linked chromosomal abnormalities Abnormalities that are transmitted from generation to generation, carried by a sex chromosome, usually an X sex chromosome.

Approximately one male in 700–1000 has an extra Y chromosome. The Y chromosome is associated with maleness, and the extra Y sex chromosome apparently heightens male secondary sex characteristics. For example, XYY males are somewhat taller than average and develop heavier beards. For these reasons, males with XYY sex chromosomal structure were once referred to as "supermales." Although the prefix *super-* often implies superior, it turns out that XYY males tend to have more problems than XY males. For example, they are often mildly delayed, particularly in language development. As part of their "excessive maleness," it was once thought that XYY males were given to aggressive criminal behaviour. When we examine prison populations, we find that the number of XYY males is "overrepresented" relative to their number in the population. However, it may be that the number of XYY males in prisons reflects their level of intelligence rather than aggressiveness. Most XYY males in prison have committed crimes against property (e.g., stealing) rather than crimes against persons (e.g., assault and battery). And when we examine XYY individuals in the general population, most do not have records of aggressive criminal behaviour (Goetz, Johnstone, & Ratcliffe, 1999; Ike, 2000).

Klinefelter syndrome A chromosomal disorder found among males that is caused by an extra X sex chromosome and characterized by infertility and mild mental retardation.

testosterone A male sex hormone produced by the testes.

About one male in 500–900 has **Klinefelter syndrome,** which is caused by an extra X sex chromosome (an XXY sex chromosomal pattern) (Fales et al., 2003). XXY males produce less of the male sex hormone—**testosterone**—than normal males. As a result, male primary and secondary sex characteristics, such as the testes, deepening of the voice, musculature, and the male pattern of body hair, do not develop properly. XXY males usually have enlarged breasts (*gynecomastia*) and are usually mildly mentally retarded, particularly in language skills. XXY males are typically treated with testosterone replacement therapy, which can foster growth of sex characteristics and elevate the mood, but the therapy does not reverse infertility.

About one girl in 2500 has a single X sex chromosome and as a result develops what is called **Turner syndrome.** The external genitals of girls with Turner syndrome are normal, but their ovaries are poorly developed, and they produce little of the female sex hormone **estrogen.** Girls with this problem are shorter than average and infertile. Because of low estrogen production, they do not develop breasts or menstruate. Researchers have connected a specific pattern of cognitive deficits with low estrogen levels: problems in visual-spatial skills, mathematics, and nonverbal memory (Bruandet Molko, Cohen, & Dehaene, 2004; Ross et al, 2000b). They have also found these problems to be somewhat reversible with estrogen therapy (Ross et al., 2000a). Other researchers have found that girls with Turner syndrome have some motor impairment (Nijhuis-van der Sanden, Smits-Engelsman, & Eling, 2000). Such motor impairment may be connected with higher verbal scores than performance scores on intelligence tests (O'Connor, Fitzgerald, & Hoey, 2000).

About one girl in 1000 has an XXX sex chromosomal structure, *Triple X syndrome.* Such girls are normal in appearance. However, they tend to show lower-than-average language skills and poorer memory for recent events. Development of external sexual organs appears normal enough, although there is increased incidence of infertility.

Genetic Abnormalities

A number of disorders have been attributed to defective genes. *Question: What kinds of disorders are caused by genetic abnormalities?*

Phenylketonuria

The enzyme disorder **phenylketonuria (PKU)** is transmitted by a recessive gene and affects about one child in 8000. Therefore, if both parents possess the gene, PKU will be transmitted to one child in four (as in Figure 2.4). Two children in four will possess the gene but will not develop the disorder. These two, like their parents, will be carriers of the disease. One child in four will not receive the recessive gene. Therefore, he or she will not be a carrier.

Children with PKU cannot metabolize an amino acid called phenylalanine. As a consequence, the substance builds up in their bodies and impairs the functioning of the central nervous system. The results are serious: mental retardation, psychological disorders, and physical problems (Antshel & Waisbren, 2003; Huijbregts et al., 2003). We have no cure for PKU, but it can be detected in newborn children through analysis of the blood or urine. Children with PKU who are placed on diets low in phenylalanine within three to six weeks after birth develop normally. The diet prohibits all meat, poultry, fish, dairy products, beans, and nuts. Fruits, vegetables, and some starchy foods are allowed. Pediatricians recommend staying on the diet at least until adolescence, and some encourage staying on it for life.

Huntington's Disease

Huntington's disease (HD) is a fatal, progressive degenerative disorder and is a dominant trait. Physical symptoms include uncontrollable muscle movements. Psychological symptoms include loss of intellectual functioning and personality change. Because the onset of HD is delayed until middle adulthood, many individuals with

Turner syndrome A chromosomal disorder found among females that is caused by having a single X sex chromosome and characterized by infertility.

estrogen A female sex hormone produced mainly by the ovaries.

phenylketonuria (PKU) (fee-nul-key-tun-UR-ee-uh) A genetic abnormality in which phenylalanine builds up and causes mental retardation.

Huntington's disease (HD) A fatal genetic neurological disorder whose onset is in middle age.

the defect have borne children only to discover years later that they and possibly half their offspring will inevitably develop it. Fortunately, the disorder is rare—affecting one in every 10 000 Canadians. Medicines are helpful with some of the symptoms of HD, but they do not cure it (Bonelli & Kapfhammer, 2003; Bonelli et al., 2003).

Sickle-Cell Anemia

sickle-cell anemia A genetic disorder that decreases the blood's capacity to carry oxygen.

Sickle-cell anemia is caused by a recessive gene and is most common among people whose families come from Africa, the Caribbean, the Eastern Mediterranean, the Middle East and Asia. In sickle-cell anemia, red blood cells take on the shape of a sickle and clump together, obstructing small blood vessels and decreasing the oxygen supply. The lessened oxygen supply can impair academic performance (Schatz, Brown, Pascual, Hsu, & DeBaun, 2001) and performance on tests of verbal skills, attention, and memory (Noll et al., 2001). Problems can also include painful and swollen joints, jaundice, and potentially fatal conditions such as pneumonia, stroke, and heart and kidney failure. Some children with sickle-cell anemia are being taught to cope with the pain the condition causes through means such as relaxation training and focusing on pleasant imagery (Gil et al., 2001).

Tay-Sachs Disease

Tay-Sachs disease A fatal genetic neurological disorder.

Tay-Sachs disease is also caused by a recessive gene. It causes the central nervous system to degenerate, resulting in death. The disorder is most commonly found among children in Jewish families of Eastern European background. About one in thirty Jewish North Americans from this background carries the recessive gene for Tay-Sachs. Children with the disorder progressively lose control over their muscles. They experience visual and auditory sensory losses, develop mental retardation, become paralyzed, and die toward the end of early childhood, by about the age of five.

Cystic Fibrosis

cystic fibrosis A fatal genetic disorder in which mucus obstructs the lungs and pancreas.

Cystic fibrosis, also caused by a recessive gene, is the most common fatal hereditary disease among European Americans. It is estimated that one in every 3,600 children born in Canada has CF (Canadian Cystic Fibrosis Association, 2007). Children with the disease suffer from excessive production of thick mucus that clogs the pancreas and lungs. Most victims die of respiratory infections in their twenties.

Sex-Linked Genetic Abnormalities

hemophilia A genetic disorder in which blood does not clot properly.

sex-linked genetic abnormalities Abnormalities resulting from genes that are found on the X sex chromosome. They are more likely to be shown by male offspring (who do not have an opposing gene from a second X chromosome) than by female offspring.

muscular dystrophy (DIS-truh-fee) A chronic disease characterized by a progressive wasting away of the muscles.

Some genetic defects, such as **hemophilia,** are carried on only the X sex chromosome. For this reason, they are referred to as **sex-linked genetic abnormalities.** These defects also involve recessive genes. Females, who have two X sex chromosomes, are less likely than males to show sex-linked disorders, because the genes that cause the disorder would have to be present on both of a female's sex chromosomes for the disorder to be expressed. Sex-linked diseases are more likely to afflict sons of female carriers, because males have only one X sex chromosome, which they inherit from their mothers. Queen Victoria was a carrier of hemophilia and transmitted the blood disorder to many of her children, who, in turn, carried it into a number of the ruling houses of Europe. For this reason, hemophilia has been dubbed the "royal disease."

One form of **muscular dystrophy,** Duchenne muscular dystrophy, is sex-linked. Muscular dystrophy is characterized by a weakening of the muscles, which can lead to wasting away, inability to walk, and sometimes death. Other sex-linked abnormalities include diabetes, colour blindness, and some types of night blindness.

Genetic Counselling and Prenatal Testing

It is now possible to detect the genetic abnormalities that are responsible for hundreds of diseases. *Question: How do health professionals determine whether children will have genetic or chromosomal abnormalities?*

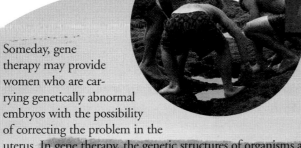

A Closer Look | *Gene Therapy*

Someday, gene therapy may provide women who are carrying genetically abnormal embryos with the possibility of correcting the problem in the uterus. In gene therapy, the genetic structures of organisms are changed by direct manipulation of their cells (Carter & Schuchman, 2001; Korf, 2003; Noguchi, 2003).

Innovations in genetic engineering have already given us screening for fatal hereditary diseases such as Huntington's disease and cystic fibrosis. The following therapies are in development:

• New vaccines for diseases such as hepatitis and herpes.

• Ways of detecting predispositions for disorders such as cancer or bipolar disorder by studying a newborn's (or fetus's) genetic code.

• Modification of the genetic codes of fetuses or children to prevent or cure disease (Carter & Schuchman, 2001). For example, a four-year-old girl recently was the first to receive new genes in an effort to cure a severe inherited immune deficiency disorder. Before treatment, the girl and her family rarely left home for fear of bringing back even a minor infection, which could have been life-threatening. Within a year after receiving gene therapy, the child's immune system responded so well that she could swim, take dancing lessons, and even go to school (Greenough, 1993).

• Insertion of foreign genes into human lymphocytes (white blood cells) to enhance the cells' ability to combat cancer and other diseases.

• Creation of new drugs from DNA.

• Treatment of hemophilia (Mannucci & Tuddenham, 2001).

Many of the ways in which science has permitted us to intervene in the reproductive process have engendered heated controversy (Gaskell, Einsiedel, Hallman, Hornig-Priest, Jackson, & Olsthoorn, 2005). Some people, including a number of religious leaders, fear that we are converting natural biological processes into a calamity that

will have profound moral consequences and change the face of our species (and others) in ways that we cannot foresee. Other people fear the invention of various kinds of biological monsters or disease agents—most of them microscopic—that we may not be able to control.

Some ethical questions that are listed on the Human Genome Project Information website (U.S. Department of Energy Office of Science, 2007) are

• What is normal and what is a disability or disorder, and who decides?

• Are disabilities diseases? Do they need to be cured or prevented?

• Does searching for a cure demean the lives of individuals presently affected by disabilities?

• Preliminary attempts at gene therapy are exorbitantly expensive. Who will have access to these therapies? Who will pay for their use?

What is there to conclude? Ugly scenarios are indeed possible, but so are splendid, health-enhancing outcomes. For example, Canadian researchers from Edmonton, Alberta, recently developed a protocol to treat type 1 diabetes with pancreatic islet cell injections. As scientists, we believe that there is no such thing as bad knowledge—only bad use of knowledge. As citizens, it is our duty to keep abreast of technical innovations and to ensure that their applications are beneficial.

Important and current information about Canadian gene therapy may be accessed through Health Canada postings (http://www.hc-sc.gc.ca/sr-sr/biotech/about-apropos/lab/gen_therap_e.html). Such scientific advancement is a global partnership. The much publicized Human Genome Project (HGP) started as an international collaboration in 1990 and ended in 2003. Its two main goals were to (a) chart the location of genes in the human genome, and (b) find the sequence of nucleotides that make up the DNA of human genes. Canada's leading source of information on genomics is Genome Canada, which has six genome centres across the country.

genetic counselling Advice concerning the probabilities that a couple's children will show genetic abnormalities.

In an effort to help parents avert these predictable tragedies, **genetic counselling** is becoming widely used, and many Canadian hospitals have specific programs dealing with genetic counselling. One such program, the *Prenatal Diagnosis and Medical Genetics program* (www.mtsinai.on.ca/pdmg), is found at Mount Sinai Hospital in Toronto, Ontario. Genetic counsellors compile information about a couple's genetic heritage to explore whether their children might develop genetic abnormalities. Couples who face a high risk of passing along genetic defects to their children sometimes elect to adopt children rather than conceive their own.

prenatal Before birth.

In addition, **prenatal** testing can indicate whether the embryo or fetus is carrying genetic abnormalities. Prenatal testing includes amniocentesis, chorionic villus sampling, ultrasound, and blood tests.

Amniocentesis

amniocentesis (AM-nee-oh-sen-TEE-sis) A procedure of drawing and examining fetal cells sloughed off into amniotic fluid to determine the presence of various disorders.

Amniocentesis is usually performed on the mother at about fourteen to sixteen weeks after conception, although many physicians now perform the procedure earlier. In this method, the health professional uses a syringe (needle) to withdraw fluid from the amniotic sac (Figure 2.6). The fluid contains cells that are sloughed off by the fetus. The cells are separated from the amniotic fluid, grown in a culture, and then examined microscopically for genetic and chromosomal abnormalities.

Figure 2.6
Amniocentesis

Amniocentesis allows prenatal identification of certain genetic and chromosomal disorders by examining genetic material sloughed off by the fetus into amniotic fluid. Amniocentesis also allows parents to learn the sex of their unborn child. Would you want to know?

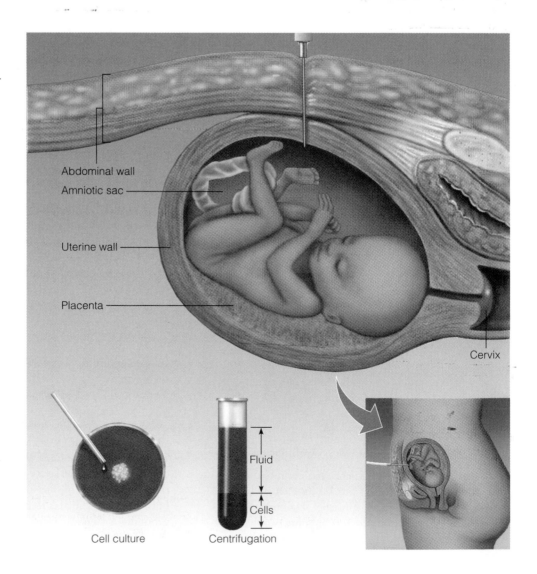

Abdominal wall

Amniotic sac

Uterine wall

Placenta

Cervix

Fluid

Cells

Cell culture   Centrifugation

Amniocentesis has become routine among Canadian women who become pregnant beyond the age of thirty-five because the chances of Down syndrome increase dramatically as women approach or pass the age of forty. But women carrying the children of aging fathers may also wish to have amniocentesis. Amniocentesis can detect the presence of well over 100 chromosomal and genetic abnormalities, including sickle-cell anemia, Tay-Sachs disease, **spina bifida,** muscular dystrophy, and Rh incompatibility in the fetus. Women (or their partners) who carry or have a family history of any of these disorders are advised to have amniocentesis performed. If the test reveals the presence of a serious disorder, the expectant parents may decide to abort the fetus. Or they may decide to continue the pregnancy and prepare themselves to raise a child who has special needs.

Amniocentesis also permits parents to learn the sex of their unborn child through examination of the sex chromosomes, but most parents learn the sex of their baby earlier by means of ultrasound. Amniocentesis carries some risk of miscarriage (about one woman in 100 who undergo the procedure will miscarry), so health professionals would not conduct it simply to learn the sex of the child.

Chorionic Villus Sampling

Chorionic villus sampling (CVS) is similar to amniocentesis but offers the advantage of diagnosing fetal abnormalities much earlier in the pregnancy. CVS is carried out between the ninth and twelfth weeks of pregnancy. A small syringe is inserted through the vagina into the **uterus.** The syringe gently sucks out a few of the threadlike projections (villi) from the outer membrane that envelops the amniotic sac and fetus. Results are available within days of the procedure. CVS has not been used as frequently as amniocentesis because many studies have shown that CVS carries a slightly greater risk of spontaneous abortion. However, more recent research suggests that the risks of the procedures are about equivalent (Simpson, 2000).

Ultrasound

For more than half a century, the military has been using sonar to locate enemy submarines. Sonar sends high-frequency sound waves into the depths of the ocean, and the waves bounce back from objects such as submarines (and whales and schools of fish and the ocean floor) to reveal their presence. Within the past generation, health professionals have also innovated the use of (very!) high-frequency sound waves to obtain information about the fetus. The sound waves, called **ultrasound,** are too high in frequency to be heard by the human ear. However, they are reflected by the fetus, and a computer can use the information to generate a picture (visual) of the fetus. The picture is referred to as a **sonogram,** from roots meaning "written with sound" (see Figure 2.7).

Ultrasound is used as an adjunct to amniocentesis or CVS to better determine the position of the fetus. In this way, the physician performing the procedure can make sure that the needle enters the sac surrounding the fetus and not the fetus itself. Ultrasound is also used to locate fetal structures when intrauterine transfusions are necessary for the survival of a fetus with Rh disease.

Ultrasound is also used to track the growth of the fetus, to determine fetal age and sex, and to detect multiple pregnancies and structural abnormalities.

spina bifida A neural tube defect that causes abnormalities of the brain and spine.

chorionic villus sampling (CORE-ee-AH-nick VIH-luss) A method for the prenatal detection of genetic abnormalities that samples the membrane enveloping the amniotic sac and fetus.

uterus The hollow organ within females in which the embryo and fetus develop.

ultrasound Sound waves too high in pitch to be sensed by the human ear.

sonogram A procedure for using ultrasonic sound waves to create a picture of an embryo or fetus.

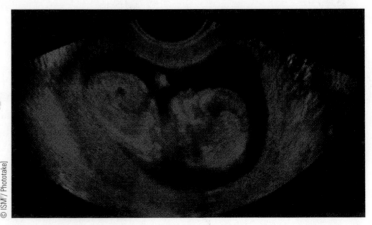

© ISM / Phototake

Figure 2.7

Sonogram of a 5-Month-Old Fetus

In the ultrasound technique, sound waves are bounced off the fetus, providing a picture, called a sonogram, that enables professionals to detect various abnormalities.

Lessons in Observation
Prenatal Assessment

click on "Prenatal Assessment" in Module 1, Section 1, in your Observing Children and Adolescents CD-ROM. You can also visit the Student Book Companion Site to watch the video, answer the questions, and e-mail your responses to your professor.

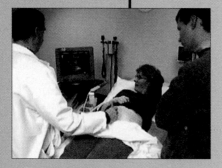

During a routine prenatal visit, Dr. Cohen performs a detailed ultrasound on Eleanor Walsh, who is in her fourth month of pregnancy.

Learning Objectives
- What is the purpose of a prenatal ultrasound?
- What does an ultrasound look like?
- What does an ultrasound tell doctors and parents about the fetus?
- What is amniocentesis?
- Why would a pregnant woman choose to have amniocentesis?
- What is the most common chromosomal disorder seen in live-born babies?

Applied Lesson
Describe the ultrasound procedure. What structures does Dr. Cohen identify, and what does their appearance tell him about the health of the baby? Describe the reasons that Dr. Cohen does not recommend an amniocentesis for Eleanor.

Critical Thinking
For what reasons might a doctor recommend that a woman under age thirty-five have an amniocentesis? What are the risks involved in this procedure? How might the doctor and mother determine whether amniocentesis is the right choice during the course of the pregnancy? What are some ethical considerations in the use of prenatal monitoring?

Blood Tests

Parental blood tests can reveal the presence of recessive genes for a variety of disorders, such as sickle-cell anemia, Tay-Sachs disease, and cystic fibrosis. When both parents carry genes for these disorders, the disorders can be detected in the fetus by means of amniocentesis or CVS.

alpha-fetoprotein (AFP) assay   A blood test that assesses the mother's blood level of alpha-fetoprotein, a substance that is linked with fetal neural tube defects.

Another kind of blood test, the **alpha-fetoprotein (AFP) assay,** is used to detect neural tube defects such as spina bifida and certain chromosomal abnormalities. Neural tube defects cause an elevation in the AFP level in the mother's blood. Elevated AFP levels are also associated with increased risk of fetal death. However, the mother's AFP level also varies with other factors. For this reason, the diagnosis of a neural tube defect is confirmed by other methods of observation, such as amniocentesis or ultrasound.

In the next section, we will see that our development is affected not only by genes but also by environmental influences.

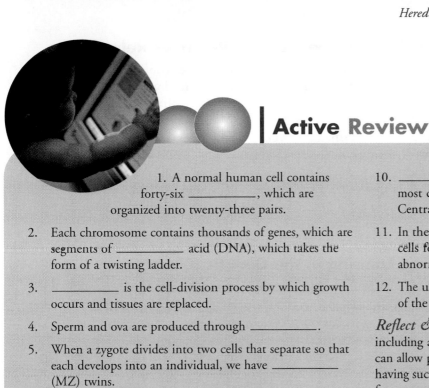

Active Review

1. A normal human cell contains forty-six _____, which are organized into twenty-three pairs.

2. Each chromosome contains thousands of genes, which are segments of _____ acid (DNA), which takes the form of a twisting ladder.

3. _____ is the cell-division process by which growth occurs and tissues are replaced.

4. Sperm and ova are produced through _____.

5. When a zygote divides into two cells that separate so that each develops into an individual, we have _____ (MZ) twins.

6. If two ova are fertilized by different sperm cells, they develop into _____ (DZ) twins.

7. People who bear one dominant gene and one recessive gene for a trait are said to be _____ of the recessive gene.

8. In _____, the twenty-first pair of chromosomes has an extra, or third, chromosome.

9. Phenylketonuria (PKU) is transmitted by a (dominant or recessive?) gene.

10. _____ anemia is caused by a recessive gene and is most common among individuals from Western and Central Africa.

11. In the prenatal testing method of _____, fetal cells found in amniotic fluid are examined for genetic abnormalities.

12. The use of _____ can form a picture ("sonogram") of the fetus.

Reflect & Relate: Many methods of prenatal testing, including amniocentesis, some blood tests, and ultrasound, can allow parents to learn the sex of their fetus. If you were having such testing, would you want to know the sex of your fetus, or would you prefer to wait? Explain.

Go to
W W W http://www.voyages1CE.nelson.com
for an interactive version of this review.

Heredity and the Environment: Nature versus Nurture

Now that we have studied heredity, we know why we have arms rather than wings and hairy skin rather than feathers. (Well, perhaps not so hairy for many of us.) But none of us is the result of heredity alone.

Question: What is the difference between our genotypes and our phenotypes? Heredity provides the biological basis for a **reaction range** in the expression of traits. Our inherited traits can vary in expression, depending on environmental conditions. In addition to inheritance, the development of our traits is influenced by nutrition, learning, exercise, and—unfortunately—accident and illness. A potential Shakespeare who is reared in poverty and never taught to read or write will not create a *Hamlet*. Our traits and behaviours represent the interaction of heredity and environment. The sets of traits that we inherit from our parents are referred to as our **genotypes.** Our actual sets of traits at any point in time are termed our **phenotypes.** Phenotypes are the product of genetic and environmental influences.

Researchers have developed a number of strategies to help sort out the effects of heredity and the environment on development. *Question: What kinds of research strategies do researchers use to sort out the effects of genetics and environmental influences on development?*

reaction range The variability in the expression of inherited traits as they are influenced by environmental factors.

genotype The genetic form or constitution of a person as determined by heredity.

phenotype The actual form or constitution of a person as determined by heredity and environmental factors.

Kinship Studies: Are the Traits of Relatives Related?

Researchers have studied the distribution of a particular behaviour pattern among relatives who differ in degree of genetic closeness. The more closely people are related, the more genes they have in common. Parents and children have a 50 percent overlap in their genetic endowments, and so do siblings (brothers and sisters), on average. Aunts and uncles have a 25 percent overlap with nieces and nephews, and so do grandparents with their grandchildren. First cousins share 12.5 percent of their genetic endowment. So, if genes are implicated in a physical trait or behaviour pattern, people who are more closely related should be more likely to share the pattern. You probably look more like a parent or brother or sister than like a cousin, and you probably look very little like a stranger.

Twin Studies: Looking in the Genetic Mirror

Monozygotic (MZ) twins share 100 percent of their genes, whereas dizygotic (DZ) twins have a 50 percent overlap, just as other siblings do. If MZ twins show greater similarity on some trait or behaviour than DZ twins do, a genetic basis for the trait or behaviour is indicated.

MZ twins resemble each other more closely than DZ twins on a number of physical and psychological traits. MZ twins are more likely to look alike and to be similar in height, even to have more similar cholesterol levels than DZ twins (Plomin, 2002). This finding holds even when the MZ twins are reared apart and the DZ twins are reared together (Bouchard & Loehlin, 2001). Other physical similarities between pairs of MZ twins may be more subtle, but they are also strong. For example, research shows that MZ twin sisters begin to menstruate about one to two months apart, whereas DZ twins begin to menstruate about a year apart. MZ twins are more alike than DZ twins in their blood pressure, brain wave patterns, and even in their speech patterns, gestures, and mannerisms (Plomin, 2002; Bouchard & Loehlin, 2001).

MZ twins resemble one another more strongly than DZ twins in intelligence and in personality traits such as sociability, anxiety, friendliness, conformity, and even happiness and the tendency to choose marriage over the single life (Johnson McGue, Krueger, & Bouchard, 2004; McCourt et al., 1999; McCrae et al., 2000). David Lykken and Mike Csikszentmihalyi (2001) suggested that we inherit a tendency toward a certain level of happiness. Despite the ups and downs of life, we tend to drift back to our usual levels of cheerfulness or irritability. It seems that our bank accounts, our levels of education, and our marital status are less influential than genes as contributors to happiness.

Heredity is also a key contributor to psychological developmental factors such as cognitive functioning, autism, and early signs of attachment (e.g., smiling, cuddling, and expression of fear of strangers) (DiLalla, Carey, Gottesman, & Bouchard, 1996; Plomin, 2002). MZ twins are more likely than DZ twins to share psychological disorders such as **autism,** depression, schizophrenia, and even vulnerability to alcoholism (Plomin, 2002). In one study on autism, the **concordance** rate for MZ twins was 96 percent. The concordance rate for DZ twins was only 24 percent (Ritvo, Freeman, Mason-Brothers, Mo, & Ritvo, 1985).

Of course, twin studies are not perfect. MZ twins may resemble each other more closely than DZ twins partly because they are treated more similarly. MZ twins frequently are dressed identically, and parents sometimes have difficulty telling them apart.

autism Refers specifically to autistic disorder (classic autism) or to five autism spectrum disorders described under the pervasive developmental disorders (PDD) diagnostic category of the Diagnostic and Statistical Manual of Mental Disorders (DSM-IV). Autism spectrum disorder is a neurological condition that causes developmental disability. It is often characterized by failure to relate to others, communication problems, intolerance of change, and ritualistic behaviour.

concordance Agreement.

One way to get around this difficulty is to find and compare MZ twins who were reared in different homes. Any similarities between MZ twins reared apart cannot be explained by a shared home environment and would appear to be largely a result of heredity. In the fascinating Minnesota Study of Twins Reared Apart (Bouchard, Lykken, McGue, Segal, & Tellegen, 1990; DiLalla, Gottesman, Carey, & Bouchard, 1999; Lykken, McGue, Tellegen, & Bouchard, 1992), researchers have been measuring the physiological and psychological characteristics of fifty-six sets of MZ adult twins who were separated in infancy and reared in different homes. The MZ twins reared apart are about as similar as MZ twins reared together on a variety of measures of intelligence, personality, temperament, occupational and leisure-time interests, and social attitudes. These traits thus would appear to have a genetic underpinning.

Adoption Studies

Adoption studies in which children are separated from their natural parents at an early age and reared by adoptive parents provide special opportunities for sorting out nature and nurture. As we will see in discussions of the origins of intelligence (Chapter 12) and of various problem behaviours (Chapters 10 and 13), psychologists look for the relative similarities between children and their adoptive and natural parents. When children who are reared by adoptive parents are nonetheless more similar to their natural parents in a trait, a powerful argument is made for a genetic role in the appearance of that trait.

Active Review

13. The sets of traits that we inherit are referred to as our (genotype or phenotype?).

14. The actual traits that we display at any point in time are the product of genetic and environmental influences and are called our (genotypes or phenotypes?).

15. Parents and children have a _____ percent overlap in their genetic endowments.

16. _____ (MZ) twins share 100 percent of their genes.

17. _____ (DZ) twins have a 50 percent overlap, as do other siblings.

Reflect & Relate: Do you know sets of twins? Are they monozygotic or dizygotic? How are they alike? How do they differ?

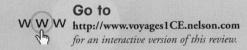

Go to
http://www.voyages1CE.nelson.com
for an interactive version of this review.

Conception: Against All Odds

Traits are determined by pairs of genes. One member of each pair comes from each parent. *Question: What process brings together the genes from each parent? That process is called conception.* Let's talk about the birds and the bees and peek through the microscope to understand how it all works.

conception The union of a sperm cell and an ovum that occurs when the chromosomes of each of these cells combine to form twenty-three new pairs.

Conception is the union of an ovum and a sperm cell. Conception, from one perspective, is the beginning of a new human life. But conception is also the end of a fantastic voyage in which one of several hundred thousand ova produced by the woman unites with one of hundreds of million sperm produced by the man in the average ejaculate.

Ova

At birth, women already contain their 400 000 or so ova. However, the ova are immature in form. The ovaries also produce the female hormones estrogen and progesterone. At puberty, in response to hormonal command, some ova begin to mature (Figure 2.8). Each month, one egg (occasionally more than one) is released from its ovarian follicle about midway through the menstrual cycle and enters a nearby **fallopian tube**. It might take three to four days for an egg to be propelled by small, hairlike structures called cilia and, perhaps, by contractions in the wall of the tube, along the few inches of the fallopian tube to the uterus. Unlike sperm, eggs do not propel themselves.

fallopian tube A tube through which ova travel from an ovary to the uterus.

If the egg is not fertilized, it is discharged through the uterus and the vagina—sloughed off—along with the **endometrium** that had formed to support an embryo, in the menstrual flow. During a woman's reproductive years, only about 400 ova (i.e., one in 1 000) will ripen and be released. How these ova are selected is a mystery.

endometrium The inner lining of the uterus.

In an early stage of development, egg cells contain forty-six chromosomes. Each developing egg cell contains two X sex chromosomes. After meiosis, each ovum contains twenty-three chromosomes, one of which is an X sex chromosome.

Ova are much larger than sperm. The chicken egg and the six-inch ostrich egg are each just one cell, although the sperm of these birds are microscopic. Human ova are barely visible to the eye, but their bulk is still thousands of times larger than that of sperm cells.

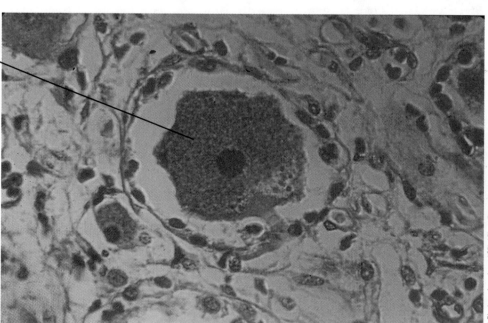

Ovum

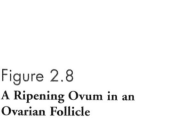

Figure 2.8

A Ripening Ovum in an Ovarian Follicle

When a female reaches puberty, some ova begin to mature. Each month one egg (occasionally more than one) is released from its ovarian follicle and enters a fallopian tube.

Canadian Birthrates by Province and Territory					
	2001-2002	2002-2003	2003-2004	2004-2005ʳ	2005-2006ᵖ
	Number of births				
Canada	328 155	330 523	337 762	338 894	343 517
Newfoundland and Labrador	4 636	4 596	4 598	4 451	4 368
Prince Edward Island	1 313	1 374	1 403	1 390	1 393
Nova Scotia	8 693	8 635	8 713	8 700	8 617
New Brunswick	6 971	7 104	7 072	6 924	6 837
Quebec	72 602	72 273	74 364	75 347	78 450
Ontario	128 947	129 256	132 874	132 769	133 170
Manitoba	13 746	13 765	13 981	13 864	13 915
Saskatchewan	11 996	11 794	12 121	12 012	12 031
Alberta	37 602	39 450	40 635	41 056	41 989
British Columbia	39 932	40 534	40 205	40 565	40 926
Yukon Territory	344	322	374	364	365
Northwest Territories	651	658	697	698	686
Nunavut	722	762	725	754	770

Source: Statistics Canada (2007).

ᵖ preliminary
ʳ revised
Note: From July 1 of one year to June 30 of the next year.

Sperm Cells

Sperm cells develop through several stages. Like ova, in one early stage, they each contain forty-six chromosomes, including one X and one Y sex chromosome. After meiosis, each sperm has twenty-three chromosomes. Half have X sex chromosomes, and the other half have Y sex chromosomes. Each sperm cell is about 1/500th of an inch long, one of the smallest types of cells in the body. Sperm with Y sex chromosomes appear to swim faster than sperm with X sex chromosomes. ***Truth or Fiction Revisited:*** This is one of the reasons that 120 to 150 boys are conceived for every 100 girls. Male fetuses suffer a higher rate of **spontaneous abortion** than females, however, often during the first month of pregnancy. Live births of boys outnumber those of girls by a ratio of only 106 to 100. Boys also have a higher incidence of infant mortality, which further equalizes the numbers of girls and boys in a population by the time they show an interest in pairing off.

spontaneous abortion
Unplanned, accidental abortion; miscarriage.

The 200 to 400 million sperm in the ejaculate may seem to be a wasteful investment, because only one sperm can fertilize an ovum. But only one in 1000 sperm will ever arrive in the vicinity of an ovum. Millions deposited in the vagina simply flow out of the woman's body because of gravity, unless she remains prone for quite some time. Normal vaginal acidity kills many more sperm. Many surviving sperm then have to swim against the current of fluid coming from the cervix (see Figure 2.9).

Sperm that survive these initial obstacles may reach the fallopian tubes sixty to ninety minutes after ejaculation. About half the sperm enter the wrong tube—that is, the tube without the egg. Perhaps 2000 enter the correct tube. Fewer still manage to swim the final two inches against the currents generated by the cilia that line the tube.

Although the journey of sperm is literally blind, it is apparently not random. ***Truth or Fiction Revisited:*** It is not true that sperm travel about at random inside the woman's reproductive tract, so that reaching the ovum is a matter of luck. Sperm

Figure 2.9

Female Reproductive Organs

Conception is something of an obstacle course. Sperm must survive the pull of gravity and vaginal acidity, risk winding up in the wrong fallopian tube, and surmount other hurdles before they reach the ovum.

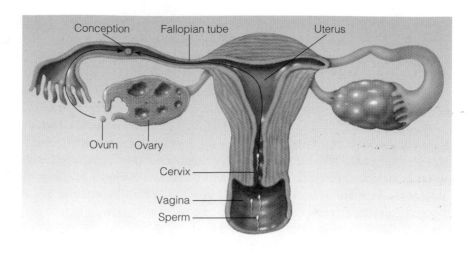

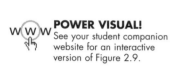
POWER VISUAL! See your student companion website for an interactive version of Figure 2.9.

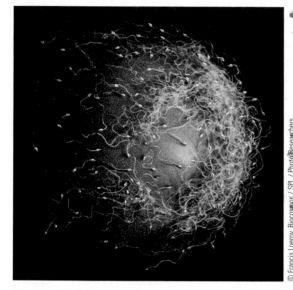

Figure 2.10

Human Sperm Swarming Around an Ovum in a Fallopian Tube

Fertilization normally occurs in a fallopian tube, not in the uterus. Thousands of sperm may wind up in the vicinity of an ovum, but only one fertilizes it. How this sperm cell is "selected" remains one of the mysteries of nature.

zona pellucida A gelatinous layer that surrounds an ovum (from roots referring to a "zone through which light can shine").

hyaluronidase An enzyme that briefly thins the zona pellucida, enabling a single sperm cell to penetrate (from roots referring to a "substance that breaks down a glasslike fluid").

cells are apparently attracted by the odor of a chemical secreted by ova. It has been shown that sperm cells have odor receptors (Donner & Babcock, 2003; Spehr et al., 2003), making it conceivable (excuse the pun) that sperm are attracted to ova by some form of a sense of smell.

Of all the sperm swarming around the egg, only one enters (see Figure 2.10). Ova are surrounded by a gelatinous layer called the **zona pellucida.** This is the layer that must be penetrated if fertilization is to occur. Many of the sperm that have completed their journey to the ovum secrete an enzyme called **hyaluronidase.** The group bombardment of the enzyme emitted by the sperm briefly thins the wall of the ova, but it enables only one sperm to penetrate. Once a sperm cell has entered, the ova walls thicken again, locking other sperm out. How this one sperm cell is "selected" is another biological mystery. Nevertheless, other sperm are unable to enter.

The chromosomes from the sperm cell line up across from the corresponding chromosomes in the egg cell. Conception finally occurs as the chromosomes combine to form twenty-three new pairs with a unique set of genetic instructions.

For couples who want children, few problems are more frustrating than the inability to conceive. Physicians often recommend that couples try to conceive on their own for six months before seeking medical assistance. The term *infertility* usually is not applied until the couple has failed to conceive for a year. We consider the problem of infertility next.

Infertility and Other Ways of Becoming Parents

About one of every six or seven Canadian couples has fertility problems (Rebar & DeCherney, 2004; http://myfertility.ca). Infertility was once viewed as a problem of the woman, but it turns out that fertility problems are pretty much equally divided, with 40 percent of the problem due to the female partner, 40 percent due to the male partner, and approximately 15 percent of cases unexplained.

Causes of Infertility

Question: What are the causes of infertility? Five major fertility problems are found among men: (1) too few sperm ("low sperm count"), (2) deformed sperm, (3) poor ability of the sperm to swim to the ovum ("low sperm motility"), (4) infectious diseases, and (5) direct trauma to the testes (Rebar & DeCherney, 2004). A low sperm count—or complete lack of sperm—is the most common male infertility problem. Men's fertility problems have a variety of causes. Among these are genetic factors, poisons found in the environment, diabetes, sexually transmitted infections (STIs), overheating of the testes (which occasionally happens among athletes, such as long-distance runners), pressure (which can be caused by certain bicycle seats—have your doctor recommend a more comfortable and less harmful seat), aging, and the use of certain prescription and illicit drugs (Rebar & DeCherney, 2004; Velez de la Calle et al., 2001). ***Truth or Fiction Revisited:*** It is true that extensive athletic activity can contribute to infertility in the male. Sometimes the sperm count is adequate, but other factors such as prostate or hormonal problems deform sperm or deprive them of their **motility.** Motility can also be impaired by the scar tissue from infections, such as STIs.

Women encounter the following four major fertility problems: (1) failure to ovulate, (2) various infections, (3) inflammation of the tissue that is sloughed off during menstruation ("endometriosis"), and (4) barriers or disorders in the passageways through which the ovum must pass (Rebar & DeCherney, 2004). The most common problem in women is irregular ovulation or lack of ovulation. This problem can have many causes, including irregularities among the hormones that govern ovulation, stress, and malnutrition. So-called fertility drugs (e.g., *clomiphene* and *pergonal*) are made up of hormones that cause women to ovulate. These drugs often cause multiple births by stimulating more than one ovum to ripen during a month (Rebar & DeCherney, 2004).

Infections may scar the fallopian tubes and other organs, impeding the passage of sperm or ova. Such infections include **pelvic inflammatory disease (PID).** PID can result from any of a number of bacterial or viral infections, including the STIs gonorrhea and chlamydia. Antibiotics are usually helpful in treating bacterial infections, but infertility can be irreversible if the infection has gone without treatment for too long.

Endometriosis can obstruct the fallopian tubes, where conception normally takes place. This problem is clear enough. But endometriosis is also believed to somehow dampen the "climate" for conception; the mechanisms involved in this effect are not as well understood. Endometriosis has become a fairly frequent cause of infertility today, because so many women are delaying childbearing to further their educations and to establish their careers. What apparently happens is this: Each month tissue develops to line the uterus in case the woman conceives. This tissue, called the endometrium, is then normally sloughed off during menstruation. However, some of it backs up into the abdomen through the same fallopian tubes that would provide a duct for an ovum. Endometrial tissue then collects in the abdomen, where it can cause a good deal of abdominal pain and also somehow impede the chances of conception. Physicians may treat endometriosis through hormone treatments that temporarily prevent menstruation or through surgery. These treatments are often successful, but they are certainly not reliable.

Let us now consider some of the methods that have been developed in recent years to help infertile couples bear children. *Question: How are couples helped to have children?*

Artificial Insemination

Multiple ejaculations of men with low sperm counts can be collected and quick-frozen. The sperm can then be injected into the woman's uterus at the time of ovulation. This is one **artificial insemination** procedure. Sperm from men with low sperm

motility   Self-propulsion.

pelvic inflammatory disease (PID)   An infection of the abdominal region that may have various causes and that may impair fertility.

endometriosis   Inflammation of endometrial tissue sloughed off into the abdominal cavity rather than out of the body during menstruation; the condition is characterized by abdominal pain and, sometimes, infertility.

artificial insemination   Injection of sperm into the uterus to fertilize an ovum.

motility can also be injected into their partners' uteruses, so that the sperm can begin their journey closer to the fallopian tubes. When a man is completely infertile or has an extremely low sperm count, his partner can be artificially inseminated with the sperm of a donor who resembles the man in physical traits. Women who want a baby but do not have a partner may also choose to have artificial insemination. So may lesbian couples. The child then bears the genes of one of the parents—the mother.

In Vitro Fertilization

in vitro fertilization
(VEE-tro) Fertilization of an ovum in a laboratory dish.

Have you heard the expression "test-tube baby"? Does it sound as though a baby develops in a test tube? Not so. Does it sound as though a baby is conceived in a test tube? Not so—but close. In this method, which is more technically known as **in vitro fertilization (IVF),** ripened ova are removed surgically from the mother and placed in a laboratory dish. The father's sperm are also placed in the dish. One or more ova are fertilized and then injected into the mother's uterus to become implanted. ***Truth or Fiction Revisited:*** It is not true that test-tube babies are grown in a laboratory dish throughout their nine-month gestation period. Instead, they are conceived in a laboratory dish or vessel and then injected into the uterus, where they must become implanted to develop successfully.

In vitro fertilization may be used when the fallopian tubes are blocked, because the ova need not travel through them. If the father's sperm are low in motility, they are sometimes injected directly into the ovum (Rebar & DeCherney, 2004). A variation known as donor IVF can be used when the intended mother does not produce ova. An ovum from another woman is fertilized and injected into the uterus of the mother-to-be.

It can take several tries to achieve a pregnancy, because only a minority of attempts lead to births. Yet several embryos may be injected into the uterus at once, heightening the odds. IVF remains costly but has become rather routine.

Donor IVF

donor IVF The transfer of a donor's ovum, fertilized in a laboratory dish, to the uterus of another woman.

The method called **donor IVF** is used when a woman does not produce ova of her own but when her uterus is apparently capable of providing an adequate environment to bring a baby to term. An ovum is harvested from another woman—the donor. It is fertilized in vitro—often by sperm from the partner of the recipient. Then, as in other cases of IVF, the fertilized ovum is placed directly into the uterus of the recipient. The embryo becomes implanted and undergoes the remainder of prenatal development in the recipient's uterus.

Surrogate Mothers

surrogate mother A woman who is artificially inseminated and carries to term a child who is then given to another woman, typically the spouse of the sperm donor.

In recent years, stories about **surrogate mothers** have filled the headlines. Surrogate mothers bring babies to term for other women who are infertile. (The word *surrogate* means "substitute.") Surrogate mothers may be artificially inseminated by the partners of infertile women, in which case the baby thus carries the genes of the father. But sometimes—as with fifty-three-year-old singer-songwriter James Taylor and his forty-seven-year-old wife—ova are surgically extracted from the biological mother, fertilized in vitro by the biological father, and then implanted in another woman's uterus, where the baby is brought to term (Byrd, 2001). Surrogate mothers are usually paid fees and sign agreements to surrender the baby. (These contracts have been annulled in some American states, however, so that surrogate mothers cannot be forced to hand over their babies.) In the case of Taylor and his wife, the surrogate mother was a friend of the family, and she delivered twins in 2001.

Biologically, surrogate motherhood might seem the mirror image of the more common artificial insemination technique in which a fertile woman is artificially inseminated with sperm from a donor. But the methods are psychologically very different. For example, sperm donors usually do not know the identity of the women who have received their sperm, nor do they follow the child's prenatal development. Surrogate mothers, however, are involved throughout the course of prenatal development.

Ethical and legal dilemmas revolve around the fact that artificially inseminated surrogate mothers have a genetic link to their babies. If they change their minds and do not want to hand the babies over to the contractual parents, there can be legal struggles.

Adoption

Many adults wishing to welcome a child into their family adopt. Although many who cannot conceive children of their own elect to adopt, adoptions occur for a variety of other reasons as well. Because adopting Canadian-born babies is difficult, some Canadians are adopting children from other regions of the world such as Asia, Africa, and Eastern Europe (see Table 2.4).

Diversity in Families
Many couples have chosen to adopt children with ethnic identities different from their own.

Adoptions by Country			
International Adoptions in Canada, Top 25 Countries			
	2005	2004	2003
China	973	1001	1112
Haiti	115	159	150
United States	102	79	74
Republic of Korea	97	97	73
Russia	88	106	92
Philippines	70	62	58
India	41	37	10
Ukraine	39	16	23
Ethiopia	31	34	14
Taiwan	30	15	26
Jamaica	22	23	43
Thailand	21	40	38
Colombia	18	38	37
Pakistan	17	7	9
Ghana	15	12	11
Congo, Dem. Rep	11	8	x
Bulgaria	10	10	11
Liberia	10	10	x
Cambodia	10	14	23
Hong Kong	8	x	x
Guyana	8	14	19
Nigeria	6	x	x
Brazil	6	x	x
El Salvador	5	x	x
St. Vincent/ Grenadines	5	x	x
Other Countries	113	183	297
Total	1871	1955	2180

x From 0 to 4
Source: Adoption Council of Canada (2006).
Note: Due to privacy considerations, CIC has suppressed and replaced cells containing fewer than five cases with the notation "x." As a result, components may not sum to total indicated.

Selecting the Sex of Your Child: Fantasy or Reality?

Just as new technologies are enhancing the chances for infertile couples to become parents, new methods seem to be leading to the day when we can choose the sex of our children.

What would happen if we could select the sex of our children? In many cultures, one sex—usually male—has been preferred over the other. Would Canadians predominantly select boys or girls? Would it all balance out in the end? Then, too, there are sex-linked diseases that show up only in sons. Would-be parents in such cases might feel more secure if they could choose to have daughters.

Question: How do people attempt to select the sex of their children? Folklore is replete with methods (Kalb, 2004). Some cultures have advised having sexual intercourse under the full moon as a way of begetting boys. The Greek philosopher Aristotle suggested making love during a north wind to conceive sons. A south wind would lead to the conception of daughters. Sour foods were once suggested for parents desirous of having boys. Those who wanted girls were advised to consume sweets. In more recent times, men who desired to father boys might be advised to wear their boots to bed. At one time it was also believed that the right testicle was responsible for siring boys. Noblemen in eighteenth-century France were thus advised to have their left testicles removed if they wanted sons. In any event, need we point out that none of these methods worked?

Methods after conception have also been used to obtain children of the desired sex, such as selective abortion and infanticide. Such practices are especially widespread in developing nations such as China and India (see the nearby "Developing in a World of Diversity" feature).

Let us consider the methods being used today to try to conceive boys or girls.

Sperm-Separation Procedures

Several sperm-separation procedures are in use. One is based on the swimming rates of X- and Y-chromosome-bearing sperm. Another reflects the finding that the two types of sperm carry different electrical charges. A more recent method relies on the fact that sperm carrying the Y sex chromosome have a bit less (about 2.8 percent less) genetic material (DNA) than sperm carrying the X sex chromosome (Kolata, 1998). Fugger and his colleagues (1998) managed to pass the hundreds of million sperm cells in an ejaculation through a "DNA detector" and separated them on this basis. Mothers have then been artificially inseminated with the chosen sperm. Still, there remains the question of reliability.

Preimplantation Genetic Diagnosis

In preimplantation genetic diagnosis (PGD), health professionals fertilize ova in vitro, leading to the conception of perhaps six to eight embryos. After a few days of cell division, a cell is extracted from each embryo. The sex chromosomal structure of the cell is examined microscopically to determine whether the embryo is female or male. The embryos of the desired sex are implanted in the woman's uterus, where one or more can grow to term, as in other uses of IVF. *Truth or Fiction Revisited:* PGD is a foolproof sex-selection method, but it is medically invasive and expensive, and successful implantation cannot be guaranteed (Kalb, 2004).

Moral and Ethical Questions

Such sex-selection methods raise momentous moral and ethical questions. Many people wonder whether people have the "right" to select the sex of their children. For some people, the word *right* has a religious meaning. That is, they think that only

God should determine the sex of a child. Others may consider the word *right* in terms of balancing the numbers of females and males within a culture. Because males tend to be preferred, sex selection can quickly lead to an overabundance of males within a society, as it may do in India (Dugger, 2001). Some—for example, the Ethics Committee of the American Society of Reproductive Medicine (2000)—consider sex selection for nonmedical reasons to be sexist. In Canada, the *Assisted Human Reproduction Act* (Bill C-13) prohibits sex selection, along with cloning people, growing human embryos for research, cloning stems cells, making changes to human DNA that would pass from one generation to the next, creating people who have animal DNA, and

Developing in a World of Diversity

Clinics' Pitch to Indian Émigrés: It's a Boy

The pitch could not be more direct. The intended audience could not be more specific. "Desire a Son?" asked an advertisement in *India Abroad,* a weekly newspaper for Indian expatriates living in the United States and Canada. "Choosing the sex of your baby: New scientific reality," declared another.

The products in question are procedures to preselect the sex of a child or to identify the sex of the fetus early in pregnancy. The market is immigrants from India, where sex-determination tests were outlawed years ago to thwart the widespread practice of aborting female fetuses.

Such ads would be illegal in India, which has struggled to discourage women from exploiting medical technology to assure themselves of giving birth to boys (Sachs, 2001). Now, Indians in the United States and Canada find themselves being courted by companies that promise to help do just that.

In conversations prompted by the appearance of the sex-selection ads, many Indian and South Asian immigrants said that traditional bias against female children runs deep. In India, sex selection is responsible for a widening sex gap, with the number of girls per boys dropping from 962 to 927 in just twenty years. The 2002 census found that in the states of Haryana and Punjab, the ratio of girls younger than age six had fallen from 95 for every 100 boys in 1991 to 90 in 2002. In Haryana, there were 86 females for every 100 males (Sachs, 2001).

In many cultures, a boy is particularly valued as a breadwinner who will support his parents in their old age; often, only a son can inherit property. A girl is seen as a burden who requires a costly dowry when she marries. The attitudes are so deeply ingrained that they often persist after immigration.

In India, recently released census figures suggested that female fetuses were being regularly aborted despite efforts to restrict access to prenatal tests (Sachs, 2001). The ban against sex-determination tests is feeble, and abortions are virtually unregulated.

Indians are not the only immigrant group to be offered sex-selection procedures so directly. Chinese immigrants in New York City can find a sex-selection clinic right in Manhattan's Chinatown, where Dr. Robert M. Nyein started offering the Ericsson sperm-separation technique as part of his gynecological practice about four years ago. Nearly all the Chinese immigrants who come to him, said Dr. Nyein, want boys. China, like India, has a long tradition of favouring male children, a tradition that has been exacerbated by the country's current one-child-per-family policy.

Source: From Susan Sachs (2001, August 15). "Clinics' Pitch to Indian Emigres: It's a Boy." *New York Times,* pp. A1, B6. © 2001 by the New York Times Co. Reprinted with permission.

buying or selling embryos, sperm, eggs, or other human reproductive material (CBC News, 2007). For example, the act states that people cannot, "for the purpose of creating a human being, perform any procedure or provide, prescribe or administer any thing that would ensure or increase the probability that an embryo will be of a particular sex, or that would identify the sex of an *in vitro* embryo, except to prevent, diagnose or treat a sex-linked disorder or disease." Yet many people believe that selecting the sex of one's children is a personal and not a social matter: "By what authority," they challenge, "do some decide whether the rest of us have acceptable reasons for selecting the sex of our children?" (Holmes-Farley, 1998).

Bill C-13 does allow for surrogate mothers, sperm donation, egg donation, and other reproductive methods to assist conception, as well as using human embryos and stem cells in research. It should come as no surprise that there is ongoing ethical debate about the interpretation and implementation of the guidelines put forth in the act. What controversies related to Bill C-13 have you heard about? Detailed information about the *Assisted Human Reproduction Act* can be found at http://www2.parl.gc.ca/HousePublications/Publication.aspx?pub=bill&doc=C-13&parl=37&ses=2&language=E&File=19.

In most of the next chapter, we will deal with issues on a smaller scale—beginning with the division of the single cell that is formed by the union of sperm cell and ovum.

Active Review

18. The union of an ovum and a sperm cell is called _____.

19. Each month, an ovum is released from its follicle and enters a nearby _____ tube.

20. Low _____ count is the most common infertility problem in the male.

21. Failure to _____ is the most frequent infertility problem in women.

Reflect & Relate: What methods do people use to try to select the sex of their children? Do you believe it is right or proper to attempt to select the sex of one's child? Support your point of view.

Go to

W W W http://www.voyages1CE.nelson.com
for an interactive version of this review.

Recite: *An Active Summary*™

1. What is meant by heredity?	Heredity defines one's nature, as determined by the biological transmission of traits and characteristics from one generation to another. Heredity is fundamental in the transmission of physical traits, and is also involved in psychological traits, including psychological disorders.
2. What are chromosomes and genes?	Chromosomes are rod-shaped structures found in cell nuclei. People normally have forty-six chromosomes organized into twenty-three pairs. Each chromosome contains thousands of genes—the biochemical materials that regulate the development of traits. Genes are segments of strands of DNA, which takes the form of a twisting ladder.
3. What happens during cell division?	In mitosis, strands of DNA break apart and are rebuilt in the new cell. Sperm and ova are produced by meiosis—or reduction division—and have twenty-three rather than forty-six chromosomes.
4. How are twins formed?	If a zygote divides into two cells that separate and each develops into an individual, we obtain monozygotic (MZ) twins, which are identical. If two ova are each fertilized by a different sperm cell, they develop into dizygotic (DZ) twins, which are fraternal twins. DZ twins run in families.
5. How do genes determine traits?	Traits are determined by pairs of genes. Mendel established laws of heredity and realized that some traits result from an "averaging" of the genetic instructions carried by the parents. However, genes can also be dominant (as in the case of brown eyes) or recessive (blue eyes). When recessive genes from both parents combine, the recessive trait is shown. People who bear one dominant gene and one recessive gene for a trait are carriers of the recessive gene. Some genetic abnormalities are caused by a single pair of genes; others by combinations of genes.
6. What kinds of disorders are caused by chromosomal abnormalities?	Chromosomal abnormalities become more likely as parents age. Mental retardation is common in many such disorders. Down syndrome is caused by an extra chromosome on the twenty-first pair. Children with Down syndrome have characteristic facial features, including a downward-sloping fold of skin at the inner corners of the eyes, and various physical health problems. Disorders that arise from abnormal numbers of sex chromosomes are called sex-linked. These include XYY males and girls with a single X sex chromosome.
7. What kinds of disorders are caused by genetic abnormalities?	Phenylketonuria (PKU) is a metabolic disorder transmitted by a recessive gene. Huntington's disease is a fatal progressive degenerative disorder and a dominant trait. Sickle-cell anemia is caused by a recessive gene and is most common among African Americans. Tay-Sachs disease is a fatal disease of the nervous system that is caused by a recessive gene and is most common among children in Jewish families of Eastern European origin. Cystic fibrosis is caused by a recessive gene and is the most common fatal hereditary disease among European North Americans. Sex-linked genetic abnormalities are carried

only on the X sex chromosome and include hemophilia, Duchenne muscular dystrophy, diabetes, and colour blindness.

8. How do health professionals determine whether children will have genetic or chromosomal abnormalities?

Prenatal testing procedures can determine the presence of various genetic and chromosomal abnormalities. Such tests include amniocentesis, chorionic villus sampling, ultrasound, and parental blood tests.

9. What is the difference between our genotypes and our phenotypes?

Our genotypes are the sets of traits that we inherit. However, inherited traits vary in expression, depending on environmental conditions. One's actual set of traits at a given point in time is one's phenotype.

10. What research strategies do researchers use to sort out the effects of genetics and environmental influences on development?

Researchers can study the distribution of a trait among relatives who differ in degree of genetic closeness. Parents and children have a 50 percent overlap in genes, as do brothers and sisters, with the exception of MZ twins, who have a 100 percent overlap. MZ twins resemble each other more closely than DZ twins in physical and psychological traits, even when reared apart. If adopted children better resemble their natural than their adoptive parents in a physical or psychological trait, that trait is likely to have a strong genetic basis.

11. What process brings together the genes from each parent?

The process is the union of a sperm and an ovum—conception. Fertilization normally occurs in a fallopian tube. If the egg is not fertilized, it is discharged. Men typically ejaculate hundreds of millions of sperm. More boys are conceived than girls, but male fetuses have a higher rate of spontaneous abortion. Chromosomes from the sperm cell align with chromosomes in the egg cell, combining to form twenty-three new pairs.

12. What are the causes of infertility?

Male fertility problems include low sperm count and motility, infections, and trauma to the testes. Female fertility problems include failure to ovulate, infections such as PID, endometriosis, and obstructions.

13. How are couples helped to have children?

Fertility drugs help regulate ovulation. Artificial insemination can be done with the sperm from multiple ejaculations of a man with a low sperm count or with the sperm of a donor. In vitro fertilization (IVF) can be used when the fallopian tubes are blocked. When the mother cannot produce ova, embryonic transplant transfers an embryo into a host uterus.

14. How do people attempt to select the sex of their children?

Methods have been developed for sorting male (Y) and female (X) sperm cells. Some methods are based on the swimming rates and other characteristics of X- and Y-chromosome-bearing sperm cells. Other methods sort sperm cells on the basis of their electrical charges or the bulk of their genetic material. The only perfectly reliable method is preimplantation genetic diagnosis.

Go to W W W http://www.voyages1CE.nelson.com *for an interactive version of this summary review.*

Key Terms

ovary *(page 52)*

ovum *(page 52)*

heredity *(page 52)*

genetics *(page 52)*

neuroticism *(page 52)*

chromosomes *(page 53)*

gene *(page 53)*

polygenic *(page 53)*

deoxyribonucleic acid (DNA) *(page 53)*

zygote *(page 53)*

mitosis *(page 53)*

mutation *(page 54)*

meiosis *(page 54)*

autosome *(page 54)*

sex chromosome *(page 54)*

monozygotic (MZ) twins *(page 55)*

dizygotic (DZ) twins *(page 55)*

ovulation *(page 55)*

allele *(page 55)*

homozygous *(page 55)*

heterozygous *(page 55)*

dominant trait *(page 55)*

recessive trait *(page 55)*

carrier *(page 56)*

multifactorial problems *(page 56)*

Down syndrome *(page 57)*

sex-linked chromosomal abnormalities *(page 60)*

Klinefelter syndrome *(page 60)*

testosterone *(page 60)*

Turner syndrome *(page 61)*

estrogen *(page 61)*

phenylketonuria (PKU) *(page 61)*

Huntington's disease *(page 61)*

sickle-cell anemia *(page 62)*

Tay-Sachs disease *(page 62)*

cystic fibrosis *(page 62)*

hemophilia *(page 62)*

sex-linked genetic abnormalities *(page 62)*

muscular dystrophy *(page 62)*

genetic counselling *(page 64)*

prenatal *(page 64)*

amniocentesis *(page 64)*

spina bifida *(page 65)*

chorionic villus sampling *(page 65)*

uterus *(page 65)*

ultrasound *(page 65)*

sonogram *(page 65)*

alpha-fetoprotein (AFP) assay *(page 66)*

reaction range *(page 67)*

genotype *(page 67)*

phenotype *(page 67)*

autism *(page 68)*

concordance *(page 68)*

conception *(page 70)*

fallopian tube *(page 70)*

endometrium *(page 70)*

spontaneous abortion *(page 71)*

zona pellucida *(page 72)*

hyaluronidase *(page 72)*

motility *(page 73)*

pelvic inflammatory disease (PID) *(page 73)*

endometriosis *(page 73)*

artificial insemination *(page 73)*

in vitro fertilization *(page 74)*

donor IVF *(page 74)*

surrogate mother *(page 74)*

Active Learning Resources

Observing Children and Adolescents CD-ROM

Want to watch a video showing what you've just learned about in this chapter? Check out the "Prenatal Assessment" video in Module 1, Section 1. Your "Lessons in Observation" feature on p. 66 provides further learning objectives, an applied lesson, and a critical thinking exercise designed to help you experience this stage of development.

Visit Your Companion Website for This Book

http://www.voyages1CE.nelson.com

Check out this companion website, where you will find online resources directly linked to your book. The website includes interactive exercises related to PQ4R and Power Visuals for mastering and reviewing key concepts as well as quizzing, chapter outlines, and much more!

CengageNOW!™

http://hed.nelson.com

Go to this site for the link to CengageNOW™, your one-stop study shop. Take a Pretest for this chapter, and CengageNOW™ will generate a personalized Study Plan based on your test results! The Study Plan will identify the topics you need to review and direct you to online resources to help you master those topics. You can then take a Posttest to help you determine the concepts you have mastered and those you still need to work on.

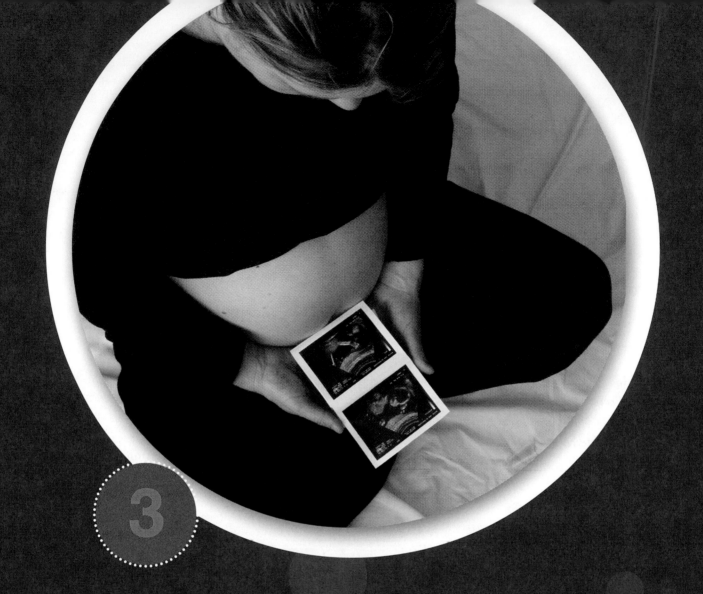

3

Prenatal Development

PREVIEW

TRUTH OR FICTION?

● ● ● ● ● ● ● ● ● ● ●

(T) (F) Newly fertilized egg cells survive without any nourishment from the mother for more than a week.

(T) (F) Your heart started beating when you were only one-fourth of an inch long and weighed a fraction of an ounce.

(T) (F) If it were not for the secretion of male sex hormones a few weeks after conception, we would all develop external sex organs that look like those of females.

(T) (F) Fetuses suck their thumbs and hiccup, sometimes for hours on end.

(T) (F) The same disease organism or chemical agent that can do serious damage to a six-week-old embryo may have no effect on a four-month-old fetus.

(T) (F) Babies can be born addicted to narcotics and other drugs.

(T) (F) It is harmless to the embryo and fetus for a pregnant woman to have a couple of glasses of wine in the evening.

Go to

http://www.voyages1CE.nelson.com
for an interactive version of this "Truth or Fiction" feature.

© Merrill Dyck/Shutterstock, Inc.

Back in 1938, when rapping was still something that hurt the knuckles, L. W. Sontag and T. W. Richards reported the results of a study in fetal behaviour. They stimulated pregnant woman with methods such as ringing a bell and measured the results on the heart rate of the fetus, as assessed by an instrument on the mother's abdomen. Many of the mothers smoked, and the researchers assessed the effects of smoking on the fetal heart rate. They also got the fetus all shook up by placing a vibrator against the mother's abdomen.

Sontag and Richards learned that powerful vibrations usually induced faster heart rates in the fetus (big surprise?), but maternal smoking had less predictable effects on the fetus. Cigarette smoke contains nicotine, which is a stimulant, but smoke also reduces the supply of oxygen in the bloodstream, and oxygen is needed to fuel bursts of activity. How could the researchers spend their time assessing the effects of maternal smoking rather than warning the mothers that their smoking was placing their fetuses at risk for low birth weight, prematurity, short attention span, academic problems, or hyperactivity? This was 1938, and little was known of the harmful effects of smoking.

In any event, Sontag and Richards also discovered that fetuses are sensitive to sound waves during the last months of pregnancy, which has led to a wave of more recent research—including research into whether **neonates** are "loyal," preferring their mothers' voices to those of strangers, and whether listening to classical music during pregnancy rather than heavy metal has noticeable effects (on the brain as well as the heart rate). Stay tuned....

Researchers are finding that the most rapid and dramatic human developments are literally "out of sight"—they take place in the uterus. Within nine months, a child develops from a nearly microscopic cell to a neonate about twenty inches long. Its weight increases by a billionfold.

We can date pregnancy from the onset of the last menstrual period before conception, which makes the normal gestation period 280 days. We can also date pregnancy from the assumed date of fertilization, which normally occurs two weeks after the beginning of the woman's last menstrual cycle. With this accounting method, the gestation period is 266 days.

Soon after conception, the single cell formed by the union of sperm and egg begins to multiply—becoming two cells, then four, then eight, and so on. During the weeks and months that follow, tissues, organs, and structures begin to form, and the fetus gradually takes on the unmistakable shape of a human being. By the time a fetus is born, it consists of hundreds of billions of cells—more cells than there are stars in the Milky Way galaxy. Prenatal development is divided into three periods: the germinal stage (approximately the first two weeks), the embryonic stage (the third through the eighth weeks), and the fetal stage (the third month through birth). Health professionals also commonly speak of prenatal development in terms of three trimesters of three months each.

The Germinal Stage: Wanderings

Let us begin by asking ... *Question: What happens during the germinal stage of prenatal development?* Within thirty-six hours after conception, the zygote divides into two cells. It then divides repeatedly as it proceeds on its journey to the uterus. Within another thirty-six hours, it has become thirty-two cells. It takes the zygote three to four days to reach the uterus. The mass of dividing cells wanders about the uterus for another three to four days before it begins to become implanted in the uterine wall. Implantation takes another week or so. The period from conception to implantation is called the **germinal stage** (see Figure 3.1).

A few days into the germinal stage, the dividing cell mass takes the form of a fluid-filled ball of cells called a **blastocyst.** A blastocyst already shows cell differentiation.

neonate A newborn baby.

germinal stage The period of development between conception and the implantation of the embryo in the uterine wall.

blastocyst A stage within the germinal period of prenatal development in which the zygote has the form of a sphere of cells surrounding a cavity of fluid.

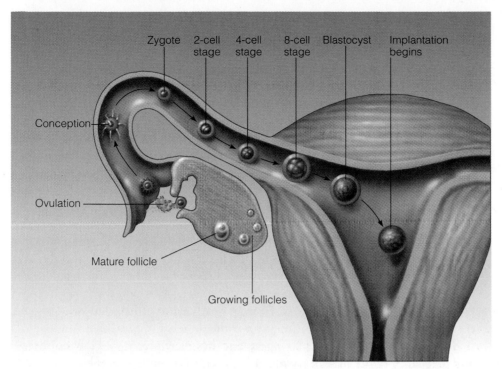

Zygote 2-cell stage 4-cell stage 8-cell stage Blastocyst Implantation begins

Conception

Ovulation

Mature follicle

Growing follicles

POWER VISUAL!
W W W See your student companion website for an interactive version of Figure 3.1.

Figure 3.1

The Ovarian Cycle, Conception, and the Early Days of the Germinal Stage
The zygote first divides about 36 hours after conception. Continuing division creates the hollow sphere of cells termed the blastocyst. The blastocyst normally becomes implanted in the wall of the uterus.

Cells begin to separate into groups that will eventually become different structures. The inner part of the blastocyst has two distinct layers of cells that form a thickened mass of cells called the **embryonic disk.** These cells will become the embryo and eventually the fetus.

The outer part of the blastocyst, or **trophoblast,** at first consists of a single layer of cells. However, it rapidly differentiates into four membranes that will protect and nourish the embryo. One membrane produces blood cells until the embryo's liver develops and takes over this function. Then the membrane disappears. Another membrane develops into the **umbilical cord** and the blood vessels of the **placenta.** A third develops into the amniotic sac, and the fourth becomes the chorion, which will line the placenta.

Without Visible Means of Support ...

Question: If the dividing mass of cells is moving through a fallopian tube and then "wandering" through the uterus for another few days, how does it obtain any nourishment?

We will make one of this book's more controversial statements: People are not chickens. Nevertheless, the dividing cluster of cells that will become the embryo and then the fetus is at first nourished only by the yolk of the egg cell, as is a chick developing in an egg. *Truth or Fiction Revisited:* It is true that newly fertilized egg cells survive without any nourishment from the mother for more than a week. They are nourished by the yolk of the ovum until they implant in the wall of the uterus. Therefore, it makes no gains in mass. The blastocyst gains mass only when it receives nourishment from the outside. In order for that to happen, it must be implanted in the wall of the uterus.

embryonic disk The plate-like inner part of the blastocyst that differentiates into the ectoderm, mesoderm, and endoderm of the embryo.

trophoblast The outer part of the blastocyst from which the amniotic sac, placenta, and umbilical cord develop.

umbilical cord A tube that connects the fetus to the placenta.

placenta (pluh-SEN-tuh) An organ connected to the uterine wall and to the fetus by the umbilical cord. The placenta serves as a relay station between mother and fetus for exchange of nutrients and wastes.

Implantation may be accompanied by some bleeding, which is usually normal enough, and results from the rupturing of small blood vessels that line the uterus. Bleeding can also be a sign of miscarriage (also called *spontaneous abortion*). However, most women who experience implantation bleeding do not miscarry but go on to have normal pregnancies and normal babies. Miscarriage usually stems from abnormalities in the developmental process. Many women miscarry early in pregnancy, but their menstrual flow appears about on schedule, so that they may not even realize they had conceived. Nearly one-third of all pregnancies result in miscarriage, most of them occurring in the first three months (Sciarra et al., 2000). Women who have miscarriages seem to experience a good deal of anxiety for several months afterward (Geller, Kerns, & Klier, 2004).

Active Review

1. A few days into the germinal stage, the dividing cell mass becomes a fluid-filled ball of cells that is called a(n) _____.

2. The outer part of the blastocyst—called the _____—differentiates into membranes that will protect and nourish the embryo.

3. The dividing cluster of cells is nourished by the yolk of the ovum before _____.

Reflect & Relate: Nearly all of us have known—or have been—pregnant women. What early signs made the women suspect that they were pregnant? How do these signs fit with what was happening in their bodies?

W W W **Go to**
www.voyages1ce.nelson.com
for an interactive version of this review.

embryonic stage The stage of prenatal development that lasts from implantation through the eighth week of pregnancy; it is characterized by the development of the major organ systems.

cephalocaudal From head to tail.

proximodistal From the inner part (or axis) of the body outward.

ectoderm The outermost cell layer of the newly formed embryo from which the skin and nervous system develop.

neural tube A hollowed-out area in the blastocyst from which the nervous system develops.

endoderm The inner layer of the embryo from which the lungs and digestive system develop.

The Embryonic Stage

The **embryonic stage** begins with implantation and covers the first two months, during which the major organ systems differentiate. *Question: What happens during the embryonic stage of prenatal development?* Development follows two general trends—**cephalocaudal** (Latin for "head to tail") and **proximodistal** (Latin for "near to far"). The apparently oversized heads of embryos and fetuses at various stages of prenatal development show that growth of the head takes precedence over the growth of the lower parts of the body (see Figure 3.2). You can also think of the body as containing a central axis that coincides with the spinal cord. The growth of the organ systems close to this axis (i.e., in *proximity* to the axis) occurs earlier than the growth of the extremities, which are farther away (i.e., *distant* from the axis). Relatively early maturation of the brain and organ systems that lie near the central axis allows these organs to play important roles in the subsequent development of the embryo and fetus.

During the embryonic stage, the outer layer of cells of the embryonic disk, or **ectoderm**, develops into the nervous system, sensory organs, nails, hair, teeth, and the outer layer of skin. At about twenty-one days, two ridges appear in the embryo and fold to compose the **neural tube**, from which the nervous system will develop. The inner layer, or **endoderm**, forms the digestive and respiratory systems, the liver, and the pancreas. A bit later in the embryonic stage, the mesoderm, a middle layer of cells,

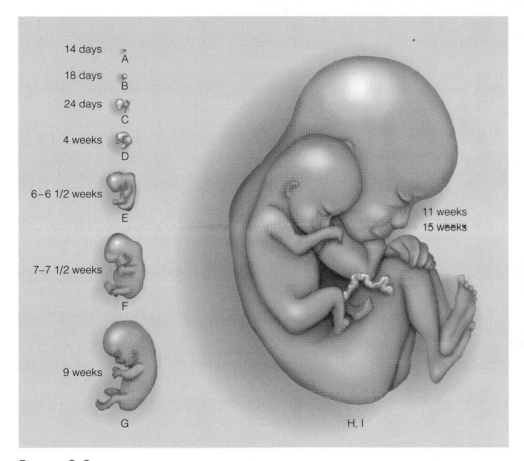

14 days A
18 days B
24 days C
4 weeks D
6–6 1/2 weeks E
7–7 1/2 weeks F
9 weeks G
11 weeks
15 weeks
H, I

Figure 3.2

Human Embryos and Fetuses at Various Stages of Development

Development proceeds in cephalocaudal and proximodistal directions. Development of the head takes precedence over development of the lower parts of the body, enabling the brain to be involved in subsequent developments.

becomes differentiated. The **mesoderm** develops into the excretory, reproductive, and circulatory systems, the muscles, the skeleton, and the inner layer of the skin.

During the third week after conception, the head and blood vessels begin to form. *Question: When does the heart begin to beat? **Truth or Fiction Revisited:*** It is true that your heart started beating when you were only one-fourth of an inch long and weighed a fraction of an ounce. The major organ systems develop within the first two months of pregnancy. The heart will continue to beat without rest every minute of every day for perhaps eighty or ninety years.

What else happens during the embryonic stage? Arm buds and leg buds begin to appear toward the end of the first month. Eyes, ears, nose, and mouth begin to take shape. By this time, the nervous system, including the brain, has also begun to develop. In accord with the principle of proximodistal development, the upper arms and legs develop before the forearms and lower legs. Next come hands and feet, followed at six to eight weeks by webbed fingers and toes. By the end of the second month, the limbs are elongating and separated. The webbing is gone. By this time the embryo is looking quite human. The head has the lovely round shape of your own, and the facial features have become quite distinct. Bear in mind that all this detail is inscribed on an embryo that is only about one inch long and weighs only about ⅓₀ of an ounce. During the second month of embryonic development, the cells in the nervous system begin to "fire" (i.e., to send messages among themselves). This is most

mesoderm The central layer of the embryo from which the bones and muscles develop.

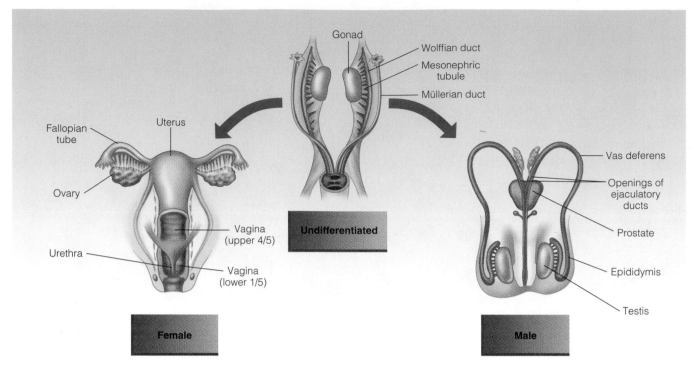

Figure 3.3

Development of the Internal Genital Organs at 5–6 Weeks Following Conception

POWER VISUAL!
W W W See your student companion website for an interactive version of Figure 3.3.

likely random cell firing; the content of such "messages" is anybody's guess. (No, the embryo isn't contemplating Shakespeare or Confucius.) By the end of the embryonic period, teeth buds have formed. The embryo's kidneys are filtering acid from the blood, and its liver is producing red blood cells.

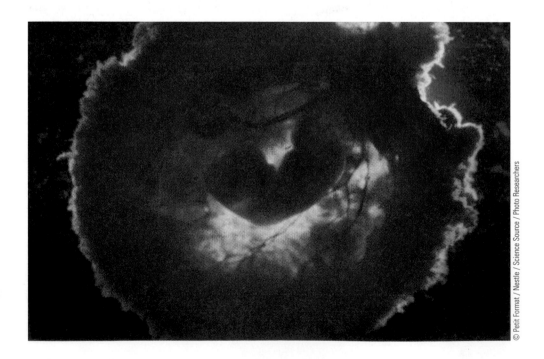

A Human Embryo at 7 Weeks
At this late part of the embryonic stage, the major organ systems have already become differentiated, except for the sex organs.

© Petit Format / Nestle / Science Source / Photo Researchers

Sexual Differentiation

By five to six weeks, the embryo is only one-quarter to one-half inch long. Nevertheless, nondescript sex organs will already have formed, including the internal and external genital organs, as shown in Figures 3.3 and 3.4. Both female and male embryos possess a pair of sexually undifferentiated gonads and two sets of primitive duct structures, the so-called Müllerian (female) ducts and the Wolffian (male) ducts. At this stage of development, both the internal and external genitals resemble primitive female structures.

By about the seventh week, the genetic code (XY or XX) begins to assert itself, causing sex organs to differentiate. Genetic activity on the Y sex chromosome causes the testes to begin to differentiate (National Center for Biotechnology Information, 2000). Ovaries begin to differentiate if the Y chromosome is absent. By about four months after conception, males and females show distinct external genital structures.

Sex Hormones and Sexual Differentiation

Prenatal sexual differentiation requires hormonal influences as well as genetic influences. Male sex hormones—**androgens**—are critical in the development of male genital organs. *Truth or Fiction Revisited:* Without androgens, all people—whether genetically female or male—would develop external sex organs that look like those of females. However, "females" with an XY sex chromosomal structure would be infertile.

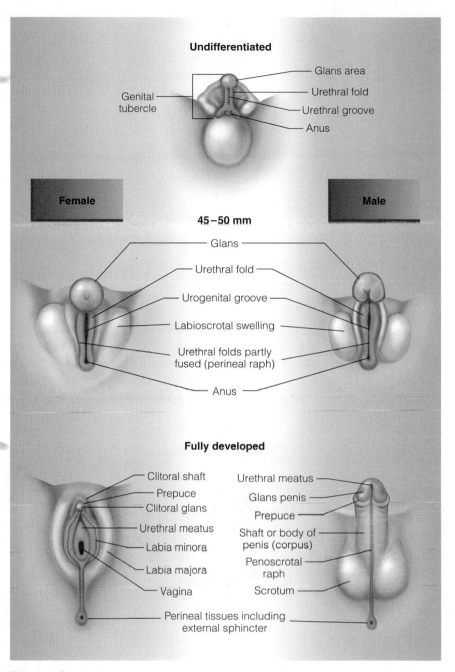

Figure 3.4

Development of the External Genital Organs from an Undifferentiated Stage at 5–6 Weeks Following Conception

POWER VISUAL!
See your student companion website for an interactive version of Figure 3.4.

Once testes have developed in the embryo, they begin to produce androgens. The most important of these is **testosterone.** Testosterone spurs the differentiation of the male (Wolffian) duct system (see Figure 3.3) and remains involved in sexual development and activity for a lifetime. Each Wolffian duct develops into a complex maze of ducts and storage facilities for sperm. At about the eighth week of prenatal development, another androgen, *dihydrotestosterone* (DHT), spurs the formation of the external male genital organs, including the penis. Yet another testicular hormone, secreted somewhat later, prevents the Müllerian ducts from developing into the female duct system. That hormone is labelled Müllerian inhibiting substance (MIS).

androgens Male sex hormones (from roots meaning "giving birth to men").

testosterone A male sex hormone—a steroid—that is produced by the testes and that promotes growth of male sexual characteristics and sperm.

Female embryos and fetuses do produce small amounts of androgens, but they are not normally enough to cause sexual differentiation along male lines. However, they do play important roles in the development of some secondary sexual characteristics in adolescence, such as the appearance of pubic and underarm hair. Androgens are also important in the sex drive of females for a lifetime (Morley & Perry, 2003; Munarriz et al., 2002). But in the female embryo and fetus, low levels of androgens are connected with degeneration of the Wolffian ducts and further development of female sexual organs. The Müllerian ducts develop into fallopian tubes, the uterus, and the inner part of the vagina. The presence of the female sex hormones is not necessary for these developments to occur, although they will become crucial in puberty.

The Amniotic Sac: A Shock Absorber

amniotic sac The sac containing the fetus.

amniotic fluid Fluid within the amniotic sac that suspends and protects the fetus.

The embryo and fetus develop suspended within a protective **amniotic sac** in the uterus. The sac is surrounded by a clear membrane and contains **amniotic fluid.** The fluid serves as a kind of natural air bag, allowing the embryo and fetus to move around without injury. It also helps to maintain an even temperature.

Questions: How does the embryo get nourishment from its mother? How does it eliminate waste products? The answers involve the placenta and the umbilical cord. The placenta is a mass of tissue that permits the embryo (and, later on, the fetus) to exchange nutrients and wastes with the mother. Unique in origin, the placenta grows from material supplied by both the mother and the embryo. The fetus is connected to the placenta by the umbilical cord. The mother is connected to the placenta by the system of blood vessels in the uterine wall.

A Closer Look | *Healthy Pregnancy*

Promotion of healthy lifestyle has become increasingly important to Canadians in recent years. In fact, if you are pregnant or planning on becoming pregnant, Health Canada has a website especially for you (http://www.phac-aspc.gc.ca/hp-gs/index.html). This site is an excellent source of information and covers many of the maternal and environmental influences on prenatal development. For women considering motherhood, topics include alcohol and pregnancy, physical activity, folic acid, and smoking. For those who are already pregnant, additional topics covered are emotional health and healthy eating.

Times Have Changed!

There was a time when expectant mothers were told to engage in as little physical activity as possible. Nowadays there is research indicating that women who are active during pregnancy may have reduced risk of gestational diabetes, hypertensive disease, and preterm birth (Evanson, Siega-Riz, Savitz, Leiferman, & Thorp, 2002; Hatch et al., 1993). In fact, physical activity during pregnancy has also been associated with enhanced psychological well-being (DaCosta, Rippen, Drista, & Ring, 2003). It comes as no surprise then that medical experts are encouraging expectant mothers to engage in some level of physical activity throughout their pregnancies. The types of activities pregnant women are suited to vary, and women need to find activities they enjoy and are comfortable with. For instance, high-intensity sports and running may be replaced with walking or aqua-fit activities. It is advised that women speak to their physicians about the type of exercise they are interested in engaging in (or continuing to engage in) during pregnancy.

How much weight women should gain during pregnancy is dictated by a woman's weight before pregnancy (Health Canada, 2007b). The Public Health Agency of Canada indicates that healthy weight gain in women with a body mass index (BMI) of twenty to twenty-seven prior to pregnancy is twenty-five to thirty-five pounds; however, a woman whose BMI prior to pregnancy is over twenty-seven should gain only fifteen to twenty-five pounds. Conversely, if a women's BMI prior to pregnancy is less than twenty, weight gain of twenty-eight to forty pounds is recommended. In the end, the expectant mother's focus should be on eating a healthy, balanced diet (getting the recommended daily intake from the various food groups detailed in Canada's newly published food guide) and adding some physical activity to her daily routine.

The Placenta: A Filtration System

Question: Do germs or drugs in the mother pass through the placenta and affect the baby? In one of the more fascinating feats of prenatal engineering, it turns out that the mother and baby have separate circulatory systems. The mother's bloodstream is her own, and the embryo's bloodstream is the embryo's. The pancake-shaped placenta contains a membrane that acts as a filter: Only certain substances can pass through it. The membrane permits oxygen and nutrients to reach the embryo from the mother. It also permits carbon dioxide (which is the gas you breathe out and plants "breathe" in) and waste products to pass to the mother from the child. Once the mother has them, she eliminates them through her lungs and kidneys. This is the good part. It also happens that a number of harmful substances can sneak through the placenta. They include various "germs" (microscopic disease-causing organisms), such as the ones that cause syphilis (a bacterium called *Treponema pallidum*), German measles, and, to some degree, AIDS. The good news here is that most pregnant women who are infected with the virus that causes AIDS (HIV) do *not* transmit it to the baby through the placenta. HIV is more likely to be transmitted through childbirth. But some drugs—aspirin, narcotics, alcohol, tranquillizers, and others—do cross the placenta and can affect the baby in one way or another.

The placenta also secretes hormones that preserve the pregnancy, prepare the breasts for nursing, and stimulate the uterine contractions that prompt childbirth. Ultimately, the placenta passes from the woman's body after the child is delivered. For this reason, it is also called the *afterbirth*.

Active Review

4. The embryo and fetus develop within a(n) _____ sac, which functions as a shock absorber, among other things.

5. Development follows two general trends: cephalocaudal and _____.

6. The (inner or outer?) layer of cells of the ectoderm develops into the nervous system, sensory organs, and the outer layer of skin.

7. Without sex hormones, all embryos would develop the appearance of being (males or females?).

8. The _____ permits the embryo to exchange nutrients and wastes with the mother.

9. The embryo and fetus are connected to the placenta by the _____.

Reflect & Relate: Are you surprised at how early the heart begins to beat and in the size of the embryo at the time? Explain.

 Go to
http://www.voyages1CE.nelson.com
for an interactive version of this review.

The Fetal Stage

The **fetal stage** lasts from the beginning of the third month until birth. *Question: What happens during the fetal stage of prenatal development?* The fetus begins to turn and respond to external stimulation at about the ninth or tenth week. By the end of the first trimester, all the major organ systems have been formed. The fingers and toes are fully formed. The eyes can be clearly distinguished, and the sex of the fetus can be determined visually.

fetal stage The stage of development that lasts from the beginning of the ninth week of pregnancy through birth; it is characterized by gains in size and weight and maturation of the organ systems.

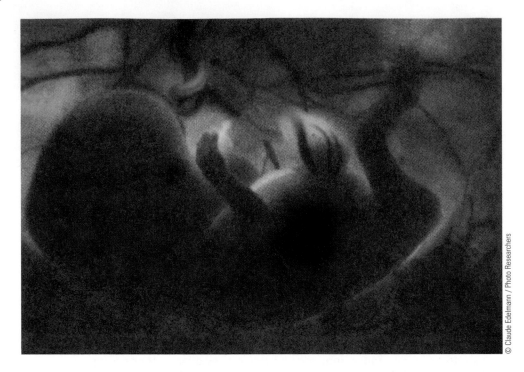

A Human Fetus at
12 Weeks
By the end of the first trimester, formation of all the major organ systems is complete. Fingers and toes are fully formed, and the sex of the fetus can be determined visually.

The second trimester is characterized by further maturation of fetal organ systems and dramatic gains in size. The brain continues to mature, contributing to the fetus's ability to regulate its own basic body functions. During the second trimester, the fetus advances from one ounce to two pounds in weight and grows four to five times in length, from about three inches to fourteen inches. Soft, downy hair grows above the eyes and on the scalp. The skin turns ruddy because of blood vessels that show through the surface. (During the third trimester, fatty layers will give the skin a pinkish hue.)

By the end of the second trimester, the fetus opens and shuts its eyes, sucks its thumb, alternates between periods of wakefulness and sleep, and perceives light and sounds. ***Truth or Fiction Revisited:*** There are also sharp spasms of the diaphragm, or fetal hiccups, which may last for hours (ask a weary pregnant woman).

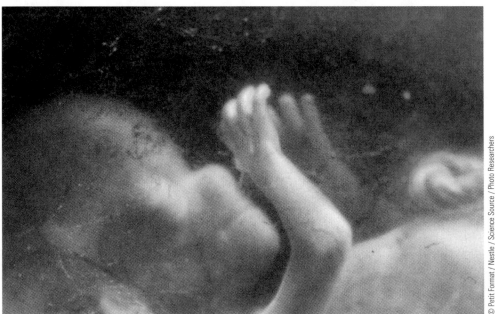

A Human Fetus at
4½ Months
At this midway point between conception and birth, the fetus is covered with fine, downy hair, called lanugo.

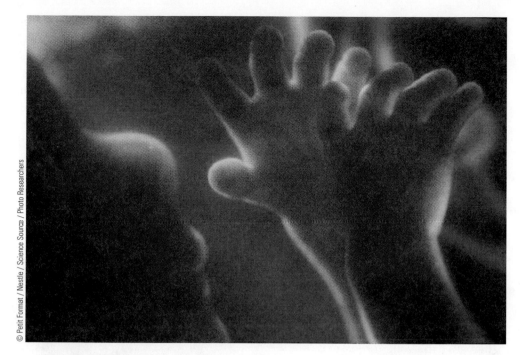

© Petit Format / Nestle / Science Source / Photo Researchers

The Hands of a Human Fetus at 5 Months
By 5 months of age, the hands have been fully formed for a month or so. At this age, the fetus may occasionally suck its thumb.

About half of babies who are born at twenty-two to twenty-five weeks of gestation will survive, and the survival rate is connected with the quality of the medical care they receive (Rogowski et al., 2004).

During the third trimester, the organ systems of the fetus continue to mature. The heart and lungs become increasingly capable of sustaining independent life. The fetus gains about five and a half pounds and doubles in length. Newborn boys average about seven and a half pounds, and newborn girls, about seven pounds.

During the seventh month, the fetus normally turns upside down in the uterus so that delivery will be headfirst. By the end of the seventh month, the fetus will have almost doubled in weight, gaining another one pound, twelve ounces, and will have increased another two inches in length. If born now, chances of survival are nearly 90 percent (Ekvall, 1993b). If born at the end of the eighth month, the odds are overwhelmingly in favour of survival.

Fetal Perception: Bach at Breakfast and Beethoven at Brunch?

Question: Why did Aunt Margaret play classical music (and put the speakers near her abdomen) when she was seven months pregnant? Although we've never met your aunt Margaret, perhaps like most expectant parents, she felt a desire to connect with her unborn child throughout the pregnancy. As beginning graduate students, we were astounded by what we thought was the naïveté of parents-to-be who listened to Bach or Beethoven or who read Shakespeare aloud to promote the cultural development of their fetuses. On second thought, exposing fetuses to music and sounds may not be so far-fetched. Why? Classic research shows that by the thirteenth week of pregnancy, the fetus responds to sound waves. In research cited at the beginning of the chapter—but repeated here so that you cannot complain we sent you searching—Sontag and Richards (1938) rang a bell near the mother, and the fetus responded with movements similar to those of the startle reflex shown after birth. During the third trimester, fetuses respond to sounds of different frequencies through a variety of movements and changes in heart rate, suggesting that by this time, they can discriminate pitch (Lecanuet, Graniere-Deferre, Jacquet, & DeCasper, 2000).

An experiment by DeCasper and Fifer (1980) is even more intriguing. In this study, women read the Dr. Seuss book *The Cat in the Hat* out loud twice daily during the final month and a half of pregnancy. After birth, their babies were given special pacifiers: Sucking on them in one way would activate recordings of their mothers' reading *The Cat in the Hat*. Sucking on them in another way would activate their mothers' reading another book—*The King, the Mice, and the Cheese*—which was written in a very different cadence. The newborns chose to hear *The Cat in the Hat*.

Concept Review 3.1 Highlights of Prenatal Development

© David M. Phillips / Photo Researchers

First Trimester

Germinal Stage

First 2 weeks

- Dividing cluster of cells enters and moves around the uterus, living off the yolk of the egg cell.
- Blastocyst becomes implanted in the wall of the uterus, possibly accompanied by implantation bleeding.

Embryonic Stage

3 weeks

- Head and blood vessels form.
- Brain begins to develop.

4 weeks

- Heart begins to beat and pump blood.
- Arm buds and leg buds appear.
- Eyes, ears, nose, and mouth form.
- Nerves begin to develop.
- Umbilical cord is functional.
- Embryo weighs a fraction of an ounce and is ½ inch long.

5–8 weeks

- Hands and feet develop with webbed fingers and toes.
- Undifferentiated sex organs appear.
- Teeth buds develop.
- Kidneys filter uric acid from the blood; liver produces blood cells.
- Bone cells appear.
- Head is half the length of the entire body.
- Embryo weighs about ⅓ of an ounce and is 1 inch long.

Fetal Stage

9–12 weeks

- All major organ systems formed.
- Fingers and toes are fully formed.
- Eyes can be clearly distinguished.
- Sex of fetus can be determined visually (e.g., by ultrasound).
- Mouth opens and closes; fetus swallows.
- Fetus responds to external stimulation.
- Fetus weighs 1 ounce and is 3 inches long.

Using similar research methods, DeCasper and his colleagues also found that newborns prefer the mother's voice to that of the father or an unfamiliar woman (DeCasper & Prescott, 1984; DeCasper & Spence, 1986, 1991). Presumably, preference for the mother's voice is established through prenatal exposure.

Is it possible that Bach at breakfast and Beethoven at brunch may not be a bad idea during the later days of pregnancy? Perhaps. It just may do more than help the food go down.

Second Trimester	
13–16 weeks	• Mother detects fetal movement. • Many reflexes present. • Fingernails and toenails form. • Head is about ¼ the length of the body.
17–20 weeks	• Hair develops on head. • Fine, downy hair (lanugo) covers body. • Fetus sucks its thumb and hiccups. • Heartbeat can be heard when listener presses head against mother's abdomen.
21–24 weeks	• Eyes open and shut. • Light and sounds can be perceived. • Fetus alternates between periods of wakefulness and sleep. • Skin looks ruddy because blood vessels show through the surface. • Survival rate low if fetus is born. • Fetus weighs about 2 pounds and is 14 inches long; growth rate is slowing down.
Third Trimester	
25–28 weeks	• Organ systems continue to mature. • Fatty layer begins to develop beneath the skin. • Fetus turns head down in the uterus. • Fetus cries, swallows, sucks its thumb. • Chances of survival good if born. • Fetus weighs 3 to 4 pounds and is 16 inches long.
29 to 36–38 weeks	• Organ systems function well. • Fatty layer continues to develop. • Fetal activity level decreases in the weeks before birth as a result of crowding. • Weight increases to an average of 7–7½ pounds; boys are about half a pound heavier than girls; length increases to about 20 inches.

© Ansell Horn / Phototake

Fetal Movements

So the fetus can hear toward the end of the pregnancy. *Question: When does the mother begin to detect fetal movements?* In the middle of the fourth month, the mother usually detects the first fetal movements (Eaton & Saudino, 1992). By twenty-nine or thirty weeks, the mother gets her kicks—that is, the fetus moves its limbs so vigorously that the mother may complain of being kicked—often at 4 a.m. (Okamoto, Sugano, & Negayama, 2003). The fetus also turns somersaults, which are clearly felt by the mother. Fortunately, the umbilical cord will not break or become dangerously wrapped around the fetus, no matter how many acrobatic feats the fetus performs.

Fetuses show different patterns of prenatal activity (Sontag, 1966). Slow squirming movements begin at about five or six months. Sharp jabbing or kicking movements begin at about the same time and increase in intensity until shortly before birth. As the fetus grows, it becomes cramped in the uterus, and movement is constricted. Many women become concerned that their fetuses are markedly less active during the ninth month than previously, but most of the time this change is normal.

There are individual differences in level of fetal activity, but a Dutch study found no sex differences in fetal movement (Robles de Medina, Visser, Huizink, Buitelaar, & Mulder, 2003). Moreover, prenatal activity predicts activity levels after birth. For instance, highly active fetuses show more advanced motor development six months after birth than do their more lethargic counterparts (Richards & Nelson, 1938).

Concept Review 3.1 (pp. 94–95) highlights key events during prenatal development.

Active Review

10. The fetal stage is characterized by _____ of organ systems and gains in size and weight.

11. Research shows that fetuses respond to sound waves by about the _____ week of pregnancy.

12. Mothers usually detect fetal movements during the _____ month.

Reflect & Relate: During the fourth month, when the baby's movements can be detected, many women have the feeling that their babies are "alive." What is your view on when the baby is alive? What standard or standards are you using to form your opinion?

WWW **Go to**
http://www.voyages1CE.nelson.com
for an interactive version of this review.

Environmental Influences on Prenatal Development

Yes, the fetus develops in a protective "bubble"—the amniotic sac. Nevertheless, the developing fetus is subject to many environmental hazards. Scientific advances have made us keenly aware of the types of things that can go wrong and what we can do to prevent these problems. In this section, we consider some of the environmental factors that have an effect on prenatal development.

Nutrition

Question: How does the nutrition of the mother affect prenatal development? We quickly bring nutrition inside, but nutrition originates outside. Therefore, it is one environmental factor in prenatal (and subsequent) development.

It is a common misconception that fetuses "take what they need" from their mothers. If this were true, pregnant women would not have to be highly concerned about their diets. But malnutrition in the mother, especially during the last trimester when the fetus should be making rapid gains in weight, has been linked to low birth weight, prematurity, stunted growth, retardation of brain development, cognitive deficiencies, and behavioural problems (Bhutta, Cleves, Casey, Cradock, & Anand, 2002; Hynes, Sheik, Wilson, & Spiegel, 2002; Christian et al., 2003).

As if pregnant women did not have enough to be concerned about, there are also risks in their being too slender or obese. Women who are overly slender risk preterm deliveries and having babies who are low in birth weight (Cnattingius, Bergstrom, Lipworth, & Kramer, 1998). Maternal obesity is linked with a higher risk of **stillbirth** (Cnattingius et al., 1998).

stillbirth The birth of a dead fetus.

Maternal malnutrition can have long-term behavioural effects (Guerrini, Thomson, & Gurling, 2007). Studies carried out in Latin America indicate that children whose mothers were malnourished during their pregnancies show deficits in motor and cognitive skills and general intelligence (Schultz, 1990). Fortunately, the effects of fetal malnutrition can be overcome by a supportive, care-giving environment. Experiments with children who suffered from fetal malnutrition show that enriched daycare programs enhance intellectual and social skills by five years of age (Ramey et al., 1992; Ramey, Campbell, & Ramey, 1999).

Evidence on supplementing the diets of pregnant women who might otherwise be deficient in their intake of calories and protein also shows modest positive effects on the motor development of the women's infants. In one study, eight-month-old children of Taiwanese women who had received prenatal calorie and protein supplements showed more advanced motor development than control children, as measured by crawling and sitting, pulling themselves to a standing position, and making stepping movements (Joos, Pollitt, Mueller, & Albright, 1983).

Pregnant women require the following food elements to maintain themselves and to give birth to healthy babies: protein, which is heavily concentrated in red meat, fish, poultry, eggs, beans, milk, and cheese; vitamin A, which is found in milk and vegetables; vitamin B, which is found in wheat germ, whole grain breads, and liver; vitamin C, which is found in citrus fruits; vitamin D, which is derived from sunshine, fish-liver oil, and vitamin D-fortified milk; vitamin E, which is found in whole grains, some vegetables, eggs, and peanuts; iron, which is concentrated heavily in meat (especially liver), egg yolks, fish, and raisins; the trace minerals zinc and cobalt, which are found in seafood; calcium, which is found in dairy products; and, yes, calories. Research also demonstrates the importance of consuming folic acid, which is found in leafy green vegetables. Women who eat a well-rounded diet do not require food supplements, but most doctors recommend them to be safe (Balluz et al., 2000). Pregnant women who take folic acid supplements reduce the risk of giving birth to babies with neural tube defects, which can cause paralysis and death (Honein, Paulozzi, Mathews, Erickson, & Wong, 2001; Lawrence et al., 2003).

Obesity during pregnancy increases the likelihood of health problems such as neural tube defects. In a study reported in the *Journal of the American Medical Association,* women who weighed 176 to 195 pounds before pregnancy were about twice as likely as women who weighed 100 to 130 pounds to bear children with neural tube defects; women who weighed 242 pounds or more were four times as likely to have children with neural tube defects (Shaw, Velie, & Schaffer, 1996). Note that these findings were for obese women only. Very tall women normally weigh more than shorter women, so the study's findings must be considered in terms of women's recommended weights for a given height. In Shaw's study, folic acid supplements did not appear to prevent neural tube defects in the babies of women who weighed more than 154 pounds. (See "A Closer Look: Healthy Pregnancy" for a discussion of nutrition, health, and activity during pregnancy.)

Teratogens and Health Problems of the Mother

teratogens Environmental influences or agents that can damage the embryo or fetus (from the Greek *teras*, meaning "monster").

Most of what the mother does for the embryo is not only remarkable but also healthful. There are exceptions, however. Consider the case of teratogens. **Teratogens** (the word derives from frightening roots meaning "giving birth to monsters") are environmental agents that can harm the embryo or fetus. Teratogens include drugs that the mother ingests, such as thalidomide (connected with birth deformities) and alcohol, and substances that the mother's body produces, such as Rh-positive antibodies. Another class of teratogens is the heavy metals, such as lead and mercury, which are toxic to the embryo. Hormones are healthful in countless ways; for example, they help maintain pregnancy. However, excessive quantities of hormones are harmful to the embryo. If the mother is exposed to radiation, that radiation can harm the embryo. Then, of course, disease-causing organisms—also called *pathogens*—such as bacteria and viruses, are also teratogens. When it comes to pathogens, bigger is better for the embryo. That is, larger pathogens are less likely to pass through the placenta and affect the embryo. But smaller pathogens sneak through, including those that cause mumps, syphilis, measles, and chicken pox. Some disorders, such as toxemia, are not transmitted to the embryo or fetus but adversely affect the environment that it develops in.

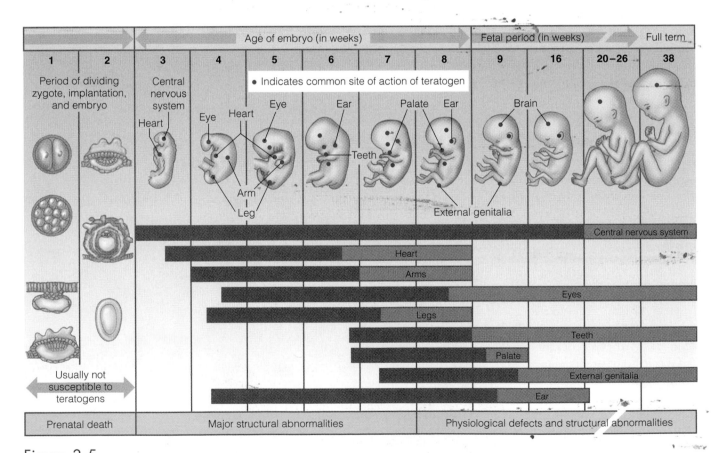

Figure 3.5

Critical Periods in Prenatal Development

Knowledge of the sequences of prenatal development allows one to understand why specific teratogens are most harmful during certain periods of prenatal development. Major structural abnormalities are most likely to occur when teratogens strike during the embryonic period.

Critical Periods of Vulnerability

Question: Does it matter when, during pregnancy, a woman is exposed to a teratogen? Exposure to particular teratogens is most harmful during **critical periods** that correspond to the times when organs are developing. ***Truth or Fiction Revisited:*** Therefore, the same disease organism or chemical agent that can do serious damage to a six-week-old embryo may have no effect on a four-month-old fetus. For example, the heart develops rapidly during the third to fifth weeks after conception. As you can see in Figure 3.5, the heart is most vulnerable to certain teratogens at this time. The arms and legs, which develop later, are most vulnerable during the fourth through eighth weeks. Because the major organ systems differentiate during the embryonic stage, the embryo is generally more vulnerable to teratogens than the fetus. But many teratogens are harmful throughout the entire course of prenatal development.

    Question: What are the effects of maternal health problems? Let us consider the effects of various health problems of the mother, beginning with sexually transmitted infections (STIs).

critical period In this usage, a period during which an embryo is particularly vulnerable to a certain teratogen.

Sexually Transmitted Infections

The STI **syphilis** is caused by the *Treponema pallidum* bacterium. It can cause miscarriage, stillbirth, or **congenital** syphilis. Routine blood tests early in pregnancy can diagnose syphilis.

    The syphilis bacterium is vulnerable to antibiotics, and rates of syphilis are currently low in Western nations. Also, the bacterium does not readily cross the placental membrane early in pregnancy. The fetus will probably not contract syphilis if an infected mother is treated with antibiotics before the fourth month of pregnancy. However, an infected woman has about a 40 percent chance of having a child who is stillborn or dies shortly after birth (Centers for Disease Control and Prevention, 2001a). If the mother is not treated, the baby has a 40 to 70 percent chance of being infected in utero and of developing congenital syphilis. About 12 percent of those infected die.

    Infected babies may show no symptoms when they are born, but they may develop symptoms within a few weeks if they are not treated. The symptoms of congenital syphilis include skin sores, a runny nose, which is sometimes bloody (and infectious), slimy patches in the mouth, inflamed bones in the arms and legs, swollen liver, jaundice, anemia, or a small head. Congenital syphilis can impair vision and hearing, damage the liver, or deform the bones and teeth. Untreated babies may develop mental retardation or have seizures.

    HIV/AIDS (human immunodeficiency virus/acquired immunodeficiency syndrome) disables the body's immune system, leaving victims prey to a variety of fatal illnesses, including respiratory disorders and cancer. HIV/AIDS is lethal unless treated with a combination of antiviral drugs. Even then, the drugs do not work for everyone, and the eventual outcome remains in doubt (Rathus, Nevid, & Fichner-Rathus, 2005).

    HIV can be transmitted by means of sexual relations, blood transfusions, sharing hypodermic needles while shooting up drugs, childbirth, and breast feeding. About one-fourth of babies born to HIV-infected mothers end up infected themselves (Coovadia, 2004). Many of them are infected during childbirth, when blood vessels in the mother and baby rupture, enabling an exchange of blood and transmission of HIV. HIV is also found in breast milk. An African study found that the probability of transmission of HIV through breast milk was about one in six (16.2 percent) (Nduati et al., 2000).

syphilis A sexually transmitted infection that, in advanced stages, can attack major organ systems.

congenital Present at birth; resulting from the prenatal environment.

HIV/AIDS Acronym for human immunodeficiency virus/acquired immuno deficiency syndrome. AIDS is a fatal, usually sexually transmitted infection that is caused by a virus (HIV); the infection cripples the body's immune system, making the person vulnerable to opportunistic diseases.

Rubella

rubella A viral infection that can cause retardation and heart disease in the embryo. Also called German measles.

Rubella (German measles) is a viral infection. Women who are infected during the first twenty weeks of pregnancy stand at least a 20 percent chance of bearing children with birth defects such as deafness, mental retardation, heart disease, or eye problems, including blindness (Food and Drug Administration, 2004; Reef, Zimmerman-Swain, & Coronado, 2004).

Many adult women had rubella as children and became immune in this way. Women who are not immune are best vaccinated before they become pregnant, although they can be inoculated during pregnancy, if necessary. Inoculation has led to a dramatic decline in the number of Canadian children born with defects caused by rubella and Canada continues to experience very low incidence of rubella and congenital rubella syndrome (0 to 0.6 per 100 000 live births) (Canadian Paediatric Society, 2004).

Toxemia

toxemia A life-threatening disease that can afflict pregnant women; it is characterized by high blood pressure.

premature Born before the full term of gestation. (Also referred to as preterm.)

Toxemia is a life-threatening disease, characterized by high blood pressure, that may afflict women late in the second or early in the third trimester. Women with toxemia often have **premature** or undersized babies. Toxemia is also a cause of pregnancy-related maternal deaths (MacKay, Berg, & Atrash, 2001). Toxemia appears to be linked to malnutrition, but the causes are unclear. Women who do not receive prenatal care are more than seven times as likely to die from toxemia as those who receive prenatal care (American College of Obstetricians and Gynecologists, 2001; Perinatal Health Indicators for Canada, 2000).

Rh Incompatibility

Rh incompatibility A condition in which antibodies produced by the mother are transmitted to the child, possibly causing brain damage or death.

In **Rh incompatibility,** antibodies produced by the mother are transmitted to a fetus or newborn infant and cause brain damage or death. Rh is a blood protein that is found in the red blood cells of some individuals. Rh incompatibility occurs when a woman who does not have this factor—and is thus Rh negative—is carrying an Rh-positive fetus, which can happen if the father is Rh positive. The negative-positive combination occurs in about 10 percent of Canadian couples and becomes a problem in some resulting pregnancies (Beaulieu, 1980). Rh incompatibility does not affect a first child because women will not have formed Rh antibodies. The chances of an exchange of blood are greatest during childbirth. If an exchange occurs, the mother produces Rh-positive antibodies to the baby's Rh-positive blood. These antibodies can enter the fetal bloodstream during subsequent deliveries, causing anemia, mental deficiency, or death.

If an Rh-negative mother is injected with Rh immunoglobulin within seventy-two hours after delivery of an Rh-positive baby, she will not develop the antibodies. A fetus or newborn child at risk of Rh disease may receive a blood transfusion to remove the mother's antibodies.

Drugs Taken by the Parents

Rh antibodies can be lethal to children, but many other substances can have harmful effects. *Question: How do drugs taken by the mother affect prenatal development?* In this section, we discuss the effects of various drugs on the unborn child—prescription drugs, over-the-counter drugs, and illegal drugs. Even commonly used medications, such as aspirin, can be harmful to the fetus. If a woman is pregnant or thinks she may be, it is advisable for her to consult her obstetrician before taking any drugs, not just prescription medications. A physician usually can recommend a safe and effective substitute for a drug that could potentially harm a developing fetus. The Hospital for Sick Children, located in Toronto, Ontario, has a website (http://www.motherisk.org) with resources and information about the use of alcohol and/or drugs during pregnancy or while breast feeding.

Thalidomide

Thalidomide was marketed in the 1960s as a treatment for insomnia and nausea. It was available in Germany and England without prescription. Within a few years, more than 10 000 babies with missing or stunted limbs were born in these countries and elsewhere as a result of their mothers' using thalidomide during pregnancy (Gillio, 1999; National Library of Medicine, 1997). Thalidomide is still in use, to treat disorders as various as dermatological problems and Kaposi's sarcoma, a form of cancer that affects many people with HIV/AIDS (Chaudhry et al., 2002).

Thalidomide provides a dramatic example of critical periods of vulnerability to various teratogens. The extremities undergo rapid development during the second month of pregnancy (see Figure 3.5). Thalidomide taken during this period almost invariably causes birth defects.

thalidomide A sedative used in the 1960s that has been linked to birth defects, especially deformed or absent limbs.

Antibiotics

Several antibiotics may be harmful to the fetus. Tetracycline, which is frequently prescribed for bacterial infections, can lead to yellowed teeth and bone abnormalities (American Pregnancy Association, 2003). Other antibiotics are implicated in hearing loss.

Hormones

Women at risk for miscarriages have been prescribed hormones such as progestin and DES to help maintain their pregnancies. **Progestin** is chemically similar to male sex hormones and can masculinize the external sex organs of female embryos. Prenatal progestin has also been linked to aggressive behaviour and masculine-typed play in girls (Keenan & Soleymani, 2001; Reinisch, Ziemba-Davis, & Sanders, 1991).

DES (short for diethylstilbestrol), a powerful estrogen, was given to many women during the 1940s and 1950s to help prevent miscarriage (Centers for Disease Control and Prevention, 2004), but it has caused cervical and testicular cancer in some of the offspring. Among daughters of DES users, about one in 1000 will develop cancer in the reproductive tract. Daughters are also more likely to have babies who are premature or low in birth weight. Daughters and sons of mothers who took DES have high rates of infertility and immune system disorders.

progestin A hormone used to maintain pregnancy that can cause masculinization of the fetus.

DES Abbreviation for diethylstilbestrol, a powerful estrogen that has been linked to cancer in the reproductive organs of children of women who used the hormone when pregnant.

Vitamins

Although pregnant women are often prescribed multivitamins to maintain their own health and to promote the development of their fetuses, too much of a good thing can be dangerous. High doses of vitamins A and D have been associated with central nervous system damage, small head size, and heart defects (National Institutes of Health, 2002). Nonetheless, Health Canada (2007) recommends that all women of childbearing age take at least 0.4 mg of folic acid, found in many multivitamins. Folic acid supplements have reduced the number of neural tube deficits in infants (Berry, Li, Erickson, Li, Moore, Wang, Mulinare, Zhao, Wong, Gindler, Hong, & Correa, 1999). Health Canada's website http://www.healthypregnancy.gc.ca is one initiative aimed at promoting healthy prenatal development.

Heroin and Methadone

Maternal addiction to heroin or methadone is linked to low birth weight, prematurity, and toxemia. These narcotics readily cross the placental membrane, and the fetuses of women who use them regularly can become addicted. ***Truth or Fiction Revisited:*** It is true that babies can be born addicted to narcotics and other substances used regularly by their mothers.

Addicted newborns may be given the narcotic shortly after birth so that they will not suffer serious withdrawal symptoms. They are then withdrawn gradually from the drug. Still, infant death, usually from respiratory problems, is more likely among children of mothers addicted to heroin or methadone. Behavioural and cognitive effects remain apparent years later. For example, infants whose mothers were on methadone are slower in motor and language development at the age of two (Hans, Henson, & Jeremy, 1992).

Marijuana (Cannabis)

Using marijuana during pregnancy apparently poses a number of risks for the fetus, including low birth weight (Visscher, Feder, Burns, Brady, & Bray, 2003). The babies of women who regularly used marijuana show increased tremors and startling, suggesting immature development of the nervous system (Dahl, Scher, Williamson, Robles, & Day, 1995).

Research into the cognitive effects of maternal prenatal use of marijuana shows mixed results. Some studies suggest that there may be no impairment (Fried & Smith, 2001). Others suggest that learning and memory may be impaired (Richardson, Ryan, Willford, Day, & Goldschmidt, 2002). One study assessed the behaviour of ten-year-olds who had been exposed prenatally to maternal marijuana use (Goldschmidt, Day, & Richardson, 2000). The study included the children of 635 mothers, aged eighteen to forty-two. Prenatal use of marijuana was significantly related to increased hyperactivity, impulsivity, and problems in paying attention (as measured by the Swanson, Noland, and Pelham checklist), increased delinquency (as measured by the Child Behavior Checklist), and increased delinquency and aggressive behaviour (as measured by teacher reports). The researchers hypothesized that the pathway between prenatal marijuana exposure and delinquency involves the effects of marijuana on attention, impairing the abilities to learn in school and to conform to social rules and norms.

Researchers have also found that maternal use of marijuana predisposes offspring to dependence on opiates (narcotics derived from the opium poppy). The fetal brain, like the adult brain, has cannabinoid receptors—called CB-1 receptors—and other structures that are altered by exposure to marijuana. The alterations make the individual more sensitive to the reinforcing properties of opiates, even in adulthood (Moreno, Trigo, Escuredo, Rodriguez de Fonseca, & Navarro, 2003).

Cocaine

Most studies suggest that prenatal exposure to cocaine can harm the child. Pregnant women who abuse cocaine increase the risk of stillbirth, low birth weight, and birth defects. The infants are often excitable and irritable or lethargic. The more heavily exposed to cocaine they are in utero, the more problems they have with jitteriness and concentration (Singer, Arendt, Minnes, Farkas, & Salvator, 2000). Later in childhood, they are more likely to show hyperactivity, disorganization, delayed cognitive development, and social problems.

One study matched fifty-six infants, aged twelve to twenty-eight months, who were exposed prenatally to cocaine with fifty-six infants who were not (Chapman, 2000a). The infants were matched according to sex, marital status of the mother, and race. All infants were administered the Mullen Scales of Early Learning, the Bayley Scales of Infant Development-II (BSID-II), and the Behavior Rating Scale of the BSID-II. Infants and toddlers who were prenatally exposed to cocaine obtained significantly lower scores in language development—differences that persisted at the ages of forty-eight to sixty-four months (Chapman, 2000b). Another study examined 458 six-year-olds, 204 of whom had been prenatally exposed to cocaine (Delaney-Black et al., 2000). Children who had been exposed were 2.4 times as likely to lag in language development as children who had not.

Infants exposed prenatally to cocaine become overly aroused by stressors and do not recover as rapidly as infants not exposed. For example, after being presented with a stressor, eight-week-old cocaine-exposed infants did not recover their normal heart rates as rapidly as control infants did (Bard, Coles, Platzman, & Lynch, 2000).

The studies with humans are correlational. That is, mothers are not randomly assigned to use cocaine; rather, they make the choice themselves. This type of research challenge is technically termed a *selection factor*. Thus, it may be that the same factors that lead mothers to use cocaine affect their children. We must also consider the confounding factors of maternal cocaine abuse with polydrug abuse and general neglect of health during pregnancy (Frank, Augustyn, Knight, Pell, & Zuckerman, 2001; Stanwood et al., 2001a). Cocaine-abusing parents often do not nurture or supervise their children adequately; some of their children do not become securely attached to their parents (Alessandri, Bendersky, & Lewis, 1998; Finch et al., 2001). By the same token, good parenting may help to counteract the effects of prenatal exposure to drugs. Research suggests that the outcome is more positive for cocaine-exposed children who are reared in a stable and caring home environment (Frank et al., 2001; Stanwood et al., 2001a).

To overcome the selection factor, numerous experiments have been conducted with laboratory animals (Chelonis, Gillam, & Paule, 2003; Lidow & Song, 2001). In one study, randomly selected pregnant rats were given cocaine during days twelve through twenty-one of gestation, whereas control rats received no cocaine (Huber, Darling, Park, & Soliman, 2001). The rat pups were then exposed to stressors such as cold-water swimming and tail flicks. The pups exposed to cocaine showed less tolerance of the stressors—as measured by behaviours such as tail twitches and convulsions—than control subjects. Another study found that such group differences in response to stressors endure into rat adulthood, that is, ninety to 120 days of age (Campbell, Bliven, Silver, Snyder, & Spear, 2000).

Some investigators have also exposed rabbit embryos to cocaine during various periods of prenatal brain development (Gabriel, Taylor, & Burhans, 2003; Stanwood et al., 2001b). The researchers found deficiencies in learning in the offspring and changes in development of a structure in the brain called the anterior cingulate cortex (ACC). The ACC is involved in the functions of attention and self-control.

Methamphetamine

An increase in methamphetamine (methylamphetamine or desoxyephedrine) use in certain regions of North America has caused surprise and concern. A recent large-scale investigation examining methamphetamine use revealed that as many as 5.2 percent of pregnant women are users (Arria, Derauf, LaGasse, Grant, Shah, Smith, Haning, Huestis, Strauss, Della Grotta, Liu, & Lester, 2006). The most accessible version of this drug is *crystal meth,* a crystalline form of the drug that is usually smoked. Although very little human research exists, preliminary work by Smith and colleagues (Smith, Yonekura, Berman, Kuo, & Berkowitz, 2003), found that methamphetamine use during pregnancy (based on retrospective reports) was associated with growth restriction in infants.

© George Steinmetz

Fetal Alcohol Syndrome (FAS)
The children of many mothers who drank alcohol during pregnancy exhibit FAS. This syndrome is characterized by developmental lags and such facial features as an underdeveloped upper jaw, a flattened nose, and widely spaced eyes.

Alcohol

What is there to say about alcohol—the social lubricant, the ubiquitous tranquillizer, the socially acceptable drug when taken in moderation? Actually, quite a bit. Because alcohol passes through the placenta, drinking by a pregnant woman poses risks for the embryo and fetus. Heavy drinking can be lethal to the fetus and neonate. It is also connected with deficiencies and deformities in growth. Some children of heavy drinkers develop **fetal alcohol syndrome,** or *FAS* (Autti-Ramo, 2002; Barr & Streissguth, 2001). Babies with FAS are often smaller than normal, and so are their brains. There are distinct facial features: widely spaced eyes, an underdeveloped upper jaw, a flattened nose. There may be malformation of the limbs, poor coordination, and cardiovascular problems. A number of psychological characteristics are connected with FAS and appear to reflect dysfunction of the brain: mental retardation, hyperactivity, distractibility, lessened verbal fluency, and learning disabilities (Autti-Ramo, 2002; Granato & Van Pelt, 2003; Steinhausen, Willms, Metzke, & Spohr, 2003). There are deficits in speech and hearing, practical reasoning, and visual-motor coordination (Adnams et al., 2001).

The facial deformities of FAS diminish as the child moves into adolescence, and most children catch up in height and weight. But the intellectual, academic, and behavioural deficits of individuals with FAS persist (Autti-Ramo, 2000). Academic and intellectual problems relative to peers range from verbal difficulties to deficiency in spatial memory (Kaemingk & Halverson, 2000; Timler & Olswang, 2001).

A Closer Look | *Fetal Alcohol Spectrum Disorder (FASD)*

Fetal alcohol spectrum disorder (FASD) is a term used to describe a range of disabilities that may affect individuals whose mothers drank alcohol while they were pregnant. FASD is a serious health and social concern for Canadians with the following diagnoses: fetal alcohol syndrome (FAS), partial fetal alcohol syndrome (pFAS), alcohol-related neurodevelopmental disorder (ARND), and alcohol-related birth defects (ARBD). According to the *It Takes a Community* report (Health Canada, 2001), about one baby out of 500 to 3000 live births will have fetal alcohol syndrome. Statistics for the range of FASD diagnoses are difficult to find for various reasons, including regional differences in description, classification, and diagnosis. Recently, however, Canadian guidelines for diagnosis of FASD were published in the *Canadian Medical Association Journal* (Chudley, Conry,

Cook, Loock, Rosales, & LeBlanc, 2005). Health Canada asserts that there is no safe amount of alcohol to consume during pregnancy, recommending that it be avoided altogether. For information on FASD, contact the FASD Information Service (Canadian Centre on Substance Abuse), an information and reference service, by calling 1-800-559-4514.

Studies find that the average academic functioning of adolescents and young adults with FAS was at the second- to fourth-grade level. Maladaptive behaviours such as poor judgment, distractibility, and difficulty perceiving social cues are common (Zevenbergen & Ferraro, 2001).

FAS is part of a broader group of fetal alcohol-related problems referred to as *fetal alcohol spectrum disorders* (Barr & Streissguth, 2001). ***Truth or Fiction Revisited:*** It cannot be guaranteed that one glass of wine a day is harmless to the embryo and fetus. Although some health professionals allow pregnant women a glass of wine with dinner, research suggests that even moderate drinkers place their offspring at increased risk for a less severe set of effects known as **fetal alcohol effect (FAE).** Pregnant women who have as few as one or two drinks a day may be more likely to miscarry and have growth-retarded babies than pregnant women who do not drink (Newburn-Cook et al., 2002; Ornoy, 2002).

The reported effects of maternal drinking, as with the effects of maternal use of cocaine, are based on correlational evidence. No researcher would randomly assign some pregnant women to drinking and others to abstention. However, researchers have randomly assigned experimental animals to intake of alcohol, and the results support the correlational evidence with humans. For example, research with animals finds that exposure to alcohol during gestation is connected with retarded growth, facial malformations characteristic of FAS, deficiencies in the immune system, and structural and chemical differences in the central nervous system (Ponnappa & Rubin, 2000). Check out the nearby "A Closer Look" feature for a Canadian perspective on FASD.

Caffeine

If you can't imagine starting your day off without your cup of coffee or tea, perhaps you may be able to relate to the following. Many pregnant women consume caffeine in the form of coffee, tea, soft drinks, chocolate, and nonprescription drugs. Until recently, the findings of research on caffeine's effects on the developing fetus had been inconsistent. Some studies report no adverse findings, but others have found that pregnant women who take in a good deal of caffeine are more likely than nonusers to have a miscarriage or a low-birth-weight baby (Signorello et al., 2001).

A Swedish study suggested that intake of caffeine during pregnancy may well be a risky business. Sven Cnattingius and his colleagues (2000) performed a population-based study of early miscarriage in Uppsala County, Sweden. They compared 562 women who had had a miscarriage at six to twelve weeks of gestation with 953 women who had not. They obtained information on caffeine intake by means of personal interviews. They also obtained information on the smoking habits of the women. Among nonsmokers, it turned out that the more caffeine the women ingested, the more likely they were to have a miscarriage, with the heaviest users of caffeine (those likely to have the equivalent of several cups of coffee a day) more than twice as likely as nonusers to have a miscarriage. (These finding are inconsistent with those of the study by Mark Klebanoff and his colleagues [1999], who found that low to moderate caffeine intake did not increase the risk of miscarriage.) Ironically, intake of caffeine in the Cnattingius study did not increase the chances of miscarriage among women who smoked. But do not think of smoking as protecting the embryo and fetus; as amply documented in the following pages, smoking is connected with multiple risks for the baby, including stillbirth.

Now, the Cnattingius study was correlational and not experimental. Thus, it could be that other factors, such as stress or fatigue, contributed both to the use of caffeine and the risk of miscarriage. But if you are going to drink coffee, tea, or colas while you are pregnant, it may be wise to select decaffeinated versions. A little caffeine may not hurt, but we cannot be certain.

fetal alcohol syndrome (FAS)
A cluster of symptoms shown by children of women who drank heavily during pregnancy, including characteristic facial features and mental retardation.

fetal alcohol effect (FAE) A cluster of symptoms less severe than those of fetal alcohol syndrome shown by children of women who drank during pregnancy.

Health Canada

Licensed under Health Canada copyright.

Why Start a New Life under a Cloud?
This Health Canada warning label dramatizes the risks posed by maternal smoking during pregnancy.

Cigarettes

Cigarette smoke contains many ingredients, including the stimulant nicotine, the gas carbon monoxide, and hydrocarbons ("tars"), which are carcinogens. Fortunately, only the first two of these, the nicotine and the carbon monoxide, pass through the placenta and reach the fetus. That's the end of the fortunate news. Nicotine stimulates the fetus, but its long-term effects are uncertain. Carbon monoxide is toxic; it decreases the amount of oxygen available to the fetus. Oxygen deprivation is connected with cognitive and behavioural problems, including impaired motor development. The cognitive difficulties include academic delays, learning disabilities, and mental retardation. Not all children of smokers develop these problems, but many do not function as well as they would have if they had not been exposed to maternal smoking.

Health Canada (2005a) reports that approximately 20 to 30 percent of pregnant women use tobacco. Pregnant women who smoke are likely to deliver smaller babies than nonsmokers (Haslam & Draper, 2001; X. Wang et al., 2002). In addition, their babies are more likely to be stillborn or to die soon after birth (Tizabi et al., 2000; X. Wang et al., 2002).

Maternal smoking may also have long-term negative effects on development. Children whose mothers smoke during pregnancy are more likely to have short attention spans, hyperactive disorders, lower cognitive and language scores, and poor grades. In one study, women who smoked during pregnancy were 50 percent more likely to have children whose intelligence test scores placed them in the mentally retarded range (scores under seventy) when the children were ten years old (Drews et al., 1996). Women who smoked at least one pack a day were 85 percent more likely to have children with cognitive delays.

Secondhand smoke also holds dangers. Men who smoke are more likely to produce abnormal sperm. Babies of fathers who smoke have higher rates of birth defects, infant mortality, lower birth weights, and cardiovascular problems (Hutchison et al., 1998). Most provinces offer counselling, support, and other services through telephone help lines (e.g., Alberta Alcohol and Drug Abuse Commission's Smokers' Help Line).

Environmental Hazards

Mothers know when they are ingesting drugs, but there are many other substances in the environment that they may take in unknowingly. These are environmental hazards to which we are all exposed, and we refer to them collectively as pollution. *Question: What are the effects of environmental hazards during pregnancy?*

Prenatal exposure to heavy metals such as lead, mercury, and zinc threatens the development of children. In one longitudinal study, newborns who had even mildly elevated levels of lead in their umbilical cord blood showed delayed mental development at one and two years of age (Bellinger, Leviton, Waternaux, Needleman, & Rabinowitz, 1987). By age six, their cognitive functioning had improved if they were no longer exposed to lead in the home. But those children who continued to be exposed to lead still showed cognitive deficits (Bellinger et al., 1991).

One study of the effects of prenatal exposure to lead recruited 442 children in Yugoslavia (Wasserman et al., 2000). Some of the children lived in a town with a smelter; the others did not. (*Smelting*—or the melting of lead-bearing scrap metal into metallic lead—is a major source of lead fume emissions.) The children received intelligence testing at the ages of three, four, five, and seven, using Wechsler and other scales. The researchers found that the children from the town with the smelter obtained somewhat lower intelligence test scores.

Experiments with rodents support the correlational findings with humans. For example, mice exposed to lead in utero do not form memories as well as those who are free of prenatal exposure to lead (de Oliveira, Viana, Antoniolli, & Marchioro, 2001). Research with rats has found that prenatal exposure to lead decreases the levels of neurotransmitters (the chemical messengers of the brain) in all areas of the brain, but especially in the hippocampus. The hippocampus is involved in memory formation.

The devastating effects of mercury on the fetus were first recognized among the Japanese who lived around Minimata Bay. Industrial waste containing mercury was dumped into the bay and accumulated in the fish, which were a major food source for local residents. Children born to women who had eaten the fish during pregnancy often were profoundly retarded and neurologically damaged (Vorhees & Mollnow, 1987). Prenatal exposure to even small amounts of mercury and other heavy metals such as cadmium and chromium can produce subtle deficits in cognitive functioning and physical health (Davidson et al., 1998; Lewis et al., 1992).

Polychlorinated biphenyls (PCBs) are chemicals used in many industrial products. Like mercury, they accumulate in fish that feed in polluted waters. Newborns whose mothers had consumed PCB-contaminated fish from Lake Michigan were smaller and showed poorer motor functioning and less responsiveness than newborns whose mothers had not eaten these fish. Furthermore, even those PCB-exposed infants who appeared normal at birth showed deficits in memory at seven months and at four years of age (Jacobson, Jacobson, Padgett, Brumitt, & Billings, 1992).

An unfortunate natural experiment in the effects of prenatal exposure to PCBs took place in Taiwan during the late 1970s, when a group of people accidentally ingested contaminated rice. Children born to mothers who ate the rice had characteristic signs of PCB poisoning, including hyperpigmented skin. The researchers (Lai, Guo, Guo, & Hsu, 2001) had the opportunity to compare the cognitive development of 118 children born to exposed mothers with that of other children in the community. The children were all followed through the age of twelve and were tested with instruments including the Bayley Scale for Infant Development, the Chinese version of the Stanford-Binet IQ Test, and two nonverbal intelligence tests. Throughout the observation period, the children of mothers who'd eaten the contaminated rice scored lower than the control children on each of these methods of measurement. It appears that prenatal exposure to PCBs has long-term harmful effects on cognitive development.

Fetal exposure to radiation in high doses can cause defects in a number of organs, including the eyes, central nervous system, and skeleton (Michel, 1989). Pregnant women who were exposed to atomic radiation during the bombing of Hiroshima and Nagasaki in World War II gave birth to babies who were more likely to be mentally retarded in addition to being physically deformed (Yamazaki & Schull, 1990). The best advice for a pregnant woman is to avoid unnecessary exposure to x-rays.

Research suggests that men exposed to heavy metals and radiation can also produce children with abnormalities (Merewood, 1991; Purvis, 1990). For example, children of fathers employed in jobs with high exposure to lead had three times more kidney tumours than children whose fathers were not exposed (Davis, 1991). Another study found a higher incidence of leukemia among children whose fathers worked in nuclear plants, where they were exposed to high levels of radiation before the children's conception ("British Study Finds," 1990).

The risks of radiation and other environmental agents to the embryo and fetus are summarized in Concept Review 3.2 (pages 108–109).

Concept Review 3.2 — Risks of Various Agents to the Embryo and Fetus

Agent	Risks
Prescription Drugs[1]	
Accutane (used to treat acne; repeated blood tests required to show that one is not pregnant or encountering drug-related problems)	Stillbirth, malformation of limbs and organs
Bendectin	Cleft palate, malformation of the heart
Carbamazepine (and other anticonvulsant drugs)	Spina bifida
Diethylstilbestrol (DES; once used to help maintain pregnancy)	Cancer of the cervix or testes
Strong general anesthesia during labour (sedation that goes beyond normal medical practice)	Anoxia, asphyxiation, brain damage
Progestin (a synthetic version of the natural hormone progesterone, which is sometimes used to help maintain pregnancy)	Masculinization of the sex organs of female embryos, possible development of "masculine" aggressiveness
Streptomycin (an antibiotic)	Deafness
Tetracycline (an antibiotic)	Malformed bones, yellow teeth
Thalidomide (several uses, including sedation)	Malformed or missing limbs
Other Drugs	
Alcohol	Fetal death, low birth weight, addiction, academic and intellectual problems, hyperactivity, distractibility, fetal alcohol syndrome (FAS), including characteristic facial features
Aspirin (high doses)	Bleeding, respiratory problems
Caffeine (the stimulant found in coffee, tea, colas, chocolate)	Stimulates fetus (not necessarily a problem in itself), miscarriage, low birth weight
Cigarette smoke (the stimulant nicotine and carbon monoxide are transmitted through the placenta)	Stimulates fetus (not necessarily a problem in itself), premature birth, low birth weight, fetal death, academic problems, hyperactivity, short attention span
Opiates (heroin, morphine, others)	Low birth weight, premature birth, addiction, toxemia
Marijuana	Tremors, startling, premature birth, birth defects, neurological problems

Agent	Risks
Vitamins[2]	
Vitamin A (high doses)	Cleft palate, damage to the eyes
Vitamin D (high doses)	Mental retardation
Pathogens (disease-causing agents)	
HIV (the virus that causes AIDS)	Physical deformity, mental retardation
Rubella (German measles)	Neurological impairment involving sensation and perception (vision, hearing), mental retardation, heart problems, cataracts
Syphilis (a sexually transmitted infection caused by the *Treponema pallidum* bacterium)	Infant mortality, seizures, mental retardation, sensory impairment (vision, hearing), liver damage, malformation of bones and teeth
Environmental Hazards	
Heavy metals (lead, mercury, zinc)	Mental retardation, hyperactivity, stillbirth, problems in memory formation
Paint fumes (heavy exposure)	Mental retardation
PCBs (polychlorinated biphenyls), dioxin, other insecticides and herbicides	Stillbirth, low birth weight, cognitive impairment, motor impairment
X-rays	Deformation of organs
Biochemical Incompatibility with Mother	
Rh antibodies	Infant mortality, brain damage

[1]Normally healthful, even life-saving drugs can be harmful to the embryo and fetus. Women should inform their physicians when they are pregnant, may be pregnant, or are planning to become pregnant.

[2]Adequate intake of vitamins is essential to the well-being of the mother and the embryo and fetus. Most obstetricians advise pregnant women to take vitamin supplements. However, too much of a good thing can be harmful. In brief, don't do "megavitamins." And when in doubt, ask your obstetrician.

Maternal Stress

Although pregnancy can be a time of immense gratification for women, it can also be a time of stress. The baby might be unplanned and unwanted. Parents might not have the financial resources or the room for the child. The mother might be experiencing physical discomforts because of the pregnancy. *Question: What, then, are the apparent effects of maternal stress on the child?*

How does a mother's emotional state affect her fetus? Emotions are psychological feeling states, but they also have physiological components. For example, they are linked to the secretion of hormones such as adrenaline. **Adrenaline** stimulates the mother's heart rate, respiratory rate, and other bodily functions. Hormones pass through the placenta and also have an effect on the fetus. Health Canada's (2007) guide to a healthy pregnancy also touches upon the topic of emotional well-being and encourages expectant mothers to relax during pregnancy and not to take on additional pressures or burdens if possible. An interesting Canadian longitudinal study examining the effects of a natural disaster on prenatal maternal stress is being conducted by researchers in Montreal. Suzanne King and David Laplante are following 150 children who were exposed in utero to the 1998 Quebec ice storm (which they term "Project Ice Storm"). Thus far, findings suggest that a major stressful event (e.g., a natural disaster and its aftermath) can have various negative impacts, affecting cognitive, language, and emotional functioning (King & Laplante, 2005; Laplante, Barr, Brunet, Galbaud du Fort, Meaney, Saucier, Zelazo, & King, 2004). While natural disasters are beyond anyone's control, this study reaffirms the importance of reducing maternal stress levels.

Parents' Age

What, then, of the parents' age? *Question: Is the parents' age connected with the outcome of pregnancy?*

In Chapter 2, we noted that aging fathers are more likely to produce abnormal sperm. The mother's age also matters. From a biological vantage point, the twenties may be the ideal age for women to bear children. Canadian fertility statistics, however, show that Canadian females are having children on average in their late twenties and early thirties (Health Canada, 2005b). Teenage mothers have a higher incidence of infant mortality and children with low birth weight (Phipps, Blume, & DeMonner, 2002; Save the Children, 2004b). Pregnancy in early teenage years may place a burden on bodies that might not have adequately matured enough to facilitate pregnancy and childbirth. Teenage mothers are also less educated and less likely to obtain prenatal care—all factors associated with high-risk pregnancy (Berg, Chang, Callaghan, & Whitehead, 2003).

What about women older than thirty? Women possess all their ova in immature form at birth. But women's fertility declines gradually until their mid-thirties, after which it declines more rapidly. Women beyond their mid-thirties may have passed the

adrenaline A hormone that generally arouses the body, increasing the heart and respiration rates.

point at which their reproductive systems function most efficiently. Over the course of thirty years, ova are exposed to the slings and arrows of an outrageous environment of toxic wastes, chemical pollutants, and radiation, thus increasing the risk of chromosomal abnormalities such as Down syndrome (Behrman, Kliegman, & Jenson, 2000). Women who wait until their thirties or forties to have children also increase the likelihood of having stillborn or preterm babies (Berg et al., 2003). But with adequate prenatal care, the risk of bearing a premature or unhealthy baby still is relatively small, even for older first-time mothers (Berg et al., 2003). This news should be encouraging for women who have delayed, or plan to delay, bearing children until their thirties or forties.

Whatever the age of the mother, the events of childbirth provide some of the most memorable moments in the lives of parents. In Chapter 4, we continue our voyage with the process of birth and the characteristics of the newborn child.

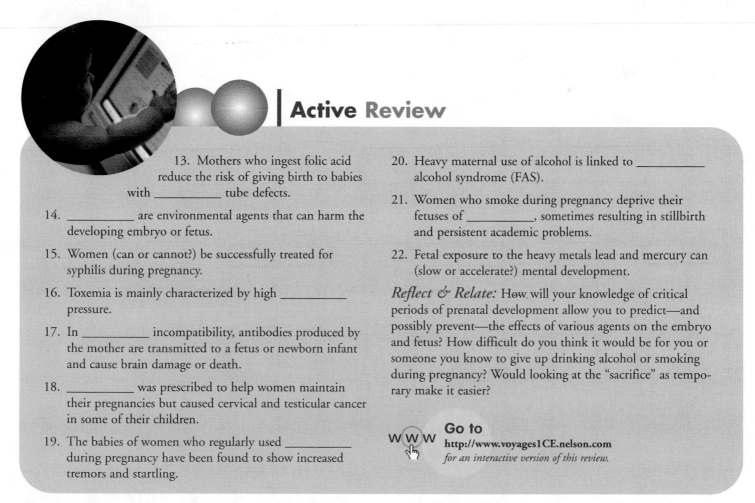

Active Review

13. Mothers who ingest folic acid reduce the risk of giving birth to babies with _____ tube defects.

14. _____ are environmental agents that can harm the developing embryo or fetus.

15. Women (can or cannot?) be successfully treated for syphilis during pregnancy.

16. Toxemia is mainly characterized by high _____ pressure.

17. In _____ incompatibility, antibodies produced by the mother are transmitted to a fetus or newborn infant and cause brain damage or death.

18. _____ was prescribed to help women maintain their pregnancies but caused cervical and testicular cancer in some of their children.

19. The babies of women who regularly used _____ during pregnancy have been found to show increased tremors and startling.

20. Heavy maternal use of alcohol is linked to _____ alcohol syndrome (FAS).

21. Women who smoke during pregnancy deprive their fetuses of _____, sometimes resulting in stillbirth and persistent academic problems.

22. Fetal exposure to the heavy metals lead and mercury can (slow or accelerate?) mental development.

Reflect & Relate: How will your knowledge of critical periods of prenatal development allow you to predict—and possibly prevent—the effects of various agents on the embryo and fetus? How difficult do you think it would be for you or someone you know to give up drinking alcohol or smoking during pregnancy? Would looking at the "sacrifice" as temporary make it easier?

Go to
WWW http://www.voyages1CE.nelson.com
for an interactive version of this review.

Recite: *An Active Summary*™

1. What happens during the germinal stage of prenatal development?

During the germinal stage, the zygote divides repeatedly but does not gain in mass. It travels through a fallopian tube to the uterus, where it implants. It then takes the form of a blastocyst. Layers of cells form within the embryonic disk. The outer part of the blastocyst differentiates into membranes that will protect and nourish the embryo.

2. If the dividing mass of cells is moving through a fallopian tube and then "wandering" through the uterus for another few days, how does it obtain any nourishment?

Before implantation, the dividing cluster of cells is nourished by the yolk of the original egg cell. Once implanted in the uterine wall, it obtains nourishment from the mother.

3. What happens during the embryonic stage of prenatal development?

The embryonic stage lasts from implantation until the eighth week of development, during which the major organ systems differentiate. Development follows cephalocaudal and proximodistal trends. The outer layer of the embryonic disk develops into the nervous system, sensory organs, nails, hair, teeth, and skin. Two ridges form the neural tube, from which the nervous system develops. The inner layer forms the digestive and respiratory systems, liver, and pancreas. The middle layer becomes the excretory, reproductive, and circulatory systems, the muscles, the skeleton, and the inner layer of the skin.

4. When does the heart begin to beat?

The heart begins to beat during the fourth week.

5. What else happens during the embryonic stage?

Toward the end of the first month, arm and leg buds appear and the face takes shape. The nervous system has also begun to develop. By the end of the second month, limbs are elongating, facial features are becoming distinct, teeth buds have formed, the kidneys are working, and the liver is producing red blood cells.

6. How do some babies develop into girls and others into boys?

By five to six weeks, the embryo has undifferentiated sex organs that resemble female structures. Testes produce male sex hormones that spur development of male genital organs and the male duct system.

7. How does the embryo get nourishment from its mother? How does it eliminate waste products?

The embryo and fetus exchange nutrients and wastes with the mother through a mass of tissue called the placenta. The umbilical cord connects the fetus to the placenta.

8. Do germs in the mother pass through the placenta and affect the baby? Do drugs?

Many do, including the germs that cause syphilis and rubella. Some drugs, including aspirin, narcotics, and alcohol, also pass through.

9. What happens during the fetal stage of prenatal development?

The fetal stage lasts from the end of the embryonic stage until birth. The fetus begins to turn at the ninth or tenth week. The second trimester is characterized by maturation of organs and gains in size. By the end of the second trimester, the fetus opens and shuts its eyes, sucks its thumb, alternates between wakefulness and sleep, and responds to light and sounds. During the third trimester, the heart and lungs become increasingly capable of sustaining independent life.

10. Why did aunt Margaret play classical music (and put the speakers near her abdomen) when she was seven months pregnant?

We can't speak for your aunt Margaret, but the fetus responds to sound waves by the thirteenth week of pregnancy. Newborn babies prefer their mother's voice to that of other women, apparently because of prenatal exposure.

11. When does the mother begin to detect fetal movements?

The mother usually detects fetal movements during the fourth month. By the end of the second trimester, the fetus turns somersaults.

12. How does the nutrition of the mother affect prenatal development?

Malnutrition in the mother has been linked to low birth weight, prematurity, stunted growth, retardation of brain development, cognitive deficiencies, and behavioural problems. Folic acid reduces the risk of neural tube defects.

13. Does it matter when, during pregnancy, a woman is exposed to a teratogen?

Yes. Exposure to particular teratogens is most harmful during critical periods—the times when certain organs are developing. The embryo is generally more vulnerable than the fetus because the major organ systems are differentiating.

14. What are the effects of maternal health problems?

Women who contract rubella may bear children who suffer from deafness, mental retardation, heart disease, or cataracts. Syphilis can cause miscarriage, stillbirth, or congenital syphilis. Babies can be infected with HIV in utero, during childbirth, or through breast feeding. Toxemia is characterized by high blood pressure and is connected with preterm or undersized babies. In Rh incompatibility, antibodies produced by the mother are transmitted to a fetus or newborn infant and cause brain damage or death.

15. How do drugs taken by the mother affect prenatal development?

Thalidomide causes missing or stunted limbs in babies. Tetracycline can cause yellowed teeth and bone problems. DES leads to high risk of cervical and testicular cancer. High doses of vitamins A and D are associated with nervous system damage and heart defects. Maternal addiction to narcotics is linked to low birth weight, prematurity, and toxemia, and fetuses can be born addicted themselves. Marijuana may cause tremors and startling in babies. Cocaine increases the risk of stillbirth, low birth weight, and birth defects. Maternal use of alcohol is linked to death of the fetus and neonate, malformations, growth deficiencies, and fetal alcohol syndrome (FAS). Caffeine is connected with miscarriage and low birth weight. Maternal cigarette smoking is linked with low birth weight, stillbirth, and mental retardation.

16. What are the effects of environmental hazards during pregnancy?

Prenatal exposure to heavy metals threatens cognitive development. Prenatal exposure to mercury is connected with neurological damage. Prenatal exposure to PCBs is connected with babies that are smaller, less responsive, and more likely to develop cognitive deficits. Fetal exposure to radiation can cause neural and skeletal problems.

17. What are the apparent effects of maternal stress on the child?

Maternal stress is linked to the secretion of hormones such as adrenaline, which pass through the placenta and affect the baby. Maternal stress may be connected with complications during pregnancy and labour, preterm or low-birth-weight babies, and irritable babies.

18. Is the parents' age connected with the outcome of pregnancy?

Yes. Teenage mothers have a higher incidence of infant mortality and children with low birth weight. Women older than thirty run an increasing risk of chromosomal abnormalities and of having stillborn or preterm babies.

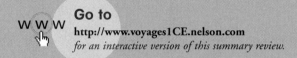

W W W **Go to**
http://www.voyages1CE.nelson.com
for an interactive version of this summary review.

Key Terms

neonate *(page 84)*
germinal stage *(page 84)*
blastocyst *(page 84)*
embryonic disk *(page 85)*
trophoblast *(page 85)*
umbilical cord *(page 85)*
placenta *(page 85)*
embryonic stage *(page 86)*
cephalocaudal *(page 86)*
proximodistal *(page 86)*
ectoderm *(page 86)*
neural tube *(page 86)*

endoderm *(page 86)*
mesoderm *(page 87)*
androgens *(page 89)*
testosterone *(page 89)*
amniotic sac *(page 90)*
amniotic fluid *(page 90)*
fetal stage *(page 91)*
stillbirth *(page 97)*
teratogens *(page 98)*
critical period *(page 99)*
syphilis *(page 99)*
congenital *(page 99)*

HIV/AIDS *(page 99)*
rubella *(page 100)*
toxemia *(page 100)*
premature *(page 100)*
Rh incompatibility *(page 100)*
thalidomide *(page 101)*
progestin *(page 101*
DES *(page 101)*
fetal alcohol syndrome *(page 105)*
fetal alcohol effect *(page 105)*
adrenaline *(page 110)*

Active Learning Resources

Observing Children and Adolescents CD-ROM

Check out your Observing Children and Adolescents CD-ROM. Observational videos cover child development from infancy to adolescence. This package will allow you to experience and learn critical concepts in the field of child development.

Visit Your Companion Website for This Book
http://www.voyages1CE.nelson.com

Check out this companion website, where you will find online resources directly linked to your book. The website includes interactive exercises related to PQ4R and Power Visuals for mastering and reviewing key concepts as well as quizzing, chapter outlines, and much more!

CengageNOW!™
http://hed.nelson.com

Go to this site for the link to CengageNOW™, your one-stop study shop. Take a Pretest for this chapter, and CengageNOW™ will generate a personalized Study Plan based on your test results! The Study Plan will identify the topics you need to review and direct you to online resources to help you master those topics. You can then take a Posttest to help you determine the concepts you have mastered and those you still need to work on.

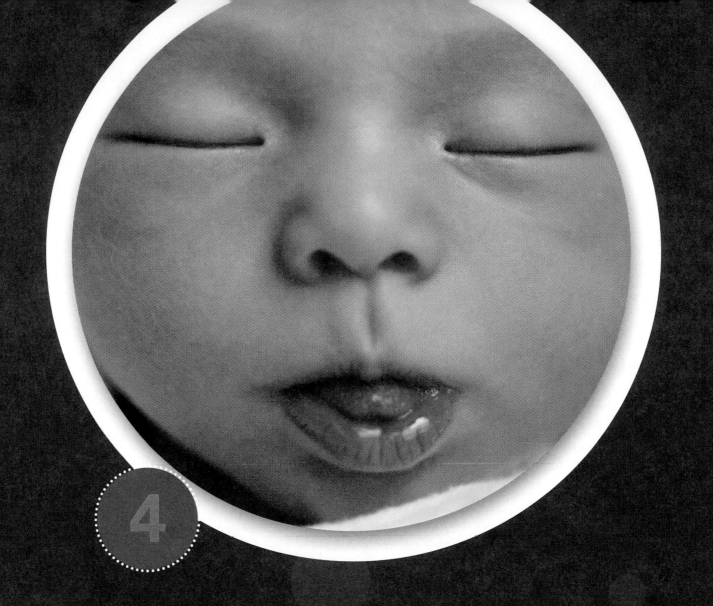

Birth and the Newborn Baby:
In the New World

PREVIEW

TRUTH OR FICTION?

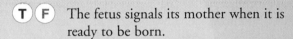

T F   The fetus signals its mother when it is ready to be born.

T F   After birth, babies are held upside down and slapped on the buttocks to stimulate independent breathing.

T F   The way that the umbilical cord is cut determines whether the baby's "belly button" will be an "innie" or an "outie."

T F   Women who give birth according to the Lamaze method do not experience pain.

T F   In Canada, one birth in five is by caesarean section.

T F   It is abnormal to feel depressed following childbirth.

T F   Parents must have extended early contact with their newborn children if adequate bonding is to take place.

T F   More children die from sudden infant death syndrome (SIDS) than from cancer, heart disease, pneumonia, child abuse, AIDS, cystic fibrosis, and muscular dystrophy combined.

Go to www

http://www.voyages1CE.nelson.com
for an interactive version of this "Truth or Fiction" feature.

© Don Mason / CORBIS

D uring the last few weeks before she gave birth, Michele explained:

> I couldn't get my mind off the pregnancy—what it was going to be like when I finally delivered Lisa. I'd had the amniocentesis, so I knew it was a girl. I'd had the ultrasounds, so all her fingers and toes had been counted, but I was still hoping and praying that everything would turn out all right. To be honest, I was also worried about the delivery. I had always been an A student, and I guess I wanted to earn an A in childbirth as well. Matt was understanding, and he was even helpful, but, you know, it wasn't him.
>
> My obstetrician was bending over backwards (*she* could bend—I couldn't), being politically correct, and talking about how *we* had gotten pregnant and about how *we* were going to have the baby. Toward the end there, I would have been thrilled if it had really been we. Or I would even have allowed Matt to do it all by himself. But the fact is it was *me*. And I was worrying about how I could even reach the steering wheel of the car in those days, much less deliver a perfect healthy child. On TV, of course, they do it without even disturbing their mascara, but I was living in the real world. And waiting, waiting, waiting. And, oh yes, did I mention waiting?

Nearly all first-time mothers struggle through the last weeks of pregnancy and worry about the mechanics of delivery. Childbirth is a natural function, of course, but so many women go to classes to learn how to do what comes naturally! They worry about whether they'll get to the hospital or birthing centre on time ("Is there gas in the car?" "Is it snowing?"). They worry about whether the baby will start breathing on its own properly. They may wonder if they'll do it on their own or need a caesarean section. And they may worry about whether it will hurt, and how much, and when they should ask for anesthetic, and, well, how to earn that A.

term A set period of time.

Close to full **term,** Michele and other women are sort of front-loaded, and they feel bent out of shape. Guess what: They are. The weight of the fetus may also be causing backaches. Will they deliver the baby naturally? Will the baby—by being born—deliver them from discomfort? "Hanging in and bearing Lisa was a wonderful experience," Michele said. "I think Matt should have had it."

Countdown . . .

Question: What events occur just before the beginning of childbirth? Early in the last month of pregnancy, the head of the fetus settles in the pelvis. This is called *dropping* or *lightening*. Because lightening decreases pressure on the diaphragm, the mother may, in fact, feel lighter.

Braxton-Hicks contractions The first, usually painless, contractions of childbirth.

The first uterine contractions are called **Braxton-Hicks contractions,** or false-labour contractions. They are relatively painless and may be experienced as early as the sixth month of pregnancy. They tend to increase in frequency as the pregnancy progresses and may serve to tone the muscles that will be used in delivery. Although they may be confused with actual labour contractions, real labour contractions are more painful and regular and are also usually intensified by walking.

A day or so before labour begins, increased pelvic pressure from the fetus may rupture superficial blood vessels in the birth canal, making blood appear in vaginal secretions. The mucus tissue that plugs the cervix and protects the uterus from infection becomes dislodged. At about this time, one woman in ten has a rush of warm liquid from the vagina. This liquid is amniotic fluid, and its discharge means that the amniotic sac has burst. The amniotic sac usually does not burst until the end of the first stage of childbirth, as described later. Indigestion, diarrhea, an ache in the small of the back, and abdominal cramps are also common signs that labour is beginning.

Truth or Fiction Revisited: The fetus may actually signal the mother when it is "ready" to be born—that is, when it is mature enough to sustain life outside the uterus. The adrenal and pituitary glands of the fetus may trigger labour by secreting hormones (Norwitz, Robinson, & Challis, 1999).

Fetal hormones stimulate the placenta (which is a gland as well as a relay station for nutrition and wastes between mother and fetus) and the uterus to secrete **prostaglandins.** Prostaglandins are the main culprits when women experience uncomfortable cramping before or during menstruation; they also serve the function of exciting the muscles of the uterus to engage in labour contractions. As labour progresses, the pituitary gland releases **oxytocin,** another hormone. Oxytocin stimulates contractions that are powerful enough to expel the fetus—although now, of course, we call it a baby.

In this chapter, we discuss the events of childbirth and the characteristics of the **neonate.** Arriving in the new world may be a bit more complex than you had thought, and it may also be that neonates can do a bit more than you had imagined.

The Stages of Childbirth

Regular uterine contractions signal the beginning of childbirth. Developmentalists speak of childbirth as occurring in three stages.

The First Stage

Question: What happens during the first stage of childbirth? In the first stage of childbirth, uterine contractions **efface** and **dilate** the cervix. This passageway needs to widen to about four inches (ten centimetres) to allow the baby to pass. The dilation of the cervix is responsible for most of the pain that is experienced during childbirth. When the cervix dilates rapidly and easily, there may be little or no discomfort.

The first stage is the long stage. Among women undergoing their first deliveries, it may last from a few hours to more than a day. Half a day to a day is about average, but for some women, the first stage is much briefer, and some last up to a couple of days. Subsequent pregnancies take less time and may be surprisingly rapid—sometimes between an hour and two hours. The first contractions are not usually all that painful and are spaced ten to twenty minutes apart. They may last from twenty to forty seconds each.

As the process continues, the contractions become more powerful, frequent, and regular. Women are usually advised to go to the hospital or birthing centre when the contractions are four to five minutes apart. Until the end of the first stage of labour, the mother is frequently in a labour room with her partner or another companion.

If the woman is to be "prepped"—that is, if her pubic hair is to be shaved—it takes place now. The prep is intended to lower the chances of infection during delivery and to facilitate the performance of an **episiotomy** (described later). A woman may be given an enema to prevent an involuntary bowel movement during labour. However, many women find prepping and enemas degrading and seek obstetricians who do not perform them routinely; in Canada the move toward more natural forms of childbirth has diminished, and in some cases eliminated, the prepping routine altogether.

During the first stage of childbirth, **fetal monitoring** may be used. One kind of monitoring is an electronic sensing device strapped around the woman's abdomen. It can measure the fetal heart rate as well as the frequency, strength, and duration of the mother's contractions. Abnormal heart rate alerts the medical staff to possible fetal distress so that appropriate steps can be taken, such as speeding up the delivery by such means as **forceps** or a **vacuum extraction tube.** The forceps is a curved instrument that fits around the baby's head and allows the baby to be pulled out of the mother's body. The vacuum extraction tube relies on suction to pull the baby through the birth canal.

prostaglandins (pross-tuh-GLAN-dins) Hormones that stimulate uterine contractions.

oxytocin (ok-see-TOE-sin) A pituitary hormone that stimulates labour contractions (from the Greek oxys, meaning "quick," and tokos, meaning "birth").

neonate A newborn child (from the Greek neos, meaning "new," and the Latin natus, meaning "born").

efface To rub out or wipe out; to become thin.

dilate To make wider or larger.

episiotomy (ih-pee-zee-AH-tuh-mee) A surgical incision in the area between the birth canal and the anus that widens the vaginal opening, preventing random tearing during childbirth.

fetal monitoring The use of instruments to track the heart rate and oxygen levels of the fetus during childbirth.

forceps A curved instrument that fits around the head of the baby and permits it to be pulled through the birth canal.

vacuum extraction tube An instrument that uses suction to pull the baby through the birth canal.

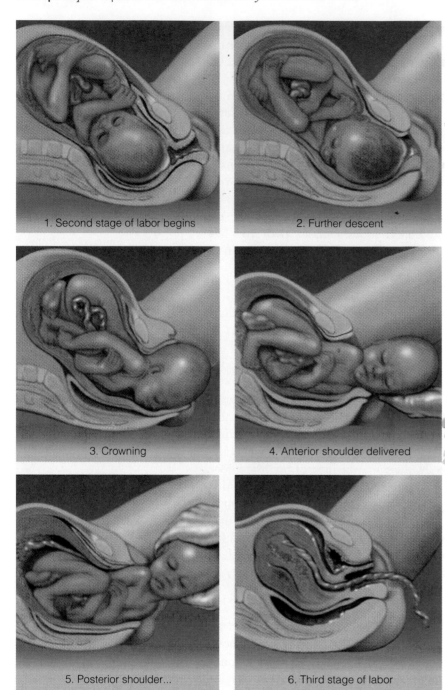

1. Second stage of labor begins

2. Further descent

3. Crowning

4. Anterior shoulder delivered

5. Posterior shoulder...

6. Third stage of labor

Figure 4.1

The Stages of Childbirth

In the first stage, uterine contractions efface and dilate the cervix to about 4 inches so that the baby may pass. The second stage begins with movement of the baby into the birth canal and ends with the birth of the baby. During the third stage, the placenta separates from the uterine wall and is expelled through the birth canal.

When the cervix is nearly fully dilated, the head of the fetus begins to move into the vagina, or birth canal. This process is called **transition.** During transition, which lasts about thirty minutes or less, contractions usually are frequent and strong.

The Second Stage

The second stage of childbirth follows transition. *Question: What occurs during the second stage of childbirth?* This stage begins when the baby appears at the opening of the vagina (referred to as the "birth canal" in this stage; see Figure 4.1). The second stage is briefer than the first stage. It may last minutes or a few hours and culminates in the birth of the baby. The woman may be taken to a delivery room for the second stage of childbirth.

The contractions of the second stage further stretch the skin surrounding the birth canal and propel the baby farther along. The baby's head is said to have crowned when it begins to emerge from the birth canal. Once crowning has occurred, the baby normally emerges completely within minutes.

The physician, nurse, or midwife may perform an episiotomy once crowning takes place. The purpose of the episiotomy is to prevent random tearing when the area between the birth canal and the anus becomes severely stretched. Women are unlikely to feel the incision because the pressure of the crowning head tends to numb the region between the vagina and the anus. The episiotomy, like prepping and the enema, is controversial and is not practised in Europe. The incision may cause itching and discomfort as it heals. In the U.S., the use of episiotomy dropped from about 70 percent in 1983 to 19 percent in 2000 (Goldberg, Holtz, Hyslop, & Tolosa, 2002). Many health professionals believe that episiotomy is warranted when the baby's shoulders are quite wide or if the baby's heart rate declines for a long period of time (Eason & Feldman, 2000). But the strongest predictor of whether a practitioner will choose to use episiotomy is not the condition of the mother or the baby but rather whether the physician normally performs an episiotomy (Robinson, Norwitz, Cohen, & Lieberman, 2000).

transition The initial movement of the head of the fetus into the birth canal.

Whether or not the physician performs an episiotomy, the passageway into the world outside is a tight fit, and the baby squeezes through. Mothers may be alarmed at the visual results of the tight fit. Sometimes the baby's head and facial features are quite bent out of shape. The baby's head can wind up elongated; its nose can be flattened or pushed to the side; and the ears can be contorted—as though this little thing had gotten caught up in a vicious prizefight. Parents understandably wonder whether their baby's features will "pop up" properly, returning to a more normal shape. Usually they need not worry.

Don't wait for the baby to be held upside down and spanked to spur breathing. That happens in old movies but not in today's hospitals and birthing centres. Today, as soon as the head emerges from the birth canal, mucus is suctioned from the baby's mouth to clear any obstructions to the passageway for breathing. The procedure may be repeated once the baby has fully emerged. ***Truth or Fiction Revisited:*** Therefore, it is not true that newborn babies are held upside down and slapped on the buttocks to stimulate independent breathing.

click on
"Birth" in Module 1,
Section 1, on your
Observing Children and
Adolescents CD-ROM. You
can also visit the Student
Book Companion Site to
watch the video, answer the
questions, and e-mail your
responses to your professor.

Lessons in Observation
Birth

Learning Objectives
• What are the different birthing options available to expectant mothers?
• What are the different stages of birth?
• What does a newborn baby look like?
• What does a newborn baby act like?
• What does the Apgar scale test for in newborn babies?
• Why do health care providers use the Apgar scale?

Applied Lesson
Describe the stages of birth. What stage is highlighted in the video?

Critical Thinking
If a baby scores low on the Apgar scale, what treatment options do parents and health-care providers have? Does the Apgar score predict the future health of a baby?

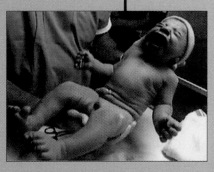

Lee delivers a healthy baby boy named Carter after labouring for more than 9 hours. The appearance of a newborn does not fit most people's definition of a "cute baby."

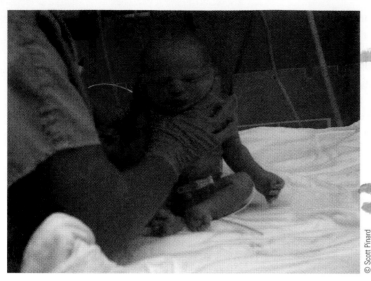

Figure 4.2

A Clamped and Severed Umbilical Cord

The stump of the cord dries and falls off in about 10 days.

When the baby is breathing adequately on its own, the umbilical cord is clamped and severed about three inches from the baby's body (Figure 4.2). At about 266 days after conception, mother and infant have finally become separate beings. The stump of the umbilical cord will dry and fall off on its own in about seven to ten days. There are exceptions. Rathus's daughter Allyn, nearly two at the time, yanked off the umbilical cord of her newborn sister, Jordan, causing a crisis but no particular harm to the baby.

Truth or Fiction Revisited: It is not true that the way the umbilical cord is cut determines whether the baby's belly button will be an "innie" or an "outie." Your belly-button status—that is, whether you have a concave navel or a protruding navel—is unrelated to the methods of your obstetrician.

You might think that it would be nice for mother and baby to hang out for a while at this juncture, but the baby is frequently whisked away by a nurse, who will perform various procedures— for example, footprinting the baby, supplying an ID bracelet, putting antibiotic ointment (erythromycin) or drops of silver nitrate into the baby's eyes to prevent bacterial infections, and giving the baby a vitamin K injection to help its blood clot properly if it bleeds (newborn babies do not manufacture vitamin K). While this goes on, the mother is in the third stage of labour.

The Third Stage

The third stage of labour is also referred to as the placental stage. It lasts from minutes to an hour or more. *Question: What happens during the third stage of childbirth?* During this stage, the placenta separates from the wall of the uterus and is expelled through the birth canal along with fetal membranes. Bleeding is normal at this time. The uterus begins to shrink, although it will take some time for it to approximate its prepregnancy size. The obstetrician now sews the episiotomy—if one has been performed.

Active Review

1. The first uterine contractions are "false" and are called _____ contractions.

2. A day or so before delivery, about one woman in ten has a rush of _____ fluid from the vagina.

3. In the first stage of childbirth, uterine contractions cause the cervix to become effaced and _____.

4. _____ occurs when the cervix is nearly fully dilated and the head of the fetus begins to move into the birth canal.

5. When the baby is breathing adequately, the _____ cord is clamped and severed.

6. During the third stage, the _____ separates from the uterine wall and is expelled.

Reflect & Relate: How do you feel about the routine performance of "prepping" and episiotomy? Why are these controversial and personal issues?

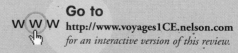

Go to
WWW http://www.voyages1CE.nelson.com
for an interactive version of this review.

Methods of Childbirth

Think of old movies in which a woman is giving birth in her home on the prairie, and a neighbour emerges heralding the good news to the anxious father and members of the community. Perhaps prairies have not hosted the majority of childbirths over the millennia, but there was a time when childbirth was a more intimate procedure, one that usually took place in the woman's home and involved her, perhaps a **midwife,** and family. This pattern is followed in many less developed nations today, but only rarely in Canada and other developed nations. Contemporary Canadian childbirths usually take place in hospitals, where they are overseen by physicians who use sophisticated instruments and **anesthetics** to protect mother and child from complications and discomfort. There is no question that modern medicine has saved lives—millions of them. However, childbearing has also become more impersonal. Some argue that modern methods wrest from women control over their own bodies. They even argue that anesthetics have denied many women the experience of giving birth—an experience that many women admit they appreciate having "muted."

In the next section, we consider a number of contemporary methods for facilitating childbirth.

midwife An individual who helps women in childbirth (from Old English roots meaning "with woman").

anesthetic An agent that produces partial or total loss of the sense of pain (from Greek roots meaning "without feeling").

Anesthesia

Painful childbirth has historically been seen as the standard for women. But during the past two centuries, the development of modern medicine and effective anesthetics has led many people to believe that women need not experience discomfort during childbirth. Today, at least some anesthesia is used in most Canadian deliveries. *Questions: How is anesthesia used in childbirth? What are its effects on the baby?*

General anesthesia achieves its anesthetic effect by putting the woman to sleep by means of a barbiturate that is injected into a vein in the hand or arm. Other drugs in common use are **tranquillizers,** oral barbiturates, and narcotics. These drugs are not anesthetics per se, but they may be used to reduce anxiety and the perception of pain without inducing sleep.

General anesthesia can have negative effects on the infant, including abnormal patterns of sleep and wakefulness and decreased attention and social responsiveness for at least the first six weeks of life (Sepkoski, Lester, Ostheimer, & Brazelton, 1992; Sepkoski, Lester, & Brazelton, 1994). The higher the dosage, the greater the effect.

A major question is whether these anesthetics have long-term effects on the child. The evidence is mixed (Brazelton, 1990a). Some studies show no long-term effects. Others, however, suggest that children whose mothers received heavy doses of anesthetics during delivery lag in their motor development and cognitive functioning at least through seven years of age (Brackbill, McManus, & Woodward, 1985).

Regional or **local anesthetics** deaden pain without putting the mother to sleep. In the pudendal block, the mother's external genitals are numbed by local injection. In the epidural block and the spinal block, anesthetic is injected into the spinal canal or spinal cord, temporarily numbing the body below the waist. Local anesthesia has minor depressive effects on the strength and activity levels of neonates shortly after birth (Eltzschig, Lieberman, & Camann, 2003; Sepkoski et al., 1992, 1994).

In contrast to the use of anesthesia, there is a trend toward **natural childbirth.** In natural childbirth, a woman uses no anesthetics. Instead, she is educated about the biological aspects of reproduction and delivery, encouraged to maintain physical fitness, and taught relaxation and breathing exercises.

general anesthesia The process of eliminating pain by putting the person to sleep.

tranquillizer A drug that reduces feelings of anxiety and tension.

local anesthetic An agent that reduces feeling in a specific area of the body.

natural childbirth A method of childbirth in which women use no anesthesia and are educated about childbirth and strategies for coping with discomfort.

© Peter Cade / The Image Bank / Getty Images

An Exercise Class for Pregnant Women
Years ago, the rule of thumb was that pregnant women were not to exert themselves. Today, it is recognized that exercise is healthful for pregnant women, because it promotes cardiovascular fitness and increases muscle strength. Fitness and strength are assets during childbirth—and at other times. (Refer to Chapter 3 for a review of fitness during pregnancy.)

Prepared Childbirth

Question: What is prepared childbirth? Most women who are pregnant for the first time expect pain and discomfort during childbirth. Certainly the popular media image of childbirth is one in which the woman sweats profusely and screams and thrashes in pain. When the French obstetrician Fernand Lamaze visited Russia, he discovered that many Russian women bore babies without anesthetics or pain. He studied their relaxation techniques and brought them to Western Europe and North America, where they became known as the **Lamaze method,** or *prepared childbirth.* Lamaze (1981) contended that women could engage in breathing and relaxation exercises that would lessen fear and pain by giving them something to do and distracting them from discomfort.

In the Lamaze method, women do not go it alone. The mother-to-be attends Lamaze classes with a "coach"—most often, her partner—who will aid her in the delivery room by doing things such as massaging her, timing the contractions, offering social support, and coaching her in patterns of breathing and relaxation. The woman is taught to breathe in a specific way during contractions. She is taught how to contract specific muscles in her body while remaining generally relaxed. The idea is that she will be able to transfer this training to the process of childbirth by remaining generally at ease while her uterine muscles contract. The procedure tones muscles that will be helpful in childbirth (such as leg muscles) and enables her to minimize tension, conserve energy, and experience less anxiety.

The woman is also educated about the process of childbirth. Her partner or another coach is integrated into the process. The woman receives more social support as a result. *Truth or Fiction Revisited:* It is not true that women who give birth according to the Lamaze method do not experience pain. But they apparently report less pain and ask for less medication when others, such as their partner, are present (Meldrum, 2003).

Social support during labour can be provided by individuals other than a woman's partner. A mother, sibling, or friend can also serve as a coach. Studies in three countries demonstrate the benefit of continuous emotional support during labour by an

Lamaze method   A childbirth method in which women are educated about childbirth, learn to relax and breathe in patterns that conserve energy and lessen pain, and have a coach (usually the mother's partner) present during childbirth. Also termed prepared childbirth.

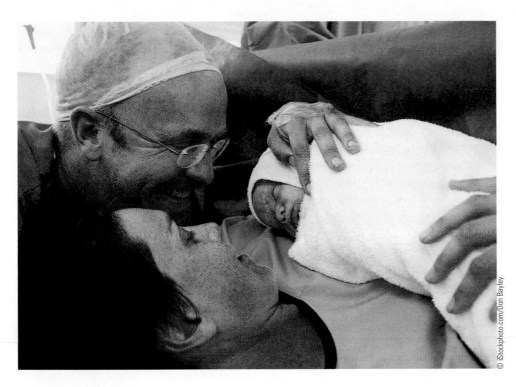

Partner in the Delivery Room
Today, the woman's partner is usually integrated into the process of childbirth. They both take pride in "their" accomplishment of childbirth.

experienced but nonprofessional female companion known as a *doula* (Kennell & McGrath, 1993; Stein, Kennell, & Fulcher, 2003). Women in Canada and elsewhere who have doulas have fewer caesarean deliveries (also called *C-sections*), require less anesthesia, and have shorter and less painful labours than women without doulas (Stein et al., 2003).

Caesarean Section

There are many controversies about the **caesarean section.** The first that comes to mind is the proper spelling. Years ago the term was spelled *Caesarean section* (note the capitalization), after the Roman emperor Julius Caesar, who was thought to have been delivered in this manner. Now, however, the more common spelling in the United States is *cesarean* (lowercased), while in Canada, we usually spell it *caesarean*. In any event, the term is usually abbreviated *C-section.*

Questions: What is the C-section? Why is it so common? In a C-section, the physician delivers the baby by abdominal surgery. He or she cuts through the abdomen and the uterus and physically removes the baby. The incisions are then sewn up. Most health professionals encourage the mother to get up and walk around on the same day as the surgery, but make no mistake about it: Doing so is usually painful. When the C-section first came into common practice, it left visible scars on the abdomen. Today, physicians usually ensure that the C-section incision is more or less hidden by the upper edge of the woman's pubic hair. This method is referred to as a "bikini cut," referring to the shape of the brief swimsuit.

Truth or Fiction Revisited: It is true that C-sections account for one in five births in Canada today (Canadian Institute for Health Information, 2007). To gain some perspective, note that C-sections accounted for 15 percent of births in 1979–1980. Why the upsurge? Some of the increase is due to advances in medicine. For example, fetal monitors now allow physicians to more readily detect fetal distress. But other factors are less "medical." Physicians also perform C-sections because they are concerned

caesarean section A method of childbirth in which the neonate is delivered through a surgical incision in the abdomen. (Also spelled cesarean.)

about the possibility of malpractice suits if something goes wrong during a vaginal delivery, and also, frankly, because they are trained to perform them whenever they suspect there *might* be a reason for them (Maternity Center Association, 2004).

Physicians prefer C-sections to vaginal delivery when they believe that normal delivery may threaten the mother or child or may simply be more difficult than desired. Typical indications that a C-section is warranted include a small pelvis in the mother, maternal weakness or fatigue (e.g., if labour has been prolonged), or a baby that is too large or in apparent distress. C-sections are also performed when the physician wants to prevent the circulatory systems of the mother and baby from mixing, as might occur when there is bleeding during vaginal delivery. C-sections in such cases help prevent transmission of genital herpes or HIV, the virus that causes AIDS (see the "A Closer Look" feature on page 94). The combination of anti-HIV drugs and C-section cuts the chance that an HIV-infected mother will transmit the virus to her baby to less than one in fifty (Coovadia, 2004). The physician may also perform a C-section when it appears that the baby is facing the wrong direction. It is normal, and safest, for babies to be born headfirst. A C-section is warranted if the baby is going to be born sideways or "backward"—that is, feet first. Some women also ask for C-sections (Cohen & Feig, 2003). This in particular has become a controversial topic, especially with certain papers using headlines like "Too Posh to Push" in reference to elective C-sections of celebrity moms such as Britney Spears, Victoria Beckham, and Elizabeth Hurley. The Society of Obstetricians and Gynaecologists of Canada promotes natural childbirth and believes surgery should occur only when there are medical reasons for it. Yet, some women want to avoid the pain of vaginal delivery, or they want to control exactly when the baby will be born (Lo, 2003). Views in support of or against C-sections are varied. An international team of researchers led by the University of Toronto's Mary Hannah (Hannah et al., 2004) found no differences in maternal outcomes after two years between women who had undergone a planned caesarean section and those who had planned on vaginal births but had caesareans due to **breech** (bottom-first) **presentation** at term. In contrast, an analysis of a large number of studies on the issue found that women who have C-sections tend to be less satisfied with the birth than women who deliver vaginally, but it is difficult to assess how much of this is tied to societal expectations and pressures.

A variety of Canadian associations' websites shed light on this debate:

- The Canadian Association of Midwives: http://www.canadianmidwives.org/electiveCS.pdf
- Society of Obstetricians and Gynaecologists of Canada (SOGC): http://www.sogc.org
- Child Birth Connection: http://www.childbirthconnection.org/article.asp?ck=10168
- Canadian Medical Association Journal (CMAJ): http://www.cmaj.ca/cgi/content/full/170/5/813
- Canadian Women's Health Network: http://www.cwhn.ca/indexeng.html

breech presentation   A position in which the fetus enters the birth canal buttocks first.

Labouring through the Birthing Options

We have considered some of the kinds of childbirth available today. Now let us ask: *Question: How can a woman decide where to deliver her baby?* Women have never had so many choices in childbirth. They have the option to labour in a pool of warm water or at home in bed, in a cozy hospital "birthing suite," or in a traditional labour room. They can choose between an obstetrician or midwife—or both. How about some aromatherapy or acupuncture, yoga or Yanni to help ease the pain and discomfort? Whatever your desire, those in the baby-delivery business want to make sure a woman's birth experience is all it can be.

There is an increasing demand in many parts of the country for nurse-midwives—trained professionals, usually women, who stay with a woman throughout her labour, supporting her and working with techniques such as massage to avoid surgery, forceps, and other interventions. There is also growing interest in doulas, laywomen with minimal training who do not perform deliveries but offer support during childbirth (Stein et al., 2003).

More and more women also want a family atmosphere for their deliveries, inviting mothers, sisters, friends, and their other children to witness the event. And unhappy with the days when obstetricians dictated every step of the way, today's mothers-to-be want control, many working through every detail of their "birth plan" with their health-care providers.

State-of-the-Art Birthing

Traditionally, labour and delivery take place in separate rooms or in the same room, after which a woman may be transferred to a recovery room and then to a hospital room for the duration of her stay. The all-in-one labour, delivery, recovery, and postpartum (LDRP) rooms aim to reduce problems for both mother and medical staff. LDRP rooms resemble high-class hotel suites but are equipped with all the medical necessities for an uncomplicated birth, and emergency facilities are generally just down the hall. Many doctors have concerns about delivering babies at freestanding birthing centres, however. Because there are no surgical facilities, if complications arise, a woman would need to be transferred elsewhere.

The Home Birth Debate

The overwhelming majority of Canadian women give birth in hospitals. In Canada, there are about 4.4 maternal deaths for every 100,000 live births (Chalmers & Wen, 2003). In developing countries, where medical resources are scarce, as many as one woman in six will die in childbirth (Save the Children, 2004b). Although these impressive numbers may be explained partly as a result of women giving birth in hospitals, home delivery can be a fairly safe option for healthy women with little risk of complications, especially if they have given birth before. A certified nurse-midwife will typically assess a woman's risk for complications and her proximity to emergency medical care before agreeing to assist with a home birth.

With all these options available, obstetricians encourage women to be informed of the risks and benefits of each before making a decision.

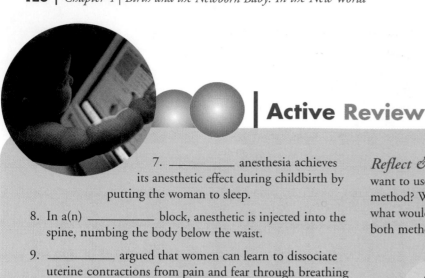

Active Review

7. _____ anesthesia achieves its anesthetic effect during childbirth by putting the woman to sleep.

8. In a(n) _____ block, anesthetic is injected into the spine, numbing the body below the waist.

9. _____ argued that women can learn to dissociate uterine contractions from pain and fear through breathing exercises and muscle-relaxation techniques.

10. A(n) _____ is performed for various reasons, including when a baby is too large to pass through the woman's pelvis, when the mother or baby is in distress, and when striving to prevent transmission of genital herpes or HIV.

Reflect & Relate: If you were delivering a child, would you want to use anesthetic medication? Would you use the Lamaze method? Why or why not? If you were a prospective partner, what would your thoughts be? What are the pros and cons of both methods?

Go to
W W W http://www.voyages1CE.nelson.com
for an interactive version of this review.

Birth Problems

Although most deliveries are unremarkable from a medical standpoint, perhaps every delivery is most remarkable from the parents' point of view. Still, a number of problems can and do occur. In this section, we discuss the effects of oxygen deprivation and the problems of preterm and low-birth-weight neonates.

Oxygen Deprivation

anoxia A condition characterized by lack of oxygen.

hypoxia A condition characterized by less oxygen than is required.

schizophrenia A severe psychological disorder that is characterized by disturbances in thought and language, perception and attention, motor activity, and mood and by withdrawal and absorption in daydreams or fantasy.

Question: What are the effects of oxygen deprivation at birth? Researchers use two terms to discuss oxygen deprivation: *anoxia* and *hypoxia*. **Anoxia** derives from roots meaning "without oxygen." **Hypoxia** derives from roots meaning "under" and "oxygen"—the point again being that the baby does not receive enough oxygen throughout pregnancy to develop properly. Prenatal oxygen deprivation can impair the development of the central nervous system, leading to a host of problems, including cognitive and motor problems and even psychological disorders (Hopkins-Golightly, Raz, & Sander, 2003). Much research has focused on the effects of oxygen deprivation on the hippocampus, a brain structure that is vital in memory formation. Children who were deprived of oxygen at birth often show the predicted problems in learning and memory, but their cognitive problems tend to be much broader, including problems in spatial relations (Hopkins-Golightly et al., 2003) and motor development (Raz et al., 1998).

Prolonged cut-off of the baby's oxygen supply during delivery can also cause psychological and physical health problems, such as early-onset **schizophrenia** and cerebral palsy (Cannon et al., 2002; van Erp et al., 2002). Most researchers now consider schizophrenia a disease of the brain, and oxygen deprivation is believed to impair the development of neural connections in the brain. And, of course, severe, prolonged oxygen deprivation is lethal.

Oxygen deprivation can be caused by maternal disorders, such as diabetes, by immaturity of the baby's respiratory system, and by accidents, some of which involve pressure against the umbilical cord during birth. The fetus and emerging baby receive oxygen through the umbilical cord. Passage through the birth canal is tight, and the umbilical cord is usually squeezed during the process. If the squeezing is temporary, the effect is like holding one's breath for a moment, and no problems are likely to ensue. (In fact, slight oxygen deprivation at birth is not unusual because the transition from the baby receiving oxygen through the umbilical cord to breathing on its own may not take place immediately after birth.) But if constriction of the umbilical cord is prolonged, developmental problems can result. Prolonged constriction is more likely during a breech presentation, when the baby's body may press the umbilical cord against the birth canal.

Fetal monitoring can help detect anoxia before it causes damage. A C-section can be performed if the fetus seems to be in distress.

Preterm and Low-Birth-Weight Infants

Because the fetus makes dramatic gains in weight during the final weeks of pregnancy, prematurity and low birth weight usually go hand in hand. *Question: What is meant by the terms* prematurity *and* low birth weight? A baby is considered premature or **preterm** when birth occurs at or before thirty-seven weeks of gestation, compared with the normal forty weeks. A baby is considered to have a low birth weight when it weighs less than five and a half pounds (about 2500 grams). When a baby is low in birth weight even though it is born at full term, it is referred to as being **small for dates.** Mothers who smoke, use other drugs, or fail to receive proper nutrition place their babies at risk of being small for dates (Ahluwalia, Merritt, Beck, & Rogers, 2001). Small-for-dates babies tend to remain shorter and lighter than their age mates (Barros, Huttly, Victora, Kirkwood, & Vaughan, 1992; Niedbala & Tsang, 1993). Preterm babies who survive are more likely than small-for-dates babies to achieve normal heights and weights.

About 7 percent of children are born preterm or low in birth weight, although the incidence varies in different racial and ethnic groups (Singh & Yu, 1995). However, among multiple births, even twins, the risk of having a preterm child rises to at least 50 percent (Kogan et al., 2000).

Risks Associated with Prematurity and Low Birth Weight

Question: What risks are connected with being born prematurely or low in birth weight? Neonates weighing between 3 1/4 and 5 1/2 pounds are seven times more likely to die than infants of normal birth weight, whereas those weighing less than 3.3 pounds are nearly 100 times as likely to die (Nadeau et al., 2003). But physical survival is only one issue connected with prematurity and low birth weight.

By and large, the lower a child's birth weight, the more poorly he or she fares on measures of neurological development and cognitive functioning throughout the school years (Anderson et al., 2003; Nadeau et al., 2003; Wood et al., 2000). Children whose birth weight was less than 750 grams fare less well between ages eleven and thirteen than children whose birth weight was 750–1499 grams (Taylor, Klein, Minich, & Hack, 2000, 2004). Both low-birth-weight groups perform more poorly than children whose birth weight was normal. There seem also to be sex differences. The cognitive functioning and school achievement of girls with low birth weight seem to improve more rapidly than those of boys with low birth weight (Hindmarsh, O'Callaghan, Mohay, & Rogers, 2000).

preterm Born at or before completion of 37 weeks of gestation.

small for dates Descriptive of neonates who are unusually small for their age.

There are also risks for motor development (Anderson et al., 2003; Foulder-Hughes & Cooke, 2003). One study compared ninety-six very low birth weight (VLBW) children with normal-term children at six, nine, twelve, and eighteen months, correcting for age according to the expected date of delivery (Jeng, Yau, Liao, Chen, & Chen, 2000). The median age at which the full-term infants began to walk was twelve months, compared with fourteen months for the VLBW infants. By eighteen months of age, all full-term infants were walking, whereas 11 percent of the VLBW infants had not yet begun to walk.

The outcomes for low-birth-weight children are variable. One research group followed a group of 1338 Dutch individuals who were born in 1983 with either a gestational age of less than thirty-two weeks or a birth weight of less than 3.3 pounds (Walther, den Ouden, & Verloove-Vanhorick, 2000). The children were assessed at the age of two years by their pediatricians and at the ages of five and nine through fourteen years by teams of investigators, including teachers and parents. All in all, only 10 percent of the group could be characterized as having a severe disability at ages nine through fourteen. However, many more children appeared to have mild to moderate problems in learning or behaviour.

Another study compared thirty-nine individuals born before thirty-five weeks of completed gestation with twenty-three full-term individuals at the ages of four, nine, and nineteen years (Tideman, 2000). Psychological tests found the cognitive development of the preterm individuals to be inferior but within normal limits compared to that of the full-term individuals at the age of four years. The difference was no longer evident by the ages of nine and nineteen. Why do the findings of this study differ from those of the Dutch study? One reason may be that the premature individuals in this study were less premature, by about three weeks.

Preschool experience appears to foster the cognitive and social development of VLBW children. Hoy and McClure (2000) compared a group of VLBW children who attended preschool with a group who did not and also with a group of normal-birth-weight children of the same age. The VLBW children who attended preschool outperformed the VLBW children who did not on measures of cognitive functioning and teacher ratings. They earned higher grades, worked harder, were more likely to participate in social interactions, and were more likely to be rated as "learns a lot." However, their performance on all measures was still exceeded somewhat by the normal-birth-weight children.

lanugo (luh-NOO-go) Fine, downy hair that covers much of the body of the neonate, especially preterm babies.

vernix An oily white substance that coats the skin of the neonate, especially preterm babies.

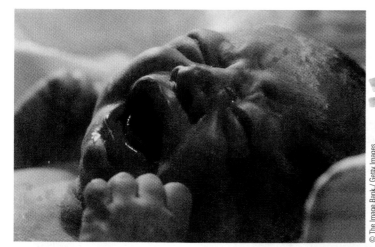

A Newborn Baby
This newborn shows lanugo and vernix, both characteristics of prematurity.

Signs of Prematurity

Preterm babies show characteristic signs of immaturity. They are relatively thin, because they have not yet formed the layer of fat that gives so many full-term children their round, robust appearance. They often have fine, downy hair, referred to as **lanugo,** and an oily white substance on the skin known as **vernix.** Lanugo and vernix disappear within a few days or weeks. If the babies are born six weeks or more before full term, their nipples will not yet have emerged. The testicles of boys born this early will not yet have descended into the scrotum. However, the nipples develop further and the testes descend after birth.

The muscles of preterm babies are immature. As a result, the babies' vital sucking and breathing reflexes are weak. The muscles of preterm babies may not be mature enough to sustain independent breathing. Also, the walls of the tiny air sacs in their lungs may tend to stick together because they do not yet secrete substances that lubricate the walls of the sacs. As a result, babies born more than a month before full term may breathe irregularly or suddenly stop breathing, evidence of a cluster of problems known as **respiratory distress syndrome.** About one baby in seven born one month early shows the syndrome. It is found more frequently among infants born still earlier (Behrman et al., 2000). Respiratory distress syndrome causes a large percentage of neonatal deaths. Preterm infants with severe respiratory stress syndrome show poorer development in cognitive, language, and motor skills and more persistent neurological abnormalities over the first two years of development than infants with less severe respiratory distress and full-term infants (Smith et al., 1999).

Major strides have been made in helping low-birth-weight children survive. Still, those who do survive often have problems, including below-average verbal ability and academic achievement and various physical, motor, perceptual, neurological, and behavioural impairments (Hoy & McClure, 2000; Luciana, 2003).

Preterm infants with very low birth weights (under 3.3 pounds) are likely to show the greatest cognitive deficits and developmental delays. Still, medical advances in recent years have reduced the severity and incidence of handicaps among babies with very low birth weights. A review of 111 studies that followed the development of VLBW babies into the preschool years and beyond reported that 75 percent had no disabilities (Escobar, Littenberg, & Petitti, 1991).

respiratory distress syndrome
A cluster of breathing problems, including weak and irregular breathing, to which preterm babies are particularly prone.

Treatment of Preterm Babies

Question: How are preterm infants treated following birth? Because of their physical frailty, preterm infants usually remain in the hospital and are placed in **incubators,** which maintain a temperature-controlled environment and afford some protection from disease. They may be given oxygen, although excessive oxygen can cause permanent eye injury.

incubator A heated, protective container in which premature infants are kept.

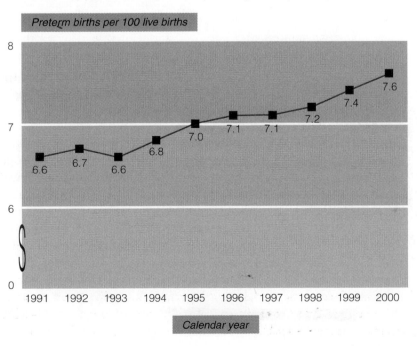

Figure 4.3
Longitudinal Preterm Birth Rates in Canada

Source: Statistics Canada. Cadadian Vital Statistics System. 1991–2000 (unlinked live birth files)
*Data for Ontario were excluded because of data quality concerns; they are presented in Appendix G Excludes live births with unknown gestational age

Parents and Preterm Neonates

One might assume that parents would be more concerned about preterm babies than babies who have gone to full term and thus would treat them better. Ironically, this is not the case. Parents often do not treat preterm neonates as well as they treat full-term neonates. For one thing, preterm neonates are less attractive than full-term babies. Preterm infants usually do not have the robust, appealing appearance of many full-term babies. Their cries are more high-pitched and grating, and they are more irritable

Developing in a World of Diversity

Maternal and Infant Mortality around the World

Modern medicine has made vast strides, but the advances are not equally spread throughout the world. Save the World, a nonprofit relief and development organization that is helping children in more than forty countries, has been tracking the likelihood that a woman will die in childbirth and that an infant will die during the first year.

As shown in Table 4.1, the likelihood of maternal mortality and infant mortality is connected with factors such as the percentage of births that are attended by trained people, the literacy rate of adult women (which is one measure of the level of education of women), and the participation of women in national government (which is one measure of the extent to which a society empowers women). The safest place for a woman to deliver and for her baby to survive appears to be Sweden, where the chances of the woman dying are about one in 30 000 and where only three infants in 1000 die during the first year. Perhaps it is no coincidence that Sweden also has nearly a 100 percent adult female literacy rate, attends all recorded births with trained per-

sonnel, and has the highest participation rate (45 percent) by women in national government. Afghanistan may have the world's most frightening statistics. One woman in six will die as the result of a pregnancy, and 165 children of 1000 will die during their first year. In Afghan society, the literacy rate for women is only 21 percent. There is little if any professional coverage of childbirth (12 percent). And in this male-dominated society, women have virtually no role in government. There is also little if any prenatal care in Afghanistan and other nations with high infant mortality rates. How do Canadians fare?

Mothers of preterm babies frequently report that they feel alienated from their babies and harbour feelings of failure, guilt, and low self-esteem. They respond less sensitively to their infants' behaviour than do mothers of full-term babies (Bugental & Happaney, 2004). Mothers of preterm infants also touch and talk to their infants less and hold them at a greater distance during feeding.

Once they come home from the hospital, preterm infants remain more

passive and less sociable than full-term infants (Garcia-Coll, Halpern, Vohr, Seifer, & Oh, 1992; Garner & Landry, 1992), so they demand less interaction with parents. However, when their parents do interact with them during the first year, they are more likely to poke at preterm babies, caress them, and talk to them, apparently in an effort to prod them out of their passivity. Mothers of preterm babies report feeling overprotective toward them. This may explain why one-year-old preterm infants explore less and stay closer to their mothers than do full-term babies of the same age.

Preterm infants fare better when they have responsive and caring parents. Longitudinal research shows that preterm children who are reared in attentive and responsive environments attain higher intelligence test scores, have higher self-esteem, show more positive social skills, and have fewer behavioural and emotional problems in childhood than do preterm children reared in less responsive homes (Kirsh, Crnic, & Greenberg, 1995).

(Bugental & Happaney, 2004; Eckerman, Hsu, Molitor, Leung, & Goldstein, 1999). The demands of caring for preterm babies can be depressing to mothers (Davis, Edwards, Mohay, & Wollin, 2003; Drewett, Blair, Emmett, Emond, & The ALSPAC Study Team, 2004). Fear of hurting preterm babies can further discourage parents from handling them, even when there is evidence that handling and massage facilitate development (Field, 2001).

Table 4.1 *Maternal Mortality and Infant Mortality around the World as Related to Access to Medical Assistance and Empowerment of Women*

Country	Lifetime Risk of Maternal Mortality	Percentage of Births Attended by Trained Personnel	Adult Female Literacy Rate (%)	Participation of Women in National Government (% of Seats Held by Women)	Infant Mortality Rate (per 1,000 Live Births)
Sweden	1 in 29 800	100	99	45	3
Austria	1 in 16 000	100	99	34	6
Denmark	1 in 9800	100	99	38	4
Canada	1 in 8700	98	99	21	5
United Kingdom	1 in 3800	99	99	18	5
South Korea	1 in 2800	100	96	6	5
United States	1 in 2500	99	99	18	5
Israel	1 in 1800	99	93	15	6
Russia	1 in 1000	99	99	8	18
China	1 in 830	76	78	22	31
North Korea	1 in 590	97	96	20	42
Turkey	1 in 480	81	77	4	36
Iran	1 in 370	90	69	4	35
Mexico	1 in 370	86	89	23	24
Egypt	1 in 310	61	44	2	35
Brazil	1 in 140	88	87	9	30
Iraq	1 in 65	72	23	8	102
India	1 in 48	43	45	9	67
Pakistan	1 in 31	20	28	22	83
Zambia	1 in 19	43	72	12	108
Afghanistan	1 in 6	12	21	—	165

Figure 4.4

Stimulating a Preterm Infant

It was once believed that preterm infants should be left as undisturbed as possible. Today, however, it is recognized that preterm infants usually profit from various kinds of stimulation.

Intervention Programs

A generation ago, preterm babies were left as undisturbed as possible. For one thing, concern was aroused by the prospect of handling such a tiny, frail creature. For another, preterm babies would not normally experience interpersonal contact or other sources of external stimulation until full term. However, experiments carried out over the past two decades have suggested that preterm infants profit from early stimulation just as full-term babies do. Preterm babies benefit from being cuddled, rocked, talked and sung to, exposed to recordings of their mothers' voices, and having mobiles placed within view. One study combined mechanical rocking with a recorded heartbeat for several fifteen-minute periods on a daily basis (Barnard & Bee, 1983). Immediately following the treatment, the infants showed increased activity levels. At a two-year follow-up, their intellectual functioning was significantly ahead of preterm babies who were not given this treatment. Other recent innovations in stimulating premature babies include massage (Field, 1992) and "kangaroo care," in which the baby spends several hours a day lying skin to skin, chest to chest, with one of its parents (Dombrowski et al., 2000). By and large, preterm infants exposed to stimulation tend to gain weight more rapidly, show fewer respiratory problems, and make greater advances in motor, intellectual, and neurological development than control infants (Caulfield, 2000; Dombrowski et al., 2000) (see Figure 4.3).

Other intervention programs help parents adjust to the birth and care of low-birth-weight infants. One such program involved ninety-two preterm infants at three sites (Als et al., 2003). The following factors contributed to superior cognitive and motor development in the infants and better adjustment in the parents: early discontinuation of intravenous feeding, hospitalization with intensive care for digestive and other problems, and individualized counselling to foster appreciation of the infant.

As we see in the "Developing in a World of Diversity" feature on page 132, maternal and infant mortality are serious problems around the world.

Active Review

11. Prenatal _____ deprivation can impair the development of the central nervous system, leading to cognitive and motor problems, even psychological disorders.

12. A baby is considered to be _____ when birth occurs at or before 37 weeks of gestation.

13. A baby has a low _____ when it weighs less than 5 1/2 pounds (about 2500 grams).

14. Research suggests that it is (helpful or harmful?) to stimulate preterm infants.

Reflect & Relate: If you had a preterm infant, do you think you would want to handle him or her as much as possible, or would you tend to leave him or her alone? Explain.

Go to
W W W http://www.voyages1CE.nelson.com
for an interactive version of this review.

The Postpartum Period

Postpartum derives from roots meaning "after" and "birth." The **postpartum period** refers to the weeks following delivery, but there is no specific limit. "Parting is such sweet sorrow," Shakespeare has Juliet tell Romeo. The "parting" from the baby is also frequently a happy experience. The family's long wait is over. Concerns about pregnancy and labour are over, fingers and toes have been counted, and despite some local discomfort, the mother finds her "load" to be lightened—most literally. However, according to the Canadian Mental Health Association (2006), between 50 and 80 percent of new mothers have periods of tearfulness, sadness, and irritability that the association refers to as the "baby blues." In this section, we discuss two issues of the postpartum period: maternal depression and bonding.

postpartum period The period that immediately follows childbirth.

Maternal Depression

Question: What kinds of problems in mood do women experience during the postpartum period? These problems include the baby blues and more serious mood disorders ("postpartum-onset mood episodes"), which occasionally include "psychotic features" (American Psychiatric Association, 2000; Canadian Mental Health Association, 2006). These problems are not limited to Canada or even to developed nations. They are far-flung, and researchers find them in China, Turkey, Guyana, Australia, and South Africa—with similar frequency (Affonso, De, Horowitz, & Mayberry, 2000; Cooper et al., 1999; Guelseren, 1999; Lee et al., 2001). In a country like Canada, where a significant portion of the population is composed of women who are recent immigrants or refugees, issues of maternal depression are also related to a lack of culturally relevant support systems (i.e., extended family and community) during and after childbirth (Vissandjée, 2001; Vissandjée, Carignan, & Bourdeau-Marchand, 1999).

Truth or Fiction Revisited: Actually, it is normal to feel depressed following childbirth. The baby blues affect most women in the weeks after delivery (American Psychiatric Association, 2000). Researchers believe that baby blues are so common because of hormonal changes that follow delivery (Kohl, 2004).

The baby blues last about ten days and are generally not severe enough to impair the mother's functioning. Don't misunderstand—the baby blues are seriously discomforting and not to be ignored, as in "Oh, you're just experiencing what most women experience." The point is that most new mothers can function through the baby blues, even though they can be pretty awful at times, partly because women know that they are transient.

A minority of women but perhaps as many as one in every five to ten encounter the more serious mood disorder frequently referred to as **postpartum depression (PPD).** PPD begins about a month after delivery and may linger for weeks, even months. PPD is technically referred to as a major depressive disorder with postpartum onset. As in other major depressive disorders, it is characterized by serious sadness, feelings of hopelessness and helplessness, feelings of worthlessness, difficulty concentrating, and major changes in appetite (usually loss of appetite) and sleep patterns (frequently insomnia). There can also be severe fluctuations in mood, with women sometimes feeling elated. Some women show obsessive concern with the well-being of their babies at this time. PPD can also interfere with the mother-baby relationship in the short term (Stanley, Murray, & Stein, 2004).

Feelings of depression before getting pregnant or during pregnancy are a major risk factor for PPD (Ritter, Hobfoll, Lavin, Cameron, & Hulsizer, 2000). It is possible that PPD, like the baby blues, is worsened by concerns about all the life changes that motherhood creates and about whether one will be a good mother (Grazioli & Terry, 2000; Grön, Wunderlich, Spitzer, Tomczak, & Riepe, 2000). Marital problems and having a

postpartum depression (PPD) More severe, prolonged depression that afflicts 10-20% of women after delivery and that is characterized by sadness, apathy, and feelings of worthlessness.

sick or unwanted baby can also heighten the likelihood and severity of PPD. Many researchers have suggested that PPD is caused by the interactions of such psychological factors as described above and physiological (mainly hormonal) factors, including a precipitous decline in estrogen (Kohl, 2004). There are major changes in body chemistry during and after pregnancy, and, interestingly, women around the world seem to experience similar disturbances in mood, even when their life experiences and support systems are radically different from those we find in North America. However, social and cultural factors also need to be considered, especially in cases of immigrant and refugee women where high rates of postpartum depression have been found (Vissandjée, 2001).

According to studies reviewed by the Canadian Mental Health Association (2006), postpartum mood episodes are accompanied by "psychotic features" in one woman in 1,000. A psychotic feature may mean a break with reality. Mothers with these features may have delusional thoughts about the infant that place the infant at risk of injury or death. Some women experience delusions that the infant is possessed by the devil, and some have "command hallucinations" to kill the infant. That is, they "hear" a command to kill the infant as though it is coming from an outside source—perhaps from an authoritative person or some kind of divine or evil spirit—even though the thought originates from within. Because of the nature of the illness, they may be unable to tell the difference, putting the infant in possible serious jeopardy. Remember, though, that these psychotic features are rather rare and that when they occur, they do not *always* place the baby at risk.

Women who experience PPD usually profit from social support and a general history of high self-esteem (Grön et al., 2000; Ogrodniczuk & Piper, 2003). They may profit from psychotherapy, even if therapy does little more than explain that many women encounter PPD and get through it. Drugs that increase estrogen levels or act as antidepressants may be of help. Most women will get over PPD on their own (without medication or support) but with greater personal cost, which may come in the form of strain on the marriage or on the mother-child relationship. Interestingly, it is reported that 50 percent of women with postpartum depression decline available support (Letourneau et al., n.d.). Letourneau and her colleagues (n.d.) found that of those who do want support, mothers in both rural and urban Canadian settings experience gaps in service availability and that their stated preferences for support differ from the types of services typically offered. Given the multifactorial nature of PPD, Letourneau et al. (2006) recommend that a variety of interventions (e.g., one-on-one support, group support, education awareness) be considered. These findings are in line with offering women of various cultural backgrounds services and supports that are culturally sensitive and appropriate.

Bonding

bonding The process of forming bonds of attachment between parent and child.

Bonding—that is, the formation of bonds of attachment between parents and their children—is essential to the survival and well-being of children. *Question: How critical is parental interaction with neonates in the formation of bonds of attachment?*

Do the first hours after birth provide a special opportunity—or a necessary opportunity—for bonding between parents and neonates? A controversial study on this issue was carried out by Marshall Klaus and John Kennell (1976). They asserted that the first few hours after birth present a "maternal-sensitive" period during which the mother is particularly disposed, largely because of hormone levels, to form a bond with the neonate.

In their study, one group of mothers was randomly assigned to standard hospital procedure in which their babies were whisked away to the nursery shortly after birth. Throughout the remainder of the hospital stay, the babies visited with their mothers only during feeding. The other group of mothers spent five hours a day with their infants during the hospital stay. The hospital staff encouraged and reassured the group of mothers who had extended contact. Follow-ups over two years suggested that extended contact benefited both the mothers and their children (Klaus & Kennell, 1978). Mothers with extended contact were more likely than control mothers to cuddle their babies, soothe them when they cried, and interact with them.

Critics note that the Klaus and Kennell studies are fraught with methodological problems (Goldberg, 1983; Thomson & Kramer, 1984). For example, we cannot separate the benefits of extended contact from those attributable to parents' knowledge that they were in a special group and from the extra attention of the hospital staff. In short, the evidence that the hours after birth are critical is tainted. There are millions of fine parent-child relationships, including adoptive relationships, in which parents did not have early access to their children (Rutter, 1981). ***Truth or Fiction Revisited:*** Despite the Klaus and Kennell studies, which made a splash in the 1970s, it is not true that parents must have extended early contact with their newborn children if adequate bonding is to take place. Most researchers view the hours after birth as just one element in a complex and prolonged bonding process.

Active Review

15. Research suggests that the (majority or minority?) of new mothers experience periods of depression.

16. Postpartum depression has been connected with a precipitous decline in the hormone _____.

17. Research (does or does not?) show that early parental interaction with neonates is critical in the formation of bonds of attachment.

Reflect & Relate: Imagine that you are visiting a friend who has just had a baby. Weepy and listless, she tells you that she's worried that she doesn't have the "right" feelings for a new mother. What do you think you would say to her? Why?

Go to
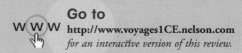 http://www.voyages1CE.nelson.com
for an interactive version of this review.

Characteristics of Neonates

Many neonates come into the world looking a bit fuzzy, but even though they are utterly dependent on others, they are probably more aware of their surroundings than you had imagined. Neonates make rapid adaptations to the world around them. In this section, we see how health professionals assess the health of neonates and describe the characteristics of neonates.

Assessing the Health of Neonates

Question: How do health professionals assess the health of neonates? The neonate's overall level of health is usually evaluated at birth according to the **Apgar scale,** developed by Virginia Apgar in 1953. Apgar scores are based on five signs of health, as shown in Table 4.2. The neonate can receive a score of zero, one, or two on each sign. The total Apgar score, therefore, can vary from zero to ten. A score of seven or above usually indicates that the baby is not in danger. A score below four suggests that the baby is in critical condition and requires medical attention. By one minute after birth, most normal babies attain scores of eight to ten (Bornstein & Lamb, 1992).

The acronym APGAR is commonly used as an aid in remembering the five criteria of the Apgar scale:

A: the general **a**ppearance or colour of the neonate
P: the **p**ulse or heart rate
G: **g**rimace (the one-point indicator of reflex irritability)
A: general **a**ctivity level or muscle tone
R: **r**espiratory effort, or rate of breathing

The **Brazelton Neonatal Behavioral Assessment Scale,** developed by pediatrician T. Berry Brazelton, measures neonates' reflexes and other behaviour patterns (Brazelton, 1990b; Brazelton, Nugent, & Lester, 1987). The test screens neonates for behavioural and neurological problems by assessing four areas of behaviour—motor behaviour, including muscle tone and most **reflexes,** response to stress, adaptive behaviour, and control over physiological state.

Apgar scale   A measure of a newborn's health that assesses appearance, pulse, grimace, activity level, and respiratory effort.

Brazelton Neonatal Behavioral Assessment Scale   A measure of a newborn's motor behaviour, response to stress, adaptive behaviour, and control over physiological state.

reflex   An unlearned, stereotypical response to a stimulus.

Table 4.2	*The Apgar Scale*		
Points	0	1	2
Appearance: Colour*	Blue, pale	Body pink, extremities blue	Entirely pink
Pulse: Heart rate	Absent (not detectable)	Slow—below 100 beats/minute	Rapid—100–140 beats/minute
Grimace: Reflex irritability	No response	Grimace	Crying, coughing, sneezing
Activity level: Muscle tone	Completely flaccid, limp	Weak, inactive	Flexed arms and legs; resists extension
Respiratory effort: Breathing	Absent (infant is apneic)	Shallow, irregular, slow	Regular breathing; lusty crying

*Note: At the time of development, the Apgar scale was being used predominantly with Caucasian infants.

Reflexes

If soon after birth you had been held gently for a few moments with your face down in comfortably warm water, you would not have drowned. Instead of breathing the water in, you would have exhaled slowly through the mouth and engaged in swimming motions. (We urge readers not to test babies for this reflex. The hazards are obvious.) This swimming response is "prewired"—innate or inborn—and it is just one of the many reflexes shown by neonates.

Questions: What are reflexes? What kinds of reflexes are shown by neonates? Reflexes are simple, unlearned, stereotypical responses that are elicited by certain types of stimulation. They do not require higher brain functions; they occur automatically, without thinking. Reflexes are the most complicated motor activities displayed by neonates. Neonates cannot roll over, sit up, reach for an object that they see, or raise their heads.

Let us return to our early venture into the water. If you had been placed into the water not a few moments but several months after birth, the results might have been very different and disastrous. After a few months, the swimming reflex, like many others, ceases to exist. However, at six to twelve months of age, infants can learn how to swim voluntarily. In fact, the transition from reflexive swimming to learned swimming can be reasonably smooth with careful guided practice.

Many reflexes have survival value. Adults and neonates, for example, will reflexively close their eyes when assaulted with a puff of air or sudden bright light. Other reflexes seem to reflect interesting facets of the evolution of the nervous system. The swimming reflex seems to suggest that there was a time when our ancestors profited from being born able to swim.

Pediatricians learn a good deal about the adequacy of neonates' **neural** functioning by testing their reflexes. The absence or weakness of a reflex may indicate immaturity (as in prematurity), slowed responsiveness (which can result from anesthetics used during childbirth), brain injury, or retardation. Let us examine some of the reflexes shown by neonates.

The rooting and sucking reflexes are basic to survival. In the **rooting reflex,** the baby turns the head and mouth toward a stimulus that strokes the cheek, chin, or corner of the mouth (Figure 4.5). The rooting reflex facilitates finding the mother's nipple in preparation for sucking. Babies will suck almost any object that touches the

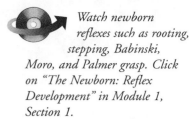

Watch newborn reflexes such as rooting, stepping, Babinski, Moro, and Palmer grasp. Click on "The Newborn: Reflex Development" in Module 1, Section 1.

neural Of the nervous system.

rooting reflex A reflex in which infants turn their mouths and heads in the direction of a stroking of the cheek or the corner of the mouth.

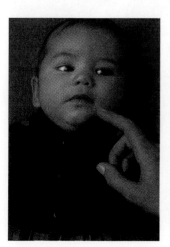

© Dan Bryant

Figure 4.5
The Rooting Reflex

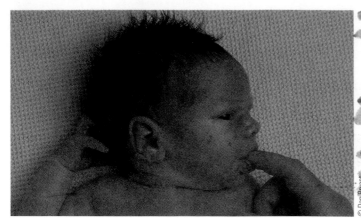

Figure 4.6
Testing the Sucking Reflex

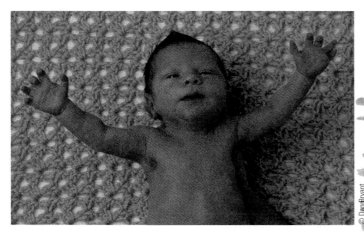

Figure 4.7
The Moro Reflex

lips. The sucking reflex grows stronger during the first days after birth and can be lost if not stimulated (Figure 4.6). As months go on, reflexive sucking becomes replaced by voluntary sucking.

In the startle or **Moro reflex,** the back arches and the legs and arms are flung out and then brought back toward the chest, with the arms in a hugging motion (Figure 4.7). The Moro reflex occurs when a baby's position is suddenly changed or support for the head and neck is suddenly lost. It can also be elicited by loud noises, by bumping the baby's crib, or by jerking the baby's blanket. The Moro reflex is usually lost by six to seven months after birth, although similar movements can be found in adults who suddenly lose support. Absence of the Moro reflex can indicate immaturity or brain damage.

During the first few weeks following birth, babies show an increasing tendency to reflexively grasp fingers or other objects pressed against the palms of their hands (Figure 4.8). In this **grasping reflex,** or palmar reflex, they use four fingers only (the thumbs are not included). The grasping reflex is stronger when babies are simultaneously startled. Most babies can support their own weight in this way. They can be literally lifted into the air as they reflexively cling with two hands. Some babies can actually support their weight with just one hand. (Please do not try this, however!) Absence of the grasping reflex may indicate depressed activity of the nervous system, which can stem from use of anesthetics during childbirth. The grasping reflex is usually lost by three to four months of age, and babies generally show voluntary grasping by five to six months. The Moro and grasping reflexes, like the swimming reflex, may suggest something about our evolutionary history.

Moro reflex A reflex in which infants arch their back, fling out their arms and legs, and draw them back toward the chest in response to a sudden change in position.

grasping reflex A reflex in which infants grasp objects that cause pressure against the palms.

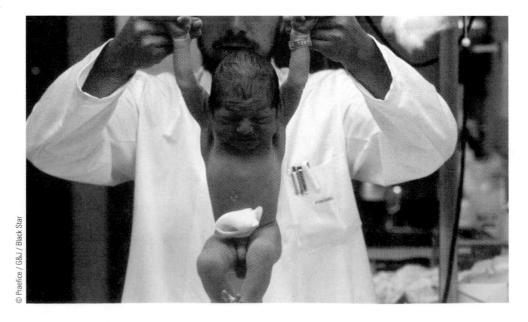

Figure 4.8
The Grasping Reflex

For example, the startle and grasping reflexes could work together to allow baby monkeys to cling to their mothers (Field, 1990).

One or two days after birth, babies show a reflex that mimics walking. When held under the arms and tilted forward so that the feet press against a solid surface, a baby will show a **stepping reflex** in which the feet advance one after the other (Figure 4.9). A full-term baby "walks" heel to toe, whereas a preterm infant is more likely to remain on tiptoe. The stepping reflex usually disappears by about three or four months of age.

In the **Babinski reflex,** the neonate fans or spreads the toes in response to stroking of the foot from heel to toes. The Babinski reflex normally disappears toward the end of the first year, to be replaced by curling downward of the toes. Persistence of the Babinski reflex may suggest defects of the lower spinal cord, lagging development of nerve cells, or other disorders.

The **tonic-neck reflex** is observed when the baby is lying on its back and turns its head to one side (Figure 4.10). The arm and leg on that side extend, while the limbs on the opposite side flex. You can see why this reflex sometimes is known as the "fencing position."

Some reflexes, such as breathing and blinking the eye in response to a puff of air, remain with us for life. Others, such as the sucking and grasping reflexes, are gradually replaced by voluntary sucking and grasping after a number of months. Still others, such as the Moro and Babinski reflexes, disappear, indicating that the nervous system is maturing on schedule.

Sensory Capabilities

In 1890, William James, one of the founders of modern psychology, wrote that the neonate must sense the world "as one great blooming, buzzing confusion." The neonate emerges from being literally suspended in a temperature-controlled environment to being—again, in James's words—"assailed by eyes, ears, nose, skin, and entrails at once." *Question: How well do neonates see, hear, and so on?* In this section, we describe the sensory capabilities of neonates, and we see that James, for all his eloquence, probably exaggerated their disorganization.

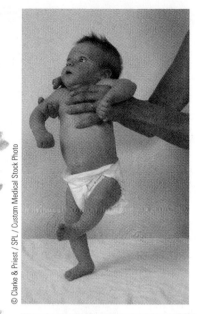

Figure 4.9
The Stepping Reflex

stepping reflex A reflex in which infants take steps when held under the arms and leaned forward so that the feet press against the ground.

Babinski reflex A reflex in which infants fan their toes when the undersides of their feet are stroked.

tonic-neck reflex A reflex in which infants turn their head to one side, extend the arm and leg on that side, and flex the limbs on the opposite side. Also known as the "fencing position."

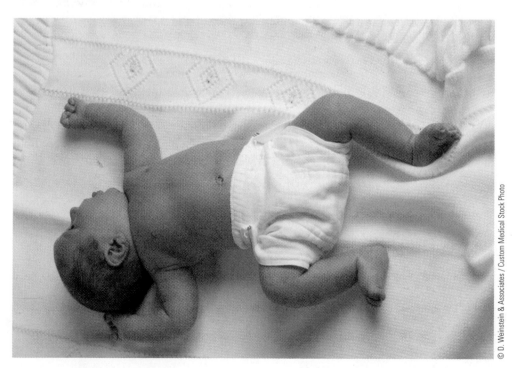

Figure 4.10
The Tonic-Neck Reflex

visual acuity   Keenness or sharpness of vision.

track   Follow.

visual accommodation   The automatic adjustments made by the lenses of the eyes to bring objects into focus.

convergence   The inward movement of the eyes as they focus on an object that is drawing nearer.

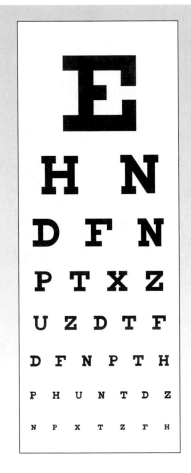

Figure 4.11
The Snellen Chart
The Snellen chart is used in eye examinations to provide an approximate measure of visual acuity.

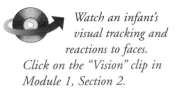

Watch an infant's visual tracking and reactions to faces.
Click on the "Vision" clip in Module 1, Section 2.

Vision

Neonates can see, but they do not possess great sharpness of vision, or **visual acuity.** Visual acuity is expressed in numbers such as 20/20 or 20/200. Think for a moment of the big E on the Snellen chart (Figure 4.11), which you have probably seen during many eye examinations. If you were to stand twenty feet from the Snellen chart and could see only the E, we would say that your vision is 20/200. This would mean that you can see from a distance of twenty feet what a person with normal vision can discriminate from a distance of 200 feet. In such a case, you would be quite nearsighted. You would have to be unusually close to an object to discriminate its details.

Expressed in these terms, investigators have arrived at various approximations of the visual acuity of neonates, with the best estimates in the neighbourhood of 20/600 (Banks & Salapatek, 1983). Neonates can best see objects that are about seven to nine inches away from their eyes. Neonates also see best through the centres of their eyes. They do not have the peripheral vision of older children. To learn how psychologists measure the visual acuity of infants, check the nearby "A Closer Look" feature.

Neonates can visually detect movement, and many neonates can **track** movement the first day after birth. In fact, they appear to prefer (i.e., they spend more time looking at) moving objects to stationary objects (Kellman & von Hofsten, 1992). In one study (Haith, 1966), one- to four-day-old neonates were exposed to moving or nonmoving lights while they sucked on a pacifier. The frequency of their sucking decreased significantly when moving lights were presented, suggesting that they preferred this visual stimulus.

Visual accommodation refers to the self-adjustments made by the lens of the eye to bring objects into focus. If you hold your finger at arm's length and bring it gradually nearer, you will feel tension in your eyes as your lenses automatically foreshorten and thicken in an effort to maintain the image in focus. When you move the finger away, the lens accommodates by lengthening and flattening to keep the finger in focus. Neonates show little or no visual accommodation; they see as if through a fixed-focus camera. Objects placed about seven to nine inches away are in clearest focus for most neonates, although this range can be somewhat expanded when lighting conditions are bright. Interestingly, this is about the distance of the face of an adult who is cradling a neonate in the arms. It has been speculated that this sensory capacity for gazing into others' eyes may promote attachment between neonates and caregivers. Visual accommodation improves dramatically within the first two months (Hainline & Abramov, 1992).

Now bring your finger toward your eyes trying to maintain a single image of the approaching finger. If you do so, it is because your eyes turn inward, or converge on the finger, resulting in a cross-eyed look and feelings of tension in the eye muscles (see Figure 4.13). **Convergence** is made possible by the coordination of the eye muscles. Neonates do not have the muscular control to converge their eyes on an object that is close to them. For this reason, one eye may be staring off to the side while the other fixates on an object straight ahead. Convergence does not occur until seven or eight weeks of age for near objects. Neonates do show some convergence for objects that are at intermediate viewing distances (Aslin, 1987).

How do psychologists determine the visual acuity of neonates? Naturally, they cannot ask babies to report how well they see, but psychologists can determine what babies are looking at and draw conclusions from this information.

One method of observing what a baby is looking at is by using a "looking chamber" of the sort used in research by Robert Fantz and his colleagues (1975) (see Figure 4.12). In this chamber, the baby lies on its back, with two panels above. Each panel contains a visual stimulus. The researcher observes the baby's eye movements and records how much time is spent looking at each panel. A similar strategy can be carried out in the baby's natural environment. Filtered lights and a movie or TV camera can be trained on the baby's eyes. Reflections from objects in the environment can then be recorded to show what the baby is looking at.

Neonates will stare at almost any nearby object for minutes—golf balls, wheels, checkerboards, bull's-eyes, circles, triangles, even lines (Maurer & Maurer, 1976). But babies have their preferences, as measured by the amount of time they spend fixating on (looking at) certain objects. For example, they will spend more time looking at black and white stripes than at grey blobs. This fact suggests one strategy for measuring visual acuity in the neonate. As black and white stripes become narrower, they eventually take on the appearance of that dull grey blob. And, as the stripes are progressively narrowed, we can assume that babies continue

to discriminate them as stripes only so long as they spend more time looking at them than at blobs.

Studies such as these suggest that neonates are very nearsighted. But we should remember that they, unlike adults or older children, are not motivated to "perform" in such experiments. If they were, they might show somewhat greater acuity.

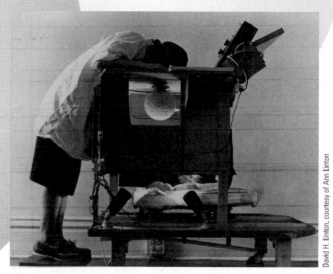

David H. Linton, courtesy of Ann Linton

Figure 4.12
The Looking Chamber

This chamber makes it easier for the researcher to observe the baby's eye movements and to record how much time the baby spends looking at a visual stimulus.

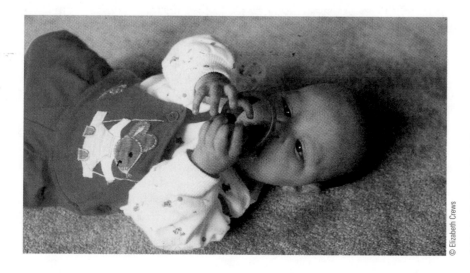

© Elizabeth Crews

Figure 4.13
Convergence of the Eyes

Neonates do not have the muscular control to converge their eyes on an object that is close to them. However, they do show some convergence for objects at intermediate viewing distances.

intensity Brightness.

saturation Richness or purity of a colour.

hue Colour.

rods In the eye, rod-shaped receptors of light that are sensitive to intensity only. Rods permit black-and-white vision.

cones In the eye, cone-shaped receptors of light that transmit sensations of colour.

The degree to which neonates perceive colour remains an open question. The research problem is that colours vary in **intensity** (i.e., brightness), **saturation** (richness), and **hue.** For this reason, when babies appear to show preference for one colour over another, we cannot be certain that they are responding to the hue. They may be responding to the difference in brightness or saturation. So, you say, simply change hues and keep intensity and saturation constant. A marvellous idea—but easier said than done, unfortunately.

Physiological observations also cast doubt on the capacity of neonates to have highly developed colour vision. There are two types of cells in the retina of the eye that are sensitive to light: rods and cones. **Rods** transmit sensations of light and dark. **Cones** transmit sensations of colour. At birth, the cones are less well developed than rods in structure.

Infants younger than one month of age do not show the ability to discriminate stimuli that differ in colour. Two-month-olds do, but they require large colour differences. By three months, infants can see most, if not all, the colours of the visible spectrum (Banks & Shannon, 1993; Brown, 1990; Teller & Lindsey, 1993).

Even at birth, babies do not just passively respond to visual stimuli. For example, babies placed in absolute darkness open their eyes wide and actively search the visual field, moving their eyes two to three times a second (Haith, 1986).

Hearing

Fetuses respond to sound months before they are born. Although myelination of the auditory pathways is not complete before birth, fetuses' middle and inner ears normally reach their mature shapes and sizes before they are born (Aslin et al., 1983). Normal neonates can also hear remarkably well, unless their middle ears are clogged with amniotic fluid. In fact, most neonates will turn their heads toward unusual sounds, such as the shaking of a rattle.

amplitude Height. The higher the amplitude of sound waves, the louder they are.

pitch The highness or lowness of a sound, as determined by the frequency of sound waves.

Neonates have the capacity to respond to sounds of different **amplitude** and **pitch.** They are more likely to respond to high-pitched sounds than to low-pitched sounds (Bergeson & Trehub, 1999; Morrongiello & Clifton, 1984; Werner & Gillenwater, 1990). By contrast, speaking or singing to infants softly, in a relatively low-pitched voice, can have a soothing effect (Papousek, Papousek, & Symmes, 1991). This may explain the widespread practice in many cultures of singing lullabies to infants to promote sleep (Trehub, Trainor, & Unyk, 1993).

It may well be that the sense of hearing plays a role in the formation of affectional bonds between neonates and their mothers that goes well beyond the soothing potential of the mothers' voices. Research indicates that neonates prefer their mothers' voices to those of other women, but they do not show similar preferences for the voices of their fathers (DeCasper & Prescott, 1984; Freeman et al., 1993). It may seem tempting to conclude that the human nervous system is prewired to respond positively to the voice of one's biological mother. However, neonates have already had several months of experience in the uterus, and, for a good part of this time, they have been capable of sensing sounds. Because they are predominantly exposed to prenatal sounds produced by their mothers, learning appears to play a role in neonatal preferences.

There is fascinating evidence that neonates are particularly responsive to the sounds and rhythms of speech, although they do not show preferences for specific languages. Neonates can discriminate between different speech sounds (Molfese, Burger-Judisch, & Hans, 1991), and they can discriminate between new sounds of speech and those that they have heard before (Brody, Zelazo, & Chaika, 1984).

Smell: The Nose Knows, and Early

Neonates can definitely discriminate distinct odours, such as those of onions and anise (licorice). They show more rapid breathing patterns and increased bodily movement in response to powerful odours. They also turn away from unpleasant odours, such as ammonia and vinegar, as early as the first day after birth (Engen & Lipsitt, 1965; Rieser, Yonas, & Wikner, 1976).

The nasal preferences of neonates are quite similar to those of older children and adults (Ganchrow, Steiner, & Daher, 1983; Steiner, 1979). When a cotton swab saturated with the odour of rotten eggs was passed beneath their noses, neonate infants spat, stuck out their tongues, wrinkled their noses, and blinked their eyes. However, they showed smiles and licking motions when presented with the odours of chocolate, strawberry, vanilla, butter, bananas, and honey.

Research by Aidan Macfarlane (1975, 1977) and others suggests that the sense of smell, like hearing, may provide a vehicle for mother-infant recognition and attachment. Macfarlane suspected that neonates may be sensitive to the smell of milk because, when held by the mother, they tend to turn toward her nipple before they have had a chance to see or touch it. In one experiment, Macfarlane placed nursing pads above and to the sides of neonates' heads. One pad had absorbed milk from the mother, and the other was clean. Neonates less than a week old spent more time turning to look at their mothers' pads than at the clean pads.

Neonates will also turn toward preferred odours. In the second phase of this research, Macfarlane suspended pads with milk from the neonates' mothers and from strangers to the sides of babies' heads. For the first few days following birth, the infants did not turn toward their mothers' pads. However, by the time they were one week old, they turned toward their mothers' pads and spent more time looking at them than at the strangers' pads. It appears that they learned to respond positively to the odour of their mothers' milk during the first few days. Afterward, a source of this odour received preferential treatment even when the infants were not nursing.

Breast-fed fifteen-day-old infants also prefer their mothers' axillary (underarm) odour to odours produced by other lactating women and by nonlactating women. Bottle-fed infants do not show this preference (Cernoch & Porter, 1985; Porter, Makin, Davis, & Christensen, 1992). The investigators explain this difference by suggesting that breast-fed infants may be more likely than bottle-fed infants to be exposed to their mothers' axillary odour. That is, mothers of bottle-fed infants usually remain clothed during feeding. Axillary odour, along with odours from breast secretions, might contribute to the early development of recognition and attachment.

Taste

Neonates are sensitive to different tastes. Research shows that neonates form facial expressions similar to those of adults in response to various kinds of fluids. Neonates swallow without showing any facial expression suggestive of a positive or negative response when distilled water is placed on their tongues (Steiner, 1979). Sweet solutions are met with smiles, licking, and eager sucking, as in Figure 4.14a (Rosenstein & Oster, 1988). Neonates apparently do discriminate among solutions with salty, sour, and bitter tastes, as suggested by different reactions in the lower part of the face (Rosenstein & Oster, 1988). Sour fluids frequently elicit pursing of the lips, nose wrinkling, and eye blinking (Figure 4.14b). Bitter solutions stimulate spitting, gagging, and sticking out of the tongue (Figure 4.14c).

Sweet solutions have a calming effect on neonates (Blass & Smith, 1992; Rosenstein & Oster, 1988; Smith et al., 1990). One study found that sweeter solutions increase the heart rate, suggesting heightened arousal, but also slow down the rate of

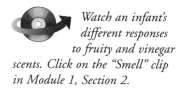
Watch an infant's different responses to fruity and vinegar scents. Click on the "Smell" clip in Module 1, Section 2.

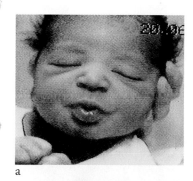
a

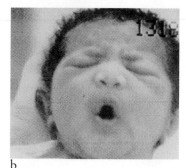
b

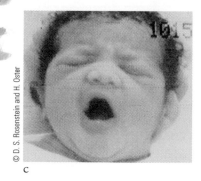
c

© D. S. Rosenstein and H. Oster

Figure 4.14

Facial Expressions Elicited by Sweet, Sour, and Bitter Solutions

Neonates are sensitive to different tastes, as shown by their facial expressions when tasting (a) sweet, (b) sour, and (c) bitter solutions.

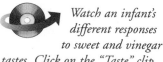
Watch an infant's different responses to sweet and vinegar tastes. Click on the "Taste" clip in Module 1, Section 2.

sucking (Crook & Lipsitt, 1976). The researchers interpret this finding to suggest an effort to savour the sweeter solution—to make the flavour last. Although we do not know why infants ingest sweet foods more slowly, this difference could be adaptive in the sense of preventing overeating. Sweet foods tend to be high in calories; eating them slowly gives infants' brains more time to respond to bodily signals that they have eaten enough and thus to stop eating. Ah, to have the wisdom of a neonate!

Touch and Pain

The sense of touch is an extremely important avenue of learning and communication for babies. Not only do the skin senses provide information about the external world, but the sensations of skin against skin also appear to provide feelings of comfort and security that may be major factors in the formation of bonds of attachment between infants and their caregivers, as we will see in Chapter 7.

Neonates are sensitive to touch. As noted earlier in this chapter, many reflexes—including the rooting, sucking, Babinski, and grasping reflexes, to name a few—are activated by pressure against the skin. However, neonates do not seem as sensitive to pain as slightly older babies are (Reisman, 1987). Considering the squeezing that takes place during childbirth, relative insensitivity to pain seems to be adaptive.

Habituation

habituate Show a decline in interest as a repeated stimulus becomes familiar.

Neonates from different ethnic groups show some differences in their behaviour. For example, compared with neonates of European descent, infants of Chinese, Japanese, and Navajo descent are less likely to fret or cry, are calmed more readily when upset, are less excitable, and **habituate** more quickly to repeated presentation of stimuli (Chisholm, 1983; Kagan, 1992). These differences are thought to reflect a variety of factors, including genetic endowment, the prenatal environment, and the mother's reproductive history (Garcia-Coll, 1990). Cultural differences in the way parents respond to their babies may strengthen early biologically based differences in emotional reactivity. For example, Japanese mothers are much more likely than American mothers to carry their infants and to sleep with them. Japanese mothers also are more apt to try to minimize their infants' crying and to emotionally indulge them (Camras, Campos, Oster, Miyake, & Bradshaw, 1992). These maternal behaviours may contribute to the lower emotional reactivity of Japanese infants.

Learning: *Really* Early Childhood "Education"

Question: Can neonates learn? The somewhat limited sensory capabilities of neonates suggest that they may not learn as rapidly as older children do. After all, we must sense clearly those things we are to learn about. However, neonates seem capable of at least two basic forms of learning: classical conditioning and operant conditioning.

Classical Conditioning of Neonates

In classical conditioning of neonates, involuntary responses are conditioned to new stimuli. In a typical study (Lipsitt, 1990), neonates were taught to blink in response to a tone. Blinking (the unconditioned response) was elicited by a puff of air directed toward the infants' eyes (the unconditioned stimulus). A tone was sounded (the conditioned stimulus) as the puff of air was delivered. After repeated pairings, sounding the tone caused the neonate to blink (the conditioned response).

Classical conditioning takes longer in neonates than in older infants. By the end of the first month, babies already have improved their ability to show classical conditioning and to retain what they have learned (Little, Lipsitt, & Rovee-Collier, 1984).

But even neonates are equipped to learn that events peculiar to their own environments (touches or other conditioned stimuli) may mean that a meal is at hand—or, more accurately, at mouth. One neonate may learn that a light switched on overhead precedes a meal. Another may learn that feeding is preceded by the rustling of a carpet of thatched leaves. The conditioned stimuli are culture specific; the capacity to learn is universal.

Operant Conditioning of Neonates

Operant conditioning, like classical conditioning, can take place in neonates. In Chapter 3, we described an experiment in which neonates learned to suck on a pacifier in such a way as to activate a recording of their mothers' reading *The Cat in the Hat* (DeCasper & Fifer, 1980; DeCasper & Spence, 1991) (Figure 4.15). The mothers had read this story aloud during the final weeks of pregnancy. In this example, the infants' sucking reflexes were modified through the reinforcement of hearing their mothers read a familiar story.

The younger the child, the more important it is that reinforcers be administered rapidly. Among neonates, it seems that reinforcers must be administered within a second after the desired behaviour is performed if learning is to occur (Millar, 1972). Infants aged six to eight months can learn if the reinforcer is delayed by two seconds, but if the delay is three seconds or more, learning does not take place (Millar, 1990).

There are large individual differences in conditionability among neonates. Some infants can be conditioned with relatively few trials, whereas others apparently cannot be conditioned at all (Fitzgerald & Brackbill, 1976). However, it would be premature to attribute differences in conditionability to differences in intelligence. Although intelligence is often loosely thought of as learning ability, conditionability is not comparable with the complex cognitive tasks that define intellectual performance in older children. Measures of intelligence in infants do not correlate well with measures of intelligence at later ages.

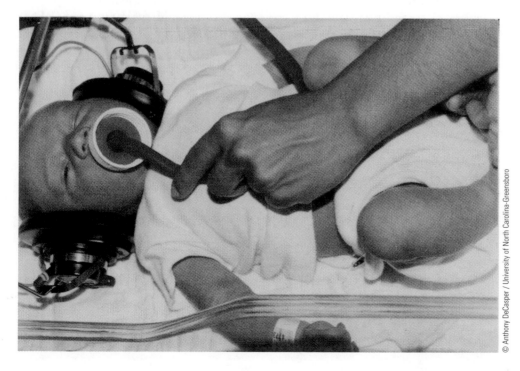

Figure 4.15

A Neonate Sucking to Hear Her Mother's Voice

Sleeping and Waking

As adults, we spend about one-third of our time sleeping. *Question: What patterns of sleep are found among neonates?* Neonates greatly outdo us, spending two-thirds of their time, or about sixteen hours per day, in sleep. And in one of life's basic challenges to parents, neonates do not sleep their sixteen hours consecutively.

A number of different states of sleep and wakefulness have been identified in neonates and infants, as shown in Table 4.3 (Berg & Berg, 1987; Colombo, Moss, & Horowitz, 1989; Wulff & Siegmund, 2001). Although individual babies differ in the amount of time they spend in each of these states, sleep clearly predominates over wakefulness in the early days and weeks of life.

Different infants require different amounts of sleep and follow different patterns of sleep, but virtually all infants distribute their sleeping throughout the day and night through a series of naps. The typical infant has about six cycles of waking and sleeping in a twenty-four-hour period (Bamford et al., 1990). The longest nap typically approaches four and a half hours, and the neonate is usually awake for a little more than one hour during each cycle.

This pattern of waking and sleeping changes rapidly and dramatically over the course of the years (Berg & Berg, 1987; Lowrey, 1986). Even after a month or so, the infant has fewer but longer sleep periods and will usually take longer naps during the night. Parents whose babies do not know the difference between night and day usually teach them the difference by playing with them during daytime hours, once feeding and caretaking chores have been carried out, and by putting them back to sleep as soon as possible when they awaken hungry during the night. Most parents do not require professional instruction in this method. At 3:00 a.m., parents are not likely to feel playful.

By the ages of about six months to a year, many infants begin to sleep through the night. Some infants start sleeping through the night even earlier (Anders, Halpern, & Hua, 1992). A number of infants begin to sleep through the night for a week or so and then revert to their wakeful ways again for a while.

REM and Non-REM Sleep

rapid-eye-movement (REM) sleep A period of sleep during which we are likely to dream, as indicated by rapid eye movements.

non-rapid-eye-movement (non-REM) sleep Periods of sleep during which we are unlikely to dream.

electroencephalograph (EEG) An instrument that measures electrical activity of the brain.

Sleep is not a consistent state. It can be divided into **rapid-eye-movement (REM) sleep** and **non-rapid-eye-movement (non-REM) sleep** (Figure 4.16). Studies with the **electroencephalograph (EEG)** show that we can subdivide non-REM sleep into

	States of Sleep and Wakefulness in Infancy	
State	**Comments**	
Quiet sleep (non-REM)	Regular breathing, eyes closed, no movement	
Active sleep (REM)	Irregular breathing, eyes closed, rapid eye movement, muscle twitches	
Drowsiness	Regular or irregular breathing, eyes open or closed, little movement	
Alert inactivity	Regular breathing, eyes open, looking around, little body movement	
Alert activity	Irregular breathing, eyes open, active body movement	
Crying	Irregular breathing, eyes open or closed, thrashing of arms and legs, crying	

four additional stages of sleep, each with its characteristic brain waves, but our discussion will be limited to REM and non-REM sleep. REM sleep is characterized by rapid eye movements that can be observed beneath closed lids. The EEG patterns produced during REM sleep resemble those of the waking state. For this reason, REM sleep is also called paradoxical sleep. However, we are difficult to awaken during REM sleep. About 80 percent of the time, adults who are roused during REM sleep report that they have been dreaming. Is the same true of neonates?

Note from Figure 4.16 that neonates spend about half their time sleeping in REM sleep. As they develop, the percentage of sleeping time spent in REM sleep declines. By six months or so, REM sleep accounts for only about 30 percent of the baby's sleep. By two to three years, REM sleep drops off to about 20 to 25 percent (Coons & Guilleminault, 1982). There is a dramatic falling-off in the total number of hours spent in sleep as we develop (Salzarulo & Fagioli, 1995). Figure 4.16 shows that the major portion of the drop-off can be attributed to lessened REM sleep.

What is the function of REM sleep in neonates? Research with humans and other animals, including kittens and rat pups, suggests that the brain requires a certain amount of activity for the creation of proteins that are involved in the development of neurons and synapses (Mirmiran, 1995; Shaffery et al., 1998). Brain activity can be stimulated by internal or external sources. In older children and adults, external sources of stimulation are provided by activity, a vast and shifting array of sensory impressions, and, perhaps, thought processes during the waking state. The neonate, however, spends its brief waking periods largely isolated from the kaleidoscope of events of the world outside and is not likely to be lost in deep thought. Thus, in the waking state, the brain may not be provided with the needed stimulation. As a compensatory measure, the neonate spends relatively more time in REM sleep, which most closely parallels the waking state in terms of brain waves. While infants are in REM sleep, internal physiological stimulation spurs the brain on to appropriate development. Preterm babies spend an even greater proportion of their time in REM sleep than full-term babies, perhaps—goes the argument—because they require relatively greater stimulation of the brain.

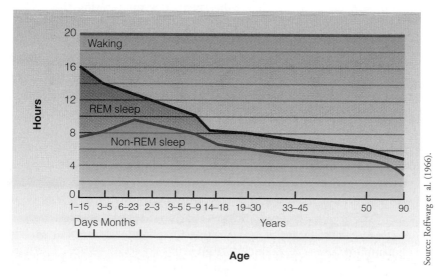

Source: Roffwarg et al. (1966).

Figure 4.16

REM Sleep and Non-REM Sleep

Neonates spend nearly 50% of their time sleeping in rapid-eye movement (REM) sleep. The percentage of time spent in REM sleep drops off to 20-25% for 2- to 3-year-olds.

Crying

No discussion of the sleeping and waking states of the neonate would be complete without mentioning crying—a comment that parents will view as an understatement. The main reason that babies cry seems to be simple enough. Studies suggest that a one-word answer often suffices: pain (Gormally et al., 2001; Isik et al., 2000).

Some parents have entered into conflict with hospital nurses who tell them not to worry when their babies are crying on the other side of the nursery's glass partition. Nurses often tell the parents that their babies must cry because crying helps clear their respiratory systems of fluids that linger from the amniotic sac and also stimulates the circulatory system.

Whether crying is healthful and necessary remains an open question, but at least some crying among babies seems to be universal. Some scholars have suggested that crying may be a primitive language, but it is not. Languages contain units and groupings of sounds that symbolize objects and events. Crying does not. Still, crying appears to be both expressive and functional. It serves as an infant's expressive response to unpleasant feelings and also stimulates caretakers to do something to help. Crying thus communicates something, even though it is not a form of language. Crying may also communicate the identity of the crier across distance. Cries have multiple markers of individuality, and they may signal to parents and other caretakers the location of their infant in a group (Gustafson, Green, & Cleland, 1994).

There are different types of cries (Gustafson & Harris, 1990). Schaffer (1971) suggested the existence of three distinct causes and patterns of crying: crying that stems from (1) hunger, (2) anger, and (3) pain. A sudden, loud, insistent cry associated with flexing and kicking of the legs may indicate colic (pain resulting from gas or other sources of distress in the digestive tract). The baby may seem to hold its breath for a few moments, then gasp and begin to cry again. Crying from colic can be severe and persistent—lasting for hours, although cries generally seem to settle into a pattern after a while (Barr, Rotman, Yaremko, Leduc, & Francoeur, 1992; Lester, Boukydis, Garcia-Coll, Hole, & Peucker, 1992). Much to the relief of parents, colic tends to disappear by the third to sixth month, as a baby's digestive system matures.

Before parenthood, many people wonder whether they will be able to recognize the meanings of their babies' various cries, but it usually does not take them long. Parents are also somewhat better than other people at interpreting the cries of unfamiliar babies, probably because of their greater experience with infant cries and caregiving (Green, Jones, & Gustafson, 1987; Gustafson & Harris, 1990).

Parents and nonparents alike, as well as children, have similar physiological responses to infant crying—increases in heart rate, blood pressure, and sweating (Frodi, 1985). Infant crying makes them feel irritated and anxious and motivates them to run to the baby to try to relieve the distress. The pitch of an infant's cries appears to provide information (Dessureau, Kurowski, & Thompson, 1998). Adults perceive high-pitched crying to be more urgent, distressing, and sick-sounding than low-pitched crying (Crowe & Zeskind, 1992; Lester et al., 1992).

Certain high-pitched cries, when prolonged, may signify health problems. For example, the cries of chronically distressed infants differ from those of normal infants in both rhythm and pitch. Patterns of crying may be indicative of such problems as chromosomal abnormalities, infections, fetal malnutrition, and exposure to narcotics (Huntington, Hans, & Zeskind, 1990; Sepkoski et al., 1993). A striking example of the link between crying and a health problem is the syndrome called *cri du chat,* French for "cry of the cat." This is a genetic disorder that produces abnormalities in the brain, atypical facial features, and a high-pitched, squeaky cry.

There are certain patterns of crying. For example, peaks of crying appear to be concentrated in the late afternoon and early evening (McGlaughlin & Grayson, 2001).

Although some cries may seem extreme and random at first, they tend to settle into a pattern that is recognizable to most parents (Green, Gustafson, & McGhie, 1998; Gustafson & Harris, 1990). Infants seem to produce about the same number of crying bouts during the first nine months or so, but the *duration* of the bouts grows briefer, by half, during this period (van IJzendoorn & Hubbard, 2000). The response of the mother apparently influences infants' crying. It turns out that the more frequently mothers ignore their infants' crying bouts in the first nine weeks, the less frequently their infants cry in the following nine-week period (van IJzendoorn & Hubbard, 2000). Please do *not* interpret this finding to mean that infant crying is best ignored. At least at first, crying communicates pain and hunger, and these are conditions that should be corrected. Persistent crying, unfortunately, can strain the mother–infant relationship (Papousek & von Hofacker, 1998).

Soothing

Now that you are an expert on the causes and patterns of crying, you might want to know the answer to the following: *Question: What can I do to stop an infant from crying?* For one thing, sucking seems to function as a built-in tranquillizer. Sucking on a **pacifier** decreases crying and agitated movement in neonates who have not yet had the opportunity to feed (Kessen, Leutzendoff, & Stoutsenberger, 1967). Therefore, the soothing function of sucking need not be learned through experience. However, sucking (drinking) a sweet solution also appears to have a soothing effect (Gormally et al., 2001; Isik, Oezek, Bilgen, & Cebeci, 2000). (Can it be that even babies are programmed to enjoy "comfort food"?)

Parents find many other ways to soothe infants—picking them up, patting, caressing, and rocking them, swaddling, and speaking to them in a low voice (Acebo & Thomas, 1992; Gustafson & Harris, 1990). Parents then usually try to find the specific cause of the distress by offering breast milk, a bottle, or a pacifier or by checking the diaper. Parents in many cultures, including those of the United States, France, and Japan, show these same responses to a crying infant (Bornstein et al., 1992b).

Learning occurs quickly during the soothing process. Parents learn by trial and error what types of embraces and movements are likely to soothe their infants. And infants learn quickly that crying is followed by being picked up or other forms of intervention.

pacifier An artificial nipple, teething ring, or similar device that soothes babies.

© SW Productions/Getty Images

Soothing
How can a crying baby be soothed? Picking the baby up, talking to it quietly, patting, stroking, and rocking all seem to have calming effects.

Parents sometimes worry that if they pick up the crying baby quickly, they are reinforcing the baby's crying. In this way, they believe, the child may become spoiled and find it progressively more difficult to engage in self-soothing to get to sleep. Fortunately, as infants mature and learn, crying tends to become replaced by less upsetting verbal requests for intervention. Among adults, of course, soothing techniques take very different forms—a bouquet of flowers or admission that one started the argument.

Sudden Infant Death Syndrome (SIDS)

Truth or Fiction Revisited: It is true that more children die from sudden infant death syndrome (SIDS) than die from cancer, heart disease, pneumonia, child abuse, AIDS, cystic fibrosis, and muscular dystrophy combined (Lipsitt, 2003). *Questions: What is SIDS? What are the risk factors for SIDS?*

Sudden infant death syndrome (SIDS)—also known as crib death—is a disorder of infancy that apparently strikes while the baby is sleeping. In a typical case, a baby goes to sleep, apparently in perfect health, and is found dead the next morning. There is no sign that the baby struggled or was in pain. The incidence of SIDS has been declining, but on average three infants a week are reported to die of SIDS in Canada (Public Health Agency of Canada, 2002), making it the most common cause of death in infants between the ages of one month and one year. Most SIDS deaths occur between two and five months of age (Lipsitt, 2003). New parents frequently live in dread of SIDS and check their babies regularly through the night to see if they are breathing. It is not abnormal, by the way, for babies occasionally to suspend breathing for a moment. The intermittent suspension of respiration is called **apnea,** and the buildup of carbon dioxide usually spurs a return to breathing. Lewis Lipsitt (2003) noted that any theory of the causes of SIDS must deal with the fact that it tends to occur between the second and fifth months, when reflexive behaviour is weakening. He suggests that babies who are less likely to move reflexively and vigorously to obtain air when their air passageways are occluded are at higher risk of SIDS.

Although it is known that SIDS does not result from suffocation or from choking on regurgitated food, its causes remain largely obscure. Currently, one of the most compelling hypotheses is that SIDS results from abnormal control of cardiac and respiratory functioning by the brain stem (Browne, Colditz, & Dunster, 2000). Still, a number of **risk factors** are associated with the disorder, and parents whose situations seem to fit the stereotypical picture may wish to take special heed. SIDS is more common among

- babies aged two to four months;
- babies who are put to sleep in the prone position (on their stomachs);
- premature and low-birth-weight infants;
- male infants;
- families of lower socioeconomic status;
- African American families (African American babies are twice as likely as European American babies to die of SIDS);
- babies of teenage mothers; and
- babies whose mothers smoked during or after pregnancy or whose mothers used narcotics during pregnancy.

Studies have found a higher risk of SIDS among babies who sleep on their stomachs (Lipsitt, 2003). And in a joint statement, the Canadian Foundation for the Study of Infant Deaths, the Canadian Institute of Child Health, the Canadian Paediatric Society, and Health Canada recommend putting normal, healthy babies down to sleep

---

sudden infant death syndrome (SIDS) The death, while sleeping, of apparently healthy babies who stop breathing for unknown medical reasons. Also called crib death.

apnea (AP-nee-uh) Temporary suspension of breathing (from the Greek a-, meaning "without," and pnoie, meaning "wind").

risk factors Variables such as ethnicity and social class that are associated with the likelihood of problems but that do not directly cause problems.

on their backs (Public Health Agency of Canada, 2002). A recent American national survey revealed that before the recommendation, 43 percent of infants were usually placed to sleep on their stomachs (prone) and 27 percent on their backs (supine). But now only 17 percent are placed in the prone position, and 56 percent are placed in the supine position (Willinger et al., 2000).

Home monitoring systems have been developed to alert parents to episodes of apnea and to give them time to intervene—for example, by using artificial respiration. However, use of home monitors can be stressful for the families (SIDS Network, 2001). Moreover, there is little evidence that SIDS rates have been reduced as a result of using monitors (SIDS Network, 2001).

What should you do about SIDS? Bear in mind that the prevention of SIDS begins during pregnancy. Smoking and using other drugs during pregnancy increases the risk of SIDS. Obtain adequate prenatal nutrition and health care. Place your baby in the supine position (on its back) to sleep. Keep current with research data on SIDS: Check with your pediatrician and check websites such as those of the Public Health Agency of Canada (http://www.phac-aspc.gc.ca/dca-dea/prenatal/sids_e.html), the Canadian Foundation for the Study of Infant Deaths (http://www.sidscanada.org), and the Canadian Paediatric Society (http://www.caringforkids.cps.ca/babies/SafeSleepForBaby.htm) for the most up-to-date information.

Back to Sleep

Each week, 3 babies die of SIDS in Canada. According to the latest research, there are things you can do to **reduce the risk** of Sudden Infant Death Syndrome (SIDS):

1. Put your baby on his or her back to sleep.
2. Make sure no one smokes around your baby.
3. Avoid putting too many clothes and covers on your baby.
4. Breastfeed your baby, it may give some protection against SIDS.

For more information call 1-800-END-SIDS (1-800-363-7437).

Health Canada — Santé Canada · The Canadian Foundation for the Study of Infant Deaths · Canadian Institute of Child Health · Canadian Paediatric Society

Additional copies of the SIDS promotional material can be ordered from (613) 954-5995.

Reducing the Risks of SIDS
Source: *Back to Sleep*, Health Canada. Reproduced with the permission of the Minister of Public Works and Government Services Canada, 2007.

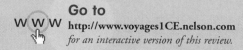

Active Review

18. In Canada today, the neonate's overall level of health is usually evaluated at birth according to the _____ scale.

19. In the _____ reflex, the baby turns its head and mouth toward a stimulus that strokes the cheek, chin, or corner of the mouth.

20. Neonates are rather (nearsighted or farsighted?).

21. Neonates (do or do not?) prefer their mothers' voices to those of other women.

22. As babies mature, they spend a (greater or smaller?) percentage of their time in REM sleep.

23. _____ is the most common cause of death in infants between the ages of one month and one year.

Reflect & Relate: Have you or a family member had to adjust to the waking and sleeping patterns of a baby? Do you think that it is normal to occasionally resent being awakened repeatedly through the night? Explain.

Go to
W W W http://www.voyages1CE.nelson.com
for an interactive version of this review.

Recite: *An Active Summary*™

1. What events occur just before the beginning of childbirth?

The first uterine contractions are called Braxton-Hicks contractions, or false labour contractions. A day or so before labour begins, some blood spotting can occur in vaginal secretions. At about this time, one woman in ten has a rush of amniotic fluid from the vagina. The initiation of labour may be triggered by secretion of hormones by the fetus. Maternal hormones stimulate contractions strong enough to expel the baby.

2. What happens during the first stage of childbirth?

Childbirth begins with the onset of regular contractions of the uterus, which cause the cervix to become effaced and dilated. The first stage may last from a few hours to more than a day. During transition, the cervix is nearly fully dilated and the head of the fetus moves into the birth canal.

3. What occurs during the second stage of childbirth?

The second stage begins when the baby appears at the opening of the birth canal. It ends with the birth of the baby. Once the baby's head emerges from the mother's body, mucus is suctioned from its mouth so that breathing is not obstructed. When the baby is breathing on its own, the umbilical cord is clamped and severed.

4. What happens during the third stage of childbirth?

During this stage, the placenta separates from the uterine wall and is expelled along with fetal membranes.

5. How is anesthesia used in childbirth? What are its effects on the baby?

General anesthetic puts the woman to sleep, but it decreases the strength of uterine contractions and lowers the responsiveness of the neonate. Regional or local anesthetics deaden pain in parts of the body without putting the mother to sleep.

6. What is prepared childbirth?

Prepared childbirth is the process whereby women learn to dissociate uterine contractions from pain and fear by associating other responses, such as relaxation, with contractions. A coach aids the mother in the delivery room.

7. What is the C-section? Why is it so common?

A caesarean section (C-section) delivers a baby surgically through the abdomen. C-sections are most likely to be advised if the baby is large or in distress or if the mother's pelvis is small or she is tired or weak. Herpes and HIV infections in the birth canal can be bypassed by C-section.

8. Can a woman decide where to deliver her baby?

Women have choices in childbirth—for example, home delivery, birthing suites, or traditional labour rooms. Birthing suites provide homelike surroundings with immediate hospital backup available.

9. What are the effects of oxygen deprivation at birth?

Prenatal oxygen deprivation can be fatal if prolonged; it can also impair development of the nervous system, leading to cognitive and motor problems.

10. What is meant by the terms *prematurity* and *low birth weight*?

A baby is preterm when birth occurs at or before thirty-seven weeks of gestation. A baby has a low birth weight when it weighs less than five and a half pounds (about 2500 grams). A baby who is low in birth weight but born at full term is said to be small for dates. The risk of having preterm babies rises with multiple births.

11. What risks are connected with being born prematurely or low in birth weight?

Risks include infant mortality and delayed neurological and motor development. Preterm babies are relatively thin and often have vernix on the skin and lanugo. Sucking and breathing reflexes may be weak. The walls of air sacs in the lungs may stick together, leading to respiratory distress.

12. How are preterm infants treated following birth?

Preterm babies usually remain in the hospital in incubators. Preterm infants profit from early stimulation just as full-term babies do. Parents often do not treat preterm neonates as well as they treat full-term neonates, perhaps because they are less attractive and have irritating, high-pitched cries.

13. What kinds of problems in mood do women experience during the postpartum period?

Women may encounter the baby blues, postpartum depression, and postpartum psychosis. These problems are found around the world and probably reflect hormonal changes following birth, although stress can play a role. High self-esteem and social support help women manage these adjustment problems.

14. How critical is parental interaction with neonates in the formation of bonds of attachment?

It may not be. Research by Klaus and Kennell suggested that the first few hours after birth present a "maternal-sensitive" period during which women's hormone levels particularly dispose them to "bond" with their neonates. However, the study confounded the effects of extra time with their babies with special attention from health professionals.

15. How do health professionals assess the health of neonates?

The neonate's overall health is usually evaluated according to the Apgar scale. The Brazelton Neonatal Behavioral Assessment Scale also screens neonates for behavioural and neurological problems.

16. What are reflexes? What kinds of reflexes are shown by neonates?

Reflexes are simple, unlearned, stereotypical responses that are elicited by specific stimuli. The rooting and sucking reflexes are basic to survival. Other key reflexes include the startle reflex, the grasping reflex, the stepping reflex, the Babinski reflex, and the tonic-neck reflex. Most reflexes disappear or are replaced by voluntary behaviour within months.

17. How well do neonates see, hear, and so on?

Neonates are nearsighted. Neonates visually detect movement, and many track movement. Fetuses respond to sound months before they are born. Neonates are particularly responsive to the sounds and rhythms of speech. The nasal preferences of neonates are similar to those of older children and adults. Neonates prefer sweet solutions and find them soothing. The sensations of skin against skin are also soothing and may contribute to formation of bonds of attachment.

18. Can neonates learn?

Yes. Neonates are capable of classical and operant conditioning. For example, they can be conditioned to blink their eyes in response to a tone.

19. What patterns of sleep are found among neonates?

Neonates spend two-thirds of their time in sleep. Nearly all neonates distribute sleep through naps. Neonates spend about half their time sleeping in REM sleep, but as time goes on, REM sleep accounts for less of their sleep. REM sleep may be connected with brain development.

20. Why do babies cry?

Babies cry mainly because of pain and discomfort. Crying may communicate the identity of the crier across distance, as well as hunger, anger, pain, and the presence of health problems.

21. What can I do to stop an infant from crying?

Pacifiers help because sucking is soothing. Parents also try picking babies up, patting, caressing, and rocking them, and speaking to them in a low voice.

22. What is SIDS? What are the risk factors for SIDS?

SIDS is a disorder of infancy that apparently strikes while the baby is sleeping. It is the most common cause of death in infants between the ages of one month and one year. SIDS is more common among babies who are put to sleep in the prone position, preterm and low-birth-weight infants, male infants, and infants whose mothers smoked during or after pregnancy or whose mothers used narcotics during pregnancy.

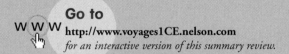

Go to
W W W http://www.voyages1CE.nelson.com
for an interactive version of this summary review.

Key Terms

term *(page 118)*
Braxton-Hicks contractions *(page 118)*
prostaglandins *(page 119)*
oxytocin *(page 119)*
neonate *(page 119)*

efface *(page 119)*
dilate *(page 119)*
episiotomy *(page 119)*
fetal monitoring *(page 119)*
forceps *(page 119)*
vacuum extraction tube *(page 119)*

transition *(page 120)*
midwife *(page 123)*
anesthetic *(page 123)*
general anesthesia *(page 123)*
tranquillizer *(page 123)*
local anesthetic *(page 123)*

Active Learning Resources

Observing Children and Adolescents CD-ROM
Want to watch videos showing what you've just learned about in this chapter? Click on the "Birth" video in Module 1, Section 1. Your Lessons in Observation feature on p. 121 provides further learning objectives, an applied lesson, and a critical thinking exercise designed to help you experience this stage of development. In CD Module 1, also check out "The Newborn: Reflex Development" video in Section 1 and the "Smell," "Taste," and "Vision" videos in Section 2.

Visit Your Companion Website for This Book
http://www.voyages1CE.nelson.com
Check out this companion website, where you will find online resources directly linked to your book. The website includes interactive exercises related to PQ4R and Power Visuals for mastering and reviewing key concepts as well as quizzing, chapter outlines, and much more!

CengageNOW!™
http://hed.nelson.com
Go to this site for the link to CengageNOW™, your one-stop study shop. Take a Pretest for this chapter, and CengageNOW™ will generate a personalized Study Plan based on your test results! The Study Plan will identify the topics you need to review and direct you to online resources to help you master those topics. You can then take a Posttest to help you determine the concepts you have mastered and those you still need to work on.

Infancy: Physical Development

PREVIEW

TRUTH OR FICTION?

●●●●●●●●●●●●

T F The head of the newborn child doubles in length by adulthood, but the legs increase in length by about five times.

T F Infants triple their birth weight within a year.

T F Breast feeding helps prevent obesity later in life.

T F A child's brain reaches half its adult weight by the age of one year.

T F The cerebral cortex—the outer layer of the brain that is vital to human thought and reasoning—is only one-eighth of an inch thick.

T F Native American Hopi infants spend the first year of life strapped to a board, yet they begin to walk at about the same time as children who are reared in other cultures.

T F Infants need to have experience crawling before they develop fear of heights.

Go to WWW

www.voyages1ce.nelson.com
for an interactive version of this "Truth or Fiction" feature.

e, the authors, are keen observers of children—of our own, that is. From our personal experiences, we have derived the following basic principles of physical development:

- Just when you think your child has finally begun to make regular gains in weight, he or she will begin to lose weight or go for months without gaining an ounce.
- No matter how early your child sits up or starts to walk, your neighbour's child will do it earlier.
- Children first roll over when one parent is watching but will steadfastly refuse to repeat it when the other parent is called in.
- Children begin to get into everything before you get childproof latches on the cabinets.
- Every advance in locomotor ability provides your child with new ways to get hurt.
- Children will display their most exciting developmental milestones when the camcorder or digital camera batteries are dead.

More seriously, in this chapter we discuss various aspects of physical development during the first two years. We examine changes in physical growth, the development of the brain and the nervous system, motor development, and the development and coordination of sensory and perceptual capabilities, such as vision and hearing.

Physical Growth and Development

What a fascinating creature the newborn is: tiny, seemingly helpless, apparently oblivious to its surroundings, yet perfectly formed and fully capable of letting its caregivers know when it is hungry, thirsty, or uncomfortable. And what a fascinating creature is this same child two years later: running, climbing, playing, talking, hugging, and kissing.

It is hard to believe that only two short years can bring about such remarkable changes. It seems that nearly every day brings a new accomplishment. Yet, as we will see, not all infants share equally in the explosion of positive developments. Therefore, we will also be enumerating some developmental problems and what can be done about them.

Sequences of Physical Development: Head First?

Question: What are the sequences of physical development? During the first two years, children make enormous strides in physical growth and development. In this section, we explore sequences of physical development, changes in height and weight, and nutrition. Three key sequences of physical development include cephalocaudal development, proximodistal development, and differentiation (see Concept Review 5.1).

Cephalocaudal Development

As noted in Chapter 3, development proceeds from the upper part of the head to the lower parts of the body. When we consider the central role of the brain, which is contained within the skull, the cephalocaudal sequence appears quite logical. The brain regulates essential functions, such as heartbeat. Through the secretion of hormones, the brain also regulates the growth and development of the body and influences basic drives, such as hunger and thirst.

The head develops more rapidly than the rest of the body during the embryonic stage. By eight weeks after conception, the head constitutes half the entire length of the embryo. The brain develops more rapidly than the spinal cord. Arm buds form before leg buds. Most newborn babies have a strong, well-defined sucking reflex, although their legs are spindly and their limbs move back and forth only in diffuse excitement or agitation. Infants can hold up their heads before they gain control over their arms, their torsos, and, finally, their legs. They can sit up before they can crawl and walk. When they first walk, they use their hands to hold on to a person or object for support.

The lower parts of the body, because they get off to a later start, must do more growing to reach adult size. ***Truth or Fiction Revisited:*** The head does double in length between birth and maturity, and the torso triples in length. The arms increase their length by about four times, and the legs and feet do so by about five times.

Proximodistal Development

Growth and development also proceed from the trunk outward—from the body's central axis toward the periphery. The proximodistal principle, too, makes sense. The brain and spinal cord follow a central axis down through the body, and it is essential that the nerves be in place for the infant to gain control over the arms and legs. Also, the life functions of the newborn baby—heartbeat, respiration, digestion, and elimination of wastes—are all carried out by organ systems close to the central axis. These must be in operation or ready to operate when the child is born.

In terms of motor development, infants gain control over their trunks and shoulders before their arms, hands, and fingers. They make clumsy swipes at objects with their arms before they can voluntarily grasp them with their hands. Infants can grab large objects before picking up tiny things with their fingers. Similarly, infants gain control over their hips and upper legs before they can direct their lower legs, feet, and toes.

Differentiation

As children mature, their physical reactions become less global and more specific. The tendency of behaviour to become more specific and distinct is called **differentiation.** If a neonate's finger is pricked or burned, he or she may withdraw the finger but also thrash about, cry, and show general signs of distress. Toddlers may also cry, show distress, and withdraw the finger, but they are less likely to thrash about wildly. Thus, the response to pain has become more specific. An older child or adult is also likely to withdraw the finger, but less likely to wail (usually) and show general distress.

differentiation The processes by which behaviours and physical structures become more specialized.

Growth Patterns in Height and Weight: Heading toward the Greek Ideal?

The most dramatic gains in height and weight occur during prenatal development. Within a span of nine months, children develop from a zygote that is about 1/100 (0.014514068) of a centimetre long to a neonate that is about 50.8 centimetres long. Weight increases by a factor of billions.

Question: What patterns of growth occur in infancy? During the first year after birth, gains in height and weight are also dramatic, although not by the standards of prenatal gains. Infants usually double their birth weight in about five months and triple it by the first birthday (Kuczmarski et al., 2000). Their height increases by about 50 percent in the first year, so a child whose length at birth was 50.8 centimetres is likely to be about 76.2 centimetres tall at twelve months. ***Truth or Fiction Revisited:*** Thus, it is true that infants triple their birth weight within a year. The gain sounds dramatic, but keep in mind that their weight increases more than a billionfold in the nine months between conception and birth.

Growth in infancy has long been viewed as a slow and steady process. Growth charts in pediatricians' offices resemble the smooth, continuous curves shown in Figure 5.1. But research suggests that infants actually grow in spurts. About 90 to 95 percent of the time, they are not growing at all. One study measured the height

Concept Review 5.1 Sequences of Physical Development

Cephalocaudal Development

Cephalocaudal means that development proceeds from the "head" to the "tail," or, in the case of humans, to the lower parts of the body. Cephalocaudal development gives the brain an opportunity to participate more fully in subsequent developments.

This photo shows that an infant gains control over its hands and upper body before gaining control over its lower body.

(c) Felix St. Clair Renard / The Image Bank / Getty Images

Proximodistal Development

Proximodistal means that development proceeds from the trunk or central axis of the body outward. The brain and spine make up the central nervous system along the central axis of the body and are functional before the infant can control the arms and legs.

In this photo you can see that the infant's arm is only slightly longer than her head. Compare this to the length of your own head and arm.

(c) Kaz Mori / Getty Images

Differentiation

As children mature, physical reactions become less global and more specific. This infant engages in diffuse motor activity. Within a few months, he will be grasping for objects and holding on to them with a more and more sophisticated kind of grasp.

This photo shows that infants engage in diffuse motion before they begin to reach and grasp.

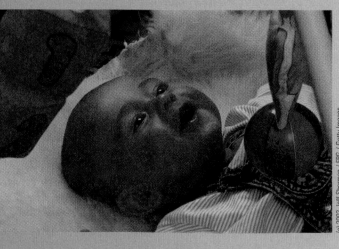
(c) 2002 Jeff Sherman / FPG / Getty Images

of infants throughout their first twenty-one months (Lampl, Veldhuis, & Johnson, 1992). The researchers found that the infants would remain the same size for two to sixty-three days and then would shoot up in length by half a centimetre to 2.5 centimetres in less than twenty-four hours. Parents who swear that their infants sometimes consume enormous amounts of food and grow overnight may not be exaggerating all that much.

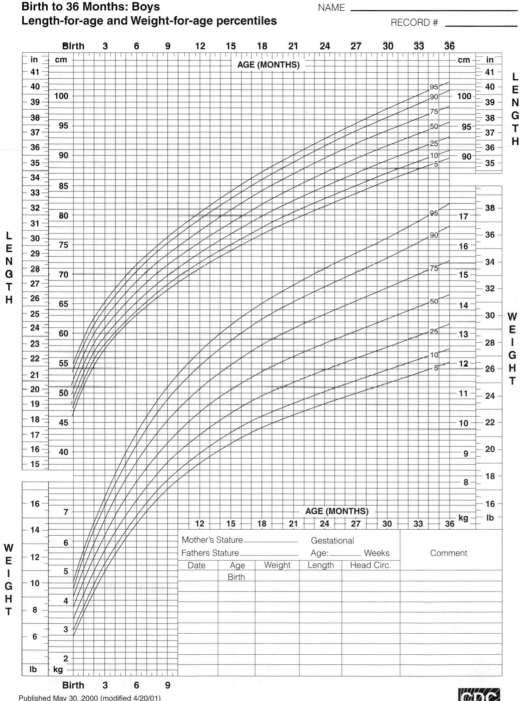

Figure 5.1

Growth Charts for Boys and Girls: Birth to 36 Months

The American National Center for Health Statistics, together with the National Center for Chronic Disease Prevention and Health Promotion, developed Growth Charts for boys and girls. These growth charts are used in Canada as well (Dietitians of Canada, Canadian Paediatric Society, The College of Family Physicians of Canada, & Community Health Nurses Association of Canada, 2004). The curves indicate the percentiles for weight and length at different ages. Lines labelled 95 show the height and weight of children who are taller and heavier than 95 percent of children of a particular age. Lines marked 50 indicate the median height and weight of a child of a given age: half their age-mates are shorter and lighter, and half are heavier and taller. Lines labelled 5 designate children who are taller and heavier than only 5 percent of children their age, and so on.

Source: National Center for Health Statistics & National Center for Chronic Disease Prevention and Health Promotion (2000).

Figure 5.1

Birth to 36 Months: Girls
Length-for-age and Weight-for-age percentiles

NAME _____

RECORD # _____

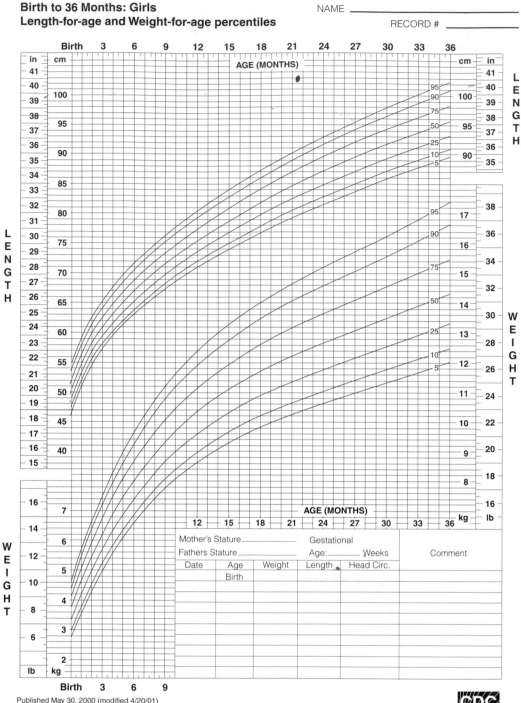

Published May 30, 2000 (modified 4/20/01)
SOURCE: Developed by the National Center for Health Statistics in collaboration with
the National Center for Chronic Disease Prevention and Health Promotion (2000)
http://www.cdc.gov/growthcharts

SAFER•HEALTHIER•PEOPLE™

Infants grow another 10.16 to 15.24 centimetres during their second year and gain another 1.81 to 3.17 kilograms. Boys generally reach half their adult height by their second birthday. Girls, however, mature more quickly than boys and are likely to reach half their adult height at the age of eighteen months (Tanner, 1989). Taller-than-average infants, as a group, tend to slow down in their growth rates. Shorter-than-average infants, as a group, tend to speed up. This is not to suggest that there is no relationship between infant and adult heights or that we all wind up in an average range. Tall infants, as a group, wind up taller than short infants, but in most cases not by as much as seemed likely during infancy.

Changes in Body Proportions

In rendering the human form, Greek classical sculptors followed the rule of the "golden section": The length of the head must equal one-eighth of the height of the body (including the head). The ideal of human beauty may be so, but the reality is that, among adults, the length of the head actually varies from about one-eighth to one-tenth the length of the entire body. Among children, the head is proportionately larger (see Figure 5.2).

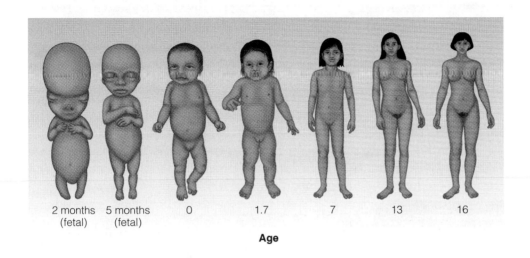

2 months (fetal)   5 months (fetal)   0   1.7   7   13   16

Age

Figure 5.2
Changes in the Proportions of the Body
Development proceeds in a cephalocaudal direction. The head is proportionately larger among younger children.

Development proceeds in a cephalocaudal manner. A few weeks after conception, an embryo is almost all head. At the beginning of the fetal stage, the head is about half the length of the unborn child. In the neonate, it is about one-fourth the length of the body. The head gradually diminishes in proportion to the rest of the body, even though it doubles in size by adulthood.

Among adults, the arms are nearly three times the length of the head. The legs are about four times as long—nearly half the length of the body. Among neonates, the arms and legs are about equal in length. Each is only about one and a half times the length of the head. By the first birthday, the neck has begun to lengthen visibly, as have the arms and legs. The arms grow more rapidly than the legs do at first (an example of the cephalocaudal trend), and by the second birthday, the arms are actually longer than the legs. The legs then grow more rapidly, soon catching up with and surpassing the arms in length.

We have described typical growth patterns. Most infants follow these patterns and thrive. Some do not. *Question: What is failure to thrive?*

Failure to Thrive

Haley is four months old. Her mother is breast-feeding her, as she puts it, "all the time," because Haley is not gaining weight. Not gaining weight for a while is normal enough, but Haley is also irritable, and she feeds fitfully, sometimes refusing the breast entirely. Her pediatrician is evaluating her for a syndrome called **failure to thrive (FTT)** .

We live in one of the world's most bountiful nations. Few have trouble accessing food. Nevertheless, a number of infants, such as Haley, show FTT, which is a serious disorder that impairs growth in infancy and early childhood (Drotar & Robinson, 2000). FTT is sometimes a fuzzy diagnosis. Historically, researchers have spoken of biologically based (or "organic") FTT versus nonbiologically based ("nonorganic") FTT. The idea is that in organic FTT, an underlying health problem accounts for the

failure to thrive (FTT) A disorder of impaired growth in infancy and early childhood characterized by failure to gain weight within normal limits.

failure to obtain or make use of adequate nutrition. Nonorganic FTT (abbreviated NOFTT in the research literature) apparently has psychological and/or social roots. In either case, the infant does not make normal gains in weight and size (Robinson, Drotar, & Boutry, 2001).

Regardless of the cause or causes, feeding problems are central. Research has shown that infants with FTT tend to be introduced to solid and finger foods later than other children. As in Haley's case, they are more likely to be described as variable eaters and less often as being hungry (Wright & Birks, 2000). FTT is linked not only to slow physical growth but also to cognitive, behavioural, and emotional problems (Boddy, Skuse, & Andrews, 2000; Mackner, Black, & Starr, 2003; Robinson et al., 2001). For example, between the ages of two and twelve months, infants with FTT express more negative feelings, vocalize less, and often refuse to make eye contact with adults (Steward, 2001). Another study found that at the age of eight and a half, children who had been diagnosed with FTT at the median age of twenty months remained smaller, were less cognitively advanced, and had more emotional and behavioural difficulties than other children (Dykman, Casey, Ackerman, & McPherson, 2001).

Many investigators believe that deficiencies in caregiver-child interaction play a major role in the development of FTT (Robinson et al., 2001). For example, compared with mothers of healthy infants, mothers of infants with FTT show fewer adaptive social interactions (they are less likely to "go with the flow") and fewer positive feelings toward their infants. The mothers also terminate feedings more arbitrarily (Robinson et al., 2001). Perhaps as a consequence, children with FTT are less likely than other children to be securely attached to their mothers (Ward, Lee, & Lipper, 2000). Why are the mothers of children with FTT less likely to help their children to feel secure? Many have a large number of children, an unstable home environment, or psychological problems of their own (Mackner et al., 2003).

Because FTT often results from a combination of factors, treatment may not be easy. Children with FTT need both nutritional support and attention to possible adjustment problems (Robinson et al., 2001). It turns out that Haley's parents will profit from both personal counselling and advice on relating to Haley.

Catch-Up Growth

A child's growth can be slowed from its genetically predetermined course by many organic factors, including illness and dietary deficiency. However, once the problem is alleviated, the child's rate of growth frequently accelerates and returns to approximate its normal deflected course. The tendency to return to one's genetically determined pattern of growth is referred to as **canalization**. Once Haley's parents receive counselling and once Haley's FTT is overcome, Haley will put on weight rapidly and catch up to the norms for her age.

canalization The tendency of growth rates to return to genetically determined patterns after undergoing environmentally induced change.

Nutrition: Fuelling Development

Most children in Canada do thrive. The overall nutritional status of Canadian children is good compared with that of children in most countries. The nutritional status of poor children has improved through federal community-based programs such as the Community Action Program for Children (CAPC) and the Canada Prenatal Nutrition Program (CPNP). Even so, infants and young children from low-income families are more likely than other children to display signs of poor nutrition, such as anemia and FTT (Conference Board of Canada, 2005; National Center for Children in Poverty, 2004). For more information on children in poverty, go to http://www.campaign2000.ca/index.html or http://www.nccp.org *Question: What are the nutritional needs of infants?*

From birth, infants should be fed either breast milk or an iron-fortified infant formula. The introduction of solid foods is not recommended until the infant can indicate hunger by leaning forward and fullness by turning away from food. These behaviours normally occur at four to six months of age. The Canadian Paediatric Society, however, recommends exclusive breast feeding for the first six months of life and suggests that healthy full-term infants be fed breast milk throughout the first year—longer if possible (Boland, 2005; WHO, 2003). For more information about infant nutrition, including guidelines for introducing solid foods, visit the Canadian Paediatric Society at http://www.cps.ca. An infant's first solid food is usually iron-enriched cereal, followed by strained fruits, then vegetables, and finally meats, poultry, and fish. Whole cow's milk is normally delayed until the infant is nine to twelve months old. Finger foods such as teething biscuits are introduced in the latter part of the first year.

The Canadian Paediatric Society, Dietitians of Canada, and Health Canada, (1998) have provided useful guidelines for infant nutrition in their *Nutrition for Healthy Term Infants* document:

- Build up to a variety of foods. Introduce new foods one at a time (three to four days between each new food), if possible, to determine whether they make a difference in the infant's behaviour. (The infant may be allergic to a new food, and introducing foods one at a time helps isolate a new food's possible effects on the infant.)
- In general, pay attention to the infant's appetite to help avoid overfeeding or underfeeding. (If the infant seems to have a poor appetite, discuss it with your pediatrician.)
- Do not restrict fat and cholesterol too much. (For example, do not substitute skim milk for whole milk.) Infants need calories and some fat.
- Do not overdo high-fibre foods.
- In general, avoid items with added sugar and salt.
- Encourage high-iron foods; infants need more iron, pound for pound, than adults do.

When in doubt, parents should check with a nutritionist, dietitian, or pediatrician. What is good for adults is not good for infants. Parents who are on low-fat, high-fibre diets to ward off cardiovascular problems, cancer, and other health problems should not assume that the same diet is healthful for infants.

Breast Feeding versus Bottle Feeding: Pros and Cons, Biological and Political

No one can argue that breast feeding is the "natural" way to nourish a baby. Of course it is. Breast feeding was the standard Canadian way of feeding infants until infant formulas were developed in the 1930s. Over the next several decades, breast feeding declined because women were entering the work force, bottle feeding was seen as "scientific," and the women's movement encouraged women to become liberated from traditional roles (Reiger, 2000). Breast feeding thus has political and social aspects as well as nutritional aspects (Law, 2000). Much of the decision of whether or not to breast-feed has to do with domestic and occupational arrangements, daycare, social support, reactions to public breast feeding, and beliefs about mother-infant bonding (Guttman & Zimmerman, 2000; Stewart-Knox, Gardiner, & Wright, 2003).

A survey of mothers or pregnant adolescents (aged twelve to nineteen) found that those who recognized the benefits of breast feeding were more likely to do it (Hannon, Willis, Bishop-Townsend, Martinez, & Scrimshaw, 2000). They reported benefits such as promoting mother-infant bonding and the infant's health. Barriers to breast feeding in this study and others (e.g., Barber, Abernathy, Steinmetz, & Charlebois, 1997; Palda, Guise, Wathen, & the Canadian Task Force on Preventive

Health Care, 2004; Stewart-Knox et al., 2003) include fear of pain, embarrassment by public exposure, and unease with the act itself. However, an influential person—such as the woman's partner or mother—often successfully encourages the mother to breast-feed (Mahoney & James, 2000; Rempel & Rempel, 2004). Community support through volunteer workers and visiting nurses also encourages women to breast-feed

Developing in a World of Diversity

Alleviating Protein-Energy Malnutrition (PEM)

Protein-energy malnutrition (PEM) is the most severe form of malnutrition. Protein is essential for growth, and food energy translates as calories. Here are a few facts about PEM from the World Health Organization (2004):

• PEM affects one child in four around the world. One-hundred fifty million children (27 percent) are underweight, and 182 million (33 percent) have stunted growth.
• More than 70 percent of children with PEM live in Asia, 26 percent live in Africa, and about 4 percent live in Latin America and the Caribbean.
• Children may encounter PEM before birth if their mother is malnourished.
• Malnutrition, also known as "the silent emergency," has contributed to about 60 percent of the 11 million deaths of children each year.
• Infants and young children are most vulnerable to growth impairment as a result of PEM because of their high protein and energy needs and their susceptibility to infection.
• Children with PEM suffer up to 160 days of illness per year.

The World Health Organization (2003b) produced step-by-step guidelines on the treatment of children with PEM in the clinical setting. The guidelines are being promoted for use worldwide by physicians, nurses, and

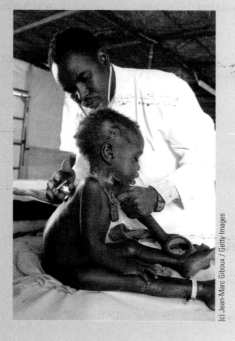

Fighting Malnutrition through Aid and Education
This doctor, who works for the Médecins sans Frontières (Doctors without Borders) organization, is tending a severely malnourished child in Maradi, Niger. Médecins sans Frontières is an independent organization that is committed to providing medical aid wherever necessary and raising awareness of the plight of the people they help.

all other frontline health workers. They include,

• educating health workers on the extent and severity of PEM;
• identifying children with severe malnutrition (symptoms include

hypoglycemia—shakiness resulting from low blood sugar levels—hypothermia, shock, dehydration, and severe anemia);
• preparing appropriate feeding formulas and food supplements;
• using antibiotics and other medicines to treat disease;
• monitoring the child's intake of food and the child's waste products, and preparing and using a weight chart;
• monitoring the child's vital signs—pulse, respiration rate, and temperature—and being aware of signs of danger;
• bathing the child; and
• involving mothers in care so that they can continue care at home, including feeding and play activities (for purposes of stimulation), and providing mothers with comprehensive instructions at discharge.

The mortality rate of children with PEM can be as high as 50 percent, but with adequate care, the rates can be reduced to less than 5 percent. For more information, contact Department of Nutrition for Health and Development
World Health Organization
1211 Geneva 27
Switzerland
Phone: 141 22 791 2624/4342
Fax: 141 22 791 4156

(Fetrick, Christensen, & Mitchell, 2003; Graffy, Taylor, Williams, & Eldridge, 2004). Better-educated women are more likely to breast-feed, even among low-income women (Hannon et al., 2000). A document titled Attachment Across Cultures, which can be found on the Public Health Agency of Canada website (http://www .attachmentacrosscultures.org/eindex.html), acknowledges that women's beliefs, values, and practices influence how they see their role in feeding and caring for their children.

In any event, breast feeding has become more popular during the past generation, largely because of increased knowledge of its health benefits, even among women at the lower end of the socioeconomic spectrum (Hannon et al., 2000). Today, most Canadian mothers—about four in five—initiate breast feeding their children (Statistics Canada, Community Health Survey, 2003). However, only about one woman in five continues to breast-feed after six months. The Canadian Paediatric Society recommends that women breast-feed exclusively for six months and continue breast feeding for up to two years and beyond (Health Canada, 2004).

Question: Why do women bottle-feed or breast-feed their children? There are several reasons why women choose one form of feeding over the other. Many women bottle-feed because they return to work after childbirth and therefore are unavailable or simply exhausted. However, early childhood educators and early childhood caregivers have an opportunity to assist mothers who wish to continue to breast-feed their children upon their return to work. Working out a flexible feeding schedule and allowing mothers to drop in for feedings during the day are ways caregivers can support breast feeding. Another support strategy is to offer mothers a choice of pumping and bottling breast milk to use at daycare. Some mothers choose to bottle-feed because it permits others (e.g., fathers, partners, caregivers) to share in feeding—around the clock. Even though bottle feeding requires preparing formulas or pumping breast milk, many women find it to be less troublesome.

Question: What are the advantages and disadvantages of breast milk? Let us begin with the positive (American Academy of Pediatrics, 2002; Health Canada, 2004; Kramer et al., 2001; Lawrence, 2001):

- Breast milk conforms to human digestion processes (i.e., it is unlikely to upset the stomach and cause infants to vomit).
- Breast milk possesses the nutrients that babies require (even though most physicians prescribe supplementary vitamins and, sometimes, minerals).
- As the infant matures, the composition of breast milk changes to help meet the infant's changing needs.
- Breast milk contains the mother's antibodies; when they are transmitted to the infant, they help to prevent problems ranging from ear infections, pneumonia, wheezing, bronchiolitis, and tetanus to chicken pox, bacterial meningitis, and typhoid fever.
- Breast milk helps protect against the form of cancer known as childhood lymphoma (a cancer of the lymph glands).
- Diarrhea can be a persistent and deadly disease for millions of infants in developing countries, and breast milk decreases the likelihood of developing serious and lingering cases of diarrhea.
- Infants who are nourished by breast milk are less likely to develop allergic responses and constipation than infants who are bottle-fed.
- Infants who are nourished by breast milk are less likely to develop obesity later in life.
- Breast feeding is associated with better neural and behavioural organization in the infant, at least in the short term (S. Hart, Boylan, Carroll, Musick, & Lampe, 2003).

Truth or Fiction Revisited: Therefore, it is true that drinking breast milk is connected with a better chance of avoiding obesity later in life. Perhaps it is because breast milk is lower in fat than whole milk.

Breast feeding also has health benefits for the mother: It reduces the risk of early breast cancer and ovarian cancer, and it builds the strength of bones, which can reduce the likelihood of the hip fractures that result from osteoporosis following menopause. Breast feeding also helps shrink the uterus after delivery.

Potential contraindications to breast feeding outlined by the Canadian Paediatric Society, Dietitians of Canada, and Health Canada (1998) include certain drugs, alcohol, environmental contaminants such as polychlorinated biphenyls (PCBs), and maternal infection (e.g., HIV). In the case of HIV, there is a downside to breast feeding. For example, one of the bodily fluids that transmits HIV (the virus that causes AIDS) is breast milk. Researchers estimate that as many as one-third of the world's infants who have HIV/AIDS were infected in this manner (Richardson, John-Stewart, Hughes, Nduati, Mbori-Ngacha, Overbaugh, & Kreiss, 2003; United Nations Special Session on AIDS, 2001). Since alcohol, drugs taken by the mother, and environmental hazards can also be transmitted to infants through breast feeding (see Chapter 3), breast milk may not always be as pure as it would seem. Moreover, in order for breast milk to contain the necessary nutrients, the mother must be adequately nourished herself. In many cases, mothers in developing countries do not eat sufficiently well to pass along proper nutrition to their infants (Crossette, 2000).

Other challenges to breast feeding include the mother's assumption of the sole responsibility for nighttime feedings. She also encounters the physical demands of producing and expelling milk, a tendency for soreness in the breasts, and the inconvenience of being continually available to meet the infant's feeding needs.

The hormones prolactin and oxytocin are involved in breast feeding. *Prolactin* means in favour of ("pro") producing milk. By a few days after delivery, prolactin stimulates the mammary glands to produce milk. Oxytocin is secreted in response to suckling and stimulates the breasts to eject milk. When breast feeding is discontinued, prolactin and oxytocin are no longer secreted, and lactation ends.

Women who are seeking help with or want more information about breast feeding can visit http://www.BreastfeedingTaskForLA.org, http://www.breastfeeding.org, http://www.breastfeeding.com, http://www.lalecheleague.org, or http://www.ILCA.org.

Active Review

1. Cephalocaudal development describes the processes by which development proceeds from the _____ to the lower parts of the body.

2. The _____ principle means that development proceeds from the trunk outward.

3. Infants usually double their birth weight in about _____ months and triple it by the first birthday.

4. Mothers of infants with failure to thrive, compared to mothers of healthy infants, show fewer (positive or negative?) feelings toward their infants.

5. After illness or dietary deficiency, children show _____, which is a tendency to return to their genetically determined pattern of growth.

6. Breast milk contains _____ that can prevent problems such as ear infections, meningitis, tetanus, and chicken pox.

Reflect & Relate: How closely did your parents pay attention to your height and weight? Did they chart it? When did you begin to think that you were average or above or below average in height and weight? What effect did your size have on your self-concept and self-esteem?

Go to
WWW www.voyages1ce.nelson.com
for an interactive version of this review.

Development of the Brain and Nervous System

Most students hearing about the nervous system for the first time often wonder what benefit to humans it is to have such a system. Who, after all, wants to be nervous? In reality, the nervous system is a system of **nerves** involved in heartbeat, visual-motor coordination, thought and language, and so on. The human nervous system is more complex than that of other animals. Although elephants and whales have heavier brains, our brains make up a larger proportion of our body weight.

Development of Neurons

The basic units of the nervous system are **neurons**. *Questions: What are neurons? How do they develop?* Neurons are cells that receive and transmit messages from one part of the body to another. The messages transmitted by neurons account for phenomena as varied as reflexes, the perception of an itch from a mosquito bite, the visual-motor coordination of a skier, the composition of a concerto, and the solution of a math problem.

People are born with about 100 billion neurons, most of which are in the brain. Neurons vary according to their functions and locations in the body. Some neurons in the brain are only a fraction of an inch in length, whereas neurons in the leg can grow several feet long. Each neuron possesses a cell body, dendrites, and an axon (see Figure 5.3). **Dendrites** are short fibres that extend from the cell body and receive incoming messages from up to 1000 adjoining transmitting neurons. The **axon** extends trunklike from the cell body and accounts for much of the difference in length in neurons. An axon can be up to several feet in length if it is carrying messages from the toes upward. Messages are released from axon terminals in the form of chemicals called **neurotransmitters.** These messages are then received by the dendrites of adjoining neurons, muscles, or glands. As the child matures, the axons of neurons grow in length, and the dendrites and axon terminals proliferate, creating vast interconnected networks for the transmission of complex messages.

Myelin

Many neurons are tightly wrapped with white, fatty **myelin sheaths** that give them the appearance of a string of white sausages. The high fat content of the myelin sheath insulates the neuron from electrically charged atoms in the fluids that encase the nervous system. In this way, leakage of the electric current being carried along the axon is minimized, and messages are conducted more efficiently.

The term **myelination** refers to the process by which axons are coated with myelin. Myelination is not complete at birth. Myelination is part of the maturation process that leads to the abilities to crawl and walk during the first year after birth. Incomplete myelination accounts for some of the helplessness of neonates. Myelination of the prefrontal matter of the brain continues into the second decade of life and is connected with advances in the capacity of working memory (Klingberg, Vaidya, Gabrieli, Moseley, & Hedehus, 1999; Paus, Zijdenbos, Worsley, Collins, Blumenthal, Giedd, Rapoport, & Evans, 1999). Breakdown of myelin is believed to be associated with Alzheimer's disease, a source of cognitive decline that usually begins in middle or late adulthood (Bartzokis, 2004; Connor, 2004).

In the disease **multiple sclerosis**, myelin is replaced by a hard, fibrous tissue that disrupts the timing of neural transmission, thus interfering with muscle control. The disorder phenylketonuria (PKU) leads to mental retardation by inhibiting the formation of myelin in the brain (Dyer, 1999). Congenital infection with HIV has been

---

nerves Bundles of axons from many neurons.

neurons Nerve cells; cells found in the nervous system that transmit messages.

dendrites The rootlike parts of a neuron that receive impulses from other neurons (from the Greek dendron, meaning "tree" and referring to the branching appearance of dendrites).

axon A long, thin part of a neuron that transmits impulses to other neurons through small branching structures called axon terminals.

neurotransmitter A chemical substance that enables the transmission of neural impulses from one neuron to another.

myelin sheath (MY-uh-lin) A fatty, whitish substance that encases and insulates neurons, permitting more rapid transmission of neural impulses.

myelination The process by which axons are coated with myelin.

multiple sclerosis A disorder in which myelin is replaced by hard fibrous tissue that impedes neural transmission.

Figure 5.3

Anatomy of a Neuron

"Messages" enter neurons through dendrites, are transmitted along the axon, and then are sent through axon terminals to muscles, glands, and other neurons. Neurons develop by means of proliferation of dendrites and axon terminals and through myelination.

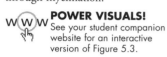
POWER VISUALS! See your student companion website for an interactive version of Figure 5.3.

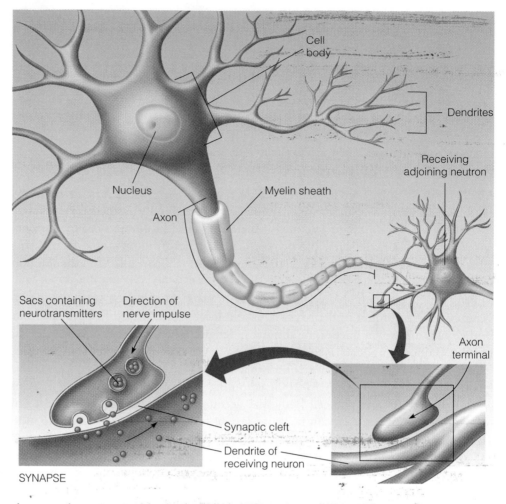

shown to be connected with abnormalities in the formation of myelin and with cognitive and motor impairment, as measured by the Bayley Scales of Infant Development (Blanchette, Smith, Fernandes-Penney, King, & Read, 2001).

Development of the Brain

Questions: What is the brain? How does the brain develop? The brain is the command centre of the developing organism. (If you like computer analogies, think of the brain as the central processing unit.) It contains neurons and provides the basis for physical, cognitive, personal, and social development.

The brain of the neonate weighs a little less than a pound—nearly one-fourth of its adult weight. *Truth or Fiction Revisited:* In keeping with the principles of cephalocaudal growth, the brain reaches a good deal more than half its adult weight by the first birthday. It actually triples in weight, reaching nearly 70 percent of its adult weight (see Figure 5.4). Let us look at the brain, as shown in Figure 5.5, and discuss the development of the structures within.

Structures of the Brain

Many nerves that connect the spinal cord to higher levels of the brain pass through the **medulla.** The medulla is vital in the control of basic functions, such as heartbeat and respiration. The medulla is part of an area called the brain stem, which may be implicated in sudden infant death syndrome (SIDS; see Chapter 4).

medulla (muh-DUH-luh) An oblong-shaped area of the hindbrain involved in heartbeat and respiration.

Above the medulla lies the **cerebellum,** which is Latin for "little brain." The cerebellum helps the child maintain balance, control motor behaviour, and coordinate eye movements with bodily sensations.

The **cerebrum** is the crowning glory of the brain. It makes possible the breadth and depth of human learning, thought, memory, and language. Only in human beings does the cerebrum constitute such a large proportion of the brain. The surface of the cerebrum consists of two hemispheres—left and right—that become increasingly wrinkled as the child develops, coming to show ridges and valleys called fissures. This surface is the cerebral cortex. The wrinkles allow a great deal of surface area to be packed into the brain. ***Truth or Fiction Revisited:*** Yes, the cerebral cortex is only one-eighth of an inch thick. Yet it is here that thought and reasoning occur. It is here that we display sensory information from the world outside and command muscles to move.

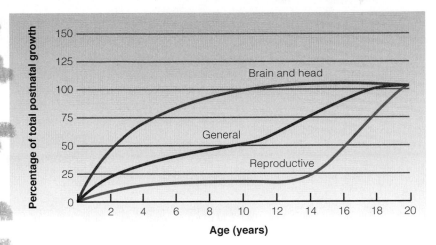

Figure 5.4

Growth of Body Systems as a Percentage of Total Postnatal Growth
The brain of the neonate weighs about one-fourth of its adult weight. In keeping with the principle of cephalocaudal growth, the brain will triple in weight by the infant's first birthday, reaching nearly 70 percent of its adult weight.

cerebellum (ser-uh-BEH-lum) The part of the hindbrain involved in muscle coordination and balance.

cerebrum (seh-REE-brum) The large mass of the forebrain, which consists of two hemispheres.

Growth Spurts of the Brain
The brain makes gains in size and weight in different ways. One way is in the formation of neurons, a process completed by birth. The first major growth spurt of the brain occurs during the fourth and fifth months of prenatal development, when neurons proliferate. A second growth spurt in the brain occurs between the twenty-fifth week of prenatal development and the end of the second year after birth. Whereas the first growth spurt of the brain is due to the formation of neurons, the second growth spurt is due primarily to the proliferation of dendrites and axon terminals.

Brain Development in Infancy
There is a clear link between what infants can do and the myelination of areas within the brain. At birth, the parts of the brain involved in heartbeat and respiration, sleeping and arousal, and reflex activity are fairly well myelinated and functional.

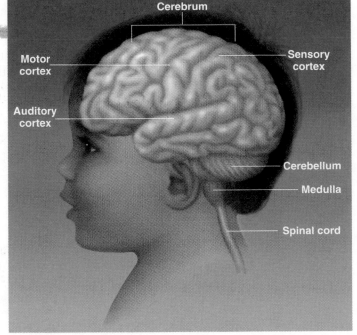

Figure 5.5

Structures of the Brain

The convolutions of the cortex increase its surface area and, apparently, its intellectual capacity. (In this case, wrinkles are good.) The medulla is involved in vital functions such as respiration and heartbeat; the cerebellum is involved in balance and coordination.

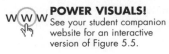 **POWER VISUALS!**
See your student companion website for an interactive version of Figure 5.5.

Myelination of motor pathways allows neonates to show stereotyped reflexes, but otherwise neonates' physical activity tends to be random and ill-organized. Myelination of the motor area of the cerebral cortex begins at about the fourth month of prenatal development. Myelin develops rapidly along the major motor pathways from the cerebral cortex during the last month of pregnancy and continues after birth. The development of intentional physical activity coincides with myelination as the unorganized movements of the neonate come under increasing control. Myelination of the nerves to muscles is largely developed by the age of two years, although research using magnetic resonance imaging (MRI) suggests that myelination continues to some degree into adolescence (Paus et al., 1999).

Although neonates respond to touch and can see and hear quite well, the areas of the cortex that are involved in vision, hearing, and the skin senses are less well myelinated at birth. As myelination progresses and the interconnections between the various areas of the cortex thicken, children become increasingly capable of complex and integrated sensorimotor activities (Tanner, 1989).

Neonates whose mothers read *The Cat in the Hat* aloud during the last few weeks of pregnancy show a preference for this story (see Chapter 3). It turns out that myelination of the neurons involved in the sense of hearing begins at about the sixth month of pregnancy—coinciding with the period in which fetuses begin to respond to sound. Myelination of these pathways is developing rapidly at term and continues until about the age of four years.

Although the fetus shows some response to light during the third trimester, it is hard to imagine what use the fetus could have for vision. It turns out that the neurons involved in vision begin to myelinate only shortly before full term, but then they complete the process of myelination rapidly. Within a short five to six months after birth, vision has become the dominant sense.

Nature and Nurture in the Development of the Brain

Development of the areas of the brain that control sensation and movement begins as a result of maturation, but sensory stimulation and physical activity during early infancy also spur their development (Grossman, Churchill, McKinney, Kodish, Otte, & Greenough, 2003; Hensch, 2003). *Question: How do nature and nurture affect the development of the brain?* Experience seems to fine-tune the unfolding of the genetic code.

Research with animals shows how sensory stimulation sparks growth of the cortex. Researchers have created rat "amusement parks" with toys such as ladders, platforms, and boxes to demonstrate the effects of enriched environments. Rats have also been provided with exploratory sessions in mazes and in fields with barriers. In these studies, "enriched" rats invariably develop heavier brains than control animals. The weight differences in part reflect greater numbers of dendrites and axon terminals (Jones, Klintsova, Kilman, Sirevaag, & Greenough, 1997; Werry, 1991). On the other hand, animals raised in darkness show shrinkage of the visual cortex, impaired vision, and impaired visual-motor coordination (Greenough, Black, & Wallace, 1987; Klintsova & Greenough, 1999).

Human brains also are affected by experience. Infants actually have more connections among neurons than adults do (Rakic, 1991). Connections that are activated by experience survive; the others do not (Casaer, 1993; Greenough, 1991; Tsuneishi & Casaer, 2000; Weinberg, 2004).

The great adaptability of the brain appears to be a double-edged sword. Adaptability allows us to develop different patterns of neural connections to meet the demands of different environments. However, lack of stimulation—especially during critical early periods of development (as we will see later)—can impair adaptability.

Brain nourishment, like early experience, plays a role in the brain achieving what is permitted by the child's genes. Inadequate nutrition in the fetus, especially during the prenatal growth spurt of the brain, has several negative effects. These include smallness in the overall size of the brain, the formation of fewer neurons, and less myelination (Bauerfeld & Lachenmeyer, 1992; Lukas & Campbell, 2000).

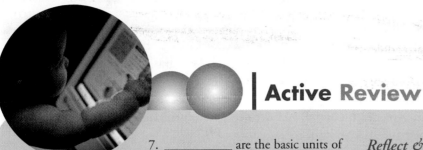

Active Review

7. _____ are the basic units of the nervous system.

8. Each neuron possesses a cell body, dendrites, and a(n) _____.

9. The brain reaches nearly _____ percent of its adult weight by the first birthday.

10. The wrinkled part of the brain, called the _____, enables the child to maintain balance and to control physical behaviour.

Reflect & Relate: Are you surprised that there is such a close connection between experience and development of the brain? How does the information presented in this section fit with the adage "Use it or lose it"?

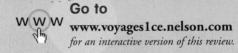

Go to

W W W **www.voyages1ce.nelson.com**
for an interactive version of this review.

Motor Development: How Moving

"Allyn couldn't walk yet at ten months, but she zoomed after me in her walker, giggling her head off." "Anthony was walking forward and backward by the age of thirteen months."

These are some of the types of comments parents make about their children's motor development. *Questions: What is motor development? How does it occur?* Motor development involves the activity of muscles, leading to changes in posture, movement, and coordination of movement with the infant's developing sensory apparatus. Motor development provides some of the most fascinating changes in infants, in part because so much seems to happen so fast—and so much of it during the first year.

Motor development, as with physical development, follows cephalocaudal and proximodistal patterns and differentiation. As noted earlier, infants gain control of their heads and upper torsos before they can effectively use their arms. This trend illustrates cephalocaudal development. Infants can also control their trunks and shoulders before they can use their hands and fingers, demonstrating the proximodistal trend.

Click on the "Gross Motor" clip in Module 1, Section 2, to see the development of gross motor skills in children of different ages. Watch the development of fine motor skills, such as gaining control of hands and fingers, in children of different ages. Click on the "Fine Motor" clip in Module 1, Section 2.

Lifting and Holding the Torso and Head: Heads Up

Neonates can move their heads slightly to the side. They can thus avoid suffocation if they are lying facedown and their noses or mouths are obstructed by bedding. At about one month, infants can raise their heads. By about two months, they can also lift their chests while lying on their stomachs.

When neonates are held, their heads must be supported. But by three to six months of age, infants generally manage to hold their heads quite well, so that supporting the head is no longer necessary. Unfortunately, infants who can normally support their heads cannot do so when they are lifted or moved about in a jerky manner; infants who are handled carelessly can thus develop neck injuries.

Control of the Hands: Getting a Grip on Things

The development of hand skills is a clear example of proximodistal development. Infants will track (follow) slowly moving objects with their eyes shortly after birth, but they will not generally reach for them. They show a grasp reflex but do not reliably reach for the objects that appear to interest them. Voluntary reaching and grasping require visual-motor coordination. By about the age of three months, infants will make clumsy swipes at objects, failing to grasp them, because their aim is poor or they close their hands too soon or too late.

Between the ages of four and six months, infants become more successful at grasping objects (Santos, Gabbard, & Goncalves, 2000). However, they may not know how to let go of an object and may hold it indefinitely, until their attention is diverted and the hand opens accidentally. Four to six months is a good age for giving children rattles, large plastic spoons, mobiles, and other brightly coloured hanging toys that can be grasped but are harmless when they wind up in the mouth.

Grasping is reflexive at first. Voluntary grasping (holding) replaces reflexive grasping by the age of three to four months. Infants first use an **ulnar grasp,** in which they hold objects clumsily between their fingers and their palm (Butterworth, Verweij, & Hopkins, 1997). By the age of four to six months, they can transfer objects back and forth between hands. The oppositional thumb comes into play at about the age of nine to twelve months. Use of the thumb gives infants the ability to pick up tiny objects in a **pincer grasp** (Figure 5.6). By about eleven months of age, infants can hold objects in each hand and inspect them in turn.

Between the ages of five and eleven months, infants adjust their hands in anticipation of grasping moving targets. They also gather information from the objects' movements to predict their future location and catch them (Wentworth et al., 2000). Think of the complex concepts it requires to explain this behaviour and how well infants perform it—without any explanation at all! Of course, I am not suggesting that infants solve problems in geometry and physics to grasp moving objects; that interpretation, as developmental psychologist Marshall M. Haith (1998) would describe it, would put a "cog in infant cognition."

Another aspect of visual-motor coordination is stacking blocks. On average, children can stack two blocks at fifteen months, three blocks at eighteen months, and five blocks at twenty-four months (Wentworth, Benson, & Haith, 2000). At about twenty-four months of age, children can also copy horizontal and vertical lines.

Locomotion: Getting a Move On

Locomotion is movement from one place to another. Children gain the capacity to move their bodies through a sequence of activities that includes rolling over, sitting up, crawling, creeping, walking, and running (see Figure 5.7). There is much variation in the ages at which infants first engage in these activities. Although the sequence mostly remains the same, some children will skip a step. For example, an infant may creep without ever having crawled.

ulnar grasp A method of grasping objects in which the fingers close somewhat clumsily against the palm.

pincer grasp The use of the opposing thumb to grasp objects between the thumb and other fingers.

© 2002 Laura Dwight

Figure 5.6
Pincer Grasp

Infants first hold objects between their fingers and palm. Once the oppositional thumb comes into play at about 9 to 12 months of age, infants are able to pick up tiny objects using what is termed a *pincer grasp.*

locomotion Movement from one place to another.

Most infants can roll over, from back to stomach and from stomach to back, by about the age of six months. They can also sit (and support their upper bodies, necks, and heads) for extended periods if they are aided by a person or placed in a seat with a strap, such as a high chair. By about seven months of age, infants usually begin to sit up by themselves.

At about eight to nine months, most infants begin to crawl, a motor activity in which they lie prone and use their arms to pull themselves along, dragging their bellies and feet behind. Creeping, a more sophisticated form of locomotion in which infants move themselves along up on their hands and knees, requires a good deal more coordination and usually appears a month or so after crawling (Figure 5.8).

There are fascinating alternatives to creeping. Some infants travel from one place to another by rolling over and over. Some lift themselves and swing their arms while in a sitting position, in effect dragging along on their buttocks. Still others do a "bear walk" in which they move on their hands and feet, without allowing their elbows and knees to touch the floor. And some, as noted, just crawl until they are ready to stand and walk from place to place while holding on to chairs, other objects, and people.

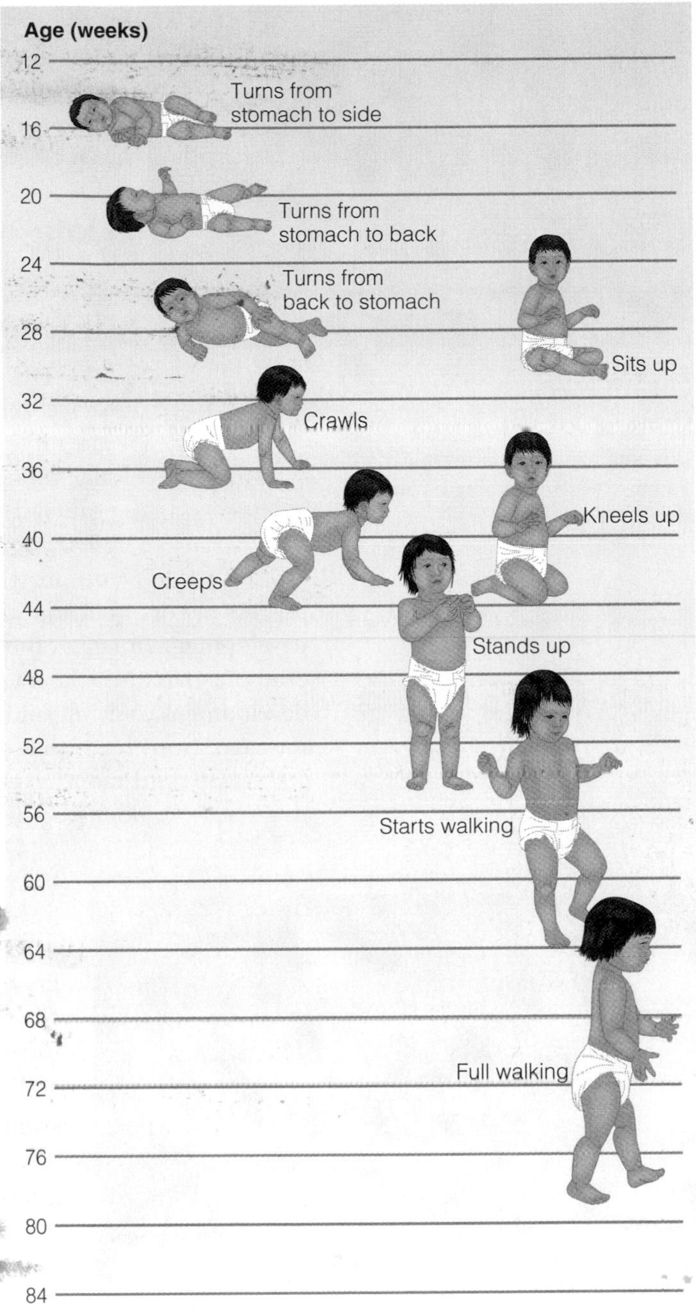

Standing overlaps with crawling and creeping. Most infants can remain in a standing position by holding on to something at the age of eight or nine months. At this age they may also be able to walk a bit when supported by adults. Such walking is voluntary and does not have the stereotyped appearance of the walking reflex described in Chapter 4. About two months later, they can pull themselves to a standing position by holding on to the sides of their cribs or other objects and can stand briefly without holding on. Soon afterward, they walk about unsteadily while holding on. By twelve to fifteen months or so, they walk by themselves, earning them the name **toddler** (Figure 5.9). Attempts to master these new motor skills are often accompanied by signs of pleasure such as smiling, laughing, and babbling (Mayes & Zigler, 1992).

Toddlers soon run about, supporting their relatively heavy heads and torsos by spreading their legs in a bow-legged fashion. Because they are top-heavy and inexperienced, they fall frequently. Some toddlers require consoling when they fall. Others spring right up and run on again with barely an interruption. Many toddlers are skillful at navigating steep and shallow slopes (Weiner & Adolph, 1993). They walk down shallow slopes but prudently elect to slide or crawl down steep ones.

Walking lends children new freedom. It allows them to get about rapidly and to grasp objects that were formerly out of reach. Give toddlers a large ball to toss and run after; it is about the least expensive and most enjoyable toy they can be given.

Age (weeks)

Turns from stomach to side

Turns from stomach to back

Turns from back to stomach

Sits up

Crawls

Kneels up

Creeps

Stands up

Starts walking

Full walking

Figure 5.7

Motor Development in Infancy

Motor development proceeds in an orderly sequence, but there is considerable variation in the timing of the marker events shown in this figure. An infant who is a bit behind will most likely develop without problems, and a precocious infant will not necessarily become a rocket scientist (or gymnast).

toddler A child who walks with short, uncertain steps. Toddlerhood lasts from about 18 to 30 months of age, thereby bridging infancy and early childhood.

Figure 5.8

Creeping

Creeping requires considerable coordination of arm and leg movements. Creeping usually appears a month or so after crawling.

Figure 5.9

Walking

By 12 to 15 months or so, babies walk by themselves, earning them the name *toddler*.

As children mature, their muscle strength, the density of their bones, and their balance and coordination improve. By the age of two years, they can climb steps one at a time, placing both feet on each step. They can run well, walk backward, kick a large ball, and jump several inches.

Nature and Nurture in Motor Development

Cross-cultural studies highlight the variation of when infants are exposed to motor opportunities in their physical environments. Infant-rearing practices vary from culture to culture (e.g., Hopkins & Westra, 1988; Seymour, 1999). For example, the Kipsigis of Kenya and the West Indians of Jamaica actively promote physical and motor development early on, and their infants generally reach such motor milestones as sitting, walking, and running before European and European North American infants do (Allen & Alexander, 1990; Hopkins & Westra, 1988; Super, 1981). Although genetic factors may be involved in the earlier motor development, environmental factors also appear to play a role. African infants excel in areas of motor development in which they have received considerable stimulation and practice. For example, parents in Africa and in cultures of African origin, such as Jamaica, stress the development of sitting and walking and provide experiences, including stretching and massage, from birth that stimulate the development of these behaviours. From the second or third months, other activities are added, such as propping infants in a sitting position, bouncing them on their feet, and exercising the stepping reflex.

Question: What are the roles of nature and nurture in motor development? Research with humans and other species leaves little doubt that both maturation (nature) and experience (nurture) are involved in motor development (Muir, 2000; Pryce, Bettschen, Bahr, & Feldon, 2001; Roncesvalles, Woollacott, & Jensen, 2001). Certain voluntary motor activities are not possible until the brain has matured in terms of myelination and the differentiation of the motor areas of the cortex. Although the neonate shows stepping and swimming reflexes, these behaviours are controlled by more primitive parts of the brain. They disappear when cortical development inhibits some functions of the lower parts of the brain, and, when they reappear, they differ in quality.

Infants also need some opportunity to experiment before they can engage in milestones such as sitting up and walking. Even so, much of these advances can apparently be attributed to maturation. ***Truth or Fiction Revisited:*** It is true that Native American Hopi infants spend the first year strapped to a board but begin to walk at about the same time as children who are reared in other cultures. In classic research, Wayne and Marsena Dennis (1940) reported on the motor development of Native American Hopi children who spent the first year strapped to a cradle board. Although denied a full year of experience in locomotion, the Hopi infants gained the capacity to walk early in their second year, at about the same time as other children. A cross-cultural study (Hindley, Filliozat, Klackenberg, Nicolet-Neister, & Sand, 1966) reported that infants in five European cities began to walk at about the same time (generally, between twelve and fifteen months), despite cultural differences in encouragement to walk.

On the other hand, evidence is mixed on whether specific training can accelerate the appearance of motor skills. For example, in a classic study with identical twins, Arnold Gesell (1929) gave one twin extensive training in hand coordination, block building, and stair climbing from early infancy. The other twin was allowed to develop on his own. At first, the trained twin had better skills, but as time passed, the untrained twin became just as skilled.

Although the appearance of motor skills can be accelerated by training (Adolph, Vereijken, & Shrout, 2003; Zelazo, 1998), the effect seems slight. Practice in the absence of neural readiness has limited results. There is also little evidence that training leads to eventual superior motor skills.

Although being strapped to a cradle board did not permanently prevent the motor development of Hopi infants, Wayne Dennis (1960) reported that infants in an Iranian orphanage were significantly retarded in their motor development. In contrast to the Hopi infants, the institutionalized infants were exposed to extreme social and physical deprivation. Under these conditions, they grew apathetic, and all aspects of development suffered. But there is also a bright side to this tale of deprivation. The motor development of similar infants in a Lebanese orphanage accelerated dramatically in response to such minimal intervention as being propped up in their cribs and being given a few colourful toys (Dennis & Sayegh, 1965).

(c) Mike Greenlar / The Image Works

A Native American Hopi Infant Strapped to a Cradle Board
Researchers have studied Hopi children who are strapped to cradle boards during their first year to see whether their motor development is delayed significantly. Once released from their boards, Hopi children make rapid advances in motor development, suggesting the importance of maturation in motor development.

Active Review

11. Infants can first raise their heads at about the age of _____ month(s).

12. Infants first use a(n) (ulnar or pincer?) grasp for holding objects.

13. Developmentalists assess infants' ability to stack blocks as a measure of their _____-motor coordination.

14. Infants (sit up or crawl?) before they (sit up or crawl?).

15. As children mature, their bones (increase or decrease?) in density.

16. Research reveals that both maturation and _____ play indispensable roles in motor development.

17. Arnold Gesell (did or did not?) find that extensive training in hand coordination, block building, and stair climbing gave infants enduring advantages over infants untrained in these skills.

Reflect & Relate: "When did your baby first sit up?" "When did he walk?" Why are people so concerned about when infants do what? Imagine that you are speaking to a parent who is concerned that her child is not yet walking at fourteen months. What would you say to the parent? When should there be cause for concern?

Go to
www.voyages1ce.nelson.com
for an interactive version of this review.

Nature provides the limits—the "reaction range"—for the expression of inherited traits. Nurture determines whether the child will develop skills that reach the upper limits of the range. Even a fundamental skill such as locomotion is determined by a complex interplay of maturational and environmental factors (Adolph et al., 2003; Thelen, 2000). There may be little purpose in trying to train children to enhance their motor skills before they are ready. Once they are ready, however, teaching and practice do make a difference. One does not become an Olympic athlete without "good genes." But one also usually does not become an Olympic athlete without high-quality training. And because motor skills are important to the self-concepts of children, good teaching is all the more important.

Sensory and Perceptual Development: Taking in the World

What a world we live in—green hills and reddish skies; rumbling trucks, murmuring brooks, and voices; the sweet and the sour; the acrid and the perfumed; the metallic and the fuzzy. What an ever-changing display of sights, sounds, tastes, smells, and touches. The pleasures of the world, and its miseries, are known to us through sensory impressions and the organization of these impressions into personal inner maps of reality. Our eyes, our ears, the sensory receptors in our noses and our mouths, our skin senses—these are our tickets of admission to the world.

In Chapter 4 we examined the sensory capabilities of the neonate. *Question: How do sensation and perception develop in the infant?* In this section, we see how infants develop the ability to integrate disjointed **sensations** into meaningful patterns of events termed **perceptions.** We see what captures the attention of infants, and we see how young children develop into purposeful seekers of information—selecting the sensory impressions they choose to capture. We focus on the development of vision and hearing because most of the research on sensory and perceptual development in infancy has been done in these areas.

We will see that many things that are obvious to us are not so obvious to infants. You may know that a coffee cup is the same whether you see it from above or from the side, but make no such assumptions about the infant. You may know that an infant's mother is the same size whether she is standing next to the infant or approaching from two blocks away, but do not assume that the infant agrees with you.

We cannot ask infants to explain why they look at some things and not at others. Nor can we ask them if their mother appears to be the same size whether she is standing close to them or far away. But investigators of childhood sensation and perception have devised clever methods to answer these questions, and their findings provide us with fascinating insights into the perceptual processes of even the neonate. They reveal that many basic perceptual competencies are present early in life.

Development of Vision: The Better to See You With
Development of Visual Acuity and Peripheral Vision
Neonates are nearsighted. The most dramatic gains in visual acuity are made between birth and six months of age, with acuity reaching about 20/50 (Cavallini, Fazzi, Viviani, Astori, Zaviero, Bianchi, & Lanzi, 2002; Haith, 1990; Skoczenski, 2002). Gains in visual acuity then become more gradual, approximating adult levels (20/20) by about three to five years of age.

Neonates also have poor peripheral vision (Cavallini et al., 2002; Skoczenski, 2002). Adults can perceive objects that are nearly ninety degrees off to the side (i.e.,

sensation The stimulation of sensory organs such as the eyes, ears, and skin and the transmission of sensory information to the brain.

perception The process by which sensations are organized into a mental map of the world.

directly to the left or right), although objects at these extremes are unclear. Neonates cannot perceive visual stimuli that are off to the side by an angle of more than thirty degrees, but their peripheral vision expands to an angle of about forty-five degrees by the age of seven weeks (Macfarlane, Harris, & Barnes, 1976). By six months of age, their peripheral vision is about equal to that of an adult.

Let us now consider the development of visual perception. In so doing, we will see that infants frequently prefer the strange to the familiar and will avoid going off the deep end—sometimes.

Visual Preferences: How Do You Capture an Infant's Attention?

Questions: What captures the attention of infants? How do visual preferences develop? Neonates look at stripes longer than at blobs. This finding has been used in much of the research on visual acuity. Classic research found that by the age of eight to twelve weeks, most infants also show distinct preferences for curved lines over straight ones (Fantz et al., 1975).

Robert Fantz (1961) also wondered whether there was something intrinsically interesting about the human face that drew the attention of infants. To investigate this question, he showed two-month-old infants the six disks illustrated in Figure 5.10. One disk contained a caricature of human features; another, newsprint; and still another, a bull's-eye. The remaining three disks were featureless but were coloured red, white, and yellow. In this study, the infants fixated significantly longer on the human face.

Subsequent studies have suggested that the infants in Fantz's (1961) study may not have preferred the human face so much because it was a face but because it had a complex, intriguing pattern of dots (eyes) within an outline. In some of these studies, infants have been shown drawings that resemble a face and other drawings that contain the same elements of a face (such as eyes, nose, and mouth) but in scrambled order. Neonates pay about an equal amount of attention to both types of drawings (Easterbrook, Kisilevsky, Hains, & Muir, 1999a; Kisilevsky, Muir, & Laplante, 1999b). But by two months of age, they begin to prefer the "real"-face to the scrambled one (Johnson, Dziurawiec, Bartrip, & Morton, 1992; Morton & Johnson, 1991).

Researchers continue to be vitally interested in infants' preferences for the human face. The preference raises fascinating questions about whether humans come into the world "prewired" to prefer human stimuli to other stimuli that are just as complex, and—if so—just what it is about human stimuli that draws attention (Easterbrook et al., 1999a, 1999b). Therefore, studies along these lines continue. Some researchers argue that neonates do not "prefer" faces because they are faces per se but because of the structure of their immature visual systems (Simion, Cassia, Turati, & Valenza, 2001). A supportive study of thirty-four neonates found that the longer fixations on facelike stimuli resulted from a larger number of brief fixations (looks) rather than from a few prolonged fixations (Cassia, Simion, & Umilta, 2001). The infants' gaze, then, was

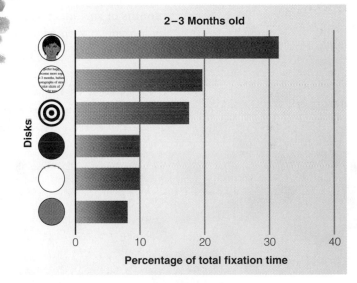

Figure 5.10

Preferences for Visual Stimuli in 2-Month-Olds

Infants appear to prefer complex to simple visual stimuli. By the time they are 2 months old, they also tend to show preference for the human face. Researchers continue to debate whether the face draws attention because of its content (i.e., being a face) or because of its stimulus characteristics (complexity, arrangement, etc.).

sort of bouncing around from feature to feature rather than "staring" at the face in general. The researchers interpreted the finding to show that the stimulus properties of the visual object are more important than the fact that it represents a human face. Even so, of course, the "immature visual system" would be providing some "prewired" basis for attending to the face.

Neonates can discriminate their mother's face from a stranger's after eight hours of mother-infant contact spread over four days (Bushnell, 2001). By three to five months of age, infants respond differently to happy, surprised, and sad faces (Muir & Hains, 1993). Moreover, infants as young as two months of age prefer attractive faces to unattractive faces (Ramsey, Langlois, Hoss, Rubenstein, & Griffin, 2004). This preference is more deeply ingrained by six months of age (Ramsey et al., 2004). Do standards of attractiveness have an inborn component, or are they learned (very!) early?

Neonates appear to direct their attention to the edges of objects. This pattern persists for the first several weeks (Bronson, 1991). When they are given the opportunity to look at human faces, one-month-old infants tend to pay most attention to the "edges"—that is, the chin, an ear, or the hairline. Two-month-old infants move in from the edge, as shown in Figure 5.11. They focus particularly on the eyes, although they also inspect other inner features, such as the mouth and nose (Nelson & Ludemann, 1989).

Some researchers (e.g., Haith, 1979) explain infants' tendencies to scan from the edges of objects inward by noting that for the first several weeks of life, infants seem to be essentially concerned with *where* things are. Their attention is captured by movement and sharp contrasts in brightness and shape, such as those that are found where the edges of objects stand out against their backgrounds. But by about two months of age, infants tend to focus on the *what* of things. They may locate objects by looking at their edges, but now they scan systematically within the boundaries of objects (Bronson, 1990, 1997).

Click on the "Vision" clip in Module 1, Section 2. At the end of this video you can watch different infants try to navigate the visual cliff.

Development of Depth Perception: On *Not* Going Off the Deep End

Infants generally respond to cues for depth by the time they are able to crawl (on average at eight to nine months of age), and most have the good sense to avoid "going off the deep end"—that is, crawling off ledges and tabletops into open space (Campos, Hiatt, Ramsey, Henderson, & Svejda, 1978). *Question: How do researchers determine whether infants will "go off the deep end"?*

In a classic study on depth perception, Eleanor Gibson and Richard Walk (1960) placed infants of various ages on a fabric-covered runway that ran across the centre of a clever device called a visual cliff (see Figure 5.12). The visual cliff is a sheet of Plexiglas that covers a cloth with a high-contrast checkerboard pattern. On one side, the cloth is placed immediately beneath the Plexiglas, and on the other, it is dropped about four feet below. Because the Plexiglas alone would easily support the infant, this is a visual cliff rather than an actual cliff. In the Gibson and Walk study, eight out of ten infants who had begun to crawl refused to venture onto the seemingly unsupported surface, even when their mothers beckoned encouragingly from the other side.

Psychologists can assess infants' emotional responses to the visual cliff long before infants can crawl. For example, Joseph Campos and his colleagues (1970) found that one-month-old infants showed no change in

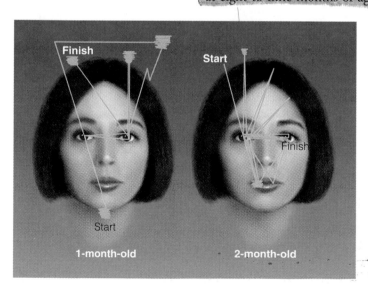

Figure 5.11

Eye Movements of 1- and 2-Month-Olds

One-month-olds direct their attention to the edges of objects. Two-month-olds "move in from the edge." When looking at a face, for example, they focus on the eyes and other inner features. How do researchers explain this change? *Source: Salapatek (1975).*

heart rate when placed facedown on the "cliff." They apparently did not perceive the depth of the cliff. At two months, infants showed decreases in heart rate when so placed, which psychologists interpret as a sign of interest. But the heart rates of nine-month-olds accelerated on the cliff, which is interpreted as a fear response. The study appears to suggest that infants may need to have some experience crawling about (and, perhaps, accumulating some bumps) before they develop fear of heights. The nine-month-olds but not the two-month-olds had had such experience. Other studies support the view that infants usually do not develop fear of heights until they can move around (Bertenthal & Campos, 1990).

Figure 5.12
The Visual Cliff

This young explorer has the good sense not to crawl out onto an apparently unsupported surface, even when Mother beckons from the other side. Do infants have to experience some of life's "bumps" before they avoid "going off the deep end"?

More recent research suggests that infants' tendencies to avoid falling off a cliff are connected with their body positions at the time (Adolph, 2000). Infants generally sit before they crawl, and by nine months of age, we can think of most of them as experienced sitters. Crawling enters the picture at about this time. Karen Adolph examined the behaviour of nineteen nine-month-old infants who were on the edge of crawling as well as on the edge of a visual cliff. The infants were placed in a sitting or crawling position and enticed to reach out for an object over the cliff. The infants were more likely to avoid the cliff when they were sitting. This suggests that different postures involve the brain in different ways and that infants' avoidance of the cliff is connected with their posture. Adolph's findings bring into question the view that avoidance of the cliff depends on general knowledge, such as fear of heights, associations between perceived depth and falling, or awareness that the body cannot be supported in empty space.

Truth or Fiction Revisited: Actually, evidence is mixed as to whether infants need to have experience crawling before they develop fear of heights. Some do not. This would appear to be a case in which survival might be wrapped up in *not* having to learn from experience.

Development of Perceptual Constancies

Questions: What are perceptual constancies? How do they develop? It may not astonish you that a twelve-inch ruler is the same length whether it is two feet or six feet away or that a door across the room is a rectangle whether closed or ajar. Awareness of these facts depends not on sensation alone but on the development of perceptual constancies. **Perceptual constancy** is the tendency to perceive an object to be the same, even though the sensations produced by the object may differ under various conditions.

Consider again the example of the ruler. When it is two feet away, its image, as focused on the retina, is a certain length. This length is the image's "retinal size." From six feet away, the twelve-inch ruler is only one-third as long in terms of retinal size, but we perceive it as being the same size because of size constancy. **Size constancy** is the tendency to perceive the same objects as being of the same size even though their

perceptual constancy The tendency to perceive objects as the same even though sensations produced by them may differ when, for example, they differ in position or distance.

size constancy The tendency to perceive objects as being the same size even though the sizes of their retinal images may differ as a result of distance.

retinal sizes vary as a function of their distance. From six feet away, a thirty-six-inch yardstick casts an image equal in retinal size to the twelve-inch ruler at two feet, but—if recognized as a yardstick—it is perceived as longer, again because of size constancy.

In a classic study of the development of size constancy, Thomas Bower (1974) conditioned two-and-a-half- to three-month-old infants to turn their heads to the left when shown a twelve-inch cube from a distance of three feet. He then presented them with three experimental stimuli: (1) a twelve-inch cube nine feet away, whose retinal size was smaller than that of the original cube; (2) a thirty-six-inch cube three feet away, whose retinal size was larger than that of the original cube; and (3) a thirty-six-inch cube nine feet away, whose retinal size was the same as that of the original cube. The infants turned their heads most frequently in response to the first experimental cube, although its retinal image was only one-third the length of that to which they had been conditioned, suggesting that they had achieved size constancy. Later studies have confirmed Bower's finding that size constancy is present in early infancy. Some research suggests that even neonates possess rudimentary size constancy (Slater, 2000; Slater, Mattock, & Brown, 1990).

	Practical Tips for Supporting Physical Development in Infancy: Suggestions for Parents and Caregivers			
There are many ways that parents and caregivers can support infants' physical development during infancy. The suggestions and information listed below are geared toward North American early childhood experiences; however, there is a great variety of experiences beyond this list depending on cultural practices and environment.				
	Newborn	1-4 months	4-8 months	8-12 months
Visual preferences	• Faces of caregivers • Human faces - eyes, mouth • Slow motion • Strong contrast • Bright colours • Patterns • Moving parts	• Human faces • Faces of individuals in environment • More complex patterns with elements, greater contrast, more colour	• *Play games to find hidden objects* • Picks up, looks at objects of various sizes, shapes, colours, hardness/ softness, textures	
Visual tracking	• Opportunities to allow infant to see from different views • Mobiles—slow motion items facing downward so infant can see them • Carry or transport infant around so infant can see surroundings • Observe reactions and change stimulus as needed			

	Newborn	1-4 months	4-8 months	8-12 months
Taste		• Objects put in mouth provide experience of different temperatures, hardness/softness, textures, tastes (need to have access to safe objects for oral exploration)	• Feeds self • *Provide finger foods, variety of texture/taste experiences*	• Feeds self; starting to use utensils • *Provide food to encourage use of utensils*
Auditory tracking	• *Provide a variety of auditory tracking signals to allow for tracking activities*			
Building memory	• *Provide stimulus* • *Observe for waning interest* • *Change stimulus* • *Utilize all senses*	• *Provide stimulus within reach of infant* • Requires longer observation time because infants' attention is held longer • *Provide change of stimulus* • *Utilize all senses* • *Provide cause-and-effect experiences*	• Active exploration • *Provide materials in a variety of contextual situations* • *Provide opportunities to reinforce child's exploration in alternative ways* • Imitation of action, gestures	• Repetition of actions • Deferred imitation • Rich imitation of actions, gestures, words • Object permanence • Combines behaviours • Tries to use objects as intended
Grasping	• Engages in "chance" grasping, and releases when tired • *Provide secure low-hanging items that encourage swatting, kicking, "chance" grasping* • *Use auditory, visual preference* • *Observe waning interest*	• Voluntary grasp; release not voluntary • Object must be in visual field • Uses all fingers to draw object into hand • *Provide safe materials for infant to explore cause and effect (no small objects that are hazardous for swallowing/choking, no sharp edges)*	• Voluntary release, pincer grasp • Transfer of objects • Pokes, prods, probes • Recognizes objects by touch	• Increased dexterity—stack, build, fix • *Provide materials that are easy to manipulate*

Table 5.1 *Practical Tips for Supporting Physical Development in Infancy: Suggestions for Parents and Caregivers*

Table 5.1 *Practical Tips for Supporting Physical Development in Infancy: Suggestions for Parents and Caregivers*

	Newborn	1-4 months	4-8 months	8-12 months
Awareness of environment	• *To help infants get a better sense of their environment, provide clear visibility; experiences that include repetition, sequence, predictability; opportunities to see materials from different perspectives, in different locations; auditory cues*	• *Provide infant with materials that are safe to put into mouth and to touch* • *Support to sit, reach, grasp* • *Ensure safe environment*	• *Provide materials that fit together, can be pulled apart, can be stacked* • *Ensure safe environment*	• Active exploration • Intensely curious about items "out of sight" • *Provide safe storage of materials*
Promote pleasure	• *In order to take advantage of sensory activities involving the whole body, expose babies to soft, varied dialogue; body-temperature water activities; massage using varied strokes, touches, media (e.g., oil, powder); varied textured surfaces to lie on*	• Self-exploration of tactile, taste experiences • Adult support required to explore water-play through motion—kicking, splashing • Manipulates objects to create sounds, movements • Listens to human speech sound (talk to babies!) • Makes speech sounds • Imitates facial expressions	• Active exploration of environment • Intensely curious	• Active repetition (games, nursery rhymes, songs) • Excitement at results
Auditory preferences	• Caregivers' voices • Low sounds • Soothing sounds • Heartbeat • Music (varied—preferably not loud or scary)	• Human voices • Repetition • Speech sounds • Turn-taking—listening, responding • Interest in music	• Listening and speaking • *Label child's actions, experiences, materials used* • *Listen to children's verbalizations and respond accordingly*	• Language • *Provide labelling of child's experiences* • *Provide expansions* • *Allow child to initiate* • *Answer child*

	Newborn	1-4 months	4-8 months	8-12 months
Symbolic representation			• Pretends using actions and objects • *Provide modelling of actions with and without objects*	• Uses objects as intended • *Provide realistic props/materials* • *Model use of props and materials* • *Uses object as dictated by object*
Mobility			• Crawls, walks holding on, climbs • *Provide a safe, unobstructed environment (get on the floor and crawl around to get a view of child's world to assess stimulation and safety of setup)*	• Fully mobile • Transports items • *Provide opportunity to cart, push, climb, run, etc.*

Practical Tips for Supporting Physical Development in Infancy: Suggestions for Parents and Caregivers

Adapted from Crowther, I. (2006), 4, 23, 55, 70, 82.

Shape constancy is the tendency to perceive an object as having the same shape even though, when perceived from another angle, the shape projected onto the retina may change dramatically. When the top of a cup or a glass is seen from above, the visual sensations are in the shape of a circle. When seen from a slight angle, the sensations are elliptical, and when seen from the side, the image resembles a straight line. However, we still perceive the rim of the cup or glass as being a circle because of our familiarity with the object. In the first few months after birth, infants see the features of their caregivers, bottles, cribs, and toys from all different angles, so that by the time they are four or five months old, a broad grasp of shape constancy seems to be established, at least under certain conditions (Slater, 2000).

shape constancy The tendency to perceive objects as being the same shape even though the shapes of their retinal images may differ when the objects are viewed from different positions.

Development of Hearing: The Better to Hear You With

Question: How does the sense of hearing develop in infancy? Neonates can crudely orient their heads in the direction of a sound (Aslin, 1987). By eighteen months of age, the accuracy of sound-localizing ability approaches that of adults (Morrongiello, Fenwick, & Chance, 1990). Sensitivity to sounds increases in the first few months of life (Aslin, 1987). As infants mature, the range of the pitch of the sounds they can sense gradually expands to include the adult's range of twenty to 20 000 cycles per second. The ability to detect differences in the pitch and loudness of sounds improves considerably throughout the preschool years (Jensen & Neff, 1993). Auditory acuity also improves gradually over the first several years (Aslin, 1987) although infants' hearing can be so acute that many parents complain their napping infants will awaken at the slightest sound. This is especially true if parents have been overprotective in attempting to keep their rooms as silent as possible. Infants who are normally exposed to a backdrop of moderate noise levels become habituated to them and are not likely to awaken unless there is a sudden, sharp noise.

habituation A process in which one becomes used to and therefore pays less attention to a repeated stimulus.

By the age of one month, infants perceive differences between speech sounds that are highly similar. In a classic study relying on the **habituation** method, infants of this age could activate a recording of "bah" by sucking on a nipple (Eimas, Sigueland, Juscyk, & Vigorito, 1971). As time went on, habituation occurred, as shown by decreased sucking in order to hear the "bah" sound. Then the researchers switched from "bah" to "pah." If the sounds had seemed the same to the infants, their lethargic sucking patterns would have continued. But they immediately sucked harder, suggesting that they perceived the difference. Other researchers have found that within another month or two, infants reliably discriminate three-syllable words such as *marana* and *malana* (Kuhl, Andruski, Chistovich, Chistovich, et al., 1997).

Infants can discriminate the sounds of their parents' voices by three and a half months of age. In one study, infants of this age were oriented toward their parents as they reclined in infant seats. The researchers (Spelke & Owsley, 1979) played recordings of the mother's or father's voice while the parents themselves remained inactive. The infants reliably looked at the parent whose voice was being played.

Young infants are capable of perceiving most of the speech sounds present in the world's languages. But after exposure to one's native language, infants gradually lose the capacity to discriminate those sounds that are not found in the native language. Before six months of age, for example, infants reared in an English-speaking environment could discriminate sounds found in Hindi (a language of India) and Salish (a Native American language). But by ten to twelve months of age, they had lost the ability to do so, as shown in Figure 5.13 (Werker, 1989).

Infants also learn at an early age to ignore small, meaningless variations in the sounds of their native language. Adults do this routinely. For example, if someone speaking your language has a head cold or a slight accent, you ignore the minor variations in the person's pronunciation and hear these variations as the same sound. But when you hear slight variations in the sounds of a foreign language, you might assume that each variation carries a different meaning and so you hear the sounds as different.

Infants can screen out meaningless sounds as early as six months of age. Patricia Kuhl and her colleagues (1997) presented American and Swedish infants with pairs of sounds in either their own language or the other one. The infants were trained to look over their shoulder when they heard a difference in the sounds and to ignore sound pairs that seemed to be the same. The infants routinely ignored variations in sounds that were part of their language, because they apparently perceived them as the same sound. But they noticed slight variations in the sounds of the other language. Another study demonstrated the same ability in infants as young as two months (Marean, Werner, & Kuhl, 1992). By their first birthday, many infants understand many words, and some may even say a word or two of their own.

Development of Coordination of the Senses: If I See It, Can I Touch It?

Neonates crudely orient their heads toward sounds and pleasant odours. In this way, they increase the probability that the sources of the sounds and odours will also be sensed through visual scanning. Young infants can also recognize that an object experienced by one sense (e.g., vision) is the same as an identical object experienced through another sense (e.g., touch). This ability has been demonstrated in infants as young as one month of age (Bushnell, 1993). One experiment demonstrating such understanding in twelve-month-olds takes advantage of the fact that children of this age prefer novel to familiar sources of stimulation. Susan Rose and Esther Orlian (1991) allowed the infants to handle, but not see, an object (e.g., a plastic triangle). Then, this object and a novel object (e.g., a plastic cross) were shown to the infants, but they were not allowed to touch them. The children spent more time looking at the novel object. This indicates that they recognized the object that they had handled, even though they were now experiencing it visually.

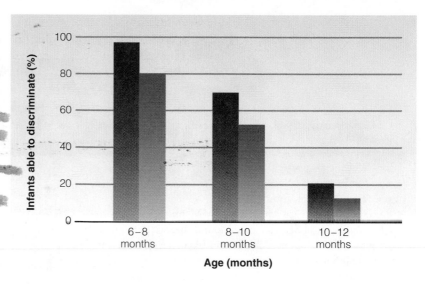

Figure 5.13

Declining Ability to Discriminate the Sounds of Foreign Languages

Infants show a decline in the ability to discriminate sounds not found in their native language. Before 6 months of age, infants from English-speaking families could discriminate sounds found in Hindi (red bars) and Salish, a Native American language (blue bars). By 10 to 12 months of age, they could no longer do so.

Children's Role in Perceptual Development

Question: Do children play an active or a passive role in perceptual development? Neonates may have more sophisticated sensory capabilities than you expected. Still, their ways of perceiving the world are largely mechanical, or passive. The description of a stimulus capturing an infant's attention seems quite appropriate. Neonates seem to be generally at the mercy of external stimuli. When a bright light strikes, they attend to it. If the light moves slowly across the plane of their vision, they track it.

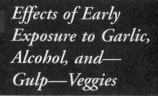

Research shows that infants begin to learn about the flavours found in their cultures through breast milk, possibly even through amniotic fluid. For example, psychologist Julie Mennella, of the Monell Chemical Senses Center, found that when women eat garlic, their infants suckle longer (Azar, 1998). It is not that the infants ingest more milk. Instead, they seem to be spending the extra time analyzing what they are tasting. They keep the milk in their mouths, pause, and perceive the flavours. Vanilla flavouring has a similar effect on suckling—enhancing the duration.

Infants ingest amniotic fluid while they are still in the womb, and this fluid also acquires a distinct smell after a woman eats garlic, according to Mennella. It would appear that the fetus detects this change in its environment.

No Direct Road to Alcohol Abuse

Does exposure to alcohol in the breast milk of mothers who drink create a disposition toward alcohol abuse in the infant? Mennella's research suggests that the truth may lie in the opposite direction. First of all, infants appear not to like the taste of alcohol in breast milk. Mennella (2001) found that infants of ages two to five months drink less breast milk when the mother has recently drunk alcohol. In fact, they ingest more breast milk once the alcohol is out of the mother's system, apparently to compensate for the lessened calorie intake at the previous feeding.

A related study by Mennella and a colleague, Pamela Garcia (2000), showed that early exposure to the odour of alcohol may also be something of a turnoff to infants. In this study, Mennella and Garcia compared the preferences of children who had been exposed to alcohol around the house during infancy with those of children who had not. All the children were about four to six years of age at the time of testing. Children who had been exposed to alcohol early were significantly more likely than the other children to dislike the odour of a bottle containing alcohol.

We do not suggest that parents drink alcohol to discourage their children from drinking later on. But the findings do seem to contradict what one might have expected.

And What about Encouraging Children to Eat Their Veggies through Early Exposure?

Many parents in North America understand the benefits of eating vegetables and bring out the jars of vegetable baby food when they are feeding their infants. Does early exposure to these foods encourage or discourage the infants to eat them?

Early exposure generally seems to have a positive effect on children's appetites for vegetables. Consider a study of four- to seven-month-old infants by Leann Birch and her colleagues (1998). The investigators repeatedly exposed infants to vegetables such as peas and green beans in the form of baby food to see whether they would subsequently eat more or less of them. Thirty-nine infants were fed the target foods once a day for ten consecutive days. During that period, their consumption of the vegetables doubled from an average of thirty-five grams to an average of seventy-two grams. Moreover, the infants became more likely to eat similar foods—that is, other vegetables. Julie Mennella and her colleagues have also found that the infants of mothers who eat more diverse diets are more willing to eat a variety of foods (cited in Azar, 1998). Moreover, studies of rodents, pigs, and sheep show that once they are weaned, young animals prefer the flavours to which they were exposed through their mothers' milk. Early exposure to the foods that are traditional within a culture may be a key to shaping an infant's food preferences.

© Jose Luis Pelaez, Inc. / CORBIS

How Do You Encourage Children to Eat Their Veggies?

Do you want to talk about cruel experimental treatments that skirt the edges of the ethical limits of the researchers? Try this one on for size. Leann Birch and her colleagues repeatedly exposed four- to seven-month-old infants to baby food consisting of vegetables. Actually, the "treatment" apparently had the effect of teaching the infants to like vegetables. In terms of what the experimenters measured, they found that the infants exposed to vegetables ate more of them during test trials.

Lessons in Observation
Sensation and Perception in Infancy

click on
"The Newborn: Sensation and Perception" in Module 1, Section 1, on your Observing Children and Adolescents CD-ROM. You can also visit the Student Book Companion Site to watch the video, answer the questions, and e-mail your responses to your professor.

To watch this video

© 2002 Laura Dwight

Vision is the least mature of a newborn's senses, but infants have a strong preference for patterns with strong contrasts and prefer human faces above all else. Here, 2-month-old Giuseppina fixates on a drawing of a face.

Learning Objectives
• What types of tests do doctors perform for testing newborn and infant senses?
• What visual preferences do newborns have?
• Do visual preferences change as a newborn becomes an infant?

Applied Lesson
Describe the different tests doctors use to check the senses in newborns and infants.

Critical Thinking
How can a newborn's capacities for vision and hearing be considered adaptive? Hint: Think about Carter's initial interaction with his mother in this video.

As time passes, broad changes occur in the perceptual processes of children, and the child's role in perception appears to become decidedly more active. Developmental psychologist Eleanor Gibson (1969, 1991) noted a number of these changes:

1. Intentional action replaces "capture" (automatic responses to stimulation). As infants mature and gain experience, purposeful scanning and exploration of the environment take the place of mechanical movements and passive responses to potent stimulation.

    Consider the scanning "strategies" of neonates. In a lighted room, neonates move their eyes mostly from left to right and back again. Mechanically, they sweep a horizontal plane. If they encounter an object that contrasts sharply with the background, their eye movements bounce back and forth against the edges. However, even when neonates awaken in a dark room, they show the stereotypical horizontal scanning pattern, with about two eye movements per second (Haith, 1990).

The stereotypical quality of these initial scanning movements suggests that they are inborn. They provide strong evidence that the neonate is neurologically prewired to gather and seek visual information. They do not reflect what we would consider a purposeful, or intentional, effort to learn about the environment.

2. *Systematic search replaces unsystematic search.* Over the first few years of life, children become more active as they develop systematic ways of exploring the environment. They come to pay progressively more attention to details of objects and people and to make finer and finer discriminations.

3. *Attention becomes selective.* Older children become capable of selecting the information they need from the welter of confusion in the environment. For example, when older children are separated from their parents in a department store, they have the capacity to systematically scan for people of their parents' height, hair colour, vocal characteristics, and so on. They are also more capable of discriminating the spot where the parents were last seen. A younger child is more likely to be confused by the welter of voices and faces and aisles and to be unable to extract essential information from this backdrop.

4. *Irrelevant information becomes ignored.* Older children gain the capacity to screen out or deploy their attention away from stimuli that are irrelevant to the task at hand. This might mean shutting out the noise of cars in the street or radios in the neighbourhood in order to focus on a book.

In short, children develop from passive, mechanical reactors to the world about them into active, purposeful seekers and organizers of sensory information. They develop from beings whose attention is diffuse and "captured" into people who make decisions about what they will attend to. This is a process that, as with so many others, appears to depend on both maturation and experience.

Let us now screen out distractions and turn our attention to consideration of the importance of maturation (nature) and experience (nurture) in perceptual development.

Nature and Nurture in Perceptual Development

The nature-nurture issue is found in perceptual development, just as it is in other dimensions of development. *Question: What is the evidence for the roles of nature and nurture in perceptual development?*

Evidence for the Role of Nature

Compelling evidence supports the idea that our inborn sensory capacities play a crucial role in our perceptual development. For one thing, neonates have already come into the world with a good number of perceptual skills. They can see nearby objects quite well, and their hearing is usually fine. They are also born with tendencies to track moving objects, to systematically scan the horizon, and to prefer certain kinds of stimuli. Preferences for different kinds of visual stimuli appear to unfold on schedule as the first months wear on. Sensory changes, as with motor changes, appear to be linked to maturation of the nervous system.

For these reasons, it seems clear that we do have certain inborn ways of responding to sensory input—certain "categories" and built-in limits—that allow us to perceive certain aspects of the world of physical reality.

Evidence for the Role of Nurture

Evidence that experience plays a crucial role in perceptual development is also compelling. We could use any of hundreds of studies with children and other species to make the point, but let us limit our discussion to a couple of examples of research with kittens and human infants.

Children and lower animals have critical periods in their perceptual development. Failure to receive adequate sensory stimulation during these critical periods can result in permanent sensory deficits (Greenough et al., 1987). For example, newborn kittens raised with a patch over one eye wind up with few or no cells in the visual area of the cerebral cortex that would normally be stimulated by light that enters that eye. In effect, that eye becomes blind, even though sensory receptors in the eye itself may fire in response to light. On the other hand, if the eye of an adult cat is patched for the same amount of time, the animal will not lose vision in that eye. The critical period apparently will have passed. Similarly, if health problems require that a child's eye must be patched for an extensive period of time during the first year, the child's visual acuity in that eye may be impaired.

Consider a study of visual acuity among twenty-eight human infants who had been deprived of all patterned visual input by cataracts in one or both eyes until they were treated at one week to nine months of age (Maurer, Lewis, Brent, & Levin, 1999). Immediately following treatment, their visual acuity was no better than that of normal neonates, suggesting that their lack of visual experience has impaired their visual development. However, their visual acuity improved rapidly over the month following treatment. They showed some improvement in as little as one hour following visual input.

And so, with perceptual development as with other dimensions of development, nature and nurture play indispensable roles. Today, few developmentalists would subscribe to either extreme. Most would agree that nature and nurture *interact* to shape perceptual development. Nature continues to guide the unfolding of the child's physical systems. Yet nurture continues to interact with nature in the development of these systems. We know that inborn physical structures, such as the nature of the cortex of the brain, place limits on our abilities to respond to the world. But we also know that experience continues to help shape our most basic physical structures. For example, sensorimotor experiences thicken the cortex of the brain. Sensory experiences are linked to the very development of neurons in the cortex, causing dendrites to proliferate and affecting myelination.

In the next chapter, we will see how nature and nurture influence the development of thought and language in infants.

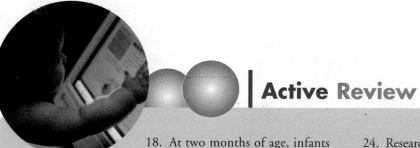

Active Review

18. At two months of age, infants tend to fixate longer on a (scrambled or real?) face.

19. Neonates direct their attention to the (centre or edges?) of objects.

20. Researchers have studied depth perception in infants through use of the visual _____.

21. Research suggests that infants have developed size constancy by about _____ months.

22. As infants develop, they have (greater or lesser?) ability to screen out meaningless sounds in their native languages.

23. As time passes during infancy, one change in perceptual development is that intentional action replaces _____ (automatic responses to stimulation).

24. Research shows that both nature and _____ are essential to perceptual development.

Reflect & Relate: What do you think it would mean if infants came into the world "prewired" to prefer the human face to other equally complex visual stimulation? Can you explain the evolutionary advantage that such prewiring would provide?

Go to
W W W **www.voyages1ce.nelson.com**
for an interactive version of this review.

Recite: *An Active Summary*™

1. What are the sequences of physical development?

Three key sequences of physical development include cephalocaudal development, proximodistal development, and differentiation.

2. What patterns of growth occur in infancy?

Infants usually double their birth weight in five months and triple it by the first birthday. Height increases by about half in the first year. Infants grow another four to six inches in the second year and gain another four to seven pounds. The head gradually diminishes in proportion to the rest of the body.

3. What is failure to thrive?

Failure to thrive (FTT) is a serious disorder that impairs growth in infancy and early childhood. FTT can have organic causes or nonorganic causes. Deficiencies in caregiver–child interaction may play a major role in FTT.

4. What are the nutritional needs of infants?

Infants require breast milk or an iron-fortified infant formula. Introduction of solid foods is recommended at four to six months. Caregivers are advised to build up to a variety of foods.

5. Why do women bottle-feed or breast-feed their children?

Breast feeding is connected with factors such as the mother's availability (most women work), knowledge of the advantages of breast feeding, and availability of alternatives to breast milk.

6. What are the advantages and disadvantages of breast milk?

Breast milk is tailored to human digestion, contains essential nutrients, contains the mothers' antibodies, helps protect against infant diarrhea, and is less likely than formula to cause allergies. However, some environmental toxins are found in breast milk.

7. What are neurons? How do they develop?

Neurons are cells that receive and transmit messages in the form of chemicals called neurotransmitters. As the child matures, axons grow in length, dendrites and axon terminals proliferate, and many neurons become wrapped in myelin, enabling them to function more efficiently.

8. What is the brain? How does the brain develop?

The brain is the command centre of the developing organism. The brain triples in weight by the first birthday, reaching nearly 70 percent of its adult weight. There are two major prenatal growth spurts: Neurons proliferate during the first growth spurt; the second spurt is due mainly to the proliferation of dendrites and axon terminals.

9. How do nature and nurture affect the development of the brain?

Sensory and motor areas of the brain begin to develop because of maturation, but sensory stimulation and motor activity also spur development. Rats raised in enriched environments develop more dendrites and axon terminals. Malnutrition is connected with a small brain, fewer neurons, and less myelination.

10. What is motor development? How does it occur?

Motor development refers to developments in the activity of muscles and is connected with changes in posture, movement, and coordination. Children gain the ability to move their bodies through a sequence of activities that includes rolling over, sitting up, crawling, creeping, walking, and running. The sequence remains stable, but some children skip a step.

11. What are the roles of nature and nurture in motor development?

Both maturation (nature) and experience (nurture) play indispensable roles in motor development. Infants need some opportunity for experimentation before they can engage in milestones such as sitting up and walking. Development of motor skills can be accelerated by training, but the effect is generally slight.

12. How do sensation and perception develop in the infant?

Neonates are nearsighted and have poor peripheral vision. Acuity and peripheral vision approximate adult levels by the age of six months.

13. What captures the attention of infants? How do visual preferences develop?

Neonates attend longer to stripes than blobs, and by eight to twelve weeks of age, they prefer curved lines over straight ones. Two-month-old infants fixate longer on the human face than on other stimuli. Some researchers argue that neonates do not prefer faces because they are faces but because they are complex images. Infants can discriminate their mother's face from a stranger's after about eight hours of contact. Neonates direct their attention to the edges of objects, but two-month-olds scan from the edges inward.

14. How do researchers determine whether infants will "go off the deep end"?

Many use the classic visual cliff apparatus. Most infants refuse to venture out over the visual cliff by the time they can crawl. Researchers have speculated that infants may need some experience crawling before they can develop fear of heights.

15. What are perceptual constancies? How do they develop?

A perceptual constancy is a tendency to perceive an object to be the same, even though it produces different sensations under different conditions. Size constancy appears to be present by two and a half to three months of age; shape constancy develops by age four to five months.

16. How does the sense of hearing develop in infancy?

Neonates reflexively orient their heads toward a sound. By eighteen months of age, infants locate sounds about as well as adults. Infants discriminate caregivers' voices by three and a half months of age. Early infants can perceive most of the speech sounds throughout the languages of the world, but by ten to twelve months of age, this ability lessens.

17. Do children play an active or a passive role in perceptual development?

Neonates seem to be at the mercy of external stimuli, but later on, intentional action replaces capture. Systematic search replaces unsystematic search, attention becomes selective, and irrelevant information gets ignored.

18. What is the evidence for the roles of nature and nurture in perceptual development?

Evidence shows that sensory changes are linked to maturation of the nervous system (nature) but that experience also plays a crucial role in perceptual development (nurture). For one thing, there are critical periods in the perceptual development of children and lower animals, such that sensory experience is required to optimize—or maintain—sensory capacities.

W W W **Go to**
www.voyages1ce.nelson.com
for an interactive version of this summary review.

Key Terms

differentiation *(page 161)*

failure to thrive (FTT) *(page 165)*

canalization *(page 166)*

nerves *(page 171)*

neurons *(page 171)*

dendrites *(page 171)*

axon *(page 171)*

neurotransmitter *(page 171)*

myelin sheath *(page 171)*

myelination *(page 171)*

multiple sclerosis *(page 172)*

medulla *(page 172)*

cerebellum *(page 173)*

cerebrum *(page 173)*

ulnar grasp *(page 176)*

pincer grasp *(page 176)*

locomotion *(page 176)*

toddler *(page 177)*

sensation *(page 180)*

perception *(page 180)*

perceptual constancy *(page 183)*

size constancy *(page 183)*

shape constancy *(page 187)*

habituation *(page 188)*

Active Learning Resources

Observing Children and Adolescents CD-ROM
Want to watch videos showing what you've just learned about in this chapter? Click on "The Newborn: Sensation and Perception" video in Module 1, Section 1. Your "Lessons in Observation" feature on p. 191 provides further learning objectives, an applied lesson, and a critical thinking exercise designed to help you experience this stage of development. Also check out the "Gross and Fine Motor Development" and "Vision" videos in CD Module 1, Section 2.

Visit Your Companion Website for This Book
http://www.voyages1CE.nelson.com
Check out this companion website, where you will find online resources directly linked to your book. The website includes interactive exercises related to PQ4R and Power Visuals for mastering and reviewing key concepts as well as quizzing, chapter outlines, and much more!

CengageNOW!™
http://hed.nelson.com
Go to this site for the link to CengageNOW™, your one-stop study shop. Take a Pretest for this chapter, and CengageNOW™ will generate a personalized Study Plan based on your test results! The Study Plan will identify the topics you need to review and direct you to online resources to help you master those topics. You can then take a Posttest to help you determine the concepts you have mastered and those you still need to work on.

6

Infancy: Cognitive Development

PREVIEW

TRUTH OR FICTION?

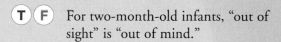

(T) (F) For two-month-old infants, "out of sight" is "out of mind."

(T) (F) A one-hour-old infant may imitate an adult who sticks out his or her tongue.

(T) (F) Psychologists can begin to measure intelligence in infancy.

(T) (F) Infant crying is a primitive form of language.

(T) (F) You can advance children's development of pronunciation by correcting their errors.

(T) (F) Children are "prewired" to listen to language in such a way that they come to understand rules of grammar.

Go to www

http://www.voyages1CE.nelson.com
for an interactive version of this "Truth or Fiction" feature.

© Rubberball / Getty Images

L aurent ... resumes his experiments of the day before. He grabs in succession a celluloid swan, a box, etc., stretches out his arm and lets them fall. He distinctly varies the position of the fall. Sometimes he stretches out his arm vertically, sometimes he holds it obliquely, in front of or behind his eyes, etc. When the object falls in a new position, he lets it fall two or three times more on the same place, as though to study the spatial relation; then he modifies the situation.

Is this the description of a scientist at work? In a way, it is. Although Swiss psychologist Jean Piaget (1963 [1936]) was describing his eleven-month-old son Laurent, children of this age frequently act like scientists, performing what Piaget called "experiments in order to see."

In this chapter we chronicle the developing thought processes of infants and toddlers—that is, their cognitive development. We focus on the sensorimotor stage of cognitive development hypothesized by Piaget. Then, we examine infant memory and imitation. We next explore individual differences in infant intelligence. Finally, we turn our attention to a remarkable aspect of cognitive development: language.

Cognitive Development: Jean Piaget

scheme   According to Piaget, an action pattern (such as a reflex) or mental structure that is involved in the acquisition or organization of knowledge.

assimilation   According to Piaget, the incorporation of new events or knowledge into existing schemes.

accommodation   According to Piaget, the modification of existing schemes in order to incorporate new events or knowledge.

Cognitive development focuses on the development of children's ways of perceiving and mentally representing the world. Piaget labelled children's concepts of the world **schemes.** He hypothesized that children try to use **assimilation** to absorb new events into existing schemes; and when assimilation does not allow the child to make sense of novel events, children try to modify existing schemes through **accommodation.** (To refresh your memory, go back to Chapter 1 for a review of Piaget's concepts.)

Piaget (1963 [1936]) hypothesized that children's cognitive processes develop in an orderly sequence, or series of stages. As is the case with motor and perceptual development, some children may be more advanced than others at particular ages, but the developmental sequence does not normally vary (Flavell, Green, & Flavell, 2002; Siegler & Alibali, 2005). Piaget identified four major stages of cognitive development: sensorimotor, preoperational, concrete operational, and formal operational. In this chapter, we discuss the sensorimotor stage.

The Sensorimotor Stage (0-24 months)

Question: What is the sensorimotor stage of cognitive development? Piaget's sensorimotor stage refers to the first two years of cognitive development, a time when these developments are demonstrated by means of sensory and motor activity. Although it may be difficult for us to imagine how we can develop and use cognitive processes in the absence of language, children do so in many ways.

During the sensorimotor stage, infants progress from responding to events with reflexes, or ready-made schemes, to goal-oriented behaviour that involves awareness of past events. During this stage, they come to form mental representations of objects and events, to hold complex pictures of past events in mind, and to solve problems by mental trial and error.

Question: What are the parts or substages of the sensorimotor stage? Piaget divided the sensorimotor stage into six substages, each of which is characterized by more complex behaviour than the preceding substage. But there is also continuity from substage to substage. Each substage can be characterized as a variation on a theme in which earlier forms of behaviour are repeated, varied, and coordinated. The approximate time periods of the substages and some characteristics of each are summarized in Concept Review 6.1.

Concept Review 6.1   The Six Substages of the Sensorimotor Stage, According to Piaget

	Substage	Comments
	1. Simple reflexes (0–1 month)	Assimilation of new objects into reflexive responses. Infants "look and see." Inborn reflexes can be modified by experience.
	2. Primary circular reactions (1–4 months)	Repetition of actions that may have initially occurred by chance but that have satisfying or interesting results. Infants "look in order to see." The focus is on the infant's body. Infants do not yet distinguish between themselves and the external world.
	3. Secondary circular reactions (4–8 months)	Repetition of schemes that have interesting effects on the environment. The focus shifts to external objects and events. There is initial cognitive awareness that schemes influence the external world.
	4. Coordination of secondary schemes (8–12 months)	Coordination of secondary schemes, such as looking and grasping to attain specific goals. There is the beginning of intentionality and means-end differentiation. We find imitation of actions not already in infants' repertoires.
	5. Tertiary circular reactions (12–18 months)	Purposeful adaptation of established schemes to specific situations. Behaviour takes on an experimental quality. There is overt trial and error in problem solving.
	6. Invention of new means through mental combinations (18–24 months)	Mental trial and error in problem solving. Infants take "mental detours" based on cognitive maps. Infants engage in deferred imitation and symbolic play. Infants' cognitive advances are made possible by mental representations of objects and events and the beginnings of symbolic thought.

Simple Reflexes

At birth, neonates assimilate objects into reflexive responses. But even within hours after birth, neonates begin to modify reflexes as a result of experience. For example, they adapt sucking patterns to the shape of the nipple. (But don't be too impressed; porpoises are born swimming and "know" to rise to the surface of the ocean to breathe.)

Simple Reflexes

The first substage covers the first month after birth. It is dominated by the assimilation of sources of stimulation into inborn reflexes such as grasping, visual tracking, crying, sucking, and crudely turning the head toward a sound.

At birth, reflexes have a stereotypical, inflexible quality. But even within the first few hours, neonates begin to modify reflexes as a result of experience. For example, infants will adapt (accommodate) patterns of sucking to the shape of the nipple and the rate of flow of fluid.

During the first month or so, infants apparently make no connection between stimulation perceived through different sensory modalities. They make no effort to grasp objects that they visually track. Crude turning toward sources of sounds and smells has a mechanical look about it that cannot be considered purposeful searching.

Primary Circular Reactions

The second substage, primary circular reactions, lasts from about one to four months of age and is characterized by the beginnings of the ability to coordinate various sensorimotor schemes. In this substage, infants tend to repeat stimulating actions that first occurred by chance. For example, they may lift their arm repeatedly to bring it into view. A circular reaction is a behaviour that is repeated. **Primary circular reactions** focus on the infant's own body rather than on the external environment. Piaget noticed the following primary circular reaction in his son Laurent:

> At two months four days, Laurent by chance discovers his right index finger and looks at it briefly. At two months eleven days, he inspects for a moment his open right hand, perceived by chance. At two months seventeen days, he follows its spontaneous movement for a moment, then examines it several times while it searches for his nose or rubs his eye.
>
> At two months twenty-one days, he holds his two fists in the air and looks at the left one, after which he slowly brings it toward his face and rubs his nose with it, then his eye. A moment later the left hand again approaches his face; he looks at it and touches his nose. He recommences and laughs five or six times in succession while moving the left hand to his face.... He laughs beforehand but begins to smile again on seeing the hand.

—Piaget (1963 [1936], pp. 96–97)

Thus, Laurent, early in the third month, visually tracks the behaviour of his hand, but his visual observations do not seem to influence their movement. At about two months twenty-one days, Laurent can apparently exert some control over his hands, because he seems to know when a hand is about to move (and entertain him). But the link between looking at and moving the hands remains weak. A few days later, however, his looking "acts" on the hands, causing them to remain in his field of vision. Sensorimotor coordination has been achieved. An action is repeated because it stimulates the infant.

In terms of assimilation and accommodation, the child is attempting to assimilate the motor scheme (moving the hand) into the sensory scheme (looking at it). But the schemes do not automatically fit. Several days of apparent trial and error pass, during which the infant seems to be trying to make accommodations so that they will fit.

Goal-directed behaviour makes significant advances during the second substage. During the month after birth, infants visually track objects that contrast with their backgrounds, especially moving objects. But this ready-made behaviour is largely automatic, so that the infant is "looking and seeing." But by the third month, infants may examine objects repeatedly and intensely, as Laurent did. It seems clear that the

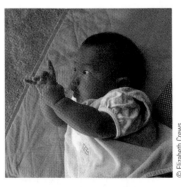

Primary Circular Reactions

In the substage of primary circular reactions, infants repeat actions that involve their bodies. The three-month-old in this picture is also beginning to coordinate visual and sensorimotor schemes—that is, looking at the hand is becoming coordinated with holding it in the field of vision.

infant is no longer simply looking and seeing but is now "looking in order to see." And by the end of the third month, Laurent seems to be moving his hands in order to look at them.

Because Laurent (and other infants) will repeat actions that allow them to see, cognitive-developmental psychologists consider sensorimotor coordination self-reinforcing. Laurent does not seem to be looking or moving his hands because these acts allow him to satisfy a more basic drive such as hunger or thirst. The desire to prolong stimulation may be just as basic.

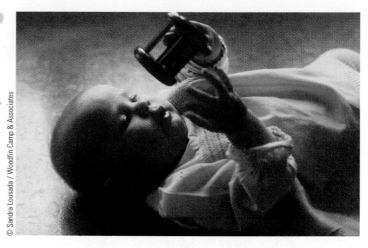

Secondary Circular Reactions

The third substage lasts from about four to eight months and is characterized by **secondary circular reactions,** in which patterns of activity are repeated because of their effect on the environment. In the second substage (primary circular reactions), infants are focused on their own bodies, as in the example given with Laurent. In the third substage (secondary circular reactions), the focus shifts to objects and environmental events. Infants may now learn to pull strings in order to make a plastic face appear or to shake an object in order to hear it rattle.

Although infants in this substage track the trajectory of moving objects, they abandon their searches when the objects disappear from view. As we will see later in this chapter, the object concepts of infants are quite limited at these ages, especially the age at which the third substage begins.

Coordination of Secondary Schemes

In the fourth substage, infants no longer act simply to prolong interesting occurrences. Now they can coordinate schemes to attain specific goals. Infants begin to show intentional, goal-directed behaviour in which they differentiate between the means of achieving a goal and the goal or end itself. For example, they may lift a piece of cloth in order to reach a toy that they had seen a parent place under the cloth earlier. In this example, the scheme of picking up the cloth (the means) is coordinated with the scheme of reaching for the toy (the goal or end).

This example indicates that the infant has mentally represented the toy placed under the cloth. Consider another example. At the age of five months, one of Piaget's daughters, Lucienne, was reaching across her crib for a toy. As she did so, Piaget obscured the toy with his hand. Lucienne pushed her father's hand aside but, in doing so, became distracted and began to play with the hand. A few months later, Lucienne did not allow her father's hand to distract her from the goal of reaching the toy. She moved the hand firmly to the side and then grabbed the toy. The mental representation of the object appears to have become more persistent. The intention of reaching the object was also maintained, and so the hand was perceived as a barrier and not as another interesting stimulus.

During the fourth substage, infants also gain the capacity to copy actions that are not in their own repertoires. Infants can now imitate many gestures and sounds that they had previously ignored. The imitation of a new facial gesture implies that infants have mentally represented their own faces and can tell what parts of their faces they are moving through feedback from facial muscles. For example, when a girl imitates her mother sticking out her tongue, it would appear that she has coordinated moving her own tongue with feedback from muscles in the tongue and mouth. In this way, imitation suggests a great deal about the child's emerging self-concept.

Secondary Circular Reactions
In the substage of secondary circular reactions, patterns of activity are repeated because of their effect on the environment. This infant shakes a rattle to produce an interesting sound.

primary circular reactions
The repetition of actions that first occurred by chance and that focus on the infant's own body.

secondary circular reactions
The repetition of actions that produce an effect on the environment.

Coordination of Secondary Schemes
During this substage, infants coordinate their behaviours to attain specific goals. This infant lifts a piece of cloth to retrieve a toy that has been placed under the cloth.

© Bob Krist / CORBIS

Tertiary Circular Reactions
In this substage, infants vary their actions in a trial-and-error fashion to learn how things work. This child is fascinated by what happens when he paints his body.

tertiary circular reactions
The purposeful adaptation of established schemes to new situations.

Tertiary Circular Reactions

In the fifth substage, which lasts from about twelve to eighteen months of age, Piaget looked on the behaviour of infants as characteristic of budding scientists. Infants now engage in **tertiary circular reactions,** or purposeful adaptations of established schemes to specific situations. Behaviour takes on a new experimental quality, and infants may vary their actions dozens of times in a deliberate trial-and-error fashion in order to learn how things work.

Piaget reported an example of tertiary circular reactions by his daughter Jacqueline. The episode was an experiment in which Piaget placed a stick outside Jacqueline's playpen, which had wooden bars (Piaget, 1963 [1936]). At first, Jacqueline grasped the stick and tried to pull it sideways into the playpen. The stick was too long and could not fit through the bars. Over a number of days of trial and error, however, Jacqueline discovered that she could bring the stick between the bars by turning it upright. In future presentations, she would immediately turn the stick upright and bring it in.

Jacqueline's eventual success with the stick was the result of overt trial and error. In the sixth substage, described next, the solution to problems is often more sudden, suggesting that children have manipulated the elements of the problems in their minds and engaged in mental trial and error before displaying the correct overt response.

Invention of New Means through Mental Combinations

The sixth substage lasts from about eighteen to twenty-four months of age. It serves as a transition between sensorimotor development and the development of symbolic thought. External exploration is replaced by mental exploration.

Recall Jacqueline's trials with the stick. Piaget cleverly waited until his other children, Lucienne and Laurent, were eighteen months old, and then he presented them with the playpen and stick problem. By waiting until eighteen months, he could attribute differences in their performance to advanced age instead of a possible warm-up effect from earlier tests. Rather than engage in overt trial and error, the eighteen-month-old children sat and studied the situation for a few moments. Then they grasped the stick, turned it upright, and brought it into the playpen with little overt effort.

Jacqueline had at first failed with the stick. She then turned it every which way, happening on a solution almost by chance. Lucienne and Laurent solved the problem fairly rapidly, suggesting that they mentally represented the stick and the bars of the playpen and perceived that the stick would not fit through as it was. They must then have rotated the mental image of the stick until they perceived a position that would allow the stick to pass between the bars.

At about eighteen months old, children may also use imitation to symbolize or stand for a plan of action. Consider how Lucienne goes about retrieving a watch chain her father placed in a matchbox. It seems that symbolic imitation serves her as a way of thinking out loud.

> I put the chain back into the box and reduce the opening. [Lucienne] is not aware of [how to open and close] the match box. [She] possesses two preceding schemes: turning the box over in order to empty it of its contents, and sliding her fingers into the slit to make the chain come out. [She] puts her finger inside and gropes to reach the chain, but fails. A pause follows during which Lucienne manifests a very curious reaction....

She looks at the slit with great attention. Then, several times in succession, she opens and shuts her mouth, at first slightly, then wider and wider! Apparently Lucienne understands the existence of a cavity.... [Lucienne then] puts her finger in the slit, and, instead of trying as before to reach the chain, she pulls so as to enlarge the opening. She succeeds and grasps the chain.

—Piaget (1963 [1936], pp. 337–338)

Development of Object Permanence

One important aspect of sensorimotor development is the appearance of **object permanence.** *Questions: What is object permanence? How does it develop?* Object permanence is the recognition that an object or person continues to exist when out of sight. Your child development textbook continues to exist when you accidentally leave it in the library after studying for the big test, and an infant's mother continues to exist even when she is in another room. Your realization that your book exists, although out of view, is an example of object permanence. If an infant acts as though its mother no

object permanence Recognition that objects continue to exist even when they are not seen.

click on "Piaget's Sensorimotor Stage" in Module 1, Section 3, on your Observing Children and Adolescents CD-ROM. You can also visit the Student Book Companion Site to watch the video, answer the questions, and e-mail your responses to your professor.

Lessons in Observation
Piaget's Sensorimotor Stage

Learning Objectives
- What is Piaget's sensorimotor stage?
- What is a primary circular reaction?
- What is a secondary circular reaction?
- In terms of Piaget's stages, what is a scheme?
- How do infants display object permanence?

Applied Lesson
Describe the substages of the sensorimotor period in terms of each of the children you see in the video. How do sensory and motor activities affect the development of cognitive skills?

Critical Thinking
Which of the infants illustrates a tertiary circular reaction? How have the other stages of the sensorimotor period helped this child reach this level?

Nine-month-old Hayden has learned that he can use one secondary circular reaction in service of another. That is, he moves the large toy (obstacle) to retrieve the more desirable toy underneath.

longer exists when she is out of sight, the infant does not have the concept of object permanence. The development of object permanence is tied into infants' general tendency to remember sensory impressions and reason about them (Aguiar & Baillargeon, 2002; Hespos & Baillargeon, 2001a, 2001b; Luo, Baillargeon, Brueckner, & Munakata, 2003; Siegler & Alibali, 2005).

Neonates show no tendency to respond to objects that are not within their immediate sensory grasp. By the age of two months, infants may show some surprise if an object (such as a toy duck) is placed behind a screen and then taken away so that when the screen is lifted, it is absent. However, they make no effort to search for the missing object. Through the first six months or so, when the screen is placed between the object and the infant, the infant behaves as though the object is no longer there (see Figure 6.1). ***Truth or Fiction Revisited:*** It is true that "out of sight" is "out of mind" for two-month-old infants. Apparently, they do not yet reliably mentally represent objects they see.

There are some interesting advances in the development of the object concept by about the sixth month (Piaget's substage 3). For example, an infant at this age will tend to look for an object that has been dropped, behaviour that suggests some form of object permanence. By this age, there is also reason to believe that the infant perceives a mental representation (image) of an object, such as a favourite toy, in response

Figure 6.1
Development of Object Permanence

To the infant who is in the early part of the sensorimotor stage, out of sight is truly out of mind. Once a sheet of paper is placed between the infant and the toy monkey (top two photos), the infant loses all interest in the toy. From evidence of this sort, Piaget concluded that the toy is not mentally represented. The bottom series of photos shows a child in a later part of the sensorimotor stage. This child does mentally represent objects and pushes through a towel to reach an object that has been screened from sight.

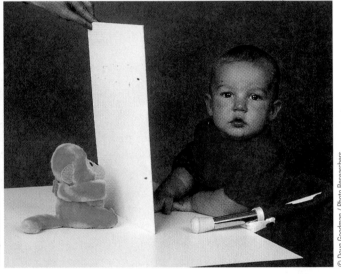

© Doug Goodman / Photo Researchers
© Doug Goodman / Photo Researchers
© 2004 George S. Zimbel
© 2004 George S. Zimbel
© 2004 George S. Zimbel

to sensory impressions of part of the object. This is shown by the infant's reaching for an object that is partly hidden.

By eight to twelve months of age (Piaget's substage 4), infants will seek to retrieve objects that have been completely hidden. But in observing his own children, Piaget (1963 [1936]) noted an interesting error known as the *A not B error.* Piaget repeatedly hid a toy behind a screen (A), and each time, his infant removed the screen and retrieved the toy. Then, as the infant watched, Piaget hid the toy behind another screen (B) in a different place. Still, the infant tried to recover the toy by pushing aside the first screen (A). It is as though the child had learned that a certain motor activity would reinstate the missing toy. The child's concept of the object did not, at this age, extend to recognition that objects usually remain in the place where they have been most recently mentally represented.

But more recent research indicates that under certain conditions, nine- to ten-month-old infants do not show the A not B error (Bremner & Bryant, 2001; Marcovitch, Zelazo, & Schmuckler, 2002). For example, if infants are allowed to search for the object immediately after seeing it hidden, the error often does not occur. But if they are forced to wait five or more seconds before looking, they are likely to commit the A not B error (Wellman, Cross, & Bartsch, 1986).

In the next chapter, we will see that most children develop object permanence before they develop emotional bonds to specific caregivers. It seems logical that infants must have permanent representations of their mothers before they will show distress at being separated from them. But wait, you say. Don't even three- or four-month-old infants cry when their mother leaves and then stop crying when she returns and picks them up? Doesn't this behaviour pattern show object permanence? Not necessarily. Infants appear to appreciate the comforts provided by their mothers and to express displeasure when they end (as when their mothers depart). The expression of displeasure frequently results in the reinstatement of pleasure (being held, fed, and spoken to). Therefore, infants may learn to engage in these protests when their mothers leave because of the positive consequences of protesting—and not because they have developed object permanence.

Nevertheless, studies by Renee Baillargeon and her colleagues (Aguiar & Baillargeon, 1999; Baillargeon, Graber, DeVos, & Black, 1990) show that some rudimentary knowledge of object permanence may be present as early as two and a half to three and a half months. In one study, Baillargeon (1987) first showed three-and-a-half- and four-and-a-half-month-olds the event illustrated in the top part of Figure 6.2. A screen rotated back and forth through a 180-degree arc like a drawbridge. After several trials, the infants showed habituation; that is, they spent less time looking at the screen. Next, a box was placed in the path of the screen, as

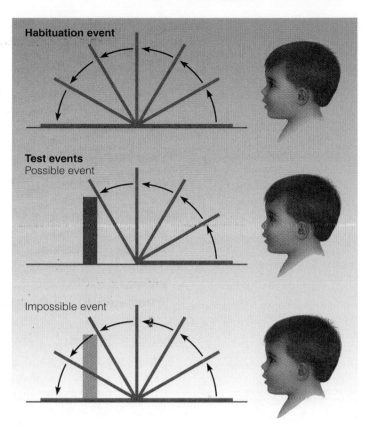

Figure 6.2

Object Permanence Before 4 Months of Age?

Renee Baillargeon (1987) used the technique shown here to demonstrate that knowledge of object permanence may exist before 4 months of age. She first showed infants a screen rotated back and forth like a drawbridge (top drawing). After infants showed habituation, a box was placed in the path of the screen. The middle drawing shows a possible event—the screen stops when it reaches the box. The bottom drawing shows an impossible event—the screen rotates through a full 180-degree arc as though the box were no longer behind it. (The experimenter had removed it, unknown to the infant.) Infants looked longer at the impossible event, indicating they realized the box still existed even when hidden behind the screen.

POWER VISUAL!
See your student companion website for an interactive version of Figure 6.2.

shown in the middle drawing of Figure 6.2. The infant could see the box at the beginning of each trial, but could no longer see it when the screen reached the box. In one condition, labelled the "possible event," the screen stopped when it reached the box. In another condition, labelled the "impossible event," the screen rotated through a full 180-degree arc, as though the box were no longer behind it. (How could this happen? Unknown to the infant, a trapdoor was released, causing the box to drop out of the way.) The infants looked longer at the "impossible event" than at the "possible" one. (Infants look longer at unexpected events.) So it seems they were surprised that the screen did not stop when it reached the box. This reaction indicates that children as young as three and a half months of age realized that the box continued to exist when it was hidden (Baillargeon, 1991). But why, then, do infants not actively look for hidden objects until about eight months of age? Piaget suggested that coordination of acts (such as removing a barrier in order to reach a toy) does not occur until the later age (Baillargeon et al., 1990).

Evaluation of Piaget's Theory

Question: What are the strengths and limitations of Piaget's theory of sensorimotor development? Piaget's theory remains a comprehensive model of infant cognition. Many of his observations of his own infants have been confirmed by others. The pattern and sequence of events he described have been observed among American, European, African, and Asian infants (Werner, 1988). Still, research has raised questions about the validity of many of Piaget's claims (Siegler & Alibali, 2005).

For one thing, most researchers now agree that cognitive development is not as tied to discrete stages as Piaget believed (Siegler & Alibali, 2005). The stage-theory approach requires that changes be discontinuous. In Piaget's theory, children's developing cognitive responses to the world would have to change relatively suddenly. Although later developments do seem to build on earlier ones, the process appears to be more gradual than discontinuous.

A second criticism of Piaget's theory is that he appears to have underestimated infants' competence (Siegler & Alibali, 2005). For example, infants display object permanence earlier than he believed (Aguiar & Baillargeon, 2002).

Finally, it is important to recognize that early cognitive development is greatly affected by children's sociocultural environments. According to Vygotsky (1987), whose theory and work will be evaluated more closely in Chapter 9, cognitive development is an interactive process, going beyond the individual.

Another example of early infant competence is provided by studies on **deferred imitation,** which is imitation of an action that may have occurred hours, days, or even weeks earlier. The presence of deferred imitation suggests that children have mentally represented behaviour patterns. Piaget believed that deferred imitation appears at about eighteen months, but others have found that infants show deferred imitation as early as nine months (Meltzoff, 1988, 2002). In Meltzoff's (1988) study, nine-month-old infants watched an adult perform behaviours such as pushing a button to produce a beep. When given a chance to play with the same objects a day later, many infants imitated the actions they had witnessed.

Let me mention one final example of infant competence that occurs much earlier than Piaget predicted. Recent research suggests that five-month-old infants may be able to grasp some basic computational concepts—*more* and *less* (see the nearby "A Closer Look" feature). In Piaget's view, this ability does not emerge until approximately two years of age.

deferred imitation   The imitation of people and events that occurred hours, days, or weeks in the past.

Psychologists Andrew Meltzoff and M. Keith Moore (1998) asserted bluntly that "the sensorimotor theory of infancy has been overthrown," but they admitted that "there is little consensus on a replacement." In an interview with a staff writer for the *Monitor* of the American Psychological Association, Meltzoff remarked that "Piaget's

A Closer Look | *Counting in the Crib? Findings from a "Mickey Mouse Experiment"*

Infants as young as five months of age may have some ability to "add" and "subtract," according to research by Karen Wynn (1992). Wynn's method was based on the fact that infants look longer at unexpected (novel) events than at expected (familiar) events. If infants are able to engage in some basic addition and subtraction, then they should look longer at a "wrong answer"—that is, at an unexpected answer—than at an expected "correct answer."

In her research, Wynn showed infants four-inch-tall Mickey Mouse dolls. (Yes, this was a "Mickey Mouse experiment," literally.) One group of infants saw a single doll. Then a screen was raised, blocking the infants' view. Some behind-the-scenes manipulation occurred so that when the screen was removed, the infants were presented with either two dolls (the unexpected or "wrong answer") or only one doll (the expected or "right answer"). They looked longer at the wrong answer. Another group of infants was initially shown two dolls. A screen was put in front of the dolls, and one doll was visibly taken from behind the screen. But some manipulation took place behind the scenes again, so that when the screen was removed, the infants were shown either one doll (the right answer) or two dolls (the wrong answer). The infants consistently looked longer at the two dolls—that is, the wrong answer.

These results suggest that infants were responsive to some change in quantity—perhaps they showed some rudimentary sense of "more" or "less." But how do we know that the infants were aware of a difference in the number of objects? Can infants somehow calculate the change in number that was produced in the experiment?

To gain some insight into infants' abilities to "count," Wynn first presented a third group of infants with a single doll. She raised the screen and visibly added one doll as the infants observed. Again, some behind-the-scenes manipulation took place so that when the screen was removed, the

infants would be presented with either two Mickeys (the right answer) or three Mickeys (the wrong answer) (see Figure 6.3). In this phase of the research, the infants stared longer at the three Mickeys than the two, suggesting that they might have somehow calculated the number of Mickeys that should have resulted from the researcher's manipulations. But again, we cannot say that the infants are adding per se. Other researchers suggest that the infants are more likely to be sensitive to simpler concepts of more and less (Gao, Levine, & Huttenlocher, 2000).

So where was Minnie?

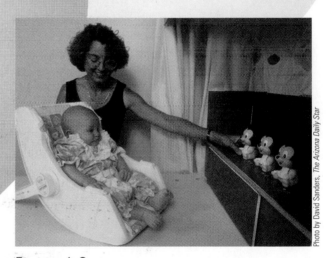

Photo by David Sanders, The Arizona Daily Star

Figure 6.3

Counting in the Crib?

Research by Karen Wynn suggests that 5-month-old infants may know when simple computations—or demonstrations involving concepts of *more* and *less*—are done correctly. The research is made possible by the fact that infants stare longer at unexpected stimuli—in this case, at a "wrong answer." Wynn conducted her research by exposing infants to Mickey Mouse dolls. She then added or removed one or more dolls behind a screen in such a way that the infant could see what was coming and going, removed the screen, and observed how long the infants gazed at "right" or "wrong" answers.

theories were critical for getting the field of [cognitive development] off the ground, ... but it's time to move on" (Meltzoff, 1997, p. 9). But move on to what exactly? Again, there is no consensus. Piaget is not so readily replaced.

Active Review

1. Piaget labelled children's concepts of the world as _____.

2. Children try to _____ new events into existing schemes.

3. Piaget's _____ stage spans the first two years of cognitive development.

4. Primary _____ reactions are characterized by repeating stimulating actions that occur by chance.

5. In _____ circular reactions, activity is repeated because of its effect on the environment.

6. _____ circular reactions are purposeful adaptations of established schemes to specific situations.

7. Object _____ is recognition that an object or person continues to exist when out of sight.

Reflect & Relate: How might an outside observer gather evidence that you and a friend or family member have "mentally represented" one another? How are you asked to demonstrate that you have mentally represented the subject matter in this textbook and in this course?

Go to
W W W http://www.voyages1CE.nelson.com
for an interactive version of this review.

Information Processing

The information-processing approach to cognitive development focuses on how children manipulate or process information coming in from the environment or already stored in the mind (Siegler & Alibali, 2005). *Question: What are infants' tools for processing information? One is memory. Another is imitation.*

Infants' Memory

Many of the cognitive capabilities of infants—recognizing the faces of familiar people, developing object permanence, and, in fact, learning in any form—depend on one critical aspect of cognitive development: their memory (Hayne & Fagen, 2003; Pascual-Leone, 2000). Even neonates demonstrate memory for stimuli to which they have been exposed previously. Neonates adjust their rate of sucking to hear a recording of their mother reading a story she had read aloud during the last weeks of pregnancy (DeCasper & Fifer, 1980; DeCasper & Spence, 1991). Remember, too, that neonates who are breast-fed are able to remember and show recognition of their mother's unique scent/odour (Cernoch & Porter, 1985).

Memory improves dramatically between two and six months of age and then again by twelve months (Rose, Feldman, & Jankowski, 2001). The improvement may indicate that older infants are more capable than younger ones of encoding (i.e., storing) information, retrieving information already stored, or both (Hayne & Fagen, 2003). As reviewed in Chapter 5, brain growth and development is connected to increased memory capacity. As infants' brains grow (synaptic growth, synaptic pruning, and myelination), their cognitive processing becomes more efficient (Case 1992, 1998). In terms of memory acquisition, the common phrase "Practice makes perfect" is pretty good advice. Neo-Piagetians like Robbie Case argue that assimilation is really practising schemes, and the practice leads to atomization. Working memory is then freed up and allows for accommodation. This may be a simplification, but you can see how the two theories are not mutually exclusive.

A fascinating series of studies by Carolyn Rovee-Collier and her colleagues (Rovee-Collier, 1993) illustrates some of these developmental changes in infant memory (see Figure 6.4). One end of a ribbon was tied to a brightly coloured mobile suspended above the infant's crib. The other end was tied to the infant's ankle, so that when the infant kicked, the mobile moved. Infants quickly learned to increase their rate of kicking. To measure memory, the infant's ankle was again fastened to the mobile after one or more days. In one study, two- and three-month-olds remembered how to make the mobile move after delays of up to three days, and three-month-olds remembered for more than a week (Greco, Rovee-Collier, Hayne, Griesler, & Early, 1986).

Infant memory can be improved if infants receive a reminder before they are given the memory test (Rovee-Collier & Shyi, 1992). In one study that used this reminder procedure, infants were shown the moving mobile on the day before the memory test, but they were not allowed to activate it. Under these conditions, three-month-olds remembered how to move the mobile after a twenty-eight-day delay (Rovee-Collier, 1993).

Imitation: Infant See, Infant Do?

Imitation is the basis for much of human learning. Deferred imitation—that is, the imitation of actions after a time delay—occurs as early as nine months of age. To help them remember the imitated act, infants are usually permitted to practise it when they learn it. But in one study, twelve-month-old infants were prevented from practising the behaviour they imitated. Yet they were able to demonstrate it four weeks later, suggesting that they had mentally represented the act (Klein & Meltzoff, 1999).

But infants have the capacity to imitate certain actions at a much earlier age. Neonates only 0.7 to 71 hours old have been found to imitate adults who open their mouths or stick out their tongues (Meltzoff & Prinz, 2002; Rizzolatti, Fadiga, Fogassi, & Gallese, 2002) (see Figure 6.5).

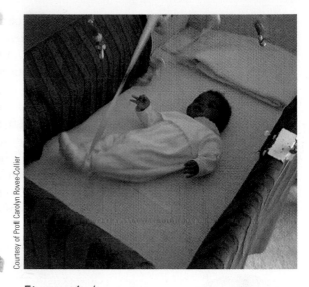

Courtesy of Prof. Carolyn Rovee-Collier

Figure 6.4
Investigating Infant Memory

In this technique, developed by Carolyn Rovee-Collier, the infant's ankle is connected to a mobile by a ribbon. Infants quickly learn to kick to make the mobile move. Two- and 3-month-olds remember how to perform this feat after a delay of a few days. If given a reminder of simply viewing the mobile, their memory lasts for 2 to 4 weeks.

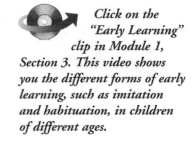

Click on the "Early Learning" clip in Module 1, Section 3. This video shows you the different forms of early learning, such as imitation and habituation, in children of different ages.

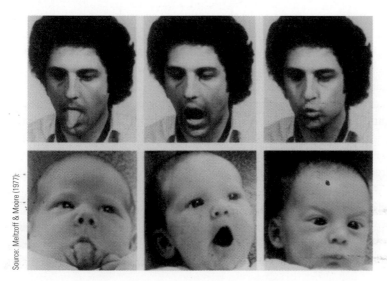

Source: Meltzoff & Moore (1977).

Figure 6.5
Imitation in Infants

These 2- to 3-week-old infants are imitating the facial gestures of an adult experimenter. How are we to interpret these findings? Can we say that the infants "knew" what the experimenter was doing and "chose" to imitate the behaviour, or is there an alternative explanation?

Before you become too impressed with this early imitative ability of neonates, you should know that some studies have not found imitation in early infancy (Abravanel & DeYong, 1991). One key factor may be the infants' age. The studies that find imitation generally have been done with very young infants—up to two weeks old—whereas the studies that do not find imitation have tended to use older infants. Therefore, the imitation of neonates is likely to be reflexive. Thus, imitation might disappear when reflexes are "dropping out" and reemerge when the infant has a firmer cognitive footing. **Truth or Fiction Revisited:** It is true that a one-hour-old infant may imitate an adult who sticks out his or her tongue. But such imitation is reflexive. That is, the infant is not observing the adult and then *deciding* to stick out his or her tongue.

Why might newborns possess some sort of imitation reflex? Answers lie in the realm of speculation. One possibility is that such a built-in response would contribute to the formation of caregiver-infant bonding and the survival of the newborn (Meltzoff & Prinz, 2002). Giacomo Rizzolatti and his colleagues (2002) wrote of the possibility of "mirror neurons," which they claimed to have found in the brains of our close genetic relatives, monkeys. Because such neurons would enhance the probability of survival as a result of caregiving, they would be maintained by evolutionary forces.

Active Review

8. The _____-processing approach to cognitive development focuses on how children manipulate or process information.

9. _____ improves dramatically between the ages of two and six months.

10. The imitation of actions after a time delay is called _____ imitation.

Reflect & Relate: Why do adolescents and adults stick their tongues out at infants? (Why not ask a few—a few adolescents and adults, that is?)

Go to
W W W http://www.voyages1CE.nelson.com
for an interactive version of this review.

Individual Differences in Intelligence among Infants

Cognitive development does not proceed in the same way or at the same pace for all infants (Rose et al., 2001). *Question: How do we measure individual differences in the development of cognitive functioning?* Efforts to understand the development of infant differences in cognitive development have relied on so-called scales of infant development or infant intelligence.

Measuring cognition or intelligence in infants is quite different from measuring it in adults. Infants cannot, of course, be assessed by asking them to explain the meanings of words, the similarity between concepts, or the rationales for social rules. One of the most important tests of intellectual development among infants contains very different kinds of items. It is the Bayley Scales of Infant Development, constructed in 1933 by psychologist Nancy Bayley and revised most recently in 2005.

The Bayley-III test currently consists of the adaptive behaviour, cognitive, language, motor, and social-emotional development domains. The adaptive behaviour domain assesses some of the following: communication, community use, functional preacademics, home living, health and safety, and leisure. The cognitive domain assesses sensorimotor development, exploration and manipulation, object relatedness, concept formation, memory, habituation, visual acuity, visual preference, and objection permanence as well as other cognitive processes. In the language domain, both expressive (babbling, gesturing, vocabulary) and receptive (i.e., understanding of morphological markers) communication are assessed. The motor domain assesses (1) fine motor skills (e.g., motor planning, prehension, manipulation, reaching, grasping) and (2) gross motor skills (e.g., standing, walking, and balance). A social-emotional domain was added to the third edition of the test. For this domain, the early signs of social-emotional growth are assessed—such as self-regulation, use of emotions, and social interactions. Table 6.1 contains sample items from the mental and motor scales and shows the ages at which 50 percent of the infants taking the test passed the items. The addition of an adaptive scale and social-emotional scale to the Bayley-III reflects a growing appreciation for a broader understanding of cognitive functioning.

Truth or Fiction Revisited: It is true that psychologists can begin to measure intelligence in infancy. However, they use measures that differ quite a bit from those used with older children and adults, and it remains unclear how well the results obtained in infancy predict intellectual functioning at later ages.

© Courtesy of the Psychological Association

The Bayley Scales of Infant Development
The Bayley scales measure the infant's mental and motor development.

Items from the Bayley Scales of Infant Development (BSID–III)		
Age	Cognitive-Scale Items	Motor-Scale Items
1 month	The infant quiets when picked up.	The infant makes a postural adjustment when put to examiner's shoulder.
2 months	When examiner presents two objects (bell and rattle) above the infant in a crib, the infant glances back and forth from one to the other.	The infant holds his or her head steady when being carried about in a vertical position.
5 months	The infant is observed to transfer an object from one hand to the other during play.	When seated at a feeding-type table and presented with a sugar pill that is out of reach, the infant attempts to pick it up.
8 months	When an object (toy) in plain view of the infant (i.e., on a table) is covered by a cup, the infant removes the cup in order to retrieve the object.	The infant raises herself or himself into a sitting position.
12 months	The infant imitates words that are spoken by the examiner.	When requested by the examiner, the infant moves from a reclining position on his or her back on the floor to a standing position.
14–16 months	The infant builds a tower with two cubes (blocks) after the examiner demonstrates the behaviour.	The infant walks alone with good coordination.

Testing Infants: Why and with What?

As you can imagine, it is no easy matter to test an infant. The items must be administered on a one-to-one basis by a patient tester, and it can be difficult to judge whether the infant is showing the targeted response. Why, then, do we test infants?

One reason is to screen infants for handicaps. A highly trained tester may be able to detect early signs of sensory or neurological problems, as suggested by development of visual-motor coordination. In addition to the Bayley scales, a number of tests, including the Brazelton Neonatal Behavioral Assessment Scale (see Chapter 4) and the Denver Developmental Screening Test, have been developed to screen infants for difficulties.

Instability of Intelligence Scores Attained in Infancy

Researchers have also tried to use infant scales to predict development, but this effort has been less than successful. *Question: How well do infant scales predict later intellectual performance?* The answer is somewhat less than clear. Certain items on the Bayley scales have been found to predict specific intellectual skills later in childhood. For example, Linda Siegel found that Bayley items measuring infant motor skills predicted subsequent fine motor and visual-spatial skills at six to eight years of age. Bayley language items also predicted language skills at the same age (Siegel, 1992).

One study found that the Bayley scales and socioeconomic status were able to predict cognitive development among low-birth-weight children from eighteen months to four years of age (Dezoete, MacArthur, & Tuck, 2003). Being female, having a longer period of gestation, and having a relatively higher birth weight were also positively associated with cognitive functioning at eighteen months and four years.

But overall or global scores on the Bayley and other infant scales apparently do not predict school grades or IQ scores among schoolchildren very well (Colombo, 1993; Storfer, 1990). Why do infant tests fail to do a good job of predicting IQ scores among school-aged children? Aside from the possibility that intellectual functioning fluctuates between the preschool and school years, it may be that the sensorimotor test items used during infancy are not that strongly related to the verbal and symbolic items used to assess intelligence at later ages.

Use of Visual Recognition Memory: An Effort to Enhance Predictability

In a continuing effort to find aspects of intelligence and cognition that might remain consistent from infancy through later childhood, a number of researchers have recently focused on visual recognition memory (Courage, Howe, & Squires, 2004). *Questions: What is visual recognition memory? How is it used?* **Visual recognition memory** is the ability to discriminate previously seen objects from novel objects. How is it used? This procedure is based on habituation, as are many of the methods for assessing perceptual development (see Chapter 5).

Let us consider longitudinal studies of this type. Susan Rose and her colleagues (Rose, Feldman, & Wallace, 1992) showed seven-month-old infants pictures of two identical faces. After twenty seconds, the pictures were replaced with one picture of a new face and a second picture of the familiar face. The amount of time the infants spent looking at each of the faces in the second set of pictures was recorded. Some infants spent more time looking at the new face than at the familiar face, suggesting that they had better memory for visual stimulation. The children were given standard IQ tests yearly from ages one through six. It was found that the children with greater visual recognition memory later attained higher IQ scores.

visual recognition memory The kind of memory shown in an infant's ability to discriminate previously seen objects from novel objects.

Rose and her colleagues (2001) also showed that, from age to age, individual differences in capacity for visual recognition memory are stable. This finding is important because intelligence—the quality that many researchers seek to predict from visual recognition memory—is also theorized to be a reasonably stable trait. Similarly, items on intelligence tests are age graded; that is, older children perform better than younger children, even as developing intelligence remains constant. So, too, with visual recognition memory. Capacity for visual recognition memory increases over the first year after birth (Rose, Feldman, & Jankowski, 2001).

A number of other studies have examined the relationship between either infant visual recognition memory or preference for novel stimulation (which is a related measure) and later IQ scores. In general, they show good predictive validity for broad cognitive abilities throughout childhood, including measures of intelligence and language ability (S. A. Rose et al., 2004).

In sum, scales of infant development may provide useful data as screening devices, as research instruments, or simply as a way to describe the things that infants do and do not do. However, their predictive power as intelligence tests has so far been disappointing. Tests of visual recognition hold better promise as predictors of later intelligence.

Many parents today spend a good deal of time trying to teach their children skills that will enhance their intelligence testing scores. No shortage of commercial products prey on parents' fears that their children might not measure up, and these products are found on the shelves of such stores as Toys "R" Us. Although these products themselves probably do no harm, parents might better spend their time reading to children, playing with them, and taking them on stimulating excursions. Even a supermarket provides ample opportunities for parents to talk with their young children about shapes and colours and temperatures and kinds of foods.

Now let us turn our attention to a fascinating aspect of cognitive development, the development of language.

Active Review

11. The Bayley Scales of Infant Development consists of _____ development domains.

12. The Brazelton Neonatal Behavioral Assessment Scale is used to screen for sensory or _____ problems.

13. _____ recognition memory refers to an infant's ability to discriminate previously seen objects from novel objects.

Reflect & Relate: When you have observed infants, what kinds of behaviours have led you to think that one is "brilliant" or another is "dull"? How do your "methods" correspond to those used by researchers who attempt to assess intellectual functioning among infants?

Go to
W W W http://www.voyages1CE.nelson.com
for an interactive version of this review.

Language Development

"The time has come," the Walrus said,
"To talk of many things
Of shoes—and ships—and sealing wax—
Of cabbages—and kings—
And why the sea is boiling hot—
And whether pigs have wings."

Lewis Carroll, *Through the Looking-Glass*

No, in his well-known children's book, Lewis Carroll wasn't quite telling the truth. The sea is not boiling hot—at least not in most places and at most times. And at the risk of alienating walrus aficionados, we will assert that walruses neither speak nor use other forms of language to communicate. But children do. Children come "to talk of many things," perhaps only rarely of sealing wax and cabbages, but certainly about the things more closely connected with their environments and their needs. Children may be unlikely to debate "whether pigs have wings," unless they are reared on an unusual farm, but they do develop the language skills that will eventually enable them to do just that. Lewis Carroll enjoyed playing with language, and we will see that children also join in that game. In physical development, the most dramatic developments come early—fast and furious—long before the child is born. Language does not come quite so early, and its development may not seem quite so fast and furious. Nevertheless, during the years of infancy, most children develop from creatures without language to little people who understand nearly all the things that are said to them and who relentlessly sputter words and simple sentences for all the world to hear. If much of the world might think that they do not yet have anything of value to say, most parents find their utterances to be just priceless.

In this section, we trace language development from early crying and cooing through the production of two-word sentences. We then consider theoretical views of language development.

Early Vocalizations

Children develop language according to an invariant sequence of steps, or stages, as outlined in Table 6.2. We begin with the **prelinguistic** vocalizations. *Question: What are prelinguistic vocalizations?* True words are symbols of objects and events. Prelinguistic vocalizations, such as cooing and babbling, do not represent objects or events. *Truth or Fiction Revisited:* Actually, infant crying is *not* a primitive form of language. Cries do not represent objects or events.

Newborn children, as parents are well aware, have an unlearned but highly effective form of verbal expression: crying and more crying. Crying is accomplished by blowing air through the vocal tract. There are no distinct well-formed sounds. Crying is about the only sound that infants make during the first month.

During the second month, infants begin **cooing.** Infants use their tongues when they coo. For this reason, coos are more articulated than cries. Coos are often vowel-like and may resemble extended "oohs" and "ahs." Cooing appears linked to feelings of pleasure or positive excitement. Infants tend not to coo when they are hungry, tired, or in pain.

Cries and coos are innate but can be modified by experience (Volterra, Caselli, Capirci, & Pizzuto, 2004). When parents respond positively to cooing by talking to their infants, smiling at them, and imitating them, cooing increases. Early parent-child "conversations," in which parents respond to coos and then pause as the infant coos, may foster infant awareness of taking turns as a way of verbally relating to other people.

Watch infants and toddlers exhibit different types of language development, from listening and cooing to forming words. Click on the "Language Development" clip in Module 1, Section 3.

prelinguistic Referring to vocalizations made by the infant before the development of language. (In language, words symbolize objects and events.)

cooing Prelinguistic, articulated vowel-like sounds that appear to reflect feelings of positive excitement.

Table 6.2	Milestones in Language Development in Infancy
Approximate Age	**Vocalization and Language**
Birth	• Cries.
12 weeks	• Cries less. • Smiles when talked to and nodded at. • Engages in squealing and gurgling sounds (cooing). • Sustains cooing for 15–20 seconds.
16 weeks	• Responds to human sounds more definitely. • Turns head, searching for the speaker. • Chuckles occasionally.
20 weeks	• Cooing becomes interspersed with consonant-like sounds. • Vocalizations differ from the sounds of mature language.
6 months	• Cooing changes to single-syllable babbling. • Neither vowels nor consonants have fixed pattern of recurrence. • Common utterances sound somewhat like ma, mu, da, or di.
8 months	• Continuous repetition (reduplication) enters into babbling. • Patterns of intonation become distinct. • Utterances can signal emphasis and emotion.
10 months	• Vocalizations mixed with sound play—gurgling, bubble blowing. • Makes effort to imitate sounds made by older people with mixed success.
12 months	• Identical sound sequences replicated more often. • Words (e.g., mamma or dadda) emerge. • Many words and requests understood (e.g., "Show me your eyes").
18 months	• Repertoire of 3–50 words. • Explosive vocabulary growth. • Babbling consists of several syllables with intricate intonation. • Little effort to communicate information. • Little joining of words into spontaneous two-word utterances. • Understands nearly everything spoken.
24 months	• Vocabulary more than 50 words, naming everything in the environment. • Spontaneous creation of two-word sentences. • Clear efforts to communicate.

Source: Table items adapted from Lenneberg (1967, pp. 128–130).
Note: Ages are approximations. Slower development does not necessarily indicate language problems. Albert Einstein did not talk until the age of 3.

By about eight months of age, cooing decreases markedly. Somewhere between six and nine months, children begin to babble. **Babbling** is the first vocalizing that sounds like human speech. In babbling, infants frequently combine consonants and vowels, as in *ba, ga,* and, sometimes, the much valued *dada* (Stoel-Gammon, 2002). At first, *dada* is purely coincidental (sorry, dads), despite the family's jubilation over its appearance.

In verbal interactions between infants and adults, the adults frequently repeat the syllables produced by their infants. They are likely to say "dadada" or "bababa" instead of simply "da" or "ba." Such redundancy apparently helps infants discriminate these sounds from others and further encourages them to imitate their parents (Goodsitt, Morse, Ver Hoeve, & Cowan, 1984).

After infants have been babbling for a few months, parents often believe that their children are having conversations with themselves. At ten to twelve months, infants tend to repeat syllables, showing what linguists refer to as **echolalia.** Parents overhear them going on and on, repeating consonant-vowel combinations ("ah-bah-bah-bah-bah"), pausing, and then switching to other combinations.

babbling The child's first vocalizations that have the sounds of speech.

echolalia The automatic repetition of sounds or words.

intonation   The use of pitches of varying levels to help communicate meaning.

Toward the end of the first year, infants are also using patterns of rising and falling **intonation** that resemble the sounds of adult speech. Elizabeth Bates and her colleagues (1987) noted that it may sound as though the infant is trying to speak the parents' language. Parents may think that their children are babbling in English or in whatever tongue is spoken in the home.

While certain behaviours develop along predetermined channels (often referred to as **canalization** because of the limitation on variance of expression of certain inherited characteristics), extreme environmental conditions (e.g., trauma or deprivation) may alter their course or impact development. Most babies tend to follow the typical sequence of language development (described above), yet experience (or lack thereof) can affect milestones.

Development of Vocabulary

receptive vocabulary   The sum total of the words whose meanings one understands.

expressive vocabulary   The sum total of the words that one can use in the production of language.

Question: How does vocabulary develop? Vocabulary development refers to the child's learning the meanings of words. In general, children's **receptive vocabulary** development outpaces their **expressive vocabulary** development (Baker & Cantwell, 1991; Lickliter, 2001). This means that at any given time, they can understand more words than they can use. One study, for example, found that twelve-month-olds could speak an average of thirteen words but could comprehend the meaning of eighty-four (Thal & Bates, 1990). In fact, infants usually understand much of what others are saying well before they themselves utter any words at all.

The Child's First Words

Ah, that long-awaited first word! What a milestone! Sad to say, many parents miss it. They are not quite sure when their infants utter their first word, often because the first word is not pronounced clearly or because pronunciation varies from usage to usage.

Developing in a World of Diversity

Babbling Here, There, and Everywhere

Babbling, like crying and cooing, appears to be inborn. Children from different cultures, where languages sound very different, all seem to babble the same sounds, including many they could not have heard (Oller, 1995, 2000). Deaf children whose parents use sign language babble with their hands and fingers, using repetitive gestures that

resemble the vocal babbling of infants who can hear (Bloom, 1998; Petittio & Marentette, 1991).

Despite the fact that babbling is innate, it is readily modified by the child's language environment. One study followed infants growing up in French-, Chinese-, and Arabic-speaking households (de Boysson-Bardies & Halle, 1994). At four to

seven months of age, the infants began to use more of the sounds in their language environment; foreign phonemes began to drop out. The role that experience plays in language development is further indicated by the fact that the babbling of deaf infants never begins to approximate the sounds of the parents' language.

The first word typically is spoken between the ages of eleven and thirteen months, but a range of eight to eighteen months is considered normal (Baker & Cantwell, 1991; Bates, Thal, & Janowsky, 1992). First words tend to be brief, consisting of one or two syllables. Each syllable is likely to consist of a consonant followed by a vowel. Vocabulary acquisition is slow at first. It may take children three or four months to achieve a vocabulary of ten to thirty words after the first word is spoken (de Villiers & de Villiers, 1999).

By about eighteen months of age, children may be producing up to fifty words. Many of them are quite familiar, such as *no, cookie, mama, hi,* and *eat.* Others, such as *all gone* and *bye-bye,* may not be found in the dictionary, but they function as words. That is, they are used consistently to symbolize the same meaning.

More than half (65 percent) of children's first words make up what Katherine Nelson (1973) referred to as "general nominals" and "specific nominals." General nominals are similar to nouns in that they include the names of classes of objects (*car, ball*), animals (*doggy, cat*), and people (*boy, girl*). But they also include both personal and relative pronouns (*she, that*). Specific nominals are proper nouns, such as *Daddy* and *Rover.* The attention of infants seems to be captured by movement. Words expressing movement are frequently found in early speech (Stockman & Vaughn-Cooke, 1992). Nelson (1973, 1981) found that of children's first fifty words, the most common were names for people, animals, and objects that move (*Mommy, car, doggy*) or that can be moved (*dolly, milk*), action words (*bye-bye*), a number of modifiers (*big, hot*), and expressive words (*no, hi, oh*).

At about eighteen to twenty-two months of age, there is a rapid burst in the number of new words learned (Reznick & Goldfield, 1992). The child's vocabulary may increase from fifty to more than 300 words in just a few months (Bates et al., 1992). This vocabulary spurt could also be called a naming explosion, because almost 75 percent of the words added during this time are nouns (Goldfield & Reznick, 1990). The rapid pace of vocabulary growth continues through the preschool years, with children acquiring an average of nine new words per day (Rice, 1989).

referential language style
Use of language primarily as a means for labelling objects.

expressive language style
Use of language primarily as a means for engaging in social interaction.

Fostering Language Development
Language growth in young children is enhanced when parents and caregivers engage the infant "in conversation" about activities and objects in the environment.

Referential and Expressive Styles in Language Development
Nelson (1981) also found that some children prefer a referential approach in their language development, whereas others take a more expressive approach. Children who show the **referential language style** use language primarily to label objects in their environments. Their early vocabularies consist mainly of nominals. Children who use an **expressive language style** use language primarily as a means for engaging in social interactions. Children with an expressive style use more pronouns and many words involved in social routines, such as *stop, more,* and *all gone.* More children use an expressive style than a referential style (Hampson, 1989), but most use a combination of the styles.

Why do some children prefer a referential style and others an expressive style? It may be that some children are naturally oriented toward objects, whereas others are primarily interested in social relationships. Nelson also found that the parents' ways of teaching children play a role. Some parents focus on labelling objects for children as soon as they notice their vocabularies expanding. Others are more oriented toward social interactions themselves, teaching their children to say "hi," "please," and "thank you."

© 2007 Laura Dwight

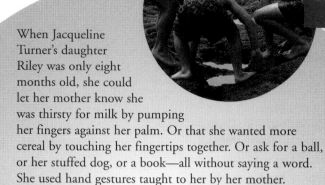

When Jacqueline Turner's daughter Riley was only eight months old, she could let her mother know she was thirsty for milk by pumping her fingers against her palm. Or that she wanted more cereal by touching her fingertips together. Or ask for a ball, or her stuffed dog, or a book—all without saying a word. She used hand gestures taught to her by her mother.

Why teach signs to a baby who is not deaf? Mrs. Turner, a Spanish-language interpreter from Beaverton, said she bought a book and video about teaching signs to babies to help eliminate the frustration Riley had in not being able to communicate, as well as Mrs. Turner's own frustration in not understanding her. "It makes her feel that she's more in control of a situation and has choices," Mrs. Turner said.

For hearing and deaf children, the ability to gesture tends to develop ahead of words. Babies can wave bye-bye to Grandma months before they can talk, for instance.

In interviews in 2003, Dr. Elizabeth Bates, one of the leading researchers in the field and the director of the Center for Research in Language at the University of California at San Diego, talked about the development of this type of communication.

"It has to do with how easily one can imitate and reproduce something with a great big fat hand as opposed to the mini, delicate hundreds of muscles that control the tongue," Dr. Bates said in the interview. "You can also see somebody using a hand, which you can't do with a tongue." The areas in the brain that control the mouth and speech and the areas that control the hands and gestures overlap a great deal and develop together, Dr. Bates added.

Teaching simple gestures, or signs, to babies before they can talk is a way to jump-start the language and communication process, and stimulate intellectual development. It can also confer a host of related benefits, including increased vocabulary, a deeper parent-child bond, enhanced self-esteem, and decreased tantrums during the "terrible twos," proponents say.

Research by Dr. Linda Acredolo and Dr. Susan W. Goodwyn has perhaps drawn the most interest. They found that second-graders who had been encouraged to use their signing system during the second year of life had an advantage of twelve IQ points over children who did not use any such system.

Also intriguing has been the work of Joseph Garcia, the author of the best-selling book and video series *Sign with Your Baby: How to Communicate with Infants before They Can Speak.* Mr. Garcia, an American Sign Language and early child development researcher, noticed that the hearing babies of deaf parents could communicate their needs and desires at a much earlier age than children of hearing parents. His research found that through signs, parent-infant communication could begin at eight months, rather than at sixteen to eighteen months, when comprehensible speech has begun to develop.

Parents who sign with their babies may be learning as much about communicating as their children. "Research shows huge individual differences in how much adults communicate with children," Dr. Bates said. "The studies out there show significant effects probably because a subset of the parents in the studies were not communicating with their kids as much as they start to when they enter these programs."

Many parents wonder whether signing will get in the way of their babies' learning how to talk. According to Mrs. Turner, who continued to sign with Riley for several months after she began speaking, what happened was just the opposite. "Once she started saying her first words, the more I used signs, the more she answered back with words," she said. Riley, now twenty months old, is very verbal and says cogent three-word sentences.

Signing can also ease a toddler's transition to speaking by reducing the frustration of trying to pronounce words like "toothbrush," or to express concepts like needing a diaper changed. For instance, even before Riley could speak, she was able to show her mother that something hurt by making the sign for pain and pointing to a part of her body. And according to Mrs. Turner, Riley understood that the word "please" would get her a favourite toy or a drink of milk more quickly, but it was difficult for her to say because of the l sound. Instead she used the sign for "please."

For Mrs. Turner, signing with a child is as much about empowerment as about communication. It provided Riley, and would provide other children, with another tool to get their needs met.

Source: From Berck, J. (2004, January 5). "Before Baby Talk, Signs and Signals." *New York Times.* Copyright © 2004 by the New York Times Co. Reprinted by permission.

Overextension

Young children try to talk about more objects than they have words for (not so surprising—so do adults, now and then). To accomplish their linguistic feats, children often extend the meaning of one word to refer to things and actions for which they do not have words (McDonough, 2002). This process is called **overextension.** In classic research, Eve Clark (1973, 1975) studied diaries of infants' language development and found that overextensions are generally based on perceived similarities in function or form between the original object or action and the new one to which the first word is being extended. She provides the example of the word *mooi*, which one child originally used to refer to the moon. The child then overextended *mooi* to designate all round objects, including the letter *o* and cookies and cakes.

Overextensions gradually pull back to their proper references as the child's vocabulary and ability to classify objects develop (McDonough, 2002). Consider the example of a child who first refers to a dog as a "bowwow." The word *bowwow* then becomes overextended to also refer to horses, cats, and cows. In effect, *bowwow* comes to mean something akin to "familiar animal." Next, the child learns to use the word *moo* to refer to cows. But *bowwow* still remains extended to horses and cats. As the child's vocabulary develops, he or she acquires the word *doggy*. So dogs and cats may now be referred to with either *bowwow* or *doggy*. Eventually, each animal has one or more correct names.

overextension Use of words in situations in which their meanings become extended or inappropriate.

Development of Sentences: Telegraphic Speech

Question: How do infants create sentences? The infant's first sentences are typically one-word utterances, but these utterances appear to express complete ideas and therefore can be thought of as sentences. Roger Brown (1973) called brief expressions that have the meanings of sentences **telegraphic speech.** Adults who write telegrams use principles of syntax to cut out all the unnecessary words. "Home Tuesday" might stand for "I expect to be home on Tuesday." Similarly, only the essential words are used in children's telegraphic speech—in particular, nouns, verbs, and some modifiers.

telegraphic speech Type of speech in which only the essential words are used.

Mean Length of Utterance

Roger Brown (1973, 1977) described telegraphic speech in terms of children's average or **mean length of utterance (MLU).** The MLU is defined as the average number of **morphemes** that children use in their sentences. Morphemes are the smallest units of meaning in a language. A morpheme may be a whole word or part of a word, such as a prefix or suffix. For example, the word *walked* consists of two morphemes: the verb *walk* and the suffix *ed*, which changes the verb to the past tense. In Figure 6.6, we see the relationship between chronological age and MLU for three children tracked by Brown: Lin, Victor, and Sarah.

mean length of utterance (MLU) The average number of morphemes used in an utterance.

morpheme The smallest unit of meaning in a language.

The patterns of growth in MLU are similar for each child, showing swift upward movement, broken by intermittent and brief regressions. Figure 6.6 also shows us something about individual differences. Lin was precocious compared to Victor and Sarah, extending her MLU at much earlier ages. However, as suggested earlier, the receptive language of all three children would have exceeded their expressive language at any given time. Also, Lin's earlier extension of MLU does not guarantee that she will show more complex expressive language than Victor and Sarah at maturity.

Let us now consider the features of two types of telegraphic speech: the holophrase and two-word utterances.

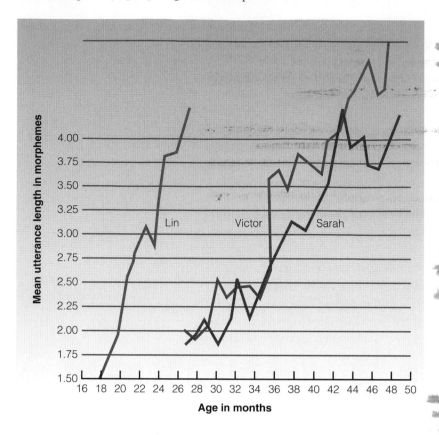

Figure 6.6

Mean Length of Utterance for Three Children

Some children begin speaking earlier than others. However, the mean length of utterance (MLU) increases rapidly once speech begins.

holophrase A single word that is used to express complex meanings.

syntax The rules in a language for placing words in proper order to form meaningful sentences (from the Latin *syntaxis*, meaning "joining together").

Holophrases

Holophrases are single words that are used to express complex meanings. For example, *Mama* may be used by the child to signify meanings as varied as "There goes Mama," "Come here, Mama," and "You are Mama." Most children readily teach their parents what they intend by augmenting their holophrases with gestures, intonations, and reinforcers. That is, they act delighted when parents do as requested and howl when they do not.

Infants are likely to combine single words with gestures as they undertake the transition from holophrases to two-word utterances (Capirci, Iverson, Pizzuto, & Volterra, 1996). For example, pointing can signify "there" before the word is used.

Two-Word Sentences

When the child's vocabulary consists of fifty to 100 words (usually somewhere between eighteen and twenty-four months of age), telegraphic two-word sentences begin to appear (Baker & Cantwell, 1991; Bates et al., 1992). In the sentence "That ball," the words *is* and *a* are implied.

Two-word sentences, although brief and telegraphic, still show understanding of **syntax** (Slobin, 2001). The child will say, "Sit chair," not "Chair sit," to tell a parent to sit in a chair. The child will say, "My shoe," not "Shoe my," to show possession. "Mommy go" means Mommy is leaving, whereas "Go, Mommy" expresses the wish for Mommy to go away.

Theories of Language Development: Can You Make a Houseplant Talk?

> Since all normal humans talk but no house pets or house plants do, no matter how pampered, heredity must be involved in language. But since a child growing up in Japan speaks Japanese whereas the same child brought up in California would speak English, the environment is also crucial. Thus, there is no question about whether heredity or environment is involved in language, or even whether one or the other is "more important." Instead, ... our best hope [might be] finding out *how* they interact.
>
> —Steven Pinker

Countless billions of children have learned the languages spoken by their parents and have passed them down, with minor changes, from generation to generation. But how do they do so? In discussing this question—and so many others—we refer to the possible roles of nature and nurture. Learning theorists have come down on the side of nurture, and those who point to a basic role for nature are said to hold a *nativist* view.

Learning-Theory Views

Question: How do learning theorists account for language development? Learning plays an obvious role in language development. Children who are reared in English-speaking homes learn English, not Japanese or Russian. Learning theorists usually explain language development in terms of imitation and reinforcement.

The Role of Imitation From a social cognitive perspective, parents serve as models. Children learn language, at least in part, by observation and imitation. It seems likely that many vocabulary words, especially nouns and verbs (including irregular verbs), are learned by imitation.

But imitative learning does not explain why children spontaneously utter phrases and sentences that they have not observed (Harris, 1990). Parents, for example, are unlikely to model utterances such as "Bye-bye sock" and "All gone, Daddy," but children do say them.

And children sometimes steadfastly avoid imitating certain language forms suggested by adults, even when the adults are insistent. Note the following exchange between two-year-old Ben and a (very frustrated) adult (Kuczaj, 1982, p. 48):

> Ben: I like these candy. I like they.
> Adult: You like them?
> Ben: Yes, I like they.
> Adult: Say them.
> Ben: Them.
> Adult: Say "I like them."
> Ben: I like them.
> Adult: Good.
> Ben: I'm good. These candy good too.
> Adult: Are they good?
> Ben: Yes. I like they. You like they?

models In learning theory, those whose behaviours are imitated by others.

Developing in a
World of Diversity

Two-Word Sentences Here, There, and ...

Two-word sentences appear at about the same age in the development of all languages (Slobin, 2001). Also, the sequence of emergence of the types of two-word utterances—for example, first, subject-verb ("Mommy go"), then verb-object ("Hit ball"), location ("Ball here"), and possession ("My ball")—is the same in languages as diverse as English, Luo (an African tongue), German, Russian, and Turkish. This is an example of the point that language develops in a series of steps that appear to be invariant. Dan Slobin interprets his findings to mean that the construction of sentences serves specific functions of communication in various languages. Slobin does not argue that there is an innate linguistic structure but rather that basic human processes of cognition, communication, and information processing are found across cultures (Slobin, 2001).

Ben is not resisting the adult because of obstinacy. He does repeat "I like them" when asked to do so. But when given the opportunity afterward to construct the object *them*, he reverts to using the subjective form *they*. At this period in his development, Ben is likely to use his (erroneous) understanding of syntax spontaneously to actively produce his own language, rather than just imitate a model.

The Role of Reinforcement B. F. Skinner (1957) allowed that prelinguistic vocalizations such as cooing and babbling may be inborn. But parents reinforce children for babbling that approximates the form of real words, such as *da*, which, in English, resembles *dog* or *daddy*. Children, in fact, do increase their babbling when it results in adults smiling at them, stroking them, and talking back to them. We have seen that as the first year progresses, children babble the sounds of their native tongues with increasing frequency; foreign sounds tend to drop out. The behaviourist explains this pattern of changing frequencies in terms of reinforcement (of the sounds of the adults' language) and **extinction** (of foreign sounds). An alternative (nonbehavioural) explanation is that children actively attend to the sounds in their linguistic environments and are intrinsically motivated to utter them.

From Skinner's perspective, children acquire their early vocabularies through **shaping.** That is, parents require that children's utterances be progressively closer to actual words before they are reinforced. In support of Skinner's position, more recent research shows that reinforcement accelerates the growth of vocabulary in young children (Whitehurst & Valdez-Menchaca, 1988). Skinner viewed multiword utterances as complex stimulus-response chains that are also taught by shaping. As children's utterances increase in length, parents foster correct word order by uttering sentences to their children and reinforcing imitation. As with Ben, when children make grammatical errors, parents recast their utterances correctly. They reinforce the children for repeating them.

But recall Ben's refusal to be shaped into correct syntax. If the reinforcement explanation of language development were sufficient, parents' reinforcement would facilitate children's learning of syntax and pronunciation. We do not have such evidence. For one thing, parents are more likely to reinforce their children for the accuracy, or "truth value," of their utterances than for their grammatical correctness (Brown, 1973). Parents, in other words, generally accept the syntax of their children's vocal efforts. The child who points down and says, "The grass is purple" is not likely to be reinforced, despite correct syntax. But the enthusiastic child who shows her empty plate and blurts out, "I eated it all up" is likely to be reinforced, despite the grammatical incorrectness of "eated." Research confirms that, although parents do expand and rephrase their children's ungrammatical utterances more than their grammatically correct ones, they do not overtly correct their children's language mistakes (Bohannon & Stanowicz, 1988; Coley, 1993; Penner, 1987).

Also, selective reinforcement of children's pronunciation might backfire. Children whose parents reward proper pronunciation but correct poor pronunciation develop vocabulary more slowly than children whose parents are more tolerant about pronunciation (Nelson, 1973). *Truth or Fiction Revisited:* Actually, the evidence suggests that correcting children's pronunciation may *slow* their vocabulary development.

Learning theory also cannot account for the invariant sequences of language development and for children's spurts in acquisition. Even the types of two-word utterances emerge in a consistent pattern in diverse cultures. Although timing differs from child to child, the types of questions used, passive versus active sentences, and so on all emerge in the same order. Yet, it is unlikely that parents around the world teach language skills in the same sequence.

extinction The decrease and eventual disappearance of a response in the absence of reinforcement.

shaping In learning theory, the gradual building of complex behaviour patterns through reinforcement of successive approximations of the target behaviour.

On the other hand, there is ample evidence that aspects of the child's language environment influence the development of language. Much of the research in this area has focused on the ways in which adults—especially mothers—interact with their children.

Studies show that language growth in young children is enhanced when mothers and other adults do the following things:

- Use a simplified form of speech known as "Motherese" (see the "A Closer Look" feature on page 211).
- Use questions that engage the child in conversation (Tamis-LeMonda & Bornstein, 2002).
- Respond to the child's expressive language efforts in a way that is "attuned"; for example, they relate their speech to the child's utterance by saying, "Yes, your doll is pretty" in response to the child's statement "My doll" (Nicely, Tamis-LeMonda, & Bornstein, 1999; Tamis-LeMonda & Bornstein, 2001).

Developing in a World of Diversity

Talking to Infants

The research on parent-infant communication usually focuses on mothers, who, despite the blurring of traditional gender roles in the West, still usually have the primary responsibility for rearing children. Mothers in different cultures show certain similarities in the way they talk to their infants, but cultural variations in their speech patterns exist as well (Tamis-LeMonda & Bornstein, 2002). One study analyzed how Argentinean, French, Japanese, and American mothers spoke to their five- and thirteen-month-old infants (Bornstein et al., 1992a). Mothers in all four cultures spoke more to older infants. When the infants were five months old, mothers' speech was more heavily laced with expressive statements such as greetings, songs, nonsense sounds, and endearing terms. As children got older, mothers in all groups provided more informa-

tion in their speech. They made statements, gave reports about the infant, mother, or environment, and asked the child questions.

But there were also variations in the speech of mothers in the four cultures that appeared to reflect cultural values and beliefs. Japanese mothers used emotionally expressive speech more often than Western mothers did, consistent with the Japanese mothers' child-rearing emphasis on social and emotional closeness and interdependence. Mothers from the three Western cultures favoured speech containing information. This may reflect Western traditions of encouraging independence (Barratt, Negayama, & Minami, 1993; Tamis-LeMonda, Bornstein, Cyphers, Toda, & Ogino, 1992).

Even within the three Western cultures, the types of information mothers provided to their infants

were different. Argentinean mothers used more direct statements, perhaps reflecting their more directive view of child rearing. U.S. mothers asked the most questions, possibly indicating an emphasis on the child as an active learner. French mothers conveyed less information in their speech than other Western mothers. French mothers placed less emphasis on stimulating achievement and more on emotional support (Bornstein et al., 1992a).

Do these variations in maternal speech affect the infant's behaviour? The answer seems to be yes. For example, at thirteen months of age, American infants are more advanced than Japanese infants in vocabulary development, possibly reflecting the more information-oriented speech of American mothers (Tamis-LeMonda et al., 1992).

- Join the child in paying attention to a particular activity or toy (Tamis-LeMonda & Bornstein, 1991).
- Gesture to help the child understand what they are saying (Gogate, Bahrick, & Watson, 2000; Iverson, Capirci, Longobardi, & Caselli, 1999).
- Describe aspects of the environment occupying the infant's current focus of attention (Tamis-LeMonda & Bornstein, 2002).
- Read to the child (Hoff-Ginsberg, 1998).
- Talk to the child a great deal (Tamis-LeMonda & Bornstein, 2002).

The Nativist View

Question: What is the nativist view of language development? The nativist view holds that innate or inborn factors cause children to attend to and acquire language in certain ways. From this perspective, children bring an inborn tendency in the form of neurological "prewiring" to language learning (Clancy & Finlay, 2001; Pinker, 1994; Werker & Desjardins, 2001).

psycholinguistic theory The view that language learning involves an interaction between environmental influences and an inborn tendency to acquire language. The emphasis is on the inborn tendency.

language acquisition device (LAD) In psycholinguistic theory, neural "prewiring" that facilitates the child's learning of grammar.

surface structure The superficial grammatical construction of a sentence.

deep structure The underlying meaning of a sentence.

Psycholinguistic Theory According to **psycholinguistic theory**, language acquisition involves an interaction between environmental influences—such as exposure to parental speech and reinforcement—and an inborn tendency to acquire language (Clancy & Finlay, 2001). Chomsky (1988, 1990) and some others labelled this innate tendency a **language acquisition device (LAD)**. Evidence for an inborn tendency is found in the universality of human language abilities; in the regularity of the early production of sounds, even among deaf children; and in the invariant sequences of language development, regardless of which language the child is learning (Bloom, 1998; Volterra et al., 2004).

The inborn tendency primes the nervous system to learn grammar. On the surface, languages differ a great deal in their vocabulary and grammar. Chomsky refers to these elements as the **surface structure** of language. However, the LAD serves children all over the world because languages share what Chomsky refers to as a "universal grammar"—an underlying **deep structure** or set of rules for transforming ideas into sentences. From Chomsky's perspective, children are genetically prewired to attend to language and to deduce the rules for constructing sentences from ideas. Consider an analogy with computers: According to psycholinguistic theory, the universal grammar that resides in the LAD is the basic operating system of the computer, whereas the particular language that a child learns to use is the word-processing program. ***Truth or Fiction Revisited:*** It is apparently true that children are prewired to listen to language in such a way that they come to understand rules of grammar.

Brain Structures Involved in Language *Question: What parts of the brain are involved in language development?* Research shows that many parts of the brain are involved in language development and that each person may have a unique pattern of organization for language ability (Rosen, Ojemann, Ollinger, & Petersen, 2000; Schwartz, Haglund, M. M., Lettich, E., & Ojemann, 2000). However, some of the key biological structures that may provide the basis for the functions of the LAD appear to be based in the left hemisphere of the cerebral cortex for nearly all right-handed people and for two out of three left-handed people (Pinker, 1994).

Although both hemispheres of the brain are involved in perception of speech (Dehaene-Lambertz, Pena, Christophe, & Landrieu, 2004), the sounds of speech elicit greater electrical activity in the left hemisphere of newborns than in the right hemisphere, as indicated by the activity of brain waves. In the left hemisphere of the cortex, the two areas most involved in speech are Broca's area and Wernicke's area (Dogil, Ackermann, Grodd, Haider, Kamp, Mayer, Riecker, & Wildgruber, 2002) (see Figure 6.7). Even in the human fetus, Wernicke's area is usually larger in the left hemisphere than in the right. Damage to either area is likely to cause an **aphasia**—that is, a disruption in the ability to understand or produce language.

Broca's area is located near the section of the motor cortex that controls the muscles of the tongue and throat and other areas of the face that are used when speaking. When Broca's area is damaged, people speak slowly and laboriously, with simple sentences—a pattern known as **Broca's aphasia.** Their ability to understand the speech of others is relatively unaffected, however. Wernicke's area lies near the auditory cortex and is connected to Broca's area by nerve fibres. People with damage to Wernicke's area may show **Wernicke's aphasia.** Although they usually speak freely and with proper syntax, their abilities to comprehend other people's speech and to think of the words to express their own thoughts are impaired. Thus, Wernicke's area seems to be essential to understanding the relationships between words and their meanings.

A part of the brain called the *angular gyrus* lies between the visual cortex and Wernicke's area. The angular gyrus "translates" visual information, such as written words, into auditory information (sounds) and sends it on to Wernicke's area. It appears that problems in the angular gyrus can give rise to *dyslexia*, or serious impairment in reading, because it becomes difficult for the reader to segment words into sounds (Pugh, Mencl, Shaywitz, Shaywitz, Fulbright, Constable, Skudlarski, Marchione, Jenner, Fletcher, Liberman, Shankweiler, Katz, Lacadie, Gore, 2000).

The Sensitive Period Numerous researchers have suggested that language learning occurs during one or more **sensitive periods**, which begin at about eighteen to twenty-four months of age and last until puberty (Clancy & Finlay, 2001). *Question: What is meant by a sensitive period for language development?* During these sensitive periods, neural development (as in the differentiating of brain structures) provides plasticity that facilitates language learning. Experience with language also alters the structure of the brain, although the exact relationships have not been discovered (Clancy & Finlay, 2001).

Evidence for a sensitive period is found in recovery from brain injuries in some people. Injuries to the hemisphere that controls language (usually the left hemisphere) can impair or destroy the ability to speak. But before puberty, children suffering left-hemisphere injuries frequently recover a good deal of speaking ability. Lenneberg (1967) suggested that in young children, left-hemisphere damage may encourage the development of language functions in the right hemisphere. But adaptation ability wanes in adolescence, when brain tissue has reached adult levels of differentiation.

The best way to determine whether people are capable of acquiring language once they have passed puberty would be to run an experiment in which one or more children were reared in such severe isolation that they were not exposed to language until puberty. Of course, such an experiment could not be run because of ethical and legal barriers.

However, the disturbing case history of Genie offers insights into the issue of whether there is a sensitive period for language development (Curtiss,

aphasia A disruption in the ability to understand or produce language.

Broca's aphasia A form of aphasia caused by damage to Broca's area and characterized by slow, laborious speech.

Wernicke's aphasia A form of aphasia caused by damage to Wernicke's area and characterized by impaired comprehension of speech and difficulty in attempting to produce the right word.

sensitive period In linguistic theory, the period from about 18 months to puberty when the brain is thought to be especially capable of learning language because of its plasticity.

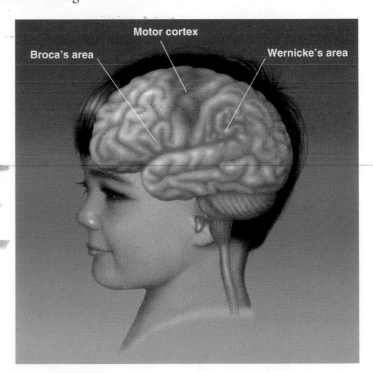

Figure 6.7

Broca's and Wernicke's Areas of the Cerebral Cortex

Broca's area and Wernicke's area of the (usually left) hemisphere are most involved in speech. Damage to either area can produce an aphasia—an impairment in the ability to understand or produce language.

A Closer Look | *"Motherese"*

One fascinating way that adults influence the language development of young children is through the use of baby talk, or "Motherese"—known more technically as *infant-directed speech (IDS)*. But "Motherese" is a limiting term because grandparents, fathers, siblings, and unrelated people, including older children, also use varieties of Motherese when talking to infants (Shute & Wheldall, 1999, 2001). Motherese occurs in languages as different as Arabic, English, Comanche, Italian, French, German, Xhosa (an African language), Japanese, and Mandarin Chinese (Fernald & Morikawa, 1993; Masataka, 1998; Papousek et al., 1991).

Researchers find that Motherese has several characteristics (Gogate et al., 2000; Trevarthen, 2003; Weppelman, Bostow, Schiffer, Elbert-Perez, & Newman, 2003):

1. Motherese is spoken more slowly and at a higher pitch than speech addressed to adults. There are distinct pauses between ideas.
2. Sentences are brief, and adults make the effort to speak in a grammatically correct manner.
3. Sentences are simple in syntax. The focus is on nouns, verbs, and just a few modifiers.
4. Key words are put at the ends of sentences and are spoken in a higher and louder voice.
5. The diminutive morpheme *y* is frequently added to nouns. *Dad* becomes *Daddy* and *horse* becomes *horsey.*
6. Motherese is repetitive. Adults repeat sentences several times, sometimes using minor variations, as in "Show me your nose." "Where is your nose?" "Can you touch your nose?" Adults also repeat children's utterances, often rephrasing them in an effort to expand children's awareness of their expressive opportunities. If the child says, "Baby shoe," the mother may reply, "Yes, that's your shoe. Shall Mommy put the shoe on baby's foot?"
7. Motherese includes a type of repetition called reduplication. *Yummy* becomes *yummy-yummy. Daddy* may alternate with *Da-da.*

8. Vocabulary is concrete, referring, when possible, to objects that are in the immediate environment. For example, stuffed lions may be referred to as "kitties." Purposeful overextension is intended to avoid confusing the child by adding too many new labels.
9. Objects may be overdescribed by being given compound labels. Rabbits may become "bunny rabbits," and cats may become "kitty cats." In this way parents may try to be sure that they are connecting with the child by using at least one label that the child will recognize.
10. Parents speak for the children, as in "Is baby tired?" "Oh, we're so tired." "We want to take our nap now, don't we?" This parent is pretending to have a two-way conversation with the child. In this way, parents seem to be trying to help their children express themselves by offering children models of sentences they can use later on.
11. Users of Motherese stay a step ahead of the child. As children's vocabularies grow and their syntax develops, adults step up their own language levels—remaining just ahead of the child. In this way, adults seem to be encouraging the child to continue to play catch-up.

And so, adults and older children use a variety of strategies to communicate with young children and to draw them out. Does it work? Does Motherese foster language development? Research on the effects of Motherese is supportive of its use. Infants as young as two days old prefer baby talk over adult talk (Trevarthen, 2003; Weppelman et al., 2003). The short, simple sentences and high pitch used in Motherese are more likely to produce a response from the child and to enhance vocabulary development than are complex sentences and those spoken in a lower pitch. Children who hear their utterances repeated and recast do seem to learn from the adults who are modelling the new expressions (Nicely et al., 1999; Tamis-LeMonda, Bornstein, & Baumwell, 2001). Repetition of children's vocalizations also appears to be one method of reinforcing vocalizing. In sum, Motherese may be of significant help in fostering children's language development.

For Better or For Worse®   **by Lynn Johnston**

"Motherese"
Adults and older children use a simplified form of language known as "Motherese" when they talk to infants. Motherese is spoken slowly and at a higher pitch than that used with adults, and it uses brief sentences that are simple in syntax.

1977; Rymer, 1993). Genie's father locked her in a small room at the age of twenty months and kept her there until she was thirteen. Her social contacts during this period were limited to her mother, who entered the room only to feed Genie, and her father, who beat her. When Genie was rescued, she weighed only about sixty pounds, did not speak, was not toilet trained, and could barely stand. Genie was placed in a foster home, where she was exposed to English for the first time in nearly twelve years. Her language development followed the normal sequence of much younger children in a number of ways, but she never acquired the proficiency of children reared under normal circumstances. Five years after her liberation, Genie's language remained largely telegraphic. She still showed significant problems with syntax—for example, failing to reverse subjects and verbs to phrase spontaneous questions. She showed confusion concerning the use of the past tense (adding *ed* to words) and had difficulty using negative helping verbs such as *isn't* and *haven't*.

Genie's language development provides some support for the sensitive-period hypothesis, although it is possible that her language problems can also be attributed to her long years of malnutrition and abuse. It is also possible that she was mentally retarded to begin with. Her efforts to acquire English after puberty were clearly laborious, and the results were substandard compared even to the language of many two- and three-year-olds.

Further evidence for the sensitive-period hypothesis is provided by a study of a deaf boy named Simon, who was observed from the ages of two and a half to nine years (Newport, 1992). Researchers reported that Simon signed in **American Sign Language (ASL)** with correct grammar, even though he had been exposed only to grammatically incorrect ASL by his parents and their friends, who also were deaf. Simon's parents and their friends had not learned to sign until they were teenagers. At that age, people often learn languages imperfectly. But Simon showed early mastery of grammatical rules that his parents used incorrectly or not at all. Simon's deduction of these rules on his own supports the view that the tendency to acquire language is inborn, and it also provides evidence that such learning occurs most readily during a sensitive period early in life.

In sum, the development of language in infancy represents the interaction of environmental and biological factors. The child brings a built-in readiness to the task of

American Sign Language (ASL) The communication of meaning through the use of symbols that are formed by moving the hands and arms. The language used by some deaf people.

language acquisition—whereas houseplants and other organisms do not. The child must also have the opportunity to hear spoken language and to interact verbally with others. In the next chapter, we will see how interaction with others affects the social development of the infant.

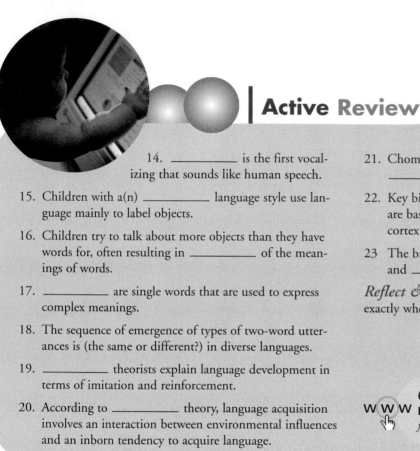

Active Review

14. _____ is the first vocalizing that sounds like human speech.

15. Children with a(n) _____ language style use language mainly to label objects.

16. Children try to talk about more objects than they have words for, often resulting in _____ of the meanings of words.

17. _____ are single words that are used to express complex meanings.

18. The sequence of emergence of types of two-word utterances is (the same or different?) in diverse languages.

19. _____ theorists explain language development in terms of imitation and reinforcement.

20. According to _____ theory, language acquisition involves an interaction between environmental influences and an inborn tendency to acquire language.

21. Chomsky refers to this inborn tendency as a language _____ device (LAD).

22. Key biological structures that provide a basis for language are based in the (left or right?) hemisphere of the cerebral cortex for most people.

23 The brain areas most involved in speech are Broca's area and _____ area.

Reflect & Relate: Why are so many parents concerned with exactly when their children learn to talk?

Go to
W W W http://www.voyages1CE.nelson.com
for an interactive version of this review.

Recite: *An Active Summary*™

1. What is the sensorimotor stage of cognitive development?

Piaget's sensorimotor stage refers to the first two years of cognitive development, during which changes are shown by means of sensory and motor activity.

2. What are the parts or substages of the sensorimotor stage?

The first substage is dominated by the assimilation of stimulation into reflexes. In the second substage, primary circular reactions, infants repeat stimulating actions that occur by chance. In the third substage, secondary circular reactions, patterns of activity are repeated because of their effects. In the fourth substage, infants intentionally coordinate schemes to attain goals. In the fifth substage, tertiary circular reactions, infants purposefully adapt established schemes to specific situations. In the sixth substage, external exploration is replaced by mental exploration.

3. What is object permanence? How does it develop?

Object permanence is recognition that an object or person continues to exist when out of sight. Through the first six months or so, when a screen is placed between an object and an infant, the infant behaves as if the object is no longer there.

4. What are the strengths and limitations of Piaget's theory of sensorimotor development?

Evidence supports the pattern and sequence of events described by Piaget. However, cognitive development may not be tied to discrete stages, as Piaget believed. Piaget also appears to have been incorrect about the ages at which infants develop various concepts.

5. What are infants' tools for processing information?

The tools include memory and imitation. Older infants are more capable of encoding and retrieving information. Neonates reflexively imitate certain behaviours, such as sticking out the tongue. Infants later show deferred imitation, suggesting that they have mentally represented actions.

6. How do we measure individual differences in the development of cognitive functioning?

Some infants develop cognitive functioning more rapidly than others. The Bayley Scales of Infant Development (BSID) consist of mental-scale and motor-scale items. A tester may be able to detect early signs of sensory or neurological problems.

7. How well do infant scales predict later intellectual performance?

Certain BSID items predict intellectual skills later in childhood, but overall scores on such scales do not predict school grades accurately.

8. What is visual recognition memory? How is it used?

Visual recognition memory is the ability to discriminate previously seen objects from novel objects. Visual recognition memory moderately predicts IQ scores in later childhood.

9. What are prelinguistic vocalizations?

Prelinguistic vocalizations do not represent objects or events and include crying, cooing, and babbling. Children from different cultures initially babble the same sounds.

10. How does vocabulary develop?	Receptive vocabulary development outpaces expressive vocabulary. The first word is typically spoken between eleven and thirteen months of age. It may take another three or four months to achieve a vocabulary of ten to thirty words. Children's first words are mostly nominals. Children with a referential language style use language mainly to label objects. Those with an expressive language style mainly seek social interactions. Infants often extend the meanings of words to refer to things and actions for which they do not have words.
11. How do infants create sentences?	Infants' early sentences are telegraphic. Two-word sentences show understanding of syntax. The kinds of two-word sentences are the same among children from diverse linguistic environments.
12. How do learning theorists account for language development?	Learning theorists explain language development in terms of imitation and reinforcement. However, children resist imitating sentences that do not fit with their awareness of grammar.
13. What is the nativist view of language development?	The nativist view holds that innate or inborn prewiring causes children to attend to and acquire language in certain ways. Psycholinguistic theory considers that language acquisition involves the interaction between environmental influences and prewiring. Chomsky argues that languages share a "universal grammar" that children are prewired to perceive and use.
14. What parts of the brain are involved in language development?	Key biological structures are based in the left hemisphere for most people: Broca's area and Wernicke's area. Damage to either area may cause a characteristic aphasia.
15. What is meant by a *sensitive period* for language development?	Lenneberg proposes that plasticity of the brain provides a sensitive period for learning language that begins at about eighteen to twenty-four months and lasts until puberty.

WWW **Go to**
http://www.voyages1CE.nelson.com
for an interactive version of this summary review.

Key Terms

scheme *(page 200)*

assimilation *(page 200)*

accommodation *(page 200)*

primary circular reactions *(page 203)*

secondary circular reactions
(page 203)

tertiary circular reactions *(page 204)*

object permanence *(page 205)*

deferred imitation *(page 208)*

visual recognition memory *(page 214)*

prelinguistic *(page 216)*

cooing *(page 216)*

babbling *(page 217)*

echolalia *(page 217)*

intonation *(page 218)*

receptive vocabulary *(page 218)*

expressive vocabulary *(page 218)*

referential language style *(page 219)*

expressive language style *(page 219)*

overextension *(page 221)*

telegraphic speech *(page 221)*

mean length of utterance (MLU)
(page 221)

morpheme *(page 221)*

holophrase *(page 222)*

syntax *(page 222)*

models *(page 223)*

extinction *(page 224)*

shaping *(page 224)*

psycholinguistic theory *(page 226)*

language acquisition device (LAD)
(page 226)

surface structure *(page 226)*

deep structure *(page 226)*

aphasia *(page 227)*

Broca's aphasia *(page 227)*

Wernicke's aphasia *(page 227)*

sensitive period *(page 227)*

American Sign Language (ASL)
(page 229)

Active Learning Resources

Observing Children and Adolescents CD-ROM

Want to watch videos showing what you've just learned about in this chapter? Click on the "Piaget's Sensorimotor Stage" video in CD Module 1, Section 3. Your "Lessons in Observation" feature on p. 189 provides further learning objectives, an applied lesson, and a critical thinking exercise designed to help you experience this stage of development. Also check out the "Early Learning" and "Language Development" videos in CD Module 1, Section 3.

Visit Your Companion Website for This Book

http://www.voyages1CE.nelson.com

Check out this companion website, where you will find online resources directly linked to your book. The website includes interactive exercises related to PQ4R and Power Visuals for mastering and reviewing key concepts as well as quizzing, chapter outlines, and much more!

CengageNOW!™

http://hed.nelson.com

Go to this site for the link to CengageNOW™, your one-stop study shop. Take a Pretest for this chapter, and CengageNOW™ will generate a personalized Study Plan based on your test results! The Study Plan will identify the topics you need to review and direct you to online resources to help you master those topics. You can then take a Posttest to help you determine the concepts you have mastered and those you still need to work on.

7

Infancy:
Social and Emotional Development

PREVIEW

TRUTH OR FICTION?

● ● ● ● ● ● ● ● ● ● ● ●

(T) (F) Infants who are securely attached to their mothers do not like to stray from them.

(T) (F) You can estimate how strongly infants are attached to their fathers if you know how many diapers per week the father changes.

(T) (F) Child abusers have frequently been the victims of child abuse themselves.

(T) (F) Children placed in daycare are more aggressive than children who are cared for in the home.

(T) (F) Fear of strangers is abnormal among infants.

(T) (F) All children are born with the same temperament. Treatment by caregivers determines whether they are difficult or easygoing.

(T) (F) Girls prefer dolls and toy animals, and boys prefer toy trucks and sports equipment only after they have become aware of the gender roles assigned to them by society.

Go to www

www.voyages1ce.nelson.com
for an interactive version of this "Truth or Fiction" feature.

© Patricia Doyle / Getty Images

Any parent who has tried to complete a task (e.g., fill out federal tax returns, bake a soufflé, soothe another child) with a young child around can appreciate Rathus's personal account of the challenges of parenting his two-year-old daughter:

> At the age of two, my daughter Allyn almost succeeded at preventing publication of a book on which I was working. When I locked myself into my study, she positioned herself outside the door and called, "Daddy, oh, Daddy." At other times she would bang on the door or cry. When I would give in (several times a day) and open the door, she would run in and say, "I want you to pick up me," and hold out her arms or climb into my lap. How would I ever finish the book?

In Rathus's case, he had several options available to him. For example, he could write outside the home. But this solution had the drawback of distancing him from his family. Another solution was to ignore his daughter and let her cry. If he refused to reinforce crying, crying would become extinguished. (And research does suggest that ignoring crying discourages it [Van Ijzendoorn & Hubbard, 2000].) There was only one problem with this solution. He didn't *want* to extinguish her efforts to get to him. **Attachment,** you see, is a two-way street.

Attachment is one of the key issues in the social and personality development of the infant. If this chapter had been written by the poet John Donne, it might have begun, "No children are islands unto themselves." Children come into this world fully dependent on others for their survival and well-being.

This chapter is about some of the consequences of that absolute dependency. It is about the social relationships between infants and caregivers and about the development of the bonds of attachment that usually—but not always—bind them. It is about the behaviours of infants that prompt social and emotional responses from adults and about the behaviours of adults that prompt social and emotional responses from infants. It is also about infants' unique and different ways of reacting socially and emotionally.

Let us first consider the issue of attachment and the factors that contribute to its development. Next, we examine some circumstances that interfere with the development of attachment: social deprivation, child abuse, and autism. Then, we turn to a discussion of daycare. Finally, we look at the development of emotions and personality in infancy, including the self-concept, temperament, and sex differences.

Attachment: Bonds That Endure

Question: What is meant by "attachment"? Attachment is what most people refer to as affection or love. Mary Ainsworth (1989), one of the preeminent researchers on attachment, defines attachment as an emotional tie formed between one animal or person and another specific individual. Attachment keeps organisms together and tends to endure. John Bowlby believes that attachment is essential to the very survival of the infant (Bowlby, 1988; Ainsworth & Bowlby, 1991). He argues that babies are born with behaviours—crying, smiling, clinging—that elicit caregiving from parents.

Babies and children try to maintain contact with caregivers to whom they are attached. They engage in eye contact, pull and tug at them, and ask to be picked up. When they cannot maintain contact, infants show behaviours suggestive of **separation anxiety.** They may thrash about, fuss, cry, screech, or whine. Parents who are seeking a few minutes to attend to their own needs sometimes see these behaviours as manipulative, and, in a sense, they are. That is, children learn that the behaviours achieve desired ends. But what is wrong with "manipulating" a loved one to end distress?

---

attachment An affectional bond between individuals characterized by a seeking of closeness or contact and a show of distress upon separation.

separation anxiety Fear of being separated from a target of attachment, usually a primary caregiver.

Watch how infants of different ages and personalities differ in their attachment styles. See also how infants of different ages react to strangers and separation from a parent. Click on the "Attachment" clip in Module 1, Section 3.

Mary D. Salter Ainsworth

Patterns of Attachment

Mary Ainsworth and her colleagues (1978) identified various patterns of attachment. Broadly, infants show either **secure attachment** or insecure attachment. Ainsworth and other investigators have found that most infants, older children, and adults in Western cultures are securely attached (Bartholomew & Horowitz, 1991; Clarke-Stewart, Goossens, & Allhusen, 2001; McCartney, Owen, Booth, Clarke-Stewart, & Vandell, 2004).

Question: What does it mean for a child to be "secure"? Think of security in terms of what infants *do*. Ainsworth developed the strange-situation method as a way of measuring the development of attachment (Figure 7.1). In this method, an infant is exposed to a series of separations and reunions with a caregiver (usually the mother) and a stranger who is a confederate of the researchers. In the strange situation, securely attached infants mildly protest their mother's departure, seek interaction upon reunion, and are readily comforted by her.

Question: What, then, is "insecurity"? Hold on! This is science, and in the science of development, we speak of insecurity as "insecure attachment." The two major types of insecure attachment are **avoidant attachment** and **ambivalent/resistant attachment.** Babies who show avoidant attachment are least distressed by their mothers' departure. They play without fuss when alone and ignore their mothers upon reunion. Ambivalent/resistant babies are the most emotional. They show severe signs of distress when their mothers leave and show ambivalence upon reunion by alternately clinging to and pushing away their mothers. Additional categories of insecure attachment have been proposed, including **disorganized-disoriented attachment** (Main & Hesse, 1990). Babies showing this pattern appear dazed, confused, or disoriented. They may show contradictory behaviours, such as moving toward the mother while looking away from her.

secure attachment A type of attachment characterized by mild distress at leave-takings, seeking nearness to an attachment figure, and being readily soothed by the figure.

avoidant attachment A type of insecure attachment characterized by apparent indifference to the leave-takings of and reunions with an attachment figure.

ambivalent/resistant attachment A type of insecure attachment characterized by severe distress at the leave-takings of and ambivalent behaviour at reunions with an attachment figure.

disorganized-disoriented attachment A type of insecure attachment characterized by dazed and contradictory behaviours toward an attachment figure.

a

b

c

d

© Mary D. S. Ainsworth

Figure 7.1

The Strange Situation

These historic photos show a twelve-month-old child in the strange situation. In (a), the child plays with toys, glancing occasionally at Mother. In (b), the stranger approaches with a toy. While the child is distracted, Mother leaves the room. In (c), Mother returns after a brief absence. The child crawls to her quickly and clings to her when picked up. In (d), the child cries when Mother again leaves the room. What pattern of attachment is this child showing?

Question: Is it better for an infant to be securely attached to its caregivers? Sure it is. Securely attached infants and toddlers are happier, more sociable with unfamiliar adults, and more cooperative with parents; get along better with peers; and are better adjusted in school than insecurely attached children (Coleman, 2003; McCartney et al., 2004; Spieker, Nelson, Petras, Jolley, & Barnard, 2003). Alan Sroufe (1998) found that insecure attachment at the age of one year predicted psychological disorders at the age of seventeen. Ainsworth and Bowlby (1991) found that infants used the mother as a secure base from which to venture out and explore the environment. Secure attachment is also connected with the experiencing of fewer negative emotions toward members of out-groups (Mikulincer & Shaver, 2001). Thus, security encourages children to explore interactions with unfamiliar people, broadening their horizons. *Truth or Fiction Revisited:* Thus, infants who are securely attached to their mothers are likely to "stray" from them in the sense that they use them as a secure base for exploration of the environment.

Developing in a
World of Diversity

Cross-Cultural Patterns of Attachment

How widespread are the patterns of attachment that we discuss in this chapter? Studies using the strange-situation method in seven European and Asian countries have found that secure attachments predominate, just as in Canada. Avoidant attachments are more common in some European countries, especially Germany, than in Canada. Although avoidant attachment is more common than ambivalent/resistant attachment in most countries, the opposite pattern has been found in Japan and Israel (van IJzendoorn & Kroonenberg, 1988; van IJzendoorn et al., 1992; Sagi, van IJzendoorn, & Koren-Karie, 1991) (Table 7.1).

Different child-rearing practices and attitudes may account for these differences in attachment patterns. For example, German parents encourage independence in the child at an early age. Compared with

Table 7.1 — *Some Patterns of Insecure Attachment and Child-Rearing Practices in Other Countries*

Country	Predominant Patterns of Insecure Attachment	Child-Rearing Practices and Attitudes (compared with some European and Asian countries)
Germany	Avoidant	• Parents are less likely to pick up a crying infant. • Parents are more likely to leave the infant alone in bed.
Japan	Ambivalent/resistant	• Parents are less likely to leave an infant with strangers. • Parents are more likely to emphasize continuous, close contact with the mother.
Israel	Ambivalent/resistant	• Parents are less likely to leave an infant with strangers. • Parents are more likely to emphasize continuous, close contact with caregivers other than the parents.

Securely attached toddlers also have longer attention spans, are less impulsive, and are better at solving problems (Granot & Mayseless, 2001; Spieker et al., 2003). At ages five and six, securely attached children are better liked by peers and teachers, are more competent, are less aggressive, and have fewer behaviour problems than insecurely attached children (Coleman, 2003; Lyons-Ruth, Alpern, & Repacholi, 1993).

Question: What are the roles of the parents in the formation of bonds of attachment?

Establishing Attachment

Attachment is one measure of the quality of care that infants receive (Coleman, 2003; Rosen & Rothbaum, 1993). The parents of babies who are securely attached are more affectionate, cooperative, and predictable in their caregiving. They respond more sensitively to their babies' smiles, cries, and other social behaviours (Harel & Scher, 2003; Rosen & Rothbaum, 1993).

Western parents, they are less likely to pick up a crying baby and more likely to leave the baby alone in bed (Grossmann & Grossmann, 1991). This pattern may be more likely to foster avoidant attachment in the child. Japanese mothers, on the other hand, emphasize close and continuous contact with their babies and rarely leave them with other caretakers (Barratt et al., 1993; Takahashi, 1990). These infants are not used to being alone or with strangers, which may account for their distressed behaviour in the strange situation.

The Israeli studies have involved children raised in a collective farm community known as a kibbutz. Parents visit and play with their children frequently during the day and evening. The children's primary care and training, however, is entrusted to a child-rearing specialist called a metapelet, who also spends the night with the children. Despite the reduced parent-child contact, kibbutz life does not seem to impair parent-child bonds of attachment (Maccoby & Feldman, 1972). Babies, however, appear to become equally attached to their metapelet (van IJzendoorn et al., 1992).

How can we explain the finding that kibbutz-reared children show a higher incidence of ambivalent/resistant attachment than avoidant attachment? As with the Japanese child, the kibbutz-reared child has close, continuous contact with its primary caretakers but little contact with strangers. For both these groups of children, then, the strange situation may produce intense distress.]

Child-Rearing Practices and Attachment
Japanese mothers emphasize close, continuous contact with their babies and rarely leave them with other caretakers. Might this account for the distress shown by Japanese babies in the strange situation?

© Bob Krist / CORBIS

A Japanese study found evidence for the "intergenerational transmission of attachment" from mother to child (Kazui, Endo, Tanaka, Sakagami, & Suganuma, 2000). For example, the children of secure mothers showed the most secure patterns of attachment themselves, as assessed by various means. The children of secure mothers interacted positively both with their mothers and with strangers, so their pattern of attachment provided a secure base for exploration.

Providing economically stressed families with support services can enhance their involvement with their infants and increase secure attachment. In one study, low-income women received child-care information and social support from home visitors during pregnancy and for a year following childbirth (Jacobson & Frye, 1991). In another study, low-income women suffering from depression received similar support services until their child was eighteen months old (Lyons-Ruth, Connell, Grunebaum, & Botein, 1990). In both instances, children whose mothers received support services showed more secure attachment than control children whose mothers had not received such services. Even something as simple as increasing the amount of physical contact between mothers and their infants appears to promote greater maternal responsiveness and more secure attachment between infant and mother (Anisfeld, Casper, Kozyce, & Cunningham, 1990). Consistent with this, Benoit and colleagues' (2001) study on mothers with infants with feeding disorders revealed that mothers who were trained to focus on training caregivers to respond sensitively to their infants (play-focused intervention) showed a significant decrease in the level of disrupted communication from pre- to postintervention sessions, displaying more responsiveness, more appropriate reading of cues, and less maltreatment.

Insecure attachment occurs more often among infants whose mothers are mentally ill or abusive (McCartney et al., 2004; van IJzendoorn et al., 1992). It is found more often among infants whose mothers are slow to meet their needs or meet them coldly (Steele, Hodges, Kaniuk, Hillman, & Henderson, 2003).

Research by Marinus van IJzendoorn and colleagues (2000) suggests that siblings tend to develop similar attachment relationships with their mothers. The study pooled data on sibling attachment from research groups in the United States, the Netherlands, and Canada to form 138 pairs of siblings. Children's security of attachment was assessed with the strange-situation procedure at twelve to fourteen months. Maternal sensitivity to infants' needs was also observed. Broad sibling attachment relationships (secure or insecure, but not necessarily the kinds of insecurity) with the mother were found to be significantly alike. It was also found that siblings of the same sex are more likely to form similar attachment relationships with their mother than are girl-boy pairs. Mothers, that is, may behave differently with daughters and sons.

Although it is tempting to seek the sources of attachment in caregivers' behaviour and personalities, that is not the whole story. Security is also connected with the baby's temperament (Mangelsdorf, Gunnar, Kestenbaum, Lang, & Andreas, 1990, 2000) (see pp. 250–252). Babies who are more active and irritable and who display more negative emotion are more likely to develop insecure attachment. Such babies may elicit parental behaviours that are not conducive to the development of secure attachment. For example, mothers of "difficult" children are less responsive to their children and report that they feel less emotionally close to them (Morrell & Steele, 2003; Stams, Juffer, & van IJzendoorn, 2002). Caregivers respond to babies' behaviour, just as the babies respond to caregivers' behaviour. The process of attachment is a two-way street.

Involvement of Fathers

Truth or Fiction Revisited It is true that you can predict how well babies are attached to their fathers if you know how many diapers the fathers change each week. Gail Ross and her colleagues (1975) found that the more diapers the father changed, the stronger the attachment. There is no magical connection between diapers and love, but the number of diapers the father changes roughly reflects his involvement in child rearing.

How involved is the average father with his children? The brief answer, in developed nations, is more so than in the past. Gender roles are blurring to some degree, and fathers can rear infants as competently and sensitively as mothers can (Grossmann et al., 2002). But studies of parents in Canada and the U.S. show that father-child interactions differ qualitatively and quantitatively from mother-child interactions (Laflamme, Pomerleau, & Malcuit, 2002; Magill-Evans & Harrison, 2001). Mothers engage in far more interactions with their infants. Most fathers spend much less time on basic child-care tasks, such as feeding and diaper changing, than mothers do. Fathers are more likely to play with their children than to feed or clean them (Laflamme et al., 2002; Lamb, Ketterlinus, & Fracasso, 1992). Fathers more often than mothers engage in physical rough-and-tumble play, such as tossing their babies into the air and poking them. Mothers are more likely to play games like patty-cake and peekaboo and to play games involving toys (Bretherton, Golby, & Halvorsen, 1993; Laflamme et al., 2002).

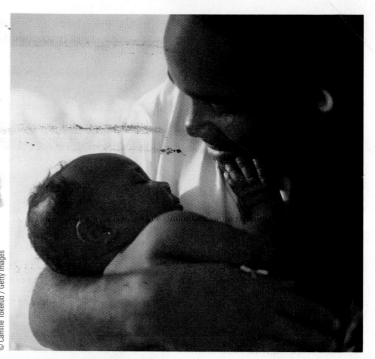

© Camille Tokerud / Getty Images

Fathers and Attachment: The "Diaper Index"
The number of diapers a father changes reflects his involvement in child rearing. Children develop strong attachments to fathers as well as mothers, especially if the father interacts positively and affectionately with the child.

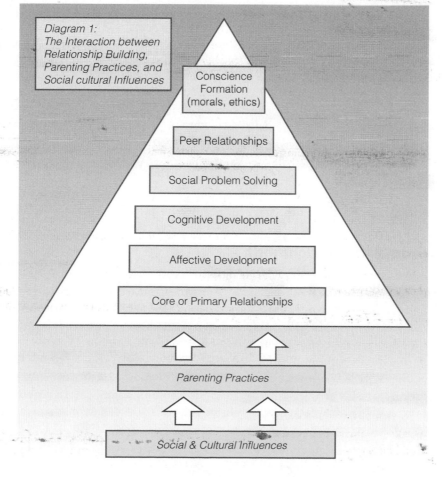

Diagram 1:
The Interaction between Relationship Building, Parenting Practices, and Social cultural Influences

Conscience Formation (morals, ethics)

Peer Relationships

Social Problem Solving

Cognitive Development

Affective Development

Core or Primary Relationships

Parenting Practices

Social & Cultural Influences

Figure 7.2

The Interaction between Relationship Building, Parenting Practices, and Sociocultural Influences

Source: Reebye et al. (n.d.).

How strongly, then, do infants become attached to their fathers? The answer depends on the quality of the time that the father spends with the baby (Easterbrook & Goldberg, 1984; Thompson, Easterbrooks, & Padilla-Walker, 2003). The more affectionate the interaction between father and infant, the stronger the attachment (R. A. Thompson et al., 2003). Infants under stress still seek out mothers more so than fathers (Lamb, Sternberg, & Prodromidis, 1992b). But when observed at their natural activities in the home and other familiar settings, they seek proximity and contact with their fathers about as often as with their mothers.

These parent-child interactions are dependent upon cultural practices. Since both Canada and the U.S. are multicultural nations, parent-child interactions vary widely and extend beyond typical Western styles of interaction. The Canadian Public Heath Agency has a document available for public access titled "Attachment Across Cultures," which covers topics that include cultural differences in parent-child attachment; beliefs, values, and practices; the impact of migration; and maintaining effective practices and culturally responsive resources. Acknowledging that these areas may impact parent-child interactions is important for educators, practitioners, and health providers working with families from a variety of backgrounds.

Stability of Attachment

Patterns of attachment tend to persist when care-giving conditions remain consistent (Karavasilis, Doyle, & Markiewicz, 2003; Main & Cassidy, 1988). But attachment patterns can change when child care changes (Thompson, 1991). Egeland and Sroufe (1981) followed a number of infants who were severely neglected and others who received high-quality care from twelve to eighteen months of age. Attachment patterns remained stable (secure) for infants receiving fine care. However, many neglected infants changed from insecurely to securely attached over the six-month period, sometimes because of a relationship with a supportive family member, sometimes because home life grew less tense. Other studies show that children can become less securely attached to caregivers when the quality of home life deteriorates (Egeland & Farber, 1984; Thompson, Lamb, & Estes, 1982).

Even when children are adopted as late as the age of four, they can become securely attached to their adoptive parents (Hodges & Tizard, 1989). Young children show resilience in their social and emotional development. Early insecurities can be overcome.

Early attachment patterns tend to endure into middle childhood, adolescence, and even adulthood (Bartholomew & Horowitz, 1991; Karavasilis et al., 2003). As Erik Erikson (1963) argued in *Childhood and Society,* it seems that positive relationships with caregivers can set the stage for positive relationships throughout life.

Stages of Attachment

Cross-cultural studies by Mary Ainsworth (1967) and others have led to a theory of stages of attachment. In one study, Ainsworth tracked the attachment behaviours of Ugandan infants. Over a nine-month period, she noted their efforts to maintain contact with the mother, their protests when separated, and their use of the mother as a base for exploring the environment. *Question: What did Ainsworth learn about the stages of attachment?* At first, the Ugandan infants showed **indiscriminate attachment.** That is, they showed no particular preferences for the mother or another familiar caregiver. Specific attachment to the mother, as evidenced by separation anxiety and other behaviours, began to develop at about four months of age and grew intensely by about seven months. Fear of strangers developed one or two months later.

indiscriminate attachment
The display of attachment behaviours toward any person.

In another study, shown in Figure 7.3, Scottish infants showed indiscriminate attachment during the first six months or so after birth (Schaffer & Emerson, 1964). Then, indiscriminate attachment waned. Specific attachments to the mother and other familiar caregivers intensified, as demonstrated by the appearance of separation anxiety, and remained at high levels through the age of eighteen months. Fear of strangers occurred a month or so after the intensity of specific attachments began to mushroom. Thus, in both this and the Ugandan study, fear of strangers followed separation anxiety and the development of specific attachments by a number of weeks. Other cross-cultural studies have found that the onset of separation anxiety occurs earliest in cultures in which mothers care for their infants almost exclusively and are in close physical contact with them for extended periods (Crowell & Waters, 1990).

Bowlby (1969) along with Ainsworth and her colleagues (1978) identified the following four phases of attachment:

1. The **initial-preattachment phase** lasts from birth to about three months and is characterized by indiscriminate attachment.
2. The **attachment-in-the-making phase** occurs at about three or four months and is characterized by preference for familiar figures.
3. The **clear-cut-attachment phase** occurs at about six or seven months to eighteen months to two years, and is characterized by intensified dependence on the primary caregiver, usually the mother.
4. Formation of a **reciprocal relationship** occurs at about eighteen months to two years onward, and is characterized by a better understanding of parents' comings and goings and ability to predict their return.

Most infants have more than one adult caregiver, however, and are likely to form multiple attachments—to the father, daycare providers, grandparents, and other caregivers, as well as to the mother. In most cultures, single attachments are the exception, not the rule (Howes & Matheson, 1992a).

initial-preattachment phase The first phase in the formation of bonds of attachment, lasting from birth to about 3 months of age and characterized by indiscriminate attachment.

attachment-in-the-making phase The second phase in the development of attachment, occurring at 3 or 4 months of age and characterized by preference for familiar figures.

clear-cut-attachment phase The third phase in the development of attachment, occurring at 6 or 7 months of age and characterized by intensified dependence on the primary caregiver.

reciprocal-relationship phase The fourth phase in the development of attachment, occurring at 18 months to 2 years onward and characterized by less protesting of separation and a better understanding of relationship duration beyond the immediate.

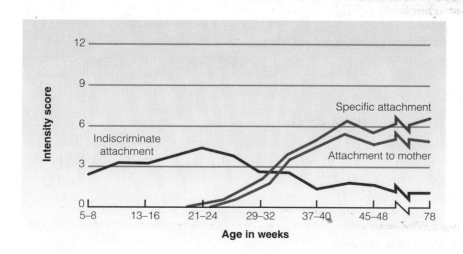

Figure 7.3
The Development of Attachment
During the first 6 months, infants tend to show indiscriminate attachment. Indiscriminate attachment then wanes while specific attachments grow intense and remain at high levels. Fear of strangers develops a month or so after the intensity of specific attachments begins to blossom.

Theories of Attachment

Attachment, as with so many other behaviour patterns, seems to develop as a result of the interaction of nature and nurture. *Question: How do different theorists emphasize nature or nurture in their explanations of the development of attachment?*

Cognitive View of Attachment

The cognitive view of attachment focuses on the contention that an infant must have developed some concept of object permanence before specific attachment becomes possible. In other words, if caregivers are to be missed when absent, the infant must perceive that they continue to exist. We have seen that infants tend to develop specific attachments at about the age of six or seven months. In support of the cognitive view, recall that rudimentary object permanence concerning physical objects develops somewhat earlier (see Chapter 6).

Behavioural View of Attachment: Caregiver as Reinforcer

Early in the century, behaviourists argued that attachment behaviours are learned through conditioning. Caregivers feed their infants and tend to their other physiological needs. Thus, infants associate their caregivers with gratification and learn to approach them to meet their needs. From this perspective, a caregiver becomes a conditioned reinforcer.

Psychoanalytic Views of Attachment: Caregiver as Love Object

Psychoanalytic theorists view the development of attachment somewhat differently from behaviourists. The caregiver, usually the mother, becomes not just a "reinforcer" but a love object who forms the basis for all later attachments.

In both the psychoanalytic and behaviourist views, the caregiver's role in gratifying the child's needs is crucial. Freud emphasized the importance of oral activities, such as eating, in the first year. Freud believed that the infant becomes emotionally attached to the mother during this time because she is the primary satisfier of the infant's needs for food and sucking.

We will revisit Erikson's theory of psychosocial development in later chapters, but the first two psychosocial stages of his developmental-life-span theory are pertinent to understanding attachment as well as self-concept (see p. 10). Erikson described psychosocial development as a series of eight stages (listed in Chapter 1). At each stage, a particular challenge needs to be overcome, and if these challenges are not properly resolved or dealt with, well, they are likely to persist or cause problems. The two stages that apply to infancy and toddlerhood are stage one, trust versus mistrust (infancy), and stage two, autonomy versus shame and doubt (toddler years). The first stage (trust versus mistrust) is very similar to the attachment theory in that it is the stage in which infants learn whether or not they can trust the adults in their environment. Either babies learn that the world is a safe and predictable place (primary needs are met), or they learn to mistrust their environment (needs are not being met or they are inconsistently dealt with). Erik Erikson believed that the first year is critical for developing a sense of trust in the mother, which thereby fosters attachment. Erikson wrote that the mother's general sensitivity to all of the child's needs (i.e., social, emotional, physical), not just the need for food, fosters the development of trust and attachment.

The Harlows' View of Attachment: The Caregiver as a Source of Contact Comfort

Harry and Margaret Harlow conducted a series of classic experiments to demonstrate that feeding is not as critical to the attachment process as Freud suggested (Harlow & Harlow, 1966). In one study, the Harlows placed rhesus monkey infants in cages with two surrogate mothers (see Figure 7.4). One "mother" was made from wire mesh, from which a baby bottle was extended. The other surrogate mother was made of soft, cuddly terry cloth. Infant monkeys spent most of their time clinging to the cloth mother, even though she did not offer food. The Harlows concluded that monkeys—and perhaps humans—have a need for **contact comfort** that is as basic as the need for food.

Ethological View of Attachment: Smiling and Imprinting

Ethologists note that for many animals, attachment is an inborn **fixed action pattern (FAP)**. The FAP of attachment, as with other FAPs, is theorized to occur in the presence of a species-specific **releasing stimulus**. According to John Bowlby, one component of the FAP of attachment in humans—and its releasing stimulus—is a baby's smile in response to a human voice or face (Bowlby, 1988; Ainsworth & Bowlby, 1991). Bowlby proposed that the baby's smile helps ensure survival by eliciting affection from caregivers. By the time the infant is two to three months of age, the human face begins to elicit a **social smile** (Emde, Gaensbauer, & Harmon, 1976). The development of smiling seems to follow the same sequence throughout the world (Werner, 1988).

contact comfort The pleasure derived from physical contact with another; a hypothesized need or drive for physical contact with another.

ethologist A scientist who studies the behaviour patterns that are characteristic of various species.

fixed action pattern (FAP) Instinct; a stereotyped behaviour pattern that is characteristic of a species and is triggered by a releasing stimulus.

releasing stimulus A stimulus that elicits a fixed action pattern (FAP).

social smile A smile that occurs in response to a human voice or face.

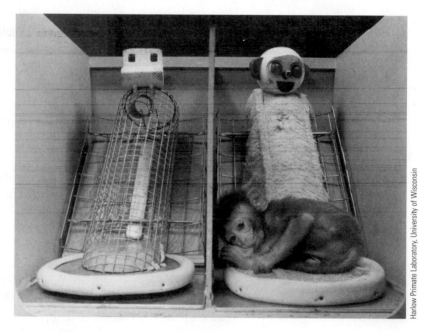

Figure 7.4

Contact Comfort: The Source of Attachment in Infant Monkeys

As shown in this classic series of photos, although this rhesus monkey infant is fed by the "wire-mesh mother," it spends most of its time clinging to a soft, cuddly "terry-cloth mother." It knows where to get a meal, but contact comfort is apparently more central to attachment than feeding in infant monkeys (and infant humans?).

© Nina Leen / Time Life Pictures / Getty Images

Figure 7.5

Imprinting: A Source of Attachment in Etiological Theory

Quite a following? Konrad Lorenz may not look like Mommy to you, but these goslings became attached to him because he was the first moving object they perceived and followed. This type of attachment process is referred to as imprinting.

In many nonhuman animals, the FAP of attachment apparently occurs during a **critical period** of life. If it does not occur then, it may never. During this period, young animals can form an instinctive attachment to caregivers if the releasing stimuli are present. Waterfowl become attached during this period to the first moving object they encounter. The image of the moving object seems to become "imprinted" on the young animal, so this process is termed **imprinting.**

Ethologist Konrad Lorenz (1962, 1981) became well known when pictures of his "family" of goslings were made public (see Figure 7.5). How did Lorenz acquire his family? He was present when the goslings hatched and during their critical period, and he allowed them to follow him. The critical period for geese and ducks begins when they first engage in locomotion and ends when they develop fear of strangers. The goslings followed Lorenz persistently, ran to him when frightened, honked with distress at his departure, and tried to overcome barriers placed between them. If you substitute crying for honking, it all sounds rather human.

critical period   A period of development during which a releasing stimulus can elicit a fixed action pattern (FAP).

imprinting   The process by which some animals exhibit the fixed action pattern (FAP) of attachment in response to a releasing stimulus. The FAP occurs during a critical period and is difficult to modify.

Ethology, Ainsworth, and Bowlby

Now let us return full circle to Mary D. Salter Ainsworth and John Bowlby (1991). At the beginning of a major retrospective article, they wrote that "the distinguishing characteristic of the theory of attachment that we have jointly developed is that it is *an ethological approach* to personality development." The theoretical aspects of their work developed almost by accident and have a broad base in the psychological and biological perspectives of their day:

> Bowlby intended his contribution as an up-to-date version of psychoanalytic object-relations theory [developed largely by Margaret Mahler], compatible with contemporary ethology [e.g., Lorenz] and evolution theory [e.g., Charles Darwin], supported by research, and helpful to clinicians in understanding and treating child and adult patients. Nevertheless, it was developmental psychologists rather than clinicians who first adopted attachment theory.
>
> —Ainsworth & Bowlby (1991)

Yet theirs is not the attachment theory of Konrad Lorenz. Yes, there are what Bowlby believed to be "releasing stimuli," such as the human face and the crying, smiling, and clinging of infants. But caregiving in humans is largely learned, not inborn. Children and infants of many other species also try to maintain contact with caregivers to whom they have grown attached. When they cannot maintain contact, they show signs of distress—honking and flapping about in geese, whining and barking in dogs, crying and fussing in children.

Ainsworth and Bowlby (1991) wrote that the critical period for attachment in humans is extended for months or years. It involves learning and perceptual and cognitive processes. The type of attachment that develops is related to the quality of the caregiver-infant relationship. Caregiving itself and infant responsiveness, such as infant smiling, appear to spur the development of attachment. Theories of attachment are reviewed in Concept Review 7.1.

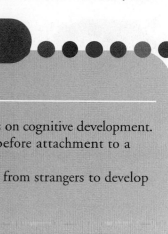

Concept Review 7.1 Theories of Attachment

Theory	Characteristics
Cognitive theory (proponent: Alan Sroufe)	• Emotional development is connected with and relies on cognitive development. • Infant must have developed object permanence before attachment to a specific other becomes possible. • Infant must be able to discriminate familiar people from strangers to develop fear of strangers.
Behaviourism (proponent: John B. Watson)	• Caregiver is a conditioned reinforcer; attachment behaviours are learned through conditioning. • Caregivers meet infants' physiological needs; thus, infants associate caregivers with gratification. • Feelings of gratification associated with meeting needs generalize into feelings of security when the caregiver is present.
Psychoanalytic theory (proponents: Sigmund Freud, Erik Erikson, Margaret Mahler)	• Caregiver is a love object who forms the basis for future attachments. • Infant becomes attached to the mother during infancy because she primarily satisfies the infant's needs for food and sucking (Freud). • First year is critical in developing a sense of trust in the mother, which, in turn, fosters feelings of attachment (Erikson).
Contact comfort (proponents: Harry and Margaret Harlow)	• Caregiver is a source of contact comfort. • Experiments with rhesus monkeys suggest that contact comfort is more crucial than feeding to attachment.
Ethological theory (proponents: Konrad Lorenz, Mary Ainsworth, John Bowlby)	• Attachment is an inborn fixed action pattern (FAP) that occurs in the presence of a species-specific releasing stimulus during a critical period of development (Lorenz). • Waterfowl become attached to the first moving object they encounter (Lorenz). • The image of the moving object becomes "imprinted" on the young animal (Lorenz). • Caregiving in humans is elicited by infants' cries of distress (Bowlby). • The human face is a releasing stimulus that elicits a baby's smile (Bowlby). • Smiling helps ensure survival by eliciting caregiving and feelings of affection (Bowlby). • Attachment in humans is a complex process that continues for months or years (Ainsworth). • The quality of attachment is related to the quality of the caregiver-infant relationship (Ainsworth). • Attachment in humans occurs in stages or phases (Ainsworth): 　1. The initial-preattachment phase: birth to about 3 months; indiscriminate attachment 　2. The attachment-in-the-making phase: 3 or 4 months; preference for familiar figures 　3. The clear-cut-attachment phase: 6 or 7 months; intensified dependence on the primary caregiver

Active Review

1. Ainsworth defines _____ as an affectional tie that is formed between one animal or person and another specific individual.

2. One of Ainsworth's contributions to the field of child development is the innovation of the _____ method of measuring attachment.

3. Broadly, infants have either secure attachment or _____ attachment.

4. Securely attached infants use the caregiver as a secure base from which to _____ the environment.

5. Ainsworth's study of Ugandan infants found that they at first show _____ attachment.

6. From the _____ perspective, a caregiver becomes a conditioned reinforcer.

7. The Harlows' research with monkeys suggests that _____ comfort is a key source of attachment.

8. Lorenz believed that attachment is an inborn _____ action pattern (FAP).

Reflect & Relate: To which caregiver are you most attached? Why?

Go to
W W W www.voyages1ce.nelson.com
for an interactive version of this review.

When Attachment Fails

We have considered effects of rearing children in a group setting (the kibbutz) on attachment. But children in the kibbutz continue to have contact with their parents. What happens when children are reared in group settings, such as some orphanages, where they have little or no contact with parents or other caregivers? What happens when parents neglect or abuse their children? In both cases, children's attachments may be impaired. In this section, we consider the effect of social deprivation and child abuse on the development of attachment.

Social Deprivation

Studies of children reared in institutions where they receive little social stimulation from caregivers are limited in that they are correlational. In other words, family factors that led to the children's placement in institutions may also have contributed to their developmental problems. Ethical considerations prevent us from conducting experiments in which we randomly assign children to social deprivation. However, experiments of this kind have been undertaken with rhesus monkeys, and the results are consistent with those of the correlational studies of children. Let us first examine these animal experiments and then turn to the correlational research involving children.

Experiments with Monkeys

The Harlows and their colleagues conducted studies of rhesus monkeys that were "reared by" wire-mesh and terry-cloth surrogate mothers. In later studies, rhesus monkeys were reared without even this questionable "social" support. They were reared without seeing any other animal, whether monkey or human.

*Question: **What are the findings of the Harlows' studies on the effects of social deprivation on monkeys?*** The Harlows (Harlow, Harlow, & Suomi, 1971) found that rhesus infants reared in this most solitary confinement later avoided contact with other monkeys. They did not engage in the characteristic playful chasing and romping. Instead, they cowered in the presence of others and failed to respond to them. Nor did they attempt to fend off attacks by other monkeys. Rather, they sat in the corner, clutching themselves and rocking back and forth. Females who later bore children tended to ignore or abuse them (Higley, Lande, & Suomi, 1989).

Can the damage done by social deprivation be overcome? When monkeys deprived for six months or more are placed with younger, three- to four-month-old females for a couple of hours a day, the younger monkeys make efforts to initiate social interaction with their deprived elders (see Figure 7.6). Many of the deprived monkeys begin to play with the youngsters after a few weeks, and many of them eventually expand their social contacts to other rhesus monkeys of various ages (Suomi, Harlow, & McKinney, 1972). Perhaps of greater interest is the related finding that socially withdrawn four- and five-year-old children make gains in their social and emotional development when they are provided with younger playmates (Furman, Rahe, & Hartup, 1979).

*Question: **What do we know about the effects of social deprivation on humans?***

Studies with Children

Institutionalized children whose material needs are met but who receive little social stimulation from caregivers encounter problems in their physical, intellectual, social, and emotional development (Grusec & Lytton, 1988; Provence & Lipton, 1962; Spitz, 1965). Spitz (1965) noted that many institutionalized children appear to develop a syndrome characterized by withdrawal and depression. They show progressively less interest in their world and become progressively inactive. Some of them die.

Consider a report of life in one institution (Provence & Lipton, 1962). Infants were maintained in separate cubicles for most of their first year to ward off infectious diseases. Adults tended to them only to feed and change their diapers. As a rule, baby bottles were propped up in the infants' cribs. Attendants rarely responded to the babies' cries, and the infants were rarely played with or spoken to. By the age of four months, the infants in this institution showed little interest in adults. They rarely tried to gain their attention, even when in distress. A few months later, some of them sat withdrawn in their cribs and rocked back and forth, almost like the Harlows' monkeys. Language deficiencies were striking. As the first year progressed, little babbling was heard within the infants' cubicles. None were speaking even one word at twelve months.

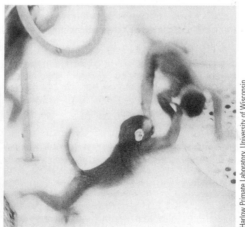

Figure 7.6
Monkey Therapists

In the left-hand photo, a 3- to 4-month-old rhesus monkey "therapist" tries to soothe a monkey who was reared in social isolation. The deprived monkey remains withdrawn. She clutches herself into a ball and rocks back and forth. The right-hand photo was taken several weeks later and shows that deprived monkeys given young "therapists" can learn to play and adjust to community life. Socially withdrawn preschoolers have similarly profited from exposure to younger peers.

Harlow Primate Laboratory, University of Wisconsin

Why do children whose material needs are met show such dramatic deficiencies? Is it because they do not receive the love and affection of a human? Or is it because they do not receive adequate sensory or social stimulation?

The answer may depend, in part, on the age of the child. Classic studies by Leon Yarrow and his colleagues (Yarrow, Goodwin, Manheimer, & Milowe, 1971; Yarrow & Goodwin, 1973) suggest that deficiencies in sensory stimulation and social interaction may cause more problems than lack of love in infants who are too young to have developed specific attachments. However, once infants have developed specific attachments, separation from their primary caregivers can lead to problems.

In the first study, the development of fifty-three adopted children was tracked over a ten-year period (Yarrow et al., 1971). The researchers compared the development of three subgroups: (1) children who were transferred to their permanent adoptive homes almost immediately after birth, (2) children who were given temporary foster mothers and then transferred to permanent adoptive homes before they were six months old, and (3) children who were transferred from temporary foster mothers to their permanent adoptive homes after they were six months old. At the age of ten, children in the first two groups showed no differences in social and emotional development. However, children in the third group showed significantly less ability to relate to other people. Perhaps their deficits resulted from being separated from their foster mothers after they had become attached to them.

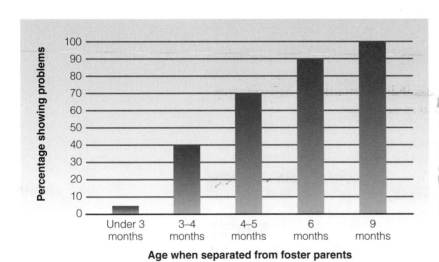

Figure 7.7

The Development of Adopted Children Separated from Temporary Foster Parents

The older the child at the time of separation, the more likely it is that behavioural disturbances will occur. *Source: Yarrow & Goodwin (1973).*

In the second study, Yarrow and Goodwin (1973) followed the development of seventy adopted children who were separated from temporary foster parents between birth and the age of sixteen months. The researchers found strong correlations between the age at which the children were separated and feeding and sleeping problems, decreased social responsiveness, and extremes in attachment behaviours (see Figure 7.7). Disturbed attachment behaviours included excessive clinging to the new mother and violent rejection of her. None of the children who were separated from the initial foster mothers before the age of three months showed moderate or severe disturbances. All the children who were separated at nine months or older did show such disturbances. Forty to ninety percent of the children separated between the ages of three and nine months showed moderate to severe disturbances. The incidence of problems increased as the age advanced.

The Yarrow studies suggest that babies in institutions, at least up to the age of three months or so, may require general sensory and social stimulation more than a specific relationship with a primary caregiver. After the age of three months, some disturbance is likely if there is instability in the caregiving staff. By the ages of six to nine months, disturbance seems to be guaranteed if there is instability in the position of primary caregiver. More recent follow-up studies have also found that children reared in institutions in early childhood and then adopted into well-functioning families have social relationship problems well into adolescence (Maclean, 2003; Rutter, Colvert, Kreppner, Beckett, Castle, Groothues,

Hawkins, O'Connor, Stevens, & Sonuga-Barke, 2007; Smyke, Dumitrescu, & Zeenah, 2002). Fortunately, there is also evidence that children show some capacity to recover from early social deprivation.

The Capacity to Recover from Social Deprivation

Studies with animals and children show that early social deprivation is linked to developmental deficits. However, other studies suggest that infants also have powerful capacities to recover from deprivation.

Kagan and Klein (1973) reported that many children may be able to recover fully from thirteen or fourteen months of deprivation. The natives in an isolated Guatemalan village believe that fresh air and sunshine will make children ill. Thus, children are kept in windowless huts until they can walk. They are played with infrequently. During their isolation, the infants behave apathetically; they are physically and socially retarded when they start to walk. But by eleven years of age, they are alert, active, and as intellectually able as Canadian children of the same age.

A classic longitudinal study of orphanage children also offers evidence of the ability of children to recover from social deprivation (Skeels, 1966). In this study, a group of nineteen-month-old apparently retarded children were placed in the care of older institutionalized girls. The girls spent a great deal of time playing with, talking to, and nurturing them. Four years after being placed with the girls, the "retarded" children made dramatic gains in intelligence test scores, whereas children remaining in the orphanage showed declines in IQ.

The children placed in the care of the older girls also appeared to be generally well adjusted. By the time Skeels reported on their progress in 1966, most were married and were rearing children of their own who showed no intellectual or social deficits. Despite this, there is growing evidence that disinhibited attachment is a common clinical pattern among children who were reared in institutions (Rutter et al., 2007). Unfortunately, many of the children who had been left in the orphanage were still in some type of institutional setting. Few of them showed normal social and emotional development. Few were functioning as independent adults.

The good news from this and other studies is that many children who have been exposed to early social deprivation can catch up in their social and emotional development and lead normal adult lives if they receive individual attention and environmental stimulation (Landesman, 1990). The bad news is that society has not yet allocated the resources to give all children the opportunity to do so.

Reactive Attachment Disorder

Reactive attachment disorder (RAD) is a diagnosis used to describe "markedly disturbed and developmentally inappropriate social relatedness in most contexts, beginning before the age of 5 years" (American Psychiatric Association, 1994, p. 116). Because both bonding (feelings that primary caregiver has toward infant) and attachment (feelings that child has toward caregiver) are impaired in RAD, children with a history of abuse are likely to receive a RAD diagnosis (Hanson & Spratt, 2000). Although many terms have been used to describe impaired attachment (disorganized, avoidant, resistant, diffused, disinhibited, indiscriminate sociability), two clinical types are described in both the *DSM-IV* and the *Tenth Revision of the International Statistical Classification of Diseases* (World Heath Organization, 1992). The first describes an emotionally withdrawn/inhibited child—one who rarely seeks or responds to comfort and fails to demonstrate preference for a caregiver. The second type is an indiscriminate/disinhibited type—a child who is overly sociable, seeking comfort and affection nonselectively (i.e., even from strangers), and fails to exhibit expected reserve with strangers. Another type of attachment disorder is the disrupted attachment disorder, reserved to describe cases where a child is suddenly separated from a primary attachment figure (e.g., because of the death of a parent or other unforeseeable circumstances) and the normal progression of grief and bereavement occur (Zeanah & Boros, 2000). Why is there so much disagreement about the diagnosis of attachment disorders? Mainly because, for accurate diagnosis, attachment problems need to be distinguished from other problems and disorders (Zilberstein, 2006).

Child Abuse and Neglect

We have considered the results of rearing children in settings in which contact with parents is reduced or absent. But living with one's parents does not guarantee that a child will receive tender loving care. Sadly, there's no place like home—for violence, that is. *Questions: What are the incidences of child abuse and neglect? What are their effects?* Consider the following incidence rates (i.e., number of child maltreatment investigations conducted in a given year by child welfare agencies) as reported in the Canadian Incidence Study of Reported Child Abuse and Neglect, 2003: Major Findings (Trocmé, Fallon, MacLaurin, Daciuk, Felstiner, Black, Tonmyr, Blackstock, Barter, Turcotte, & Cloutier, 2005):

- An estimated 235 315 child maltreatment investigations were conducted in Canada (a rate of 38.33 investigations per 1000 children aged 0–15 years).
- About 49 percent (114 607 or 18.67 investigations per 1000 children) of the investigations were found to be substantiated.
- The most common form of substantiated child maltreatment is neglect (34 percent), followed by exposure to family violence (26 percent), physical abuse (23 percent), emotional harm (14 percent), and sexual abuse (3 percent).

Fifty-one percent of boys and forty-one percent of girls are the victims of substantiated cases of child maltreatment. Boys are more likely than girls to be the victims of physical abuse, but only between the ages of eight and eleven years. The mother (54 percent) is more likely than the father (48 percent) to be the aggressor (Trocmé et al., 2005).

Child Abuse
Flyers such as this one are designed to bring awareness to the public and to reach out to parents who may be in crises.

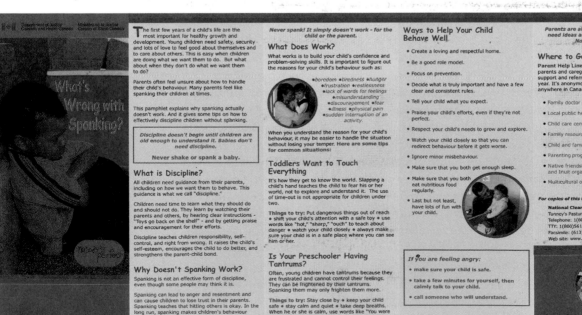

There are five types of child maltreatment listed in "Child Maltreatment in Canada," a publication of the National Clearinghouse on Family Violence (2006):

- **Physical abuse:** The application of unreasonable force by an adult or youth to any part of a child's body.
- **Sexual abuse:** Involvement of a child, by an adult or youth, in any act of sexual gratification, or exposure of a child to sexual contact, activity, or behaviour.
- **Neglect:** Failure by a parent or caregiver to provide the physical or psychological necessities of life to a child.
- **Emotional harm:** Adult behaviour that harms a child psychologically, emotionally, or spiritually.
- **Exposure to family violence:** Circumstances that allow a child to be aware of violence occurring between a caregiver and his or her partner or between other family members.

It is fair to assume that only a proportion of maltreatment incidences are actually reported. Prevalence rates based on an Ontario community-based survey revealed that 33 percent of males and 27 percent of females reported experiences of physical and/or sexual abuse during childhood (MacMillan, Fleming, Trocmé, Boyle, Wong, Racine, Beardslee, & Offord, 1997).

Sexual Abuse of Children

About 3 percent of Canadian children are victims of sexual abuse each year (Minister of Public Works and Government Services Canada, 2005). Sexual abuse of children can be difficult to detect or define (Haugaard, 2000) because adults interact with children in many ways that involve touching, and sometimes they touch the genital organs, as when they are bathing or changing children. They may (literally) sleep with their children and may wander around in the nude near them. Most of these behaviour patterns are innocent enough, but some adults fondle children's genital organs, kiss them in sexual ways, or have sexual intercourse with them. These behaviours fit the definition of child sexual abuse.

Effects of Child Abuse

Abused children show a high incidence of personal and social problems and psychological disorders (Letourneau, Schoenwald, & Sheidow, 2004). In general, abused children are less securely attached to their parents. They are less intimate with their peers and are more aggressive, angry, and noncompliant than other children (DeAngelis, 1997; Parker & Herrera, 1996; Rothbart & Ahadi, 1994; Shields, Ryan, & Cicchetti, 2001). They rarely express positive emotions, have lower self-esteem, and show impaired cognitive functioning, leading to poorer performance in school (Shonk & Cicchetti, 2001). When they reach adulthood, they are more likely to act aggressively toward their intimate partners (Malinosky-Rummell & Hansen, 1993). As they mature, maltreated children are at greater risk for delinquency, academic failure, and substance abuse (Eckenrode, Laird, & Doris, 1993; Haapasalo & Moilanen, 2004).

There is no single concrete identifiable syndrome—cluster of symptoms—that indicates a history of physical abuse, neglect, or sexual abuse (Saywitz, Mannarino, Berliner, & Cohen, 2000). More generally, however, there seems to be little doubt that victims of child sexual abuse develop a higher incidence of psychological and physical health problems than other children (Saywitz et al., 2000). Child sexual abuse, as with physical abuse, also appears to have lingering effects on relationships in adulthood. For one thing, sexually abused children are more likely to engage in risky sexual behaviour later in life (Letourneau et al., 2004; Noll, Trickett, & Putnam, 2000). Abusive experiences at the hands of adults also colour children's expectation of other adults.

Causes of Child Abuse

A number of factors contribute to the probability that parents will abuse their children. They include situational stress, a history of child abuse in at least one of the parents' families of origin, lack of adequate coping and problem-solving skills, deficiency in child-rearing skills, unrealistic expectations of what a child should be able to do at a given developmental level, and substance abuse (Maluccio & Ainsworth, 2003; Merrill, Crouch, Thomsen, & Guimond, 2004).

Stress has many sources, including such life changes as parental conflict and divorce or separation, the loss of a job, moving, and the birth of a new family member. Unemployment seems to be a particularly predisposing life change: The incidence of child abuse increases among the unemployed (Straus & Smith, 1990; Wolfner & Gelles, 1993).

Stress is created by crying infants themselves (Green et al., 1987). Ironically, infants who are already in pain of some kind and relatively difficult to soothe may be more likely to be abused (Frodi, 1985). Abusive parents may find the cries of their infants to be particularly aversive, and so the infants' crying may precipitate abusive behaviour (Schuetze & Zeskind, 2001; Schuetze, Zeskind, & Eiden, 2003). Ironically, mothers who are deeply depressed or using cocaine may neglect crying infants because they perceive the cries to be less aversive (Schuetze & Zeskind, 2001; Schuetze et al., 2003). Children who act disobediently, inappropriately, or unresponsively are also at greater risk of abuse (Bugental & Happaney, 2004). Why? Parents tend to become frustrated and irritated when their children show prolonged signs of distress or misbehaviour. Abusive mothers are more likely than nonabusive mothers to assume that their children's misbehaviour is intentional, even when it is not (Bugental & Happaney, 2004). Within our culture, intentional misconduct is seen as more deserving of punishment than incidental misconduct. Abusive mothers also tend to believe that they have little control over their child's misbehaviour (Bugental & Happaney, 2004).

What of the role of failure of attachment in abuse? The parents of preterm children have more difficulty becoming attached to them (see Chapter 4). One reason may be that the early parent-infant relationship is interrupted by hospital procedures. Preterm children are more likely than their full-term counterparts to be abused (Crittenden & Ainsworth, 1989). With prematurity, of course, we are not only dealing with possible failures in attachment. Preterm children are also more likely to develop illnesses and other problems. As a consequence, they may cry more frequently and generally make more demands on their parents.

Truth or Fiction Revisited: It is true that child abusers have frequently been the victims of child abuse themselves (Ertem et al., 2000; White & Smith, 2004). Yet most people who were abused as children do not abuse their own children (Kaufman & Zigler, 1992). Still, many adults who were victims of child abuse worry that they are destined to abuse their own children. One study found that abused mothers who broke the cycle were more likely to have received emotional support from a nonabusive adult during childhood, to have participated in therapy at some point, and to have had a supportive mate (Egeland, Jacobvitz, & Sroufe, 1988).

Question: Why does child abuse run in families? There are a number of reasons (White & Smith, 2004). One is that parents serve as role models for their children. As noted by Murray Straus (1995), "Spanking teaches kids that when someone is doing something you don't like and they won't stop doing it, you hit them." If children grow up observing their parents using violence as a means of coping with stress and feelings of anger, they are less likely to learn to diffuse anger through techniques such as humour, verbal expression of feelings, reasoning, or even counting to ten to let the anger pass.

Exposure to violence in their own homes may lead some children to accept family violence as a norm. They may see nothing wrong with it. Certainly, parents can find any number of "justifications" for violence—if they seek them. One is the adage, "Spare the rod, spoil the child." Another is the belief that they are hurting their children "for their own good"—to discourage behaviour that is likely to get them into trouble. Still another "justification" for child abuse is the sometimes cloudy distinction between the occasional swat on the rear end and spanking. Child abusers may argue that all parents hit their children (which is not true), and they may claim not to understand why outsiders are making such a fuss about private family behaviour. Child abusers who were subjected to abuse also may harbour the (incorrect) belief that "everyone does it."

The patterns of attachment of the perpetrators of child abuse have also been studied. One study, for example, found that nonfamilial perpetrators of sexual child abuse were significantly less likely to have a secure attachment style in their relationships (Jamieson & Marshall, 2000).

In any event, child abuse must be conceptualized and dealt with as a crime of violence. Whether or not child abusers happen to be victims of abuse themselves, child abusers are criminals and children must be protected from them.

What to Do

Dealing with child abuse is a frustrating task. Social agencies and the courts can find it as difficult to distinguish between spanking and abuse as many abusers do. Because of the belief in this country that parents have the right to rear their children as they wish, police and the courts have also historically tried to avoid involvement in domestic quarrels and family disputes. However, the alarming incidence of child abuse has spawned new efforts at detection and prevention. In Canada, each province and territory has laws that mandate professionals such as educators, psychologists, nurses, and physicians to report suspected child maltreatment. With the exception of Newfoundland, Saskatchewan, Prince Edward Island, and the Northwest Territories, where suspected cases of child maltreatment are reported to the RCMP, the provinces and territories report suspected cases to the local Child Protection Services (CPS).

A number of techniques have been developed to help prevent child abuse. One approach focuses on strengthening parenting skills among the general population (Altepeter & Walker, 1992). The introduction of parent-education classes in high school is an example of this approach.

Another approach targets groups at high risk for abuse, such as poor, single teen mothers (Kaufman & Zigler, 1992; Roberts, Wasik, Casto, & Ramey, 1991). In some programs, for example, home visitors help new parents develop skills in caregiving and home management (Duggan et al., 2004).

A third technique focuses on presenting information about abuse and providing support to families. For instance, many locales have child abuse hotlines. Private citizens who suspect child abuse may call for advice. Parents who are having difficulty controlling aggressive impulses toward their children are encouraged to call. Some hotlines are serviced by groups such as Parents Anonymous, whose members have had similar difficulties and can help callers diffuse feelings of anger in less harmful ways.

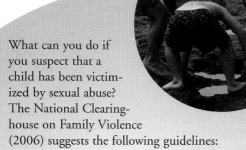

What can you do if you suspect that a child has been victimized by sexual abuse? The National Clearinghouse on Family Violence (2006) suggests the following guidelines:

• Act on the suspicion quickly (i.e., do not wait for days or weeks).

• Keep the best interest of the child in mind, and protect the child from any further harm (i.e., keep the child from returning to the abusive or neglectful situation).

• Write down what you have been told and by whom, your observations and what you did.

• If the child has disclosed maltreatment, reassure the child that it was right to do so, as he or she may have mixed feelings and/or feel loyalty to the perpetrator.

• Try to learn as much as you can about the situation and context, and find out if the child is currently at risk (e.g., is experiencing ongoing exposure to the perpetrator), but do not interview the child about details. That is the responsibility of the CPS.

• Contact the local CPS and report the situation. Provide identifying data and your contact information.

• In consultation with CPS, consider immediate medical assessment/treatment of physical problems and referral to local emergency health services or sexual assault teams, etc.

• Consider referral to a mental health professional for assessment/treatment of any psychological or psychiatric problems.

• Short term and long-term safety plans for the child should be prepared in collaboration with CPS.

Here are some Canadian resources:

Centre of Excellence for Child Welfare
http://www.cecw-cepb.ca
Faculty of Social Work
University of Toronto
246 Bloor Street W.
Toronto, ON M5S 1A1
Fax: (416) 946-8846

Child Welfare League of Canada
http:www.cwlc.ca
75 Albert Street, Suite 1001
Ottawa, ON K1P 5E7
Tel: (613) 235-4412

First Nations Child & Family Caring Society of Canada (FNCFCS)
http://www.fncfcs.com
1001-75 Albert Street
Ottawa, ON K1P 5E7
Tel: (613) 230-5885

National Clearinghouse on Family Violence
http://www.phac-aspc.gc.ca/nc-cn
Family Violence Prevention Unit
Public Health Agency of Canada
200 Eglantine Driveway
Jeanne Mance Building, AL: 1909D1
Tunney's Pasture
Ottawa, ON K1A 0K9
Tel: 1-800-267-1291

Another helpful measure is increased publicity on the dimensions of the child abuse problem. The public may also need more education about where an occasional swat on the behind ends and child abuse begins. Perhaps the format for such education could be something like, "If you are doing such and such, make no mistake about it—you are abusing your child."

Active Review

9. The Harlows found that rhesus infants reared in isolation later (sought or avoided?) contact with other monkeys.

10. Spitz noted that many institutionalized children appear to develop a syndrome characterized by _____ and depression.

11. Relatively more deaths occur from (physical abuse or neglect?).

Reflect & Relate: What would you do if you learned that the child of a neighbour was being abused? What would you do if you were a teacher and learned that a child in your class was being abused?

Go to

W W W www.voyages1ce.nelson.com

for an interactive version of this review.

Emotional Development

Emotions colour our lives. We are green with envy, red with anger, blue with sorrow. Positive emotions such as love can fill our days with pleasure. Negative emotions such as fear, depression, and anger can fill us with dread and make each day a chore. *Question: What are emotions?* An **emotion** is a state of feeling that has physiological, situational, and cognitive components. Physiologically, when emotions are strong, our hearts may beat more rapidly and our muscles may tense. Situationally, we may feel fear in the presence of a threat and joy or relief in the presence of a loved one. Cognitively, fear is accompanied by the idea that we are in danger.

emotion A state of feeling that has physiological, situational, and cognitive components.

Theories of the Development of Emotions

Question: How do emotions develop? A number of theories concerning the development of emotions have been offered. Basically, they break down into two camps. The first, proposed originally by Katherine Bridges (1932), holds that we are born with a single emotion and that other emotions become differentiated as time passes. The second, proposed by Carroll Izard (1991, 1992), holds that all emotions are present and adequately differentiated at birth. However, they are not shown all at once. Instead, they emerge in response to the child's developing needs and maturational sequences.

Bridges's and Sroufe's Theories

On the basis of her observations of babies, Bridges proposed that newborns experience one emotion—diffuse excitement. By the age of three months, two other emotions have differentiated from this general state of excitement—a negative emotion, distress, and a positive emotion, delight. By six months of age, fear, disgust, and anger will have developed from distress. By twelve months, elation and affection will have differentiated from delight. Jealousy develops from distress, and joy develops from delight—both during the second year.

Alan Sroufe (1979) has advanced Bridges's theory by focusing on the ways in which cognitive development provides a basis for emotional development. Jealousy, for example, could not become differentiated without some understanding of object permanence (the continuing existence of people and objects) and possession. Similarly, infants usually show distress at the mother's departure after they have developed object permanence. Fear of strangers cannot occur without the perceptual ability to discriminate familiar people from others.

Izard's Theory

Carroll Izard (1991, 1992) proposed that infants are born with discrete emotional states. However, the timing of their appearance is linked to the child's cognitive development and social experiences. For example, Izard and his colleagues (1987a) reported that two-month-old babies receiving inoculations showed distress, whereas older infants showed anger.

Izard's view may sound similar to Sroufe's. Both suggest an orderly unfolding of emotions that become more specific as time passes. However, in keeping with Izard's view, researchers have found that a number of different emotions appear to be demonstrated by infants at ages earlier than those suggested by Bridges and Sroufe. In one study of emotions shown by babies during the first three months, 95 percent of the mothers interviewed reported observing joy; 84 percent, anger; 74 percent, surprise; and 58 percent, fear (Johnson, Emde, Pannabecker, Stenberg, & Davis, 1982). These figures are based on mothers' reports, and it is possible that the infants were actually showing more diffuse emotions (Murphy, 1983).

Izard (1983) claimed to have found many discrete emotions at the age of one month by using his Maximally Discriminative Facial Movement Scoring System. Figure 7.8 shows some infant facial expressions that Izard believes are associated with the basic emotions of anger/rage, enjoyment/joy, fear/terror, and interest/excitement. Izard and his colleagues reported that facial expressions indicating interest, disgust, and pain are present at birth. They and others have observed expressions of anger and sadness at two months of age, expressions of surprise at four months, and expressions of fear at seven months (Izard & Malatesta, 1987). However, some researchers have suggested that this type of research is

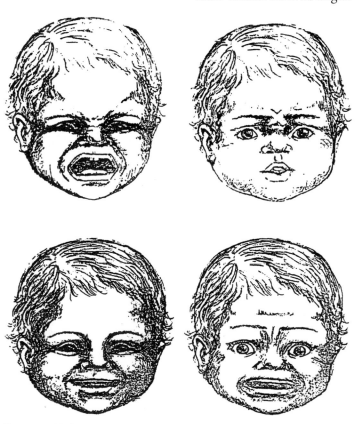

Figure 7.8

Illustrations from Izard's Maximally Discriminative Facial Movement Scoring System

What emotion do you think is being experienced by each of these infants? *Source: Izard (1983).*

fraught with problems. First, observers cannot always accurately identify the emotions shown in slides or drawings of infant facial expressions (Oster, Hegley, & Nagel, 1992). Second, we cannot know the exact relationship between a facial expression and an infant's inner feelings, which, of course, are private events (Camras, Sullivan, & Michel, 1993). In other words, even if the drawings accurately represent young infants' facial expressions, we cannot be certain that the drawings express the specific emotions that they would suggest if the expressions were exhibited by older children and adults. With development, children start to experience complex emotions (e.g., shame, guilt, pride), the types of emotions that require some sort of automatic understanding of the self (Lewis, Alessandri, & Sullivan, 1992; Saarni, Mumme, & Campos, 1998). This type of expansion in emotional development is intricately connected to cognitive growth and processes—hence the name *self-conscious emotions*. For example, children must be able to understand others' feelings and evaluations in order to experience embarrassment.

Table 7.2	*The Development of Emotional and Behavioural Control in Infants and Toddlers*	
	Development of emotional and behavioural control	Effects of the environment
Infants	• Develop self-soothing and self-stimulating strategies • Develop arousal and sleep-wake patterns that relate to the environment • Begin voluntary efforts to control own motor activity and behaviours • Begin voluntary efforts to contact other people and objects and to engage in sustained interactions with them	• Chaotic, overstimulating, or understimulating environment impedes development of adaptive arousal and wake-sleep patterns • Caregiver warmth and responsiveness assists developmental of differentiated emotional responses • Caregiver warmth, consistency, and responsiveness to child's signals support feelings of security and development of awareness of control • Caregiver responsive interaction with infant establishes early understanding of social interaction and communication patterns (turn-taking, etc.)
Toddlers	• Experience more complex emotions • Develop early impulse control (can comply with simple directions and restrictions) • Develop language and increasing awareness of own desires (can form and carry out intentions) • Can regulate some types of activities by imitating others • Use social referencing to judge own actions and environmental events	• Caregiver sensitivity to child's needs and individual characteristics supports the development of inner control • Environments arranged for safe independent action and self-testing, with opportunities for positive experiences with objects and peers, support the development of inner control • Positive models of behaviour support the development of self-regulated control • Positive and responsive guidance that is consistent but respects autonomy and encourages responsibility and self-controls supports self-regulation

Source: Bronson (2000).

In sum, researchers agree that a handful of emotions are shown by infants during the first few months. They agree that other emotions develop in an orderly manner. They agree that emotional development is linked to cognitive development and social experience. They do not agree on exactly when specific emotions are first shown or whether discrete emotions are present at birth.

Emotional Development and Patterns of Attachment

Research by Grazyna Kochanska (2001) links emotional development with various histories of attachment. Kochanska, in a longitudinal study of 112 children at ages nine, fourteen, twenty-two, and thirty-three months, studied the development of fear, anger, and joy using laboratory situations designed to evoke these emotions. Patterns of attachment were assessed using the strange-situation method. Differences in emotional development could first be related to attachment at the age of fourteen months. Resistant children were most fearful and least joyful. Fear was their most powerful emotion. They frequently responded with distress even in episodes designed to evoke joy. When they were assessed repeatedly over time, it became apparent that securely attached children were becoming significantly less angry. By contrast, the negative emotions of insecurely attached children rose: Avoidant children grew more fearful, and resistant children became less joyful. At thirty-three months of age, securely attached children were less likely to show fear and anger, even when they were exposed to situations designed to elicit these emotions.

Enough disagreement. Let us focus on an emotion that we can all agree is little fun: fear. We focus on a common fear of infants: the fear of strangers.

Fear of Strangers

Here is an example of how attachment and emotions interplay. Rathus recounts, "When Jordan was one year old, her mother and I decided we had to get a nanny for a few hours a day so that we could teach, write, breathe, and engage in other life activities. We hired a graduate student in social work who had a mild, engaging way about

Stranger Anxiety
Infants in many cultures develop a fear of strangers, known as stranger anxiety, at about 6 to 9 months of age. This infant shows clear signs of distress when held by a stranger, even though Mother is close by. How would you behave around an infant who does not know you to minimize his or her stranger anxiety?

© 2002 Laura Dwight

her. She nurtured Jordan and played with her for about four months, during which time Jordan came to somewhat grudgingly accept her—most of the time. Still, Jordan was never completely comfortable with her and frequently let out a yowl as if buildings were collapsing around her, although the nanny did nothing except attempt to soothe her in a calm, consistent manner."

Jordan had a nanny and she had fear of strangers. Unfortunately, she met the nanny during the period after she had developed this fear. The fear was eventually to subside, as these fears do, but during her entire encounter with the nanny, the nanny wondered what she was doing wrong. The answer, of course, was simple: She was existing, within sight of Jordan. Worse yet, Jordan's parents were not there to protect her from this vicious foe.

Was Jordan's response to her nanny "normal"? *Question: Is fear of strangers normal?* **Truth or Fiction Revisited:** Development of fear of strangers—sometimes termed **stranger anxiety**—is normal. Most (but not all) infants develop it. Stranger anxiety appears at about six to nine months of age in many different cultures, including those of the United States, Great Britain, Guatemala, and Zambia (Smith, 1979). By four or five months of age, infants smile more in response to their mothers than to strangers. At this age, infants may compare the faces of strangers and their mothers, looking back and forth. Somewhat older infants show marked distress by crying, whimpering, gazing fearfully, and crawling away. Fear of strangers may peak between nine and twelve months of age and decline in the second year or reach a second peak between the ages of eighteen and twenty-four months and then decline in the third year (Thompson & Limber, 1990).

stranger anxiety A fear of unfamiliar people that emerges between 6 and 9 months of age. Also called fear of strangers.

Children who have developed fear of strangers show less distress in response to strangers when their mothers are present. Babies are less likely to show fear of strangers when they are held by their mothers than when they are placed a few feet away (Thompson & Limber, 1990). Children also are less likely to show fear of strangers when they are in familiar surroundings, such as their homes, than when they are in the laboratory (Sroufe, Waters, & Matas, 1974).

In terms of proximity, the fear response to strangers is the mirror image of attachment. Children attempt to remain near people to whom they are attached. However, the closer they are to strangers, the greater their signs of distress (Boccia & Campos, 1989). They are most distressed when the strangers touch them. For this reason, if you find yourself in a situation in which you are trying to comfort an infant who does not know you, it may be more effective to talk in a friendly and soothing manner from a distance. Reconsider rushing in and picking up the child. Your behaviour with an unfamiliar child can also make a difference. Studies have found that adults who are active and friendly—who gesture, smile, and offer toys—receive more positive response from six- to eighteen-month-olds than do strangers who are quiet and passive (Bretherton, Stolberg, & Kreye, 1981; Mangelsdorf, 1992).

Social Referencing: What Should I Do Now?

Social referencing is the seeking out of another person's perception of a situation to help us form our own view of it (Hertenstein & Campos, 2004; Moses, Baldwin, Rosicky, & Tidball, 2001). In novel situations, adolescents and adults frequently observe how others behave and pattern their behaviour after them. For example, people who are not afraid may help children reduce their fears. Essentially, the models provide information about how to act in a frightening situation.

social referencing Using another person's reaction to a situation to form one's own assessment of it.

Question: When does social referencing develop? Infants also display social referencing, as early as six months of age. They use caregivers' facial expressions or tone of voice to provide clues on how to respond (Hertenstein & Campos, 2004; Saarni, Mumme, & Campos, 1998)). In one study, for example, eight-month-old infants were friendlier to a stranger when their mothers exhibited a friendly facial expression in the stranger's presence than when she displayed a worried expression (Boccia & Campos, 1989).

Infants also use their caregivers' facial expressions to help them interpret ambiguous situations. Do you recall our discussion of the visual cliff in Chapter 6? Most infants are reluctant to cross over to the deep side of the cliff. James Sorce and his colleagues (1985) adjusted the deep side of a visual cliff so that it was neither very deep nor very shallow. In this situation, one-year-old babies initially hesitated and looked back and forth at the drop-off and at their mother's face. If the mother's facial expression exhibited joy or interest, most infants crossed the deep side. But if the mother looked fearful or angry, few infants crossed.

Emotional Regulation: Keeping on an Even Keel

emotional regulation Techniques for controlling one's emotional states.

Infants use emotional signals from an adult to help them cope with uncertainty. Another important feature of early emotional development is *emotional regulation* (Kopp, 1992; Rothbart, Ellis, & Posner, 2004). *Question: What is emotional regulation?* **Emotional regulation** refers to the ways in which young children control their own emotions. Even young infants display certain behaviours to control unpleasant emotional states. They may look away from a disturbing event or suck their thumbs (Rothbart et al., 2004). Caregivers play an important role in helping infants learn to regulate their emotions. Early in life, a two-way communication system develops in which the infant signals the caregiver that help is needed and the caregiver responds. Claire Kopp (1989, p. 347) gave an example of how this system works:

> A thirteen-month-old, playing with a large plastic bottle, attempted to unscrew the cover, but could not. Fretting for a short time, she initiated eye contact with her mother and held out the jar. As her mother took it to unscrew the cover, the infant ceased fretting.

Evidence from a Japanese study suggests that the children of secure mothers are not only likely to be securely attached themselves but are also likely to regulate their own emotions in a positive manner (Kazui et al., 2000). A German longitudinal study (Zimmermann, Maier, Winter, & Grossmann, 2001) related emotional regulation in adolescence with patterns of attachment during infancy, as assessed using the strange-situation method. Forty-one adolescents, age sixteen and seventeen years, were placed in complex problem-solving situations with friends. It turned out that those adolescents who were secure as infants were most capable of regulating their emotions to interact cooperatively with their friends. Yet another study (Volling, 2001) addressed the relationship between attachment in infancy and emotional regulation in an interaction with a distressed sibling at the age of four. Of forty-five preschoolers in the study, those who had an insecure-resistant infant-mother attachment at the age of one year engaged in more conflict with their siblings and showed greater hostility at the age of four.

Active Review

12. Bridges proposed that we are born with a single emotion: diffuse _____.

13. The (majority or minority?) of infants develop fear of strangers.

14. Social _____ is the seeking out of another person's perception of a situation to help us form our own view of it.

15. Emotional _____ refers to the ways in which young children control their own emotions.

Reflect & Relate: Have you ever been in a novel situation and been uncertain about what to do? How about when you entered adolescence or began your first college/university class? Did you observe other people's reactions to the situation in an effort to determine what to do? This behaviour is termed social referencing. At what age do humans begin to use social referencing?

Go to
W W W www.voyages1ce.nelson.com
for an interactive version of this review.

Personality Development

An individual's **personality** refers to his or her distinctive ways of responding to people and events. In this section, we examine important aspects of personality development in the infant years. First, we look at the emergence of the self-concept. We then turn to a discussion of temperament. Finally, we consider sex differences in behaviour.

personality An individual's distinctive ways of responding to people and events.

The Self-Concept

At birth, we may find the world to be a confusing blur of sights, sounds, and inner sensations. Yet, the "we" may be missing, at least for a while. When our hands first come into view, there is little evidence that we realize that that hand "belongs" to us and that we are somehow separate and distinct from the world outside.

Questions: What is the self-concept? How does it develop? The **self-concept** is the sense of self. It appears to emerge gradually during infancy. At some point, infants understand the hand they are moving in and out of sight is "their" hand. At some point, they understand that their own bodies extend only so far and that at a certain point, external objects and the bodies of others begin.

self-concept One's impression of oneself; self-awareness.

Self-Awareness
In the middle of the second year, infants begin to develop self-awareness, which has a powerful effect on social and emotional development.

separation-individuation
The child's increasing sense of becoming separate from and independent of the mother.

Development of the Self-Concept

Psychologists have devised ingenious methods to assess the development of the self-concept among infants. One of these is the mirror technique. This technique involves the use of a mirror and a dot of rouge. Before the experiment begins, the researcher observes the infant for baseline data on how frequently the infant touches his or her nose. Then the mother places rouge on the infant's nose, and the infant is placed before a mirror. Not until about the age of eighteen months do infants begin to touch their own noses upon looking in the mirror (Butterworth, 1990; Schneider-Rosen & Cicchetti, 1991).

Nose touching suggests that children recognize themselves and that they have a mental picture of themselves that allows them to perceive that the dot of rouge is an abnormality. By thirty months, most infants can also point to pictures of themselves, and they begin to use their own name spontaneously (Bullock & Lutkenhaus, 1990; Stipek, Gralinski, & Kopp, 1990).

Self-awareness has a powerful impact on social and emotional development (Asendorpf & Baudonniere, 1993; Lewis, 1991). Knowledge of the self permits the child to develop notions of sharing and cooperation. In one study, for example, two-year-olds who had a better developed sense of self were more likely to cooperate with other children (Brownell & Carriger, 1990).

Self-awareness also makes possible the development of "self-conscious" emotions such as embarrassment, envy, empathy, pride, guilt, and shame (Lewis, 1990). One illustration of the development of these "self-conscious" emotions comes from a study by Deborah Stipek and her colleagues (1992). They found that children older than twenty-one months often seek their mother's attention and approval when they have successfully completed a task, whereas younger toddlers do not.

Psychoanalytic Views of the Self-Concept

Margaret Mahler, a psychoanalyst, has proposed that development of self-concept comes about through a process of **separation-individuation,** which lasts from about five months until three years of age (Mahler, Pine, & Bergman, 1975). Separation involves the child's growing perception that her mother is separate from herself. Individuation refers to the child's increasing sense of independence and autonomy.

The word *autonomy* may remind you of a similar view proposed by Erik Erikson that was discussed in Chapter 1. In Erikson's second psychosocial stage of development—the autonomy versus shame and doubt stage—toddlers begin to exercise some autonomy in their day-to-day functions. With better motor and muscle control and increased verbal skills, toddlers attempt to be more independent (you might be familiar with the term the *terrible twos*). However, if toddlers' search for autonomy is met with unrealistic demands (requiring a toddler to sit through a two-hour movie without talking) or with harsh criticism, toddlers may develop a sense of shame and doubt. Erikson states that the major developmental task of the child from ages two to three is acquiring a sense of autonomy and independence from parents. Remember that Freud, too, believed that children of this age are gaining greater independence and control. His focus, however, was primarily on such bodily functions as toileting behaviour. As a parent, Rinaldi recalls when her two children were between the ages of two and three and how toilet training took over her family's lives for a very short, intense period of time.

One of the ways toddlers demonstrate their growing autonomy, much to the dismay of their parents, is by refusing to comply with parental requests or commands, such as refusing to go "pee in the potty." Studies of toddlers and preschoolers between the ages of one and a half and five years have found that as children grow older, they adopt more skillful ways of expressing resistance to parental requests (Klimes-Dougan, 1993;

Kuczynski & Kochanska, 1990). For example, young toddlers are more likely to ignore a parent's request or defy it ("No, I won't," accompanied by foot stamping). Older toddlers and preschoolers are more likely to make excuses ("I'm not hungry") or engage in negotiations ("Can I just eat some of my vegetables?"). This change in response demonstrates that children's level of sophistication in social exchanges is increasing.

Temperament: Easy, Difficult, or Slow to Warm Up?

Question: What is meant by the temperament of a child? Each child has a characteristic way of reacting and adapting to the world. The term **temperament** refers to stable individual differences in styles of reaction that are present early in life. Many researchers believe that temperament forms the basic core of personality and that there is a strong genetic component to temperament (e.g., Goldsmith et al., 2003; Oniszcenko et al., 2003; Plomin, 2000).

The child's temperament includes many aspects of behaviour. Alexander Thomas and Stella Chess, in their well-known New York Longitudinal Study, followed the development of temperament in 133 girls and boys from birth to young adulthood (Chess & Thomas, 1991; Thomas & Chess, 1989) and identified nine characteristics of temperament. Other researchers (e.g., Gartstein, Slobodskaya, & Kinsht, 2003) have identified other characteristics. These include:

- activity level;
- smiling/laughter;
- regularity in child's biological functions, such as eating and sleeping;
- approach or withdrawal from new situations and people;
- adaptability to new situations;
- sensitivity to sensory stimulation;
- intensity of responsiveness;
- quality of mood—generally cheerful or unpleasant;
- distractibility;
- attention span and persistence;
- soothability; and
- distress to limitations.

Questions: What types of temperament do we find among children? How do they develop?

Types of Temperament

Thomas and Chess (1989) found that from the first days of life, many of the children in their study could be classified into one of three types of temperament: "easy" (40 percent of their sample), "difficult" (10 percent), and "slow to warm up" (15 percent). Only 65 percent of the children studied by Chess and Thomas fit into one of the three types of temperament. Some of the differences among these three types of children are shown in Table 7.3. As you can see, the easy child has regular sleep and feeding schedules, approaches new situations (such as a new food, a new school, or a stranger) with enthusiasm and adapts easily to them, and is generally cheerful. It is obvious why such a child would be relatively easy for parents to raise. Some children are more inconsistent and show a mixture of temperament traits. For example, a toddler may have a pleasant disposition but be frightened of new situations.

The difficult child, on the other hand, has irregular sleep and feeding schedules, is slow to accept new people and situations, takes a long time to adjust to new routines, and responds to frustrations with tantrums and loud crying. Parents find this type of child more difficult to deal with. The slow-to-warm-up child falls somewhere

temperament Individual differences in styles of reaction that are present early in life.

To watch different temperaments in infants (difficult, easy, and slow-to-warm-up) click on "Temperament" in Module 1, Section 3.

between the other two. These children have somewhat irregular feeding and sleeping patterns and do not react as strongly as difficult children. They initially respond negatively to new experiences and adapt slowly only after repeated exposure.

Stability of Temperament

How stable is temperament? ***Truth or Fiction Revisited:*** Children are not all born with the same temperament. Thomas and Chess found that many children have one of three kinds of temperament from the first days of life. Evidence also indicates that there is at least moderate consistency in the development of temperament from infancy onward (Pauli-Pott, Mertesacker, & Beckmann, 2003; Rothbart et al., 2004). The infant who is highly active and cries in novel situations often becomes a fearful toddler. An anxious, unhappy toddler tends to become an anxious, unhappy adolescent. The child who refuses to accept new foods during infancy may scream when getting the first haircut, refuse to leave a parent's side during the first day of kindergarten, and have difficulty adjusting to college as a young adult. Difficult children in general are at greater risk for developing psychological disorders and adjustment problems later in life (Pauli-Pott et al., 2003; Rothbart et al., 2004). A longitudinal study tracked the progress of infants with a difficult temperament from one and a half through twelve years of age (Guerin, Gottfried, & Thomas, 1997). Temperament during infancy was assessed by the mother. Behaviour patterns were assessed by both parents during the third year through the age of twelve and by teachers from the ages of six to eleven. A difficult temperament correlated significantly with parental reports of behavioural problems from ages three to twelve, including problems with attention span and aggression. Teachers concurred that children who had shown difficult temperaments during infancy were more likely to be aggressive later on and to have shorter attention spans.

Types of Temperament			
Temperament Category	**Easy**	**Difficult**	**Slow to Warm Up**
• Regularity of biological functioning	• Regular	• Irregular	• Somewhat irregular
• Response to new stimuli	• Positive approach	• Negative withdrawal	• Negative withdrawal
• Adaptability to new situations	• Adapts readily	• Adapts slowly or not at all	• Adapts slowly
• Intensity of reaction	• Mild or moderate	• Intense	• Mild
• Quality of mood	• Positive	• Negative	• Initially negative; gradually more positive

Sources: Chess & Thomas (1991); Thomas & Chess (1989).

Differences in Temperament Differences in temperament emerge in early infancy. The photo on the left shows the positive reactions of a five-month-old girl being fed a new food for the first time. The photo on the right shows the very different response of another girl of about the same age when she is introduced to a new food.

Goodness of Fit: The Role of Environment

The environment also affects the development of temperament. An initial biological predisposition to a certain temperament may be strengthened or weakened by the parents' reaction to the child. Consider the following: Parents may react to a difficult child by becoming less available and less responsive (Spangler, 1990). They may insist on imposing rigid care-giving schedules, which in turn can cause the child to become even more difficult to handle (Power, Gershenhorn, & Stafford, 1990). This example illustrates a discrepancy, or poor fit, between the child's behaviour style and the parents' expectations and behaviours.

On the other hand, parents may respond in such a way as to modify a child's initial temperament in a more positive direction. Take the case of Carl, who in early life was one of the most difficult children in the New York Longitudinal Study:

> Whether it was the first solid foods in infancy, the beginning of nursery and elementary school, first birthday parties, or the first shopping trip, each experience evoked stormy responses, with loud crying and struggling to get away. However, his parents learned to anticipate Carl's reactions, knew that if they were patient, presented only one or a few new situations at a time, and gave him the opportunity for repeated exposure, Carl would finally adapt positively. Furthermore, once he adapted, his intensity of responses gave him a zestful enthusiastic involvement, just as it gave his initial negative reactions a loud and stormy character. His parents became fully aware that the difficulties in raising Carl were due to his temperament and not to their being "bad parents." The father even looked on his son's shrieking and turmoil as a sign of lustiness. As a result of this positive parent-child interaction, Carl never became a behaviour problem.
>
> —Chess & Thomas (1984, p. 263)

goodness of fit Agreement between the parents' expectations of or demands on the child and the child's temperamental characteristics.

This example demonstrates **goodness of fit** between the behaviours of child and parent. A key factor is the parents' realization that their youngster's behaviour does not mean that the child is weak or deliberately disobedient, or that they are bad parents. This realization helps parents modify their attitudes and behaviours toward the child, whose behaviour may in turn change in the desired direction (Chess & Thomas, 1984, 1991).

Sex Differences

All cultures make a distinction between females and males and have beliefs and expectations about how they ought to behave. For this reason, a child's sex is a key factor in shaping its personality and other aspects of development. *Questions: How do girls and boys differ in their social, emotional, and other behaviours?*

Lessons in Observation
Gender

click on "Gender" in Module 1, Section 3, on your Observing Children and Adolescents CD-ROM. You can also visit the Student Book Companion Site to watch the video, answer the questions, and e-mail your responses to your professor.

To watch this video

Learning Objectives
• What are gender roles?
• Why do children seem to engage in gender-typed behaviour?
• How do adults encourage gender-typed behaviour through expectations and gifts?
• Do children show preference for same-sex playmates, or do they play with others regardless of sex?

Applied Lesson
Describe how parental expectations and gifts can influence gender-typed behaviour in children.

Critical Thinking
How might parents try to raise their children in a more "gender-free" environment? Do you think a child raised in a relatively gender-free environment will develop differently from other children?

Researchers believe that children may be born with gender-typed preferences but that peers and adults also encourage these behaviours. Does this toddler girl's desire to feed her doll reflect her genetic code, learning from peers, learning from adults, or all three?

Behaviours of Infant Girls and Boys

Girls are more advanced in their motor development: They sit, crawl, and walk earlier than boys do (Matlin, 1999). Female and male infants are quite similar in their responses to sights, sounds, tastes, smells, and touch. Although a few studies have found that infant boys are more active and irritable than girls, others have not (Cossette, Malcuit, & Pomerleau, 1991; Matlin, 1999). Girls and boys also are similar in their social behaviours. They are equally likely to smile at people's faces, for example, and do not differ in their dependency on adults (Maccoby & Jacklin, 1974; Matlin, 1999). One area in which girls and boys begin to differ early in life is their preference for certain toys and play activities. By twelve to eighteen months of age, girls prefer to play with dolls, doll furniture, dishes, and toy animals, whereas boys prefer transportation toys (trucks, cars, airplanes, and the like), tools, and sports equipment (Alexander, 2003; Hanna, 1993; Snow, Jacklin, & Maccoby, 1983). There are also a handful of studies that have found that females exposed prenatally to androgens (a hormone typically produced by testes) showed increased preference for masculine-type toys (e.g., Berenbaum & Hines, 1992; Slijper, 1984).

Truth or Fiction Revisited: Thus, it appears to be fiction that children play with gender-typed toys only after they have become aware of the gender roles assigned to them by society. It may well be the case that (most) girls prefer dolls and toy animals and that (most) boys prefer toy trucks and sports equipment before they have been socialized—even before they fully understand whether they themselves are female or male. Researchers continue to try to sort out the effects of nature and nurture in children's gender-related preferences.

Adults' Behaviours toward Infant Girls and Boys

Adults respond differently to girls and boys. For example, in some studies, adults are presented with an unfamiliar infant who is dressed in boys' clothes and has a boy's name, whereas other adults are introduced to a baby who is dressed in girls' clothing and has a girl's name. (In reality, it is the same baby who simply is given different names and clothing.) When adults believe they are playing with a girl, they are more likely to offer "her" a doll; when they think the child is a boy, they are more likely to offer a football or a hammer. "Boys" are also encouraged to engage in more physical activity than are "girls" (Stern & Karraker, 1989). Perhaps it is no wonder that infants labelled as "girls" are perceived as littler and softer (as well as nicer and more beautiful) than infants labelled as "boys" (Vogel, Lake, Evans, & Karraker, 1991).

Parents' Behaviours toward Sons and Daughters

Do parents treat infant sons and daughters differently? Yes, as did the adults with the unfamiliar babies, parents are more likely to encourage rough-and-tumble play in their sons than in their daughters. Fathers are especially likely to do so (Eccles et al., 2000; Fagot, Rodgers, & Leinbach, 2000). On the other hand, parents talk more to infant daughters than to infant sons. They smile more at daughters, are more emotionally expressive toward them, and focus more on feelings when talking to them (Martin, Ruble, & Szkrybalo, 2002; Powlishta, Sen, Serbin, Poulin-Dubois, & Eichstedt, 2001).

Perhaps the most obvious way in which parents treat their baby girls and boys differently is in their choice of clothing, room furnishings, and toys. Infant girls are likely to be decked out in a pink or yellow dress, embellished with ruffles and lace, whereas infant boys wear blue or red (Eccles et al., 2000; Powlishta et al., 2001). Parents provide baby girls and boys with different bedroom decorations and toys. Examination of the contents of rooms of children from five months to six years of age found that boys' rooms were often decorated with animal themes and with blue bedding and curtains. Girls' rooms featured flowers, lace, ruffles, and pastels. Girls owned more dolls; boys had more vehicles, military toys, and sports equipment.

Adults Treat Infant Girls and Boys Differently
Perhaps the most obvious way in which parents treat their baby girls and boys differently is in their choice of clothing, toys, and room furnishings. If you were to meet this infant, would you have any doubt as to his or her sex?

© Raphael Van Butsele / Getty Images

Other studies find that parents react favourably when their preschool daughters play with "toys for girls" and their sons play with "toys for boys." Parents and other adults show more negative reactions when girls play with toys for boys and boys play with toys for girls (Fagot et al., 2000; Martin et al., 2002). In general, fathers are more concerned than mothers that their children engage in activities viewed as "appropriate" for their sex.

Parents thus attempt to influence their children's behaviour during infancy and lay the foundation for development in early childhood.

Active Review

16. Psychologists devised the mirror technique to assess development of the self-_____.

17. The child's _____ refers to the stable individual differences in styles of reaction that are present very early in life.

18. The three basic types of temperament are easy, difficult, and _____ to warm up.

19. Girls prefer to play with dolls, whereas boys show a preference to play with transportation toys as early as _____ months of age.

Reflect & Relate: Have you known infants who were easygoing or difficult? How did their temperaments affect their relationships with their parents?

Go to
W W W www.voyages1ce.nelson.com
for an interactive version of this review.

Daycare

Looking for a word that strikes a fierce debate in the hearts of thousands of Canadian parents? Try *daycare*. Just under 60 percent of women employed in Canada in 2002 had young children (Minister of Industry, 2006). Only a relatively small percentage of Canadian families fit the conventional model where the father works and the mother stays at home and cares for the children. As a result, hundreds of thousands of Canadian parents are preoccupied with trying to find proper child care. While certainly a simplification of a continuing issue in Canada, there are those who strongly believe there should be a national child-care program. Child care, however, is under provincial or territorial jurisdiction. Clearly, the issue of implementing a national child-care policy is a complicated one because it is affected by both federal decision making and funding, as well as by provincial decision making and funding. What does that mean for Canadian parents? It means there is great diversity in child-care quality and choices based on where they live and what resources they have access to (e.g., familial support, income, community supports, provincial legislation).

When both parents spend the day on the job, the children—at least young children—must be taken care of by others. What happens to them? *Questions: Does daycare affect children's bonds of attachment with their parents? Does it affect their social and cognitive development?*

How Does Daycare Affect Bonds of Attachment?

Many parents wonder whether daycare will affect their children's attachment to them. Are such concerns valid? This issue has been hotly debated. Some studies have found that infants who are in daycare full-time (more than twenty hours a week) are somewhat more likely than children without daycare experience to show insecure attachment (Baydar & Brooks-Gunn, 1991). Some American psychologists in the early nineties concluded from these studies that a mother who works full-time puts her infant at risk for developing emotional insecurity (Belsky, 1990a, 1990b). Others note that infants whose mothers work may be less distressed by her departure in the strange situation and less likely to seek her out when she returns. Also keep in mind that the likelihood of insecure attachment is not much greater in infants placed in daycare than in those cared for in the home. Most infants in both groups are securely attached (Booth, Kelly, Spieker, & Zuckerman, 2003; Sagi, Koren-Karie, Gini, Ziv, & Joels, 2002).

How Does Daycare Influence Social and Cognitive Development?

Daycare has mixed effects on children's social and cognitive development. Infants with daycare experience are more peer oriented and play at higher developmental levels than do home-reared infants. Children in daycare are more likely to share their toys. They are more independent, self-confident, outgoing, and affectionate as well as more helpful and cooperative with peers and adults (Clarke-Stewart, 1991; Field, 1991b). Participation in daycare is also associated with better school performance during the elementary school years, especially for children from poor families (Caughy, DiPietro, & Strobino, 1994).

A study funded by the National Institute on Child Health and Human Development (NICHD) compared the development of children in "high-quality" daycare with that of children in low-quality daycare and with that of children reared in the home by their mothers. The quality of the daycare was defined in terms of the richness of the learning environment (availability of toys, books, and other materials), the

Children in Daycare
High-quality daycare often has a positive influence on children's social and cognitive development.

ratio of caregivers to children (high quality meant more caregivers), the amount of individual attention received by the child (more was better), and the extent to which caregivers talked to the children and asked them questions (again, more was better). The researchers found high-quality daycare resulted in scores on tests of language and cognitive skills that rivalled those of the children reared in the home by their mothers (Belsky, Weinraub, Owen, & Kelly, 2001).

Yet some studies find that children placed in daycare are less cooperative and more aggressive toward peers and adults than children who are reared in the home. Consider the findings of an NICHD study that went off like an H-bomb among parents. One finding was that the more time preschoolers spent in child care, the more likely they were to display behavioural problems in kindergarten (Belsky et al., 2001). The more time spent away from their mothers, the more likely they were to be rated as defiant, aggressive, and disobedient once they got to kindergarten. *Truth or Fiction Revisited:* It is therefore true that children who attend daycare programs are more aggressive than children who do not. However, as we will see, the differences are not huge and the reasons are unclear.

Seventeen percent of children who were in child care for more than thirty hours a week received higher scores on rating items such as "gets in lots of fights," "is cruel," "talks too much," "exhibits explosive behaviour," "argues a lot," and "demands a lot of attention." Only 6 percent of children who were in child care for fewer than ten hours a week had these problems. Children who were cared for in traditional daycare settings—by a grandmother, by a nanny, even by their fathers—received the troublesome ratings. Was Mom the only answer?

The study also held some good news. For example, it found that children who are enrolled in high-quality daycare show cognitive benefits compared with children who are in lower-quality daycare or who spend more time in the home with their mothers. Canadian parents and consumers of child care need to be aware that a great deal of the context for the majority of the child-care research (such as the NICHD papers) is the United States, which does not have as broad a spectrum of social and family policy as Canada (Friendly, 2004). For example, the extension of paid parental leave in Canada to one year in 2000 has resulted in more parents staying home that first year (Friendly, 2004; Marshall, 2003). In her Centre of Excellence for Early Childhood paper, Martha Friendly, coordinator and senior research associate at the Child Care Resource and Research Unit at the University of Toronto, made the following summary about child care: "High-quality child care, provided by well-educated, sensitive early childhood educators, well-supported and accompanied by a good mix of other family policies, is a benefit, not a danger, to the social and cognitive development across the economic spectrum" (p. 3). She also reminds us that child care in the U.S. is different from child care in other countries such as Sweden and Canada.

A Closer Look | *Finding Child Care You (and Your Child) Can Live With*

It is normal to be anxious. You are thinking about selecting a daycare centre or a private home for your child, and you have a lot at stake. So of course this is an anxiety-provoking task, but you need not be overwhelmed. You can go about the task with a checklist that can guide your considerations. Above all, don't be afraid to open your mouth and ask questions, even pointed, challenging questions. If the daycare provider does not like questions or if the provider does not answer them satisfactorily, *you want your child someplace else.* So much for the preamble. Here is the checklist. (Source: Government of Alberta, 2007.)

1. Does the daycare centre have a licence? Who issued the licence? What did the daycare centre have to do to acquire the licence? (You can also call the licensing agency to obtain the answer to the last question.) Licences must be posted.
2. How many children are cared for by the centre? How many caregivers are there? Remember this nursery rhyme:
   There was an old woman who lived in a shoe.
   She had so many children she didn't know what to do.
   All right, the rhyme is sexist and ageist and maybe even shoe-ist. But it suggests that it is important for caregivers not to be overburdened by too many children, especially infants. Know your provincial regulations for child-care services. Each province will have some sort of licensing standards and regulations. In Alberta, for example, one primary caregiver is required for every three children under the age of thirteen months. One primary staff member is required for every four children between thirteen and eighteen months. And the

ratio for children from nineteen to thirty-five months is one adult per six children.

3. Caregiver training is very important. Are child-care staff trained at the required provincial levels of certification? How were the caregivers hired? How were they trained? Did the centre check references? What were the minimum educational credentials? Did the centre check them out? Do the caregivers have any education or training in the behaviour and needs of children? Do the caregivers seem to be proactive and attempt to engage the children in activities and educational experiences? Or are they inactive unless a child cries or screams? Many child-care centres find that one of their most challenging tasks is to find and keep qualified child-care workers, as the job is very demanding and the wages paid are not as competitive as in other fields
4. Is the environment child-proofed and secure? Can children stick their fingers in electrical sockets? Are toys and outdoor equipment in good condition? Are sharp objects within children's reach? Can anybody walk in off the street? What is the history of children being injured or otherwise victimized in this daycare centre? Is the daycare provider hesitant about answering any of these questions?
5. Are children fed? If infants, how often? When are meals served? Snacks? What do they consist of? Will your child find them appetizing or go hungry? Some babies are placed in daycare at six months or younger, and parents will need to know what formulas are used. Does the food prepared and/or served meet Canada's Food Guide for children? Do caregivers sit with children during meals?

A Closer Look | *(continued)*

6. Is it possible for you to meet the caregivers who will be taking care of your child? If not, why not?

7. With what children will your child interact and play?

8. Does the centre seem to have an enriching environment? Do you see books, toys, games, and educational objects strewn about? Do the toys, games, books, and activities suit the ages of all the children? Are they reflective of the multicultural context in which children live and of their own ethnic/racial/cultural backgrounds?

9. Check the facility and equipment. Are there facilities and objects such as swings and tricycles that will enhance your child's physical and motor development? Are children supervised when they play with these things, or are they pretty much left on their own?

10. Does the centre's schedule coincide with your needs?

11. Is the centre located conveniently for you? Does it appear to be in a safe location or to have adequate security arrangements? (Let me emphasize that you have a right to ask whether people can walk in unannounced to where the children are. It's a fair question. You can also ask what they would do if a stranger broke into the place.)

12. Are parents permitted to visit unannounced? They should be.

13. Do you like the overall environment and feel of the centre or home? Listen to your "gut."

Although we have listed many important items, this list is not exhaustive. In order to learn about child care and your provincial or territorial government's guidelines and its checklist, visit its website. For example, Ontario's Ministry of Children and Youth Services provides tips for parents looking for nonparental child care and the pros and cons of choosing one type of care over another (http://www.children.gov.on.ca). On its website, Alberta Children's Services has provided parents with guidelines on how to find quality care, in addition to free booklets for parents looking into daycare centres or family day homes.

Although the study found a connection between time spent away from mothers and aggression, disobedience, and defiance in kindergarten, the reasons for these problems were not clear. For example, was it the time spent away from mothers that brought on the problems, or did the problems stem from other factors, such as the stresses encountered by families who need two incomes?

A number of the researchers on the team added that if other information yielded by the study had been presented, the reaction might have been different. Note the following:

- Although 17 percent of kindergartners who had been in child care acted more assertively and aggressively, that percentage is actually the norm for the general population of children. (And 9 percent of the children who spent most of their time with their mothers were also rated by teachers as showing more troubling behaviours.)

- The nature of family–child interactions had a greater effect on children's behaviour than the number of hours spent in child care.

- Some aspects of aggressiveness—and the fact that infants who had been in daycare may demand more attention as kindergartners—may be adaptive responses to being placed in a situation where many children are competing for limited resources.

- In addition, the researchers admitted that the statistics are modest: Yes, 17 percent acted aggressively and assertively, but only a few of them exhibited above-average behaviour problems. Moreover, the problems were not that serious.

In any case, millions of parents do not have the option of deciding *whether* to place their children in daycare; their only choice is *where* to do so. The "A Closer Look" feature on page 243 may help guide you to make the choice that is right for you.

Active Review

20. The (minority or majority?) of mothers in Canada work outside the home.

21. Infants with daycare experience play at (higher or lower?) developmental levels than do home-reared babies.

22. Belsky and his colleagues found that once children are in school, those who had spent more time in daycare were rated by teachers, caregivers, and mothers as being (more or less?) aggressive toward other children.

Reflect & Relate: What are your concerns about placing children in daycare? How do your concerns fit with the evidence on the effects of daycare?

 Go to
www.voyages1ce.nelson.com
for an interactive version of this review.

Recite: *An Active Summary*™

1. What is meant by "attachment"?

An attachment is an enduring emotional tie between one animal or person and another specific individual. Children try to maintain contact with persons to whom they are attached.

2. What does it mean for a child to be "secure"?

Most infants in Canada are securely attached. In the strange situation, securely attached infants mildly protest their mothers' departure and are readily comforted by them.

3. What, then, is "insecurity"?

The two major types of insecure attachment are avoidant attachment and ambivalent/resistant attachment. Infants with avoidant attachment are least distressed by their mothers' departure. Infants with ambivalent/resistant attachment show severe distress when their mothers leave but are ambivalent upon reunion.

4. Is it better for infants to be securely attached to their caregivers?

Yes, securely attached infants are happier, more sociable, and more cooperative. They use the mother as a secure base from which to explore the environment. At ages five and six, securely attached children are preferred by peers and teachers and are more competent.

5. What are the roles of the parents in the formation of bonds of attachment?

High-quality care contributes to security. Parents of securely attached infants are more likely to be affectionate and sensitive to their needs. Security of attachment is related to infants' temperaments as well as to caregivers' behaviour.

6. What did Ainsworth learn about the stages of attachment?

The initial-preattachment phase lasts from birth to about three months and is characterized by indiscriminate attachment. The attachment-in-the-making phase occurs at about three or four months and is characterized by preference for familiar figures. The clear-cut-attachment phase occurs at about six or seven months and is characterized by dependence on the primary caregiver.

7. How do different theorists emphasize nature or nurture in their explanation of the development of attachment?

Cognitive theorists suggest that an infant must develop object permanence before specific attachment is possible. Behaviourists suggest that infants become attached to caregivers because caregivers meet their bodily needs. Psychoanalysts suggest that the primary caregiver becomes a love object. The Harlows' experiments with monkeys suggest that contact comfort is a key to attachment. Ethologists view attachment as an inborn fixed action pattern (FAP) that occurs during a critical period in response to a releasing stimulus.

8. What are the findings of the Harlows' studies on the effects of social deprivation on monkeys?

The Harlows found that rhesus infants reared in isolation confinement later avoided contact with other monkeys. Females who later had offspring tended to ignore or abuse them.

9. What do we know about the effects of social deprivation on humans?

Institutionalized children who receive little social stimulation encounter problems in development. Many develop withdrawal and depression. Deficiencies in sensory stimulation and social interaction may cause more problems than lack of love per se. Infants have much capacity to recover from deprivation.

10. What are the incidences of child abuse and neglect? What are their effects?

Nearly 114 607 Canadian children are neglected or abused each year, and neglect results in more serious harm than abuse. Maltreated children are less intimate with peers and are more aggressive, angry, and noncompliant than other children.

11. Why does child abuse run in families?

Abusive parents serve as role models. Exposure to violence in the home may lead children to accept family violence as the norm. Some parents rationalize that they are hurting their children "for their own good"—to discourage problematic behaviour.

12. Does daycare affect children's bonds of attachment with their parents? Does it affect their social and cognitive development?

Infants with daycare experience are more independent, self-confident, outgoing, affectionate, and more cooperative with peers and adults. Children in high-quality daycare outperform children who remain in the home in terms of cognitive development. Children in daycare are more aggressive than other children, but Clarke-Stewart suggests that some aggression may indicate independence, not maladjustment.

13. What are emotions?

Emotions are states of feeling that have physiological, situational, and cognitive components.

14. How do emotions develop?

Bridges proposed that we are born with one emotion—diffuse excitement—and that other emotions differentiate over time. Sroufe focused on the ways in which cognitive development can provide the basis for emotional development. Izard proposed that infants are born with several emotional states but that their appearance is linked to cognitive development and social experiences.

15. Is fear of strangers normal?

Fear of strangers is normal in that most infants develop it at about the age of six to nine months.

16. When does social referencing develop?

Infants display social referencing as early as six months of age, when they use caregivers' facial expressions or tones of voice for information on how to respond in novel situations.

17. What is emotional regulation?

Emotional regulation is emotional self-control. Caregivers help infants learn to regulate their emotions. The children of secure mothers are more likely to regulate their emotions positively.

18. What is the self-concept? How does it develop?

The self-concept is the sense of self. Findings using the mirror technique suggest that the self-concept develops by about eighteen months of age. Self-awareness enables the child to develop concepts of sharing and cooperation and "self-conscious" emotions such as embarrassment, envy, empathy, pride, guilt, and shame.

19. What is meant by the temperament of a child?

The term *temperament* refers to stable individual differences in styles of reaction to the world that are present early in life. These reactions include activity level, regularity, approach or withdrawal, adaptability, response threshold, response intensity, quality of mood, distractibility, attention span, and persistence.

20. What types of temperament do we find among children? How do they develop?

Thomas and Chess found that most infants can be classified as having easy, difficult, or slow-to-warm-up temperaments. Temperament remains moderately consistent from infancy through young adulthood.

21. How do girls and boys differ in their social, emotional, and other behaviours?

Female infants sit, crawl, and walk earlier than boys do. By twelve to eighteen months of age, girls prefer to play with dolls and similar toys, whereas boys prefer transportation toys and gear.

Go to
W W W **www.voyages1ce.nelson.com**
for an interactive version of this summary review.

Key Terms

attachment *(page 236)*

separation anxiety *(page 236)*

secure attachment *(page 237)*

avoidant attachment *(page 237)*

ambivalent/resistant attachment
(page 237)

disorganized-disoriented attachment
(page 237)

indiscriminate attachment *(page 242)*

initial-preattachment phase
(page 243)

attachment-in-the-making phase
(page 243)

clear-cut-attachment phase *(page 243)*

reciprocal-relationship phase
(page 243)

contact comfort *(page 245)*

ethologist *(page 245)*

fixed action pattern (FAP) *(page 245)*

releasing stimulus *(page 245)*

social smile *(page 245)*

critical period *(page 246)*

imprinting *(page 246)*

emotion *(page 257)*

stranger anxiety *(page 261)*

social referencing *(page 261)*

emotional regulation *(page 262)*

personality *(page 263)*

self-concept *(page 263)*

separation-individuation *(page 264)*

temperament *(page 265)*

goodness of fit *(page 268)*

Active Learning Resources

Observing Children and Adolescents CD-ROM

Want to watch a video showing what you've just learned about in this chapter? Click on the "Gender" video in Module 1, Section 3. Your "Lessons in Observation" feature on p. 253 provides further learning objectives, an applied lesson, and a critical thinking exercise designed to help you experience this stage of development. Also check out the "Temperament" and "Attachment" videos in CD Module 1, Section 3.

Visit Your Companion Website for This Book
http://www.voyages1CE.nelson.com

Check out this companion website, where you will find online resources directly linked to your book. The website includes interactive exercises related to PQ4R and Power Visuals for mastering and reviewing key concepts as well as quizzing, chapter outlines, and much more!

CengageNOW!™
http://hed.nelson.com

Go to this site for the link to CengageNOW™, your one-stop study shop. Take a Pretest for this chapter, and CengageNOW™ will generate a personalized Study Plan based on your test results! The Study Plan will identify the topics you need to review and direct you to online resources to help you master those topics. You can then take a Posttest to help you determine the concepts you have mastered and those you still need to work on.

8

Early Childhood: Physical Development

PREVIEW

TRUTH OR FICTION?

T F Some children are left-brained, and others are right-brained.

T F Children's levels of motor activity increase during the preschool years.

T F Sedentary parents are more likely to have "couch potatoes" for children.

T F Julius Caesar, Michelangelo, Tom Cruise, and Oprah have something in common? (Hint: They don't all have book clubs.)

T F A disproportionately high percentage of math whizzes are left-handed.

T F Some diseases are normal.

T F Infections are the most common cause of death among children in Canada.

T F It is dangerous to awaken a sleepwalker.

T F More-competent parents toilet train their children by their second birthday.

Go to WWW

www.voyages1ce.nelson.com
for an interactive version of this "Truth or Fiction" feature.

© Ariel Skelley / BLEND

L
ukas is a two-year-old boy having lunch in his high chair. He is not without ambition. He begins by shoving fistfuls of hamburger into his mouth. He picks up his cup with both hands and drinks milk. Then he starts banging his spoon on his tray and his cup. He kicks his feet against the chair. He throws hamburger onto the floor.

Compare Lukas's behaviour with that of Matteo, age three and a half, who is getting ready for bed. Matteo carefully pulls his plastic train track apart and places each piece in the box. Then he walks to the bathroom, brings his stool over to the sink, and stands on it. He takes down his toothbrush and toothpaste, opens the cap, squeezes toothpaste on the brush, and begins to brush his teeth (Rowen, 1973).

Lukas and Matteo are in early childhood, the years from two to six—also known as the preschool period. During early childhood, physical growth is slower than it was in infancy. Children become taller and leaner, and by the end of early childhood, they look more like adults than infants. An explosion of motor skills occurs as children become stronger, faster, and better coordinated.

Language improves enormously, and children can carry on conversations with others. As cognitive skills develop, a new world of make-believe or "pretend" play emerges. Curiosity and eagerness to learn are hallmarks of the preschool years.

Increased physical and cognitive capabilities enable the child to emerge from total dependence on parents and caregivers to become part of the broader world outside the family. Peers take on an increasingly important role in the life of the preschooler. Children begin to acquire a sense of their own abilities and shortcomings.

We learn about all these developments of early childhood—physical, cognitive, social, and personal—in Chapters 8, 9, and 10.

Growth Patterns

During the preschool years, physical and motor development proceeds, literally, by leaps and bounds. While toddlers like Lukas are occupied with grasping, banging, and throwing things, three-year-olds like Matteo are busy manipulating objects and exercising their newly developing fine motor skills. *Question: What changes occur in height and weight during early childhood?*

Height and Weight

Following the dramatic gains in height of the first two years, the growth rate slows down during the preschool years (Kuczmarski et al., 2000). Girls and boys tend to gain about two to three inches in height per year throughout early childhood. Weight gains also remain fairly even, at about four to six pounds per year (see Figure 8.1). Children become increasingly slender during early childhood, as they gain in height and lose some of their "baby fat." Boys as a group are only slightly taller and heavier than girls in early childhood (Figure 8.1). Noticeable variations in growth patterns also occur from child to child.

Development of the Brain

Question: How does the brain develop during early childhood? The brain develops more quickly than any other organ in early childhood. At two years of age, for example, the brain already has attained 75 percent of its adult weight. By the age of five, the brain has reached 90 percent of its adult weight, even though the total body weight of the five-year-old is barely one-third of what it will be as an adult (Tanner, 1989).

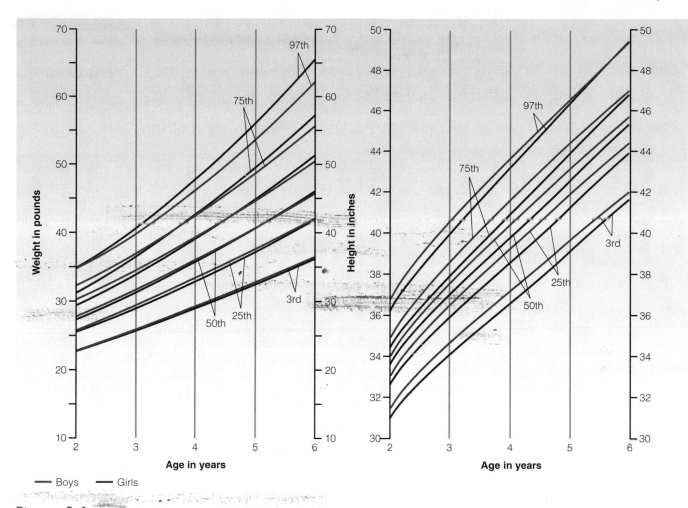

Figure 8.1

Growth Curves for Height and Weight, Ages 2 to 6 Years

The numbers on the curves indicate the percentiles for height and weight at different ages. The growth rate slows down during early childhood. As in infancy, boys are only slightly taller and heavier than girls. Variations in growth patterns from child to child are evident. *Source: Kuczmarski et al. (2000, Figures 9-12).*

The increase in brain size is due in part to the continuing process of myelination of nerve fibres (for a review, see Chapter 5). Completion of the myelination of the neural pathways that link the cerebellum to the cerebral cortex facilitates the development of fine motor skills (Nelson & Luciana, 2001; Paus et al., 1999). The cerebellum is involved in balance and coordination, and the young child's balancing abilities increase dramatically as myelination of these pathways nears completion.

Brain Development and Visual Skills

Brain development is also linked to improvements in the ability to attend to and process visual information (Yamada et al., 2000). These skills are critical in learning to read (Bornstein, 1992). The parts of the brain that enable the child to sustain attention and screen out distractions become increasingly myelinated between the ages of about four and seven (Nelson & Luciana, 2001). As a result, most children are ready to focus on schoolwork between these ages.

The speed with which children process visual information improves throughout childhood, reaching adult levels at the beginning of adolescence (Paus et al., 1999;

Wilson, Nettelbeck, Turnbull, & Young, 1992). The child's ability to systematically scan visual material also improves in early childhood. For example, one classic study presented children with pairs of pictures of similar-looking houses and asked the children whether or not the houses were identical (Vurpillot, 1968). Four-year-olds almost never showed thorough, systematic visual scanning of the features of the houses, but nine-year-olds often did so.

Right Brain, Left Brain?

It has become popular to speak of people as being "right-brained" or "left-brained." We have even heard it said that some instructional methods are aimed at the right brain (they are presented in an emotionally laden, esthetic way), whereas others are aimed at the left brain (they are presented in a logical and straightforward manner).

Question: What does it mean to be left-brained or right-brained? The notion is that the hemispheres of the brain are involved in different kinds of intellectual and emotional functions and responses. Research does suggest that in right-handed individuals, the left hemisphere is relatively more involved in intellectual undertakings that require logical analysis and problem solving, language, and mathematical computation (Baum & Dwivedi, 2003; Cabeza, Locantore, & Anderson, 2003; Corballis, Funnell, & Gazzaniga, 2002; Lukashevich, Machinskaya, & Shklovskii, 2002; Shenal & Harrison, 2003). The other hemisphere (usually the right hemisphere) tends to be superior in visual-spatial functions (it is better at putting puzzles together), recognition of faces, discrimination of colours, esthetic and emotional responses, understanding metaphors, and creative mathematical reasoning.

Truth or Fiction Revisited: Actually, it is not true that some children are left-brained and others are right-brained. Brain functions are not split up so precisely, as has been popularly believed. The functions of the left and right hemispheres overlap to some degree, and the hemispheres also tend to respond simultaneously when we focus our attention on one thing or another. They are aided in "cooperation" by the myelination of the **corpus callosum**—a thick bundle of nerve fibres that connects the hemispheres (Kinsbourne, 2003). Myelination of the corpus callosum proceeds rapidly during early and middle childhood and is largely complete by the age of eight. By that time, children can better integrate logical and emotional functioning.

corpus callosum The thick bundle of nerve fibres that connects the left and right hemispheres of the brain.

plasticity The tendency of new parts of the brain to take up the functions of injured parts.

Plasticity of the Brain

Many parts of the brain have specialized functions. Specialization allows our behaviour to be more complex. But specialization also means that injuries to certain parts of the brain can result in loss of these functions.

Fortunately, the brain also shows **plasticity** (Bouma, 2001; Holland, 2004). *Question: What is meant by "plasticity of the brain"?* "Plasticity" means that the brain frequently can compensate for injuries to particular areas. This compensatory ability is greatest at about one to two years of age and then gradually declines, although it may not be completely gone, even in adulthood (Kolb, Gibb, & Gorny, 2001; Stiles, 2001). When we suffer damage to the areas of the brain that control language, we may lose the ability to speak or understand language. However, other areas of the brain may assume these functions in young children who suffer such damage. As a result, they sometimes dramatically regain the ability to speak or comprehend language (Booth & Burman, 2001). In adolescence and adulthood, regaining such functions is much more difficult and may be all but impossible.

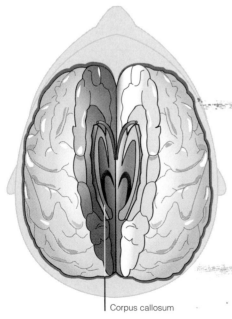

Corpus callosum

Figure 8.2
The Corpus Callosum

The corpus callosum is a structure of the human brain that connects the left and right cerebral hemispheres.

A number of factors are involved in the brain's plasticity (Giedd, 2003). The first is "sprouting," or the growth of new dendrites. To some degree, new dendrites can allow for the rearrangement of neural circuits. The second factor is the redundancy of neural connections. In some cases, similar functions are found at two or more sites in the brain, although they are developed to different degrees. If one site is damaged, the other may be able to develop to perform the function.

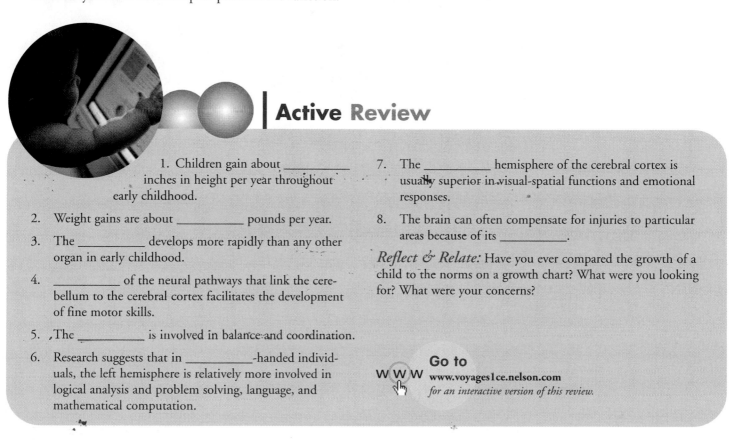

Active Review

1. Children gain about _____ inches in height per year throughout early childhood.

2. Weight gains are about _____ pounds per year.

3. The _____ develops more rapidly than any other organ in early childhood.

4. _____ of the neural pathways that link the cerebellum to the cerebral cortex facilitates the development of fine motor skills.

5. The _____ is involved in balance and coordination.

6. Research suggests that in _____ -handed individuals, the left hemisphere is relatively more involved in logical analysis and problem solving, language, and mathematical computation.

7. The _____ hemisphere of the cerebral cortex is usually superior in visual-spatial functions and emotional responses.

8. The brain can often compensate for injuries to particular areas because of its _____.

Reflect & Relate: Have you ever compared the growth of a child to the norms on a growth chart? What were you looking for? What were your concerns?

Go to
W W W www.voyages1ce.nelson.com
for an interactive version of this review.

Motor Development

The preschool years witness an explosion of motor skills, as children's nervous systems mature and their movements become more precise and coordinated. The development of various gross and fine motor skills permits preschoolers to learn and discover new things about themselves and their environments. In the preschool years, children typically learn culture-specific motor skills such as riding a tricycle, playing soccer with siblings, helping make dinner and hopping for playing hopscotch. *Question: How do motor skills develop in early childhood?*

Gross Motor Skills

During the preschool years, children make great strides in the development of **gross motor skills,** which involve the large muscles used in locomotion (see Table 8.1). At about the age of three, children can balance on one foot. By age three or four, they can walk up stairs as adults do, by placing a foot on each step. If presented with the materials in their family/community contexts, then by age four or five, children can skip and pedal a tricycle (Crowther, 2006). Older preschoolers are better able to coordinate two tasks, such as singing and running at the same time, than are younger preschoolers (Whitall, 1991). In general, preschool children appear to acquire motor

gross motor skills Skills employing the large muscles used in locomotion.

	Development of Gross Motor Skills in Early Childhood		
2 Years (24–35 Months)	**3 Years (36–47 Months)**	**4 Years (48–59 Months)**	**5 Years (60–71 Months)**
• Runs well straight ahead • Walks up stairs, two feet to a step • Kicks a large ball • Jumps a distance of 4–14 inches • Throws a small ball without falling • Pushes and pulls large toys • Hops on one foot, two or more hops • Tries to stand on one foot • Climbs on furniture to look out of window	• Goes around obstacles while running • Walks up stairs, one foot to a step • Kicks a large ball easily • Jumps from the bottom step • Catches a bounced ball, using torso and arms to form a basket • Goes around obstacles while pushing and pulling toys • Hops on one foot, up to three hops • Stands on one foot • Climbs nursery-school apparatus	• Turns sharp corners while running • Walks down stairs, one foot to a step • Jumps from a height of 12 inches • Throws a ball overhand • Turns sharp corners while pushing and pulling toys • Hops on one foot, four to six hops • Stands on one foot for 3–8 seconds • Climbs ladders • Skips on one foot • Rides a tricycle well	• Runs lightly on toes • Jumps a distance of 3 feet • Catches a small ball, using hands only • Hops 2 to 3 yards forward on each foot • Stands on one foot for 8–10 seconds • Climbs actively and skillfully • Skips on alternate feet • Rides a bicycle with training wheels

Note: The ages are averages and are based on white, middle-class North American norms; there are individual variations, and once again we highlight that other cultural experiences and activities also exist to promote motor development.

skills by teaching themselves and observing the behaviour of other children. The opportunity to play with other children seems more important than adult instruction at this age.

Throughout early childhood, girls and boys are not far apart in their motor skills. Girls are somewhat better at tasks requiring balance and precision of movement. Boys, on the other hand, show some advantage in throwing and kicking (McDevitt & Ormrod, 2002).

Individual differences are more impressive than sex differences throughout early and middle childhood. Some children develop motor skills earlier than others. Some are genetically predisposed to developing better coordination or more strength than others. Motivation and practice also are important in children's acquisition of motor skills. Motor experiences in infancy may affect the development of motor skills in early childhood. For example, children with early crawling experience perform better than noncrawlers on tests of motor skills in the preschool years (McEwan, Dihoff, & Brosvic, 1991).

Physical Activity

Preschool children spend quite a bit of time in physical activity. One study found that preschoolers spend an average of more than twenty-five hours a week in large muscle activity (Campbell, Eaton, & McKeen, 2002). Younger preschoolers are more likely than older preschoolers to engage in physically oriented play, such as grasping, banging, and mouthing objects (D. W. Campbell et al., 2002). Consequently, they need more space and less furniture in a preschool or daycare setting. Although this is an exciting time for preschoolers to explore the world around them, with exploration may come some injuries. It is estimated that 20 000 to 30 000 Canadian children each year require medical attention due to playground injuries (Safe Kids Canada, 2005).

Truth or Fiction Revisited: It is not true that motor activity increases during the preschool years. Motor activity level begins to decline after two or three years of age. Children become less restless and are able to sit still longer (D. W. Campbell et al., 2002; Eaton, McKeen, & Campbell, 2001). Between the ages of two and four, children in free play show an increase in sustained, focused attention.

Rough-and-Tumble Play

One form of physical and social activity often observed in young children is known as **rough-and-tumble play.** Rough-and-tumble play consists of running, chasing, fleeing, wrestling, hitting with an open hand, laughing, and making faces. Rough-and-tumble play is not the same as aggressive behaviour. Aggression involves hitting with fists, pushing, taking, grabbing, and angry looks. Unlike aggression, rough-and-tumble play helps develop both physical and social skills in children (D. W. Campbell et al., 2002; Pellegrini & Perlmutter, 1988).

Play fighting and chasing activities are found among young children in societies around the world (Whiting & Edwards, 1988). But the particular form that rough-and-tumble play takes is influenced by culture and environment. For example, rough-and-tumble play among girls is quite common among the Pilaga Indians and the !Kung of Botswana but less common among girls in North America. In North America, rough-and-tumble play usually occurs in groups made up of the same sex. However, !Kung girls and boys engage in rough-and-tumble play together. And among the Pilaga, girls often are matched against the boys.

Individual Differences in Activity Level

Children differ widely in their activity levels. Some children are much more active than others.

Truth or Fiction Revisited: It is true that sedentary parents are more likely to have "couch potatoes" for children. Physically active children are more likely to have physically active parents. In a study of four- to seven-year-olds (Moore et al., 1991), children of active mothers were twice as likely to be active as children of inactive mothers. Children of active fathers were three and a half times as likely to be active as children of inactive fathers.

Several reasons may explain this relationship. First, active parents may serve as role models for activity. Second, sharing of activities by family members may encourage activity. Parents who are actively engaged in chores or use walking as their main means of getting around their city, town, or village may involve their children in these types of naturally occurring physical activities. By the same token, couch-potato parents who prefer to view tennis on television rather than play it may be more likely to share this sedentary activity with their children. A third factor is that active parents may encourage and support their children's participation in physical activity. Finally, a tendency to be active or inactive may be transmitted genetically, as shown by evidence from twin studies (see Chapter 2) (Saudino & Eaton, 1993; Stevenson, 1992). Genetic and environmental factors apparently interact to determine a child's activity level.

Health Canada endorses physical activity as part of a healthy lifestyle, and has produced physical activity guides aimed specifically at children and their families. A complete set of resources and links to the guides can be found at the Public Health Agency of Canada website (http://www.phac-aspc.gc.ca/pau-uap/paguide/child_youth/index.html).

Gross Motor Skills
During the preschool years, children make great strides in the development of gross motor skills. By age 4 or 5, they can pedal a tricycle quite skillfully.

rough-and-tumble play
Play fighting and chasing.

Rough-and-Tumble Play
Play fighting and chasing activities—known as rough-and-tumble play—are found among young children in societies around the world.

Fine Motor Skills
Control over the wrists and fingers enables children to hold a pencil, play a musical instrument, and, as shown in this photograph, play with stacking toys.

fine motor skills   Skills employing the small muscles used in manipulation, such as those in the fingers.

Fine Motor Skills

Fine motor skills develop gradually and lag behind gross motor skills. This is yet another example of the proximodistal trend in development (see Chapters 3 and 5). Fine motor skills involve the small muscles used in manipulation and coordination. Control over the wrists and fingers enables children to hold a pencil properly, dress themselves, and stack blocks (see Table 8.2). Preschoolers can labour endlessly in attempting to tie their shoelaces and get their jackets zipped. There are terribly frustrating (and funny) scenes of children alternating between steadfastly refusing to allow a parent to intervene and requesting the parent's help. Activities that require manipulation (cutting, reproducing shapes) and artwork (e.g., exposure to different colours, pencils, paints, crayons, etc.) with experimentation and practice are ideal activities to engage children in the preschool years. Parents and educators can make the most of materials found in children's immediate environments.

Children's Drawings

The development of drawing in young children is closely linked to the development of both motor and cognitive skills. Children first begin to scribble during the second year of life. Initially, they seem to make marks for the sheer joy of it (Eisner, 1990).

Question: Are children's scribbles the result of random motor activity? Rhoda Kellogg (1959, 1970) studied more than 1 million drawings made by children. She found a meaningful pattern in the scribbles. She identified twenty basic scribbles that she considered the building blocks of all art: vertical, horizontal, diagonal, circular, curving, waving or zigzagging lines, and dots (see Figure 8.3).

Developing in a World of Diversity

Sex Differences in Motor Activity

Question: Do girls and boys differ in their activity levels during early childhood? During early childhood, boys tend to be more active than girls, at least in some settings (Campbell & Eaton, 1999; D. W. Campbell et al., 2002). Boys spend more time than girls in large muscle activities. Boys tend to be more fidgety and distractible than girls and to spend less time focusing on tasks (McGuinness, 1990).

Why are boys more active and restless than girls? One theory is that boys of a given age are less mature physically than girls of the same age. Children tend to become less active as they develop. Therefore, the sex difference in activity level may really be a maturational difference (Eaton & Yu, 1989). However, parental encouragement and reward of motor activity in boys and discouragement of such behaviour in girls may be involved as well (Fredricks & Eccles, 2002).

Boys also are more likely than girls to engage in rough-and-tumble play (Moller, Hymel, & Rubin, 1992; Pellegrini, 1990). What might account for this sex difference? Some psychologists suggest that the reasons might be partly based in biology (Collaer & Hines, 1995; Maccoby, 1990a, 1991). Others argue that the socializing influences of the family and culture at large promote play differences among girls and boys (Caplan & Larkin, 1991; Golombok & Hines, 2004; Meyer, Murphy, Cascardi, & Birns, 1991).

Development of Fine Motor Skills in Early Childhood			
2 Years (24-35 Months)	**3 Years (36-47 Months)**	**4 Years (48-59 Months)**	**5 Years (60-71 Months)**
• Builds tower of 6 cubes • Copies vertical and horizontal lines • Imitates folding of paper • Prints on easel with a brush • Places simple shapes in correct holes	• Builds tower of 9 cubes • Copies circle and cross • Copies letters • Holds crayons with fingers, not fist • Strings 4 beads using a large needle • Uses pencil with correct hand grip • Strings 10 beads using a large needle	• Builds tower of 10 or more cubes • Copies square • Prints simple words • Imitates folding paper three times	• Builds 3 steps from 6 blocks, using a model • Copies triangle and star • Prints first name and numbers • Imitates folding of piece of square paper into a triangle • Traces around a diamond drawn on paper • Ties shoes

Note: The ages are averages; there are individual variations.

Children go through four stages as they progress from making scribbles to drawing pictures. These are the **placement, shape, design,** and **pictorial stages** (see Figure 8.4). Two-year-olds place their scribbles in various locations on the page (e.g., in the middle of the page or near one of the borders). By age three, children are starting to draw basic shapes: circles, squares, triangles, crosses, X's, and odd shapes. As soon as they can draw shapes, children begin to combine them in the design stage. Between ages four and five, the child reaches the pictorial stage, in which designs begin to resemble recognizable objects.

Children's early drawings tend to be symbolic of a broad category rather than specific. For example, a child might draw the same simple building whether she is asked to draw a school or a house (Tallandini & Valentini, 1991). Children between three and five years old usually do not start out to draw a particular thing. They are more likely to first see what they have drawn and then name it (Winner, 1989). As motor and cognitive skills improve beyond the age of five, children become able to draw an object they have in mind (Matthews, 1990). They improve at copying figures (Karapetsas & Kantas, 1991; Pemberton, 1990). Fine motor skills become more refined with age for several reasons: typical neurological development, practice, and experience.

Handedness

Truth or Fiction Revisited: Yes, Julius Caesar, Michelangelo, Tom Cruise, and Oprah do have something in common. They are all left-handed. *Questions: When does handedness emerge? How many children are left-handed?* **Handedness** emerges during infancy. By the age of two to three months, a rattle placed in the infant's hand is held longer with the right hand than with the left (Fitzgerald et al., 1991). By four months of age, most infants show a clear-cut right-hand preference in exploring objects using the sense of touch (Streri, 2002). Preference for grasping with the right or left hand increases markedly between the ages of seven and eleven months (Hinojosa, Sheu, & Michel, 2003). Handedness becomes more strongly established during the early childhood years (McManus et al., 1988). Most people are right-handed, although studies vary as to how many are left-handed.

Figure 8.3

The 20 Basic Scribbles (Really)

By the age of 2, children can scribble. Rhoda Kellogg has identified these 20 basic scribbles as the building blocks of the young child's drawings. *Source: Kellogg (1970).*

placement stage An early stage in drawing, usually found among 2-year-olds, in which children place their scribbles in various locations on the page (such as in the middle or near a border).

shape stage A stage in drawing, attained by age 3, in which children draw basic shapes such as circles, squares, triangles, crosses, X's and odd shapes.

design stage A stage in drawing in which children begin to combine shapes.

pictorial stage A stage in drawing attained between ages 4 and 5 in which designs begin to resemble recognizable objects.

handedness The tendency to prefer using the left or right hand in writing and other activities.

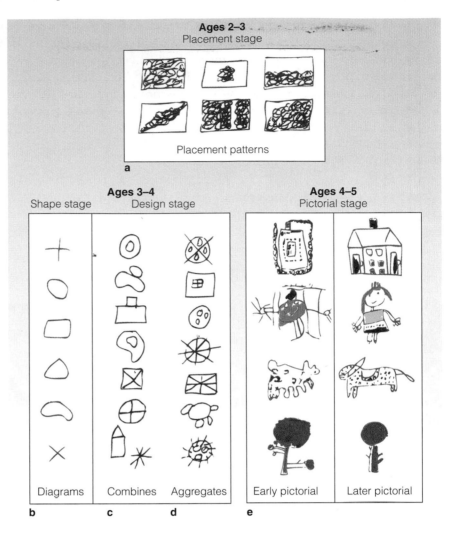

Figure 8.4

Four Stages in Children's Drawings

Children go through four stages in drawing pictures. (a) They first place their scribbles in various locations on the page. (b) They then draw basic shapes and (c, d) combine shapes into designs. Finally, (e) they draw recognizable objects. *Source: Kellogg (1970).*

Left-Handedness: Is It Gauche to Be Left-Handed? Myths and Realities

Question: Are there problems connected with being left-handed? Being a "lefty" was once regarded as a deficiency. The language still swarms with slurs on lefties. We speak of "left-handed compliments," of having "two left feet," of strange events as "coming out of left field." The word *sinister* means "left-hand or unlucky side" in Latin. *Gauche* is a French word that literally means "left," although in English it is used to mean awkward or ill-mannered. The English word *adroit,* meaning "skillful," derives from the French *à droit,* literally translated as "to the right." Also consider positive usages such as "being righteous" or "being on one's right side."

Being left-handed is not gauche or sinister, but left-handedness may matter because it appears to be connected with language problems, such as dyslexia and stuttering, and with health problems, such as migraine headaches and allergies (Andreou, Krommydas, Gourgoulianis, Karapetsas, & Molyvdas, 2002; Geschwind & Galaburda, 1987; Ostatnikova et al., 2002). Left-handedness is also apparently connected with psychological disorders, including schizophrenia and depression (Elias, Saucier, & Guylee, 2001; Rosenbaum, 2000; Shaw, Claridge, & Clark, 2001).

There may be advantages to being left-handed. ***Truth or Fiction Revisited:*** A disproportionately high percentage of math whizzes are in fact left-handed. In a series of studies, Camilla Benbow (O'Boyle & Benbow, 1990) related handedness to scores on the math part of the Scholastic Assessment Test (SAT) among twelve- and thirteen-year-olds. Twenty percent of the highest-scoring group was left-handed. Only 10 percent of the general population is left-handed, so it appears that left-handed children are more than adequately represented among the most academically gifted.

To watch this video

click on **"Gross Motor"** and **"Fine Motor"** in Module 2, Section 1, on your Observing Children and Adolescents CD-ROM. You can also visit the Student Book Companion Site to watch the video, answer the questions, and e-mail your responses to your professor.

Lessons in Observation
Gross and Fine Motor Skills

Learning Objectives
- What is the difference between gross motor skills and fine motor skills?
- How do gross motor skills improve as children age?
- How does Olivia's attempt to catch a ball illustrate the proximodistal trend in motor development?
- What activities help prepare children for writing and drawing?

Applied Lesson
Describe the different stages of climbing and how each stage represents an advancement in gross motor skills.

Critical Thinking
How might parents help their child improve fine motor development? At what stage(s) should a parent introduce new toys and activities?

Although 3 1/2-year-old Olivia can kick a ball, she has to use her torso and arms formed into a basket to catch a ball.

Fine motor activities, such as building things with blocks, help children improve their skills and prepare them for drawing and writing.

Left-handedness (or use of both hands) has also been associated with success in athletic activities such as handball, fencing, boxing, basketball, and baseball (Coren, 1992; Dane & Erzurumluoglu, 2003). Higher frequencies of left-handedness are also found among musicians, architects, and artists (Natsopoulos, Kiosseoglou, & Xeromeritou, 1992; O'Boyle & Benbow, 1990). Two of the greatest artists in history—Leonardo da Vinci and Michelangelo—were left-handed.

In the next section, we consider how it can be that left-handedness is associated with both talent and giftedness on the one hand (excuse the pun!) and with problems and deficits on the other. What are the origins of handedness?

Theories of Handedness

The origins of handedness apparently have a genetic component (Geschwind, 2000; McManus, 2003). Left-handedness runs in families. In the English royal family, the Queen Mother, Queen Elizabeth II, and Prince Charles and Prince William are all left-handed (Rosenbaum, 2000). If both of your parents are right-handed, your chances of being right-handed are about 92 percent. If one of your parents is left-handed, your chances of being right-handed drop to about 80 percent. And if both of your parents are left-handed, your chances of also being left-handed are about 50 percent (Rosenbaum, 2000).

On the other hand, identical (monozygotic) twins frequently are different in handedness (Sommer, Ramsey, Mandl, & Kahn, 2002). One explanation is that monozygotic twins are sometimes mirror opposites (Sommer et al., 2002). If this is so, the disagreement on handedness among monozygotic twins would not contradict a role for genetics in handedness.

In any case, handedness develops early. An ultrasound study found that about 95 percent of fetuses suck their right thumbs rather than their left (Hepper, Shahidullah, & White, 1990).

Interestingly, handedness is also found in species other than humans—for example, chimpanzees and parrots (yes, parrots). It appears that hand preferences in chimpanzees are heritable, as they are in humans but that environmental factors can modify inborn preferences—in chimps as well as in humans (Hopkins, Dahl, & Pilcher, 2001).

Active Review

9. (Girls or Boys?) are somewhat better at tasks requiring balance and precision of movement.

10. (Girls or Boys?) show some advantage in throwing and kicking.

11. Motor activity begins to (increase or decrease?) after two or three years of age.

12. During early childhood, (girls or boys?) tend to be more active.

13. Left-handed people have a (higher or lower?) incidence of language problems and psychological disorders compared with right-handed people.

Reflect & Relate: Think of left-handed people you know (perhaps including yourself). Do they seem to be awkward in any activities? Explain. Do you know anyone who was "changed" from a lefty to a righty? Why was the change made? How was it done? Was it successful? Explain.

Go to

W W W **www.voyages1ce.nelson.com**
for an interactive version of this review.

In sum, left-handed children are not necessarily clumsier than right-handed children. They are, however, somewhat more prone to allergies. Academically, left-handedness is associated with positive as well as negative outcomes. Because handedness may reflect the differential development of the hemispheres of the cortex, there is no point in struggling to write with the nondominant hand. After all, would training right-handed children to write with their left hands help them in math?

Nutrition

Nutrition affects both physical and behavioural development. *Question: What are children's nutritional needs and their eating behaviour like in early childhood?*

Nutritional Needs

As children move from infancy into the preschool years, their nutritional needs change. True, they still need to consume the basic foodstuffs: proteins, fats, carbohydrates, minerals, and vitamins. But more calories are required as children get older. For example, the average four- to six-year-old needs 1800 calories, compared with only 1300 for the average one- to three-year-old (Ekvall, 1993a). However, preschoolers grow at a slower rate than infants. This means that preschoolers need fewer calories per pound of body weight.

Patterns of Eating

During the second and third years, a child's appetite typically decreases and becomes erratic, often causing parents great worry. But it must be remembered that because the child is growing more slowly now, he or she needs fewer calories. Also, young children who eat less at one meal typically compensate by eating more at another (Shea, Stein, Basch, Contento, & Zybert, 1992). Children may develop strong (and strange) preferences for certain foods (Cooke, Wardle, & Gibson, 2003). As parents, we both have experienced preschoolers who at one time during their third year wanted to eat nothing but Spaghetti-O's (first author's daughter) or cinnamon toast (second author's daughter).

Using Health Canada's (2007) *Eating Well with Canada's Food Guide* for the entire family is helpful since most children model and adapt the same eating patterns as their families. Unfortunately, many Canadian children (and adults) consume excessive amounts of sugar and salt, which can be harmful to their health. Infants seem to be born liking the taste of sugar, although they are fairly indifferent to salty tastes. But preference for both sweet and salty foods increases if children are repeatedly exposed to them during childhood (Sullivan & Birch, 1990). Parents also serve as role models in the development of food preferences. If a parent—especially the parent who usually prepares meals—displays an obvious dislike for vegetables, children may develop a similar dislike (Hannon, Bowen, Moinpour, & McLerran, 2003). The message to parents is clear: The eating habits you create will probably last. Children eat according to the eating customs of their family, and these traditions are a valued aspect of their culture. Learning to appreciate a variety of foods as prepared by various ethnic and cultural groups is another way to engage and interest children in nutrition and eating (Health Canada, 2002). Kumar and Wandel (2006) studied nutrition challenges among immigrant children and youth in Norway and discovered that breast feeding and weaning practices as well as the adoption of Western customs are important variables when considering the nutrition practices of immigrant families.

Canada's Food Guide
The recently revised Canada's Food Guide (2007) provides useful information for parents and children on healthy eating habits and is available at http://www.hc-sc.gc.ca/fn-an/food-guide-aliment/index_e.html.

Other helpful tips for parents and educators wanting to know more about nutrition for preschoolers are detailed in the online publication *Canada's Food Guide to Healthy Eating: Focus on Preschoolers,* which states that

- preschoolers are curious and may experiment with their food;
- preschoolers want to be independent yet they require structure (wanting a favourite cup or plate sound familiar?); and
- preschoolers imitate those around them.

What is the best way to get children to eat their green peas or spinach or other healthful foods they may dislike? (Notice that it is rarely dessert that the child refuses to eat.) According to Leann Birch, bribing or rewarding a child to eat a new food does not help and may backfire. She recommends instead that adults encourage the child to taste tiny amounts of the food eight or ten times within a period of a few weeks so that it becomes more familiar (cited in Kutner, 1993). Perhaps familiarity with food breeds content and not contempt.

Table 8.3	*Examples of One Child-Sized Serving*
Grain Products	1/2–1 slice of whole wheat bread 15–30 g cold whole grain cereal 75–175 mL (1/3–3/4 cup) hot cereal 1/4–1/2 bagel, pita, or bun 1/2–1 muffin 50–125 mL (1/4–1/2 cup) pasta or rice 4–8 soda crackers
Vegetables and Fruit	1/2–1 medium-sized vegetable or fruit 50–125 mL (1/4–1/2 cup) fresh, frozen, or canned vegetables or fruit 125–250 mL (1/2–1 cup) salad 50–125 mL (1/4–1/2 cup) juice
Milk Products	25–50 g cheese 75–175 g (1/3–3/4 cup) yogurt 175 g (3/4 cup) Kefir 250 mL (1 cup) of fortified soy beverage Preschoolers should consume a total of 500 mL (2 cups) of milk every day.
Meat and Alternatives	25–50 g meat, fish, or poultry 1 egg 50–125 mL (1/4–1/2 cup) beans 50–100g (1/4–1/3 cup) tofu 15–30 mL (1–2 Tbsp.) peanut butter

Source: Health Canada (2002).

"He just learned in school that potato chips are vegetables."

© WM Hoest Enterprises, Inc. Reprinted with special permission of King Features Syndicate.

Food Aversions
Strong preferences—and aversions—for certain foods may develop in early childhood.

Active Review

14. During the second and third years, a child's appetite typically (increases or decreases?).

Go to
www.voyages1ce.nelson.com
for an interactive version of this review.

Reflect & Relate: Did you ever try to convince a two- or three-year-old to eat something? What did you do? What were the consequences?

Health and Illness

Almost all children get ill now and then. Some seem to be ill every other week or so. Most of these illnesses are minor, and children seem to eventually outgrow many of them, including ear infections. However, some illnesses are more serious. Fortunately, we have ways of preventing or curing a great many of them.

Questions: How healthy are children in Canada and in other countries? What are some of the illnesses and environmental hazards encountered during early childhood?

Minor Illnesses

Minor illnesses refer to respiratory infections, such as colds, and to gastrointestinal upsets, such as nausea, vomiting, and diarrhea. ***Truth or Fiction Revisited:*** These diseases are normal—statistically speaking—in the sense that most children come down with them. They typically last a few days or less and are not life threatening. Although diarrheal illness in Canada is usually mild, it is a leading killer of children in developing countries (Save the Children, 2004b).

Canadian children between the ages of one and three generally average eight to nine minor illnesses a year. Between the ages of four and ten, this drops to about four to six illnesses a year. You may be surprised to learn that being ill can have some beneficial effects on children's development. It can lead to the creation of antibodies that may prevent them from coming down with the same illnesses later, say, in adulthood, when the illnesses can be more harmful.

A Closer Look | Ten Things You Need to Know about Immunizations

1. *"Why should my child be immunized?"* Children need immunizations (shots) to protect them from dangerous childhood diseases. These diseases can have serious complications and even kill children.

2. *"What diseases do childhood vaccines prevent?"*
   - Measles
   - Mumps
   - Polio
   - Diphtheria
   - Varicella (chickenpox)
   - *Haemophilus influenzae* type b (Hib disease—a major cause of bacterial meningitis)
   - Pneumococcal disease (causes bacterial meningitis and blood infections)
   - Rubella (German measles)
   - Hepatitis B
   - Pertussis (whooping cough)
   - Tetanus (lockjaw)

3. *"How many shots does my child need?"* The following vaccinations are recommended by age two and can be given over five visits to a doctor or clinic:
   4 doses of diphtheria, tetanus, & pertussis vaccine (DTaP)
   4 doses of Hib vaccine
   3 doses of polio vaccine
   3 doses of hepatitis B vaccine
   3 doses of pneumococcal vaccine
   1 dose of measles, mumps, & rubella vaccine (MMR)
   1 dose of varicella vaccine

4. *"Do these vaccines have any side effects?"* Side effects can occur with any medicine, including vaccines. Depending on the vaccine, these can include slight fever, rash, or soreness at the site of injection. Slight discomfort is normal and should not be a cause for alarm. Your health care provider can give you additional information.

5. *"Can they cause serious reactions?"* Yes, but serious reactions to vaccines are extremely rare. The risks of serious disease from not vaccinating are far greater than the risks of serious reaction to a vaccination.

6. *"What do I do if my child has a serious reaction?"* If you think your child is experiencing a persistent or severe reaction, call your doctor or get the child to a doctor right away. Write down what happened and the date and time it happened. Ask your doctor, nurse, or health department to file a Vaccine Adverse Event Report.

7. *"Why can't I wait until school to have my child immunized?"* Children under five are especially susceptible to disease because their immune systems have not built up the necessary defences to fight infection. By immunizing on time (by age two), you can protect your child from disease and also help protect others at school or daycare.

8. *"Why is a vaccination health record important?"* A vaccination health record helps you and your health care provider keep your child's vaccinations on schedule. If you move or change providers, having an accurate record might prevent your child from repeating vaccinations he or she has already had. A shot record should be started when your child receives his or her first vaccination and updated with each vaccination visit.

9. *"Where can I get free vaccines?"* Although this varies across provinces and territories, most vaccinations can be obtained free of charge from health clinics affiliated with regional health authorities.

10. *"Where can I get more information?"* You can contact the Canadian Coalition for Immunization Awareness & Promotion (CCIAP):
    c/o Canadian Public Health Association
    400-1565 Carling Avenue
    Ottawa, Ontario K1Z 8R1
    Tel: (613) 725-3769 ext. 139 or 170; Fax: (613) 725-9826
    E-mail: immunize@cpha.ca or your local health authority for regional information website:
    http://www.immunize.cpha.ca/english/links/canhlth.htm

Table 8.4 *Publicly Funded Immunization Programs by Province/Territory*

Publicly funded immunization programs			
Province/Territory	2005 Status	2007 Status	Comments
British Columbia	Good	Good	Provides coverage for all five recommended vaccines, but meningococcal vaccine is not given according to CPS and NACI recommendations.
Alberta	Excellent	Excellent	Provides coverage for all five recommended vaccines according to CPS and NACI recommendations.
Saskatchewan	Good	Good	Provides coverage for all five recommended vaccines, but meningococcal vaccine is not given according to CPS and NACI recommendations.
Manitoba	Good	Good	Provides coverage for all five recommended vaccines, but meningococcal and pneumococcal vaccines are not given according to CPS and NACI recommendations.
Ontario	Good	Good	Provides coverage for all five recommended vaccines, but meningococcal vaccine is not given according to CPS and NACI recommendations.
Quebec	Fair	Good	Provides coverage for all five recommended vaccines, but meningococcal and pneumonoccal vaccines are not given according to CPS and NACI recommendations.
New Brunswick	Good	Good	Provides coverage for all five recommended vaccines, but meningococcal vaccine is not given according to CPS and NACI recommendations.
Nova Scotia	Good	Good	Provides coverage for all five recommended vaccines, but meningococcal vaccine is not given according to CPS and NACI recommendations.
Prince Edward Island	Good	Fair	Provides coverage for four of the five recommended vaccines. Meningococcal vaccine is not given according to CPS and NACI recommendations. A fee is applied for the administration of the Influenza vaccine for infants aged 6–23 months.
Newfoundland and Labrador	Good	Good	Provides coverage for all five recommended vaccines, but meningococcal vaccine is not given according to CPS and NACI recommendations.
Yukon	Fair	Good	Provides coverage for all five recommended vaccines, but meningococcal and pneumonoccal vaccines are not given according to CPS and NACI recommendations.
Northwest Territories	Fair	Good	Provides coverage for all five recommended vaccines, but meningococcal vaccine is not given according to CPS and NACI recommendations.
Nanavut	Fair	Good	Provides coverage for all five recommended vaccines, but meningococcal vaccine is not given according to CPS and NACI recommendations.

Source: Canadian Paediatric Society (2007).

Major Illnesses

Advances in immunization along with the development of antibiotics and other medications have dramatically reduced the incidence of serious and potentially fatal childhood diseases in Canada. Because most preschoolers and schoolchildren have been inoculated against major childhood illnesses such as rubella (German measles), measles, tetanus, mumps, whooping cough, diphtheria, and polio, these diseases no longer pose the threat they once did. Still, immunization is far from universal. The recommended immunization schedule of the Canadian Paediatric Society is shown in Tables 8.5a and b. There are three main contraindications to vaccines approved in Canada: (1) anaphylaxis to a component of the vaccine (severe allergic reaction to vaccine), (2) significant immunosuppression (live vaccines) in individuals with severely compromised immune systems, and (3) pregnancy (live vaccines) as detailed in the *Vaccine Safety and Adverse Events Following Immunization Guide* (found at http://www.phac-aspc.gc.ca/publicat/cig-gci/index.html). Despite these recommendations, there are some parents who choose not to immunize their children for a host of reasons (e.g., fear or concerns about immunizations, against cultural or religious beliefs, etc.). While certain daycares and schools request that children's immunization records be kept up-to-date, immunization practice is at the discretion of the parents or guardians.

Table 8.5a	Routine Immunization for Infants and Children

The range of recommended ages is indicated for the listed vaccines, routinely administered to children through the age of sixteen years. For age groups that warrant special effort to administer recommended doses that were not previously given, catch-up immunization is indicated.

Age at vaccination	DTaP-IPV	Hib	MMR	Var	HB	Pneu-C-7	Men-C	Tdap	Int
Birth					Infancy 3 doses				
2 months	●	✦				⊠	⊙		
4 months	●	✦			★	⊠	(⊙)		
6 months	●	✦				⊠	⊙		6–23 months
12 months			■	●		⊠ 12–15 months	or ⊙ if not yet given		⊗ 1–2 doses
18 months	●	✦	■		or				
4–6 years	●		or ■						
14–16 years					Preteen/ teen 2–3 doses		⊙ if not yet given	▲	

Source: Canadian Paediatric Society (2007).

Table 8.5b	Routine Immunization Schedule for Children < 7 Years of Age Not Immunized in Early Infancy								
Timing	DTaP-IPV	Hib	MMR	Var	HB	Pneu-C-7	Men-C	Tdap
First visit	⊙	✦	■	●	★	⊠	⊙	
2 months later	⊙	(✦)	■		★	(⊠)	(⊙)	
2 months later	⊙					(⊠)		
6–12 months later	⊙	(✦)			★			
4–6 years of age	⊙							
14–16 years of age								

( ) Symbols with brackets around them imply that these doses may not be required, depending upon the age of the child or adult.

⊙ **Diphtheria, tetanus, acellular pertussis and inactivated polio virus vaccine (DTaP-IPV):** DTaP-IPV(± Hib) vaccine is the preferred vaccine for all doses in the vaccination series, including completion of the series in children who have received one or more doses of DPT (whole cell) vaccine (e.g., recent immigrants) In Tables 1 and 2, the 4–6 year dose can be omitted if the fourth dose was given after the fourth birthday.

✦ **Haemophilus influenzae type b conjugate vaccine (Hib):** the Hib schedule shown is for the *Haemophilus* b capsular polysaccharide—polyribosylribitol phosphate (PRP) conjugated to tetanus toxoid (PRP-T). For catch up, the number of doses depends on the age at which the schedule is begun. Not usually required past age 5 years.

■ **Measles, mumps, and rubella vaccine (MMR):** a second dose of MMR is recommended for children at least 1 month after the first dose for the purpose of better measles protection. For convenience, options include giving it with the next scheduled vaccination at 18 months of age or at school entry (4–6 years) (depending on the provincial/territorial policy) or at any intervening age that is practical. In the catch-up schedule (Table 8.5b), the first dose should not be given until the child is ≥ 12 months old. MMR should be given to all susceptible adolescents and adults.

● **Varicella vaccine (Var):** children aged 12 months to 12 years should receive one dose of varicella vaccine. Susceptible individuals ≥ 13 years of age should receive two doses at least 28 days apart.

★ **Hepatitis B vaccine (HB):** hepatitis B vaccine can be routinely given to infants or pre-adolescents, depending on the provincial/territorial policy. For infants born to chronic carrier mothers, the first dose should be given at birth (with hepatitis B immunoglobulin); otherwise the first dose can be given at 2 months of age to fit more conveniently with other routine infant immunization visits. The second dose should be administered at least 1 month after the first dose, and the third at least 2 months after the second dose, but these may fit more conveniently into the 4- and 6-month immunization visits. A two-dose schedule for adolescents is an option.

⊠ **Pneumococcal conjugate vaccine — 7 valent (Pneu-C-7):** recommended for all children under 2 years of age. The recommended schedule depends on the age of the child when vaccination is begun.

▪ **Pneumococcal polysaccharide — 23-valent (Pneu-P-23):** recommended for all adults ≥ 65 years of age.

⊙ **Meningococcal C conjugate vaccine (Men-C):** recommended for children under 5 years of age, adolescents, and young adults. The recommended schedule depends on the age of the individual and the conjugate vaccine used. At least one dose in the primary infant series should be given after 5 months of age. If the provincial/territorial policy is to give Men-C to persons ≥ 12 months of age, one dose is sufficient.

▲ **Diphtheria, tetanus, acellular pertussis vaccine — adult/adolescent formulation (Tdap):** a combined adsorbed "adult type" preparation for use in people ≥ 7 years of age; contains less diphtheria toxoid and pertussis antigens than preparations given to younger children and is less likely to cause reactions in older people.

▯ **Diphtheria, tetanus vaccine (Td):** a combined adsorbed "adult type" preparation for use in people ≥ 7 years of age; contains less diphtheria toxoid antigen than preparations given to younger children and is less likely to cause reactions in older people. It is given to adults not immunized in childhood as the second and third doses of their primary series and subsequent booster doses; Tdap is given only once under these circumstances as it is assumed that previously unimmunized adults will have encountered *Bordetella pertussis* and have some prexisting immunity.

⊗ **Influenza vaccine (Inf):** recommended for all children 6–23 months of age and all persons ≥ 65 years of age. Previously unvaccinated children < 9 years of age require two doses of the current season's vaccine with an interval of at least 4 weeks. The second dose within the same season is not required if the child received one or more doses of influenza vaccine during the previous influenza season.

⬢ **IPV Inactivated polio virus**

Although many of the major childhood diseases have been largely eradicated in Canada and other industrialized nations, they remain fearsome killers of children in developing countries. Around the world, more than 13 million children die each year. Two-thirds of these children die of just six diseases: pneumonia, diarrhea, measles, tetanus, whooping cough, and tuberculosis (Save the Children, 2004b). Air pollution from the combustion of fossil fuels for heating and cooking gives rise to many respiratory infections, which are responsible for nearly one death in five among children who are younger than five years of age (Save the Children, 2004b). Around the world, diarrhea kills nearly 2 million children under the age of five. Diarrheal diseases are almost completely related to unsafe drinking water and a general lack of sanitation and hygiene. Children's immune systems and detoxification mechanisms are not as strong as those of adults, and they are thus more vulnerable to chemical, physical, and biological hazards in the water, soil, and air (Save the Children, 2004b).

Lead is a particularly harmful pollutant. Many youngsters are exposed to lead in early childhood, often by eating chips of lead paint from their homes or by breathing in dust from the paint. Infants fed formula made with tap water also are at risk of lead poisoning because the pipes that carry water into homes sometimes contain lead. Lead causes neurological damage and may result in lowered cognitive functioning and other developmental delays in early childhood (Nation & Gleaves, 2001; Needleman & Bellinger, 2001). To help you assess the risk of lead poisoning in children younger than six years of age, see the nearby "A Closer Look" feature.

A Closer Look | Lead Poisoning: Assessing the Risk

In the U.S., Medicaid rules advise physicians to ask the following questions to assess the risk of lead poisoning in children six months to six years old:

- Does your child have any toys with made with lead-based paint?

- Does your child live in or regularly visit a house, a day-care centre, or a nursery school that was built before 1960 and has peeling or chipping paint?

- Does your child live in a home built before 1960 that is being remodelled or renovated?

- Does your child live near a heavily travelled major highway where soil and dust may be contaminated with lead?

- Have any of your children or their playmates had lead poisoning?

- Does your child often come in contact with an adult who works with lead—in construction, welding, plumbing, pottery, or other trades?

- Does your child live near a lead smelter, a battery-recycling plant, or other industrial site likely to release lead?

- Does your home plumbing have lead pipes or copper with lead solder joints?

If the answer to any of these questions is yes, a child has a substantial risk of being exposed to lead and should receive a blood lead test. If the answers to all questions are no, the child has a low risk but, according to American officials, should nevertheless be tested for lead poisoning at twelve months of age and again, if possible, at twenty-four months.

In Canada, toy recalls posted at www.healthycanadians.ca have listed toy items that have been recalled due to surface paints on the recalled products containing lead in excess of allowable safe limit.

Source: Pear (1993).

Low-cost measures such as vaccines, antibiotics, and a technique called **oral rehydration therapy** could prevent most of these deaths. Oral rehydration therapy involves giving a simple homemade salt and sugar solution to a child who is dehydrated from diarrhea. One promising step is that most children in developing countries are now immunized against tuberculosis, measles, polio, diphtheria, tetanus, and whooping cough (Save the Children, 2004b).

oral rehydration therapy A treatment involving administration of a salt and sugar solution to a child who is dehydrated from diarrhea.

Accidents

Truth or Fiction Revisited: It is not true that infections are the most common cause of death among children in Canada (see Table 8.6). In fact, accidents cause more deaths in Canadian children than the next two most frequent causes combined (Public Health Agency, 1997). Common unintentional injuries are motor vehicle accidents, drowning, poisoning, mishaps or injuries during play, swallowing objects, and falls (Parents Canada, 2005).

Accidents are the major killer of children in most countries of the world, except for those developing nations still racked by high rates of malnutrition and disease. Injuries are responsible for nearly half the deaths of children one to four years of age and for more than half the deaths of children aged five to fourteen. Boys are more likely than girls to incur accidental injuries at all ages and in all socioeconomic groups.

Accidental injuries occur most often among low-income children. Poor children are five times as likely to die from fires and more than twice as likely to die in motor vehicle accidents (National Center for Injury Prevention and Control, 2004a). The high accident rate of low-income children may result partly from living in dangerous housing and neighbourhoods. Poor parents also are less likely than higher-income parents to take such preventive measures as using infant safety seats, fastening children's seat belts, installing smoke detectors, or having the telephone number of a poison control centre. The families of children who are injured are frequently more disorganized and under more stress than other families. Injuries often occur when family members are distracted and children are under minimal supervision.

Automobile Safety
Automobile accidents are the most common cause of death in young children in Canada. All provinces now require child-restraint seats in automobiles. These laws have contributed to a reduction in child deaths and injuries.

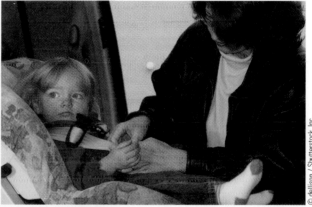

© dellison / Shutterstock, Inc.

	10 Leading Causes of Death, 1997, Canada: Both Sexes	
Rank	Ages 1 to 4	Ages 5 to 9
1	Unintentional injury	Unintentional injury
2	Congenital anomalies	Fatal cancers
3	Fatal cancers	Diseases of the nervous systems
4	Diseases of the nervous system	Congenital anomalies
5	Diseases of the circulatory system	Endocrine diseases
6	Respiratory diseases	Diseases of the circulatory system
7	Homicide	Homicide
8	Infectious and parasitic diseases	Infectious and parasitic diseases
9	Endocrine diseases	Diseases of the digestive system
10	Diseases of the digestive system	Respiratory diseases

Source: Adapted from Public Health Agency of Canada (2000).

Province/Territory	2005 Status	2007 Status	Comments
British Columbia	Poor	Good	Effective July 1, 2008, car booster seats will be mandatory for all children 9 years and under who weigh at least 18 kg and stand less than 145 cm tall. Some public awareness programs exist.
Alberta	Poor	Fair	No legislation on booster seats. Children under 6 years weighing less than 18 kg must be properly secured in a front-facing child safety seat. Examining the possibility of legislation for booster seats for children under 8 years weighing less than 37 kg. Some public educations programs exist.
Saskatchewan	Fair	Fair	Children under 18 kg must be in a child restraint system, but there is no specific booster seat legislation. Has public education programs and a program to provide child safety seats to those who cannot afford them.
Manitoba	Poor	Fair	Children under 5 years weighing less than 22 kg must be properly secured in an approved child safety seat. No legislation for booster seats, though it is under review.
Ontario	Excellent	Excellent	Booster seats required for children under 8 years who weigh 18–26 kg and stand less than 145 cm tall. More drivers required to use child care seats when travelling with toddlers, such as babysitters and grandparents as well as primary caregivers. Education and incentive programs exist.
Quebec	Fair	Good	Children with a sitting height (from the seat to the top of the head) of under 63 cm must use a restraint system or booster cushion. Public awareness programs exist.
New Brunswick	Poor	Fair	No legislation on booster seats. Children under 5 years weighing less than 18 kg must be properly secured in a front-facing child safety seat. Some public education programs exist.
Nova Scotia	Poor	Excellent	Anyone transporting children must properly secure them in an infant seat, child seat, or booster seat. Children weighing more than 18 kg who are younger than 9 years and/or less than 145 cm tall must be in a booster seat. Public education programs and incentives exist.
Prince Edward Island	Poor	Fair	Children weighing 18–23 kg must be secured by a seat belt assembly or a booster seat. No specific booster seat legislation. Some public education programs exist.
Newfoundland and Labrador	Poor	Good	Effective July 1, 2008, booster seats will be mandatory for all children 8 years and under who weigh between 18 and 37 kg, and who are less than 145 cm tall. A public awareness campaign will be implemented.

Table 8. *Booster seat legislation*

Source: Canadian Paediatric Society (2007).

			Booster seat legislation
Yukon	Good	Fair	Children under 6 years must be secured in a child restraint system. Has various requirements depending on a child's weight. Some public education programs exist.
Northwest Territories	Poor	Fair	No legislation on booster seats. Children weighing less than 18 kg msut be properly secured in a front-facing child safety seat. Some public education programs exist.
Nanavut	Poor	Fair	No legislation on booster seats. Children weighing less than 18 kg must be properly secured in a front-facing child safety seat. A review of legislation in other jurisdictions is under way.

Source: Canadian Paediatric Society (2007).

Prevention of Accidental Injury

Legislation has helped to reduce certain injuries in children (National Center for Injury Prevention and Control, 2004a). Approximately 10 000 children under the age of twelve are injured in automobile collisions every year in Canada (Transport Canada, 2001). Child safety seats are required in automobiles, and their use has decreased deaths resulting from automobile injuries. Most large cities in North America now also have laws requiring installation of window guards in high-rise apartment buildings. In a number of countries, the risks of injury to children have been reduced because of legislation requiring manufacturers to meet safety standards for such items as toys and flammable clothing.

Oral Health

A child's teeth begin developing long before birth when they are in the prenatal stage. By the time most children reach the age of thirty months, all the primary teeth (twenty baby teeth) are in place (see Figure 8.5). The Canadian Dental Association recommends that parents brush their children's teeth as soon as they appear, and in fact that they clean babies' mouths with a gentle toothbrush even before teeth appear to get into the habit of good oral hygiene. The Canadian Dental Association (2005) encourages the assessment of an infant's teeth within six months of the first teeth eruptions. The Canadian Paediatric Society recommends the following good practices for oral hygiene in early childhood:

- Avoid feeding child sticky or sugary snacks.
- Take your child to the dentist when he or she is about one year old, and every six months afterward.
- Brush teeth twice a day, especially before bedtime.
- Don't share toothbrushes. Germs can easily pass from one person to another.
- Rinse the toothbrush well with water after each use and let it air dry.
- Replace a toothbrush every few months, when the bristles become flattened with use.

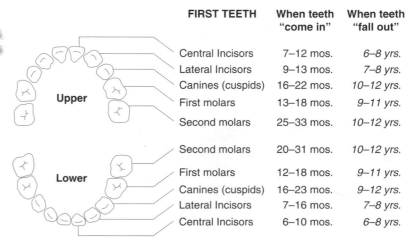

FIRST TEETH	When teeth "come in"	When teeth "fall out"
Upper		
Central Incisors	7–12 mos.	*6–8 yrs.*
Lateral Incisors	9–13 mos.	*7–8 yrs.*
Canines (cuspids)	16–22 mos.	*10–12 yrs.*
First molars	13–18 mos.	*9–11 yrs.*
Second molars	25–33 mos.	*10–12 yrs.*
Lower		
Second molars	20–31 mos.	*10–12 yrs.*
First molars	12–18 mos.	*9–11 yrs.*
Canines (cuspids)	16–23 mos.	*9–12 yrs.*
Lateral Incisors	7–16 mos.	*7–8 yrs.*
Central Incisors	6–10 mos.	*6–8 yrs.*

Figure 8.5
First Teeth

Active Review

15. The most frequent cause of death of children in Canada is _____.

16. How many children under the age of ten are injured in automobile collisions every year in Canada?

Reflect & Relate: What environmental hazards have you recently become more aware of in your community, if any?

W W W **Go to**
www.voyages1ce.nelson.com
for an interactive version of this review.

Sleep

Question: How much sleep is needed during early childhood? Children in the early years do not need as much sleep as infants. Most preschoolers sleep ten to eleven hours in a twenty-four-hour period (National Sleep Foundation, 2004) (see Table 8.8). A common pattern includes nine to ten hours at night and a nap of one to two hours. In Canada, the young child's bedtime routine typically includes putting on pyjamas, brushing teeth, and being read a story. Many young children also take a so-called **transitional object**—such as a favoured blanket or a stuffed animal—to bed with them (Morelli, Oppenheim, Rogoff, & Goldsmith, 1992). Such objects apparently help children make the transition to greater independence and separation from their parents.

But we're not ending the topic here, because it sounds much too easy. As too many parents know, getting children to sleep can be a major challenge of parenthood. Many children resist going to bed or going to sleep (Christophersen & Mortweet, 2003). A Japanese study suggests that getting to sleep late can be a problem because preschoolers tend not to make up fully for lost sleep (Kohyama, Shiiki, Ohinata-Sugimoto, & Hasegawa, 2002). But resisting sleep is a run-of-the-mill problem. In the next section we focus on more serious problems, called *sleep disorders*.

transitional object A soft, cuddly object often carried to bed by a child to ease the separation from parents.

		Sleep Obtained by Children during a 24-Hour Period		
% of	Infants	Preschoolers	Younger School-Aged Children	Older School-Aged Children
Bottom 25%	11 hours or less	9.9 hours or less	9 hours or less	8.9 hours or less
Middle 50%	11.1–14.9 hours	10–11 hours	9.1–10 hours	9–9.9 hours
Upper 25%	15 hours or more	11.1 hours or more	10.1 hours or more	10 hours or more

Source: National Sleep Foundation (2004).

Sleep Disorders

Question: What kinds of problems or disorders disrupt sleep during early childhood? In this section we focus on the sleep disorders of sleep terrors, nightmares, and sleepwalking.

Sleep Terrors and Nightmares

First, a few words about terms: **Sleep terrors** are more severe than the anxiety dreams we refer to as nightmares. For one thing, sleep terrors usually occur during deep sleep. **Nightmares** take place during lighter rapid-eye-movement (REM) sleep, when about 80 percent of normal dreams occur. In fact, nightmares sort of qualify as "normal" dreams—because of their frequency, not because of their desirability!

Deep sleep alternates with lighter REM sleep. Sleep terrors, sometimes referred to as *night terrors,* tend to occur early during the night, when periods of deep sleep are longest. Nightmares tend to occur more often in the morning hours when periods of REM sleep tend to lengthen (Christophersen & Mortweet, 2003; Stores & Wiggs, 2001). Children have several periods of REM sleep a night and may dream in each one of them.

Sleep terrors usually begin in childhood or early adolescence and are outgrown by late adolescence. They are often but not always associated with stress, such as moving to a new neighbourhood, attending school for the first time, adjusting to parental divorce, or being caught up in a war zone (Krippner & McIntyre, 2003; Schredl, 2001). Children are also more likely to experience nightmares during stressful periods (Schredl, 2001). Children with sleep terrors may wake up suddenly with a surge in heart and respiration rates, talk incoherently, and thrash about. Children are not completely awake during sleep terrors and may fall back into more restful sleep. Fortunately, the incidence of sleep terrors wanes as children develop and spend less time in deep sleep. They are all but absent among adults.

Children who have frequent nightmares or sleep terrors may come to fear going to sleep. They may show distress at bedtime, refuse to get into their pyjamas, and insist that the lights be kept on during the night. As a result, they can develop **insomnia.** Children with frequent nightmares or sleep terrors need their parents' understanding and affection. They also profit from a regular routine in which they are expected to get to sleep at the same time each night (Christophersen & Mortweet, 2003). Yelling at them over their "immature" refusal to have the lights out and return to sleep will not alleviate their anxieties.

sleep terrors Frightening dreamlike experiences that occur during the deepest stage of non-REM sleep, shortly after the child has gone to sleep.

nightmares Frightening dreams that occur during REM sleep, often in the morning hours.

insomnia One or more of a number of sleep problems—difficulty falling asleep, difficulty remaining asleep during the night, and waking early.

Developing in a World of Diversity

Cross-Cultural Differences in Sleeping Arrangements

The commonly accepted practice in middle-class Canadian families is for infants and children to sleep in separate beds and, when finances permit, in separate rooms from their parents. Child-care experts in Canada have generally endorsed this practice. Sleeping in the same room, they warn, can lead to problems such as the development of overdependence, the difficulty of breaking the habit when the child gets older, and even accidental sexual stimulation of the child (Morelli et al., 1992).

Yet, in many other cultures, children sleep with their mothers for the first few years of life, often in the same bed (Javo, Ronning, & Heyerdahl, 2004). This practice, known as co-sleeping, occurs in cultures that are technologically advanced, such as Austria (Rothrauff, Middlemiss, & Jacobson, 2004) and Japan (Takahashi, 1990), and in those that are less technologically sophisticated, such as that of the indigenous Sami people of Norway (Javo et al., 2004).

Getting Their Z's

In North America, most parents believe that it is harmful or at least inappropriate for parents to sleep with their children; however, since Canada is a multicultural nation there is great variety in parenting practices and sleep preferences. Parents in many other cultures are more relaxed about sleeping arrangements.

Twenty to forty percent of Canadian infants and preschoolers regularly resist going to bed (Johnson, 1991), but this resistance seldom occurs in cultures that practice co-sleeping. Some psychologists believe that the resistance shown by some young Canadian children at bedtime is

caused by the stress of separating from parents. This view is supported by the finding that young children who sleep with or near their parents are less likely to use transitional objects or to suck their thumbs at night than are children who sleep alone (Morelli et al., 1992; Wolf & Lozoff, 1989).

Research does not reveal harmful effects for co-sleeping. For example, an Austrian study found no significant differences between children's sleeping arrangements and their subsequent social development (Rothrauff et al., 2004). Among the Norwegian Sami, children not only slept with their parents but also—unlike other Norwegians—regulated their own sleeping and eating schedules. Sami parents were less tolerant of aggressive behaviour in their children than Norwegian parents were. The outcome of all these cultural approaches was connected with relatively greater social independence among Sami children.

Sleepwalking

somnambulism Sleep-walking (from the Latin somnus, meaning "sleep," and ambulare, meaning "to walk").

Sleepwalking, or **somnambulism,** is much more common among children than adults. As with sleep terrors, sleepwalking tends to occur during deep sleep (stages 3 and 4) (Stores & Wiggs, 2001). Onset is usually between the ages of three and eight.

During medieval times, people believed that sleepwalking was a sign of possession by evil spirits. Psychoanalytic theory suggests that sleepwalking allows people the chance to express feelings and impulses they would inhibit while awake. But children who sleepwalk have not been shown to have any more trouble controlling impulses than other children do. Moreover, what children do when they sleepwalk is usually too boring to suggest exotic motivation. They may rearrange toys, go to the bathroom, or go to the refrigerator and have a glass of milk. Then they return to their rooms and go back to bed. Their lack of recall in the morning is consistent with sleep terrors, which also occur during deep sleep. Sleepwalking episodes are brief; most tend to last no longer than half an hour.

There are some myths about sleep walking—for example, that sleepwalkers' eyes are closed, that they will avoid harm, and that they will become violently agitated if they are awakened during an episode. All of these notions are false. Sleepwalkers' eyes are usually open, although they may respond to onlooking parents as furniture to be walked around and not as people. Children may incur injury when sleepwalking, just as they may when awake. ***Truth or Fiction Revisited:*** It is also not true that it is dangerous to awaken a sleepwalker. Children may be difficult to rouse when they are sleepwalking, just as during sleep terrors. But if they are awakened, they are more likely to show confusion and disorientation (again, as during sleep terrors) than violence.

Today, sleepwalking in children is assumed to reflect immaturity of the nervous system, not acting out of dreams or psychological conflicts. As with sleep terrors, the incidence of sleepwalking drops as children develop. It may help to discuss persistent sleep terrors or sleepwalking with a health professional.

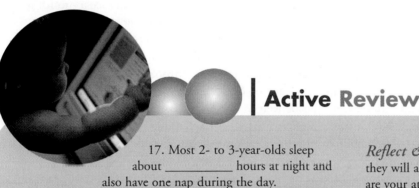

Active Review

17. Most 2- to 3-year-olds sleep about _____ hours at night and also have one nap during the day.

18. (Nightmares or Sleep terrors?) usually occur during deep sleep.

19. _____ is also referred to as *somnambulism.*

Reflect & Relate: Critical thinkers insist on evidence before they will accept beliefs, even widely held cultural beliefs. What are your attitudes toward children sleeping with their parents? Are your attitudes supported by research evidence? Explain.

 W W W **Go to**
www.voyages1ce.nelson.com
for an interactive version of this review.

Elimination Disorders

The elimination of waste products occurs reflexively in neonates. As children develop, their task is to learn to inhibit the reflexes that govern urination and bowel movements. The process by which parents teach their children to inhibit these reflexes is referred to as toilet training. The inhibition of eliminatory reflexes makes polite conversation possible. *Questions: When are children considered to be gaining control over elimination too slowly? What can be done to help them gain control?*

Truth or Fiction Revisited: It is not true that more competent parents toilet train their children by their second birthday. Most Western children are toilet trained between the ages of twenty-four and forty-eight months (Liebert & Fischel, 1990; Scheres & Castellanos, 2003). They may have accidents at night for another year or so.

In toilet training, as in so many other areas of physical growth and development, maturation plays a crucial role, but so does cultural practice and expectations. It is

Toilet Training
If parents wait until the third year to begin toilet training, the process usually goes relatively rapidly and smoothly.

rare to find a North American child who is toilet trained in his or her first year, even when parents devote a great deal of time and energy to the task. If parents wait until the third year to begin toilet training, the process usually runs smoothly.

An end to diaper changing is not the only reason parents are motivated to toilet train their children. Parents often experience pressure from grandparents, other relatives, and friends who point out that so-and-so's children were all toilet trained before the age of _____. (You fill it in. Choose a number that will make most of us feel like inadequate parents.) Parents, in turn, may pressure their children to become toilet trained. And so toilet training can become a major arena for parent-child conflict. Children who do not become toilet trained within reasonable time frames are said to have *enuresis, encopresis,* or both.

Enuresis

enuresis (en-you-REE-sis) Failure to control the bladder (urination) once the normal age for control has been reached.

Give it a name like **enuresis** (en-you-REE-sis), and suddenly it looms like a serious medical problem rather than a bit of an annoyance. Enuresis is the failure to control the bladder (urination) once the "normal" age for achieving control of the bladder has been reached. Conceptions as to the normal age vary. The American Psychiatric Association (2000) is reasonably lenient on the issue and places the cutoff age at five years. The frequency of "accidents" is also an issue. The American Psychiatric Association does not consider such accidents enuresis unless they occur at least twice a month for five- and six-year-olds or once a month for children who are older.

bed-wetting Failure to control the bladder during the night. (Frequently used interchangeably with enuresis, although bed-wetting refers to the behaviour itself and enuresis is a diagnostic category, related to the age of the child.)

A nighttime accident is referred to as **bed-wetting.** Nighttime control is more difficult to achieve than daytime control. At night, children must first wake up when their bladders are full. Only then can they go to the bathroom.

Bed-wetting is more common among boys than girls. Nearly 15 percent of children five years and under wet their beds at night (Canadian Paediatric Society, 2005; Greene, 2003). The incidence drops as age increases. A study of 3,344 Chinese children found that these children appeared to attain control a bit earlier: 7.7 percent obtained nocturnal urinary control by the age of two, 53 percent by the age of three, and 93 percent by the age of five (Liu, Sun, Uchiyama, Li, & Okawa, 2000b). As with North American studies, girls achieved control earlier than boys.

Causes of Enuresis

Enuresis can have organic causes, such as infections of the urinary tract or kidney problems (Greene, 2003). Numerous psychological explanations of enuresis have also been advanced. Psychoanalytic theory suggests that enuresis is a way of expressing hostility toward parents (because of their harshness in toilet training) or a form of symbolic masturbation. These views are largely unsubstantiated. Learning theorists point out that enuresis is most common among children whose parents attempted to train them early. Early failures might have conditioned anxiety over attempts to control the bladder. Conditioned anxiety, then, prompts rather than inhibits urination.

Situational stresses seem to play a role. Children are more likely to wet their beds when they are entering school for the first time, when a sibling is born, or when they are ill. There may also be a genetic component, in that the concordance rate for enuresis is higher among monozygotic twins than among dizygotic twins (Barabas, 1990).

It has also been noted that bed-wetting tends to occur during the deepest stage of sleep. This is also the stage when sleep terrors and sleepwalking take place. For this reason, bed-wetting could be considered a sleep disorder. Like sleepwalking, bed-wetting could reflect immaturity of certain parts of the nervous system. Just as children outgrow sleep terrors and sleepwalking, they tend to outgrow bed-wetting. In most cases, bed-wetting resolves itself by adolescence, but usually by the age of eight.

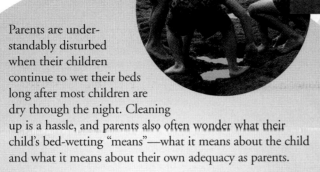

Parents are understandably disturbed when their children continue to wet their beds long after most children are dry through the night. Cleaning up is a hassle, and parents also often wonder what their child's bed-wetting "means"—what it means about the child and what it means about their own adequacy as parents.

Bed-wetting may only "mean" that the child is slower than most children to keep his or her bed dry through the night. It may mean nothing at all about the child's intelligence or personality or about the parents' capabilities.

Certainly a number of devices (alarms) can be used to teach the child to awaken in response to bladder pressure. Medications also can be used to help the child retain fluids through the night. Before turning to these methods, however, methods such as the following may do the trick (Greene, 2003; Needlman, 2000):

- **Limit fluid intake late in the day.** Less pressure on the bladder makes it easier to control urinating, but do not risk depriving the child of liquids. On the other hand, it makes sense to limit fluid intake in the evening, especially at bedtime. Drinks with caffeine, such as colas, coffee, and tea, act as diuretics, making it more difficult to control urination. So it is helpful to cut down on them after lunch.

- **Wake the child during the night.** Waking the child at midnight or 1:00 in the morning may make it possible for him or her to go to the bathroom and urinate. Children may complain and say that they don't have to go, but often they will. Praise the child for making the effort.

- **Try a night-light.** Many children fear getting up in the dark and trying to find their way to the bathroom. A night-light can make the difference. If the bathroom is far from the child's bedroom, it may be helpful to place a chamber pot in the bedroom. The child can empty the pot in the morning.

- **Maintain a consistent schedule so that the child can form helpful bedtime and nighttime habits.** Having a regular bedtime not only helps ensure that your child gets enough sleep but also enables the child to get into a routine of urinating before going to bed and keeps the child's internal clock in sync with the clock on the wall. Habits can be made to work for the child rather than against the child.

- **Use a "sandwich" bed.** A sandwich bed? This is simply a plastic sheet, covered with a cloth sheet, covered with yet another plastic sheet, and then still another cloth sheet. If the child wets his or her bed, the top wet sheet and plastic sheet can be pulled off, and the child can get back into a comfortable dry bed. In this way, the child develops the habit of sleeping in a dry bed. Moreover, the child learns how to handle his or her "own mess" by removing the wet sheets.

- **Have the child help clean up.** The child can throw the sheets into the wash and, perhaps, operate the washing machine. The child can make the bed, or at least participate. These behaviours are not punishments; they help connect the child to the reality of what is going on and what needs to be done to clean things up.

- **Reward the child's successes.** Parents risk becoming overly punitive when they pay attention only to the child's failures. Ignoring successes also allows them to go unreinforced. When the child has a dry night, or half of a dry night, make a note of it. Track successes on a calendar. Connect them with small treats, such as more TV time or time with you. Make a "fuss"—that is, a positive fuss. Also consider rewarding partial successes, such as the child's getting up after beginning to urinate so that there is less urine in the bed.

- **Have a positive attitude.** ("Accentuate the positive.") Talk with your child about "staying dry" rather than "not wetting." Communicate the idea that you have confidence that things will get better. (They almost always do.)

Encopresis

Soiling, or **encopresis,** is lack of control over the bowels. Soiling, like enuresis, is more common among boys. However, the overall incidence of soiling is lower than that of enuresis. About 1 to 2 percent of children at the ages of seven and eight have continuing problems controlling their bowels (Liebert & Fischel, 1990).

encopresis Failure to control the bowels once the normal age for bowel control has been reached. Also called *soiling*.

Soiling, in contrast to enuresis, is more likely to occur during the day. Thus, it can be acutely embarrassing to the child.

Encopresis stems from both physical causes, such as chronic constipation, and psychological factors (Cox et al., 1998; McGrath et al., 2000; Needlman, 2001). Soiling may follow harsh punishment of toileting accidents, especially in children who are already anxious or under stress. Punishment may cause the child to tense up on the toilet, but moving one's bowels requires that one relax the anal sphincter muscles. Harsh punishment also focuses the child's attention on soiling. The child then begins to ruminate about soiling, so that soiling, punishment, and worrying about future soiling become a vicious cycle.

We now leave our exploration of physical development in early childhood and begin an examination of cognitive development.

Active Review

20. In toilet training, maturation (does or does not?) play a crucial role.

21. Bed-wetting is more common among (girls or boys?).

22. A common physical cause of encopresis is _____.

Reflect & Relate: Why do you think so many parents become upset when their children are a bit behind others in toilet training? Do you think it is bad if it takes three or four years for a child to learn to use the toilet reliably? If so, why?

Go to
W W W **www.voyages1ce.nelson.com**
for an interactive version of this review.

Recite: *An Active Summary*™

1. What changes occur in height and weight during early childhood?

Children gain about two to three inches in height and four to six pounds in weight per year in early childhood. Boys are slightly larger than girls.

2. How does the brain develop during early childhood?

The brain develops more quickly than any other organ in early childhood, in part because of myelination. Myelination enhances children's ability to attend to and process visual information, enabling them to read and to screen out distractions.

3. What does it mean to be left-brained or right-brained?

The left hemisphere is relatively more involved in logical analysis and problem solving, language, and mathematical computation. The right hemisphere is usually superior in visual-spatial functions, esthetic and emotional responses, and creative mathematical reasoning. Nevertheless, the functions of the left and right hemispheres are not independent.

4. What is meant by "plasticity of the brain"?

Plasticity means that the brain compensates for injuries to particular areas. Two factors involved in the brain's plasticity are the growth of new dendrites and the redundancy of neural connections.

5. How do motor skills develop in early childhood?

In the preschool years, children make great strides in the development of gross motor skills, which involve the large muscles. Girls are somewhat better at tasks requiring balance and precision; boys have some advantage in throwing and kicking. Fine motor skills develop gradually. The most active children generally show less well developed motor skills. After two or three years of age, children become less restless and are more able to sustain attention during play.

6. Do girls and boys differ in their activity levels during early childhood?

Boys tend to be more active than girls in large muscle activities. Boys are more fidgety and distractible, perhaps because they are less mature physically.

7. Are children's scribbles the result of random motor activity?

Apparently not. Kellogg identified twenty scribbles that she considers the building blocks of art. She theorizes that children undergo four stages of progressing from scribbles to drawing pictures.

8. When does handedness emerge? How many children are left-handed?

By six months, most infants show clear-cut hand preferences, which become still more established during early childhood. More than 90 percent of children are right-handed.

9. Are there problems connected with being left-handed?

Left-handedness may be connected with language problems and some health problems. Yet a disproportionately large number of artists, musicians, and mathematicians are left-handed.

10. What are children's nutritional needs and their eating behaviour like in early childhood?

The typical four- to six-year-old needs 1800 calories a day, compared with 1300 for the average one- to three-year-old. During the second and third years, children's appetites typically wane and grow erratic. Many children eat too much sugar and salt, which can harm their health.

11. How healthy are children in Canada and in other countries? What are some of the illnesses and environmental hazards encountered during early childhood?

The incidence of minor illnesses, such as colds, nausea and vomiting, and diarrhea, is high. Although diarrheal illness is usually mild in Canada, it is a leading killer of children in developing countries. Immunization and antibiotics reduce the incidence of serious childhood diseases. Air pollution contributes to respiratory infections. Diarrheal diseases are almost completely related to unsafe drinking water and lack of sanitation.

12. How much sleep is needed during early childhood?

Most two- and three-year-olds sleep about ten hours at night and nap during the day.

13. What kinds of problems or disorders disrupt sleep during early childhood?

Sleep terrors are more severe than nightmares. Sleep terrors and sleepwalking usually occur during deep sleep. Sleepwalkers' eyes are usually open, and if sleepwalkers are awakened, they may show confusion and disorientation but are unlikely to be violent.

14. When are children considered to be gaining control over elimination too slowly? What can be done to help them gain control?

Most Canadian children are toilet trained by about age three or four but continue to have "accidents" at night for another year or so. Enuresis (bedwetting) is the failure to control the bladder once a child has reached the "normal" age for doing so—placed at five years of age by the American Psychiatric Association. Encopresis (soiling) is lack of control over the bowels. Enuresis is apparently connected with physical immaturity and stress. Encopresis can stem from physical causes, such as constipation, and psychological factors.

WWW Go to www.voyages1ce.nelson.com *for an interactive version of this summary review.*

Key Terms

Active Learning Resources

Observing Children and Adolescents CD-ROM

Want to watch videos showing what you've just learned about in this chapter? Click on the "Gross Motor" and "Fine Motor" videos in Module 2, Section 1. Your "Lessons in Observation" feature on p. 271 provides further learning objectives, an applied lesson, and a critical thinking exercise designed to help you experience these stages of development.

Visit Your Companion Website for This Book
http://www.voyages1CE.nelson.com

Check out this companion website, where you will find online resources directly linked to your book. The website includes interactive exercises related to PQ4R and Power Visuals for mastering and reviewing key concepts as well as quizzing, chapter outlines, and much more!

CengageNOW!™
http://hed.nelson.com

Go to this site for the link to CengageNOW™, your one-stop study shop. Take a Pretest for this chapter, and CengageNOW™ will generate a personalized Study Plan based on your test results! The Study Plan will identify the topics you need to review and direct you to online resources to help you master those topics. You can then take a Posttest to help you determine the concepts you have mastered and those you still need to work on.

Early Childhood: Cognitive Development

PREVIEW

TRUTH OR FICTION?

T **F**   A preschooler's having imaginary play-mates is a sign of loneliness or psychological problems.

T **F**   Two-year-olds tend to assume that their parents are aware of everything that is happening to them, even when their parents are not present.

T **F**   "Because Mommy wants me to" may be a perfectly good explanation—for a three-year-old.

T **F**   Children's levels of intelligence—not just their knowledge—are influenced by early learning experiences.

T **F**   A highly academic preschool education provides children with advantages in school later on.

T **F**   One- and two-year-olds are too young to remember past events.

T **F**   During her third year, a girl explained that she and her mother had finished singing a song by saying, "We singed it all up."

T **F**   Three-year-olds usually say, "Daddy goed away" instead of "Daddy went away" because they *do* understand rules of grammar.

Go to www

www.voyages1ce.nelson.com
for an interactive version of this "Truth or Fiction" feature.

For those of you who work with young children, have young children of your own, or occasionally come in contact with young children, you will appreciate this next recollection by Rathus. He recounts how he was confused when his daughter Allyn, at the age of two and a half, insisted that he continue to play "Billy Joel" on the stereo. Put aside the question of her taste in music. His problem stemmed from the fact that when Allyn asked for Billy Joel, the name of the singer, she could be satisfied only by his playing the song "Moving Out." When "Moving Out" had ended and the next song, "The Stranger," had begun to play, she would insist that he play "Billy Joel" again. "That *is* Billy Joel," he would protest. "No, no," she would insist, "I want Billy Joel!"

Finally, it occurred to him that, for her, "Billy Joel" symbolized the song "Moving Out," not the name of the singer. Of course his insistence that the second song was also "Billy Joel" could not satisfy her! She was conceptualizing Billy Joel as a property of a particular song, not as the name of a person who could sing many songs. Children between the ages of two and four tend to show confusion between symbols and the objects they represent. They do not yet recognize that words are arbitrary symbols for objects and events and that people can use different words. They tend to think of words as inherent properties of objects and events.

In this chapter we discuss cognitive development during early childhood. First, we examine Piaget's preoperational stage of cognitive development. Piaget largely viewed cognitive development in terms of maturation; however, in the section on factors in cognitive development, we will see that social and other factors foster cognitive development by placing children in "the zone," as Vygotsky might have put it. Next, we consider other aspects of cognitive development, such as how children acquire a "theory of mind" and develop memory. Finally, we continue our exploration of language development.

Jean Piaget's Preoperational Stage (2–7 years)

According to Piaget, the **preoperational stage** of cognitive development lasts from about age two to age seven. Be warned: Any resemblance between the logic of a preschooler and your own may be purely coincidental.

Symbolic Thought

Question: How do children in the preoperational stage think and behave? Preoperational thought is characterized by the use of symbols to represent objects and relationships among them. Perhaps the most important kind of symbolic activity of young children is language. But we will see that children's early use of language leaves something to be desired in the realm of logic.

Children begin to scribble and draw pictures in the early years. These drawings are symbols of objects, people, and events in children's lives. Symbolism is also expressed as symbolic or pretend play, which emerges during these years.

Symbolic or Pretend Play: "We Could Make Believe"

Children's **symbolic play**—the "let's pretend" type of play—may seem immature to busy adults meeting the realistic demands of the business world, but it requires cognitive sophistication (Lytle, 2003; Nichols & Stich, 2000; Nielsen & Dissanayake, 2000). In fact, pretend play has been found to be associated with higher levels of negotiation in sibling exchanges and to more internal state language (both skills that children will need throughout their lifetimes) (Howe, Petrakos, & Rinaldi, 1998).

Piaget (1962) wrote that pretend play usually begins in the second year, when the child begins to symbolize objects. The ability to engage in pretend play is based on the use and recollection of symbols—that is, on mental representations of things

preoperational stage The second stage in Piaget's scheme, characterized by inflexible and irreversible mental manipulation of symbols.

symbolic play Play in which children make believe that objects and toys are other than what they are. Also termed *pretend play*.

children have experienced or heard about. At nineteen months, Allyn picked up a pine cone and looked it over. Her babysitter said, "That's a pine cone." Allyn pretended to lick it, as if it were an ice cream cone.

Children first engage in pretend play at about twelve or thirteen months of age. They make believe that they are performing familiar activities, such as sleeping or feeding themselves. By age fifteen to twenty months, they can shift their focus from themselves to others. A child may thus pretend to feed a doll. By thirty months, he or she can make believe that the other object takes an active role. The child may now pretend that the doll is feeding itself (Campbell, 1990; McCune, 1993; Thyssen, 2003).

The quality of preschoolers' pretend play has implications for subsequent development. For example, preschoolers who engage in violent pretend play are less empathic, less likely to help other children, and more likely to engage in antisocial behaviour later on (Dunn & Hughes, 2001). Preschoolers who engage in more elaborate pretend play are also more likely to do well in school later on (Stagnitti, Unsworth, & Rodger, 2000). The quality of pretend play is also connected with preschoolers' creativity and their ability to relate to peers (Farver, Kim, & Lee-Shin, 2000).

Imaginary friends are one example of pretend play. At age two, Allyn acquired an imaginary playmate named Loveliness. He told Allyn to do lots of things—move things from here to there, get food for him, and so on. At times, Allyn was overheard talking to Loveliness in her room. As many as 65 percent of preschoolers have such friends, and they are more common among firstborn and only children (Gleason, Sebanc, & Hartup, 2003).

Truth or Fiction Revisited: It is not true that having imaginary playmates is a sign of loneliness or psychological problems (and we're not saying this just because one of us has admitted to having an imaginary playmate in childhood). Having an imaginary playmate does not mean that the child is having difficulty in real relationships (Gleason, 2004; Taylor, 1999). In fact, children with imaginary companions are less aggressive, more cooperative—they often nurture the imaginary friend (Gleason, 2002)—and more creative. They have more real friends, show greater ability to concentrate, and are more advanced in language development (Taylor, 1999).

Another interesting way that children make sense of the world around them is the sometimes used strategy of magical thinking. Children occasionally use magical thinking (also referred to as *wishful thinking*) to explain occurrences that do not have realistic explanations (Subbotsky, 2004; Woolley, Phelps, Davis, & Mandell, 1999).

© Brian Milne/First Light

Symbolic Play

Symbolic play—also called *pretend play*—usually begins in the second year, when the child begins to form mental representations of objects. This girl may engage in a sequence of play acts such as making her teddy bears sit down at the table and offering them a make-believe cup of tea.

Operations: "Transformers" of the Mind

Any resemblance between the logic of children aged two to seven and your own may be purely coincidental. *Question: How do we characterize the logic of the preoperational child?* **Operations** are mental acts (or schemes) in which objects are changed or transformed and then can be returned to their original states. Mental operations are flexible and reversible.

Consider the example of planning a move in checkers. A move requires knowledge of the rules of the game. The child who plays the game well (as opposed to just making moves) is able to picture the results of the move—how, in its new position,

operations Flexible, reversible mental manipulations of objects, in which objects can be mentally transformed and then returned to their original states.

the piece will support or be threatened by other pieces and how other pieces might be left undefended by the move. Playing checkers well requires that the child be able to picture, or focus on, different parts of the board and on relationships between pieces at the same time. By considering several moves, the child shows flexibility. By picturing the board as it would be after a move and then as it is, the child shows reversibility.

Having said all this, let us return to the fact that this section is about preoperational children—children who cannot yet engage in flexible and reversible mental operations. Young children's logic reflects the fact that their ability to perform operations is "under construction." The preoperational stage is thus characterized by features such as egocentrism, immature notions about what causes what, confusion between mental and physical events, and the ability to focus on only one dimension at a time.

Egocentrism: It's All about Me

egocentrism Putting oneself at the centre of things such that one is unable to perceive the world from another person's point of view. Egocentrism is normal in early childhood but is a matter of choice, and rather intolerable, in adults. (Okay, we sneaked an editorial comment into a definition. Dr. Samuel Johnson also did that.)

Sometimes the attitude "It's all about me" is a sign of early childhood, not of selfishness. One consequence of one-dimensional thinking is **egocentrism.** *Question: What is egocentrism?* Egocentrism, in Piaget's use of the term, does not mean that preoperational children are selfish (although, of course, they may be). It means that they do not understand that other people may have different perspectives on the world.

Truth or Fiction Revisited: Two-year-olds may, in fact, assume that their parents are aware of everything that is happening to them, even when their parents are not present. They may view the world as a stage that has been erected to meet their needs and amuse them. When Allyn—still at the age of two and a half—was asked to recount a trip to the store with her mother, she answered, "You tell me." It did not occur to her that Rathus could not see the world through her eyes.

Piaget used the "three-mountains test" (see Figure 9.1) to show that egocentrism literally prevents young children from taking the viewpoints of others. In this demonstration, the child sits at a table before a model of three mountains. The mountains differ in colour. One has a house on it, and another a cross at the summit.

Piaget then placed a doll elsewhere on the table and asked the child what the doll sees. The language abilities of very young children do not permit them to provide verbal descriptions of what can be seen from where the doll is situated, so they can answer in one of two ways. They can either select a photograph taken from the proper vantage point, or they can construct another model of the mountains, as they would be seen by the doll. The results of an experiment with the three-mountains test suggest that five- and six-year-olds usually select photos or build models that correspond to their own viewpoints (Laurendeau & Pinard, 1970).

Figure 9.1

The Three-Mountains Test
Piaget used the three-mountains test to learn whether children at certain ages are egocentric or can take the viewpoints of others.
Source: Piaget & Inhelder (1969).

Causality: Why? Because.

Preoperational children's responses to questions such as "Why does the sun shine?" show other facets of egocentrism. At the age of two or so, they may answer that they do not know or change the subject. *Truth or Fiction Revisited:* Three-year-olds may report themselves as doing things because they want to do them or "Because Mommy wants me to." In egocentric fashion, this explanation of behaviour is extended to inanimate objects. The sun may thus be thought of as shining because it wants to shine or because someone (or something) else wants it to shine. In this case, the sun's behaviour is thought of as being caused by will—perhaps the sun's wish to bathe the child in its rays or the child's wish to remain warm. In either case, the answer puts the child at the centre of the conceptual universe. The sun becomes an instrument similar to a light bulb.

Piaget labels this type of structuring of cause and effect **precausal**. *Question: What is precausal thinking?* Preoperational children believe that things happen for reasons and not by accident. However, unless preoperational children know the natural causes of an event, their reasons are likely to have an egocentric favour and not be based on science. Consider the question "Why does it get dark outside?" The preoperational child usually does not have knowledge of the earth's rotation and is likely to answer something like "So I can go to sleep."

Another example of precausal thinking is **transductive reasoning**. In transductive reasoning, children reason by going from one specific isolated event to another. For example, a three-year-old may argue that she should go on her swings in the backyard *because* it is light outside or that she should go to sleep *because* it is dark outside. That is, separate specific events, daylight and going on the swings (or being awake) are thought of as having cause-and-effect relationships.

Preoperational children also show **animism** and **artificialism** in their attributions of causality. In animistic thinking, they attribute life and intentions to inanimate objects, such as the sun and the moon. ("Why is the moon gone during the day?" "It is afraid of the sun.") Artificialism assumes that environmental features such as rain and thunder have been designed and made by people. In *Six Psychological Studies*, Piaget (1967 [1964]) wrote that "Mountains 'grow' because stones have been manufactured and then planted. Lakes have been hollowed out, and for a long time the child believes that cities are built [before] the lakes adjacent to them" (p.28). Table 9.1 shows other examples of egocentrism, animism, and artificialism. It is important to note that animism and artificialism are culturally influenced, therefore the examples in Table 9.1 are not absolutes.

precausal A type of thought in which natural cause-and-effect relationships are attributed to will and other preoperational concepts. (For example, the sun sets because it is tired.)

transductive reasoning Reasoning from the specific to the specific. (In deductive reasoning, one reasons from the general to the specific; in inductive reasoning, one reasons from the specific to the general.)

animism The attribution of life and intentionality to inanimate objects.

artificialism The belief that environmental features were made by people.

Table 9.1 *Highlights of Preoperational Thought*

Type of Thought	Sample Questions	Typical Answers
Egocentrism (placing oneself at the centre of things such that one is unable to perceive the world from another's point of view)	Why does it get dark out? Why does the sun shine? Why is there snow? Why is grass green? What are TV sets for?	So I can go to sleep. To keep me warm. For me to play in. Because that's my favourite colour. To watch my favourite shows and cartoons.
Animism (attributing life and consciousness to physical objects)	Why do trees have leaves? Why do stars twinkle? Why does the sun move in the sky? Where do boats go at night?	To keep them warm. Because they're happy and cheerful. To follow children and hear what they say. They sleep like we do.
Artificialism (assuming that environmental events are human inventions)	What makes it rain? Why is the sky blue? What is the wind? What causes thunder? How does a baby get in Mommy's tummy?	Someone emptying a watering can. Somebody painted it. A man blowing. A man grumbling. Just make it first. (How?) You put some eyes on it, then put on the head.

Confusion of Mental and Physical Events: On "Galaprocks" and Dreams That Are Real

What would you do if someone asked you to pretend you were a galaprock? Chances are you might inquire what a galaprock is and how it behaves. So might a five-year-old child. But a three-year-old might not think that such information is necessary (Gottfried, Hickling, Totten, Mkroyan, & Reisz, 2003). Have you seen horror movies in which people's dreams become real? It could be said that preoperational children tend to live in such worlds—although, for them, that world is normal and not horrible.

Question: Why do young children think they can pretend to be galaprocks without knowing what galaprocks are? According to Piaget, the preoperational child has difficulty making distinctions between mental and physical phenomena. Children between the ages of two and four show confusion between symbols and the things that they represent. Egocentrism contributes to the assumption that their thoughts exactly reflect external reality. They do not recognize that words are arbitrary and that people can use different words to refer to things. In *Play, Dreams, and Imitation in Childhood,* Piaget (1962 [1946]) asked a four-year-old child, "Could you call this table a cup and that cup a table?" "No," the child responded. "Why not?" "Because," explained the child, "you can't drink out of a table!"

Another example of the preoperational child's confusion of the mental and the physical is the tendency to believe that dreams are real. Dreams are cognitive events that originate within the dreamer but seem to be perceived through the dreamer's senses. These facts are understood by seven-year-olds, but many four-year-olds believe that dreams are real (Meyer & Shore, 2001). They think that their dreams are visible to others and that dreams come from the outside. It is as though they were watching a movie (Crain, 2000).

Focus on One Dimension at a Time: Mental Blinders

To gain further insight into preoperational thinking, consider these two problems: Imagine that you pour water from a low, wide glass into a tall, thin glass, as in Figure 9.2(b). Now, does the tall, thin glass contain more than, less than, or the same amount of water as the low, wide glass? We won't keep you in suspense. If you said the same (with possible minor exceptions for spillage and evaporation), you were correct.

a   b   c

Figure 9.2

Conservation

(a) The boy in this illustration agreed that the amount of water in two identical containers is equal. (b) He then watched as water from one container was poured into a tall, thin container. (c) When asked whether the amounts of water in the two containers are now the same, he says no.

Now that you're on a roll, here's another problem. If you flatten a ball of clay into a pancake, do you wind up with more, less, or the same amount of clay? If you said the same, you are correct once more.

To arrive at the correct answers to these questions, you must understand the law of **conservation.** *Question: What is conservation (i.e., in terms of the cognitive development of the child)?* The law of conservation states that properties of substances such as volume, mass, and number remain the same—or are conserved—even if you change their shape or arrangement.

Now, preoperational children are not conservationists. This does not mean that they throw out half-eaten meals (although they do so often enough). It means that they tend to focus on only one aspect of a problem at a time.

Conservation requires the ability to focus on two aspects of a situation at once, such as height and width. The preoperational boy in Figure 9.2(c) focuses or *centres* on only one dimension at a time, a characteristic of thought that Piaget called **centration.** Asked which glass has more water, he points to the tall glass. Why? When he looks at the glasses, he is swayed by the fact that the thinner glass is taller.

The preoperational child's failure to show conservation also comes about because of a characteristic of thought known as **irreversibility.** That is, the child fails to realize that an action such as pouring water from the tall glass to the squat glass can be reversed, restoring things to their original condition.

If all this sounds rather illogical, that is because it is illogical—or, to be precise, preoperational. But if you have any doubts concerning its accuracy, borrow a three-year-old and try the water experiment for yourself. Or you can check the "Lessons in Observation" video feature on page 322. The video shows children participating in the experiment.

After you have tried the experiment with the water, try this experiment on conservation of number. Make two rows with four pennies in each, about half an inch apart. As the three-year-old child is watching, move the pennies in the second row to about an inch apart, as in Figure 9.3. Then ask the child which row has more pennies. What do you think the child will say? Why?

conservation In cognitive psychology, the principle that properties of substances such as weight and mass remain the same (are conserved) when superficial characteristics such as their shapes or arrangement are changed.

centration Focusing on one dimension of a situation while ignoring others.

irreversibility Lack of recognition that actions can be reversed.

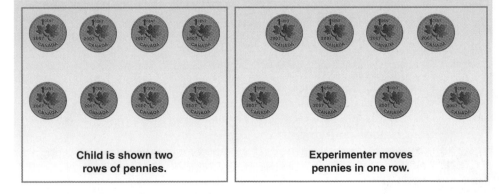

Child is shown two rows of pennies.   **Experimenter moves pennies in one row.**

Figure 9.3

Conservation of Number

In this demonstration, we begin with two rows of pennies that are spread out equally, as shown in the left-hand part of the drawing. Then one row of pennies is spread out more, as shown in the drawing on the right-hand side. We then ask the child, "Do the two rows still have the same number of pennies?" Do you think that a preoperational child will conserve the number of pennies or focus on the length of the longer row in arriving at an answer?

Figure 9.4

Class Inclusion

A typical 4-year-old child will say there are more dogs than animals in the example.

class inclusion The principle that one category or class of things can include several subclasses.

Class Inclusion

Class inclusion, as we are using it here, does not refer to whether a class is open to children from diverse backgrounds. We are talking about an aspect of conceptual thinking that you most likely take for granted: including new objects or categories in broader mental classes or categories.

Class inclusion also requires children to focus on two aspects of a situation at once. Class inclusion means that one category or class of things includes other subclasses. For example, the class "animals" includes the subclasses of dogs and cats.

In one of Piaget's class-inclusion tasks, the child is shown several objects from two subclasses of a larger class (see Figure 9.4). For example, a four-year-old child is shown pictures of four cats and six dogs. She is asked whether there are more dogs or more animals. Now, she knows what dogs and cats are. She also knows that they are both animals. What do you think she will say? Preoperational children typically answer that there are more dogs than animals (Piaget, 1963). That is, they do not show class inclusion.

Why do children make this error? According to Piaget, the preoperational child cannot think about the two subclasses and the larger class at the same time. Therefore, he or she cannot easily compare them. The child views dogs as dogs, or as animals, but finds it difficult to see them as both dogs and animals at once (Rabinowitz, Howe, & Saunders, 2002; Siegal, 2003).

click on
"Piaget's Preoperational Stage" in Module 2, Section 2, on your Observing Children and Adolescents CD-ROM. You can also visit the Student Book Companion Site to watch the video, answer the questions, and e-mail your responses to your professor.

Lessons in Observation
Piaget's Preoperational Stage

Learning Objectives

• How do pretend play and symbolic representation illustrate Piaget's preoperational stage of development?
• How do children show egocentrism?
• What is the meaning of conservation in Piaget's theory?
• How do children show failure to conserve?

Applied Lesson

How do preoperational inflexibility and irreversibility affect the children's failure to conserve in this video?

Critical Thinking

How did Piaget's experimental procedures and task demands influence the responses of children in conservation tasks?

Preoperational children, such as this young girl, fail to conserve volume. She believes that there is more liquid in the taller glass because she is focusing on height alone.

Developing in a World of Diversity

Cognitive Development and Concepts of Ethnicity and Race

What is the connection between cognitive development and the development of concepts about people from different ethnic and racial backgrounds? When is it most useful to intervene to help children develop open attitudes toward people from different backgrounds?

From interviews of 500 African American, Asian American, Latino and Latina American, and Native American children, psychologists Stephen Quintana (1998) and L. Rabasca (2000) concluded that children undergo four levels of understanding of ethnicity and race. Between the ages of three and six, children generally think about racial differences in physical terms. They do not necessarily see race as a fixed or stable attribute. They may think that a person could change his or her race by means of surgery or tanning in the sun.

From the ages of six to ten, children generally understand that race is a matter of ancestry that affects not only physical appearance but also one's language, diet, and leisure activities. But understanding at this stage is literal, or concrete. For example, children believe that being Mexican American means that one speaks Spanish and eats

How Stable a Trait Is Ethnicity in the Eyes of Children?
According to research by Quintana, children between the ages of three and six tend to think about racial differences in physical terms. They do not necessarily see race as a fixed or stable attribute. They may think that people can change their race by means of surgery or suntanning.

Mexican-style food. Interethnic friendships are likely to develop among children of this age group.

From the age of about ten to age fourteen, children tend to link ethnicity with social class. They become aware of connections between race and income, race and neighbourhood, and race and affirmative action.

During adolescence, many individuals begin to take pride in their ethnic heritage and experience a sense of belonging to their ethnic group. They are less open to intergroup relationships than younger children are.

Quintana's research found that middle childhood and early adolescence (the ages six to fourteen) are probably the best times to fend off the development of prejudice by teaching children about people from different cultural backgrounds. "That's when [children are] able to go beyond the literal meaning of the words and address their own observations about race and ethnicity," he noted (cited in Rabasca, 2000). Children at these ages also tend to be more open to forming relationships with children from different backgrounds than they are during adolescence.

An alternative approach to racial learning is put forth in The First R: How Children Learn Race and Racism (Van Ausdale & Feagin, 2001), which highlights the importance of how children create their own meanings of race based on their cognitive development and personal experiences in their social worlds.

© Ariel Skelley/Getty Images

Evaluation of Piaget

Piaget was an astute observer of the cognitive processes of young children. But more recent research questions the accuracy of his age estimates concerning children's failures (or apparent failures) to display certain cognitive skills. For example, Margaret Donaldson (1979) argued that the difficulty young children have with the three-mountains test may not be due to egocentrism. Instead, she attributes much of the problem to the demands that this particular approach makes on the child. Donaldson believes that the three-mountains test presents a lifeless scene, one devoid of people and human motives. By contrast, she has found that when children are asked to place a boy doll behind tabletop screens so that it cannot be "seen" by police dolls, three-and-a-half-year-olds succeed most of the time.

Comparison Chart of Perspectives			
Construct	Behaviourist-derived	Cognitive constructivist (Piaget)	Social constructivist (Vygotsky)
Knowledge	Fixed body of knowledge to acquire	Changing body of knowledge, individually constructed in social world	Changing body of knowledge, mutually constructed with others
Learning What	Acquisition of facts, skills, concepts	Active constructivism, restructuring prior knowledge	Collaborative construction of socially/culturally defined knowledge and values
Learning How	Through drill and guided practice	Through multiple opportunities and diverse processes to connect what is already known	Through socially and culturally constructed opportunities, tying to students' experience
Learning Where	Within individual's head	In interaction with others and environment	In collaboration with others through the social/cultural setting
Teaching	Transmission, presentation, telling (sage on the stage)	Challenge thinking toward more complete understanding (guide on the side)	Construct knowledge with students by sharing expertise and understanding (actuator of learning)
Motivation	Rewards, grades, jobs	Self-development, competence	Collective individual development through collaboration
Role of Teacher	Manager, supervisor	Facilitator, guide	Mediator, mentor, actuator
Role of Teacher Actions	Encourage on-time task completion, correct wrong answers	Create opportunities for interacting with meaningful ideas, materials, others	Construct with students opportunities for interacting with meaningful ideas, materials, others
Role of Peers	Not usually considered or rigidly structured	Not necessarily encouraged, but can stimulate thinking, raise questions	Assume part of knowledge construction, contribute to definition of knowledge, help define opportunities for learning

Comparison Chart of Perspectives

Construct	Behaviourist-derived	Cognitive constructivist (Piaget)	Social constructivist (Vygotsky)
Role of Student	Passive receptor of information	Active construction within mind	Active construction with others and self-negotiating meaning
	Worker	Generator, constructor	Cogenerator, coconstructor, reformulator
	Active listener, direction follower	Active thinker, explainer, Interpreter, questioner	Active thinker, explainer, interpreter, inquirer, social participator
Student View of Self	Rememberer/forgetter, algorithm follower, worker	Sense-maker, problem solver	Sense-maker, problem solver, socially appropriate member of collective
Evidence of Learning	Products	Process of inquiry	Process of inquiry, socially competent participation in collective
	Performance: answers on worksheets, standardized tests	Performance: explanation of reasoning	Performance: explanation of reasoning, social performance over multiple sites
	Assessed in single setting at one or periodic points	Ongoing assessment	Ongoing assessment over multiple sites
Purpose of School	Transmit, reproduce a common body of knowledge	Create new knowledge, learn strategies to continue learning	Create new knowledge, learn strategies to continue learning
			Prepare individuals as social members with expanding repertoires of appropriate ways of interacting

Source: Wink & Putney (2002).

Concept Review 9.1

Features of Preoperational Cognition, According to Piaget

Symbolic thought 	• Child uses symbols to represent objects and relationships. • Child engages in symbolic play. • Symbolic play grows more frequent and complex. • Child may have imaginary friend(s). • Mental operations are inflexible and irreversible.
Egocentrism 	• Child does not take viewpoint of others. • Child may be lacking in empathy for others. • Piaget used three-mountains test to assess egocentrism.
Precausal thinking	• Child believes things happen for a reason. • Child engages in transductive reasoning ("Should sleep because it's dark outside"). • Child shows animism (attributes life and will to inanimate objects). • Child shows artificialism (assumes environmental features are made by people).
Confusion of mental and physical events 	• Child assumes thoughts reflect external reality. • Child believes dreams are real.
Focus on one dimension at a time 	• Child does not understand law of conservation. • Child centres on one dimension at a time. • Child does not show appropriate class inclusion (may not include dogs as animals).

Note: Researchers find that the demand characteristics of testing and young children's developments in language and counting ability may lead to an underestimate of their general cognitive abilities.

Language development may also play a role in tests of children's egocentrism and other aspects of cognitive development. Young children may not quite understand what is being asked of them in the three-mountains test, even though they may proceed to select the (wrong) photograph rather quickly. Let us give you an example. Rathus was interested in knowing whether Allyn, at age two years nine months, thought that her mother could see her from another room. He asked, "Can Mommy see you now?" "Sure," said Allyn, "if she wants to." Allyn thought he was asking whether her mother could have permission to see her, not whether her mother had the capacity to see Allyn from behind a wall.

Newer studies indicate that the young child's understanding of causality is somewhat more sophisticated than Piaget believed (Hickling & Wellman, 2001). Again, much depends on how the task is presented. When four- to seven-year-olds are asked the kind of open-ended questions that Piaget used (e.g., "Where did the ocean come from?"), they give artificialistic responses, such as "The ocean comes from sinks." But when asked direct questions ("Do you think people made the oceans?"), most will correctly respond that people do not make natural things such as oceans or flowers, but they do make objects such as cups and TVs (Gelman & Kremer, 1991).

The demands of the standard conservation task may also present a misleading picture of the child's knowledge. Piaget and other experimenters filled identical beakers with the same amount of water and then poured water from one of the beakers into a beaker of another shape. Before pouring the water, the experimenter typically asked the child whether both beakers have the same amount of water and instructed the child to watch the pouring carefully. A variation on this experiment by Susan Rose and Marion Blank (1974) suggested that this approach can push the child to expect a change.

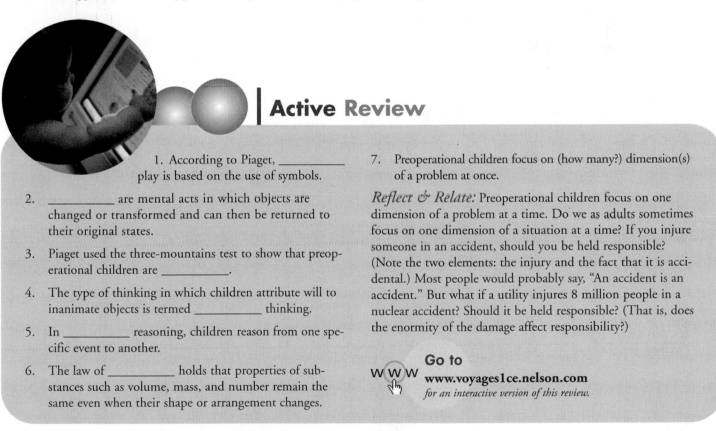

Active Review

1. According to Piaget, _____ play is based on the use of symbols.

2. _____ are mental acts in which objects are changed or transformed and can then be returned to their original states.

3. Piaget used the three-mountains test to show that preoperational children are _____.

4. The type of thinking in which children attribute will to inanimate objects is termed _____ thinking.

5. In _____ reasoning, children reason from one specific event to another.

6. The law of _____ holds that properties of substances such as volume, mass, and number remain the same even when their shape or arrangement changes.

7. Preoperational children focus on (how many?) dimension(s) of a problem at once.

Reflect & Relate: Preoperational children focus on one dimension of a problem at a time. Do we as adults sometimes focus on one dimension of a situation at a time? If you injure someone in an accident, should you be held responsible? (Note the two elements: the injury and the fact that it is accidental.) Most people would probably say, "An accident is an accident." But what if a utility injures 8 million people in a nuclear accident? Should it be held responsible? (That is, does the enormity of the damage affect responsibility?)

Go to

W W W **www.voyages1ce.nelson.com**
for an interactive version of this review.

Language Development: Why "Daddy Goed Away"

Children's language skills grow enormously during the preschool years. By the fourth year, children are asking adults and each other questions, taking turns talking, and engaging in lengthy conversations. *Question: What language developments occur during early childhood?* Some milestones of language development that occur during early childhood are shown in Table 9.3. Let us consider a number of them.

Age	Characteristics	Typical Sentences
2½ years	• There is rapid increase in vocabulary, with new additions each day. • There is no babbling. • Intelligibility is still not very good. • Child uses 2–3 words in sentences. • Child uses plurals. • Child uses possessives. • Child uses past tense. • Child uses some prepositions.	• Two cups. • Sarah's car. • It broke. • Keisha in bed.
3 years	• Child has vocabulary of some 1000 words. • Speech nears 100% intelligibility. • Articulation of *l* and *r* is frequently faulty. • Child uses 3–4 words in sentences. • Child uses yes–no questions. • Child uses *wh* questions. • Child uses negatives. • Child embeds one sentence within another.	• Will I go? • Where is the doggy? • I not eat yucky peas. • That's the book Mommy buyed me.
4 years	• Child has vocabulary of 1500–1600 words. • Speech is fluent. • Articulation is good except for *sh, z, ch,* and *j* sounds. • Child uses 5–6 words in sentences. • Child coordinates two sentences.	• I went to Allie's and I had cookies.

Table 9.x *Development of Language Skills in Early Childhood*

To watch children's development of language, click on the "Language Development" clip in Module 2, Section 2.

Development of Vocabulary: Words, Words, and More Words

The development of vocabulary proceeds at an extraordinary pace during early childhood. Preschoolers learn an average of nine new words per day (Rice, 1989). But how can this be possible when each new word has so many potential meanings? Consider the following example. A toddler observes a small black dog running through the park. His older sister points to the animal and says, "doggy." The word *doggy* could mean this particular dog, or all dogs, or all animals. It could refer to one part of the dog (e.g., its tail) or to its behaviour (running, barking) or to its characteristics (small, black) (Waxman, 2002, 2003). Does the child consider all these possibilities before determining what doggy actually means?

Studies have generally shown that word learning, in fact, does not occur gradually but is better characterized as a **fast-mapping** process in which the child quickly attaches a new word to its appropriate concept (Waxman, 2002, 2003; Wilkinson et al., 2003). The key to fast mapping seems to be that children are equipped with early cognitive biases or constraints that lead them to prefer certain meanings over others (Waxman, 2002, 2003).

fast mapping A process of quickly determining a word's meaning, which facilitates children's vocabulary development.

One bias that children have is assuming that words refer to whole objects and not to their component parts or their characteristics, such as colour, size, or texture (Bloom, 2002). This inclination is known as the **whole-object assumption**. In the example given at the beginning of the section, this bias would lead the young child to assume that "doggy" refers to the dog rather than to its tail, its colour, or its barking.

Children also seem to hold the bias that objects have only one label. Therefore, novel terms must refer to unfamiliar objects and not to familiar objects that already have labels. This is the **contrast assumption,** which is also known as the *mutual exclusivity assumption* (Bloom, 2002; Waxman, 2002, 2003). How might this bias help children figure out the meaning of a new word? Suppose that a child is shown two objects, one of which has a known label ("doggy") and one of which is an unknown object. Let us further suppose that an adult now says "Look at the lemur." If the child assumes that "doggy" and "lemur" each can refer to only one object, the child would correctly figure out that "lemur" refers to the other object and is not just another name for "doggy." Several studies have found evidence of this bias in children, which facilitates their word learning (Au & Glusman, 1990; Merriman & Schuster, 1991; Waxman & Senghas, 1992).

Vocabulary Development
When this adult points to the goat and says "goat," the child assumes that "goat" refers to the whole animal, rather than to its horns, fur, size, or colour. This bias, known as the *whole-object assumption*, helps children acquire a large vocabulary in a relatively short period of time.

(photo credit: Lawrence Migdale / Stock Boston)

Development of Grammar: Toward More Complex Language

Somewhat similar to the naming explosion in the second year is a "grammar explosion," which occurs during the third year (de Villiers & de Villiers, 1999). Children's sentence structure expands to include the words missing in telegraphic speech. During the third year, children usually add to their vocabulary an impressive array of articles (*a, an, the*), conjunctions (*and, but, or*), possessive adjectives (*your, her*), pronouns (*she, him, one*), and prepositions (*in, on, over, around, under, through*). Usually between the ages of three and four, children show knowledge of rules for combining phrases and clauses into complex sentences. An early example of a complex sentence is "You goed and Mommy goed, too." Table 9.4 shows some interesting examples of one of Rathus's daughter's use of language during the third year.

Overregularization

One of the more intriguing language developments—**overregularization**—is apparently based on the simple fact that children acquire grammatical rules as they learn language. At young ages they tend to apply these rules rather strictly, even in cases that call for exceptions (de Villiers & de Villiers, 1999; Stemberger, 2004). Consider the formation of the past tense and plurals in English. We add *d* or *ed* to regular verbs and *s* or *es* to regular nouns. Thus, *walk* becomes *walked* and *doggy* becomes *doggies*. But then there are irregular verbs and irregular nouns. For example, *sit* becomes *sat* and *go* becomes *went*. *Sheep* remains *sheep* (plural) and *child* becomes *children*.

whole-object assumption
The assumption that words refer to whole objects and not to their component parts or characteristics.

contrast assumption The assumption that objects have only one label. Also known as the mutual exclusivity assumption (if a word means one thing, it cannot mean another).

overregularization The application of regular grammatical rules for forming inflections (e.g., past tense and plurals) to irregular verbs and nouns.

Examples of Allyn's Speech during the Third Year

- Objecting to something said to her: "No, that is not a good talk to say. I don't like that."
- Describing her younger sister: "Jordan is very laughy today."
- On the second floor of her home: "This is not home. This is upstairs."
- Objecting to her father's departure: "Stay here for a couple of whiles."
- Directing her father to turn up the stereo: "Make it a big louder, not a small louder."
- Use of the plural number: "I see two policemans."
- Use of the past tense: "I goed on the choo-choo."
- Requesting a nickel: "Give me another money."
- Explaining that she and her mother are finished singing a song: "We singed it all up."
- Requesting an empty cup: "Give me that. I need it to drink nothing."
- Use of the possessive case: "That car is blue, just like us's."
- When she wants her father to hold her: "I want you to pick up me."
- Directing her father to turn on the stereo: "Push the button and make it too loud." (A minute later): "Make it more louder."
- Refusing to answer a question: "I don't want you to ask that to me."
- Confessing what she did with several coins: "I taked those money and put it on the shelf."

Allyn, Age 2½

Courtesy of Spencer A. Rathus, author

At first, children learn a small number of these irregular constructions by imitating their parents. Two-year-olds tend to form them correctly temporarily. Then they become aware of the syntactic rules for forming the past tense and plurals in English. As a result, they tend to make charming errors (Stemberger, 2004). ***Truth or Fiction Revisited:*** It is true that a two-and-a-half-year-old girl said, "We singed it all up" after she and her mother had finished singing a song. Some three- to five-year-olds are more likely to say, "Mommy sitted down" than "Mommy sat down." They are likely to talk about the "sheeps" they "seed" on the farm and about all the "childs" they ran into at the playground. ***Truth or Fiction Revisited:*** It is also true that a three-year-old is likely to say, "Daddy goed away" rather than "Daddy went away" because the child does understand rules of grammar. The child is correctly applying a rule for forming the past tense of regular verbs to an irregular verb.

Some parents recognize that their children were forming the past tense of irregular verbs correctly and that they then began to make errors. The thing to remember is that overregularization represents an advance in the development of syntax. Overregularization reflects accurate knowledge of grammar—not faulty language development. (Really.) In another year or two, *mouses* will be boringly transformed into *mice*, and Mommy will no longer have *sitted* down. Parents might as well enjoy overregularization while they can.

In a classic experiment designed to show that preschool children are not just clever mimics in their formation of plurals but have actually grasped rules of grammar, Berko (1958) showed children pictures of nonexistent animals (see Figure 9.5). She first showed them a single animal and said, "This is a wug." Then she showed them a picture of two animals and said, "Now there are two of them. There are two _____," asking the children to finish the sentence. Ninety-one percent of the children said "wugs," giving the correct plural of the bogus word.

This is a wug.   **Now there are two of them.**   **There are two _____.**

Figure 9.5
Wugs

Wugs? Why not? Many bright, sophisticated college students have not heard of "wugs." What a pity. Here are several wugs—actually, make-believe animals used in a study to learn whether preschool children can use rules of grammar to form the plurals of unfamiliar nouns.

Asking Questions

Children's first questions are telegraphic and characterized by a rising pitch at the end, which signifies a question mark in English (Rowland & Pine, 2000). "More milky?" for example, can be translated into "May I have more milk?," "Would you like more milk?," or "Is there more milk?," depending on the context. It is usually toward the latter part of the third year that the *wh* questions appear. Consistent with the child's general cognitive development, certain *wh* questions (*what, who,* and *where*) appear earlier than others (*why, when, which,* and *how*) (de Villiers & de Villiers, 1999). *Why* is usually too philosophical for a two-year-old, and *how* is too involved. Two-year-olds are also likely to be now-oriented, so that *when* is of less than immediate concern. By the fourth year, most children are spontaneously producing *why, when,* and *how* questions. These *wh* words are initially tacked on to the beginnings of sentences. "Where Mommy go?" can stand for "Where is Mommy going?," "Where did Mommy go?," or "Where will Mommy go?," and its meaning must be derived from context. Later on, the child will add the auxiliary verbs *is, did,* and *will* to indicate whether the question concerns the present, past, or future.

Passive Sentences

Passive sentences, such as "The food is eaten by the dog," are difficult for two- and three-year-olds to understand, and so young preschoolers almost never produce them. In a fascinating study of children's comprehension (Strohner & Nelson, 1974), two- to five-year-olds used puppets and toys to act out a number of sentences that were read to them. Two- and three-year-olds in the study made errors in acting out passive sentences (e.g., "The car was hit by the truck") 70 percent of the time. Older children had less difficulty interpreting the meanings of passive sentences correctly. However, most children usually do not produce passive sentences spontaneously even at the ages of five and six.

Pragmatics: Preschoolers Can Be Practical

Pragmatics in language development refers to the practical aspects of communication. Children are showing pragmatism when they adjust their speech to fit the social situation. For example, children show greater formality in their choice of words and syntax when they are role-playing high-status figures, such as teachers or physicians, in their games. They also say "please" more often when making requests of high-status people (Owens, 1990). Children also show pragmatism in their adoption of Motherese when they are addressing a younger child.

pragmatics The practical aspects of communication, such as adaptation of language to fit the social situation.

Pragmatism provides another example of the ways in which cognitive and language development are intertwined. As we saw earlier in the chapter, preschoolers tend to be egocentric; that is, they show some difficulty in taking the viewpoints of other people. A two-year-old telling another child "Gimme my book," without specifying which book, is not just assuming that the other child knows what she herself knows.

A Closer Look | Canada's Languages: A Multilingual Nation

Learning a second language is common for Canadian children. Canada's two official languages are English and French, but Canada, in fact, has a large number of language groups, as revealed by the 2001 census. The majority of Canadians (59 percent) listed English as their mother tongue; 23 percent listed French; and just under 1 percent listed both French and English. However, just about 18 percent listed "other" as their first language (Allen, 2004).

In contemporary Canadian society, learning more than one language and being bilingual is considered an asset. However, this has not always been the case. Language-based research in the '50s and '60s led to erroneous conclusions about the pros and cons of bilingual or multilingual education—that learning more than one language could be detrimental to overall language development. Present-day research confirms what many multilingual nations around the world already know—that learning more than one language can be enriching, not restrictive, in the long term. But understanding bilingual or multilingual language acquisition is complex (Bialystok & Herman, 1999). Canadian bilingualism researcher Ellen Bialystok, a professor of psychology at York University, is interested in the relationships between bilingualism and cognitive development, language proficiency, and reading. Her work has great practical relevance for many Canadian children who are growing up in multicultural settings. While there are some noted benefits of bilingualism (e.g., it speeds up the development of cognitive functions dealing with attention and inhibition), bilingual education is affected by cultural communities and the opportunities within those communities to engage in bilingual or multilingual practice (Bialystok, 2001; Bialystok, McBride-Chang, & Luk, 2005).

The reasons parents choose bilingual education are varied. In Alberta, for example, bilingual schools are quite common, and parents have an opportunity to send their children to publicly funded schools that offer nonofficial language instruction in Cree, Hebrew, Ukrainian, or

Chinese, for example. This educational approach allows for cultural stability for children whose second language acquisition can include the child's native language (e.g., Chinese) as well as Canada's primary languages. However, instruction in nonofficial languages is not always possible or readily available.

Let's turn our attention to the issue of French immersion. Table 9.5 shows the percentage of students in English-language school systems who are currently enrolled in French immersion programs in Canada. French-immersion students tend to do as well as (or better than) their English-only-program peers in main subject areas (Allen, 2004; Holobow, Genesee & Lambert, 1991; Turnbull, Hart, & Lapkin, 2003). There have been many explanations put forth for this. It has been suggested that French-immersion students are more likely to be from high socioeconomic status backgrounds and to have parents with postsecondary education. However, even when these factors are controlled for, French-immersion students outperform their monolinguistic (English-only) peers on certain reading achievement tests. There are other issues to consider. For example, selection and attrition in French-immersion programs may influence reading performance. An additional caution put forth by language researchers is that looking for global advantages or universal effects of bilingualism may be misleading (Bruck & Genesee, 1995) since there may be fundamental differences between bilingual and monolingual students and their home environments. From a practical perspective, being able to function well in one or both of Canada's official languages is a realistic goal for many Canadian children when supported by communities (parents, teachers, administrators, and governments).

She is also overestimating the clearness of her communication and how well she is understood (Beal & Flavell, 1983). Once children can perceive the world through the eyes of others, however, they advance in their abilities to make themselves understood to others. Now the child recognizes that the other child will require a description of the book or of its location to carry out the request. Between the ages of three and five, egocentric speech gradually disappears and there is rapid development of pragmatic skills. The child's conversation shows increasing sensitivity to the listener, as, for example, in allowing turn taking (Baker & Cantwell, 1991).

The Relationship between Language and Cognition

Language and cognitive development are strongly interwoven (Rakison & Oakes, 2003; Waxman, 2002, 2003). For example, the child gradually gains the capacity to discriminate between animals on the basis of distinct features, such as size, patterns of movement, and the sounds they make. At the same time, the child is also acquiring words that represent broader categories, such as mammal and animal.

But it's chicken and egg time. Which comes first? *Question: What is the relationship between language and cognition?* Does the child first develop concepts and then acquire the language to describe them, or does the child's increasing language ability lead to the development of new concepts?

Does Cognitive Development Precede Language Development?

Jean Piaget (1976) believed that cognitive development precedes language development. He argued that children must first understand concepts before they can use words that describe the concepts. Object permanence emerges toward the end of the first year. Piaget believed that words that relate to the disappearance and appearance of people and objects (such as *all gone* and *bye-bye*) are used only after the emergence of object permanence.

	English-Language School System Students Enrolled in French Immersion Programs	
	Enrolled in French immersion	Enrolled in immersion and had started before grade 4 (early immersion)
	Percentage of students	
Newfoundland and Labrador	7	57
Prince Edward Island	20	59
Nova Scotia	12	21
New Brunswick	32	39
Quebec	22	74
Ontario	6	57
Manitoba	6	90
Saskatchewan	3	87
Alberta	4	80
British Columbia	2	55

Source: Statistics Canada (2000b).

From Piaget's perspective, children learn words in order to describe classes or categories that they have already created (Nelson, 1982). Children can learn the word *doggy* because they have already perceived the characteristics that distinguish dogs from other things.

Some studies support the notion that cognitive concepts may precede language. For example, the vocabulary explosion that occurs at about eighteen months of age is related to the child's ability to group a set of objects into two categories, such as "dolls" and "cars" (Gopnik & Meltzoff, 1987, 1992). Both developments may reflect the child's understanding that objects belong in categories. Other studies (Brownell, 1988; Ogura, 1991) show that as children make the transition from one- to two-word sentences, they also begin to string together sequences of play activities (such as placing a doll in bed, covering it with a blanket, and rocking it). These transitions seem to indicate a basic change from "oneness" to "twoness" that is occurring in the child's cognitive development (Bates et al., 1987).

Does Language Development Precede Cognitive Development?

Although many theorists argue that cognitive development precedes language development, others reverse the causal relationship and claim that children create cognitive classes in order to understand things that are labelled by words (Clark, 1983). When children hear the word *dog*, they try to understand it by searching for characteristics that separate dogs from other things. Research with four-and-a-half-year-olds shows that descriptions of events can prompt children to create categories in which to classify occurrences (Nazzi & Gopnik, 2000).

The Interactionist View: Outer Speech and Inner Speech

Today, most developmentalists find something of value in each of these cognitive views (Rakison & Oakes, 2003; Waxman, 2002). In the early stages of language development, concepts often precede words, so that many of the infant's words describe classes that have already developed. Later, however, language is not merely the servant of thought; language influences thought.

Lev Vygotsky also made key contributions to our understanding of the relationships between concepts and words. Vygotsky believed that during most of the first year, vocalizations and thought are separate but that during the second year, thought and speech—cognition and language—combine forces. "Speech begins to serve intellect and thoughts begin to be spoken" (Vygotsky, 1962, p. 43). Usually during the second year, children discover that objects have labels. Learning labels becomes more active, more self-directed. At some point, children ask what new words mean. Learning new words clearly fosters the creation of new categories and classes. An interaction develops in which classes are filled with labels for new things, and labels nourish the blossoming of new classes.

inner speech Vygotsky's concept of the ultimate binding of language and thought. Inner speech originates in vocalizations that may regulate the child's behaviour and become internalized by age 6 or 7.

Vygotsky's concept of **inner speech** is a key feature of his position. At first, according to Vygotsky, children's thoughts are spoken aloud. You can overhear three-year-olds giving themselves instructions as they play with toys. At this age their vocalizations may serve to regulate their behaviour. But language gradually becomes internalized. What was spoken aloud at four and five becomes an internal dialogue by six or seven. This internal dialogue, or inner speech, is the ultimate binding of language and thought. Inner speech is involved in the development of planning and self-regulation and seems to facilitate learning. Vygotsky's ideas about the self-regulative function of language have inspired psychological treatment approaches for children with self-control problems. For example, hyperactive children can be taught to use self-directed speech to increase self-control (Crain, 2000).

And so language is inextricably bound not only to thought but also to aspects of personality and social behaviour in the young child. It is to these areas of development that we turn in Chapter 10.

Active Review

8. Word learning does not occur gradually but is better characterized as a fast-_____ process.

9. The _____-object assumption refers to the fact that young children assume that words refer to whole objects and not to their component parts or to their characteristics, such as colour or texture.

10. Young children also tend to assume that objects have _____ (how many?) label(s).

11. Therefore, they have the _____ assumption, which holds that novel terms must refer to unfamiliar objects and not to familiar objects that already have labels.

12. Vygotsky's concept of _____ speech refers to the fact that what was spoken aloud at four and five becomes an internal dialogue by six or seven.

Reflect & Relate: What are some of the new words you are learning by reading this book? Do the words you chose to list have a single meaning or multiple meanings? How does their number of meanings affect your acquisition of these words? (Consider the examples of conservation, scaffold, and mapping.)

WWW **Go to**
www.voyages1ce.nelson.com
for an interactive version of this summary review.

Theory of Mind: What Is the Mind? How Does It Work?

Adults appear to have a commonsense understanding of how the mind works. This understanding, known as a **theory of mind,** allows us to explain and predict behaviour by referring to mental processes. For example, we understand that we can acquire knowledge through our senses or through hearsay. We understand the distinction between external and mental events and between how things appear and how they really are. We are able to infer the perceptions, thoughts, and feelings of others. We understand that mental states affect behaviour (Flavell et al., 2002; Siegal, 2003).

theory of mind A commonsense understanding of how the mind works.

Question: What are children's ideas about how the mind works? Piaget might have predicted that preoperational children are too egocentric and too focused on misleading external appearances to have a theory of mind. But research has shown that even preschool-aged children can accurately predict and explain human action and emotion in terms of mental states. They are beginning to understand where knowledge comes from. And they have a rudimentary ability to distinguish appearance from reality (Wellman, 2002; Wellman & Liu, 2004; Wellman, Cross, & Watson, 2001). Let us consider these developments.

False Beliefs: Just Where Are Those Crayons?

One important indication of the young child's understanding that mental states affect behaviour is the ability to understand false beliefs. This concept involves children's ability to separate their beliefs from those of another person who has false knowledge of a situation. It is illustrated in a study of three-year-olds by Louis Moses and John Flavell (1990). The children were shown a videotape in which a girl named Cathy found some crayons in a bag. When Cathy left the room briefly, a clown entered the room. The clown removed the crayons from the bag, hid them in a drawer, and put rocks in the bag instead. When Cathy returned, the children were asked whether Cathy thought there were going to be rocks or crayons in the bag. Most of the three-year-olds incorrectly answered "rocks," demonstrating their difficulty in understanding that the other person's belief would be different from their own (see Figure 9.6). But by the age of four to five years, children do not have trouble with this concept and correctly answer "crayons" (Flavell, 1993; Flavell, Flavell, Green, & Moses, 1990). At this age, they also start to understand that beliefs may be held with differing degrees of certainty (Moore, Pure, & Furrow, 1990).

Another intriguing demonstration of the false belief concept comes from studies of children's ability to deceive others. For example, Beate Sodian and her colleagues (1991) asked children to hide a toy truck driver in one of five cups in a sandbox so that another person could not find it. The child was given the opportunity to deceive the other person by removing real trails in the sand and creating false ones. Once again, four-year-olds acted in ways that were likely to mislead the other person. Younger children did not.

From the research we have considered, it is tempting to conclude that an understanding of false belief and deception does not emerge until age four (Peskin, 1992; Ruffman, Olson, Ash, & Keenan, 1993). But some studies have found that under certain conditions, children at age three and even younger may show some knowledge of these concepts. One condition involves asking three-year-olds specific questions about their beliefs and those of the other person (Lewis & Osborne, 1990).

The ability to understand false beliefs is related to the development of executive functioning, including working memory, ability to pay sustained attention to problems, and self-control (Flynn, O'Malley, & Wood, 2004; Hala, Hug, & Henderson, 2003; Ziv & Frye, 2003).

Origins of Knowledge: Where Does It Come From?

Another aspect of theory of mind is how we acquire knowledge. *Questions: Do children understand where their knowledge comes from? If so, how early do they show this ability?*

Figure 9.6

False Beliefs

John Flavell and his colleagues showed preschoolers a videotape in which a girl named Cathy found crayons in a bag (a). When Cathy left the room, a clown entered, removed the crayons from the bag, hid them in a drawer (b), and filled the bag with rocks (c). When asked whether Cathy thought there would be rocks or crayons in the bag, most 3-year-olds said "rocks." Most 4-year-olds correctly answered "crayons," showing the ability to separate their own beliefs from those of someone who has erroneous knowledge of a situation.

By age three, most children begin to realize that people gain knowledge about something by looking at it (Pratt & Bryant, 1990). By age four, children understand that particular senses provide information about only certain qualities of an object—for example, we come to know an object's colour through our eyes, but we learn about its weight by feeling it (O'Neill & Chong, 2001). In a study by Daniela O'Neill and Alison Gopnik (1991), three-, four-, and five-year-olds learned about the contents of a toy tunnel in three different ways: They saw the contents, were told about them, or felt them. The children then were asked to state what was in the tunnel and also how they knew what was in the tunnel. Although four- and five-year-olds had no trouble identifying the sources of their knowledge, the three-year-olds did. For example, after feeling but not seeing a ball in the tunnel, a number of three-year-olds told the experimenter that they could tell it was a blue ball. The children apparently did not realize that it was impossible to discover the ball's colour just by feeling it.

The Appearance-Reality Distinction: Appearances Are More Deceiving at Some Ages than at Others

Questions: Is seeing believing? What do preoperational children have to say about that? One of the most important things children must acquire in developing a theory of mind is a clear understanding of the difference between real events on the one hand and mental events, fantasies, and misleading appearances on the other hand (Bialystock & Senman, 2004; Flavell et al., 2002). This is known as the **appearance-reality distinction**.

Piaget's view was that children do not differentiate reality from appearances or mental events until the age of seven or eight. But more recent studies have found that children's ability to distinguish between the two emerges in the preschool years. Children as young as age three can distinguish between pretend actions and real actions, between pictures of objects and the actual objects, and between toy versions of an object and the real object (Wellman, 2002). By the age of four, children make a clear distinction between real items (such as a cup) and imagined items (such as an imagined cup or an imagined monster) (Harris, Brown, Marriott, Whittall, & Harmer, 1991).

Despite these accomplishments, preoperational children still show some difficulties in recognizing the difference between reality and appearances. According to Flavell and his colleagues (2000), this is because children of this age still have only a limited understanding of **mental representations**. They have trouble understanding that a real object or event can take many forms in our minds. For example, in a study by Marjorie Taylor and Barbara Hort (1990), children from the ages of three to five were shown a variety of objects that had misleading appearances, such as an eraser that looked like a cookie. Children initially reported that the eraser looked like a cookie. But once they learned that it was actually an eraser, they tended to report that it looked like an eraser, ignoring its cookie-like appearance. Apparently, the children could not mentally represent the eraser as both being an eraser and looking like a cookie.

Three-year-olds also apparently cannot understand changes in their mental states. In one study (Gopnik & Slaughter, 1991), three-year-olds were shown a crayon box. They consistently said they thought crayons were inside. The box was opened, revealing birthday candles, not crayons. When the children were asked what they had thought was in the box before it was opened, they now said "candles."

Children two and a half to three years old also find it difficult to understand the relationship between a scale model and the larger object or space that it represents (DeLoache, 2002; Sharon & DeLoache, 2003). Perhaps this is because the child cannot conceive that the model can be two things at once: both a representation of something and an object in its own right.

appearance-reality distinction The difference between real events on the one hand and mental events, fantasies, and misleading appearances on the other hand.

mental representations The mental forms that a real object or event can take, which may differ from one another. (Successful problem solving is aided by accurate mental representation of the elements of the problem.)

Active Review

13. Moses and Flavell used crayons and a clown to learn whether preschoolers can understand _____ beliefs.

14. By age three, most children begin to realize that people gain knowledge about things through the _____.

Reflect & Relate: Think of research on the origins of knowledge—on where knowledge comes from. Can you relate this area of research to arguments we might find among adults about sources of knowledge such as experience versus revelation?

WWW **Go to**
www.voyages1ce.nelson.com
for an interactive version of this summary review.

Development of Memory: Creating Files and Retrieving Them

Even newborns have some memory skills, and memory improves substantially throughout the first two years of life (Flavell et al., 2002). *Question: What sorts of memory skills do children possess in early childhood?*

Memory Tasks: Recognition and Recall

Two of the basic tasks used in the study of memory are recognition and recall. Recognition is the easiest type of memory task. For this reason, multiple-choice tests are easier than fill-in-the-blank or essay tests. In a **recognition** test, one simply indicates whether a presented item has been seen before or which of a number of items is paired with a stimulus (as in a multiple-choice test). Children are capable of simple recognition during early infancy; they recognize their mother's nursing pads, her voice, and her face. To test recognition memory in a preschooler, you might show the child some objects and then present those objects along with some new ones. The child is then asked which objects you showed the first time.

Recall is more difficult than recognition. In a **recall** task, children must reproduce material from memory without any cues. If I ask you to name the capital of Wyoming, that is a test of recall. A recall task for a preschooler might consist of showing him or her some objects, taking them away, and asking the child to name the objects from memory.

When preschoolers are presented with objects, words, or TV shows, they typically recognize more later on than they can recall (Holliday, 2003; Oates, Blades, & Gunter, 2002). In fact, younger preschoolers are almost as good as older ones in recognizing objects they have seen. But they are not nearly as good at recall (Holliday, 2003). In Figure 9.7, compare the ability of three- and four-and-a-half-year-olds to recognize and recall various objects from a life-size playhouse (Jones, Swift, & Johnson, 1988). (We will discuss the "activities" part of this figure later.)

Competence of Memory in Early Childhood

Until recently, most studies of children's memory were conducted in laboratory settings. The tasks had little meaning for the children. The results appeared to show that the memories of young children are deficient relative to those of older children. But

recognition A memory task in which the individual indicates whether presented information has been experienced previously.

recall A memory task in which the individual must reproduce material from memory without any cues.

parents often tell you that their children have excellent memories for events. It turns out that they are right. More recently, psychologists have focused their research on children's memory for meaningful events and activities.

Truth or Fiction Revisited: It is not true that one- and two-year-olds are too young to remember past events. Preschoolers' memories are apparently quite impressive (Nelson, 1990, 1993). Children as young as eleven and a half months of age can remember organized sequences of events they have just experienced (Bauer & Mandler, 1992). Even after a delay of six weeks, sixteen-month-old children can reenact a sequence of events they experienced only one time, such as placing a ball in a cup, covering it with another cup, and shaking the resulting "rattle" (Bauer & Mandler, 1990). By the age of four years, children can remember events that occurred at least a year and a half earlier (Fivush & Hammond, 1990).

Katherine Nelson (1990, 1993) interviewed children between the ages of two and five to study their memory for recurring events in their lives, such as having dinner, playing with friends, and going to birthday parties. She found that even three-year-olds can present coherent, orderly accounts of familiar events. Furthermore, young children seem to form **scripts,** which are abstract, generalized accounts of these repeated events. For example, in describing what happens during a birthday party, a child might say, "You play games, open presents, and eat cake" (Fivush, 2002). Details of particular events often are omitted. However, an unusual experience, such as a devastating hurricane, may be remembered in detail for many years (Fivush, Sales, Goldberg, Bahrick, & Parker, 2004).

Young children begin forming scripts after experiencing an event only once. The script becomes more elaborate with repeated experiences. As might be expected, older preschoolers form detailed scripts more quickly than younger preschoolers (Fivush, 2002).

Even though children as young as one and two years of age can clearly remember events, these memories seldom last into adulthood. This memory of specific events—known as **autobiographical memory**—appears to be linked to the development of language skills, as children begin to talk with their parents and others about past events (Nelson & Fivush, 2004).

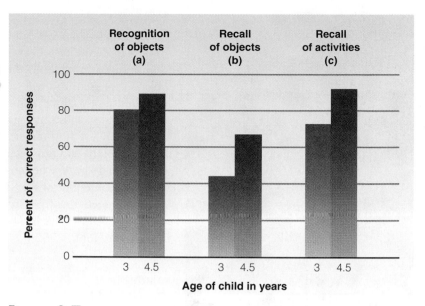

Figure 9.7

Recognition and Recall Memory

Preschoolers can recognize previously seen objects (a) better than they can recall them (b). They are also better at recalling their activities (c) than at recalling objects (b). Older preschoolers (green bars) have better memories than younger ones (gold bars).
Source: Jones et al. (1988).

scripts Abstract generalized accounts of familiar repeated events.

autobiographical memory The memory of specific episodes or events.

Factors Influencing Memory

Question: What factors affect memory in early childhood? The factors that affect memory include what the child is asked to remember, the interest level of the child, the availability of retrieval cues or reminders, and what memory measure we are using. Let us discuss each of these in turn.

Childhood Memory
Despite his youth, this boy will most likely remember this traumatic experience in detail for years to come.

Types of Memory

Preschoolers' memories for activities are better than their memories for objects. Return to Figure 9.6. Compare children's accuracy in recalling the activities they engaged in while in the playhouse with their accuracy in recalling the objects they used. You will see that children were much better at recalling their activities (e.g., washing a shirt, chopping ice) than they were at recalling specific objects, such as shirts and icepicks (Jones et al., 1988).

Children also find it easier to remember events that follow a logical order than events that do not occur in a particular order. For instance, three- and five-year-olds have a better memory for the activities involved in making pretend cookies out of Play-Doh (you put the ingredients in the bowl, then mix the ingredients, then roll out the dough, and so on) than they do for the activities involved in sand play, which can occur in any order (Fivush, Kuebli, & Clubb, 1992).

Interest Level

There is nothing new about the idea that we pay more attention to the things that interest us. The world is abuzz with signals, and we tend to remember those to which we pay attention. Attention opens the door to memory.

Interest level and motivation also contribute to memory among young children (Ghetti & Alexander, 2004; Sales, Fivush, & Peterson, 2003). In one study, for example, three-year-old boys were more interested in playing with toys such as cars and rockets, whereas three-year-old girls were more interested in playing with dolls, dishes, and teddy bears. Later, the children showed better recognition and recall for the toys in which they were interested (Renninger, 1990). Even by this age, gender-role expectations may exert their influence on cognitive development.

Retrieval Cues

To retrieve information (a file) from your computer's storage, you have to remember its name or some part of it. Then you can use a Find routine. The name is the retrieval cue. In the same way, we need retrieval cues to find things in our own memories.

Although young children can remember a great deal, they depend more than older children do on cues provided by adults to help them retrieve their memories. Consider the following interchange between a mother and her two-year-old child (Hudson, 1990, p. 186):

Mother: What did we look for in the grass and in the bushes?

Child: Easter bunny.

Mother: Did we hide candy eggs outside in the grass?

Child: (nods)

Mother: Remember looking for them? Who found two? Your brother?

Child: Yes, brother.

Preschoolers whose parents elaborate on the child's experiences and ask questions that encourage the child to contribute information to the narrative remember an episode better than children whose parents simply provide reminders (Nelson & Fivush, 2004). Parental assistance is more important under some conditions than others. For example, when four-year-olds were internally motivated to remember items needed to prepare their own bag lunches, they did equally well with or without parental coaching. But when the task was simply to recall a series of items, they did better with parental assistance (Rogoff & Mistry, 1990).

Types of Measurement

What we find is in part determined by how we measure it. Children's memory is often measured or assessed by asking them to say what they remember. But verbal reports, especially from preschoolers, appear to underestimate children's memory (Mandler, 1990). In one longitudinal study, children's memory for certain events was tested at age two and a half and again at age four. Most of the information recalled at age four had not been mentioned at age two and a half, indicating that when they were younger, the children remembered much more than they reported (Fivush & Hammond, 1990).

What measures might be more accurate than verbal report? One study found that when young children were allowed to use dolls to reenact an event, their recall was much better than when they gave a verbal report of the event (Goodman, Rudy, Bottoms, & Aman, 1990).

Memory Strategies: Remembering to Remember

Question: How do we remember to remember?

When adults and older children are trying to remember things, they use strategies to help their memory. One common strategy is mental repetition, or **rehearsal.** If you are trying to remember a new friend's phone number, for example, you might repeat it several times. Another strategy is to organize into categories things to be remembered. Many students outline textbook chapters to prepare for an exam. This is a way of organizing information in a meaningful way, which makes it easier to learn and remember (Kail, 1990). Similarly, if you are going to buy some things at the grocery store, you might mentally group together items that belong to the same category: dairy items, produce, household cleaners, and so on.

But preschool children generally do not appear to use memory strategies on their own initiative. Most young children do not spontaneously engage in rehearsal until about five years of age (Small, 1990). They also rarely group objects into related categories to help them remember. By about age five, many children have learned to verbalize information silently to themselves—counting in their heads, for example, instead of aloud. This strategy improves their ability to remember visual information (Adler, 1993).

But even very young children are capable of using some simple and concrete memory aids to help them remember. They engage in behaviours such as looking, pointing, and touching when trying to remember. For example, in a study by Judith DeLoache and her colleagues (1985), eighteen- to twenty-four-month-old children observed as the experimenter hid a Big Bird doll under a pillow. Then they were given attractive toys to play with and, after a short period of time, were asked to find the hidden object. During the play interval, the children frequently looked or pointed at the hiding place or repeated the name of the hidden object. These behaviours suggest the beginning of the use of strategies to prompt the memory.

Young children can also be taught to successfully use strategies they might not use on their own. For example, six-year-old children who are trained to rehearse show a marked improvement in their ability to recall items on a memory test (Small, 1990). Similarly, requiring preschoolers to sort objects into categories enhances memory (Lange & Pierce, 1992; Schneider & Pressley, 1989). Even three- and four-year-olds will use rehearsal and labelling if they are instructed to try to remember something (Fabricius & Cavalier, 1989; Weissberg & Paris, 1986).

rehearsal Repetition.

©Photodisc/Getty Images

Helping Young Children Remember
Memory functioning in early childhood—and at other ages—is aided when adults provide cues to help children remember. Adults can help by elaborating on the child's experiences and asking questions that encourage the child to contribute information.

The preschooler's use of memory strategies is not nearly as sophisticated as that of the school-aged child. The use of memory strategies and the child's understanding of how memory works advance greatly in middle childhood. For a fun application of some of the material we have just covered you might enjoy reading *Wilfred Gordon MacDonald Partridge* by Mem Fox. It is a children's book that deals with a child grappling with the idea of memories while building a friendship with a senior adult with Alzheimer's disease.

Active Review

15. Children are capable of simple (recognition or recall?) during infancy.

16. Memory for events in one's life is referred to as _____ memory.

17. Preschoolers' memories for activities are (better or worse?) than their memories for objects.

18. Interest level is (positively or negatively?) connected with ability to remember.

19. Using mental repetition to remember is termed _____.

Reflect & Relate: How do you prepare for a test? How do you remember lists of new vocabulary words, for example? What strategies does your textbook author (that's us!) use to help you remember the subject matter in this course?

Go to
WWW **www.voyages1ce.nelson.com**
for an interactive version of this review.

Factors in Cognitive Development: On Being in "the Zone" (of Proximal Development)

Very much like Piaget, Vygotsky believed that children construct their own understanding and are not passive agents in their own development (Budrova & Leong, 2007). Vygotsky's four basic principles are "(1) children construct knowledge, (2) development cannot be separated from its social context, (3) learning can lead development, and (4) language plays a central role in mental development" (Budrova & Leong, 2007, p. 9).

Question: What are some of the factors that influence cognitive development in early childhood? One of the most important factors is scaffolding, Vygotsky's concept of social supports for cognitive development. Other factors include social and family factors—family income, the parents' educational level, family size, parents' mental health, and stressful family events such as divorce, job loss, or illness (Bradley, Burchinal, & Casey, 2001). In this section, we consider Vygotsky's theory, the home environment, preschool education, and television.

Scaffolding and the Zone of Proximal Development: Zoning for Cognitive Development

Parental responsiveness and interaction with the child are key ingredients in the child's cognitive development. One component of this social interaction is **scaffolding** (see Chapter 1). A scaffold is a temporary structure used for holding workers during building construction. Similarly, cognitive scaffolding refers to temporary support provided by a parent or teacher to a learning child. The guidance provided by the adult decreases as the child becomes more skilled and capable of carrying out the task without help (Davis, 2003; Gregory & Whiren, 2003).

scaffolding Vygotsky's term for temporary cognitive structures or methods of solving problems that help the child as he or she learns to function independently.

A related concept is Vygotsky's (1978) **zone of proximal development (ZPD).** The zone refers to the gap between what the child is capable of doing now and what she or he could do with help from others. Adults or older children can best guide the child through this zone by gearing their assistance to the child's capabilities (Davis, 2003; Flavell et al., 2002).

The concepts of scaffolding and the zone of proximal development are illustrated in a study in which three- and five-year-old children were given the task of sorting doll furniture into the rooms where they belonged (Freund, 1990). Children who were allowed to interact with their mothers performed at a higher level than children who worked alone. Furthermore, mothers adjusted the amount of help they gave to fit the child's level of competence. They gave younger children more detailed, concrete suggestions than they gave older children. When the experimenters made the task more difficult, mothers gave more help to children of both ages.

In another study, K. Alison Clarke-Stewart and Robert Beck (1999) had thirty-one children who were five years old observe a videotaped film segment with their mother, talk about it with her, and then retell the story to an experimenter. They found that the quality of the stories, as retold by the children, was related to the scaffolding strategies the mothers used. Children whose mothers focused the children's attention on the tape, asked their children to talk about it, and discussed the feelings of the characters told better stories than children whose mothers did not use such scaffolding strategies and children in a control group who did not discuss the story at all. Children's understanding of the characters' emotional states was most strongly connected with the number of questions the mother asked and her correction of the child's misunderstandings of what he or she saw.

In a longitudinal study, Catherine Haden and her colleagues (2001) observed twenty-one mother-child pairs as they engaged in specially constructed tasks when the children were thirty, thirty-six, and forty-two months of age. They analyzed the children's recall of their performance one and three days afterward at all three ages. It turned out that the children best recalled those aspects of the tasks they had both worked on and discussed with their mothers. Recall under these circumstances exceeded recall when the activities were (1) handled jointly but talked about only by the mother or (2) handled jointly but not discussed.

Being at HOME: The Effect of the Home Environment

Bettye Caldwell developed a measure for evaluating children's home environments labelled, appropriately enough, HOME—an acronym for Home Observation for the Measurement of the Environment. With this method, researchers directly observe parent-child interaction in the home. The HOME inventory contains six subscales, as shown in Table 9.6. The HOME inventory items are better predictors of young children's later IQ scores than social class, mother's IQ, or infant IQ scores (Bradley, 1989; Luster & Dubow, 1992).

Truth or Fiction Revisited: It is true that early learning experiences affect children's levels of intellectual functioning. In a longitudinal study, Caldwell and her colleagues observed children from poor and working-class families over a period of years, starting at six months of age. The HOME inventory was used at the early ages, and standard IQ tests were given at ages three and four. The children of mothers who were emotionally and verbally responsive, who were involved with their children, and who provided appropriate play materials and a variety of daily experiences during the early years showed advanced social and language development even at six months of age (Parks & Bradley, 1991). These children also attained higher IQ scores at ages three and four and higher achievement test scores at age seven (Bradley, 1989). Other studies support the view that being responsive to preschoolers, stimulating them, and

zone of proximal development (ZPD) Vygotsky's term for the situation in which a child carries out tasks with the help of someone who is more skilled, frequently an adult who represents the culture in which the child develops.

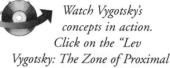

Watch Vygotsky's concepts in action. Click on the "Lev Vygotsky: The Zone of Proximal Development and Scaffolding" clip in Module 3, Section 2.

encouraging independence is connected with higher IQ scores and greater school achievement later on (Molfese, DiLalla, & Bunce, 1997; Steinberg, Brown, & Dornbusch, 1996; Suzuki & Valencia, 1997). Victoria Molfese and her colleagues (1997) found that the home environment was the single most important predictor of scores on IQ tests among children aged three to eight.

Scales of the HOME Inventory

Scale	Sample Items
Parental emotional and verbal responsiveness	• The parent spontaneously vocalizes to the child during the visit. • The parent responds to the child's vocalizations with vocal or other verbal responses.
Avoidance of restriction and punishment	• The parent does not shout at the child. • The parent does not interfere with the child's actions or restrict the child's movements more than three times during the visit.
Organization of the physical environment	• The child's play environment seems to be safe and free from hazards.
Provision of appropriate play materials	• The child has a push or a pull toy. • The child has one or more toys or pieces of equipment that promote muscle activity. • The family provides appropriate equipment to foster learning.
Parental involvement with child	• The parent structures the child's play periods. • The parent tends to keep the child within his or her visual range and looks at the child frequently.
Opportunities for variety in daily stimulation	• The child gets out of the house at least four times a week. • The parent reads stories to the child at least three times a week.

The Home Environment
The home environment of the young child is linked to intellectual development and later academic achievement. Key aspects of the home environment include the parents' involvement and encouragement of the child, the availability of toys and learning materials, and the variety of experiences to which the child is exposed.

(c) Syd Johnson / The Image Works

Developing in a World of Diversity

Cultural Variation in the Home Environment

Research in various cultures and among various ethnic groups supports the view that the early environment of the child is linked to IQ scores and academic achievement. (Whiteside-Mansell, Bradley, Tresch Owen, Randolph, & Cauce, 2003). For example, Marc Bornstein and Catherine Tamis-LeMonda (1989) studied the responsiveness of Japanese and American mothers toward their babies during the first half of the first year. They noted how often mothers responded to their infants' vocalizations or other behaviours by talking, touching, picking up, patting, feeding, and so forth. Maternal responsiveness was positively linked to Japanese children's IQ scores at the age of two and a half and to American children's scores at age four. Similar results were found in a collaborative project involving six different longitudinal studies and three ethnic groups in the United States (Bradley et al., 1989). In this project, three aspects of the home environment during the first three years of life were related to higher IQ scores at age three for European American, African American, and Mexican American children. These sources of stimulation were the availability of toys and learning materials, the parents' involvement and encouragement of the child, and the variety of experiences to which the child was exposed.

Effects of Early Childhood Education: Does It Give Preschoolers a Head Start?

How important are academic experiences in early childhood? Do they facilitate cognitive development? Research suggests that preschool education enables children to get an early start on achievement in school.

Preschool Education for Economically Disadvantaged Children

Children growing up in poverty generally perform less well on standardized intelligence tests, and they are at greater risk for school failure (Caputo, 2003). As a result, a number of preschool programs in Canada, including Head Start, target families with low incomes. While the programs and services offered by Head Start programs across the country vary, they typically include services such as preparation for school, Aboriginal culture and traditions (if program is for Aboriginal children and families), parent support groups and classes, and health nutrition and physical development. Generally, children in these programs are exposed to letters and words, numbers, books, exercises in drawing, pegs and pegboards, puzzles, and toy animals and dolls in addition to other materials and activities that middle-class children usually take for granted. Many programs encourage parental involvement in the program itself.

The Government of Canada established Aboriginal Head Start in 1995 to support child development and school readiness initiatives for Aboriginal children living in urban centres and large northern communities. The main objectives of these locally run programs is to support culture and language, education, health promotion, nutrition, social support, and parent education and involvement (Health Canada, 2005a). For more information about Aboriginal Head Start programs, visit: http://www .hc-sc.gc.ca/fnih-spni/famil/develop/ahsor-papa_intro_e.html. Here are some websites of local Canadian Head Start programs:

- Ottawa: http://www.aboriginalcanada.com/headstart
- ABC Head Start Society (Edmonton): http://www.abcheadstart.org
- Toronto: http://www.nativechild.org/SitePages/?section=4&page=61

The Ontario government has published two major reports dealing with early childhood development: *The Early Years: Reversing the Brain Drain* (1999) and *The Early Years Report II: Putting Science into Action* (2007). These reports have examined Ontario communities' initiatives in early childhood development programs that support parents in the following ways:

- "Providing good advice and support in respect to nourishment, nurturing and stimulation for young children through play-based learning;
- Providing support to parents of young children;
- Offering nonparental care (day care) which supports early child development and parenting capacity; and
- Improving the community's capacity to support early child development programs" (p. 115).

A key conclusion from the report is that parents need and want nonparental care to varying degrees. What McCain and Mustard (1999) recommended for Ontario are the following: (1) early childhood development and parenting centres in communities that are available and accessible for all families, (2) improved maternity/parental leave benefits to parents, (3) family-friendly workplaces, and (4) tax incentives for the development of new early child development programs in communities. It's now been several years since this report was submitted. How do you think your province stacks up in delivering these key services and benefits to young families?

Truth or Fiction Revisited: It is true that an academic preschool can provide children with advantages in school. Studies of Head Start and other intervention programs provide convincing evidence that environmental enrichment can significantly enhance the cognitive development of economically disadvantaged children (Wilson, 2004; Zigler & Styfco, 2001). The initial effects can be dramatic. In the Milwaukee Project, poor children of low-IQ mothers were provided with enriched daycare from the age of six months. By the late preschool years, their IQ scores averaged about 121, compared with an average of ninety-five for children from similar backgrounds who did not receive daycare (Garber, 1988). In addition to positively influencing IQ scores, Head Start and other programs also lead to gains in school readiness tests and achievement tests (Wilson, 2004; Zigler, 1999). Programs that involve and educate the parents are particularly beneficial (Webster-Stratton, Reid, & Hammond, 2001b).

Preschool intervention programs can have long-term effects on life outcomes for poor children (Caputo, 2003). During the elementary and high school years, graduates of preschool programs are less likely to have been left back or placed in classes for slow learners. They are more likely to graduate from high school, go on to college, and earn higher incomes. They are less likely to be delinquent, unemployed, or on welfare (Schweinhart & Weikart, 1993; Zigler & Styfco, 2001).

One of the tragic contributors to the perpetuation of the cycle of poverty is the incidence of pregnancy among single teenage girls. Pregnancy in these cases usually means that the young mother's formal education comes to an end. These children are then destined to be reared by poorly educated mothers. Some researchers have found that girls from preschool education programs are less likely to become single mothers

(Schweinhart & Weikart, 1993). Others have found that girls who attended preschool intervention programs became pregnant as frequently as matched controls but were more likely to return to school after giving birth (Haskins, 1989).

It appears that the long-term benefits of preschool intervention programs are greatest when intervention continues into elementary school (Farran, 1990). The Maryland-based Success for All program, for example, runs from preschool through third grade. It combines academic tutoring with a family support team to engage parental involvement (Madden, Slavin, Karweit, Dolan, & Wasik, 1991). First- through third-graders in the program outperform control children in reading achievement. Similar results have been found for Chicago's Child-Parent Centers, which enroll children from preschool through at least third grade and which use methods similar to those used by Success for All. Children in the program have higher reading scores, are more likely to graduate from high school, and are less likely to be held back a grade than children who have attended only preschool or who have no preschool experience (Chira, 1992b; Reynolds, 1993).

Preschool Education for Middle-Class Children: Too Much Pressure?

According to some educators, academic environments in the preschool years will benefit advantaged as well as disadvantaged children (Rescorla, 1991a). Others argue that formal academic instruction and strong pressures to achieve, especially on the part of middle-class parents, may impair children's learning and social-emotional development (Elkind, 1990, 1991).

A series of studies by Kathy Hirsch-Pasek, Marion Hyson, and Leslie Rescorla examined the effects of strong academic pressures on preschool children. They studied middle-class children attending a variety of preschools, ranging from those with a highly academic orientation (e.g., class periods of formal instruction in math, computers, and French) to those that were more child oriented and less academic (strong free-play emphasis, no direct instruction). Not surprisingly, those parents who placed a strong value on early academics sent their children to the academically oriented schools (Rescorla, 1991b). They also enrolled their children in music, art, and sports lessons outside school and were directive and controlling when interacting with their children (Hyson, 1991). What is the effect of this "hothouse" approach on the child? Parental academic expectations had a positive but short-lived effect. That is, higher parental expectations were linked to an increase in academic skills in preschool. However, by kindergarten the other children had caught up. Furthermore, the children of the parents with high expectations were less creative, showed more anxiety when performing tasks, and tended to think less positively about school (Hirsh-Pasek, 1991; Hirsh-Pasek, Hyson, & Rescorla, 1990).

Television: Window on the World or Prison within a False World?

How many people do you know who do not have a TV set? Canadian children aged two to eleven spend an average of 14.4 hours a week watching television (Statistics Canada http://www.statcan.ca.login.ezproxy.library.ualberta.ca/english/kits/winner /2001/tv/inthelife.htm). In the U.S., by the time the average child turns three, he or she already watches two to three hours of television a day (Palmer, 2003).

© Mary Kate Denny/PhotoEdit

Head Start
Preschoolers enrolled in Head Start programs have made dramatic increases in both readiness for elementary school and intelligence test scores. Head Start and other similar programs can also have long-term effects on education and employment outcomes.

Sesame Street

Sesame Street is viewed regularly by an estimated 50–60% of children between the ages of 2 and 3 years in the United States. Research shows that regular viewing of the program improves children's cognitive and language skills.

Television has great potential for teaching a variety of cognitive skills, social behaviours, and attitudes. In Chapter 10, we will explore the effects of television on children's social behaviours and attitudes (uh-oh). Here, we focus on television's effect on cognitive development in early childhood. In many ways, television provides children with an important window on the outside world and on the cognitive skills required to succeed in that world.

Educational Television

In the U.S., the Children's Television Act requires that networks devote a number of hours per week to educational television. The resultant programs have been shown to have mild to moderate positive effects on preschoolers' cognitive development, more so with girls than with boys (Calvert & Kotler, 2003). Why is this relevant for Canadians? Because the reality is that Canadians access American programming, and that U.S. shows make up a good portion of what is broadcast in Canada. Even though the Canadian Broadcasting Act requires Canadian content in programming, we are nonetheless exposed to a great deal of non-Canadian material. Hence, the inclusion of studies conducted with American children is provided below.

Sesame Street is the most successful TV program designed to educate children. Begun in 1969, *Sesame Street* was developed with the goal of promoting the intellectual growth of preschoolers, particularly those of lower socioeconomic status. *Sesame Street* is viewed by an estimated 50 to 60 percent of American preschoolers, including children of various ethnic backgrounds and levels of family income (Comstock & Paik, 1991).

Several large-scale evaluations of the effects of *Sesame Street* have concluded that regular viewing of the program increases children's learning of numbers, letters, and cognitive skills such as sorting and classification (Fisch, Truglio, & Cole, 1999). These effects are found for African American and European American children, girls and boys, and urban, suburban, and rural children.

Longitudinal research by Mabel Rice and her colleagues (1990) showed that regularly viewing *Sesame Street* between the ages of three and five leads to improved vocabulary at age five. Viewing cartoons, on the other hand, may not benefit vocabulary development. Follow-up studies have found that children learn the most from segments that give them time to respond, clap, or sing along; from segments that are repeated in a show and throughout the season; and from those skits that they find more entertaining (Chira, 1989).

Helping Children Use Television Wisely[1]

Overall, television appears to have some positive effects on cognitive development. But there is more to life than television. Let us share some ideas on how parents can help their children reap the benefits of television without allowing it to take over their lives.

General Suggestions

• Encourage children to watch educational programming.

• Help them choose among cartoon shows. Not all are filled with violence. Nick Jr's *Dora the Explorer* and *The Backyardigans* may help foster intellectual and social development.

• Encourage your children to sit with you when you are watching educational programming.

• If your child is spending too much time in front of the tube, keep a chart with the child of his or her total activities, including TV, homework, and play with friends. Discuss what to eliminate and what to substitute.

• Set a weekly viewing limit.

• Rule out TV at certain times, such as before breakfast or on school nights.

• Make a list of alternative activities— riding a bicycle, reading a book, working on a hobby.

• Encourage the entire family to choose a program before turning the TV set on. Turn the set off when the show is over.

TV, TV Everywhere—How Do We Teach Children to Stop to Think?
Parents can have a positive effect on children's cognitive processing of the information they glean from TV programs and commercials.

Coping with Violence

• Watch at least one episode of programs the child watches to see how violent they are.

• When viewing TV together, discuss the violence with the child. Talk about why the violence happened and how painful it is. Discuss how conflict can be resolved without violence.

• Explain to the child how violence on TV shows is faked.

• Encourage children to watch programs with characters who cooperate, help, and care for each other. Such programs can influence children in a positive way.

Applying TV to Real Life

• Ask children to compare what they see on the screen with people, places, and events they know firsthand, have read about, or have studied in school.

• Tell children what is real and what is make-believe on TV—the use of stunt people, dream sequences, and animation.

• Explain to the child your values with regard to sex, alcohol, and drugs.

Understanding Advertising

• Explain to children that the purpose of advertising is to sell products.

• On shopping trips, let children see that toys that look big, fast, and exciting on the screen are disappointingly small and slow close up.

• Talk to the child about nutrition. If the child can read package labels, allow the child to choose a breakfast cereal from those in which sugar levels are low.

1. Sources: Huston et al. (1992); Rosenkoetter, Rosenkoetter, Ozretich, & Acock. (2004).

© photoalto/First Light

What about the effects of television on other aspects of cognitive behaviour in the young child? There is some evidence that watching television is negatively connected with impulse control. One study (Desmond, Singer, & Singer, 1990) found that heavy TV viewing is associated with greater restlessness in children. Other research, however, indicates that exposure to such educational programs as *Sesame Street, Electric Company,* and *Mister Rogers' Neighborhood* may actually increase impulse control and concentration among preschoolers (Cole et al., 2003).

Television is a powerful medium, and this power can be used to good effect. For example, it can be used to show the harmful effects of prejudice and to decrease feelings of prejudice by showing people from different backgrounds working together to solve problems in constructive ways (Cole et al., 2003; Persson & Musher-Eizenman, 2003).

It has been suggested that television may stifle the imagination, but at least among preschoolers, television appears to have little or no effect on children's imagination (Comstock & Paik, 1991). The type of TV show may have something to do with this. Moreover, this research may not be assessing certain ways in which television affects the child's imagination. Take these conclusions with a grain of salt. Interested readers (and other readers) may profit from reviewing the suggested guidelines for helping children use television wisely in the nearby "A Closer Look" feature.

Commercials

Critics are concerned that the cognitive limitations of young children make them particularly susceptible to commercial messages, which can be potentially misleading and even harmful. Preschoolers do not understand the selling intent of advertising, and they often are unable to tell the difference between commercials and program content (Palmer, 2003; Pine & Nash, 2002). Exposure to commercials does not make the child a sophisticated consumer. In fact, children who are heavy TV viewers are more likely than light viewers to believe commercials' claims.

Commercials that encourage children to choose nutritionally inadequate foods—such as sugared breakfast cereals, candy, and fast foods—are harmful to children's nutritional beliefs and diets. Young children do not understand that sugary foods are detrimental to health, nor do they understand disclaimers in ads that, for example, state that sugared cereals should be part of a balanced breakfast (Palmer, 2003; Pine & Nash, 2002).

Television and Inactivity

Watching television, of course, is a sedentary activity. Parents might prefer that children spend more time exercising, but television also functions as an engrossing babysitter. However, research does show that children who watch more television gain more body fat from the preschool years through adolescence (Proctor et al., 2003). The research is correlational, to be sure; that is, children choose (or are allowed) to watch more or less television. They are not randomly assigned to view various amounts of television. Thus, it may be that the same factors that lead them to choose more television also lead them to put on more body fat. On the other hand, there may be little harm (and much good!) in encouraging children to spend more time in physical activity.

Active Review

20. Cognitive _____ refers to temporary support provided by a parent or teacher to a child who is learning to perform a task.

21. Caldwell and her colleagues found that the children of parents who are emotionally and verbally _____ show advanced social and language development.

22. Molfese and her colleagues found that the _____ was the single most important predictor of scores on IQ tests among children.

23. Head Start programs (can or cannot?) significantly enhance the cognitive development of economically disadvantaged children.

24. During the elementary and high school years, graduates of preschool programs are (more or less?) likely to have been left back or placed in classes for slow learners.

25. The average Canadian child spends _____ hours watching television each week.

Reflect & Relate: What was your early home environment like? How do you think it would have appeared in terms of the factors described in Table 9.6? How can you use the information in this section to create a home environment for your own children?

How much television did you watch as a child? Can you think of things you learned by watching television? Can you imagine developing in a world without television? Explain.

Go to
W W W **www.voyages1ce.nelson.com**
for an interactive version of this review.

Recite: *An Active Summary*™

1. How do children in the preoperational stage think and behave?

Piaget's preoperational stage lasts from about age two to age seven and is characterized by the use of symbols to represent objects and relationships. Pretend play is based on the use and recollection of symbols or on mental representations of things. By thirty months, children can pretend that objects are active.

2. How do we characterize the logic of the preoperational child?

Preoperational thinking is characterized by egocentrism, precausal thinking, confusion between mental and physical events, and ability to focus on only one dimension at a time.

3. What is egocentrism?

Egocentrism is inability to see the world from the perspective of others. Young children often view the world as a stage that is meant to meet their needs.

4. What is precausal thinking?

Young children's thinking is egocentric, animistic, and artificialistic. In transductive reasoning, children reason by going from one instance of an event to another.

5. Why do young children think they can pretend to be galaprocks without knowing what galaprocks are?

Preoperational children have difficulty distinguishing between mental and physical events. Egocentrism contributes to their belief that their thoughts reflect reality.

6. What is conservation (i.e., in terms of the cognitive development of the child)?

The law of conservation holds that properties of substances such as volume, mass, and number stay the same (are conserved) even if their shape or arrangement changes. Conservation requires focusing on two aspects of a situation at once.

7. What are some of the factors that influence cognitive development in early childhood?

Some of the most important factors include scaffolding and the zone of proximal development, as envisioned by Vygotsky. Others include social and family factors such as family income, parents' educational level, family size, and the presence of stressful family events such as divorce, job loss, or illness. The children of responsive parents who provide appropriate play materials and stimulating experiences show gains in social and language development. Head Start programs enhance economically disadvantaged children's cognitive development, academic skills, and readiness for school.

8. What are children's ideas about how the mind works?

As children's theory of mind develops, children come to understand that there are distinctions between external and mental events and between appearances and realities.

9. Do children understand where their knowledge comes from? If so, how early do they show this ability?

By age three, most children begin to realize that people gain knowledge through the senses. By age four, children understand which sense is required to provide information about qualities such as colour (vision) and weight (touch).

10. Is seeing believing? What do preoperational children have to say about that?

Although Piaget believed that children do not differentiate reality from appearances or mental events until the age of seven or eight, research finds that preschoolers can do so.

11. What sorts of memory skills do children possess in early childhood?

Preschoolers recognize more items than they can recall. Autobiographical memory is linked to language skills. By the age of four, children can remember events that occurred a year and a half earlier. Young children seem to form scripts, which are abstract, generalized accounts of events.

12. What factors affect memory in early childhood?

Factors affecting memory include what the child is asked to remember, interest level and motivation, the availability of retrieval cues, and the memory measure being used.

13. How do we remember to remember?

Preschoolers engage in behaviours such as looking, pointing, and touching when trying to remember. Preschoolers can be taught to use strategies such as rehearsal and grouping of items that they might not use on their own.

14. What language developments occur during early childhood?

Preschoolers acquire about nine new words per day. Word learning often occurs rapidly through fast mapping. During the third year, children usually add articles, conjunctions, possessive adjectives, pronouns, and prepositions. Between the ages of three and four, children combine phrases and clauses into complex sentences. Preschoolers tend to overregularize irregular verbs and noun forms as they acquire rules of grammar.

15. What is the relationship between language and cognition?

Piaget believed that children learn words in order to describe classes or categories they have created. Other theorists argue that children create classes to understand things that are labelled by words. Vygotsky believed that during most of the first year, vocalizations and thought are separate. But usually during the second year, cognition and language combine forces. To Vygotsky, inner speech is the ultimate binding of language and thought.

Key Terms

preoperational stage *(page 316)*

symbolic play *(page 316)*

operations *(page 317)*

egocentrism *(page 318)*

precausal *(page 319)*

transductive reasoning *(page 319)*

animism *(page 319)*

artificialism *(page 319)*

conservation *(page 321)*

centration *(page 321)*

irreversibility *(page 321)*

class inclusion *(page 322)*

fast mapping *(page 328)*

whole-object assumption *(page 329)*

contrast assumption *(page 329)*

overregularization *(page 329)*

pragmatics *(page 331)*

inner speech *(page 334)*

theory of mind *(page 335)*

appearance-reality distinction *(page 337)*

mental representations *(page 337)*

recognition *(page 338)*

recall *(page 338)*

scripts *(page 339)*

autobiographical memory *(page 339)*

rehearsal *(page 341)*

scaffolding *(page 342)*

zone of proximal development (ZPD) *(page 343)*

Go to
W W W www.voyages1ce.nelson.com
for an interactive version of this summary review.

Active Learning Resources

Observing Children and Adolescents CD-ROM
Want to watch videos showing what you've just learned about in this chapter? Click on the "Piaget's Preoperational Stage" video in Module 2, Section 2. Your "Lessons in Observation" feature on p. XXX provides further learning objectives, an applied lesson, and a critical thinking exercise designed to help you experience this stage of development. Also check out the "Language Development" video in CD Module 2, Section 2, and the "Lev Vygotsky" clip in CD Module 3, Section 2.

Visit Your Companion Website for This Book
http://www.voyages1CE.nelson.com
Check out this companion website, where you will find online resources directly linked to your book. The website includes interactive exercises related to PQ4R and Power Visuals for mastering and reviewing key concepts as well as quizzing, chapter outlines, and much more!

CENGAGENOW™

CengageNOW!™
http://hed.nelson.com
Go to this site for the link to CengageNOW™, your one-stop study shop. Take a Pretest for this chapter, and CengageNOW™ will generate a personalized Study Plan based on your test results! The Study Plan will identify the topics you need to review and direct you to online resources to help you master those topics. You can then take a Posttest to help you determine the concepts you have mastered and those you still need to work on.

Early Childhood:
Social and Emotional Development

PREVIEW

TRUTH OR FICTION?

● ● ● ● ● ● ● ● ● ● ●

(T)(F) Parents who are restrictive and demand mature behaviour wind up with rebellious children, not mature children.

(T)(F) There is no point in trying to reason with a four-year-old.

(T)(F) Firstborn children are more highly motivated to achieve than later-born children.

(T)(F) Children who are physically punished are more likely to be aggressive.

(T)(F) Children who watch two to four hours of TV a day will see 8000 murders and another 100 000 acts of violence *by the time they have finished elementary school.*

(T)(F) Children mechanically imitate the aggressive behaviour they view in the media.

(T)(F) The most common fear among preschoolers is fear of social disapproval.

(T)(F) A two-and-a-half-year-old may know that she is a girl but still think that she can grow up to be a daddy.

Go to w w w

www.voyages1ce.nelson.com
for an interactive version of this "Truth or Fiction" feature.

© Tom Prettyman / PhotoEdit

Sekou and Mona are both two and a half years old. They are standing at the water table in the preschool classroom. Mona is filling a plastic container with water and spilling it out. She watches the water splash down the drain. Sekou watches and then goes to get another container. He, too, fills his container with water and spills it out. The children stand side by side. They empty and refill their plastic pails; they glance at each other and exchange a few words. They continue playing like this for several minutes, until Mona drops her pail and runs off to ride the tricycle. Soon after, Sekou also loses interest and finds something else to do.

Meanwhile, four-and-a-half-year-olds Karasi and Anwar are building in the block corner, making a huge rambling structure that they have decided is a spaceship. They talk animatedly as they work, negotiating who should be captain of the ship and who should be the space alien. Anwar and Karasi take turns adding blocks. They continue to build, working together and talking as they play (Campbell, 1990).

These observations illustrate some of the changes that occur in social development while in an early childhood education context. Toddlers often spend time watching and imitating each other, but they do not interact very much. Older preschoolers are more likely to take turns, work cooperatively toward a goal, and share. They often engage in fantasy play that involves adopting adult roles.

In this chapter, we examine some of the changes that occur in social and emotional development in early childhood. We consider the roles played by parents, siblings, and peers. We examine child's play, helping and sharing, and aggression. Then we look at personality and emotional development. We begin with the development of the self-concept, move on to Erikson's stage of initiative versus guilt, and explore the changing nature of children's fears. Finally, we discuss the development of gender roles and sex differences in behaviour.

Influences on Development: Parents, Siblings, and Peers

Young children usually spend most of their time within the family. Most parents attempt to foster certain behaviours in their children. They want them to develop a sense of responsibility and conform to family routines. They want them to develop into well-adjusted individuals. They want them to acquire social skills. In other words, they want to ensure healthy social and emotional development. How do parents go about trying to achieve these goals? What part do siblings play? How do a child's peers influence social and emotional development?

Dimensions of Child Rearing and Parenting Styles

Parents have different approaches to rearing their children. *Question: What are the dimensions of child rearing?* Investigators of parental patterns of child rearing in Western countries have found it useful to classify them according to two broad dimensions: parental acceptance and involvement (warmth–coldness) and control (restrictiveness–permissiveness) (Baumrind, 1989, 1991a, 1991b). Warm parents and cold parents can be either restrictive or permissive. It is important to note that child rearing practices are greatly influenced by cultural practices as well. Providing parents with information about effective parenting practices is an essential part of healthy family development.

Acceptance and Parental Involvement (Warmth–Coldness)

Warm parents are affectionate toward their children. They tend to hug and kiss them and smile at them frequently. Warm parents are caring and supportive of their children. They generally behave in ways that communicate their enjoyment in being with the children. Parents who engage in warm exchanges are less likely than parents with colder tendencies to use physical discipline (Wade & Kendler, 2001).

Parents who tend to be cold may not enjoy being with their children and may have few feelings of affection for them. They are likely to complain about their behaviour, saying that they are naughty or have "minds of their own." Parents with a warmer style may also say that their children have "minds of their own," but, in contrast, they are frequently proud of and entertained by their children's stubborn behaviour. Even when they are irked by it, they usually focus on attempting to change it, instead of rejecting the children.

It requires no stretch of the imagination to conclude that it is better to be warm than cold toward children (Grusec, 2002). The children of parents who are warm and accepting are more likely to develop internalized standards of conduct—a moral sense or conscience (Grusec, 2002; Grusec, Goodnow, & Kuczynski, 2000). Parental warmth is also related to the child's social and emotional well-being (Karavasilis et al., 2003; Leung, McBride-Chang, & Lai, 2004; Wang & He, 2002).

Where does parental warmth come from? Some of it reflects parental beliefs about how best to rear children, and some reflects parents' tendencies to imitate the behaviour of their own parents. But research by E. Mavis Hetherington and her colleagues (Feinberg, Neiderhiser, Howe, & Hetherington, 2001) suggests that genetic factors may be involved as well.

Parental Control (Restrictiveness–Permissiveness)

Parents must generally decide how restrictive they will be. How will they respond when children make excessive noise, play with dangerous objects, damage property, mess up their rooms, hurt others, go nude, or masturbate? Parents who are restrictive tend to impose rules and to watch their children closely.

Truth or Fiction Revisited: It is not true that parents who are strict and demand mature behaviour wind up with rebellious children. Consistent control and firm enforcement of rules can have positive consequences for the child, particularly when combined with strong support and affection (Grusec, 2002). This parenting style is termed the *authoritative style*. On the other hand, if "restrictiveness" means physical punishment, interference, or intrusiveness, it can have negative effects such as disobedience, rebelliousness, and lower levels of cognitive development (Grusec, 2002).

Permissive parents impose few if any rules and supervise their children less closely. They allow their children to do what is "natural"—make noise, treat toys carelessly (although they may also extensively childproof their homes to protect their children and the furniture), and experiment with their own bodies. They may also allow their children to show some aggression, intervening only when another child is in danger. Parents may be permissive for different reasons. Some parents believe that children need the freedom to express their natural urges. Others may simply be uninterested and uninvolved.

Cross-cultural research suggests that in Spain and Brazil the permissive parenting style is connected with higher self-esteem and adjustment than other parenting styles (Martínez, Musitu, Garcia, & Camino, 2003). The investigators suggested that these cultures may be somewhat more "laid back" than "Anglo-Saxon" cultures and that there is a better fit between indulgence of children and their adjustment in Latino/Latina cultures.

How Parents Set Boundaries

Regardless of their general approaches to child rearing, most if not all parents impose boundaries now and then, even if only when they are teaching their children not to run into the street or to touch a hot stove. *Question: What techniques do parents use to set boundaries for children's behaviour?* Parents tend to use the methods of *induction, power assertion*, and *withdrawal of love.*

Inductive Techniques

inductive Characteristic of disciplinary methods, such as reasoning, that attempt to foster an understanding of the principles behind parental demands.

Inductive methods aim to impart knowledge that will enable children to generate desirable behaviour in similar situations. The main inductive technique is "reasoning," or explaining why one kind of behaviour is good and another is not. Reasoning with a one- or two-year-old can be basic. "If you touch the hot stove, it will hurt" qualifies as reasoning with toddlers. "It hurts!" is an explanation, although a brief one. *Truth or Fiction Revisited:* Thus, there *is* a point in trying to reason with a four-year-old. The inductive approach helps the child understand moral behaviour and fosters prosocial behaviour such as helping and sharing (Grusec, 2002; Grusec & Lytton, 1988).

Power-Assertive Methods

Power-assertive methods include physical punishment and denial of privileges. Parents often justify physical punishment with sayings such as "Spare the rod, spoil the child." Parents may insist that power assertion is necessary because their children are noncompliant. However, the use of power-assertive methods is related to parental authoritarianism as well as to (negative) children's behaviour (Chen et al., 2000; Clark & Ladd, 2000). Parental power assertion is associated with children's lower acceptance by peers, poorer grades, and higher rates of antisocial behaviour (Chang, Schwartz, Dodge, & McBride-Chang, 2003). The more parents use power-assertive techniques, the less children appear to develop internal standards of moral conduct. Parental punishment and rejection is often linked with aggression and delinquency (Grusec, 2002; Putallaz, Costanzo, Grimes, & Sherman, 1998).

© Joel Gordon Photography

Inductive Reasoning
Inductive methods for imposing limits attempt to teach children the principles they should use in guiding their own behaviour. This mother is using the inductive technique of reasoning.

Withdrawal of Love

Some parents control children by threatening them with withdrawal of love. They isolate or ignore misbehaving children. Because most children need parental approval and contact, loss of love can be more threatening than physical punishment. Withdrawal of love may foster compliance, but it may also instill guilt and anxiety (Grusec, 2002).

Preschoolers more readily comply when asked to *do* something than when asked to *stop doing* something (Kochanska, Coy, & Murray, 2001). One way to manage children who are doing something wrong or bad is to involve them in something else.

How Parents Transmit Values and Standards

Traditional views of the ways in which children acquire values and standards for behaviour focus on parenting styles (Grusec et al., 2000, 2002). However, many other factors are involved, including the characteristics of a particular child, the child's situation, and other aspects of parental behaviour.

Psychologist Diana Baumrind (1989, 1991b) focused on the relationship between parenting styles and the development of competent behaviour in young children. She used the two dimensions of child rearing we have just examined: warmth–coldness and restrictiveness–permissiveness. She developed a classification of four parenting styles based on whether parents are high or low on each of the two dimensions, as seen in Table 10.2. *Question: What are the parenting styles involved in the transmission of values and standards?*

The Development of Emotional and Behavioural Control in Preschoolers	
Development of emotional and behavioural control	Effects of the environment
• Increasingly capable of true internal control of emotions and behaviour • Needs less continuous adult support and guidance to maintain control (shifting from external to internal control) • More interest in interacting with other children and being accepted by them • Capable of cooperative interactions with peers • Able to use internalized rules, strategies, and plans to guide behaviour (though not necessarily consciously) • Internalizing standards for appropriate behaviour and emotional expression • Can use language to assist and guide self-regulation	• Caregiver guidance techniques and styles that support responsibility, inner control, and positive interactions with others support the development of self-regulation • Adult and peer modelling influence children's patterns of interaction, self-control, and developing standards for appropriate behaviour • Opportunities for positive interactions with peers (e.g., adult monitoring of peer interactions, mediating disputes, if necessary, in a problem-solving way, and an expressed value for cooperative interactions) increase positive self-regulation

Source: Bronson (2000).

Authoritative Parents

The parents of the most capable children are rated as high on both dimensions of behaviour (see Table 10.2). They make strong efforts to set boundaries and impose reasonable limits for their children (i.e., they are high on control), and they make strong demands for maturity. However, they also reason with their children and show them strong support and feelings of love. Baumrind applies the label **authoritative** to these parents to suggest that they have a clear vision of what they want their children to do but they also respect their children and provide them with warmth.

authoritative A child-rearing style in which parents are restrictive and demanding yet communicative and warm.

Baumrind's Patterns of Parenting		
Parenting Style	Parental Behaviour Patterns	
	Control	Acceptance & Involvement
Authoritative	High	High
Authoritarian	High	Low
Permissive–indulgent	Low	High
Indifferent–uninvolved	Low	Low

authoritarian A child-rearing style in which parents demand submission and obedience from their children but are not very communicative and warm.

permissive–indulgent A child-rearing style in which parents are not controlling and restrictive but are warm.

rejecting–neglecting A child-rearing style in which parents are neither restrictive and controlling nor supportive and responsive.

Compared to other children, the children of authoritative parents tend to show self-reliance and independence, high self-esteem, high levels of activity and exploratory behaviour, and social competence. They are highly motivated to achieve and do well in school (Baumrind, 1989, 1991b; Grusec, 2002; Kaufmann et al., 2000). With regard to attachment, researchers have found the authoritative parenting style to be positively associated with secure attachment in children (Karavasilis, Doyle, & Makiewicz, 2003; Nair & Murray, 2005).

Authoritarian Parents

"Because I say so" could well be the motto of parents that Baumrind labels **authoritarian.** These parents tend to look on obedience as a high virtue. Authoritarian parents believe in strict guidelines for determining what is right and wrong. They demand that their children accept these guidelines without question. Like authoritative parents, they are controlling. Unlike authoritative parents, their enforcement methods rely on coercion. Moreover, authoritarian parents do not communicate well with their children. They do not show respect for their children's viewpoints, and most researchers find them to be generally cold and rejecting. However, among some ethnic groups—such as Egyptians living in Canada—authoritarianism reflects cultural values, and these authoritarian parents are also warm and reasonably flexible (Grusec, 2002; Rudy & Grusec, 2001).

In Baumrind's research, the sons of authoritarian parents were relatively hostile and defiant and the daughters were low in independence and dominance (Baumrind, 1989). Other researchers have found that children of authoritarian parents are less competent socially and academically than children of authoritative parents. Children of authoritarian parents also tend to be conflicted, anxious, and irritable. They are less friendly and spontaneous in their social interactions (Grusec, 2002). As adolescents, they may be conforming and obedient but have lower self-reliance and self-esteem (Lamborn, Mounts, Steinberg, & Dornbusch, 1991). These findings appear to hold up across cultures and across the years. A Turkish study of 279 students found that students from authoritarian families were less likely to have secure attachment and self-esteem and more likely to be anxious than students from authoritative families (Suemer & Guengoer, 1999).

© Image Source / Royalty-Free / CORBIS

Permissive Parents

Baumrind found two types of parents who are permissive, as opposed to restrictive. One type is labelled permissive–indulgent and the other, rejecting–neglecting. **Permissive–indulgent** parents are rated low in their attempts to control their children and in their demands for mature behaviour. They are easygoing and unconventional. Their brand of permissiveness is accompanied by high nurturance (warmth and support).

Rejecting–neglecting parents are also rated low in their demands for mature behaviour and their attempts to control their children. But unlike indulgent parents, they are low in support and responsiveness.

The neglectful parenting style is associated with poor outcomes for children. By and large, the children of neglectful parents are the least competent, responsible, and mature and the most prone to problem behaviours. They tend to have low self-esteem, to be

Permissive Parents

Some parents are considered permissive—they demand little of their children in terms of mature behaviour or control. Permissive–indulgent parents still provide plenty of warmth and support for their children, whereas rejecting–neglecting parents tend to neglect or ignore their children.

insecurely attached to caregivers, and to be anxious (Suemer & Guengoer, 1999). Children of permissive–indulgent parents, like those of neglectful parents, show less competence in school and more deviant behaviour (e.g., misconduct and substance abuse) than children of more restrictive, controlling parents. But children from permissive–indulgent homes, unlike those from neglectful homes, are fairly high in social competence and self-confidence (Baumrind, 1991a).

Effects of the Situation and the Child on Parenting Styles

Parenting styles are not just a one-way street, from parent to child. Parenting styles also depend partly on the situation and partly on the characteristics of the child (Grusec, 2002; Grusec et al., 2000). *Question: How do the situation and the child influence parenting styles?*

One example of how the situation affects the parenting style is that parents are more likely to use power-assertive techniques than social withdrawal for dealing with aggressive behaviour (Mills & Rubin, 1990). Parents prefer power assertion over induction when they believe that children understand the rules they have violated, are capable of acting appropriately, and are responsible for their bad behaviour (Dix, Ruble, & Zambarino, 1989). Stressful life events, marital discord, and emotional problems all contribute to parental use of power assertion (Campbell, Pierce, March, & Ewing, 1991).

Children's behaviours and temperamental characteristics also influence adults. In one intriguing experiment (Anderson, Christian, & Luce, 1986), mothers of typically functioning boys and mothers of boys with behaviour problems interacted with boys of both types. Both groups of mothers were more negative and controlling when dealing with the boys with behaviour problems. Thus, the child's behaviour may elicit certain responses from parents. Recent parenting research embraces the notion of mutuality in parent–child relations. That is, it asserts that the parent–child relationship is a bidirectional one (Lollis & Kuczynski, 1997).

Baumrind's research suggests that we can make an effort to avoid some of the pitfalls of being authoritarian or overly permissive. Some recommended techniques that parents can use to help control and guide their children's behaviour are listed in Table 10.3.

Advice for Parents in Guiding Children's Behaviour

Do . . .	Don't . . .
• Reward good behaviour with praise, smiles, hugs.	• Pay attention only to a child's misbehaviour.
• Give clear, simple, realistic rules appropriate to the child's age.	• Issue too many rules or enforce them haphazardly.
• Enforce rules with reasonable consequences.	• Try to control behaviours solely in the child's domain, such as thumb sucking, which can lead to frustrating power struggles.
• Ignore annoying behaviour such as whining and tantrums.	
• Childproof the house, putting dangerous and breakable items out of reach. Then establish limits.	• Nag, lecture, shame, or induce guilt.
	• Yell or spank.
• Be consistent.	• Be overly permissive.

Sources: Windell (1991); Schmitt (1991).

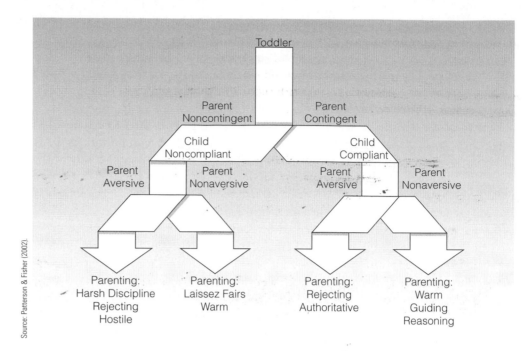

Source: Patterson & Fisher (2002).

Figure 10.1
The Compliance Process

Influence of Siblings: Brothers and Sisters Matter

A recent Canadian census (Statistics Canada, 2004) states that the average number of children per Canadian family is 1.1. Of Canadian (and North American) families with children, however, most have at least two children (Dunn, 2004). (A rise in one-child families or in blended families is occurring in Western countries though.) In many cases, children spend more time with their siblings in the early years than they spend with their parents (Volling, 2003).

Question: What kinds of influences do siblings have on social and personal development in early childhood? Siblings make a unique contribution to one another's social, emotional, and cognitive development (Roberts & Blanton, 2001). They serve many functions, including giving physical care, providing emotional support and nurturance, offering advice and direction, serving as role models, providing social interaction that helps develop social skills, and making demands and imposing restrictions (Howe, Rinaldi, Jennings, & Petrakos, 2002; Roberts & Blanton, 2001). They also advance each other's cognitive development, as shown in research concerning false beliefs and the theory of mind (Cutting & Dunn, 1999; Peterson, 2001; Ruffman, Perner, & Parkin, 1999).

In early childhood, when siblings spend a great deal of time together, their interactions are often emotionally loaded and marked by both positive aspects (cooperation, teaching, nurturance) and negative aspects (conflict, control, competition) (Howe, Rinaldi, Jennings, & Petrakos, 2002; Howe, Petrakos, & Rinaldi, 1998; Volling, 2003). By and large, older siblings are more nurturant but also more dominating than younger siblings. Younger siblings are more likely to imitate older siblings and to accept their direction. At the ripe old age of two, Rinaldi's younger daughter raced onto the soccer field and attempted to intercept play to the surprise of her brother and his five-year-old teammates. She was convinced she was part of Team Blizzard, and was not pleased when her mother quickly escorted her back to her spectator blankie on the sidelines.

© Myrleen Ferguson Cate/PhotoEdit

Siblings
Siblings make a unique contribution to one another's social, emotional, and cognitive development. In many cultures, older girls are expected to care for younger siblings.

However, older siblings may also imitate younger siblings, especially when parents remark in front of the older child "how cute" the baby is being. At the age of two years five months, Rathus's daughter Allyn would pretend that she could not talk every once in a while, just like her five-month-old sister, Jordan.

In many cultures, older girls are expected to care for younger siblings (Volling, 2003). Younger siblings, therefore, frequently turn to older sisters when the mother is unavailable.

Parents often urge their children to stop fighting among themselves. There are times when these conflicts look deadly (and occasionally they are). It is important to note, however, that garden-variety conflict among siblings can have positive outcomes. (Really.) It appears that conflict between siblings enhances their social competence, their development of self-identity (who they are and what they stand for), and their ability to rear their own children in a healthful manner (Bedford, Volling, & Avioli, 2000; Rinaldi & Howe, 1998). When adults look back on their childhood conflicts with their siblings, their memories of them are often positive (Bedford et al., 2000).

As siblings move from early childhood through middle childhood and into adolescence, the nature of their relationship changes in at least two ways (Volling, 2003). First, as siblings grow more competent and their developmental statuses become similar, their relationship becomes more egalitarian. In other words, as later-born siblings grow older and become more self-sufficient, they need and accept less nurturance and direction from older siblings. Second, sibling relationships become less intense as children grow older. The exercise of power and the amount of conflict declines. The extent of warmth and closeness diminishes somewhat as well, although the attachment between siblings remains fairly strong throughout adolescence.

Other factors also affect the development of sibling relationships. For example, there is more conflict between siblings in families in which the parents treat the children differently (Volling, 2003). Conflict between siblings is also greater when the relationship between the parents or between the parents and children is not harmonious (Rinaldi & Howe, 2003; Volling, 2003). It should also come as no surprise that children who have a difficult temperament have more trouble getting along with their siblings (Dunn, 1993).

Canadian Parents

The importance of early child–parent relationships has been emphasized in theories of attachment (Ainsworth, 1989; Ainsworth & Bowlby, 1991), social information processing (Dodge, Bates, & Pettit, 1990), and social interaction (Fisher, Ellis, & Chamberlain, 1999). In the child development literature, Baumrind's (1971) parenting style dimensions (authoritative, authoritarian, and permissive) continue to be relevant constructs to understanding individual differences in parenting practices. To date, there is considerable research that has emphasized the positive benefits of authoritative parenting styles on children as they grow up (e.g., Grusec, 2002). In contrast, authoritarian and permissive styles have been linked to less positive outcomes for children (Kaufmann et al., 2000). The majority of parenting research has been conducted with mothers. Unfortunately, little research has focused on fathers' parenting styles, and as a result little is known about how mothers' and fathers' parenting styles are connected. Family systems theory frames the family as an interdependent unit, and therefore both mothers' and fathers' parenting practices must be simultaneously considered in order to gain a better understanding of child functioning (Hinde & Stevenson-Hinde, 1988). Consistent parenting practices have been found to be associated with more reliable and harmonious parenting, while incompatible parenting approaches have been found to be sources of conflict and stress for parents (Gable, Crnic, & Belsky, 1994).

In a Canadian study on parenting styles, Rinaldi, Gates, & Urichuk (2007) investigated mothers' and fathers' reports of their own as well as their partners' parenting styles, and assessed the relationship between parenting practices and toddlers' social

individualist A person who defines himself or herself in terms of personal traits and gives priority to his or her own goals.

behaviour. Mothers and fathers of twenty-seven toddlers participated. All families consisted of two parents living together with their children. Mothers' and fathers' self-reported parenting styles were low to moderately correlated on the permissiveness and authoritative parenting dimensions, respectively. Parents' reports of their own and their partners' parenting styles yielded moderate correlations (i.e., they tended to be similar to one another) and suggested that parents are for the most part congruent in

Developing in a World of Diversity

Individualism, Collectivism, and Patterns of Child Rearing

Much of the research on parenting styles has been done with middle-class Western families. But parenting styles must be viewed within the context of particular cultures. Socialization methods that appear authoritarian or punitive by middle-class standards may be used more frequently among poor families from ethnic minority groups to prepare children to cope with the hazards of daily life. Placing a high value on unquestioned obedience might be considered overly restrictive in a quiet middle-class neighbourhood but warranted now and then in a more dangerous inner city environment (Baldwin, Baldwin, & Cole, 1990). Poor families in other

countries also tend to use authoritarian child-rearing styles.

A study by Kobayashi-Winata and Power (1989) compared child-rearing practices of middle-class Japanese and American parents whose children ranged in age from four to seven. In both groups of families, the most compliant children had parents who provided opportunities for appropriate behaviour and who used relatively little punishment. But American parents were more likely to rely on external punishments such as sending children to their room, whereas Japanese parents more often used verbal commands, reprimands, and explanations (see Table 10.4).

These differences in disciplinary practices apparently reflect cultural differences. Cross-cultural research reveals that people in many Western cultures tend to be individualistic (Ayyash-Abdo, 2001; French et al., 2001). On the other hand, many people from cultures in Africa, Asia, and Central and South America tend to be collectivistic (Abe-Kim, Okazaki, & Goto, 2001; Basic Behavioral Science Task Force, 1996).

Individualists tend to define themselves in terms of their personal identities and to give priority to their personal goals (Triandis, 1995). When asked to complete the statement "I am ... ," they are likely to respond in

Table 10.4	Cultural Values and Child-Rearing Techniques in North America and Japan	
Culture	**Parental Value**	**Child-Rearing Practices**
North American middle class	• Early socialization	• Expect child to follow more rules
	• Independence	• Listen to child's opinion
	• Individualism	• Use external punishment (e.g., send child to his or her room)
Japanese middle class	• Group harmony	• Make fewer demands
	• Dependence on others	• Be more indulgent
		• Use verbal commands
	• Conformity	• Use reprimands and explanations

rating each other's parenting practices. In looking at toddler behaviour, the more favourbale authoritative style of parenting was found to be associated with toddlers' adaptive skills. While fathers' authoritarian parenting style was correlated to behaviour challenges, it was mothers' permissive style that was associated with behavioural symptoms. These findings suggest that although mothers and fathers share similarities in parenting, they have unique experiences with their children.

collectivist A person who defines himself or herself in terms of relationships to other people and groups and gives priority to group goals.

terms of their personality traits ("I am outgoing," "I am artistic") or their occupations ("I am a nurse," "I am a systems analyst") (Triandis, 1990). In contrast, **collectivists** tend to define themselves in terms of the groups to which they belong and to give priority to the group's goals (Triandis, 1995). They feel complete in terms of their relationships with others (Markus & Kitayama, 1991) (see Figure 10.2). They are more likely than individualists to conform to group norms and judgments (Abe-Kim et al., 2001; Phalet & Schoenpflug, 2001). When asked to complete the statement "I am ... ," they are more likely to respond in terms of their family, sex, religion, or ethnicity ("I am a father," "I am a Buddhist," "I am Japanese") (Triandis, 1990, 1994).

It must be mentioned, however, that individuals from within the same country can belong to different "cultures" in terms of individualistic and collectivist tendencies. In Lebanon, for example, Ayyash-Abdo (2001) found that college students who spoke French or English were more likely to be individualistic than those who spoke mainly Arabic. Moreover, traditional Islamic values were also connected with collectivism.

Other studies reveal additional differences in the child-rearing techniques of American and Japanese parents that appear to foster the American emphasis on early socialization and independence and the Japanese focus on group harmony and dependence on others. For example, in one study, American mothers of preschoolers expected their children to follow more rules but were also more likely to listen to their children's opinions. Japanese mothers, in contrast, made fewer demands on their children and were more indulgent (Power, Kobayashi-Winata, & Kelley, 1992).

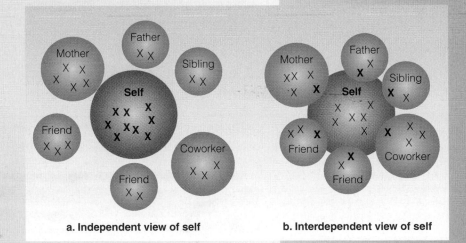

a. Independent view of self

b. Interdependent view of self

Figure 10.2

The Self in Relation to Others from the Individualist and Collectivist Perspectives

(a) To an individualist, the self is separate from other people. (b) To a collectivist, the self is complete only in terms of relationships to other people. (Based on Markus & Kitayama, 1991.) Are there differences in the ways in which people in individualist and collectivist cultures rear their children?

Adjusting to the Birth of a Sibling

The birth of a sister or brother is often a source of stress for young children because of changes in family relationships and the environment (Volling, 2003). When a new baby comes into the home, the mother pays relatively more attention to it and spends much less time in playful activities with the older child. No wonder the child may feel displaced and resentful of the affection lavished on the newborn. These feelings are illustrated by the comments of a three-year-old who worried that his new sister would take all of his mother's love and not leave enough for him (Campbell, 1990).

Children show a mixture of negative and positive reactions to the birth of a sibling. These include **regression** to babyish behaviours, such as increased clinging, crying, and toilet accidents. Anger and naughtiness may increase as well. But the same children will often show increased independence and maturity, insisting on feeding or dressing themselves and helping to take care of the baby (Volling, 2003).

What can parents do to help a young child cope with the arrival of a new baby? For one thing, they can prepare the child by explaining in advance what is to come. In one study, preschoolers who attended a sibling preparation class with their mothers showed fewer signs of **sibling rivalry** (Fortier, Carson, Will, & Shubkagel, 1991). Parental support is extremely important as well. Children show less distress following the birth of a sibling when the parents give them lots of affection, encouragement, and praise and spend time doing things with them (Gottlieb & Mendelson, 1990).

regression A return to behaviours characteristic of earlier stages of development.

sibling rivalry Jealousy or rivalry among brothers and sisters.

Birth Order: Not Just Where in the World but Also Where in the Family

Interestingly (to us anyway), both Rathus and Rinaldi, the authors of this text, are only children. We experienced what we imagine are most of the rewards and, yes, punishments of being an only child. First and perhaps foremost, we were each the little king and queen of our respective households. Rathus enjoyed all the resources his family had to offer: a relatively good allowance (with which he bought a comic book a day—*Superman* did nothing that escaped his young attention) and lots of parental attention. He recalls never knowing that his family was poor because he got most of what he wanted.

Rinaldi's experience of being an only child also allowed her a lot of parental attention. Although surrounded by many close cousins and friends, she enjoyed relating to adults, sometimes more so than to other children. And there were times when she had sibling envy—she wanted an older sister, one that would lend her cool clothes and play Charlie's Angels with her. Rathus also recalls being lonely at home and wishing that he had a sister or a brother. But these are the experiences of only two individuals, and it is difficult to know how accurately they are recalled. So let's be more scientific about it. *Question: What does the research say about the effects of being a firstborn or an only child?*

Many differences in personality and achievement have been observed among firstborn and only children compared with later-born children. *Truth or Fiction Revisited:* It is true that firstborn children, as a group, are more highly motivated to achieve than later-born children. As a group, firstborn and only children perform better academically (that applies to both authors, too, of course) and are more cooperative (not so sure about that one). They are also helpful (true for Rinaldi), adult-oriented (more true for Rathus), and less aggressive (true for both of us) (Braza et al., 2000; Paulhus, Trapnell, & Chen, 1999; Zajonc, 2001). They obtain higher standardized test scores, including SAT scores (Zajonc & Mullally, 1997). An adoptee study found that first-reared children, regardless of their biological birth order, were more conscientious than later-reared children (Beer & Horn, 2000). As part of their achievement orientation, firstborn children also see themselves as being more in control of their successes (Phillips & Phillips, 2000). On the negative side, firstborn and only children may show greater anxiety (both Rinaldi & Rathus fall into that category) and are less self-reliant (hmm...we wonder).

Interviews with the parents of 478 children ranging in age from three to nine years found that firstborn children are more likely than later-born children to have imaginary playmates (Bouldin & Pratt, 1999). Rinaldi had an imaginary playmate when she was four years old—in fact, she made up an imaginary older sister. Also, Allyn, Rathus's firstborn, had an imaginary playmate named Loveliness, while his second-born (Jordan) and third-born (Taylor) may have been too busy coping with older siblings to have imaginary playmates.

Later-born children may learn to act aggressively to compete for the attention of their parents and older siblings. They must also deal with the fact that they do not come first (Downey, 2001). Perhaps for that reason, their self-concepts tend to be lower than those of firstborn or only children. But the social skills they acquire from dealing with their family position seem to translate into greater popularity with peers. They tend to be more rebellious, liberal, and agreeable than firstborn children—factors connected with their popularity (Paulhus et al., 1999; Zweigenhaft & Von Ammon, 2000).

Differences in personality and achievement among firstborn and later-born children may be linked to contrasting styles in parenting. Firstborn children start life as only children. For a year or more, they receive the full attention of parents. Even after other children come along, parents still tend to relate more often to the first child. Parents continue to speak at levels appropriate for the firstborn. Parents impose tougher restrictions on firstborn children and make greater demands of them. Parents are more highly involved in their activities. Firstborn children are often recruited to help teach younger siblings (Zajonc, 2001). As we can testify, being asked to teach something (often) prompts one to learn something about it.

By and large, parents are more relaxed and flexible with later-born children. Children are aware of the greater permissiveness often given to later-born children and may complain about it. (Endlessly.) Why are parents more indulgent with later-born children? They have probably gained some self-confidence in child rearing. They see that the firstborn child is turning out just fine. (All right, the firstborn child *usually* turns out to be just fine, and sometimes "just fine" needs to be qualified as "*just fine much of the time.*") Parents may therefore assume that later-born children will also turn out, well, just fine. In any event, Rinaldi and her husband found themselves being more relaxed with their daughter (second-born) than with their son (firstborn).

There is a more negative interpretation of parents' relative "relaxation" in rearing later-born children. Parents have just so many resources, in terms of time, energy, and, yes, money. As new children come along, they dilute the resources so that not as much can be devoted to them (Downey, 2001).

All right, then, siblings hold key places in child development. *Question: What is the influence of peers on social and personal development in early childhood?*

Peer Relationships

The importance of **peers** in the development of the young child is widely recognized. As children move into the preschool years, they spend more time in the company of other children. Peer interactions serve many functions. Children learn social skills in the peer group—sharing, helping, taking turns, dealing with conflict. They learn how to lead and how to follow. Physical and cognitive skills develop through peer interactions. Finally, peers are a source of emotional support (Bukowski, 2003; Grusec, 2002; Parker & Gottman, 1989).

peers Children of the same age. (More generally, people of similar background and social standing.)

Friendship

Friendship takes on different meanings as children develop. Preschoolers focus on sharing toys and activities. Five- to seven-year-olds report that friends are children with whom they have "fun." Sharing confidences becomes important in late childhood and in adolescence.

Tom Prettyman / PhotoEdit

Infants first show positive interest in one another at about six months. If they are placed on the floor facing each other, they will smile, occasionally imitate one another, and often touch one another. Social interaction increases over the next few months, but during the first year, contacts between infants tend to be brief (Hartup, 1992b; Howes, 1987). In the second year, children show more interest in each other and interact by playing with each other's toys. But they still show relatively little social interaction. By about two years of age, however, children imitate one another's play and engage in social games such as follow the leader (Brownell, 1990; Eckerman & Stein, 1990; Hanna & Meltzoff, 1993). Also by the age of two, children have established preferences for a few particular playmates (Strayer, 1990).

The preferences of toddlers for certain other children is an early sign of friendship (Collins & Gunnar, 1990). Friendship extends beyond casual interactions. It is characterized by shared positive experiences and feelings of attachment (Grusec, 2002; Park, Lay, & Ramsay, 1993). Even early friendships are fairly stable. One- to six-year-olds tend to maintain their friendships from one year to the next, some for as long as three years (Howes, 1988). On the other hand, parental conflict can spill over into peer conflict. Children of fighting parents are less tolerant of the bumps and bruises of peer relationships (Du Rocher Schudlich, Shamir, & Cummings, 2004).

Preschool children behave somewhat differently toward their friends than toward ordinary playmates. Friends, compared with nonfriends, show higher levels of interaction, helpful behaviour, more smiling and laughing, and more frequent cooperation and collaboration (Costin & Jones, 1992; Rubin & Coplan, 1992). Conflicts between young friends are less intense and are resolved more readily than other conflicts (Hartup, 1992a).

What are children's conceptions of friendships? When preschoolers are asked what they like about their friends, they typically mention the toys and activities they share (Hartup, 1993). Five- to seven-year-olds usually report that their friends are the children with whom they do things and have fun (Berndt & Perry, 1986). Not until late childhood and adolescence do friends' traits and notions of trust, communication, and intimacy become key aspects of friendship.

Developing in a World of Diversity

The Case of the (In)Visible Father

Certainly over the past two centuries, forces such as urbanization, industrialization, and government-funded welfare programs have contributed to illegitimacy and fathers' abandonment of families. Developmentalists conceptualize responsible fatherhood as providing children with financial support, care-giving (feeding and bathing children, tucking them in, reading to them, spending time with them), emotional support, and legal paternity (Coley, 2001; Doherty, Kouneski, & Erickson, 1996). It's not happening—at least not for many children in North America. Family structure is connected with level of income. For example, couple families have a higher median total income than lone-parent families. Many single fathers give lip service to intending to support and care for their children (Johnson, 2000), but studies show that most drop out as their children go through early childhood (Coley & Chase-Lansdale, 1999).

On the other hand, many fathers are more deeply involved than ever before in the day-to-day lives of their children (Cabrera, Tamis-LeMonda,

Bradley, Hofferth, & Lamb, 2000). They do more child care and housework, even though mothers are usually thought of as the primary caregivers and homemakers. This shift is connected with the blurring of traditional gender roles and with the fact that most mothers are in the work force—often in better-paying positions than their husbands. Moreover, after divorce, a growing number of fathers obtain custody or share custody of their children.

Fathers may play a distinctive role in promoting their children's social and emotional development (Denham & Kochanoff, 2002; Isley, O'Neil, & Parke, 1996; Parke, 1996). While both mothers' and fathers' socialization practices have been correlated, certain paternal traits (e.g., endorsement of authoritarian control) are linked to externalizing problems in children (Calzada, Eyberg, Rich, & Querido, 2004). Some researchers report mothers are more responsive and engage in more care-giving and comforting than fathers, whereas fathers engage in more high intensity play (Lamb, 1996; Volling, McElwain, Notaro, & Herrera, 2002). However, most

studies that include fathers rely heavily on self-report data, whereas there are a greater number of observational mother–child studies. The small number of studies that have actually compared mothers and fathers (with both sons and daughters) on the same measures have yielded equivocal results. To really understand the nature of father–child relationships, a multi-level and dynamic approach is needed (Parke, 2002). Research of paternal involvement with children has suggested that we should focus on three components: interaction, availability, and responsibility (Lamb et al., 1996)

Rebekah Levine Coley (2001) noted that none of these statistics, in themselves, indicate whether the presence of the father *matters*. She acknowledges that theories of child development generally find significant roles for the father but argues that research is needed to fill in some blanks. For example, what exactly is the father's influence on the child's cognitive development, educational attainment, and social and personal development?

Active Review

1. Investigators of child rearing find it useful to classify parents according to two dimensions: warmth-coldness and _____.

2. _____ methods of enforcing restrictions attempt to give children knowledge that will enable them to generate desirable behaviour patterns in similar situations.

3. _____ parents are both warm and restrictive.

4. _____ parents believe that obedience is a virtue for its own sake.

5. (Firstborn or Later-born?) children are most highly motivated to achieve.

Reflect & Relate: Where do you fit into your family of origin? Are you a firstborn or only child? Were you born later? How does your own development and personality fit in with the stereotypes discussed in this section?

Go to
WWW www.voyages1ce.nelson.com
for an interactive version of this review.

Social Behaviours: In the World, Among Others

During the early childhood years, children make tremendous strides in the development of social skills and behaviour. Their play activities increasingly involve other children. They learn how to share, cooperate, and comfort others. But young children, like adults, are complex beings. They can be aggressive at times but also loving and helpful. Some key developments in early childhood are the growing abilities to control negative emotions and behaviours, talk about mental states, take various perspectives, carry out various roles in dramatic play, internalize standards of behaviour, and start to follow prosocial rules. In the following section we will see how these developments take place.

Play—Child's Play, That Is

Question: What do developmentalists know about child's play?

While children play, developmentalists work to understand just how they do so. They have found that play has many characteristics. It is meaningful, pleasurable, voluntary, and internally motivated (Jennings & Dietz, 2003). Play is fun! But play also serves many important functions in the life of the young child (Azar, 2002). Play helps children develop motor skills and coordination. It contributes to social development, because children learn to share play materials, take turns, and try on new roles through **dramatic play.** It supports the development of such cognitive qualities as curiosity, exploration, symbolic thinking, and problem solving (Singer & Singer, 2001). Play may even help children learn to control impulses (Azar, 2002).

To watch children's different styles of play, click on the "Play" clip in Module 2, Section 3.

dramatic play Play in which children enact social roles; made possible by the attainment of symbolic thought. A form of *pretend play.*

Play and Cognitive Development

Play both contributes to and expresses milestones in cognitive development. Jean Piaget (1962) identified kinds of play, each characterized by increasing cognitive complexity:

- Functional play. Beginning in the sensorimotor stage, the first kind of play involves repetitive motor activity, such as rolling a ball or running and laughing.
- Symbolic play. Also called pretend play, imaginative play, or dramatic play, symbolic play emerges toward the end of the sensorimotor stage and increases during early childhood. In symbolic play, children create settings and characters and scripts (Lytle, 2003; Nichols & Stich, 2000; Nielsen & Dissanayake, 2000).
- Constructive play. Constructive play is common in early childhood. Children use objects or materials to draw something or make something, such as a tower of blocks.
- Formal games. The most complex form of play, according to Piaget, involves formal games with rules. These include board games, which are sometimes enhanced or invented by children, and games involving motor skills, such as marbles and hopscotch, ball games involving sides or teams, and video games. Such games may involve social interaction as well as physical activity and rules. People play such games for a lifetime. Mildred Parten, whom we discuss next, focused on the social dimensions of play.

Parten's Types of Play

In classic research on children's play, Mildred Parten (1932) observed the development of six types of play among two- to five-year-old nursery school children: unoccupied play, solitary play, onlooker play, parallel play, associative play, and cooperative play (see Table 10.5). Solitary play and onlooker play are considered

Table 10.5   *Parten's Categories of Play*

Category	Nonsocial or Social?	Description
Unoccupied play	Nonsocial	Children do not appear to be playing. They may engage in random movements that seem to be without a goal. Unoccupied play appears to be the least frequent kind of play in nursery schools.
Solitary play	Nonsocial	Children play with toys by themselves, independently of the children around them. Solitary players do not appear to be influenced by children around them. They make no effort to approach them.
Onlooker play	Nonsocial	Children observe other children who are at play. Onlookers frequently talk to the children they are observing and may make suggestions, but they do not overtly join in.
Parallel play	Social	Children play with toys similar to those of surrounding children. However, they treat the toys as they choose and do not directly interact with other children.
Associative play	Social	Children interact and share toys. However, they do not seem to share group goals. Although they interact, individuals still treat toys as they choose. The association with the other children appears to be more important than the nature of the activity. They seem to enjoy each other's company.
Cooperative play	Social	Children interact to achieve common, group goals. The play of each child is subordinated to the purposes of the group. One or two group members direct the activities of others. There is also a division of labour, with different children taking different roles. Children may pretend to be members of a family, animals, space monsters, and all sorts of creatures.

© Michael Newman / PhotoEdit

Associative Play
Associative play is a form of social play in which children interact and share toys.

nonsocial play Forms of play (solitary play or onlooker play) in which play is not influenced by the play of nearby children.

social play Play in which children interact with and are influenced by the play of others. Examples include parallel play, associative play, and cooperative play.

types of **nonsocial play**—that is, play in which children do not interact socially. Nonsocial play occurs more often in two- and three-year-olds than in older preschoolers. Parallel play, associative play, and cooperative play are considered **social play.** In each case, children are influenced by other children as they play. Parten found that associative play and cooperative play become common by age five. More recent research continues to show that they are more likely to be found among older and more experienced preschoolers (Howes & Matheson, 1992b). Furthermore, girls are somewhat more likely than boys to engage in social play (Zheng & Colombo, 1989).

But there are exceptions to these age trends in social play. Nonsocial play can involve educational activities that foster cognitive development. In fact, many four- and five-year-olds spend a good deal of time in parallel constructive play. For instance, they may work on puzzles or build with blocks near other children. Parallel constructive players are frequently perceived by teachers to be socially skillful and are popular with their peers (Coplan, Rubin, Fox, Calkins, & Stewart, 1994; Rubin, 1982). Some toddlers are also more capable of social play than one might expect, given their age. Two-year-olds with older siblings or with a great deal of group experience may engage in advanced forms of social play. Nina Howe and colleagues (Howe et al., 1998; Howe, Petrakos, Rinaldi, & LeFebvre, 2005) have found that children's attempts to construct shared meanings in exchanges were associated with pretense and internal-state language. As well, high levels of pretend play were correlated with higher levels of negotiation skills in sibling interactions.

Learning through Play: A Vygotskian Perspective

We have discussed Lev Vygotsky's sociocultural theory of cognitive development in other chapters. It is fitting to discuss Vygostky's influence on early childhood educators' understanding of play as well. Both researchers and practitioners adhering to a Vygotskian approach would argue that play has a key purpose in the lives of children. In particular, play (1) creates a zone of proximal development, (2) eases the separation of thought from actions and objects, (3) aids the development of self-regulation, (4) impacts motivation, and (5) helps decentration (Bordova & Leong, 2007). One fascinating conclusion is that play allows children to grow by engaging them in higher levels of attention, symbolizing, and problem solving. Play is serious business.

Sex Differences in Play

Question: Are there 'boys' toys and girls' toys? It appears that there are. The reasons are a bit harder to pin down.

Lisa Serbin and her colleagues (2001) explored infants' visual preferences for gender-stereotyped toys using the time-honoured assumption that infants spend more time looking at objects that are of greater interest. They found that, by eighteen months of age, both girls and boys showed significant preferences for gender-stereotyped toys. Although preferences for gender-typed toys are well developed by the ages of fifteen to thirty-six months, girls are more likely to stray from the stereotypes (Bussey & Bandura, 1999; Frey & Ruble, 1992). Girls ask for and play with "boys' toys" such as cars and trucks more often than boys choose dolls and other "girls' toys." These cross-role activities may reflect the greater prestige of "masculine" activities and traits in American culture. Therefore, a boy's playing with "girls' toys" might be seen as his taking on an inferior role. A girl's playing with "boys' toys" might be interpreted as having an understandable desire for power or esteem.

Girls and boys differ not only in toy preferences but also in their choice of play environments and activities. During the preschool and early elementary school years, boys prefer vigorous physical outdoor activities such as climbing, playing with large vehicles, and rough-and-tumble play. In middle childhood, boys spend more time than girls in large play groups of five or more children and spend more time in competitive play (Crombie & Desjardins, 1993; Van Brunschot, Zarbatany, & Strang, 1993). Girls are more likely to engage in arts and crafts and domestic play. Their activities are more closely directed and more structured by adults than are boys' activities (Campbell, Shirley, & Caygill, 2002). Girls spend more time than boys playing with just one other child or with a small group of children (Crombie & Desjardins, 1993; Van Brunschot et al., 1993).

Why do children show these early preferences for gender-stereotyped toys and activities? Although one cannot rule out the possibility of biological factors, such as boys' slightly greater strength and activity levels and girls' slightly greater physical maturity and coordination, note that these differences are just that—slight. On the other hand, parents and other adults treat girls and boys differently from birth onward. They consistently provide gender-stereotyped toys and room furnishings and encourage gender typing in children's play activities and even household chores (Leaper, 2002). Children, moreover, tend to seek out information on which kinds of toys and play are "masculine" or "feminine" and then conform to the label (Martin & Ruble, 2004).

Some studies find that children who "cross the line" by exhibiting an interest in toys or activities considered appropriate for the other sex are often teased, ridiculed, rejected, or ignored by their parents, teachers, other adults, and peers. Boys are more likely to be criticized than girls (Fagot & Hagan, 1991; Garvey, 1990). On the other hand, one study of fifty preschoolers—twenty-five girls and twenty-five boys—found

© Philip James Corwin / CORBIS

Girls Enjoying a Game of Baseball
Although preferences for gender-typed toys are well established by the age of 3, girls are more likely than boys to stray from the stereotypes, as in this photograph of a girl playing the masculine-typed game of baseball.

that most children believed that their peers should not be excluded from gender-typed play activities on the basis of sex (Theimer, Killen, & Stangor, 2001). That is, most believed that it was wrong in terms of equality and fairness to prevent girls from playing with trucks and boys from playing with dolls. Perhaps the inconsistency in research findings has something to do with the difference between what preschoolers are observed to do and what they say. (Why should children be more consistent than the rest of us?)

Another well-documented factor involving sex and play is that girls prefer the company of girls, whereas boys prefer to play with boys. This phenomenon is found in a wide variety of cultures and ethnic groups, and it appears early in life. Children begin to prefer playmates of the same sex by the age of two, with girls developing this preference somewhat earlier than boys (Fagot, 1990; Hay, Payne, & Chadwick, 2004; Strayer, 1990). The tendency to associate with peers of the same sex becomes stronger during middle childhood (Bukowski, Gauze, Hoza, & Newcomb, 1993a; Crombie & Desjardins, 1993). Perhaps you remember a period during your childhood when you and your friends found members of the other sex absolutely loathsome and wanted nothing to do with them.

Question: Why do children choose to associate with peers of their own sex? Eleanor Maccoby (1990b) believed that two factors are involved. One is that boys' play is more oriented toward dominance, aggression, and rough play. The second is that boys are not very responsive to girls' polite suggestions. Maccoby suggested that girls avoid boys because they want to protect themselves from boys' aggression and because they find it unpleasant to interact with unresponsive people. Boys may avoid the company of girls because they see girls as inferior (Caplan & Larkin, 1991).

Another view is that children simply "like" peers of their own sex more than peers of the other sex (Bukowski et al., 1993a). But in the field of psychology, "simple liking" is usually based on similarity in interests. Children who prefer dolls to transportation toys may prefer to associate with children who share their preference.

Prosocial Behaviour: It Could Happen, and Does

prosocial behaviour
Behaviour intended to benefit another without expectation of reward.

Prosocial behaviour, sometimes known as *altruism,* is behaviour intended to benefit another without expectation of reward. Prosocial behaviour includes helping and comforting others in distress, sharing, and cooperating (Strayer & Roberts, 2004). Rinaldi has seen her son often trying to help his preschool peers. She remembers seeing him sharing his toys, often at his own expense. He had many sad times when toys or favours he gave were not returned or when toys were broken by others. *Question: How does prosocial behaviour develop?*

Even in the first year, children begin to share. They spontaneously offer food and objects to others (Hay & Murray, 1982). In the second year, children continue to share objects, and they also begin to comfort distressed companions and help others with

Whom Do You Want to Play With?
During early and middle childhood, children tend to prefer the company of children of their own sex. Why?

tasks and chores (Hay, Caplan, Castle, & Stimson, 1991; Zahn-Waxler, Radke-Yarrow, & Wagner, 1992).

By the preschool and early school years, children frequently engage in prosocial behaviour. Some types of prosocial behaviour occur more often than others. One study observed four- and seven-year-olds at home and found that helping occurred more often than sharing, affection, and reassuring (Grusec, 1991). Research suggests that the development of prosocial behaviour is linked to the development of other capabilities in the young child, such as empathy and perspective taking.

Question: What can adults do to support the development of prosocial behaviours? Primary adults in the lives of children have a critical role to play in fostering prosocial behaviours. Adult behaviours that have been found to encourage prosocial behaviour are empathic care-giving, prosocial modelling, and the provision of clear rules when negative or coercive behaviours are used (Bronson, 2000). Furthermore, adults (parents, caregivers, educators) can coach children through appropriate sibling or peer interactions. Modelling is an excellent tool for adults to use—whether they are modelling or communicating about caring actions and values, using prosocial reasoning to explain and guide behaviour, or employing positive reinforcement of prosocial behaviours (while avoiding physical punishment and criticism) (Bronson, 2000). Finally, empowering children by assigning them age- and skill-appropriate social responsibilities is a recommended educational strategy.

Empathy: "I Feel Your Pain"

Empathy is sensitivity to the feelings of others. It is the ability to understand and share another person's feelings and is connected with sharing and cooperation. A survey of American and Japanese mothers of preschoolers found that both groups reported that cooperativeness and interpersonal sensitivity were the most desirable characteristics in young children (Olson, Kashiwagi, & Crystal, 2001).

empathy Ability to share another person's feelings.

Children respond emotionally from infancy when others are in distress (Strayer & Roberts, 2004). Infants frequently begin to cry when they hear other children crying (Eisenberg, Wolchik, Goldberg, & Engel, 1992). However, this early agitated response may be largely reflexive. Even so, crying might signal the development of empathy.

Empathy appears to promote prosocial behaviour and to decrease aggressive behaviour, and these links are evident by the second year (Hastings, Zahn-Waxler, Robinson, Usher, & Bridges, 2000; Strayer & Roberts, 2004). During the second year, many children approach other children and adults who are in distress and try to help them. They may hug a crying child or tell the child not to cry. Toddlers who are rated as emotionally unresponsive to the feelings of others are more likely to behave aggressively throughout the school years (Olson, Bates, Sandy, & Lanthier, 2000).

There is evidence that girls show more empathy than boys (Eisenberg et al., 1992; Strayer & Roberts, 2004). The difference may arise because girls are socialized to be more attuned to others' emotions than boys are (Strayer & Roberts, 2004), but genetic factors may also play a role in the sex difference.

Perspective Taking: Standing in Someone Else's Shoes

According to Piaget, children in the preoperational stage tend to be egocentric. That is, they tend not to be able to see things from the vantage points of others. It turns out that various cognitive abilities, such as being able to see another person's perspective, are related to knowing when someone is in need or distress (Carlo, Knight, Eisenberg, & Rotenberg, 1991). Perspective-taking skills improve with age, and so do prosocial skills. Among children of the same age, those with better developed perspective-taking ability also show more prosocial behaviour and less aggressive behaviour (Bengtsson & Johnson, 1992; Eisenberg & Miller, 1990; Hastings et al., 2000).

Influences on Prosocial Behaviour

Yes, altruistic behaviour is usually defined as prosocial behaviour that occurs in the absence of or expectation of rewards. Nevertheless, prosocial behaviour is influenced by rewards and punishments.[1] Observations of nursery school children show that the peers of children who are cooperative, friendly, and generous respond more positively to them than they do to children whose behaviour is self-centred (Hartup, 1983). Children who are rewarded in this way for acting prosocially are likely to continue these behaviours (Eisenberg et al., 1992).

Some children at early ages are made responsible for doing household chores and caring for younger siblings. They are taught helping and nurturance skills, and their performances are selectively reinforced by other children and adults. Whiting and Edwards (1988) reported that children who are given such tasks are more likely to show prosocial behaviours than children who are not.

There is evidence that children can acquire sharing behaviour by observing models who help and share. In one experiment in sharing, twenty-nine to thirty-six-month-olds were more likely to share toys with playmates who first shared toys with them (Levitt, Weber, Clark, & McDonnell, 1985). That is, the children appeared to model—and reciprocate—the sharing behaviour of their peers.

It also appears that children's prosocial behaviour is influenced by the kinds of interactions they have with their parents. For example, prosocial behaviour and empathy are enhanced in children who are securely attached to their parents and in children whose mothers show a high degree of empathy (Clark & Ladd, 2000; Strayer & Roberts, 2004).

Parenting styles also affect the development of prosocial behaviour. Prosocial behaviour is fostered when parents use inductive techniques such as explaining how behaviour affects others ("You made Josh cry. It's not nice to hit"). Parents of prosocial children are more likely to expect mature behaviour from their children. They are less likely to use power-assertive techniques of discipline (Strayer & Roberts, 2004).

Development of Aggression: The Dark Side of Social Interaction

Children, like adults, are complex beings. Not only can they be loving and altruistic, but they can also be aggressive. (More contradictions.) Some children, of course, are more aggressive than others. Aggression refers to behaviour intended to cause pain or hurt to another person.

Question: How does aggression develop? Aggressive behaviours, as with other social behaviours, seem to follow developmental patterns. For one thing, the aggression of preschoolers is frequently instrumental or possession oriented (Parke & Slaby, 1983). That is, young children tend to use aggression to obtain the toys and things they want, such as a favoured seat at the table or in the car. But older preschoolers are more likely to resolve their conflicts over toys by sharing rather than fighting (Caplan, Vespo, Pedersen, & Hale, 1991). Anger and aggressive behaviour in preschoolers usually causes other preschoolers to reject them (Henry et al., 2000; Walter & LaFreniere, 2000).

By age six or seven, aggression becomes hostile and person oriented. Children taunt and criticize each other and call each other names; they also attack one another physically.

---

[1]It reminds us of these lines from Walt Whitman's "Song of Myself": "Do I contradict myself? / Very well then I contradict myself. / (I am large, I contain multitudes.)" Be tolerant of contradictions. You will find them all around you for the rest of your life.

Aggressive behaviour appears to be generally stable and predictive of a wide variety of social and emotional difficulties in adulthood (Mesman, Bongers, & Koot, 2001; Nagin & Tremblay, 2001; National Research Council, 1993). Boys are more likely than girls to show aggression from childhood through adulthood, a finding that has been documented in many cultures (Kupersmidt, Bryant, & Willoughby, 2000; Nagin & Tremblay, 2001). In longitudinal research, Sheryl Olson and her colleagues (2000) found that toddlers who were perceived as difficult and defiant were more likely to behave aggressively throughout the school years. A longitudinal study of more than 600 children found that aggressive eight-year-olds tended to remain more aggressive than their peers twenty-two years later, at age thirty (Eron, Huesmann, & Zelli, 1991). Aggressive children of both sexes were more likely to have criminal convictions as adults, to abuse their spouses, and to drive while drunk.

Theories of Aggression

Question: What causes aggression in children? What causes some children to be more aggressive than others? Aggression in childhood appears to result from a complex interplay of biological factors and environmental factors such as reinforcement and modelling.

Evolutionary Theory

Is aggression "natural"? In his theory of evolution, Charles Darwin noted that more individuals are produced than can find food and survive into adulthood. Therefore, there is a struggle for survival. Individuals who possess characteristics that give them an advantage in this struggle are more likely to reach reproductive maturity and contribute their genes to the next generation. In many species, then, whatever genes are linked to aggressive behaviour are more likely to be transmitted to new generations.

Biological Factors

Recent evidence suggests that genetic factors may be involved in aggressive behaviour, including criminal and antisocial behaviour (Leve, Winebarger, Fagot, Reid, & Goldsmith, 1998; McGuffin et al., 2001; Plomin, 2001b). A classic longitudinal study of more than 14 000 adoptees in Denmark found that biological sons of criminal fathers had elevated crime rates even when adopted at birth and reared by law-abiding parents (Mednick, Moffitt, & Stack, 1987).

If genetics is involved in aggression, genes may do their work at least in part through the male sex hormone testosterone. Testosterone is apparently connected with feelings of self-confidence, high activity levels, and—the negative side—aggressiveness (Dabbs, Bernieri, Strong, Campo, & Milun, 2001; Pope et al., 2000; A. Sullivan, 2000). Males are more aggressive than females, and males have higher levels of testosterone than females (Pope et al., 2000). Studies show, for example, that nine- to eleven-year-old boys with conduct disorders are likely to have higher testosterone levels than their less aggressive peers (Booth, Johnson, Granger, Crouter, & McHale, 2003; Chance, Brown, Dabbs, & Casey, 2000).

Another biologically based factor that may indirectly influence the development of aggression is a child's temperament. Children who are impulsive, uninhibited, and relatively fearless may be more likely to elicit punitive, aggressive reactions from parents (Bates, Bayles, Bennett, Ridge, & Brown, 1991; National Research Council, 1993). In a literally vicious cycle, aggressive parental reactions may contribute to the development of aggression in children. Intriguingly, both permissiveness and harsh discipline is ineffective in parenting children, reaffirming the importance of parent support and education programs (Patterson & Fish, 2002; Straus, 1991).

Cognitive Factors

Aggressive boys are more likely than nonaggressive boys to incorrectly interpret the behaviour of other children as potentially harmful (Dodge, Laird, Lochman, Zelli, & Conduct Problems Prevention Research Group U.S., 2002). This bias may make the aggressive child quick to respond aggressively in social situations. Research with somewhat older children—781 fourth- and fifth-graders—also found a strong role for cognitive factors (Erdley & Asher, 1998). Children who believed in the legitimacy of aggression were more likely to say that they would behave aggressively when they were presented with hypothetical social provocations.

Aggressive children are also often found to be lacking in empathy and the ability to see things from the perspective of other people (Hastings et al., 2000). They fail to conceptualize the experiences of their victims, and so they are less likely to inhibit their aggressive impulses.

Social Learning

Social cognitive explanations of aggression focus on the role of environmental factors such as reinforcement and observational learning. Children, like adults, are most likely to be aggressive when they are frustrated in attempts to gain something they want, such as attention or a toy. When children repeatedly push, shove, and hit in order to grab toys or break into line, other children usually let them have their way (Cole, Mills, Dale, & Jenkins, 1991). Children who are thus rewarded for acting aggressively are likely to continue to use aggressive means, especially if they do not have alternative means to achieving their ends.

Aggressive children may also associate with peers who value their aggression and encourage it (Cairns & Cairns, 1991; Perry, Perry, & Boldizar, 1990). These children have often been rejected by less aggressive peers, a fact that decreases their motivation to please less aggressive children and reduces their opportunity to learn social skills (Arnold, Homrok, Ortiz, & Stowe, 1999; Henry et al., 2000; Walter & LaFreniere, 2000).

Parents may also encourage aggressive behaviour, sometimes inadvertently. Gerald Patterson (1982, 1995) and his colleagues examined families in which parents use coercion as the primary means for controlling children's behaviour. In a typical pattern, parents threaten, criticize, and punish a "difficult" or "impossible" child. The child then responds by whining, yelling, and refusing to comply until the parents give in. Both parents and children are relieved when the cycle ends. Thus, when the child misbehaves again, the parents become yet more coercive and the children yet more defiant, until parents or children give in. A study of 156 children found that this cycle of behaviour, observed in the home when children were eighteen months of age, predicted childhood aggression at the age of five in both sexes, as assessed by teacher ratings (Fagot & Leve, 1998). A study with 407 five-year-olds also found that the Patterson model predicts aggressive behaviour in both sexes (Eddy, Leve, & Fagot, 2001).

Children learn not only from the effects of their own behaviour but also from observing the behaviour of others. They may model the aggressive behaviour of their peers, their parents, or their communities at large (Linares et al., 2001; Putallaz et al., 1998). Children are more apt to imitate what their parents do than to heed what they say. If adults say they disapprove of aggression but smash furniture or hit each other when frustrated, children are likely to develop the notion that this is the way to handle frustration.

Truth or Fiction Revisited: It is true that children who are physically punished are more likely to be aggressive themselves (American Psychological Association, 1993; Putallaz et al., 1998; Shields & Cicchetti, 2001). Physically aggressive parents serve as models for aggression and also stoke their children's anger.

Media Influences

Real people are not the only models of aggressive behaviour in children's lives. A classic study by Bandura and his colleagues (1963) suggested that televised models had a powerful influence on children's aggressive behaviour. One group of preschool children observed a film of an adult model hitting and kicking an inflated Bobo doll, whereas a control group saw an aggression-free film. The experimental and control children were then left alone in a room with the same doll as hidden observers recorded their behaviour. The children who had observed the aggressive model showed significantly more aggressive behaviour toward the doll themselves (see Figure 10.3). Many children imitated bizarre attack behaviours devised for the model in this experiment—behaviours that they would not have thought up themselves.

The children exposed to the aggressive model also showed aggressive behaviour patterns that had not been modelled. Therefore, observing the model not only led to imitation of modelled behaviour patterns but also apparently **disinhibited** previously learned aggressive responses. The results were similar whether children observed human or cartoon models on film.

The Bandura study was a setup—an experimental setup, to be sure, but still a setup. It turns out that television is one of children's major sources of informal observational learning. It also turns out that television is a fertile source of aggressive models throughout much of the world (Villani, 2001). Children are routinely

disinhibit To stimulate a response that has been suppressed (inhibited) by showing a model engaging in that response without aversive consequences.

Figure 10.3

Photos from Albert Bandura's Classic Experiment in the Imitation of Aggressive Models

Research by Albert Bandura and his colleagues has shown that children frequently imitate the aggressive behaviour they observe. In the top row, an adult model strikes a clown doll. The second and third rows show a boy and a girl imitating the aggressive behaviour.

Albert Bandura / Dept. of Psychology, Stanford University

exposed to scenes of murder, beating, and sexual assault—just by turning on the TV set. ***Truth or Fiction Revisited:*** It is true that children who watch two to four hours of TV a day will see 8000 murders and another 100 000 acts of violence *by the time they have finished elementary school* (Eron, 1993). Are children less likely to be exposed to violence by watching only G-rated movies? No. One study found that virtually all G-rated animated films have scenes of violence, with a mean duration of nine to ten minutes per film (Yokota & Thompson, 2000). Other media that contain violence include movies, rock music and music videos, advertising, video games, and the Internet (Villani, 2001).

In any event, most organizations of health professionals agree that media violence does contribute to aggression (Holland, 2000; Villani, 2001). This relationship has been found for girls and boys of different ages, social classes, ethnic groups, and cultures. Consider a number of ways in which depictions of violence make such a contribution:

- *Observational learning.* Children learn from observation (Holland, 2000). TV violence supplies *models* of aggressive "skills," which children may acquire. Classic experiments show that children tend to imitate the aggressive behaviour they see in the media (Bandura et al., 1963) (see Figure 10.3).
- *Disinhibition.* Punishment inhibits behaviour. Conversely, media violence may disinhibit aggressive behaviour, especially when media characters "get away" with violence or are rewarded for it.
- *Increased arousal.* Media violence and aggressive video games increase viewers' level of arousal. That is, television "works them up." We are more likely to be aggressive under high levels of arousal.
- *Priming of aggressive thoughts and memories.* Media violence "primes" or arouses aggressive ideas and memories (Bushman, 1998).
- *Habituation.* We become "habituated to," or used to, repeated stimuli. Repeated exposure to TV violence may decrease viewers' sensitivity to real violence (Holland, 2000).

A joint statement issued by the American Medical Association, the American Academy of Pediatrics, the American Psychological Association, and the American Academy of Child and Adolescent Psychiatry (Holland, 2000) made some additional points:

- Children who see a lot of violence are more likely to view violence as an effective way of settling conflicts. Children exposed to violence are more likely to assume that violence is acceptable.
- Viewing violence can decrease the likelihood that one will take action on behalf of a victim when violence occurs.
- Viewing violence may lead to real-life violence. Children exposed to violent programming at a young age are more likely to be violent themselves later on in life.

The Canadian Paediatric Society urges Canadian children to watch less television and be more active. Specific recommendations to help parents curb their children's TV viewing habits include the following (Canadian Paediatric Society, 2007b):

• Limit daily TV viewing to one hour for preschoolers.
• Try to watch television with children.
• Turn off the television during meals, when visitors arrive, and during study time.
• Allow older children to plan their weekly viewing schedule in advance.
• Help children understand the difference between fantasy and real-life situations.
• Support media literacy education in the schools.

Violent video games are also connected with aggressive behaviour. Craig Anderson and Karen Dill (2000) found that playing violent video games increases aggressive thoughts and behaviour in the laboratory. It was also connected with a history of juvenile delinquency. However, males are relatively more likely than females to act aggressively after playing violent video games and are more likely to view the world as a hostile place. Students who obtain higher grades are also less likely to behave aggressively following exposure to violent media games. Thus, cultural stereotyping of males and females, possible biological sex differences, and moderating variables such as academic achievement also come into play when we are talking about the effects of media violence. There is no simple one-to-one connection between media violence and violence in real life. ***Truth or Fiction Revisited:*** Therefore, it is *not* true that children mechanically imitate the aggressive behaviour they view in the media. But exposure to violence in the media increases the probability of violence in viewers in several ways.

There seems to be a circular relationship between exposure to media violence and aggressive behaviour (Anderson & Dill, 2000; Eron, 1982; Funk, Buchman, Myers, & Jenks, 2000). Yes, TV violence and violent video games contribute to aggressive behaviour, but aggressive youngsters are also more likely to seek out this kind of "entertainment."

The family constellation also affects the likelihood that children will imitate the violence they see on TV. Studies find that parental substance abuse, paternal physical punishments, and single motherhood contribute to the likelihood of aggression in early childhood (Brook, Zheng, Whiteman, & Brook, 2001; Chang et al., 2003; Gupta, Nwosa, Nadel, & Inamdar, 2001). Parental rejection further increases the likelihood of aggression in children (Eron, 1982). These family factors suggest that the parents of aggressive children are absent or unlikely to help young children understand that the kinds of socially inappropriate behaviours they see in the media are not for them. A harsh home life may also confirm the TV viewer's vision of the world as a violent place and further encourage reliance on television for companionship. In Chapter 9, we saw how parents can help children understand that the violence they view in the media is not real and not to be imitated.

Active Review

6. In _____ play, children play with toys by themselves.

7. In _____ play, children interact and share toys.

8. Preschoolers tend to prefer to play with children of the (other or same?) sex.

9. _____ is another term for prosocial behaviour.

10. Preschoolers tend to (admire or reject?) aggressive peers.

11. Aggressive behaviour is linked with the hormone _____.

12. _____ theorists explain aggressive behaviour in terms of reinforcement and observational learning.

13. The observation of aggression in the media tends to (inhibit or disinhibit?) aggressive behaviour in children.

Reflect & Relate: Do you believe that violence in the media causes aggression? (What does the word *cause* mean?) Media violence is everywhere—not only in R-rated films but also in G-rated films and in video games. There are connections between media violence and aggression, but not everyone who witnesses media violence behaves aggressively. So how do we explain the connections between violence in the media and aggression?

Go to
W W W www.voyages1ce.nelson.com
for an interactive version of this review.

Personality and Emotional Development

In the early childhood years, children's personalities start becoming more defined. Their sense of self—who they are and how they feel about themselves—continues to develop and becomes more complex. They begin to acquire a sense of their own abilities and their increasing mastery of the environment. As they move out into the world, they also face new experiences that may cause them to feel fearful and anxious. Let's explore some of these facets of personality and emotional development.

The Self

self-concept One's impression of oneself; self-awareness.

The sense of self, or the **self-concept,** emerges gradually during infancy. Infants and toddlers visually begin to recognize themselves and differentiate themselves from other individuals such as their parents.

Question: How does the self develop during early childhood? In the preschool years, children continue to develop their sense of self. Almost as soon as they begin to speak, they describe themselves in terms of certain categories, such as age groupings (baby, child, adult) and sex (girl, boy). These self-definitions that refer to concrete external traits have been called the **categorical self** (Damon & Hart, 1992; Lewis & Brooks-Gunn, 1979).

categorical self Definitions of the self that refer to concrete external traits.

Children as young as three years are able to describe themselves in terms of behaviours and internal states that appear to occur frequently and are fairly stable over time (Eder, 1989, 1990). For example, in response to the question "How do you feel when you're scared?" young children frequently respond, "Like running away" (Eder, 1989). Or in answer to the question "How do you usually act around grown-ups?" a typical response might be, "I mostly been good with grown-ups." Thus, even preschoolers seem to understand that they have stable characteristics that endure over time.

self-esteem The sense of value, or worth, that people attach to themselves.

One aspect of the self-concept is **self-esteem,** the value or worth that people attach to themselves. Children who have a good opinion of themselves during the preschool years show secure attachment and have mothers who are sensitive to their needs (Cassidy, 1988;

Mueller & Tingley, 1990). These children are also more likely to engage in prosocial behaviour (Cauley & Tyler, 1989).

By the age of four, children begin to make evaluative judgments about two different aspects of themselves (Harter, 1990a; Harter & Pike, 1984). One is their cognitive and physical competence (e.g., being good at puzzles, counting, swinging, tying shoes), and the second is their social acceptance by peers and parents (e.g., having lots of friends, being read to by Mom). But preschoolers do not yet make a clear distinction between different areas of competence. For example, a child of this age is not likely to report being good in school but poor in physical skills. One is either "good at doing things" or one is not (Harter & Pike, 1984).

During middle childhood, personality traits become increasingly important in children's self-definitions. Children then are also able to make judgments about their self-worth in many different areas of competence, behavioural conduct, appearance, and social relations.

Initiative versus Guilt

As preschool children continue to develop a separate sense of themselves, they increasingly move out into the world and take the initiative in learning new skills. Erik Erikson refers to these early childhood years as the third stage of his psychosocial model theory of development, termed *initiative versus guilt.*

Children in this stage strive to achieve independence from their parents and master adult behaviours. They are curious, trying new things and testing themselves. These qualities are illustrated in the following account of a day in the life of a five-year-old (Crain, 2000):

> In a single day, he decided to see how high he could build his blocks, invented a game that consisted of seeing who could jump the highest on his parents' bed, and led the family to a new movie containing a great deal of action and violence.

During these years, children learn that not all of their plans, dreams, and fantasies can be realized. Adults prohibit children from doing certain things, and children begin to internalize these adult rules. Fear of violating the rules may cause the child to feel guilty and may curtail efforts to master new skills. Parents can help children develop and maintain a healthy sense of initiative by encouraging their attempts to learn and explore and by not being unduly critical and punitive.

Fears: The Horrors of Early Childhood

In Erik Erikson's view, fear of violating parental prohibitions can be a powerful force in the life of a young child. *Question: What sorts of fears do children have in the early years?*

Both the frequency and the content of fears change as children move from infancy into the preschool years. The number of fears seems to peak between two and a half and four years and then tapers off (Miller, Boyer, & Rodoletz, 1990b).

The preschool period is marked by a decline in fears of loud noises, falling, sudden movement, and strangers. *Truth or Fiction Revisited:* Fear of social disapproval is *not* the most common fear among preschoolers. Preschoolers are most likely to have fears that revolve around animals, imaginary creatures, the dark, and personal safety (Finch & McIntosh, 1990; Ollendick & King, 1991; Wenar, 1990). The fantasies of young children frequently involve stories they are told and media imagery. Frightening images of imaginary creatures can persist. Many young children are reluctant to have the lights turned off at night for fear that these creatures may harm them in the dark. Imaginary creatures also threaten personal safety.

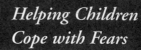

Helping Children Cope with Fears

A number of methods have been developed to help children cope with fears. Professionals who work with children today are most likely to use such behaviour modification methods as *counterconditioning, operant conditioning,* and *participant modelling.* Each method is based on principles of learning.

Counterconditioning

Counterconditioning exposes children gradually to the sources of their fears while they are engaging in behaviour that is incompatible with fear. Fear includes bodily responses such as rapid heart rate and respiration rate. Thus, doing things that reduce the heart and respiration rates is incompatible with fear.

In a classic study, Mary Cover Jones (1924) used counter-conditioning to eliminate a fear of rabbits in a two-year-old boy named Peter. Jones arranged for a rabbit to be gradually brought closer to Peter while the boy engaged in some of his favourite activities, such as munching merrily away on candy and cookies. Peter, to be sure, cast a wary eye in the rabbit's direction, but he continued to eat. Jones suspected that if she brought the rabbit too close too quickly, the cookies left on Peter's plate and those already eaten might have decorated the walls. But gradually the animal could be brought nearer without upsetting the boy. Eventually, Peter could eat and touch the rabbit at the same time. Jones gave the child a treat. Having the child play with a game or favourite toy or asking the child to talk about a favourite book or TV hero are other methods of relaxing the child.

Operant-Conditioning Techniques

In operant conditioning, children are guided into desirable behaviours and then reinforced for engaging in them. In using behaviour modification in the classroom, good behaviour is reinforced and misbehaviour is ignored.

Parents and other adults use operant techniques all the time. They may teach children how to draw letters of the alphabet by guiding their hand and saying "Good!" when the desired result is obtained. When children fear touching a dog, parents frequently take their hands and guide them physically in petting the animal. Then they say something reinforcing, such as "Look at that big girl/boy petting that doggy!" or "Isn't the puppy nice and soft?" In one study, two young girls with nighttime fears were successfully treated by being praised for sleeping in their own beds (Ollendick, Hagopian, & Huntzinger, 1991).

Participant Modelling

In participant modelling, children first observe live models or filmed or taped models (ideally, children similar in age) engage in the behaviour that evokes fear. Then they imitate the behaviour of the models. In an often cited experiment on participant modelling, Bandura and his colleagues (1969) found that participant modelling helped people who were afraid of snakes. Figure 10.4 shows children and adults in the Bandura study who imitated unafraid models.

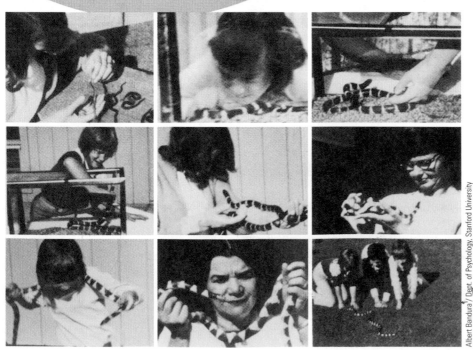

Albert Bandura / Dept. of Psychology, Stanford University

Figure 10.4

Participant Modelling

Participant modelling helps children overcome fears through principles of observational learning. In these photos, children with a fear of snakes observe then imitate models who are unafraid. Parents often try to convince children that something tastes good by eating it in front of them and saying, "Mmm!"

But real objects and situations also cause many children to fear for their personal safety, such as lightning, thunder and other loud noises, the dark, high places, sharp objects and being cut, blood, unfamiliar people, strange people, stinging and crawling insects, and other animals.

During middle childhood, children's fears become more realistic. They become less fearful of imaginary creatures, but fears of bodily harm and injury remain fairly common. Children grow more fearful of failure and criticism in school and in social relationships (Finch & McIntosh, 1990; Ollendick & King, 1991; Wenar, 1990).

Girls report more fears and higher levels of anxiety than boys (Ollendick, King, & Frary, 1989; Ollendick, Yule, & Ollier, 1991). Whether these findings reflect actual differences in fears and anxieties or differences in the willingness of girls and boys to report "weaknesses" is a matter of debate (Finch & McIntosh, 1990).

Active Review

14. Self-definitions that refer to concrete external traits are called the _____ self.

15. Self-_____ is the value or worth that people attach to themselves.

16. Children who are _____ attached tend to have high self-esteem.

17. Erikson referred to early childhood as the stage of _____ versus guilt.

18. Early childhood fears tend to revolve around personal _____.

19. (Boys or Girls?) report more fears and higher levels of anxiety.

Reflect & Relate: Do you remember any fears from early childhood? Have they faded over the years?

Go to
W W W www.voyages1ce.nelson.com
for an interactive version of this review.

Development of Gender Roles and Sex Differences

I am woman, hear me roar . . .

I am strong

I am invincible

I am woman

These lyrics are from the song "I Am Woman" by Helen Reddy and Ray Burton. They capture the attention because they run counter to the **stereotype** of the woman as vulnerable and in need of the protection of a man. The stereotype of the vulnerable woman, as with all stereotypes, is a fixed, oversimplified, and often distorted idea about a group of people—in this case, women. The stereotype of the chivalrous, protective man is also a stereotype. *Questions: What are stereotypes and gender roles? How do they develop?*

stereotype A fixed, conventional idea about a group.

gender role A complex cluster of traits and behaviours that are considered stereotypical of females and males.

Cultural stereotypes of males and females involve broad expectations of behaviour that we call **gender roles.** In our culture, the feminine gender-role stereotype includes such traits as dependence, gentleness, helpfulness, warmth, emotionality, submissiveness, and home orientation. The masculine twentieth-century gender-role stereotype includes aggressiveness, self-confidence, independence, competitiveness, and competence in business, math, and science.

Gender-role stereotypes appear to develop through a series of stages. First, children learn to label the sexes. At about two to two and a half years of age, they become quite accurate in identifying pictures of girls and boys (Fagot & Leinbach, 1993). By age three, they display knowledge of gender stereotypes for toys, clothing, work, and activities (Campbell, Shirley, & Candy, 2004). For example, children of this age generally agree that boys play with cars and trucks, help their fathers, and tend to hit others. They also agree that girls play with dolls, help their mothers, and do not hit others.

Showing distress apparently becomes gender-typed so that preschoolers judge it to be acceptable for girls. One study found that preschool boys but not girls were rejected by their peers when they showed distress (Walter & LaFreniere, 2000). The same study found that peers rejected preschoolers of both sexes when they displayed too much anger.

Children become increasingly traditional in their stereotyping of activities, occupational roles, and personality traits between the ages of three and about nine or ten (Levy, Sadovsky, & Troseth, 2000; Powlishta et al., 2001). For example, traits such as "cruel" and "repairs broken things" are viewed as masculine and traits such as "often is afraid" and "cooks and bakes" are seen as feminine. A study of fifty-five middle-class, primarily European American children, aged thirty-nine to eighty-four months, found that they considered men to be more competent in traditionally masculine-typed occupations (such as occupations in science and transportation) and women to be more competent in traditionally feminine-typed occupations (such as nursing and teaching) (Levy et al., 2000). The children equated competence with income: They believed that men earned more money in the masculine-typed jobs but that women earned more in the feminine-typed jobs.

Stereotyping levels off or declines slightly beyond the preschool years (Martin & Ruble, 2004). Older children and adolescents apparently become somewhat more flexible in their perceptions of males and females. They retain the broad stereotypes but also perceive similarities between the sexes and recognize that there are individual differences. They are more capable of recognizing the arbitrary aspects of gender categories and more willing to try behaviours that typify the other sex (Katz & Walsh, 1991).

Children and adolescents show some chauvinism by perceiving their own sex in a somewhat better light. For example, girls perceive other girls as nicer, more hardworking, and less selfish than boys. Boys, on the other hand, think that they are nicer, more hardworking, and less selfish than girls (Etaugh, Levine, & Mennella, 1984).

Sex Differences

Clearly, females and males are anatomically different. And according to the gender-role stereotypes we have just examined, people believe that they also differ in their behaviours, personality characteristics, and abilities. *Question: How different are females and males in terms of cognitive and social and emotional development?*

Sex differences in infancy are small and rather inconsistent. In this chapter, we have reviewed sex differences during early childhood. Young girls and boys display some differences in their choices of toys and play activities. Boys engage in more rough-and-tumble play and are also more aggressive. Girls tend to show more empathy and to report more fears. Girls show greater verbal ability than boys, whereas boys show greater visual–spatial ability than girls. *Question: What are the origins of sex differences in behaviour?* Different views have been proposed.

Theories of the Development of Sex Differences

Like mother, like daughter; like father, like son—at least often, if not always. Why is it that little girls (often) grow up to behave according to the cultural stereotypes of what it means to be female? Why is it that little boys (often) grow up to behave like male stereotypes? Let's have a look at various explanations of the development of sex differences.

The Roles of Evolution and Heredity

According to evolutionary psychologists such as David Buss (2000) and David Schmitt (2003), sex differences were fashioned by natural selection in response to problems in adaptation that were repeatedly encountered by humans over thousands of generations. The story of the survival of our ancient ancestors is now etched in our genes. Genes that bestow attributes that increase an organism's chances of surviving to produce viable offspring are most likely to be transmitted to future generations. We thus possess the genetic codes for traits that helped our ancestors survive and reproduce. These traits include structural sex differences, such as those found in the brain, and differences in body chemistry, such as hormones.

Consider a sex difference. Males tend to place relatively more emphasis on physical appearance in mate selection than females do, whereas females tend to place relatively more emphasis on personal factors such as financial status and reliability (Buss, 2000; Buss & Schmitt, 1993; Schmitt. 2003). Why? Evolutionary psychologists believe that evolutionary forces favour the survival of women who seek status in their mates and men who seek physical allure because these preferences provide reproductive advantages. Some physical features such as cleanliness, good complexion, clear eyes, strong teeth and healthy hair, firm muscle tone, and a steady gait are found to be universally appealing to both males and females (Buss, 1999). Perhaps such traits have value as markers of better reproductive potential in prospective mates. According to the "parental investment model," a woman's appeal is more strongly connected with her age and health, both of which are markers of reproductive capacity. The value of men as reproducers, however, is more intertwined with factors that contribute to a stable environment for child rearing, such as social standing and reliability (Buss & Schmitt, 1993). For such reasons, these qualities may have grown relatively more alluring to women over the millennia.

This theory is largely speculative, however, and not fully consistent with all the evidence. Women, as men, are attracted to physically appealing partners, and women tend to marry men similar to them in physical attractiveness and socioeconomic standing.

But evolution has also led to the development of the human brain. As we will see in the next section, the organization of the brain apparently plays a role in gender typing.

Organization of the Brain

The organization of the brain is largely genetically determined, and it at least in part involves prenatal exposure to sex hormones (Collins, Maccoby, Steinberg, Hetherington, & Bornstein, 2000; Maccoby, 2000). The hemispheres of the brain are specialized to perform certain functions. In most people, the left hemisphere is more involved in language skills, whereas the right hemisphere is specialized to carry out visual–spatial tasks.

Both males and females have a left hemisphere and a right hemisphere. They also share other structures in the brain, but the question is whether they use them in quite the same way. Consider the hippocampus, a brain structure that is involved in the formation of memories and the relay of incoming sensory information to other parts of the brain. Matthias Riepe and his colleagues have studied the ways in which humans and rats use the hippocampus when they are navigating mazes. Males use the hippocampus in both hemispheres when they are navigating (Grön et al., 2000). Women, however, rely on the hippocampus in the right hemisphere in concert with the right prefrontal cortex—an area of the brain that evaluates information and makes plans. Researchers have also found that females tend to rely on landmarks when they are finding their way ("Go a block past Ollie's Noodle Shop, turn left, and go to the corner past Café Lalo"). Men rely more on geometry, as in finding one's position in terms of coordinates or on a map ("You're at the corner of Yonge and Eglinton, and you want to get to King and Bay, so head south...") (Grön et al., 2000). Riepe and colleagues (Grön et al., 2000) speculated that a female's prefrontal activity represents the conscious effort to keep landmarks in mind. The "purer" hippocampal activity in males might represent a more geometric approach.

Some psychological activities, such as the understanding and production of language, are regulated by structures in the left hemisphere—particularly Broca's area and Wernicke's area. But emotional and esthetic responses, along with some other psychological activities, are more or less regulated in the right hemisphere. Brain-imaging research suggests that the left and right hemispheres of males may be more specialized than those of females (Shaywitz et al., 1995). For example, if you damage the left hemisphere of a man's brain, you may cause greater language difficulties than if you cause similar damage in a woman. The right hemisphere is thought to be relatively more involved in spatial relations tasks, and damage in this hemisphere is more costly to a male's spatial relations skills than to a female's.

If the brain hemispheres of women "get along better" than those of men—that is, if they better share the regulation of various cognitive activities—we may have an explanation of why women frequently outperform men in language tasks that involve some spatial organization, such as spelling, reading, and enunciation. Yet men, with more specialized spatial-relations skills, could be expected to generally outperform women at visualizing objects in space and reading maps.

Sex Hormones

There is no question that sex hormones and other chemical substances stoke the prenatal differentiation of sex organs (Davis, Grattan, & McCarthy, 2000). Toward the end of the embryonic stage, androgens—male sex hormones—are sculpting male genital organs. These chemicals may also "masculinize" or "feminize" the brain; in other words, they may give rise to behavioural tendencies that are consistent with gender-role stereotypes (Collaer & Hines, 1995; Crews, 1994).

Studies with animals have found evidence for a role for sex hormones and other substances (Collaer & Hines, 1995; Crews, 1994). Let's return to navigation. Research shows that male rats generally outperform females in maze learning, a task that relies on spatial skills. However, if you expose female rats to male sex hormones during prenatal development (as would be the case if they are sharing the uterus with a number of male siblings) or shortly after birth, they will learn maze routes as quickly as males do. They will also exhibit other stereotypical masculine behaviours, including roaming great distances and marking large territories (Vandenbergh, 1993).

The greater frequency of aggressive behaviour and rough-and-tumble play in boys may also be linked to biological factors. Prenatal sex hormones—particularly testosterone—may create predispositions that are consistent with gender-role stereotypes (Jacklin, 1989; Money, 1987).

Let us also consider psychological views of the development of sex differences.

To watch this video

click on **"Gender"** in Module 2, Section 3, on your Observing Children and Adolescents CD-ROM. You can also visit the Student Book Companion Site to watch the video, answer the questions, and e-mail your responses to your professor.

When asked "What doll takes care of the babies?" children typically respond in a stereotypical manner by pointing to the female doll.

Lessons in Observation
Gender

Learning Objectives
- At what age do children begin expressing stereotypical ideas about gender?
- What is the difference between gender identity and gender role?
- At what age do children seem to first understand that their own sex will remain stable?
- Are preschool children flexible or inflexible when it comes to their ideas concerning gender-typed behaviour?

Applied Lesson
Describe the concepts of *gender identity, gender stability,* and *gender constancy.* How do they develop, according to Kohlberg? Does research support Kohlberg's view of when children should show preferences for gender-typed toys and activities?

Critical Thinking
If a child is reared without gender-typed toys in the household or if the child's parents avoid giving the child gender-typed messages about what kinds of behaviours are appropriate, how might that child's views on gender differ from those of his or her classmates? Are classmates likely to respond flexibly to his or her views of gender?

Concept Review 10.1 — Theories of the Development of Sex Differences

Nature and Gender Typing

Theories of the development of sex differences deal with the roles of evolution, heredity, and biology in gender typing.

Perspective	Key Points	Comments
Evolution and heredity	Psychological sex differences were fashioned by natural selection in response to challenges that humans faced repeatedly over thousands of generations.	Evolutionary theorists believe that sex differences in aggression are natural. They suggest that a woman's allure is strongly connected with her age and health, which are markers of reproductive capacity, but the value of men as reproducers is also connected with factors that create a stable environment for child rearing.
Organization of the brain	The hemispheres of the brain are more specialized in males than in females.	Sex differences in brain organization might explain why women tend to excel in language skills and men in visual–spatial tasks.
Sex hormones	Sex hormones may prenatally "masculinize" or "feminize" the brain by creating predispositions consistent with gender roles.	Male rats are generally superior to females in maze-learning ability, a task that requires spatial skills. Aggressiveness appears to be connected with testosterone.

© Sylvie Villeger/Photo Researchers, Inc.
© Kathy Sloane/Photo Researchers, Inc.

Nurture and Gender Typing

The nurture and gender typing approach deals with theories in psychology—for example, learning theory, and cognitive theory—and related research.

Perspective	Key Points	Comments
Social cognitive theory	Children learn what is masculine or feminine by observational learning.	Parents and others tend to reinforce children for gender-appropriate behaviour.
Cognitive-developmental theory	Gender typing is connected with the development of the concepts of gender identity, gender stability, and gender constancy.	Research evidence shows that children develop gender-typed preferences and behaviours before development of gender stability and gender constancy.
Gender-schema theory	Cultures tend to organize social life around polarized gender roles. Children accept these scripts and try to behave in accord with them.	Research evidence suggests that polarized female–male scripts pervade our culture. For example, children tend to distort their memories to conform to the gender schema.

Social Cognitive Theory

Social cognitive theorists attempt to straddle the gulf between behaviourism and cognitive perspectives on human development. As such, they pay attention both to the roles of rewards and punishments (reinforcement) in gender typing and to the ways in which children learn from observing others and then decide what behaviours are appropriate for them. Children learn much about what society considers "masculine" or "feminine" by observing and imitating models of the same sex. These models may be their parents, other adults, children, even TV characters.

The importance of observational learning was shown in an experiment conducted by Kay Bussey and Albert Bandura (1984). In this study, children obtained information on how society categorizes behaviour patterns by observing how often they were performed either by men or by women. While children of ages two to five observed them, female and male adult role models exhibited different behaviour patterns, such as choosing a blue or a green hat, marching or walking across a room, and repeating different words. Then the children were given a chance to imitate the models. Girls were twice as likely to imitate the woman's behaviours as the man's, and boys were twice as likely to imitate the man's behaviours as the woman's.

Socialization also plays a role in gender typing. Parents, teachers, other adults—even other children—provide children with information about the gender-typed behaviours they are expected to display (Sabattini & Leaper, 2004). Children are rewarded with smiles and respect and companionship when they display "gender-appropriate" behaviour. Children are punished with frowns and "yucks" and loss of friends when they display behaviour considered inappropriate for their sex.

Boys are encouraged to be independent, whereas girls are more likely to be restricted and given help. Boys are allowed to roam farther from home at an earlier age and are more likely to be left unsupervised after school (Leaper, 2002).

Fathers are more likely than mothers to communicate norms for gender-typed behaviours to their children (Leaper, 2002). Mothers are usually less demanding. Fathers tend to encourage their sons to develop instrumental behaviour (i.e., behaviour that gets things done or accomplishes something) and their daughters to develop warm, nurturant behaviour. Fathers are likely to cuddle daughters. By contrast, they are likely to toss their sons into the air and use hearty language with them, such as "How're yuh doin', Tiger?" and "Hey, you, get your keister over here." Rinaldi's husband, being a nontraditionalist, tosses their young daughter into the air, which raises objections from relatives who criticize him for being too rough. This, of course, has led him to modify his behaviour. He has learned to toss their daughter into the air only when the relatives are not around.

Elementary school children show less stereotyping if their mothers frequently engage in traditionally "masculine" household and child-care tasks such as yard work, washing the car, taking children to ball games, or assembling toys (Powlishta et al., 2001). Many daughters have mothers who serve as career-minded role models. Maternal employment is associated with less polarized gender-role concepts for girls and boys (Leaper, 2002; Powlishta et al., 2001). The daughters of employed women also have higher educational and career aspirations than daughters of unemployed women, and they are more likely to choose careers that are nontraditional for women.

Social cognitive theory has helped outline the ways in which rewards, punishments, and modelling foster gender-typed behaviour. But *how* do rewards and punishment influence behaviour? Do reinforcers mechanically increase the frequency of behaviour, or, as suggested by cognitive theories, do they provide us with concepts that in turn guide our behaviour? Let's consider two cognitive approaches to gender typing that address these matters: cognitive-developmental theory and gender-schema theory.

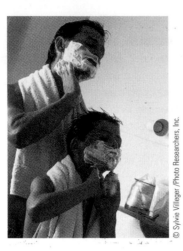

Acquiring Gender Roles

What psychological factors contribute to the acquisition of gender roles? Psychoanalytic theory focuses on the concept of identification. Social cognitive theory focuses on imitation of the behaviour patterns of same-sex adults and reinforcement by parents and peers.

Cognitive-Developmental Theory

Lawrence Kohlberg (1966) proposed a cognitive-developmental view of gender typing. According to this perspective, children play an active role in gender typing (Martin & Ruble, 2004). They form concepts about gender and then fit their behaviour to the concepts. These developments occur in stages and are entwined with general cognitive development.

According to Kohlberg, gender typing involves the emergence of three concepts: *gender identity, gender stability,* and *gender constancy.* The first step in gender typing is attaining **gender identity.** Gender identity is the knowledge that one is male or female. At two years, most children can say whether they are boys or girls. By the age of three, many children can discriminate anatomic sex differences (Bem, 1989; Campbell et al., 2004).

At around age four or five, most children develop the concept of **gender stability,** according to Kohlberg. They recognize that people retain their sexes for a lifetime. Girls no longer believe they can grow up to be daddies, and boys no longer think they can become mommies. ***Truth or Fiction Revisited:*** Because most two-and-a-half-year-olds have not developed gender stability, a girl of this age may know that she is a girl but think that she can grow up to be a daddy.

By the age of five to seven years, Kohlberg believes that most children develop the more sophisticated concept of **gender constancy.** Children with gender constancy recognize that sex does not change, even if people modify their dress or behaviour. A woman who cuts her hair short remains a woman. A man who dons an apron and cooks dinner remains a man.

We could relabel gender constancy "conservation of gender," highlighting the theoretical debt to Jean Piaget. Indeed, researchers have found that the development of gender constancy is related to the development of conservation (Serbin & Sprafkin, 1986). According to cognitive-developmental theory, once children have established concepts of gender stability and constancy, they seek to behave in ways that are consistent with their sexes (Martin & Ruble, 2004).

Cross-cultural studies in the United States, Samoa, Nepal, Belize, and Kenya (Munroe, Shimmin, & Munroe, 1984) have found that the concepts of gender identity, gender stability, and gender constancy emerge in the order predicted by Kohlberg (Leonard & Archer, 1989; Munroe et al., 1984). Children may achieve gender constancy earlier than Kohlberg stated, however. Many three- and four-year-olds show some understanding of the concept (Bem, 1989; Leonard & Archer, 1989).

gender identity Knowledge that one is female or male. Also, the name of the first stage in Kohlberg's cognitive-developmental theory of the assumption of gender roles.

gender stability The concept that one's sex is a permanent feature.

gender constancy The concept that one's sex remains the same despite superficial changes in appearance or behaviour.

Kohlberg's theory also has difficulty accounting for the age at which gender-typed play emerges. Girls show preferences for dolls and soft toys and boys for hard transportation toys by the age of one and a half to three (Alexander, 2003; Campbell et al., 2004; Powlishta et al., 2001). At this age, children are likely to have a sense of gender identity, but gender stability and gender constancy remain a year or two away. Does gender identity alone motivate a child to assume gender-typed behaviour patterns, or are biological forces also at work? Kohlberg's theory also does not explain why the concept of gender plays such a prominent role in children's classification of people and behaviour (Bem, 1983; Jacklin & McBride-Chang, 1991). Another cognitive view, gender-schema theory, attempts to address these concerns.

Gender-Schema Theory

Sandra Bem's **gender-schema theory** proposes that children use sex as one way of organizing their perceptions of the world (Campbell et al., 2004; Martin & Ruble, 2004). A gender schema is a cluster of concepts about male and female physical traits, behaviours, and personality traits. For example, consider the dimension of *strength-weakness.* Children learn that strength is linked to the male gender-role stereotype and weakness to the female stereotype. They also learn that some dimensions, such as strength–weakness, are more relevant to one gender than the other—in this case, to males. A boy will learn that the strength he displays in weight training or wrestling affects the way others perceive him. But most girls do not find this trait to be important to others, unless they are competing in gymnastics, tennis, swimming, or other sports. Even so, boys are expected to compete in these sports and girls are not. A girl is likely to find that her gentleness and neatness are more important in the eyes of others than her strength.

From the viewpoint of gender-schema theory, gender identity alone can inspire "gender-appropriate" behaviour. As soon as children understand the labels "girl" and "boy," they seek information concerning gender-typed traits and try to live up to them. A boy may fight back when provoked because boys are expected to do so. A girl may be gentle and kind because that is expected of girls. Both boys' and girls' self-esteem will depend on how they measure up to the gender schema.

Studies indicate that children do possess information according to a gender schema. For example, boys show better memory for "masculine" toys, activities, and occupations, whereas girls show better memory for "feminine" toys, activities, and occupations (Martin & Ruble, 2004). However, gender-schema theory does not answer the question of whether biological forces also play a role in gender typing.

gender-schema theory The view that one's knowledge of the gender schema in one's society (the behaviour patterns that are considered appropriate for men and women) guides one's assumption of gender-typed preferences and behaviour patterns.

Psychological Androgyny

Let's be aboveboard about it. We have made several subtle suggestions about being male and about being female in this chapter. We have acknowledged that there is probably something biological involved in it—including brain organization and baths in bodily fluids that are brimming with sex hormones. But we have probably also suggested that we may put too much stock in what is "masculine" and what is "feminine" and that we may often do boys and girls more harm than good when we urge them to adhere to strict cultural stereotypes.

Cultural stereotypes tend to polarize females and males. They tend to push females and males to the imagined far ends of a continuum of gender-role traits (Rathus et al., 2005). It is common to label people as being either masculine or feminine. It is also common to assume that the more feminine people are, the less masculine they are, and vice versa. That is, the female U.S. Marines helicopter pilot is not usually conceptualized as wearing lipstick or baking. The tough male business executive is not usually conceptualized as changing diapers and playing peek-a-boo. An "emotional" boy who also shows the "feminine" traits of nurturance and tenderness is probably thought of as less masculine than other boys. Outspoken, competitive girls are likely to be seen as not only masculine but also unfeminine.

But many psychologists today think masculinity and femininity are independent personality dimensions. That is, people (male or female) who obtain high scores on measures of masculine traits can also score high on feminine traits (Ward, 2000). *Question: What is psychological androgyny?* People with both stereotypical feminine and masculine traits are termed **psychologically androgynous** (from the Greek roots *andr,* meaning man, and *gyne,* meaning woman). *Only* people high in masculine traits are typed as masculine. *Only* people high in feminine traits are typed as feminine. People who show neither strong feminine nor masculine traits are termed undifferentiated (Bem, 1993).

psychological androgyny
Possession of both stereotypical feminine and masculine traits.

Some psychologists suggest that it is worthwhile to promote psychological androgyny in children because they will then possess both the feminine and masculine traits that are valued in our culture (Hyde, Krajnik, & Skuldt-Niederberger, 1991). A good deal of evidence suggests that androgynous children and adolescents are relatively well adjusted, apparently because they can summon a wider range of traits to meet the challenges in their lives. For example, compared with their masculine, feminine, or undifferentiated peers, androgynous children and adolescents have better social relations, superior adjustment, greater creativity (Norlander, Erixon, & Archer, 2000), and more willingness to pursue occupations stereotyped as "belonging" to the other sex (Hebert, 2000).

As reviewed by Rathus (remember him?) and his colleagues (2005), some feminist scholars criticize the concept of psychological androgyny because it is defined in terms of "masculine" and "feminine" personality traits, which tends to lend them reality. Some feminists would prefer to see the stereotypes recognized as culturally induced and then dissolved.

The changes in physical, cognitive, social, and emotional development reviewed in the last three chapters lay the groundwork for the next major period in development: the middle childhood years. We will explore those years in the next three chapters, beginning with physical development in Chapter 11.

Active Review

20. Cultural stereotypes of males and females involve broad expectations for behaviour that are called gender _____.

21. The organization of the brain involves prenatal exposure to _____ hormones.

22. Brain imaging suggests that the hemispheres of the brain are more specialized in (males or females?).

23. (Mothers or Fathers?) are more likely to communicate norms for gender-typed behaviours to children.

24. Kohlberg proposes that the emergence of three concepts guides gender typing: gender identity, gender stability, and gender _____.

25. Gender-_____ theory proposes that children blend their self-concepts with the gender schema of their culture.

Reflect & Relate: Do you see yourself as being traditionally feminine, traditionally masculine, or psychologically androgynous? Have the gender roles and stereotypes of our culture created opportunities or conflicts for you? Explain.

Go to
W W W www.voyages1ce.nelson.com
for an interactive version of this review.

Recite: *An Active Summary*™

1. What are the dimensions of child rearing?

Parental approaches to child rearing can be classified according to the independent dimensions of warmth–coldness and restrictiveness–permissiveness. Consistent control and firm enforcement of rules can have positive consequences for the child.

2. What techniques do parents use to restrict their children's behaviour?

Parents tend to use inductive methods, power assertion, and withdrawal of love to enforce rules. Inductive methods use "reasoning," or explaining why one sort of behaviour is good and another is not.

3. What parenting styles are involved in the transmission of values and standards?

The main methods are authoritative, authoritarian, and permissive. Authoritative parents are restrictive but warm and tend to have the most competent and achievement-oriented children. Authoritarian parents are restrictive and cold. The sons of authoritarian parents tend to be hostile and defiant; daughters are low in independence. Children of neglectful parents show the least competence and maturity.

4. How do the situation and the child influence parenting styles?

Parents tend to prefer power-assertive techniques when they believe that children understand the rules they have violated and are capable of acting appropriately. Stress contributes to the use of power assertion.

5. What kinds of influences do siblings have on social and personal development in early childhood?

Siblings provide care-giving, emotional support, advice, role models, social interaction, restrictions, and cognitive stimulation. However, they are also sources of conflict, control, and competition. Younger siblings usually imitate older siblings.

6. What does the research say about the effects of being a firstborn or an only child?

Firstborn and only children are generally more highly motivated to achieve, more cooperative, more helpful, more adult oriented, and less aggressive. Later-born children tend to be more aggressive, have lower self-esteem, and greater social skills with peers.

7. What is the influence of peers on social and personal development in early childhood?

Children learn social skills from peers—such as sharing, helping, taking turns, and coping with conflict. Peers foster development of physical and cognitive skills and provide emotional support. Preschoolers' friendships are characterized by shared activities and feelings of attachment.

8. What do developmentalists know about child's play?

Play is meaningful, pleasurable, and internally motivated and develops motor, social, and cognitive skills. It may help children deal with conflict and anxiety. Parten followed the development of six types of play among two to five-year-olds: unoccupied play, solitary play, onlooker play, parallel play, associative play, and cooperative play.

9. Are there boys' toys and girls' toys?

It seems so. Children show preferences for gender-stereotyped toys by fifteen to thirty months of age. Boys' toys commonly include transportation toys (cars and trucks) and weapons; girls' toys more often include dolls. Boys in early childhood prefer vigorous outdoor activities and rough-and-tumble play. Girls are more likely to engage in arts and crafts. Preferences for toys may involve the interaction of biological factors and socialization.

10. Why do children choose to associate with peers of their own sex?

Preschool children generally prefer playmates of their own sex partly because of shared interest in activities. Boys' play is more oriented toward dominance, aggression, and rough play.

11. What can adults do to support the development of prosocial behaviours?

There are many ways for adults to support the development of prosocial behaviours. Three important adult behaviours are empathic caregiving, prosocial modelling, and providing children with clear rules regarding appropriate and inappropriate behaviours. Adults also facilitate prosocial behaviour development by assigning children age- and skill-appropriate social tasks and responsibilities.

12. How does prosocial behaviour develop?

Prosocial behaviour—altruism—begins to develop in the first year, when children begin to share. Development of prosocial behaviour is linked to the development of empathy and perspective taking. Girls show more empathy than boys do.

13. How does aggression develop?

The aggression of preschoolers is frequently instrumental or possession oriented. By age six or seven, aggression becomes hostile and person oriented. Aggressive behaviour appears to be generally stable and predictive of problems in adulthood.

14. What causes aggression in children?

Genetic factors may be involved in aggressive behaviour. Genes may be expressed in part through the male sex hormone testosterone. Impulsive and relatively fearless children are more likely to be aggressive. Aggressive boys are more likely than nonaggressive boys to incorrectly assume that other children mean them ill. Social cognitive theory suggests that children become aggressive as a result of frustration, reinforcement, and observational learning. Aggressive children are often rejected by less aggressive peers. Children who are physically punished are more likely to behave aggressively. Observing aggressive behaviour teaches aggressive skills, disinhibits the child, and habituates children to violence.

15. How does the self develop during early childhood?

Self-definitions that refer to concrete external traits are called the categorical self. Children as young as three years can describe themselves in terms of characteristic behaviours and internal states. Secure attachment and competence contribute to the development of self-esteem.

16. What sorts of fears do children have in the early years?

Preschoolers are most likely to fear animals, imaginary creatures, and the dark; the theme involves threats to personal safety. Girls report more fears than boys do.

17. What are stereotypes and gender roles? How do they develop?

A stereotype is a fixed conventional idea about a group. Females are stereotyped as dependent, gentle, and home oriented. Males are stereotyped as aggressive, self-confident, and independent. Cultural expectations of females and males are called gender roles.

18. How different are females and males in terms of cognitive and social and emotional development?

Males tend to excel in math and spatial-relations skills, whereas girls tend to excel in verbal skills. Stereotypical gender preferences for toys and play activities are in evidence at an early age. Males are more aggressive and more interested in sex than females. The extent of all these sex differences is under debate.

19. What are the origins of sex differences in behaviour?

Testosterone may specialize the hemispheres of the brain—more so in males than in females, explaining why females excel in verbal skills that require some spatial organization, such as reading. Males might be better at specialized spatial-relations tasks. Male sex hormones are connected with greater maze-learning ability in rats and with aggressiveness. Social cognitive theorists explain the development of gender-typed behaviour in terms of observational learning and socialization. According to Kohlberg's cognitive-developmental theory, gender-typing involves the emergence of three concepts: gender identity, gender stability, and gender constancy. According to gender-schema theory, preschoolers attempt to conform to the cultural gender schema.

20. What is psychological androgyny?

People with both stereotypical feminine and masculine traits are said to be psychologically androgynous. Theorists differ as to whether it is beneficial to promote psychological androgyny.

W W W **Go to** www.voyages1ce.nelson.com
for an interactive version of this summary review.

Key Terms

inductive *(page 360)*

authoritative *(page 361)*

authoritarian *(page 362)*

permissive–indulgent *(page 362)*

rejecting–neglecting *(page 362)*

individualist *(page 366)*

collectivist *(page 367)*

regression *(page 368)*

sibling rivalry *(page 368)*

peers *(page 369)*

dramatic play *(page 372)*

nonsocial play *(page 374)*

social play *(page 374)*

prosocial behaviour *(page 376)*

empathy *(page 377)*

disinhibit *(page 381)*

self-concept *(page 384)*

categorical self *(page 384)*

self-esteem *(page 384)*

stereotype *(page 387)*

gender role *(page 388)*

gender identity *(page 394)*

gender stability *(page 394)*

gender constancy *(page 394)*

gender-schema theory *(page 395)*

psychological androgyny *(page 396)*

Active Learning Resources

Observing Children and Adolescents CD-ROM
Want to watch videos showing what you've just learned about in this chapter? Click on the "Gender" video in Module 2, Section 3. Your "Lessons in Observation" feature on p. 391 provides further learning objectives, an applied lesson, and a critical thinking exercise designed to help you experience this stage of development. Also check out the "Play" video in CD Module 2, Section 3.

Visit Your Companion Website for This Book
http://www.voyages1ce.nelson.com
Check out this companion website, where you will find online resources directly linked to your book. The website includes interactive exercises related to PQ4R and Power Visuals for mastering and reviewing key concepts as well as quizzing, chapter outlines, and much more!

CengageNOW!™
http://hed.nelson.com
Go to this site for the link to CengageNOW™, your one-stop study shop. Take a Pretest for this chapter, and CengageNOW™ will generate a personalized Study Plan based on your test results! The Study Plan will identify the topics you need to review and direct you to online resources to help you master those topics. You can then take a Posttest to help you determine the concepts you have mastered and those you still need to work on.

11

Middle Childhood: Physical Development

PREVIEW

TRUTH OR FICTION?

(T)(F) Children outgrow "baby fat."

(T)(F) The typical North American child is exposed to about 10 000 food commercials each year.

(T)(F) Most Canadian children are physically fit.

(T)(F) Hyperactivity is caused by chemical food additives.

(T)(F) Stimulants are often used to treat children who are already hyperactive.

(T)(F) Some children who are intelligent and provided with enriched home environments cannot learn how to read or do simple math problems.

Go to

www.voyages1ce.nelson.com
for an interactive version of this "Truth or Fiction" feature.

t is six-year old Jessica's first day of school. During recess, she runs to the climbing apparatus in the schoolyard and climbs to the top. As she reaches the top, she announces to the other children, "I'm coming down." She then walks to the parallel bars, goes halfway across, lets go, and tries again.

Zach and Kael are eight-year-olds. They are riding their bikes up and down the street. Zach tries riding with no hands on the handlebars. Kael starts riding fast, standing up on the pedals. Zach shouts, "Boy, you're going to break your neck!" (adapted from Rowen, 1973).

Middle childhood is a time for learning many new motor skills. Success in both gross and fine motor skills reflects children's increasing physical maturity, their opportunities to learn, and personality factors such as their persistence and self-confidence. Competence in motor skills enhances children's self-esteem and their acceptance by their peers.

In this chapter, we examine physical and motor development during middle childhood. We also discuss children with certain disabilities.

Growth Patterns

Question: What patterns of growth occur in middle childhood? Gains in height and weight are fairly steady throughout middle childhood. But notable variations in growth patterns also occur from child to child.

Height and Weight

Following the growth trends begun in early childhood, boys and girls continue to gain a little over two inches in height per year during the middle childhood years. This pattern of gradual gains does not vary significantly until children reach the adolescent **growth spurt** (see Figure 11.1). The average gain in weight between the ages of six and twelve is about five to seven pounds a year. During these years, children continue to become less stocky and more slender (Kuczmarski et al., 2000).

Most deviations from these average height and weight figures are quite normal. Individual differences are more marked in middle childhood than they were earlier. For example, most three-year-olds are within eight to ten pounds and four inches of each other. But by the age of ten, children's weights may vary by as much as thirty to thirty-five pounds, and their heights may vary by as much as six inches.

growth spurt A period during which growth advances at a dramatically rapid rate compared with other periods.

Nutrition and Growth

In middle childhood, average body weight doubles. Children also expend a good deal of energy as they engage in physical activity and play. To fuel this growth and activity, children need to eat more than they did in the preschool years. The average four- to six-year-old needs about 1800 calories per day. But the average seven- to ten-year-old requires 2000 calories a day (Ekvall, 1993a).

Nutrition involves much more than calories, as we will see in the section on childhood obesity. The federal government has a food guide that suggests that it is healthful to eat fruits and vegetables, fish, poultry (without skin), and whole grains and to limit intake of fats, sugar, and starches. However, the food offered to children in school and elsewhere tends to be heavy on sugar, animal fats, and salt (Bauer, Yang, & Austin, 2004). In addition, food portions have grown over the past couple of decades, particularly for salty snacks, desserts, soft drinks, fruit drinks, french fries, hamburgers, cheeseburgers, and Mexican food (Nielsen & Popkin, 2003). The largest portions are eaten at fast food restaurants.

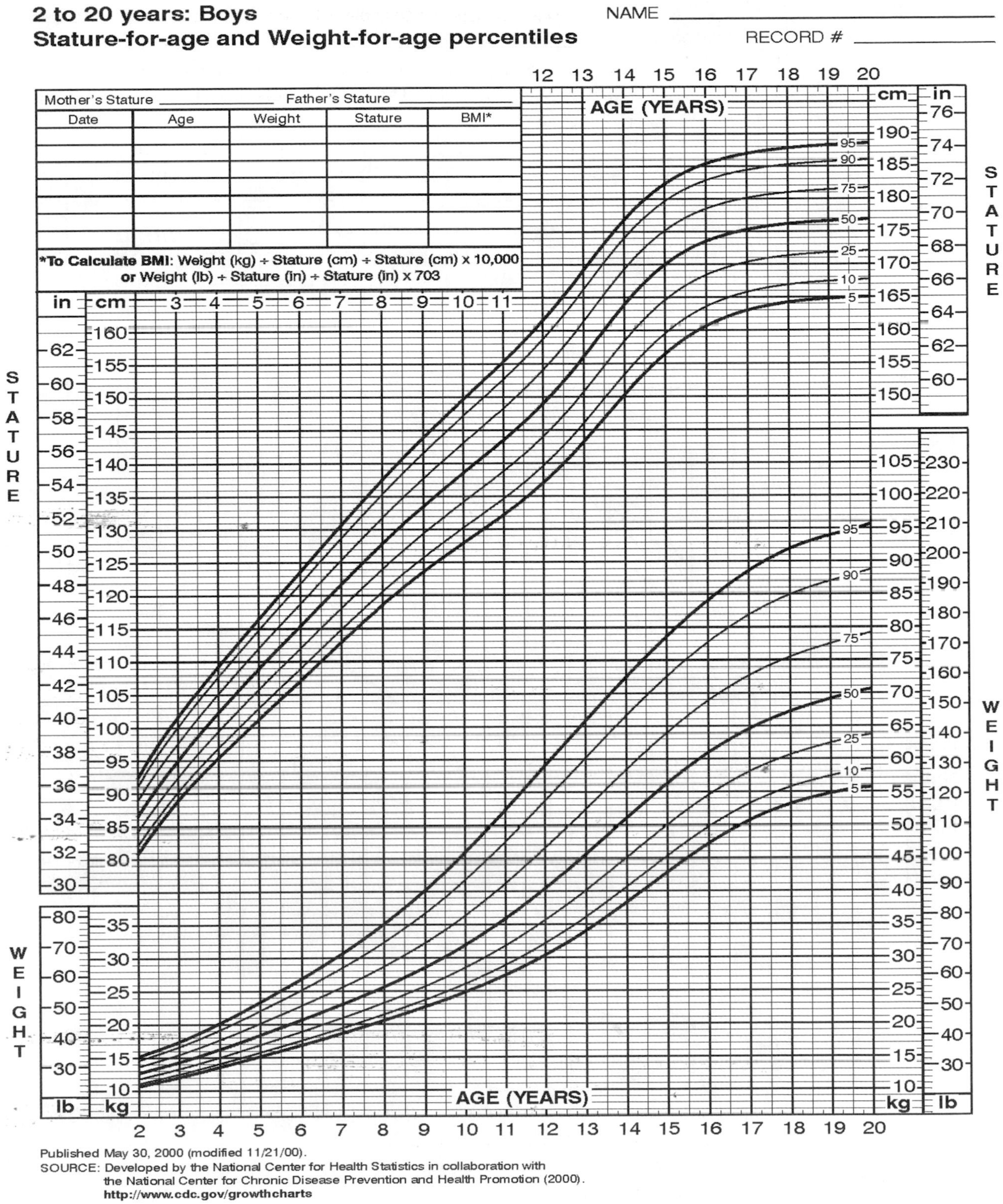

2 to 20 years: Boys
Stature-for-age and Weight-for-age percentiles

NAME _____

RECORD # _____

Published May 30, 2000 (modified 11/21/00).
SOURCE: Developed by the National Center for Health Statistics in collaboration with
the National Center for Chronic Disease Prevention and Health Promotion (2000).
http://www.cdc.gov/growthcharts

Figure 11.1

Growth Curves for Height and Weight

Gains in height and weight are fairly steady during middle childhood. Boys continue to be slightly heavier and taller than girls through 9 or 10 years of age. Girls then begin their adolescent growth spurt and surpass boys in height and weight until about age 13 or 14.

Published May 30, 2000 (Modified 10/16/00).

Source: *Developed by the National Center for Health Statistics in collaboration with the National Center for Chronic Disease Prevention and Health Promotion (2000) http:/:www.cdc.gov/growthcharts*

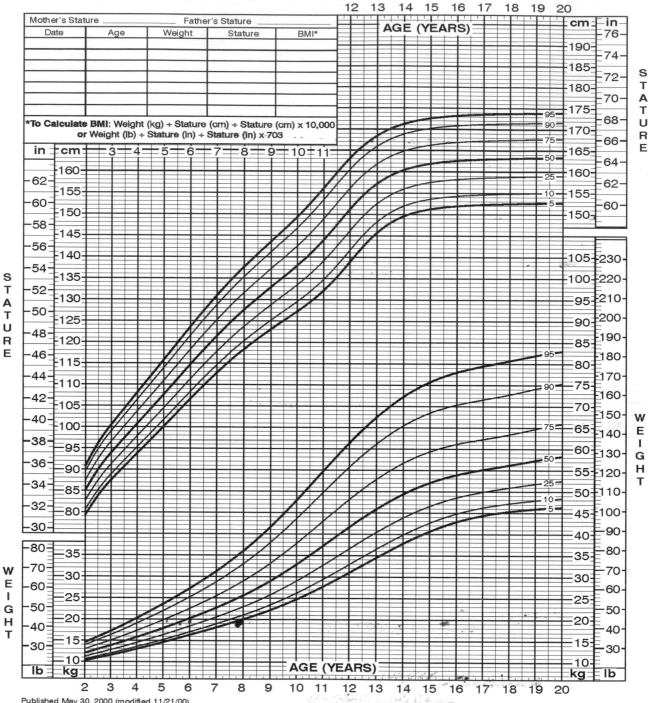

2 to 20 years: Girls
Stature-for-age and Weight-for-age percentiles

NAME _____

RECORD # _____

Published May 30, 2000 (modified 11/21/00).
SOURCE: Developed by the National Center for Health Statistics in collaboration with
the National Center for Chronic Disease Prevention and Health Promotion (2000).
http://www.cdc.gov/growthcharts

Figure 11.1

Published May 30, 2000 (Modified 10/16/00).

Source: *Developed by the National Center for Health Statistics in collaboration with the National Center for Chronic Disease Prevention and Health Promotion (2000) http/:www.cdc.gov/growthcharts*

Nutrition and social class are also connected. Consider two studies of African American mothers and daughters. Daughters living at the poverty line were likely to be fed diets high in fats and fast foods (Miklos, Brahler, Baer, & Dolan, 2004). Middle-class mothers, however, were concerned about the weight of their daughters and encouraged physical activity as a means of weight control. The mothers also tended to limit consumption of snack foods and sugar-laden carbonated beverages. Instead, they encouraged their daughters to drink water (V. J. Thompson et al., 2003).

Sex Similarities and Differences in Physical Growth

Figure 11.1 also reveals that boys continue to be slightly heavier and taller than girls through the age of nine or ten. Girls then begin their adolescent growth spurt and surpass boys in height and weight until about age thirteen or fourteen. At that time, boys are approaching the peak of their adolescent growth spurt, and they become taller and heavier than girls (Malina & Bouchard, 1991).

The steady gain in height and weight during middle childhood is paralleled by an increase in muscular strength for both girls and boys (Malina & Bouchard, 1991). The relative proportion of muscle and fatty tissue is about the same for boys and girls in early middle childhood. But this begins to change at about age eleven, as males develop relatively more muscle tissue and females develop more fatty tissue (Michael, 1990).

Childhood Obesity

Obesity is a disorder characterized by the excessive accumulation of fat. *Questions: How many children in Canada are obese? Why are they obese?* Most authorities define obesity as a body weight in excess of 20 percent of the norm. According to Statistics Canada (Shields, 2006), one-quarter of Canadian children are overweight and/or obese (see Figure 11.2). Despite the current emphasis on fitness and health in our society, the prevalence of obesity has increased among all races and in both sexes, in children as well as adults (Mokdad et al., 2000; Muntner, He, Cutler, Wildman, & Whelton, 2004). Since the 1970s, the incidence of obesity has increased by more than 50 percent among children aged six to eleven years and by nearly 40 percent among children aged twelve to seventeen years (Bar-Or et al., 1998). In Canada, the Canadian Broadcasting Corporation (CBC) and the National Film Board of Canada (NFB) have partnered to create some high-quality educational material to inform and empower students of the obesity crisis in our schools. The material may be found at http://www.cbc.ca/weightoftheworld.

Truth or Fiction Revisited: Although parents often assume that heavy children will "outgrow" their "baby fat"—especially once they hit the growth spurt of adolescence—it is not so. Most overweight children become overweight adults (Lucas, 1991; Tiwary & Holguin, 1992). By contrast, only about 40 percent of normal-weight boys and 20 percent of normal-weight girls become obese adults.

There are also social-emotional risk factors associated with obesity. Some research suggests that heavy children are often rejected by their peers (Bell & Morgan, 2000; Jackson, 1992). They usually perform poorly in sports, which can provide a source of prestige for slimmer children (Kirkcaldy, Shephard, & Siefen, 2002). As obese children approach adolescence, they become even less popular because they are less likely to be found attractive by peers of the other sex. It is no surprise, then, that obese children tend to like their bodies less than children of normal weight (Vander Wal & Thelen, 2000). Moreover, overweight adolescents are more likely to be depressed and anxious than peers who are normal in weight (Kirkcaldy et al., 2002).

Childhood obesity can also lead to high blood pressure, as we see in the nearby "A Closer Look" feature.

obesity A medical term describing individuals who are at least 20 percent above the ideal weight for their height, age, and sex.

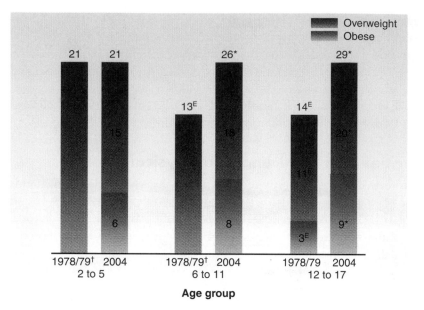

Figure 11.2

Percentage of Overweight or Obese by Age Group, Household Population Aged 2 to 17, Canada Excluding Territories, 1978/79 and 2004

Sources: *1978/79 Canada Health Survey; 2004 Canadian Community Health Survey: Nutrition.*

Data sources: *1978/79 Canada Health Survey, 2004 Canadian Community Health Survey. Nutrition*
† Obesity estimate has a coefficient of variation greater than 33.3%, therefore, it cannot be released and the combined overweight/obesity prevalence is shown.
*Significantly different from estimate for 1978/79 (p <0 05)
E Coefficient of variation 16.6% to 33.3% (interpret with caution)

Causes of Obesity

Obesity runs in families (Baker, Whisman, & Brownell, 2000; Fogelholm, Nuutinen, Pasanen, Myohanen, & Saatela, 1999; Maffeis, Talamini, & Tato, 1999; Statistics Canada, 2000; Treuth, Butte, Adolph, & Puyau, 2004). Research provides convincing evidence that heredity plays a role in obesity (Devlin, Yanovski, & Wilson, 2000). One study found that some people inherit a tendency to burn up extra calories, whereas others inherit a tendency to turn their extra calories into fat (C. Bouchard, Lykken, McGue, Segal, & Tellegen, 1990). Another study showed that identical twins have a similar body weight in adulthood whether they had been reared together or apart (Stunkard, Harris, Pedersen, & McClearn, 1990). In this study, childhood experiences appeared to have little effect on adult weight.

adipose tissue Fat.

Obesity has also been related to the quantity of fat cells, or **adipose tissue,** that we have. We may have some tendency to inherit different numbers of fat cells. The hunger drive is connected with the quantity of fat accumulated in these cells. The blood-sugar level is relatively high after one has eaten; then it drops as time elapses. As the blood-sugar level declines, the well of fat in fat cells is tapped to nourish the person, and the cells shrivel up. Eventually—and in some cases, "eventually" happens sooner than we might like!—the hypothalamus learns of the deficit and stirs the hunger drive (Woods, Schwartz, Baskin, & Seeley, 2000).

Children who have more fat cells than other children feel hungry sooner, even if they are the same weight. Perhaps the possession of more fat cells means that more signals are being transmitted to the hypothalamus in the brain. Children (and adults) who are overweight and those who were once overweight usually have more fat cells than individuals who have always weighed less. This abundance is no blessing. Childhood obesity may cause the adolescent or adult dieter to feel persistent hunger, even after they have levelled off at a weight they prefer.

Evidence that genetic and physiological factors are involved in obesity does not mean that the environment plays no role (Baker et al., 2000). Family, peers, and other environmental factors are likely to influence children's dietary behaviour (Bauer et al., 2004; Burke, Beilin, & Dunbar, 2001; Weber Cullen et al., 2001). Parents,

Health Canada Physical Activity Chart
The Health Canada Physical Activity Chart is a worksheet that children can use to track how active they are in their day-to-day lives.

for example, may be models of poor exercise habits, may encourage overeating, and may keep the wrong kinds of food in the house (Treuth et al., 2004). The reality of life in the twenty-first century is that many children and adults spend a significant portion of work and leisure time in sedentary activities such as using the computer (e.g., instant messaging, emailing, blogging), watching TV, sitting at a desk, playing video games, and talking on the phone.

More specifically, watching television also plays a role in the development of obesity (Brownell & Horgen, 2003). A large-scale longitudinal study showed that children who watched television for twenty-five or more hours per week during the middle childhood years were more likely to become obese as adolescents (Dietz, 1990; Dietz & Gortmaker, 1985). The influence of TV watching is at least threefold. First, children tend to consume snacks while watching. Second, television bombards children with commercials for fattening foods, such as candy and potato chips (Strasburger, 2001). Third, watching television is a sedentary activity. We burn fewer calories sitting than engaging in physical activity. Children who are heavy TV viewers are less physically active overall (Strasburger, 2001; Trost, Sirard, Dowda, Pfeiffer, & Pate, 2003). ***Truth or Fiction Revisited:*** It is true that North American children are exposed to about 10 000 food commercials per year—the bulk of them for fast foods (such as Burger King and Pizza Hut), highly sweetened cereals, soft drinks, and candy bars (Brownell & Horgen, 2003; Wadden, Brownell, & Foster, 2002).

Treating High Blood Pressure in Middle Childhood

Adiva was only eight years old when her doctors prescribed blood pressure medication. Her parents were not happy. "It was scary to think that this small child who wasn't even ten years old was going to have to be taking medication," her mother said. "You think about high blood pressure as an illness of adults" (cited in Carroll, 2004).

Blood pressure is rising among youth, as reported in the *Journal of the American Medical Association* (Muntner et al., 2004). As a result, doctors are prescribing antihypertensive medications to children and teenagers more often. The hope is that by catching and treating high blood pressure early, lives will be saved.

The rise in blood pressure is at least in part related to the increasing number of children who are overweight. The high intake of fast foods among children is also a likely factor. These foods are typically high in salt, which stimulates the body to retain water and in this way increases blood pressure. Children are also taking in more sugar, because they drink more soda and less milk than they did a generation ago (Carroll, 2004).

New guidelines published in the journal *Pediatrics* suggest that doctors start checking blood pressure in children as young as three years old (National High Blood Pressure Education Program Working Group, 2004). It is further recommended that most children with moderate to high blood pressure be encouraged to eat a healthful diet and exercise. But children whose blood pressure appears to be currently harmful are to be placed on medication.

As with adults, doctors may choose not to use medications right away. Lifestyle changes are preferable. But for those with high blood pressure who cannot or will not bring their blood pressure under control with these changes, medicine may prevent damage to the kidneys, heart, and eyes. And for those with extremely high blood pressure, medicine may be begun before lifestyle changes have the opportunity to take effect. These children are at risk for enlarged hearts or kidney function deterioration. Adiva's parents agreed to try the medication immediately because Adiva already showed minor organ damage.

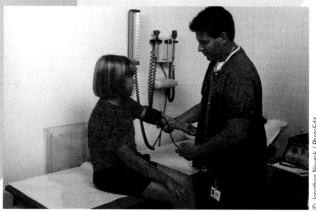

© Jonathon Nourok / PhotoEdit

Assessing Blood Pressure
Yes, some people develop high blood pressure in middle childhood. Health professionals prefer to treat high blood pressure in children with lifestyle changes, including diet and exercise. However, when organs are in danger or when lifestyle changes do not work, medication may be advised.

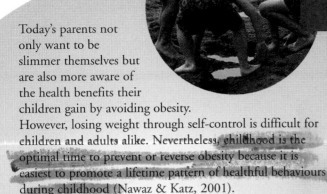

A Closer Look | *Helping Children Lose Weight*

Today's parents not only want to be slimmer themselves but are also more aware of the health benefits their children gain by avoiding obesity. However, losing weight through self-control is difficult for children and adults alike. Nevertheless, childhood is the optimal time to prevent or reverse obesity because it is easiest to promote a lifetime pattern of healthful behaviours during childhood (Nawaz & Katz, 2001).

Physical Activity, Weight, and Fitness
Get kids away from those TV sets! One way parents can motivate their children to engage in regular physical activity is to find time for family outdoor activities that promote weight control and fitness.

Cognitive behavioural methods show promise in helping children lose weight (Epstein et al., 2000; Wadden & Stunkard, 2002) by (1) improving nutritional knowledge, (2) reducing calories, (3) introducing exercise, and (4) modifying behaviour. Behavioural methods involve tracking the child's caloric intake and weight, keeping the child away from temptations, setting a good example, and systematically using praise and other rewards. The most successful weight-loss programs for children combine exercise, decreased caloric intake, behaviour modification, and emotional support from parents. Here are some suggestions from the literature:

- Teach children about nutrition—calories, protein, vitamins, minerals, fibre, food groups, and so on. Indicate which foods may be eaten in nearly unlimited quantities (e.g., green vegetables) and which foods should be eaten only sparingly (cakes, cookies, soft drinks sweetened with sugar, and so on).

- Do not insist that the entire family sit down at the same time for a large meal. Allow your child to eat only when hungry. This will break the tyranny of the clock—the expectation that he or she must be hungry because it is noon or six p.m.

- Substitute low-calorie foods for high-calorie foods. Calories translate into pounds.

- Do not push your child to "finish the plate." Allow children to stop eating when they feel full. Serve recommended food portions, not supersized portions.

- Prepare low-calorie snacks for your child to eat throughout the day. Children who feel deprived and desperate for food may go on a binge.

- Do not cook, eat, or display fattening foods when the child is at home. The sight and aroma of such foods can be tantalizing.

- Involve the child in more activities. When children are busy, they are less likely to think about food. (And physical activity burns calories.)

- Involve your child in making healthy food choices when grocery shopping. It is preferable to take a list organized by food categories from each of Canada's Food Guide groups. Try to avoid the aisles with ice cream, cakes, and candies.

- Ask relatives and friends not to offer fattening or empty-calorie treats when you visit.

- Do not allow snacking in front of the TV set or computer, or while playing video games, reading, or engaging in any other activity. Allowing children to snack while watching TV makes eating a mindless habit. Also, limit the amount of time spent in sedentary activities each day.

- Involve the child in calorie-burning exercise, such as swimming or prolonged bicycle riding. Exercise will burn calories, increase the child's feelings of competence and self-esteem, improve cardiovascular condition, and, possibly, promote lifetime exercise habits.

- Reward the child for steps in the right direction, such as eating less or exercising more. Praise is a powerful reward, but children also respond to tangible rewards such as a new toy. (See Health Canada's physical activity chart at the website mentioned below.)

- Do not assume that it is a catastrophe if the child slips and goes on a binge. Talk over what triggered the binge with the child to avert similar problems in the future. Remind the child that tomorrow is a new day and a new start.

- If you and your children are overweight, consider losing weight together. It is more effective for overweight children and their parents to diet and exercise together than for children to go it alone.

For further information and activities for active and healthy living, refer to Health Canada's Family Guide to Physical Activity for Children (six to nine years of age) and "Gotta Move!" Interactive Magazine for Children (six to nine years of age at http://www.phac-aspc.gc.ca/pau-uap/fitness/downloads.html.)

Stressors and emotional reactions also play roles in prompting children to eat (Lindel & Laessle, 2002). Overeating may occur in response to severe stresses, such as bickering in the home, parental divorce, or the birth of a sibling. Family celebrations and arguments are quite different, but both can lead to overeating or breaking a diet. Efforts to curb food intake may also be hampered by negative-feeling states, such as anxiety and depression (McGuire, Wing, Klem, Lang, & Hill, 1999; Stice, Akutagawa, Gaggar, & Agras, 2000). The rule of thumb here seems to be something like this: If life is awful, try chocolate (or french fries or pizza or whatever).

For some suggestions on how parents can help their children (and themselves) lose weight, see the nearby "A Closer Look" feature.

Active Review

1. Gains in height and weight are generally (abrupt or steady?) throughout middle childhood.

2. Children gain a little over _____ inches in height per year during middle childhood.

3. They gain about _____ pounds a year.

4. (Boys or Girls?) are slightly heavier and taller through the age of nine or ten.

5. Boys begin to become more muscular than girls at about the age of _____.

6. About _____ percent of Canadian children are obese.

7. Children (do or do not?) tend to outgrow "baby fat."

8. Obesity (does or does not?) run in families.

Reflect & Relate: How were obese children treated by their peers in your elementary school? Were you sensitive to these children's feelings, or were you part of the problem?

Go to
W W W **www.voyages1ce.nelson.com**
for an interactive version of this review.

Motor Development

Question: What changes in motor development occur in middle childhood? The school years are marked by increases in the child's speed, strength, agility, and balance (Abdelaziz, Harb, & Hisham, 2001; Loovis & Butterfield, 2000). These developments, in turn, lead to more skillful performance of motor activities, such as skipping.

Gross Motor Skills

To watch the progression of gross motor skills as children reach middle childhood, click on the "Gross Motor" clip in Module 3, Section 1.

Throughout middle childhood, children show steady improvement in their ability to perform various gross motor skills (Abdelaziz et al., 2001; Laszlo, 1990). School-aged children are usually eager to participate in group games and athletic activities that require the movement of large muscles, such as catching and throwing balls. As seen in Concept Review 11.1, children are hopping, jumping, and climbing by age six or so; and by age six or seven, they are usually capable of pedalling and balancing on a bicycle. By the ages of eight to ten, children are showing the balance, coordination, and strength that allow them to engage in gymnastics and team sports.

During these years, the muscles are growing stronger, and the pathways that connect the cerebellum to the cortex are becoming increasingly myelinated. Experience also plays an indispensable role in refining many sensorimotor abilities, especially at championship levels, but individual differences that seem inborn are also present. Some people, for example, have better visual acuity or better depth perception than others. For reasons such as these, they will have an edge in playing the outfield or hitting a golf ball.

One of the most important factors in athletic performance is **reaction time,** or the amount of time required to respond to a stimulus. Reaction time is basic to the child's timing of a swing of the bat to meet the ball. Reaction time is basic to adjusting to a fly ball or hitting a tennis ball. Reaction time is also involved in children's responses to cars and other (sometimes deadly) obstacles when they are riding their bicycles or running down the street.

reaction time The amount of time required to respond to a stimulus.

Reaction time gradually improves (i.e., *decreases*) from early childhood to about age eighteen (Abdelaziz et al., 2001; Bard, Hay, & Fleury, 1990). However, individual differences can be large (Largo et al., 2001). Reaction time begins to increase in the adult years. Even so, some seventy-five-year-olds still outperform children. Baseball and volleyball may be "child's play," but, everything else being equal, adults will respond to the ball more quickly.

Fine Motor Skills

By the age of six to seven years, children can usually tie their shoelaces and hold their pencils as adults do (see Concept Review 11.1). Their abilities to fasten buttons, zip zippers, brush teeth, wash themselves, and coordinate a knife and fork all develop during the early school years and improve during childhood (Abdelaziz et al., 2001; Cratty, 1986).

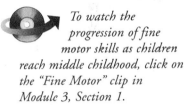

To watch the progression of fine motor skills as children reach middle childhood, click on the "Fine Motor" clip in Module 3, Section 1.

Sex Similarities and Differences in Motor Development

Question: Are there sex differences in motor skills? Throughout the middle years, boys and girls perform similarly in most motor activities. Boys show slightly greater overall strength and, in particular, more forearm strength (with dominant arm), which aids them in swinging a bat or throwing a ball (Butterfield & Loovis, 1993; Williams, Haywood, & Painter, 1996).

Girls, on the other hand, show somewhat greater limb coordination and overall flexibility, which is valuable in dancing, balancing, and gymnastics (Abdelaziz et al., 2001; Cratty, 1986). Girls with a certain type of physique seem particularly well suited to gymnastics. Those who are short, lean, and small-boned make the best gymnasts, according to Olympic coaches, because they displace gravity most effectively. This may explain why female gymnasts are considered old for the sport by the time they reach their late teens. By then, they have often grown taller and their body contours have filled out (Adler & Starr, 1992; Press, 1992).

At puberty, sex differences in motor performance favouring boys become progressively greater (Smoll & Schultz, 1990). What factors might account for the development of sex differences in physical performance? In their review of the literature, Thomas and French (1985) concluded that the slight sex differences in motor performance before puberty are not large enough to be attributed to biological variables. (The one exception may be throwing, a skill that boys excel in from an early age.) Boys are more likely than girls to receive encouragement, support, and opportunities for participation in sports (Geary, 1998). Even during the preschool years, parents emphasize physical activity in boys more than in girls. By middle childhood, boys are involved in competitive games and in games of longer duration more so than girls. They also engage in more vigorous activity than girls (A. M. Thompson, Baxter-Jones, Mirwald, & Bailey, 2003).

At puberty, when boys begin to excel in such areas as running, the long jump, sit-ups, and grip strength, boys' greater size and strength confer a biological advantage. But some environmental factors that operated in middle childhood may exert even greater importance in puberty. "Tomboy" behaviour in girls is less socially accepted in adolescence than it was in middle childhood. Therefore, girls may become less interested in participating in athletic activities and may be less motivated to do well in the ones in which they do engage (Geary, 1998; Thomas & French, 1985). By the ages of twelve or thirteen, girls are less likely than boys to perceive themselves as competent and interested in physical exercise and activity (Ferguson, Yesalis, Pomrehn, & Kirkpatrick, 1989; Whitehead & Corbin, 1991).

Concept Review 11.1 — Development of Motor Skills during Middle Childhood

Age	Skills
Gross Motor Skills	
6 years	• Hops, jumps, climbs
7 years	• Balances on and pedals a bicycle
8 years	• Has good body balance
9 years	• Engages in vigorous bodily activities, especially team sports such as hockey, baseball, football, soccer, and basketball
10 years	• Balances on one foot for 15 seconds; catches a fly ball
12 years	• Displays some awkwardness as a result of asynchronous bone and muscle development
Fine Motor Skills	
6-7 years	• Ties shoelaces
	• Throws ball by using wrist and finger release
	• Holds pencil with fingertips (i.e., tripod grasp)
	• Provides greater detail in drawing and uses colour purposefully
	• Human figures become more detailed in drawings
	• Follows simple mazes
	• May be able to hit a ball with a bat
8-9 years	• Spaces words when writing
	• Writes and prints accurately and neatly
	• Copies a diamond shape correctly
	• Swings a hammer well
	• Sews and knits
	• Shows good hand-eye coordination

© Jacksonville Journal Courier / The Image Works

© Monika Graff / The Image Works

In any event, physical activity decreases with age between middle childhood and adolescence in both sexes (R. A. Thompson et al., 2003). However, physical activities become increasingly stereotyped by children as being masculine (e.g., football) or feminine (e.g., dance) (Meaney, Dornier, & Owens, 2002).

Exercise and Fitness

The health benefits of exercise for both adults and children are well known. Exercise reduces the risk of heart disease, stroke, diabetes, and certain forms of cancer (Georgiades et al., 2000; Hakim et al., 1998; Hu et al., 2000; Stampfer, Hu, Manson, Rimm, & Willett, 2000; Taylor-Tolbert et al., 2000). Exercise confers psychological benefits as well. Physically active adolescents have a better self-image and better coping skills than those who are inactive (Kirkcaldy et al., 2002).

Questions: Are children in Canada physically fit? If not, why not? Adults in Canada are becoming more conscientious about exercising and staying fit. **Truth or Fiction Revisited:** However, most children in Canada are not physically fit. The Canadian Paediatric Society reports that most schools offer half of the recommended provincial requirements (approximately two hours per week) for physical education (Healthy Active Living Committee, 2002). In fact, it has been deduced that most Canadian children are moderately to vigorously active during physical education class for only about nine to thirty-two minutes per week (Beaumont, 2006). Based on the National Longitudinal Survey of Children and Youth data, it appears that 38 percent of acceptable-weight children and 34 percent of overweight/obese children are physically active (Statistics Canada, 2003). Check out how your province or territory fares in its promotion of physical activity in Table 11.1.

School authorities shall ensure that all students in grades 1 to 9 are physically active for a minimum of 30 minutes daily through activities that are organized by the school.

Guiding Principles:

Schools have the responsibility of creating and nurturing a learning environment for students that supports the development of a lifelong habit of daily physical activity and healthy lifestyles. Daily physical activities (DPA) should

- vary in form and intensity;
- take into account each student's ability;
- consider resources available within the school and the larger communities; and
- allow for student choice.

Procedures:

1. School authorities have the flexibility to use instructional and/or noninstructional hours to implement DPA.
   a. Physical education classes are an appropriate strategy to meet the DPA requirement.
   b. DPA should be offered in as large a block of time as possible but can be offered in time segments adding up to the minimum thirty minutes per day; e.g., two fifteen minute blocks of time for a total of thirty minutes
   c. DPA can be incorporated throughout the day and integrated into other subject areas.
2. School authorities will monitor the implementation of DPA to ensure that all students are active for a minimum of thirty minutes daily.
3. Exemptions from DPA may be granted by the principal under the following conditions:
   a. religious beliefs – upon written statement from parent to the principal;
   b. medical reasons – certification to principal by a medical practitioner indicating in which activities the student is not able to participate.

Source: Alberta Education (2006).

Figure 11.3

An Example of a Provincial Policy Statement: Alberta Education's Daily Physical Activity (DPA) Policy Statement

	Obesity Prevention and Promotion of Physical Activity	
Province/Territory	Status	Comments
British Columbia	Good	Physical education is mandatory for grades K–10, must be 10% of time. Daily physical activity not mandatory. Junk food will be banned in schools by spring 2007.
Alberta	Good	Physical activity mandatory for grades 1–10 for 30 minutes a day. One course mandatory for high school graduation. Province has initiated work on child and youth nutrition guidelines.
Saskatchewan	Good	Physical activity mandatory for grades 1–9 for 150 minutes a week. Some physical activity mandatory for high school students. Saskatchewan in Motion aims to ensure all schools have a minimum of 30 minutes' activity daily. Nutrition recommendations for schools are in progress.
Manitoba	Good	Physical activity mandatory in grades 1–9 but not necessarily daily. At least two credits in physical education needed for high school graduation. Healthy schools initiative encourages healthy eating and physical activity. School nutrition guidelines published in 2006. Pilot project on healthy choices for vending machines.
Ontario	Good	Physical activity mandatory through grade 8 for 20 minutes daily. One course mandatory for high school graduation. Junk food banned from elementary schools. Programs include Eat Smart for cafeterias and funding for communities to introduce healthy food choices in schools.
Quebec	Good	Mandatory physical education to be taught by qualified teachers for grades K–12. Minimum two hours per week in elementary schools. Vending machines banned in elementary schools.
New Brunswick	Good	Physical activity mandatory for grades K–8 from 100 to 150 minutes weekly. Healthier Eating and Nutrition in Public Schools policy recommends healthy food choices and bans junk food.
Nova Scotia	Good	Physical activity mandatory for grades K–9 for at least 150 minutes weekly. Food and Nutrition Policy for Nova Scotia Public Schools. Junk food will be phased out by 2009. Active Kids, Healthy Kids strategy promotes healthier lifestyles.
Prince Edward Island	Good	Physical education mandatory for grades K–9 but not necessarily daily, and optional for grades 10–12. Has developed an Eating Strategy for Island Children.
Newfoundland	Good	Physical education mandatory for grades 1–9 but not necessarily daily, and some required for grades 10–12. New guidelines and healthy schools strategy resulted in healthier options for vending machines. Unhealthy foods must be removed by 2008.
Yukon	Good	Physical education required for grades K–10, must be 10% of time. Daily physical exercise not mandatory. Some programs to encourage healthier choices for beverages.
Northwest Territories	Good	Mandatory 30 minutes of daily physical activity. High school students must do at least one physical education course. School nutrition program in development.
Nunavut	Good	Mandatory 30 minutes of daily physical activity. School nutrition improvements under consideration.

Source: Canadian Paediatric Society (2007a).

What are some possible reasons for this low rate of activity? Again, one obvious culprit is watching television. Students who watch relatively little television have less body fat and are more physically fit than those who watch for several hours per day (Armstrong et al., 1998). According to Belfry (1996), the average Canadian child watches more than twenty-six hours of TV and engages in up to thirty hours of sedentary activity at school each week.

Cardiac and muscular fitness, both in childhood and adulthood, is developed by participation in continuous exercise such as running, walking quickly, swimming laps, bicycling, or jumping rope for intervals of several minutes at a time (Michael, 1990). Unfortunately, some schools and parents tend to focus on sports such as baseball and football, which are less apt to promote fitness (Brody, 1990a).

As you might expect, children who engage in exercise and are physically fit have more positive attitudes toward physical activity and are more likely to perceive its benefits (Brustad, 1991; Desmond et al., 1990; Ferguson et al., 1989). Children with high levels of physical activity are more likely to have parents who encourage their children to exercise and who actively exercise themselves (Stucky-Ropp & DiLorenzo, 1992). How, then, can more children be motivated to engage in regular physical activity? Here are some suggestions for parents (Bjorklund & Bjorklund, 1989; Brody, 1990a, 1990b):

- Find time for family outdoor activities that promote fitness: walking, swimming, bicycling, skating.
- Reduce the amount of time spent watching television.
- Encourage outdoor play during daylight hours after school.
- Do not assume that your child gets sufficient exercise by participating in a team sport. Many team sports involve long periods of inactivity.

Organized sports for children are enormously popular, but many children lose their enthusiasm and drop out. Participation in sports declines steadily after the age of ten (Seefeldt, Ewing, & Walk, 1991). Why? Sometimes children are pushed too hard, too early, or too quickly by parents or coaches. Children may thus feel frustrated or inferior, and they are sometimes injured (Brody, 1990a; Kolata, 1992). Hence, parents are advised not to place excessive demands for performance on their children. Let them progress at their own pace. Encourage them to focus on the fun and health benefits of physical activity and sports, not on winning. Nonetheless, if children prefer not to be involved in team or individual sports it does not have to mean the end of being physical active—there are many economical and easy ways to stay active, as outlined in "Gotta Move!," a physical activity guide developed by Health Canada especially for children aged six through nine.

A Closer Look

Community Approach to Fitness

A school community approach that involves children, parents, schools, and community programs that help children be active and make healthy food choices is best. Recently, several provinces have made efforts to get junk food out of schools. In 2005 Canadian elementary schools became "pop-free." In Ontario, the provincial government required school boards to replace pop and chips in their vending machines with milk, juice, nuts, and granola. In New Brunswick, junk food was banned from elementary school cafeterias, vending machines, canteens, and fundraising schemes. British Columbia is considering similar legislation, while Quebec is reviewing a tax on junk food (CBC News, 2006).

Active Review

9. During middle childhood, children show (abrupt or steady?) improvement in gross motor skills.

10. By the age of about _____, children show the balance, coordination, and strength that allow them to engage in gymnastics and team sports.

11. Reaction time gradually (increases or decreases?) from early childhood to about age eighteen.

12. (Boys or Girls?) tend to show greater overall strength.

13. (Boys or Girls?) show somewhat greater coordination and flexibility.

14. Most children in Canada tend to be physically (fit or unfit?).

Reflect & Relate: When did you become "good at" things such as riding a bicycle, skating, or team sports? Did these activities provide an opportunity for fulfillment and social approval for you, or were they a source of anxiety? Did you approach these activities with pleasure or shy away from them? Explain.

Go to
http://psychology.wadsworth.com/
rathus_voyages2e
for an interactive version of this review.

Children with Disabilities

Certain disabilities of childhood are most apt to be noticed in the middle childhood years, when the child enters school. The school setting requires that a child sit still, pay attention, and master a number of academic skills. But some children have difficulty with one or more of these demands. In this section we focus on children with various disabilities. Table 11.2 highlights the types of disabilities that can affect a child's functioning, especially in school. Let's consider attention-deficit/hyperactivity disorder and learning disabilities in greater depth.

Table 11.2	*Types of Exceptionalities*
Overall intellectual functioning	• Intellectual disabilities (Chapter 12)
Learning disabilities[1]	• Reading disability (dyslexia) (this chapter) • Mathematics disability (dyscalculia) (this chapter) • Disorder of written expression
Speech disorders	• Articulation disorder • Voice disorders • Fluency disorders
Physical disabilities	• Visual impairment • Hearing impairment • Paralysis
Social and emotional disorders	• Attention-deficit/hyperactivity disorder (this chapter) • Autism spectrum disorders (Chapter 7) • Conduct disorders (Chapter 13) • Childhood depression (Chapter 13) • Childhood anxiety (Chapter 13)

[1]The American Psychiatric Association (2000) uses the term *learning disorder* rather than *learning disability*. Most educators appear to prefer the term *learning disability*.

Attention-Deficit/Hyperactivity Disorder (AD/HD)

Scott, age 7, is extremely restless and distractible in class. Every few minutes, he is out of his seat, exploring something on a bookshelf or looking out the window. When in his seat, he swings his legs back and forth, drums his fingers on the table, shifts around, and keeps up a high level of movement. He speaks rapidly, and his ideas are poorly organized, although his intelligence is normal. During recess, Scott is aggressive and violates many of the playground rules. Scott's behaviour at home is similar to his behaviour in school. He is unable to concentrate on any activity for more than a few minutes. Scott has attention-deficit/hyperactivity disorder.
—Halgin & Whitbourne (1993, p. 335)

Many parents think that their children do not pay enough attention to them—that they tend to run around as the whim strikes and to do things in their own way. Some inattention, especially at early ages, is to be expected. *Question: How does run-of-the-mill failure to "listen" to adults differ from attention-deficit/hyperactivity disorder?* In **attention-deficit/hyperactivity disorder (AD/HD)**, the child shows

attention-deficit/hyperactivity disorder (AD/HD) A behaviour disorder characterized by excessive inattention, impulsiveness, and hyperactivity.

hyperactivity Excessive restlessness and overactivity; one of the primary characteristics of attention-deficit/hyperactivity disorder (AD/HD). Not to be confused with misbehaviour or with normal high-activity levels that occur during childhood.

developmentally inappropriate or excessive inattention, impulsivity, and **hyperactivity** (American Psychiatric Association, 2000; Nigg, 2001). A more complete list of problems is shown in Table 11.3. The degree of hyperactive behaviours is crucial, because many normal children are labelled overactive and fidgety from time to time. In fact, if talking too much were the sole criterion for AD/HD, the label would have applied to many of us.

The onset of AD/HD occurs by age seven. The behaviour pattern must have persisted for at least six months for the diagnosis—a category used by the American Psychiatric Association (2000)—to apply. The hyperactivity and restlessness of some children with AD/HD impair their ability to function in school. They simply cannot sit still. They also have difficulty getting along with others. Their disruptive and noncompliant behaviour often elicits punishment from parents. AD/HD is quite common. It is diagnosed in about 1 to 5 percent of school-aged children and is one of the most common causes of childhood referrals to mental health clinics. AD/HD is many times more common in boys than in girls. For some Canadian statistics related to AD/HD, check out the AD/HD Foundation of Canada website: http://www.adhdfoundation.ca/goals/adhd_ld_stats.htm.

Some psychologists and educators argue that AD/HD is overdiagnosed—that many children who do not toe the line in school are falsely diagnosed with AD/HD and medicated to encourage more acceptable behaviour. Research does suggest that those who diagnose children with AD/HD tend to be "suggestible." That is, they are more likely to diagnose children with the disorder when told—for example, by teachers and parents—that the children do not adequately control their behaviour (Simonson & Glenn, 2001).

Provincial education jurisdictions do not list AD/HD as a distinct category of exceptionality (Friend, Bursuck, & Hutchinson, 1998). However, Canadian children with AD/HD may qualify for services under other categories of exceptionality such as behavioural disorders and learning disabilities.

© David Young-Wolff/PhotoEdit

A Girl with Attention-Deficit/Hyperactivity Disorder
Hyperactive children are continually on the go, as if their "motors" are constantly running. The psychological disorder we refer to as hyperactivity is not to be confused with the normal high energy levels of children. However, it is sometimes—*sometimes*—difficult to tell where one ends and the other begins.

Causes of AD/HD

Question: What are the causes of AD/HD? Because AD/HD is in part characterized by excessive motor activity, many theorists focus on possible physical causes. For one thing, AD/HD tends to run in families, for both girls and boys with the disorder (Faraone et al., 2000). AD/HD is also found to coexist with other psychological disorders and problems, ranging from anxiety and depression to tics (Souza, Serra, Mattos, & Franco, 2001; Spencer et al., 2001). At least some children with AD/HD appear to have an inherited defect in the body's thyroid hormone system (Hauser et al., 1993). AD/HD also appears to be more prevalent in children who have suffered from encephalitis (Anderson & Cohen, 1991). Recordings of brain waves frequently show abnormalities as well (Hechtman, 1991).

Evidence such as this has led some investigators to suggest that children diagnosed with AD/HD suffer from "minimal brain damage" or "minimal brain dysfunction,"

Kind of Problem	Specific Patterns of Behaviour
Lack of attention	• Fails to attend to details or makes careless errors in schoolwork, and so on • Has difficulty sustaining attention in schoolwork or play activities • Does not appear to pay attention to what is being said • Fails to follow through on instructions or to finish work • Has trouble organizing work and other activities • Avoids work or activities that require sustained attention • Loses work tools (e.g., pencils, books, assignments, toys) • Becomes readily distracted • Is forgetful in daily activities
Hyperactivity	• Fidgets with hands or feet or squirms in his or her seat • Leaves seat in situations in which remaining seated is required, such as in the classroom • Constantly runs around or climbs on things; "runs like a motor" • Has difficulty playing quietly • Shows excessive motor activity when asleep • Talks excessively
Impulsivity	• Often acts without thinking • Shifts from activity to activity • Cannot organize tasks or work • Requires constant supervision • Often "calls out" in class • Does not wait his or her turn in line, games, and so on

Symptoms of Attention-Deficit/Hyperactivity Disorder (AD/HD)

Source: Adapted from American Psychiatric Association (2000).

These labels, of course, do not add much to efforts to locate and remedy possible damage. A study by Alan Zametkin and his colleagues (1990) found that individuals with AD/HD have reduced activity in those areas of the brain that control attention and movement.

It has also been hypothesized that the chemical additives in processed food are largely responsible for hyperactivity. ***Truth or Fiction Revisited:*** However, studies of the so-called Feingold diet, which removes food additives from children's food, have *not* supported this hypothesis (Ekvall, Ekvall, & Mayes, 1993; Hynd & Hooper, 1992).

Joel T. Nigg (2001) noted that AD/HD is widely thought to be caused by inhibitory processes that do not work efficiently. That is, children with AD/HD do not inhibit, or control, impulses that most children are capable of controlling. But Nigg noted that *inhibition* is defined in somewhat different ways by different theorists. In an article published in *Psychological Bulletin*, Nigg distinguished between inhibition that is under the executive control of the brain—a sort of cognitive-neurological inhibition—and inhibition that is normally motivated by emotions such as anxiety and fear (e.g., anxiety about disappointing a teacher or fear of earning poor grades). Nigg argued that AD/HD is unlikely to reflect failure to respond to feelings of anxiety or fear. He believes that the disorder is more likely due to a lack of executive control but admits that the precise nature of this control—for example, specification of possible neurological aspects—remains poorly understood.

Treatment and Outcome

stimulants Drugs that increase the activity of the nervous system.

Truth or Fiction Revisited: **Stimulants** such as Ritalin (methylphenidate), Dexedrine (dextroamphetamine), and Cylert (pemoline) are often used to treat hyperactive children; in fact, they are the most widespread treatment for AD/HD. *Question: Why are children with AD/HD treated with stimulants?* It may seem ironic that stimulants would be used with children who are already overly active. The rationale is that the activity of the hyperactive child stems from inability of the cerebral cortex to inhibit more primitive areas of the brain (Keating, McClellan, & Jarvis, 2001; Nigg, 2001). The drugs block the reuptake (reabsorption) of two neurotransmitters in the brain: dopamine and noradrenaline. Keeping more of these neurotransmitters active has the effect of stimulating the cerebral cortex and facilitating cortical control of primitive areas of the brain (Keating et al., 2001). This interpretation is supported by evidence that caffeine—the stimulant found in coffee, tea, colas, and chocolate (yes, chocolate)—also helps children control hyperactivity (Leon, 2000; Rezvani & Levin, 2001).

Children with AD/HD who are given stimulants show increased attention span, improved cognitive and academic performance (Evans, Smith, Bukstein, Gnagy, Greiner, Altenderfer, Baron-Myak, 2001), less activity (Klorman, Brumaghim, Fitzpatrick, Borgstedt, & Strauss, 1994), and a reduction in disruptive, annoying, and aggressive behaviours (Evans et al., 2001). The use of stimulants is controversial, however. Some critics argue that stimulants suppress gains in height and weight, do not contribute to academic gains, and lose effectiveness over time (Green, 1991; Whalen & Henker, 1997). Another concern is that stimulants are overused or misused in an attempt to control normal high-activity levels of children at home or in the classroom. Supporters of stimulant treatment argue that many children with AD/HD are helped by medication. They counter that the suppression of growth appears to be related to the dosage of the drug and that low doses seem to be about as effective as large doses (Evans et al., 2001).

Another approach that shows some promise in treating children with AD/HD is cognitive behavioural therapy. This approach attempts to increase the child's self-control and problem-solving abilities through modelling, role-playing, and self-instruction. A Spanish study found that it was possible to teach many children with AD/HD to "stop and think" before giving in to angry impulses and behaving in an aggressive manner (Miranda & Presentacion, 2000). However, it should be noted that the recent Multimodal Treatment Study, which was sponsored by the National Institute of Mental Health, found that "medical management"—meaning use of stimulant medication—was superior in effectiveness to cognitive behavioural therapy (Greene & Ablon, 2001; Whalen, 2001). Even so, the Multimodal Treatment Study did not match treatments to the needs of the individual child with AD/HD (Abikoff, 2001; Whalen, 2001). It is possible that some children will do best with stimulants alone, others with cognitive behavioural therapy, and still others with a combination of the two (Abikoff, 2001; Greene & Ablon, 2001).

Many but not all children appear to "outgrow" AD/HD. Some longitudinal studies have found that at least two-thirds of children with AD/HD continue to exhibit one or more of the core symptoms in adolescence and adulthood (Barkley, 2004; Nigg, Goldsmith, & Sachek, 2004). Problems in attention, conduct, hyperactivity, and learning frequently continue.

Learning Disabilities

Nelson Rockefeller served as vice president of the United States under Gerald Ford. He was intelligent and well educated. Yet despite the best of tutors, he could never master reading. Rockefeller had **dyslexia.** *Truth or Fiction Revisited:* It is true that some children who are intelligent and who are provided with enriched home environments cannot learn how to read or do simple math problems. Many such children have *learning disabilities.*

Question: What are learning disabilities? Dyslexia is one type of **learning disability.** The term *learning disabilities* refers to a group of disorders characterized by inadequate development of specific academic, language, and speech skills (see Concept Review 11.2). Children with learning disabilities may show problems in math, writing, or reading. Some have difficulties in articulating sounds of speech or in understanding spoken language. Others have problems in motor coordination. Children are usually considered to have a learning disability when they are performing below the level expected for their age, despite at least average cognitive abilities, when there is no evidence of other handicaps such as vision or hearing problems, cognitive delays, or socioeconomic disadvantages (Joshi, 2003; Lyon, Shaywitz, & Shaywitz, 2003). However, some psychologists and educators, such as Frank Vellutino (Vellutino, 2001; Vellutino, Fletcher, Snowling, & Scanlon, 2004), argue that too much emphasis is placed on the discrepancy between intelligence and reading achievement. This criticism was found in Canadian research as well. For example, Klassen (2002) acknowledges that Canadian researchers are arguing for a shift in learning-disability identification practice. Currently, pseudo-word decoding, word identification, and reading comprehension are considered key measures of identifying students with reading difficulties.

Below is the official definition of learning disabilities as laid out by the Learning Disabilities Association of Canada (2002):

"Learning Disabilities" refer to a number of disorders which may affect the acquisition, organization, retention, understanding or use of verbal or nonverbal information. These disorders affect learning in individuals who otherwise demonstrate at least average abilities essential for thinking and/or reasoning. As such, learning disabilities are distinct from global intellectual deficiency.

Learning disabilities result from impairments in one or more processes related to perceiving, thinking, remembering or learning. These include, but are not limited to: language processing; phonological processing; visual-spatial processing; processing speed; memory and attention; and executive functions (e.g. planning and decision-making).

Learning disabilities range in severity and may interfere with the acquisition and use of one or more of the following:

- oral language (e.g. listening, speaking, understanding);

- reading (e.g. decoding, phonetic knowledge, word recognition, comprehension);

- written language (e.g. spelling and written expression); and

- mathematics (e.g. computation, problem solving).

Learning disabilities may also involve difficulties with organizational skills, social perception, social interaction and perspective taking.

dyslexia   A reading disorder characterized by problems such as letter reversals, mirror reading, slow reading, and reduced comprehension (from the Greek roots dys, meaning "bad," and lexikon, meaning "of words").

learning disabilities   A group of disorders characterized by inadequate development of specific academic, language, and speech skills.

Learning disabilities are lifelong. The way in which they are expressed may vary over an individual's lifetime, depending on the interaction between the demands of the environment and the individual's strengths and needs. Learning disabilities are suggested by unexpected academic underachievement or achievement which is maintained only by unusually high levels of effort and support.

Learning disabilities are due to genetic and/or neurobiological factors or injury that alters brain functioning in a manner which affects one or more processes related to learning. These disorders are not due primarily to hearing and/or vision problems, socioeconomic factors, cultural or linguistic differences, lack of motivation or ineffective teaching, although these factors may further complicate the challenges faced by individuals with learning disabilities. Learning disabilities may coexist with various conditions including attentional, behavioural and emotional disorders, sensory impairments or other medical conditions.

Concept Review 11.2 Types of Learning Disabilities

According to the Learning Disabilities Association of Canada, learning disabilities range in severity and may interfere with the acquisition and use of one or more of the following:

Reading Disability (e.g., decoding, phonetic knowledge, word recognition, comprehension)
- As measured by a standardized test that is given individually, the child's ability to read (accuracy or comprehension) is substantially less than what one would expect considering his or her age, level of intelligence, and educational experiences.
- The reading disorder materially interferes with the child's academic achievement or daily living.
- If there is also a sensory or perceptual defect, the reading problems are worse than one would expect with it.

Mathematics Disability (dyscalculia, dealing with computation, and problem solving)
- As measured by a standardized test that is given individually, the child's mathematical ability is substantially less than what one would expect considering his or her age, level of intelligence, and educational experiences.
- The mathematics disorder materially interferes with the child's academic achievement or daily living.
- If there is also a sensory or perceptual defect, the problems in mathematics are worse than one would expect with it.

Disorder of Written Expression (spelling and written expression)
- As measured by assessment of functioning or by a standardized test that is given individually, the child's writing ability is substantially less than what one would expect considering his or her age, level of intelligence, and educational experiences.
- The problems in writing grammatically correct sentences and organized paragraphs materially interfere with the child's academic achievement or daily living.
- If there is also a sensory or perceptual defect, the problems in writing are worse than one would expect with it.

Oral Language (e.g., listening, speaking, understanding)
- As measured by assessment of functioning or by a standardized test that is given individually, the child's verbal ability is substantially less than what one would expect considering his or her age, level of intelligence, and educational experiences.

Source: Learning Disabilities Association of Canada (2002).

For success, individuals with learning disabilities require early identification and timely specialized assessments and interventions involving home, school, community and workplace settings. The interventions need to be appropriate for each individual's learning disability subtype and, at a minimum, include the provision of:

- specific skill instruction;
- accommodations;
- compensatory strategies; and
- self-advocacy skills.

Children with learning disabilities frequently display other problems as well. They are more likely than other children to have AD/HD (Faraone et al., 2000; Lindgren et al., 2002). They do not communicate as well with their peers, have poorer social skills, show more behaviour problems in the classroom, and are more likely to experience emotional problems (Frith, 2001; Lyon et al., 2003).

For most children with learning disabilities, the disorder persists through life. But with early recognition and appropriate remediation, many individuals can learn to overcome or compensate for their learning disability (Vellutino et al., 2004).

To illustrate some of the theoretical and treatment issues involved in learning disabilities, let us consider reading disabilities. As with other learning disabilities, reading disability is puzzling because there may be every indication that the child ought to be able to read. Some dyslexic children are at least average in intelligence. Their vision and hearing check out as normal. However, problems in developing reading skills persist (Lyon et al., 2003).

It has been estimated that dyslexia affects anywhere from 5 to 17.5 percent of children (Shaywitz, 1998). Most studies show that dyslexia is much more common in boys than in girls. Figure 11.4 is a writing sample of a child with dyslexia.

In childhood, treatment of dyslexia focuses on remediation (Shaywitz, 1998). Children are given highly structured exercises to help them become aware of how to blend sounds to form words, such as identifying word pairs that rhyme and do not rhyme. Later in life, the focus tends to be on accommodation rather than on remediation (Shaywitz, 1998). For example, college students with dyslexia may be given extra time to do the reading involved in taking tests. Interestingly, college students with dyslexia are frequently excellent at word recognition. Even so, they continue to show problems in decoding new words.

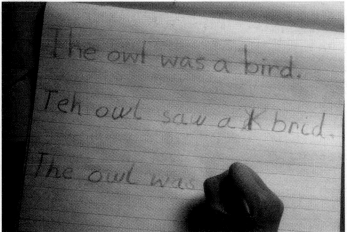

Figure 11.4

Writing Sample of a Child with Dyslexia

Dyslexic children have trouble perceiving letters in their correct orientation. They may perceive letters upside down (confusing *w* with *m*) or reversed (confusing *b* with *d*). This perceptual difficulty may lead to rotations or reversals in their writing, as shown here.

Origins of Dyslexia

Question: What are the origins of dyslexia? Current views of dyslexia focus on the ways in which neurological problems may contribute to the perceptual (psychological) problems we find in dyslexic individuals (Nicolson, Fawcett, & Dean, 2001; Shaywitz & Shaywitz, 2003).

We will return to neurological problems in a minute. Let's first note that genetic factors appear to be associated with dyslexia (Fernandez & State, 2004; Plomin & Walker, 2003). In support of this view, it is known that dyslexia runs in families. It has been estimated that 25 to 65 percent of children who have one dyslexic parent are dyslexic themselves (Shaywitz, 1998). About 40 percent of the siblings of children with dyslexia are also dyslexic.

Genetic factors may give rise to neurological problems. The problems can involve "faulty wiring" in the left hemisphere of the brain, which is usually involved in language functions. A part of the brain called the *angular gyrus* lies in the left hemisphere between the visual cortex and Wernicke's area. The angular gyrus "translates" visual information, such as written words, into auditory information (sounds) and sends it on to Wernicke's area. Problems in the angular gyrus may give rise to reading problems because it becomes difficult for the reader to associate letters with sounds (Shaywitz & Shaywitz, 2003; Vellutino et al., 2004). For example, we develop habits of seeing an *f* or a *ph* or a *gh* and saying or hearing an *f* sound in our brains. Dyslexic individuals find it more difficult to go from the visual stimulus to the right sound.

Genetic or other factors may also be expressed through prenatal exposure to the male hormone testosterone. A high level of prenatal testosterone slows growth in the left hemisphere (Geshwind & Galaburda, 1987; Shaywitz & Shaywitz, 2003). Males are normally exposed to higher levels of testosterone during pregnancy than females, because their testes secrete it. The common finding that males are more likely than females to be dyslexic can be seen as supporting this hypothesis.

In sum, dyslexia would appear to stem from neurological problems in the brain, not from faulty learning or other psychological problems (such as unconscious conflict). The site of the neurological problems appears to involve structures that are involved in translating visual symbols into sounds. The precise origins of these neurological problems remain to be discovered. *Question: Should children with exceptionalities receive their education in the regular classroom?*

Educating Children with Disabilities

In Canada, all children are eligible for public education. In contrast, in the United States, special educational programs have been created to meet the needs of schoolchildren with mild to moderate disabilities. These disabilities include learning disabilities, emotional disturbance, intellectual disabilities, and physical disabilities such as blindness, deafness, or paralysis. A question that stirs a great deal of debate is *From where should children with learning disabilities receive instruction (i.e., should they be fully integrated)?* Evidence is mixed on whether placing children with exceptionalities in separate classes can also stigmatize them and segregate them from other children. Special-needs classes also negatively influence teacher expectations. Neither the teacher nor the students themselves come to expect very much. This negative expectation becomes a self-fulfilling prophecy, and the exceptional students' achievements suffer. The Canadian process of inclusion and education of students with exceptionalities differs from the American system. With the adoption of the Constitution Act in 1982 (which includes the Canadian Charter of Rights and Freedom), the rights of peoples with disabilities is embedded within the Constitution. Another unique feature of the Canadian system is that all provinces and territories have their own education or school act governing education within its jurisdiction. Despite individual provinces and territories overseeing their own special education services, all educational policy must coincide with the Charter of Rights (Smith & Foster, 1996).

The websites of the provincial ministries of education can offer further information:

- Alberta Learning: http://www.learning.gov.ab.ca
- British Columbia Ministry of Education, Skills and Training: http://www.gov.bc.ca/bced/
- Manitoba Ministry of Education: http://www.edu.gov.mb.ca
- New Brunswick Ministry of Education: http://www.gnb.ca/0000
- Newfoundland and Labrador Ministry of Education: http://www.ed.gov.nl.ca/edu
- Northwest Territories Ministry of Education, Culture and Employment: http://www.ece.gov.nt.ca
- Nova Scotia Ministry of Education and Culture: http://www.ednet.ns.ca
- Nunavut Ministry of Education: http://www.gov.nu.ca/education/eng
- Ontario Ministry of Education and Training: http://www.edu.gov.on.ca
- Prince Edward Island Ministry of Education: http://www.gov.pe.ca/education
- Ministère de l'Éducation du Québec: http://www.gov.pe.ca/education
- Saskatchewan Ministry of Education: http://www.sasked.gov.sk.ca
- Yukon Ministry of Education: http://www.education.gov.yk.ca

inclusion Students with exceptionalities are fully included in school programs and activities.

Historically, students with disabilities received their educational programming in either self-contained classes or resource rooms. Today, the majority of students with disabilities spend a great deal of their time in the general education classroom. Proponents of the inclusion model prefer *fully* including students with special needs in general education programs. Presently, several professional organizations and advocacy groups such as the Council for Exceptional Children (CEC), the Canadian National Association for the Blind (CNIB), the Family Network for Deaf Children, and the Learning Disabilities Association of Canada (LDAC) advocate for an inclusive education model with a continuum of services (Smith, Polloway, Patton, Dowdy, & Heart, 2001)

Although the goals of **inclusion** are laudable, observations of the results are mixed. Some studies indicate that children with disabilities may achieve more when they are fully included (e.g., Truesdell & Abramson, 1992). But other studies suggest that many children with disabilities do not fare well in regular classrooms (Brady, Swank, Taylor, & Freiberg, 1988; Chira, 1993). According to the *Advancing the Inclusion of Persons with Disabilities* (Human Resources Development Canada, 2004) report, the majority of Canadian students with disabilities attend a regular school (64 percent), with 26 percent attending a regular school *with* special education classes, 6.4 percent attending a special education school, and 2.3 percent attending another type of educational institution. While some argue that rather than inspiring them to greater achievements, regular classrooms can be overwhelming for many students

Inclusion
Today, most students with mild disabilities spend at least part of their school day in regular classrooms. The goals of inclusion include providing broader educational opportunities for students with exceptionalities and fostering interactions with nondisabled children.

with disabilities (Chalfant, 1989), there is evidence that higher-performing students with disabilities appear to gain more from regular classes; however, the same evidence shows that lower-performing students gain more from segregated classes (Cole et al., 1991). Clearly, interpreting the research related to this topic is not simple. One confounding factor that muddies our interpretation of inclusion research is the amount of support and resources different school districts receive for implementing full inclusion models.

Researchers need to learn more about what types of teacher training and preparation for students without exceptionalities can ease the way for children with exceptionalities in the regular classroom. We also need to find out what sorts of supplementary educational experiences will round out the educational and social experiences of children who are fully included (Murphy & Hicks-Stewart, 1991; Simmons, Fuchs, & Fuchs, 1991). Promising findings have revealed that both students with and without exceptionalities benefit from inclusion (Human Resources Development Canada, 2004; Giangreco, Dennis, Cloniger, Edelman, & Schattman, 1993; McDonnell, Wilcox, & Hardman, 1991). Proper funding and supports for full inclusion are in great demand and are cited as a reason that a portion of Canadian children with disabilities (4 percent) are not in school (Human Resources Development Canada, 2004). Exciting new research and work with children with exceptionalities is taking place across Canada and will continue to inform policy and practice in the schools.

Nevertheless, we can focus on the adequacy of teaching methods. For example, in an experiment on instructing children with learning disabilities, Alice Wilder and Joanna Williams (2001) recruited ninety-one students (fifty-nine boys and thirty-two girls) from special-education classrooms in New York City. The city's board of education had certified the students as having a learning disability. Most children had obtained IQ scores of at least 85. The study attempted to determine whether special instruction could help the students pick out the themes in stories. A story was read aloud and students were then asked to consider questions such as,

- Who was the main character?
- What was his/her problem?
- What did he/she do?
- What happened at the end of the story?
- Was what happened good or bad?
- Why was it good or bad?

Students receiving this form of instruction were more capable of identifying the themes and applying them to everyday life than children who received more traditional instruction. The investigators concluded that this sort of "theme identification" program enables children with severe learning disabilities to profit from instruction that is geared toward abstract thinking and understanding. Perhaps we can generalize to note that these results seem to be underscoring the fact that "good teaching helps"—often, if not always. (Why isn't this kind of teaching "traditional instruction"?)

Perhaps any method that carefully assesses the child's skills, identifies deficits, and creates and follows precise plans for remediating these deficits can be of help. Having said that, it seems that no method identified to date provides learning-disabled children with the levels of skills that so many other children apply with ease. But reading and other academic skills are important in everyday life in our society, and any advance would appear to be better than none.

Our examination of educational programs for children with exceptionalities leads us next into an investigation of cognitive development in middle childhood and the conditions that influence it. We address this topic in Chapter 12.

Active Review

15. Children with _____ (AD/HD) show developmentally inappropriate or excessive inattention, impulsivity, and hyperactivity.

16. AD/HD is more common among (boys or girls?).

17. AD/HD (does or does not?) tend to run in families.

18. Children with AD/HD are likely to be treated with (stimulants or tranquillizers?).

19. Learning _____ are a group of disorders characterized by inadequate development of specific academic, language, and speech skills.

20. Difficulty learning to read is called _____.

21. Current views of dyslexia focus on the ways that _____ problems contribute to the perceptual problems we find in dyslexic children.

22. Dyslexia (does or does not?) tend to run in families.

Reflect & Relate: Did you know any children with disabilities who were "mainstreamed" in your classes? How were they treated by other students? How were they treated by teachers? Do you believe that inclusion was helpful for them?

 Go to
W W W **http://psychology.wadsworth.com/ rathus_voyages2e**
for an interactive version of this review.

Recite: *An Active Summary*™

1. What patterns of growth occur in middle childhood?

Children tend to gain a little over two inches in height and five to seven pounds in weight per year during middle childhood. Children become more slender. Boys are slightly heavier and taller than girls through the ages of nine or ten, when girls begin the adolescent growth spurt. At around age eleven, boys develop relatively more muscle tissue and females develop more fatty tissue.

2. What portion of children in Canada are obese? Why are they obese?

About one-fourth of Canadian children are obese, and the prevalence of obesity has been increasing. Obese children usually do not "outgrow" "baby fat." During childhood, heavy children are often rejected by their peers. Heredity plays a role in obesity. Children with high numbers of fat cells feel food-deprived sooner than other children. Obese parents may encourage overeating by keeping fattening foods in the home. Sedentary habits also foster obesity.

3. What changes in motor development occur in middle childhood?

Middle childhood is marked by increases in speed, strength, agility, and balance. Children show regular improvement in gross motor skills and are often eager to participate in athletic activities, such as ball games that require movement of large muscles. Muscles grow stronger, and pathways that connect the cerebellum to the cortex become more myelinated. Reaction time gradually decreases. Fine motor skills also improve, with six- to seven-year-olds tying shoelaces and holding pencils as adults do.

4. Are there sex differences in motor skills?

Boys have slightly greater overall strength, whereas girls have better coordination and flexibility, which is valuable in dancing, balancing, and gymnastics. Boys generally receive more encouragement than girls to excel in athletics.

5. Are children in Canada physically fit? If not, why not?

Most children in Canada are not physically fit. One reason is the amount of time spent watching television.

6. How does run-of-the-mill failure to "listen" to adults differ from attention-deficit/hyperactivity disorder?

Attention-deficit/hyperactivity disorder (AD/HD) involves inattention, impulsivity, and hyperactivity. AD/HD impairs children's ability to function in school. AD/HD tends to be overdiagnosed and overmedicated.

7. What are the causes of AD/HD?

AD/HD runs in families and coexists with other problems. Abnormalities may suggest brain damage. Children with AD/HD do not inhibit impulses that most children control, suggesting poor executive control in the brain.

8. Why are children with AD/HD treated with stimulants?

Stimulants are used to stimulate the cerebral cortex to inhibit more primitive areas of the brain. Stimulants increase the attention span and academic performance of children with AD/HD, but there are side effects and the medications may be used too often. Cognitive behavioural therapy can also help teach children self-control.

9. What are learning disabilities?

Learning disabilities are characterized by inadequate development of specific academic, language, and speech skills. Children may be diagnosed with a learning disability when their performance is below that expected for their age and level of intelligence. Learning disabilities tend to persist.

10. What are the origins of dyslexia?

Current views of dyslexia focus on the ways that neurological problems may contribute to perceptual problems. Dyslexic children frequently show behaviours found among children with brain damage, such as short attention spans and difficulty sitting still. Genetic factors appear to be involved because dyslexia runs in families. There may be "faulty wiring" in the left hemisphere of the brain, which is usually involved in language.

11. Should children with exceptionalities receive their education in the regular classroom?

Research evidence on this question is mixed. Some studies suggest that children with exceptionalities achieve more when they are included. Other studies suggest that many children with exceptionalities find regular classrooms overwhelming. These issues are tied to the continuum of services and supports available for inclusive practices.

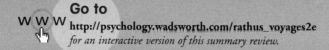

Go to
W W W http://psychology.wadsworth.com/rathus_voyages2e
for an interactive version of this summary review.

Key Terms

growth spurt *(page 404)*

obesity *(page 407)*

adipose tissue *(page 408)*

reaction time *(page 413)*

attention-deficit/hyperactivity disorder (AD/HD) *(419)*

hyperactivity *(page 420)*

stimulants *(page 422)*

dyslexia *(page 423)*

learning disabilities *(page 423)*

inclusion *(page 427)*

Active Learning Resources

Observing Children and Adolescents CD-ROM
Want to watch videos showing what you've just learned about in this chapter? Check out the "Gross Motor" and "Fine Motor" clips in Module 3, Section 1.

Visit Your Companion Website for This Book
http://www.voyages1CE.nelson.com
Check out this companion website, where you will find online resources directly linked to your book. The website includes interactive exercises related to PQ4R and Power Visuals for mastering and reviewing key concepts as well as quizzing, chapter outlines, and much more!

***CengageNOW!*™**
http://hed.nelson.com
Go to this site for the link to CengageNOW™, your one-stop study shop. Take a Pretest for this chapter, and CengageNOW™ will generate a personalized Study Plan based on your test results! The Study Plan will identify the topics you need to review and direct you to online resources to help you master those topics. You can then take a Posttest to help you determine the concepts you have mastered and those you still need to work on.

Middle Childhood: Cognitive Development

PREVIEW

TRUTH OR FICTION?

● ● ● ● ● ● ● ● ● ● ● ●

(T)(F) Don't try the "Yes, but" defence with a five-year-old. If you did it, you're guilty, even if it was an accident.

(T)(F) Memorizing the alphabet requires that children keep twenty-six chunks of information in mind at once.

(T)(F) An IQ is a score on a test.

(T)(F) Two children can answer exactly the same items on an intelligence test correctly, yet one can be above average in intelligence and the other below average.

(T)(F) Highly intelligent children are creative.

(T)(F) Adopted children are more similar in intelligence to their adoptive parents than to their biological parents.

(T)(F) Bilingual children encounter more academic problems than children who speak only one language.

Go to W W W

www.voyages1CE.nelson.com
for an interactive version of this "Truth or Fiction" feature.

D id you hear the one about the judge who pounded her gavel and yelled, "Order! Order in the court!"? "A hamburger and french fries, Your Honour," responded the defendant.

Or how about this one? "I saw a man-eating lion at the zoo." "Big deal! I saw a man eating snails at a restaurant."

Or how about, "Make me a glass of chocolate milk!"? "Poof! You're a glass of chocolate milk."

These children's jokes are based on ambiguities in the meanings of words and phrases. Most seven-year-olds will find the joke about order in the court funny and can recognize that the word *order* has more than one meaning. The jokes about the man-eating lion and chocolate milk will strike most children as funny at about the age of eleven, when they can understand ambiguities in grammatical structure.

Children make enormous strides in their cognitive development during the middle childhood years. Their thought processes and language become more logical and more complex. In this chapter, we follow the course of cognitive development in middle childhood. First, we examine Piaget's cognitive-developmental view. We then consider the information-processing approach that has been stimulated by our experience with that high-tech phenomenon, the computer. We next examine the development of intelligence, various ways of measuring it, and the roles of heredity and environment in shaping it. Finally, we turn to the development of language.

Piaget: The Concrete-Operational Stage

concrete operations The third stage in Piaget's scheme, characterized by flexible, reversible thought concerning tangible objects and events.

According to Piaget, the typical child is entering the stage of **concrete operations** by the age of seven. *Question: What is meant by the stage of concrete operations?* In the stage of concrete operations, which lasts until about the age of twelve, children show the beginnings of the capacity for adult logic. However, their thought processes, or operations, generally involve tangible objects rather than abstract ideas. This is why we refer to their thinking as "concrete."

reversibility According to Piaget, recognition that processes can be undone, leaving things as they were before. Reversibility is a factor in conservation of the properties of substances.

The thinking of the concrete-operational child is characterized by **reversibility** and flexibility. Consider adding the numbers two and three to get five. Adding is an operation. The operation is reversible in that the child can then subtract two from five to get three. There is flexibility in that the child can also subtract three from five to get the number two. To the concrete-operational child, adding and subtracting are not just rote activities. The concrete-operational child recognizes that there are relationships among numbers—that operations can be carried out according to rules. This understanding lends concrete-operational thought flexibility and reversibility.

Concrete-operational children are less *egocentric*. Their abilities to take on the roles of others and to view the world and themselves from other people's perspectives are greatly expanded. They recognize that people see things in different ways because of different situations and different sets of values.

decentration Simultaneous focusing (centring) on more than one aspect or dimension of a problem or situation.

Compared with preoperational children, who can focus on only one dimension of a problem at a time, concrete-operational children can engage in **decentration**. That is, they can focus on multiple parts of a problem at once. Decentration has implications for conservation and other intellectual undertakings.

Conservation

Concrete-operational children show understanding of the laws of conservation. The seven-year-old girl in Figure 12.1 (on page 196) would say that the flattened ball still has the same amount of clay. If asked why, she might reply, "Because you can roll it up again like the other one." This answer shows reversibility.

The concrete-operational girl knows that objects can have several properties or dimensions. Things that are tall can also be heavy or light. Things that are red can also be round or square, or thick or thin. Knowledge of this principle allows the girl to *decentre* and to avoid focusing on only the diameter of the clay pancake. By attending to both the height and the width of the clay, she recognizes that the loss in height compensates for the gain in width.

Researchers have found that children do not develop conservation in all kinds of tasks simultaneously (Kreitler & Kreitler, 1989). For example, conservation of mass usually develops first, followed by conservation of weight and conservation of volume. Piaget theorized that the gains of the concrete-operational stage are so tied to specific events that achievement in one area does not necessarily transfer to achievement in another.

Lessons in Observation
Piaget's Concrete-Operational Stage

click on "Piaget's Concrete-Operational Stage" in Module 3, Section 2, on your Observing Children and Adolescents CD-ROM. Also see your Student Workbook for more activities, key terms, and concepts. You can also visit the Student Book Companion Site to watch the video, answer the questions, and e-mail your responses to your professor.

Children in Piaget's concrete-operational stage can not only understand that both glasses contain the same amount of water no matter what shape the glass is but can also explain why.

Learning Objectives
- What is the concrete-operational stage of cognitive development?
- How do conservation tasks help illustrate whether or not a child has reached the concrete-operational stage?
- What is the difference between logical and intuitive approaches to problem solving?
- How is reversibility related to ability to engage in concrete operations?

Applied Lesson
Imagine that you are showing a preoperational child 100 rolls of 100 pennies each and a $100 bill. You ask the child which is more money. What do you think the child will say? Why? Now imagine that you ask the same question of a concrete-operational child. Would you expect the same answer? Why or why not? Now do some thinking of your own: Which is less expensive: a $3000 computer or a $12 000 car? Explain your answer in as much detail as you like.

Critical Thinking
Recall the video that you watched in Chapter 9: "Piaget's Preoperational Stage" in Module 2, Section 2. Describe the differences in reasoning between the younger children in Chapter 9 and the children in the current chapter. How has the reasoning of the children in the current chapter advanced over that of the children shown in the video that accompanies Chapter 9?

Figure 12.1

Conservation of Mass

This girl is in the concrete-operational stage of cognitive development. She has rolled two clay balls. In the photo on the left, she agrees that both have the same amount (mass) of clay. In the photo on the right, she (gleefully) flattens one clay ball. When asked whether the two pieces still have the same amount of clay, she says yes.

© Judy Allen Biggs

Transitivity

Question of the day: If your parents are older than you are and you are older than your children, are your parents older than your children? (How do you know?)

We have posed some tough questions in this book, but the one about your parents is a real ogre. The answer, of course, is yes. But how did you arrive at this answer? If you said yes simply on the basis of knowing that your parents are older than your children (e.g., fifty-eight and fifty-six compared with five and three), your answer did not require concrete-operational thought. One aspect of concrete-operational thought is the principle of **transitivity:** If A exceeds B in some property (say, age or height) and if B exceeds C, then A must also exceed C.

Researchers can assess whether or not children understand the principle of transitivity by asking them to place objects in a series, or order, according to some property or trait, such as lining up one's family members according to age, height, or weight. Placing objects in a series is termed **seriation.** Let's consider some examples with pre-operational and concrete-operational children.

Piaget frequently assessed children's abilities at seriation by asking them to place ten sticks in order of size. Children who are four to five years of age usually place the sticks in a random sequence, or in small groups, as in small, medium, or large. Six- to seven-year-old children, who are in transition between the preoperational and concrete-operational stages, may arrive at proper sequences. However, they usually do so by trial and error, rearranging their series a number of times. In other words, they are capable of comparing two sticks and deciding that one is longer than the other, but their overall perspective seems limited to the pair they are comparing at the time and does not seem to encompass the entire array.

But consider the approach of seven- and eight-year-olds who are capable of concrete operations. They go about the task systematically, usually without error. For the ten sticks, they look over the array, then select either the longest or shortest and place it at the point from which they will build their series. Then they select the next longest (or shortest) and continue in this fashion until the task is complete.

Knowledge of the principle of transitivity allows concrete-operational children to go about their task unerringly. They realize that if stick A is longer than stick B and stick B is longer than stick C, then stick A is also longer than stick C. After putting stick C in place, they need not double-check in hope that it will be shorter than stick A; they *know* it will be.

transitivity The principle that if A is greater than B in a property and B is greater than C, then A is greater than C.

seriation Placing objects in an order or series according to a property or trait.

Concrete-operational children also have the decentration capacity to allow them to seriate in two dimensions at once. Consider a seriation task used by Piaget and his longtime colleague Barbel Inhelder. In this test, children are given forty-nine leaves and asked to classify them according to size and brightness (from small to large and from dark to light) (see Figure 12.2). As the grid is completed from left to right, the leaves become lighter. As it is filled In from top to bottom, the leaves become larger. Preoperational six-year-olds can usually order the leaves according to size or brightness, but not both simultaneously. But concrete-operational children of age seven or eight can work with both dimensions at once and fill in the grid properly.

A number of researchers have argued that children can seriate earlier than Piaget believed and that Piaget's results reflected the demand characteristics of his experiments (Blevins-Knabe, 1987; Siegler & Alibali, 2005). This may be so, but the *sequence* of developments in seriation and transitivity seems to have been captured fairly well by Piaget.

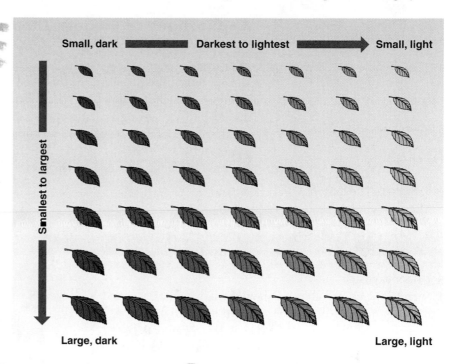

Figure 12.2

A Grid for Demonstrating the Development of Seriation

To classify these 49 leaves, children must be able to focus on two dimensions at once: size and lightness. They must also recognize that if quantity A exceeds quantity B and quantity B exceeds quantity C, then quantity A must also exceed quantity C. This relationship is called the *principle of transitivity*.

Class Inclusion

Another example of an operation is **class inclusion,** which we learned about in Chapter 9. In the example in Chapter 9 (see page 322), a four-year-old was shown pictures of four cats and six dogs. When asked whether there were more dogs or more animals, she said more dogs. This preoperational child apparently could not focus on the two subclasses (dogs, cats) and the larger subclass (animals) at the same time. But concrete-operational children can focus on two dimensions (in this case, classes and subclasses) at the same time. Therefore, they are more likely to answer the question about the dogs and the animals correctly (Chapman & McBride, 1992). But their thought remains concrete in that they will give you the correct answer if you ask them about dogs and animals (or daffodils and flowers) but not if you attempt to phrase the question in terms of abstract symbols, such as A, B_1, and B_2. Aspects of concrete-operational thinking are summarized in Concept Review 12.1.

As with other areas of cognitive development, researchers have taken issue with Piaget's views of the ages at which class-inclusion skills develop, and they have argued that language continues to pose hazards for the children being tested. One review of the literature on class inclusion suggests that many children cannot answer standard class-inclusion questions correctly until they are ten years or older (Winer, 1980).

class inclusion The principle that one category or class of things includes several subclasses.

Applications of Piaget's Theory to Education

Question: Can we apply Piaget's theory of cognitive development to educational practices? It seems that we can (Crain, 2000; Davis, 1991). Piaget pointed out some applications himself. First, he believed that learning involves active discovery. Therefore, teachers should not simply try to impose knowledge on the child but should find interesting and stimulating materials. Kamii, Lewis & Kirkland (2001) examined the usefulness of manipulatives (e.g., tanagrams, counters, cards used in games) in helping children acquire logiomathematical knowledge. They noted that a rigid use of manipulatives e.g., tangrams, counters, playing cards—without the pos-

Concept Review 12.1 Aspects of Concrete-Operational Thinking

Conservation

Concrete-operational children show conservation of *mass* and *number*. As you may remember, the girl on the right shows conservation of the mass of the clay. Refer to Figure 9.3 (p. 321), which shows the experiment using pennies to test conservation of number. A concrete-operational child will conserve number and say that both panels have the same number of pennies. Preoperational children will say that the wider row has more.

© Judy Allen Biggs

Child is shown two rows of pennies.

Experimenter moves pennies in one row.

Seriation

A concrete-operational child understands the principle of transitivity (if A > B and B > C, then A > C). Therefore, the child can place the sticks in order from longest to shortest.

Class Inclusion

Here are 10 animals, including 6 dogs. When asked whether there are more dogs or animals, the preoperational child, focusing on one aspect of the problem at a time, may see that there are more dogs than cats and say, "Dogs." The concrete-operational child is more likely to recognize that the class "animals" includes both "dogs" and "cats" and thus will answer, "Animals."

sibility of exploration and problem solving, and without any teacher guidance/intervention, is limited. If a child is struggling with a problem, the authors recommend that a simpler problem be given (and the child be allowed to work through that one) rather than the "missing step" being pointed out to the child. Second, instruction should be geared to the child's level of development. When teaching a concrete-operational child about fractions, for example, the teacher should not just lecture but should allow the child to divide concrete objects into parts. Third, Piaget believed that learning to take into account the perspectives of others is a key ingredient in the development of both cognition and morality. Accordingly, he thought that teachers should promote group discussions and interactions among their students.

Evaluation of Piaget's Theory

Although Piaget's theory has led many psychologists to recast their concepts of children, it has also met with criticism on several grounds. As noted in Chapters 6 and 9, some researchers have shown that Piaget underestimated children's abilities. Modified task demands suggest that children are capable of conservation and other concrete-operational tasks earlier than Piaget believed. Cognitive skills may develop more independently and continuously than Piaget thought—not in stages. For example, conservation does not arrive all at once. Children develop conservation for mass, weight, and volume at different ages. The onset of conservation can be seen in terms of the gradual accumulation of problem-solving abilities instead of in terms of suddenly changing cognitive structures (Flavell et al., 2002). However, the sequences of development—which are at the core of Piaget's theory—continue to appear to remain the same. In sum, Piaget's theoretical edifice has been rocked, but it has not been dashed to rubble.

In the next section, we revisit Piaget and examine his views on children's decisions about right and wrong. Then we consider the views of Lawrence Kohlberg on the same topic.

Active Review

1. Concrete-operational children are (more or less?) egocentric than preoperational children.

2. The principle of _____ holds that if A exceeds B and B exceeds C, then A must exceed C.

3. Class _____ involves the ability to recognize that one class of things (A) can include subclasses (B$_1$ and B$_2$).

Reflect & Relate: Ariel becomes angry that one of her best friends, Azarah, has told other friends a secret she confided in her. Ariel is hurt, and in retaliation spreads malicious rumours about Azarah at school. Shannon makes a mistake at the nuclear energy plant where she works, causing a nuclear accident in which a great deal of radiation is released, killing 300 people within a week and shortening the lives of more than 1 million people because of cancer. Which person has done something naughtier—Ariel or Shannon? Explain your viewpoint. (Now you are ready to read the next section.)

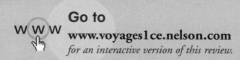

Go to
www.voyages1ce.nelson.com
for an interactive version of this review.

Moral Development: The Child as Juror

Moral development is a complex issue with both cognitive and behavioural aspects. On a cognitive level, moral development concerns the basis on which children judge that an act is right or wrong. In this section, we examine the contributions of Jean Piaget and Lawrence Kohlberg to our understanding of children's moral development.

Piaget and Kohlberg argued that moral reasoning undergoes the same cognitive-developmental pattern around the world. The moral considerations that children weigh at a given age are likely to reflect the values of the social and cultural settings in which they are being reared. However, moral reasoning is also theorized to reflect the orderly unfolding of cognitive processes (Narvaez, Getz, Rest, & Thoma, 1999). Moral reasoning is related to the child's overall cognitive development. *Question: How does Piaget view the development of moral reasoning?*

Piaget's Theory of Moral Development

For years, Piaget observed children playing games such as marbles and making judgments on the seriousness of the wrongdoing of characters in stories. On the basis of these observations, he concluded that children's moral judgments develop in two major overlapping stages: *moral realism* and *autonomous morality* (Piaget, 1932).

The Stage of Moral Realism

The first stage is usually referred to as the stage of **moral realism,** or of **objective morality.** During this stage, which emerges at about the age of five, children consider behaviour to be correct when it conforms to authority or to the rules of the game. When asked why something should be done in a certain way, the five-year-old may answer, "Because that's the way to do it" or "Because my mommy says so."

At about the age of five, children perceive rules as embedded in the structure of things. Rules, to them, reflect ultimate reality, hence the term *moral realism*. Rules and right and wrong are seen as absolute. They are not seen as deriving from people to meet social needs.

Another consequence of viewing rules as embedded in the fabric of the world is **immanent justice,** or automatic retribution. Punishment is perceived as structurally connected to wrongdoing. Therefore, punishment is inevitable. Five- or six-year-old children who lie or steal usually believe that they will be found out or at least punished for their acts. If they trip and scrape their knees, they may assume that this accident represents punishment for a transgression.

Truth or Fiction Revisited: It is true that you are guilty in the eyes of a five-year-old even if your behaviour was an accident. Preoperational children tend to focus on only one dimension at a time. Therefore, they judge the wrongness of an act only in terms of the amount of damage done, not in terms of the intentions of the wrong-doer. Children in the stage of moral realism are tough jurors indeed. They do not excuse the person who harms by accident. As an illustration, consider children's response to Piaget's story about the broken cups. Piaget told children a story in which one child breaks fifteen cups accidentally and another child breaks one cup deliberately. Which child is naughtiest? Which should be punished most? Children in the stage of moral realism typically say that the child who did the most damage is the naughtiest and should be punished most. The amount of damage is more important than the child's intentions (Piaget, 1932).

The Stage of Autonomous Morality

Piaget found that when children reach the ages of nine to eleven, they begin to show **autonomous morality.** Their moral judgments tend to become more *autonomous,* or

---

Children in middle childhood often judge in terms of rules rather than circumstances and human needs. To watch the video, click on the "Moral Development" clip in Module 3, Section 3.

moral realism   According to Piaget, the stage during which children judge acts as moral when they conform to authority or to the rules of the game. Morality at this stage is perceived as embedded in the structure of the universe.

objective morality   The perception of morality as objective—that is, as existing outside the cognitive functioning of people; a characteristic of Piaget's stage of moral realism.

immanent justice   The view that retribution for wrong-doing is a direct consequence of the wrongdoing, reflective of the belief that morality is embedded within the structure of the universe.

autonomous morality   The second stage in Piaget's cognitive-developmental theory of moral development. In this stage, children base moral judgments on the intentions of the wrongdoer and on the amount of damage done. Social rules are viewed as agreements that can be changed.

self-governed. Children come to view social rules as arbitrary agreements that can be changed, no longer automatically viewing obedience to authority figures as right. They realize that circumstances can require breaking rules.

Children who show autonomous morality are capable of flexible operational thought. They can focus simultaneously on multiple dimensions, and so they consider not only social rules but also the motives of the wrongdoer.

Children in this stage also show a greater capacity to take the point of view of others, to empathize with them. Decentration and increased empathy prompt children to weigh the intentions of the wrongdoer more heavily than the amount of damage done. The child who deliberately broke one cup may be seen as deserving of more punishment than the child who accidentally broke fifteen cups. Children become capable of considering mitigating circumstances. Accidents are less likely to be considered crimes.

Piaget assumed that autonomous morality usually develops as a result of cooperative peer relationships. But he also believed that parents could help foster autonomous morality by creating egalitarian relationships with their children and explaining the reasons for social rules. As we will see in the next section, knowledge of social rules is also a key factor in Lawrence Kohlberg's theory of moral development.

Moral Realism
It looks bad, but Mom asked them to find her car keys. Mom wasn't thinking of having them go through her purse, however. If they break things or drop them on the floor in the effort, are the children being "bad"? Children in the stage of moral realism might well say yes because they focus on the damage done, not on the intentions of the wrongdoer.

Kohlberg's Theory of Moral Development

Question: What is Kohlberg's theory of moral development? Lawrence Kohlberg (1981, 1985) advanced the cognitive-developmental theory of moral development by elaborating on the kinds of information children use and on the complexities of moral reasoning. Before we discuss Kohlberg's views, read the tale that Kohlberg used in his research, and answer the questions that follow.

> In Europe a woman was near death from a special kind of cancer. There was one drug that the doctors thought might save her. It was a form of radium that a druggist in the same town had recently discovered. The drug was expensive to make, but the druggist was charging 10 times what the drug cost him to make. He paid $200 for the radium and charged $2000 for a small dose of the drug. The sick woman's husband, Heinz, went to everyone he knew to borrow the money, but he could only get together about $1000, which was half of what it cost. He told the druggist that his wife was dying and asked him to sell it cheaper or let him pay later. But the druggist said: "No, I discovered the drug and I'm going to make money from it." So Heinz got desperate and broke into the man's store to steal the drug for his wife.
>
> —Kohlberg (1969)

When posed with Kohlberg's question about whether or not Heinz was right or wrong to steal the drug to save his wife's life, many adolescents have different answers than younger children who are governed by rules and consequences. To watch the video, click on "Moral Development" in Module 3, Section 3.

Kohlberg emphasized the importance of being able to view the moral world from the perspective of another person (Carpendale, 2000). Look at this situation from Heinz's perspective. What do you think? Should Heinz have tried to steal the drug? Was he right or wrong? As you can see from Table 12.1, the issue is more complicated than a simple yes or no. Heinz is caught in a moral dilemma in which legal or social rules (in this case, laws against stealing) are pitted against a strong human need (Heinz's desire to save his wife). According to Kohlberg's theory, children and adults arrive at yes or no answers for different reasons. These reasons can be classified according to the level of moral development they reflect.

Children (and adults) are faced with many moral dilemmas. Consider cheating in school. When children fear failing a test, they may be tempted to cheat. Different children may decide not to cheat for different reasons. One child may simply fear getting caught. A second child may decide that it is more important to live up to his or her moral principles than to get the highest possible grade. In each case, the child's decision is not to cheat. However, the cognitive processes behind each decision reflect different levels of reasoning.

Kohlberg's Levels and Stages of Moral Development

Stage of Development	Examples of Moral Reasoning That Support Heinz's Stealing the Drug	Examples of Moral Reasoning That Oppose Heinz's Stealing the Drug
Level I: Preconventional—Typically Begins in Early Childhood[1]		
Stage 1: Judgments guided by obedience and the prospect of punishment (the consequences of the behaviour)	It is not wrong to take the drug. Heinz did try to pay the druggist for it, and it is worth only $200, not $2000.	Taking things without paying is wrong because it is against the law. Heinz will get caught and go to jail.
Stage 2: Naively egoistic, instrumental orientation (things are right when they satisfy people's needs)	Heinz ought to take the drug because his wife really needs it. He can always pay the druggist back.	Heinz should not take the drug. If he gets caught and winds up in jail, it won't do his wife any good.
Level II: Conventional—Typically Begins in Middle Childhood		
Stage 3: Good-boy/good-girl orientation (moral behaviour helps others and is socially approved)	Stealing is a crime, so it is bad, but Heinz should take the drug to save his wife or else people would blame him for letting her die.	Stealing is a crime. Heinz should not just take the drug because his family will be dishonoured and they will blame him.
Stage 4: Law-and-order orientation (moral behaviour is doing one's duty and showing respect for authority)	Heinz must take the drug to do his duty to save his wife. Eventually, he has to pay the druggist for it, however.	If we all took the law into our own hands, civilization would fall apart, so Heinz should not steal the drug.
Level III: Postconventional—Typically Begins in Adolescence[2]		
Stage 5: Contractual, legalistic orientation (one must weigh pressing human needs against society's need to maintain social order)	This thing is complicated because society has a right to maintain law and order, but Heinz has to take the drug to save his wife.	I can see why Heinz feels he has to take the drug, but laws exist for the benefit of society as a whole and cannot simply be cast aside.
Stage 6: Universal ethical principles orientation (people must follow universal ethical principles and their own conscience, even if it means breaking the law)	In this case, the law comes into conflict with the principle of the sanctity of human life. Heinz must take the drug because his wife's life is more important than the law.	If Heinz truly believes that stealing the drug is worse than letting his wife die, he should not take it. People have to make sacrifices to do what they think is right.

[1]Tends to be used less often in middle childhood.
[2]May not develop at all.

As a stage theorist, Kohlberg argued that the developmental stages of moral reasoning follow the same sequence in all children. Children progress at different rates, and not all children (or adults) reach the highest stage. But children must experience Stage 1 before they enter Stage 2, and so on. According to Kohlberg, there are three levels of moral development and two stages within each level.

Let's return to Heinz and see how responses to the questions we have posed can reflect different levels and stages of moral development.

The Preconventional Level

In the **preconventional level**, children base their moral judgments on the consequences of their behaviour. For instance, Stage 1 is oriented toward obedience and punishment. Good behaviour means being obedient, which allows one to avoid punishment. According to Stage 1 reasoning, Heinz could be urged to steal the drug because he did ask to pay for it first. But he could also be urged not to steal the drug so that he will not be sent to jail (see Table 12.1).

In Stage 2, good behaviour allows people to satisfy their own needs and, perhaps, the needs of others. A Stage 2 reason for stealing the drug is that Heinz's wife needs it. Therefore, stealing the drug—the only way of attaining it—is not wrong. A Stage 2 reason for not stealing the drug would be that Heinz's wife might die even if he does so. Thus, he might wind up in jail needlessly.

In a study of American children aged seven through sixteen, Kohlberg (1963) found that Stage 1 and 2 types of moral judgments were offered most frequently by seven- and ten-year-olds. There was a steep falling off of Stage 1 and 2 judgments after age ten.

The Conventional Level

In the **conventional level** of moral reasoning, right and wrong are judged by conformity to conventional (family, religious, societal) standards of right and wrong. According to the Stage 3 "good-boy/good-girl orientation," it is good to meet the needs and expectations of others. Moral behaviour is what is "normal"—what the majority does. From the Stage 3 perspective, Heinz should steal the drug because that is what a "good husband" would do. It is "natural" or "normal" to try to help one's wife. Or Heinz should not steal the drug because "good people do not steal." Stage 3 judgments also focus on the role of sympathy—on the importance of doing what will make someone else feel good or better.

In Stage 4, moral judgments are based on rules that maintain the social order. Showing respect for authority and duty is valued highly. From this perspective, one could argue that Heinz must steal the drug, because it is his duty to save his wife. He would pay the druggist when he could. Or one could argue that Heinz should not steal the drug, because he would be breaking the law. He might also be contributing to the breakdown of the social order. Many people do not develop beyond the conventional level.

Kohlberg (1963) found that Stage 3 and 4 types of judgments emerge during middle childhood. They are all but absent among seven-year-olds. However, they are reported by about 20 percent of ten-year-olds (and by higher percentages of adolescents). A critique of Kohlberg's theory by Richard Shweder and Carol Gilligan is presented in Chapter 15.

The Postconventional Level

In the **postconventional level**, moral reasoning is based on the person's own moral standards. If this level of reasoning develops at all, it is found among adolescents and adults (see Table 12.1).

preconventional level
According to Kohlberg, a period during which moral judgments are based largely on expectations of rewards or punishments.

conventional level
According to Kohlberg, a period during which moral judgments largely reflect social rules and conventions.

postconventional level
According to Kohlberg, a period during which moral judgments are derived from moral principles and people look to themselves to set moral standards.

Active Review

4. Piaget believed that children's moral judgments develop in two stages: moral realism and _____ morality.

5. Preoperational children judge the wrongness of an act in terms of (the amount of damage done or the intentions of the wrongdoer?).

6. In Kohlberg's _____ level, children base their moral judgments on the consequences of their behaviour.

7. In the _____ level, right and wrong are judged by conformity to conventional (family, religious, societal) standards of right and wrong.

Reflect & Relate: Do you believe that Heinz should have taken the drug without paying? Why or why not? What does your reasoning suggest about your level of moral development?

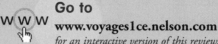

Go to
www.voyages1ce.nelson.com
for an interactive version of this review.

Information Processing: Learning, Remembering, Problem Solving

Question: What is the difference between Piaget's view of cognitive development and the information-processing approach? Whereas Piaget looked on children as budding scientists, psychologists who view cognitive development in terms of **information processing** see children (and adults) as akin to computer systems. Sort of. Children, like computers, attain information (input) from the environment, store it, retrieve it, manipulate it, and then respond to it overtly (output). One goal of the information-processing approach is to learn how children store, retrieve, and manipulate information—how their "mental programs" develop. Information-processing theorists also study the development of children's strategies for processing information (Bjorklund & Rosenblum, 2001; Pickering, 2001).

Although something may be gained from thinking of children in terms of computers, children, of course, are not computers. Children are self-aware and capable of creativity and intuition

Key elements in information processing include

- development of selective attention—development of children's abilities to focus on the elements of a problem and find solutions;
- development of capacity for storage and retrieval of information—development of the capacity of memory and of children's understanding of the processes of memory and how to strengthen and use memory; and
- development of strategies for processing information—development of ability to solve problems, for example, by finding the correct formula and applying it.

Development of Selective Attention

A key cognitive process is the ability to pay attention to relevant features of a task. The ability to focus one's attention and screen out distractions advances steadily through middle childhood (Miller, Birnbaum, & Durbin, 1990a). Preoperational children engaged in problem solving tend to focus (or centre) their attention on one element of the problem at a time—a major reason that they lack conservation. Concrete-operational children, by contrast, can attend to multiple aspects of the problem at once, permitting them to conserve number, volume, and so on.

An experiment by Strutt and colleagues (1975) illustrates how selective attention and the ability to ignore distraction develop during middle childhood. The researchers asked children between six and twelve years of age to sort a deck of cards as quickly as possible on the basis of the figures depicted on each card (e.g., circle versus square). In one condition, only the relevant dimension (i.e., form) was shown on each card. In another condition, a dimension not relevant to the sorting was also present (e.g., a horizontal or vertical line in the figure). In a third condition, *two* irrelevant dimensions were present (e.g., a star above or below the figure, in addition to a horizontal or vertical line in the figure). As seen in Figure 12.3, the irrelevant information interfered with sorting ability for all age groups, but older children were much less affected than younger children. In the next section we will learn more about how children gain the ability to store and retrieve information.

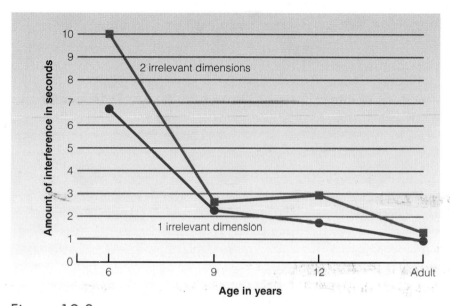

Figure 12.3

Development of the Ability to Ignore Distractions

Strutt and his colleagues demonstrated how the ability to ignore distraction develops during middle childhood. The effect of irrelevant dimensions on sorting speed was determined by subtracting the speed of the sort in the no-irrelevant-dimension condition from the speed of the other two conditions. As shown here, irrelevant information interfered with sorting ability for all age groups, but older children were less affected than younger ones. *Source: Strutt et al. (1975).*

Developments in the Storage and Retrieval of Information

Question: What is meant by the term memory? Keep in mind that the word **memory** is not a scientific term, even though psychologists and other scientists may use it for the sake of convenience. Psychologists usually use the term to refer to the processes of storing and retrieving information. Many but not all psychologists divide memory functioning into three major processes or structures: *sensory memory, working memory (short-term memory),* and *long-term memory* (Figure 12.4).

memory The processes by which we store and retrieve information.

Figure 12.4

The Structure of Memory

Many psychologists divide memory into three processes or "structures." Sensory information enters the registers of sensory memory, where memory traces are held briefly before decaying. If we attend to the information, much of it is transferred to working memory (also called short-term memory), where it may decay or be displaced if it is not transferred to long-term memory. We usually use rehearsal (repetition) or elaborative strategies to transfer memories to long-term memory. Once in long-term memory, memories can be retrieved through appropriate search strategies. But if information is organized poorly or if we cannot find cues to retrieve it, it may be "lost" for all practical purposes.

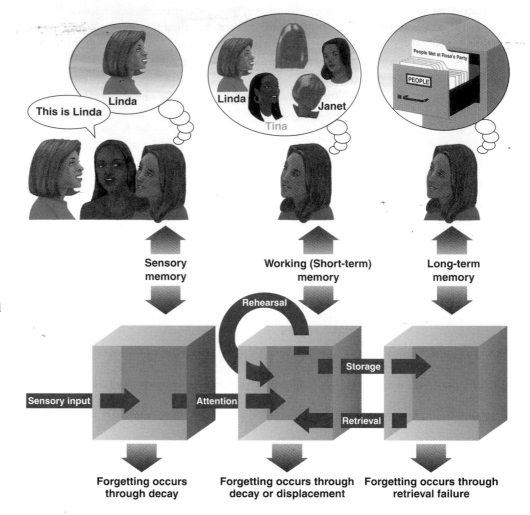

POWER VISUALS!
See your student companion website for an interactive version of Figure 12.4.

sensory memory The structure of memory first encountered by sensory input. Information is maintained in sensory memory for only a fraction of a second.

sensory register Another term for sensory memory.

working memory The structure of memory that can hold a sensory stimulus for up to 30 seconds after the trace decays. Also called *short-term memory*.

Sensory Memory

When we look at an object and then blink our eyes, the visual impression of the object lasts for a fraction of a second in what is called **sensory memory,** or the **sensory register.** Then the "trace" of the stimulus decays. The concept of sensory memory applies to all the senses. For example, when we are introduced to somebody, the trace of the sound of the name also decays, but as we will see in the next section, we can maintain the name in memory by focusing on it.

Working Memory (Short-Term Memory)

When children focus their attention on a stimulus in the sensory register, it tends to be retained in **working memory** (also called *short-term memory*) for up to thirty seconds after the trace of the stimulus decays. Ability to maintain information in short-term memory depends on cognitive strategies and on basic capacity to continue to perceive a vanished stimulus. Memory function in middle childhood seems largely adultlike in organization and strategies and shows only gradual improvement in a quantitative sense through early adolescence (Alloway ,Gathercole, Willis, & Adams, 2004; Gathercole, Pickering, Ambridge, & Wearing, 2004a).

Auditory stimuli can be maintained longer in short-term memory than can visual stimuli. For this reason, one strategy for promoting memory is to **encode** visual stimuli as sounds, or auditory stimulation. Then the sounds can be repeated out loud or mentally. For example, in Figure 12.4, mentally repeating the sound of Linda's name helps the other girl remember it. That is, the sounds can be **rehearsed.**

encode   To transform sensory input into a form that is more readily processed.

rehearse   Repeat.

Capacity of Short-Term Memory The basic capacity of the short-term memory can be described in terms of the number of "bits" or chunks of information that can be kept in memory at once. To remember a new phone number, for example, one must keep seven chunks of information in short-term memory simultaneously—that is, one must rehearse them consecutively.

Classic research shows that the typical adult can keep about seven chunks of information—plus or minus two—in short-term memory at a time (Miller, 1956). As measured by the ability to recall digits, the typical five- to six-year-old can work on two chunks of information at a time. The ability to recall a series of digits improves throughout middle childhood, and adolescents can keep about seven chunks of information in short-term memory at the same time (Cowan, Nugent, Elliott, Ponomarev, & Saults, 1999; Cowan, Nugent, Elliott, & Saults, 2000; Gathercole, Pickering, Knight, & Stegmann, 2004b).

The information-processing view focuses on children's capacity for memory and their use of cognitive strategies, such as the way in which they focus their attention (Gathercole et al., 2004a, 2004b). Certain Piagetian tasks require several cognitive strategies instead of one. Young children frequently fail at such tasks because they cannot simultaneously hold many pieces of information in their short-term memories. Put another way, preschoolers can solve problems that have only one or two steps, whereas older children can retain information from earlier steps as they proceed to subsequent steps.

But how do young children remember the alphabet, which is twenty-six chunks of information? *Truth or Fiction Revisited:* It is not true that learning the alphabet requires keeping twenty-six chunks of information in mind at once. Children usually learn the alphabet by **rote learning**—simple associative learning based on repetition. After the alphabet is repeated many, many times, M triggers the letter N, N triggers O, and so on. The typical three-year-old who has learned the alphabet by rote will not be able to answer the question "What letter comes after N?" However, if you recite "H, I, J, K, L, M, N" with the child and then pause, the child is likely to say, "O, P." The three-year-old will probably not realize that he or she can find the answer by using the cognitive strategy of reciting the alphabet, but many five- or six-year-olds will.

rote learning   Learning by repetition.

Long-Term Memory

Think of **long-term memory** as a vast storehouse of information containing names, dates, places, what Shareef did to you in second grade, what Alyssa said about you when you were twelve. Long-term memories may last days, years, or, for practical purposes, a lifetime.

Questions: How much information can be stored in long-term memory? How is it "filed"? There is no known limit to the amount of information that can be stored in long-term memory. From time to time it may seem that we have forgotten, or lost, a long-term memory, such as the names of elementary or high school classmates. But it is more likely that we simply cannot find the proper cues to help us retrieve the information. It is "lost" in the same way as when we misplace an object but know that it is still in the house. It remains there somewhere for the finding.

How is information transferred from short-term memory to long-term memory? Rehearsal is one method. Older children are more likely than younger children to use rehearsal (Cowan et al., 2003; Hutton & Towse, 2001; Saito & Miyake, 2004). But pure rehearsal, with no attempt to make information meaningful by linking it to past learning, is no guarantee that the information will be stored permanently.

long-term memory   The memory structure capable of relatively permanent storage of information.

elaborative strategy   A method for increasing retention of new information by relating it to well-known information.

semantic code   A code based on the meaning of information.

A more effective method than simple rehearsal is to purposefully relate new material to well-known information. Relating new material to well-known material is known as an **elaborative strategy** (Siegler & Alibali, 2005). English teachers encourage children to use new vocabulary words in sentences to help them remember them. This is an example of an elaborative strategy. In this way, children are building extended **semantic codes** that will help them retrieve the words' meanings in the future.

Before we proceed to the next section, here's a question for you. Which of the following words is spelled correctly: *retreival* or *retrieval?* The spellings sound alike, so an acoustic code for reconstructing the correct spelling would not be of help. But a semantic code, such as the spelling rule "i before e except after c," would allow you to reconstruct the correct spelling: retr*ie*val. This is why children are taught rules and principles. Of course, whether these rules are retrieved in the appropriate situation is another issue.

Organization in Long-Term Memory

As children's knowledge of concepts advances, the storehouse of their long-term memory becomes gradually organized according to categories. Preschoolers tend to organize their memories by grouping objects that share the same function (Lucariello & Nelson, 1985; Towse, 2003). "Toast" may be grouped with "peanut butter sandwich," because both are edible. Only during the early elementary school years are toast and peanut butter likely to be joined under the concept of food.

When items are correctly categorized in long-term memory, children are more likely to recall accurate information about them. For instance, do you "remember" whether whales breathe underwater? If you did not know that whales are mammals or if you knew nothing about mammals, a correct answer might depend on some remote instance of rote learning. If children have incorrectly classified whales as fish, they might search their "memories" and construct the incorrect answer that whales breathe underwater. Correct categorization, in sum, expands children's knowledge and allows them to retrieve information more readily.

But it has also been shown that when the knowledge of children in a particular area surpasses that of adults, the children show superior capacity to store and retrieve related information. For example, chess experts are superior to amateurs at remembering where chess pieces had been placed on the board (Gobet & Simon, 2000; Saariluoma, 2001). This may not surprise you, until you learn that in these studies, the experts were eight- to twelve-year-old children and the amateurs were adults.

Development of Recall Memory

Recall memory involves retrieval of information from memory. As children develop, their capacity for recalling information increases (Gathercole et al., 2004a, 2004b). Improvement in memory is linked to their ability to quickly process (i.e., scan and categorize) information. Children's memory is a good overall indicator of their cognitive ability (Hutton & Towse, 2001).

In an experiment on categorization and memory, researchers placed objects that fell into four categories (furniture, clothing, tools, fruit) on a table before second- and fourth-graders (Hasselhorn, 1992). The children were allowed three minutes to arrange the pictures as they wished and to remember as many as they could. Fourth-graders were more likely to categorize, and recall, the pictures than second-graders.

Research also reveals that children are more likely to accurately recall information when they are strongly motivated to do so (Roebers, Moga, & Schneider, 2001). Fear of poor grades can encourage recall even in middle childhood. The promise of rewards also helps.

Development of Metacognition and Metamemory

Question: What do children understand about the functioning of their cognitive processes and, more particularly, their memory? Children's knowledge and control of their cognitive abilities is termed **metacognition.** The development of metacognition is shown by the ability to formulate problems, awareness of the processes required to solve a problem, activation of cognitive strategies, maintaining focus on the problem, and checking answers.

When a sixth-grader decides which homework assignments to do first, memorizes the names of all past prime ministers for tomorrow's test, and then tests herself to see which ones she needs to study more, she is displaying metacognition. Teaching students metacognitive skills improves their performance in reading and other areas of education (Flavell et al., 2002; Stright, Neitzel, Sears, & Hoke-Sinex, 2001).

Metamemory is one aspect of metacognition. It more specifically refers to children's awareness of the functioning of their memory. Older children show greater insight into how memory works (Hashimoto, 1991). For example, young elementary school students frequently announce that they have memorized educational materials before they have actually done so. Older students are more likely to accurately assess their knowledge (Paris & Winograd, 1990). As a result, older children store and retrieve information more effectively than younger children (Siegler & Alibali, 2005).

Older children also show more knowledge of strategies that can be used to facilitate memory. Preschoolers will usually use rehearsal if someone else suggests that they do, but not until about the age of six or seven do children use rehearsal on their own (Flavell et al., 2002). Older elementary school children also become better at adapting their memory strategies to fit the characteristics of the task at hand (Siegler & Alibali, 2005; Towse, Hitch, & Hutton, 2002).

As children develop, they also are more likely to use selective rehearsal to remember important information. That is, they exclude the meaningless mass of perceptions milling about them by confining rehearsal to what they are trying to remember. Selectivity in rehearsal is found more often among fifteen- and eighteen-year-olds than among eleven-year-olds (Bray, Hersh, & Turner, 1985; Bray, Huffman, & Fletcher, 1999).

If you are trying to remember a new phone number, you would know to rehearse it several times or to write it down before setting out to do math problems. However, five-year-olds, asked whether it would make a difference if they jotted the number down before or after doing the math problems, do not reliably report that doing the problems first would matter. Ten-year-olds, however, are aware that new mental activities (the math problems) can interfere with old ones (memorizing the telephone number) and usually suggest jotting the number down before doing the math problems.

Your metamemory is advanced to the point, of course, where you recognize that it would be poor judgment to read this book while watching MuchMusic or fantasizing about your next vacation. Isn't it?

We have seen that children's memory improves throughout middle childhood. But how good is the memory of children for observed or experienced events? For a discussion of this controversial issue, turn to the nearby "A Closer Look" feature.

Observe children's rehearsal strategies as they mature. To watch the video, click on the "Rehearsal Strategies" clip in Module 3, Section 2.

metacognition Awareness of and control of one's cognitive abilities, as shown by the intentional use of cognitive strategies in solving problems.

metamemory Knowledge of the functions and processes involved in one's storage and retrieval of information (memory), as shown by use of cognitive strategies to retain information.

Children's Eyewitness Testimony

Jean Piaget distinctly "remembered" an attempt to kidnap him from his baby carriage as he was being wheeled along the Champs Élysées. He recalled the excited throng, the abrasions on the face of the nurse who rescued him, the police officer's white baton, and the flight of the assailant. Although they were graphic, Piaget's memories were false. Years later, the nurse admitted that she had made up the tale.

Children are often called on to testify about events they have seen or experienced, often involving child abuse (Koriat, Goldsmith, Schneider, & Nakash-Dura, 2001). But how reliable is children's testimony?

Even preschoolers can recall and describe personally experienced events, although the accounts may be sketchy (Bruck, Ceci, & Hembrooke, 2002; Roebers & Schneider, 2002). However, there are many individual differences. Consequently, the child witness is typically asked questions to prompt information. But such questions may be "leading"— that is, they may suggest an answer. For example, "What happened at school?" is not a leading question, but "Did your teacher touch you?" is.

Can children's testimony be distorted by leading questions? It appears that by the age of ten or eleven, children are no more suggestible than adults, but younger children are more likely to be misled (Bruck & Ceci, 1999; Krackow & Lynn, 2003).

One hotly debated question is whether children can be led into making false reports of abuse (Krackow & Lynn, 2003). There is no simple answer to this question, as illustrated by a study carried out by Gail Goodman and

How Reliable Is Children's Eyewitness Testimony?
This question remains hotly debated. By age 10 or 11, children may be no more suggestible than adults. The findings for younger children are inconsistent, however.

her colleagues (Goodman & Clarke-Stewart, 1991). They interviewed five- and seven-year-old girls following a routine medical checkup that included genital and anal exams for half the girls. Most of the children who experienced genital and anal touching failed to mention it when simply asked what happened during the exam. But when asked specific leading questions ("Did the doctor touch you there?"), thirty-one of thirty-six girls mentioned the experience. Of the thirty-six girls who did not have genital and anal exams, none reported any such experience when asked what happened during the exam. When asked the leading questions, three falsely reported being touched in these areas, illustrating the dilemma faced by investigators of sexual abuse. Although children may not reveal genital contact until specifically asked, asking may influence some children to give a false report.

Research indicates that repeated questioning may lead children to make up events that never happened to them (Roebers & Schneider, 2002). In one study, preschoolers were questioned each week for eleven weeks about events that either had or had not happened to them (Ceci, 1993). By the eleventh week, 58 percent of the children reported at least one false event as true.

What, then, are investigators to do when the only witnesses to criminal events are children? Ceci (1993) recommended that interviewers avoid leading or suggestive questions to minimize influencing the child's response. It might also be useful to ask the child whether he or she actually saw what happened or merely heard about it. Young children do not always make this distinction on their own (Principe & Ceci, 2002).

Active Review

8. Ability to screen out distractions (increases or decreases?) through middle childhood.

9. When children focus on stimuli, they can keep them in _____ memory for about thirty seconds.

10. Children can remember visual stimuli longer when they _____ it as sounds.

11. Repetition of sounds or other stimuli is known as _____ learning.

12. _____ rehearsal is relation of new information to things that are already known.

13. _____ refers to children's awareness of the functioning of their memory processes.

Reflect & Relate: I asked, "How is information transferred from short-term memory to long-term memory?" How is the process analogous to placing information in a computer's "memory" into a computer's "storage" device? What happens if you forget to "save" information in the computer's memory?

 Go to
W W W **www.voyages1ce.nelson.com**
for an interactive version of this review.

Intellectual Development, Creativity, and Achievement

At an early age, we gain impressions of how intelligent we are compared to other family members and schoolmates. We think of some people as having more **intelligence** than others. We associate intelligence with academic success, advancement on the job, and appropriate social behaviour.

Question: What is intelligence? Despite our sense of familiarity with the concept of intelligence, intelligence cannot be seen, touched, or measured physically. For this reason, intelligence is subject to various interpretations. Theories about intelligence are some of the most controversial issues in psychology today.

Psychologists generally distinguish between **achievement** and **intelligence**. Achievement is what a child has learned—the knowledge and skills that have been gained by experience. Achievement involves specific content areas such as English, history, and math. Educators and psychologists use achievement tests to measure what children have learned in academic areas. The strong relationship between achievement and experience seems obvious. We are not surprised to find that a student who has taken French but not Spanish does better on a French achievement test than on a Spanish achievement test.

The meaning of *intelligence* is more difficult to pin down (Neisser et al., 1996). Most psychologists would agree that intelligence provides the cognitive basis for academic achievement. Intelligence is usually perceived as a child's underlying *competence* or *learning ability*, whereas achievement involves a child's acquired competencies or *performance*. Most psychologists would also agree that many of the competencies underlying intelligence manifest themselves during middle childhood, when most children are first exposed to formal schooling. Psychologists disagree, however, about the nature and origins of a child's underlying competence or learning ability.

Theories of Intelligence

Let us consider some theoretical approaches to intelligence. Then we will see how researchers and practitioners actually assess intellectual functioning.

intelligence A complex and controversial concept, defined by David Wechsler as the "capacity ... to understand the world [and the] resourcefulness to cope with its challenges." Intelligence implies the capacity to make adaptive choices (from the Latin inter, meaning "among," and legere, meaning "to choose").

achievement That which is attained by one's efforts and presumed to be made possible by one's abilities.

Factor Theories

factor A condition or quality that brings about a result—in this case, "intelligent" behaviour. A cluster of related items, such as those found on an intelligence or personality test.

Many investigators have viewed intelligence as consisting of one or more major mental abilities, or **factors**. *Question: What are "factor theories" of intelligence?* In 1904, the British psychologist Charles Spearman suggested that the various behaviours that we consider intelligent have a common, underlying factor: *g*, or "general intelligence." He thought that *g* represented broad reasoning and problem-solving abilities. He supported this view by noting that people who excel in one area generally show the capacity to excel in others. But he also noted that even the most capable people seem more capable in some areas—perhaps in music or business or poetry—than in others. For this reason, he also suggested that *s*, or specific capacities, accounts for a number of individual abilities.

This view seems to make sense. Most of us know children who are good at math but poor in English and vice versa. Nonetheless, some link—*g*—seems to connect different mental abilities. Few if any people surpass 99 percent of the population in one mental ability yet are surpassed by 80 or 90 percent of the population in other abilities.

factor analysis A statistical technique that allows researchers to determine the relationships among a large number of items, such as test items.

To test his views, Spearman developed **factor analysis**, a statistical technique that allows researchers to determine which items on tests seem to be measuring the same things. Researchers continue to find a key role for *g* in performance on many intelligence tests. A number of researchers (e.g., Colom, Flores-Mendoza, & Rebollo, 2003; Conway, Kane, & Engle, 2003) have found evidence that connects *g* with *working memory*—that is, the ability to keep various elements of a problem in mind at once. Contemporary psychologists continue to use the term *g*, as in speaking of the extent to which a particular test measures *g* (Gignac & Vernon, 2003; Lubinski, 2004; Rushton, Skuy, & Fridjhon, 2003).

The American psychologist Louis Thurstone (1938) used factor analysis and concluded that intelligence consists of several specific factors, which he termed *primary mental abilities*, including visual-spatial abilities, perceptual speed, numerical ability, the ability to learn the meanings of words, ability to bring to mind the right word rapidly, and ability to reason. Thurstone suggested, for example, that we might be able to rapidly develop lists of words that rhyme but might not be particularly able to solve math problems.

The Triarchic Theory of Intelligence

triarchic Governed by three. Descriptive of Sternberg's view that intellectual functioning has three aspects: context of the action/behaviour, the individuals' experience with the task, and the information-processing strategies applied by individuals.

Psychologist Robert Sternberg (Sternberg, 2000; Sternberg, Lautrey, & Lubart, 2003) constructed a three-pronged, or **triarchic,** theory of intelligence that is similar to a view proposed by the Greek philosopher Aristotle (Tigner & Tigner, 2000). *Question: What is Sternberg's triarchic model of intelligence?* The three prongs of Sternberg's theory are context, experience, and information processing.

One component of Sternberg's triarchic model is the *contextual component*. That is, whether or not behaviour is intelligent is highly dependent on the context. Both Aristotle and Sternberg speak of practical intelligence, or "street smarts." Practical intelligence enables people to adapt to the demands of their environment, including the social environment.

A second component of Sternberg's model is termed the *experiential component*. Here Sternberg was interested in (1) novelty, creativity, and insight and (2) automatization. Providing children with relatively novel tasks and assessing how they perform and solve these tasks provides psychologists and educators with practical information. Psychologists who believe that creativity is separate from analytical intelligence (academic ability) find only a moderate relationship between academic ability and creativity (Simonton, 2000). However, to Sternberg, creativity is a basic facet of intelligence. Creative intelligence is defined by the abilities to cope with novel situations and to profit from experience. Creativity allows us to relate novel situations to familiar situations (i.e., to perceive

Information-Processing Component

(academic ability)

Abilities to solve problems, compare and contrast, judge, evaluate, and criticize

Experimental Component

(creativity and insight)

Abilities to invent, discover, suppose, or theorize

Contextual Component

("street smarts")

Abilities to adapt to the demands of one's environment, apply knowledge in practical situations

Figure 12.5

Sternberg's Triarchic Theory of Intelligence

Robert Sternberg views intelligence as three-pronged—as having contextual, experimental, and componential components.

similarities and differences) and fosters adaptation. Sternberg also believes, however, that there is some usefulness in the automatization of everyday routines and practices as well.

A third component of the triarchic model is the *componential* (or *information-processing skills*) component, also sometimes referred to as *analytical intelligence.* This component enables us to solve problems and acquire new knowledge. Information-processing theorists such as Sternberg believe that how we process stimuli and cues; generate, evaluate, and implement strategies to solve problems; and evaluate outcomes (i.e., do we learn from our mistakes, or do we repeat them?) tells us a great deal about our intellectual potential.

The Theory of Multiple Intelligences

Psychologist Howard Gardner (1983, 2003a, 2003b), like Robert Sternberg, believes that intelligence—or intelligences—reflects more than academic ability. *Question: What is meant by multiple intelligences?* Gardner refers to each kind of intelligence in his theory as "an intelligence" because the kinds differ in quality (see Figure 12.6). He also believes that each intelligence is based in a different part of the brain.

Figure 12.6

Gardner's Theory of Multiple Intelligences

Howard Gardner argued that there are many intelligences, not just one, including bodily talents as expressed through dancing or gymnastics. Each "intelligence" is presumed to have its neurological base in a different part of the brain. Each is an inborn talent that must be developed through educational experiences if it is to be expressed.

Three of Gardner's intelligences are familiar enough: verbal ability, logical-mathematical reasoning, and spatial intelligence (visual-spatial skills). But Gardner also includes bodily-kinesthetic intelligence (as shown by dancers and gymnasts), musical intelligence, interpersonal intelligence (as shown by empathy and ability to relate to others), and personal knowledge (self-insight). Occasionally, individuals show great "intelligence" in one area—such as the genius of the young Mozart with the piano or the island girl who can navigate her small boat to hundreds of islands by observing the changing patterns of the stars—without notable abilities in others. Gardner (2001) recently added "naturalist intelligence" and "existential intelligence." Naturalist intelligence refers to the ability to look at natural events, such as various kinds of animals and plants or the stars above, and develop insights into their nature and the laws that govern their behaviour. Existential intelligence involves dealing with the

Concept Review 12.2 Theories of Intelligence

Theory	Basic Information	Comments
General versus specific factors (main proponent: Charles Spearman)	• Created factor analysis to study intelligence • Strong evidence for general factor (*g*) in intelligence • *s* factors are specific abilities, skills, talents	• Concept of *g* remains in use today—a century later
Primary mental abilities (proponent: Louis Thurstone) 	• Used factor analysis • Found many "primary" abilities • All abilities/factors academically oriented	• Other researchers (e.g., Guilford) claim to have found hundreds of factors • The more factors claimed, the more they overlap
Triarchic theory (proponent: Robert Sternberg)	• Intelligence as three-pronged—with contextual, experiential, and componential components • Componential (or information-processing) component of intelligence analogous to academic ability	• Coincides with views of Aristotle • Critics do not view creativity as a component of intelligence
Multiple intelligences (proponent: Howard Gardner)	• Theorized distinct "intelligences" • Includes academic intelligences, personal and social intelligences, talents, and philosophical intelligences • Theorizes different bases in brain for different intelligences	• Continues to expand number of "intelligences" • Critics see little value to theorizing "intelligences" rather than aspects of intelligence • Most critics consider musical and bodily skills to be special talents, not "intelligences"

larger philosophical issues of life. According to Gardner, one can compose symphonies or advance mathematical theory yet be average in, say, language and personal skills. (Are not some academic "geniuses" foolish in their personal lives?)

Critics of Gardner's view agree that people function more intelligently in some areas of life than others. They also agree that many people have special talents, such as bodily-kinesthetic talents, even if their overall intelligence is average. But they question whether such special talents are "intelligences" (Neisser et al., 1996). Language skills, reasoning ability, and ability to solve math problems seem to be more closely related than musical or gymnastic talent to what most people mean by "intelligence."

The various theories of intelligence are reviewed in Concept Review 12.2. We do not yet have the final word on the nature of intelligence, but we would like to share with you David Wechsler's definition of intelligence. Wechsler is the originator of the most widely used series of contemporary intelligence tests, and he defined intelligence as the "capacity of an individual to understand the world [and the] resourcefulness to cope with its challenges" (Wechsler, 1975, p. 139). To Wechsler, intelligence involves accurate representation of the world and effective problem solving (adapting to one's environment, profiting from experience, selecting the appropriate formulas and strategies, and so on).

A Closer Look | "Emotional Intelligence"

Psychologists Peter Salovey and John Mayer developed the theory of emotional intelligence, which was popularized by the *New York Times* writer Daniel Goleman (1995). The theory holds that social and emotional skills are a form of intelligence, just as academic skills are. Emotional intelligence resembles two of Gardner's "intelligences"—intrapersonal skills and interpersonal skills (including insight into the feelings of other people). It is also involved with self-insight and self-control—the ability to recognize and regulate one's moods (Salovey, Stroud, Woolery, & Epel, 2002).

The theory suggests that self-awareness and social awareness are best learned during childhood (Richburg & Fletcher, 2002). Failure to develop emotional intelligence is connected with poor ability to cope with stress, depression, and aggressive behaviour (Salovey et al., 2002; Wang, 2002). Moreover, childhood experiences may even mould the brain's emotional responses to life's challenges.

No one argues that self-awareness, self-control, empathy, and cooperation are unimportant. But critics of the theory of emotional intelligence argue that schools may not have the time (or the competence) to teach these skills and that emotional intelligence may not really be a kind of intelligence at all. *Is* emotional intelligence a form of intelligence? Psychologist Ulric Neisser (1997) says that "the skills that Goleman describes ... are certainly important for determining life outcomes, but nothing is to be gained by calling them forms of intelligence." Indian psychologist Nutankumar Thingujam (2002) is not as generous as Neisser. Thingujam argues that there is little agreement among psychologists on exactly what emotional intelligence is and that the quality of tests designed to measure emotional intelligence is "questionable" at best.

Measurement of Intellectual Development

There may be disagreements about the nature of intelligence, but thousands of intelligence tests are administered by psychologists and educators every day.

The Stanford-Binet Intelligence Scale (SBIS) and the Wechsler scales for preschool children, school-aged children, and adults are the most widely used and well-respected intelligence tests. The SBIS and Wechsler scales yield scores called **intelligence quotients (IQs)**. *Truth or Fiction Revisited:* An IQ is in fact a score on a test. The concept of intelligence per se is more difficult to define. The SBIS and Wechsler scales have been carefully developed and revised over the years. Each of them has been used to make vital educational decisions about children. In many cases, children whose test scores fall below or above certain scores require individualized program plans or adapted curriculum in order to meet their particular needs (i.e., cognitive delays, giftedness).

It must be noted just as emphatically that each test has been accused of discriminating against ethnic minorities (such as First Nations and ESL children in Canada; African and Latino/Latina American children in the U.S.), the foreign-born, and the children of the socially and economically disadvantaged (Beiser & Gotowiec, 2000; Harris, Tulsky, & Schultheis, 2003; Okazaki & Sue, 2000). Because of the controversy surrounding IQ tests, probably no single test should be used to make important decisions about a child. Decisions about children should be made only after a comprehensive assessment (which may involve a battery of tests, among other tools) is given by a qualified psychologist, in consultation with parents and teachers. *Question: What is the Stanford-Binet Intelligence Scale?*

The Stanford-Binet Intelligence Scale

The SBIS originated in the work of Frenchmen Alfred Binet and Theodore Simon about a century ago. The French public school system sought an instrument to identify children who were unlikely to profit from the regular classroom so that they could receive special attention. The Binet-Simon scale came into use in 1905. Since then, it has undergone revision and refinement.

The Binet-Simon scale yielded a score called a **mental age (MA)**. The MA shows the intellectual level at which a child is functioning. A child with an MA of six is functioning, intellectually, like the average six-year-old child. In taking the test, children earned months of credit for each correct answer. Their MA was determined by adding the months of credit they attained.

Louis Terman adapted the Binet-Simon scale for use with American children. Because Terman carried out his work at Stanford University, he renamed the test the Stanford-Binet Intelligence Scale. The first version of the SBIS was published in 1916. The SBIS yielded an intelligence quotient, or IQ, rather than an MA. The SBIS today can be used with children from the age of two onward up to adults. Table 12.2 shows the kinds of items that define typical performance at various ages.

The IQ states the relationship between a child's mental age and his or her actual or **chronological age (CA)**. The ratio reflects the fact that the same MA score has different meanings for children of different ages. That is, an MA of eight is an above-average score for a six-year-old but a below-average score for a ten-year-old.

The IQ is computed by the formula IQ = (Mental Age / Chronological Age) x 100, or

$$IQ = \frac{\text{Mental Age (MA)}}{\text{Chronological Age (CA)}} \times 100$$

---

intelligence quotient (IQ) (1) Originally, a ratio obtained by dividing a child's score (or "mental age") on an intelligence test by his or her chronological age. (2) In general, a score on an intelligence test.

mental age (MA) The accumulated months of credit that a person earns on the Stanford-Binet Intelligence Scale.

chronological age (CA) A person's age.

Table 12.2	Items Similar to Those on the Stanford-Binet Intelligence Scale	
Age	**Item**
2 years	1. Children show knowledge of basic vocabulary words by identifying parts of a doll, such as the mouth, ears, and hair. 2. Children show counting and spatial skills along with visual-motor coordination by building a tower of four blocks to match a model.
4 years	1. Children show word fluency and categorical thinking by filling in the missing words when they are asked questions such as 　　"Father is a man; mother is a _____?" 　　"Hamburgers are hot; ice cream is _____?" 2. Children show comprehension by answering correctly when they are asked questions such as 　　"Why do people have automobiles?" 　　"Why do people have medicine?"
9 years	1. Children can point out verbal absurdities, as in this question: "In an old cemetery, scientists unearthed a skull which they think was that of George Washington when he was only five years of age. What is silly about that?" 2. Children display fluency with words, as shown by answering these questions: 　　"Can you tell me a number that rhymes with snore?" 　　"Can you tell me a colour that rhymes with glue?"
Adult	1. Adults show knowledge of the meanings of words and conceptual thinking by correctly explaining the differences between word pairs such as "sickness and misery," "house and home," and "integrity and prestige." 2. Adults show spatial skills by correctly answering questions such as "If a car turned to the right to head north, in what direction was it heading before it turned?"

According to this formula, a child with an MA of six and a CA of six would have an IQ of 100. Children who can handle intellectual problems and older children will have IQs above 100. For instance, an eight-year-old who does as well on the SBIS as the average ten-year-old will attain an IQ of 125. Children who do not answer as many items correctly as other children of their age will attain MAs that are lower than their CAs. Their IQ scores will be below 100.

Truth or Fiction Revisited: It is true that two children can answer exactly the same items on an intelligence test correctly, yet one can be above average in intelligence and the other below average. The younger of the two is considered to be more intelligent. Today, IQ scores on the SBIS are derived by comparing children's and adults' performances with those of other people of the same age. People who get more items correct than average attain IQ scores above 100, and people who answer fewer items correctly attain scores below 100.

Question: How do the Wechsler scales differ from the Stanford-Binet test?

The Wechsler Scales

David Wechsler (1975) developed a series of scales for use with school-aged children (Wechsler Intelligence Scale for Children; WISC), younger children (Wechsler Preschool and Primary Scale of Intelligence; WPPSI), and adults (Wechsler Adult Intelligence Scale; WAIS). These tests have been repeatedly revised. For example, the current version of the WISC is the WISC-IV (Wechsler, 2003).

The Wechsler scales group test questions into subtests (such as those shown in Table 12.3). Each subtest measures a different intellectual task. For this reason, the test compares a person's performance on one type of task (such as defining words) with another (such as using blocks to construct geometric designs). The Wechsler scales thus suggest children's strengths and weaknesses and provide overall measures of intellectual functioning.

Table 12.3	Kinds of Items Found on Wechsler's Intelligence Scales		
Verbal Comprehension Items[1]	**Perceptual Reasoning Items**	**Working Memory Items**	**Processing Speed Items**
Information: "What is the capital of Canada?" "Who was Shakespeare?" Comprehension: "Why do we have postal codes?" "What does 'A stitch in time saves 9' mean?" Similarities: "How are good and bad alike?" "How are peanut butter and jelly alike?" Vocabulary: "What does *canal* mean?" Word Reasoning: "Identify a common concept being described with a series of clues presented."	Picture completion: Pointing to the missing part of a picture Picture Concepts: Presented with two or three rows of pictures and must pick one picture from each row to form a group with a common characteristic Block Design: Copying pictures of geometric designs using multicoloured blocks Matrix Reasoning: Looking at incomplete matrices and choosing the missing piece from various options presented.	Digit Span: Recalling a series of random numbers Letter-Number Sequence: Recalling numbers and letters that are read aloud in sequence Arithmetic: "If 3 candy bars cost 25 cents, how much will 18 candy bars cost?"	Coding: Rapid scanning and drawing of symbols that are associated with numbers Symbol Search: Looking for a specific symbol in an array of symbols Cancellation: Scanning random and structured arrangements in order to find target pictures

[1]Items for verbal subtests are similar but not identical to actual test items on the Wechsler intelligence scales.

For six and a half decades, Wechsler described some subtests as measuring verbal tasks and others as assessing performance tasks (Kaufman, Flanagan, Alfonso & Mascolo, 2006). In general, verbal subtests require knowledge of verbal concepts, whereas performance subtests (see Figure 12.7) require familiarity with spatial-relations concepts. Wechsler's older test scales permitted the computation of verbal and performance IQs. Nontechnically oriented college students often obtain higher verbal than performance IQs. The latest edition of the Wechsler scales, the WISC-IV, contains fifteen subtests, ten of which form the core battery, which yield a Full Scale

IQ (FS-IQ). Unlike its predecessor, the WISC-III, the WISC-IV no longer has a Verbal and Performance IQ. It now has the following core battery subtests: Verbal Comprehension Index (VCI), Perceptual Reasoning Index (PRI), Working Memory Index (WMI), and Processing Speed Index (PSI).

Figure 12.8 on page 220 indicates the labels that Wechsler assigned to various IQ scores and the approximate percentages of the population who attain IQ scores at those levels. As you can see, most children's IQ scores cluster around the average. Only about 5 percent of the population have IQ scores above 130 or below 70.

Question: Many psychologists and educators consider standard intelligence tests to be culturally biased. What is that controversy about?

Picture arrangement

These pictures tell a story, but they are in the wrong order. Put them in the right order so that they tell a story.

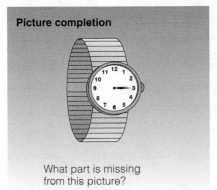

Picture completion

What part is missing from this picture?

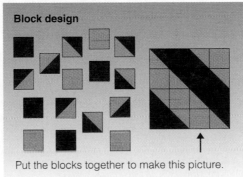

Block design

Put the blocks together to make this picture.

POWER VISUALS!
See your student companion website for an interactive version of Figure 12.7.

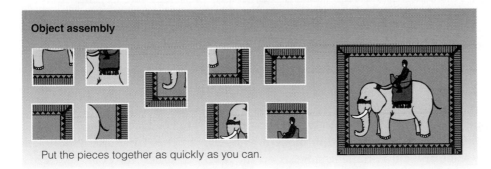

Object assembly

Put the pieces together as quickly as you can.

Figure 12.7

Performance Items on an Intelligence Test

This figure shows a number of items that resemble those found on the Wechsler Intelligence Scale for Children.

The Testing Controversy

> I was almost one of the testing casualties. At 15 I earned an IQ test score of 82, three points above the track of the special education class. Based on this score, my counsellor suggested that I take up bricklaying because I was "good with my hands." My low IQ, however, did not allow me to see that as desirable.
> —Robert Williams (1974, p. 32)

This testimony, offered by African American psychologist Robert Williams, echoes the sentiments of many psychologists. A survey of psychologists and educational specialists found that most consider intelligence tests to be at least somewhat biased against African Americans and members of lower social classes (Snyderman & Rothman, 1990). To fill in a bit more historical background, let's note that during the 1920s, intelligence tests were used to prevent many Europeans and others from immigrating to the United States. For example, testing pioneer H. H. Goddard assessed 178 newly arrived immigrants at Ellis Island and claimed that most of the Hungarians, Italians, and Russians were "feeble-minded." It was apparently of little concern to Goddard that these immigrants, by and large, did not understand English—the language in which the tests were administered! Because of a history of abuse of intelligence testing, some states have outlawed the use of IQ tests as the sole standard for placing children in special-education classes. In Canada, our practices are somewhat different; however, we, too, often use information gleaned from intelligence tests to help make educational recommendations. In fact, we have often used American norms (because Canadian norms were nonexistent or not readily available) in calculating subscale scores on the Wechsler scales.

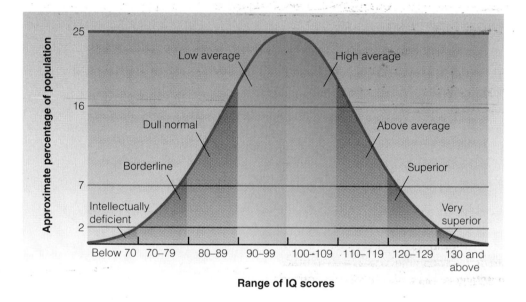

Figure 12.8

Variations in IQ Scores

IQ scores vary according to a bell-shaped, or "normal," curve. Scores tend to bunch around the central score (100) and then to decrease in frequency as they move upward and downward.

cultural bias A factor hypothesized to be present in intelligence tests that provides an advantage for test takers from certain cultural or ethnic backgrounds but that does not reflect true intelligence.

culture-free Descriptive of a test in which cultural biases have been removed. On such a test, test takers from different cultural backgrounds would have an equal opportunity to earn scores that reflect their true abilities.

On the other hand, supporters of standard intelligence tests point out that they appear to do a good job of measuring Spearman's *g* (Frey & Detterman, 2004) and cognitive skills that are valued in modern high-tech societies (Anastasi, 1988). The old vocabulary and arithmetic subtests on the Wechsler scales, for example, clearly reflect achievement in language skills and computational ability. Although the broad types of achievement measured by these tests reflect intelligence, they might also reflect cultural familiarity with the concepts required to answer questions correctly. In particular, the tests seem to reflect middle-class European American culture in the United States (Allen & Majidi-Ahi, 1991; Okazaki & Sue, 2000).

If scoring well on intelligence tests requires a certain type of cultural experience, the tests are said to have a **cultural bias.** Children reared to speak Cree would be at a disadvantage, not because of differences in intelligence but because of cultural differences (Helms, 1992). For this reason, psychologists have tried to construct **culture-free,** or culture-fair, intelligence tests. It is important to conduct culturally competent and fair evaluations. Inappropriate assessment of culturally diverse students can lead to misdiagnoses, misguided interventions, or failure to intervene when necessary. Some problems in assessment stem from (Castillo, Quintana, & Zamarripa, 2000) (1) historical bias in the development of psychological assessment procedures, (2) disproportionate representation of children from diverse linguistic and cultural backgrounds as research participants or researchers themselves, and (3) ecological or contextual factors. *Question: How can we address this bias in our system?* One step is for practitioners to become familiar with professional standards for assessing culturally diverse children (APA and CPA guidelines). Psychologists should (1) assess their own cultural self-knowledge and cultural competence; (2) review and, where appropriate, include key elements in culturally competent assessment; (3) be aware of the strengths and limitations of assessment instruments, scales, and inventories; (4) research and implement alternate assessment strategies; and finally (5) be sensitive to the continuing evolution of intellectual assessment (Rodriguez, 2000). Ideally, as part of the assessment, psychologists should become familiar with the primary cultural characteristics of the child. In addition, they should evaluate proficiency in the child's native language as well as in English if possible.

Some tests do not rely on expressive language at all. For example, Cattell's (1949) Culture-Fair Intelligence Test evaluates reasoning ability through the child's comprehension of the rules that govern a progression of geometric designs, as shown in Figure 12.9.

Unfortunately, culture-free tests have not lived up to their promise. First, middle-class children still outperform lower-class children on them (Rushton et al., 2003). Middle-class children, for example, are more likely to have basic familiarity with materials such as blocks and pencils and paper. They are more likely than disadvantaged children to have arranged blocks into various designs (practice relevant to the Cattell test). Second, culture-free tests do not predict academic success as well as other intelligence tests, and scholastic aptitude remains the central concern of educators.

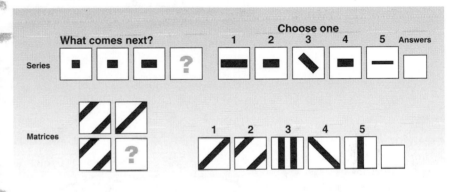

Figure 12.9

Sample Items from Cattell's Culture-Fair Intelligence Test

Culture-fair tests attempt to exclude items that discriminate on the basis of cultural background rather than intelligence.

Is it possible that there is no such thing as a culture-free intelligence test (Humphreys, 1992)? Motivation to do well, for example, might also be a cultural factor. Because of lifestyle differences, some children from low-income families may not share the motivation of middle-class children to do well on tests (Zigler & Seitz, 1982).

Patterns of Intellectual Development

Sometimes you have to run rapidly to stay in the same place—at least in terms of taking intelligence tests. That is, the "average" taker of an intelligence test obtains an IQ score of 100. However, that person must answer more questions correctly as childhood progresses in order to obtain the same score. Even though his or her intelligence is "developing" at a typical pace, he or she continues to obtain the same score. *Question: Putting test scores aside, how does intelligence develop?*

Rapid advances in intellectual functioning occur during childhood. Within a few years, children gain the ability to symbolize experiences and manipulate symbols to solve increasingly complex problems. Their vocabularies leap, and their sentences become more complex. Their thought processes become increasingly logical and abstract, and they gain the capacity to focus on two or more aspects of a problem at once.

Intellectual growth seems to occur in at least two major spurts. The first growth spurt occurs at about the age of six. This spurt coincides with entry into a school system and also with the shift from preoperational to concrete-operational thought. The school experience may begin to help crystallize intellectual functioning at this time. The second spurt occurs at about age ten or eleven.

Once they reach middle childhood, however, children appear to undergo relatively more stable patterns of gains in intellectual functioning, although there are still spurts (Deary, Whiteman, Starr, Whalley, & Fox, 2004). As a result, intelligence tests gain greater predictive power. In a classic study by Marjorie Honzik and colleagues (1948), intelligence test scores taken at the age of nine correlated strongly (10.90) with scores at the age of ten and more moderately (10.76) with scores at the age of eighteen. Testing at age eleven even shows a moderate to high relationship with scores at the age of seventy-seven (Deary et al., 2004).

Despite the increased predictive power of intelligence tests during middle childhood, individual differences exist. In the classic Fels Longitudinal Study (see Figure 12.10), two groups of children (Groups 1 and 3) made reasonably consistent gains in intelligence test scores between the ages of ten and seventeen, whereas three groups showed declines. Group 4, children who had shown the most intellectual promise at age ten, went on to show the most precipitous decline, although they still wound up in the highest 2 to 3 percent of the population (McCall, Applebaum, & Hogarty, 1973). Many factors influence changes in intelligence test scores, including changes in the child's home environment, social and economic circumstances, educational experiences, even B vitamins such as folic acid (Deary et al., 2004).

Although intelligence test scores change throughout childhood, many children show reasonably consistent patterns of below-average or above-average performance. In the next section, we discuss children who show consistent patterns of extreme scores—low and high.

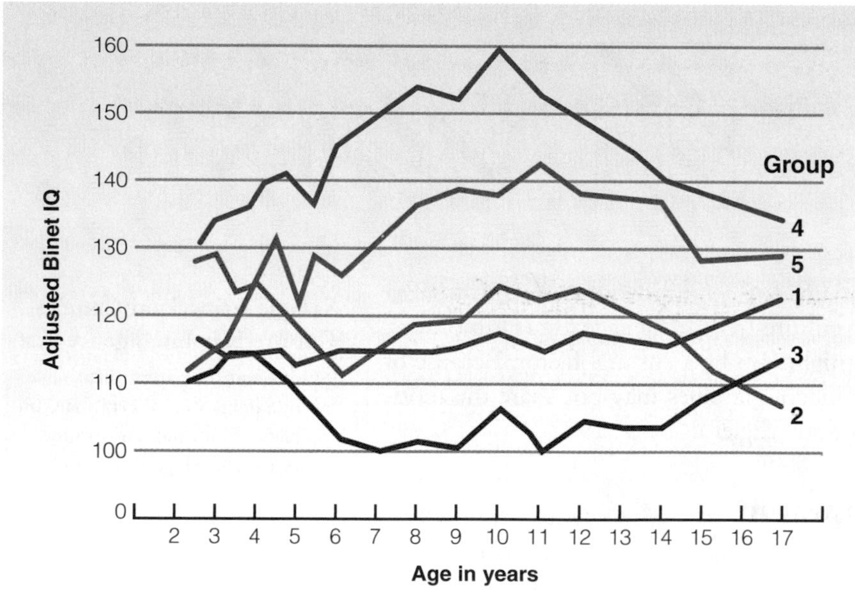

Differences in Intellectual Development

The average IQ score in Canada is close to 100. About half the children in Canada attain IQ scores in the broad average range from 90 to 110 (see Figure 12.8). Nearly 95 percent attain scores between 70 and 130. But what of the other 5 percent? Children who attain IQ scores below 70 are generally labelled "intellectually deficient" or as exhibiting cognitive delays. Children who attain scores of 130 or above are usually labelled "gifted."

These labels—these verbal markers of extreme individual differences—lead to certain expectations of children. Ironically, the labels can place heavy burdens on children and parents.

Intellectual Disability

Question: What is a cognitive disability? A cognitive disability is usually assessed as mild, moderate, or severe based on an intelligent quotient (IQ) below 75 and delays in adaptive functioning. The Canadian Association for Community Living

Figure 12.10

Five Patterns of Change in IQ Scores for Children in the Fels Longitudinal Study

In the Fels Longitudinal Study, IQ scores remained stable between the ages of 2½ and 17 for only 1 of 5 groups—Group 1.
Source: McCall et al. (1973).

(http://www.cacl.ca/english/index.html) is an association composed of family members and others working for the benefit of persons of all ages who have an intellectual disability. According to the American Association on Mental Retardation (2004), "Mental retardation is a disability characterized by significant limitations both in intellectual functioning and in adaptive behaviour as expressed in conceptual, social, and practical adaptive skills." Mental retardation involves an IQ score of no more than 70 to 75. An interesting difference between Canadian and U.S. practice is that the term *mental retardation* is not commonly used in Canada any longer.

Most of the children (more than 80 percent) who exhibit cognitive delays fall within the "mild cognitive delays" category. Children with mild cognitive disability are the most capable of adjusting to the demands of educational institutions and, eventually, to society at large. Many children with mild cognitive delays can have their educational needs met within an inclusive classroom setting.

Children with Down syndrome are most likely to fall within the moderate cognitive disability range. Children with a moderate cognitive disability can learn to speak, dress, feed, and clean themselves, and, eventually, to engage in useful work under supportive conditions, as in a sheltered workshop. However, they usually do not acquire skills in reading and arithmetic. Children with severe cognitive disabilities may not acquire speech and self-help skills and may remain highly dependent on others for survival throughout their lives.

What causes cognitive impairments? Some of the causes of impairment are biological. Cognitive delays, for example, can stem from chromosomal abnormalities, such as Down syndrome; genetic disorders, such as phenylketonuria (PKU); and brain damage (American Association on Mental Retardation, 2004). Brain damage can have many origins, including accidents during childhood and problems during pregnancy. For example, maternal alcohol abuse, malnutrition, or diseases during pregnancy can lead to cognitive impairment in the fetus.

At the University of Alberta, researchers at the J. P. Das Developmental Disabilities Centre conduct research related to the education and provision of services for persons with cognitive disabilities, learning disabilities, and multiple handicaps. The centre provides resources for parents and teachers interested in learning more or supporting children with developmental delays. Check out its website and its publication, *The Developmental Disabilities Bulletin*, at: http://www.ualberta.ca/~jpdasddc/INDEX.html.

There is also **cultural-familial delay,** in which the child is biologically normal but does not develop age-appropriate behaviours at the normal pace because of social isolation of one kind or another. For example, the later-born children of impoverished families may have little opportunity to interact with adults or play with stimulating toys. As a result, they may not develop sophisticated language skills or the motivation to acquire the kinds of knowledge that are valued in a technology-oriented society.

Naturally, we wish to encourage all children to develop to the maximum of their capacities—including children with cognitive disabilities. As a rule of thumb, keep in mind that IQs are scores on tests. They are not perfectly reliable, meaning that they can and do change somewhat from testing to testing. Thus, it is important to focus on children's current levels of achievement in the academic and self-help skills that we wish to impart; by doing so, we can try to build these skills gradually and coherently, step by step.

Children with cultural-familial delay can change dramatically when we provide enriched learning experiences, especially at early ages. The early childhood programs described in the McCain and Fraser (1999) Ontario Report on Early Learning or the American Head Start programs, for example, have enabled children at cultural-familial risk to function at above-average levels.

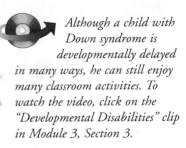

Although a child with Down syndrome is developmentally delayed in many ways, he can still enjoy many classroom activities. To watch the video, click on the "Developmental Disabilities" clip in Module 3, Section 3.

cultural-familial delay
Substandard intellectual performance that is presumed to stem from lack of opportunity to acquire the knowledge and skills considered important within a cultural setting.

(c) Matthew Peyton / Getty Images

A Fashion Prodigy

Fashion designer Esteban Cortazar made his fashion debut with a 9-piece collection at the age of 13 and was the youngest designer to ever show at Fashion Week in New York City. By the age of 20, he had given five major fashion shows. Cortazar's creativity and giftedness began at an early age, as it does in many other gifted and visionary people.

creativity The ability to generate novel solutions to problems. A trait characterized by flexibility, ingenuity, and originality.

Giftedness

Question: What does it mean to be gifted? Giftedness involves more than excellence on the tasks provided by standard intelligence tests. In determining who is gifted, most educators include children who have outstanding abilities, are capable of high performance in a specific academic area, such as language or mathematics, or who show creativity, leadership, distinction in the visual or performing arts, or bodily talents, as in gymnastics and dancing. Robert Sternberg (2003) presented a "WICS" model of giftedness, which seems to be a play on the letters in the WISC-IV. Sternberg describes giftedness as involving wisdom, intelligence, and creativity—synthesized (assembled together). He claims that giftedness basically involves expertise. In gifted children, it involves expertise in development.

According to the Special Education Coding Criteria 2006/2007 put forth by the special programs branch of Alberta Education, children who are gifted demonstrate "exceptional potential and/or performance across a wide range of abilities in one or more of the following areas: general intellectual, specific academic, creative thinking, social, musical, artistic, and kinaesthetic" (p. 5).

Question: What are the socioeconomic and ethnic differences in intelligence? As you can see in the nearby "Developing in a World of Diversity" feature, there are also socioeconomic and ethnic differences in IQ.

Creativity and Intellectual Development

Question: What is creativity? To illustrate something about the nature of creativity, let us ask you a rather ordinary question: What does the word *duck* mean? Now let us ask you a somewhat more interesting question: How many meanings can you find for the word *duck*? Arriving at a single correct answer to the question might earn you points on an intelligence test. Generating many answers to the question, as we will see, may be a sign of creativity as well as of the knowledge of the meanings of words. **Creativity** is the ability to do things that are novel and useful (Sternberg, 2001). Creative children and adults can solve problems to which there are no preexisting solutions, no tried and tested formulas (Mumford, 2003; Simonton, 2000). Creative children share a number of qualities (Sternberg & Lubart, 1995, 1996):

- They take chances. (They may use sentence fragments in essays, and they may colour outside the lines in their colouring books.)
- They refuse to accept limitations and try to do the impossible.
- They appreciate art and music (which sometimes leaves them out among their peers).
- They use the materials around them to make unique things.
- They challenge social norms. (Creative children are often independent and non-conformist, but independence and nonconformity do not necessarily make a child creative. Creative children may be at odds with their teachers because of their independent views. Faced with the task of managing large classes, teachers often fall into preferences for quiet, submissive, "good" children.)
- They take unpopular stands (which sometimes gives them the appearance of being oppositional, when they are expressing their genuine ideas and feelings).
- They examine ideas that other people accept at face value. (They come home and say, "——said that yada yada. What's that all about?")

Developing in a World of Diversity

Socioeconomic and Ethnic Differences in IQ

What is your own ethnic background? Are there any stereotypes about how people from your ethnic background perform in school or on IQ tests? If so, what is your reaction to these stereotypes? Why?

Research suggests that differences in IQ exist between socioeconomic and ethnic groups (Beiser & Gotowiec, 2000; Neisser et al., 1996; Wright, Taylor, & Ruggiero, 1996). Lower-class children obtain IQ scores some 10 to 15 points lower than those obtained by middle- and upper-class children. African American children tend to obtain IQ scores about 15 points lower than those obtained by their European American peers (Neisser et al., 1996). Latino and Latina American and Native American children also tend to score below the norms for European Americans (Neisser et al., 1996). Native children scored significantly lower IQ scores (using the Wechsler scales) than their non-Native counterparts (Besir & Gotowiec, 2000). While in another Canadian study of Inuit children of Arctic Quebec using a less culturally biased nonverbal intelligence test (in this study, the Raven's Coloured Progressive Matrices), the group of children fared better than the U.S. norms and about the same as their southern Quebec counterparts (Wright, Taylor & Ruggiero, 1996). There have been noted ethnic differences in psychological research, and so the question that is asked frequently is why? The answer is still hotly debated today. Discussion about relationships between intelligence, race, and genetics is a controversial topic in psychology (Sternberg, Grigorenko, & Kidd, 2005; Templer, 2006).

Several studies of IQ have confused social class with ethnicity because larger proportions of African Americans, Latino and Latina Americans, and Native Americans have lower socioeconomic status (Neisser et al., 1996). When we limit our observations to particular ethnic groups, we still find an effect for social class. That is, middle-class European Americans outscore lower-class European Americans. Middle-class African Americans, Latino and Latina Americans, and Native Americans also outscore their less affluent counterparts. In the study by Beiser and colleagues that found differences in IQ scores of Native and non-Native children, however, when biopsychosocial variables (maternal and child health, SES, English-

Are intelligence tests culturally appropriate? Steinberg and colleagues caution researchers about drawing conclusions about intelligence and its relation to race, ethnicity, or gender.

© Winnipeg Free Press - Marc Gallant/CP Images

language skills, parental attitudes toward school) were controlled for, the differences disappeared. Sternberg and Grigorenko (2006) argue that intelligence cannot be interpreted apart from its cultural context.

Attributions for success may also be involved. Research shows that Asian students and their mothers tend to attribute academic successes to hard work (Randel, Stevenson, & Witruk, 2000). American mothers, in contrast, are more likely to attribute children's academic successes to "natural" ability (Basic Behavioral Science Task Force, 1996). Asians are more likely to believe that they can work to make good scores happen. Sue and Okazaki (1990) agreed. They argued that because Asian Americans have been discriminated against in blue-collar careers, they have come to emphasize the value of education. In Japan, emphasis on succeeding through hard work is illustrated by the increasing popularity of cram schools, or *juku*, which prepare Japanese children for entrance exams to private schools and colleges (Ruiz & Tanaka, 2001). More than half of all Japanese schoolchildren are enrolled in these schools, which meet after the regular school day is over.

Looking to other environmental factors, Steinberg and his colleagues (1996) claimed that parental encouragement and supervision in combination with peer support for academic achievement partially explain the superior performances of European Americans and Asian Americans compared with African Americans and Latino and Latina Americans.

More recently, Sternberg and colleagues (2005) have argued that because there is little consensus among intelligent theorists on what intelligence is, researchers should be cautious about drawing conclusions about intelligence and its relation to race, ethnicity, or gender.

One of Rinaldi's colleagues and one of Rathus's former professors (both of whom shall remain nameless) each remarked that there is nothing new under the sun, only new combinations of existing elements. Many psychologists agree. They see creativity as the ability to make unusual, sometimes remote, associations to the elements of a problem to generate new combinations. An essential aspect of a creative response is the leap from the elements of the problem to the novel solution. A predictable solution is not creative, even if it is hard to reach.

Question: What is the relationship between creativity and intelligence? The answer to this question depends on how one defines intelligence. If one accepts Sternberg's model, creativity is one of three aspects of intelligence (along with analytical thinking and practical intelligence). From this perspective, creativity overlaps with intelligence. ***Truth or Fiction Revisited:*** However, otherwise, it is not necessarily true that highly intelligent children are creative.

Some scientists argue that creativity and innovation require high levels of general intelligence (Heilman, Nadeau, & Beversdorf, 2003), but the tests we use to measure intelligence and creativity tend to show only a moderate relationship between global intelligence test scores and measures of creativity (Simonton, 2000; Sternberg & Williams, 1997). A Canadian study found that gifted children, aged nine to eleven, as a group, were more creative than less intelligent children (Kershner & Ledger, 1985). But not all the gifted children were more creative than their less intelligent peers. In terms of Gardner's theory of multiple intelligences, we can note that some children who have only average intellectual ability in some areas, such as logical analysis, can excel in areas that are considered more creative, such as music or art.

Children mainly use *convergent thinking* to arrive at the correct answers on intelligence tests. In **convergent thinking,** thought is limited to present facts; the problem solver narrows his or her thinking to find the best solution. (A child uses convergent thinking to arrive at the right answer to a multiple-choice question or to a question on an intelligence test.)

Creative thinking tends to be *divergent* rather than convergent (Vartanian, Martindale, & Kwiatkowski, 2003). In **divergent thinking,** the child associates freely to the elements of the problem, allowing "leads" to run a nearly limitless course. (Children use divergent thinking when they are trying to generate ideas to answer an essay question or to find keywords to search on the Internet.) Tests of creativity determine how flexible, fluent, and original a person's thinking is. Here, for example, is an item from a test used by Getzels and Jackson (1962) to measure associative ability, a factor in creativity: "Write as many meanings as you can for each of the following words: (a) duck; (b) sack; (c) pitch; (d) fair." Those who write several meanings for each word, rather than only one, are rated as potentially more creative.

Another measure of creativity might ask children to produce as many words as possible that begin with *t* and end with *n* within a minute. Still another item might give people a minute to classify a list of names in as many ways as possible. For example, in how many ways can you classify the following group of names?

Martha   Paul   Jeffry   Sally   Pablo   Joan

Sometimes arriving at the right answer involves both divergent and convergent thinking. When presented with a problem, a child may first use divergent thinking to generate many possible solutions to the problem. Convergent thinking may then be used to select likely solutions and reject others.

Intelligence tests such as the Stanford-Binet and Wechsler scales require children to focus in on the single right answer. On intelligence tests, ingenious responses that differ from the designated answers are marked wrong. Tests of creativity, by contrast, are oriented toward determining how flexible and fluent one's thinking can be. Such

convergent thinking   A thought process that attempts to focus in on the single best solution to a problem.

divergent thinking   A thought process that attempts to generate multiple solutions to problems. Free and fluent association to the elements of a problem.

tests include items such as suggesting improvements or unusual uses for a familiar toy or object, naming things that belong in the same class, producing words similar in meaning, and writing different endings for a story (Meador, 1992).

Determinants of Intellectual Development

Questions: What are the roles of nature (heredity) and nurture (environmental influences) on the development of intelligence? All right, we won't keep you in suspense: After a review of the literature, we conclude that there is ample evidence for both genetic and environmental influences on intelligence (Dickens & Flynn, 2001). Moreover, many of the same studies—in particular, kinship studies and studies of adopted children—appear to provide evidence for both genetic and environmental influences.

Consider the problems in attempting to decide whether a child's performance on an intelligence test is influenced mainly by nature or nurture—that is, by genetic or environmental factors. If a superior child has superior parents, do we attribute the superiority to heredity or to the environment provided by these parents? Similarly, if a dull child lives in an impoverished home, do we attribute the dullness to the genetic potential transmitted by the parents or to the lack of intellectual stimulation in the environment?

No research strategy for attempting to ferret out genetic and environmental determinants of IQ is flawless. Still, a number of ingenious approaches have been devised. The total weight of the evidence provided through these approaches may be instructive.

Genetic Influences

Various strategies have been devised for research into genetic factors, including kinship studies and studies of adopted children.

If heredity is involved in human intelligence, closely related people ought to have more similar IQs than distantly related or unrelated people, even when they are reared separately. Figure 12.11 shows the averaged results of more than 100 studies of IQ and heredity in human beings (T. J. Bouchard et al., 1990). The IQ scores of identical (monozygotic— MZ) twins are more alike than the scores for any other pairs, even when the twins have been reared apart. The average correlation for MZ twins reared together is 10.85; for those reared apart, it is 10.67. Correlations between the IQ scores of fraternal (dizygotic—DZ) twins, siblings, and parents and children are generally comparable, as is their degree of genetic relationship. The correlations tend to vary from about 10.40 to 10.59. Correlations between the IQ scores of children and their natural parents (10.48) are higher than those between children and adoptive parents (10.18). ***Truth or Fiction Revisited:*** Actually, adopted children are more similar in intelligence to their biological parents than to their adoptive parents, which is suggestive of the role of genetic factors in intellectual functioning.

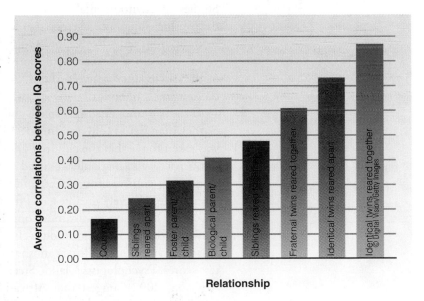

Figure 12.11

Findings of Studies of the Relationship between IQ Scores and Heredity

The data are a composite of studies summarized in *Science* magazine (T. J. Bouchard et al., 1990). By and large, correlations grow stronger for persons who are more closely related. Persons reared together or living together have more similar IQ scores than persons reared or living apart. Such findings support both genetic and environmental hypotheses of the origins of intelligence.

heritability The degree to which the variations in a trait from one person to another can be attributed to, or explained by, genetic factors.

All in all, studies suggest that the **heritability** of intelligence is between 40 and 60 percent (T. J. Bouchard et al., 1990; Neisser et al., 1996). In other words, about half the variations (the technical term is *variance*) in IQ scores can be accounted for by heredity. This is *not* the same as saying that you inherited about half of your intelligence. The implication of such a statement would be that you "got" the other half of your intelligence somewhere else. Rather, it means that about half of the difference between your IQ score and the IQ scores of other people can be explained in terms of genetic factors.

Let's return to Figure 12.11 for a moment. Note that genetic pairs (such as MZ twins) reared together show higher correlations between IQ scores than similar genetic pairs (such as other MZ twins) who were reared apart. This finding holds for MZ twins, siblings, parents, children, and unrelated people. *For this reason, the same group of studies that suggests that heredity plays a role in determining IQ scores also suggests that environment plays a role.*

When children are separated from their biological parents at early ages, one can argue that strong relationships between their IQ scores and those of their natural parents reflect genetic influences. Strong relationships between their IQs and those of their adoptive parents, on the other hand, might reflect environmental influences. Several projects involving adopted children in Colorado, Texas, and Minnesota (Coon, Fulker, & DeFries, 1990; Scarr, 1993; Turkheimer, 1991) have found a stronger relationship between the IQ scores of adopted children and their biological parents than between the IQ scores of adopted children and their adoptive parents.

These studies, then, also point to a genetic influence on intelligence. Nevertheless, the environment also has an impact.

Environmental Influences

Studies of environmental influences on IQ use several research strategies, including discovering situational factors that affect IQ scores, exploring children's abilities to rebound from early deprivation, and exploring the effects of positive early environments.

In some cases, we need look no further than the testing situation to explain some of the discrepancy between the IQ scores of middle-class children and those of children from economically disadvantaged backgrounds. In one study (Zigler et al., 1982), the examiner simply made children as comfortable as possible during the test. Rather than being cold and impartial, the examiner was warm and friendly, and care was taken to see that the children understood the directions. As a result, the children's test anxiety was markedly reduced and their IQ scores were six points higher than those for a control group treated in a more indifferent manner. Disadvantaged children made relatively greater gains from the procedure. By doing nothing more than making testing conditions more optimal for all children, we can narrow the IQ gap between low-income and middle-class children.

Stereotype vulnerability is another aspect of the testing situation, and it also affects test scores. Psychologists Claude Steele and Joshua Aronson (Steele & Aronson, 2000; Aronson, 2002) suggest that African American children carry an extra burden on intelligence tests. They worry that they risk confirming their group's negative stereotype by doing poorly. Their concern creates performance anxiety, which distracts them from the questions, hurting their scores.

In Chapter 7, we discussed a longitudinal study of at-risk orphanage children that provided striking evidence that children can recover from early deprivation. In the orphanage, nineteen-month-old children were placed with surrogate mothers who provided a great deal of intellectual and social stimulation. Four years later, the children showed dramatic gains in IQ.

Children whose parents are responsive and provide appropriate play materials and varied experiences during the early years attain higher IQ and achievement test scores (Bradley et al., 2001; Espy, Molfese, & DiLalla, 2001). Graduates of Head Start and other preschool programs show significant gains in later educational outcomes (Zigler & Styfco, 2001).

Although kinship studies and studies of adoptees suggest that there is a genetic influence on intelligence, they also suggest a role for environmental influences. For example, an analysis of a large number of twin and kinship studies showed that the older twins and other siblings become, the less alike they are on various measures of intelligence and personality (McCartney, Harris, & Bernjeri, 1990). This appears to be due to increasing exposure to different environments and experiences outside the family.

Many psychologists believe that heredity and environment interact to influence intelligence (Lubinski & Benbow, 2000; Winner, 2000). An impoverished environment may prevent some children from living up to their potential. An enriched environment may encourage others to realize their potential, minimizing possible differences in heredity.

Perhaps we need not be concerned with how much of a person's IQ is due to heredity and how much is due to environmental influences. Psychology has traditionally supported the dignity of the individual. It might be more appropriate for us to try to identify children of *all* races whose environments place them at high risk for failure and to do what we can to enrich them.

Active Review

14. Spearman suggested that the behaviours we consider intelligent have a common factor, which he labelled _____.

15. Gardner argues for the existence of _____ intelligences, each of which is based in a different area of the brain.

16. The IQ states the relationship between a child's _____ age and chronological age.

17. The Wechsler scales have subtests that assess _____ tasks.

18. If scoring well on an IQ test requires a certain type of cultural experience, the tests are said to have a cultural _____.

19. The first spurt in intellectual growth occurs at about the age of _____.

20. Children tend to use (convergent or divergent) thinking when they are thinking creatively.

21. Studies find that there is a stronger relationship between the IQ scores of adopted children and their (adoptive or biological?) parents than between the IQ scores of adopted children and their (adoptive or biological?) parents.

Reflect & Relate: As you look back on your own childhood, can you point to any kinds of family or educational experiences that seem to have had an impact on your intellectual development? Would you say that your background, overall, was deprived or enriched? In what ways?

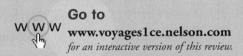
Go to
www.voyages1ce.nelson.com
for an interactive version of this review.

Language Development and Literacy

Question: How does language develop in middle childhood? Children's ability to understand and use language becomes increasingly sophisticated in middle childhood. Children learn to read as well. Many children are exposed to a variety of linguistic experiences other than standard English, and these experiences have important ramifications for language development. In this section, we examine each of these topics.

Vocabulary and Grammar

By the age of six, the child's vocabulary has expanded to 10 000 words, give or take a few thousand. By seven to nine years of age, most children realize that words can have different meanings, and they become entertained by riddles and jokes that require semantic sophistication. (Remember the jokes at the beginning of the chapter?) By the age of eight, or nine, children are able to form "tag questions," in which the question is tagged onto the end of a declarative sentence (Dennis, Sugar, & Whitaker, 1982). "You want more ice cream, don't you?" and "You're sick, aren't you?" are examples of tag questions.

Children also make subtle advances in articulation and in the capacity to use complex grammar. For example, preschool-aged children have difficulty understanding passive sentences such as "The truck was hit by the car." But children in the middle years have less difficulty interpreting the meanings of passive sentences correctly (Whitehurst, 1982). Children can learn to produce passive sentences in early childhood, but the teaching must be intensive (Tomasello, Brooks, & Stern, 1998); there is also no point to the exercise, except as a method of studying language development.

During these years, children develop the ability to use connectives, as illustrated by the sentence "I'll eat my spinach, but I don't want to." They also learn to form indirect object-direct object constructions (e.g., "She showed her sister the toy").

Reading Skills and Literacy

In many ways, reading is a key to unlocking the benefits society has to offer. Good readers find endless pleasure in literature, reading and rereading favourite poetic passages. Reading makes textbook learning possible. Reading also permits us to identify subway stops, to consider the contents of food packages, to assemble barbecue grills and children's swing sets, and to learn how to use a microcomputer.

Millions of people around the world are not literate and therefore cannot enjoy many of the benefits of contemporary knowledge and society (United Nations Statistics Division, 2004). But do you find it surprising to know that 42 percent of Canadians are classified as semiliterate (The National, 2006)? That means they would have difficulty reading instructions that accompany medicine or reading traffic signs and emergency safety regulations in buildings. Most Canadians, fortunately, learn to read when they enter school. However, Statistics Canada (Knighton & Bussière, 2006) reports that the higher a student's reading proficiency is, the more likely he or she is to graduate from high school (see Table 12.4). And high school graduation is an important milestone. *Question: What cognitive skills are involved in reading?*

Integration of Auditory and Visual Information

Reading is a complex process that depends on perceptual, cognitive, and linguistic processes (Siegel, 1993). It relies on skills in the integration of visual and auditory information. Accurate awareness of the sounds in the child's language is an extremely important factor in subsequent reading achievement (Caravolas & Bruck, 2000; Dufva, Niemi, & Voeten, 2001). Reading also requires the ability to make basic visual discriminations (Cunningham, Perry, & Stanovich, 2001). In reading, for example,

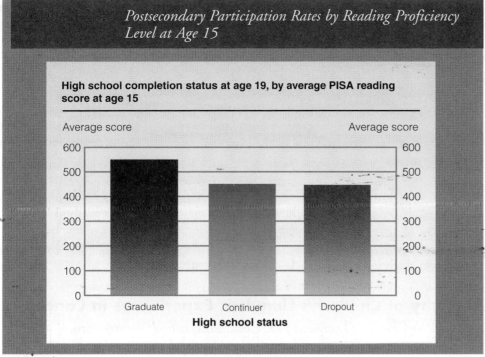

Postsecondary Participation Rates by Reading Proficiency Level at Age 15

High school completion status at age 19, by average PISA reading score at age 15

Note: Reading literacy was assessed through a two-hour written test completed at school. Student responses to test items were used to develop a reading score expressed on a scale with an average of 500 points. *Source: Knighton & Bussière (2006).*

children must "mind their *p*'s and *q*'s." That is, in order to recognize letters, children must be able to perceive the visual differences between letters such as *b* and *d* and *p* and *q*.

During the preschool years, neurological maturation and experience combine to allow most children to make visual discriminations between different letters with relative ease. Those children who can recognize and name the letters of the alphabet by kindergarten age are better readers in the early school grades (Kirby, Parrila, & Pfeiffer, 2003; Siegler & Alibali, 2005).

How do children acquire familiarity with their own written languages? More and more today, Canadian children are being exposed to TV programs and video games such as *Sesame Street* and *Leap Frog*, but these are relatively recent educational innovations. Children are also exposed to books, street signs, names of stores and restaurants, and the writing on packages, especially at the supermarket. Some children, of course, have more books in the home than others do. Children from affluent homes where books and other sources of stimulation are plentiful learn to read more readily than children from impoverished homes. But regardless of income level, reading storybooks with parents in the preschool years helps prepare a child for reading (Baker, Mackler, Sonnenschein, & Serpell, 2001; Clarke-Stewart, 1998). Children who read at home during the school years also show better reading skills in school and more positive attitudes toward reading.

Methods of Teaching Reading

When they read, children integrate visual and auditory information (they associate what they see with sounds), whether they are reading by the *word-recognition method* or the *phonetic method*. If they are using the **word-recognition method,** they must be able to associate visual stimuli such as *cat* and *Robert* with the sound combinations that produce the spoken words "cat" and "Robert." This capacity is usually acquired by *rote learning,* or extensive repetition.

Reading
Children who read at home during the school years show better reading skills in school and more positive attitudes toward reading.

word-recognition method
A method for learning to read in which children come to recognize words through repeated exposure to them.

© First Light

phonetic method   A method for learning to read in which children decode the sounds of words based on their knowledge of the sounds of letters and letter combinations.

In the **phonetic method,** children first learn to associate written letters and letter combinations (such as *ph* or *sh*) with the sounds they are meant to indicate. Then they sound out words from left to right, decoding them. The phonetic method has the obvious advantage of giving children skills that they can use to decode (read) new words (Bastien-Toniazzo & Jullien, 2001; Dufva et al., 2001). However, some children learn more rapidly at early ages through the word-recognition method. The phonetic method can also slow them down when it comes to familiar words. Most children and adults, in fact, tend to read familiar words by the word-recognition method (regardless of the method of their original training) and to make some effort to sound out new words.

Which method is superior? A controversy rages over the issue, and we cannot resolve it here. But let us note that some words in English can be read only by the word-recognition method—consider the words *one* and *two*. This method is useful when it comes to words such as *danger, stop, poison,* and the child's name, because it helps provide children with a basic **sight vocabulary.** But decoding skills must be acquired so that children can read new words on their own.

sight vocabulary   Words that are immediately recognized on the basis of familiarity with their overall shapes, rather than decoded.

Diversity of Children's Linguistic Experiences in Canada

Although we have already reviewed some of the literature regarding learning a second language in our Early Childhood: Cognitive Development chapter (Chapter 9), we will present some additional information about second language acquisition here.

Most people throughout the world speak two or more languages. Most countries have minority populations whose languages differ from the national tongue. Nearly all Europeans are taught English and the languages of neighbouring nations. Consider the Netherlands: Dutch is the native tongue, but all children are also taught French, German, and English and are expected to become fluent in each of them. Interestingly, a recent report put forth by the Canadian Council on Learning (2007) documents that almost half of Canadian Francophones speak English, whereas only 10 percent of Anglophones speak French. (The report also lists economic, cognitive, and cultural benefits of English-French bilingualism in Canada.)

Question: What does research reveal about the advantages and disadvantages of bilingualism? **Truth or Fiction Revisited:** It is *not* true that bilingual children encounter more academic problems than children who speak only one language. Nevertheless, a century ago, it was widely believed that children reared in bilingual homes were delayed in their cognitive and language development. The theory was that mental capacity is limited, so people who store two linguistic systems are crowding their mental abilities. It is true that there is some "mixing" of languages by bilingual children (J. L. Patterson, 2000), but they can generally separate the two languages from an early age (Mueller & Hulk,

Bilingualism
Most people throughout the world speak two or more languages. It was once thought that children reared in bilingual homes were retarded in their cognitive and language development, but today most linguists consider it advantageous for children to be bilingual.

2001). Moreover, a reanalysis of older studies in bilingualism shows that the observed bilingual children often lived in poor families and received little education. Yet these bilingual children were compared to middle-class monolingual children. In addition, achievement and intelligence tests were conducted in the monolingual child's language, which was the second language of the bilingual child (Reynolds, 1991). Lack of education and inadequate testing methods, rather than bilingualism per se, accounted for the apparent differences in achievement and intelligence.

Today most linguists consider it advantageous for children to be **bilingual.** Knowledge of more than one language expands children's awareness of different cultures and broadens their perspectives (Cavaliere, 1996). There is even evidence that bilingualism contributes to the complexity of the child's cognitive processes (Bialystock, 1999). For example, bilingual children are more likely to understand that the symbols used in language are arbitrary. Monolingual children are more likely to think erroneously that the word *dog* is somehow intertwined with the nature of the beast. Bilingual children therefore have somewhat more cognitive flexibility. Second, learning a second language does not crowd children's available "cognitive space." Instead, learning a second language has been shown to increase children's expertise in their first (native) language. For example, research evidence reveals that learning French enhances knowledge of the structure of English among Canadian children whose native language is English (Lambert, Genesee, Holobow, & Chartrand, 1991).

bilingual Using or capable of using two languages with nearly equal or equal facility.

Active Review

22. Reading relies on skills in the integration of _____ and auditory information.

23. In using the _____ method of reading, children associate written letters and letter combinations (such as *ph* or *sh*) with the sounds they indicate.

24. Bilingual children generally (can or cannot?) separate the two languages at an early age.

25. Today most linguists consider it a(n) (advantage or disadvantage?) to be bilingual.

Reflect & Relate: Did you grow up speaking a language other than English in the home? If so, what special opportunities and problems were connected with the experience?

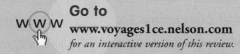

Go to
www.voyages1ce.nelson.com
for an interactive version of this review.

Recite: *An Active Summary*™

1. What is meant by the stage of concrete operations?

In the stage of concrete operations, children begin to show the capacity for adult logic with tangible objects. Concrete-operational thinking is characterized by reversibility, flexibility, and decentration. Concrete-operational children show understanding of conservation, transitivity, and class inclusion.

2. Can we apply Piaget's theory of cognitive development to educational practices?

Piaget believed that learning involves active discovery. Thus, teachers should not impose knowledge on the child but should find materials to interest and stimulate the child. Instruction should be geared to the child's level of development.

3. How does Piaget view the development of moral reasoning?

Piaget theorized two stages of moral development: moral realism and autonomous morality. The earlier stage emerges at about the age of five and judges behaviour as right when it conforms to rules. Five-year-olds see rules as embedded in the structure of things and believe in immanent justice. Preoperational children focus on one dimension at a time—in this case, the amount of damage and not the intentions of the wrongdoer. Children begin to show autonomous morality in middle childhood. At that time, they view social rules as agreements that can be changed.

4. What is Kohlberg's theory of moral development?

Kohlberg believed that there are three levels of moral development and two stages within each level. In the preconventional level, children base moral judgments on the consequences of behaviour. In the conventional level, right and wrong are judged by conformity to conventional standards. In the post-conventional level, moral reasoning is based on one's own values.

5. What is the difference between Piaget's view of cognitive development and the information-processing approach?

Information-processing theorists aim to learn how children store, retrieve, and manipulate information—how their "mental programs" develop. One key cognitive process is selective attention—attending to the relevant features of a task—which advances steadily through middle childhood.

6. What is meant by the term *memory*?

Memory refers to the storage and retrieval of information. Many psychologists divide memory functioning into three major processes: sensory memory, working memory, and long-term memory. Maintenance of information in working memory depends on cognitive strategies such as encoding and rehearsing stimuli. Older children process information more efficiently.

7. How much information can be stored in long-term memory? How is it "filed"?

There is no known limit to the capacity of long-term memory. Information is transferred from short-term memory to long-term memory by rehearsal and elaboration. Children organize their long-term memory into categories. Correct categorization expands knowledge and allows for efficient retrieval.

8. What do children understand about the functioning of their cognitive processes and, more particularly, their memory?

Awareness and conscious control of cognitive abilities is termed *metacognition*, as evidenced by ability to formulate problems, awareness of how to solve them, use of rules and strategies, ability to remain focused, and ability to check answers. *Metamemory* refers to children's awareness of the workings of their memory. By six or seven, children know to use rehearsal to remember things.

9. What is intelligence?

Intelligence provides the basis for academic achievement. It is a child's underlying competence or learning ability.

10. What are "factor theories" of intelligence?

Spearman suggested that the behaviours we consider intelligent have a common, underlying factor: *g*. But *s*, or specific capacities, account for some individual abilities. Thurstone used factor analysis to define several primary mental abilities.

11. What is Sternberg's triarchic model of intelligence?

Sternberg proposes a three-pronged theory of intelligence, including contextual, experiential and componential (information-processing).

12. What is meant by multiple intelligences?

Gardner believes that people have multiple "intelligences," each of which is based in a different part of the brain. Some of these—verbal ability, logical-mathematical reasoning, and spatial intelligence—involve academic ability. Others—for example, bodily-kinesthetic intelligence, musical intelligence, interpersonal intelligence, and personal knowledge—strike other psychologists as special talents or other skills.

13. What is the Stanford-Binet Intelligence Scale?

The SBIS assumes that intelligence increases with age, so older children must answer more items correctly than younger children to obtain a comparable score—which Binet referred to as a mental age (MA). A comparison of a child's mental age with his or her chronological age (CA)—(MA/CA)—yields an intelligence quotient (IQ). The average IQ score is defined as 100.

14. How do the Wechsler scales differ from the Stanford-Binet test?

The Wechsler scales group test questions into subtests that measure different types of intellectual tasks. Some tasks are mainly verbal, whereas others rely more on spatial-relations skills. Wechsler innovated a deviation IQ.

15. Many psychologists and educators consider standard intelligence tests to be culturally biased. What is that controversy about?

Most psychologists and educational specialists believe that intelligence tests are at least somewhat biased against non-European races and members of lower social classes. In addition to underlying competence, they reflect knowledge of the language and culture in which the test is administered.

16. Putting test scores aside, how does intelligence develop?

During middle childhood, thought processes become more logical and abstract. Children gain the capacity to focus on two or more aspects of a problem at once. The first intellectual spurt occurs at about the age of six and coincides with entry into school. The second spurt occurs at age ten or eleven. Intelligence tests gain greater predictive power during middle childhood.

17. What is cognitive disability?

Cognitive disability (or mental retardation as it is still referred to in the United States) refers to limitations in intellectual functioning that are characterized by an IQ score of no more than 70 to 75. Some causes of retardation are biological, but there is also cultural-familial retardation.

18. What does it mean to be gifted?

Giftedness is demonstrated through outstanding abilities, high performance in a specific academic area, such as language or mathematics, leadership, distinction in the arts, or bodily talents. Gifted children tend to be successful as adults.

19. What are the socioeconomic and ethnic differences in intelligence?

Lower-class children obtain lower IQ scores than more affluent children. Children from most ethnic minority groups obtain IQ scores below those obtained by the majority group.

20. What is creativity?

Creativity is the ability to do things that are novel and useful. Creative children take chances, refuse to accept limitations, and appreciate art and music.

21. What is the relationship between creativity and intelligence?

The relationship between intelligence test scores and measures of creativity are only moderate. Children mainly use *convergent* thinking to arrive at the correct answers on intelligence tests. Creative thinking tends to be *divergent* rather than convergent.

22. What are the roles of nature (heredity) and nurture (environmental influences) on the development of intelligence?

The closer the relationship between people, the more alike their IQ scores. The IQ scores of adopted children are more like those of their biological parents than those of their adoptive parents. Research also finds situational influences on IQ scores, including motivation, familiarity with testing materials, and the effects of enriched environments.

23. How does language develop in middle childhood?

In middle childhood, language use becomes more sophisticated, including understanding that words can have multiple meanings. There are advances in articulation and use of grammar.

24. What cognitive skills are involved in reading?

Reading relies on skills in the integration of visual and auditory information. During the preschool years, neurological maturation and experience combine to allow most children to make visual discriminations between letters with relative ease.

25. What does research reveal about the advantages and disadvantages of bilingualism?

Research shows that children can generally separate two languages from an early age and that most Americans who first spoke another language in the home also speak English well. Knowledge of more than one language expands children's knowledge of different cultures.

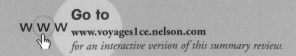

Go to

W W W www.voyages1ce.nelson.com

for an interactive version of this summary review.

Key Terms

concrete operations *(page 434)*

reversibility *(page 434)*

decentration *(page 434)*

transitivity *(page 436)*

seriation *(page 436)*

class inclusion *(page 437)*

moral realism *(page 440)*

objective morality *(page 440)*

immanent justice *(page 440)*

autonomous morality *(page 440)*

preconventional level *(page 443)*

conventional level *(page 443)*

postconventional level *(page 443)*

memory *(page 445)*

sensory memory *(page 446)*

sensory register *(page 446)*

working memory *(page 446)*

encode *(page 447)*

rehearse *(page 447)*

rote learning *(page 447)*

long-term memory *(page 447)*

elaborative strategy *(page 448)*

semantic code *(page 448)*

metacognition *(page 449)*

metamemory *(page 449)*

intelligence *(page 451)*

achievement *(page 451)*

factor *(page 452)*

factor analysis *(page 452)*

triarchic *(page 452)*

intelligence quotient (IQ) *(page 456)*

mental age (MA) *(page 456)*

chronological age (CA) *(page 456)*

cultural bias *(page 460)*

culture-free *(page 460)*

cultural-familial delay *(page 463)*

creativity *(page 464)*

convergent thinking *(page 466)*

divergent thinking *(page 466)*

heritability *(page 468)*

word-recognition method *(page 471)*

phonetic method *(page 472)*

sight vocabulary *(page 472)*

bilingual *(page 473)*

Active Learning Resources

Observing Children and Adolescents CD-ROM

Want to watch videos showing what you've just learned about in this chapter? Click on the "Piaget's Concrete Operational Stage" video in Module 3, Section 2. Your "Lessons in Observation" feature on p. 195 provides further learning objectives, an applied lesson, and a critical thinking exercise designed to help you experience this stage of development. Also check out the "Rehearsal Strategies" and "Suggestibility" videos in CD Module 3, Section 2, and the "Developmental Disabilities" and "Moral Development" clips in Module 3, Section 3.

Visit Your Companion Website for This Book

http://www.voyages1CE.nelson.com

Check out this companion website, where you will find online resources directly linked to your book. The website includes interactive exercises related to PQ4R and Power Visuals for mastering and reviewing key concepts as well as quizzing, chapter outlines, and much more!

CengageNOW!™

http://hed.nelson.com

Go to this site for the link to CengageNOW™, your one-stop study shop. Take a Pretest for this chapter, and CengageNOW™ will generate a personalized Study Plan based on your test results! The Study Plan will identify the topics you need to review and direct you to online resources to help you master those topics. You can then take a Posttest to help you determine the concepts you have mastered and those you still need to work on.

Middle Childhood: Social and Emotional Development

PREVIEW

TRUTH OR FICTION?

● ● ● ● ● ● ● ● ● ●

(T) (F) Children's self-esteem tends to rise in middle childhood.

(T) (F) Parents who are in conflict should stay together "for the sake of the children."

(T) (F) The daughters of employed women are more achievement oriented and set higher career goals for themselves than the daughters of unemployed women.

(T) (F) In middle childhood, popular children tend to be attractive and relatively mature for their age.

(T) (F) Teachers who have higher expectations of students may elicit greater achievements from them.

(T) (F) Some children—like some adults—blame themselves for all the problems in their lives, whether they deserve the blame or not.

(T) (F) It is better for children with school phobia to remain at home until the origins of the problem are uncovered and resolved.

Go to WWW

www.voyages1CE.nelson.com
for an interactive version of this "Truth or Fiction" feature.

A college student taking a child development course had the following conversation with a nine-year-old girl named Sarjeet:

Student: Sarjeet, how was school today?

Sarjeet: Oh, it was all right. I don't like it a lot.

Student: How come?

Sarjeet: Ming and Talia won't talk to me. I told Ming I thought her dress was very pretty, and she pushed me out of the way. That made me so mad.

Student: That wasn't nice of them.

Sarjeet: No one is nice except for Lexie. At least she talks to me.

Here is part of a conversation between a different college student and her nine-year-old cousin Mona:

Mona: My girlfriend Heather at school has the same glasses as you. My girlfriend, no, not my girlfriend—my *friend*—my friend picked them up yesterday from the doctor, and she wore them today.

Student: What do you mean—not your girlfriend but your friend? Is there a difference?

Mona: Yeah, my friend. 'Cause Keisha is my girlfriend.

Student: But what's the difference between Heather, your friend, and Keisha, your girlfriend?

Sue: Well, Keisha is my best friend, so she's my girlfriend. Heather isn't my best friend, so she's just a friend.

—Adapted from Rowen (1973)

In the years from age six to age twelve, the child's social world expands. As illustrated by the remarks of these nine-year-old girls, peers take on greater importance and friendships deepen (Hamm, 2000). Entry into school exposes the child to the influence of teachers and to a new peer group. Relationships with parents change as children develop greater independence. Some children will face adjustments resulting from the divorce and remarriage of parents. During these years, major advances occur in children's ability to understand themselves. Their knowledge of social relationships and their skill in developing such relationships increase as well (Collins, 1984; Davis, 2001). Some children, unfortunately, develop problems during these years, although some are able to cope with life's stresses better than others.

In this chapter, we discuss each of these areas. First, we examine major theories of social and emotional development in the middle years. Next, we examine the development of self-concept and the development of relationships with parents and peers. Then we turn to the influences of the school. Finally, we look at some of the social and emotional problems that can arise in middle childhood.

Theories of Social and Emotional Development in Middle Childhood

Question: What are some features of social and emotional development in middle childhood? The major theories of personality have had less to say about this age group than about the other periods of childhood and adolescence. Nevertheless, common threads emerge. These include the development of skills, the importance of interpersonal relationships, and the expansion of self-understanding.

Psychoanalytic Theory

According to Freud, children in the middle years are in the **latency stage**. Freud believed that sexual feelings remain repressed (unconscious) during this period. Children use this period to focus on developing intellectual, social, and other culturally valued skills.

Erikson, like Freud, sees the major developmental task of middle childhood as the acquisition of cognitive and social skills. Erikson labels this stage **industry versus inferiority**. To the extent that children are able to master the various tasks and challenges of the middle years, they develop a sense of industry or competence. But if a child has difficulties in school or with peer relationships, a sense of inferiority may result.

© Gabe Palmer/CORBIS

Development of Skills
According to psychoanalytic theory, the major development task of middle childhood is to acquire cognitive, social, physical, and other culturally valued skills. Children who develop valued skills tend to have high self-esteem and to be admired by peers.

Social Cognitive Theory

Social cognitive theory focuses on the continued importance of rewards and modelling in middle childhood. During these years, children depend less on external rewards and punishments and increasingly regulate their own behaviour (Crain, 2000).

How do children acquire moral and social standards for judging their own behaviour? One mechanism is direct reward and punishment. For example, parents may praise children when they share their toys with younger siblings. In time, they incorporate the importance of sharing into their own value systems.

Another mechanism for acquiring self-evaluative standards is modelling. Children in the middle years are exposed to an increasing variety of models. Not only parents but also teachers, other adults, peers, and symbolic models (such as TV characters or the hero or heroine in a story) can serve as influential models (Bandura, 2002).

Cognitive-Developmental Theory and Social Cognition

Cognitive-developmental theory stresses the importance of the child's growing cognitive capacities. According to Piaget, middle childhood coincides with the stage of concrete operations and is partly characterized by a decline in egocentrism and an expansion of the capacity to view the world and oneself from other people's perspectives. This cognitive advance not only enhances the child's intellectual functioning but also has a major effect on the child's social relationships (Mischo, 2004; Zan & Hildebrandt, 2003).

Question: What is the relationship between social cognition and perspective taking? **Social cognition** refers to the development of children's knowledge about the social world. It focuses on the child's understanding of the relationship between the self and others. A key aspect of the development of social cognition is the ability to assume the role or perspective of another person. Robert Selman and his colleagues (Selman, 1980, 1989; Selman & Schultz, 1989) devised a method to study

latency stage In psychoanalytic theory, the fourth stage of psychosexual development, characterized by repression of sexual impulses and development of skills.

industry versus inferiority
The fourth stage of psychosocial development in Erikson's theory, occurring in middle childhood. Mastery of tasks leads to a sense of industry, whereas failure produces feelings of inferiority.

social cognition Development of children's understanding of the relationship between the self and others.

the development of perspective-taking skills in childhood. They presented children with a social dilemma such as the following:

> Holly is an 8-year-old girl who likes to climb trees. She is the best tree climber in the neighborhood. One day while climbing down from a tall tree, she falls off the bottom branch but does not hurt herself. Her father sees her fall. He is upset and asks her to promise not to climb trees anymore. Holly promises. Later that day, Holly and her friends meet Sean. Sean's kitten is caught up in a tree and can't get down. Something has to be done right away, or the kitten may fall. Holly is the only one who climbs trees well enough to reach the kitten and get it down, but she remembers her promise to her father.
>
> —Selman (1980, p. 36)

The children then were asked a series of questions designed to test their ability to take the role of another person (e.g., "How will Holly's father feel if he finds out she climbed the tree?"). Based on the children's responses to these questions, Selman and his colleagues described five levels of perspective-taking skills in childhood (Selman, 1976) (see Table 13.1).

		Levels of Perspective Taking
Level	**Approximate Age (Years)**	**Comments**
0	3–6	Children are still egocentric and do not realize that other people have perspectives different from their own. A child of this age will typically say that Holly will save the kitten because she likes kittens and that her father will be happy because he likes kittens too. The child assumes that everyone feels as she does.
1	5–9[a]	Children understand that people in different situations may have different perspectives. The child still assumes that only one perspective is "right." A child might say Holly's father would be angry if he did not know why she climbed the tree. But if she told him why, he would understand. The child recognizes the father's perspective may differ from Holly's because of lack of information. But once he has the information, he will assume the "right" (i.e., Holly's) perspective.
2	7–12	The child understands that people may think or feel differently because they have different values or ideas. The child also recognizes that others are capable of understanding the child's own perspective. Therefore, the child is better able to anticipate reactions of others. The typical child of this age might say that Holly knows that her father will understand why she climbed the tree and that he therefore will not punish her.
3	10–15	The child finally realizes that both she and another person can consider each other's point of view at the same time. The child may say something similar to this: Holly's father will think that she shouldn't have climbed the tree. But once he has heard her side of the story, he would feel that she was doing what she thought was right. Holly realizes that her father will consider how she felt.
4	12 and older	The child realizes that mutual perspective taking does not always lead to agreement. The perspectives of the larger social group also must be considered. A child of this age might say that society expects children to obey their parents and therefore that Holly should realize why her father might punish her.

[a]Yes, there is overlap between the stages in terms of children's ages.
Source: Selman (1976).

Research supports Selman's developmental progression in perspective taking (Dixon & Moore, 1990; Fox, 1991; Nakkula & Nikitopoulos, 2001). Also, as you might expect, children with better perspective-taking skills tend to be more skilled at negotiating and peer relations (Fitzgerald & White, 2003; Strough, Berg, & Meegan, 2001; Zhang & Lin, 1999).

Development of the Self-Concept in Middle Childhood

Question: How does the self-concept develop during middle childhood? In early childhood, children's self-concepts, or self-definitions, focus on concrete external traits, such as appearance, activities, and living situations. But as children undergo the cognitive developments of middle childhood, their more abstract internal traits, or personality characteristics, begin to play a role in their self-definition. Social relationships and group memberships also take on significance (Damon, 2000; Damon & Hart, 1992).

An investigative method called the Twenty Statements Test bears out this progression and also highlights the relationships between the self-concept and general cognitive development. According to this method, children are given a sheet of paper with the question "Who am I?" and twenty spaces in which to write answers. Consider the answers of a nine-year-old boy and an eleven-year-old girl:

> The nine-year-old boy: My name is Raj K. I have brown eyes. I have brown hair. I have brown eyebrows. I'm 9 years old. I LOVE? sports. I have 7 people in my family. I have great? eye site. I have lots! of friends. I live on 1923 Pinecrest Drive. I'm going on 10 in September. I'm a boy. I have a uncle that is almost 7 feet tall. My school is Pinecrest. My teacher is Mrs. V. I play hockey! I'm also the smartest boy in the class. I LOVE! food. I love fresh air. I LOVE school.

> The eleven-year-old girl: My name is A. I'm a human being. I'm a girl. I'm a truthful person. I'm not pretty. I do so-so in my studies. I'm a very good cellist. I'm a very good pianist. I'm a little bit tall for my age. I like several boys. I like several girls. I'm old-fashioned. I play tennis. I am a very good musician. I try to be helpful. I'm always ready to be friends with anybody. Mostly I'm good, but I lose my temper. I'm not well liked by some girls and boys. I don't know if boys like me or not.

> —Montemayor & Eisen (1977, pp. 317–318)

Only the nine-year-old lists his age and address, discusses his family, and focuses on physical traits, such as eye colour, in his self-definition. The nine-year-old mentions his likes, which can be considered rudimentary psychological traits, but they are tied to the concrete, as would be expected of a concrete-operational child.

The nine- and eleven-year-olds both list their competencies. The eleven-year-old's struggle to bolster her self-esteem—her insistence on her musical abilities despite her qualms about her attractiveness—shows a greater concern with internal traits, psychological characteristics, and social relationships.

Research also finds that females are somewhat more likely than males to define themselves in terms of the groups to which they belong (Madson & Trafimow, 2001). A Chinese study found that children with siblings are more likely to define themselves in terms of group membership than are only children (Wang, Leichtman, & White, 1998).

Self-Esteem

self-esteem The sense of value or worth that people attach to themselves.

One of the most critical aspects of self-concept is **self-esteem,** the value or worth that people attach to themselves. A positive self-image is crucial to psychological adjustment in children and adults (Chen, Chen, & Kaspar, 2001; Feinberg, Neiderhiser, Simmens, Reiss, & Hetherington, 2000). *Question: How does self-esteem develop during middle childhood?*

As children enter middle childhood, their self-concepts become more differentiated and they are able to evaluate their self-worth in many different areas (Tassi, Schneider, & Richard, 2001). Preschoolers do not generally make a clear distinction between different areas of competence. They are either "good at doing things" or not. At one time, it was assumed that before age eight, children could differentiate between only two broad facets of self-concept. One involved general competence, and the other, social acceptance (Harter & Pike, 1984). It was also believed that an overall, or general, self-concept did not emerge until the age of eight. But research indicates that even as early as five to seven years of age, children are able to make judgments about their performance in seven different areas: physical ability, physical appearance, peer relationships, parent relationships, reading, mathematics, and general school performance. They also display an overall, or general, self-concept (Eccles et al., 1993; Marsh, Craven, & Debus, 1991).

Truth or Fiction Revisited: Children's self-esteem actually *declines* throughout middle childhood, reaching a low point at about age twelve or thirteen; then it increases during adolescence (Harter, 1990b, 1990c; Pomerantz, Frey, Greulich, & Ruble, 1993). What accounts for the decline? Because young children are egocentric, their initial self-concepts may be unrealistic. As children become older, they compare themselves with other children and adjust their self-concepts. For most children, the comparison results in a more critical self-appraisal and the consequent decline in self-esteem.

Do girls or boys have a more favourable self-image? The answer depends on the area (Quatman & Watson, 2001). Girls tend to have more positive self-concepts regarding reading and general academics than boys do, whereas boys tend to have more positive self-concepts in math, physical ability, and physical appearance (Eccles, 1999; Eccles et al., 1993; Marsh et al., 1991). Cross-cultural studies in China (Dai, 2001), Finland (Lepola, Vaurus, & Maeki, 2000), and Germany (Tiedemann, 2000) also find that girls tend to have higher self-concepts in writing and that boys tend to have higher self-concepts in math.

Why do girls and boys differ in their self-concepts? Socialization and gender stereotypes appear to affect the way females and males react to their achievements. For example, girls predict that they will do better on tasks that are labelled "feminine," and boys predict better performance for themselves when tasks are labelled "masculine" (Rathus et al., 2005).

Authoritative parenting apparently contributes to children's self-esteem (Baumrind, 1991a, 1991b; Furnham & Cheng, 2000; Hickman, Bartholomae, & McKenry, 2000). Children with a favourable self-image tend to have parents who are restrictive, involved, and loving. Children with low self-esteem are more likely to have authoritarian or rejecting-neglecting parents.

High self-esteem in children is related to their closeness to parents, especially as found in father-son and mother-daughter relationships (Fenzel, 2000). Close relationships between parents are also associated with positive self-concepts in children (Bagley, Bertrand, Bolitho, & Mallick, 2001; Maejima & Oguchi, 2001).

Peers also play a role in children's self-esteem. Social acceptance by peers is related to self-perceived competence in academic, social, and athletic domains (Cole, 1991). Parents and classmates have an equally strong effect on children's sense of self-worth in the middle years. Close friends and teachers have somewhat less influence in shaping self-esteem (Harter, 1987).

Self-esteem may also have a genetic component, which would contribute to its stability (S. McGuire, Manke, Saudino, Reiss, Hetherington, & Plomin, 1999). In any event, self-esteem, once established, seems to endure. One longitudinal study, for example, found that children's self-esteem remained stable from the ages of seven to eleven years (Hoglund & Bell, 1991). Most children will encounter failure, but high self-esteem may contribute to the belief that they can master adversity. Low self-esteem may become a self-fulfilling prophecy: Children with low self-esteem may not carve out much to boast about.

Authoritative Parenting and Self-Esteem
Research suggests that parental demands for mature behaviour, imposition of restrictions, and warmth help children develop behaviour patterns that are connected with self-esteem.

Learned Helplessness

One outcome of low self-esteem in academics is known as **learned helplessness.** *Question: What is learned helplessness, and how does it develop in middle childhood?* Learned helplessness refers to an acquired belief that one is unable to obtain the rewards that one seeks. "Helpless" children tend to quit following failure, whereas children who believe in their own ability tend to persist in their efforts or change their strategies (Zimmerman, 2000). One reason for this difference is that helpless children believe that success is due more to ability than to effort and that they have little ability in a particular area. Consequently, persisting in the face of failure seems futile (Bandura, Barbaranelli, Vittorio Caprara, & Pastorelli, 2001; Carr, Borkowski, & Maxwell, 1991). "Helpless" children typically perform more poorly in school and on standardized tests of intelligence and achievement (Chapman, Skinner, & Baltes, 1990; Welton & Rinaldi, 2007).

learned helplessness An acquired (hence, learned) belief that one is unable to control one's environment.

Sex and Learned Helplessness

It is unclear whether girls or boys exhibit more learned helplessness in middle childhood (Boggiano & Barrett, 1991; Valas, 2001). But a sex difference does emerge in mathematics (Stipek & Gralinski, 1991). Jacquelynne Eccles and her colleagues have been carrying out longitudinal studies of children of elementary school and high school age (Anderman et al., 2001; Eccles et al., 1991). They have found that even when girls are performing as well as boys in math and science, they have less confidence in their ability. Why? Parents' expectations that children will do well (or poorly) in a given area influence both the children's self-perceptions and their performance. Parents tend to hold the stereotyped view that girls have less math ability than boys. This is true regardless of their own daughter's actual performance in math. Because of lower parental expectations, girls may shy away from math and not develop their math skills as much as boys do (Eccles et al., 1991). This is an example of the self-fulfilling prophecy.

To watch this video

click on
"Self-Concept" in Module 3, Section 3, on your Observing Children and Adolescents CD-ROM. You can also visit the Student Book Companion Site to watch the video, answer the questions, and e-mail your responses to your professor.

© Royalty-Free/CORBIS

At age 4½ Christopher describes himself by listing objects and possessions in his house.

Lessons in Observation
Self-Concept

Learning Objectives
• What is a self-concept?
• How does the self-concept develop over time?
• When do children begin to incorporate personal traits into their self-descriptions?

Applied Lesson
How would you describe yourself? What information do you choose to include? Why?

Critical Thinking
You cannot see or touch a self-concept. How do researchers study the self-concept? Are you satisfied with their methods? Why or why not?

Active Review

1. Erikson labels middle childhood the stage of _____ versus inferiority.

2. According to Piaget, middle childhood coincides with the stage of _____ operations.

3. A key aspect of the development of social cognition is the ability to take the _____ of another person.

4. Children's self-esteem (increases or decreases?) during middle childhood.

5. (Authoritarian or Authoritative?) parenting contributes to high self-esteem in children.

Reflect & Relate: Are you "responsible" for your own self-esteem, or does your self-esteem pretty much vary with the opinion that others have of you? Why is this an important question?

Go to
W W W www.voyages1CE.nelson.com
for an interactive version of this review.

The Family

Question: What kinds of influences are exerted by the family during middle childhood? In middle childhood, the family continues to play a key role in socializing the child, even though peers, teachers, and other outsiders begin to play a greater role (Maccoby, 1984; Peterson, 2001). In this section, we examine developments in parent-child relationships during the middle years. We also look at the effects of living in different types of family environments: the family environment provided by lesbian and gay parents and the experience of living in families with varying marital arrangements (e.g., original two parents, single parent, stepparent). We also consider the effects of parental employment.

Parent-Child Relationships

Parent-child interactions focus on some new concerns during the middle childhood years. These include school-related matters, assignment of chores, and peer activities (Collins, Maccoby, Steinberg, Hetherington, & Bornstein, 2003; DeLuccie & Davis, 1991).

During the middle years, parents do less monitoring of children's activities and provide less direct feedback than they did in the preschool years. In middle childhood, children do more monitoring of their own behaviour. Although the parents still retain control over the child, control is gradually transferred from parent to child, a process known as **coregulation** (Maccoby, 2002; Wahler, Herring, & Edwards, 2001). Children no longer need to be constantly reminded of dos and don'ts as they begin to internalize the standards of their parents.

Children and parents spend less time together in middle childhood than in the preschool years. But as in early childhood, children spend more of this time with their mothers than with their fathers (Russell & Russell, 1987). Mothers' interactions with school-aged children continue to revolve around caregiving and household tasks, whereas fathers are more involved in recreational activities, especially with sons (Collins & Russell, 1991).

In the later years of middle childhood (ages ten to twelve), children evaluate their parents more critically than they do in the early years (Reid, Ramey, & Burchinal, 1990). This shift in perception may reflect the child's developing cognitive ability to view relationships in more complex ways (Selman, 1989). But throughout middle childhood, children rate their parents as their best source of emotional support, rating them more highly than friends (Reid et al., 1990). And emotional support is more valuable than economics during middle childhood (Santinello & Vieno, 2002).

coregulation A gradual transferring of control from parent to child, beginning in middle childhood.

Lesbian and Gay Parents

"Where did you get that beautiful necklace?" I asked the little girl in the pediatrician's office.

"From my moms," she answered.

It turned out that her family consisted of two women, each of whom had a biological child, one girl and one boy. *Question: What are the effects of having lesbian or gay parents?*

Research on **lesbian** and **gay** parenting has fallen into two general categories: the general adjustment of children and whether the children of lesbian and gay parents are more likely than other children to be lesbian or gay themselves. Research by Charlotte Patterson and her colleagues has generally found that the psychological adjustment of children of lesbian and gay parents—whether conceived by intercourse,

lesbian A female who is interested romantically and sexually in other females.

gay An adjective describing a male who is interested romantically and sexually in other males. (Also used more broadly to refer to both lesbians and gay males.)

through donor insemination, or adopted—is comparable to that of children of heterosexual parents (Chan, Raboy, & Patterson, 1998; C. J. Patterson, 1992, 2000, 2002, 2003, 2006; Tasker, 2005). One study by Patterson (1992) essentially found no significant differences in development. A review written somewhat later (C. J. Patterson, 2000) concluded that despite the stigma attached to homosexuality, lesbians and gay men frequently create and sustain positive family relationships. An article by Tasker (2005) concurred with Patterson's finding that the psychological development of children with lesbian or gay parents are similar. However, she also underscores that variations in family form, children's awareness of lesbian and gay relationships, heterosexism, and homophobia are important issues for children. A good Canadian resource site is Egale Canada (http://www.egale.ca/index.asp), whose purpose is to advance equality and justice for lesbian, gay, bisexual, and transidentified people and their families across Canada.

Now let's consider the sexual orientation of the children of lesbian and gay parents. In doing so, we begin a generation back with the research of psychiatrist Richard Green. In a classic study, Green (1978) observed thirty-seven children and young adults, aged three to twenty years old, who were being reared—or had been reared—by lesbians or **transsexuals.** All but one of the children reported or recalled preferences for toys, clothing, and friends (male or female) that were typical for their sex and age. All of the thirteen older children who reported sexual fantasies or sexual behaviour were heterosexually oriented. In a subsequent study, Green and his colleagues (1986) compared the children of European American mothers who were currently single, fifty of whom were lesbians and forty of whom were heterosexual. Boys from the two groups showed no significant differences in intelligence test scores, sexual orientation, gender-role preferences, relationships with family and peer groups, and adjustment to life with a single parent. Girls showed slight differences, including somewhat more flexibility in gender roles. Green concluded that the mother's sexual orientation had no connection with parental fitness. A study by Patterson and her colleagues (Brodzinsky, Patterson, & Vaziri, 2002) suggested that many adoption agencies now agree with Green's conclusions.

Another review by Patterson (2003) addressed the personal and social development of children with lesbian and gay parents. Patterson found that the sexual orientation of the children was generally heterosexual. When parents had gotten divorced and created families with same-sex partners because of their sexual orientations, their children experienced a period of adjustment that entailed some difficulties—as do children when heterosexual parents get divorced. Children who are adopted by lesbian or gay parents tend to be well adjusted. The point here—reinforcing Green's findings—is that wanting the child is more important to the child's adjustment than the sexual orientation of the parents.

transsexual A person who would prefer to be a person of the other sex and who may undergo hormone treatments and/or cosmetic surgery to achieve the appearance of being a member of the other sex.

Generation X or Generation Ex? What Happens to Children Whose Parents Get Divorced?

To many in Canada, the 2000s are the "Generation X" years—the period that those born in the late sixties and early seventies are at their peak. However, it may be more accurate to think of this time as that of "Generation Ex"—that is, a generation characterized by ex-partners. Their children are also a part of Generation Ex, which is large, although stabilizing. More than 70 000 divorces were recorded in Canada in 2003 (a slight rise from 2002). That same year, the total divorce rate for all Canadians, by the thirtieth wedding anniversary, was 38.3 per 100 marriages. The divorce rate varies depending on how long couples have been together. In 2003, the peak divorce rate occurred after three years of marriage: Out of

1,000 marriages, 26.2 ended in divorce (Statistics Canada, 2005). *Question: What are the effects of divorce on children?*

In considering the effects of divorce on family members—both children and adults—Amato (2000) suggested that researchers consider whether the effects are due to divorce or to "selection factors." For example, are the effects on children due to divorce per se, to marital conflict, to inadequate parental problem-solving ability, or to changes in financial status? Also, do children undergo a temporary crisis and gradually adjust, or do stressors persist indefinitely? For example, three years after the divorce, feelings of sadness, shock, disbelief, and desire for parental reunion tend to decline, but even ten years later, children tend to retain anger toward the parent they hold responsible for the breakup.

Parents who get divorced are often in conflict about many things, and one of them typically involves how to rear the children. Because the children often hear their parents fighting over child rearing, the children may come to blame themselves for the split. Young children, who are less experienced than adolescents, are more likely to blame themselves. Young children also worry more about uncharted territory—the details of life after the breakup. Adolescents are relatively more independent and have some power to control their day-to-day lives.

Most children live with their mothers after a divorce (Ulloa & Ulibarri, 2004). Some fathers remain fully devoted to their children despite the split, but others tend to spend less time with their children as time goes on. This pattern is especially common when fathers create other families, such that the children of their new partners are competing with their biological children. Not only does the drop-off in paternal attention deprive children of activities and social interactions, but it also saps their self-esteem: "Why doesn't Daddy love me anymore? What's wrong with me?"

There is no question that divorce has challenging effects on children (Ellis, 2000). The children of divorce are more likely to have conduct disorders, lower self-esteem, drug addictions, and poor grades in school (Chao et al., 2001; O'Connor, Caspi, DeFries, & Plomin, 2000). Their physical health may decline, at least temporarily (Troxel & Matthews, 2004). There are individual differences, but, by and large, the fallout for children is worst during the first year after the breakup. Children tend to rebound after a couple of years or so (Malone et al., 2004).

A parental breakup is connected with a decline in the quality of parenting. A longitudinal study by E. Mavis Hetherington and her colleagues (Hetherington, 1987, 1989; Hetherington, Stanley-Hagan, & Anderson, 1989) tracked the adjustment of children who were four years old at the time of the divorce; the follow-ups occurred two months, one year, two years, and six years after the divorce. The investigators found that the organization of family life deteriorates. The family is more likely to eat meals pickup style, as opposed to sitting together. Children are less likely to get to school or to sleep on schedule. Divorced mothers have a more difficult time setting limits and enforcing restrictions on sons' behaviour. Divorced parents are significantly less likely to show the authoritative behaviours that foster competence. They make fewer demands for mature behaviour, communicate less, and show less nurturance and warmth. Their disciplinary methods become inconsistent.

Cross-cultural studies show that children of divorce in other cultures experience problems similar to those experienced by children in North America (Boey, Omar, & Phillips, 2003). A study in China matched 58 children of divorce with 116 children from intact families according to sex, age, and social class. Children of divorce were more likely than the other children to make somatic complaints ("My stomach hurts," "I feel nauseous"), demonstrate lower social competence, and behave aggressively (Liu et al., 2000a). Another Chinese study found that divorce impairs the quality of parent-child relationships, interferes with concern over the children's education, and creates financial woes (Sun, 2001). A third Chinese study showed that divorce compromises the academic and social functioning of children in their sample (Zhou, Bray, Kehle, & Xin, 2001).

A study of children and their mothers in Botswana, Africa, had similar results (Maundeni, 2000). Divorce led to economic hardship for most mothers and children. Lack of money made some children feel inferior to other children. Financial worries and feelings of resentment and betrayal led to social and emotional problems among both children and mothers.

Back to North America: Boys seem to have a harder time than girls coping with divorce, and they take a longer time to recover (Grych, Fincham, Jouriles, & McDonald, 2000; Malone et al., 2004). In the Hetherington study, boys whose parents were divorced showed more social, academic, and conduct problems than boys whose parents were married. These problems sometimes persisted for six years. Girls, by contrast, tended to regain functioning within two years.

K. Alison Clarke-Stewart and her colleagues (2000) compared the well-being of children in families headed by a separated or divorced mother with the well-being of about 170 children reared in intact families. As a group, the children who were being reared in two-parent families exhibited fewer problematic behaviours, more social skills, and higher IQ test scores. They were more securely attached to their mothers. But then the researchers factored in the mother's level of education, her socioeconomic status, and her psychological well-being. Somewhat surprisingly, the differences between the children in the two groups (one-parent versus intact families) almost vanished. The researchers concluded that at least in this study, it was not the parental breakup per se that caused the problems among the children. Instead, the difficulties were connected with the mother's psychological status (such as feelings of depression), income, and level of education. Other research confirms that maternal depression following divorce contributes to adjustment problems in the children (Hammen, 2003).

By and large, research shows that the following sources of support help children cope with divorce: social support from the immediate family, support from the

© Royalty-Free / CORBIS

Generation Ex: Ex-Husband, Ex-Wife, Ex-Family, Ex-Security
A good half of marriages today end in divorce, and divorce turns life topsy-turvy for children. Younger children tend to erroneously blame themselves for the dissolution of the family, but children in middle childhood come to see things more accurately. Children of divorce tend to develop problems, many of which fade as time passes. Should parents in conflict stay together for the sake of the children? The answer seems to be that the children will not be better off if the parents continue to fight in front of them.

extended family, support of friends, membership in a religious community, communication among family members, and financial security (Greeff & Van Der Merwe, 2004; Rogers, 2004).

Some children of divorce profit from psychological treatment. Many programs include parents. The usefulness of a program that includes the mother was studied with 240 children, aged nine to twelve (Wolchik et al., 2000). The program addressed the quality of the mother-child relationship, ways of disciplining the child, ways of coping with interparental conflict, and the nature of the father-child relationship. Children were also helped to handle stressors (by thinking of them as difficult but not impossible) and to not blame themselves. Children's adjustment showed improvement at completion of the program and at a six-month follow-up. In Canada, there are programs for families in transition (FIT) that may help with reducing parental conflict, strengthening relationships between parents, helping children adjust to loss, improving parent-child relationships, and creating successful stepfamilies. The Family Services Association of Toronto (http://www.fsatoronto.com/programs/families.html) provides one such program. Other communities across Canada offer these types of services as well.

Life in Stepfamilies: His, Hers, Theirs, and ...

Most divorced people remarry, usually while the children are young. The rule of thumb about the effects of living in stepfamilies is that there is no rule of thumb. Living in a stepfamily may have no measurable psychological effects (Coleman, Ganong, & Fine, 2000). Stepparents may claim stepchildren as their own (Marsiglio, 2004). One study of the effects of stepparenting on middle-schoolers found that good stepmother-stepchild relationships were linked with less aggressive behaviour in both boys and girls and with higher self-esteem among stepdaughters (Clingempeel & Segal, 1986). But not everything comes up roses in stepfamilies. There are some risks. Infanticide (killing infants) is a rarity in the United States, but the crime occurs sixty times as often in stepfamilies as in families with biological kinship (Daly & Wilson, 2000). There is also a significantly higher incidence—by a factor of eight—of sexual abuse by stepparents than by natural parents.

Why do we find these risks in stepfamilies? According to evolutionary psychologists, people often behave as though they want their genes to flourish in the next generation. Thus, it could be that stepparents are less devoted to rearing other people's children. They may even see "foreign" children as competitors for resources for their own children. Or a stepfather may see a woman's possession of children by another man as lessening her capacity to bear and rear his children (Brody, 1998a). Evolutionary psychologists then often stray into research that describes how dominant males in many species do away with the offspring of females that have been sired by other males. (We're not going there.)

"All Right, We Fight—Should We Remain Married 'for the Sake of the Children'?"

Questions: What is best for the children? Should parents who bicker remain together for their children's sake? Let's have it out at once. We are going to address this issue from a psychological perspective only. Many readers believe—for moral reasons—that marriage and family life must be permanent, no matter what. Readers will have to consider the moral aspects of divorce in the light of their own value systems.

So—from a purely psychological perspective—what should bickering parents do? The answer seems to depend largely on how they behave in front of the children. Research shows that parental bickering—especially severe fighting—is linked to the same kinds of problems that children experience when their parents get separated or divorced (Furstenberg & Kiernan, 2001; Troxel & Matthews, 2004). Moreover, when children are exposed to marital conflict, they display a biological "alarm reaction": their heart rate, blood pressure, and sweating rise sharply (El-Sheikh & Harger, 2001). The bodily response is stronger yet when children blame themselves for parental conflict, as is common among younger children.

One study analyzed data from 727 children, aged four to nine years, from intact families and followed them six years later, when many of the families had undergone separation or divorce (Morrison & Coiro, 1999). Both separation and divorce were associated with increases in behaviour problems in children, regardless of the amount of conflict between the parents. However, in the marriages that remained intact, high levels of marital conflict were associated with yet more behaviour problems in the children. Message? Although separation and divorce are connected with adjustment problems in children, the outcome can be even worse for children when conflicted parents stay together. The problems caused by parents in conflict are further highlighted by studies that show that many psychological problems seen in the children of divorce were present before the breakup (Furstenberg & Kiernan, 2001; Kelly, 2000).

Because of the stresses experienced by children caught up in marital conflict, E. Mavis Hetherington suggested that "divorce is often a positive solution to destructive family functioning" (1989, p. 857). ***Truth or Fiction Revisited:*** From a psychological perspective, when bickering parents stay together "for the sake of the children," the children encounter stress.

What Are the Effects of Maternal Employment?

Let's be honest here. Why doesn't the caption read "What are the effects of parental employment?" The answer is that the vestiges of sexism run rampant in society. When things go wrong with children in families where both parents must work—or choose to work—the tendency remains to blame the mother. However, research shows that maternal employment is actually connected with few problems with children; it is also connected with more egalitarian attitudes. (Go, Mom!)

The Effects of Maternal Employment

Why is this section labelled "The Effects of Maternal Employment"? Why not "Parental Employment" or "Paternal Employment"? Perhaps because of the traditional (although changing) role of women as homemakers.

Even so, the past half-century has witnessed one of the most dramatic social changes in the history of North America. The work force participation rate of mothers with a youngest child between the ages of six and fifteen years old ranges from 74.4 percent in Newfoundland to 85.5 percent in Manitoba, with a Canadian average of 80.7 percent (Friendly, Beach, & Turiano, 2002). Family lifestyles have changed as more women combine maternal and occupational roles. *Question: What are the effects of maternal employment on children?* Do problems arise when mother is not available for round-the-clock love and attention?

A study by Judy Lupart, Canada research chair at the University of Alberta, and her colleagues, Elizabeth Cannon and Jo Ann Tefler (2004), found that adolescent males and females are conflicted about work and child rearing. They believe that both men and women should contribute equally to the daily income; however, this conflicts with the view that young children need their mothers most of the time. It is no wonder that adults making decisions about family choices, work, and education may feel pressured and overwhelmed.

Many psychologists and educators—and lay commentators—have been concerned about the effects of maternal employment on children. Part of the brouhaha has been based on traditionalist, moralistic values, which argue that the mother ought to

Province/Territory	Youngest child less than 3 years old		Youngest child 3–5 years old		Youngest child 6–15 years old	
	No. of mothers in the work force	%	No. of mothers in the work force	%	No. of mothers in the work force	%
Newfoundland and Labrador	7800	65.5	7300	71.6	24 200	77.3
Prince Edward Island	2900	80.6	2100	84.0	7700	86.5
Nova Scotia	16 300	76.2	12 500	76.7	45 200	81.6
New Brunswick	12 900	71.3	12 200	79.7	33 800	81.8
Quebec	141 600	74.1	114 700	78.5	360 000	82.7
Ontario	249 800	69.4	194 100	75.6	609 300	83.7
Manitoba	21 600	63.9	16 400	76.3	54 300	85.0
Saskatchewan	19 300	67.0	14 000	76.9	45 500	87.2
Alberta	63 200	62.5	42 800	68.7	151 700	81.0
British Columbia	65 900	64.3	54 600	75.7	184 400	79.4
Northwest Territories[1]	n/a	n/a	n/a	n/a	n/a	n/a
Nunavut[1]	n/a	n/a	n/a	n/a	n/a	n/a
Yukon Territory[1]	n/a	n/a	n/a	n/a	n/a	n/a
Canada[1] (calculated)	601 300	68.9	470 700	75.8	1 516 100	82.6

Work Force Participation of Mothers by Age Group of Youngest Child 2005 (rounded estimate)

[1] 2005 information for the Northwest Territories, Nunavut, and Yukon not available. Therefore, totals do not include these territories. For the most recent information for these territories, visit Statistics Canada's website.
Source: Friendly, Beach, & Turiano (2002).

remain in the home. But concern has also been based on research findings that suggest that maternal employment (and nonmaternal care) have some negative effects on children (Belsky, 2001). In our daycare section in Chapter 7, we reviewed the Canadian data indicating that quality outside-the-home child care is not detrimental to children's development, and in fact may be beneficial.

Political and moral arguments aside, there is little evidence that maternal employment harms children (Gottfried, Bathurst, & Gottfried, 1994; Harvey, 1999). Elizabeth Harvey (1999) and other researchers (Han, Waldfogel, & Brooks-Gunn, 2001) have examined data from the National Longitudinal Survey of Youth on the effects of early parental employment on children. The effects were minimal. Neither the timing nor the continuity of early maternal employment was consistently related to children's development. Harvey did find that working a greater number of hours was linked with slightly lower scores on measures of cognitive development through the age of nine and with slightly lower academic achievement scores before the age of seven. However, there was no connection between maternal employment and children's behaviour problems, compliance, or self-esteem. And now for the pluses: Harvey found that early parental employment was beneficial for single mothers and lower-income families. Why? It brought in cash, and increasing family income has positive effects on children's development.

Other researchers have found other family benefits for maternal employment. Maternal employment appears to benefit school-aged children by fostering greater independence and encouraging responsibility and competence (Hoffman & Youngblade, 1998). Both the sons and daughters of employed women appear to be more flexible in their gender-role stereotypes (Wright & Young, 1998). For example, sons of working women are more helpful with housework. ***Truth or Fiction Revisited:*** Daughters of employed women are more achievement oriented and do set higher career goals for themselves than daughters of nonworking women. Children with employed mothers also view their mothers as more competent.

There are other interesting findings on maternal employment. For example, Hoffman and Youngblade (1998) studied a sample of 365 mothers of third- and fourth-graders in an industrialized Midwestern (U.S.) city. They discovered that working-class full-time homemakers were more likely to be depressed than employed mothers. Feelings of depression were related to permissive and authoritarian parenting styles, suggesting that many financially stressed homemakers do not have the emotional resources to give their children the best possible rearing. Among middle-class mothers, employment was not related to mood or style of parenting. Greater family financial resources apparently lift the mood.

Employed mothers and their partners are more egalitarian in their distribution of household chores and in breadwinning. The fathers spend more time with the children than in single-earner families (Gottfried et al., 1994). Mothers with fulfilling work are happier with their lives (Jackson, 2000; Zaslow, Rabinovich, & Suwalsky, 1991). Happier mothers have better adjusted children (Scarr, 1998; Wright & Young, 1998).

Active Review

6. During the middle years, parents do (more or less?) monitoring of children's activities and provide less direct feedback than they did in the preschool years.

7. The children of lesbian and gay parents are most likely to be (heterosexual or homosexual?) in their sexual orientation.

8. Children of divorce most often experience (upward or downward?) movement in financial status.

9. Most children of divorce live with their (mothers or fathers?).

10. (Boys or Girls?) seem to have a harder time coping with divorce.

Reflect & Relate: Have you known children whose families have undergone divorce? What were (or are) the effects on the children?

Go to
W W W www.voyages1CE.nelson.com
for an interactive version of this review.

Peer Relationships

Families exert the most powerful influences on a child during his or her first few years. But as children move into middle childhood, their activities and interests become directed farther away from home. *Question: What is the influence of peers during middle childhood?* Peers take on increasing importance in middle childhood. Let us explore the ways in which peers socialize one another. Then we examine factors in peer acceptance and rejection. Finally, we see how friendships develop.

Peers as Socialization Influences

Peer relationships are a major part of growing up. Peers exert powerful socialization influences and pressures to conform (Hanlon, Bateman, Simon, O'Grady, & Carswell, 2004; Keddie, 2004). Even highly involved parents can provide children only with experience relating to adults. Children profit from experience relating to peers because peers have interests and skills that reflect being part of the same generation as the child. Peers differ as individuals, however. For all these reasons, peer experiences broaden children (Molinari & Corsaro, 2000).

Peers guide children and afford practice in sharing and cooperating, in relating to leaders, and in coping with aggressive impulses, including their own. Peers can be important confidants (Dunn, Davies, O'Connor, & Sturgess, 2001). Peers, like parents, help children learn what types of impulses—affectionate, aggressive, and so on—they can safely express and with whom. Children who are at odds with their parents can turn to peers as sounding boards. They can compare feelings and experiences they would not bring up in the home. When children share troubling ideas and experiences with peers, they often learn that friends have similar concerns. They realize that they are normal and not alone (Wentzel, Barry, & Caldwell, 2004).

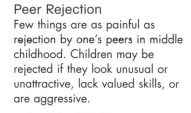

Find out how children rate their peers in terms of likability. To watch the video, click on the "Peer Acceptance" clip in Module 3, Section 3.

Peer Acceptance and Rejection

Acceptance or rejection by peers is of major importance in childhood because problems with peers are a harbinger of maladjustment later on (Wentzel et al., 2004). What are the characteristics of popular and rejected children?

Truth or Fiction Revisited: Popular children do tend to be attractive and relatively mature for their age, although attractiveness seems to be more important for girls than for boys (Jackson, 1992; Langlois et al., 2000). Socially speaking, popular children are friendly, nurturant, cooperative, helpful, and socially skillful (Chen et al., 2001; Newcomb, Bukowski, & Pattee, 1993). Popular children tend to lavishly dispense praise (Landau & Milich, 1990). Popular children have higher self-esteem than other children, which tends to reflect success in academics or valued extracurricular activities such as sports (Chen et al., 2001). Later-born children are more likely to be popular than firstborns, perhaps because they develop greater social skills (Hartup, 1983).

Children who show behavioural and learning problems, who are aggressive, and who disrupt group activities are more likely to be rejected by peers (Walter & LaFreniere, 2000). However, aggressive children who are also highly popular may be excused for their aggressive ways (Rose, Swenson, & Carlson, 2004). Moreover, aggressive children are more likely to seek out aggressive friends (A. J. Rose et al., 2004).

Although pressure to conform to group norms and standards can be powerful, most rejected children do not shape up. Instead, they tend to remain lonely—on the fringes of the group (Wentzel et al., 2004). Fortunately, training in social skills seems to help increase children's popularity (Cashwell, Skinner, & Smith, 2001; Webster-Stratton et al., 2001b).

Peer Rejection
Few things are as painful as rejection by one's peers in middle childhood. Children may be rejected if they look unusual or unattractive, lack valued skills, or are aggressive.

© Nancy Richmond / The Image Works

Development of Friendships

Question: How do children's concepts of friendship develop? In the early years of middle childhood, friendships are based on geographic closeness or proximity. Friendships are relatively

© Jason Stitt/Shutterstock, Inc.

Friendship, Friendship … A Perfect "Blendship"?
Children's concepts of friendship develop over time. In middle childhood, friendship is generally seen in terms of what children do for each other. These children are beginning to value loyalty and intimacy.

superficial—quickly formed, easily broken. What matters are shared activities and who has the swing set or sandbox. Five- to seven-year-olds usually report that their friends are the children with whom they share activities (Berndt & Perry, 1986; Epstein, 1989). There is little reference to friends' traits.

Between the ages of eight and eleven, children show increased recognition of the importance of friends meeting each other's needs and possessing desirable traits (Zarbatany, McDougall, & Hymel, 2000). Children at these ages are more likely to say that friends are nice to one another and share interests as well as things. During these years, children increasingly pick friends who are similar to themselves in behaviour and personality. Trustworthiness, mutual understanding, and a willingness to share personal information characterize friendships in middle childhood and beyond (Hamm, 2000; Rotenberg et al., 2004). Girls tend to develop closer friendships than boys (Zarbatany et al., 2000). Girls are more likely to seek confidants—girls with whom they can share their inmost feelings.

Robert Selman (1980) described five stages in children's changing concepts of friendship (see Table 13.3). The stages correspond to the five levels of perspective-taking skills discussed earlier in the chapter.

Friends behave differently with each other than they do with children who are not their friends. School-aged friends are more verbal, attentive, expressive, relaxed, and mutually responsive to each other during play than are children who are only acquaintances (Field et al., 1992). Cooperation occurs more readily between friends than between other groupings, as might be expected. But intense competition can also occur among friends, especially among boys (Hartup, 1993). When conflicts occur between friends, they tend to be less intense and are resolved in ways that maintain positive social interaction (Hartup, 1993; Laursen, 1993).

In one study, 696 fourth- and fifth-grade children responded to thirty hypothetical situations involving conflict with a friend (Rose & Asher, 1999). It was found that those children who responded to conflict by seeking revenge were least likely to have friendships or close friendships. Sex differences were also found. Girls were generally more interested in resolving conflicts than boys were. In another study, Rinaldi and Heath (2006) examined (1) the reports of conflict strategies and goals in response to hypothetical conflict situations, (2) generation of solutions to hypothetical conflicts, and (3) conflict in observed dyadic exchanges in a group of Canadian children with high and low depressive symptoms. These authors found that the two groups differed on the types of conflict strategies but not conflict goals chosen in hypothetical social problem-solving tasks. Also, children reporting depressive symptoms typically chose less effective strategies to solving social problems. In observed dyadic exchanges, the high depressive symptoms group employed more negative strategies than the low depressive symptoms group. Social and emotional functioning in the schools is being considered more closely than ever before, and understanding relationships as an integral part of education is being championed by Canadian researchers (e.g., Hymel, Schonert-Reichl, & Miller, 2006).

Children in middle childhood typically will tell you that they have more than one "best" friend (Berndt, Miller, & Park, 1989). One study found that nine-year-olds

	Table 13.3	*Stages in Children's Concepts of Friendship*		
Stage	Name	Approximate Age (Years)	Comments	
0	Momentary physical interaction	3–6	Children remain egocentric and unable to take one another's point of view. Thus, their concept of a friend is one who likes to play with the same things they do and who lives nearby.	
1	One-way assistance	5–9	Children realize that their friends may have different thoughts and feelings than they do, but they place their own desires first. They view a friend as someone who does what they want.	
2	Fairweather cooperation	7–12	Friends are viewed as doing things for one another (reciprocity), but the focus remains on each individual's self-interest rather than on the relationship per se.	
3	Intimate and mutual sharing	10–15	The focus is on the relationship itself, rather than on the individuals separately. The function of friendship is viewed as mutual support over a long period of time, rather than concern about a given activity or self-interest.	
4	Autonomous interdependence	12 and older	Children understand that friendships grow and change as people change. They realize that they may need different friends to satisfy different personal and social needs.	

Source: Selman (1980).

reported having an average of four best friends (Lewis & Feiring, 1989). Best friends tend to be more similar to each other than other friends (Epstein, 1989).

In middle childhood, girls and boys do not differ in number of best friends (Benenson, 1990; Krappmann, Oswald, Weiss, & Uhlendorff, 1993). Boys tend to play in larger groups than girls, however. By middle childhood, children's friendships are almost exclusively with others of the same sex, continuing the trend of sex segregation (Hartup, 1993; Krappmann et al., 1993).

During middle childhood, contact with members of the other sex is strongly discouraged by peers. Maccoby's (1998) review of children's in-school relationships revealed that children's best friends are almost always the same sex as themselves. It has been documented in some studies that children crossing the "sex boundary" was especially unpopular with their peers (Sroufe, Bennett, Englund, Urban, & Shulman,

Active Review

11. As children move into middle childhood, their activities and interests become directed (closer to or farther away from?) the home.

12. Popular children tend to be attractive and relatively (mature or immature?) for their age.

13. (Firstborn or Later-born?) children are more likely to be popular.

14. During middle childhood, contact with members of the other sex is (encouraged or discouraged?) by peers.

Reflect & Relate: What do you look for in a friend? What "stage" are you in, according to Table 13.3?

Go to

W W W **www.voyages1CE.nelson.com**
for an interactive version of this review.

1993). It should come as no surprise then that Serbin, Powlishta, and Gulko, (1993) found that 95 percent of elementary school children preferred same-sex peers.

The School

Question: What are the effects of the school on children's social and emotional development? The school exerts a powerful influence on many aspects of the child's development. Schools, like parents, set limits on behaviour, make demands for mature behaviour, attempt to communicate, and are oriented toward nurturing positive physical, social, and cognitive development. The schools, like parents, have a direct influence on children's IQ scores, achievement motivation, and career aspirations (Landau, 2004; Woolfolk-Hoy, 2004). As in the family, schools influence social and moral development (Landau, 2004; Woolfolk-Hoy, 2004).

Schools are also competitive environments, and children who do too well—and students who do not do well enough—can suffer from the resentment or the low opinion of others. An Italian study placed 178 male and 182 female eight- to nine-year-old elementary school students in competitive situations (Tassi et al., 2001). It was found that when the students were given the task of trying to outperform one another, competition led to social rejection by students' peers. On the other hand, when the students were simply asked to do the best they could, high rates of success led to admiration by one's peers.

In this section, we consider children's transition to school and then examine the effects of the school environment and of teachers.

Entry into School: Getting to Know You

An increasing number of children attend preschool. Almost half have had some type of formal prekindergarten experience (Landau, 2004; Woolfolk-Hoy, 2004). But most children first experience full-time schooling when they enter kindergarten or first grade. Children must master many new tasks when they start school. They will have to meet new academic challenges, learn new school and teacher expectations, and fit into a new peer group. They must learn to accept extended separation from parents and develop increased attention, self-control, and self-help skills.

What happens to children during the transition from home, child care, or preschool to elementary school may be critical for the eventual success or failure of their educational experience. This is particularly true for low-income children. Families of children living in poverty may be less able to supply both the material and emotional supports that help the child adjust successfully to school (Landau, 2004; Woolfolk-Hoy, 2004).

How well prepared are children to enter school? Discussions of school readiness must consider at least three critical factors:

• the diversity and inequity of children's early life experiences;
• individual differences in young children's development and learning; and
• the degree to which schools establish reasonable and appropriate expectations of children's capabilities when they enter school.

You may be surprised to know that kindergarten is not mandatory for children in all provinces. For example, in the province of Alberta, parents may choose not to place their child into a half-day kindergarten program. In contrast, in other provinces like New Brunswick and Nova Scotia, kindergarten is compulsory. In Canada, parents have the choice of placing their children in half-day programs, full-day programs, and also in preschool or junior kindergarten programs depending on where they live.

Nearly half the teachers thought that children entered school less ready to learn than children had been five years earlier. Most of the teachers said that children often lacked the language skills needed to succeed. This report and others (Landau, 2004; Woolfolk-Hoy, 2004) concluded that poor health care and nutrition and lack of adequate stimulation and support by parents place many children at risk for academic failure even before they enter school.

Magnuson, Meyers, Ruhm, and Waldfogel (2004) found that children who attended a school-based preschool program in the year before school entry performed better on assessments of reading and math skills upon beginning kindergarten, after

P/T	Program	Enrollment (5-Year-Olds If Not Specified)	Spending (2005/2006)	Other Features
Newfoundland	• Part-time	• 4956	Total n/a $7879 per K–12 student	• Kinderstart, a kindergarten orientation program for 4-year-olds
PEI	• Part-time • Delivered as part of regulated child-care centres	• 1409	Total $3.1M $2193 per child	
New Brunswick	• Full primary school day • Very limited provision for 4-year-olds • Compulsory	• 9056 (public only)	Total n/a $5967 per FTE K–12 student[1]	• 4 Plus program available for at-risk populations in Halifax • Pre-primary pilot program
Nova Scotia	• Full primary school day • Compulsory	• 7451	Total n/a $6911 per child	
Quebec	• Full-day—5-year-olds • Part-day—4-year-olds (There are two separate programs for 4-year-olds: pre-maternelle and passe-partout. Both of these were initiated for low-income children, though this is no longer the programs' sole clientele)	• 5-year-olds—69 000 (public), 4735 (private) • 4-year-olds—6103 pre-maternelle, 8500 passe-partout	Total n/a • $1728 per 5-year-old • $2124 per 4-year-old (pre-maternelle) • $1020 per 4-year-old (passe-partout)	• Kindergarten for 4-year-olds is no longer being developed but only maintained, as 4-year-olds may attend full-time child care

Table 13.4 *Selected Characteristics of Kindergarten Programs by Province or Territory*

[1] This is the 2003/04 figure. No information available for 2005/06.

Table 13.4   Selected Characteristics of Kindergarten Programs by Province or Territory

P/T	Program	Enrollment (5-Year-Olds If Not Specified)	Spending (2005/2006)	Other Features
Ontario	• Part-day, every day in most urban boards; full-day alternate day in some rural boards (all French and some Catholic boards have full-day for 5-year-olds and 4-year-olds) • Almost all boards provide kindergarten for 4-year-olds although it is not mandated	2005/06 • 5-year-olds—127 571 • 4-year-olds—113 053	Total • 5-year-olds— $535.9M • 4-year-olds— $504.9M • $4320 per 5-year-old • $4320 per 4-year-old (part-day rate)	• Both public and Catholic school systems • Best Start, Ontario's maternal, newborn, and early child development resource centre
Manitoba	• Part-day in most boards • Limited provision for 4-year-olds	• 5-year-olds—12 034 public, 761 funded independent • 4-year-olds—2127 public • 375 funded independent	Total n/a • $4233 (est.) per 5-year-old • Per four—n/a	
Saskatchewan	• Part-day 5-year-olds • 3- and 4-year-olds, vulnerable children in targeted communities (limited enrollment)	• 5-year-olds—10 552 • 4-year-olds—1600 (estimate—includes some 3-year-olds)	Total n/a • $2478 per 5-year-old (rural) • $2397 in Regina/ Saskatoon • $3022 per 4-year-old	• Provision is at the discretion of school boards • Both "public" and Catholic school systems
Alberta	• Part-day 5-year-olds • 2 1/2- to 4-year-olds with disabilities	• 5-year-olds—43 463[1] • 4-year-olds—n/a • 3-year-olds—n/a	Total n/a $2544 per child	• Can be delivered in public schools or by Early Childhood Services • Both public and Catholic school systems

Source: Friendly, Beach, & Turiano (2002).

P/T	Program	Enrollment (5-Year-Olds If Not Specified)	Spending (2005/2006)	Other Features
		Selected Characteristics of Kindergarten Programs by Province or Territory		
British Columbia	• Part-day 5-year-olds, some full-day special populations • Limited provision for 4-year-olds	• 35 319 (public only)	Total • $111 465 360 • $5520 per FTE child • $2760 per part-time child	
Northwest Territories	• Part-day or full-day 5-year-olds (decision is made by the Divisional Educational Council or the District Education Authority)	• 647[1]	Total • $4 206 000 • $13 400 (per FTE K–12 student)[2]	• Both public and Catholic school systems
Nunavut	• Part-day 5-year-olds	• 700	Total n/a • $10 521 (per FTE K–12 student)	• Kindergarten is delivered in Inuktitut
Yukon	• Full-day and part-day 5-year-olds • Limited provision for 4-year-olds	• 5-year-olds—374 • 4-year-olds—30	Total n/a • $12 581 (per K–12 student)	• Both public and Catholic school systems

[1] Includes both part-time and full-time students; breakdown unavailable.
[2] This amount excludes capital.
Source: Friendly, Beach, & Turiano (2002).

controlling for a host of family background and other factors that might be associated with selection into early-education programs and relatively high academic skills. This advantage persisted into the spring of kindergarten and first grade.

A study by the U.S. Department of Education concluded that schools could do a better job of easing the transition to kindergarten (Love, Logue, Trudeau, & Thayer, 1992). The researchers surveyed schools in 1003 school districts and also visited eight schools. The average school reported that between 10 and 20 percent of incoming kindergartners had difficulty adjusting to kindergarten. Adjusting to the academic demands of school was reported to be the area of greatest difficulty. Children whose families were low in socioeconomic status had a more difficult time adjusting than other children, particularly in academics. Sad to say, children who enter school with deficits in language and math skills generally continue to show deficits in these areas during at least the first years of school (Landau, 2004; Woolfolk-Hoy, 2004). Is this also a concern for Canadians? A Canadian study by Kirby, Parrila, and Pfeiffer (2003) conducted with kindergarten children revealed that phonological awareness and naming speed predicted subsequent reading development over the course of the elementary school years quite well. Are children to acquire these prekindergarten skills at home, in preschool, in formal or informal programs? The choice for the most part is up to parents.

The School Environment: Setting the Stage for Success or ...

Question: What are the characteristics of a good school? Research summaries (Landau, 2004; Snowden & Gorton, 2002) indicate that an effective school has the following characteristics:

- an active, energetic principal;
- an atmosphere that is orderly but not oppressive;
- empowerment of teachers—that is, teachers participating in decision making;
- teachers who have high expectations that children will learn;
- a curriculum that emphasizes academics;
- frequent assessment of student performance; and
- empowerment of students—that is, students participating in setting goals, making classroom decisions, and engaging in cooperative learning activities with other students.

Certain aspects of the school environment are important as well. One key factor is class size. Smaller classes permit students to receive more individual attention and to express their ideas more often (Landau, 2004). Smaller classes lead to increased achievement in mathematics and reading in the early primary grades. Smaller classes are particularly useful in teaching the "basics"—reading, writing, and arithmetic—to elementary school students at risk for academic failure (Landau, 2004; Woolfolk-Hoy, 2004). Another component, being termed as the "fourth *r*"—the relationship factor—is often overlooked in educational settings; however, it is clearly an area that warrants serious attention (Hymel et al., 2006). The nearby "A Closer Look" feature provides insight into the problem of aggression and bullying in our schools.

Teachers: Setting Limits, Making Demands, Communicating Values, and Teaching the Subject Matter

The influence of the schools is mainly due to teachers. Teachers, like parents, set limits, make demands, communicate values, and foster development. Teacher-student relationships are more limited than parent-child relationships, but teachers still have the opportunity to serve as powerful role models and dispensers of reinforcement. After all, children spend several hours each weekday in the presence of teachers.

Teacher Influences on Student Performance

Many aspects of teacher behaviour are related to student achievement (Landau, 2004). Achievement is enhanced when teachers expect students to master the curriculum, allocate most of the available time to academic activities, and manage the classroom environment effectively. Students learn more in classes when actively instructed or supervised by teachers than when working on their own. The most effective teachers ask questions, give personalized feedback, and provide opportunities for drill and practice, as opposed to straight lecturing.

Student achievement also is linked to the emotional climate of the classroom (Landau, 2004). Students do not do as well when teachers rely heavily on criticism, ridicule, threats, or punishment. Achievement is high in classrooms with a pleasant, friendly atmosphere but not in classrooms with extreme teacher warmth.

Nine-year-old Gabrielle did not want to go to school. As with many other children who refuse to go to school, she showed anxiety at the thought of leaving home. But Gabrielle was not experiencing separation anxiety from her family. It turns out that she had gotten into a disagreement with Shoshana, and Shoshana had told her she would beat her mercilessly if she showed up at school again. To highlight her warning, Shoshana had shoved Gabrielle across the hall.

Gabrielle was a victim of bullying. Shoshana was a bully. Gabrielle did not know it, but there was something of an irony. Shoshana was also bullied from time to time by a couple of girls at school.

Was there something unusual about all this? Not really. Boys are more likely than girls to be bullies, but many girls engage in bullying (Baldry, 2003; Griffin & Gross, 2004; Richter & Barbara, 2003). All in all, it is estimated that 10 percent of students have been exposed to extreme bullying, and that 70 to 75 percent of students overall have been bullied (Elias & Zins, 2003; Richter & Barbara, 2003; Swearer & Cary, 2003).

Bullying has devastating effects on the school atmosphere. It transforms the perception of school as a safe place into one of a violent place (Laufer & Harel, 2003; Nansel, Haynie, & Simons-Morton, 2003). Even bullies come to perceive the school as a violent environment (Laufer & Harel, 2003). Bullying also impairs adjustment to junior high, where bullying is sometimes carried out by older children against younger children (Nansel et al., 2003). It especially impairs adjustment for children who speak another language in the home, who tend to be picked on more often (Yu, Huang, Schwalberg, Overpeck, & Kogan, 2003).

Many but not all bullies have some things in common. For one thing, their achievement tends to be lower than average, such that peer approval (or deference from peers) might be more important to them than academics (Laufer & Harel, 2003; Pereira, Mendonça, Neto, Valente, & Smith, 2004). Bullies are more likely to come from homes of lower socioeconomic status (Baldry, 2003; Pereira et al., 2004). Many of these homes are characterized by violence between parents (Baldry, 2003).

Numerous studies have also investigated the personalities of bullies. One American study compared middle-school (grades six through eight) bullies to matched control students (Coolidge, DenBoer, & Segal, 2004). Bullying was associated with more frequent diagnoses of conduct disorder, oppositional defiant disorder, attention-deficit/hyperactivity disorder, and depression. Bullies were also more likely to have personality problems, such as assuming that others were predisposed to harming them. They also showed more problems in impulse control.

Is there any "cure" for bullying? School systems and families have a stake in controlling bullying, and sometimes setting strict limits on bullies is of help. But much—or most—bullying goes unreported, sometimes because children are embarrassed to admit they are being bullied, sometimes because they fear retaliation by the bully. Many children simply learn to accommodate or avoid bullies until they are out of school (Hunter & Boyle, 2004). Then they go their separate ways.

Canadians are taking the lead in anti-bullying prevention, intervention, research, and education. Debra Pepler from York University and her colleagues have been involved in establishing PREVNet (Promoting Relationships and Eliminating Violence), a network of Canadian researchers and child/youth-focused national organizations with the vision of stopping bullying in Canada. PREVNet is funded through the Networks of Centres of Excellence New Initiative program. Within PREVNet, Canadian researchers and education advocates have begun a dialogue to promote safe and healthy relationships for all Canadian children and youth. As Pepler and Craig (2000) point out, the following messages about bullying need to be communicated:

- Bullying is wrong and hurtful.
- Bullying is a relationship problem.
- Promoting relationships and eliminating violence are everyone's responsibility.

For in-depth discussion of these key messages, visit http://www.nce.gc.ca/nces-rces/prevnet_e.htm. Other sources of information include

- http://www.bullying.org,
- http://www.cipb.ca/index.html
- http://www.cyberbullying.ca

© Cindy Charles / Photoedit

Bullying
For victims of bullying, the school can become a violent place rather than a safe one. Although many schools and families try to control bullying, much of it goes unreported.

Pygmalion effect A self-fulfilling prophecy; an expectation that is confirmed because of the behaviour of those who hold the expectation.

self-fulfilling prophecy An event that occurs because of the behaviour of those who expect it to occur.

sexism Discrimination or bias against people based on their sex.

Teacher Expectations

There is a saying that "You find what you're looking for." Consider the so-called **Pygmalion effect** in education. In Greek mythology, the amorous sculptor Pygmalion breathed life into a beautiful statue he had carved. Similarly, in the musical *My Fair Lady*, a reworking of the Pygmalion legend, Henry Higgins fashions a great lady from the lower-class Eliza Doolittle.

Teachers also try to bring out positive traits that they believe dwell within their students. ***Truth or Fiction Revisited:*** A classic experiment by Robert Rosenthal and Lenore Jacobson (1968) suggested that teacher expectations can become **self-fulfilling prophecies.** As reported in *Pygmalion in the Classroom,* Rosenthal and Jacobson (1968) first gave students a battery of psychological tests. Then they informed teachers that a handful of the students, although average in performance to date, were about to blossom forth intellectually in the current school year.

Now, in fact, the tests had indicated nothing in particular about the "chosen" children. These children had been selected at random. The purpose of the experiment was to determine whether changing teacher expectations could affect student performance. As it happened, the identified children made significant gains in intelligence test scores.

In subsequent research, however, results have been mixed. Some studies have found support for the Pygmalion effect (Madon et al., 2001). Others have not. A review of eighteen such experiments found that the Pygmalion effect was most pronounced when the procedure for informing teachers of the potential in the target student had greatest credibility (Raudenbusch, 1984). A fair conclusion would seem to be that teacher expectations sometimes, but not always, affect students' motivation, self-esteem, expectations for success, and achievement.

These findings have serious implications for children from ethnic minority and low-income families. There is some indication that teachers expect less academically from children in these groups (Landau, 2004; Woolfolk-Hoy, 2004). Teachers with lower expectations for certain children may spend less time encouraging and interacting with them.

What are some of the ways that teachers can help motivate *all* students to do their best? Anita Woolfolk-Hoy (2004) suggested the following:

- Make the classroom and the lesson interesting and inviting.
- Ensure that students can profit from social interaction.
- Make the classroom a safe and pleasant place.
- Recognize that students' backgrounds can give rise to diverse patterns of needs.
- Help students take appropriate responsibility for their successes and failures.
- Encourage students to perceive the links between their own efforts and their achievements.
- Help students set attainable short-term goals.

Sexism in the Classroom

Although girls were systematically excluded from formal education for centuries, today we might not expect to find **sexism** among teachers. Teachers, after all, are generally well educated. They are also trained to be fair minded and sensitive to the needs of their young charges in today's changing society.

However, we may not have heard the last of sexism in our schools. According to a review of more than 1000 publications about girls and education, girls are treated unequally by their teachers, their male peers, the school curriculum, and standardized tests (American Association of University Women, 1992). Among the conclusions of the reviewers were these (Chira, 1992a):

- Teachers pay less attention to girls than boys.
- Girls are subjected to increasing **sexual harassment**—unwelcome verbal or physical conduct of a sexual nature—from male classmates. Many teachers continue to tolerate such behaviour.
- School textbooks still stereotype or ignore women. Students learn almost nothing in school about problems such as discrimination and sexual abuse.
- Some standardized tests, such as the SAT in the U.S., are biased against girls, hurting their chances of getting into college and getting scholarships.

sexual harassment Unwelcome verbal or physical conduct of a sexual nature.

In a widely cited study, Myra and David Sadker (1994) observed students in fourth-, sixth-, and eighth-grade classes in four states and in the District of Columbia. Teachers and students were European American and African American, urban, suburban, and rural. In almost all cases, the findings were depressingly similar. Boys generally dominated classroom communication, whether the subject was math (a traditionally "masculine" area) or language arts (a traditionally "feminine" area). Boys, in fact, were eight times more likely than girls to call out answers without raising their hands. So far, it could be said, we have evidence of a sex difference, but not of sexism. However, teachers were less than impartial in responding to boys and girls when they called out. Teachers, male and female, were significantly more likely to accept calling out from boys. Girls were significantly more likely, as the song goes, to receive "teachers' dirty looks"—or to be reminded that they should raise their hands and wait to be called on. Boys, it appears, are expected to be impetuous, but girls are reprimanded for "unladylike behaviour." Sad to say, until they saw tapes of themselves, the teachers generally were unaware that they were treating girls and boys differently.

Waiting to Be Called On
Who is the teacher most likely to call on? Some studies say that teachers may unconsciously favour the boy and call on him before the girl.

Other studies show that elementary and secondary teachers give more active teaching attention to boys than to girls. They call on boys more often, ask them more questions, talk to and listen to them more, give them lengthier directions, and praise and criticize them more often (Landau, 2004; Snowden & Gorton, 2002; Woolfolk-Hoy, 2004).

Others argue the exact opposite—that we are not connecting with our boys early enough. In early childhood education and elementary school programs, most teachers are females, and that means boys have very few role models. In fact, there is growing concern by some researchers and professionals that boys struggle in early education (Gurian & Stevens, 2005; Kindlon & Thompson, 2002; Pollack, 2002; Sadker & Sadker, 2002). Rather than see this as a "girls versus boys" issue, it would be more helpful to view education as providing all students (male or female) with opportunities to learn and express themselves in a safe and caring environment. Easier said than done, right?

Active Review

15. Children whose families are (high or low?) in socioeconomic status have a more difficult time adjusting to school.

16. (Smaller or Larger?) classes facilitate learning during middle childhood.

17. An experiment by Rosenthal and Jacobson suggests that teacher expectations can become _____ prophecies.

18. (Boys or Girls?) tend to be favoured by teachers in the classroom.

Reflect & Relate: Do you remember what it was like for you to enter school at kindergarten or first grade? Did you experience some adjustment problems? What were they?

Go to

W W W **www.voyages1CE.nelson.com**
for an interactive version of this review.

Social and Emotional Problems

There is sparse Canadian data on the prevalence of emotional and behavioural difficulties in the schools, and what little documentation we do have shows that Canadian rates fall considerably below reported U.S. rates. From American sources, a significant percentage of children (10 to 15 percent) experience emotional and behavioural difficulties (Briggs-Gowan et al., 2001; Roberts et al., 1998), and rates nearly double once children enter educational settings, with reports of 15 percent of preschool and 20 percent of school-aged children demonstrating difficulties (Dogra et al., 2002; Kramer & Garralda, 2000). In comparison, two different Canadian survey studies report that 0.49 to 0.79 percent of the school-aged population experience E/BD (Dworet & Rathgeber, 1998; Weber, 1994). Clearly, definitions influence prevalence rates; therefore, Canadian rates vary from province to province. Many school-aged children who suffer from emotional or behavioural problems could profit from professional treatment, but most of them are unlikely to receive help. What are some of the more common psychological problems of middle childhood? In previous chapters, we examined attention-deficit/hyperactivity disorder (AD/HD) and learning disabilities. Here, we focus on those problems more likely to emerge during middle childhood: conduct disorders, depression, and anxiety. We use the terminology in the *Diagnostic and Statistical Manual* (DSM-IV) of the American Psychiatric Association (2000) because it is the most widely used index of psychological disorders.

Conduct Disorders

David is a sixteen-year-old high school dropout. He has just been arrested for the third time in two years for stealing video equipment and computers from people's homes. Acting alone, David was caught in each case when he tried to sell the stolen items. In describing his actions in each crime, David expressed defiance and showed a lack of remorse. In fact, he bragged about how often he had gotten away with similar crimes.

—Adapted from Halgin & Whitbourne (1993, p. 335)

David has **a conduct disorder.** *Questions: What are conduct disorders? What can we do about them?* Children with conduct disorders, like David, persistently break rules or violate the rights of others. They exhibit behaviours such as lying, stealing, fire setting, truancy, cruelty to animals, and fighting (American Psychiatric Association, 2000). To receive this diagnosis, children must engage in the behaviour pattern for at least six months. Conduct disorders typically emerge by eight years of age and are much more prevalent in boys.

Children with conduct disorders are often involved in sexual activity before puberty and smoke, drink, and abuse other substances (American Psychiatric Association, 2000). They have a low tolerance for frustration and may have temper flare-ups. They tend to blame other people for their scrapes (Schultz & Shaw, 2003). They believe that they are misunderstood and treated unfairly. Academic achievement is usually below grade level, but intelligence is usually at least average. Many children with conduct disorders are also diagnosed with AD/HD (Decker, McIntosh, Kelly, A. M., Nicholls, & Dean, 2001; Drabick, Gadow, Carlson, & Bromet, 2004; Hudziak, 2001).

Conduct disorders tend to endure. One longitudinal study found that children who show conduct disorders in kindergarten through third grade have more contacts with police in adolescence (Spivack, Marcus, & Swift, 1986). Children with conduct disorders are more likely to be antisocial and to abuse substances as adults (Ihle, Esser, Schmidt, & Blanz, 2000).

conduct disorders Disorders marked by persistent breaking of the rules and violations of the rights of others.

Origins of Conduct Disorders

Conduct disorders may have a genetic component (Hudziak, 2001). They are more likely to be found among the biological parents than the adoptive parents of adopted children with such problems (Langbehn & Cadoret, 2001). Other contributors include antisocial family members, deviant peers, inconsistent discipline, parental insensitivity to the child's behaviour, physical punishment, and family stress (Curtner-Smith, 2000; Eddy & Chamberlain, 2000; Kilgore, Snyder, & Lentz, 2000; Straus, 2000).

Treatment of Conduct Disorders

The treatment of conduct disorders is challenging, but it would seem that cognitive-behavioural techniques involving parent training hold promise (Cavell, 2001; Kazdin, 2000; Kazdin & Wassell, 2000; O'Reilly & Dillenburger, 2000). Children with conduct disorders profit from interventions in which their behaviour is monitored closely, there are consequences (such as time-outs) for unacceptable behaviour, physical punishment is avoided, and positive social behaviour is rewarded. That is, rather than just targeting noncompliant behaviour, it is useful to attend to children when they are behaving properly and to reward them for doing so (Cavell, 2001).

Other approaches include teaching aggressive children methods for coping with feelings of anger that will not violate the rights of others. One promising cognitive-behavioural method teaches children social skills and how to use problem solving to manage interpersonal conflicts (Webster-Stratton et al., 2001b). Desirable social skills include asking other children to stop annoying behaviour rather than hitting them. Children are also taught to "stop and think" before engaging in aggressive behaviour. They are encouraged to consider the outcomes of their behaviour and find acceptable ways to reach their goals.

© Bill Aron/PhotoEdit

Treating Conduct Disorder
Treatment of conduct disorder is a complex process involving monitoring the behaviour of the child, creating negative consequences (such as time-outs) for unacceptable behaviour, avoiding physical punishment, and rewarding positive social behaviour.

Childhood Depression

> Kristin, an eleven-year-old, feels "nothing is working out for me." For the past year, she has been failing in school, although she previously had been a B student. She has trouble sleeping, feels tired all the time, and has started refusing to go to school. She cries easily and thinks her peers are making fun of her because she is "ugly and stupid." Her mother recently found a note written by Kristin that said she wanted to jump in front of a car "to end my misery."
>
> —Adapted from Weller & Weller (1991, p. 655)

Childhood is the happiest time of life, correct? Not necessarily. Many children are happy enough—protected by their parents and unencumbered by adult responsibilities. From the perspective of aging adults, their bodies seem made of rubber and free of aches. Their energy is apparently boundless.

Yet many children, like Kristin, are depressed. *Questions: What is depression? What can we do about it?* Depressed children may feel sad, blue, down in the dumps. They may show poor appetite, insomnia, lack of energy and inactivity, loss of self-esteem, difficulty concentrating, loss of interest in people and activities they usually enjoy, crying, feelings of hopelessness and helplessness, and thoughts of suicide (American Psychiatric Association, 2000).

But many children do not recognize depression in themselves until the age of seven or so. Part of the problem is cognitive developmental. The capacity for concrete operations apparently contributes to children's abilities to perceive internal feeling states (Glasberg & Aboud, 1982).

When children cannot report their feelings, depression is inferred from behaviour. Depressed children in middle childhood engage in less social activity and have poorer social skills than peers (American Psychiatric Association, 2000). In some cases, childhood depression is "masked" by conduct disorders, physical complaints, academic problems, and anxiety.

It has been estimated that between 5 and 9 percent of children are seriously depressed in any given year (American Psychiatric Association, 2000). In a recent study conducted in the Montreal area, out of 315 participants from grades four, five, and six, 18.1 percent reported depressive symptoms (Rinaldi, 2002). Those students who identified more depressive symptoms tended to choose less effective social problem strategies. Depression occurs equally often in girls and boys during childhood but is more common among women later in life. Children with depression frequently continue to have depressive episodes as adolescents and adults.

Origins of Depression

The origins of depression are complex and varied. Psychological and biological explanations have been proposed.

Some social cognitive theorists explain depression in terms of relationships between competencies (knowledge and skills) and feelings of self-esteem. Children who gain academic, social, and other competencies usually have high self-esteem. Perceived low levels of competence are linked to helplessness, low self-esteem, and depression. A four-year longitudinal study of 631 elementary school children found that problems in academics, socializing, physical appearance, and sports could predict feelings of depression: (Cole, Jacquez, & Maschman, 2001). Conversely, it was found that self-perceived competence in these areas was negatively related to feelings of depression four years later (Cole et al., 2001). That is, competence appears to "protect" children from depression.

© Johnathan M. Thomas/Shutterstock, Inc.

Childhood Depression Depressed children may complain of poor appetite, insomnia, lack of energy, difficulty concentrating, loss of interest in other people and activities they used to like, and feelings of worthlessness. But many depressed children do not recognize feelings of sadness. In some cases, childhood depression is "masked" by physical complaints, academic problems, and anxiety—even conduct disorders.

Children who have not developed competencies because of lack of opportunity, inconsistent parental reinforcement, and so on may develop feelings of helplessness and hopelessness. Similarly, a study by Reinecke and DuBois (2001) found that stressful life events, daily hassles, and poor problem-solving ability give rise to helplessness and hopelessness. These ideas, in turn, triggered depression. In contrast, social support and self-confidence tend to protect children from depression (Reinecke & DuBois, 2001). Some competent children might not credit themselves because of excessive parental expectations. Or children may be perfectionistic themselves. Perfectionistic children may be depressed because they cannot meet their own standards.

Children in elementary school are likely to be depressed because of situational stresses, such as family problems. Among middle-schoolers, however, we find cognitive contributors to depression. For example, a study of 582 Chinese children from Hong Kong secondary schools found that cognitive distortions, such as minimizing accomplishments and blowing problems out of proportion, were associated with feelings of depression (Leung & Poon, 2001). A European study found that ruminating about problems (going over them again and again—and again), blaming oneself for things that are not one's fault, and blowing problems out of proportion are linked with depression (Garnefski, Kraaij, & Spinhoven, 2001).

A tendency to blame oneself (an *internal* attribution) or others (an *external* attribution) is called a child's **attributional style.** Certain attributional styles can contribute to helplessness and hopelessness and hence to depression (Kagan, MacLeod, & Pote, 2004; Runyon & Kenny, 2002).

Truth or Fiction Revisited: It is true that some children blame themselves for all the problems in their lives, whether they deserve the blame or not. Research shows that children who are depressed are more likely to attribute the causes of their failures to *internal, stable,* and *global* factors—factors they are relatively helpless to change (Lewinsohn, Rohde, Seeley, Klein, & Gotlib, 2000b). Helplessness triggers depression. Consider the case of two children who do poorly on a math test. Sanjay thinks, "I'm a jerk! I'm just no good in math! I'll never learn." Gianmarco thinks, "That test was tougher than I thought it would be. I'll have to work harder next time." Sanjay is perceiving the problem as *global* (he's "a jerk") and *stable* (he'll "never learn"). Gianmarco perceives the problem as *specific* rather than global (related to the type of math test the teacher makes up) and as *unstable* rather than stable (he can change the results by working harder). In effect, Sanjay thinks, "It's me" (an internal attribution). By contrast, Gianmarco thinks, "It's the test" (an external attribution). Depressed children tend to explain negative events in terms of internal, stable, and global causes. As a result, they, like Sanjay, are more likely than Gianmarco to be depressed.

When it comes to attributions, children can endorse an incremental view of ability, in which they believe that ability can and does improve with effort, while others endorse an entity view of ability, where they believe that ability is relatively permanent and unchangeable (Dweck, 2000). Over time, individuals develop predictable patterns of attributions and expectations for future performance in academic, sports, and leisure activities as well as social ability. Certain children develop a mastery orientation, which is the belief that one is capable of accomplishing challenging tasks. Others, unfortunately, as we discussed at the beginning of the chapters, develop a general belief that they are incapable of accomplishing tasks and feel they have little to no control over their environment (i.e., learned helplessness).

There is also evidence of genetic factors in depression (Nurnberger et al., 2001; Sullivan et al., 2000). For example, the children of depressed parents are at greater risk for depression and other disorders (Hudziak, 2001; Jang, Livesley, Taylor, Stein, & Moon, 2004; Korszun et al., 2004). The agreement rate for depression is about 75 percent for identical twins compared with only 19 percent for fraternal twins

attributional style The way in which one is disposed toward interpreting outcomes (successes or failures), as in tending to place blame or responsibility on oneself or on external factors.

serotonin A neurotransmitter that is implicated in depression.

(Weller & Weller, 1991). On a neurological level, evidence suggests that depressed children (and adults) "underutilize" the neurotransmitter **serotonin** (Yatham et al., 2000). Learned helplessness is linked to lower serotonin levels in the brains of humans and rats (Wu et al., 1999).

Treatment of Depression

Parents and teachers can do a good deal to alleviate relatively mild feelings of depression among children. They can involve children in enjoyable activities, encourage the development of skills, offer praise when appropriate, and point out when children are being too hard on themselves. But if feelings of depression persist, treatment is called for.

Psychotherapy for depression tends to be mainly cognitive behavioural these days, and it is often straightforward. Children (and adolescents) are encouraged to do enjoyable things and build social skills. They are made aware of their tendencies to minimize their accomplishments, catastrophize their problems, and overly blame themselves for shortcomings (e.g., Ellis & Dryden, 1996).

We noted that many depressed children underutilize the neurotransmitter serotonin. Antidepressant medication (selective serotonin reuptake inhibitors, or SSRIs), such as Luvox, Prozac, and Zoloft, increase the action of serotonin in the brain and are sometimes used to treat childhood depression. Studies of their effectiveness yield a mixed review, ranging from something like "deadly dangerous" to "often effective" (Harris, 2004; Wagner & Ambrosini, 2001; Walkup et al., 2003). Walkup and his colleagues (2003) found that SSRIs are effective much of the time. However, in 2004, the U.S. Food and Drug Administration warned that there may be a link between use of SSRIs and suicidal thinking in children (Harris, 2004).

Childhood depression is frequently accompanied by anxiety (Masi et al., 2004), as we will see in the next section. Social and emotional problems that tend to emerge in middle childhood are summarized in Concept Review 13.1.

Childhood Anxiety

generalized anxiety disorder (GAD) An anxiety disorder in which anxiety appears to be present continuously and is unrelated to the situation.

phobia An irrational, excessive fear that interferes with one's functioning.

separation anxiety disorder (SAD) An extreme form of otherwise normal separation anxiety that is characterized by anxiety about separating from parents; SAD often takes the form of refusal to go to school.

obsessive-compulsive disorder (OCD) An anxiety disorder characterized by obsessions (recurring thoughts or images that seem beyond control) and compulsions (irresistible urges to repeat an act, such as hand washing or checking that one has put one's homework in one's backpack).

Children show many kinds of anxiety disorders, and these disorders are accompanied by depression in 50 to 60 percent of children (Masi et al., 2004). Yet many children show anxiety disorders, such as **generalized anxiety disorder (GAD),** in the absence of depression (Masi et al., 2004). Other anxiety disorders shown by children include **phobias** such as **separation anxiety disorder (SAD)** and stage fright.

Obsessive-Compulsive Disorder

A cross-cultural study compared anxiety disorders in 862 German children and 975 Japanese children between the ages of eight and twelve (Essau, Sakano, Ishikawa, & Sasagawa, 2004). The German children were significantly more likely to report generalized anxiety, separation anxiety, social phobias, and **obsessive-compulsive disorder (OCD)**. The Japanese children were more likely to report physical complaints and phobias in the realm of bodily injury. In both nations, girls were more likely than boys to report anxieties.

Separation Anxiety Disorder

It is normal for children to show anxiety when they are separated from their caregivers. Separation anxiety is a normal feature of the child–caregiver relationship and begins during the first year. But the sense of security that is usually provided by bonds of attachment encourages children to explore their environments and become progressively independent of caregivers. *Question: What is separation anxiety disorder?*

SAD is diagnosed when separation anxiety is persistent and excessive, when it is inappropriate for the child's developmental level, and when it interferes with the activities or development tasks—most important, attending school. Six-year-olds ought to be able to enter first grade without anxiety-related nausea and vomiting and without dread that they or their parents will come to harm. Children with SAD tend to cling to their parents and follow them around the house. They may voice concerns about death and dying and insist that someone stay with them while they are falling asleep. They may complain of nightmares, stomach-aches, and nausea and vomiting on school days. They may plead with their parents not to leave the house, or they may throw tantrums.

SAD may occur before middle childhood, preventing adjustment to daycare or nursery school. In adolescence, refusal to attend school is often connected with academic and social problems, in which cases, the label of SAD would not apply. SAD usually becomes a significant problem in middle childhood because that is when children are expected to adjust to school. The disorder may persist into adulthood, leading to an exaggerated concern about the well-being of one's children and spouse and difficulty tolerating any separation from them.

SAD frequently develops after a stressful life event, such as illness, the death of a relative or pet, or a change of schools or homes. Zana's problems followed the death of her grandmother:

> Zana's grandmother died when Zana was seven years old. Her parents decided to permit her request to view her grandmother in the open coffin. Zana took a tentative glance from her father's arms across the room, and then asked to be taken out of the room. Her five-year-old sister took a leisurely close-up look, with no apparent distress.
>
> Zana had been concerned about death for two or three years by this time, but her grandmother's passing brought on a new flurry of questions: "Will I die?" "Does everybody die?" and so on. Her parents tried to reassure her by saying, "Grandma was very, very old, and she also had a heart condition. You are very young and in perfect health. You have many, many years before you have to start thinking about death."
>
> Zana also could not be alone in any room in her house. She pulled one of her parents or her sister along with her everywhere she went. She reported nightmares about her grandmother and, within a couple of days, insisted on sleeping in the same room with her parents. Fortunately, Zana's fears did not extend to school. Her teacher reported that Zana spent some time talking about her grandmother, but her academic performance was apparently unimpaired.
>
> Zana's parents decided to allow Zana time to "get over" the loss. Zana gradually talked less and less about death, and by the time three months had passed, she was able to go into any room in her house by herself. She wanted to continue to sleep in her parents' bedroom, however. So her parents "made a deal" with her. They would put off the return to her own bedroom until the school year had ended (a month away), if Zana would agree to return to her own bed at that time. As a further incentive, a parent would remain with her until she fell asleep for the first month. Zana overcame the anxiety problem in this fashion with no additional delays.

—From Rathus's files

Concept Review 13.1 — Social and Emotional Problems That May Emerge During Middle Childhood

Problem	Behaviour Patterns	Comments
Conduct disorders 	• Precocious sexual activity, substance abuse • Truancy, stealing, lying, and aggression	• More common in boys • Child blames others for problems • Probably connected with genetic factors • Other contributors—antisocial family members, deviant peers, inconsistent discipline, physical punishment, family stress • Tends to be stable throughout adolescence and into adulthood • Frequently accompanied by AD/HD
Childhood depression 	• Feelings of sadness, poor appetite, insomnia, lack of energy and inactivity, loss of self-esteem, difficulty concentrating, loss of interest in people and activities, crying, feelings of hopelessness and helplessness, and thoughts of suicide • Can be masked by conduct disorders, physical complaints, academic problems, and anxiety	• Occurs about equally in both sexes • Connected with lack of competencies (knowledge and skills) • Connected with situational stresses, such as divorce • Connected with feelings of helplessness and hopelessness • Connected with cognitive factors such as perfectionism, rumination, minimization of achievements, blowing problems out of proportion, and a negative attributional style—internal, stable, and global attributions for failures • Possibly connected with genetic factors • Connected with "underutilization" of the neurotransmitter serotonin • Frequently accompanied by anxiety
Childhood anxiety: • Phobias (e.g., separation anxiety disorder, stage fright, school phobia) • Panic disorder • Generalized anxiety disorder • Obsessive–compulsive disorder • Stress disorders	• Persistent, excessive worrying • Fear of the worst happening • Anxiety inappropriate for child's developmental level • Physical symptoms such as stomach-aches, nausea, and vomiting • Nightmares • Concerns about death and dying	• More common in girls • Genetic factors implicated • Frequently develops after stressful life events, such as divorce, illness, death of relative or pet, or change of schools or homes • Often overlaps with—but not the same as—school refusal • Frequently accompanied by depression

Separation Anxiety Disorder, School Phobia, and School Refusal

*Question: **What are the connections between separation anxiety disorder, school phobia, and school refusal?*** SAD is similar to but not the same as *school phobia.* SAD is an extreme form of separation anxiety. It is characterized by anxiety about separating from parents and may be expressed as **school phobia**—which means *fear* of school—or of refusal to go to school (which can be based on fear or other factors). Separation anxiety—fear—is not behind all instances of school refusal. Some children refuse school because they perceive it as unpleasant, unsatisfying, or hostile—and sometimes it is. Some children are concerned about doing poorly in school or being asked to answer questions in class (in which case, they might be suffering from the social phobia of stage fright). High parental expectations to perform may heighten concern. Other children may refuse school because of problems with classmates (Ishikawa, Oota, & Sakano, 2003).

There is a strong but incomplete overlap between SAD and school refusal. First, epidemiological studies indicate that SAD affects about 4 to 5 percent of children and that it is more common among girls (American Psychiatric Association, 2000; Masi, Mucci, & Millepiedi, 2001). School refusal is reported in about 75 percent of children with SAD, and SAD is reported to occur in as many as 80 percent of those children who refuse to go to school.

*Question: **What can we do about school phobia or school refusal?***

Treatment of School Phobia or School Refusal

Truth or Fiction Revisited: It is usually *not* better for children with school phobia to remain at home until the origins of the problem are uncovered and resolved. A phobia is an irrational or overblown fear—out of proportion to any danger in the situation. Therefore, one need not protect the child from school phobia. Most professionals agree that the first rule in the treatment of school phobia is this: Get the child back into school. The second rule is: Get the child back into school. The third rule ... Even without investigating the "meanings" of the child's refusal to attend school, many of the "symptoms" of the disorder disappear once the child is back in school on a regular basis.

Put it this way. There is nothing wrong with trying to understand why a child refuses to attend school. Knowledge of the reasons for refusal can help parents and educators devise strategies for assisting the child to adjust. But should such understanding *precede* insistence that the child return to school? Perhaps not.

Here are some things parents can do to get a child back into school (Brody, 1991):

- Do not accede to the child's demands to stay home. If the child complains of being tired or ill, tell the child he or she may feel better at school and can rest there if necessary.
- Discuss the problem with the child's teacher, principal, and school nurse.

Separation Anxiety

School phobia is often a form of separation anxiety. This boy is afraid to be separated from his mother. He imagines that something terrible will happen to her (or to him) when they are apart. Many mornings he complains of a tummy ache or of being too tired to go to school.

school phobia   Fear of attending school, marked by extreme anxiety at leaving parents.

- If there is a specific school-related problem, such as a strict teacher, help the child find ways to handle the situation. But finding ways to handle such problems can be accomplished while the child is in school. It is not necessarily the case that parents should wait until all such problems are ironed out before insisting that the child return to school.
- Reward the child for attending school. (Yes, perhaps parents shouldn't "have to" reward children for doing what is normally expected, but do you want them in school or not?)

What if these measures do not work? How do professionals help? A variety of therapeutic approaches have been tried, and it would appear that cognitive-behavioural approaches are the most effective (Masi et al., 2001; Shortt, Barrett, & Fox, 2001). One cognitive-behavioural method is counterconditioning to reduce the child's fear. (As noted in Chapter 10, Mary Cover Jones used this method to reduce Peter's fear of rabbits.) Others are operant-conditioning approaches, such as rewarding the child for attending school.

Comprehensive treatment programs involving a cluster of cognitive-behavioural techniques are advised. In one study, the cognitive-behavioural methods of systematic desensitization, modelling, cognitive restructuring, and the shaping and rewarding of school attendance were used to treat SAD in seven children (Kearney & Silverman, 1990). Six of the seven children were attending school full-time after treatment and at a six-month follow-up.

When possible, the children's parents are taught to apply cognitive-behavioural methods. One study assessed the effectiveness of so-called family-based group cognitive-behavioural treatment (FGCBT) for anxious children (Shortt et al., 2001). It included seventy-one children between the ages of six and ten who were diagnosed with either SAD, GAD, or social phobia (e.g., stage fright). The children and their families were assigned at random to FGCBT or to a ten-week waiting list ("We'll get to you in ten weeks"), which was the control group. The effectiveness of the treatment was evaluated after treatment and at a twelve-month follow-up. The researchers found that nearly 70 percent of the children who had completed FGCBT were no longer diagnosable with anxiety disorders, compared with 6 percent of the children on the waiting list. Even at the twelve-month follow-up, 68 percent of children remained diagnosis free.

Antidepressant medication has been used—often in conjunction with cognitive-behavioural methods—with a good deal of success (Murphy, Bengtson, Tan, Carbonell, & Levin, 2000; Pine et al., 2001; Walkup et al., 2001). Antidepressants can have side effects, however, such as abdominal discomfort (Burke & Baker, 2001). Moreover, some professionals fear that they can trigger suicidal thoughts in children (Mosholder, 2004). However, drugs in themselves do not teach children how to cope with situations. Many health professionals suggest that the drugs—in this case, antidepressants—are best used only when psychological treatments have proven to be ineffective (Masi et al., 2001).

Daniel Pine and his colleagues (2001) reported a study on the treatment of 128 anxious children, aged six to seventeen years. Like those in the Shortt study, they were diagnosed with a social phobia (such as stage fright), SAD, or GAD. All the children had received psychological treatment for three weeks without improvement. The children were assigned at random to receive an antidepressant (fluvoxamine) or a placebo (a "sugar pill") for eight weeks. Neither the children, their parents, their teachers, nor the researchers knew which child had received which treatment. After eight weeks, the children's anxiety was evaluated. Forty-eight of sixty-three children (76 percent) who had received the antidepressant had improved significantly, compared with nineteen of sixty-five children (29 percent) who had received the placebo.

It seems unfortunate to depart middle childhood following a discussion of social and emotional problems. Most children in developed nations come through middle childhood quite well, in good shape for the challenges and dramas of adolescence.

Developing in a World of Diversity

Problems? No Problem. (For Some Children)

Perhaps all children encounter some stress. But some children bear a heavy burden. The cumulative effect of stressors such as poverty, parental discord, abuse, or neglect places children at high risk of maladjustment (Davies & Windle, 2001). But some children are more resilient than others. They adapt and thrive despite stress (Masten, 2001). Consider the results of a study of a multiracial group of children born in Hawaii (Werner, 1990). One-third of the children were considered at risk because they had stressful births and were reared in poverty by a family marked by marital discord, mental illness, or alcoholism. Two of three of the high-risk children developed adjustment problems, but one-third overcame their childhoods to become competent, confident, and caring adults.

How do resilient children differ from those who are more vulnerable to stress? Two key factors appear to be the child's personality and social support.

Personality Characteristics

Genetics and temperament may play key roles in children's resilience (Collins et al., 2003; Maccoby, 2002). At one year of age, resilient children are securely attached to their mothers. At age two, they are independent and easygoing, even if they are abused or neglected. Not only is the easygoing child less likely to be the target of negative behaviour from parents, but he or she is also better able to cope with stress. By three and a half years of age, resilient children are cheerful, persistent, flexible, and capable of seeking help from adults. In middle childhood, they distance themselves from turmoil and show independence. They believe they can make good things happen (Griffin, Scheier, Botvin, & Diaz, 2001; Sandler, 2001).

Social Support

Support from others—parents, grandparents, siblings, peers, or teachers—helps children cope with stress (Davies & Windle, 2001; Greeff & Van Der Merwe, 2004; Letourneau et al., 2001). Social support is particularly important for children who live in poverty. The 2006 Report Card on Child and Family Poverty in Canada is not good: Close to one child out of every six lives in poverty in Canada. What makes this especially troubling is that the rate has gone up since 1989.

Who is especially vulnerable? Fifty-two percent of low-income children are in households headed by single women. In addition, children of recent immigrant families (49 percent) and of visibility minorities (34 percent) are overrepresented in Canadian poverty rates (Statistics Canada, 2001).

A protective factor for many poor children from ethnic minority groups is the presence of extended families (that may include grandparents) who live with them or nearby. Extended families provide economic, social, and emotional support for children (Murry, Bynum, Brody, Willert, & Stephens, 2001). Grandmothers, in particular, play a key role. Extended families enable single mothers to attend school or work and increase the quality of child care (Cebello & Olson, 1993; Oyserman, Radin, & Benn, 1993; Wadsworth & McLoyd, 1993).

The message is that many, many children do well despite adversity. In fact, Ann Masten (2001) characterized such an outcome as somewhat "ordinary." Hey, kids: Just do it!

For more information, check out the Canadian Psychology Foundation website: http://www .kidshavestresstoo.org/khst_docs/ index.php.

Active Review

19. Conduct disorders are more likely to be found among the (biological or adoptive?) parents of adopted children with conduct disorders.

20. Self-perceived competence appears to (protect children from or make children vulnerable to) feelings of depression.

21. Depressed children tend to (underutilize or overutilize?) the neurotransmitter serotonin in the brain.

22. Separation _____ disorder is similar to but not exactly the same as *school phobia*.

23. Separation anxiety (is or is not?) behind all instances of school refusal.

Reflect & Relate: Have you known children with conduct disorders, depression, or separation anxiety disorder (or school phobia)? Do you have any thoughts about the origins of the problems? Were the problems treated? What happened to the children?

Go to

W W W **www.voyages1CE.nelson.com**
for an interactive version of this review.

Recite: *An Active Summary*™

1. What are some features of social and emotional development in middle childhood?

Social development in middle childhood involves the development of skills, changes in interpersonal relationships, and the expansion of self-understanding. Freud viewed the period as the latency stage; Erikson saw it as the stage of industry versus inferiority. Social cognitive theorists note that children now depend less on external rewards and punishments and increasingly regulate their own behaviour. Cognitive-developmental theory notes that concrete operations enhance social development.

2. What is the relationship between social cognition and perspective taking?

In middle childhood, children become more capable of taking the role or perspective of another person. Selman theorizes that children move from egocentricity to seeing the world through the eyes of others in five stages.

3. How does the self-concept develop during middle childhood?

In early childhood, children's self-concepts focus on concrete external traits. In middle childhood, children begin to include abstract internal traits. Social relationships and group membership assume importance.

4. How does self-esteem develop during middle childhood?

In middle childhood, competence and social acceptance contribute to self-esteem, but self-esteem tends to decline because the self-concept becomes more realistic. Authoritative parenting fosters self-esteem.

5. What is learned helplessness, and how does it develop in middle childhood?

Learned helplessness is the acquired belief that one cannot obtain rewards. "Helpless" children tend not to persist in the face of failure. Girls tend to feel more helpless in math than boys do, largely because of gender-role expectations.

6. What kinds of influences are exerted by the family during middle childhood?

In middle childhood, the family continues to play a key role in socialization. Parent-child interactions focus on school-related issues, chores, and peers. Parents do less monitoring of children; "coregulation" develops.

7. What are the effects of having lesbian or gay parents?

Children of lesbian and gay parents by and large develop as well as children of heterosexual parents. The sexual orientation of these children is generally heterosexual.

8. What are the effects of divorce on the children?

Divorce disrupts children's lives and usually lowers the family's financial status. Children are likely to greet divorce with sadness, shock, and disbelief. Children of divorce fare better when parents cooperate on child rearing. Children's adjustment is related to the mother's coping ability.

9. What is best for the children? Should parents who bicker remain together for their children's sake?

In terms of the child's psychological adjustment, the answer seems to be not necessarily. Children appear to suffer as much from marital conflict as from divorce per se.

10. What are the effects of maternal employment on children?

Having both parents in the work force may be related to relative lack of supervision. However, there is little evidence that maternal employment harms children. Maternal employment fosters greater independence and flexibility in gender-role stereotypes.

11. What is the influence of peers during middle childhood?

Peers take on increasing importance and exert pressure to conform. Peer experiences also broaden children. Peers afford practice in social skills, sharing, relating to leaders, and coping with aggressive impulses. Popular children tend to be attractive and mature for their age.

12. How do children's concepts of friendship develop?

Early in middle childhood, friendships are based on proximity. Between the ages of eight and eleven, children become more aware of the value of friends as meeting each other's needs and having traits such as loyalty. At this age, peers tend to discourage contact with members of the other sex.

13. What are the effects of the school on children's social and emotional development?

Schools make demands for mature behaviour and nurture positive physical, social, and cognitive development. Readiness for school is related to children's early life experiences, individual differences in development and learning, and the schools' expectations.

14. What are the characteristics of a good school?

An effective school has an energetic principal, an orderly atmosphere, empowerment of teachers and students, high expectations for children, and solid academics. Teachers' expectations can become self-fulfilling prophecies. Many girls suffer from sexism and sexual harassment in school. Math and science are generally stereotyped as masculine, and language arts as feminine.

15. What are conduct disorders? What can we do about them?

Children with conduct disorders persistently break rules or violate the rights of others. There may be a genetic component to such disorders, but sociopathic models in the family, deviant peers, and inconsistent discipline all contribute. Parental training in cognitive-behavioural methods holds promise for treating these disorders.

16. What is depression? What can we do about it?

Depressed children tend to complain of poor appetite, insomnia, lack of energy, and feelings of worthlessness. Depressed children tend to blame themselves excessively for shortcomings. Psychotherapy tends to make children aware of their tendencies to minimize their accomplishments and overly blame themselves for shortcomings. Antidepressants are sometimes helpful but controversial.

17. What is separation anxiety disorder?

Separation anxiety disorder (SAD) is diagnosed when separation anxiety is persistent and excessive and interferes with daily life. Children with SAD tend to cling to parents and may refuse to attend school.

18. What are the connections between separation anxiety disorder, school phobia, and school refusal?

SAD is an extreme form of otherwise normal separation anxiety and may take the form of school phobia. But children can refuse school for other reasons, including finding school to be unpleasant or hostile.

19. What can we do about school phobia or school refusal?

The most important aspect of treatment is to insist that the child attend school. Cognitive-behavioural therapy and medicine may also be of use.

W W W **Go to** www.voyages1CE.nelson.com
for an interactive version of this summary review.

Key Terms

latency stage *(page 481)*

industry versus inferiority
(page 481)

social cognition *(page 481)*

self-esteem *(page 484)*

learned helplessness *(page 485)*

coregulation *(page 487)*

lesbian *(page 487)*

gay *(page 487)*

transsexual *(page 488)*

Pygmalion effect *(page 504)*

self-fulfilling prophecy *(page 504)*

sexism *(page 504)*

sexual harassment *(page 505)*

conduct disorders *(page 507)*

attributional style *(page 509)*

serotonin *(page 510)*

generalized anxiety disorder (GAD)
(page 510)

phobia *(page 510)*

separation anxiety disorder (SAD)
(page 510)

obsessive-compulsive disorder
(OCD) *(page 510)*

school phobia *(page 513)*

Active Learning Resources

Observing Children and Adolescents CD-ROM
Want to watch videos showing what you've just learned about in this chapter? Click on the "Self-Concept" video in Module 3, Section 3. Your "Lessons in Observation" feature on p. 445 provides further learning objectives, an applied lesson, and a critical thinking exercise designed to help you experience this stage of development. Also check out the "Peer Acceptance and Rejection" video in CD Module 3, Section 3.

Visit Your Companion Website for This Book
http://www.voyages1CE.nelson.com
Check out this companion website, where you will find online resources directly linked to your book. The website includes interactive exercises related to PQ4R and Power Visuals for mastering and reviewing key concepts as well as quizzing, chapter outlines, and much more!

CengageNOW!™
Go to this site for the link to CengageNOW™, your one-stop study shop. Take a Pretest for this chapter, and CengageNOW™ will generate a personalized Study Plan based on your test results! The Study Plan will identify the topics you need to review and direct you to online resources to help you master those topics. You can then take a Posttest to help you determine the concepts you have mastered and those you still need to work on.

14

Adolescence: Physical Development

PREVIEW

TRUTH OR FICTION?

● ● ● ● ● ● ● ● ● ● ●

T **F** Canadian adolescents are growing taller than their parents.

T **F** Girls are fertile immediately after their first menstrual period.

T **F** Boys and girls who mature early have higher self-esteem than those who mature late.

T **F** Most adolescents in Canada are unaware of the risks of HIV/AIDS.

T **F** Substance abuse is the leading cause of death among male adolescents in Canada.

T **F** You can never be too rich or too thin.

T **F** Some female undergraduates control their weight by going on cycles of binge eating followed by self-induced vomiting.

T **F** Substance use and abuse is on the rise among high school students.

Go to w w w

www.voyages1ce.nelson.com
for an interactive version of this "Truth or Fiction" feature.

© David Stoecklein/CORBIS

hen will it happen?"

"Why is my voice acting so funny?"

"How tall will I be?"

"Why do I get pimples?"

"Why am I getting hairy?"

"Why is mine not like his?"

"What's happening to me?"

Perhaps no other period of life is as exciting—and as bewildering—as adolescence. Except for infancy, more changes occur during adolescence than during any other time of life.

In our society, adolescents are neither children nor adults. Adolescents may be old enough to reproduce and may be as large as their parents, yet they are required to remain in school through age sixteen, may not be allowed to get driver's licences until they are sixteen or seventeen, and cannot attend R-rated films unless accompanied by an adult. Given the restrictions placed on adolescents, their growing yearning for independence, and a sex drive heightened by high levels of sex hormones, it is not surprising that adolescents occasionally are in conflict with their parents.

The capacity to think abstractly and hypothetically emerges during the teenage years. This ability gives rise to a stream of seemingly endless "Who am I?" questions, as adolescents search for a sense of identity and ponder the possible directions their adult lives may take.

Question: What is adolescence? Adolescence is a transitional period between childhood and adulthood, a coming of age. A century ago, most children in Canada assumed adult responsibilities early. Adolescence began to emerge as a distinct stage of development between childhood and adulthood when the demands of an increasingly complex society required a longer period of education and delayed entry into the labour force. It is no longer easy for Canadian adolescents to know when they have made the transition to adulthood. One legally becomes an adult at different ages, depending on whether one is enlisting in the armed services, buying a drink, driving a car, voting, or getting married.

The idea that adolescence is an important and separate developmental stage was proposed by G. Stanley Hall (1904), an early American psychologist. Hall believed that adolescence is marked by intense turmoil. He used the German term *Sturm und Drang* ("storm and stress") to refer to the conflicts and stresses of adolescence. According to Hall, adolescents swing back and forth between happiness and sadness, overconfidence and self-doubt, dependence and independence. Hall believed that adolescent mood swings and conflicts with parents are a necessary part of growing up. He thought that children have to rebel against their parents and their parents' values to make the transition to adulthood. Although Hall views adolescence as universal and biological "storm and stress," he acknowledged the importance of individual differences as well as the influence of culture on adolescents' experiences with this period (Arnett, 1999).

Sigmund Freud (1964 [1933]) placed relatively little emphasis on adolescence, because he believed that the first five years of life are the most critical. According to Freud, we enter the **genital stage** of psychosexual development at puberty. Sexual feelings are initially aimed at the parent of the other sex, but they become transferred, or displaced, onto other adults or adolescents of the other sex. Anna Freud (1969), Freud's daughter, saw adolescence as a turbulent period resulting from an increase in the sex drive. The adolescent tries to keep surging sexual impulses in check and redirects

genital stage In psychoanalytic theory, the fifth and final stage of psychosexual development in which gratification is attained through sexual intercourse with an individual of the other sex.

them from the parents to more acceptable outlets. The result is unpredictable behaviour, defiance of parents, confusion, and mood swings. Anna Freud, like G. Stanley Hall, believed that adolescent turmoil is a part of normal development.

But adolescence need not be a time of "storm and stress." Contemporary theorists no longer see adolescent storm and stress as inevitable (Griffin, 2001; Susman et al., 2003). Instead, they see adolescence as a period when biological, cognitive, social, and emotional functioning are reorganized.

Some theorists even argue that the concept of adolescence as a period of storm and stress marginalizes adolescents (Griffin, 2001). Seeing young people as "troubled" or "troubling" encourages adults to eye them warily and to not take their problems seriously. It is more useful to try to understand adolescents' problems and find ways of helping them cope.

Even if adolescence does not necessarily involve storm and stress, adolescents face the challenge of adapting to numerous biological, cognitive, social, and emotional changes. In this chapter, we focus on the biological and physical changes of adolescence. Let us begin—as adolescence begins—with *puberty*. *Questions: What is puberty? What happens during puberty?*

Is Adolescence a Period of Storm and Stress?
Research challenges the view that "storm and stress" are either normal or beneficial for adolescents. Neither violent mood swings nor deep-rooted parental conflicts appear inevitable, and most teenagers report feeling happy with their lives.

Puberty: The Biological Eruption

Puberty is defined as a stage of development characterized by reaching sexual maturity and the ability to reproduce. The onset of adolescence coincides with the advent of puberty. Puberty, however, is a biological concept, whereas adolescence is a psychosocial concept with biological correlates.

Puberty is controlled by a complex **feedback loop** involving the **hypothalamus, pituitary gland,** gonads—ovaries in females and testes in males—and hormones. The hypothalamus sends signals to the pituitary gland, which, in turn, releases hormones that control physical growth and the functioning of the gonads. The gonads respond to pituitary hormones by increasing their production of sex hormones (androgens and estrogens). The sex hormones further stimulate the hypothalamus, thus perpetuating the feedback loop.

The sex hormones also trigger the development of both the primary and secondary sex characteristics. The **primary sex characteristics** are the structures that make reproduction possible. In girls, these structures are the ovaries, vagina, uterus, and fallopian tubes. In boys, they are the penis, testes, prostate gland, and seminal vesicles. The **secondary sex characteristics** are physical indicators of sexual maturation that do not involve the reproductive structures; these include breast development, deepening of the voice, and the appearance of facial, pubic, and underarm hair. Let us now explore the physical changes of puberty, starting with the growth spurt and then examining other pubertal changes in boys and girls involving the primary and secondary sex characteristics. *Question: What happens during the adolescent growth spurt?*

The Adolescent Growth Spurt: Changed Forever

The stable growth patterns in height and weight that characterize early and middle childhood come to an abrupt end with the adolescent growth spurt. Girls start to spurt in height sooner than boys, at an average age of a little more than ten. Boys start to spurt about two years later, at an average age of about twelve. Girls and boys reach

puberty The biological stage of development characterized by changes that lead to reproductive capacity. Puberty signals the beginning of adolescence.

feedback loop A system in which glands regulate each other's functioning through a series of hormonal messages.

hypothalamus A pea-sized structure above the pituitary gland that is involved in the regulation of body temperature, motivation (e.g., hunger, thirst, sex), and emotion.

pituitary gland The body's "master gland," which is located in the lower central part of the brain and which secretes many hormones essential to development, such as oxytocin, prolactin, and growth hormone.

primary sex characteristics The structures that make reproduction possible.

secondary sex characteristics Physical indicators of sexual maturation—such as changes to the voice and growth of bodily hair—that do not directly involve reproductive structures.

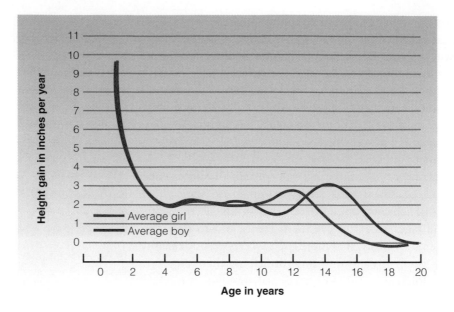

Figure 14.1

Spurts in Growth

Girls begin the adolescent growth spurt about 2 years earlier than boys. Girls and boys reach their periods of peak growth about 2 years after the spurt begins—at about 12 and 14 years old, respectively.

their periods of peak growth in height about two years after the growth spurt begins, at about twelve and fourteen years old, respectively (see Figure 14.1). The spurt in height for both girls and boys continues for about another two years at a gradually declining pace. Boys grow more than girls do during their spurt, averaging nearly four inches per year during the fastest year of the spurt compared with slightly over three inches per year for girls. Overall, boys add an average of fourteen and a half inches to their height during the spurt and girls add a little over thirteen inches (Tanner, 1991a).

Adolescents begin to spurt in weight about half a year after they begin to spurt in height. The period of peak growth in weight occurs about a year and a half after the onset of the spurt. As is the case with height, the growth spurt in weight then continues for a little more than two years for both girls and boys. As you can see in Figure 14.2, girls are taller and heavier than boys from about age nine or ten until about age thirteen or fourteen because their growth spurt occurs earlier. Once boys begin their growth spurt, they catch up with girls and eventually become taller and heavier.

Because the spurt in weight lags the spurt in height, many adolescents are relatively slender compared with their preadolescent and postadolescent stature. However, adolescents tend to eat enormous quantities of food to fuel their growth spurts. Active fourteen- and fifteen-year-old boys may consume 5,000 to 6,000 calories a day without becoming obese. If they were to eat this much twenty years later, they might gain upward of 100 pounds per year. Little wonder that adults fighting the dismal battle of the bulge stare at adolescents in amazement as they inhale pizza for lunch and go out later for burgers and fries!

Girls' and boys' body shapes begin to differ in adolescence. For one thing, boys' shoulders become broader than those of girls, whereas the hip dimensions of both sexes do not differ much. Thus, girls have relatively broader hips compared with their shoulders, whereas the opposite is true for boys. A girl's body shape is also more rounded than that of a boy. This is because, during puberty, girls gain almost twice as much fatty tissue as boys do, whereas boys gain twice as much muscle tissue as girls. Thus, a larger proportion of a male's body weight is composed of his muscle mass, whereas a relatively larger part of a female's body weight is composed of fatty tissue.

Individual Differences in the Growth Spurt

The figures given in this discussion are averages. Few of us begin or end our growth spurts right on the mark. Children who spurt earlier are likely to wind up with somewhat shorter legs and longer torsos, whereas children who spurt late are somewhat longer legged. However, there are no significant differences between early and late spurters in the total height attained at maturity (Tanner, 1991a).

Regardless of the age at which the growth spurt begins, there is a moderate to high correlation between a child's height at the onset of adolescence and at maturity (Tanner, 1989). Are there exceptions? Of course. However, everything else being equal, a tall child has a reasonable expectation of becoming a tall adult, and vice versa.

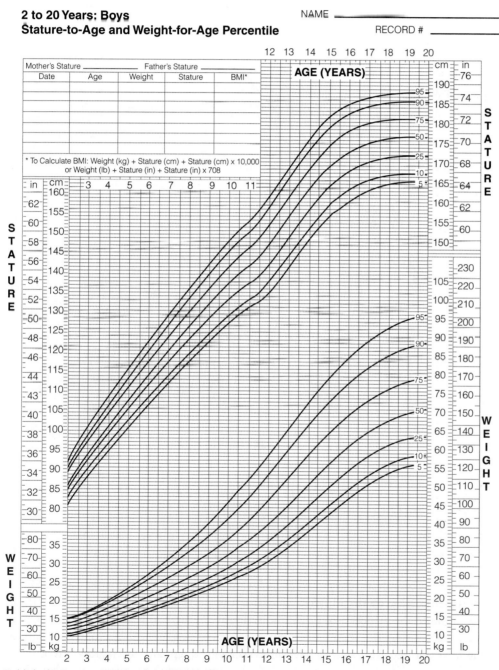

2 to 20 Years: Boys
Stature-to-Age and Weight-for-Age Percentile

Published May 30, 2000 (modified 11/21/00)
Source: *Developed by the National Center for Health Statistics in collaboration with the National Center for Chronic Desease Prevention and Health Promotion (2000) http://www.cdc.gov/growthcharts*

Figure 14.2

Growth Curves for Height and Weight

Girls are taller and heavier than boys from about age 9 or 10 until about age 13 because their growth spurt occurs earlier. Once boys begin their growth spurt, they catch up with girls and eventually become taller and heavier.

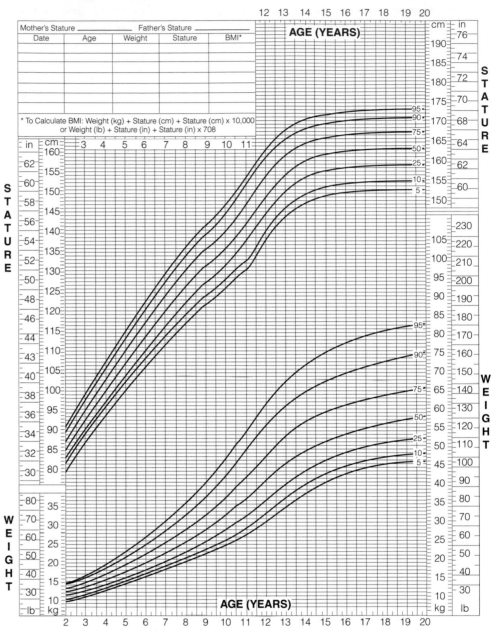

2 to 20 Years: Girls
Stature-to-Age and Weight-for-Age Percentile

Figure 14.2
Growth Curves for Height and Weight

Published May 30, 2000 (modified 11/21/00)
Source: *Developed by the National Center for Health Statistics in collaboration with the National Center for Chronic Desease Prevention and Health Promotion (2000) http://www.cdc.gov/growthcharts*

asynchronous growth
Imbalanced growth, such as the growth that occurs during the early part of adolescence and causes many adolescents to appear gawky.

Asynchronous Growth: On Being Gawky

Adolescents are often referred to as awkward and gawky. A major reason for this is **asynchronous growth**—different parts of the body grow at different rates. In an exception to the principle of proximodistal growth, the hands and feet mature before the arms and legs do. As a consequence, adolescent girls and boys may complain of big hands or feet. And, in an apparent reversal of the cephalocaudal growth trend, legs reach their peak growth before the shoulders and chest. This means that boys stop growing out of their pants about a year before they stop growing out of their jackets (Tanner, 1989).

The Secular Trend in Growth

During the past century, children in the Western world have grown dramatically more rapidly and have wound up taller than children from earlier times. This historical trend toward increasing adult height, which also has been accompanied by an earlier onset of puberty, is known as the **secular trend.** Figure 14.3 shows that Swedish boys and girls grew more rapidly in 1938 and 1968 than they did in 1883 and ended up several inches taller. At the age of fifteen, the boys were more than six inches taller and the girls were more than three inches taller, on average, than their counterparts from the previous century (Tanner, 1989). The occurrence of a secular trend in height and also in weight has been documented in nearly all European countries and Canada.

> **secular trend** A historical trend toward increasing adult height and earlier puberty.

Truth or Fiction Revisited: It turns out that children from middle- and upper-class families in industrialized countries, including Canada, have now stopped growing taller, whereas their poorer counterparts continue to make gains in height from generation to generation (Tanner, 1989). Why?

Nutrition apparently plays an important role. Although each generation has stopped gaining on the last, children from middle- and upper-class families are nevertheless taller and heavier than their age-mates from lower-class families. But these data in themselves are not very convincing. For example, it could be argued that genetic factors provide advantages that increase the chances for financial gain as well as for greater height and weight. Perhaps, however, individuals who have had nutritional and medical advantages have simply reached their full genetic potential in height. Continued gains among families of lower socioeconomic status suggest that poorer children are still benefiting from improved nutrition.

We now examine some of the other changes that occur during puberty. You will notice that there are wide individual differences in the timing of the events of puberty. In a group of teenagers of the same age and sex, you may well find some who have completed puberty, others who have not even started, and others who are somewhere in between.

Pubertal Changes in Boys

At puberty, the pituitary gland stimulates the testes to increase their output of testosterone, leading to further development of the male genitals. The first visible sign of puberty is accelerated growth of the testes, which begins at an average age of about eleven and a half, although a range of ages of plus or minus two years is considered perfectly normal. Testicular growth further accelerates testosterone production and other pubertal changes. The penis begins a spurt of accelerated growth about a year later, and still later, pubic hair begins a growth spurt.

Underarm hair appears at about age fifteen. Facial hair is at first a fuzz on the upper lip. An actual beard does not develop for another two to three years. The beard and chest hair continue to develop past the age of twenty.

At fourteen or fifteen, the voice deepens because of growth of the "voice box," or **larynx,** and the lengthening of the vocal cords. The developmental process is gradual, and adolescent boys sometimes encounter an embarrassing cracking of the voice.

> **larynx** The part of the throat that contains the vocal cords.

Testosterone also triggers the development of acne, which afflicts between 75 and 90 percent of adolescents (Goldstein, 2004; Lowrey, 1986). Severe acne is manifested by multiple pimples and blackheads on the face, chest, and back. Although boys are more prone to acne than girls, we cannot say that girls suffer less from it. In our society, a smooth complexion has a higher value for girls than for boys, and girls with acne that boys would consider mild may suffer terribly.

Males are capable of producing erections in early infancy (and some male babies are born with erections), but the phenomenon is not frequent until age thirteen or fourteen. Adolescent males may experience unwanted and unprovoked erections.

semen The fluid that contains sperm and substances that nourish and help transport sperm.

nocturnal emission Emission of seminal fluid while asleep.

gynecomastia Enlargement of breast tissue in males.

epiphyseal closure The process by which the cartilage that separates the long end (epiphysis) of a bone from the main part of the bone turns to bone.

mammary glands Glands that secrete milk.

labia The major and minor lips of the female genitalia.

clitoris A female sex organ that is highly sensitive to sexual stimulation but not directly involved in reproduction.

Many boys worry that they will be caught with erections when walking between classes or when asked to stand before the class. The organs that produce **semen** grow rapidly, and boys typically ejaculate seminal fluid by age thirteen or fourteen—about a year and a half after the penis begins its growth spurt—although here, too, there is much individual variation. About a year later, boys begin to have **nocturnal emissions,** also called wet dreams because of the myth that emissions accompany erotic dreams. However, nocturnal emissions and erotic dreams need not coincide. Mature sperm are found in ejaculatory emissions by about the age of fifteen. And so ejaculation is not adequate evidence of reproductive capacity. Ejaculatory ability in boys usually precedes the presence of mature sperm by at least a year.

Nearly half of all boys experience enlargement of the breasts, or **gynecomastia,** which usually declines in a year or two. Gynecomastia stems from the small amount of female sex hormones secreted by the testes. When gynecomastia persists or becomes distressful, it can be treated with drugs, such as tamoxifen (Derman et al., 2003).

At age twenty or twenty-one, men stop growing taller because testosterone causes **epiphyseal closure**, which prevents the long bones from making further gains in length. And so, puberty for males draws to a close. The changes of puberty in males are summarized in Concept Review 14.1.

Pubertal Changes in Girls

In girls, the pituitary gland signals the ovaries to vastly increase estrogen production at puberty. Estrogen may stimulate the growth of breast tissue ("breast buds") as early as the age of eight or nine, but the breasts usually begin to enlarge during the tenth year. The development of fatty tissue and ducts elevates the areas of the breasts surrounding the nipples and causes the nipples themselves to protrude. The breasts typically reach full size in about three years, but the **mammary glands** do not mature fully until a woman has a baby.

Estrogen also promotes the growth of the fatty and supporting tissue in the hips and buttocks, which, along with the widening of the pelvis, causes the hips to become rounded. Growth of fatty deposits and connective tissue varies considerably. For this reason, development of breasts and hips differs.

Beginning at about the age of eleven, girls' adrenal glands produce small amounts of androgens which, along with estrogen, stimulate the growth of pubic and underarm hair. Excessive androgen production can darken or increase the amount of facial hair. Androgens and estrogen have other functions as well.

Estrogen causes the **labia,** vagina, and uterus to develop during puberty, and androgens cause the **clitoris** to develop. The vaginal lining varies in thickness according to the amount of estrogen in the bloodstream.

Estrogen typically brakes the female growth spurt some years before testosterone brakes that of males. Girls deficient in estrogen during their late teens may grow quite tall, but most girls reach their heights because of normal, genetically determined variations.

Concept Review 14.1 Stages of Pubertal Development in Males

Age of Onset (Years)	Characteristics
Between 9 and 15	• Testicles begin to grow. • Skin of the scrotum becomes redder and coarser. • Straight pubic hairs begin to appear at the base of the penis. • Muscle mass develops, and the boy begins to grow taller. • Areola (the dark area around the nipple) grows larger and darker.
Between 11 and 16	• Penis begins to grow longer. • Testicles and scrotum continue to grow. • Pubic hair becomes coarser and more curled and spreads to cover the area between the legs. • Body gains in height. • Shoulders broaden. • Hips narrow. • Larynx enlarges, and voice deepens. • Sparse facial and underarm hair appears.
Between 11 and 17	• Penis begins to increase in circumference as well as in length (although more slowly). • Testicles continue to increase in size. • Texture of the pubic hair becomes more adultlike. • Growth of facial and underarm hair increases. • First ejaculation occurs. • Gynecomastia occurs in nearly half of all boys. • Increased skin oils may produce acne.
Between 14 and 18	• Body nears final adult height, genitals achieve adult shape and size, pubic hair spreads to thighs and upward toward the belly. • Chest hair appears. • Facial hair reaches full growth. • Further increases in height, body hair, and muscle growth and strength may continue into the early 20s.

This review is a general guideline. Changes may appear sooner or later than shown and do not always appear in the indicated sequence.

Source: From *The Kinsey Institute New Report on Sex*, 1990, pp. 272-273. Reprinted by permission of The Kinsey Institute for Research in Sex, Gender, and Reproduction, Inc.

Menarche

Menarche (first menstruation) commonly occurs between the ages of eleven and fourteen. But it is quite normal for menarche to occur as early as age nine or as late as age sixteen (Golub, 1992). In the middle 1800s, European girls first menstruated

menarche The onset of menstruation.

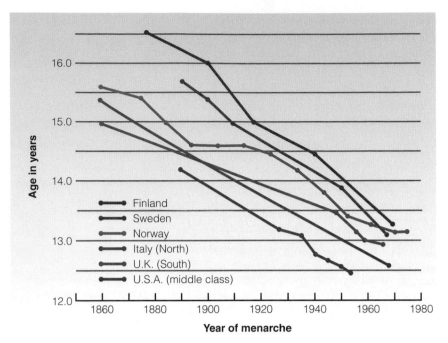

Figure 14.3

The Decline in Age at Menarche

The age at menarche has been declining since the mid-1800s among girls in Western nations, apparently because of improved nutrition and health care. Menarche may be triggered by the accumulation of a critical percentage of body fat.

Source: Tanner (1989).

at about the age of sixteen, as shown in Figure 14.3. During the past century and a half, however, the processes of puberty have occurred at progressively earlier ages in Western nations, an example of the secular trend in development. By the 1960s, the average age of menarche in North America had plummeted to its current figure of twelve and a half (Frisch, 1991; Tanner, 1991b).

No single theory of the onset of puberty has found wide acceptance. In any event, the average age of the advent of puberty for girls and boys appears to have levelled off in recent years. The precipitous drop suggested in Figure 14.3 seems to have come to an end.

What accounts for the earlier age of puberty? One hypothesis is that girls must reach a certain body weight to trigger pubertal changes such as menarche. Body fat could trigger the changes because fat cells secrete the protein leptin. Leptin would then signal the brain to secrete a cascade of hormones that raise estrogen levels in the body. Menarche comes later to girls who have a lower percentage of body fat, such as athletes (Frisch, 1997). Injections of leptin also cause laboratory animals to reach sexual maturity early (Angier, 1997).

The average body weight for triggering menarche depends on the girl's height. For girls who are five feet to five and a half feet tall, the average triggering weight is between ninety-seven and 114 pounds (Frisch, 1991). Today's children are larger than the children of the early twentieth century, probably because of improved nutrition and health care. It seems that the age threshold for reaching menarche may have been attained because the average age has levelled off in recent years.

Hormonal Regulation of the Menstrual Cycle

Testosterone levels remain fairly stable in boys, although they decline gradually in adulthood. However, estrogen and progesterone levels vary markedly and regulate the menstrual cycle. Following menstruation—the sloughing off of the endometrium—estrogen levels increase, leading once more to the growth of endometrial tissue. ***Truth or Fiction Revisited:*** It is usually not true that girls can become pregnant after they have their first menstrual period. Girls usually begin to ovulate only twelve to eighteen months after menarche. A ripe ovum is released by the ovary when estrogen reaches peak blood levels. Then the inner lining of the uterus thickens in response to the secretion of progesterone. In this way, it gains the capacity to support an embryo if fertilization should occur. If the ovum is not fertilized, estrogen and progesterone levels drop suddenly, triggering menstruation once again.

The average menstrual cycle is twenty-eight days, but variation between girls and in the same girl is common. Girls' cycles are often irregular for a few years after menarche but later tend to assume patterns that are reasonably regular. Most menstrual cycles during the first two years or so after menarche occur without ovulation having taken place. But keep in mind that in any given individual cycle, an ovum may be produced, making pregnancy possible. So it is possible to become pregnant shortly after the onset of menarche.

The Psychological Impact of Menarche

In different times, in different places, menarche has had different meanings. The Manus of New Guinea greet menarche with elaborate ceremony (Golub, 1992). The other girls of the village sleep in the menstruating girl's hut. They feast and have parties. In the West, menstruation has historically received a mixed response. The menstrual flow itself has generally been seen, erroneously, as polluting, and the frequent discomforts of menstruation have led many menstruating women to be stereotyped as irrational (Rathus et al., 2005). Menarche itself has generally been perceived as the event in which a girl suddenly develops into a woman, but because of taboos and prejudice against menstruating women, girls historically matured in ignorance of menarche.

Girls' attitudes toward menarche reflect their level of education as well as certain physical realities. A Hong Kong study of 1573 Chinese high school students found a mixed response to the onset of menstruation (Tang et al., 2003). The average age of menarche was 11.67 years. Although most of the girls reported that menstruation was annoying (it involved some discomfort for them, along with the need to dispose of the menstrual flow), two in three reported feeling more "grown up" and four in ten felt that they had become more feminine. Girls who felt positively about menarche were more likely to be educationally prepared to welcome it as a natural event, have a positive body image, and reject traditional negative attitudes.

Most Canadian girls currently receive advance information about menstruation, not only from family and girlfriends but also from school health classes. The old horror stories are pretty much gone, at least in mainstream society. However, most girls experience at least some menstrual discomfort and need to discreetly dispose of the menstrual flow (Costos et al., 2002; Rathus et al., 2005). Most girls can separate pride in "becoming women" from the realities of some discomfort and the fact that menarche usually means that the girl will not be growing much taller, because of the braking effects of estrogen. The changes of puberty in females are summarized in Concept Review 14.2.

Early versus Late Maturers: Does It Matter When You Arrive, as Long as You Do?

Rathus recalls Al from his high school days. When Al entered the ninth grade, he was all of fourteen, but he was also about six feet three inches tall, with broad shoulders and arms thick with muscle. His face was cut from rock, and his beard was already dark. Al paraded down the hallways with an entourage of male and female admirers. When there were shrieks of anticipation, you could bet that Al was coming around the corner. Al was given a wide berth in the boys' room. He would have to lean back when he combed his waxed hair up and back—otherwise, his head would be too high for the mirror. At that age, Rathus and his friends liked to tell themselves that Al was not all that bright. (This stereotype is unfounded, as we will see.) Nevertheless, they were envious of Al.

Al had arrived.

Al had matured early, and he had experienced the positive aspects of maturing early. What causes some children to mature earlier or later than others? Genetic, dietary, and health factors all seem to influence the timing of puberty. And one controversial new theory suggests that childhood stress may trigger early puberty in girls. *Question: What are the effects of early or late maturation on adolescents?*

Concept Review 14.2 Stages of Pubertal Development in Females

Age of Onset (Year)	Characteristics
Between 8 and 11	• Pituitary hormones stimulate ovaries to increase production of estrogen. • Internal reproductive organs begin to grow.
Between 9 and 15	• First the areola and then the breasts increase in size and become more rounded. • Pubic hair becomes darker and coarser. • Growth in height continues. • Body fat rounds body contours. • A normal vaginal discharge becomes noticeable. • Sweat and oil glands increase in activity, and acne may appear. • Internal and external reproductive organs and genitals grow, making the vagina longer and the labia more pronounced.
Between 10 and 16	• Areola and nipples grow, often forming a second mound sticking out from the rounded breast mound. • Pubic hair begins to grow in a triangular shape and to cover the centre of the pubic area. • Underarm hair appears. • Menarche occurs. • Internal reproductive organs continue to develop. • Ovaries may begin to release mature eggs capable of being fertilized. • Growth in height slows.
Between 12 and 19	• Breasts near adult size and shape. • Pubic hair fully covers the pubic area and spreads to the top of the thighs. • Voice may deepen slightly (but not as much as in males). • Menstrual cycles become more regular. • Further changes in body shape may occur into the early 20s.

This review is a general guideline. Changes may appear sooner or later than shown and do not always appear in the indicated sequence.

Source: From *The Kinsey Institute New Report on Sex*, 1990, pp. 264-265. Reprinted by permission of The Kinsey Institute for Research in Sex, Gender, and Reproduction, Inc.

Early and Late Maturation in Boys

Research findings about boys who mature early are mixed, but the weight of the evidence suggests that the effects of early maturation are generally positive (Graber et al., 2004; Weichold et al., 2003). Late-maturing boys may feel conspicuous because they are among the last of their peers to lose their childhood appearance.

Early-maturing boys tend to be more popular than their late-maturing peers and more likely to be leaders in school (Ge et al., 2001b; Graber et al., 2004; O'Sullivan et al., 2000; Weichold et al., 2003). Early-maturing boys in general are also more

Early and Late Maturation in Boys
The effects of early maturation in boys are generally positive. Late-maturing boys may feel conspicuous because they are among the last of their peers to lose their childhood appearance.

poised, relaxed, and good-natured. Their edge in sports and the admiration of their peers heighten their sense of self-worth. Some studies have suggested that the stereotype of the mature tough-looking boy as dumb is just that—a stereotype.

On the negative side, early maturation may hit some boys before they are psychologically prepared to live up to the expectations of those who admire their new bodies. Coaches may expect too much of them in sports, and peers may want them to fight their battles for them (Ge et al., 2001b; O'Sullivan et al., 2000). Sexual opportunities may create demands before they know how to respond to them (Lam et al., 2002). Some early maturers may therefore worry about living up to the expectations of others.

Late maturers have the "advantage" of avoiding these early pressures. They are not rushed into maturity. On the other hand, late-maturing boys often feel dominated by early-maturing boys. They have been found to be more dependent and insecure. Although they are smaller and weaker than early maturers, they may be more likely to get involved in disruptive behaviour and substance abuse (Ge et al., 2001b; Graber et al., 2004; Weichold et al., 2003).

But there are individual differences. Although some late maturers appear to fight their physical status and get into trouble, others adjust and find acceptance through academic achievement, music, clubs, and other activities. The benefits of early maturation appear to be greatest among lower-income adolescents, because physical prowess is valued more highly among these youngsters. Middle- and upper-income adolescents are also likely to place more value on the types of achievements—academic and so on—available to late-maturing boys (Graber et al., 2004; Weichold et al., 2003).

Early and Late Maturation in Girls
The situation is somewhat reversed for girls. Whereas early maturation poses distinct advantages for boys, the picture is mixed for girls. Adolescents tend to be concerned if they differ from their peers. ***Truth or Fiction Revisited:*** Although boys who mature early usually have higher self-esteem than those who mature late, the same may not hold true for girls.

Rinaldi recounts a different story from her last year in elementary school. She recalls Marnie, a classmate who entered the sixth grade as a mature eleven-year-old. She stood out because she was taller than most of the girls and some of the boys in her grade and because she was one of the first girls to start developing breasts and wearing what was called a "training" bra. Unlike Al, Marnie did not walk around with her head held high; also in contrast to Al, she tried to hide her maturational changes by wearing baggy tops. She received a great deal of unwanted attention from the boys in her class and glares from some of the girls in her class.

Early-maturing girls may feel awkward, because they are among the first of their peers to begin the physical changes of puberty. They outgrow not only their late-maturing female counterparts but also their male age-mates. With their tallness and their developing breasts, they quickly become conspicuous. Boys of their age may tease them about their breasts and their height. Tall girls of dating age frequently find that shorter boys are reluctant to approach them or be seen with them. Occasionally, tall girls walk with a slight hunch, as if trying to minimize their height. All in all, early-maturing girls are at greater risk for a host of psychological problems and substance abuse than girls who mature later on (Ge et al., 2003; Hayward, 2003; Kaltiala-Heino et al., 2003; Wiesner & Ittel, 2002).

Many girls who mature early feel less positive about their puberty and have a poorer body image than those who mature later (Williams & Currie, 2000). These negative feelings are more pronounced for girls who are in elementary school, where they are conspicuous, but less pronounced in high school, where others are catching up.

Adolescent girls are quite concerned about their body shapes. Early maturers who are taller and heavier than other girls their age do not conform to the current cultural emphasis on thinness. Thus, they have more negative feelings about their bodies. Early maturation in girls is associated with a variety of other problems. Early-maturing girls obtain lower grades in school and have more conduct problems, a greater incidence of substance abuse, and a higher incidence of emotional disturbance, including depression (Ge et al., 2000a; Lanza & Collins, 2002; Stice et al., 2001). They are literally larger targets for deviant peer pressure (Lanza & Collins, 2002). They engage in sexual intercourse at an earlier age (Lam et al., 2002; Magnusson, 2001). Sexual activity is connected with association with older peers and interest from older boys. Their concern about their body shape also appears to heighten the risk of developing eating disorders (Kaltiala-Heino et al., 2001; Striegel-Moore et al., 2003).

The parents of early-maturing girls may increase their vigilance and restrictiveness. Increased restrictiveness can lead to new child-parent conflicts. A study of 302 African American adolescent-mother pairs found that mothers and their early-maturing daughters had more heated discussions than mothers and their later-maturing daughters had (Sagrestano et al., 1999). Sad to say, girls who mature early are also more likely to experience child sexual abuse (Kaltiala-Heino et al., 2001; Romans et al., 2001). The early-maturing girl can thus be a target of inappropriate parental attention and develop severe conflicts about her body as a result.

Body Image in Adolescence

Our *body image* refers to how physically attractive we perceive ourselves to be and to how we feel about our body. Adolescents are quite concerned about their physical appearance, particularly in early adolescence when the rapid physical changes of puberty are occurring (Striegel-Moore et al., 2003; Williams & Currie, 2000).

Question: How do adolescents feel about their bodies? By the age of eighteen, girls and boys are more satisfied with their bodies than they were in the earlier teen years. In a five-year longitudinal study, Holsen and colleagues (2001) investigated the relationship between body image and depressed mood in 645 adolescents at ages thirteen, fifteen, and eighteen. On average, girls reported having a more negative body image and feeling more depressed about their bodies at all three ages. Dissatisfaction with body image led to feelings of depression among both sexes (Holsen et al., 2001). Adolescent females in our society tend to be more preoccupied with body weight and slimness than adolescent males (Lowry et al., 2002; McCabe & Ricciardelli, 2001). Unlike females, however, many adolescent males want to put weight *on* and build their muscle mass (McCabe & Ricciardelli, 2001; Vartanian et al., 2001). Compared with adolescent boys, adolescent girls have a less positive body image and are more dissatisfied with their weight; the majority are likely to diet—either to have dieted or to be on a diet currently (Holsen et al., 2001; Lowry et al., 2002; Stice & Bearman, 2001). And girls are more likely to suffer from eating disorders, as we will see later in the chapter.

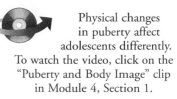

Physical changes in puberty affect adolescents differently. To watch the video, click on the "Puberty and Body Image" clip in Module 4, Section 1.

© Anna Peisl/Getty Images

Body Image
Adolescent females in our society are much more preoccupied with appearance, body weight, and slimness than are adolescent males. Why?

Active Review

1. G. Stanley Hall proposed that adolescence is a period of storm and _____.

2. Puberty is controlled by a(n) _____ loop involving hormones.

3. The gonads produce _____ hormones (androgens and estrogens).

4. Girls begin their _____ spurt in height at about ten, and boys spurt about two years later.

5. _____ growth may produce gawkiness in adolescents.

6. Males stop growing taller because testosterone causes _____ closure.

7. _____ brakes the female growth spurt.

8. (Boys or Girls?) are more likely to benefit from early maturation.

9. (Boys or Girls?) are more likely to have a positive body image.

Reflect & Relate: Was your adolescence a period of storm and stress? If so, what factors contributed to the turbulence?

Go to
www.voyages1ce.nelson.com
for an interactive version of this review.

Emerging Sexuality and the Risks of Sexually Transmitted Infections

Several TV series aimed at and about adolescents (e.g., Degrassi: Next Generation; Laguna Beach; One Tree Hill) portray adolescents as being sexually active. As we noted in our discussion of puberty, many or most adolescents are preoccupied with sex to some degree. These preoccupations are fuelled by a powerful sex drive. And many or most adolescents are not quite sure about what to do with these pressing urges. Should they masturbate? Should they pet? Should they engage in sexual intercourse? Parents and sex educators often say no, or wait. Yet it can seem that "Everyone's doing it." In Chapter 16 we will discuss various sexual outlets and sexual orientation. Here, we focus on the risks of sexually transmitted infections.

Given a body that is suddenly sexually mature, a high sex drive, vulnerability to peer pressure, and limited experience in handling temptation, teenagers are at particular risk for sexually transmitted infections (STIs). Sexually active adolescents have higher rates of STIs than any other age group. Each year, an estimated 3 million adolescents—one of every six—contracts a sexually transmitted infection (Centers for Disease Control and Prevention, 2001a). *Question: What kinds of sexually transmitted infections are there?* Chlamydia (a bacterial infection of the vagina or urinary tract that can result in sterility) is the most commonly occurring STI in adolescents, followed by gonorrhea, genital warts, genital herpes, syphilis, and **HIV/AIDS**. While chlamydia is the most commonly reported/tested STI, we are now aware that taken together, the various forms of HPV comprise one of the most common family of viruses and the world's most commonly sexually transmitted infection (http://www.sexualityandu.ca). Because of its lethality, HIV/AIDS tends to capture most of the headlines. However, other STIs are more widespread, and some of them can also be deadly.

Nearly 4 million new chlamydia infections occur each year (Centers for Disease Control and Prevention, 2002a). The incidence of chlamydia infections is especially high among teenagers and college students (Centers for Disease Control and Prevention, 2001a; Public Health Agency of Canada, 2006). Chlamydia is a major cause of pelvic inflammatory disease (PID), which often leads to infertility.

Each year in the United States, there are about 1 million new infections of genital warts, which are caused by the *human papillomavirus* (HPV) (Centers for Disease Control and Prevention, 2003). Unfortunately, Health Canada does not have HPV data because it is not documented nationally. One local study by McGill University researchers found HPV to exist in 22 percent of 498 female university students (Richardson, Franco, Pintos et al., 2000). The scary part is that according to the HPV information website (http://www.hpvinfo.ca), 87 percent of Toronto high school students have never heard of HPV, and yet their chances of contacting some type of HPV in their lifetime is quite high. It is estimated that more than half of the sexually active adolescent women in some cities in the United States are infected with genital warts. Although the warts may appear in visible areas of the skin, most cases appear in areas that cannot be seen, such as on the cervix in women or in the urethra in men. Within a few months, warts are usually found in the genital and anal regions. Women who initiate sexual intercourse before the age of eighteen and who have many sex partners are particularly susceptible to infection.

A survey of first-year college students found a great deal of ignorance about genital warts (Baer et al., 2000). The findings were ironic: Although nearly all (96 percent of the males and 95 percent of the females) had heard of genital warts, only 4 percent of the males and 12 percent of the females knew that HPV caused them. Moreover, students were generally ignorant of the modes of transmission of both genital

HIV/AIDS HIV stands for human immunodeficiency virus, the virus that causes AIDS. AIDS stands for acquired immunodeficiency syndrome, a condition that cripples the body's immune system, making the person vulnerable to diseases that would not otherwise be as threatening.

warts and HPV. Ignorance in this case is danger rather than bliss because HPV is linked to certain cancers (Cannistra & Niloff, 1996; Josefsson et al., 2000). There are many different types of HPV viruses, and some types, referred to as *carcinogenic*, can cause precancerous lesions, cervical cancer, and other genital cancers. http://www.sexualityandu.ca is a wonderful Canadian site with information on sexual health and well-being.

Other informative web links:

- Division of Sexual Health Promotion and STD Prevention and Control: http://www.phac-aspc.gc.ca/std-mts
- "Health information you can trust." Funded by and in partnership with Health Canada: http://www.canadian-health-network.ca
- Planned Parenthood Federation of Canada (information on reproductive health and an e-mail newsletter): http://www.ppfc.ca
- Credible and up-to-date information and education on sexual health: http://www.sexualityandu.ca

 Listen to different teenagers discuss the reasons behind adolescent risk taking. To watch the video, click on the "Risk Taking" clip on Module 4, Section 2.

Risk Factors

Adolescents often take risks, with harmful consequences for their health and well-being. *Question: What factors place adolescents at risk for contracting STIs?*

First, and most obvious, is sexual activity itself. Over the past thirty years, the age of first sexual experience has been dropping. The average age of first sexual intercourse is sixteen, but in some inner city areas, it is twelve. By the age of nineteen, between 70 and 90 percent of adolescents have initiated sexual intercourse (Dailard, 2001; Felton & Bartoces, 2002).

A second risk factor for contracting STIs is sex with multiple partners. About one in five high school students engages in sex with four or more different partners (Dailard, 2001).

A third factor is failure to use condoms. In recent surveys, two-thirds of sexually active adolescents reported not using condoms or using them inconsistently (Dailard, 2001).

A fourth factor is substance abuse (United Nations Special Session on AIDS, 2001). Adolescents who abuse drugs are also more likely to engage in other risky behaviours, such as sex without condoms (Morales, 2003; Santelli et al., 2004; Voisin, 2003).

HIV/AIDS and other STIs are described in Table 14.1.

HIV/AIDS

HIV/AIDS is the most devastating of STIs; if left untreated, it is lethal. (And the long-term prospects of those who do receive treatment remain unknown.) HIV—the virus that causes AIDS—is spreading rapidly around the world, and, by the end of the twentieth century, it had infected more than 40 million people worldwide (United Nations Special Session on AIDS, 2001). More than 25 percent of all Canadians with HIV are in their twenties (Canada Public Health Agency, 2006; Centers for Disease Control and Prevention, 2003). Because HIV has a long incubation period—up to a decade and longer—many of these young adults were infected as teenagers.

Overview of Sexually Transmitted Infections (STIs)

STI and Cause	Methods of Transmission	Symptoms	Diagnosis	Treatment
Acquired immunodeficiency syndrome (AIDS); caused by human immunodeficiency virus (HIV)	• Sexual intercourse • Injection of contaminated blood • From mother to child during childbirth or breast feeding	• Flulike symptoms • Chronically swollen lymph nodes and intermittent weight loss, fever, fatigue, and diarrhea • May be asymptomatic for many years • "Opportunistic" infections	• Blood, saliva, and urine tests can detect HIV antibodies in the bloodstream • Other tests detect the virus itself	• A "cocktail" of antiviral drugs reduces the amount of HIV in the blood
Bacterial vaginosis; caused by *Gardnerella vaginalis* bacterium and other bacteria	• Sexual contact	• In women, a vaginal discharge, genital irritation, and mild pain during urination • In men, inflammation of the penis, urethritis, and cystitis • May be asymptomatic	• Culture and examination of bacteria	• Oral treatment with metronidazole (Flagyl)
Candidiasis (moniliasis, thrush, "yeast infection"); caused by *Candida albicans*, a yeastlike fungus	• Sexual contact • Sharing a washcloth or towel with an infected person	• In women, vulval itching, discharge, soreness or swelling of genital tissues • In men, itching and burning on urination, or inflammation of the penis	• Diagnosis usually made on basis of symptoms	• Vaginal suppositories, creams, or tablets containing miconazole, clotrimazole, or teraconazole
Chlamydia and nongonococcal urethritis (NGU); caused by *Chlamydia trachomatous* bacterium in women and by several bacteria in men	• Vaginal, oral, or anal sexual activity	• In women, frequent and painful urination, abdominal pain and inflammation, and vaginal discharge • In men, burning or painful urination, slight discharge; may be asymptomatic	• The Abbott Testpack analyzes a cervical smear in women	• Antibiotics

Overview of Sexually Transmitted Infections (STIs)

STI and Cause	Methods of Transmission	Symptoms	Diagnosis	Treatment
Genital herpes; caused by herpes simplex virus type 2 (HSV-2)	• Vaginal, oral, or anal sexual activity • Most contagious during outbreaks	• Painful, reddish bumps around the genitals • Bumps become blisters or sores that fill with pus and break, shedding viral particles • Burning urination, fever, aches and pains, swollen glands, and vaginal discharge possible	• Clinical inspection of sores • Culture and examination of fluid drawn from sore	• Antiviral drugs may provide relief and prompt healing but are not cures
Genital warts (venereal warts); caused by human papillomavirus (HPV)	• Sexual contact • Other forms of contact, as with infected towels or clothing	• Painless warts resembling cauliflowers on the genitals or anus or in the rectum	• Clinical inspection • Pap tests	• Removal by freezing, podophyllin, burning, and surgery
Gonorrhea ("clap," "drip"); caused by gonococcus bacterium (*Neisseria gonorrhoea*)	• Vaginal, oral, or anal sexual activity	• In men, thick discharge, burning urination • In women, may be symptom free or there may be increased discharge, burning urination, irregular menstruation	• Clinical inspection • Culture of sample discharge	• Antibiotics
Pubic lice ("crabs"); caused by *Pthirus pubis* (an insect, not a crab)	• Sexual contact • Contact with infested towel, sheet, or toilet seat	• Intense itching in pubic area and other hairy regions to which lice can attach	• Clinical examination	• Drugs containing pyrethrins or piperonal butoxide (e.g., NIX, A200, RID, Triple X)

		Overview of Sexually Transmitted Infections (STIs)		
STI and Cause	Methods of Transmission	Symptoms	Diagnosis	Treatment
Syphilis; caused by *Treponema pallidum*	• Vaginal, oral, or anal sexual activity	• Hard, round painless chancre (sore) appears at site of infection within 2 to 4 weeks • May progress through additional stages if not treated • Potentially lethal	• Clinical examination or examination of fluid from a chancre • Blood test (the VDRL)	• Antibiotics
Trichomoniasis ("trich"); caused by *Trichomonas vaginalis*, a protozoan (one-celled animal)	• Almost always transmitted sexually	• In women, a discharge, itching, or burning in vulva • Mild urethritis in men • May be asymptomatic	• Microscopic examination of vaginal secretions • Examination of culture of sample	• Metronidazole (Flagyl)

Young gay males and homeless and runaway youths have elevated risk for HIV/AIDS. Anal intercourse is a likely route of transmission of HIV and is often practiced by gay males (Valleroy et al., 2000). Homeless and runaway adolescents are likely to engage in unprotected sex with several partners. Injecting drugs is another risk factor for HIV/AIDS because sharing needles with infected individuals can transmit HIV.

Women account for a minority of cases of HIV/AIDS in Canada but are more likely than males to be infected with HIV in many places around the world. A United Nations study in Europe, Africa, and Southeast Asia has found that sexually active teenage girls have higher rates of HIV infection than older women or young men (United Nations Special Session on AIDS, 2001). A number of erroneous assumptions about HIV/AIDS have had a disproportionately negative effect on women. They include the notions that HIV/AIDS is primarily a disease of gay men and people who inject drugs and that it is difficult to contract HIV/AIDS through male-female intercourse. However, the primary mode of HIV transmission worldwide is male-female intercourse. Among Canadian women, male-female intercourse is the major source of infection by HIV.

Truth or Fiction Revisited: Studies regarding knowledge, attitudes, and beliefs about HIV/AIDS find that even children in the early school years are aware of HIV/AIDS. Nearly all high school students know that HIV/AIDS is transmitted by sexual intercourse, but about half do not modify their sexual practices as a result of fear of the disease (Santelli et al., 2000). Adolescents often deny the threat of HIV/AIDS to them. As one high school girl said, "I can't believe that anyone I would have sex with would be infected." Guess what: Some are. ***Question: Given the threat of HIV/AIDS and other STIs, what can be done to prevent STIs?***

Prevention of Sexually Transmitted Infections

Prevention and education strategies are the primary weapons against STIs.

What should be the goals of a school-based program designed to prevent STIs? Increasing knowledge certainly is important (United Nations Special Session on AIDS, 2001). Adolescents need to learn about the transmission, symptoms, and consequences of STIs. They need to learn about "safer sex" techniques, including abstinence, and, if they are sexually active, the use of condoms. Educating young people to use condoms is associated with lower levels of infection around the globe (Ford et al., 2000; Fylkesnes et al., 2001). See the nearby "A Closer Look" feature on preventing HIV/AIDS and other STIs.

But knowledge alone may not change behaviour (Parsons et al., 2000). For example, many female adolescents lack power in their relationships. Males are likely to pressure them into unwanted or unprotected sexual relations (Friedman et al., 2001; Garcia-Moreno & Watts, 2000). Other goals of educational programs should include enhancing the adolescent's sense of control over the prevention of AIDS and modifying sexual and drug behaviours associated with acquiring the disease. As with programs designed to prevent substance abuse, the development of effective decision-making and social skills may be critical in programs designed to prevent STIs (United Nations Special Session on AIDS, 2001). Health Canada's (2003) *Canadian Guidelines for Sexual Health Education* use the Information, Motivational, and Behavioural Skills (IMB) model as a conceptual guide for promoting adolescent sexual health education. Plainly, sexual heath education is about more than just providing young people with relevant sexual knowledge; it also requires motivating youth to use their knowledge and engage in healthy practices, and helping youth acquire behavioural skills that will promote sexual health.

What Is the Risk of Their Contracting a Sexually Transmitted Infection? Young people generally know of the risks of HIV/AIDS, but knowledge of risks does not always translate into safe behaviour. Young people have heard of chlamydia and of genital warts, but they tend to underestimate the effects of these STIs.

How does one protect oneself from being infected with a sexually transmitted infection (STI)? Doing so can be awkward. It can be difficult. But it is also extremely important. Consider the comments of one young woman:

> It's one thing to talk about "being responsible about [STIs]" and a much harder thing to do it at the very moment. It's hard to imagine murmuring into someone's ear at a time of passion, "Would you mind slipping on this condom or using this cream just in case one of us has [an STI]?" Yet it seems awkward to bring it up beforehand, if it's not yet clear between us that we want to make love with one another.
>
> —Boston Women's Health Book Collective (1992, pp. 311-312)

Because discussing STIs with a partner can be a daunting task, some people wing it. They admit that they just hope for the best. But even if they do bring up the topic, they need to recognize that many people—perhaps most people—do not know whether they are infected with an STI, especially the organisms that cause chlamydia, gonorrhea, and AIDS. In any event, putting blinders on is not the answer. What can we do to prevent STIs? A number of things.

1. *Use sex education in the school.* Over 85 percent of Canadian parents agreed that sexual health education should be provided in the school (SIECAN, 2005).

2. *Assert the prevalence and harmful nature of STIs.* Many young people—and many older people—try not to think about the threats posed by STIs. The first, and perhaps most important, step in protecting yourself is psychological: keeping STIs in mind—refusing to play the dangerous game that involves pretending (at least for the moment) that they do not exist. The other measures involve modifying behaviour.

3. *Just say no—that is, remain abstinent.* One way of curtailing the transmission of infections is abstinence. But what does *abstinence* mean? The term can be limited to avoiding engaging in sexual intercourse with another

person. Hugging, light kissing (without exchanging saliva), and petting (without contacting semen or vaginal fluids) are usually safe, although readers may argue about whether these behaviours are consistent with the definition of abstinence.

4. *Limit yourself to a monogamous relationship with a partner who is not infected.* It is safe to engage in sexual intercourse in a monogamous relationship with a person who does not have an STI. The question is, How can you be certain that your partner is free of STIs and faithful? Adolescents who are unwilling to abstain from sexual intercourse or to limit themselves to one partner can still do things to make sex safer—that's saf*er*, not absolutely safe.

5. *Be picky.* Limit sexual activity to people you know well. Ask yourself whether these individuals are likely to have done things that could infect them with HIV or other disease organisms.

6. *Check out your partner's genitals.* Examine your partner's genitals for unpleasant odours, discharges, blisters, rashes, warts, and lice while engaged in foreplay. These are all possible symptoms of STIs.

7. *Wash the genitals.* Washing yourself beforehand helps protect your partner. Washing with soap and water afterward may kill or remove some pathogens. Urinating afterward might be of some help, particularly to men, because the acidity of urine can kill some pathogens in the urethra.

8. *Use latex condoms.* Latex condoms protect both partners from exchanging infected bodily fluids. Condoms are particularly effective in preventing transmission of gonorrhea, syphilis, and HIV.

9. *Talk to a doctor.* Use of antibiotics and antiviral medications after unprotected sex can guard against some bacterial and viral infections, even HIV. Adolescents should check with a doctor immediately if they think they may have been exposed to STIs.

10. *Have regular medical checkups.* These include blood tests. In this way, you can learn about and treat a number of disorders—particularly chlamydia and gonorrhea, the symptoms of which can go unnoticed.

Active Review

10. _____ is the most common sexually transmitted infection in adolescents.

11. Infection by _____ is linked to development of cancer of the cervix.

12. HIV is the virus that causes _____.

13. A (minority or majority?) of sexually active adolescents use condoms consistently.

Reflect & Relate: Do you—or did you—know any adolescents who contracted STIs? How? Were they aware at the time of the existence of the STIs and how they are transmitted? Have these STIs caused problems for those who were infected? Explain.

Go to
W W W **www.voyages1ce.nelson.com**
for an interactive version of this review.

Health in Adolescence

Adolescents are young and growing. Most seem sturdy. Injuries tend to heal quickly. *Question: How healthy are Canadian adolescents?* The good news is that most Canadian adolescents are healthy. Few are chronically ill or miss school. However, about 10 to 30 percent of the adolescent population are nonetheless impacted by serious and chronic illnesses (Health Canada, 2004[1]). Canadian teenagers may be less healthy than their parents were at the same age. The reason is not an increase in the incidence of infectious diseases or other physical illnesses. Rather, the causes are external and rooted in lifestyle and risky behaviour: stress and anxiety, excessive drinking, substance abuse, reckless driving, violence, disordered eating behaviour, and, as we have seen, unprotected sexual activity (Centers for Disease Control and Prevention, 2000b; Galambos & Tilton-Weaver, 1998; Health Canada, 2004).

Drinking and Driving: A Deadly Mix
The majority of adolescent deaths are due to accidents, most of them involving motor vehicles. Alcohol is often involved in accidental deaths.

Risk Taking in Adolescence

Although risk taking sometimes is viewed as a normal part of adolescent development, risk taking can be detrimental to the adolescent's health (Boyce, 2004; Galambos & Tilton-Weaver, 1998; U.S. Department of Health and Human Services, 2001). Let us look at some of the health risks of adolescence. We start by examining causes of death in adolescence. We then turn to the remaining two major health problems faced by teens: eating disorders and substance abuse. The third major health problem facing teens, sexually transmitted infections (STIs), was discussed in the previous section.

[1]Trends in the Health of Canadian Youth is a report based on the data collected through the 1989/90, 1993/94, and 1997/98 survey cycles for the World Health Organization Cross-National Collaborative Study: Health Behaviours in School-Age Children (HBSC). The trend comparisons report on data collected from among 11-, 13-, and 15-year-olds in Canada. This report includes data from a selection of other countries as well as data from grade 6, 7, 8, 9, and 10 students in Canada.

Causes of Death

Although adolescents are healthy as a group, a number of them die. *Questions: What are the causes of death among adolescents?* Death rates are low in adolescence, although they are higher for older adolescents than for younger ones. For example, each year about twice as many fifteen- to seventeen-year-olds as twelve- to fourteen-year-olds die (National Center for Injury Prevention and Control, 2004a). Death rates are nearly twice as great for male adolescents as for female adolescents. A major reason for this is that males are more likely to take risks that end in death as a result of accidents, suicide, or homicide (National Center for Injury Prevention and Control, 2004a). These three causes of death account for 75 percent of all adolescent deaths. *Truth or Fiction Revisited:* It is not true that substance abuse is the leading cause of death among male adolescents in Canada.

Unintentional injuries are the leading cause of death among children and youth in Canada (Boyce, 2004). And in the U.S., most of these involve motor vehicles (National Center for Injury Prevention and Control, 2004a). Alcohol is often involved in accidental deaths. Alcohol-related motor vehicle accidents are the leading cause of death for fifteen- to twenty-four-year-olds. Alcohol frequently is implicated in other causes of unintentional injuries or death, including drowning and falling (Steptoe et al., 2004).

Nutrition: An Abundance of Food

osteoporosis A condition involving progressive loss of bone tissue.

menopause The cessation of menstruation, typically occurring between ages 48 and 52.

Physical growth occurs more rapidly in the adolescent years than at any other time after birth, with the exception of the first year of life. *Questions: What are the nutritional needs of adolescents? What do adolescents actually eat?* To fuel the adolescent growth spurt, the average girl needs to consume about 2200 calories per day and the average boy needs about 3000 calories (Lowry et al., 2002). The nutritional needs of adolescents vary according to their stage of pubertal development. For example, at the peak of their growth spurt, adolescents use twice as much calcium, iron, zinc, magnesium, and nitrogen as they do during the other years of adolescence (Rockett et al., 2001). Calcium intake is particularly important for females to build up their bone density and help prevent a serious condition known as **osteoporosis** later in life. Osteoporosis, a progressive loss of bone, affects millions of women, particularly after **menopause.** But most teenagers—both girls and boys—do not consume enough calcium. Adolescents also are likely to obtain less vitamin A, thiamine, and iron but more fat, sugar, protein, and sodium than recommended (Rockett et al., 2001).

© Nico Kai/Getty Images

Nutritional Needs—or Should We Say *Habits*—of Adolescents
Teenagers require lots of calories to fuel the adolescent growth spurt. They may consume large amounts of fast food and junk food, which is high in calories and fat but not always nutritious.

One reason for adolescents' nutritional deficits is irregular eating patterns. Breakfast is often skipped, especially by girls who are watching their weight (Lowry et al., 2002). Teenagers are more likely to miss meals or eat away from home than they were in childhood (Thompson et al., 2004). They may consume large amounts of fast food and junk food, which is high in fat and calories but not very nutritious (Nielsen & Popkin, 2003; Thompson et al., 2004).

Junk food is connected with being overweight, and being overweight in adolescence can lead to chronic illness and earlier death in adulthood, even for teens who later lose weight (Pinhas-Hamiel & Zeitler, 2000). One study reported that overweight boys were more likely than boys of normal weight to die of heart disease, strokes, and cancer before the age of seventy (Must et al., 1992). Women who were overweight as teens had more difficulty with tasks such as climbing stairs, lifting, and walking by the age of seventy.

An Abundance of Eating Disorders: When Dieting Turns Deadly

The North American ideal has slimmed down to the point where most North American females of "average" weight (we are not talking here about those who are overweight!) are dissatisfied with the size and shape of their bodies (McLaren, 2002; Striegel-Moore et al., 2003). The wealthier your family, the more unhappy you are likely to be with your body (McLaren, 2002). Perhaps, then, it is no surprise that dieting has become the normal way of eating for most adolescent females (Lowry et al., 2002)! Plumpness has been valued in many preliterate societies, and Western paintings of previous centuries suggest that there was a time when physically well-rounded women were the ideal. But in contemporary Western culture, slim is in (Lowry et al., 2002).

Adolescents are highly concerned about their bodies. Puberty brings rapid changes, and adolescents wonder what they will look like once the flood of hormones has ebbed. In Chapter 15 we will see that adolescents also tend to think that others are paying a great deal of attention to their appearance. Because of the cultural emphasis on slimness and the psychology of the adolescent, adolescents—especially female adolescents—are highly vulnerable to eating disorders. *Question: What are eating disorders?* The eating disorders of *anorexia nervosa* and *bulimia nervosa* are characterized by gross disturbances in patterns of eating.

Anorexia Nervosa

All right: More adolescent girls diet than not. What's wrong with that? After all, there's the saying "You can never be too rich or too thin." ***Truth or Fiction Revisited:*** Most teens are not worried about a fat bank account, but one can certainly be too skinny, as in **anorexia nervosa**. Anorexia nervosa is a life-threatening eating disorder characterized by extreme fear of being too heavy, dramatic weight loss, a distorted body image, and resistance to eating enough to reach or maintain a healthful weight. Note the case of Rachel:

anorexia nervosa An eating disorder characterized by irrational fear of weight gain, distorted body image, and severe weight loss.

> I wanted to be a runner. Runners were thin, and I attributed this to dieting, not training. So I began restricting my diet: No butter, red meat, pork, dessert, candy, or snacking. If I ate any of the forbidden items, I obsessed about it and felt guilty for days.
>
> As a high school freshman, I wanted to run with the fastest girls, so I trained hard, really hard, and ate less. Lunch was lettuce sandwiches, carrots, and an apple. By my senior year, I was number three on the team, and lunch was a bagel and an orange.
>
> I maintained a rigid schedule—running cross country and track, having a seat on student council, volunteering, and maintaining a 3.9 GPA throughout high school—while starving myself (1000 calories per day), trying to attain the impossible perfection I thought couldn't be far away if I only slimmed down a little bit more.
>
> Several teammates were concerned, but I shrugged them off, saying family members were tall and slender; I was a health nut; I didn't like fatty foods; I was a vegetarian; I didn't like sweets; I wasn't hungry; I wasn't starving.

A psychiatrist didn't help at all. I went in, sat on the couch and told her what she wanted to hear: I would eat more, run less, stop restricting myself, and quit obsessing about being thin. I was very good at knowing exactly what to tell others.

I dropped ten pounds my freshman year—from 125 to 115 pounds. I was five feet, eight inches tall and wore a size five. I hated my body, so I starved myself and ran like a madwoman.

In quiet moments, I was sad and worried about what might be going on inside me.

I was already taking birth control to regain my menstrual cycle; my weight was 15 percent below what was recommended for my height; I was always cold; I had chest pains and an irregular heartbeat; my hair was limp and broke off; my skin was colorless.

It wasn't until I came to the University of Iowa and joined the varsity women's cross country team that I began to see what I was doing to myself. A teammate had an eating problem. Every time I saw her, I felt sick to my stomach. She had sunken cheeks, eyes so big they swallowed her face. She was an excellent student and a college-level varsity athlete. Many people wondered at her determination, but I understood. She used the same excuses I did.

For one sick instant, I wondered if I would be happier if I were that thin. That is when I started to realize I was slowly killing myself.

At the urging of my coach, I saw the team nutritionist who recommended a psychiatrist who felt no pity for me and made me take a brutally honest look at who I was and why I was starving myself. She didn't accept any of my excuses. She helped me realize that there are other things to think about besides food and body image. About this time I decided to quit the cross country team. The pressure I felt to be thin and competition at the college level were too much when I needed to focus on getting well.

After two months of therapy, my weight had dropped again. I'm not sure how far because I refused to step on a scale, but my size five pants were falling off. My psychiatrist required weekly weigh-ins.

I wasn't putting into practice any of the things my nutritionist and counselor suggested. They told me that if I wanted to have children someday I needed to eat. They warned me of osteoporosis at age thirty. Then my psychiatrist scared me to death. She told me I needed to start eating more or I would be checked into the hospital and hooked up to an IV. That would put me on the same level as my Iowa teammate. I had looked at her with such horror and never realized that I was in the same position.

My psychiatrist asked how my family would feel if they had to visit me in the hospital because I refused to eat. It was enough to make me think hard the next time I went through the food service lines.

Of course, I didn't get better the next day. But it was a step in the right direction. It's taken me three years to get where I am now. At five foot, eight and three-fourth inches (I even grew as I got healthier) and 145 pounds, I look and feel healthier, have better eating and exercise habits, and I don't obsess about food as much as I used to. On rare occasions, I think about controlling my food intake. My eating disorder will haunt me for the rest of my life. If I'm not careful, it could creep back.

Rachel, like other people with anorexia nervosa, weighed less than 85 percent of her recommended body weight, and "desirable" body weights are already too slender for many individuals. Anorexia nervosa afflicts males as well as females, but females with eating disorders outnumber males. Most studies put the female-to-male ratio at 10 to 1 or greater, but some find a smaller sex difference (Goode, 2000; Kjelsås et al., 2004; Striegel-Moore & Cachelin, 2001). By and large, anorexia nervosa afflicts women during adolescence and young adulthood (Winzelberg et al., 2000). The typical person with anorexia is a young European American female of higher socioeconomic status (Striegel-Moore et al, 2003). Affluent females have greater access to fitness centres and health clubs and are more likely to read the magazines that idealize slender bodies and shop in the boutiques that cater to females with svelte figures. All in all, they are regularly confronted with unrealistically high standards of slimness that make them extremely unhappy with their own physiques (McLaren, 2002). We know that the incidences of anorexia nervosa and bulimia nervosa have increased markedly in recent years.

Females with anorexia nervosa can drop 25 percent or more of their weight within a year. Severe weight loss triggers abnormalities in the endocrine system (i.e., with hormones) that prevent ovulation (Nielsen & Palmer, 2003). General health declines. Nearly every system in the body is affected. There are problems with the respiratory system (Key et al., 2001) and with the cardiovascular system (Mont, 2003). Females with anorexia are at risk for premature development of osteoporosis, a condition characterized by loss of bone density that usually afflicts people in late adulthood (Wentz et al., 2003; Wong et al., 2004). Given these problems, it is not surprising that the mortality rate for anorexic females is approximately 4 to 5 percent.

In one common pattern, the girl sees that she has gained some weight after menarche, and she resolves that she must lose it. But even after the weight is gone, she maintains her pattern of dieting and, in many cases, exercise at a fever pitch. Dieting and exercise continue as she plunges toward her recommended weight—according to weight charts—and even after those who care about her tell her that she is becoming all skin and bones. Denial is a huge part of anorexia nervosa. Anorexic girls deny they are losing too much weight. They deny any health problems, pointing to their feverish exercise routines as evidence. Distortion of the body image is a major feature of the disorder. Others see anorexic females as skin and bones, whereas anorexic women fix their gaze in the mirror and believe that they are looking at a body that is too heavy.

Ironically, individuals with anorexia do not literally distance themselves from food. They may become as preoccupied with food as they are with their own body shape. They may devour cookbooks (rather than food), shop for their families, and prepare gourmet feasts—for other people, that is.

An Adolescent with Anorexia Nervosa
Anorexia nervosa is a life-threatening eating disorder in which an individual—most often an adolescent or young adult female—has a distorted body image and consequently refuses to eat. She may lose 25 percent of her body weight in a year and impair the health of nearly all her bodily systems.

Bulimia Nervosa

Bulimia nervosa is sort of a companion disorder to anorexia nervosa, as we see in the case of Nicole:

> Nicole awakens in her cold dark room and already wishes it was time to go back to bed. She dreads the thought of going through this day, which will be like so many others in her recent past. She asks herself the question every morning, "Will I be able to make it through the day without being totally obsessed by thoughts of food, or will I blow it again and spend the day [binge eating]"? She tells herself that today she will begin a new life, today she will start to live like a normal human being. However, she is not at all convinced that the choice is hers.

—Boskind-White & White (1983, p. 29)

So, does Nicole begin a new life today? No. Despite her pledge to herself, Nicole begins the day with eggs and toast—butter included. Then she downs cookies; bagels smothered with cream cheese, butter, and jelly; doughnuts; candy bars; bowlfuls of cereal and milk—all in less than an hour. When her body cries, "No more!" she turns to the next step: purging. Purging also is a routine. In the bathroom, she ties back her hair. She runs the shower to mask noise, drinks some water, and makes herself throw everything up. Afterward she makes another pledge to herself: "Starting tomorrow, I'm going to change." Will she change? In truth, she doubts it.

bulimia nervosa An eating disorder characterized by cycles of binge eating and vomiting as a means of controlling weight gain.

Bulimia nervosa, Nicole's eating disorder, is symptomized by recurrent cycles of binge eating and purging. Binge eating often follows on the heels of food restriction—that is, dieting (Williams, 2004). There are various methods of purging. Nicole vomited. Other avenues include strict dieting or fasting, laxatives, and demanding, prolonged exercise regimes. Individuals with eating disorders, such as Rachel and Nicole, tend to be perfectionistic about their bodies. They will not settle for less than their idealized body shape and weight (Kaye et al., 2004). Bulimia, like anorexia, is connected with endocrine problems: One study found that nearly half the females with bulimia nervosa have irregular menstrual cycles (Gendall et al., 2000).

Bulimia nervosa, like anorexia nervosa, tends to afflict women during adolescence and young adulthood (Lewinsohn et al., 2000b; Williams, 2004). *Truth or Fiction Revisited:* It is true that some college women—and other young women—control their weight by going on cycles of binge eating followed by self-induced vomiting. Eating disorders are upsetting and dangerous in themselves, of course, but they are also connected with depression (Stice, Hayward et al., 2000). However, it seems that depression is more likely to co-occur with eating disorders than for either one to cause the other (Wade et al., 2000). *Question: What are the origins of eating disorders?*

Perspectives on Eating Disorders

Health professionals have done a great deal of research into the origins of eating disorders. Yet they will be the first to admit that many questions about these disorders remain unanswered (Striegel-Moore & Cachelin, 2001).

According to some psychoanalysts, anorexia nervosa may symbolize a young woman's efforts to cope with sexual fears, especially the possibility of becoming pregnant. They interpret the female's behaviour as an attempt to regress to prepubescence. Anorexia nervosa prevents some adolescents from separating from their families and assuming adult responsibilities. Their breasts and hips flatten once more because of the loss of fatty tissue. In the adolescent's fantasies, perhaps, she remains a sexually undifferentiated child.

Many parents are obsessed with encouraging their children—especially their infants—to eat adequately. Thus, some observers suggest that children may refuse to eat as a way of battling with their parents. ("You have to eat something!" "I'm not hungry!") It often seems that warfare does occur in the families of adolescents with eating disorders. Parents in such families are often unhappy and have their own issues with eating and dieting. They also "act out" against their daughters—letting them know that they consider them unattractive and, before the development of the eating disorder, letting them know that they think they should lose weight (Baker et al., 2000; Cooper et al., 2001).

A particularly disturbing risk factor for eating disorders in adolescent females is a history of child abuse, particularly sexual abuse (Jacobi et al., 2004; Williams & Gleaves, 2003). One study found a history of childhood sexual abuse in about half of women with bulimia nervosa, as opposed to a rate of about 7 percent among women without the disorder (Deep et al., 1999). Another study compared forty-five pairs of sisters, one of whom was diagnosed with anorexia nervosa (Karwautz et al., 2001). Those with anorexia were significantly more likely to be exposed to high parental expectations *and* to sexual abuse.

Some social cognitive theorists believe that weight loss acquires strong reinforcement value through its provision of feelings of personal perfectibility (Vitousek & Manke, 1994). But "perfection" is an unreachable goal for most individuals. Miss America, the annually renewed American role model, has also been slenderizing herself over the years. The pageant began in 1922. Over the past eighty years, the winner has added only 2 percent in height but has lost twelve pounds in weight. In the early days of the 1920s, Miss America's weight relative to her height yielded a body mass index (BMI[1]) of 20 to 25, which is considered normal by the World Health Organization (WHO). WHO labels people as malnourished when their BMIs are lower than 18.5. However, recent Miss Americas come in at a BMI near 17 (Rubinstein & Caballero, 2000). So Miss America adds to the woes of "normal" young women and even to those of young women who hover near the WHO "malnourished" borderline. As the cultural ideal slenderizes, women with recommended body weights, according to the health charts, feel overweight, and overweight women feel gargantuan (Winzelberg et al., 2000).

Many individuals with eating disorders, such as Rachel, are involved in activities that demand weight limits, such as dancing, acting, and modelling (Ravaldi et al., 2003). Gym enthusiasts and male wrestlers also feel the pressure to stay within an "acceptable" weight range (Ravaldi et al., 2003). Men, like women, experience pressure to create an ideal body, one with power in the upper torso and a trim abdomen.

Eating disorders tend to run in families, which raises the possibility of genetic involvement (Bellodi et al., 2001; Kaye et al., 2004; Speranza et al., 2001). Genetic factors do not directly cause eating disorders, but they appear to involve obsessionistic and perfectionistic personality traits (Kaye et al., 2004). In a society in which so much attention is focused on the ideal of the slender body, these personality traits encourage dieting (Wade et al., 2000). Anorexia also often co-occurs with depression (Lewinsohn et al., 2000b; Wade et al., 2000). Perfectionistic people are likely to be disappointed in themselves, giving rise to feelings of depression. But it may also be that both anorexia and depression share genetic factors. Genetically inspired perfectionism, cultural emphasis on slimness, self-absorption, and family conflict may create a perfect recipe for development of eating disorders (Kaye et al., 2004).

Treatment and Prevention

Treatment of eating disorders—particularly anorexia nervosa—is a great challenge (Stein et al., 2001). The disorders are connected with serious health problems, and the low weight of individuals with anorexia is often life-threatening. Many children and adolescent girls are admitted to the hospital for treatment against their will (Watson et al., 2000). Denial is a feature of anorexia nervosa, and many girls do not recognize—or do not admit—that they have a problem. When the individual with anorexia does not—or cannot—eat adequately through the mouth, measures such as nasogastric (tube) feeding may be used.

---

[1] You can calculate your body mass index as follows. Write down your weight in pounds. Multiply it by 703. Divide the product by your height in inches squared. For example, if you weigh 160 lbs and are 5 feet 8 inches tall, your BMI is $(160 \times 703)/68^2$, or 24.33. A BMI of more than 25 is defined as overweight.

Antidepressants are frequently used in the treatment of eating disorders. Eating disorders are frequently accompanied by depression, and it may be that the common culprit in eating disorders and depression is a lower than normal level of the neurotransmitter serotonin. Antidepressants such as Prozac and Zoloft enhance the activity of serotonin in the brain, often increasing food intake in anorexic individuals and decreasing binge eating in bulimic people. In one study, ten of eleven anorexic females showed significant weight gain after fourteen weeks of treatment with an antidepressant, and they maintained the gain at a sixty-four-week follow-up (Santonastaso et al., 2001). They were also evaluated as being significantly less depressed and perfectionistic. Other researchers combine antidepressants with nutritional supplements (Barbarich et al., 2004).

Because family problems are commonly connected with eating disorders, family therapy is often used to treat these disorders (Diamond & Siqueland, 2001; Lock & Le Grange, 2001). Family therapy has positive outcomes in many cases, but it is not an appropriate setting for dealing with childhood sexual abuse.

Cognitive-behavioural therapy has been used to help anorexic and bulimic individuals challenge their perfectionism and distorted body images. It has also been used to systematically reinforce appropriate eating behaviour. But let's remember that all of this is connected with cultural attitudes that idealize excessive thinness. "Prevention" will have to address cultural values as well as potential problems in individual adolescents.

Substance Abuse and Dependence: Where Does It Begin? Where Does It End?

Think of Canada as a cafeteria with brightly coloured drugs glimmering on the shelves and in the trays. In almost any high school in any part of the country, adolescents will tell you that drugs are available. In fact, so will many middle-schoolers. And so will some elementary school children. Credit adolescents who do not use drugs. They generally refuse them as a matter of choice, not because of lack of supply. The drugs are there, and some of the most harmful drugs are perfectly legal, at least for adults.

Children and adolescents use drugs not only to cope with medical problems but also to deal with daily tensions, run-of-the-mill depression, even boredom. Many adolescents use drugs for the same reasons that adults do, but they also use them because they are imitating peers or rebelling against parents who beg them not to (Jarvis, 2004; Oman et al., 2002). They use drugs to experience pleasure, to deaden pain, and to earn prestige among peers.

Adolescents frequently get involved with drugs that cripple their ability to attend school or to pay attention when they do (Bryant et al., 2003). Alcohol and other drugs are also linked with reckless, sometimes deadly, behaviour (Oman et al., 2002). Alcohol is the BDOC—that is, the Big Drug on Campus. It is the most widely used substance in high schools and on college campuses (Johnston et al., 2004). Marijuana is no slacker either. Nearly half of high school students have tried it by the time they graduate (Johnston et al., 2004).

Where does the use of a drug or substance end and substance abuse begin? *Questions: What is substance abuse? What is substance dependence?* According to the American Psychiatric Association (2000), **substance abuse** is the ongoing use of a substance despite the social, occupational, psychological, or physical problems it causes. When adolescents miss school or fail to complete assignments because they are intoxicated or "sleeping it off," they are abusing alcohol. The amount they drink is not the issue; the problem is the role that the substance plays in their lives.

substance abuse A persistent pattern of use of a substance characterized by frequent intoxication and impairment of physical, social, or emotional well-being.

© Bill Aron/PhotoEdit

Substance dependence is more serious than substance abuse. An adolescent who is dependent on a substance loses control over using it and may organize his or her life around getting the substance and using it. Substance dependence also changes the body. Having it in one's body becomes the norm so that the adolescent may experience tolerance, withdrawal symptoms, or both. **Tolerance** develops as the body becomes habituated to the substance; as a result, the adolescent has to use progressively higher doses to achieve the same effects. A number of substances are physically addictive, so that when the addicted adolescent stops using it or lowers the dosage, characteristic withdrawal symptoms occur; this is also known as **abstinence syndrome.** When addicted individuals lower their intake of alcohol, they may experience symptoms such as tremors (shakes), high blood pressure, rapid heart and pulse rate, anxiety, restlessness, and weakness. Many adolescents who begin to use substances such as alcohol for pleasure wind up using them to escape the abstinence syndrome.

Why, you might wonder, are psychologists and educators so concerned about substance abuse? It is not just a moral issue. Drugs are not "bad" simply because they are illegal. Children and adolescents are not advised to avoid them simply because they are underage. Drugs can have serious harmful effects on health. Consider the effects of some depressants, stimulants, and hallucinogens.

Effects of Depressants

Question: What are the effects of depressants? All depressants slow the activity of the nervous system. Beyond that, they have different cognitive and biological effects. Depressants include alcohol, narcotics derived from the opium poppy (heroin, morphine, and the like), and **sedatives** (such as barbiturates and methaqualone).

Research shows that alcohol lessens inhibitions, meaning that adolescents may do things when drinking that they would otherwise resist (de Wit et al., 2000; Feola et al., 2000). Ingesting five or more drinks in a row—that is, *binge drinking*—is connected with bad grades and risky behaviour, including risky (unprotected, promiscuous) sex, acts of aggression, and accidents (Bryant et al., 2003; Santelli et al., 2004). Small amounts of alcohol can be stimulating, but high doses have a sedative effect, which is why alcohol is labelled a depressant. Alcohol is also an intoxicant: It

Substance Use and Abuse
It is important to distinguish between the use and abuse of substances. Many adolescents occasionally experiment with substances such as alcohol and marijuana.

substance dependence A persistent pattern of use of a substance that is accompanied by physiological addiction.

tolerance Habituation to a drug such that increasingly higher doses are needed to achieve similar effects.

abstinence syndrome A characteristic cluster of symptoms that results from a sudden decrease in the level of usage of a substance.

sedatives Drugs that soothe or quiet restlessness or agitation.

distorts perceptions, impairs concentration, hinders coordination, and slurs the speech. The media pay more attention to deaths resulting from heroin and cocaine overdoses, but hundreds of college students die each year from causes related to drinking, including accidents and overdoses (Li et al., 2001). (Yes, a person can die from drinking too much at one time.)

Adolescent drinking often leads to drinking as an adult, and chronic drinking can lead to serious physical disorders such as cirrhosis or cancer of the liver. Chronic heavy drinking has been linked to cardiovascular disorders. Heavy drinking increases the risk of breast cancer among women and may harm the embryo if she is pregnant (Rathus et al., 2005).

Heroin is a depressant that is derived from the opium poppy. Like morphine and other opioids, its major medical use is relief from pain. But it can also provide a euphoric "rush," which is why many experimenters are tempted to use it again. Heroin is addictive, and regular users develop tolerance.

Barbiturates are depressants with various legitimate medical uses, such as relief from pain, anxiety, and tension, and treatment of insomnia, high blood pressure, and epilepsy, but people can become rapidly dependent on them. These drugs are used illegally by adolescents because of their relaxing effects and their ability to produce a mild euphoria. Depressants have additive effects; therefore, mixing barbiturates and other depressants is risky.

Effects of Stimulants

Question: What are the effects of stimulants? Using stimulants is like stepping on the body's accelerator pedal. Stimulants speed up the heartbeat and other bodily functions. They can also keep people awake and alert, but at the expense of some wear and tear. Nicotine, cocaine, and amphetamines are the most commonly used stimulants.

Nicotine is found in cigars, cigarettes, and chewing tobacco. Nicotine causes the release of the hormone adrenaline, which ramps up the heart, disrupts its rhythm, and causes the liver to pour sugar into the blood (Jarvis, 2004). Nicotine, like other stimulants, also raises the rate at which the body burns calories and lowers the appetite, so some adolescents smoke as a means of weight control (Jarvis, 2004). Nicotine is also the chemical that addicts people to tobacco (Canadian Cancer Society, 2006; American Lung Association, 2000). The abstinence syndrome from nicotine includes symptoms such as drowsiness and loss of energy (the stimulant is gone, after all), palpitations of the heart (irregular heartbeats), sweating, tremors, lightheadedness and dizziness, insomnia, headaches, and digestive problems (irregular bowel movements and cramps). Annually, nearly 45 000 Canadians die from tobacco-related problems (Canadian Lung Association, 2006). Cigarette smoke contains carbon monoxide, which causes shortness of breath, and hydrocarbons ("tars"), which are responsible for most respiratory diseases and cases of lung cancer (American Lung Association, 2004). Pregnant smokers increase the risk of miscarriage, stillbirths, preterm births, and low-birth-weight babies (American Lung Association, 2004).

The stimulant cocaine produces feelings of euphoria, relieves pain, boosts self-confidence, and reduces the appetite. Cocaine has biological as well as psychological effects: It accelerates the heart rate, spikes the blood pressure, constricts the arteries of the heart, and thickens the blood—a combination that can cause cardiovascular and respiratory collapse (Moliterno et al., 1994). Cocaine has caused the deaths of several young athletes who used it to boost performance and confidence. Because cocaine is a stimulant, overdoses can cause restlessness, insomnia, and tremors.

During World War II, amphetamines were used by soldiers to keep them awake at night. Truck drivers use them to drive through the night. Amphetamines are widely known to students as enablers of all-night cram sessions. Many dieters rely on them to reduce their appetites. Tolerance for amphetamines develops rapidly, and adolescents can become dependent on them, especially when they use them to self-medicate for depression. Regular use of the powerful amphetamine called methamphetamine may be physically addictive (Volkow et al., 2001a, 2001b), but the extent to which amphetamines cause physical addiction has been a subject of controversy. High doses of amphetamines, as with high doses of cocaine, can cause restlessness and insomnia, irritability, and loss of appetite. In recent years, methamphetamine has been the new drug of choice for youth (street names: speed, meth, chalk, ice, crystal, crystal meth, jib) because of its low cost, ease of manufacture, and availability (Centre for Addiction and Mental Health, 2007).

Effects of Hallucinogens

Question: What are the effects of hallucinogens? **Hallucinogens** give rise to perceptual distortions called hallucinations. The hallucinator may believe that the hallucination cannot be real, yet it assaults the senses so strongly that it is confused with reality. Marijuana, Ecstasy, LSD, and PCP are examples of hallucinogenic drugs.

Marijuana is derived from the *Cannabis sativa* plant. It is typically smoked, although it can be eaten. Many adolescents report that marijuana helps them relax and elevates their mood. Adolescents who use marijuana report greater sensory awareness, self-insight, creativity, and empathy for other people's feelings. Smokers become highly attuned to bodily sensations, especially their heartbeat, which tends to accelerate. They experience visual hallucinations, as in time seeming to slow down so that a song might seem to go on indefinitely. But strong intoxication can disorient and frighten some smokers.

Marijuana carries a number of health risks. For example, it impairs the perceptual-motor coordination used in driving. It impairs short-term memory and slows learning (Ashton, 2001). Although it causes positive mood changes in many people, some experience anxiety and confusion (Johns, 2001). There is no question that adolescents can become psychologically dependent on marijuana. However, research also suggests that regular users can experience tolerance and an abstinence syndrome, which are signs of physical addiction (American Psychiatric Association, 2000; Johns, 2001).

Ecstasy—also known as MDMA (an abbreviation for its chemical formula)—is a popular "party drug" or "club drug." Its chemical formula has similarities to amphetamines, stimulants, and mescaline, the hallucinogenic drug (Concar, 2002; Freese et al., 2002). As a result, Ecstasy gives users the boost of a stimulant—making them somewhat more alert and suffusing them with feelings of elation and self-confidence. As a mild hallucinogen, it also removes users a bit from reality. The combination appears to free them to some degree from inhibitions and cognitive awareness of the possible consequences of risky behaviour, such as unprotected sex. Ecstasy can also impair working memory (not helpful in studying), increase anxiety, and lead to depression (Cassaday et al., 2003; Navarro & Maldonado, 2002; Parrott, 2003; Taffe et al., 2002).

LSD is the acronym for lysergic acid diethylamide, another hallucinogenic drug.

Regular use of hallucinogens can cause psychological dependence and tolerance, but people are not known to become physically addicted to them. High doses can impair coordination and judgment (driving on hallucinogenic drugs poses grave risks), change the mood, and cause hallucinations and paranoid delusions (belief that one is in danger or being observed or followed).

Various drugs and their effects are summarized in Table 14.2.

Prevalence of Substance Abuse

Ongoing Health Canada surveys of high school students find that drug use between 1998 and 2002 remained fairly stable, except for increased marijuana use in Grade 10 boys and decreased use of LSD for both males and females (Saab, 2004).

hallucinogens Drugs that give rise to hallucinations.

Question: How widespread is substance abuse among adolescents? Self-reported lifetime use of illicit drugs among eighth-graders increased from 19 percent in 1991 to 31 percent in 1996 and then declined to 23 percent in 2003.[2] The increase among twelfth-graders was from 44 percent in 1991 to a high of 55 percent in 1999; then, use declined to 51 percent in 2003. ***Truth or Fiction Revisited:*** Actually, substance use and abuse among high school students seems to be experiencing a slight decline.

The occurrence of binge drinking, in which five or more drinks in a row are consumed, is of particular concern. Binge drinking is connected with occasional deaths from alcohol overdose and with reckless behaviours, such as engaging in sex without use of condoms. According to a 1998 health report (Galambos & Tilton-Weaver, 1998), 52 percent of males and 35 percent of females (aged fifteen to nineteen) reported binge drinking at least once in a given year. Those percentages increased to 73 percent for males and 51 percent for females in the twenty to twenty-four age demographic.

About 3 percent of high school students have used steroids. Steroids, which build muscle mass, are typically used by high school males in an effort to improve athletic performance, although some users also want to improve their physical appearance.

Drugs and Their Effects

Drug	Type	How Taken	Desired Effects	Tolerance	Abstinence Syndrome	Side Effects
Alcohol	Depressant	By mouth	Relaxation, euphoria, lowered inhibitions	Yes	Yes	Impaired coordination, poor judgment, hangover[3]
Heroin	Depressant	Injected, smoked, by mouth	Relaxation, euphoria, relief from anxiety and pain	Yes	Yes	Impaired coordination and mental functioning, drowsiness, lethargy[3]
Barbiturates and methaqualone	Depressants	By mouth, injected	Relaxation, sleep, euphoria, lowered inhibitions	Yes	Yes	Impaired coordination and mental functioning, drowsiness, lethargy[3]

[3] Overdose can result in death.

[2]"Lifetime use" refers to whether the individual ever used the drug. Individuals who report experimenting with the drug even once would fall into this category. The University of Michigan group uses "30-day prevalence"—that is, whether the individual has used the drug within the past month—to arrive at estimates of more regular usage.

Drugs and Their Effects

Drug	Type	How Taken	Desired Effects	Tolerance	Abstinence Syndrome	Side Effects
Amphetamines	Stimulants	By mouth, injected	Alertness, euphoria	Yes	?	Restlessness, loss of appetite, convulsions, strokes, psychotic symptoms
Methamphetamine (methylamphetamine or desoxyephedrine)	Stimulants	Insufflation, inhalation, or suppository	Euphoria, excitement	?	?	?
Cocaine	Stimulant	By mouth, snorted, injected	Euphoria, self-confidence	Yes	Yes	Restlessness, loss of appetite, convulsions, strokes, psychotic symptoms
Nicotine (cigarettes)	Stimulant	By tobacco (smoked, chewed, or sniffed)	Relaxation, stimulation, weight control	Yes	Yes	Cancer, heart disease, lung and respiratory diseases
Marijuana	Hallucinogen	Smoked, by mouth	Relaxation, perceptual distortions, enhancement of experience	?	?	Impaired coordination, learning, respiratory problems, panic
MDMA ("Ecstasy")	Stimulant/ hallucinogen	By mouth	Alertness, self-confidence, hallucinations	?	?	Impaired memory, increased heart rate, anxiety, confusion, possible depression
LSD, PCP	Hallucinogen	By mouth	Perceptual distortions, vivid hallucinations	Yes	No	Impaired coordination, psychotic symptoms, panic

Factors in Substance Abuse and Dependence

Question: What factors are associated with substance abuse and dependence?
Adolescents often become involved with substance abuse and dependence through experimental use (Chassin et al., 2000; Lewinsohn et al., 2000a). Why do children and adolescents experiment with alcohol and other drugs? There are any number of reasons (Jarvis, 2004; Oman et al., 2002). Some are conforming to peer pressure; acceptance by peers means doing what the peers do. Some are rebelling against moral or social constraints. Others are in it for the experience. Of these, some are simply curious; they want to see what effects the drugs will have. Others are trying to escape from boredom or from the pressures of school or the neighbourhood. Some, of course, are looking for pleasure or excitement. Some youngsters are imitating what they see their own parents doing.

Social cognitive theorists suggest that children and adolescents usually try drugs because someone has recommended them or because they have observed someone else using them. But whether or not they continue to use the drug depends on factors such as whether use is reinforced by peer approval. The drug can also be reinforcing by enhancing the user's mood or by reducing unpleasant emotions such as anxiety and tension. For individuals who are addicted, the prevention of the abstinence syndrome is reinforcing. Carrying the substance and obtaining a "rainy day" supply are reinforcing because the child or adolescent does not have to worry about being caught short.

Disapproval of Drug Use by Twelfth-Graders, 1975 versus 2003		
Do You Disapprove of People (Who Are 18 or Older) Doing Each of the Following	Percentage Disapproving Class of 1975	Percentage Disapproving Class of 2003
Try marijuana once or twice	47	53
Smoke marijuana regularly	72	79
Try LSD once or twice	83	86
Take LSD regularly	94	94
Try MDMA (Ecstasy) once or twice	—	85
Try cocaine once or twice	81	89
Take cocaine regularly	93	96
Try crack once or twice	—	87
Take crack regularly	—	91
Try heroin once or twice	92	94
Take heroin regularly	97	97
Try amphetamines once or twice	75	86
Take amphetamines regularly	92	94
Try barbiturates once or twice	78	88
Take barbiturates regularly	93	94
Try one or two drinks of an alcoholic beverage (beer, wine, liquor)	22	27
Take one or two drinks nearly every day	68	69
Take four or five drinks nearly every day	89	86
Have five or more drinks once or twice each weekend	60	64
Smoke one or more packs of cigarettes per day	68	75
Take steroids	—	86

Adapted from Johnston et al. (2004, Table 7).]

Why, you may wonder, do children and adolescents use drugs when their health education courses inform them that they are harmful? Do they not believe their teachers? Some do; some don't. But the reinforcement value of the substances occurs *now, today.* The harmful effects are frequently long term or theoretical.

Associating with peers who use drugs and who tolerate drug use is one of the strongest predictors of adolescent drug use and abuse (Jarvis, 2004; Oman et al., 2002). Children are highly vulnerable to peer pressure in the early teen years. If they are closely involved with a drug-abusing group, they may feel pressured to join in. Adolescents who are extensively involved with peers, especially to the exclusion of their families, are at greater risk for drug use.

© Bonnie Kamin/PhotoEdit

Smoking
The "Monitoring the Future" survey finds that about 70 percent of twelfth-graders disapprove of smoking a pack or more of cigarettes a day, yet about 31 percent of students have smoked a cigarette within the past 30 days. Why do young people smoke when they know that smoking is harmful?

Parenting styles play a role. Having open lines of communication with a parent helps inhibit drug use. The authoritative pattern of child rearing appears to protect children from substance abuse (Baumrind, 1991b; Dorius et al., 2004; Saab, 2004). Heavy drug use is most likely to occur in families with permissive or neglecting-rejecting parenting styles.

Adolescent drug users often experience school problems. They do poorly in school, and their academic motivation is low (Bryant et al., 2003). Certain psychological characteristics are associated with drug use, including anxiety and depression, antisocial behaviour, and low self-esteem (Beitchman et al., 2001; Dierker et al., 2001; Donohue et al., 2004; Moeller et al., 2001). But because signs of maladjustment often emerge before drug abuse begins, it can be difficult to sort out cause and effect (Donohue et al., 2004).

Biological factors are apparently involved in determining which experimenters will continue to use a drug and which will not. Children may inherit genetic predispositions toward abuse of specific substances, including depressants, stimulants, and hallucinogens (Agrawal et al., 2004; Buck et al., 2004; Fromme et al., 2004; Herman et al., 2003; Shenassa et al., 2003). The biological children of alcoholics who are reared by adoptive parents are more likely to abuse alcohol than are the biological children of the adoptive parents.

Treatment and Prevention

Question: How can we treat and prevent substance abuse? Health professionals, educators, police departments, and laypeople have devised many approaches to the prevention and treatment of substance abuse and dependence among adolescents. However, treatment has been a frustrating endeavour, and it is not clear which approaches are most effective (Deas & Thomas, 2001). In many cases, adolescents with drug dependence really do not want to discontinue the substances they are abusing. Many are referred to treatment by parents or school systems, but they deny the negative impact of drugs on their lives. They may belong to a peer group that frowns on prevention or treatment programs. When addicted adolescents come for treatment, helping them through a withdrawal syndrome may be straightforward enough. But once their bodies no longer require the substance to feel "normal," they may return to the social milieu that fosters substance abuse and be unable to find strong reasons for living a life without drugs. The problem of returning to abuse and dependence following treatment—that is, the problem of *relapse*—can thus be more troublesome than the problems involved in initial treatment (Dasinger et al., 2004; Kaminer, 2001).

Many adolescents with substance abuse problems also have psychological disorders or serious family problems. When treatment programs focus only on substance abuse and do little to treat the psychological disorder or relationships in the family, the outcome of treatment tends to suffer (Beitchman et al., 2001; Rohde et al., 2001).

The ability of teenagers to deal with the physical changes of adolescence and to engage in health-promoting behaviours depends in part on their growing cognitive abilities. We examine development in that area in Chapter 15.

Active Review

14. Death rates are greater for (male or female?) adolescents.

15. Most adolescent deaths are due to _____.

16. _____ is a life-threatening eating disorder characterized by intense fear of being overweight, a distorted body image, and refusal to eat.

17. Bulimia nervosa is characterized by recurrent cycles of binge eating followed by _____.

18. Anorexia nervosa and bulimia nervosa (do or do not?) tend to run in families.

19. Eating disorders are connected with traits such as _____.

20. Substance _____ is the repeated use of a substance despite the fact that it is causing or compounding social, occupational, psychological, or physical problems.

21. Substance dependence is characterized by loss of control over the substance, tolerance, and a(n) _____ syndrome.

22. _____ is the most commonly used substance by adolescents.

23. _____ is the agent that creates physiological dependence on tobacco.

24. High school seniors are more likely to disapprove of (experimental or regular?) drug use.

Reflect & Relate: How widespread were eating disorders and substance abuse in your own high school? Did you notice sex differences in the rates of these two problems? How did these problems begin? What are some ways in which parents and educators might help adolescents avoid them?

Go to

W W W **www.voyages1ce.nelson.com**
for an interactive version of this review.

Recite: *An Active Summary*™

1. What is adolescence?

Adolescence is a transitional period between childhood and adulthood. G. Stanley Hall believed that adolescence is marked by "storm and stress." Current views challenge the idea that storm and stress are normal or beneficial.

2. What is puberty? What happens during puberty?

Puberty is a stage of physical development that is characterized by reaching sexual maturity. Puberty is controlled by a feedback loop involving glands. Sex hormones trigger the development of primary and secondary sex characteristics.

3. What happens during the adolescent growth spurt?

Girls spurt sooner than boys. Boys tend to spurt up to four inches per year, and girls, up to three inches per year. During their growth spurts, boys catch up with girls and grow taller and heavier. Boys' shoulders become broader, and girls develop broader and rounder hips. More of a male's body weight is made up of muscle. Adolescents may look gawky because of asynchronous growth. Boys typically ejaculate by age thirteen or fourteen. Female sex hormones regulate the menstrual cycle.

4. What are the effects of early or late maturation on adolescents?

The effects of early maturation are generally positive for boys and often negative for girls. Early-maturing boys tend to be more popular. Early-maturing girls become conspicuous, often leading to sexual approaches, deviant behaviour, and a poor body image.

5. How do adolescents feel about their bodies?

Girls are generally more dissatisfied with their bodies than boys are. By age eighteen, dissatisfaction tends to decline.

6. What kinds of sexually transmitted infections are there?

Sexually transmitted infections (STIs) include bacterial infections such as chlamydia, gonorrhea, and syphilis; viral infections such as HIV/AIDS, HPV, and genital herpes; and some others.

7. What factors place adolescents at risk for contracting STIs?

The factors include sexual activity with multiple partners and without condoms, and substance abuse. Sharing hypodermic needles with an infected person can also transmit HIV.

8. Given the threat of HIV/AIDS and other STIs, what can be done to prevent STIs?

Prevention involves education about STIs, along with advice concerning abstinence or "safer sex."

9. How healthy are Canadian adolescents?

Most Canadian adolescents are healthy, but 10 to 30 percent of the adolescent population is nonetheless affected by serious or chronic illnesses.

10. What are the causes of death among adolescents?

Death rates are greater for older adolescents and for male adolescents. Accidents, suicide, and homicide account for about three in four deaths among adolescents.

11. What are the nutritional needs of adolescents? What do adolescents actually eat?

The average girl needs about 2200 calories per day, and the average boy needs about 3000 calories. Adolescents need high quantities of elements such as calcium, iron, zinc, magnesium, and nitrogen. Adolescents usually need more vitamins than they take in but less sugar, fat, protein, and sodium.

12. What are eating disorders?

The eating disorders include anorexia nervosa and bulimia nervosa. Anorexia nervosa is characterized by fear of being overweight, a distorted body image, and refusal to eat. Bulimia nervosa is characterized by recurrent cycles of binge eating followed by purging. Eating disorders mainly afflict females.

13. What are the origins of eating disorders?

Some psychoanalysts suggest that anorexia represents efforts to remain pre-pubescent. One risk factor for eating disorders in adolescent females is a history of child abuse. Eating disorders may develop because of fear of gaining weight resulting from cultural idealization of the slim female. Genetic factors may connect eating disorders with perfectionistic personality styles.

14. What is substance abuse? What is substance dependence?

Substance abuse is use of a substance despite the social, occupational, psychological, or physical problems it causes. Substance dependence is characterized by loss of control over the substance and is typified by tolerance and withdrawal symptoms.

15. What are the effects of depressants?

Depressants are addictive substances that slow the activity of the nervous system. Alcohol lowers inhibitions, relaxes, and intoxicates. Heroin can provide a strong euphoric "rush." Barbiturates relieve anxiety and tension.

16. What are the effects of stimulants?

Stimulants accelerate the heartbeat and other bodily functions and depress the appetite. Nicotine is the stimulant in tobacco. The stimulant cocaine produces euphoria and bolsters self-confidence, but it occasionally causes respiratory and cardiovascular collapse. Adolescents use amphetamines to remain awake for cram sessions.

17. What are the effects of hallucinogens?

Hallucinogens give rise to perceptual distortions called hallucinations. Marijuana helps some adolescents relax and elevates the mood, but it impairs perceptual-motor coordination and short-term memory. LSD ("acid") produces vivid hallucinations.

18. How widespread is substance abuse among adolescents?

About half of high school seniors have tried illicit drugs. Marijuana use seems to be on the rise. Most students have tried alcohol, and many use it regularly. About 30 percent of high school seniors have engaged in binge drinking.

19. How many adolescents disapprove of use of drugs?

Adolescents are more likely to disapprove of regular or excessive drug use than experimental drug use. Most high school seniors disapprove of regular use of LSD, cocaine, crack, heroin, amphetamines, barbiturates, and smoking.

20. What factors are associated with substance abuse and dependence?

Substance abuse and dependence usually begin with experimental use in adolescence. Adolescents may experiment because of curiosity, conformity to peer pressure, parental use, rebelliousness, and a desire to escape from boredom or pressure and to seek excitement or pleasure. Some individuals may also have a genetic predisposition toward dependence on certain substances.

21. How can we treat and prevent substance abuse?

It may be relatively simple to help an adolescent through an abstinence syndrome (the process is called detoxification); it is more difficult to prevent relapse.

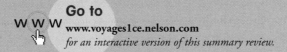

Go to
W W W **www.voyages1ce.nelson.com**
for an interactive version of this summary review.

Key Terms

genital stage *(page 522)*
puberty *(page 523)*
feedback loop *(page 523)*
hypothalamus *(page 523)*
pituitary gland *(page 523)*
primary sex characteristics *(page 523)*
secondary sex characteristics *(page 523)*
asynchronous growth *(page 526)*
secular trend *(page 527)*
larynx *(page 527)*

semen *(page 528)*
nocturnal emission *(page 528)*
gynecomastia *(page 528)*
epiphyseal closure *(page 528)*
mammary glands *(page 528)*
labia *(page 528)*
clitoris *(page 528)*
menarche *(page 529)*
HIV/AIDS *(page 536)*
osteoporosis *(page 544)*

menopause *(page 544)*
anorexia nervosa *(page 545)*
bulimia nervosa *(page 548)*
substance abuse *(page 550)*
substance dependence *(page 551)*
tolerance *(page 551)*
abstinence syndrome *(page 551)*
sedatives *(page 551)*
hallucinogens *(page 553)*

Active Learning Resources

Observing Children and Adolescents Observing Children and Adolescents CD-ROM
Want to watch videos showing what you've just learned about in this chapter? Check out the "Puberty and Body Image" and "Risk Taking" clips in Module 4, Sections 1 and 2.

Visit Your Companion Website for This Book
http://www.voyages1CE.nelson.com
Check out this companion website, where you will find online resources directly linked to your book. The website includes interactive exercises related to PQ4R and Power Visuals for mastering and reviewing key concepts as well as quizzing, chapter outlines, and much more!

CengageNOW!™
http://hed.nelson.com
Go to this site for the link to CengageNOW™, your one-stop study shop. Take a Pretest for this chapter, and CengageNOW™ will generate a personalized Study Plan based on your test results! The Study Plan will identify the topics you need to review and direct you to online resources to help you master those topics. You can then take a Posttest to help you determine the concepts you have mastered and those you still need to work on.

15

Adolescence: Cognitive Development

PREVIEW

TRUTH OR FICTION?

● ● ● ● ● ● ● ● ● ● ●

T F Many adolescents see themselves as being on stage.

T F It is normal for male adolescents to think of themselves as action heroes and to act as though they are made of steel.

T F Adolescent boys outperform adolescent girls in mathematics.

T F Most adolescents make moral decisions based on their own ethical principles and may choose to disobey the laws of the land if they conflict with their principles.

T F The transition from elementary school is more difficult for boys than for girls.

T F Adolescents who work after school obtain lower grades.

Go to WWW
www.voyages1CE.nelson.com
for an interactive version of this "Truth or Fiction" feature.

am a college student of extremely modest means. Some crazy psychologist interested in something called "formal-operational thought" has just promised to pay me $20 if I can make a coherent logical argument for the proposition that the federal government should under no circumstances ever give or lend more to needy college students. Now what could people who believe *that* possibly say by way of supporting that argument? Well, I suppose they *could* offer this line of reasoning....

—Flavell et al. (2002)

This "college student of extremely modest means" is thinking like an adolescent, quite differently from an elementary school child and differently from most junior high-school students. Children in the concrete-operational stage are bound by the facts as they are. They are not given to hypothetical thinking, to speculation about what might be. They are mainly stuck in what *is*. But the adolescent, like the adult, can ponder abstract ideas and see the world *as it could be*. Our "college student of extremely modest means" recognizes that a person can find arguments for causes in which he or she does not believe.

In this chapter, we learn about cognitive development in adolescence. We focus first on aspects of intellectual development, including Piaget's stage of formal operations, adolescent egocentrism, and sex differences. We then turn to moral development, focusing on the views of Kohlberg and Gilligan. We conclude with a look at some areas that are strongly tied to cognitive development: school, vocational development, and work experience.

formal operations The fourth stage in Piaget's cognitive-developmental theory, characterized by the capacity for flexible, reversible operations concerning abstract ideas and concepts, such as symbols, statements, and theories.

The Adolescent in Thought: My, My, How "Formal"

The growing intellectual capabilities of adolescents change the way they approach the world. The cognitive changes of adolescence influence how adolescents view themselves and their families and friends and how they deal with broader social and moral questions. *Question: What is cognitive development during adolescence like, according to Piaget's stage of formal operations?*

Piaget's Stage of Formal Operations

The stage of **formal operations** is the top level in Piaget's theory. Children or adolescents in this stage have reached cognitive maturity, even if some rough edges remain. Yet for many children in developed nations, the stage of formal operations can begin quite early—at about the time of puberty, eleven or twelve years old. But some children reach this stage somewhat later, and some not at all.

Formal Operations
The ability to deal with the abstract and the hypothetical and the capacity to engage in deductive reasoning are the key features of formal-operational thought. Formal-operational thinking allows adolescents to engage in scientific reasoning.

Piaget describes the accomplishments of the stage of formal operations in terms of the individual's increased ability to classify objects and ideas, engage in logical thought, and hypothesize—just as researchers make hypotheses in their investigations. The adolescent in the stage of formal operations can think about abstract ideas and about concrete objects. The adolescent can group and classify symbols, statements, even theories—just as we classify certain views of child development as psychoanalytic theories, learning theories, or sociocultural theories, even if they differ quite a bit in their particulars. Formal operations are flexible and reversible. Adolescents are thus capable of following and formulating arguments from their premises to their conclusions and back once more, even if they do not believe in them. Hypothetical thinking, the use of symbols to represent other symbols, and deductive reasoning allow the adolescent to more fully comprehend the real world and to play with the world that dwells within the mind alone.

Hypothetical Thinking

In formal-operational thought, children—or, should we say, adolescents?—discover the concept of "what might be" rather than "what is." Adolescents can project themselves into situations that transcend their immediate experience, **and**, for this

click on
"Abstraction and Hypothetical Propositions" in Module 4, Section 2, on your Observing Children and Adolescents CD-ROM. You can also visit the Student Book Companion Site to watch the video, answer the questions, and e-mail your responses to your professor.

Lessons in Observation
Piaget's Formal-Operational Stage:
Abstraction and Hypothetical Propositions

Learning Objectives
• What is Piaget's stage of formal operations?
• What is hypothetical reasoning?
• How do preadolescents and adolescents tend to differ in the ways in which they answer hypothetical questions?

Applied Lesson
How has your own ability to reason hypothetically changed as you have matured? Do you reason at different levels in different kinds of situations?

Critical Thinking
Explain the different ways in which preadolescents and adolescents address the question "What if people had no thumbs?" Describe how these different answers illustrate the idea of Piaget's stage of formal operations.

Researchers asked children and adolescents of different ages, "What if people had no thumbs?" Formal-operational adolescents, such as the young man on the left, can mentally picture the situation and answer hypothetically, contrasting it with reality. The younger boy on the right still answers in terms of his own reality and has difficulty hypothesizing a world without thumbs.

reason, they may become wrapped up in lengthy fantasies. Many adolescents can explore endless corridors of the mind, perceiving what would happen as one decision leads to another point where a choice presents itself—and then still another decision is made. Adolescents become aware that situations can have different outcomes. They can think ahead, systematically trying out various possibilities in their minds.

A Closer Look | *The Puzzle and the Pendulum*

If you hang a weight from a string and set it swinging back and forth, you have a pendulum. Bärbel Inhelder and Jean Piaget (1959) used a pendulum to explore ways in which children of different ages go about solving problems.

The researchers showed children several pendulums, with different lengths of string and with different weights at their ends, as in Figure 15.1. They attached the strings to rods and sent the weights swinging. They dropped the weights from various heights and pushed them with different amounts of force. The question they posed—the puzzle—was, What determines how fast the pendulum will swing back and forth?

The researchers had varied four factors:

- the amount of weight;
- the length of the string;
- the height from which the weight was released; and
- the force with which the weight was pushed.

The answer lies either in one of these factors or in some combination of them. That is, one factor, two factors, three factors, or all four factors could determine the speed of the pendulum.

One could try to solve this problem by deduction based on principles of physics, and experienced physicists might prefer a deductive, mathematical approach. However, one can also solve the problem by trying out each possible combination of factors and observing the results. This is an empirical approach. Because children (and most adults) are not physicists, they will usually take the empirical approach.

Of the children observed by Inhelder and Piaget, those between the ages of eight and thirteen could not arrive at the correct answer. The fault lay largely in their approach, which was only partly systematic. They made some effort to account for the various factors but did not control carefully for every possibility. For example, one child compared a pendulum with a light weight and a short string to a pendulum with a heavy weight and a long string.

The fourteen- and fifteen-year-olds generally sat back and reflected before doing anything. Then, in contrast to the younger children, who haphazardly varied several factors at once, the older children tried to exclude each factor systematically. You could say that they used the "process of elimination," as we often do with multiple-choice tests. Not all of the fourteen- to fifteen-year-olds solved the problem; but as a group, their approach was more advanced and more likely to succeed.

According to Inhelder and Piaget, the approach of the fourteen- and fifteen-year-olds typified formal-operational thought. The approach of the eight- to thirteen-year-olds typified concrete-operational thought. As with many other aspects of Piaget's views and methods, we have to be flexible about Piaget's age estimates for ability to solve the problem. Robert Siegler and his associates (1973), for example, were able to train ten-year-olds to approach the problem systematically and isolate the correct answer (drum roll!): the length of the string. Thus, education and training can influence the development of cognitive skills.

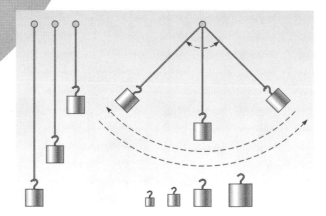

Figure 15.1
The Pendulum Problem

What determines how fast the pendulum will swing back and forth? The amount of weight? The length of the string? The height from which the weight is released? The force with which the weight is pushed? Or a combination of the above? Formal-operational children attempt to exclude each factor systematically.

You may think of scientists as people in white lab coats, with advanced degrees and a devotion to exploring uncharted territory. And some are like that, of course. But many more wear blue jeans and experiment with their hair and ways of relating to people whom they find attractive. Many adolescents in the stage of formal operations consider themselves disinterested in science, yet they conduct research daily to see whether their hypotheses about themselves and their friends and teachers are correct. These are not laboratory experiments that involve calipers or Bunsen burners. It is more common for adolescents to explore uncharted territory by trying on different clothes and "attitudes" to see which work best for them.

Adolescents, who can look ahead to multiple outcomes, may also see many possibilities for themselves. Some recognize that they can, to a large extent, fashion themselves according to their own images of what they are capable of becoming. In terms of career decisions, the wealth of possible directions leads some adolescents to experience anxiety about whether they will pick the career that really *is* them and to experience a sense of loss about the possibility that they may be able to choose only one.

This capacity to look ahead, to fashion futures, also frequently leads to **utopian** thinking. Just as adolescents can foresee many possibilities for themselves, they can also imagine different outcomes for suffering humanity. "What if" thinking enables adolescents to fashion schemes for putting an end to hunger, disease, and international strife.

utopian Referring to an ideal vision of society.

Sophisticated Use of Symbols

Children in elementary school can understand what is meant by abstract symbols such as 1 and 2. They can also perform operations in which numbers are manipulated—added, subtracted, and so on. But now consider x, that unknown (and sometimes elusive) quantity in algebra. x may be a familiar letter of the alphabet, but its designation as a symbol for an unknown quantity is a formal abstract operation. One symbol (an x) is being made to stand for something just as abstract (the unknown). Children up to the age of eleven or twelve or so usually cannot fully understand this concept, even if they can be taught the mechanics of solving for x in simple equations. But older, formal-operational children show a sophisticated grasp of the nature of symbols. They can grasp intuitively what is meant by x. Formal-operational children, or adolescents, can perform mental operations with symbols that stand for nothing in their own experience.

© Tom McHugh / Photo Researchers

A Mammal That Requires Some Deductive Reasoning!
The Australian duck-billed platypus has a bill like, well, a duck rather than a warm furry nose. It is also hairless and reproduces by laying eggs. However, formal-operational thought—and another fact—allow us to deduce that the platypus is a mammal. How? Like this: *Premise:* All animals that feed their young with breast milk are mammals. *Observation:* Platypuses feed their young with breast milk. *Conclusion:* Therefore, platypuses are mammals.

These symbols include those used in geometry. Adolescents work with points that have no dimensions, lines that have no width and that are infinite in length, and circles that are perfectly round, even though they may never find them in nature. Ability to manipulate these symbols will eventually permit them to do work in theoretical physics or math or to obtain jobs in engineering or architecture. They learn to apply symbols to the world of tangible objects and materials.

Formal-operational individuals can also understand, appreciate, and sometimes produce metaphors. Metaphors are figures of speech in which words or phrases that ordinarily signify one thing are applied to another. We find metaphors in literature, but consider how everyday figures of speech enhance our experience: *squeezing* out a living, *basking in the sunshine* of fame or glory, *hanging by a thread, jumping* to conclusions, and so on.

The moral judgments of many adolescents and adults are based on formal-operational thought. That is, they derive their judgments about what is right and wrong in specific situations by reasoning deductively from general moral principles. Their capacity for decentration also allows them to take a broad view of the situation. They can focus on many aspects of a situation at once in making judgments and solving moral dilemmas.

Enhanced cognitive abilities can backfire when adolescents adamantly advance their religious, political, and social ideas without recognition of the subtleties and practical issues that might give pause to adults. For example, let's begin with the premise, "Industries should not be allowed to pollute the environment." We then discover that Industry A pollutes the environment. An adolescent may argue to shut down Industry A, at least until it stops polluting. The logic is reasonable and the goal is noble enough, but Industry A may be indispensable to the nation at large, or many thousands of people may be put out of work if it is shut down. Other people might prefer to seek some kind of compromise.

Adolescents' new intellectual powers often present them with what seem to be crystal-clear solutions to the world's problems, and they may become intolerant of the relative stodginess of their parents. Their utopian images of how to reform the world make them unsympathetic to their parents' earthbound pursuit of a livelihood and other mundane matters.

Reevaluation of Piaget's Theory

Piaget's account of formal operations has received quite a bit of support. There appears to be little question that unique changes do occur in the nature of reasoning between preadolescence and adolescence (U. Mueller et al., 1999, 2001). For example, research strongly supports Piaget's view that the capacity to reason deductively does not emerge until adolescence (U. Mueller et al., 1999, 2001).

But note that formal-operational thought is not a universal step in cognitive development. The ability to solve abstract problems, such as those found in algebra and the pendulum problem, is more likely to be developed in technology-oriented Western societies or in major cities than in less well developed areas or nations (Flavell et al., 2002; Siegler & Alibali, 2005). Moreover, formal-operational thought may occur later than Piaget thought, if at all. For example, many early adolescents (ages thirteen to sixteen) still perform better on concrete problems than on abstract ones (Markovitz & Vachon, 1990). Reviews of the literature suggest that formal-operational thought is found among only 40 to 60 percent of first-year college students (Flavell et al., 2002; Siegler & Alibali, 2005). Also, the same individual may do well on one type of formal-operational task and poorly on another. We are more likely to use formal-operational thought in our own academic specialties. Some of us are formal-operational in math or science but not in the study of literature, and vice versa. Piaget (1972) recognized that adolescents may not always demonstrate formal-operational thought because they are unfamiliar with a particular task.

Adolescent Egocentrism: Centre Stage

Did you think that egocentrism was limited to the thought of preschool children, who show difficulty taking the perspective of other people in the three-mountains test? Wrong. Yes, teenagers are capable of hypothetical thinking, and they can argue for causes in which they do not believe (if you pay them enough to do so). However, they also can show a somewhat different brand of egocentrism in a number of ways. Adolescents comprehend the ideas of other people but have difficulty sorting out those things that concern other people from the things that concern themselves. *Question: How is adolescent egocentrism shown in the imaginary audience and in the personal fable?*

The Imaginary Audience

Many adolescents fantasize about becoming the next Canadian Idol or movie stars who are adored by millions. The concept of the **imaginary audience** achieves part of that fantasy—sort of. It places the adolescent on stage—surrounded by critics, however, more than by admirers. Adolescents assume that other people are concerned with their appearance and behaviour, more so than they really are (Bell & Bromnick, 2003; Elkind, 1967, 1985; Flavell et al., 2002; Vartanian, 2001). ***Truth or Fiction Revisited:*** Thus, it is true that adolescents generally see themselves as being on stage—with countless eyes peering in on them. This self-perception may account for the common adolescent intense desire for privacy. The concept of the imaginary audience helps explain why teenagers are so preoccupied with their appearance. It helps explain why the mirror is the constant companion of the teenager, who grooms endlessly, searches out every facial blemish, and agonizes over every zit. Being caught up with the mirror seems to peak sometime during eighth grade and declines over the remainder of adolescence.

The Imaginary Audience
Adolescents tend to feel that other people are continuously scrutinizing their appearance and behaviour. This may explain why so many adolescents worry about every facial blemish and spend long hours grooming.

Whereas some researchers view the emergence of the imaginary audience purely in cognitive-developmental terms, others believe that many adolescents are responding to increased social scrutiny (Bell & Bromnick, 2003; Kelly et al., 2002). One research group attributes the imaginary audience more to social anxiety than to cognitive development (Kelly et al., 2002).

The Personal Fable

Spiderman and Charlie's Angels, stand aside! Because of the **personal fable,** many adolescents become action heroes, at least in their own minds. If the imaginary audience puts adolescents on stage, the personal fable justifies their being there. The personal fable, another aspect of adolescent egocentrism, is the belief that one's thoughts and emotions are special and unique. It also refers to the common adolescent belief that one is all but invulnerable, like Superman or Superwoman. ***Truth or Fiction Revisited:*** It is normal for male adolescents to think of themselves as action heroes and to act as though they are made of steel.

The personal fable is connected with such behaviours as showing off and risk taking (Galanaki, 2001; Goossens et al., 2002). Many adolescents assume that they can smoke with impunity. Cancer? "It can't happen to me." They drive recklessly. They engage in spontaneous unprotected sexual activity, assuming that sexually transmitted infections (STIs) and unwanted pregnancies happen to other people, not to them. Ronald King (2000), of the HIV Community Coalition of Washington, D.C., put it this way: "All youth—rich, poor, black, white—have this sense of invincibility, invulnerability." Adolescents are more likely than their parents to minimize their assessment of risks (Flavell et al., 2002; Galanaki, 2001). Adolescents are not alone in experiencing some egocentrism, it appears as though emerging adults (roughly those who are between the ages of eighteen and twenty-five) also engage in risky behaviours, because they think that negative consequences are more likely to happen to others than to themselves (Arnett, 2000).

The specialness and uniqueness of the adolescent experience? Many adolescents believe that their parents and other adults—even their peers—could never feel what they are feeling or know the depth of their passions. "You just don't understand me!" claims the adolescent. But, at least often enough, we do.

imaginary audience The belief that others around us are as concerned with our thoughts and behaviours as we are; one aspect of adolescent egocentrism.

personal fable The belief that our feelings and ideas are special and unique and that we are invulnerable; one aspect of adolescent egocentrism.

Sex Differences in Cognitive Abilities

Although females and males do not differ in overall intelligence, starting in childhood, sex differences do appear in certain cognitive abilities (Halpern, 2004). *Question: What are the sex differences in cognitive abilities?* Females are somewhat superior to males in verbal ability. Males, on the other hand, seem somewhat superior in visual-spatial ability. The picture for mathematics ability is more complex, with females excelling in some areas and males excelling in others. Let's take a closer look at these sex differences.

Verbal Ability

Verbal abilities include a large number of language skills, such as reading, spelling, grammar, oral comprehension, and word fluency. As a group, females surpass males in verbal ability (Halpern, 2003, 2004). These differences show up early. Girls seem to acquire language faster than boys. They make more prelinguistic vocalizations, utter their first word sooner, and develop larger vocabularies. Males are more likely than females to be dyslexic (Halpern, 2003, 2004). They also are more likely to have other reading problems, such as reading below grade level.

Why do females excel in verbal abilities? For one thing, parents talk more to their infant daughters than to their infant sons (see Chapter 7). This encouragement of verbal interaction may be connected with girls' relative verbal precocity. Because of this early language advantage, girls may rely more on verbal skills to interact with people, thus furthering their abilities in this area (Halpern & LaMay, 2000). How do we account for sex differences in reading? Biological factors such as the organization of the brain may play a role, but do not discount cultural factors. One issue is whether a culture stamps reading as a gender-neutral, masculine, or feminine activity (Goldstein, 2005). Consider Nigeria and England. Reading is looked on as a masculine activity in these nations, and boys traditionally surpass girls in reading ability (and other academic skills). In Canada and the United States, however, reading tends to be stereotyped as feminine, and girls tend to excel in reading in these nations. People of all ages and all cultures tend to apply themselves more diligently to pursuits that they believe are "meant" for them—whether it is the life of the nomad, ballet, ice hockey, or reading.

Visual-Spatial Ability

Visual-spatial ability refers to the ability to visualize objects or shapes and to mentally manipulate and rotate them. As you can imagine, this ability is important in such fields as art, architecture, and engineering. Boys begin to outperform girls on many types of visual-spatial tasks starting at age eight or nine, and the difference persists into adulthood (Collaer & Nelson, 2002; Ecuyer-Dab & Robert, 2004; Halpern 2004; Parsons et al., 2004). The sex difference is greatest on mental rotation tasks (see Figure 15.2), which require imagining how objects will look if they are rotated in space (Delgado & Prieto, 2004).

What is the basis for the sex difference in visual-spatial skills? A number of biological and environmental explanations have been offered. One biological theory that has received some attention is that visual-spatial ability is influenced by sex-linked recessive genes on the X sex chromosome. But this theory has not been supported by research (Halpern & LaMay, 2000).

Some researchers link visual-spatial performance to evolutionary theory and sex hormones. For example, male humans, as with many other male mammals, have a larger "home range." This may be related to a genetic tendency to create and defend a territory, and the size of the home range is connected with spatial ability (Ecuyer-Dab &

Robert, 2004). Also, high levels of prenatal androgens have been linked to better performance on visual-spatial and arithmetic tasks among four- and six-year-old girls (Finegan et al., 1992; Jacklin et al., 1988). One study (Kimura & Hampson, 1992) found that women performed better on visual-spatial tasks when their estrogen levels were low than when their estrogen levels were high. (By contrast, they were better at tasks involving verbal skills when estrogen levels were high.)

A number of environmental theories have also been proposed to account for the sex difference in visual-spatial skills. One theory is based on the assumption that, just as reading is considered feminine in our culture, visual-spatial activities are stereotyped as masculine. (Just think of such visual-spatial activities as throwing a football, basketball, or baseball or building model planes and cars.) If we further assume that individuals perform better on cognitive tasks that match their self-image, then females and males with more masculine self-concepts should perform better on visual-spatial tasks (Halpern, 2004). It turns out that college women and men whose self-descriptions include many stereotypical masculine traits or few stereotypical feminine traits perform better on visual-spatial tasks (Signorella & Frieze, 1989). (Yes, I hear you saying that these data are correlational and not experimental. Therefore, whatever influences lead to seeing oneself as masculine or feminine could also lead to differential performance on visual-spatial tasks.)

A related environmental theory is that gender stereotypes influence the spatial experiences of children. Gender-stereotyped "boys' toys," such as blocks, Lego, and Transformers sets, provide more practice with spatial skills than gender-stereotyped "girls' toys." Boys are also more likely to engage in sports, which involve moving balls and other objects through space. Boys are allowed to travel farther from home than girls are, providing greater opportunities for exploration—and a greater "home range" (Halpern, 2004). It is no secret that participation in spatially related activities is associated with better performance on visual-spatial tasks (Newcombe & Dubas, 1992; Voyer et al., 2000).

a. Spatial visualization
Embedded-figure test. Study the figure on the left. Then cover it up and try to find where it is hidden in the figure on the right. The left-hand figure may need to be shifted in order to locate it in the right-hand figure.

b. Spatial perception
Water-level test. Examine the glass of water on the left. Now imagine that it is slightly tilted, as on the right. Draw in a line to indicate the location of the water level.

c. Mental rotation
Mental-rotation test. If you mentally rotate the figure on the left, which of the five figures on the right would you obtain?

Answers: a. 1: Orient the pattern as if it were a tilted capital M, with the left portion along the top of the white triangle. 2: This pattern fits along the right sides of the two black triangles on the left. 3: Rotate this figure about 100° to the right, so that it forms a Z, with the top line coinciding with the top line of the top white triangle. **b.** The line should be horizontal, not tilted. **c.** 1: c; 2: d.

Figure 15.2

Examples of Tests Used to Measure Visual-Spatial Ability

No sex differences are found on the spatial visualization tasks in part (a). Boys do somewhat better than girls on the tasks measuring spatial perception in part (b). The sex difference is greatest on the mental rotation tasks in part (c). What are some possible reasons for these differences?

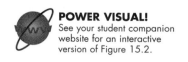

POWER VISUAL! See your student companion website for an interactive version of Figure 15.2.

Mathematical Ability

Historically, male adolescents generally outperform females in mathematics (Halpern, 2004; Leahey & Guo, 2001), and research suggests that visual-spatial skills—which are frequently superior among males—are connected with performance in the areas of geometry and word problems (Delgado & Prieto, 2004). In Lachance's & Mazzocco's (2006) recent longitudinal analysis of sex differences in math and spatial abilities in primary school children, they did not find any sex differences on standardized math tests or in any specific mathematical or spatial skills. One possibility presented by the authors is that cohort effects (remember this term from Chapter 1) indicate that sex differences in math may be diminishing over generations—at least in the primary levels. The same has not been found in the secondary levels, however. Certain authors have found that while students tend to be quite similar in the elementary years, males tend to gain an edge in the secondary school years (Leahey & Guo, 2001; Mau & Lynn, 2000). Until recently, reviewers of the research on sex differences in math concluded that sex differences appear in adolescence, but in a review of 100 studies involving more than 3 million individuals, Janet Hyde and her colleagues (1990) found a slight superiority for girls in computational skills in the elementary and middle-school years. Boys began to perform better in word problems in high school and college. There were no sex differences in understanding math concepts at any age. Among groups of more highly selected individuals, such as college students or mathematically precocious youth, differences were larger and favoured males. ***Truth or Fiction Revisited:*** Critical thinkers will see that the statement "Adolescent boys outperform adolescent girls in mathematics" is too broad to be accurate. Boys show superiority in geometry and word problems, but not in computational skills.

Although the reasons for sex differences in math may reflect a complex interaction of nature and nurture, most Canadians have different expectations for boys and girls, and these expectations may increase sex differences in math ability (Anderman et al., 2001). Consider a few of the reasons that boys are likely to feel more "at home" with math (Anderman et al., 2001; Fredricks & Eccles, 2002; Halpern 2004):

- Mom may be more likely than Dad to help Missy write an essay, but Dad is more likely to be called on to help her with her homework with fractions, decimals, and algebra.
- Male teachers are more likely to teach advanced math courses—algebra, geometry, calculus, and the like.
- Teachers tend to spend more time with boys in math and to expect more from them.
- Girls receive less encouragement and support than boys from parents and peers for studying math.
- Most parents in North America, China, and Japan believe that boys are better at math than girls.
- Parents are more likely to buy math and science books for boys than girls.

Given such experiences with math, we should not be surprised by the following:

- By junior high school, boys see themselves as being better in math than girls, even when their skills are identical (Watt & Bornholt, 2000).
- By junior high school, students perceive math as being part of the male domain (Correll, 2001; Watt & Bornholt, 2000).
- By junior high school, boys are more likely to perceive math as playing a useful role in their lives (Fredricks & Eccles, 2002).

- Whereas boys are likely to have a positive self-concept in terms of math, girls are more likely to experience anxiety about math (Osborne, 2001).
- High school and college women take fewer math courses than males do and are less likely to pursue careers in math or related fields, even when they excel in them (Watt & Bornholt, 2000).

In Sum

What, then, shall we conclude about sex differences in cognitive abilities? First, it appears that girls show greater verbal ability than boys do but that boys show greater visual-spatial and math skills (Bailey, 2003; Halpern 2003). However, sex differences in cognitive skills are *group differences*, not individual differences. That is, the difference in, say, reading skills between a male who reads well and a male who is dyslexic is greater than the average group sex difference in reading ability. Moreover, despite group differences, millions of females exceed the average male in math and visual-spatial skills; numerous males exceed the average Canadian female in writing, spelling, and articulation; and many Canadian women perform well in domains that had once been considered masculine, such as medicine and law.

Interestingly, cognitive sex differences in part reflect cultural expectations (Fredricks & Eccles, 2002). In North America, visual-spatial and math skills are stereotyped as masculine, whereas reading skills are stereotyped as feminine. Women who are given just a few hours of training in spatial skills—for example, rotating geometric figures or studying floor plans—perform as well as men do on tests of these skills (Baenninger & Elenteny, 1997; Lawton & Morrin, 1999). But in one study, girls performed more poorly on a difficult math test when they were told that the test had been shown to result in sex differences in scores—an experimental manipulation that may have made them more anxious about their performance (O'Brien & Crandall, 2003).

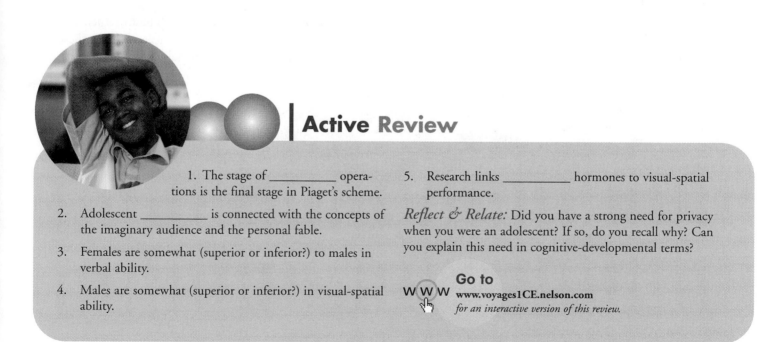

Active Review

1. The stage of _____ operations is the final stage in Piaget's scheme.

2. Adolescent _____ is connected with the concepts of the imaginary audience and the personal fable.

3. Females are somewhat (superior or inferior?) to males in verbal ability.

4. Males are somewhat (superior or inferior?) in visual-spatial ability.

5. Research links _____ hormones to visual-spatial performance.

Reflect & Relate: Did you have a strong need for privacy when you were an adolescent? If so, do you recall why? Can you explain this need in cognitive-developmental terms?

Go to

W W W **www.voyages1CE.nelson.com**
for an interactive version of this review.

The Adolescent in Judgment: Moral Development

postconventional level
According to Kohlberg, a period during which moral judgments are derived from moral principles and people look to themselves to set moral standards.

reciprocity The principle that actions have mutual effects and that people depend on one another to treat each other morally.

Moral development in adolescence is a complex issue, with cognitive and behavioural aspects. As noted in Chapter 12, children in early childhood tend to view right and wrong in terms of rewards and punishments. *Question: What are Kohlberg's views on moral reasoning in adolescence?* Lawrence Kohlberg referred to such judgments as *preconventional.* In middle childhood, *conventional* thought tends to emerge, and children usually begin to judge right and wrong in terms of social conventions, rules, and laws (see Table 12.1 on page 442). In adolescence, many—not all—individuals become capable of formal-operational thinking, which allows them to derive conclusions about what they should do in various situations by reasoning from ethical principles. And many of these individuals engage in *postconventional* moral reasoning. They *deduce* proper behaviour just as they might deduce that a platypus is a mammal because platypuses feed their young with breast milk (see page 569).

Figure 15.3

The Case of Heinz

In Europe a woman was near death from a special kind of cancer. There was one drug that the doctors thought might save her. It was a form of radium that a druggist in the same town had recently discovered. The drug was expensive to make, but the druggist was charging 10 times what the drug cost him to make. He paid $200 for the radium and charged $2000 for a small dose of the drug. The sick woman's husband, Heinz, went to everyone he knew to borrow the money, but he could get together only about $1000, half of what it cost. He told the druggist that his wife was dying and asked him to sell it cheaper or let him pay later. But the druggist said, "No, I discovered the drug and I'm going to make money from it." So Heinz got desperate and broke into the man's store to steal the drug for his wife. *Source: Kohlberg (1969).*

The Postconventional Level

In the **postconventional level,** moral reasoning is based on the person's own moral standards. Recall the case of Heinz (Figure 15.3). Moral judgments are derived from personal values, not from conventional standards or authority figures. In the contractual, legalistic orientation of Stage 5, it is recognized that laws stem from agreed-on procedures and that many rights have great value and should not be violated (see Table 15.1). But under exceptional circumstances, such as in the case of Heinz, laws cannot bind the individual. A Stage 5 reason for stealing the drug might be that it is the right thing to do, even though it is illegal. Conversely, it could be argued that if everyone in need broke the law, the legal system and the social contract would be destroyed.

Stage 6 thinking relies on supposed universal ethical principles, such as those of human life, individual dignity, justice, and **reciprocity.** Behaviour that is consistent with these principles is considered right. If a law is seen as unjust or contradicts the right of the individual, it is wrong to obey it.

Table 15.1 *Kohlberg's Postconventional Level of Moral Development*		
Stage	Examples of Moral Reasoning That Support Heinz's Stealing the Drug	Examples of Moral Reasoning That Oppose Heinz's Stealing the Drug
Stage 5: *Contractual, legalistic orientation*: One must weigh pressing human needs against society's need to maintain social order.	This thing is complicated because society has a right to maintain law and order, but Heinz has to take the drug to save his wife.	I can see why Heinz feels he has to take the drug, but laws exist for the benefit of society as a whole and cannot simply be cast aside.
Stage 6: *Universal ethical principles orientation*: People must follow universal ethical principles and their own conscience, even if it means breaking the law.	In this case, the law comes into conflict with the principle of the sanctity of human life. Heinz must take the drug because his wife's life is more important than the law.	If Heinz truly believes that stealing the drug is worse than letting his wife die, he should not take it. People have to make sacrifices to do what they think is right.

In the case of Heinz (Figure 15.3), it could be argued from the perspective of Stage 6 that the principle of preserving life takes precedence over laws prohibiting theft. Therefore, it is morally necessary for Heinz to steal the drug, even if he must go to jail. Note that it could also be asserted, from the principled orientation, that if Heinz finds the social contract or the law to be the highest principle, he must remain within the law, despite the consequences.

Stage 5 and 6 moral judgments were virtually absent among the seven- and ten-year-olds in Kohlberg's (1963) sample of American children. They increased in frequency during the early and middle teens. By age sixteen, Stage 5 reasoning was shown by about 20 percent of adolescents and Stage 6 reasoning was demonstrated by about 5 percent of adolescents. However, Stage 3 and 4 judgments were made more frequently at all ages—seven through sixteen—studied by Kohlberg and other investigators (Colby et al., 1983; Rest, 1983) (see Figure 15.4). ***Truth or Fiction Revisited:*** It is *not* true that most adolescents make moral decisions based on their own ethical principles. Postconventional moral reasoning appears in adolescence *if it appears at all, but most adolescents reason at lower levels.*

Cross-Cultural and Sex Differences in Moral Development

Cultural background is a powerful shaper of moral reasoning. Kohlberg found postconventional thinking among a minority of American adolescents, and it was all but absent among adolescents in villages in Mexico, Taiwan, Turkey (Kohlberg, 1969), and the Bahamas (White et al., 1978). Reviews of the literature conclude

Postconventional Thought
Rosa Parks smiles in this photo taken on December 21, 1956, after the U.S. Supreme Court banned segregation on city public transit. On December 1 of the previous year, Ms. Parks energized the civil rights movement with a simple act of unlawful protest: She refused to surrender her seat on a public bus to a European American man. In her own words, "I did not get on the bus to get arrested. I got on the bus to go home." Nevertheless, Parks's own postconventional thinking—her own sense of what was right and wrong—took precedence over the law at the time.

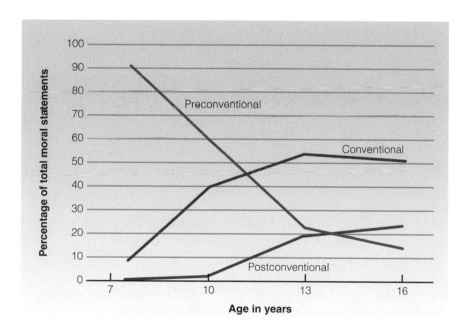

Figure 15.4

Age and Type of Moral Judgment

The incidence of preconventional reasoning declines from greater than 90 percent of moral statements at age seven to less than 20 percent of moral statements at age sixteen. Conventional moral statements increase with age between the ages of 7 and 13 but then level off to account for 50-60 percent of moral statements at ages 13 and 16. Postconventional moral statements are all but absent at ages 7 and 10 but account for about 20-25 percent of moral statements at ages 13 and 16.

Source: Kohlberg (1963).

that postconventional reasoning is more likely to be found in urban cultural groups and in middle-class populations but that it is rarely seen in traditional folk cultures (Dawson, 2002; Snarey, 1994).

Another cross-cultural study indicates that the moral reasoning of children from Western industrialized countries such as Germany, Poland, and Italy is similar to that of American children from urban areas (Boehnke et al., 1989). On the other hand, the moral reasoning of American children and Israeli city children is more self-oriented and less oriented to the needs of others than the reasoning of Israeli kibbutz children (Eisenberg et al., 1990). These differences are consistent with the differences in the children's social environments. The kibbutz is a collective farm community that emphasizes cooperative relationships and a communal philosophy.

A similar pattern has been found in comparisons of middle-class American and Hindu Indian children and adults. Hindu Indians are more likely to show a caring orientation in making moral judgments, whereas Americans more often demonstrate a justice orientation. These findings are consistent with the greater emphasis that Hindu Indian culture puts on the importance of taking responsibility for others (Miller, 1994; Miller & Bersoff, 1992).

Cultural psychologist Richard Shweder has put forth an alternative to Kohlberg's coding. Shweder classifies moral reasoning as postconventional when individuals base their reasoning on any form of universal moral obligation (Shweder et al., 1997, 1998). The coding proposed by Shweder involves the ethic of autonomy (individuals are the primary moral authority as long as no harm is done to others); the ethic of community (individuals are members of social groups to which they have commitments and obligations; moral reasoning is based on roles and responsibilities in family and community); and the ethic of divinity (individuals are spiritual entities affected by divine authority; moral reasoning is based on traditional religious authority). With Shweder's scheme, more people are at the postconventional reasoning level.

Sex Differences in Moral Development

Some researchers claim that males reason at higher levels of moral development than females in terms of responses to Heinz's dilemma. For example, Kohlberg and Kramer (1969) reported that the average stage of moral development for men was Stage 4, which emphasizes justice, law, and order. The average stage for women was reported to be Stage 3, which emphasizes caring and concern for others.

Carol Gilligan (Gilligan, 1977, 1982; Gilligan & Attanucci, 1988) argues that this sex difference reflects patterns of socialization. Gilligan provides two examples of responses to Heinz's dilemma. Eleven-year-old Jake views the dilemma as a math problem. He sets up an equation showing that life has greater value than property. Heinz should thus steal the drug. Eleven-year-old Amy, on the other hand, notes that both stealing the drug and letting Heinz's wife die would be wrong. Amy searches for alternatives, such as getting a loan, stating that it would profit Heinz's wife little if he went to jail and was no longer around to help her.

Gilligan argued that Kohlberg's theory is biased in favour of a justice orientation. Although Gilligan sees Amy's pattern of reasoning as being as sophisticated as Jake's, it would be rated as showing a lower level of moral development in Kohlberg's "justice-oriented" system. Gilligan asserts that Amy, like other girls, has been socialized into focusing on the needs of others and foregoing simplistic judgments of right and wrong. Jake, by contrast, has been socialized into making judgments based on logic. To him, clear-cut conclusions are to be derived from a set of premises. Amy was aware of the logical considerations that struck Jake, of course. However, she processed them as one source of information—not as the sole acceptable source. It is ironic that

Amy's empathy, a trait that has "defined the 'goodness' of women," marks Amy "as deficient in moral development" (Gilligan, 1982, p. 18).

Gilligan's work was monumental—it forced researchers in many areas of psychology to reconsider and reevaluate theories based solely on a limited sample (i.e., white males).

Despite their differences, Kohlberg and Gilligan agree that in making moral judgments, females are more likely to show a caring orientation, whereas males are more likely to assume a justice orientation. But other researchers find that concerns with caring and justice coexist in the judgments of both sexes and that girls do not reason at lower levels than boys (Clopton & Sorell, 1993; Kahn, 1992; Knox et al., 2004).

Moral Behaviour and Moral Reasoning: Is There a Relationship?

Is there a relationship between moral cognitive development and moral behaviour? Are individuals whose moral judgments are more mature more likely to engage in moral behaviour? The answer seems to be yes; many studies have found positive relationships between a person's level of moral development and his or her behaviour (Cheung et al., 2001; Greenberg, 2002; Palmer & Hollin, 2000).

Individuals whose moral reasoning is at Stage 2 cheat, steal, and engage in other problem behaviours more often than peers whose moral reasoning is at higher stages (Greenberg, 2002; Richards et al., 1992). Adolescents with higher levels of moral reasoning are more likely to exhibit moral behaviour, including altruistic behaviour (Eisenberg et al., 1991; D. Hart et al., 2003).

Experiments have also been conducted in the hope of advancing moral reasoning as a way of decreasing immoral behaviour. A number of studies have found that group discussion of moral dilemmas elevates delinquents' level of moral reasoning (Smetana, 1990). Is moral behaviour affected as well? In one study, discussions of moral dilemmas improved moral reasoning and reduced incidents of, for example, school tardiness, behaviour referrals, and police and court contacts among adolescents with behavioural problems (Arbuthnot & Gordon, 1988).

Evaluation of Kohlberg's Theory

Evidence supports Kohlberg's view that the moral judgments of children develop in sequence (Boom et al., 2001; Dawson, 2002), even though most children do not reach postconventional thought. Postconventional thought, when it is found, first occurs during adolescence.

Why doesn't postconventional moral reasoning appear until age thirteen or so? A number of studies suggest that formal-operational thinking is a prerequisite and that education likely plays a role (Dawson, 2002; Patenaude et al., 2003). Postconventional reasoning appears to require the capacities to understand abstract moral principles and to empathize with the views and feelings of others. However, neither formal-operational thought nor education guarantees the development of postconventional moral judgments.

Consistent with Kohlberg's theory, children do not appear to skip stages as they progress (Dawson, 2002). The thrust of moral development is from lower to higher stages.

Kohlberg believed that the stages of moral development follow the unfolding of innate sequences and are therefore universal. But he may have underestimated the influence of social, cultural, and educational institutions (Dawson, 2002; Nucci, 2002). Parents are also important. Inductive disciplinary methods, including discussions of the

Parents Influence Children's Moral Development
Parents help advance their children's moral development when they discuss moral dilemmas with them. Most adolescents respect their parents' views.

feelings of others, advance moral reasoning (Dawson, 2002; Eisenberg & Valiente, 2002; Palmer & Hollin, 2001).

Postconventional thinking is all but absent in developing societies—and infrequent in the United States (Snarey, 1994). Perhaps postconventional reasoning reflects Kohlberg's personal ideals and not a natural, universal stage of development. Stage 6 reasoning is based on the acceptance of supposedly universal ethical principles. The principles of freedom, justice, equality, tolerance, integrity, and reverence for human life have high appeal for most American adolescents, who are reared to idealize these principles.

As we look around the world—and at many of the horrors of the new millennium—we find that principles such as freedom and tolerance of differences are not universally revered. They may reflect Western cultural influences more than the cognitive development of the child. In some cultures, for instance, violation of the dominant religious tradition is a capital offence, and freedom to worship—or not to worship—is unheard of. In his later years, Kohlberg (1985) dropped Stage 6 reasoning from his theory in recognition of these problems.

Active Review

6. In Kohlberg's _____ level, moral reasoning is based on the person's own moral standards.

7. Many studies have found (positive or negative?) relationships between the child's level of moral development and moral behaviour.

Reflect & Relate: What is your stage of moral development, according to Kohlberg? How do you know? How do you feel about it?

Go to
W W W **www.voyages1CE.nelson.com**
for an interactive version of this review.

The Adolescent in School

How can we emphasize the importance of the school to the development of the adolescent? Adolescents are highly influenced by the opinions of their peers and their teachers. Their self-esteem rises or falls consistently with the pillars of their skills. *Question: How do adolescents make the transition from elementary school to middle, junior high, or high school?*

Making the Transition from Elementary School

Students make at least one and sometimes two transitions to a new school before they complete high school. Think back to your own school days. Did you spend the years from kindergarten to eighth grade in one building and then move on to high school? Did you instead attend elementary school through sixth grade and then go to junior high for grades seven through nine before starting high school? Or did you complete kindergarten through grade five in one school, then attend a middle school for grades six to eight, and then move on to high school for grades nine through twelve? Of course the transitions vary according to province, and sometimes even within a city, so here are various Canadian experiences.

The transition to middle, junior high, or high school generally involves a shift from a smaller neighbourhood elementary school with self-contained classrooms to a larger, more impersonal setting with many more students and with different teachers for different classes (Fenzel, 2000). These changes may not fit very well with the developmental needs of early adolescents. For example, adolescents express a desire for increased autonomy, yet teachers in junior high typically allow less student input and exert more behavioural control than teachers in elementary school (Tobbell, 2003). Moreover, in the shift to the new school, students move from being the "top dog" (i.e., the oldest and most experienced students) to being the "bottom dog." These changes are not the only ones facing the early adolescent. Many youngsters are also going through the early stages of pubertal development at about the same time they move to a new school.

How well do students adjust to the transition to a new school? Much of the research has examined children's experiences as they move from elementary school to junior high school. The transition to the new school setting often is accompanied by a decline in grades and in participation in school activities. Students may also experience a drop in self-esteem and an increase in psychological distress (Rudolph et al., 2001; Tobbell, 2003).

Truth or Fiction Revisited: The transition from elementary school appears to be more difficult for girls than for boys. In one study, girls who switched to a junior high for seventh grade showed a decrease in self-esteem, whereas girls who stayed in their kindergarten through eighth-grade school did not. Boys' self-esteem did not change when they switched to junior high (Simmons & Blyth, 1987). The difference may reflect the fact that girls are more likely to be undergoing puberty at about this time. Girls at this age are also likely to earn the attention of boys in higher grades, whereas younger boys are not likely to be of much interest to older girls. Girls experience major life changes, and children who experience several life changes at once find it more difficult to adjust to a new school (Tobbell, 2003).

But transition need not be that stressful. Students who are in greater control of their lives tend to do better with the transition (Rudolph et al., 2001). Elementary and junior high schools can help ease the transition to high school. Some junior high schools create a more intimate, caring atmosphere by, for instance, establishing smaller schools within the school building. Others have "bridge programs" during the summer between middle school and high school. The programs introduce students to the new school culture and strengthen their academic skills. Others still, offer buddy mentor programs, where new students are paired with more senior students to help them through the first few weeks of school and help with orientation. One longitudinal study followed the progress of students who received a two-year

© Chris Clinton/Getty Images

The Transition from Elementary School
The transition to junior high or high school is not always easy. The transition coincides with the biological forces of puberty and concerns about how one will turn out—physically, that is. It is not surprising that some children experience a decline in grades and self-esteem.

Are These Adolescents on the Path to Dropping out of School?

The consequences of dropping out of school can be harsh. High school dropouts earn less and are more likely to be unemployed. Programs have been developed to prevent dropping out, but potential dropouts must first be identified.

social-decision-making and problem-solving program in elementary school. When followed in high school four to six years later, these students showed higher levels of prosocial behaviour and fewer conduct problems than students who had not been in the program (Elias et al., 1991).

Dropping Out of School

School is a key path to success in our society, but not all adolescents complete high school. *Questions: What are the consequences of dropping out of school? Why do adolescents drop out?*

Completing high school is one of the most critical developmental tasks facing adolescents. The consequences of dropping out can be grim indeed. High school dropouts are more likely to be unemployed (Harding, 2003; Lever et al., 2004). When employed, they earn lower salaries. Research suggests that each year of education, from grade school through graduate school, adds about 16 percent to an individual's lifetime earnings (Passell, 1992). (This is a good incentive for you not only to complete university but also to consider graduate work!) Dropouts are also more likely to show problem behaviours, including delinquency, criminal behaviour, and substance abuse (Ellickson et al., 2001; Lane & Cherek, 2001). However, it is sometimes difficult to disentangle the consequences of dropping out from its causes. A pattern of delinquent behaviour, for example, might precede as well as follow dropping out.

Good News

There is some good news regarding Canadian dropout rates: They are declining (see Figures 15.5 and 15.6). The 2004-2005 dropout rate was reported at 9.8 percent (down from 16.7 percent in 1990-1991) (Bowlby, 2005). As Figure 15.6 demonstrates, more males than females drop out of school. The reasons for dropping out

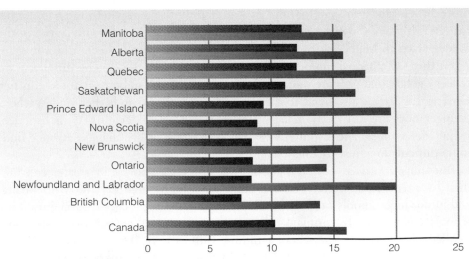

Figure 15.5

High School Dropouts as a Percentage of All 20- to 24-Year-Olds

Source: Bowlby, G. (2005).

■ Average of 2002 –2003 to 2004 – 2005 school years
■ Average of 1990 –1991 to 1992 – 1993 school years

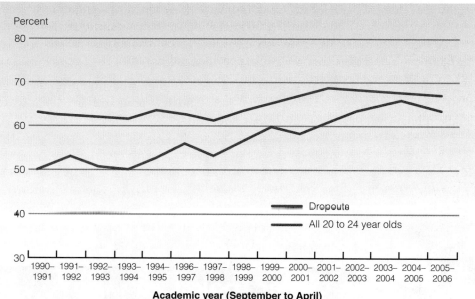

Figure 15.6

Thousands of High School Dropouts, by Gender, Canada, 1990-1991 to 2004-2005

Source: Bowlby, G. (2005).

vary according to sex. For males, reasons cited for dropping out include school disengagement and wanting to earn money. For females, dropout rates are highly related to teenage pregnancy (Bowlby, 2005). Children from lower-income households have higher dropout rates (Harding, 2003; Leventhal & Brooks-Gunn, 2004). When income levels are held constant, ethnic differences in school dropout rates are reduced (National Center for Education Statistics, 2002).

Excessive school absence and reading below grade level are two of the earliest and strongest predictors of school dropout (Lever et al., 2004). Other risk factors include low grades, poor problem-solving ability, low self-esteem, problems with teachers, dissatisfaction with school, substance abuse, being old for one's grade level, and being male (Christenson & Thurlow, 2004; Gelinas et al., 2000). The Canadian Youth in Transition Surveys found additional factors that influence high school and university dropout rates, such as the school's characteristics, the student's level of engagement in school life, and the student's experience in first year of university. Adolescents who adopt adult roles early, especially marrying at a young age or becoming a parent, are also more likely to drop out (Jimerson et al., 2000). But not all dropouts come from low-income families. Middle-class youth who feel bored with school, alienated, or strongly pressured to succeed also are at risk (Battin-Pearson, 2000; Lee & Burkam, 2003).

Preventing Dropping Out

Many programs have been developed to prevent school dropout. Successful programs have some common characteristics (Christenson & Thurlow, 2004; Lee & Burkam, 2003; Lever et al., 2004):

- early preschool intervention (examples are early childhood compensatory education, such as Head Start);
- identification and monitoring of high-risk students throughout the school years;
- small class size, individualized instruction, and counselling;
- strong vocational components that link learning and community work experiences;
- involvement of adults from families or community organizations;

- positive school climate, which makes students feel like part of a community; and
- clear and reasonable educational goals (if you don't know where you're going, how you get there isn't very important), student accountability for behaviour, and motivational systems that involve penalties and rewards.

Most intervention efforts are usually not introduced until students are on the verge of dropping out—when it is usually too late. And few programs are designed to handle students who have already dropped out.

A Closer Look | *Beyond the Classroom: How Parents Can Help Teenagers Improve Their Academic Performance*

Some adolescents profit more from education than others. Why do some adolescents perform better than others in the classroom? Certainly intelligence plays a role. So does the adequacy of the school and the teachers. Surveys of high school students suggest that the behaviour and attitudes of parents and teenagers play key roles as well (Bacete & Remirez, 2001; Steinberg, 1996). A study by psychologist Laurence Steinberg and his colleagues cut across the ethnic spectrum. It included 20,000 African American, Asian American, Latino and Latina American, and European American students from California and Wisconsin; the investigation is recounted in Steinberg's 1996 book *Beyond the Classroom*.

One problem that is connected with poor school performance is that many parents, according to Steinberg, are "disconnected" from their children's lives. Note some of his findings:

- Half the students said it would not upset their parents if they brought home grades of C or worse.
- Forty percent of students said that their parents never attended school functions.
- One-third of the students said that their parents did not even know how they were doing in school.
- One-third said that they primarily spent the day "goofing off" with their friends.
- Only one-third of students said that they had daily conversations with their parents.

Steinberg and his co-researchers, Bradford Brown and Sanford Dornbusch, also looked at the situation from the parents' point of view. Many parents said that they would like to be involved in their children's school and leisure activities but that they are just too busy. By the time the children enter high school, many parents admit looking on education as the school's job, not theirs. In fact, half of the parents surveyed admitted that they did not know who their children's friends were or where their children went (and what they did) after school.

So what can parents do to help their teenagers improve their academic performance? Turns out, it's pretty simple. Steinberg makes some recommendations. First and foremost, parents need to be more involved with their teenagers. For example, parents can

- communicate regularly with their teenagers about school and personal matters;
- use consistent discipline (as opposed to being dictatorial or too permissive);
- regularly attend school functions; and
- consult with their children's teachers and follow through on their suggestions.

Parents may also have to contend with their teenagers' peers. Although some teenagers encourage others to do well in school, Steinberg (1996) found that many peers have a harmful effect on grades. For example, nearly one in five said that he or she did not do as well as possible for fear of earning the disapproval of peers! Parents may effectively deal with fear of peer disapproval by encouraging their children to focus on their long-term goals, such as a career or college, and reminding them that their current group of peers may not be playing much of a role in their future lives.

Active Review

8. At the junior high school level, teachers typically exert (more or less?) behavioural control than elementary school teachers.

9. Students undergoing the transition from elementary school are more likely to experience a (rise or drop?) in self-esteem.

10. (Boys or Girls?) appear to be more negatively affected by the junior high transition.

11. High school dropouts are (more or less?) likely to be unemployed as adults.

12. (Boys or Girls?) are more likely to drop out of high school.

Reflect & Relate: Do you know people who dropped out of high school? Why did they drop out? What were the consequences of dropping out?

Go to
WWW www.voyages1CE.nelson.com
for an interactive version of this review.

The Adolescent at Work: Career Development and Work Experience

Deciding what job or career we will pursue after completion of school is one of the most important choices we make. *Question: How do adolescents make career choices?*

Career Development

When Rinaldi was a child, she wanted to be an ophthalmologist or a lawyer. She became a psychologist and professor. Her son at age two wanted to be a paleontologist, then at age five, an NHL hockey player or soccer star. The dream changes every year.

Rinaldi's course of career development is more typical than her son's will probably be. Children's career aspirations may not be practical at first. They become increasingly realistic—and often more conventional—as children mature and gain experience. In adolescence, ideas about the kind of work one wants to do tend to become more firmly established, or crystallized, but a particular occupation may not be chosen until the university years or afterward (Rottinghaus et al., 2003; Sullivan & Hansen, 2004). Nonetheless, a study conducted by Bardick and colleagues (Bardick et al. 2006) from the University of Lethbridge, found that junior high students are able to think about future planning and hope to combine educational and vocational streams by studying and working part-time.

Many factors influence choice of a career, including abilities and personality traits (Holland, 1996; Rottinghaus et al., 2003). Consider two individuals: Eve and Jacques. Eve has excellent mathematical and mechanical abilities. She is practical and somewhat materialistic. Jacques has excellent artistic ability. He is expressive and creative. Which one do you think is more likely to choose a career in computer engineering? Which one is more likely to become a graphic designer? Life experiences, job opportunities, parental expectations, and economic factors play roles as well. Perhaps Eve's family owns a small business, and she works there on weekends and vacations throughout high school and college. Her parents make it clear that when they retire, they would like Eve to take over the business. Perhaps she will choose to follow in their footsteps rather than become a computer engineer. Jacques would like to become a graphic designer, but perhaps his family does not have the resources to send him to college. Perhaps his girlfriend becomes pregnant. Jacques may take the best job he can find given his background—a retail sales position—to help support his new family. Like many others, Jacques may not make a career decision at all (Hardin et al., 2001). He may sort of fall into his job because it was there when he needed it.

Holland's Career Typology

Psychologists have devised approaches to matching personality traits with careers to predict adjustment in a given career. John Holland's (1997) RIASEC method, as used in his Vocational Preference Inventory, matches six personality types to various kinds of careers: realistic, investigative, artistic, social, enterprising, and conventional (see Figure 15.7). Within each "type" of career, some are more sophisticated than others and require more education and training. Other vocational tests include the Strong Interest Inventory and the Myers-Briggs Type Indicator.

Realistic people, according to Holland, are concrete in thinking. They are mechanically oriented. They tend to be best adjusted in occupations that involve motor activity. Examples of such occupations include unskilled labour, such as attending gas stations; farming; and the skilled trades, such as auto repairs, electrical work, plumbing, or construction work.

Investigative people are abstract in their thinking. They are creative and tend to be introverted but open to new experience (Larson et al., 2002). They tend to do well in college and university teaching and in research positions.

Artistic people also tend to be creative and open to new experience (Larson et al., 2002). As a group, they are emotional, interested in the emotional life, and intuitive. They tend to be happiest in the visual and the performing arts.

Socially oriented people tend to be outgoing (extraverted) and concerned for social welfare. They are often agreeable and have a need for affiliation (Larson et al., 2002). They gravitate toward occupations in teaching (kindergarten through high school), counselling, and social work.

Enterprising people tend to be adventurous. They tend to be outgoing and dominant (Larson et al., 2002). They gravitate toward industrial roles that involve leadership and planning. They climb the ladder in government and social organizations.

Conventional people thrive on routine. They are not particularly imaginative. They have needs for order, self-control, and social approval. They gravitate toward occupations in banking, accounting, clerical work, and the military.

Cross-cultural research finds these personality types among African Americans, Latino and Latina Americans, Asian Americans, Native Americans, and European Americans (Day & Rounds, 1998; Hardin et al., 2001). Many people combine several types. A copywriter in an advertising agency might be both artistic and enterprising. Clinical and counselling psychologists tend to be investigative, artistic, and socially oriented. Military people and beauticians tend to be realistic and conventional. But military leaders who plan major operations and form governments are also enterprising; and individuals who create new hairstyles and fashions are also artistic. Holland's Vocational Preference Inventory assesses these personality types, as do various vocational tests that are used in high schools and colleges.

All in all, more than 20 000 occupations are found in *The Dictionary of Occupational Titles*, which is compiled by the U.S. Department of Labour. But most young people choose from a relatively small range of occupations on the basis of their personalities, experiences, and opportunities (Arbona, 2000; Herr, 2001). Many sort of fall into jobs that are offered to them or follow career paths that are blazed by parents or role models in the community (Nauta & Kokaly, 2001; Wahl & Blackhurst, 2000).

C

These people have clerical or numerical skills. They like to work with data, to carry out other people's directions, or to carry things out in detail.

R

These people have mechanical or athletic abilities. They like to work with machines and tools, to be outdoors, or to work with animals or plants.

I

These people like to learn new things. They enjoy investigating and solving problems and advancing knowledge.

E

These people like to work with people. They like to lead and influence others for economic or organizational gains.

S

This group enjoys working with people. They like to help others, including the sick. They enjoy informing and enlightening people.

A

This group is highly imaginative and creative. They enjoy working in unstructured situations. They are artistic and innovative.

Figure 15.7

Assessing an Adolescent's Career Type by Attending a "Job Fair"

Adolescents can be given insight into where they might fit in the career world by picturing themselves at a job fair such as the one pictured here. Students and employers have a chat. As time passes, they discover mutual interests and begin to collect in groups accordingly. Adolescents can consider the types of people in the six groups by reading the descriptions for each. Then they can ask themselves, "Which group would I most like to join?" What does their answer suggest about the career choices that might be of greatest interest to them?

Sex Differences in Career Development

One fact of life in the new millennium is that the rate of participation of women in the labour force is approaching that of men (Statistics Canada, 2007). Most young women expect to be employed following their education. The more education a woman has, the more likely she is to be employed.

Question: Does gender affect career choice? To some degree, women and men still choose different types of careers, and these career choices are influenced by traditional gender-role stereotypes (Correll, 2001). Because of the complex interaction of tradition, personal preference, biology, and opportunity, women still make up the majority of kindergarten through high school teachers and nurses but a relatively small percentage of truck drivers and upper-level management (Becker, 2002). However, the

© Dan McCoy / Rainbow

An Architectural Engineer
More women today are pursuing careers traditionally dominated by males. The number of men pursuing traditionally female-dominated careers also has increased but not to the same extent. What might account for the discrepancy in shifts to "non-traditional" careers by women and men?

occupational gender typing
Judgments that certain occupations are more appropriate for one sex than the other.

numbers of women in medical and law schools now rival those of men (Glater, 2001). But math, science, and engineering continue to look very much like male domains.

A study of children of ages eight, twelve, and sixteen years found that younger children were relatively more likely to want to enter occupations that were traditionally consistent with their gender identity (Miller & Budd, 1999). Boys were more likely than girls to engage in **occupational gender typing.** Other studies have found that girls engage in more complex reasoning about the types of careers they will pursue (Segal et al., 2001). In a sense, they have to reason deeply if they are going to forge ahead, because social expectations remain stacked in favour of males. One program used to help connect young girls between the ages of eleven and eighteen with sciences and engineering is the SCIberMENTOR program developed by researchers at the University of Alberta, the University of Calgary, and the Alberta Women's Science Network. It is an e-mail mentoring program that matches girls with female science and engineering students at Alberta universities and practising female scientists and engineers. It was first implemented in November 2001, and to date approximately 350 mentor-mentee partnerships exist (http://www.scibermentor.ca/index.html).

Research by Albert Bandura and his colleagues (2001) suggested that girls who have more confidence in their ability to function in the business world—that is, higher self-efficacy expectations—are more likely to select nontraditional careers. Intellectually gifted girls are more likely than their less gifted peers to break out of the shackles of traditional career expectations (Mendez, 2000).

Cross-cultural research involving Italian, American, and Bulgarian children suggests that Italian children are most likely to engage in occupational gender typing and that Bulgarian children are least likely to engage in occupational gender typing (Trice, 2000).

Adolescents in the Work Force

Annika, age sixteen, has a job at a coffee chain located in the suburb of a central Canadian city. She has already saved $1000 toward a car by working at the café after school and on weekends. But contrary to popular belief, the income of young Canadians has actually decreased over the past two decades (Boyd & Norris, 1999).

Life experiences help shape vocational development. One life experience that is common among Canadian teenagers is holding a job. *Questions: How many Canadian adolescents hold jobs? What are the pros and cons of adolescents working?*

Prevalence of Adolescent Employment

According to a report by Franke (2003), about 15 percent of youth aged fifteen through twenty-four work and go to school. These figures differ from American data detailing that about half of all high school sophomores, two-thirds of juniors, and almost three-quarters of seniors have a job during the school year (Bachman et al., 2003).

Millions of adolescents in the United States between the ages of fourteen to eighteen are legally employed. But perhaps another 2 to 3 million are working illegally (Bachman et al., 2003; Holloway, 2004). Some of these teenagers are paid in cash so that their employers can avoid paying taxes or minimum wages. Others work too many hours, work late hours on school nights, or work at hazardous jobs. Some are younger than fourteen and are too young to be legally employed except on farms.

Pros and Cons of Adolescent Employment

The potential benefits of adolescent employment include developing a sense of responsibility, self-reliance, and discipline; learning to appreciate the value of money and education; acquiring positive work habits and values; and enhancing occupational aspirations. On the other hand, the meaning of work for adolescents—at least for middle-class adolescents—seems to have changed. Most adolescents who work do not do so to help support their families or to put money away for college. Although adolescents of lower socioeconomic status work mainly to supplement the family income (Leventhal et al., 2001), most middle-class adolescents use their income for personal purchases, such as clothing, CDs and DVDs, sports equipment, stereos, TVs, and car payments (Bachman et al., 2003). The proportion of earnings devoted to future university expenses or family expenses is small.

In addition, most employed adolescents are in service and retail jobs that have low pay, high turnover, little authority, and little chance for advancement. They typically perform simple, repetitive tasks requiring no special skills, minimal supervision, and little interdependence with other workers (Mortimer & Johnson, 1998). Some question the benefits of such jobs.

Truth or Fiction Revisited: Once again, based largely on American data, adolescents who work after school, as a group, do obtain lower grades. Research indicates that the effects of teenage employment may be harmful, particularly for students who work long hours. Students who work lengthy hours—more than eleven to thirteen hours per week—report lower grades, higher rates of drug and alcohol use, more delinquent behaviour, lower self-esteem, and higher levels

© Ariel Skelley / CORBIS

Teenagers and Work
What are the pros and cons of part-time employment during adolescence?

	Female			Male		
	No Job	Job	Difference	No Job	Job	Difference
	Female and Male Students' Daily Activity Breakdown					
	Average hours per day					
High school						
Time spent on:						
Personal care	11.2	10.3	−0.9	10.9	10.5	−0.4
Leisure	6.8	6.5	−0.3	7.7	6.2	−1.5
Paid work	0.2	0.7	0.5	0.1	1.9	1.8
Education	4.4	4.8	0.4	4.4	4.4	0.0
Unpaid work	1.4	1.7	0.3	0.9	1.1	0.2
Postsecondary						
Time spent on:						
Personal care	10.1	9.4	−0.7	10.1	9.4	−0.7
Leisure	5.3	5.5	0.2	7.0	5.6	0.8
Paid work	0.4	2.6	2.2	0.8	2.3	1.5
Education	6.4	5.1	−1.3	4.8	5.1	0.3
Unpaid work	1.8	1.6	−0.2	1.2	1.5	0.3

Source: Franke (2003).

of psychological problems than students who do not work or who work only a few hours (Brandstätter & Farthofer, 2003; Holloway, 2004; Quirk et al., 2001; Stone & Mortimer, 1998). Grades and time spent on homework drop for students who work long hours. Use of drugs and alcohol increases. Adolescents who work longer hours also spend less time in family activities, are monitored less by their parents, and are granted more freedom with day-to-day decisions (Oettinger, 1999; Singh, 1998; Singh & Ozturk, 2000).

Perhaps the most prudent course is for parents and educators to limit the number of hours adolescents work. Some are tightening their regulations on the number of hours teenagers can work during the school year.

Throughout this chapter, we have seen that the intellectual, moral, and vocational development of adolescents is influenced by parents and peers. Adolescents' relationships with family and friends, along with other aspects of their social and emotional development, are the topic of the final chapter.

Active Review

13. Children's career aspirations become increasingly _____ as they mature and gain experience.

14. Career choices of males and females are still to some degree influenced by traditional _____-role stereotypes.

15. (Boys or Girls?) are more likely to engage in occupational gender typing.

16. In Canada, the (majority or minority?) of high school students have a job during the school year.

Reflect & Relate: When you were in high school, did you have a job after school or on weekends? How did working affect your grades, your social life, and your social maturation?

Go to
W W W **www.voyages1CE.nelson.com**
for an interactive version of this review.

Recite: *An Active Summary*™

1. What is cognitive development during adolescence like, according to Piaget's stage of formal operations?

In Western societies, formal-operational thought begins at about the time of puberty. The major achievements of the stage involve classification, logical thought (deductive reasoning), and the ability to hypothesize. Adolescents can project themselves into situations that transcend their experience and become wrapped up in fantasies.

2. How is adolescent egocentrism shown in the *imaginary audience* and in the *personal fable?*

The imaginary audience concept is the belief that others around us are concerned with our thoughts and behaviours, giving rise to the desire for privacy. The personal fable is the belief that our feelings and ideas are special and that we are invulnerable, which may underlie adolescent risk taking.

3. What are the sex differences in cognitive abilities?

Females tend to excel in verbal ability. Males tend to excel in visual-spatial ability and math. Boys are more likely than girls to have reading problems. Sex differences in visual-spatial skills have been linked to biological factors and to gender stereotypes.

4. What are Kohlberg's views on moral reasoning in adolescence?

In the postconventional level, according to Kohlberg, moral reasoning is based on the person's own moral standards.

5. How do adolescents make the transition from elementary school to middle, junior high, or high school?

The transition to middle, junior high, or high school generally involves a shift from a smaller neighbourhood elementary school to a larger, more impersonal setting. The transition is often accompanied by a decline in grades and a drop in self-esteem.

6. What are the consequences of dropping out of school? Why do adolescents drop out?

High school dropouts are more likely to be unemployed and earn lower salaries. Dropouts are more likely to show delinquent behaviours. Truancy and reading below grade level predict school dropout.

7. How do adolescents make career choices?

Children's career aspirations are often not practical at first but become increasingly realistic as children mature and gain experience. Factors that influence choice of a career include abilities and personality traits.

8. Does gender affect career choice?

To some degree, women's and men's career choices are still influenced by traditional gender-role stereotypes.

9. How many Canadian adolescents hold jobs? What are the pros and cons of adolescents working?

Approximately 15 percent of Canadians between the ages of fifteen and twenty-four combine work and school. The benefits of adolescent employment include developing a sense of responsibility, self-reliance, and discipline, and learning to appreciate the value of money and education. But students who work also report lower grades and other problems.

W W W **Go to**
www.voyages1CE.nelson.com
for an interactive version of this summary review.

Key Terms

formal operations *(page 566)*

utopian *(page 569)*

imaginary audience *(page 571)*

personal fable *(page 571)*

postconventional level *(page 576)*

reciprocity *(page 576)*

occupational gender typing *(page 588)*

Active Learning Resources

Observing Children and Adolescents CD-ROM
Want to watch videos showing what you've just learned about in this chapter? Click on the "Piaget's Formal-Operational Stage" video in Module 4, Section 2. Your "Lessons in Observation" feature on p. 519 provides further learning objectives, an applied lesson, and a critical thinking exercise designed to help you experience this stage of development.

Visit Your Companion Website for This Book
http://www.voyages1CE.nelson.com
Check out this companion website, where you will find online resources directly linked to your book. The website includes interactive exercises related to PQ4R and Power Visuals for mastering and reviewing key concepts as well as quizzing, chapter outlines, and much more!

CengageNOW!™
http://hed.nelson.com
Go to this site for the link to CengageNOW™, your one-stop study shop. Take a Pretest for this chapter, and CengageNOW™ will generate a personalized Study Plan based on your test results! The Study Plan will identify the topics you need to review and direct you to online resources to help you master those topics. You can then take a Posttest to help you determine the concepts you have mastered and those you still need to work on.

16

Adolescence:
Social and Emotional Development

PREVIEW

TRUTH OR FICTION?

(T)(F) Adolescents imitate their peers' clothing, speech, hairstyles, and ideals.

(T)(F) Males are more concerned about occupational choices than females are.

(T)(F) Adolescents are in a constant state of rebellion against their parents.

(T)(F) Most adolescents' friends are "bad influences."

(T)(F) 47 000 Canadian teenagers become pregnant each year.

(T)(F) Only a minority of adolescents engage in delinquent behaviour.

(T)(F) Suicide is the leading cause of death among adolescents.

(T)(F) Adolescents reach adulthood at age twenty-one.

Go to

www.voyages1CE.nelson.com
for an interactive version of this "Truth or Fiction" feature.

© Ryan McVay/Getty Images

What am I like as a person? Complicated! I'm sensitive, friendly and out-going, though I can also be shy, self-conscious, and even obnoxious. I'd *like* to be friendly and tolerant all of the time. That's the kind of person I *want* to be, and I'm disappointed when I'm not. I'm responsible, even studious every now and then, but on the other hand I'm a goof-off too, because if you're too studious, you won't be popular. I'm a pretty cheerful person, especially with my friends, where I can even get rowdy. But I'm usually pretty stressed-out at home, or sarcastic, since my parents are always on my case. They expect me to get all A's. It's not fair! I worry about how I probably *should* get better grades. But I'd be mortified in the eyes of my friends. Sometimes I feel phony, especially around boys. Say I think some guy might be interested in asking me out. I try to act different, like Madonna. I'll be flirtatious and fun-loving. And then everybody else is looking at me like they think I'm totally weird! Then I get self-conscious and embarrassed and become radically introverted, and I don't know who I really am! But I don't really care what they think anyway. I just want to know what my close friends think. I can be my true self with my close friends. I can't be my real self with my parents. They don't understand me. They treat me like I'm still a kid. That gets confusing, though. I mean, which am I—a kid or an adult? It's scary, too, because I don't have any idea what I want to be when I grow up. I mean, I have lots of *ideas.* My friend Sheryl and I talk about whether we'll be teachers or lawyers, veterinarians, maybe mothers. I know I *don't* want to be a waitress or a secretary. But how do you decide all of this? I mean, I think about it a lot, but I can't resolve it.

—Adapted from Harter (1990c, pp. 352–353)

This self-description by a fifteen-year-old girl illustrates a key aspect of the adolescent years: the search for an answer to the question "Who am I?" She is struggling to reconcile contradictory traits and behaviours to determine the "real me." She is preoccupied not only with her present self but also with what she wants to become. What were *your* concerns at this age?

In this chapter, we explore social and emotional development in adolescence. We begin with the formation of identity and related changes in self-concept and self-esteem. We consider adolescents' relationships with their parents and their peers. We consider the emergence of sexual behaviours and attitudes and focus on the issue of teenage pregnancy. We address the problems of juvenile delinquency and suicide. Then, as we bring our present voyage to a close, we explore what some developmentalists consider a new stage in human development: emerging adulthood.

Development of Identity and the Self-Concept: "Who Am I?" (And Who Else?)

Adolescence is a key period in the lifelong process of defining just who we are—and who we are not. In Chapter 1 and throughout the social and emotional development chapters, we have reviewed the various stages of Erik Erikson's influential theory of psychosocial development. The stage that is related to adolescence is his stage of identity versus role diffusion, which we delve into here. We then turn to James Marcia's expansion of Erikson's theory and explore his four identity statuses. Next, we consider sex and cultural perspectives on identity development. Finally, we look at the development of self-concept and self-esteem during adolescence.

Erikson's View of Identity Development

Question: What does Erikson have to say about the development of identity during adolescence? Erikson's fifth stage of psychosocial development is called identity versus role diffusion. The primary task of this stage is for adolescents to develop

ego identity: a sense of who they are and what they stand for. Individuals are faced with making choices about their future occupation, their ideological view of the world (including political and religious beliefs), their sexual orientation, and their gender-role behaviours. The ability to engage in formal-operational thinking helps adolescents make these choices. Because thought is no longer tied to concrete experience, adolescents can weigh the options available to them, even though they may not have directly experienced any of them (Kahlbaugh & Haviland, 1991; Schwartz, 2001).

In the identity versus role diffusion stage, a search for identity involves the formation of a self-concept in which past, present, and future are brought together to form a unified whole. Failure to find identity, according to Erikson, can lead to self-doubt, role diffusion, role confusion, or a self-destructive one-sided preoccupation or activity. The building blocks of identity occur in childhood, but identity must be based on more than the sum of childhood identifications.

An important aspect of identity development is what Erikson (1968) referred to as a **psychological moratorium.** This can be described as a time-out period during which adolescents experiment with different roles, values, beliefs, and relationships. During this moratorium period, adolescents often experience an **identity crisis.** Erikson defined the identity crisis as a turning point in development during which one examines one's values and makes decisions about life roles. Which college should I choose? Which career? Should I become sexually active or not? If so, with whom? Adolescents may feel overwhelmed by the many options before them and by the need to make choices that inevitably will reduce their future alternatives (Crain, 2000).

Truth or Fiction Revisited: In their search for identity, many—not all—adolescents join "in" groups, slavishly imitating their peers' clothing, speech, hairstyles, and ideals. They may become intolerant of outsiders (Erikson, 1963). Those who successfully resolve their identity crisis develop a strong sense of who they are and what they stand for. Those who fail to resolve the crisis may continue to be intolerant of people who are different and continue to blindly follow people who adhere to conventional ways.

"Identity Statuses": Searching for the Self, Making a Commitment

Building on Erikson's approach, James Marcia (Marcia, 1991; Marcia et al., 1993) identified four identity statuses. *Question: What are Marcia's "identity statuses"?* The statuses represent the four possible combinations of the dimensions of *exploration* and *commitment* that Erikson believed were critical to the development of identity (Schwartz, 2001) (see Concept Review 16.1). **Exploration** involves active questioning and searching among alternatives in the quest to establish goals, values, or beliefs. **Commitment** is a stable investment in one's goals, values, or beliefs.

Role diffusion is the least developmentally advanced status. This category includes individuals who do not have commitments and who are not in the process of trying to form them (Kroger, 2003; Snarey & Bell, 2003). This stage often is characteristic of children before they reach high school and in the early high school years. Older adolescents who remain diffused may drift through life in a carefree, uninvolved way or they may be unhappy and lonely. Some individuals in the diffusion status are apathetic and adopt an "I don't care" attitude. Others are angry, alienated, and rebellious and may reject socially approved goals, values, and beliefs (Kroger, 2003; Snarey & Bell, 2003).

In the **foreclosure** status, individuals have made commitments without ever seriously considering alternatives. These commitments usually are established early in life and often are based on identification with parents, teachers, or other authority figures who have made a strong impression on the child. For example, a college student may

ego identity According to Erikson, one's sense of who one is and what one stands for.

psychological moratorium A time-out period when adolescents experiment with different roles, values, beliefs, and relationships.

identity crisis A turning point in development during which one examines one's values and makes decisions about life roles.

 For many, the sense of identity solidifies in adolescence. To watch the video, click on the "Identity Formation" clip in Module 4, Section 3.

exploration Active questioning and searching among alternatives in the quest to establish goals, values, or beliefs.

commitment A stable investment in one's goals, values, or beliefs.

role diffusion An identity status that characterizes those who have no commitments and who are not in the process of exploring alternatives.

foreclosure An identity status that characterizes those who have made commitments without considering alternatives.

unquestioningly prepare for a career that has been chosen for him by his parents. In other cases, the adolescent may uncritically adopt the lifestyle of a religious cult or extremist political group, as shown in a study of native Belgians and Belgian immigrants (Saroglou & Galand, 2004). Foreclosed individuals tend to be more authoritarian and inflexible than individuals in other identity statuses (Saroglou & Galand, 2004).

moratorium An identity status that characterizes those who are actively exploring alternatives in an attempt to form an identity.

The **moratorium** identity status refers to a person who is actively exploring alternatives in an attempt to make choices with regard to occupation, ideological beliefs, and so on (Kroger, 2003; Snarey & Bell, 2003). Individuals in the moratorium status often are anxious and intense and have ambivalent feelings toward their parents as they struggle to work toward commitment (Kroger, 2003).

Concept Review 16.1 The Four Identity Statuses of James Marcia

Commitment	Exploration	
	Yes	No
Yes	**Identity Achievement** • Most developed in terms of identity • Has experienced a period of exploration • Has developed commitments • Has a sense of personal well-being, high self-esteem, and self-acceptance • Cognitively flexible • Sets goals and works toward achieving them	**Foreclosure** • Has commitments without considering alternatives • Commitments based on identification with parents, teachers, or other authority figures • Often authoritarian and inflexible
No	**Moratorium** • Actively exploring alternatives • Attempting to make choices with regard to occupation, ideological beliefs, and so on • Often anxious and intense • Ambivalent feelings toward parents and authority figures	**Identity Diffusion** • Least developed in terms of identity • Lacks commitments • Not trying to form commitments • May be carefree and uninvolved or unhappy and lonely • May be angry, alienated, rebellious

What Is the Identity Status of These Adolescents?

Identity achievement refers to those who have experienced a period of exploration and have developed relatively firm commitments. Individuals who have achieved a clear sense of identity show a number of strengths. They have a sense of personal well-being in the form of high self-esteem and self-acceptance. They are cognitively flexible and show high levels of moral reasoning. They are able to set goals and work toward achieving them (Kroger, 2003; Snarey & Bell, 2003).

identity achievement An identity status that characterizes those who have explored alternatives and have developed commitments.

Development of Identity Statuses

Before high school, children show little interest in questions related to identity. Most of them are either in role diffusion or foreclosure statuses. During the high school and college years, adolescents increasingly move from the diffusion and foreclosure statuses to the moratorium and achievement statuses (Kroger, 2003; Snarey & Bell, 2003). The greatest gains in identity formation occur in university or college (Waterman, 1985, 1999). Undergraduate students are exposed to a broad spectrum of lifestyles, belief systems, and career choices. These experiences spur consideration of identity issues. Are you one of the undergraduate students who have changed majors once or twice (or more)? If so, you have most likely experienced the moratorium identity status, which is common among college students. You should be comforted by the results of studies that show that college seniors have a stronger sense of identity than first-year students. The identity commitments of older students are likely to result from successfully resolving crises experienced during the moratorium (Lewis, 2003).

> For me, I'm exploring who I am—trying to find out more who I am, because I'm not really sure anymore. Because up till about seventh grade, I was just a kid. I was me, and I never really thought about it. But now I've thought about it a lot more, and I'm starting to have to make decisions about who I want to be.
> —Conrad, age 13 (in Bell, 1998, p.72)

Ethnicity and Development of Identity

Question: What are the connections between ethnicity and other sociocultural factors—such as sex—and identity?

The development of self-identity is a key task for all adolescents. The task is more complex for adolescents who are members of ethnic minority groups (Phinney, 2000). Adolescents who belong to the dominant culture—in this country, European Canadians of Christian heritage—are usually faced with assimilating one set of cultural values into their identities. However, adolescents who belong to ethnic minority groups, such as Chinese, Muslim, and Jewish Canadians, confront two sets of cultural values—the values of the dominant culture and those of their particular ethnic group (Phinney et al., 2000; Spencer et al., 2000). If the cultural values conflict, the adolescent needs to sort out the values that are most meaningful to him or her and incorporate them into his or her identity. Some adolescents do it cafeteria style: They take a little bit of this and a little bit of that. For example, artificial means of birth control are well publicized in the culture at large, and a young Catholic woman may decide to use them even though doing so conflicts with her religion's teachings, although she may not tell her priest or her family.

Another problem in forging a sense of identity is that adolescents from ethnic minority groups often experience prejudice and discrimination. Furthermore, their cultural heroes may be ignored. A relative scarcity of successful role models can also be a problem, particularly for youth who live in poverty (Spencer et al., 2000). Identifying too strongly with the dominant culture may lead to rejection by the minority group. On the other hand, rejecting the dominant culture's values for those of the minority group may limit opportunities for advancement in the larger society. Biracial adolescents—those with parents from two different racial or ethnic groups—wrestle not only with these issues but also with issues relating to their dual cultural heritage (Gibbs & Hines, 1992; Spencer et al., 2000).

Question: Are there stages in developing an ethnic identity—that is, a sense of belonging to an ethnic group? Researchers find it useful to hypothesize three stages in the development of **ethnic identity** (Phinney, 1989; Umaña-Taylor et al., 2004). The first is **unexamined ethnic identity.** It is similar to Marcia's ego identity statuses of diffusion or foreclosure. In some cases, the early adolescent has not given much thought to ethnic identity issues (diffusion). In other instances, the young adolescent may have adopted an identity either with the dominant group or with the minority group based on societal or parental values but without much exploration or thought. This represents a foreclosed status. In the second stage, the adolescent embarks on an **ethnic identity search.** This stage, similar to Marcia's moratorium stage, may be based on a key incident that makes the adolescent aware of his or her ethnicity. During this stage, the adolescent may explore his or her ethnic culture, intensely participating in cultural events, reading, and talking to others. In the third stage, individuals have an **achieved ethnic identity.** This involves a clear, confident acceptance of oneself as a member of one's ethnic group.

As minority youth move through adolescence, they are increasingly likely to explore their own ethnicity and to acquire an achieved ethnic identity status. For example, only about one-third of ethnic minority eighth-graders were found to show evidence of ethnic identity search, compared with half of ethnic minority tenth-graders (Phinney, 1989; Phinney & Tarver, 1988). A longitudinal study (Phinney & Chavira, 1992) found movement from lower to higher stages of ethnic identity between sixteen and nineteen years of age. And undergraduates show higher levels of ethnic identity achievement than eleventh- or twelfth-graders (Phinney, 1992).

ethnic identity A sense of belonging to an ethnic group.

unexamined ethnic identity The first stage of ethnic identity development; similar to the diffusion or foreclosure identity statuses.

ethnic identity search The second stage of ethnic identity development; similar to the moratorium identity status.

achieved ethnic identity The final stage of ethnic identity development; similar to the identity achievement status.

How Does Ethnic Identity Develop?
According to Phinney, adolescents undergo a three-stage process of the development of ethnic identity: unexamined ethnic identity, ethnic identity search, and achieved ethnic identity. Adolescents from ethnic minority groups may be faced with conflicting values: those of their ethnic group and those of the dominant culture.

Gender Roles and Development of Identity

And what of gender roles? *Question: Does the development of ego identity differ in males and females?* Erikson believed that there were differences, and it seems that they reflected the times in which he wrote. Erikson wrote that the development of ego identity involves the development of a general outlook on life and the making of a commitment to an occupation or career. Individuals develop intimate relationships involving emotional attachment and sexual love in the following stage, that of intimacy versus isolation. But this sequence more accurately describes the traditional development of males. Gender roles influence the "possible selves" contemplated by males and females (Anthis et al., 2004).

Erikson (1968, 1975) compared the importance of interpersonal relationships, careers, and philosophies of life in males and females. He concluded that relationships were more important to women's development of identity, whereas occupational and ideological matters were relatively more important to men's. He believed that a young woman's identity was intimately bound up with her roles as wife and mother. Erikson, like most thinkers of his day, saw a woman's primary roles as related to her home life. In sum, it was normal for men to develop their identities before they developed (meaningful) intimate relationships. But women might develop their identities simultaneously with the development of intimate relationships.

However, the evidence from numerous studies suggests that females approach identity formation in a manner that is comparable to that of males (Archer, 1992; Murray, 1998). In one study, both men and women claimed that the interpersonal area was the most important (Bilsker et al., 1988). ***Truth or Fiction Revisited:*** Other studies (Archer, 1985, 1992) have found that adolescent females and males are equally concerned about occupational choices, but females are more likely to integrate occupational and family plans (Berzonsky, 2004). This sex difference may persist because females continue to assume primary responsibility for child rearing, even though most women are employed outside the home (Anthis et al., 2004).

What about the timing of identity development in women and men? Both begin identity formation in adolescence. Those women who have uninterrupted careers tend to complete the task of identity achievement in late adolescence. Women who are full-time homemakers or who defer employment until their children are in school are more likely to develop a strong sense of personal identity after their children reach school age (Patterson et al., 1992).

Finally, men appear to develop identity before intimacy, as Erikson suggested. Some women also develop identity before intimacy, whereas others achieve intimacy before identity or achieve them concurrently (Schiedel & Marcia, 1985). Brown and Gilligan's work (1993) *Meeting at the Crossroads: Women's Psychology and Girls' Development* is a documentation of the female journey through adolescence. These authors suggest that females in Western society "lose" their voice in adolescence. Harter and colleagues conceptualized level of voice as being a complicated construct tied to a development of self-concept. In a study led by Harter, male and female high school students' self-reported level of voice with parents, teachers, classmates, and close friends revealed no gender differences (Harter et al., 1998).

Development of the Self-Concept in Adolescence

The adolescent preoccupation with developing a sense of identity is part of a broader process of redefining the way adolescents view themselves. ***Question: How does the self-concept develop during adolescence?*** Before adolescence, children describe themselves primarily in terms of their physical characteristics and their actions. As they approach adolescence, children begin to incorporate psychological characteristics and social relationships into their self-descriptions. Adolescents tend to describe themselves in terms of distinct and enduring personality traits (Damon, 1991).

The self-concept also becomes more differentiated; adolescents add more categories to their self-description. Also, self-descriptions begin to vary according to adolescents' social roles. Like the fifteen-year-old at the beginning of the chapter, adolescents may describe themselves as anxious or sarcastic with parents but as caring, talkative, and cheerful with friends. Such contradictions and conflicts in self-description reach their peak at about age fourteen and then begin to decline in later adolescence (Harter & Monsour, 1992). The more advanced formal-operational skills of the older adolescent allow him or her to integrate the many apparently contradictory elements of the self. For example, the older adolescent might say, "I'm very adaptable. When I'm around my friends, who think that what I say is important, I'm very talkative; but around my family, I'm quiet because they're not interested enough to really listen to me" (Damon, 1991, p. 988).

Developing in a World of Diversity

Ethnicity, Gender Roles, and Self-Esteem

What opinions do adolescents hold of themselves? Our self-esteem tends to reflect our competencies and also the opinions of others. There are also connections to ethnicity and gender roles.

Ethnicity and Self-Esteem during Adolescence

Question: Are there ethnic differences in the development of self-esteem during adolescence? Erik Erikson (1968) believed that minority adolescents are likely to form poor self-concepts because they internalize society's negative views. Kiang, Yip, Gonzales-Backen, Witkow, and Fuligni (2006), in a study of American youth of Mexican and Chinese descent, found that adolescents with a higher ethnic regard reported being happier. Canadian researchers Gaudet, Clément, and Deuzeman (2005) found that for first- and second-generation Lebanese Canadians, there was a positive correlation between Canadian identity and depression. Similarly, Clément, Michaud, and Noels (1998) found that for minority Francophones, having support from the majority group but not from other Francophones correlated to depression. This work suggests that a strong ethnic

identity may be related to higher levels of adjustment (Gaudet et al., 2005). It is argued that, in Canada, a multiculturalism approach allows ethnic and minority groups to maintain their ethnic identity while exploring the majority culture.

Other research has examined the relationship between self-esteem and the stages of development of ethnic identity. Jean Phinney and her colleagues interviewed Latino and Latina American, Asian American, African American, and European American students in high school and college. Those who showed higher stages of ethnic identity also had higher self-esteem (Phinney & Alipuria, 1990; Phinney et al., 1992). The association between self-esteem and ethnic identity was stronger for the minority youth than for the European Americans. Self-esteem is apparently related to the extent to which adolescents have learned to understand and accept their ethnicity (Phinney & Rosenthal, 1992).

Gender Roles and Self-Esteem during Adolescence

Question: Are there sex differences in self-esteem during adolescence? Adolescent girls generally show lower self-esteem than boys (Quatman &

Watson, 2001). An American national survey of 3000 children in grades four through ten indicates that the sex gap in self-esteem increases between the grade school and high school years (American Association of University Women, 1992). At eight and nine years of age, 60 percent of the girls and 67 percent of the boys were self-confident and assertive. But by the ages of sixteen and seventeen, only 29 percent of girls, compared to 46 percent of boys, retained their positive self-esteem.

Why is the decrease in self-esteem greater for girls? One factor may be the physical changes of adolescence, which are central to the development of self-esteem in adolescence. Although physical appearance is a concern for both girls and boys, it is relatively more important for girls.

Others attribute the drop in girls' self-esteem to the negative messages that girls receive in school. In the words of one report, "Students sit in classes that day in and day out deliver the message that women's lives count far less than men's" (American Association of University Women, 1992, p. 67).

Susan Harter examined the development of the self-concept over the course of adolescence and the impact of cognitive growth on changes in self-concept using Fischer's (1980) neo-Piagetian theory of cognitive development. She argued that early adolescents' self-portraits include personal attributes, competencies, social skills, and affects that differ across relationships and situations. Then during middle adolescence, there is a further proliferation of selves. But adolescents acquire the capacity to relate single abstractions to one another—to compare and contrast them. The awareness of these contradictions may cause intrapsychic conflict (i.e., who is the real me?). By late adolescence, single abstractions are integrated into higher-order abstractions about the self. With this new capacity, potential contradictory characteristics are no longer seen as a source of conflict. During adolescence, self-concepts become more trait focused, but the traits become more abstract because adolescents may describe themselves in less tangible characteristics as they start to deal with the notion of actual self and possible selves. The most widely used measure of self-image in adolescence is Harter's Self-Perception Profile for Adolescents (1988, 1999). The scale consists of nine subscales of five items each: (1) scholastic competence, (2) social acceptance, (3) athletic competence, (4) physical appearance, (5) job competence, (6) romantic appeal, (7) behavioural conduct, (8) close friendship, and (9) global self-worth.

© David R. Frazier/DANITA DELIMONT

Development of Self-Esteem during Adolescence
Self-esteem tends to dip during early adolescence as young people face the differences between their real self and their ideal self. However, self-esteem tends to improve with emotional support from family and peers.

Self-Esteem in Adolescence: Bottoming? Rising?

Question: What happens to self-esteem during adolescence? **Self-esteem** tends to decline as the child progresses from middle childhood to about the age of twelve or thirteen (Harter & Whitesell, 2003). What might account for the drop-off? The growing cognitive maturity of young adolescents makes them increasingly and painfully aware of the disparity between their ideal self and their real self. The sense of discrepancy between the real self and ideal self is especially great in the area of physical appearance. Physical appearance contributes more to the development of self-esteem during adolescence than any other characteristic (Galliher et al., 2004).

After hitting a low point at about age twelve or thirteen, self-esteem gradually improves throughout adolescence (Harter & Whitesell, 2003). Perhaps adolescents adjust their notions of the ideal self to better reflect reality. Also, as adolescents develop academic, physical, and social skills, they may gradually grow less self-critical (Shirk et al., 2003).

For most adolescents, low self-esteem produces temporary discomfort (Harter & Whitesell, 2003). For others, low self-esteem has serious psychological and behavioural consequences. For example, low self-esteem is often found in teenagers who are depressed or suicidal (Shirk et al., 2003).

Emotional support from parents and peers is important in the development of self-esteem during adolescence. Adolescents who feel that they are highly regarded by family and friends are more likely to have positive feelings about themselves than are those who feel they are lacking such support (Roberts et al., 2000; Santos & Lopes, 2003). In early adolescence, support from parents is equally as important as peer support. By late adolescence, peer support carries more weight.

self-esteem The sense of value or worth that people attach to themselves.

Active Review

1. Erikson's fifth (adolescent) stage of psychosocial development is called _____ versus role diffusion.

2. Erikson defined a psychological _____ as a time-out during which adolescents experiment with different roles, values, beliefs, and relationships.

3. According to Marcia, identity _____ refers to adolescents who have experienced a period of exploration and developed relatively firm commitments.

4. Girls generally show (higher or lower?) self-esteem than boys during adolescence.

Reflect & Relate: Does your ethnic background play an important role in your self-identity? Explain.

Go to

W W W **www.voyages1ce.nelson.com**
for an interactive version of this review.

Although peers have significant influence in an adolescent's life, this video illustrates the importance of parental influence for teens. To watch the video, click on the "Peers—Domain Influences" clip in Module 4, Section 3. Also check out the "Cliques, Crowds, and Conformity" clip in the same section.

Relationships with Parents and Peers

Adolescents coping with the task of establishing a sense of identity and direction in their lives are heavily influenced by both their parents and peers. *Question: How do relationships with one's parents and peers change during the course of the teenage years?*

Relationships with Parents

During adolescence, children spend much less time with their parents than they did during childhood. In one study, children ranging in age from nine to fifteen years carried electronic pagers for a week and reported what they were doing each time they were signalled by the pagers (Larson & Richards, 1991). The amount of time spent with family dramatically declined as the age of the children increased. The fifteen-year-olds spent half as much time with their families as the nine-year-olds. For older boys, the time with family was replaced by time spent alone, whereas older girls spent more time alone or with friends.

Adolescents continue to interact more with their mothers than with their fathers, continuing the pattern begun in childhood. Teenagers engage in more conflicts with their mothers, but they also view their mothers as being more supportive, as knowing them better, and as being more likely to accept the teenager's opinions (Collins & Russell, 1991; Noller & Callan, 1990). On the other hand, good relations with fathers strongly contribute to the psychological well-being of adolescents (Flouri & Buchanan, 2003).

The decrease in time spent with family may reflect the adolescent's striving to become more independent from his or her parents. A certain degree of distancing from parents may be adaptive for adolescents as they engage in the tasks of forming relationships outside the family and entering adulthood. But greater independence does not mean that adolescents become emotionally detached from their mothers and fathers. Adolescents continue to maintain a great deal of love, loyalty, and respect for their parents (Montemayor & Flannery, 1991). And adolescents who feel close to their parents are more likely to show greater self-reliance and independence, higher self-esteem, better school performance, and fewer psychological and social problems (Flouri & Buchanan, 2003; Steinberg, 1996).

The relationship between parents and teens is not always rosy, of course. Early adolescence, in particular, is characterized by increased bickering and disagreements and by a decrease in shared activities and expressions of affection (Smetana et al., 2003).

Conflict is greatest during puberty and declines in later adolescence (Smetana et al., 2003). Conflicts typically centre on the everyday details of family life, such as chores, homework, curfews, personal appearance, finances, and dating. Conflicts may arise in these areas because adolescents believe that personal issues—such as choice of clothes and friends—that were previously controlled by parents should now come under their own control (Smetana et al., 2003). But parents, especially mothers, continue to believe that they should retain control in most areas, such as encouraging adolescents to do their homework and clean their rooms. And so conflicts arise. As adolescents get older, however, they and their parents are more likely to compromise (Smetana et al., 2003). On the other hand, many studies confirm that parents and adolescents are quite similar in their values and beliefs regarding social, political, religious, and economic issues (Paikoff & Collins, 1991). Disagreements in these areas are relatively few. Even though the notion of a generation gap between adolescents and their parents may persist as a popular stereotype, there is little evidence to support it. ***Truth or Fiction Revisited:*** Adolescents are not in a constant state of rebellion against their parents.

During adolescence, most teenagers and their parents establish a balance between adolescent independence and continued family connectedness. Although some conflict is inevitable, it usually is not severe (Smetana et al., 2003). As adolescents grow older, parents are more likely to relax controls and are less likely to use punishment (Smetana et al., 2003). Although parent-child relationships change, most adolescents feel that they are close to and get along with their parents (Galambos, 1992). Adolescents do not usually reject their parents' values, although they develop a less idealized view of their parents (Silverberg et al., 1992).

Parenting Styles

Children's development is affected by the degree to which their parents show warmth and set limits on the child's behaviour. Differences in parenting styles continue to influence the development of adolescents as well (Galambos et al., 2003). Adolescents from authoritative homes—whose parents are willing to exert control and explain the reasons for doing so—show more competent behaviour than any other group of teenagers. They are more self-reliant, do better in school, have better mental health, and show the lowest incidence of psychological problems and misconduct, including drug use.

Relationships with Peers

The transition from childhood to adolescence is accompanied by a shift in the relative importance of parents and peers. Although relationships with parents generally remain positive, the role of peers as a source of activities, influence, and support increases markedly during the teen years. For example, parents are perceived as the most frequent providers of social and emotional support by fourth-graders. But by seventh grade, friends of the same sex are seen to be as supportive as parents. And by tenth grade, same-sex friends are viewed as providing more support than parents (Furman & Buhrmester, 1992).

What Happens to Relationships with Parents during Adolescence? Parent-adolescent relationships become redefined during adolescence, as most adolescents strive for independence. There are often conflicts about choices of friends and clothing and how and where adolescents spend their time. But despite conflict, most adolescents continue to love and respect their parents.

The Development of Friendship in Adolescence
Adolescents tend to spend more time with their friends than with their families. They look for one or more close friends, or confidants. They also tend to belong to *cliques* and *crowds*. All serve different but overlapping functions.

Friendships in Adolescence

Friendships occupy an increasingly important place in the lives of adolescents. Adolescents have more friends than younger children do (Feiring & Lewis, 1991). Most adolescents have one or two "best friends" and several good friends. Teenagers see their friends frequently, usually several hours a day (Hartup, 1993). And when teenagers are not with their friends, you can often find them talking with each other on the phone. In fact, Rathus frequently warned his children that he would take them in for major surgery— telephonectomy—unless they got the phones out of their ears by themselves. The warning went unheard (because the children were on the phone). Rathus therefore solved the problem by having a separate line installed for the children and investing heavily in the local telephone company.

Friendships in adolescence differ in important ways from the friendships of childhood. For one thing, adolescents are much more likely to stress the importance of acceptance, intimate self-disclosure, and mutual understanding in their friendships (González et al., 2004). For example, one eighth-grade girl described her best friend this way: "I can tell her things, and she helps me talk. And she doesn't laugh at me if I do something weird—she accepts me for who I am" (Berndt & Perry, 1990, p. 269). Second, adolescents stress loyalty and trustworthiness as important aspects of friendship more than younger children do (González et al., 2004; Rotenberg et al., 2004). For example, they may say that a friend will "stick up for you in a fight" and will not "talk about you behind your back." Finally, adolescents are more likely than younger children to share with friends and are less likely to compete with them.

Adolescents and their friends are similar in many respects. They typically are the same age and the same race. They almost always are the same sex. Even though romantic attachments increase during the teen years, most adolescents still choose members of their own sex as best friends (Hartup, 1993). Friends are likely to share certain behavioural similarities. They often are alike in their school attitudes, educational aspirations, and school achievement. Friends also tend to have similar attitudes about drinking, drug use, and sexual activity (Hartup, 1993; Youniss & Haynie, 1992).

Friendship contributes to a positive self-concept and psychological adjustment. Adolescents who have a close friend have higher self-esteem than adolescents who do not. Teenagers who have intimate friendships are also more likely to show advanced stages of identity development (Berndt, 1992; Bukowski et al., 1993b).

Ethnicity, Sex, and Adolescent Friendships

Children are more likely to choose friends from their own ethnic group than from others (Hamm, 2000). This pattern strengthens in adolescence (Hartup, 1993). Adolescents from ethnic minority groups grow aware of the differences between their culture and the dominant culture. Peers from their own ethnic group provide a sense of camaraderie that reduces the pain of feeling isolated from the dominant culture (Spencer et al., 1990).

Intimacy and closeness appear to be more central to the friendships of girls than of boys both in childhood and in adolescence (Berndt & Perry, 1990; Schraf & Hertz-Lazarowitz, 2003). Both female and male adolescents describe girls' friendships as more intimate than boys' friendships (Hartup, 1993). Girls spend more time with their friends than boys do (Schraf & Hertz-Lazarowitz, 2003); view close friendships as more important than adolescent boys do; and report putting more effort into improving the depth and quality of the relationship than boys do. Adolescent and adult females also are more likely than males to disclose secrets, personal problems, thoughts, and feelings to their friends (Dindia & Allen, 1992; Schraf & Hertz-Lazarowitz, 2003).

Friendship networks among girls are smaller and more exclusive than friendship networks among boys (Schraf & Hertz-Lazarowitz, 2003). That is, girls tend to have one or two close friends, whereas boys tend to congregate in larger, less intimate groups. The activities of girls' and boys' friendship networks differ as well. Girls are more likely to engage in unstructured activities such as talking and listening to music. Boys, on the other hand, are more likely to engage in organized group activities, games, and sports.

Peer Groups

In addition to forming close friendships, most adolescents also belong to one or more larger peer groups. *Question: What kinds of adolescent peer groups are there?* Such groups include *cliques* and *crowds* (Brown, 1990). **Cliques** consist of five to ten individuals who hang around together and share activities and confidences. **Crowds** are larger groups who may or may not spend much time together and are identified by the particular activities or attitudes of the group. Crowds are usually given labels by other adolescents. Think back on your high school days. Different groups of individuals are commonly given labels such as "jocks," "brains," "druggies," "nerds," and so on. The most negatively labelled groups ("druggies," "rejects," and so on) show higher levels of alcohol and drug use, delinquency, and depression than other groups (Downs & Rose, 1991).

Adolescent peer groups differ from childhood peer groups. For one thing, the time spent with peers increases. Amount of time that adolescents spend with same-sex friends is highest in early adolescence, while time spent with cross-sex friends is greater in later adolescence (Johnson, 2004). High school students spend more than half their time with peers and only about 15 percent of their time with parents or other adults (Csikszentmihalyi & Larson, 1984).

A second difference between adolescent and childhood peer groups is that adolescent peer groups function with less adult guidance or control (Brown, 1990). Childhood peer groups stay closer to home, under the watchful eye of parents. Adolescent peer groups are more likely to congregate in settings with less adult supervision (the school) or with no supervision.

A third change in adolescent peer groups is the addition of peers of the other sex. This sharply contrasts with the sex segregation of childhood peer groups (Brown, 1990). Association with peers of the other sex may lead to dating and romantic relationships.

Dating and Romantic Relationships

Question: When do romantic relationships develop? Romantic relationships begin to appear during early and middle adolescence, and most adolescents start dating or going out by the time they graduate from high school (Florsheim, 2003). The development of dating typically takes the following sequence: putting oneself in situations where peers of the other sex will probably be present (e.g., hanging out at the mall), taking part in group activities that include peers of the other sex (e.g., school dances or parties), participating in group dating (e.g., joining a mixed-sex group at the movies), and then engaging in traditional two-person dating (Connolly et al., 2004).

Dating serves a number of important functions. First and foremost, people date to have fun. High school students rate time spent with a person of the other sex as the time when they are happiest (Csikszentmihalyi & Larson, 1984). Dating, especially

clique A group of five to ten individuals who hang around together and who share activities and confidences.

crowd A large, loosely organized group of people who may or may not spend much time together and who are identified by the activities of the group.

in early adolescence, also serves to enhance prestige with one's peers. Dating gives adolescents additional experiences in learning to relate positively to different people. Finally, dating provides preparation for adult courtship activities (Florsheim, 2003).

Dating relationships tend to be casual and short-lived in early adolescence. In late adolescence, relationships tend to become more stable and committed (Connolly et al., 2000). It is therefore not surprising that eighteen-year-olds are more likely than fifteen-year-olds to mention love, trust, and commitment when describing their romantic relationships (Feiring, 1993).

Peer Influence

Parents often worry that their teenage children will fall in with the wrong crowd and be persuaded by their peers to engage in behaviours that are self-destructive or go against the parents' wishes (Brown et al., 1993). How much influence do peers have on each other? Does peer pressure cause adolescents to adopt behaviours and attitudes of which their parents disapprove? Peer pressure actually is fairly weak in early adolescence. It peaks during mid-adolescence and declines in late adolescence, after about age seventeen (Brown et al., 1993; Reis & Youniss, 2004).

Why do peers increase in influence during adolescence? One suggestion is that peers provide a standard by which adolescents measure their behaviour as they begin to develop independence from the family (Foster-Clark & Blyth, 1991). Another reason is that peers provide social, emotional, and practical support in times of trouble (Kirchler et al., 1991; Pombeni et al., 1990).

It was once the conventional wisdom that peer influence and parental influence were in conflict, with peers exerting pressure on adolescents to engage in negative behaviours such as alcohol and drug use. Research paints a more complex picture. For one thing, we have seen that adolescents often maintain close and warm relationships with their parents. ***Truth or Fiction Revisited:*** It is not true that most adolescents' friends are bad influences. Parents and peers usually are complementary rather than competing influences on teenagers (Brown et al., 1993; Galambos et al., 2003; Reis & Youniss, 2004).

Parents and peers also seem to exert influence in somewhat different domains. Adolescents are more likely to conform to peer standards in matters pertaining to style and taste, such as clothing, hairstyles, speech patterns, and music (Camarena, 1991). They are much more likely to agree with their parents on many serious issues, such as moral principles and future educational and career goals (Savin-Williams & Berndt, 1990).

Adolescents influence each other both positively and negatively. Brown and his colleagues found that peer pressure to finish high school and achieve academically were stronger than pressures to engage in areas of misconduct, such as drug use, sexual activity, and minor delinquency (Brown et al., 1993). Moreover, teenagers were much less inclined to succumb to peer pressure to engage in antisocial activity than in neutral activity.

On the other hand, a ten-year study of 20 000 ninth- through twelfth-graders did find that some adolescents encourage one another to do well in school (Steinberg, 1996). Yet more often than not, adolescents discouraged one another from doing well or from doing too well. One in five reported not trying to perform as well as possible for fear of earning the disapproval of peers. Then, too, half reported that they never discussed schoolwork and grades with their friends.

It is true that adolescents who smoke, drink, use drugs, and engage in sexual activity often have friends who also engage in these behaviours. But we must keep in mind that adolescents tend to choose friends and peers who are similar to them to begin with. Peers reinforce behaviour patterns and predispositions that may have existed before the individual joined the group. This is true for positive behaviours, such as academic achievement, as well as for negative behaviours, such as drug use (Brown, 1990).

A number of other factors affect the susceptibility of adolescents to peer influence. One of these is sex. Girls appear to be slightly more concerned with peer acceptance than boys, but boys are more likely than girls to conform to pressures to engage in misconduct (Camarena, 1991; Foster-Clark & Blyth, 1991). Parenting style is also related to susceptibility to peer pressure. Authoritative parenting appears to discourage negative peer influence, whereas authoritarian and permissive parenting seem to encourage it (Foster-Clark & Blyth, 1991; Fuligni & Eccles, 1993).

Active Review

5. Adolescents interact more with their (mothers or fathers?).

6. Adolescents generally (do or do not?) love and respect their parents.

7. The role of peers (increases or decreases?) markedly from childhood to adolescence.

8. Children are more likely to choose friends from (their own or other?) ethnic groups.

Reflect & Relate: How did your relationships with family members change during adolescence? Did you make the changes or simply respond to them? Were the changes for the better or for the worse? Explain.

 Go to
W W W www.voyages1ce.nelson.com
for an interactive version of this review.

Sexuality: When? What? (How?) Who? Where? and Why?—Not to Mention, "Should I?"

> My first sexual experience occurred in a car after the high school junior prom. We were both virgins, very uncertain but very much in love. We had been going together since eighth grade. The experience was somewhat painful. I remember wondering if I would look different to my mother the next day. I guess I didn't because nothing was said.
>
> —Adapted from Morrison et al. (1980, p. 108)

Because of the flood of sex hormones, many or most adolescents experience a powerful sex drive. In addition, they are bombarded with sexual messages in the media, including scantily clad hip-grinding, crotch-grabbing pop stars; print ads for barely there underwear; and countless articles on "How to tell if your boyfriend has been (whatever)" and "The 10 things that will drive your girlfriend wild." Teenagers are strongly motivated to follow the crowd, yet they are also influenced by the views of their parents and teachers. So what is a teen to do? What *do* Canadian teens do? *Question: What are some patterns of sexual behaviour in adolescence?*

According to one Canadian health report, **the average age** that respondents had sexual intercourse for the first time was at 16 1/2 years of age for both males and females (Rotermann, 2005). Sexual activity in adolescence can take many forms. In this section, we consider masturbation, oral sex, homosexuality, heterosexuality, and the use of contraceptives.

Masturbation

masturbation Sexual self-stimulation.

Masturbation, or sexual self-stimulation, is the most common sexual outlet in adolescents. Even before children conceive of sexual experiences with others, they may learn that touching their own genitals can produce pleasure.

Surveys indicate that most adolescents masturbate at some time. The well-known Kinsey studies, published in the mid-twentieth century (Kinsey et al., 1948, 1953), suggested that masturbation was nearly universal among male adolescents but less common among adolescent females. This sex difference is confirmed in nearly every survey (Baumeister et al., 2001; Larsson & Svedin, 2002; Laumann et al., 1994; Schwartz, 1999). Some researchers attribute the sex difference in masturbation to a stronger sex drive for males, because of higher amounts of testosterone (Baumeister et al., 2001; Peplau, 2003). Others attribute the sex difference to the greater social constraints that are often placed on females (Fine, 2002).

Oral Sex

There has been a slight increase in oral sex practices among adolescents from 1994 to 2002 (see Table 16.1). Although rates in the younger teen population are hard to track, a study by Boekeloo and Howard (2002) of twelve- to fifteen-year olds found that 18 percent had engaged in oral sex. While most adolescents perceive oral sex to be a type of "safer" sex, health educators and professionals are concerned about communicating the message to youth that oral sex is not without its risks (refer to Table 16.1).

Table 16.1	*Percentage of Canadian Grade 9 and 11 Students Reporting Engaging in Oral Sex at Least Once, 1994, 2002*	
	1994	2002
Grade 9		
Male	27%	32%
Female	21%	28%
Grade 11		
Male	48%	53%
Female	47%	52%

Sources: *Boyce, Doherty, Fortin, & MacKinnon (2003); Warren & King (1994).*

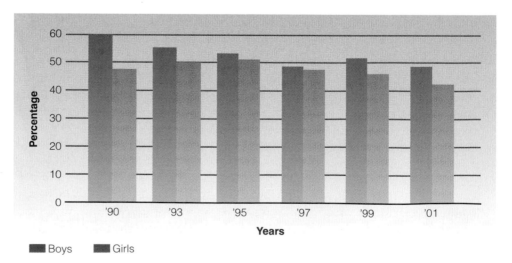

Figure 16.1

Sex Facts in Canada, 2006

Sexual Orientation

Most people, including the great majority of adolescents, have a *heterosexual* orientation. That is, they are sexually attracted to and interested in forming romantic relationships with people of the other sex. However, some people have a **homosexual** orientation. That is, they are attracted to and interested in forming romantic relationships with people of their own sex. Males with a homosexual orientation are referred to as *gay males*. Females with a homosexual orientation are referred to as *lesbians*. However, males and females with a homosexual orientation are sometimes categorized together as "gay people," or "gays." *Bisexual* people are attracted to both females and males.

homosexual Referring to an erotic orientation toward members of one's own sex.

The concept of *sexual orientation* is not to be confused with *sexual activity*. For example, engaging in sexual activity with people of one's own sex does not necessarily mean that one has a homosexual orientation. Sexual activity between males sometimes reflects limited sexual opportunities.

According to Ritch Savin-Williams and Lisa Diamond (2000), the development of sexual identity in gay males and lesbians involves four steps:

1. Attraction to members of the same sex
2. Self-labelling as gay or lesbian
3. Sexual contact with members of the same sex
4. Disclosure of one's sexual orientation to other people

Development of Gay Male or Lesbian Sexual Orientation
Students at the Stratford (Connecticut) High School get together weekly after classes to talk about sexuality and antigay bigotry. Many gay males and lesbians become aware of their sexual orientations during adolescence but fear coming out because of societal pressures. These types of classes try to help create a more positive environment for gay and lesbian students.

By and large, the researchers found a ten-year gap between initial attraction to members of one's own sex, which tended to occur at about the age of eight or nine, and disclosure of one's orientation to other people, which usually occurred at about age eighteen.

Coming Out

Gay and lesbian adolescents often face special challenges. The process of "coming out"—that is, accepting one's homosexual orientation and declaring it to others—may be a long and painful struggle (Bagley & D'Augelli, 2000; Crockett & Silbereisen, 2000). Gay adolescents may be ostracized and rejected by family and friends. Depression and suicide rates are higher among gay youth than among heterosexual adolescents:

> Sexual orientation emerges strongly during early adolescence. Youths with emerging identities that are gay, lesbian, or bisexual, living in generally hostile climates, face particular dilemmas. They are well aware that in many secondary schools the words *fag* and *dyke* are terms of denigration and that anyone who is openly gay, lesbian, or bisexual is open to social exclusion and psychological and physical persecution. Some of their families too will express negative feelings about people who are gay, lesbian, or bisexual; youths in such families may be victimized if they disclose that they are not heterosexual.
>
> —Bagley & D'Augelli (2000)

It has been estimated that as many as one in three gay, lesbian, or bisexual adolescents has attempted suicide (Hershberger & D'Augelli, 2000). Adolescents with a homosexual orientation often engage in substance abuse, run away from home, and do poorly in school (Kilpatrick et al., 2000). These factors also heighten the risk of suicide among gay, lesbian, and bisexual adolescents (Goldfried, 2001; Hershberger & D'Augelli, 2000).

"Coming out to others" sometimes means an open declaration to the world. More often, an adolescent feels more comfortable telling a couple of close friends than his or her parents. Before they inform family members, gay adolescents often anticipate their family's negative reactions, including denial, anger, and rejection (Bagley & D'Augelli, 2000). Yet some families are more accepting. Perhaps they had suspicions and prepared themselves for the news. Then, too, many families are initially rejecting but often eventually come to at least grudging acceptance that an adolescent is gay.

The Origins of Sexual Orientation

Surveys find that about 3 percent of males and 2 percent of females in North America identify themselves as being gay (Ellis, Robb, & Burke, 2005; Laumann et al., 1994). Theories of the origins of sexual orientation look both at nature and nurture—the biological makeup of the individual and environmental influences. Several theories bridge the two. *Question: What do we know about the origins of gay male and lesbian sexual orientations?*

Learning theorists look for the roles of factors such as reinforcement and observational learning. From this perspective, reinforcement of sexual behaviour with members of one's own sex—as in reaching orgasm with them when members of the other sex are unavailable—might affect one's sexual orientation. Similarly, childhood sexual abuse by someone of the same sex could lead to fantasies about sex with people of one's own sex and affect sexual orientation. Observation of others engaged in enjoyable male-male or female-female sexual encounters could also affect the development of sexual orientation. But critics point out that most individuals become aware of their sexual orientation before they experience sexual contacts with other people of either sex (Laumann et al., 1994; Savin-Williams & Diamond, 2000). Moreover, in a society that largely condemns homosexuality, young people are unlikely to believe that a homosexual orientation will have positive effects for them.

Although gay people are less likely than heterosexual people to have children, sexual orientation nevertheless tends to run in families. There is some evidence for genetic factors in sexual orientation (Bailey, 2003; Bailey et al., 2000; Dawood et al., 2000; Rahman & Wilson, 2003). One study found that 22 percent of the brothers of fifty-one gay men were gay or bisexual, although one would expect to find only 3 percent of the brothers to also be gay if the relationship were just coincidental (Pillard & Weinrich, 1986). Twin studies support a role for genetics. About 52 percent of identical (monozygotic) twin pairs are "concordant" (in agreement) for a gay male sexual orientation, compared with 22 percent for fraternal (dizygotic) twins (Bailey & Pillard, 1991). You may recall that monozygotic twins fully share their genetic heritage, whereas dizygotic twins, like other pairs of siblings, have a 50 percent overlap.

Sex hormones promote the development of male and female sex organs and regulate the menstrual cycle. They also have both activating and organizing effects on sexual behaviour. That is, they fuel the sex drive and affect *whom* one will find to be sexually attractive. Sex hormones are thus likely candidates for influencing the development of sexual orientation (Lalumière et al., 2000).

It has been demonstrated repeatedly that sex hormones predispose lower animals, such as rats, to stereotypical masculine or feminine mating patterns. Does this mean that gay males and lesbians differ from heterosexuals in their levels of sex hormones? Among gay male and lesbian adolescents and adults, the answer is apparently not. Sexual orientation has not been reliably connected with adolescent or adult levels of sex hormones (Friedman & Downey, 2001). But sex hormones may influence the developing human embryo and fetus (Dessens et al., 1999; Friedman & Downey, 2001).

We have to conclude by confessing that much about the development of sexual orientation remains speculative. There are possible roles for prenatal exposure to certain hormones. Exposure to these hormones, in turn, may be related to genetic factors, use of drugs (prescribed and illicit), even maternal stress. Even the possibility that childhood experiences play a role has not been ruled out. But the interactions among these factors largely remain a mystery. Nor is there reason to believe that the development of sexual orientation must follow the same path in everyone.

Male-Female Sexual Behaviour

Surveys show that since the early 1990s, the percentage of high school students who have engaged in sexual intercourse has been gradually declining (see Figure 16.1). Nevertheless, between 40 and 50 percent of students have had sexual intercourse, and male high school students are somewhat more likely than girls to be sexually active. The incidences of kissing, "making out," oral sex, and sexual intercourse all increase with age.

Most teenagers do not plan their first sexual experience. Rather, they perceive it as simply happening to them (Browning et al., 2000; O'Donnell et al., 2003). *Question: Why do some teenagers initiate sexual activity at an early age, whereas others wait until later?* Let us consider some of the determinants of early sexual behaviour.

Effects of Puberty

The hormonal changes of puberty probably are partly responsible for the onset of sexual activity. In boys, levels of testosterone are associated with sexual behaviour. In girls, however, testosterone levels are linked to sexual interests but not to sexual behaviour. Social factors may therefore play a greater role in regulating sexual behaviour in girls than in boys (Browning et al., 2000; O'Donnell et al., 2003).

The physical changes associated with puberty also may serve as a trigger for the onset of sexual activity. For example, the development of secondary sex characteristics such as breasts in girls and muscles and deep voices in boys may make them more sexually attractive. Early-maturing girls are more likely to have older friends, which may draw them into early sexual relationships.

Parental Influences

Teenagers who have close relationships with their parents are less likely to initiate sexual activity at an early age (Meschke et al., 2000). Adolescents who communicate well with their parents also delay the onset of sexual activity (McBride et al., 2003; National Campaign to Prevent Teen Pregnancy, 2003). If these youngsters do have sexual intercourse, they are more likely to use birth control and to have fewer sexual partners (McBride et al., 2003; National Campaign to Prevent Teen Pregnancy, 2003).

The double standard of sexuality in our society—that premarital sexual activity is acceptable for boys but not for girls—seems to influence the way in which parental communication affects sexual behaviours in teenagers. The message for daughters appears to be "Don't do it," whereas the message for sons is "It's okay to do it as long as you take precautions."

Peer Influences

Peers also play an important role in determining the sexual behaviour of adolescents. One of the most powerful predictors of sexual activity for both female and male adolescents is the sexual activity of their best friends (Meschke et al., 2000; O'Donnell et al., 2003).

When teenagers are asked why they do not wait to have sexual intercourse until they are older, the main reason reported is usually peer pressure (O'Donnell et al., 2003). Peers, especially those of the same sex, also serve as a key source of sex education for adolescents. Adolescents report that they are somewhat more likely to receive information about sex from friends and media sources—TV shows, films, magazines, and the Internet—than from sex education classes or their parents (Kaiser Family Foundation et al., 2003).

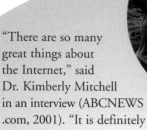

A Closer Look

"There are so many great things about the Internet," said Dr. Kimberly Mitchell in an interview (ABCNEWS.com, 2001). "It is definitely something that parents should encourage children to use, but we also think that parents should be aware of what is going on." What was "going on" was online sexual solicitation. This means that children were being approached sexually by strangers online.

Sixty percent of Canadian students use the Internet according to Cyberbullying.ca (http://www.cyberbullying.ca), a Canadian-created resource site. A preliminary study published in the Journal of the American Medical Association (Mitchell et al., 2001) found that nearly one in five (19 percent) youths who regularly used the Internet reported receiving some kind of sexual query or invitation from a stranger. According to this study, "some of the unwanted behaviour included simple requests like 'What do you look like?' to 'What is your bra size?'" The telephone survey of 1501 randomly selected youth, aged ten through seventeen, also found that 25 percent of the youth who were solicited were highly upset by the experience.

Certain background information and behaviour tended to put some children at greater risk of being solicited than others. The risk of being solicited was greater for girls than for boys and for older teens than for preteens. The risk was higher for youth who had experienced a death in the family, had moved to a new home, or whose parents were separated or divorced or recently unemployed. The risk was also higher for youth who participated in chat rooms, posted personal information, made rude or nasty comments, chatted about sex with strangers, or visited adult websites.

Mitchell further reported that only about one-third of the youths' parents used any kind of filtering device to protect their children from unwanted solicitations—or to prevent them from visiting sex-oriented websites. Mitchell suggests that many parents do not use such devices because of "the ambiguity in them"—that is, their purposes and methodology are unclear to many parents.

What to Do

Parents can do several things to protect their children from online solicitation:

- Warn children not to give out personal information, such as telephone numbers, addresses, or names, online.

- Warn children not to give out their location, such as the name of their school, their favourite haunts, and so on.

- Set the home computer in an open area such as the living room or kitchen, rather than hiding it away in a bedroom or basement area.

- Report solicitations and questionable behaviour to the police or to the Internet service provider.

© Royalty-Free/CORBIS

Online Solicitation
Nearly one in five adolescents who use the Internet has received a sexual query or invitation from a stranger. Time to heed the parental warning about not talking to strangers—even online.

Teenage Pregnancy

The title of this section is "loaded." It suggests that there is a problem with teenage pregnancy. So let's toss in a couple of caveats at the beginning. First, throughout most of history, even most of the (short) history of Canada, girls often became pregnant in their teens. Second, throughout most cultures in the world today, girls are becoming pregnant in their teens (Save the Children, 2004b). Why, then, do we bother with a section on this topic? The answer is that in Canada today, most adolescents who become pregnant are unmarried. Moreover, most teenage pregnancies are unwanted. Most adolescents in Canada and many other developed nations choose to defer pregnancy until after they have completed part or all of their education. Some people defer pregnancy until they are well into their careers—in their late twenties, their thirties, even their forties. So it is in our place and time that we have a topic called "Teenage Pregnancy," implying that there is a problem with it.

Question: In this cultural setting, why do teenage girls become pregnant? There are many, many reasons. For one thing, adolescent girls typically get little advice in school or at home about how to deal with boys' sexual advances. Another reason is failure to use contraception. Some initiate sex at very early ages, when they are least likely to use contraception (Felton & Bartoces, 2002; O'Donnell et al., 2003). Most adolescent girls do not have access to contraceptive devices. Among those who do, fewer than half use them reliably (Centers for Disease Control and Prevention, 2000b; Dailard, 2001).

Some teenage girls purposefully get pregnant to try to force their partners to make a commitment to them. Some are rebelling against their parents or the moral standards of their communities. But most girls are impregnated because they and their partners do not know as much about reproduction and contraception as they think they do or because they miscalculate the odds of getting pregnant. Even those who have been to all the sex education classes and who have access to family planning clinics slip up now and then, especially if their partners push them or do not want to use condoms. Figure 16.2 shows that the percentage of sexually active high school students who use condoms reliably has been increasing since the early 1990s, but even so, we seem to be levelling off at an unacceptable 50 percent for girls and 65 percent for boys.

Truth or Fiction Revisited: Canada's teen pregnancy rate is lower than the U.S. and New Zealand rate, but in comparison to other industrialized nations is relatively high (Canadian Institute of Child Health, 2000). Over 47 000 Canadian adolescents (between the ages of fifteen and nineteen) become pregnant each year (CICH, 2000). The rate of teenage pregnancy between 1984 and 1994 actually increased in Canada (see Figure 16.3), a trend that is opposite in other industrialized nations. The rate in young First Nations adolescent girls is especially high, at 38 times the national average (CICH, 2000). In countries where there has been a decrease in teenage pregnancies, some speculation has been that the drop-off may reflect findings that sexual activity among teenagers has levelled off and that relatively more adolescents are using contraception consistently (see Figure 16.2). Researchers at the Centers for Disease Control and Prevention attribute the drop-off in careless sex to educational efforts by schools, the media, religious institutions, and communities ("Less sex," 2004).

Nearly half of pregnant teenagers will get an abortion. Most others will become single mothers. Pregnancy rates are higher among adolescents of lower socioeconomic status and among those from ethnic minority groups ("Less sex," 2004).

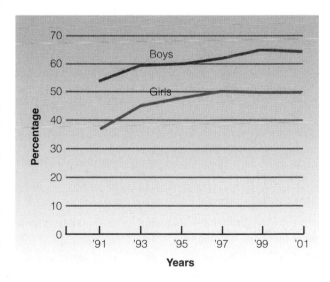

Figure 16.2

Percentage of Sexually Active Students in Grades 9–12 Who Report Using a Condom the Last Time They Had Sexual Intercourse

Sources: Centers for Disease Control and Prevention, the Alan Guttmacher Institute, and the Child Trends Databank, as reported in the *New York Times*, March 7, 2004. Reprinted by permission of the New York Times Co.

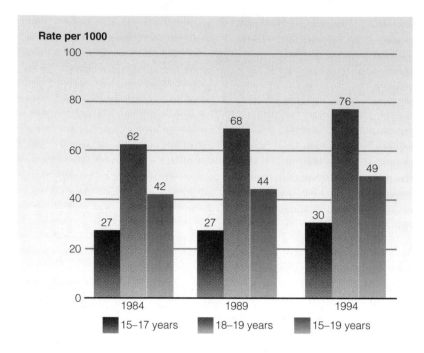

Figure 16.3a

Trends in Pregnancy and Birthrates among Women, Aged 15-19, in Canada

Source: Wadhera, S. et al (Statistics Canada) 1997 Teenage Pregnancies *Health Reports* Vol 9 No 3.

Consequences of Teenage Pregnancy

Question: What are the consequences of teenage pregnancy? Again, some caveats: The outcome of teenage pregnancies for young women who want their babies and have the resources to nurture them are generally good (Rathus et al., 2005). Females tend to be healthy in late adolescence, and again—historically speaking—people might wonder why we raise this issue at all.

We raise it because the medical, social, and economic costs of *unplanned* or *unwanted* pregnancies among adolescents are enormous both to the mothers and to the children. The problems begin with the pregnancy itself. Adolescent mothers are more likely to experience medical complications during the months of pregnancy and their labour is likely to be prolonged. The babies are at greater risk of being premature and of low birth weight. These medical problems are not necessarily due to the age of the mother but rather to the fact that teenage mothers—especially those who dwell at the lower end of the socioeconomic spectrum—are less likely to have access to prenatal care or to obtain adequate nutrition (Fraser et al., 1995).

The education of the teenage mother also suffers. She is less likely than her peers to graduate from high school or move on to college (Centers for Disease Control and Prevention, 2000b). Her deficit in education means that she earns less and is in greater need of public assistance. Few teenage mothers obtain reliable assistance—financial or emotional—from the babies' fathers. The fathers typically cannot support themselves, much less a family. Their marriages—if they are married—are more likely to be unstable, and they often have more children than they intended (Bunting & McAuley, 2004).

Figure 16.3

Live Births to Teenage Mothers, Ages 15–19 Years, Selected Countries, 1995*

*Based on Progress of Nations Report, 1998, as cited by Laboratory Centre for Disease Control, Health Canada.

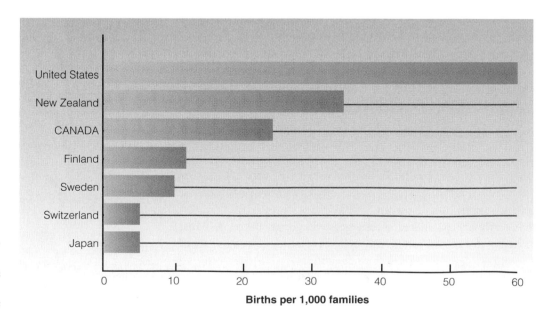

A Closer Look | *Parents and Youth: Agreeing about Sexual Health*

Although clashes over sex education often focus on parents who fear schools have been too permissive in teaching about sexuality, a recent survey suggests that the overwhelming majority of parents want schools to provide more, not less, sex education once children reach their teenage years. And they want discussions to cover a wide array of topics: abstinence, avoiding pregnancy, sexually transmitted infections, abortion, even sexual orientation.

Canadian survey research (e.g., McKay, Pietrusiak, & Holowaty, 1998; Weaver, Byers, Sears, Cohen, & Randall, 2002) reveals that both parents and youth want sexual health education taught in the schools. Most believe that community and family should share the responsibility for sexual health education (McKay, 2004). Talk to Me Sexuality Education for Parents (http://www.phac-aspc.gc.ca /publicat/ttm-pm/attitudes_e.html), a Public Health Agency of Canada-sponsored website, offers parents information about how to talk openly with their adolescents about sexual health. http://www.sexualityandu.ca is another current Canadian resource for parents, youth, and teachers. While good resources are available, it should be noted that open communication and discussion of health (i.e., physical, sexual, emotional, etc.) needs to be ongoing with children throughout their development, not just in adolescence.

Other Websites and Resources

Canadian Guidelines for Sexual Health Education: http://www.phac-aspc.gc.ca/publicat/cgshe-ldnemss/ cgshe_toc.htm

Beyond the basics: A sourcebook on sexual and reproductive health education: http://www.cfsh.ca/ppfc/media/ sourcebook2006contentwithform.pdf

Division of Sexual Health Promotion and STD Prevention and Control: http://www.phac-aspc.gc.ca/std-mts

"Health info for every body" (funded by and in partnership with Health Canada): http://www.canadian-health-network.ca

Common questions about sexual health education: http://sieccan.org/health_questions.html

What Parents Want in Sex Education Courses
Parents overwhelmingly favour sex education. Nearly all want these courses to educate about sexually transmitted infections, reproduction, STIs, AIDS, birth control, abstinence, sexual orientation, and sexual abuse.

Guided searches and FAQs on numerous subjects including sexual orientation, STIs, and planned parenthood (funded by and in partnership with Health Canada): http://www.canadian-health-network.ca/ 1sexuality_reproductive_health.html

Talk to Me Sexuality Education for Parents: http://www.phac-aspc.gc.ca/publicat/ttm-pm/sti_e.html

Planned Parenthood Federation of Canada (information on reproductive health and an e-mail newsletter): http://www.ppfc.ca

Guides for parents on teen sexuality: http://www.plannedparenthood.org/parents

Planned Parenthood: http://www.plannedparenthood.org

Sexuality education gateway for educators that includes online activities, lesson plans, and teaching advice: http://www.safehealthyschools.org/sexualityeducation/ gateway.htm

Although the most attention has been directed toward teenage mothers, young fathers bear an equal responsibility for teenage pregnancies. The consequences of parenthood for adolescent fathers are similar to those for adolescent mothers. Teenage fathers tend to have lower grades in school than their peers, and they enter the work force at an earlier age (Neville & Parke, 1991).

Children born to teenage mothers also are at a disadvantage. As early as the preschool years, they show lower levels of cognitive functioning and more behavioural and emotional problems. Boys appear to be more affected than girls. By adolescence, offspring of teenage mothers are doing more poorly in school, and they are more likely to become teenage parents themselves (Coley & Chase-Lansdale, 1998). Again, these problems seem to result not from the mother's age but from the socially and economically deprived environments in which teen mothers and their children often live.

Support for Pregnant Teenagers

A number of programs have been designed to promote positive social, economic, health, and developmental outcomes for pregnant teenagers and their children (Paikoff & Brooks-Gunn, 1991). These programs usually include prenatal care. Teen mothers who receive prenatal care are more likely to have healthy babies (Save the Children, 2004b).

Supportive services for teenage parents include family planning services, child-care services, and education about parenting skills, work skills, and life options. Some programs have achieved moderate success in improving the lives of adolescent parents. Teenagers who participate in such programs have fewer children in the long run. They are less likely to drop out of high school and more likely to become economically self-sufficient. Their babies are also healthier (Coley & Chase-Lansdale, 1998).

Research also shows that teenage mothers fare better when they have the support of their families and of the father of the child (Bunting & McAuley, 2004). Although teenage fathers usually have quite limited resources, mother and child appear to have greater psychological well-being when the father remains in their lives.

Preventing Teenage Pregnancy

The past several decades have seen a dramatic increase in programs to help prevent teenage pregnancies. Prevention efforts include educating teenagers about sexuality and contraception and providing contraceptive and family planning services (Santelli et al., 2003). An overwhelming majority of Canadian parents want their children to have sex education in the public schools (see the nearby "A Closer Look" feature).

How successful are sex education programs? The better programs increase students' knowledge about sexuality. Despite fears that sex education will increase sexual activity in teenagers, some programs seem to delay the onset of sexual activity (Santelli et al., 2003). Among teenagers who already are sexually active, sex education is associated with the increased use of effective contraception.

School-based clinics that distribute contraceptives and contraceptive information to students have been established in some school districts in the United States—but not without controversy. In high schools that have such clinics, birthrates often drop significantly (Blake et al., 2003). For more information about Canadian resources, the Canadian Federation of Sexual Health (http://www.cfsh.ca) lists local support groups by province.

Active Review

9. _____ is the most common sexual outlet in adolescents.

10. A(n) _____ orientation is defined as being attracted to and interested in forming romantic relationships with people of one's own sex.

11. It is believed that prenatal exposure to sex _____ may play a key role in sexual orientation.

12. Teenagers who have close relationships with their parents are (more or less?) likely to initiate sexual activity at an early age.

13. The top reason usually given by adolescents for why they did not wait to have sexual intercourse is _____ pressure.

Reflect & Relate: How important a part of your adolescence (or that of your peers) was sexuality? Did any of your peers experience problems related to their sexuality during adolescence? Did they resolve these problems? If so, how?

Go to
W W W www.voyages1ce.nelson.com
for an interactive version of this review.

Juvenile Delinquency

Did you ever commit a delinquent act in your teen years? If you said yes, then you are like most adolescents. In one large-scale study, for example, four out of five eleven- to seventeen-year-olds reported that they had at some time engaged in a delinquent behaviour (Dryfoos, 1990). ***Truth or Fiction Revisited:*** Therefore, it is not true that only a minority of adolescents engage in delinquent behaviour.

Question: What is juvenile delinquency? The term **juvenile delinquency** covers a broad range of illegal activities committed by a child or adolescent. At the most extreme end, it includes serious behaviours such as homicide, rape, and robbery, which are considered criminal acts regardless of the age of the offender. Other less serious offences, such as truancy, underage drinking, running away from home, and sexual promiscuity, are considered illegal only when performed by minors. Hence, these are termed **status offences** (Siegel, 2004). Youth crime rates in Canada decreased throughout the 1990s, and then generally increased from 1999 to 2003, and finally declined again in 2005 (Gannon, 2005). Something interesting to note is that since the introduction of the Youth Criminal Justice Act (YCJA) in 2003, the proportion of youth that are formally charged by police has dropped considerably (from 56 percent in 2002 to 43 percent in 2005) (Gannon, 2005).

juvenile delinquency
Conduct of a child or adolescent characterized by illegal activities.

status offences   Offences considered illegal only when performed by minors, such as truancy and underage drinking.

© Tom & Dee Ann McCarthy / CORBIS

Adolescent Delinquency
Although most adolescents reported they had engaged in some sort of delinquent behaviour, female adolescents are more likely to commit "status offences," whereas male adolescents are more likely to commit crimes of violence.

Antisocial and criminal behaviours show a dramatic increase in many societies during adolescence and then taper off during adulthood.

Many delinquent acts do not result in arrest or conviction. And when adolescents are arrested, their cases may be disposed of informally, such as by referral to a mental health agency, without the juvenile's being formally declared delinquent in a juvenile court (Siegel, 2004). One thing is clear: Before the age of forty, the mortality rate for delinquents is twice that for other people (Laub & Vaillant, 2000). The "excess" deaths are generally a result of accidents, violence, and substance abuse.

Economic factors may help to explain higher delinquency rates among youth. Low family income, poor housing, and other socioeconomic deprivations increase the risk of delinquency for all adolescents (Campbell et al., 2001; Siegel, 2004; Vermeiren et al., 2004).

Sex Differences in Juvenile Delinquency

Question: What are the sex differences in delinquent behaviour? Boys are much more likely than girls to engage in most delinquent behaviours. About four boys are arrested for every girl, but the sex difference is as much as eight to one for serious crimes (Siegel, 2004). Boys are more apt to commit crimes of violence, whereas girls are more likely to commit status offences such as truancy or running away (Siegel, 2004). Some social scientists believe that the sex difference in the commission of violent crimes reflects the pressure of evolutionary forces. This view holds that females have inherited a "lower threshold for fear" because they are the ones who become mothers, and maternal survival is necessary for reproductive success (Campbell et al., 2001).

Even though the delinquent behaviour of female adolescents is less frequent and less severe than that of males, girls are more likely than boys to be arrested for being runaways. One obvious explanation for this fact is that girls may actually be more likely than boys to run away from home. Another possibility is that the juvenile justice system has a double standard in this area, viewing females' running away as a more serious problem than males' running away and thus treating female offenders more harshly (Siegel, 2004).

Who Are the Delinquents? What Are They Like?

Question: Who is most likely to engage in delinquent behaviour? Many risk factors are associated with juvenile delinquency. No one variable stands out as being most critical. Most likely, a combination of several factors increases the odds of a child showing delinquent behaviour (Lynam et al., 2000; Vander Ven et al., 2001). The direction and timing of these factors is not always clear-cut. For example, poor school performance is related to delinquency (Vermeiren et al., 2004). But does school failure lead to delinquency, or is delinquency the cause of the school failure?

Even if the causal paths are less than clear, a number of factors are associated with delinquency. Children who show aggressive, antisocial, and hyperactive behaviour at an early age are more likely to show delinquent behaviour in adolescence (Loeber et al., 1999). Delinquency also is associated with having a lower verbal IQ, immature moral reasoning, low self-esteem, feelings of alienation, and impulsivity (Lynam et al., 2000). Other personal factors include poor school performance, little interest in school or religion, early substance abuse, early sexuality, and delinquent friends (Ge et al., 2001c; Junger et al., 2001; Laub & Vaillant, 2000). On a cognitive level, aggressive delinquents tend to approve of violence as a way of dealing with social provocations and to misinterpret other people's intentions as hostile when they are not (Shahinfar et al., 2001).

Family factors are also powerful predictors of delinquent behaviour. The families of juvenile delinquents are often characterized by lax and ineffective discipline, low levels of affection, and high levels of family conflict, physical abuse, severe parental punishment, and neglect (Siegel, 2004; Vermeiren et al., 2004). The parents and siblings of juvenile delinquents have frequently engaged in antisocial, deviant, or criminal behaviour themselves (Mednick et al., 1990; Rowe et al., 1992). One American study found that more than half of all juvenile delinquents imprisoned in state institutions had immediate family members who had also been incarcerated (Butterfield, 1992). This finding has sparked a lively debate about the possible role of genetic factors in criminal behaviour. One point of view is that, although most factors that increase the risk of delinquency are environmental, some children may be genetically more vulnerable than others. For example, hyperactivity, one of the risk factors for delinquency, may have a genetic basis (Zigler et al., 1992).

Prevention and Treatment of Juvenile Delinquency

Many approaches have been tried to prevent delinquent behaviour or to deal with it early (Clark, 2001; Siegel, 2004). *Question: What are some of these approaches, and how effective are they?*

One type of approach focuses on the individual adolescent offender. Such programs may provide training in moral reasoning, social skills, problem-solving skills, or a combination of these. In some cases, these programs have the positive effect of reducing subsequent antisocial or delinquent behaviour during short-term follow-ups of six months to a year. But long-term outcomes are not as promising (Guerra & Slaby, 1990). A problem with such approaches is that they focus on individual offenders rather than on the larger social systems in which juvenile delinquents are embedded.

Another approach tries to deal with various social systems, such as the family, peer groups, school, or community (Chamberlain & Reid, 1998; Perkins-Dock, 2001). Examples of such interventions are family therapy approaches; school-based strategies involving teams of students, parents, teachers, and staff; and various community- and neighbourhood-based programs. These broader multisystem approaches appear to be more successful in reducing problem behaviours and improving family relations of delinquent adolescents (American Psychological Association, 1993; Siegel, 2004).

One other promising approach starts with the very young child and is aimed at promoting a host of positive child outcomes, not just delinquency prevention. This approach consists of the early childhood intervention programs, such as Head Start. The preschoolers who participated in several of these programs have been tracked longitudinally through adolescence. These follow-ups show several encouraging outcomes, including reductions in aggressive and delinquent behaviour (Dryfoos, 1990; Zigler et al., 1992).

Active Review

14. Offences that are illegal only when performed by minors are called _____ offences.

15. Boys are (more or less?) likely than girls to engage in most delinquent behaviours.

16. Children who show aggressive, antisocial, and hyperactive behaviour at an early age are (more or less?) likely to show delinquent behaviour in adolescence.

Reflect & Relate: Were there any juvenile delinquents in your high school? What behaviour patterns led to the label? What happened to them? Do you know what they are doing now?

Go to
W W W **www.voyages1ce.nelson.com**
for an interactive version of this review.

Suicide: When the Adolescent Has Everything to Lose

Adolescence is such an exciting time of life. For many, the future is filled with promise. Many count the days until they graduate high school, until they enter college. Many enjoy thrilling fantasies of what might be.

And then there are those who take their own lives. *Questions: How many adolescents commit suicide? Why do they do so?* Since 1960, the suicide rate has more than tripled for young people, aged five to nineteen. In Canada, about ten in 100 000 adolescents between the ages of fifteen and nineteen commit suicide each year.

Truth or Fiction Revisited: Suicide is the third leading cause of death among adolescents (National Center for Injury Prevention and Control, 2004b). What prompts young people to take their own lives? Who is most at risk?

Risk Factors in Suicide

Most suicides among adolescents and adults are linked to feelings of depression and hopelessness (Sampaio et al., 2000). Jill Rathus and her colleagues (Miller at al., 2000; Velting et al., 2000) have found that suicidal adolescents experience four areas of psychological problems: (1) confusion about the self, (2) impulsiveness, (3) emotional instability, and (4) interpersonal problems. Some suicidal teenagers are high-achieving, rigid perfectionists who have set impossibly high expectations for themselves (Miller et al., 2000; Wu et al., 2001). Many teenagers throw themselves into feelings of depression and hopelessness by comparing themselves negatively with others, even when the comparisons are inappropriate (Barber, 2001). ("Yes, maybe it's not astrophysics, but you did get accepted into medicine, and it's a great program.")

Adolescent suicide attempts are more common after stressful life events, especially events that entail loss of social support, as in the death of a parent or friend, breaking up with a boyfriend or girlfriend, or a family member leaving home (Cooper et al., 2002). Other contributors to suicidal behaviour include concerns over sexuality, pressures to achieve in school, problems at home, and substance abuse (Miller et al., 2000; Wu et al., 2001). It is not always a stressful event itself that precipitates suicide but the adolescent's anxiety or fear of being "found out" for something, such as failing a course or getting arrested (Cooper et al., 2002). Adolescents who consider suicide are apparently less capable of solving problems, especially their social problems, than other adolescents (Miller et al., 2000). Young people contemplating suicide are thus less likely to find productive ways of changing the stressful situation.

Most young people who commit suicide send out signals about their intentions (National Center for Injury Prevention and Control, 2004b). Sad to say, these signals are often overlooked, sometimes because parents and other people do not recognize them (MacDonald, 1999; Wu et al., 2001). Sometimes adolescents do not receive help until after they've attempted suicide, and sometimes not even then (Gili-Planas et al., 2001; Wu et al., 2001). Here are some clues that a teenager may be at risk (Hendin et al., 2001; Maine et al., 2001):

- changes in eating and sleeping patterns;

- difficulty concentrating on schoolwork;

- a sharp decline in school performance and attendance;

- loss of interest in previously enjoyed activities;

- giving away prized possessions;

- complaints about physical problems when no medical basis can be found;

- withdrawal from social relationships;

- personality or mood changes;

- talking or writing about death or dying;

- abuse of drugs or alcohol;

- an attempted suicide;

- availability of a handgun;

- a precipitating event such as an argument with parents, a broken romantic relationship, academic difficulties, loss of a friend, or trouble with the law;

- knowing or hearing about another teenager who has committed suicide (which can lead to so-called cluster suicides); and

- threatening to commit suicide.

Here are some things you can do if you notice one or more of these warning signs (Omer & Elitzur, 2001; Shneidman, 1998):

- Make an appointment for the adolescent with a helping professional, or suggest that the adolescent go *with* you to obtain professional help *now.*

Adolescents May Have "So Much to Live for," But ...
Suicide is a key cause of death for adolescents. When adolescents experience conflicts and dips in self-esteem, when they have failed at something, when they fear they will be found out for something, their thoughts may turn to suicide. How can you determine whether an adolescent is considering suicide? What can you do about it?

- Draw the adolescent out. Ask questions such as "What's going on?" "Where do you hurt?" "What would you like to see happen?" (Shneidman, 1998). Questions such as these may encourage those at risk to express frustrated needs and thus provide some relief.

- Be empathetic. Show that you understand how upset the adolescent is.

- Suggest that actions other than suicide might solve the problem, even if they are not evident at the time.

- Ask how the adolescent intends to commit suicide. Adolescents with concrete plans and a weapon at hand are at greater risk. Ask if you might hold on to the weapon for a while. Sometimes the adolescent says yes.

- Extract a promise that the adolescent will not commit suicide before seeing you again. Arrange a concrete time and place to meet. Get professional help as soon as you are apart.

Suicide tends to run in families (National Center for Injury Prevention and Control, 2004b). Many suicide attempters have family members with serious psychological problems, and many have family members who have taken their lives. How do we account for the correlation? Do genetic factors play a role, possibly leading to psychological disorders, such as depression, that are connected with suicide? Could it be that a socially impoverished family environment infuses several family members with feelings of hopelessness? Or does the suicide of one family member simply give others the idea that suicide is the way in which one manages problems? Perhaps these possibilities and others—such as poor problem-solving ability—form a complex web of contributing factors.

Ethnicity, Sex, and Suicide

Rates of suicide and suicide attempts vary among different ethnic groups. Aboriginal youth have the highest suicide rate in Canada. Suicide occurs five to six times more often among First Nations groups than non-Aboriginal youth. (Health Canada, 2005c).

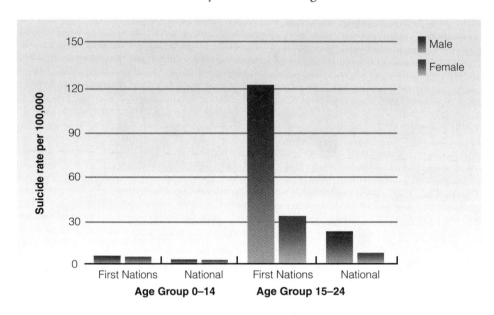

Chandler and Lalonde conducted a longitudinal study between 1987 and 1992 of suicide rates among First Nations youth in B.C., and concluded that suicide rates vary considerably among First Nation communities. They also found that suicide rates were tied to a community's control over self-government, land claims, education, health services, cultural facilities, and police and fire services.

Figure 16.4

Suicide Death Rates by Age Group, First Nations and Canadian Populations, 1989–1993

About three times as many adolescent females as males attempt suicide, but about four times as many males succeed (National Center for Injury Prevention and Control, 2004b). In part, males are more likely to "succeed" in their suicide attempts because of the methods they choose (Lubell et al., 2004; Skogman et al., 2004). The methods preferred by males are more deadly and more rapid: Most males shoot themselves; females more often use drugs, such as overdoses of tranquillizers or sleeping pills (Joseph et al., 2003). Females often do not take enough of these chemicals. It also takes a while for them to work, enabling others to find them and intervene.

Although the risk factors for suicide are similar for males and females, the relative importance of these factors differs. The likelihood of a teenage girl committing suicide is greatest if she suffers from depression (Joseph et al., 2003). But the best predictor of suicide for teenage boys is a prior suicide attempt (National Center for Injury Prevention and Control, 2004b). The nearby "A Closer Look" feature describes some of the warning signs of suicide and some things you can do if you notice them in a friend or family member.

Active Review

17. Suicide is a (rare or common?) cause of death among older teenagers.

18. Most suicides among adolescents and adults are linked to feelings of _____.

19. Suicide (does or does not?) tend to run in families.

Reflect & Relate: Do you know anyone who has committed suicide or thought about committing suicide? What pressures or disappointments was the person experiencing at the time? Did anybody intervene? How?

 Go to
www.voyages1ce.nelson.com
for an interactive version of this review.

Epilogue: Emerging Adulthood—Bridging Adolescence and the Life Beyond

When our mothers were our age, they were engaged. They at least had some idea what they were going to do with their lives. I, on the other hand, will have a dual degree in majors that are ambiguous at best and impractical at worst (English and political science), no ring on my finger, and no idea who I am, much less what I want to do. Under duress, I will admit that this is a pretty exciting time. Sometimes, when I look out across the wide expanse that is my future, I can see beyond the void. I realize that having nothing ahead to count on means I now have to count on myself; that having no direction means forging one of my own. —Kristen, age 22

—Page (1999, pp. 18, 20)

Well, Kristen has some work to do: She needs to forge her own direction. Just think: What if Kristen had been born into the caste system of old England or India, into a traditional Islamic society, or into Canada or the United States of the 1950s, where the TV sitcom *Father Knows Best* was perennially in the top ten? Kristen would have had a sense of direction—that's certain. But, of course, it would have been the sense of direction society or tradition created for her, not her own.

But Kristen was not born into any of these societies. She was born into the open and challenging Canada of the current generation. She has the freedom to become whatever the interaction of her genetic heritage and her educational and social opportunities will enable her to become—and the opportunities are many. With freedom comes the need to make choices. When we need to make choices, we profit from information. Kristen is in the process of accumulating information about herself and about the world outside. According to psychologist Jeffrey Arnett (2000), she is in *emerging adulthood.* In earlier days, adolescents made a transition, for better or worse, directly into adulthood. Now many of them—especially those in affluent nations with abundant opportunities—spend time in what some theorists think of as a new period of development.

Question: How do we define adulthood? There's a question. Legally, adulthood has many ages, depending on what you want to do. In the U.S., the age of consent to marry varies from state to state, but in general, marriage is permitted in the teens. The age for drinking legally is eighteen or nineteen depending on which province you call home. The age for obtaining a driver's learning permit varies between fourteen and sixteen. By and large, however, adulthood is usually defined in terms of what people do rather than how old they are. *Truth or Fiction Revisited:* Adolescents do not necessarily reach adulthood at age twenty-one. Over the years, people who write about human development have considered marriage a key criterion of attaining adulthood (Schlegel, 1998). Other criteria in use today include holding a full-time job and living independently (not with one's parents). Today, the transition to adulthood is mainly marked by adjustment issues, such as deciding on one's values and beliefs, accepting self-responsibility, becoming financially independent, and establishing an equal relationship with one's parents (Arnett, 2001; Jensen et al., 2004). Marriage is no longer necessarily a crucial marker for entering adulthood (Arnett, 1998).

Adulthood itself has been divided into stages, and the first of these, young adulthood, has been largely seen as the period of life when people focus on establishing their careers or pathways in life. It has been acknowledged that the transition to adulthood could be slow or piecemeal, with many individuals in their late teens and early twenties remaining dependent on their parents and reluctant or unable to make enduring commitments, in terms of either identity formation or the development of intimate relationships. The question is whether we can speak of the existence of another stage of development, one that bridges adolescence and young adulthood. A number of developmental theorists, including Arnett (2000), argue that we can. *Question: What is "emerging adulthood"?*

Emerging adulthood is theorized to be a distinct period of development that straddles the ages of eighteen through twenty-five; it is found in societies that allow young people an extended opportunity to explore their roles in life. These tend to be affluent societies, such as those found in developed nations, our own among them. Parents in Canada are often affluent enough to continue to support their children throughout university studies and in graduate school. When parents cannot do the job, the government often steps in to help, for example, through student loans. These supports allow young people the luxury of sorting out identity issues and creating meaningful life plans—even if some still do not know where they are going after they graduate from college. Should they know who they are and what they are doing by the age of twenty-one or twenty-two? Are they spoiled? These are value judgments that may or may not be on the mark. But let us note that many adults change their careers several times, partly because they did not sort out who they were and where they were going at an early age. On the other hand, even in Canada, many people cannot obtain the supports necessary for sojourning in emerging adulthood.

Erik Erikson (1968) did not use the term *emerging adulthood,* but he did recognize that developed nations tend to elongate the period of adolescence. Erikson used the term *moratorium* to describe the extended quest for identity among people who dwell in adolescence. Erikson and other theorists also believed that it was more meaningful for the individual to take the voyage to identity rather than foreclose it by adopting the viewpoints of other people. Although there are pluses to taking time to formulate one's identity, there are downsides. For example, remaining dependent on parents can compromise an individual's self-esteem. Taking out loans for graduate school means that there is more to pay back; many individuals mortgage their own lives as they invest in their futures. Women who focus on their educations and their careers may marry later and bear children later. Although many people appreciate children more when they bear them later in life, they also become less fertile as the years wend their ways, and they may find themselves in a race with their "biological clocks."

© Tom Stewart / CORBIS

"Emerging Adulthood": A New Stage of Human Development?

Some researchers suggest that affluent societies like ours have spawned a new stage of development, emerging adulthood, which involves an extended period of self-exploration, during which one remains financially dependent.

Young people in Canada seem to be generally aware of the issues involved in defining the transition from adolescence to adulthood. Arnett (2000) reported what individuals in their late teens and early twenties say when they are asked whether they think they have become adults. About three in five say something like, "In some respects yes and in other respects no." Many think that they have developed beyond the conflicts and exploratory voyages of adolescence, but they may have not yet obtained the ability to assume the financial and interpersonal responsibilities they associate with adulthood.

And then, of course, there are those who remain adolescents forever.

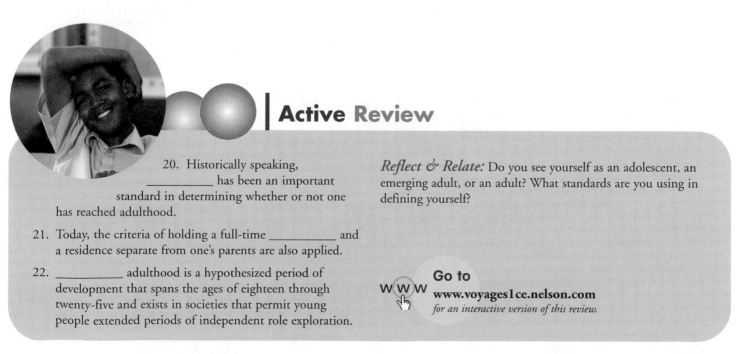

Active Review

20. Historically speaking, _____ has been an important standard in determining whether or not one has reached adulthood.

21. Today, the criteria of holding a full-time _____ and a residence separate from one's parents are also applied.

22. _____ adulthood is a hypothesized period of development that spans the ages of eighteen through twenty-five and exists in societies that permit young people extended periods of independent role exploration.

Reflect & Relate: Do you see yourself as an adolescent, an emerging adult, or an adult? What standards are you using in defining yourself?

W W W **Go to**
www.voyages1ce.nelson.com
for an interactive version of this review.

Recite: *An Active Summary*™

1. What does Erikson have to say about the development of identity during adolescence?

Erikson's adolescent stage of psychosocial development is identity versus role diffusion. The primary task of this stage is for adolescents to develop a sense of who they are and what they stand for.

2. What are Marcia's "identity statuses"?

The identity statuses represent the four combinations of the dimensions of exploration and commitment: identity diffusion, foreclosure, moratorium, and identity achievement.

3. What are the connections between ethnicity and other sociocultural factors—such as sex— and identity?

Development of identity is more complicated for adolescents who belong to ethnic minority groups. Youth from minority groups are faced with two sets of cultural values and may need to reconcile and incorporate elements of both.

4. Are there stages in developing an ethnic identity—that is, a sense of belonging to an ethnic group?

Researchers propose a three-stage model of the development of ethnic identity: unexamined ethnic identity, an ethnic identity search, and an achieved ethnic identity. As minority youth move through adolescence, they are increasingly likely to explore and achieve ethnic identity.

5. Does the development of ego identity differ in males and females?

Erikson proposed that interpersonal relationships are more important to women's identity than occupational and ideological issues, but current research suggests that adolescent females and males are equally concerned about careers.

6. How does the self-concept develop during adolescence?

Adolescents incorporate psychological traits and social relationships into their self-descriptions.

7. Are there sex differences in self-esteem during adolescence?

As a group, adolescent girls show lower self-esteem than boys. One reason for the sex difference may involve the physical changes of adolescence, which are related to physical appearance—a factor that is relatively more important for girls. Another factor may be sexism—that is, the negative messages that many girls receive in school.

8. What happens to self-esteem during adolescence?

Self-esteem tends to decline as the child progresses from middle childhood into early adolescence, perhaps because of increasing recognition of the disparity between the ideal self and the real self. Then self-esteem gradually improves.

9. How do relationships with one's parents and peers change during the course of the teenage years?

During adolescence, children spend much less time with parents than during childhood. Although adolescents become more independent of their parents, they generally continue to love and respect them. The role of peers increases markedly during the teen years. Adolescents are more likely than younger children to stress intimate self-disclosure and mutual understanding in friendships.

10. What kinds of adolescent peer groups are there?

The two major types of peer groups are cliques and crowds. Adolescent peer groups also include peers of the other sex.

11. When do romantic relationships develop?

Romantic relationships begin to appear during early and middle adolescence. Dating is a source of fun; it enhances prestige; and it provides experience in relationships. Dating is also a preparation for adult courtship.

12. What are some patterns of sexual behaviour in adolescence?

Masturbation is the most common sexual outlet in adolescents. Some adolescents have a homosexual orientation. The process of "coming out" may be a long and painful struggle.

13. What do we know about the origins of gay male and lesbian sexual orientations?

From a learning theory point of view, early reinforcement of sexual behaviour influences sexual orientation. Researchers have found evidence for genetic and hormonal factors in sexual orientation.

14. Why do some teenagers initiate sexual activity at an early age, whereas others wait until later?

Early onset of puberty is connected with earlier sexual activity. Adolescents who have close relationships with parents are less likely to initiate sexual activity early. Peer pressure is a powerful contributor to sexual activity.

15. In this cultural setting, why do teenage girls become pregnant?

Many girls who become pregnant receive little advice about how to resist sexual advances. Most of them do not have access to contraception. Most misunderstand reproduction or miscalculate the odds of conception.

16. What are the consequences of teenage pregnancy?

Teenage mothers are more likely to have medical complications during pregnancy and birth, largely because of inadequate medical care. The babies are more likely to be premature and to have low birth weight. Teenage mothers have a lower standard of living and a greater need for public assistance. Their children have more academic and emotional problems.

17. What is juvenile delinquency?

Juvenile delinquency refers to illegal activities committed by a child or adolescent. Behaviours, such as drinking, that are considered illegal when performed by minors are called status offences.

18. What are the sex differences in delinquent behaviour?

Boys are more likely than girls to engage in most delinquent behaviours. Boys are more apt to commit crimes of violence, whereas girls are more likely to commit status offences.

19. Who is most likely to engage in delinquent behaviour?

Risk factors associated with juvenile delinquency include poor school performance, delinquent friends, early aggressive or hyperactive behaviour, substance abuse, low verbal IQ, low self-esteem, impulsivity, and immature moral reasoning. The parents and siblings of delinquents have frequently engaged in antisocial behaviour themselves.

20. How many adolescents commit suicide? Why do they do so?

Suicide is the third leading cause of death among older teenagers. Most suicides among adolescents and adults are linked to stress, feelings of depression, identity problems, impulsivity, and social problems. Girls are more likely to attempt suicide, whereas boys are more likely to "succeed."

21. How do we define *adulthood?*

Historically, marriage has been an important criterion in defining adulthood. Today, the focus is more on holding a full-time occupation and maintaining a residence separate from parents.

22. What is "emerging adulthood"?

Emerging adulthood is a period of development, spanning the ages of eighteen to twenty-five, in which young people engage in extended role exploration. Emerging adulthood can occur in affluent societies that grant young people the luxury of developing their identities and their life plans.

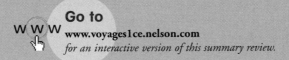

W W W **Go to**
www.voyages1ce.nelson.com
for an interactive version of this summary review.

Key Terms

ego identity *(page 597)*

psychological moratorium *(page 597)*

identity crisis *(page 597)*

exploration *(page 597)*

commitment *(page 597)*

role diffusion *(page 597)*

foreclosure *(page 597)*

moratorium *(page 598)*

identity achievement *(page 599)*

ethnic identity *(page 600)*

unexamined ethnic identity *(page 600)*

ethnic identity search *(page 600)*

achieved ethnic identity *(page 600)*

self-esteem *(page 603)*

clique *(page 607)*

crowd *(page 607)*

masturbation *(page 610)*

homosexual *(page 611)*

juvenile delinquency *(page 619)*

status offences *(page 619)*

Active Learning Resources

Observing Children and Adolescents CD-ROM

Want to watch videos showing what you've just learned about in this chapter? Check out the "Identity Formation," "Peers—Domain Influences," and "Cliques, Crowds, and Conformity" clips in Module 4, Section 3.

Visit Your Companion Website for This Book
http://www.voyages1CE.nelson.com

Check out this companion website, where you will find online resources directly linked to your book. The website includes interactive exercises related to PQ4R and Power Visuals for mastering and reviewing key concepts as well as quizzing, chapter outlines, and much more!

CengageNOW!™
http://hed.nelson.com

Go to this site for the link to CengageNOW™, your one-stop study shop. Take a Pretest for this chapter, and CengageNOW™ will generate a personalized Study Plan based on your test results! The Study Plan will identify the topics you need to review and direct you to online resources to help you master those topics. You can then take a Posttest to help you determine the concepts you have mastered and those you still need to work on.

Answers to Active Reviews

Chapter 1
1. Puberty
2. Development
3. Development
4. Theories
5. Freud
6. Eight
7. Operant
8. Piaget
9. Processing
10. Ecological
11. Sociocultural
12. Nature
13. Discontinuous
14. Hypothesis
15. Naturalistic
16. Case
17. Cause
18. Control
19. Longitudinal
20. Sectional

Chapter 2
1. Chromosomes
2. Deoxyribonucleic
3. Mitosis
4. Meiosis
5. Monozygotic, identical
6. Dizygotic, fraternal
7. Carriers
8. Down syndrome
9. Recessive
10. Sickle-cell
11. Amniocentesis
12. Ultrasound
13. Genotype
14. Phenotype
15. 50
16. Monozygotic, identical
17. Dizygotic, fraternal
18. Conception, fertilization
19. Fallopian
20. Sperm
21. Ovulate

Chapter 3
1. Blastocyst
2. Trophoblast
3. Implantation
4. Amniotic
5. Proximodistal
6. Outer
7. Females
8. Placenta
9. Umbilical cord
10. Maturation
11. Thirteenth
12. Fourth
13. Neural
14. Teratogens
15. Can
16. Blood
17. Rh
18. DES
19. Marijuana
20. Fetal
21. Oxygen
22. Slow

Chapter 4
1. Braxton-Hicks
2. Amniotic
3. Dilated
4. Transition
5. Umbilical
6. Placenta
7. General
8. Epidural, spinal
9. Lamaze
10. Caesarean section, C-section
11. Oxygen
12. Preterm
13. Birth weight
14. Helpful
15. Majority
16. Estrogen
17. Does not
18. Apgar
19. Rooting
20. Nearsighted
21. Do
22. Smaller
23. Sudden infant death syndrome (SIDS)

Chapter 5
1. Head, brain
2. Proximodistal
3. Five
4. Positive
5. Canalization
6. Antibodies
7. Neurons
8. Axon
9. 70
10. Cerebellum
11. One
12. Ulnar
13. Visual
14. Sit up, crawl
15. Increase
16. Experience, practice, nurture
17. Did not
18. Real
19. Edges
20. Cliff
21. 2 to 3
22. Greater
23. Capture
24. Nurture

Chapter 6
1. Schemata
2. Assimilate
3. Sensorimotor
4. Circular
5. Secondary
6. Tertiary
7. Permanence
8. Information
9. Memory
10. Deferred
11. Mental and Motor
12. Neurological
13. Visual
14. Babbling
15. Referential
16. Overextension
17. Holophrases
18. The same
19. Learning
20. Psycholinguistic
21. Acquisition
22. Left
23. Wernicke's

Chapter 7
1. Attachment
2. Strange situation
3. Insecure
4. Explore
5. Indiscriminate
6. Behavioural, behaviourist, learning
7. Contact
8. Fixed
9. Avoided
10. Withdrawal
11. Neglect
12. Excitement
13. Majority
14. Referencing
15. Regulation
16. Self-concept
17. Temperament
18. Slow
19. 12–18 months
20. Majority
21. Higher
22. More

Chapter 8
1. 2 to 3
2. 4 to 6
3. Brain
4. Myelination
5. Cerebellum
6. Right
7. Right
8. Plasticity
9. Girls
10. Boys
11. Decrease
12. Boys
13. Higher
14. Decreases
15. Unintentional injuries, accidents
16. 10 000
17. 10
18. Sleep terrors
19. Sleepwalking
20. Does
21. Boys
22. Constipation

Chapter 9
1. Symbolic, pretend
2. Operations
3. Egocentric
4. Animistic
5. Transductive
6. Conservation
7. One
8. Mapping
9. Whole
10. One
11. Contrast
12. Inner
13. False
14. Senses
15. Recognition
16. Autobiographical, episodic
17. Better
18. Positively
19. Rehearsal, rote rehearsal, rote learning
20. Scaffolding
21. Responsive
22. Home environment
23. Can
24. Less
25. 14.4 hours

Chapter 10
1. Restrictiveness– permissiveness
2. Inductive
3. Authoritative
4. Authoritarian
5. First
6. Solitary
7. Associative
8. Same
9. Altruism
10. Reject
11. Testosterone
12. Social cognitive, social learning
13. Disinhibit
14. Categorical
15. Esteem
16. Securely
17. Initiative
18. Safety
19. Girls
20. Roles, role stereotypes
21. Sex

22. Males
23. Fathers
24. Constancy
25. Schema

Chapter 11
1. Steady
2. 2
3. 5 to 7
4. Boys
5. 11
6. 25
7. Do not
8. Does
9. Steady
10. 8 to 10
11. Decreases
12. Boys
13. Girls
14. Unfit
15. Attention-deficit/ hyperactivity disorder
16. Boys
17. Does
18. Stimulants
19. Disabilities, disorders
20. Dyslexia
21. Neurological
22. Does

Chapter 12
1. Less
2. Transitivity
3. Inclusion
4. Autonomous
5. The amount of damage done
6. Preconventional
7. Conventional
8. Increases
9. Working, short-term

10. Encode, rehearse
11. Rote
12. Elaborative
13. Metamemory
14. *g*
15. Multiple
16. Mental
17. Verbal comprehension, perceptual reasoning, working memory, and processing speed.
18. Bias
19. 6
20. Divergent
21. Biological, Adoptive
22. Visual
23. Phonetic
24. Can
25. Advantage

Chapter 13
1. Industry
2. Concrete
3. Perspective, viewpoint
4. Decreases
5. Authoritative
6. Less
7. Heterosexual
8. Downward
9. Mothers
10. Boys
11. Farther away from
12. Mature
13. Later-born
14. Discouraged
15. Low
16. Smaller
17. Self-fulfilling
18. Boys

19. Biological
20. Protect children from
21. Underutilize
22. Anxiety
23. Is not

Chapter 14
1. Stress
2. Feedback
3. Sex
4. Growth
5. Asynchronous
6. Epiphyseal
7. Estrogen
8. Boys
9. Boys
10. Chlamydia
11. Human papillomavirus, HPV, genital warts
12. Acquired immunodeficiency syndrome, AIDS
13. Minority
14. Male
15. Accidents
16. Anorexia nervosa
17. Purging
18. Do
19. Perfectionism, obsessiveness, depression
20. Abuse
21. Abstinence, withdrawal
22. Alcohol
23. Nicotine
24. Regular

Chapter 15
1. Formal
2. Egocentrism
3. Superior
4. Superior

5. Sex
6. Postconventional
7. Positive
8. More
9. Drop
10. Girls
11. More
12. Boys
13. Realistic, practical, conventional
14. Gender
15. Boys
16. Minority (15 percent)

Chapter 16
1. Identity, ego identity
2. Moratorium
3. Achievement
4. Lower
5. Mothers
6. Do
7. Increases
8. Their own
9. Masturbation
10. Homosexual, gay male or lesbian
11. Hormones
12. Less
13. Peer
14. Status
15. More
16. More
17. Common
18. Depression, helplessness, hopelessness
19. Does
20. Marriage
21. Job
22. Emerging

Glossary

abstinence syndrome A characteristic cluster of symptoms that results from a sudden decrease in the level of usage of a substance.

accommodation According to Piaget, the modification of existing schemes to permit the incorporation of new events or knowledge.

achieved ethnic identity The final stage of ethnic identity development; similar to the identity achievement status.

achievement That which is attained by one's efforts and presumed to be made possible by one's abilities.

adaptation According to Piaget, the interaction between the organism and the environment. It consists of two processes: assimilation and accommodation.

adipose tissue Fat.

adrenaline A hormone that generally arouses the body, increasing the heart and respiration rates.

allele A member of a pair of genes.

alpha-fetoprotein (AFP) assay A blood test that assesses the mother's blood level of alpha-fetoprotein, a substance that is linked with fetal neural tube defects.

ambivalent/resistant attachment A type of insecure attachment characterized by severe distress at the leave-takings of and ambivalent behaviour at reunions with an attachment figure.

American Sign Language (ASL) The communication of meaning through the use of symbols that are formed by moving the hands and arms. The language used by some deaf people.

amniocentesis (AM-nee-oh-sen-TEE-sis) A procedure of drawing and examining fetal cells sloughed off into amniotic fluid to determine the presence of various disorders.

amniotic fluid Fluid within the amniotic sac that suspends and protects the fetus.

amniotic sac The sac containing the fetus.

amplitude Height. The higher the amplitude of sound waves, the louder they are.

androgens Male sex hormones (from roots meaning "giving birth to men").

anesthetic An agent that produces partial or total loss of the sense of pain (from Greek roots meaning "without feeling").

animism The attribution of life and intentionality to inanimate objects.

anorexia nervosa An eating disorder characterized by irrational fear of weight gain, distorted body image, and severe weight loss.

anoxia A condition characterized by lack of oxygen.

Apgar scale A measure of a newborn's health that assesses appearance, pulse, grimace, activity level, and respiratory effort.

aphasia A disruption in the ability to understand or produce language.

apnea (AP-nee-uh) Temporary suspension of breathing (from the Greek *a-*, meaning "without," and *pnoie,* meaning "wind").

appearance–reality distinction The difference between real events on the one hand and mental events, fantasies, and misleading appearances on the other hand.

artificial insemination Injection of sperm into the uterus to fertilize an ovum.

artificialism The belief that environmental features were made by people.

assimilation According to Piaget, the incorporation of new events or knowledge into existing schemes.

asynchronous growth Imbalanced growth, such as the growth that occurs during the early part of adolescence and causes many adolescents to appear gawky.

attachment An affectional bond between individuals characterized by a seeking of closeness or contact and a show of distress upon separation.

attachment-in-the-making phase The second phase in the development of attachment, occurring at 3 or 4 months of age and characterized by preference for familiar figures.

attention-deficit/hyperactivity disorder (AD/HD) A behaviour disorder characterized by excessive inattention, impulsiveness, and hyperactivity.

attributional style The way in which one is disposed toward interpreting outcomes (successes or failures), as in tending to place blame or responsibility on oneself or on external factors.

authoritarian A child-rearing style in which parents demand submission and obedience from their children but are not very communicative and warm.

authoritative A child-rearing style in which parents are restrictive and demanding yet communicative and warm.

autism A developmental disorder characterized by extreme aloneness and failure to relate to others, communication problems, intolerance of change, and ritualistic behaviour. One of the autism spectrum disorders.

autism spectrum disorders (ASDs) Developmental disorders—including autism, Asperger's syndrome, Rett's disorder, and childhood disintegrative disorder—that are characterized by impairment in communication skills, social interactions, and repetitive, stereotyped behaviour. Also referred to as *pervasive developmental disorders.*

autobiographical memory The memory of specific episodes or events.

autonomous morality The second stage in Piaget's cognitive-developmental theory of moral development. In this stage, children base moral judgments on the intentions of the wrongdoer and on the amount of damage done. Social rules are viewed as agreements that can be changed.

autosome Either member of a pair of chromosomes (with the exception of sex chromosomes).

avoidant attachment A type of insecure attachment characterized by apparent indifference to the leave-takings of and reunions with an attachment figure.

axon A long, thin part of a neuron that transmits impulses to other neurons through small branching structures called axon terminals.

babbling The child's first vocalizations that have the sounds of speech.

Babinski reflex A reflex in which infants fan their toes when the undersides of their feet are stroked.

bed-wetting Failure to control the bladder during the night. (Frequently used interchangeably with *enuresis,* although *bed-wetting* refers to the behaviour itself and *enuresis* is a diagnostic category, related to the age of the child.)

behaviour modification The systematic application of principles of learning to change problem behaviours or encourage desired behaviours.

behaviourism John B. Watson's view that a science or theory of development must study observable behaviour only and investigate relationships between stimuli and responses.

bilingual Using or capable of using two languages with nearly equal or equal facility.

blastocyst A stage within the germinal period of prenatal development in which the zygote has the form of a sphere of cells surrounding a cavity of fluid.

bonding The process of forming bonds of attachment between parent and child.

Braxton-Hicks contractions The first, usually painless, contractions of childbirth.

Brazelton Neonatal Behavioral Assessment Scale A measure of a newborn's motor behaviour, response to stress, adaptive behaviour, and control over physiological state.

breech presentation A position in which the fetus enters the birth canal buttocks first.

Broca's aphasia A form of aphasia caused by damage to Broca's area and characterized by slow, laborious speech.

bulimia nervosa An eating disorder characterized by cycles of binge eating and vomiting as a means of controlling weight gain.

caesarean section A method of childbirth in which the neonate is delivered through a surgical incision in the abdomen. (Also spelled *cesarean.*)

canalization The tendency of growth rates to return to genetically determined patterns after undergoing environmentally induced change.

carrier A person who carries and transmits characteristics but does not exhibit them.

case study A carefully drawn biography of an individual.

categorical self Definitions of the self that refer to concrete external traits.

centration Focusing on one dimension of a situation while ignoring others.

cephalocaudal From head to tail.

cerebellum (ser-uh-BEH-lum) The part of the hindbrain involved in muscle coordination and balance.

cerebrum (seh-REE-brum) The large mass of the forebrain, which consists of two hemispheres.

child A person undergoing the period of development from infancy through puberty.

chorionic villus sampling (CORE-ee-AH-nick VIH-luss) A method for the prenatal detection of genetic abnormalities that samples the membrane enveloping the amniotic sac and fetus.

chromosomes Rod-shaped structures composed of genes that are found within the nuclei of cells.

chronological age (CA) A person's age.

chronosystem The environmental changes that occur over time and have an impact on the child (from the Greek *chronos,* meaning "time").

classical conditioning A simple form of learning in which one stimulus comes to bring forth the response usually brought forth by a second stimulus by being paired repeatedly with the second stimulus.

class inclusion The principle that one category or class of things can include several subclasses.

clear-cut-attachment phase The third phase in the development of attachment, occurring at 6 or 7 months of age and characterized by intensified dependence on the primary caregiver.

clique A group of five to ten individuals who hang around together and who share activities and confidences.

clitoris A female sex organ that is highly sensitive to sexual stimulation but not directly involved in reproduction.

cognitive-developmental theory The stage theory that holds that the child's abilities to mentally represent, or perceive, the world and solve problems unfold as a result of the interaction of experience and the maturation of neurological structures.

cohort effect Similarities in behaviour among a group of peers that stem from the fact that group members are approximately of the same age. (A possible source of misleading information in cross-sectional research.)

collectivist A person who defines herself or himself in terms of relationships to other people and groups and gives priority to group goals.

commitment A stable investment in one's goals, values, or beliefs.

conception The process of becoming pregnant; the process by which a sperm cell joins with an ovum to begin a new life (i.e., when the chromosomes of each of these cells combine to form 23 new pairs).

concordance Agreement.

concrete operations The third stage in Piaget's scheme, characterized by flexible, reversible thought concerning tangible objects and events.

conditioned response (CR) A learned response to a previously neutral stimulus.

conditioned stimulus (CS) A previously neutral stimulus that elicits a response because it has been paired repeatedly with a stimulus that already elicited that response.

conduct disorders Disorders marked by persistent breaking of the rules and violations of the rights of others.

cones In the eye, cone-shaped receptors of light that transmit sensations of colour.

congenital Present at birth; resulting from the prenatal environment.

conservation In cognitive psychology, the principle that properties of substances such as weight and mass remain the same (are conserved) when superficial characteristics such as their shapes or arrangement are changed.

contact comfort The pleasure derived from physical contact with another; a hypothesized need or drive for physical contact with another.

contrast assumption The assumption that objects have only one label. Also known as the *mutual exclusivity assumption* (if a word means one thing, it cannot mean another).

control group A group made up of participants in an experiment who do not receive the treatment but for whom all other conditions are comparable to those of participants in the experimental group.

conventional level According to Kohlberg, a period during which moral judgments largely reflect social rules and conventions.

convergence The inward movement of the eyes as they focus on an object that is drawing nearer.

convergent thinking A thought process that attempts to focus in on the single best solution to a problem.

cooing Prelinguistic, articulated vowellike sounds that appear to reflect feelings of positive excitement.

coregulation A gradual transferring of control from parent to child, beginning in middle childhood.

corpus callosum The thick bundle of nerve fibres that connects the left and right hemispheres of the brain.

correlation coefficient A number ranging from +1.00 to −1.00 that expresses the direction (positive or negative) and strength of the relationship between two variables.

creativity The ability to generate novel solutions to problems. A trait characterized by flexibility, ingenuity, and originality.

critical period A period of development during which a releasing stimulus can elicit a fixed action pattern (FAP); a period during which an embryo is particularly vulnerable to a certain teratogen.

cross-sectional research The study of developmental processes by taking measures of children of different age groups at the same time.

cross-sequential research An approach that combines the longitudinal and cross-sectional methods by following individuals of different ages for abbreviated periods of time.

crowd A large, loosely organized group of people who may or may not spend much time together and who are identified by the activities of the group.

cultural bias A factor hypothesized to be present in intelligence tests that provides an advantage for test takers from certain cultural or ethnic backgrounds but that does not reflect true intelligence.

culture-free Descriptive of a test in which cultural biases have been removed. On such a test, test takers from different cultural backgrounds would have an equal opportunity to earn scores that reflect their true abilities.

cystic fibrosis A fatal genetic disorder in which mucus obstructs the lungs and pancreas.

decentration Simultaneous focusing (centring) on more than one aspect or dimension of a problem or situation.

deep structure The underlying meaning of a sentence.

deferred imitation The imitation of people and events that occurred hours, days, or weeks in the past.

dendrites The rootlike parts of a neuron that receive impulses from other neurons (from the Greek *dendron,* meaning "tree" and referring to the branching appearance of dendrites).

deoxyribonucleic acid (DNA) Genetic material that takes the form of a double helix composed of phosphates, sugars, and bases.

dependent variable A measure of an assumed effect of an independent variable.

DES Abbreviation for diethylstilbestrol, a powerful estrogen that has been linked to cancer in the reproductive organs of children of women who used the hormone when pregnant.

design stage A stage in drawing in which children begin to combine shapes.

development The processes by which organisms unfold features and traits, grow, and become more complex and specialized in structure and function.

differentiation The processes by which behaviours and physical structures become more specialized.

dilate To make wider or larger.

disinhibit To stimulate a response that has been suppressed (inhibited) by showing a model engaging in that response without aversive consequences.

disorganized–disoriented attachment A type of insecure attachment characterized by dazed and contradictory behaviours toward an attachment figure.

divergent thinking A thought process that attempts to generate multiple solutions to problems. Free and fluent association to the elements of a problem.

dizygotic (DZ) twins Twins that derive from two zygotes; fraternal twins.

dominant trait A trait that is expressed.

donor IVF The transfer of a donor's ovum, fertilized in a laboratory dish, to the uterus of another woman.

Down syndrome A chromosomal abnormality characterized by mental retardation and caused by an extra chromosome in the 21st pair.

dramatic play Play in which children enact social roles; made possible by the attainment of symbolic thought. A form of *pretend play.*

dyslexia A reading disorder characterized by problems such as letter reversals, mirror reading, slow reading, and reduced comprehension (from the Greek roots *dys,* meaning "bad," and *lexikon,* meaning "of words").

echolalia The automatic repetition of sounds or words.

ecological systems theory The view that explains child development in terms of the reciprocal influences between children and the settings that make up their environment.

ecology The branch of biology that deals with the relationships between living organisms and their environment.

ectoderm The outermost cell layer of the newly formed embryo from which the skin and nervous system develop.

efface To rub out or wipe out; to become thin.

ego identity According to Erikson, one's sense of who one is and what one stands for.

egocentrism Putting oneself at the centre of things such that one is unable to perceive the world from another person's point of view. Egocentrism is normal in early childhood but is a matter of choice in adults.

elaborative strategy A method for increasing retention of new information by relating it to well-known information.

electroencephalograph (EEG) An instrument that measures electrical activity of the brain.

elicit (i-LI-sut) To bring forth; evoke.

embryonic disk The platelike inner part of the blastocyst that differentiates into the ectoderm, mesoderm, and endoderm of the embryo.

embryonic stage The stage of prenatal development that lasts from implantation through the eighth week of pregnancy; it is characterized by the development of the major organ systems.

emotion A state of feeling that has physiological, situational, and cognitive components.

emotional regulation Techniques for controlling one's emotional states.

empathy Ability to share another person's feelings.

empirical Based on observation and experimentation.

encode To transform sensory input into a form that is more readily processed.

encopresis Failure to control the bowels once the normal age for bowel control has been reached. Also called *soiling.*

endoderm The inner layer of the embryo from which the lungs and digestive system develop.

endometriosis Inflammation of endometrial tissue sloughed off into the abdominal cavity rather than out of the body during menstruation; the condition is characterized by abdominal pain and, sometimes, infertility.

endometrium The inner lining of the uterus.

enuresis (en-you-REE-sis) Failure to control the bladder (urination) once the normal age for control has been reached.

epiphyseal closure The process by which the cartilage that separates the long end (epiphysis) of a bone from the main part of the bone turns to bone.

episiotomy (ih-pee-zee-AH-tuh-mee) A surgical incision in the area between the birth canal and the anus that widens the vaginal opening, preventing random tearing during childbirth.

equilibration The creation of an equilibrium, or balance, between assimilation and accommodation as a way of incorporating new events or knowledge.

estrogen A female sex hormone produced mainly by the ovaries.

ethnic groups Groups of people distinguished by cultural heritage, race, language, and common history.

ethnic identity A sense of belonging to an ethnic group.

ethnic identity search The second stage of ethnic identity development; similar to the moratorium identity status.

ethologist A scientist who studies the behaviour patterns that are characteristic of various species.

ethology The study of behaviours that are specific to a species.

exosystem Community institutions and settings that indirectly influence the child, such as the school board and the parents' workplaces (from the Greek *exo,* meaning "outside").

experiment A method of scientific investigation that seeks to discover cause-and-effect relationships by introducing independent variables and observing their effects on dependent variables.

experimental group A group made up of participants who receive a treatment in an experiment.

exploration Active questioning and searching among alternatives in the quest to establish goals, values, or beliefs.

expressive language style Use of language primarily as a means for engaging in social interaction.

expressive vocabulary The sum total of the words that one can use in the production of language.

extinction The decrease and eventual disappearance of a response in the absence of reinforcement.

factor A condition or quality that brings about a result. A cluster of related items, such as those found on an intelligence or personality test.

factor analysis A statistical technique that allows researchers to determine the relationships among a large number of items, such as test items.

failure to thrive (FTT) A disorder of impaired growth in infancy and early childhood characterized by failure to gain weight within normal limits.

fallopian tube A tube through which ova travel from an ovary to the uterus.

fast mapping A process of quickly determining a word's meaning, which facilitates children's vocabulary development.

feedback loop A system in which glands regulate each other's functioning through a series of hormonal messages.

fetal alcohol effect (FAE) A cluster of symptoms less severe than those of fetal alcohol syndrome shown by children of women who drank moderately during pregnancy.

fetal alcohol syndrome (FAS) A cluster of symptoms shown by children of women who drank heavily during pregnancy, including characteristic facial features and mental retardation.

fetal monitoring The use of instruments to track the heart rate and oxygen levels of the fetus during childbirth.

fetal stage The stage of development that lasts from the beginning of the ninth week of pregnancy through birth; it is characterized by gains in size and weight and maturation of the organ systems.

fine motor skills Skills employing the small muscles used in manipulation, such as those in the fingers.

fixed action pattern (FAP) Instinct; a stereotyped behaviour pattern that is characteristic of a species and is triggered by a "releasing stimulus"; an instinct.

forceps A curved instrument that fits around the head of the baby and permits it to be pulled through the birth canal.

foreclosure An identity status that characterizes those who have made commitments without considering alternatives.

formal operations The fourth stage in Piaget's cognitive-developmental theory, characterized by the capacity for flexible, reversible operations concerning abstract ideas and concepts, such as symbols, statements, and theories.

gay An adjective describing a male who is interested romantically and sexually in other males. (Also used more broadly to refer to both lesbians and gay males.)

gender The psychological state of being female or being male, as influenced by cultural concepts of gender-appropriate behaviour. Compare and contrast the concept of gender with *anatomic sex,* which is based on the physical differences between females and males.

gender constancy The concept that one's sex remains the same despite superficial changes in appearance or behaviour.

gender identity Knowledge that one is female or male. Also, the name of the first stage in Kohlberg's cognitive-developmental theory of the assumption of gender roles.

gender role A complex cluster of traits and behaviours that are considered stereotypical of females and males.

gender-schema theory The view that one's knowledge of the gender schema in one's society (the behaviour patterns that are considered appropriate for men and women) guides one's assumption of gender-typed preferences and behaviour patterns.

gender stability The concept that one's sex is a permanent feature.

gene The basic unit or building block of heredity. Genes are composed of deoxyribonucleic acid (DNA).

general anesthesia The process of eliminating pain by putting the person to sleep.

generalized anxiety disorder (GAD) An anxiety disorder in which anxiety appears to be present continuously and is unrelated to the situation.

genetic counselling Advice concerning the probabilities that a couple's children will show genetic abnormalities.

genetics The branch of biology that studies heredity.

genital stage In psychoanalytic theory, the fifth and final stage of psychosexual development in which gratification is attained through sexual intercourse with an individual of the other sex.

genotype The genetic form or constitution of a person as determined by heredity.

germinal stage The period of development between conception and the implantation of the embryo in the uterine wall.

goodness of fit Agreement between the parents' expectations of or demands on the child and the child's temperamental characteristics.

grasping reflex A reflex in which infants grasp objects that cause pressure against the palms.

gross motor skills Skills employing the large muscles used in locomotion.

growth The processes by which organisms increase in size, weight, strength, and other traits as they develop.

growth spurt A period during which growth advances at a dramatically rapid rate compared with other periods.

gynecomastia Enlargement of breast tissue in males.

habituate Show a decline in interest as a repeated stimulus becomes familiar.

habituation A process in which one becomes used to and therefore pays less attention to a repeated stimulus.

hallucinogens Drugs that give rise to hallucinations.

handedness The tendency to prefer using the left or right hand in writing and other activities.

hemophilia A genetic disorder in which blood does not clot properly.

heredity The transmission of traits and characteristics from parent to child by means of genes.

heritability The degree to which the variations in a trait from one person to another can be attributed to, or explained by, genetic factors.

heterozygous Having two different alleles.

HIV/AIDS HIV stands for *human immunodeficiency virus,* the virus that causes AIDS. AIDS stands for *acquired immunodeficiency syndrome,* a condition that cripples the body's immune system, making the person vulnerable to diseases that would not otherwise be as threatening.

holophrase A single word that is used to express complex meanings.

homosexual Referring to an erotic orientation toward members of one's own sex.

homozygous Having two identical alleles.

hue Colour.

Huntington's disease A fatal genetic neurological disorder whose onset is in middle age.

hyaluronidase An enzyme that briefly thins the zona pellucida, enabling a single sperm cell to penetrate (from roots referring to a "substance that breaks down a glasslike fluid").

hyperactivity Excessive restlessness and overactivity; one of the primary characteristics of attention-deficit/hyperactivity disorder (AD/HD). Not to be confused with misbehaviour or with normal high-activity levels that occur during childhood.

hypothalamus A pea-sized structure above the pituitary gland that is involved in the regulation of body temperature, motivation (e.g., hunger, thirst, sex), and emotion.

hypothesis (high-PAH-thuh-sis). A Greek word meaning "groundwork" or "foundation" that has come to mean a specific statement about behaviour that is tested by research.

hypoxia A condition characterized by less oxygen than is required.

identity achievement An identity status that characterizes those who have explored alternatives and have developed commitments.

identity crisis A turning point in development during which one examines one's values and makes decisions about life roles.

imaginary audience The belief that others around us are as concerned with our thoughts and behaviours as we are; one aspect of adolescent egocentrism.

immanent justice The view that retribution for wrongdoing is a direct consequence of the wrongdoing, reflective of the belief that morality is embedded within the structure of the universe.

imprinting The process by which some animals exhibit the fixed action pattern (FAP) of attachment in response to a releasing stimulus. The FAP occurs during a critical period and is difficult to modify.

inclusion Students with exceptionalities are fully included in school programs and activities.

incubator A heated, protective container in which premature infants are kept.

independent variable A condition in a scientific study that is manipulated (changed) so that its effects can be observed.

indiscriminate attachment The display of attachment behaviours toward any person.

individualist A person who defines himself or herself in terms of personal traits and gives priority to his or her own goals.

inductive Characteristic of disciplinary methods, such as reasoning, that attempt to foster an understanding of the principles behind parental demands.

industry versus inferiority The fourth stage of psychosocial development in Erikson's theory, occurring in middle childhood. Mastery of tasks leads to a sense of industry, whereas failure produces feelings of inferiority.

infancy The period of very early childhood, characterized by lack of complex speech; the first 2 years after birth.

initial-preattachment phase The first phase in the formation of bonds of attachment, lasting from birth to about 3 months of age and characterized by indiscriminate attachment.

inner speech Vygotsky's concept of the ultimate binding of language and thought. Inner speech originates in vocalizations that may regulate the child's behaviour and become internalized by age 6 or 7.

insomnia One or more of a number of sleep problems—difficulty falling asleep, difficulty remaining asleep during the night, and waking early.

intelligence A complex and controversial concept, defined by David Wechsler as the "capacity ... to understand the world [and the] resourcefulness to cope with its challenges." Intelligence implies the capacity to make adaptive choices (from the Latin *inter,* meaning "among," and *legere,* meaning "to choose").

intelligence quotient (IQ) (1) Originally, a ratio obtained by dividing a child's score (or "mental age") on an intelligence test by his or her chronological age. (2) In general, a score on an intelligence test.

intensity Brightness.

intonation The use of pitches of varying levels to help communicate meaning.

in vitro fertilization Fertilization of an ovum in a laboratory dish.

irreversibility Lack of recognition that actions can be reversed.

juvenile delinquency Conduct of a child or adolescent characterized by illegal activities.

Klinefelter syndrome A chromosomal disorder found among males that is caused by an extra X sex chromosome and characterized by infertility and mild mental retardation.

labia The major and minor lips of the female genitalia.

Lamaze method A childbirth method in which women are educated about childbirth, learn to relax and breathe in patterns that conserve energy and lessen pain, and have a coach (usually the father) present during childbirth. Also termed *prepared childbirth.*

language acquisition device (LAD) In psycholinguistic theory, neural "prewiring" that facilitates the child's learning of grammar.

lanugo (luh-NOO-go) Fine, downy hair that covers much of the body of the neonate, especially preterm babies.

larynx The part of the throat that contains the vocal cords.

latency stage In psychoanalytic theory, the fourth stage of psychosexual development, characterized by repression of sexual impulses and development of skills.

learned helplessness An acquired (hence, *learned*) belief that one is unable to control one's environment.

learning disabilities A group of disorders characterized by inadequate development of specific academic, language, and speech skills.

lesbian A female who is interested romantically and sexually in other females.

life crisis An internal conflict that attends each stage of psychosocial development. Positive resolution of early life crises sets the stage for positive resolution of subsequent life crises.

local anesthetic An agent that reduces feeling in a specific area of the body.

locomotion Movement from one place to another.

longitudinal research The study of developmental processes by taking repeated measures of the same group of children at various stages of development.

long-term memory The memory structure capable of relatively permanent storage of information.

macrosystem The basic institutions and ideologies that influence the child, such as the American ideals of freedom of expression and equality under the law (from the Greek *makros*, meaning "long" or "enlarged").

mammary glands Glands that secrete milk.

masturbation Sexual self-stimulation.

maturation The unfolding of genetically determined traits, structures, and functions.

mean length of utterance (MLU) The average number of morphemes used in an utterance.

medulla (muh-DUH-luh) An oblong-shaped area of the hindbrain involved in heartbeat and respiration.

meiosis The form of cell division in which each pair of chromosomes splits so that one member of each pair moves to the new cell. As a result, each new cell has 23 chromosomes.

memory The processes by which we store and retrieve information.

menarche The onset of menstruation.

menopause The cessation of menstruation, typically occurring between ages 48 and 52.

mental age (MA) The accumulated months of credit that a person earns on the Stanford–Binet Intelligence Scale.

mental representations The mental forms that a real object or event can take, which may differ from one another. (Successful problem solving is aided by accurate mental representation of the elements of the problem.)

mesoderm The central layer of the embryo from which the bones and muscles develop.

mesosystem The interlocking settings that influence the child, such as the interaction of the school and the larger community when children are taken on field trips (from the Greek *mesos*, meaning "middle").

metacognition Awareness of and control of one's cognitive abilities, as shown by the intentional use of cognitive strategies in solving problems.

metamemory Knowledge of the functions and processes involved in one's storage and retrieval of information (memory), as shown by use of cognitive strategies to retain information.

microsystem The immediate settings with which the child interacts, such as the home, the school, and one's peers (from the Greek *mikros*, meaning "small").

midwife An individual who helps women in childbirth (from Old English roots meaning "with woman").

mitosis The form of cell division in which each chromosome splits lengthwise to double in number. Half of each chromosome combines with chemicals to retake its original form and then moves to the new cell.

models In learning theory, those whose behaviours are imitated by others.

monozygotic (MZ) twins Twins that derive from a single zygote that has split into two; identical twins. Each MZ twin carries the same genetic code.

moral realism According to Piaget, the stage during which children judge acts as moral when they conform to authority or to the rules of the game. Morality at this stage is perceived as embedded in the structure of the universe.

moratorium An identity status that characterizes those who are actively exploring alternatives in an attempt to form an identity.

Moro reflex A reflex in which infants arch their back, fling out their arms and legs, and draw them back toward the chest in response to a sudden change in position.

morpheme The smallest unit of meaning in a language.

motility Self-propulsion.

motor development The development of the capacity for movement, particularly that made possible by changes in the nervous system and the muscles.

multifactorial problems Problems that stem from the interaction of heredity and environmental factors.

multiple sclerosis A disorder in which myelin is replaced by hard fibrous tissue that impedes neural transmission.

muscular dystrophy (DIS-truh-fee) A chronic disease characterized by a progressive wasting away of the muscles.

mutation A sudden variation in a heritable characteristic, as by an accident that affects the composition of genes.

mutism Inability or refusal to speak.

myelination The process by which axons are coated with myelin.

myelin sheath (MY-uh-lin) A fatty, whitish substance that encases and insulates neurons, permitting more rapid transmission of neural impulses.

natural childbirth A method of childbirth in which women use no anesthesia and are educated about childbirth and strategies for coping with discomfort.

naturalistic observation A method of scientific observation in which children (and others) are observed in their natural environments.

nature The processes within an organism that guide that organism to develop according to its genetic code.

negative correlation A relationship between two variables in which one variable increases as the other variable decreases.

negative reinforcer A reinforcer that, when removed, increases the frequency of a response.

neonate A newborn baby (from the Greek *neos*, meaning "new," and the Latin *natus*, meaning "born").

nerves Bundles of axons from many neurons.

neural Of the nervous system.

neural tube A hollowed-out area in the blastocyst from which the nervous system develops.

neurons Nerve cells; cells found in the nervous system that transmit messages.

neuroticism A personality trait characterized by anxiety and emotional instability.

neurotransmitter A chemical substance that enables the transmission of neural impulses from one neuron to another.

nightmares Frightening dreams that occur during REM sleep, often in the morning hours.

nocturnal emission Emission of seminal fluid while asleep.

non-rapid-eye-movement (non-REM) sleep Periods of sleep during which we are unlikely to dream.

nonsocial play Forms of play (solitary play or onlooker play) in which play is not influenced by the play of nearby children.

nurture The processes external to an organism that nourish it as it develops according to its genetic code or that cause it to swerve from its genetically programmed course. Environmental factors that influence development.

obesity A disorder characterized by excessive accumulation of fat.

object permanence Recognition that objects continue to exist even when they are not seen.

objective morality The perception of morality as objective—that is, as existing outside the cognitive functioning of people; a characteristic of Piaget's stage of moral realism.

observational learning The acquisition of expectations and skills by means of observing others.

obsessive-compulsive disorder (OCD) An anxiety disorder characterized by *obsessions* (recurring thoughts or images that seem beyond control) and *compulsions* (irresistible urges to repeat an act, such as hand washing or checking that one has put one's homework in one's backpack).

occupational gender typing Judgments that certain occupations are more appropriate for one sex than the other.

operant conditioning A simple form of learning in which an organism learns to engage in behaviour that is reinforced.

operations Flexible, reversible mental manipulations of objects, in which objects can be mentally transformed and then returned to their original states.

oral rehydration therapy A treatment involving administration of a salt and sugar solution to a child who is dehydrated from diarrhea.

osteoporosis A condition involving progressive loss of bone tissue.

ovary A female reproductive organ, located in the abdomen, that produces female reproductive cells (ova).

overextension Use of words in situations in which their meanings become extended or inappropriate.

overregularization The application of regular grammatical rules for forming inflections (e.g., past tense and plurals) to irregular verbs and nouns.

ovulation The releasing of an ovum from an ovary.

ovum (pl. ova) A female reproductive cell.

oxytocin (ok-see-TOE-sin) A pituitary hormone that stimulates labour contractions (from the Greek *oxys,* meaning "quick," and *tokos,* meaning "birth").

pacifier An artificial nipple, teething ring, or similar device that soothes babies.

peers Children of the same age. (More generally, people of similar background and social standing.)

pelvic inflammatory disease (PID) An infection of the abdominal region that may have various causes and that may impair fertility.

perception The process by which sensations are organized into a mental map of the world.

perceptual constancy The tendency to perceive objects as the same even though sensations produced by them may differ when, for example, they differ in position or distance.

permissive–indulgent A child-rearing style in which parents are not controlling and restrictive but are warm.

personal fable The belief that our feelings and ideas are special and unique and that we are invulnerable; one aspect of adolescent egocentrism.

personality An individual's distinctive ways of responding to people and events.

phenotype The actual form or constitution of a person as determined by heredity and environmental factors.

phenylketonuria (PKU) (fee-nul-key-tun-UR-ee-uh) A genetic abnormality in which phenylalanine builds up and causes mental retardation.

phobia An irrational, excessive fear that interferes with one's functioning.

phonetic method A method for learning to read in which children decode the sounds of words based on their knowledge of the sounds of letters and letter combinations.

pictorial stage A stage in drawing attained between ages 4 and 5 in which designs begin to resemble recognizable objects.

pincer grasp The use of the opposing thumb to grasp objects between the thumb and other fingers.

pitch The highness or lowness of a sound, as determined by the frequency of sound waves.

pituitary gland The body's "master gland," which is located in the lower central part of the brain and which secretes many hormones essential to development, such as oxytocin, prolactin, and growth hormone.

PKU Phenylketonuria. A genetic abnormality in which a child cannot metabolize phenylalanine, an amino acid, which consequently builds up in the body and causes mental retardation. If treated with a special diet, retardation is prevented.

placement stage An early stage in drawing, usually found among 2-year-olds, in which children place their scribbles in various locations on the page (such as in the middle or near a border).

placenta (pluh-SEN-tuh) An organ connected to the uterine wall and to the fetus by the umbilical cord. The placenta serves as a relay station between mother and fetus for exchange of nutrients and wastes.

plasticity The tendency of new parts of the brain to take up the functions of injured parts.

polygenic Resulting from many genes.

positive correlation A relationship between two variables in which one variable increases as the other variable increases.

positive reinforcer A reinforcer that, when applied, increases the frequency of a response.

postconventional level According to Kohlberg, a period during which moral judgments are derived from moral principles and people look to themselves to set moral standards.

postpartum depression (PPD) More severe, prolonged depression that afflicts 10–20 percent of women after delivery and that is characterized by sadness, apathy, and feelings of worthlessness.

postpartum period The period that immediately follows childbirth.

pragmatics The practical aspects of communication, such as adaptation of language to fit the social situation.

precausal A type of thought in which natural cause-and-effect relationships are attributed to will and other preoperational concepts. (For example, the sun sets because it is tired.)

preconscious In psychoanalytic theory, that which is not in awareness but is capable of being brought into awareness by focusing of attention.

preconventional level According to Kohlberg, a period during which moral judgments are based largely on expectations of rewards or punishments.

prelinguistic Referring to vocalizations made by the infant before the development of

language. (In language, words symbolize objects and events.)

premature Born before the full term of gestation. (Also referred to as *preterm.*)

prenatal Before birth.

prenatal period The period of development from conception to birth (from roots meaning "prior to birth").

preoperational stage The second stage in Piaget's scheme, characterized by inflexible and irreversible mental manipulation of symbols.

preterm Born at or before completion of 37 weeks of gestation.

primary circular reactions The repetition of actions that first occurred by chance and that focus on the infant's own body.

primary sex characteristics The structures that make reproduction possible.

progestin A hormone used to maintain pregnancy that can cause masculinization of the fetus.

prosocial behaviour Behaviour intended to benefit another without expectation of reward.

prostaglandins (pross-tuh-GLAN-dins) Hormones that stimulate uterine contractions.

proximodistal From the inner part (or axis) of the body outward.

psycholinguistic theory The view that language learning involves an interaction between environmental influences and an inborn tendency to acquire language. The emphasis is on the inborn tendency.

psychological androgyny Possession of both stereotypical feminine and masculine traits.

psychological moratorium A time-out period when adolescents experiment with different roles, values, beliefs, and relationships.

psychosexual development In psychoanalytic theory, the process by which libidinal energy is expressed through different erogenous zones during different stages of development.

psychosocial development Erikson's theory, which emphasizes the importance of social relationships and conscious choice throughout the eight stages of development.

puberty The biological stage of development characterized by changes that lead to reproductive capacity. Puberty signals the beginning of adolescence.

punishment An unpleasant stimulus that suppresses behaviour.

Pygmalion effect A self-fulfilling prophecy; an expectation that is confirmed because of the behaviour of those who hold the expectation.

rapid-eye-movement (REM) sleep A period of sleep during which we are likely to dream, as indicated by rapid eye movements.

reaction range The variability in the expression of inherited traits as they are influenced by environmental factors.

reaction time The amount of time required to respond to a stimulus.

recall A memory task in which the individual must reproduce material from memory without any cues.

receptive vocabulary The sum total of the words whose meanings one understands.

recessive trait A trait that is not expressed when the gene or genes involved have been paired with dominant genes. Recessive traits are transmitted to future generations and expressed if they are paired with other recessive genes.

reciprocal-relationship phase The fourth phase in the development of attachment, occurring at 18 months to 2 years onward and characterized by less protesting of separation and a better understanding of relationship duration beyond the immediate.

reciprocity The principle that actions have mutual effects and that people depend on one another to treat each other morally.

recognition A memory task in which the individual indicates whether presented information has been experienced previously.

referential language style Use of language primarily as a means for labelling objects.

reflex An unlearned, stereotypical response to a stimulus.

regression A return to behaviours characteristic of earlier stages of development.

rehearsal Repetition.

rehearse Repeat.

reinforcement The process of providing stimuli following a response, which has the effect of increasing the frequency of the response.

rejecting–neglecting A child-rearing style in which parents are neither restrictive and controlling nor supportive and responsive.

releasing stimulus A stimulus that elicits a fixed action pattern (FAP).

respiratory distress syndrome A cluster of breathing problems, including weak and irregular breathing, to which preterm babies are particularly prone.

reversibility According to Piaget, recognition that processes can be undone, leaving things as they were before. Reversibility is a factor in conservation of the properties of substances.

Rh incompatibility A condition in which antibodies produced by the mother are transmitted to the child, possibly causing brain damage or death.

risk factors Variables such as ethnicity and social class that are associated with the likelihood of problems but that do not directly cause problems.

rods In the eye, rod-shaped receptors of light that are sensitive to intensity only. Rods permit black-and-white vision.

role diffusion An identity status that characterizes those who have no commitments and who are not in the process of exploring alternatives.

rooting reflex A reflex in which infants turn their mouths and heads in the direction of a stroking of the cheek or the corner of the mouth.

rote learning Learning by repetition.

rough-and-tumble play Play fighting and chasing.

rubella A viral infection that can cause retardation and heart disease in the embryo. Also called *German measles.*

saturation Richness or purity of a colour.

scaffolding Vygotsky's term for temporary cognitive structures or methods of solving problems that help the child as he or she learns to function independently.

scheme According to Piaget, an action pattern (such as a reflex) or mental structure that is involved in the acquisition or organization of knowledge.

schizophrenia A severe psychological disorder that is characterized by disturbances in thought and language, perception and attention, motor activity, and mood and by withdrawal and absorption in daydreams or fantasy.

school phobia Fear of attending school, marked by extreme anxiety at leaving parents.

scripts Abstract generalized accounts of familiar repeated events.

secondary circular reactions The repetition of actions that produce an effect on the environment.

secondary sex characteristics Physical indicators of sexual maturation—such as changes to the voice and growth of bodily hair—that do not directly involve reproductive structures.

secular trend A historical trend toward increasing adult height and earlier puberty.

secure attachment A type of attachment characterized by mild distress at leave-takings, seeking nearness to an attachment figure, and being readily soothed by the figure.

sedatives Drugs that soothe or quiet restlessness or agitation.

self-concept One's impression of oneself; self-awareness.

self-esteem The sense of value or worth that people attach to themselves.

self-fulfilling prophecy An event that occurs because of the behaviour of those who expect it to occur.

semantic code A code based on the meaning of information.

semen The fluid that contains sperm and substances that nourish and help transport sperm.

sensation The stimulation of sensory organs such as the eyes, ears, and skin and the transmission of sensory information to the brain.

sensitive period In linguistic theory, the period from about 18 months to puberty when the brain is thought to be especially capable of learning language because of its plasticity.

sensory memory The structure of memory first encountered by sensory input. Information is maintained in sensory memory for only a fraction of a second.

sensory register Another term for sensory memory.

separation anxiety Fear of being separated from a target of attachment, usually a primary caregiver.

separation anxiety disorder (SAD) An extreme form of otherwise normal separation anxiety that is characterized by anxiety about separating from parents; SAD often takes the form of refusal to go to school.

separation–individuation The child's increasing sense of becoming separate from and independent of the mother.

seriation Placing objects in an order or series according to a property or trait.

serotonin A neurotransmitter that is implicated in depression.

sex chromosome A chromosome in the shape of a Y (male) or X (female) that determines the sex of the child.

sexism Discrimination or bias against people based on their sex.

sex-linked chromosomal abnormalities Abnormalities that are transmitted from generation to generation, carried by a sex chromosome, usually an X sex chromosome.

sex-linked genetic abnormalities Abnormalities resulting from genes that are found on the X sex chromosome. They are more likely to be shown by male offspring (who do not have an opposing gene from a second X chromosome) than by female offspring.

sexual harassment Unwelcome verbal or physical conduct of a sexual nature.

shape constancy The tendency to perceive objects as being the same shape even though the shapes of their retinal images may differ when the objects are viewed from different positions.

shape stage A stage in drawing, attained by age 3, in which children draw basic shapes such as circles, squares, triangles, crosses, *X*'s, and odd shapes.

shaping In learning theory, a procedure for teaching complex behaviour patterns by means of reinforcing small steps toward the target behaviour.

sibling rivalry Jealousy or rivalry among brothers and sisters.

sickle-cell anemia A genetic disorder that decreases the blood's capacity to carry oxygen.

SIDS See *sudden infant death syndrome.*

sight vocabulary Words that are immediately recognized on the basis of familiarity with their overall shapes, rather than decoded.

size constancy The tendency to perceive objects as being the same size even though the sizes of their retinal images may differ as a result of distance.

sleep terrors Frightening dreamlike experiences that occur during the deepest stage of non-REM sleep, shortly after the child has gone to sleep.

small for dates Descriptive of neonates who are unusually small for their age.

social cognition Development of children's understanding of the relationship between the self and others.

social cognitive theory A cognitively oriented learning theory that emphasizes observational learning in the determining of behaviour.

social play Play in which children interact with and are influenced by the play of others. Examples include parallel play, associative play, and cooperative play.

social referencing Using another person's reaction to a situation to form one's own assessment of it.

social smile A smile that occurs in response to a human voice or face.

socialization A process through which children are encouraged to adopt socially desirable behaviour patterns through a system of guidance, rewards, and punishments.

somnambulism Sleepwalking (from the Latin *somnus,* meaning "sleep," and *ambulare,* meaning "to walk").

sonogram A procedure for using ultrasonic sound waves to create a picture of an embryo or fetus.

spina bifida A neural tube defect that causes abnormalities of the brain and spine.

spontaneous abortion Unplanned, accidental abortion; miscarriage.

stage theory A theory of development characterized by hypothesizing the existence of distinct periods of life. Stages follow one another in an orderly sequence.

standardized test A test of some ability or trait in which an individual's score is compared to the scores of a group of similar individuals.

status offences Offences considered illegal only when performed by minors, such as truancy and underage drinking.

stepping reflex A reflex in which infants take steps when held under the arms and leaned forward so that the feet press against the ground.

stereotype A fixed, conventional idea about a group.

stillbirth The birth of a dead fetus.

stimulants Drugs that increase the activity of the nervous system.

stimulus A change in the environment that leads to a change in behaviour.

stranger anxiety A fear of unfamiliar people that emerges between 6 and 9 months of age. Also called *fear of strangers.*

substance abuse A persistent pattern of use of a substance characterized by frequent intoxication and impairment of physical, social, or emotional well-being.

substance dependence A persistent pattern of use of a substance that is accompanied by physiological addiction.

sudden infant death syndrome (SIDS) The death, while sleeping, of apparently healthy babies who stop breathing for unknown medical reasons. Also called *crib death.*

surface structure The superficial grammatical construction of a sentence.

surrogate mother A woman who is artificially inseminated and carries to term a child who is then given to another woman, typically the spouse of the sperm donor.

symbolic play Play in which children make believe that objects and toys are other than what they are. Also termed *pretend play.*

syntax The rules in a language for placing words in proper order to form meaningful sentences (from the Latin *syntaxis,* meaning "joining together").

syphilis A sexually transmitted infection that, in advanced stages, can attack major organ systems.

Tay-Sachs disease A fatal genetic neurological disorder.

telegraphic speech Type of speech in which only the essential words are used.

temperament Individual differences in styles of reaction that are present early in life.

teratogens Environmental influences or agents that can damage the embryo or fetus (from the Greek *teras,* meaning "monster").

term A set period of time.

tertiary circular reactions The purposeful adaptation of established schemes to new situations.

testosterone A male sex hormone—a steroid—that is produced by the testes and that promotes growth of male sexual characteristics and sperm.

thalidomide A sedative used in the 1960s that has been linked to birth defects, especially deformed or absent limbs.

theory A formulation of relationships underlying observed events. A theory involves assumptions and logically derived explanations and predictions.

theory of mind A commonsense understanding of how the mind works.

time lag The study of developmental processes by taking measures of children of the same age group at different times.

time-out A behaviour-modification technique in which a child who misbehaves is temporarily placed in a drab, restrictive environment in which reinforcement is unavailable.

toddler A child who walks with short, uncertain steps. Toddlerhood lasts from about 18 to 30 months of age, thereby bridging infancy and early childhood.

tolerance Habituation to a drug such that increasingly higher doses are needed to achieve similar effects.

tonic-neck reflex A reflex in which infants turn their head to one side, extend the arm and leg on that side, and flex the limbs on the opposite side. Also known as the "fencing position."

toxemia A life-threatening disease that can afflict pregnant women; it is characterized by high blood pressure.

track Follow.

tranquillizer A drug that reduces feelings of anxiety and tension.

transductive reasoning Reasoning from the specific to the specific. (In deductive reasoning, one reasons from the general to the specific; in inductive reasoning, one reasons from the specific to the general.)

transition The initial movement of the head of the fetus into the birth canal.

transitional object A soft, cuddly object often carried to bed by a child to ease the separation from parents.

transitivity The principle that if A is greater than B in a property and B is greater than C, then A is greater than C.

transsexual A person who would prefer to be a person of the other sex and who may undergo hormone treatments and/or cosmetic surgery to achieve the appearance of being a member of the other sex.

treatment In an experiment, a condition received by participants so that its effects may be observed.

triarchic Governed by three. Descriptive of Sternberg's view that intellectual functioning has three aspects: context of the action/behaviour, the individuals' experience with the task, and the information-processing strategies applied by individuals.

trophoblast The outer part of the blastocyst from which the amniotic sac, placenta, and umbilical cord develop.

Turner syndrome A chromosomal disorder found among females that is caused by having a single X sex chromosome and characterized by infertility.

ulnar grasp A method of grasping objects in which the fingers close somewhat clumsily against the palm.

ultrasound Sound waves too high in pitch to be sensed by the human ear.

umbilical cord A tube that connects the fetus to the placenta.

unconditioned response (UCR) An unlearned response; a response to an unconditioned stimulus.

unconditioned stimulus (UCS) A stimulus that elicits a response from an organism without learning.

unconscious In psychoanalytic theory, that which is not available to awareness by simple focusing of attention.

unexamined ethnic identity The first stage of ethnic identity development; similar to the diffusion or foreclosure identity statuses.

uterus The hollow organ within females in which the embryo and fetus develop.

utopian Referring to an ideal vision of society.

vacuum extraction tube An instrument that uses suction to pull the baby through the birth canal.

variables Quantities that can vary from child to child or from occasion to occasion, such as height, weight, intelligence, and attention span.

vernix An oily white substance that coats the skin of the neonate, especially preterm babies.

visual accommodation The automatic adjustments made by the lenses of the eyes to bring objects into focus.

visual acuity Keenness or sharpness of vision.

visual recognition memory The kind of memory shown in an infant's ability to discriminate previously seen objects from novel objects.

Wernicke's aphasia A form of aphasia caused by damage to Wernicke's area and characterized by impaired comprehension of speech and difficulty in attempting to produce the right word.

whole-object assumption The assumption that words refer to whole objects and not to their component parts or characteristics.

word-recognition method A method for learning to read in which children come to recognize words through repeated exposure to them.

working memory The structure of memory that can hold a sensory stimulus for up to 30 seconds after the trace decays. Also called *short-term memory*.

zona pellucida A gelatinous layer that surrounds an ovum (from roots referring to a "zone through which light can shine").

zone of proximal development (ZPD) Vygotsky's term for the situation in which a child carries out tasks with the help of someone who is more skilled, frequently an adult who represents the culture in which the child develops.

zygote A new cell formed from the union of a sperm and an ovum (egg cell); a fertilized egg.

References

AAP Media Alert on Breastfeeding (1999, February 11). *AAP reaffirms breastfeeding stance following fictional TV show.* Available at http://www.aap.org/visit/brmdalt.htm

ABCNEWS.com (2001, June 19). *Study: One in five kids solicited online.* Available at http://www.ABCNEWS.com

Abdelaziz, Y. E., Harb, A. H., & Hisham, N. (2001). *Textbook of clinical pediatrics.* Philadelphia: Lippincott Williams & Wilkins.

Abe-Kim, J., Okazaki, S., & Goto, S. G. (2001). Unidimensional versus multidimensional approaches to the assessment of acculturation for Asian American populations. *Cultural Diversity and Ethnic Minority Psychology, 7*(3), 232–246.

Abikoff, H. (2001). Tailored psychosocial treatments for ADHD: The search for a good fit. *Journal of Clinical Child Psychology, 30*(1), 122–125.

Abravanel, E., & DeYong, N. G. (1991). Does object modeling elicit imitative-like gestures from young infants? *Journal of Experimental Child Psychology, 52,* 22–40.

Acebo, C., & Thomas, E. B. (1992). Crying as social behavior. *Infant Mental Health Journal, 13,* 67–82.

Adler, J., & Starr, M. (1992, August 10). Flying high now. *Newsweek,* pp. 20–21.

Adler, T. (1993, June). Kids' memory improves if they talk to themselves. *APA Monitor,* p. 8.

Adnams, C. M., et al. (2001). Patterns of cognitive-motor development in children with fetal alcohol syndrome from a community in South Africa. *Alcoholism: Clinical and Experimental Research, 25*(4), 557–562.

Adolph, K. E. (2000). Specificity of learning: Why infants fall over a veritable cliff. *Psychological Science, 11*(4), 290–295.

Adolph, K. E., Vereijken, B., & Shrout, P. E. (2003). What changes in infant walking and why. *Child Development, 74*(2), 475–497.

Adoption Council of Canada (2006, August 17). International adoptions down in 2005. Available at http://adoption.ca

Affonso, D. D., De, A. K., Horowitz, J. A., & Mayberry, L. J. (2000). An international study exploring levels of postpartum depressive symptomatology. *Journal of Psychosomatic Research, 49*(3), 207–216.

Agency for Healthcare Research and Quality (2004, April). Chronic illnesses. In *Child Health Research Findings, Program Brief,* AHRQ Publication 04-P011. Rockville, MD: Agency for Healthcare Research and Quality. Available at http://www.ahrq.gov/research/childfind/chfchrn.htm

Agrawal, A., Neale, M. C., Prescott, C. A., & Kendler, K. S. (2004). Cannabis and other illicit drugs: Comorbid use and abuse/dependence in males and females.

Behavior Genetics, 34(3), 217–228.

Aguiar, A., & Baillargeon, R. (1999). 2.5-month-old infants' reasoning about when objects should and should not be occluded. *Cognitive Psychology, 39*(2), 116–157.

Aguiar, A., & Baillargeon, R. (2002). Developments in young infants' reasoning about occluded objects. *Cognitive Psychology, 45*(2), 267–336.

Ahluwalia, I. B., Merritt, R., Beck, L. F., & Rogers, M. (2001). Multiple lifestyle and psychosocial risks and delivery of small for gestational age infants. *Obstetrics and Gynecology, 97*(5), 649–656.

Ainsworth, M. D. S. (1967). *Infancy in Uganda: Infant care and the growth of love.* Baltimore: Johns Hopkins University Press.

Ainsworth, M. D. S. (1989). Attachments beyond infancy. *American Psychologist, 44,* 709–716.

Ainsworth, M. D. S., Blehar, M. C., Waters, E., & Wall, S. (1978). *Patterns of attachment: A psychological study of the Strange Situation.* Hillsdale, NJ: Erlbaum.

Ainsworth, M. D. S., & Bowlby, J. (1991). An ethological approach to personality development. *American Psychologist, 46*(4), 333–341.

Alberta Education (2006). *Guide to education: ECS to grade 12,* 44–45. Alberta, Canada: Author.

Alessandri, S. M., Bendersky, M., & Lewis, M. (1998). Cognitive functioning in 8- to 18-month old drug-exposed infants. *Developmental Psychology, 34*(3), 565–573.

Alexander, G. M. (2003). An evolutionary perspective of sex-typed toy preferences: Pink, blue, and the brain. *Archives of Sexual Behavior, 32*(1), 7–14.

Allen, L., & Majidi-Ahi, S. (1991). Black American children. In J. T. Gibbs, L. N. Huang, & Associates (Eds.), *Children of color: Psychological interventions with minority youth.* San Francisco: Jossey-Bass.

Allen, M. (2004). Does French immersion improve reading achievement? *Canadian Social Trends.* Ottawa, ON: Statistics Canada.

Allen, M. C., & Alexander, G. R. (1990). Gross motor milestones in preterm infants: Correction for degree of prematurity. *Journal of Pediatrics, 116,* 955–959.

Alloway, T. P., Gathercole, S. E., Willis, C., & Adams, A. (2004). A structural analysis of working memory and related cognitive skills in young children. *Journal of Experimental Child Psychology, 87*(2), 85–106.

Als, H., et al. (2003). A three-center, randomized, controlled trial of individualized developmental care for very low birth weight preterm infants: Medical, neurodevelopmental, parenting, and caregiving effects. *Journal of Developmental and Behavioral Pediatrics, 24*(6), 399–408.

Altepeter, T. S., & Walker, C. E. (1992). Prevention of physical abuse of children through parent training. In D. J. Willis, E. W. Holden, & M. Rosenberg (Eds.), *Prevention of child maltreatment.* New York: Wiley.

Amato, P. R. (2000). The consequences of divorce for adults and children. *Journal of Marriage and the Family, 62*(4), 1269–1287.

Amato, P. R. (2001). Children of divorce in the 1990s: An update of the Amato and Keith (1991) meta-analysis. *Journal of Family Psychology, 15*(3), 355–370.

American Academy of Pediatrics (2002, February 7). *A woman's guide to breastfeeding.* Available at http://www.aap.org/family/brstguid.htm

American Association of University Women (1992). *How schools shortchange women: The AAUW report.* Washington, DC: AAUW Educational Foundation.

American Association on Mental Retardation (2004, August 22). *Mental retardation: Definition, classification, and systems of supports* (10th ed.). Available at http://www.aamr.org

American College of Obstetricians and Gynecologists (2001, March 31). *Pregnancy-related mortality from preeclampsia and eclampsia.* ACOG Press. Available at http://www.acog.com/

American Infertility Association (2002). Cited in J. E. Brody (2002a, January 1), What women must know about fertility, *New York Times,* p. F6.

American Lung Association (2000). *Smoking fact sheet.* Available at http://www.lungusa.org

American Lung Association (2004). *American Lung Association State of Tobacco Control 2003 Fact Sheet.* Available at http://www.lungusa.org/site/apps/nl/content3

American Pregnancy Association (2003). *Acne treatment during pregnancy.* Available at http://www.americanpregnancy.org/pregnancyhealth/acnetreatment.html

American Psychiatric Association (1994). *Diagnostic and statistical manual of mental disorders* (4th ed.). Washington, DC: Author.

American Psychiatric Association (2000). *Diagnostic and statistical manual of mental disorders (DSM-IV-TR).* Washington, DC: Author.

American Psychiatric Association (2001, May 18). African-American youngsters inadequately treated for ADHD. *Psychiatric News, 36*(10), 17. Also available at http://pn.psychiatryonline.org/cgi/content/full/36/10/17-a

American Psychological Association (1992). Ethical principles of psychologists and code of conduct. *American Psychologist, 47,* 1597–1611.

American Psychological Association (1993).

Violence and youth. Washington, DC: Author.

Anastasi, A. (1988). *Psychological testing* (6th ed.). New York: Macmillan.

Anderman, E. M., et al. (2001). Learning to value mathematics and reading: Relations to mastery and performance-oriented instructional practices. *Contemporary Educational Psychology, 26*(1), 76–95.

Anders, T. F., Halpern, L. F., & Hua, J. (1992). Sleeping through the night: A developmental perspective. *Pediatrics, 90*, 554–560.

Anderson, C. A., & Dill, K. E. (2000). Video games and aggressive thoughts, feelings, and behavior in the laboratory and in life. *Journal of Personality and Social Psychology, 78*(4), 772–790.

Anderson, G. M., & Cohen, D. J. (1991). The neurology of childhood neuropsychiatric disorders. In M. Lewis (Ed.), *Child and adolescent psychiatry: A comprehensive textbook*. Baltimore: Williams & Wilkins.

Anderson, P., et al. (2003). Neurobehavioral outcomes of school-age children born extremely low birth weight or very preterm in the 1990s. *Journal of the American Medical Association, 289*(24), 3264–3272.

Anderson, S. R., Christian, W. P., & Luce, S. C. (1986). Transitional residential programming for autistic individuals. *Behavior Therapist, 9*, 205–211.

Andreou, G., Krommydas, G., Gourgoulianis, K. I., Karapetsas, A., & Molyvdas, P. A. (2002). Handedness, asthma, and allergic disorders: Is there an association? *Psychology, Health, and Medicine, 7*(1), 53–60.

Angier, N. (1997). Chemical tied to fat control could help trigger puberty. *New York Times*, pp. C1, C3.

Anisfeld, E., Casper, V., Kozyce, M., & Cunningham, N. (1990). Does infant carrying promote attachment? An experimental study of the effects of increased physical contact on the development of attachment. *Child Development, 61*, 1617–1627.

Anisfeld, M. (1991). Review: Neonatal imitation. *Developmental Review, 11*, 60–97.

Anthis, K. S., Dunkel, C. S., & Anderson, B. (2004). Gender and identity status differences in late adolescents' possible selves. Journal of *Adolescence, 27*(2), 147–152.

Antshel, K. M., & Waisbren, S. E. (2003). Timing is everything: Executive functions in children exposed to elevated levels of phenylalanine. *Neuropsychology, 17*(3), 458–468.

Arbona, C. (2000). Practice and research in career counseling and development. *Career Development Quarterly, 49*(2), 98–134.

Arbuthnot, J., & Gordon, D. A. (1988). Crime and cognition: Community applications of sociomoral reasoning development. *Criminal Justice and Behavior, 15*(3), 379–393.

Archer, S. L. (1985). Career and/or family: The identity process for adolescent girls. *Youth and Society, 16*, 289–314.

Archer, S. L. (1992). A feminist's approach to identity research. In G. R. Adams, T. P. Gullotta, & R. Montemayor (Eds.), *Adolescent identity formation*. Newbury Park, CA: Sage.

Armstrong, C. A., et al. (1998). Children's television viewing, body fat, and physical fitness. *American Journal of Health Promotion, 12*(6), 363–368.

Arnett, J. J. (1998). Learning to stand alone: The contemporary American transition to adulthood in cultural and historical context. *Human Development, 41*(5–6), 295–315.

Arnett, J. J. (2000). Emerging adulthood. *American Psychologist, 55*(5), 469–480.

Arnett, J. J. (2001). Conceptions of the transition to adulthood: Perspectives from adolescence through midlife. *Journal of Adult Development, 8*(2), 133–143.

Arnett, J. J. (1999). Adolescent storm and stress, reconsidered. *American Psychologist, 54*(5), 317–326.

Arnett, J. J. (2000). Optimistic bias in adolescent and adult smokers and non-smokers. *Addictive Behaviours, 125*(4), 625–632.

Arnold, D. H., Homrok, S., Ortiz, C., & Stowe, R. M. (1999). Direct observation of peer rejection acts and their temporal relation with aggressive acts. *Early Childhood Research Quarterly, 14*(2), 183–196.

Aronson, J. (2002). Stereotype threat: Contending and coping with unnerving expectations. In J. Aronson (Ed.), *Improving academic achievement: Impact of psychological factors on education* (pp. 279–301). San Diego: Academic Press.

Arria, A. M., Derauf, C., LaGasse, L. L., Grant, P., Shah, R., Smith, L., Haning, W., Huestis M., Strauss, A., Della Grotta, S., Liu, J., & Lester, B. (2006). Methamphetamine and other substance use during pregnancy: Preliminary estimates from infant development, environment, and lifestyle (IDEAL) study. *Maternal and Child Health Journal, 10*, 293–302.

Arthur, B. I., Jr., et al. (1998). Sexual behaviour in Drosophila is irreversibly programmed during critical period. *Current Biology, 8*(21), 1187–1190.

Asendorpf, J. B., & Baudonniere, P. (1993). Self-awareness and other-awareness: Mirror self-recognition and synchronic imitation among unfamiliar peers. *Developmental Psychology, 29*, 88–95.

Ashton, C. H. (2001). Pharmacology and effects of cannabis: A brief review. *British Journal of Psychiatry, 178*, 101–106.

Aslin, R. N. (1987). Visual and auditory development in infancy. In J. D. Osofsky (Ed.), *Handbook of infant development* (2nd ed.). New York: Wiley.

Aslin, R. N., Pisoni, D. B., & Juscyk, P. W. (1983). Auditory development and speech perception in infancy. In P. H. Mussen (Ed.), *Handbook of child psychology*, v. 2, *Infancy and experimental psychobiology*. New York: Wiley.

Au, T. K., & Glusman, M. (1990). The principle of mutual exclusivity in word learning: To honor or not to honor? *Child Development, 61*, 1474–1490.

Autti-Ramo, I. (2000). Twelve-year follow-up of children exposed to alcohol in utero. *Developmental Medicine and Child Neurology, 42*(6), 406–411.

Autti-Ramo, I. (2002). Foetal alcohol syndrome: a multifaceted condition. *Developmental Medicine and Child Neurology, 44*(2), 141–144.

Ayyash-Abdo, H. (2001). Individualism and collectivism: The case of Lebanon. *Social Behavior and Personality, 29*(5), 503–518.

Azar, B. (1998). What predicts which foods we eat? A genetic disposition for certain tastes may affect people's food preferences. *APA Monitor, 29*, 1.

Azar, B. (2002). It's more than fun and games. *Monitor on Psychology, 33*(3), 50–51.

Bagley, C., Bertrand, L., Bolitho, F., & Mallick, K. (2001). Discrepant parent-adolescent views on family functioning: Predictors of poorer self-esteem and problems of emotion and behaviour in British and Canadian adolescents. *Journal of Comparative Family Studies, 32*(3), 393–403.

Bacete, F. G., & Remirez, J. R. (2001). Family and personal correlates of academic achievement. *Psychological Reports, 88*(2), 533–547.

Bachman, J. G., Safron, D. J., Sy, S. R., & Schulenberg, J. E. (2003). Wishing to work: New perspectives on how adolescents' part-time work intensity is linked to educational disengagement, substance use, and other problem behaviours. *International Journal of Behavioral Development, 27*(4), 301–315.

Baenninger, M. A., & Elenteny, K. (1997). Cited in B. Azar (1997), *Environment can mitigate differences in spatial ability, APA Monitor, 28*(6), 28.

Baer, H., Allen, S., & Braun, L. (2000). Knowledge of human papillomavirus infection among young adult men and women: Implications for health education and research. *Journal of Community Health: The Publication for Health Promotion and Disease Prevention, 25*(1), 67–78.

Bagley, C., & D'Augelli, A. R. (2000). Suicidal behaviour in gay, lesbian, and bisexual youth. *British Medical Journal, 320*, 1617–1618.

Bailey, J. M. (2003). *The man who would be queen: The science of gender-bending and transsexualism*. Washington, DC: Joseph Henry Press.

Bailey, J. M., Dunne, M. P., & Martin, N. G. (2000). Genetic and environmental influences on sexual orientation and its correlates in an Australian twin sample. *Journal of Personality and Social Psychology, 78*(3), 524–536.

Bailey, J. M., & Pillard, R. C. (1991). A genetic study of male sexual orientation. *Archives of General Psychiatry, 48*, 1089–1096.

Baillargeon, R. (1987). Object permanence in 3½- and 4½-month-old infants. *Developmental Psychology, 23*, 655–664.

Baillargeon, R. (1991). Reasoning about the height and location of a hidden object in 41/2- and 61/2-month-old infants. *Cognition, 38*, 13–42.

Baillargeon, R., Graber, M., DeVos, J., & Black, J. (1990). Why do young infants fail to search for hidden objects? *Cognition, 36*, 255–284.

Baker, C. W., Whisman, M. A., & Brownell,

K. D. (2000). Studying intergenerational transmission of eating attitudes and behaviors: Methodological and conceptual questions. *Health Psychology, 19*(4), 376–381.

Baker, L., & Cantwell, D. P. (1991). The development of speech and language. In M. Lewis (Ed.), *Child and adolescent psychiatry: A comprehensive textbook.* Baltimore: Williams & Wilkins.

Baker, L., Mackler, K., Sonnenschein, S., & Serpell, R. (2001). Parents' interactions with their first-grade children during storybook reading and relations with subsequent home reading activity and reading achievement. *Journal of School Psychology, 39*(5), 415–438,

Balaban, E. (2004). Neurobiology: Why voles stick together. *Nature, 429,* 711–712.

Baldry, A. C. (2003). Bullying in schools and exposure to domestic violence. *Child Abuse and Neglect, 27*(7), 713–732.

Baldwin, A. L., Baldwin, C., & Cole, R. E. (1990). Stress-resistant families and stress-resistant children. In J. Rolf, A. Masten, D. Cicchetti, K. Nuechterlein, & S. Weintraub (Eds.), *Risk and protective factors in the development of psychopathology.* Cambridge: Cambridge University Press.

Balluz, L. S., et al. (2000). Vitamin and mineral supplement use in the United States: Results from the Third National Health and Nutrition Examination Survey. *Archives of Family Medicine, 9,* 258.

Ballweg, R. (2001). Story related in "Can you be too rich or too thin?" *Well & Good, 3.* University of Iowa Health Care. Available at http://www.uihealthcare.com/news/wellandgood/2001issue3/eatingdisorders.html

Bamford, F. N., et al. (1990). Sleep in the first year of life. *Developmental Medicine and Child Neurology, 32,* 718–724.

Bandura, A. (1986). *Social foundations of thought and action: A social-cognitive theory.* Englewood Cliffs, NJ: Prentice-Hall.

Bandura, A. (2002). Social cognitive theory in cultural context. *Applied Psychology: An International Review, 51*(2), 269–290.

Bandura, A., Barbaranelli, C., Vittorio Caprara, G., & Pastorelli, C. (2001). Self-efficacy beliefs as shapers of children's aspirations and career trajectories. *Child Development, 72*(1), 187–206.

Bandura, A., Blanchard, E. B., & Ritter, B. (1969). The relative efficacy of desensitization and modeling approaches for inducing behavioral, affective, and cognitive changes. *Journal of Personality and Social Psychology, 13,* 173–199.

Bandura, A., & Locke, E. A. (2003). Negative self-efficacy and goal effects revisited. *Journal of Applied Psychology, 88*(1), 87–99.

Bandura, A., Ross, S. A., & Ross, D. (1963). Imitation of film-mediated aggressive models. *Journal of Abnormal and Social Psychology, 66,* 3–11.

Banks, M. S., & Salapatek, P. (1983). Infant visual perception. In P. H. Mussen (Ed.), *Handbook of child psychology,* v. 2, *Infancy and experimental psychobiology.* New York: Wiley.

Banks, M. S., & Shannon, E. (1993). Spatial and chromatic visual efficiency in human neonates. In C. E. Granrud (Ed.), *Visual perception and cognition in infancy.* Hillsdale, NJ: Erlbaum.

Barabas, G. (1990). Physical disorders. In M. Lewis & S. M. Miller (Eds.), *Handbook of developmental pathology.* New York: Plenum.

Barbarich, N. C., et al. (2004). Use of nutritional supplements to increase the efficacy of fluoxetine in the treatment of anorexia nervosa. *International Journal of Eating Disorders, 35*(1), 10–15.

Barber, J. G. (2001). Relative misery and youth suicide. *Australian and New Zealand Journal of Psychiatry, 35*(1), 49–57.

Barber, C. M., Abernathy, T., Steinmetz, B., & Charlebois, J. (1997). Using a breastfeeding prevalence survey to identify a population for targeted programs. *Canadian Journal of Public Health, 88,* 242–245.

Bard, C., Hay, L., & Fleury, M. (1990). Timing and accuracy of visually directed movements in children: Control of direction and amplitude components. *Journal of Experimental Child Psychology, 50,* 102–118.

Bard, K. A., Coles, C. D., Platzman, K. A., & Lynch, M. E. (2000). The effects of prenatal drug exposure, term status, and caregiving on arousal and arousal modulation in 8-week-old infants. *Developmental Psychobiology, 36*(3), 194–212.

Bardick, A. D., Bernes, K. B., Magnusson, K. C., & Witko, K. D. (2006). Junior high school students' career plans for the future. *Journal of Career Development, 32*(2), 50–271.

Barkley, R. A. (2004). Adolescents with attention-deficit/hyperactivity disorder: An overview of empirically based treatments. *Journal of Psychiatric Practice, 10*(1), 39–56.

Barnard, K. E., & Bee, H. L. (1983). The impact of temporally patterned stimulation on the development of preterm infants. *Child Development, 54,* 1156–1167.

Bar-Or, O., et al. (1998). Physical activity, genetic, and nutritional considerations in childhood weight management. *Medicine and Science in Sports and Exercise, 30*(1), 2–10.

Barr, H. M., & Streissguth, A. P. (2001). Identifying maternal self-reported alcohol use associated with fetal alcohol spectrum disorders. *Alcoholism: Clinical and Experimental Research, 25*(2) 283–287.

Barr, R. G., Rotman, A., Yaremko, J., Leduc, D., & Francoeur, T. E. (1992). The crying of infants with colic: A controlled empirical description. *Pediatrics, 90,* 14–21.

Barratt, M. S., Negayama, K., & Minami, T. (1993). The social environments of early infancy in Japan and the United States. *Early Development and Parenting, 2,* 51–64.

Barrile, M., Armstrong, E. S., & Bower, T. G. R. (1999). Novelty and frequency as determinants of newborn preference. *Developmental Science, 2*(1), 47–52.

Barros, F. C., Huttly, S. R. A., Victora, C. G., Kirkwood, B. R., & Vaughan, J. P. (1992). Comparison of the causes and consequences of prematurity and intrauterine growth retardation: A longitudinal study in southern Brazil. *Pediatrics, 90,* 238–244.

Bartholomew, K., & Horowitz, L. M. (1991). Attachment styles among young adults: A test of a four-category model. *Journal of Personality and Social Psychology, 61*(2), 226–244.

Bartzokis, G. (2004). Age-related myelin breakdown: A developmental model of cognitive decline and Alzheimer's disease. *Neurobiology of Aging, 25*(1), 5–18.

Basic Behavioral Science Task Force of the National Advisory Mental Health Council (1996). Basic behavioral science research for mental health: Sociocultural and environmental practices. *American Psychologist, 51,* 722–731.

Bastien-Toniazzo, M., & Jullien, S. (2001). Nature and importance of the logographic phase in learning to read. *Reading and Writing, 14*(1–2), 119–143.

Bates, E. A. (2004). Explaining and interpreting deficits in language development across clinical groups: Where do we go from here? *Brain and Language, 88*(2), 248–253.

Bates, E., O'Connell, B., & Shore, C. (1987). Language and communication in infancy. In J. D. Osofsky (Ed.), *Handbook of infant development* (2nd ed.). New York: Wiley.

Bates, E., Thal, D., & Janowsky, J. S. (1992). Early language development and its neural correlates. *Handbook of Neuropsychology, 7,* 69–110.

Bates, J. E., Bayles, K., Bennett, D. S., Ridge, B., & Brown, M. M. (1991). Origins of externalizing behavior problems at eight years of age. In D. J. Pepler & K. H. Rubin (Eds.), *The development and treatment of childhood aggression.* Hillsdale, NJ: Erlbaum.

Battin-Pearson, S., et al. (2000). Predictors of early high school dropout: A test of five theories. *Journal of Educational Psychology, 92*(3), 568–582.

Bauer, K. W., Yang, Y. W., & Austin, S. B. (2004). "How can we stay healthy when you're throwing all of this in front of us?" Findings from focus groups and interviews in middle schools on environmental influences on nutrition and physical activity. *Health Education and Behavior, 31*(1), 33–46.

Bauer, P. J., & Mandler, J. M. (1990). Remembering what happened next: Very young children's recall of event sequences. In R. Fivush & J. A. Hudson (Eds.), *Knowing and remembering in young children.* Cambridge: Cambridge University Press.

Bauer, P. J., & Mandler, J. M. (1992). Putting the horse before the cart: The use of temporal order in recall of events by one-year-old children. *Developmental Psychology, 28,* 441–452.

Bauerfeld, S. L., & Lachenmeyer, J. R. (1992). Prenatal nutritional status and intellectual development. In B. B. Lahey & A. E. Kazdin (Eds.), *Advances in clinical child psychology,* v. 14. New York: Plenum.

Baum, S. R., & Dwivedi, V. D. (2003). Sensitivity to prosodic structure in left-and right-hemisphere-damaged individuals. *Brain and*

Language, 87(2), 278–289.

Baumeister, R. F., Catanese, K. R., & Vohs, K. D. (2001). Is there a gender difference in strength of sex drive? Theoretical views, conceptual distinctions, and a review of relevant evidence. *Personality and Social Psychology Review, 5*(3), 242–273.

Baumrind, D. (1971). Current patterns of parental authority. *Developmental Psychology, 4*(1, Pt. 2), 1–103.

Baumrind, D. (1989). Rearing competent children. In W. Damon (Ed.), *Child development today and tomorrow.* San Francisco: Jossey-Bass.

Baumrind, D. (1991a). The influence of parenting style on adolescent competence and substance use. *Journal of Early Adolescence, 11,* 56–95.

Baumrind, D. (1991b). Parenting styles and adolescent development. In J. Brooks-Gunn, R. Lerner, & A. C. Petersen (Eds.), *Encyclopedia of adolescence.* New York: Garland.

Baydar, N., & Brooks-Gunn, J. (1991). Effects of maternal employment and child-care arrangements on preschoolers' cognitive and behavioral outcomes: Evidence from the Children of the National Longitudinal Survey of Youth. *Developmental Psychology, 27,* 932–945.

Beal, C. R., & Flavell, J. H. (1983). Young speakers' evaluation of their listeners' comprehensions in a referential communication task. *Child Development, 54,* 148–153.

Beaulieu, M. D. (1980). Screening for D (Rh) sensitization in pregnancy. Available at http://www.phac-aspc.gc.ca/publicat/clinic-clinique/pdf/s1c11e.pdf

Beaumont, J. (2006). *Childhood obesity part 1: Is your child out of shape?* Available at http://www.lycos.ca/health-&-fitness/fitness/childhood_obesity_part_1.html

Becker, E. (2002, January 24). Study finds a growing gap between managerial salaries for men and women. *New York Times,* p. A24.

Bedford, V. H., Volling, B. L., & Avioli, P. S. (2000). Positive consequences of sibling conflict in childhood and adulthood. *International Journal of Aging and Human Development, 51*(1), 53–69.

Beer, J. M., & Horn, J. M. (2000). The influence of rearing order on personality development within two adoption cohorts. *Journal of Personality, 68*(4), 789–819.

Behrman, R. E., Kliegman, R. M., & Jenson, H. B. (2000). *Nelson review of pediatrics* (2nd ed.). Philadelphia: W. B. Saunders.

Beiser, M., & Gotowiec, A. (2000). Accounting for native/non-native differences in IQ scores. *Psychology in the Schools, 37*(3), 237–252.

Beitchman, J. H., et al. (2001). Comorbidity of psychiatric and substance use disorders in late adolescence: A cluster analytic approach. *American Journal of Drug and Alcohol Abuse, 27*(3), 421–440.

Belfry, J. (1996). Canadian children face activity and fitness crisis. *Interaction* (Fall 1996). Available at http://www.cfc-efc.ca/docs/cccf/00010_en.htm

Bell, J. H., & Bromnick, R. D. (2003). The social reality of the imaginary audience: A ground theory approach. *Adolescence, 38*(150), 205–219.

Bell, R. (1998). *Changing bodies, changing lives* (3rd ed.). New York: Times Books.

Bell, S. K., & Morgan, S. B. (2000). Children's attitudes and behavioral intentions toward a peer presented as obese: Does a medical explanation for the obesity make a difference? *Journal of Pediatric Psychology, 25*(3), 137–145.

Bellinger, D., et al. (1991). Low-level lead exposure and children's cognitive function in the preschool years. *Pediatrics, 87,* 219–227.

Bellinger, D., Leviton, A., Waternaux, C., Needleman, H. L., & Rabinowitz, M. (1987). Longitudinal analysis of prenatal and postnatal lead exposure and early cognitive development. *New England Journal of Medicine, 316,* 1037–1043.

Bellodi, L., et al. (2001). Morbidity risk for obsessive-compulsive spectrum disorders in first-degree relatives of patients with eating disorders. *American Journal of Psychiatry, 158,* 563–569.

Belsky, J. (1990a). Developmental risks associated with infant day care: Attachment insecurity, noncompliance and aggression? In S. Cherazi (Ed.), *Psychosocial issues in day care.* New York: American Psychiatric Press.

Belsky, J. (1990b). The "effects" of infant day care reconsidered. In N. Fox & G. G. Fein (Eds.), *Infant day care: The current debate.* Norwood, NJ: Ablex.

Belsky, J. (2001). Emanuel Miller Lecture: Developmental risks (still) associated with early child care. *Journal of Child Psychology and Psychiatry and Allied Disciplines, 42*(7), 845–859.

Belsky, J., Weinraub, M., Owen, M., & Kelly, J. (2001, April). Quantity of child care and problem behavior. In J. Belsky (Chair), *Early childcare and children's development prior to school entry.* Symposium conducted at the 2001 Biennial Meetings of the Society for Research in Child Development, Minneapolis, MN.

Bem, S. L. (1983). Gender schema theory and its implications for child development: Raising gender-aschematic children in a gender-schematic society. *Signs, 8,* 598–616.

Bem, S. L. (1989). Genital knowledge and gender constancy in preschool children. *Child Development, 60,* 649–662.

Bem, S. L. (1993). *The lenses of gender.* New Haven, CT: Yale University Press.

Benenson, J. F. (1990). Gender differences in social networks. *Journal of Early Adolescence, 10,* 472–495.

Bengtsson, H., & Johnson, L. (1992). Perspective taking, empathy, and prosocial behavior in late childhood. *Child Study Journal, 22,* 11–22.

Benoit, D., Madigan, S., Lecce, S., Shea, B., & Goldberg, S. (2001). Atypical maternal behavior toward feeding-disordered infants before and after intervention. *Infant Mental Health Journal, 22*(6), 611–626.

Berck, J. (2004, January 5). *Before baby talk: Signs and signals.* Available at http://www.nytimes.com

Berenbaum, S. A., & Hines, M. (1992). Early androgens are related to childhood sex-typed toy preferences. *Psychological Science, 3,* 203–206.

Berg, C. J., Chang, J., Callaghan, W. M., & Whitehead, S. J. (2003). Pregnancy-related mortality in the United States, 1991–1997. *Obstetrics and Gynecology, 101,* 289–296.

Berg, W. K., & Berg, K. M. (1987). Psychophysiological development in infancy: State, startle, and attention. In J. D. Osofsky (Ed.), *Handbook of infant development* (2nd ed.). New York: Wiley.

Bergeson, T. R., & Trehub, S. E. (1999). Mothers' singing to infants and preschool children. *Infant Behavior and Development, 22*(1), 51–64.

Berglund, E., Eriksson, M., & Johansson, I. (2001). Parental reports of spoken language skills in children with Down syndrome. *Journal of Speech, Language, and Hearing Research, 44*(1), 179–191.

Berko, J. (1958). The child's learning of English morphology. *Word, 14,* 150–177.

Berndt, T. J. (1992). Friendship and friends' influence in adolescence. *Current Directions in Psychological Science, 1,* 156–159.

Berndt, T. J., Miller, K. E., & Park, K. E. (1989). Adolescents' perceptions of friends and parents' influence on aspects of their school adjustment. *Journal of Early Adolescence, 9,* 419–435.

Berndt, T. J., & Perry, T. B. (1986). Children's perceptions of friendships as supportive relationships. *Developmental Psychology, 22,* 640–648.

Berndt, T. J., & Perry, T. B. (1990). Distinctive features and effects of early adolescent friendships. In R. Montemayor, G. R. Adams, & T. P. Gullotta (Eds.), *From childhood to adolescence: A transitional period?* Newbury Park, CA: Sage.

Berry, R. J., Li, Z., Erickson, J. D., Li, S., Moore, C. A., Wang, H., Mulinare, J., Zhao, P., Wong, L.-Y. C., Gindler, J., Hong, S.-X., & Correa, A. (1999). Prevention of neural-tube defects with folic acid in China. *New England Journal of Medicine, 341,* 1485–1490.

Bertenthal, B. I., & Campos, J. J. (1990). A systems approach to the organizing effects of self-produced locomotion during infancy. In C. Rovee-Collier & L. Lipsitt (Eds.), *Advances in infancy research,* v. 6. Norwood, NJ: Ablex.

Berzonsky, M. C., Kuk, L. S., & Storer, C. J. (1993, March). Identity development, autonomy, and personal effectiveness. Paper presented at the meeting of the Society for Research in Child Development, New Orleans, LA.

Berzonsky, M. D. (2004). Identity style, parental authority, and identity commitment. *Journal of Youth and Adolescence, 33*(3), 213–220.

Bhutta, A. T., Cleves, M. A., Casey, P. H.,

Cradock, M. M., & Anand, K. J. S. (2002). Cognitive and behavioral outcomes of school-aged children who were born preterm: A meta-analysis. *Journal of the American Medical Association, 288,* 728–737.

Bialystock, E. (1999). Cognitive complexity and attentional control in the bilingual mind. *Child Development, 70*(3), 636–644.

Bialystok, E. (2001). *Bilingualism in development: Language, literacy, and cognition.* New York: Cambridge University Press.

Bialystok, E. (2005). Consequences of bilingualism for cognitive development. In J. Kroll & A. M. B. de Groot (Eds.), *Handbook of bilingualism: Psycholinguistic approaches* (pp. 417–432). New York: Oxford University Press.

Bialystok, E., & Herman, J. (1999). Does bilingualism matter for early literacy? *Bilingualism: Language and Cognition, 2*(1), 35–44.

Bialystok, E., McBride-Chang, C., & Luk, G. (2005). Bilingualism, language proficiency, and learning to read in two writing systems. *Journal of Educational Psychology, 97*(4), 580–590.

Bialystok, E., & Senman, L. (2004). Executive processes in appearance-reality tasks: The role of inhibition of attention and symbolic representation. *Child Development, 75*(2), 562–579.

Bigelow, B. J. (2001). Relational scaffolding of school motivation: Developmental continuities in students' and parents' ratings of the importance of school goals. *Journal of Genetic Psychology, 162*(1), 75–92.

Bilsker, D., Schiedel, D., & Marcia, J. E. (1988). Sex differences in identity status. *Sex Roles, 18,* 231–236.

Birch, L. L., Gunder, L., Grimm-Thomas, K., & Laing, D. G. (1998). Infants' consumption of a new food enhances acceptance of similar foods. *Appetite, 30*(3), 283–295.

Bjarnason, D. (2006). Canada's shame. The National, May 24, 2006. Available at http://www.cbc.ca/news/background/education/canada-shame.html

Bjorklund, D. F., & Bjorklund, B. R. (1989, June). Physically fit families. *Parents' Magazine,* p. 215.

Bjorklund, D. F., & Rosenblum, K. E. (2001). Children's use of multiple and variable addition strategies in a game context. *Developmental Science, 4*(2), 184–194.

Black, M. M., Dubowitz, H., & Starr, R. H., Jr. (1999). African American fathers in low-income, urban families: Development, behavior, and home environments of their 3-year-old children. *Child Development, 70,* 967–978.

Blake, S. M., Ledsky, R., Goodenow, C., Sawyer, R., Lohrmann, D., & Windsor, R. (2003). Condom availability programs in Massachusetts high schools: Relationships with condom use and sexual behavior. *American Journal of Public Health, 93,* 955–962.

Blanchette, N., Smith, M. L., Fernandes-Penney, A., King, S., & Read, S. (2001). Cognitive and motor development in children with vertically transmitted HIV infection. *Brain and Cognition, 46*(1–2), 50–53.

Blass, E. M., & Smith, B. A. (1992). Differential effects of sucrose, fructose, glucose, and lactose on crying in 1- to 3-day-old human infants: Qualitative and quantitative considerations. *Developmental Psychology, 28,* 804–810.

Blevins-Knabe, B. (1987). Development of the ability to insert into a series. *Journal of Genetic Psychology, 148,* 427–441.

Bloom, L. (1998). Language acquisition in its developmental context. In W. Damon (Ed.), *Handbook of child psychology,* v. 2 (5th ed.). New York: Wiley.

Bloom, P. (2002). Mind reading, communication, and the learning of names for things. *Mind and Language, 17*(1–2), 37–54.

Boccia, M., & Campos, J. J. (1989). Maternal emotional signals, social referencing, and infants' reactions to strangers. In N. Eisenberg (Ed.), *New directions for child development, No. 44, Empathy and related emotional responses.* San Francisco: Jossey-Bass.

Boddy, J., Skuse, D., & Andrews, B. (2000). The developmental sequelae of nonorganic failure to thrive. *Journal of Child Psychology and Psychiatry and Allied Disciplines, 41*(8), 1003–1014.

Boehnke, K., Silbreisen, R. K., Eisenberg, N., Reykowski, J., & Palmonari, A. (1989). The development of prosocial motivation: A cross-national study. *Journal of Cross-Cultural Psychology, 20,* 219–243.

Boekeloo, B. O., & Howard, D. E. (2002). Oral sexual experience among young adolescents receiving general health examination. *American Journal of Health Behavior, 26,* 306–314.

Boey, C. C. M., Omar, A., & Phillips, J. A. (2003). Correlation among academic performance, recurrent abdominal pain and other factors in year-6 urban primary-school children in Malaysia. *Journal of Paediatrics and Child Health, 39*(5), 352–357.

Boggiano, A. K., & Barrett, M. (1991). Strategies to motivate helpless and mastery-oriented children: The effect of gender-based expectancies. *Sex Roles, 25,* 487–510.

Bohannon, J. N., III, & Stanowicz, L. (1988). The issue of negative evidence: Adult responses to children's language errors. *Developmental Psychology, 24,* 684–689.

Bohn, A. P. (2003). Familiar voices: Using Ebonics communication techniques in the primary classroom. *Urban Education, 38*(6), 688–707.

Boland, M. (2005). Exclusive breastfeeding should continue to six months. *Paediatrics & Child Health, 10*(3), 148.

Bonelli, R. M., et al. (2003). Ziprasidone in Huntington's disease: The first case reports. *Journal of Psychopharmacology, 17*(4), 459–460.

Bonelli, R. M., & Kapfhammer, H. (2003). Why minocycline is helpful in Huntington's disease. *Journal of Psychopharmacology, 17*(4), 461.

Boom, J., Brugman, D., & van der Heijden, P. G. M. (2001). Hierarchical structure of moral stages assessed by a sorting task. *Child Development, 72*(2), 535–548.

Booth, A., Johnson, D. R., Granger, D. A., Crouter, A. C., & McHale, S. (2003). Testosterone and child and adolescent adjustment: The moderating role of parent-child relationships. *Developmental Psychology, 39*(1), 85–98.

Booth, C. L., Kelly, J. F., Spieker, S. J., & Zuckerman, T. G. (2003). Toddlers' attachment security to child-care providers: The Safe and Secure Scale. *Early Education and Development, 14*(1), 83–100.

Booth, J. R., & Burman, D. D. (2001). Development and disorders of neurocognitive systems for oral language and reading. *Learning Disability Quarterly, 24*(3), 205–215.

Borden, M. C., & Ollendick, T. H. (1992). The development and differentiation of social subtypes in autism. In B. B. Lahey & A. E. Kazdin (Eds.), *Advances in clinical child psychology,* v. 14. New York: Plenum.

Bordova, E., & Leong, D. J. (2007). *Tools of the mind: The Vygotskian approach to early childhood education.* Upper Saddle River, NJ: Pearson.

Bornstein, M. H. (1992). Perceptual development in infancy, childhood, and old age. In M. H. Bornstein & M. E. Lamb (Eds.), *Developmental psychology: An advanced textbook* (3rd ed.). Hillsdale, NJ: Erlbaum.

Bornstein, M. H., et al. (1992a). Functional analysis of the contents of maternal speech to infants of 5 and 13 months in four cultures: Argentina, France, Japan, and the United States. *Developmental Psychology, 28,* 593–603.

Bornstein, M. H., et al. (1992b). Maternal responsiveness to infants in three societies: The United States, France, and Japan. *Child Development, 63,* 808–821.

Bornstein, M. H., Tamis-LeMonda, C. S., Tal, J., Ludemann, P., et al. (1992b). Maternal responsiveness to infants in three societies: The United States, France, and Japan. *Child Development, 63,* 808–821.

Bornstein, M. H., & Lamb, M. E. (1992a). *Development in infancy: An introduction* (3rd ed.). New York: McGraw-Hill.

Bornstein, M. H., et al. (1992b). Maternal responsiveness to infants in three societies: The United States, France, and Japan. *Child Development, 63,* 808–821.

Bornstein, M. H., & Tamis-LeMonda, C. S. (1989). Maternal responsiveness and cognitive development in children. In M. H. Bornstein (Ed.), *New directions for child development, No. 43, Maternal responsiveness: Characteristics and consequences.* San Francisco: Jossey-Bass.

Boskind-White, M., & White, W. C. (1983). *Bulimarexia: The binge/purge cycle.* New York: Norton.

Boston Women's Health Book Collective (1992). *The new our bodies, ourselves.* New York: Simon & Schuster.

Bouchard, C., et al. (1990). The response to long-term overfeeding in identical twins. *New England Journal of Medicine, 322,* 1477–1482.

Bouchard, T. J., Jr., & Loehlin, J. C. (2001). Genes, evolution, and personality. *Behavior Genetics, 31*(3), 243–273.

Bouchard, T. J., Jr., Lykken, D. T., McGue, M., Segal, N. L., & Tellegen, A. (1990). Sources of human psychological differences: The Minnesota study of twins reared apart. *Science, 250,* 223–228.

Bouldin, P., & Pratt, C. (1999). Characteristics of preschool and school-age children with imaginary companions. *Journal of Genetic Psychology, 160*(4), 397–410.

Bouma, A. (2001). Hersenkronkels in neuropsychologisch perspectief. *Psycholoog, 36*(2), 50–55.

Bower, T. G. R. (1974). *Development in infancy.* San Francisco: W. H. Freeman.

Bowlby, J. (1969). Disruption of affectional bonds and its effects on behavior. *Canada's Mental Health Supplement, 59,* 12.

Bowlby, J. (1988). *A secure base.* New York: Basic Books.

Bowlby, G. (2005). Provincial drop-out rates: Trends and consequences. *Education Matters: Insights on Education, Learning and Training in Canada, 2*(4). Available at http://www.statcan.ca/english/freepub/81–004-XIE/2005004/drop.htm

Boyce, W. (2004). Young people in Canada: Their health and well-being. Ottawa, ON: Health Canada.

Boyce, W., Doherty, M., Fortin, C., & MacKinnon, D. (2003). Canadian youth, sexual health and HIV/AIDS study: Factors influencing knowledge, attitudes and behaviours. Toronto: Council of Ministers of Education, Canada.

Boysson-Bardies, B. de, & Halle, P. A. (1994). Speech development: Contributions of cross-linguistic studies. In A. Vyt et al. (Eds.), *Early child development in the French tradition: Contributions from current research.* Hillsdale, NJ: Lawrence Erlbaum Associates.

Brackbill, Y., McManus, K., & Woodward, L. (1985). *Medication in maternity: Infant exposure and maternal information.* Ann Arbor: University of Michigan Press.

Bradley, R. H. (1989). HOME measurement of maternal responsiveness. In M. H. Bornstein (Ed.), *New directions for child development, No. 43, Maternal responsiveness: Characteristics and consequences.* San Francisco: Jossey-Bass.

Bradley, R. H., Burchinal, M. R., & Casey, P. H. (2001). Early intervention: The moderating role of the home environment. *Applied Developmental Science, 5*(1), 2–8.

Bradley, R. H., et al. (1989). Home environment and cognitive development in the first 3 years of life: A collaborative study involving six sites and three ethnic groups in North America. *Developmental Psychology, 25,* 217–235.

Brady, M. P., Swank, P. R., Taylor, R. D., & Freiberg, H. J. (1988). Teacher-student interactions in middle school mainstreamed classes: Differences with special and regular students. *Journal of Educational Research, 81,* 332–340.

Brandstätter, H., & Farthofer, A. (2003). Influence of part-time work on university students' academic performance. *Zeitschrift für Arbeits- und Organisationspsychologie, 47*(3), 134–145.

Bray, N. W., Hersh, R. E., & Turner, L. A. (1985). Selective remembering during adolescence. *Developmental Psychology, 21,* 290–294.

Bray, N. W., Huffman, L. F., & Fletcher, K. L. (1999). Developmental and intellectual differences in self-report and strategy use. *Developmental Psychology, 35*(5), 1223–1236.

Braza, F., et al. (2000). Efecto de los hermanos en la flexibilidad de comportamiento de ninos preescolares. *Revista Mexicana de Psicologia, 17*(2), 181–190.

Brazelton, T. B. (1990a). Forward: Observations of the neonate. In C. Rovee-Collier & L. P. Lipsitt (Eds.), *Advances in infancy research,* v. 6. Norwood, NJ: Ablex.

Brazelton, T. B. (1990b). Saving the bathwater. *Child Development, 61,* 1661–1671.

Brazelton, T. B., Nugent, J. K., & Lester, B. M. (1987). Neonatal behavior assessment scale. In J. D. Osofsky (Ed.), *Handbook of infant development* (2nd ed.). New York: Wiley.

Bremner, A., & Bryant, P. (2001). The effect of spatial cues on infants' responses in the AB task, with and without a hidden object. *Developmental Science, 4*(4), 408–415.

Bremner, J. D. (2003). Long-term effects of childhood abuse on brain and neurobiology. *Child and Adolescent Psychiatric Clinics of North America, 12*(2), 271–292.

Bremner, J. D., et al. (2003). Cortisol response to a cognitive stress challenge in posttraumatic stress disorder (PTSD) related to childhood abuse. *Psychoneuroendocrinology, 28*(6), 733–750.

Bretherton, I., Golby, B., & Halvorsen, C. (1993, March). Fathers as attachment and caregiving figures. Paper presented at the meeting of the Society for Research in Child Development, New Orleans, LA.

Bretherton, I., Stolberg, U., & Kreye, M. (1981). Engaging strangers in proximal interaction: Infants' social initiative. *Developmental Psychology, 17,* 746–755.

Bridges, K. (1932). Emotional development in early infancy. *Child Development, 3,* 324–341.

Briggs-Gowan, M. J., Carter, A. S., Skuban, E. M., & Horwitz, S. M. (2001). Prevalence of social-emotional and behavioral problems in a community sample of 1- and 2-year-old children. *Journal of the American Academy of Child and Adolescent Psychiatry, 40,* 811–819.

"British study finds leukemia risk in children of A-plant workers" (1990, February 18). *New York Times,* p. A27.

Brody, J. E. (1990a, May 24). Preventing children from joining yet another unfit generation. *New York Times,* p. B14.

Brody, J. E. (1990b, May 31). Children in sports: Tailoring activities to their abilities and needs will avoid pitfalls. *New York Times,* p. B8.

Brody, J. E. (1991, September 4). Averting a crisis when the offspring show symptoms of school phobia. *New York Times,* p. B7.

Brody, J. E. (1998, February 10). Genetic ties may be factor in violence in stepfamilies. *New York Times,* pp. F1, F4.

Brody, L. R., Zelazo, P. R., & Chaika, H. (1984). Habituation-dishabituation to speech in the neonate. *Developmental Psychology, 20,* 114–119.

Brodzinsky, D. M., Patterson, C. J., & Vaziri, M. (2002). Adoption agency perspectives on lesbian and gay prospective parents: A national study. *Adoption Quarterly, 5*(3), 5–23.

Bronfenbrenner, U. (1973). The dream of the kibbutz. In *Readings in human development.* Guilford, CT: Dushkin.

Bronfenbrenner, U. (1977). Toward an experimental ecology of human development. *American Psychologist, 32,* 513–531.

Bronfenbrenner, U. (1979). *The ecology of human development: Experiments by nature and design.* Cambridge, MA: Harvard University Press.

Bronfenbrenner, U. (1989). Ecological systems theory. In R. Vasta (Ed.), *Annals of child development,* v. 6. Greenwich, CT: JAI Press.

Bronfenbrenner, U. (2002). Preparing a world for the infant in the twenty-first century: The research challenge. In J. Gomes-Pedro, J. K. Nugent, et al. (Eds.), *The infant and family in the twenty-first century* (pp. 45–52). New York: Brunner-Routledge.

Bronfenbrenner, U., & Evans, G. W. (2000). Developmental science in the 21st century: Emerging questions, theoretical models, research designs and empirical findings. *Social Development, 9*(1), 115–125.

Bronson, G. W. (1990). Changes in infants' visual scanning across the 2- to 14-week age period. *Journal of Experimental Child Psychology, 49,* 101–125.

Bronson, G. W. (1991). Infant differences in rate of visual encoding. *Child Development, 62,* 44–54.

Bronson, G. W. (1997). The growth of visual capacity: Evidence from infant scanning patterns. *Advances in Infancy Research, 11,* 109–141.

Bronson, M. B. (2000). *Self-regulation in early childhood: Nature and nurture.* New York: Guilford.

Brook, J. S., Zheng, L., Whiteman, M., & Brook, D. W. (2001). Aggression in toddlers: Associations with parenting and marital relations. *Journal of Genetic Psychology, 162*(2), 228–241.

Brown, A. M. (1990). Development of visual sensitivity to light and color vision in human infants: A critical review. *Vision Research, 30,* 1159–1188.

Brown, B. B., Mounts, N., Lamborn, S. D., & Steinberg, L. (1993). Parenting practices and peer group affiliation in adolescence. *Child Development, 64,* 467–482.

Brown, R. (1973). *A first language: The early stages.* Cambridge, MA: Harvard University Press.

Brown, R. (1977). Introduction. In C. A. Snow & C. Ferguson (Eds.), *Talking to children.* New York: Cambridge University Press.

Browne, C. A., Colditz, P. B., & Dunster, K. R. (2000). Infant autonomic function is altered by maternal smoking during pregnancy. *Early Human Development, 59*(3), 209–218.

Brownell, C. A. (1988). Combinatorial skills: Converging developments over the second year. *Child Development, 59,* 675–685.

Brownell, C. A. (1990). Peer social skills in toddlers: Competencies and constraints illustrated by same-age and mixed-age interaction. *Child Development, 61,* 838–848.

Brownell, C. A., & Carriger, M. S. (1990). Changes in cooperation and self-other differentiation during the second year. *Child Development, 61,* 1164–1174.

Brownell, K. D., & Horgen, K. B. (2003). *Food fight: The inside story of America's obesity crisis—and what we can do about it.* New York: McGraw-Hill.

Browning, J. R., Hatfield, E., Kessler, D., & Levine, T. (2000). Sexual motives, gender, and sexual behavior. *Archives of Sexual Behavior, 29*(2), 135–153.

Bruandet, M., Molko, N., Cohen, L., & Dehaene, S. (2004). A cognitive characterization of dyscalculia in Turner syndrome. *Neuropsychologia, 42*(3), 288–298.

Bruck, M., & Ceci, S. J. (1999). The suggestibility of children's memory. *Annual Review of Psychology, 50,* 419–439.

Bruck, M., Ceci, S. J., & Hembrooke, H. (2002). The nature of children's true and false narratives. *Developmental Review, 22*(3), 520–554.

Bruck M., & Genesee, F. (1995). Phonological awareness in young second language learners. *Journal of Child Language, 22,* 307–324.

Brunswick, A. F. (1999). Structural strain: An ecological paradigm for studying African American drug use. *Drugs and Society, 14*(1–2), 5–19.

Brustad, R. J. (1991). Children's perspectives on exercise and physical activity: Measurement issues and concerns. *Journal of School Health, 61,* 228–230.

Bryant, A. L., Schulenberg, J. E., O'Malley, P. M., Bachman, J. G., & Johnston, L. D. (2003). How academic achievement, attitudes, and behaviors relate to the course of substance use during adolescence: A 6-year, multiwave national longitudinal study. *Journal of Research on Adolescence, 13*(3), 361–397.

Buck, K. J., et al. (2004). Serotonin 5-HT-sub-2 receptors and alcohol: Reward, withdrawal and discrimination. *Alcoholism: Clinical and Experimental Research, 28*(2), 211–216.

Bugental, D. B., & Happaney, K. (2004). Predicting infant maltreatment in low-income families: The interactive effects of maternal attributions and child status at birth. *Developmental Psychology, 40*(2), 234–243.

Bukowski, W. M. (2003). Peer relationships. In M. H. Bornstein, L. Davidson, C. L. M. Keyes, & K. A. Moore (Eds), *Well-being: Positive development across the life course* (pp. 221–233). Mahwah, NJ: Lawrence Erlbaum Associates.

Bukowski, W. M., Gauze, C., Hoza, B., & Newcomb, A. F. (1993a). Differences and consistency between same-sex and other-sex peer relationships during early adolescence. *Developmental Psychology, 29,* 255–263.

Bukowski, W. M., Hoza, B., & Boivin, M. (1993b). Popularity, friendship, and emotional adjustment during early adolescence. In B. Laursen (Ed.), *New directions in child development, No. 60, Close friendships in adolescence.* San Francisco: Jossey-Bass.

Bullock, M., & Lutkenhaus, P. (1990). Who am I? Self-understanding in toddlers. *Merrill-Palmer Quarterly, 36,* 217–238.

Bunting, L., & McAuley, C. (2004). Teenage pregnancy and motherhood: The contribution of support. *Child and Family Social Work, 9*(2), 207–215.

Burke, J. M., & Baker, R. C. (2001). Is fluvoxamine safe and effective for treating anxiety disorders in children? *Journal of Family Practice, 50*(8), 719.

Burke, V., Beilin, L. J., & Dunbar, D. (2001). Family lifestyle and parental body mass index as predictors of body mass index in Australian children: A longitudinal study. *International Journal of Obesity and Related Metabolic Disorders, 25*(2), 147–157.

Bushman, B. J. (1998). Priming effects of media violence on the accessibility of aggressive constructs in memory. *Personality and Social Psychology Bulletin, 24*(5), 537–545.

Bushnell, E. W. (1993, June). A dual-processing approach to cross-modal matching: Implications for development. Paper presented at the Society for Research in Child Development, New Orleans, LA.

Bushnell, I. W. R. (2001). Mother's face recognition in newborn infants: Learning and memory. *Infant and Child Development, 10*(1–2), 67–74.

Buss, D. M. (1999). Adaptive individual differences revisited. *Journal of Personality, 67*(2), 259–264.

Buss, D. M. (2000). The evolution of happiness. American Psychologist, 55, 15–23.

Buss, D. M., & Schmitt, D. P. (1993). Sexual strategies theory: An evolutionary perspective on human mating. *Psychological Review, 100,* 204–232.

Bussey, K., & Bandura, A. (1984). Influence of gender constancy and social power on sex-linked modeling. *Journal of Personality and Social Psychology, 47,* 1292–1302.

Bussey, K., & Bandura, A. (1999). Social cognitive theory of gender development and differentiation. *Psychological Review, 106*(4), 676–713.

Butterfield, F. (1992, January 1). Studies find a family link to criminality. *New York Times,* pp. A1, A8.

Butterfield, S. A., & Loovis, E. M. (1993). Influence of age, sex, balance, and sport participation on development of throwing by children in grades K-8. *Perceptual and Motor Skills, 76,* 459–464.

Butterworth, G. (1990). Self-perception in infancy. In D. Cicchetti & M. Beeghly (Eds.), *The self in transition.* Chicago: University of Chicago Press.

Butterworth, G., Verweij, E., & Hopkins, B.

(1997). The development of prehension in infants: Halverson revisited. *British Journal of Developmental Psychology, 15*(2), 223–236.

Byrd, V. (2001, April 23). Passages. *People,* p. 87.

Cabeza, R., Locantore, J. K., & Anderson, N. D. (2003). Lateralization of prefrontal activity during episodic memory retrieval: Evidence for the production-monitoring hypothesis. *Journal of Cognitive Neuroscience, 15*(2), 249–259.

Cabrera, N. J., Tamis-LeMonda, C. S., Bradley, R. H., Hofferth, S., & Lamb, M. E. (2000). Fatherhood in the twenty-first century. *Child Development, 71,* 127–136.

Cairns, R. B., & Cairns, B. D. (1991). Social cognition and social networks: A developmental perspective. In D. J. Pepler & K. H. Rubin (Eds.), *The development and treatment of childhood aggression.* Hillsdale, NJ: Erlbaum.

Call, J. (2001). Object permanence in orangutans (Pongo pygmaeus), chimpanzees (Pan troglodytes), and children (Homo sapiens). *Journal of Comparative Psychology, 115*(2), 159–171.

Calvert, S. L., & Kotler, J. A. (2003). Lessons from children's television: The impact of the Children's Television Act on children's learning. *Journal of Applied Developmental Psychology, 24*(3), 275–335.

Calzada, E. J., Eyberg, S. M., Rich, B., & Querido, J. G. (2004). Parenting disruptive preschoolers: Experiences of mothers and fathers. *Journal of Abnormal Child Psychology, 32,* 203–213.

Camarena, P. M. (1991). Conformity in adolescence. In R. M. Lerner, A. C. Petersen, & J. Brooks-Gunn (Eds.), *Encyclopedia of adolescence.* New York: Garland.

Campbell, A., Muncer, S., & Bibel, D. (2001). Women and crime: An evolutionary approach. *Aggression and Violent Behavior, 6*(5), 481–497.

Campbell, A., Shirley, L., & Candy, J. (2004). A longitudinal study of gender-related cognition and behaviour. *Developmental Science, 7*(1), 1–9.

Campbell, A., Shirley, L., & Caygill, L. (2002). Sex-typed preferences in three domains: Do two-year-olds need cognitive variables? *British Journal of Psychology, 93*(2), 203–217.

Campbell, D. W., & Eaton, W. O. (1999). Sex differences in the activity level of infants. *Infant and Child Development, 8*(1), 1–17.

Campbell, D. W., Eaton, W. O., & McKeen, N. A. (2002). Motor activity level and behavioural control in young children. *International Journal of Behavioral Development, 26*(4), 289–296.

Campbell, J. O., Bliven, T. D., Silver, M. M., Snyder, K. J., & Spear, L. P. (2000). Effects of prenatal cocaine on behavioral adaptation to chronic stress in adult rats. *Neurotoxicology and Teratology, 22*(6), 845–850.

Campbell, S. B. (1990). *Behavior problems in preschool children: Clinical and developmental issues.* New York: Guilford.

Campbell, S. B., Pierce, E. W., March, C. L., & Ewing, L. J. (1991). Noncompliant behavior, overactivity, and family stress as predictors of negative maternal control with preschool children. *Development and Psychopathology, 3,* 175–190.

Campos, J. J., Hiatt, S., Ramsey, D., Henderson, C., & Svejda, M. (1978). The emergence of fear on the visual cliff. In M. Lewis & L. Rosenblum (Eds.), *The origins of affect.* New York: Plenum.

Campos, J. J., Langer, A., & Krowitz, A. (1970). Cardiac responses on the visual cliff in prelocomotor human infants. *Science, 170,* 196–197.

Camras, L. A., Campos, J. J., Oster, H., Miyake, K., & Bradshaw, D. (1992). Japanese and American infants' responses to arm restraint. *Developmental Psychology, 28,* 578–583.

Camras, L. A., Sullivan, J., & Michel, G. (1993, Fall). Do infants express discrete emotions? Adult judgments of facial, vocal, and body actions. *Journal of Nonverbal Behavior, 17,* 171–186.

Canadian Council on Learning (2007). French-immersion education in Canada. Available at http://www.ccl-cca.ca/CCL/Reports/LessonsInLearning

Canadian Cystic Fibrosis Association (2007). About cystic fibrosis. Available at http://www.cysticfibrosis.ca/page.asp?id=1

Canadian Dental Association (2005). Dental care for children. Available at http://www.cda-adc.ca/en/oral_health/cfyt/dental_care_children/index.asp

Canadian Down Syndrome Society (2007). Characteristics and health concerns for people with Down syndrome. Available at http://www.cdss.ca/site/resources/down_syndrome/characteristics_and_health_concerns.php

Canadian Institute for Health Information (2007). *Giving birth in Canada: Region trends from 2001–2002 to 2005–2006.* Toronto, ON: Author.

Canadian Lung Association (2006). Available at www.lung.ca

Canadian Mental Health Association (2006). Post partum depression. Available at http://www.cmha.ca/bins/content_page.asp?cid=3-86-87-88&lang=1

Canadian Paediatric Society (2004). Canadian paediatric surveillance program: 2004 results. Available at http://www.cps.ca/english/cpsp/About/2004Results.pdf

Canadian Paediatric Society (2005). Bedwetting. Available at http://www.caringforkids.cps.ca/behaviour/Bedwetting.htm

Canadian Paediatric Society (2007a). *Are we doing enough? A status report on Canadian public policy and child and youth health* (p. 7). Ottawa, ON.

Canadian Paediatric Society (2007b). Impact of media use on children and youth. Available at http://www.cps.ca/English/statements/PP/pp03-01.htm

Canadian Paediatric Society, Dietitians of Canada, & Health Canada (1998). *Nutrition for health term infants.* Ottawa: Minister of Public Works and Government Services.

Canadian Psychological Association (2000).

Canadian code of ethics for psychologists (3rd ed.) Ottawa: Author.

Cannistra, S. A., & Niloff, J. M. (1996). Cancer of the uterine cervix. *New England Journal of Medicine, 334,* 1030–1038

Cannon, G. S., Idol, L., & West, J. F. (1992). Educating students with mild handicaps in general classrooms: Essential teaching practices for general and special educators. *Journal of Learning Disabilities, 25,* 300–317.

Cannon, T. D., et al. (2002). Fetal hypoxia and structural brain abnormalities in schizophrenic patients, their siblings, and controls. *Archives of General Psychiatry, 59*(1), 35–41.

Capirci, O., Iverson, J. M., Pizzuto, E., & Volterra, V. (1996). Gestures and words during the transition to two-word speech. *Journal of Child Language, 23*(3), 645–673.

Caplan, M., Vespo, J., Pedersen, J., & Hale, D. F. (1991). Conflict and its resolution in small groups of one and two-year-olds. *Child Development, 62,* 1513–1524.

Caplan, P. J., & Larkin, J. (1991). The anatomy of dominance and self-protection. *American Psychologist, 46,* 536.

Capone, G. T. (2001). Down syndrome: Advances in molecular biology and the neurosciences. *Journal of Developmental and Behavioral Pediatrics, 22*(1), 40–59.

Caputo, R. K. (2003). Head Start, other preschool programs, and life success in a youth cohort. *Journal of Sociology and Social Welfare, 30*(2), 105–126.

Caravolas, M., & Bruck, M. (2000). Vowel categorization skill and its relationship to early literacy skills among first-grade Quebec-French children. *Journal of Experimental Child Psychology, 76*(3), 190–221.

Carey, G., & DiLalla, D. L. (1994). Personality and psychopathology: Genetic perspectives. *Journal of Abnormal Psychology, 103,* 32–43.

Carlo, G., Knight, G. P., Eisenberg, N., & Rotenberg, K. (1991). Cognitive processes and prosocial behaviors among children: The role of affective attributions and reconciliations. *Developmental Psychology, 27,* 456–461.

Caron, A. J., Caron, R. F., & Carlson, V. R. (1979). Infant perception of the invariant shape of objects varying in slant. *Child Development, 50,* 716–721.

Carpendale, J. I. M. (2000). Kohlberg and Piaget on stages and moral reasoning. *Developmental Review, 20*(2), 181–205.

Carr, M., Borkowski, J. G., & Maxwell, S. E. (1991). Motivational components of underachievement. *Developmental Psychology, 27,* 108–118.

Carroll, C. (2004, August 10). Starting young in treating high blood pressure. Available at http://www.nytimes.com

Carter, J. E., & Schuchman, E. H. (2001). Gene therapy for neurodegenerative diseases: Fact or fiction? *British Journal of Psychiatry, 178,* 392–394.

Casaer, P. (1993). Old and new facts about perinatal brain development. *Journal of Child Psychology and Psychiatry, 34,* 101–109.

Case, R. (1992). The mind's staircase. Hillsdale, NJ: Erlbaum.

Case, R. (1998). The development of central conceptual structures. In D. Kuhn & R. Siegler (Eds.), *Handbook of child psychology: Vol. 2. Cognition, perception and language* (5th ed.). New York: Wiley.

Cashwell, T. H., Skinner, C. H., & Smith, E. S. (2001). Increasing second-grade students' reports of peers' prosocial behaviors via direct instruction, group reinforcement, and progress feedback: A replication and extension. *Education and Treatment of Children, 24*(2), 161–175.

Cassaday, H. J., et al. (2003). Intraventricular 5,7-dihydroxytryptamine lesions disrupt acquisition of working memory task rules but not performance once learned. *Progress in Neuro-Psychopharmacology and Biological Psychiatry, 27*(1), 147–156.

Cassia, V. M., Simion, F., & Umilta, C. (2001). Face preference at birth: The role of an orienting mechanism. *Developmental Science, 4*(1), 101–108.

Cassidy, J. (1988). Child-mother attachment and the self in six-year-olds. *Child Development, 59,* 121–134.

Castillo, E. M., Quintana, S. M., Zamarripa, M. X. (2000). Cultural and linguistic issues. In E. S. Shapiro & T. R. Kratochwill (Eds.), *Conducting school-based assessments of child and adolescent behavior* (pp. 274–308). New York: Guilford Press.

Cataudella, J. (1999). When women came to Queen's. *Canadian Medical Association Journal, 161*(5), 575–576.

Cattell, R. B. (1949). *The culture-fair intelligence test.* Champaign, IL: Institute for Personality and Ability Testing.

Caughy, M. O., DiPietro, J. A., & Strobino, D. M. (1994). Day-care participation as a protective factor in the cognitive development of low-income children. *Child Development, 65*(2), 457–471.

Cauley, K., & Tyler, B. (1989). The relationship of self-concept to prosocial behavior in children. *Early Childhood Research Quarterly, 4,* 51–60.

Caulfield, R. (2000). Beneficial effects of tactile stimulation on early development. *Early Childhood Education Journal, 27*(4), 255–257.

Cavaliere, F. (1996). Bilingual schools face big political challenges. *APA Monitor, 27*(2), 36.

Cavallini, A., Fazzi, E., Viviani, V., Astori, M. G., Zaviero, S., Bianchi, P. E., & Lanzi, G. (2002). Visual acuity in the first two years of life in healthy term newborns: An experience with the Teller Acuity Cards. *Functional Neurology: New Trends in Adaptive and Behavioral Disorders, 17*(2), 87–92.

Cavell, T. A. (2001). Updating our approach to parent training. I. The case against targeting noncompliance. *Clinical Psychology: Science and Practice, 8*(3), 299–318.

CBC News (2006). Junk food in schools. Available at http://www.cbc.ca/news/background/food/junkfood_schools.html

CBC News (2007, April 23). Genetics and reproduction: Regulating "assisted human reproduction." Available at http://cbc.ca/

news/background/genetics_reproduction/ rgtech.html

Cebello, R., & Olson, S. L. (1993, March). The role of alternative caregivers in the lives of children from poor, single-parent families. Paper presented at the meeting of the Society for Research in Child Development, New Orleans, LA.

Ceci, S. J. (1993, August). Cognitive and social factors in children's testimony. Master lecture presented at the meeting of the American Psychological Association, Toronto.

Centers for Disease Control and Prevention (2000a). *Health, United States, 2000.* National Center for Health Statistics and National Immunization Program, National Immunization Survey. Atlanta, GA: Centers for Disease Control and Prevention.

Centers for Disease Control and Prevention (2000b, June 9). Youth risk behavior surveillance: United States, 1999. *Morbidity and Mortality Weekly Report, 49*(SS05), 1–96.

Centers for Disease Control and Prevention (2001a, December 3). *Sexually transmitted disease surveillance 2000.* Atlanta, GA: Division of STD Prevention, National Center for HIV, STD, and TB Prevention.

Centers for Disease Control and Prevention (2001b). 10 Things you need to know about immunizations. Available at http://www .cdc.gov/nip/publications/fs/gen/ shouldknow.htm

Centers for Disease Control and Prevention (2002a). *Laboratory guidelines screening tests to detect Chlamydia trachomatis and Neisseria gonorrhoeae infections.* Atlanta, GA: Division of Sexually Transmitted Diseases, National Center for HIV, STD, and TB Prevention. Available at http://www.cdc.gov/STD/ LabGuidelines/default.htm

Centers for Disease Control and Prevention (2002b). Cited in J. E. Brody (2002, January 1), What women must know about fertility, *New York Times,* F6.

Centers for Disease Control and Prevention (2003). *HIV/AIDS surveillance report: U.S. HIV and AIDS cases reported through December 2002, 14*(2). Atlanta, GA: Centers for Disease Control and Prevention.

Centers for Disease Control and Prevention (2004). DES update: Health care providers. Available at http://www.cdc.gov/des/hcp/ index.html

Central Intelligence Agency (2004, September 17). *The World Factbook.* Available at http://www.cia.gov/cia/publications/ factbook/geos/us.html#People

Centre for Addiction and Mental Health (2003). Methamphetamine. Available at http://www.camh.net/About_Addiction_ Mental_Health/Drug_and_Addiction_ Information/methamphetamine_dyk.html

Cernoch, J., & Porter, R. (1985). Recognition of maternal axillary odors by infants. *Child Development, 56,* 1593–1598.

Chalfant, J. C. (1989). Learning disabilities: Policy issues and promising approaches. *American Psychologist, 44,* 392–398.

Chalmers, B. & Wen, S. W. (2003). Women's

health surveillance report (pp. 59–60). Canadian Institute for Health Information, 2003. Available at http://www.phac-aspc .gc.ca/publicat/whsr-rssf/pdf/CPHI_ WomensHealth_e.pdf

Chamberlain, P., & Reid, J. B. (1998). Comparison of two community alternatives to incarceration for chronic juvenile offenders. *Journal of Consulting and Clinical Psychology, 66*(4), 624–633.

Chan, R. W., Raboy, B., & Patterson, C. J. (1998). Psychosocial adjustment among children conceived via donor insemination by lesbian and heterosexual mothers. *Child Development, 69*(2), 443–457.

Chance, S. E., Brown, R. T., Dabbs, J. M., Jr., & Casey, R. (2000). Testosterone, intelligence and behavior disorders in young boys. *Personality and Individual Differences, 28*(3) 437–445.

Chandler, M., & Lalonde, C. (1998). Cultural continuity as a hedge against suicide in Canada's First Nations, *Transcultural Psychiatry, 35*(2), 191–219.

Chang, L., Schwartz, D., Dodge, K., & McBride-Chang, C. (2003). Harsh parenting in relation to child emotion regulation and aggression. *Journal of Family Psychology, 17*(4), 598–606.

Chao, Q., Wang, P., & He, N. (2001). Comparative research on self-concept of middle school students from complete and divorced families. *Chinese Journal of Clinical Psychology, 9*(2), 143.

Chapman, J. K. (2000a). Developmental outcomes in two groups of infants and toddlers: Prenatally cocaine exposed and noncocaine exposed—Part 1. *Infant-Toddler Intervention, 10*(1), 19–36.

Chapman, J. K. (2000b). Developmental outcomes in two groups of young children: Prenatally cocaine exposed and noncocaine exposed—Part 2. *Infant-Toddler Intervention, 10*(2), 81–96.

Chapman, M., & McBride, M. C. (1992). Beyond competence and performance: Children's class inclusion strategies, superordinate class cues, and verbal justifications. *Developmental Psychology, 28,* 319–327.

Chapman, M., Skinner, E. A., & Baltes, P. B. (1990). Interpreting correlations between children's perceived control and cognitive performance: Control, agency, or means-ends beliefs? *Developmental Psychology, 26,* 246–253.

Chassin, L., Presson, C. C., Pitts, S. C., & Sherman, S. J. (2000). The natural history of cigarette smoking from adolescence to adulthood in a Midwestern community sample: Multiple trajectories and their psychological correlates. *Health Psychology, 19,* 223–231.

Chassin, L., Presson, C. C., Rose, J. S., & Sherman, S. J. (2001). From adolescence to adulthood: Age-related changes in beliefs about cigarette smoking in a Midwestern community sample. *Health Psychology, 20*(5), 377–386.

Chaudhry, V., et al. (2002). Thalidomide-

induced neuropathy. *Neurology, 59*(12), 1872–1875.

Chelonis, J. J., Gillam, M. P., & Paule, M. G. (2003). The effects of prenatal cocaine exposure on reversal learning using a simple visual discrimination task in rhesus monkeys. *Neurotoxicology and Teratology, 25*(4), 437–446.

Chen, X., Chen, H., & Kaspar, V. (2001). Group social functioning and individual socioemotional and school adjustment in Chinese children. *Merrill-Palmer Quarterly, 47*(2), 264–299.

Chen, X., et al. (2000). Maternal authoritative and authoritarian attitudes and mother-child interactions and relationships in urban China. International *Journal of Behavioral Development, 24*(1), 119–126.

Chess, S., & Thomas, A. (1984). *Origins and evolution of behavior disorders: From infancy to early adult life.* New York: Brunner/Mazel.

Chess, S., & Thomas, A. (1991). Temperament. In M. Lewis (Ed.), *Child and adolescent psychiatry: A comprehensive textbook.* Baltimore: Williams & Wilkins.

Cheung, C., Chan, W., Lee, T., Liu, S., & Leung, K. (2001). Structure of moral consciousness and moral intentions among youth in Hong Kong. *International Journal of Adolescence and Youth, 9*(2–3), 83–116.

Chez, M. G., et al. (2004). Frequency of EEG abnormalities in age-matched siblings of autistic children with abnormal sleep EEG patterns. *Epilepsy and Behavior, 5*(2), 159–162.

Chira, S. (1989, November 15). "Sesame Street" at 20: Taking stock of learning. *New York Times,* p. B13.

Chira, S. (1991, December 8). Report says too many aren't ready for school. *New York Times,* p. B18.

Chira, S. (1992a, February 12). Bias against girls is found rife in schools, with lasting damage. *New York Times,* pp. A1, B6.

Chira, S. (1992b, March 4). New Head Start studies raise question on help: Should fewer get more? *New York Times,* p. B9.

Chira, S. (1993, May 19). When disabled students enter regular classrooms. *New York Times,* pp. A1, B8.

Chisholm, J. S. (1983). *Navajo infancy.* New York: Aldine deGruyter.

Chomsky, N. (1988). *Language and problems of knowledge.* Cambridge, MA: MIT Press.

Chomsky, N. (1990). On the nature, use, and acquisition of language. In W. G. Lycan (Ed.), *Mind and cognition.* Oxford: Blackwell.

Christenson, S. L., & Thurlow, M. L. (2004). School dropouts: Prevention considerations, interventions, and challenges. *Current Directions in Psychological Science, 13*(1), 36–39.

Christian, P., et al. (2003). Effects of alternative maternal micronutrient supplements on low birth weight in rural Nepal: Double blind randomised community trial. *British Medical Journal, 326,* 571.

Christophersen, E. R., & Mortweet, S. L. (2003). Establishing bedtime. In E. R.

Christophersen & S. L. Mortweet (Eds.), *Parenting that works: Building skills that last a lifetime* (pp. 209–228). Washington, DC: American Psychological Association.

Chudley, A. E., Conry, J., Cook, J. L., Loock, C., Rosales, T., & Leblanc, N. (2005). Fetal alcohol spectrum disorder: Canadian guidelines for diagnosis. *Canadian Medical Association Journal, 172* (5 suppl), S1–S21.

Ciotti Gardenier, N., MacDonald, R., & Green, G. (2004). Comparison of direct observational methods for measuring stereo-typic behavior in children with autism spec-trum disorders. *Research in Developmental Disabilities, 25*(2), 99–118.

Clancy, B., & Finlay, B. (2001). Neural correlates of early language learning. In M. Tomasello & E. Bates (Eds.), *Language development: The essential readings.* Malden, MA: Blackwell.

Clark, E. V. (1973). What's in a word? On the child's acquisition of semantics in his first language. In E. Moore (Ed.), *Cognitive development and the acquisition of language.* New York: Academic Press.

Clark, E. V. (1975). Knowledge, context, and strategy in the acquisition of meaning. In D. P. Date (Ed.), *Georgetown University roundtable on language and linguistics.* Wash-ington, DC: Georgetown University Press.

Clark, K. E., & Ladd, G. W. (2000). Connect-edness and autonomy support in parent-child relationships: Links to children's socioemo-tional orientation and peer relationships. *Developmental Psychology, 36*(4), 485–498.

Clark, L. A., Kochanska, G., & Ready, R. (2000). Mothers' personality and its interac-tion with child temperament as predictors of parenting behavior. *Journal of Personality and Social Psychology, 79*(2), 274–285.

Clark, M. D. (2001). Influencing positive behavior change: Increasing the therapeutic approach of juvenile courts. *Federal Probation, 65*(1), 18–27.

Clark, R. (1983). *Family life and school achieve-ment: Why poor black children succeed or fail.* Chicago: University of Chicago Press.

Clarke-Stewart, K. A. (1991). A home is not a school: The effects of child care on chil-dren's development. *Journal of Social Issues, 47,* 105–123.

Clarke-Stewart, K. A. (1998). Reading with children. *Journal of Applied Developmental Psychology, 19*(1), 1–14.

Clarke-Stewart, K. A., & Beck, R. J. (1999). Maternal scaffolding and children's narrative retelling of a movie story. *Early Childhood Research Quarterly, 14*(3), 409–434.

Clarke-Stewart, K. A., Goossens, F. A., & All-husen, V. D. (2001). Measuring infant-mother attachment: Is the Strange Situation enough? *Social Development, 10*(2), 143–169.

Clarke-Stewart, K. A., Vandell, D. L., McCartney, K., Owen, M. T., & Booth, C. (2000). Effects of parental separation and divorce on very young children. *Journal of Family Psychology, 14*(2), 304–326.

Clément, R., Michaud, C., & Noels, K. A. (1998). Effets acculturatifs du support social en situation de contact intergroup. [Acculturative effects of social support in an intergroup contact situation]. *Revue Québécoise de Psychologie, 19,* 189–210.

Clingempeel, W. G., & Segal, S. (1986). Stepparent-stepchild relationships and the psychological adjustment of children in stepmother and stepfather families. *Child Development, 57,* 474–484.

Clopton, N. A., & Sorell, G. T. (1993). Gender differences in moral reasoning. *Psychology of Women Quarterly, 17,* 85–101.

Cnattingius, S., Bergstrom, R., Lipworth, L., & Kramer, M. S. (1998). Prepregnancy weight and the risk of adverse pregnancy outcomes. *New England Journal of Medicine, 338,* 147–152.

Cnattingius, S., et al. (2000). Caffeine intake and the risk of first-trimester spontaneous abortion. *New England Journal of Medicine, 343*(25), 1839–1845.

Cohen, E., & Feig, C. (2003, July 22). Delivery debate: Vaginal or C-section? More women are selecting surgery without a medical reason. Available at http://www.CNN.com

Colby, A., Kohlberg, L. G., J., & Lieberman, M. (1983). A longitudinal study of moral judg-ment. *Monographs of the Society for Research in Child Development, 48*(4, Serial No. 200).

Cole, C., et al. (2003). The educational impact of Rechov Sumsum/Shara'a Simsim: A Sesame Street television series to promote respect and understanding among children living in Israel, the West Bank, and Gaza. *International Journal of Behavioral Development, 27*(5), 409–422.

Cole, D. A. (1991). Change in self-perceived competence as a function of peer and teacher evaluation. *Developmental Psychology, 27,* 682–688.

Cole, D. A., Jacquez, F. M., & Maschman, T. L. (2001). Social origins of depressive cogni-tions: A longitudinal study of self-perceived competence in children. *Cognitive Therapy and Research, 25*(4), 377–395.

Cole, K. N., Mills, P. E., Dale, P. S., & Jenkins, J. R. (1991). Effects of preschool integration for children with disabilities. *Exceptional Children, 58,* 36–45.

Coleman, M., Ganong, L. H., & Fine, M. (2000). Reinvestigating remarriage: Another decade of progress. *Journal of Marriage and the Family, 62*(4), 1288–1307.

Coleman, M., Ganong, L. H., Killian, T., & McDaniel, A. K. (1999). Child support obligations: Attitudes and rationale. *Journal of Family Issues, 20*(1), 46–68.

Coleman, P. K. (2003). Perceptions of parent-child attachment, social self-efficacy, and peer relationships in middle childhood. *Infant and Child Development, 12*(4), 351–368.

Coley, J. D. (1993, March). Parental feedback to child labeling as input to conceptual development. Paper presented at the meeting of the Society for Research in Child Development, New Orleans, LA.

Coley, R. L. (2001). (In)visible men: Emerging research on low-income, unmarried, and minority fathers. *American Psychologist, 56*(9), 743–753.

Coley, R. L., & Chase-Lansdale, P. L. (1998). Adolescent pregnancy and parenthood: Recent evidence and future directions. *American Psychologist, 53*(2), 152–166.

Coley, R. L., & Chase-Lansdale, P. L. (1999). Stability and change in paternal involvement among urban African American fathers. *Journal of Family Psychology, 13,* 1–20.

Collaer, M. L., & Hines, M. (1995). Human behavioral sex differences: A role for gonadal hormones during early develop-ment? *Psychological Bulletin, 118,* 55–107.

Collaer, M. L., & Nelson, J. D. (2002). Large visuospatial sex difference in line judgment: Possible role of attentional factors. *Brain and Cognition, 49*(1), 1–12.

Collins, W. A. (1984). Conclusion: The status of basic research on middle childhood. In W. A. Collins (Ed.), *Development during middle childhood: The years from six to twelve.* Washington, DC: National Academy Press.

Collins, W. A., & Gunnar, M. R. (1990). Social and personality development. *Annual Review of Psychology, 41,* 387–416.

Collins, W. A., Maccoby, E. E., Steinberg, L., Hetherington, E. M., & Bornstein, M. H. (2000). Contemporary research on par-enting: The case for nature and nurture. *American Psychologist, 55*(2), 218–232.

Collins, W. A., Maccoby, E. E., Steinberg, L., Hetherington, E. M., & Bornstein, M. H. (2003). Contemporary research on par-enting: The case for nature and nurture. In M. E. Hertzig & E. A. Farber (Eds.), *Annual progress in child psychiatry and child development: 2000–2001* (pp. 125–153). New York: Brunner-Routledge.

Collins, W. A., & Russell, G. (1991). Mother-child and father-child relationships in middle childhood and adolescence: A developmental analysis. *Developmental Review, 11,* 99–136.

Colom, R., Flores-Mendoza, C., & Rebollo, I. (2003). Working memory and intelligence. *Personality and Individual Differences, 34*(1), 33–39.

Colombo, J. (1993). *Infant cognition.* Newbury Park, CA: Sage.

Colombo, J., Moss, M., & Horowitz, F. D. (1989). Neonatal state profiles: Reliability and short-term predictions of neurobehavioral status. *Child Development, 60,* 1102–1110.

Comstock, G., & Paik, H. (1991). *Television and the American child.* San Diego: Academic Press.

Concar, D. (2002, April 20). Ecstasy on the brain. Available at http://www.NewScientist.com

Conde-Agudelo, A., & Beliz·n, J. M. (2000). Maternal morbidity and mortality associ-ated with interpregnancy interval: Cross sectional study. *British Medical Journal, 321,* 1255–1259.

Conel, J. L. (1959). *The postnatal development of the human cerebral cortex.* Cambridge, MA: Harvard University Press.

Conference Board of Canada (2005). Decision time for Canada: Let's make poverty history. *2005 Report Card on Child Poverty in Canada.*

Connolly, J., Craig, W., Goldberg, A., & Pepler, D. (2004). Mixed-gender groups, dating, and romantic relationships in early adolescence. *Journal of Research on Adolescence, 14*(2), 185–207.

Connolly, J., Furman, W., & Konarski, R. (2000). The role of peers in the emergence of heterosexual romantic relationships in adolescence. *Child Development, 71*(5), 1395–1408

Connor, J. R. (2004). Myelin breakdown in Alzheimer's disease: A commentary. *Neurobiology of Aging, 25*(1), 45–47.

Constantino, J. N., et al. (2004). The factor structure of autistic traits. *Journal of Child Psychology and Psychiatry, 45*(4), 719–726.

Conway, A. R. A., Kane, M. J., & Engle, R. W. (2003). Working memory capacity and its relation to general intelligence. *Trends in Cognitive Sciences, 7*(12), 547–552.

Cooke, L., Wardle, J., & Gibson, E. L. (2003). Relationship between parental report of food neophobia and everyday food consumption in 2–6-year-old children. *Appetite, 41*(2), 205–206.

Coolidge, F. L., DenBoer, J. W., & Segal, D. L. (2004). Personality and neuropsychological correlates of bullying behavior. *Personality and Individual Differences, 36*(7), 1559–1569.

Coon, H., Fulker, D. W., & DeFries, J. C. (1990). Home environment and cognitive ability of 7-year-old children in the Colorado adoption project: Genetic and environmental etiologies. *Developmental Psychology, 26,* 459–468.

Coons, S., & Guilleminault, C. (1982). Development of sleep-wake patterns and non-rapid-eye-movement sleep stages during the first six months of life in normal infants. *Pediatrics, 69,* 793–798.

Cooper, J., Appleby, L., & Amos, T. (2002). Life events preceding suicide by young people. *Social Psychiatry and Psychiatric Epidemiology, 37*(6), 271–275.

Cooper, M., Galbraith, M., & Drinkwater, J. (2001). Assumptions and beliefs in adolescents with anorexia nervosa and their mothers. *Eating Disorders: The Journal of Treatment and Prevention, 9*(3), 217–223.

Cooper, P. J., et al. (1999). Postpartum depression and the mother-infant relationship in a South African peri-urban settlement. *British Journal of Psychiatry, 175,* 554–558.

Coovadia, H. (2004). Antiretroviral agents: How best to protect infants from HIV and save their mothers from AIDS. *New England Journal of Medicine, 351*(3), 289–292.

Coplan, R. J., Rubin, K. H., Fox, N. A., Calkins, S. D., & Stewart, S. L. (1994). Being alone, playing alone, and acting alone: Distinguishing among reticence, and passive-, and active-solitude in young children. *Child Development, 65,* 129–137.

Corballis, P. M., Funnell, M. G., & Gazzaniga, M. S. (2002). Hemispheric asymmetries for simple visual judgments in the split brain. *Neuropsychologia, 40*(4), 401–410.

Corcoran, J. (2000). Ecological factors associated with adolescent sexual activity. *Social Work in Health Care, 30*(4), 93–111.

Corcoran, J. (2001). Multi-systemic influences on the family functioning of teens attending pregnancy prevention programs. *Child and Adolescent Social Work Journal, 18*(1), 37–49.

Coren, S. (1992). *The left-hander syndrome.* New York: Free Press.

Correll, S. J. (2001). Gender and the career choice process: The role of biased self-assessments. *American Journal of Sociology, 106*(6), 1691–1730.

Cossette, L., Malcuit, G., & Pomerleau, A. (1991). Sex differences in motor activity during early infancy. *Infant Behavior and Development, 14,* 175–186.

Costin, S, E,, & Jones, D. C. (1992). Friendship as a facilitator of emotional responsiveness and prosocial interventions among young children. *Developmental Psychology, 28,* 941–947.

Costos, D., Ackerman, R., & Paradis, L. (2002). Recollections of menarche: Communication between mothers and daughters regarding menstruation. *Sex Roles, 46*(1–2), 49–59.

Courage, M. L., Howe, M. L., & Squires, S. E. (2004). Individual differences in 3.5-month-olds' visual attention: What do they predict at 1 year? *Infant Behavior and Development, 27*(1), 19–30.

Cowan, N., et al. (2003). Children's working-memory processes: A response-timing analysis. *Journal of Experimental Psychology: General, 132*(1), 113–132.

Cowan, N., Nugent, L. D., Elliott, E. M., Ponomarev, I., & Saults, J. S. (1999). The role of attention in the development of short-term memory: Age differences in the verbal span of apprehension. *Child Development, 70*(5), 1082–1097.

Cowan, N., Nugent, L. D., Elliott, E. M., & Saults, J. S. (2000). Persistence of memory for ignored lists of digits: Areas of developmental constancy and change. *Journal of Experimental Child Psychology, 76*(2), 151–172.

Cox, D. J., Borowitz, S., Kovatchev, B., & Ling, W. (1998). Contribution of behavior therapy and biofeedback to laxative therapy in the treatment of pediatric encopresis. *Annals of Behavioral Medicine, 20*(2), 70–76.

Crain, W. C. (2000). *Theories of development: Concepts and applications* (4th ed.). Englewood Cliffs, NJ: Prentice Hall.

Cratty, B. (1986). *Perceptual and motor development in infants and children* (3rd ed.). Englewood Cliffs, NJ: Prentice Hall.

Crews, D. (1994). Animal sexuality. *Scientific American, 270*(1), 108–114.

Crittenden, P. M., & Ainsworth, M. D. S. (1989). Child maltreatment and attachment theory. In D. Cicchetti & V. Carlson (Eds.), *Child maltreatment: Theory and research on the causes and consequences of child abuse and neglect.* Cambridge: Cambridge University Press.

Crockett, L. J., & Silbereisen, R. K. (Eds.) (2000). *Negotiating adolescence in times of social change.* Cambridge: Cambridge University Press.

Crombie, G., & Desjardins, M. J. (1993, March). Predictors of gender: The relative importance of children's play, games, and personality characteristics. Paper presented at the meeting of the Society for Research in Child Development, New Orleans, LA.

Crook, C. K., & Lipsitt, L. P. (1976). Neonatal nutritive sucking: Effects of taste stimulation upon sucking rhythm and heart rate. *Child Development, 47,* 518–522.

Crossette, B. (2000, August 29). Researchers raise fresh issues in breast-feeding debate. Available at http://www.nytimes.com

Crowe, H. P., & Zeskind, P. S. (1992). Psychophysiological and perceptual response to infant cries varying in pitch: Comparison of adults with low and high scores on the child abuse potential inventory. *Child Abuse and Neglect, 16,* 19–29.

Crowell, J. A., & Waters, E. (1990). Separation anxiety. In M. Lewis and S. M. Miller (Eds.), *Handbook of developmental psychopathology.* New York: Plenum.

Crowther, I. (2006). *Child development: A primer.* Toronto, ON: Nelson.

Csikszentmihalyi, M., & Larson, R. (1984). *Being adolescent.* New York: Basic Books.

Cunningham, A. E., Perry, K. E., & Stanovich, K. E. (2001). Converging evidence for the concept of orthographic processing. *Reading and Writing, 14*(5–6), 549–568.

Curtiss, S. (1977). *Genie: A psycholinguistic study of a modern-day "wild child."* New York: Academic Press.

Curtner-Smith, M. E. (2000). Mechanisms by which family processes contribute to school-age boy's bullying. *Child Study Journal, 30*(3), 169–186,

Cutting, A. L., & Dunn, J. (1999). Theory of mind, emotion understanding, language, and family background: Individual differences and interrelations. *Child Development, 70*(4), 853–865.

Cystic Fibrosis Foundation (2004, April 30). What is CF? Available at http://www.cff.org

Dabbs, J. M., Jr., Bernieri, F. J., Strong, R. K., Campo, R., & Milun, R. (2001). Going on stage: Testosterone in greetings and meetings. *Journal of Research in Personality, 35*(1) 27–40.

DaCosta, D., Rippen, N., Drista, M., & Ring, A. (2003). Self-reported leisure-time physical activity during pregnancy and relationship to psychological well-being. *Journal of Psychosomatic Obstetrics & Gynecology, 24*(2), 111–119.

Dahl, R. E., Scher, M. S., Williamson, D. E., Robles, N., & Day, N. (1995). A longitudinal study of prenatal marijuana use: Effects on sleep and arousal at age 3 years. *Archives of Pediatric and Adolescent Medicine, 149,* 145–150.

Dai, D. Y. (2001). A comparison of gender differences in academic self-concept and motivation between high-ability and average Chinese adolescents. *Journal of Secondary Gifted Education, 13*(1), 22–32.

Dailard, C. (2001, February). *Sex education:*

Politicians, parents, teachers and teens. Guttmacher Report on Public Policy. New York: Alan Guttmacher Institute.

Daley, S. (1991, January 19). Girls' self-esteem is lost on way to adolescence, new study finds. *New York Times,* pp. B1, B6.

Daly, M., & Wilson, M. (2000). Genetic ties may be factor in violence in stepfamilies. *American Psychologist, 55*(6), 679–680.

Damon, W. (2000). Setting the stage for the development of wisdom: Self-understanding and moral identity during adolescence. In W. S. Brown (Ed.), *Understanding wisdom: Sources, science, and society* (pp. 339–360). Philadelphia: Templeton Foundation Press.

Damon, W., & Hart, D. (1992). Self-understanding and its role in social and moral development. In M. H. Bornstein & M. E. Lamb (Eds.), *Developmental psychology: An advanced textbook.* Hillsdale, NJ: Erlbaum.

Dana, R. H. (2002). Mental health services for African Americans: A cultural/racial perspective. *Cultural Diversity and Ethnic Minority Psychology, 8*(1), 3–18.

Dane, S., & Erzurumluoglu, A. (2003). Sex and handedness differences in eye-hand visual reaction times in handball players. *International Journal of Neuroscience, 113*(7), 923–929.

Dasinger, L. K., Shane, P. A., & Martinovich, Z. (2004). Assessing the effectiveness of community-based substance abuse treatment for adolescents. *Journal of Psychoactive Drugs, 36*(1), 27–33.

Davidson, P. W., et al. (1998). Effects of prenatal and postnatal methylmercury exposure from fish consumption on neurodevelopment: Outcomes at 66 months of age in the Seychelles Child Development Study. *Journal of the American Medical Association, 280,* 701–707.

Davidson, P. W., et al. (1998). Effects of prenatal and postnatal methylmercury exposure from fish consumption on neurodevelopment: Outcomes at 66 months of age in the Seychelles Child Development Study. *Journal of the American Medical Association, 280,* 701–707.

Davies, P. T., & Windle, M. (2001). Interparental discord and adolescent adjustment trajectories: The potentiating and protective role of intrapersonal attributes. *Child Development, 72*(4), 1163–1178.

Davis, A. (1991). Piaget, teachers and education: Into the 1990s. In P. Light, S. Sheldon, & M. Woodhead (Eds.), *Learning to think.* New York: Routledge.

Davis, A. (2003). Educational implications. In A. Slater & G. Bremner (Eds.), *An introduction to developmental psychology* (pp. 415–433). Malden, MA: Blackwell.

Davis, A. M., Grattan, D. R., & McCarthy, M. M. (2000). Decreasing GAD neonatally attenuates steroid-induced sexual differentiation of the rat brain. *Behavioral Neuroscience, 114*(5), 923–933.

Davis, H. A. (2001). The quality and impact of relationships between elementary school

students and teachers. *Contemporary Educational Psychology, 26*(4), 431–453.

Davis, L., Edwards, H., Mohay, H., & Wol-lin, J. (2003). The impact of very premature birth on the psychological health of mothers. *Early Human Development, 73*(1–2), 61–70.

Dawood, K., Pillard, R. C., Horvath, C., Revelle, W., & Bailey, J. M. (2000). Familial aspects of male homosexuality. *Archives of Sexual Behavior, 29*(2), 155–163.

Dawson, T. L. (2002). New tools, new insights: Kohlberg's moral judgement stages revisited. *International Journal of Behavioral Development, 26*(2), 154–166.

Day, S. X., & Rounds, J. (1998). Universality of vocational interest structure among racial and ethnic minorities. *American Psychologist, 53,* 728–736.

DeAngelis, T. (1997). Abused children have more conflicts with friends. *APA Monitor, 28*(6), 32.

Deary, I. J., Whiteman, M. C., Starr, J. M., Whalley, L. J., & Fox, H. C. (2004). The impact of childhood intelligence on later life: Following up the Scottish mental surveys of 1932 and 1947. *Journal of Personality and Social Psychology, 86*(1), 130–147.

Deas, D., & Thomas, S. E. (2001). An overview of controlled studies of adolescent substance abuse treatment. *American Journal on Addictions, 10*(2), 178–189.

de Boysson-Bardies, B., & Halle, P. A. (1994). Speech development: Contributions of cross-linguistic studies. In A. Vyt et al. (Eds.), *Early child development in the French tradition: Contributions from current research.* Hillsdale, NJ: Lawrence Erlbaum Associates.

DeCasper, A. J., & Fifer, W. P. (1980). Of human bonding: Newborns prefer their mothers' voices. *Science, 208,* 1174–1176.

DeCasper, A. J., & Prescott, P. A. (1984). Human newborns' perception of male voices: Preference, discrimination, and reinforcing value. *Developmental Psychobiology, 17,* 481–491.

DeCasper, A. J., & Spence, M. J. (1986). Prenatal maternal speech influences newborns' perception of speech sounds. *Infant Behavior and Development, 9,* 133–150.

DeCasper, A. J., & Spence, M. J. (1991). Auditorily mediated behavior during the perinatal period: A cognitive view. In M. J. Weiss & P. R. Zelazo (Eds.), *Infant attention* (pp. 142–176). Norwood, NJ: Ablex.

Decker, S. L., McIntosh, D. E., Kelly, A. M., Nicholls, S. K., & Dean, R. S. (2001). Comorbidity among individuals classified with attention disorders. *International Journal of Neuroscience, 110*(1–2), 43–54.

Deep, A. L., et al. (1999). Sexual abuse in eating disorder subtypes and control women: The role of comorbid substance dependence in bulimia nervosa. *International Journal of Eating Disorders, 25*(1), 1–10.

Dehaene-Lambertz, G., Pena, M., Christophe, A., & Landrieu, P. (2004). Phoneme

perception in a neonate with a left sylvian infarct. *Brain and Language, 88*(1), 26–38.

Delaney-Black, V., et al. (2000). Expressive language development of children exposed to cocaine prenatally: Literature review and report of a prospective cohort study. *Journal of Communication Disorders, 33*(6), 463–481.

Delgado, A. R., & Prieto, G. (2004). Cognitive mediators and sex-related differences in mathematics. *Intelligence, 32*(1), 25–32.

DeLoache, J. S. (2002). The symbol-mindedness of young children. In W. Hartup & R. A. Weinberg (Eds.), *Child psychology in retrospect and prospect: In celebration of the 75th anniversary of the Institute of Child Development* (pp. 73–101). Mahwah, NJ: Lawrence Erlbaum Associates.

DeLoache, J. S., Cassidy, D. J., & Brown, A. L. (1985). Precursors of mnemonic strategies in very young children's memory. *Child Development, 56,* 125–137.

DeLuccie, M. F., & Davis, A. J. (1991). Father-child relationships from the preschool years through mid-adolescence. *Journal of Genetic Psychology, 152,* 225–238.

Denham, S. A., & Kochanoff, A. T. (2002). Parental contributions to preschoolers' understanding of emotions. *Marriage & Family Review, 34,* 311–343.

Dennis, M., Sugar, J., & Whitaker, H. A. (1982). The acquisition of tag questions. *Child Development, 53,* 1254–1257.

Dennis, W. (1960). Causes of retardation among institutional children: Iran. *Journal of Genetic Psychology, 96,* 47–59.

Dennis, W., & Dennis, M. G. (1940). The effect of cradling practices upon the onset of walking in Hopi children. *Journal of Genetic Psychology, 56,* 77–86.

Dennis, W., & Sayegh, Y. (1965). The effect of supplementary experiences upon the behavioral development of infants in institutions. *Child Development, 36,* 81–90.

de Oliveira, F. S., Viana, M. R., Antoniolli, A. R., & Marchioro, M. (2001). Differential effects of lead and zinc on inhibitory avoidance learning in mice. *Brazilian Journal of Medical and Biological Research, 34*(1), 117–120.

Derman, O., Kanbur, N. O., & Kutluk, T. (2003). Tamoxifen treatment for pubertal gynecomastia. *International Journal of Adolescent Medicine and Health, 15*(4), 359–363.

des Jardins, K. (2001, May). Going for the girl. *Parenting Magazine.*

Department of Justice Canada (2004). Assisted Human Reproduction Act [not in force]. Available at http://laws.justice.gc.ca/en/A-13.4/index.html

Desmond, R. J., Singer, J. L., & Singer, D. G. (1990). Family mediation: Parental communication patterns and the influences of television on children. In J. Bryant (Ed.), *Television and the American family.* Hillsdale, NJ: Erlbaum.

Dessens, A. B., et al. (1999). Prenatal exposure to anticonvulsants and psychosexual development. *Archives of Sexual Behavior, 28*(1), 31–44.

Dessureau, B. K., Kurowski, C. O., & Thompson, N. S. (1998). A reassessment of the role of pitch and duration in adults' responses to infant crying. *Infant Behavior and Development, 21*(2), 367–371.

de Villiers, J. G., & de Villiers, P. A. (1999). Language development. In M. H. Bornstein & M. E. Lamb (Eds.), *Developmental psychology: An advanced textbook* (4th ed.) (pp. 313–373). Mahwah, NJ: Lawrence Erlbaum Associates.

Devlin, M. J., Yanovski, S. Z., & Wilson, G. T. (2000). Obesity: What mental health professionals need to know. *American Journal of Psychiatry, 157*(6), 854–866.

DeVries, R. (2000). Vygotsky, Piaget, and education: A reciprocal assimilation of theories and educational practices. *New Ideas in Psychology, 18*(2–3), 187–213.

de Wit, H., Crean, J., & Richards, J. B. (2000). Effects of d-amphetamine and ethanol on a measure of behavioral inhibition in humans. *Behavioral Neuroscience, 114*(4), 830–837.

Dezoete, J. A., MacArthur, B. A., & Tuck, B. (2003). Prediction of Bayley and Stanford-Binet scores with a group of very low birthweight children. *Child: Care, Health and Development, 29*(5), 367–372.

Diamond, G., & Siqueland, L. (2001). Current status of family intervention science. *Child and Adolescent Psychiatric Clinics of North America, 10*(3), 641–661.

Dickens, W. T., & Flynn, J. R. (2001). Heritability estimates versus large environmental effects: The IQ paradox resolved. *Psychological Review, 108*(2), 346–369.

Dierker, L. C., et al. (2001). Association between psychiatric disorders and the progression of tobacco use behaviors. *Journal of the American Academy of Child and Adolescent Psychiatry, 40*(10), 1159–1167.

Dietitians of Canada, Canadian Paediatric Society, College of Family Physicians of Canada, & Community Health Nurses Association of Canada (2004). Public policy statement: The use of growth charts for assessing and monitoring growth in Canadian infants and children. *Canadian Journal of Dietetic Practice and Research, 65*(1), 22–32.

Dietz, W. H. (1990). You are what you eat: What you eat is what you are. *Journal of Adolescent Health Care, 11,* 76–81.

Dietz, W. H., Jr., & Gortmaker, S. L. (1985). Do we fatten our children at the television set? Obesity and television viewing in children and adolescents. *Pediatrics, 75,* 807–812.

DiLalla, D. L., Carey, G., Gottesman, I. I., & Bouchard, T. J., Jr. (1996). Heritability of MMPI personality indicators of psychopathology in twins reared apart. *Journal of Abnormal Psychology, 105,* 491–499.

DiLalla, D. L., Gottesman, I. I., Carey, G., & Bouchard, T. J., Jr. (1999). Heritability of MMPI Harris-Lingoes and Subtle-Obvious subscales in twins reared apart. *Assessment, 6*(4), 353–366.

DiMatteo, M. R., et al. (1996). Cesarean childbirth and psychosocial outcomes: A meta-analysis. *Health Psychology, 15,* 303–314.

Dindia, K., & Allen, M. (1992). Sex differences in self-disclosure: A meta-analysis. *Psychological Bulletin, 112,* 106–124.

Division of Reproductive Health, National Center for Chronic Disease Prevention and Health Promotion; Division of Applied Public Health Training, Epidemiology Program Office; Division of Vital Statistics, National Center for Health Statistics; and an EIS Officer, Centers for Disease Control and Prevention (2000). Contribution of assisted reproduction technology and ovulation-inducing drugs to triplet and higher-order multiple births, United States, 1980–1997. *Morbidity and Mortality Weekly Report, 49,* 535–538.

Dix, T., Ruble, D. N., & Zambarino, R. J. (1989). Mother's implicit theories of discipline: Child effects, parental effects, and the attribution process. *Child Development, 60,* 1373–1392.

Dixon, J. A., & Moore, C. F. (1990). The development of perspective taking: Understanding differences in information and weighting. *Child Development, 61,* 1502–1513.

Dobbinson, S., Perkins, M., & Boucher, J. (2003). The interactional significance of formulas in autistic language. *Clinical Linguistics and Phonetics, 17*(4–5), 299–307.

Dodge, K. A., Bates, J. E., & Pettit, G. S. (1990). Mechanisms in the cycle of violence. *Science, 250,* 1678–1683.

Dodge, K. A., Laird, R., Lochman, J. E., Zelli, A., & Conduct Problems Prevention Research Group U.S. (2002). Multidimensional latent-construct analysis of children's social information processing patterns: Correlations with aggressive behavior problems. *Psychological Assessment, 14*(1), 60–73.

Dogil, G., Ackermann, H., Grodd, W., Haider, H., Kamp, H., Mayer, J., Riecker, A., & Wildgruber, D. (2002). The speaking brain: A tutorial introduction to fMRI experiments in the production of speech, prosody, and syntax. *Journal of Neurolinguistics, 15*(1), 59–90.

Dogra, A., Parkin, A., Gale, F., & Frake, C. (2002). *A multidisciplinary handbook of child and adolescent mental health for frontline professionals.* London: Jessica Kingsley.

Doherty, W. J., Kouneski, E. F., & Erickson, M. F. (1996). *Responsible fathering: An overview and conceptual framework.* Washington, DC: U.S. Department of Health and Human Services. Retrieved June 7, 2001, from http://fatherhood.hhs .gov/concept.htm

Dombrowski, M. A. S., et al. (2000). Kangaroo skin-to-skin care for premature twins and their adolescent parents. *American Journal of Maternal/Child Nursing, 25*(2), 92–94.

Donaldson, M. (1979). *Children's minds.* New York: Norton.

Donner, F., & Babcock, D. F. (2003). Smelling the roses? *Science, 299,* 1993–1994.

Donohue, B., et al. (2004). Psychometric evaluation of self and collateral timeline follow-back reports of drug and alcohol use in a sample of drug-abusing and conduct-disordered adolescents and their parents. *Psychology of Addictive Behaviors, 18*(2), 184–189.

Donovan, C. (2000, May 30). *Confronting teen pregnancy.* Washington Post, p. Z17.

Dorius, C. J., Bahr, S. J., Hoffmann, J. P., & Harmon, E. L. (2004). Parenting practices as moderators of the relationship between peers and adolescent marijuana use. *Journal of Marriage and Family, 66*(1), 163–178.

Downey, D. B. (2001). Number of siblings and intellectual development: The resource dilution explanation. *American Psychologist, 56*(6/7), 497–504.

Downs, W. R., & Rose, S. R. (1991). The relationship of adolescent peer groups to the incidence of psychosocial problems. *Adolescence, 26,* 473–492.

Drabick, D. A. G., Gadow, K. D., Carlson, G. A., & Bromet, E. J. (2004). ODD and ADHD symptoms in Ukrainian children: External validators and comorbidity. *Journal of the American Academy of Child and Adolescent Psychiatry, 43*(6), 735–743.

Drasgow, E., Halle, J. W., & Phillips, B. (2001). Effects of different social partners on the discriminated requesting of a young child with autism and severe language delays. *Research in Developmental Disabilities, 22*(2), 125–139.

Drewett, R., Blair, P., Emmett, P., Emond, A., & The ALSPAC Study Team (2004). Failure to thrive in the term and preterm infants of mothers depressed in the postnatal period: A population-based birth cohort study. *Journal of Child Psychology and Psychiatry and Allied Disciplines, 45*(2), 359–366.

Drews, C. D., et al. (1996, April). Pediatrics. Cited in "Smokers more likely to bear retarded babies, study says," *New York Times* (1996, April 10), p. B7.

Drotar, D., & Robinson, J. (2000). Developmental psychopathology of failure to thrive. In A. J. Sameroff et al. (Eds.), *Handbook of developmental psychopathology* (2nd ed.). Dordrecht, Netherlands: Kluwer Academic.

Dryfoos, J. G. (1990). *Adolescents at risk: Prevalence and prevention.* London: Oxford University Press.

DuBois, D. L., & Hirsch, B. J. (1990). School and neighborhood friendship patterns of blacks and whites in early adolescence. *Child Development, 61,* 524–536.

Dufva, M., Niemi, P., & Voeten, M. J. M. (2001). The role of phonological memory, word recognition, and comprehension skills in reading development: From preschool to grade 2. *Reading and Writing, 14*(1–2), 91–117.

Duggan, A., Fuddy, L., McFarlane, E., Burrell, L., Windham, A., Higman, S., & Sia, C. (2004). Evaluating a statewide home visiting program to prevent child abuse in at-risk families of newborns: Fathers' participation and outcomes. *Child Maltreatment: Journal of the American Professional Society on the Abuse of Children, 9*(1), 3–17.

Dugger, C. W. (2001, April 22). *Abortion in India is tipping scales sharply against girls.* Available at http://www.nytimes.com

Dunn, J. (1993). *Young children's close relationships: Beyond attachment.* Newbury Park, CA: Sage.

Dunn, J. (2004). Sibling relationships. In P. K. Smith & C. H. Hart (Eds.), *Handbook of child social development* (pp. 223–237). Malden, MA: Blackwell.

Dunn, J., Davies, L. C., O'Connor, T. G., & Sturgess, W. (2001). Family lives and friendships: The perspectives of children in step-, single-parent, and nonstep families. *Journal of Family Psychology, 15*(2), 272–287.

Dunn, J., & Hughes, C. (2001). "I got some swords and you're dead!": Violent fantasy, antisocial behavior, friendship, and moral sensibility in young children. *Child Development, 72*(2), 491–505.

Du Rocher Schudlich, T. D., Shamir, H., & Cummings, E. M. (2004). Marital conflict, children's representations of family relationships, and children's dispositions towards peer conflict strategies. *Social Development, 13*(2), 171–192.

Dweck, C. S. (2000). *Self-theories: Their role in motivation, personality, and development.* Philadelphia: Psychology Press.

Dworet, D. H., & Rathgeber, A. J. (1998). Confusion reigns: Definitions of behaviour exceptionalities in Canada. *Exceptionality Education Canada, 8*(1), 3–19.

Dyer, C. A. (1999). Pathophysiology of phenylketonuria. *Mental Retardation and Developmental Disabilities Research Reviews, 5*(2), 104–112.

Dykman, R. A., Casey, P. H., Ackerman, P. T., & McPherson, W. B. (2001). Behavioral and cognitive status in school-aged children with a history of failure to thrive during early childhood. *Clinical Pediatrics, 40*(2), 63–70.

Eason, E., & Feldman, P. (2000). Much ado about a little cut: Is episiotomy worthwhile? *Obstetrics and Gynecology, 95*(4), 616–618.

Easterbrook, M. A., & Goldberg, W. A. (1984). Toddler development in the family: Impact of father involvement and parenting characteristics. *Child Development, 55,* 740–752.

Easterbrook, M. A., Kisilevsky, B. S., Hains, S. M. J., & Muir, D. W. (1999a). Faceness or complexity: Evidence from newborn visual tracking of facelike stimuli. *Infant Behavior and Development, 22*(1), 17–35.

Easterbrook, M. A., Kisilevsky, B. S., Muir, D. W., & Laplante, D. P. (1999b). Newborns discriminate schematic faces from scrambled faces. Canadian *Journal of Experimental Psychology, 53*(3), 231–241.

Eaton, W. O., McKeen, N. A., & Campbell, D. W. (2001). The waxing and waning of movement: Implications for psychological development. *Developmental Review, 21*(2), 205–223.

Eaton, W. O., & Saudino, K. J. (1992). Prenatal activity level as a temperament dimension? Individual differences and developmental functions in fetal movement. *Infant Behavior and Development, 15,* 57–70.

Eaton, W. O., & Yu, A. P. (1989). Are sex differences in child motor activity a function of sex differences in maturational status? *Child Development, 60,* 1005–1011.

Eberhardy, F. (1967). The view from "the couch." *Journal of Child Psychological Psychiatry, 8,* 257–263.

Eccles, J. S. (1999). The development of children ages 6 to 14. *Future of Children, 9*(2), 30–44.

Eccles, J. S., et al. (1991, August). Expectancy effects are alive and well on the home front: Influences on, and consequences of, parents' beliefs regarding their daughters' and sons' abilities and interests. Paper presented at the meeting of the American Psychological Association, San Francisco.

Eccles, J. S., et al. (1993). Development during adolescence. *American Psychologist, 48,* 90–101.

Eccles, J. S., Freedman-Doan, C., Frome, P., Jacobs, J., & Yoon, K. S. (2000). Gender-role socialization in the family: A longitudinal approach. In T. Eckes & H. M. Trautner (Eds.), *The developmental social psychology of gender* (pp. 333–360). Mahwah, NJ: Lawrence Erlbaum Associates.

Eckenrode, J., Laird, M., & Doris, J. (1993). School performance and disciplinary problems among abused and neglected children. *Developmental Psychology, 29,* 53–62.

Eckerman, C. O., Hsu, H.-C., Molitor, A., Leung, E. H. L., & Goldstein, R. F. (1999). Infant arousal in an en-face exchange with a new partner: Effects of prematurity and perinatal biological risk. *Developmental Psychology, 35*(1), 282–293.

Eckerman, C. O., & Stein, M. R. (1990). How imitation begets imitation and toddlers' generation of games. *Developmental Psychology, 26,* 370–378.

Ecuyer-Dab, I., & Robert, M. (2004). Spatial ability and home-range size: Examining the relationship in Western men and women (Homo sapiens). *Journal of Comparative Psychology, 118*(2), 217–231.

Eder, R. A. (1989). The emergent personologist: The structure and content of 3½-, 5½-, and 7½-year-olds' concepts of themselves and other persons. *Child Development, 60,* 1218–1228.

Eder, R. A. (1990). Uncovering young children's psychological selves: Individual and developmental differences. *Child Development, 61,* 849–863.

Eddy, J. M., & Chamberlain, P. (2000). Family management and deviant peer association as mediators of the impact of treatment condition on youth antisocial behavior. *Journal of Consulting and Clinical Psychology, 68*(5), 857–863.

Eddy, J. M., Leve, L. D., & Fagot, B. I. (2001). Coercive family processes: A replication and extension of Patterson's Coercion Model. *Aggressive Behavior, 27*(1), 14–25.

Egeland, B., & Farber, E. A. (1984). Infant-mother attachment: Factors related to its development and changes over time. *Child Development, 55,* 753–771.

Egeland, B., Jacobvitz, D., & Sroufe, L. A. (1988). Breaking the cycle of abuse. *Child Development, 59,* 1080–1088.

Egeland, B., & Sroufe, L. A. (1981). Attachment and early maltreatment. *Child Development, 52,* 44–52.

Eimas, P. D., Sigueland, E. R., Juscyk, P., & Vigorito, J. (1971). Speech perception in infants. *Science, 171,* 303–306.

Eisenberg, N., Hertz-Lazarowitz, R., & Fuchs, I. (1990). Prosocial moral judgment in Israeli kibbutz and city children: A longitudinal study. *Merrill-Palmer Quarterly, 36,* 273–285.

Eisenberg, N., & Miller, P. (1990). The development of prosocial behavior versus nonprosocial behavior in children. In M. Lewis & S. M. Miller (Eds.), *Handbook of developmental psychopathology.* New York: Plenum.

Eisenberg, N., Miller, P. A., Shell, R., McNalley, S., & Shea, C. (1991). Prosocial development in adolescence: A longitudinal study. *Developmental Psychology, 27,* 849–857.

Eisenberg, N., & Valiente, C. (2002). Parenting and children's prosocial and moral development. In M. H. Bornstein (Ed.), *Handbook of parenting,* v. 5, *Practical issues in parenting* (2nd ed.) (pp. 111–142). Mahwah, NJ: Lawrence Erlbaum Associates.

Eisenberg, N., Wolchik, S. A., Goldberg, L., & Engel, I. (1992). Parental values, reinforcement, and young children's prosocial behavior: A longitudinal study. *Journal of Genetic Psychology, 153*(1), 19–36.

Eisner, E. W. (1990). The role of art and play in children's cognitive development. In E. Klugman & S. Smilansky (Eds.), *Children's play and learning: Perspectives and policy implications.* New York: Teachers College Press.

Ekvall, S. W. (Ed.) (1993a). *Pediatric nutrition in chronic diseases and developmental disorders: Prevention, assessment, and treatment.* New York: Oxford.

Ekvall, S. W. (1993b). Prenatal growth in pregnancy. In S. W. Ekvall (Ed.), *Pediatric nutrition in chronic diseases and developmental disorders: Prevention, assessment, and treatment.* New York: Oxford.

Ekvall, S. W., Ekvall, V., & Mayes, S. D. (1993). Attention deficit hyperactivity disorder. In S. W. Ekvall (Ed.), *Pediatric nutrition in chronic diseases and developmental disorders: Prevention, assessment, and treatment.* New York: Oxford.

Elias, L. J., Saucier, D. M., & Guylee, M. J. (2001). Handedness and depression in university students: A sex by handedness interaction. *Brain and Cognition, 46*(1–2), 125–129.

Elias, M. J., Gara, M. A., Schuyler, T. F., Brandon-Muller, L. R., & Sayette, M. A. (1991). The promotion of social competence: Longitudinal study of a preventative school-based program. *American Journal of Orthopsychiatry, 61,* 409–417.

Elias, M. J., & Zins, J. E. (2003). Bullying, other forms of peer harassment, and victimization in the schools: Issues for school psychology research and practice. *Journal of*

Applied School Psychology, 19(2), 1–5.

Elkind, D. (1967). Egocentrism in adolescence. *Child Development, 38,* 1025–1034.

Elkind, D. (1985). Egocentrism redux. *Developmental Review, 5,* 218–226.

Elkind, D. (1990). Academic pressures: Too much, too soon—The demise of play. In E. Klugman & S. Smilansky (Eds.), *Children's play and learning: Perspectives and policy.* New York: Teachers College Press.

Elkind, D. (1991). Early childhood education. In M. Lewis (Ed.), *Child and adolescent psychiatry: A comprehensive textbook.* Baltimore: Williams & Wilkins.

Ellickson, P. L., Tucker, J. S., & Klein, D. J. (2001). High-risk behaviors associated with early smoking: Results from a 5-year follow-up. *Journal of Adolescent Health, 28*(6), 465–473.

Ellis, A., & Dryden, W. (1996). *The practice of rational emotive behavior therapy.* New York: Springer.

Ellis, E. M. (2000). *Divorce wars: Interventions with families in conflict.* Washington, DC: American Psychological Association.

Ellis, L., Robb, B., & Burke, D. (2005). Sexual orientation in United States and Canadian college students. *Archives of Sexual Behavior, 34,* 569–581.

El-Sheikh, M., & Harger, J. (2001). Appraisals of marital conflict and children's adjustment, health, and physiological reactivity. *Developmental Psychology, 37*(6), 875–885.

Eltzschig, H., Lieberman, E., & Camann, W. (2003). Regional anesthesia and analgesia for labor and delivery. *New England Journal of Medicine, 348*(4), 319–332.

Emde, R. N., Gaensbauer, T. J., & Harmon, R. J. (1976). *Emotional expression in infancy: A biobehavioral study.* New York: International Universities Press.

Engen, T., & Lipsitt, L. P. (1965). Decrement and recovery of responses to olfactory stimuli in the human neonate. *Journal of Comparative and Physiological Psychology, 59*(2), 312–316.

Epstein, J. L. (1989). The selection of friends: Changes across the grades and in different school environments. In T. J. Berndt & G. W. Ladd (Eds.), *Peer relationships in child development.* New York: Wiley.

Epstein, L. H., et al. (2000). Problem solving in the treatment of childhood obesity. *Journal of Consulting and Clinical Psychology, 68*(4), 717–721.

Erdley, C. A., & Asher, S. R. (1998). Linkages between children's beliefs about the legitimacy of aggression and their behavior. *Social Development, 7*(3), 321–339.

Erel, O., Oberman, Y., & Yirmiya, N. (2000). Maternal versus nonmaternal care and seven domains of children's development. *Psychological Bulletin, 126*(5), 727–747.

Erikson, E. H. (1963). *Childhood and society.* New York: Norton.

Erikson, E. H. (1968). *Identity: Youth and crisis.* New York: Norton.

Erikson, E. H. (1975). *Life history and the historical moment.* New York: Norton.

Eron, L. D. (1982). Parent-child interaction, television violence, and aggression of children. *American Psychologist, 37,* 197–211.

Eron, L. D. (1993). Cited in T. DeAngelis (1993), It's baaack: TV violence, concern for kid viewers, *APA Monitor, 24*(8), 16.

Eron, L. D., Huesmann, L. R., & Zelli, A. (1991). The role of parental variables in the learning of aggression. In D. J. Pepler & K. H. Rubin (Eds.), *The development and treatment of childhood aggression.* Hillsdale, NJ: Erlbaum.

Ertem, I. O., Leventhal, J. M., & Dobbs, S. (2000). Intergenerational continuity of child physical abuse: How good is the evidence? *Lancet, 356,* 814–819.

Escobar, G. J., Littenberg, B., & Petitti, D. B. (1991). Outcome among surviving very low birthweight infants: A meta-analysis. *Archives of Disease in Childhood, 66,* 204–211.

Espy, K. A., Molfese, V. J., & DiLalla, L. F. (2001). Effects of environmental measures on intelligence in young children: Growth curve modeling of longitudinal data. *Merrill-Palmer Quarterly, 47*(1), 42–73.

Essau, C. A., Sakano, Y., Ishikawa, S., & Sasagawa, S. (2004). Anxiety symptoms in Japanese and in German children. *Behaviour Research and Therapy, 42*(5), 601–612.

Etaugh, C., Levine, D., & Mennella, A. (1984). Development of sex biases in children: 40 years later. *Sex Roles, 10,* 911–922.

Ethics Committee of the American Society of Reproductive Medicine (2000, June 7). Sex selection and preimplantation genetic diagnosis. Available at http://www.humrep .oupjournals.org/cgi/content/abstract/15/ 9/1879

Evans, G. W. (2004). The environment of childhood poverty. *American Psychologist, 59*(2), 77–92.

Evans, S. W., Smith, B. H., Bukstein, O., Gnagy, E. M., Greiner, A. R., Altenderfer, L., Baron-Myak, C. (2001). Dose-response effects of methylphenidate on ecologically valid measures of academic performance and classroom behavior in adolescents with ADHD. *Experimental and Clinical Psychopharmacology, 9*(2), 163–175.

Evenson, K. R., Siega-Riz, A. M., Savitz, D. A., Leiferman, J. A., & Thorp Jr., J. M. (2002). Vigorous leisure activity and pregnancy outcome. *Epidemiology, 13,* 653–659.

Fabricius, W. V., & Cavalier, L. (1989). The role of causal theories about memory in young children's memory strategy choice. *Child Development, 60,* 298–308.

Fagot, B. I. (1990). A longitudinal study of gender segregation: Infancy to preschool. In F. F. Strayer (Ed.), *Social interaction and behavioral development during early childhood.* Montreal: La Maison D'Ethologie de Montreal.

Fagot, B. I., & Hagan, R. (1991). Observations of parent reactions to sex-stereotyped behaviors: Age and sex effects. *Child Development, 62,* 617–628.

Fagot, B. I., & Leinbach, M. D. (1993). Gender-role development in young children: From discrimination to labeling. *Developmental Review, 13,* 205–224.

Fagot, B. I., & Leve, L. D. (1998). Teacher ratings of externalizing behavior at school entry for boys and girls: Similar early predictors and different correlates. *Journal of Child Psychology and Psychiatry and Allied Disciplines, 39*(4), 555–566.

Fagot, B. I., Rodgers, C. S., & Leinbach, M. D. (2000). Theories of gender socialization. In T. Eckes & H. M. Trautner (Eds.), *The developmental social psychology of gender* (pp. 65–89). Mahwah, NJ: Lawrence Erlbaum Associates.

Fales, C. L., et al. (2003). Working memory and relational reasoning in Klinefelter syndrome. *Journal of the International Neuropsychological Society, 9*(6), 839–846.

Fantz, R. L. (1961). The origin of form perception. *Scientific American, 204,* 66–72.

Fantz, R. L., Fagan, J. F., III, & Miranda, S. B. (1975). Early visual selectivity. In L. B. Cohen & P. Salapatek (Eds.), *Infant perception: From sensation to cognition,* v. 1. New York: Academic Press.

Faraone, S. V., et al. (2000). Family study of girls with attention deficit hyperactivity disorder. *American Journal of Psychiatry, 157*(7), 1077–1083.

Farran, D. C. (1990). Effects of intervention with disadvantaged and disabled children: A decade review. In S. J. Meisels & J. P. Shonkoff (Eds.), *Handbook of early childhood intervention.* Cambridge: Cambridge University Press.

Farver, J. A. M., Kim, Y. K., & Lee-Shin, Y. (2000). Within cultural differences: Examining individual differences in Korean American and European American preschoolers' social pretend play. *Journal of Cross-Cultural Psychology, 31*(5), 583–602.

Feinberg, M. E., Neiderhiser, J. M., Howe, G., & Hetherington, E. M. (2001). Adolescent, parent, and observer perceptions of parenting: Genetic and environmental influences on shared and distinct perceptions. *Child Development, 72*(4), 1266–1284.

Feinberg, M. E., Neiderhiser, J. M., Simmens, S., Reiss, D., & Hetherington, E. M. (2000). Sibling comparison of differential parental treatment in adolescence: Gender, self-esteem, and emotionality as mediators of the parenting-adjustment association. *Child Development, 71*(6), 1611–1628.

Feiring, C. (1993, March). Developing concepts of romance from 15 to 18 years. Paper presented at the meeting of the Society for Research in Child Development, New Orleans, LA.

Feiring, C., & Lewis, M. (1991). The transition from middle to early adolescence: Sex differences in the social network and perceived self-competence. *Sex Roles, 24,* 489–509.

Felton, G. M., & Bartoces, M. (2002). Predictors of initiation of early sex in Black and White adolescent females. *Public Health Nursing, 19*(1), 59–67.

Fenzel, L. M. (2000). Prospective study of changes in global self-worth and strain during the transition to middle school. *Journal of Early Adolescence, 20*(1), 93–116.

Feola, T. W., de Wit, H., & Richards, J. B. (2000). Effects of d-amphetamine and alcohol on a measure of behavioral inhibition in rats. *Behavioral Neuroscience, 114*(4), 838–848.

Ferguson, K. J., Yesalis, C. E., Pomrehn, P. R., & Kirkpatrick, M. B. (1989). Attitudes, knowledge, and beliefs as predictions of exercise intent and behavior in schoolchildren. *Journal of School Health, 59,* 112–115.

Fernald, A., & Morikawa, H. (1993). Common themes and cultural variations in Japanese and American mothers' speech to infants. *Child Development, 64,* 637–656.

Fernandez, T., & State, M. (2004). Genetics and genomics of neurobehavioral disorders. *Journal of the American Academy of Child Psychiatry, 43*(3), 370–371.

Fetrick, A., Christensen, M., & Mitchell, C. (2003). Does public health nurse home visitation make a difference in the health outcomes of pregnant clients and their offspring? *Public Health Nursing, 20*(3), 184–189.

Field, T. M. (1990). *Infancy: The developing child.* Cambridge, MA: Harvard University Press.

Field, T. M. (1991a). Adolescent mothers and their young children. In R. M. Lerner, A. C. Petersen, & J. Brooks-Gunn (Eds.), *Encyclopedia of adolescence.* New York: Garland.

Field, T. M. (1991b). Quality infant day-care and grade school behavior and performance. *Child Development, 62,* 863–870.

Field, T. M. (1991c). Young children's adaptations to repeated separations from their mothers. *Child Development, 62,* 539–547.

Field, T. M. (1992). Interventions in early infancy. *Infant Mental Health Journal, 13*(4), 329–336.

Field, T. M. (2001). Massage therapy facilitates weight gain in preterm infants. *Current Directions in Psychological Science, 10*(2), 51–54.

Field, T. M., et al. (1992). Behavior state matching during interactions of preadolescent friends versus acquaintances. *Developmental Psychology, 28,* 242–250.

Finch, A. J., & McIntosh, J. A. (1990). Assessment of anxieties and fears in children. In A. LaGreca (Ed.), *Through the eyes of a child.* Boston: Allyn & Bacon.

Finch, B. K., Vega, W. A., & Kolody, B. (2001). Substance use during pregnancy in the state of California, USA. *Social Science and Medicine, 52*(4), 571–583.

Fine, M. (2002). Sexuality, schooling, and adolescent females: The missing discourse of desire. In *The Jossey-Bass reader on gender in education* (pp. 375–406). San Francisco, CA: Jossey-Bass.

Finegan, J. K., Niccols, G. A., & Sitarenios, G. (1992). Relations between prenatal testosterone levels and cognitive abilities at 4 years. *Developmental Psychology, 28,* 1075–1089.

Fisch, S., Truglio, R. T., & Cole, C. F. (1999).

The impact of Sesame Street on preschool children: A review and synthesis of 30 years' research. *Media Psychology, 1*(2), 165–190.

Fisher, P. A., Ellis, B. H., & Chamberlain, P. (1999). Early intervention foster care: A model for preventing risk in young children who have been maltreated. *Children's Services: Social Policy, Research, and Practice, 2,* 159–182.

Fitzgerald, D. P., & White, K. J. (2003). Linking children's social worlds: Perspective-taking in parent-child and peer contexts. *Social Behavior and Personality, 31*(5), 509–522.

Fitzgerald, H. E., & Brackbill, Y. (1976). Classical conditioning in infancy: Development and constraints. *Psychological Bulletin, 83,* 353–376.

Fitzgerald, H. E., et al. (1991). The organization of lateralized behavior during infancy. In H. E. Fitzgerald, B. M. Lester, & M. W. Yogman (Eds.), *Theory and research in behavioral pediatrics.* New York: Plenum.

Fivush, R. (2002). Scripts, schemas, and memory of trauma. In N. L. Stein et al. (Eds.), *Representation, memory, and development: Essays in honor of Jean Mandler* (pp. 53–74). Mahwah, NJ: Lawrence Erlbaum Associates.

Fivush, R., & Hammond, N. R. (1990). Autobiographical memory across the preschool years: Toward reconceptualizing childhood amnesia. In R. Fivush & J. A. Hudson (Eds.), *Knowing and remembering in young children.* Cambridge: Cambridge University Press.

Fivush, R., Kuebli, J., & Clubb, P. A. (1992). The structure of events and event representations: A developmental analysis. *Child Development, 63,* 188–201.

Fivush, R., Sales, J, M., Goldberg, A., Bahrick, L., & Parker, J. (2004). Weathering the storm: Children's long-term recall of Hurricane Andrew. *Memory, 12*(1), 104–118.

Flavell, J. H. (1993). Young children's understanding of thinking and consciousness. *Current Directions in Psychological Science, 2,* 40–43.

Flavell, J. H., Flavell, E. R., Green, F. L., & Moses, L. J. (1990). Young children's understanding of fact beliefs versus value beliefs. *Child Development, 61,* 915–928.

Flavell, J. H., Green, F. L., & Flavell, E. R. (2000). Development of children's awareness of their own thoughts. *Journal of Cognition and Development, 1*(1), 97–112.

Flavell, J. H., Miller, P. H., & Miller, S. A. (2002). *Cognitive development* (4th ed.). Upper Saddle River, NJ: Prentice Hall.

Florsheim, P. (Ed.) (2003). *Adolescent romantic relations and sexual behavior: Theory, research, and practical implications.* Mahwah, NJ: Lawrence Erlbaum Associates.

Flouri, E., & Buchanan, A. (2003). The role of father involvement and mother involvement in adolescents' psychological well-being. *British Journal of Social Work, 33*(3), 399–406.

Flynn, E., O'Malley, C., & Wood, D. (2004). A longitudinal, microgenetic study of the emergence of false belief understanding and

inhibition skills. *Developmental Science, 7*(1), 103–115.

Fogelholm, M., Nuutinen, O., Pasanen, M., Myohanen, E., & Saatela, T. (1999). Parent-child relationship of physical activity patterns and obesity. *International Journal of Obesity and Related Metabolic Disorders, 23,* 1262–1268.

Food and Drug Administration (2004, July 20). Decreasing the chance of birth defects. Available at http://www.fda.gov/fdac/features/996_bd.html

Ford, K., Wirawan, D. N., Reed, B. D., Muliawan, P., & Sutarga, M. (2000). AIDS and STD knowledge, condom use, and HIV/STD infection among female sex workers in Bali, Indonesia. *AIDS Care, 12*(5), 523–534.

Forness, S. R., & Kavale, K. A. (2000). Emotional or behavioral disorders: Background and current status of the E/BD terminology and definition. *Behavioral Disorders, 25*(3), 264–269.

Fortier, J. C., Carson, V. B., Will, S., & Shubkagel, B. L. (1991). Adjustment to a newborn: Sibling preparation makes a difference. *Journal of Obstetric, Gynecologic, and Neonatal Nursing, 20,* 73–79.

Foster-Clark, F. S., & Blyth, D. A. (1991). Peer relations and influences. In R. M. Lerner, A. C. Petersen, & J. Brooks-Gunn (Eds.), *Encyclopedia of adolescence.* New York: Garland.

Foulder-Hughes, L., & Cooke, R. (2003). Do mainstream schoolchildren who were born preterm have motor problems? *British Journal of Occupational Therapy, 66*(1), 9–16.

Fox, R. (1991). Developing awareness of mind reflected in children's narrative writing. *British Journal of Developmental Psychology, 9,* 281–298.

Frank, D. A., Augustyn, M., Knight, W. G., Pell, T., & Zuckerman, B. (2001). Growth, development, and behavior in early childhood following prenatal cocaine exposure: A systematic review. *Journal of the American Medical Association, 285*(12), 1613–1625.

Franke, S. (2003). Studying and working: The busy lives of students with paid employment. *Canadian Social Trends, Spring 2003,* 22–25. Ottawa, ON: Statistics Canada.

Fraser, A. M., Brockert, J. E., & Ward, R. H. (1995). Association of young maternal age with adverse reproductive outcomes. *New England Journal of Medicine, 332,* 1113–1117.

Fredricks, J. A., & Eccles, J. S. (2002). Children's competence and value beliefs from childhood through adolescence: Growth trajectories in two male-sex-typed domains. *Developmental Psychology, 38,* 519–533.

Freeman, M. S., Spence, M. J., and Oliphant, C. M. (1993, June). Newborns prefer their mothers' low-pass filtered voices over other female filtered voices. Paper presented at the meeting of the American Psychological Society, Chicago.

Freese, T. E., Miotto, K., & Reback, C. J. (2002). The effects and consequences of selected club drugs. *Journal of Substance*

Abuse Treatment, 23(2), 151–156.

French, D. C., Rianasari, M., Pidada, S., Nelwan, P., & Buhrmester, D. (2001). Social support of Indonesian and U.S. children and adolescents by family members and friends. *Merrill-Palmer Quarterly, 47*(3), 377–394.

Freud, A. (1969). Adolescence as a developmental disturbance. In G. Kaplan & S. Leborici (Eds.), *Adolescence: Psychosocial perspectives.* New York: Basic Books.

Freud, S. (1964). New introductory lectures. In standard edition of *The complete psychological works of Sigmund Freud,* v. 22. London: Hogarth. (Originally published in 1933).

Freund, C. S. (1990). Maternal regulation of children's problem-solving behavior and its impact on children's performance. *Child Development, 61,* 113–126.

Frey, K. S., & Ruble, D. N. (1992). Gender constancy and the "cost" of sex-typed behavior: A test of the conflict hypothesis. *Developmental Psychology, 28,* 714–721.

Frey, M. C., & Detterman, D. K. (2004). Scholastic assessment or g? The relationship between the scholastic assessment test and general cognitive ability. *Psychological Science, 15*(6), 373–378.

Fried, P. A., & Smith, A. M. (2001). A literature review of the consequences of prenatal marijuana exposure: An emerging theme of a deficiency in aspects of executive function. *Neurotoxicology and Teratology, 23*(1), 1–11.

Friedman, R. C., & Downey, J. I. (2001). The Oedipus complex and male homosexuality. In P. Hartocollis (Ed.), *Mankind's Oedipal destiny: Libidinal and aggressive aspects of sexuality* (pp. 113–138). Madison, CT: International Universities Press.

Friedman, S. R., et al. (2001). Correlates of anal sex with men among young adult women in an inner city minority neighborhood. *AIDS, 15*(15), 2057–2060.

Friend, M., Bursuck, W., & Hutchinson, N. (1998). *Including exceptional students: A practical guide for classroom teachers.* Scarborough, ON: Allyn and Bacon.

Friendly, M. (2004). Voice from the field: Policy implications of child development research for early childhood education and care policy. In R. E. Tremblay, R. G. Barr, R. D. Peters (Eds.), *Encyclopedia on early childhood development* [online]. Montreal, QC: Centre of Excellence for Early Childhood Development. Available at http://www.execellence-earlychildhood.ca/documents/FriendlyANF.pdf

Friendly, M., Beach, J., & Turiano, M. (2002). *Early childhood education and care in Canada in 2001.* Toronto, ON: Childcare Resource and Research Unit, University of Toronto.

Frisch, R. E. (1991). Puberty and body fat. In R. M. Lerner, A. C. Petersen, & J. Brooks-Gunn (Eds.), *Encyclopedia of adolescence.* New York: Garland.

Frisch, R. (1997). Speech reported in N. Angier (1997), Chemical tied to fat control could help trigger puberty, *New York Times,* pp. C1, C3.

Frith, U. (2001). What framework should we use for understanding developmental disorders? *Developmental Neuropsychology, 20*(2), 555–563.

Frodi, A. M. (1985). When empathy fails: Infant crying and child abuse. In B. M. Lester & C. F. Z. Boukydis (Eds.), *Infant crying.* New York: Plenum.

Fromme, K., et al. (2004). Biological and behavioral markers of alcohol sensitivity. *Alcoholism: Clinical and Experimental Research, 28*(2), 247–256.

Fugger, E. F., et al. (1998, September 9). Human reproduction. Cited in G. Kolata (1998, September 9), *Researchers report success in method to pick baby's sex,* available at http://www.nytimes.com

Fuligni, A. J., & Eccles, J. S. (1993). Perceived parent-child relationships and early adolescents' orientation toward peers. *Developmental Psychology, 29,* 622–632.

Funk, J. B., Buchman, D., Myers, M., & Jenks, J. (2000, August 7). *Asking the right question in research on violent electronic games.* Paper presented at the annual meeting of the American Psychological Association, Washington, DC.

Furman, W., & Buhrmester, D. (1992). Age and sex differences in perceptions of networks of personal relationships. *Child Development, 63,* 103–115.

Furman, W., Rahe, D., & Hartup, W. W. (1979). Social rehabilitation of low-interactive preschool children by peer intervention. *Child Development, 50,* 915–922.

Furnham, A., & Cheng, H. (2000). Perceived parental behaviour, self-esteem, and happiness. *Social Psychiatry and Psychiatric Epidemiology, 35*(10), 463–470.

Furstenberg, F. F., & Kiernan, K. E. (2001). Delayed parental divorce: How much do children benefit? *Journal of Marriage and the Family, 63*(2), 446–457.

Fylkesnes, K., et al. (2001). Declining HIV prevalence and risk behaviours in Zambia: Evidence from surveillance and population-based surveys. *AIDS, 15*(7), 907–916.

Gable, S., Crnic, K., & Belsky, J. (1994). Co-parenting within the family system: Influences on children's development. *Family Relations, 43*(4), 380–386.

Gabriel, M., Taylor, C., & Burhans, L. (2003). In utero cocaine, discriminative avoidance learning with low-salient stimuli, and learning-related neuronal activity in rabbits (Oryctolagus cuniculus). *Behavioral Neuroscience, 117*(5), 912–926.

Galambos, N. L. (1992). Parent-adolescent relations. *Current Directions in Psychological Science, 1,* 146–149.

Galambos, N. L., Barker, E. T., & Almeida, D. M. (2003). Parents do matter: Trajectories of change in externalizing and internalizing problems in early adolescence. *Child Development, 74*(2), 578–594.

Galambos, N. L., & Tilton-Weaver, L. C. (1998). Multiple-risk behaviour in adolescents and young adults. *Health Reports, Autumn 1998, 10*(2), 9–20.

Galanaki, E. (2001). The "imaginary audience" and the "personal fable" in relation to risk behavior and risk perception during adolescence. *Psychology: The Journal of the Hellenic Psychological Society, 8*(4), 411–430.

Galliher, R. V., Rostosky, S. S., & Hughes, H. K. (2004). School belonging, self-esteem, and depressive symptoms in adolescents: An examination of sex, sexual attraction status, and urbanicity. *Journal of Youth and Adolescence, 33*(3), 235–245.

Ganchrow, J. R., Steiner, J. E., & Daher, M. (1983). Neonatal facial expressions in response to different qualities and intensities of gustatory stimuli. *Infant Behavior and Development, 6,* 189–200.

Gannon, M. (2005). Crime statistics in Canada, 2005. Available at http://www.statcan.ca/english/freepub/85-002-XIE/85-002-XIE2006004.pdf

Gao, F., Levine, S. C., & Huttenlocher, J. (2000). What do infants know about continuous quantity? *Journal of Experimental Child Psychology, 77*(1), 20–29.

Garbarino, J. (1982). *Children and families in the social environment.* New York: Aldine deGruyter.

Garber, H. L. (1988). *The Milwaukee Project: Preventing mental retardation in children at risk.* Washington, DC: Association on Mental Retardation.

Garcia-Coll, C. T. (1990). Developmental outcome of minority infants: A process-oriented look into our beginnings. *Child Development, 61,* 270–289.

Garcia-Coll, C. T., Halpern, L. F., Vohr, B. R., Seifer, R., & Oh, W. (1992). Stability and correlates of change of early temperament in preterm and full-term infants. *Infant Behavior and Development, 15,* 137–153.

Garcia-Moreno, C., & Watts, C. (2000). Violence against women: Its importance for HIV/AIDS. *AIDS, 14*(Suppl. 3), S253-S265.

Gardner, H. (1983). *Frames of mind: The theory of multiple intelligences.* New York: Basic Books.

Gardner, H. (2001, April 5). *Multiple intelligence.* New York Times, p. A20.

Gardner, H. (2003a). My way. In R. J. Sternberg (Ed.), *Psychologists defying the crowd: Stories of those who battled the establishment and won* (pp. 79–88). Washington, DC: American Psychological Association.

Gardner, H. (2003b). Three distinct meanings of intelligence. In R. J. Sternberg et al. (Eds.), *Models of intelligence: International perspectives* (pp. 43–54). Washington, DC: American Psychological Association.

Garnefski, N., Kraaij, V., & Spinhoven, P. (2001). De relatie tussen cognitieve copingstrategieen en symptomen van depressie, angst en suiecidaliteit. *Gedrag and Gezondheid: Tijdschrift voor Psychologie and Gezondheid, 29*(3), 148–158.

Garner, P. W., & Landry, S. H. (1992). Preterm infants' affective responses in independent versus toy-centered play with their mothers. *Infant Mental Health Journal, 13,* 219–230.

Gartstein, M. A., Slobodskaya, H. R., & Kinsht, I. A. (2003). Cross-cultural differences in temperament in the first year of life: United States of America (U.S.) and Russia. *International Journal of Behavioral Development, 27*(4), 316–328.

Garvey, C. (1990). *Developing child*. Cambridge, MA: Harvard University Press.

Gaskell, G., Einsiedel, E., Hallman, W., Hornig-Priest, S., Jackson, J., & Olsthoorn, J. (December 2005). Social values and the governance of science. *Science, 310*, 1908–1909

Gathercole, S. E., Pickering, S. J., Ambridge, B., & Wearing, H. (2004a). The structure of working memory from 4 to 15 years of age. *Developmental Psychology, 40*(2), 177–190.

Gathercole, S. E., Pickering, S. J., Knight, C., & Stegmann, Z. (2004b). Working memory skills and educational attainment: Evidence from national curriculum assessments at 7 and 14 years of age. *Applied Cognitive Psychology, 18*(1), 1–16.

Gaudet, S., Clément, R., & Deuzeman, K. (2005). Daily hassles, ethnic identity and psychological adjustment among Lebanese-Canadians. *International Journal of Psychology, 40*(3), 157–168.

Ge, X., Conger, R. D., & Elder, G. H., Jr. (2001a). Pubertal transition, stressful life events, and the emergence of gender differences in adolescent depressive symptoms. *Developmental Psychology, 37*(3), 404–417.

Ge, X., Conger, R. D., & Elder, G. H., Jr. (2001b). The relation between puberty and psychological distress in adolescent boys. *Journal of Research on Adolescence, 11*(1), 49–70.

Ge, X., Donnellan, M. B., & Wenk, E. (2001c). The development of persistent criminal offending in males. *Criminal Justice and Behavior, 26*(5), 731–755.

Ge, X., et al. (2003). It's about timing and change: Pubertal transition effects on symptoms of major depression among African American youths. *Developmental Psychology, 39*(3), 430–439.

Geary, D. C. (1998). *Male, female: The evolution of human sex differences*. Washington, DC: American Psychological Association.

Gelinas, I., et al. (2000). Etude des liens entre le risque d'abandon scolaire, les strategies d'adaptation, le rendement scolaire et les habiletes scolaires. *Revue Canadienne de Psycho-Education, 29*(2), 223–240.

Geller, P. A., Kerns, D., & Klier, C. M. (2004). Anxiety following miscarriage and the subsequent pregnancy: A review of the literature and future directions. *Journal of Psychosomatic Research, 56*(1), 35–45.

Gelman, S. A., & Kremer, K. E. (1991). Understanding natural cause: Children's explanations of how objects and their properties originate. *Child Development, 62*, 396–414.

Gendall, K. A., Bulik, C. M., Joyce, P. R., McIntosh, V. V., & Carter, F. A. (2000). Menstrual cycle irregularity in bulimia nervosa: Associated factors and changes with treatment. *Journal of Psychosomatic Research, 49*(6), 409–415.

Georgiades, A., et al. (2000). Effects of exercise and weight loss on mental stress-induced cardiovascular responses in individuals with high blood pressure. *Hypertension, 36*, 171–176.

Geschwind, D. H. (2000). Interview cited in D. E. Rosenbaum (2000, May 16), On left-handedness, its causes and costs, *New York Times*, pp. F1, F6.

Geschwind, N., & Galaburda, A. M. (1987). *Cerebral lateralization: Biological mechanisms, associations, and pathology*. Cambridge, MA: MIT Press.

Gesell, A. (1928). *Infancy and human growth*. New York: Macmillan.

Gesell, A. (1929). Maturation and infant behavior patterns. *Psychological Review, 36*, 307–319.

Getzels, J. W., & Jackson, P. W. (1962). *Creativity and intelligence*. New York: Wiley.

Gewirtz, J. L., & Pelaez-Nogueras, M. (1992). B. F. Skinner's legacy to human infant behavior and development. *American Psychologist, 47*, 1411–1422.

Ghetti, S., & Alexander, K. W. (2004). "If it happened, I would remember it": Strategic use of event memorability in the rejection of false autobiographical events. *Child Development, 75*(2), 542–561.

Giangreco, M. F., Dennis, R., Cloninger, C., Edelman, S., & Schattman, R. (1993). "I've counted Jon": Transformational experiences of teachers educating students with disabilities. *Exceptional Children, 59*, 359–372.

Gibbs, J. T., & Hines, A. M. (1992). Negotiating ethnic identity: Issues for black-white biracial adolescents. In M. P. P. Root (Ed.), *Racially mixed people in America*. Newbury Park, CA: Sage.

Gibson, E. J. (1969). *Principles of perceptual learning and development*. New York: Appleton-Century-Crofts.

Gibson, E. J. (1991). *An odyssey in learning and perception*. Cambridge, MA: MIT Press.

Gibson, E. J., & Walk, R. D. (1960). The visual cliff. *Scientific American, 202*, 64–71.

Giedd, J. N. (2003). The anatomy of mentalization: A view from developmental neuroimaging. *Bulletin of the Menninger Clinic, 67*(2), 132–142.

Gignac, G., & Vernon, P. A. (2003). Digit symbol rotation: A more g-loaded version of the traditional digit symbol subtest. *Intelligence, 31*(1), 1–8.

Gil, K. M., et al. (2001). Daily coping practice predicts treatment effects in children with sickle cell disease. *Journal of Pediatric Psychology, 26*(3), 163–173.

Gili-Planas, M., Roca-Bennasar, M., Ferrer-Perez, V., & Bernardo-Arroyo, M. (2001). Suicidal ideation, psychiatric disorder, and medical illness in a community epidemiological study. *Suicide and Life-Threatening Behavior, 31*(2), 207–213.

Gilligan, C. (1977). In a different voice: Women's conceptions of self and morality. *Harvard Educational Review, 47*, 481–517.

Gilligan, C. (1982). *In a different voice*. Cambridge, MA: Harvard University Press.

Gilligan, C., & Attanucci, J. (1988). Two moral orientations: Gender differences and similarities. *Merrill-Palmer Quarterly, 34*, 223–237.

Gillio, R. G. (1999). Bitter pills: Inside the hazardous world of legal drugs. *Journal of the American Medical Association, 281*, 469.

Glasberg, R., & Aboud, F. (1982). Keeping one's distance from sadness: Children's self-reports of emotional experience. *Developmental Psychology, 18*, 287–293.

Glater, J. D. (2001, March 16). Women are close to being majority of law students. *New York Times*, pp. A1, A16.

Gleason, T. R. (2002). Social provisions of real and imaginary relationships in early childhood. *Developmental Psychology, 38*(6), 979–992.

Gleason, T. R. (2004). Imaginary companions and peer acceptance. *International Journal of Behavioral Development, 28*(3), 204–209.

Gleason, T. R., Sebanc, A. M., & Hartup, W. W. (2003). Imaginary companions of preschool children. In M. E. Hertzig & E. A. Farber (Eds.), *Annual progress in child psychiatry and child development: 2000–2001* (pp. 101–121). New York: Brunner-Routledge.

Gobet, F., & Simon, H. A. (2000). Five seconds or sixty? Presentation time in expert memory. *Cognitive Science, 24*(4), 651–682.

Goetz, M. J., Johnstone, E. C., & Ratcliffe, S. G. (1999). Criminality and antisocial behaviour in unselected men with sex chromosomes abnormalities. *Psychological Medicine, 29*(4), 953–962.

Gogate, L. J., Bahrick, L. E., & Watson, J. D. (2000). A study of multimodal motherese: The role of temporal synchrony between verbal labels and gestures. *Child Development, 71*(4), 878–894.

Goldberg, J, Holtz, D., Hyslop, T., & Tolosa, J. E. (2002). Has the use of routine episiotomy decreased? Examination of episiotomy rates from 1983 to 2000. *Obstetrics and Gynecology, 99*(3), 395–400.

Goldberg, S. (1983). Parent-infant bonding: Another look. *Child Development, 54*, 1355–1382.

Goldfield, B. A., & Reznick, J. S. (1990). Early lexical acquisition: Rate, content, and the vocabulary spurt. *Journal of Child Language, 17*, 171–183.

Goldfried, M. R. (2001). Integrating gay, lesbian, and bisexual issues into mainstream psychology. *American Psychologist, 56*(11), 977–988.

Goldschmidt, L., Day, N. L., & Richardson, G. A. (2000). Effects of prenatal marijuana exposure on child behavior problems at age 10. *Neurotoxicology and Teratology, 22*(3), 325–336.

Goldsmith, H. H., Kagan, J., Dunn, J., Kopp, C. B., Neufeld, S. J., Mascolo, M. F., Fischer, K. W., & Li, J. (2003). Part III: Genetics and development. In R. J. Davidson et al. (Eds.), *Handbook of affective sciences*. London: Oxford University Press.

Goldstein, E. B. (2005). *Cognitive psychology: Connecting mind, research, and everyday experience*. Belmont, CA: Wadsworth.

Goldstein, I. (2004). Androgen physiology in

sexual medicine. *Sexuality and Disability, 22*(2), 165–169.

Goleman, D. J. (1995). *Emotional intelligence.* New York: Bantam Books.

Golombok, S., & Hines, M. (2004). Sex differences in social behavior. In P. K. Smith & C. H. Hart (Eds.), *Blackwell handbook of childhood social development* (pp. 117–136). Malden, MA: Blackwell.

Golub, S. (1992). *Periods: From menarche to menopause.* Newbury Park, CA: Sage.

González, Y. S., Moreno, D. S., & Schneider, B. H. (2004). Friendship expectations of early adolescents in Cuba and Canada. *Journal of Cross-Cultural Psychology, 35*(4), 436–445.

Goode, E. (2000, June 25). Thinner: The male battle with anorexia. *New York Times,* p. MH8.

Goodman, G. S., & Clarke-Stewart, A. (1991). Suggestibility in children's testimony: Implications for sexual abuse investigations. In J. Doris (Ed.), *The suggestibility of children's recollections.* Washington, DC: American Psychological Association.

Goodman, G. S., Rudy, L., Bottoms, B. L., & Aman, C. (1990). Children's concerns and memory: Issues of ecological validity in the study of children's eyewitness testimony. In R. Fivush & J. A. Hudson (Eds.), *Knowing and remembering in young children.* Cambridge: Cambridge University Press.

Goodsitt, J. V., Morse, P. A., Ver Hoeve, J. N., & Cowan, N. (1984). Infant speech recognition in multisyllabic contexts. *Child Development, 55,* 903–910.

Goossens, L., Beyers, W., Emmen, M., & Aken, M. A. G. van (2002). The imaginary audience and personal fable: Factor analyses and concurrent validity of the "New Look" measures. *Journal of Research on Adolescence, 12*(2), 193–215.

Gopnik, A., & Meltzoff, A. N. (1987). The development of categorization in the second year and its relation to other cognitive and linguistic developments. *Child Development, 58,* 1523–1531.

Gopnik, A., & Meltzoff, A. N. (1992). Categorization and naming: Basic-level sorting in eighteen-month-olds and its relation to language. *Child Development, 63,* 1091–1103.

Gopnik, A., & Slaughter, V. (1991). Young children's understanding of changes in their mental states. *Child Development, 62,* 98–110.

Gormally, S., et al. (2001). Contact and nutrient caregiving effects on newborn infant pain responses. *Developmental Medicine and Child Neurology, 43*(1), 28–38.

Gottfried, A. E., Bathurst, K., & Gottfried, A. W. (1994). Role of maternal and dual-earner employment in children's development: A longitudinal study. In A. E. Gottfried & A. W. Gottfried (Eds.), *Redefining families: Implications for children's development.* New York: Plenum.

Gottfried, G. M., Hickling, A. K., Totten, L. R., Mkroyan, A., & Reisz, A. (2003). To be or not to be a galaprock: Preschoolers' intuitions about the importance of knowledge and

action for pretending. *British Journal of Developmental Psychology, 21*(3), 397–414.

Gottlieb, L. N., & Mendelson, M. J. (1990). Parental support and firstborn girls' adaptation to the birth of a sibling. *Journal of Applied Developmental Psychology, 11,* 29–48.

Government of Alberta (2007). Finding quality child care. Available at http://www.child.gov .ab.ca/whatwedo/childcare/page.cfm?pg= Finding%20Quality%20Child%20Care

Graber, J. A., Seeley, J. R., Brooks-Gunn, J., & Lewinsohn, P. M. (2004). Is pubertal timing associated with psychopathology in young adulthood? *Journal of the American Academy of Child and Adolescent Psychiatry, 43*(6), 718–726.

Graffy, J., Taylor, J., Williams, A., & Eldridge, S. (2004). Randomised controlled trial of support from volunteer counsellors for mothers considering breast feeding. *British Medical Journal, 328*(7,430), 26–29.

Granato, A., & Van Pelt, J. (2003). Effects of early ethanol exposure on dendrite growth of cortical pyramidal neurons: Inferences from a computational model. *Developmental Brain Research, 142*(2), 223–227.

Granot, D., & Mayseless, O. (2001). Attachment security and adjustment to school in middle childhood. *International Journal of Behavioral Development, 25*(6), 530–541.

Grazioli, R., & Terry, D. J. (2000). The role of cognitive vulnerability and stress in the prediction of postpartum depressive symptomatology. *British Journal of Clinical Psychology, 39*(4), 329–347.

Greco, C., Rovee-Collier, C., Hayne, H., Griesler, P., & Early, L. (1986). Ontogeny of early event memory: II. Encoding and retrieval by 2- and 3-month-olds. *Infant Behavior and Development, 9,* 461–472.

Greeff, A. P., & Van Der Merwe, S. (2004). Variables associated with resilience in divorced families. *Social Indicators Research, 68*(1), 59–75.

Green, J. A., Gustafson, G. E., & McGhie, A. C. (1998). Changes in infants' cries as a function of time in a cry bout. *Child Development, 69*(2), 271–279.

Green, J. A., Jones, L. E., & Gustafson, G. E. (1987). Perception of cries by parents and nonparents: Relation to cry acoustics. *Developmental Psychology, 23,* 370–382.

Green, R. (1978). Sexual identity of 37 children raised by homosexual or transsexual parents. *American Journal of Psychiatry, 135,* 692–697.

Green, R., Mandel, J. B., Hotvedt, M. E., Gray, J., & Smith, L. (1986). Lesbian mothers and their children: A comparison with solo parent heterosexual mothers and their children. *Archives of Sexual Behavior, 15,* 167–184.

Green, W. H. (1991). Principles of psychopharmacotherapy and specific drug treatments. In M. Lewis (Ed.), *Child and adolescent psychiatry: A comprehensive textbook.* Baltimore: Williams & Wilkins.

Greenberg, J. (2002). Who stole the money, and when? Individual and situational determinants of employee theft. *Organizational*

Behavior and Human Decision Processes, 89(1), 985–1003.

Greene, A. (2003). Bedwetting. U.S. National Library of Medicine and the National Institutes of Health. Available at http://www .nlm.nih.gov/medlineplus/ency/article/ 001556.htm

Greene, R. W., & Ablon, J. S. (2001). What does the MTA study tell us about effective psychosocial treatment for ADHD? *Journal of Clinical Child Psychology, 30*(1), 114–121.

Greenough, B. S. (1993, April 5). Breaking the genetic code. *Newsweek,* pp. 10–11.

Greenough, W. T. (1991). Experience as a component of normal development: Evolutionary considerations. *Developmental Psychology, 27,* 14–17.

Greenough, W. T., Black, J. E., & Wallace, C. S. (1987). Experience and brain development. *Child Development, 58,* 539–559.

Gregory, K. M., & Whiren, A. (2003). The effect of verbal scaffolding on the complexity of preschool children's block constructions. In D. E. Lytle (Ed.), *Play and educational theory and practice* (pp. 117–133). Westport, CT: Praeger Publishers/Greenwood Publishing.

Griffin, C. (2001). Imagining new narratives of youth: Youth research, the "new Europe" and global youth culture. *Childhood: A Global Journey of Child Research, 8*(2), 147–166.

Griffin, K. W., Scheier, L. M., Botvin, G. J., & Diaz, T. (2001). Protective role of personal competence skills in adolescent substance use: Psychological well-being as a mediating factor. *Psychology of Addictive Behaviors, 15*(3), 194–203.

Griffin, R. S., & Gross, A. M. (2004). Childhood bullying: Current empirical findings and future directions for research. *Aggression and Violent Behavior, 9*(4), 379–400.

Grön, G., Wunderlich, A. P., Spitzer, M., Tomczak, R., & Riepe, M. W. (2000). Brain activation during human navigation: Gender-different neural networks as substrate of performance. *Nature Neuroscience, 3*(4), 404–408.

Grosenick, J. K., George, N. L., & George, M. P. (1991). Public school services for behaviorally disordered students: Program practices in the 1980s. *Behavioral Disorders, 16,* 87–96.

Grossman, A. W., Churchill, J. D., McKinney, B. C., Kodish, I. M., Otte, S. L., Greenough, W. T. (2003). Experience effects on brain development: Possible contributions to psychopathology. *Journal of Child Psychology and Psychiatry and Allied Disciplines, 44*(1), 33–63.

Grossmann, K., et al. (2002). The uniqueness of the child-father attachment relationship: Fathers' sensitive and challenging play as a pivotal variable in a 16-year longitudinal study. *Social Development, 11*(3), 307–331.

Grossmann, K., & Grossmann, K. E. (1991). Newborn behavior, the quality of early parenting, and later toddler-parent relationships in a group of German infants. In J. K. Nugent, B. M. Lester, & T. B. Brazelton (Eds.), *The cultural context of infancy* (v. 2).

Norwood, NJ: Ablex.

Grusec, J. E. (1991). Socializing concern for others in the home. *Developmental Psychology, 27,* 338–342.

Grusec, J. E. (2002). Parenting socialization and children's acquisition of values. In M. H. Bornstein (Ed.), *Handbook of parenting, v. 5, Practical issues in parenting* (2nd ed.) (pp. 143–167). Mahwah, NJ: Lawrence Erlbaum Associates.

Grusec, J. E., Davidov, M., & Lundell, L. (2002). Prosocial and helping behavior. In P. Smith & C. H. Hart (Eds.), *Blackwell handbook of childhood social development* (pp. 457–474). Malden, MA: Blackwell.

Grusec, J. E., Goodnow, J. J., & Kuczynski, L. (2000). New directions in analyses of parenting contributions to children's acquisition of values. *Child Development, 71*(1), 205–211.

Grusec, J. E., & Lytton, H. (1988). *Social development: History, theory, and research.* New York: Springer-Verlag.

Grych, J. H., Fincham, F. D., Jouriles, E. N., & McDonald, R. (2000). Interparental conflict and child adjustment: Testing the mediational role of appraisals in the cognitive-contextual framework. *Child Development, 71*(6), 1648–1661.

Guelseren, L. (1999). Dogum sonrasi depresyon: Bir goezden gecirme. *Turk Psikiyatri Dergisi, 10*(1), 58–67.

Guerin, D. W., Gottfried, A. W., & Thomas, C. W. (1997). Difficult temperament and behaviour problems: A longitudinal study from 1.5 to 12 years. *International Journal of Behavioral Development, 21*(1), 71–90.

Guerra, N. G., & Slaby, R. G. (1990). Cognitive mediators of aggression in adolescent offenders: Intervention. *Developmental Psychology, 26,* 269–277.

Guerrero, M. C. M. de, & Villamil, O. S. (2000). Activating the ZPD: Mutual scaffolding in L2 peer revision. *Modern Language Journal, 84*(1), 51–68.

Guerrini, I., Thomson, A. D., & Gurling, H. D. (2007). The importance of alcohol misuse, malnutrition and genetic susceptibility on brain growth and plasticity. *Neuroscience and Biobehavioral Reviews, 31,* 212–220.

Gupta, V. B., Nwosa, N. M., Nadel, T. A., & Inamdar, S. (2001). Externalizing behaviors and television viewing in children of low-income minority parents. *Clinical Pediatrics, 40*(6), 337–341.

Gurian, M., & Stevens, K. (2005). *The minds of boys: Saving our sons from falling behind in school and life.* San Francisco, CA: Jossey-Bass.

Gustafson, G. E., Green, J. A., & Cleland, J. W. (1994). Robustness of individual identity in the cries of human infants. *Developmental Psychobiology, 27*(1), 1–9.

Gustafson, G. E., & Harris, K. L. (1990). Women's responses to young infants' cries. *Developmental Psychology, 26*(1), 144–152.

Gutknecht, L. (2001). Full-genome scans with autistic disorder: A review. *Behavior Genetics, 31*(1), 113–123.

Guttman, N., & Zimmerman, D. R. (2000). Low-income mothers' views on breast-feeding. *Social Science and Medicine, 50*(10), 1457–1473.

Haapasalo, J., & Moilanen, J. (2004). Official and self-reported childhood abuse and adult crime of young offenders. *Criminal Justice and Behavior, 31*(2), 127–149.

Haden, C. A., Ornstein, P. A., Eckerman, C. O., & Didow, S. M. (2001). Mother-child conversational interactions as events unfold: Linkages to subsequent remembering. *Child Development, 72*(4), 1016–1031.

Haenen, J. (2001). Outlining the teaching-learning process: Piotr Gal'perin's contribution. *Learning and Instruction, 11*(2), 157–170.

Hainline, L., & Abramov, I. (1992). Assessing visual development: Is infant vision good enough? In C. Rovee-Collier & L. P. Lipsitt (Eds.), *Advances in infancy research* (v. 7). Norwood, NJ: Ablex.

Haith, M. M. (1966). The response of the human newborn to visual movement. *Journal of Experimental Child Psychology, 3,* 235–243.

Haith, M. M. (1979). Visual cognition in early infancy. In R. B. Kearsly & I. E. Sigel (Eds.), *Infants at risk: Assessment of cognitive functioning.* Hillsdale, NJ: Erlbaum.

Haith, M. M. (1986). Sensory and perceptual processes in early infancy. *Journal of Pediatrics, 109,* 158–171.

Haith, M. M. (1990). Progress in the understanding of sensory and perceptual processes in early infancy. *Merrill-Palmer Quarterly, 36,* 1–26.

Haith, M. M. (1998). Who put the cog in infant cognition? Is rich interpretation too costly? *Infant Behavior and Development, 21*(2), 167–179.

Hakim, A. A., et al. (1998). Effects of walking on mortality among nonsmoking retired men. *New England Journal of Medicine, 338,* 94–99.

Hala, S., Hug, S., & Henderson, A. (2003). Executive function and false-belief understanding in preschool children: Two tasks are harder than one. *Journal of Cognition and Development, 4*(3), 275–298.

Halgin, R. P., & Whitbourne, S. K. (1993). *Abnormal psychology.* Fort Worth, TX: Harcourt Brace Jovanovich.

Hall, G. S. (1904). *Adolescence: Its psychology and its relation to physiology, anthropology, sociology, sex, crime, religion, and education.* Englewood Cliffs, NJ: Prentice Hall.

Halpern, D. F. (2003). Sex differences in cognitive abilities. *Applied Cognitive Psychology, 17*(3), 375–376.

Halpern, D. F. (2004). A cognitive-process taxonomy for sex differences in cognitive abilities. *Current Directions in Psychological Science, 13*(4), 135–139.

Halpern, D. F., & LaMay, M. L. (2000). The smarter sex: A critical review of sex differences in intelligence. *Educational Psychology Review, 12*(2), 229–246.

Hamm, J. V. (2000). Do birds of a feather flock together? The variable bases for African American, Asian American, and European American adolescents' selection of similar friends. *Developmental Psychology, 36*(2), 209–219.

Hammen, C. (2003). Social stress and women's risk for recurrent depression. *Archives of Women's Mental Health, 6*(1), 9–13.

Hammer, C. S., Miccio, A. W., & Wagstaff, D. A. (2003). Home literacy experiences and their relationship to bilingual preschoolers' developing English literacy abilities: An initial investigation. *Language, Speech, and Hearing Services in Schools, 34*(1), 20–30.

Hampson, J. (1989, April). Elements of style: Maternal and child contributions to expressive and referential styles of language acquisition. Paper presented at the meeting of the Society for Research in Child Development, Kansas City, MO.

Han, W., Waldfogel, J., & Brooks-Gunn, J. (2001). The effects of early maternal employment on later cognitive and behavioral outcomes. *Journal of Marriage and the Family, 63*(2), 336–354.

Hanlon, T. E., Bateman, R. W., Simon, B. D., O'Grady, K. E., & Carswell, S. B. (2004). Antecedents and correlates of deviant activity in urban youth manifesting behavioral problems. *Journal of Primary Prevention, 24*(3), 285–309.

Hanna, E. (1993, March). *Sex differences in play and imitation in toddlers.* Paper presented at the meeting of the Society for Research in Child Development, New Orleans, LA.

Hanna, E., & Meltzoff, A. N. (1993). Peer imitation by toddlers in laboratory, home, and day care contexts: Implications for social learning and memory. *Developmental Psychology, 29,* 701–710.

Hannah, H., Whyte, W., Hannah, S., Hewson, K., Amankwah, M., Cheng, A., Gafni, P., Guselle, M., Helewa, E., Hodnett, E. D., Hutton, E., Kung, R., McKay, D., Ross, S., Saigal, S., & Willan, A. (2006). Maternal outcomes at 2 years after planned cesarean section versus planned vaginal birth for breech presentation at term: The international randomized Term Breech Trial. *American Journal of Obstetrics and Gynecology, 191*(3), 917–927.

Hannon, P., Bowen, D. J., Moinpour, C. M., & McLerran, D. F. (2003). Correlations in perceived food use between the family food preparer and their spouses and children. *Appetite, 40*(1), 77–83.

Hannon, P., Willis, S. K., Bishop-Townsend, V., Martinez, I. M., & Scrimshaw, S. C. (2000). African-American and Latina adolescent mothers' infant feeding decisions and breastfeeding practices: A qualitative study. *Journal of Adolescent Health, 26*(6), 399–407.

Hans, S. L., Henson, L. C., & Jeremy, R. J. (1992). The development of infants exposed in utero to opioid drugs. In C. W. Greenbaum & J. G. Auerbach (Eds.), *Longitudinal studies of children at psychological risk: Cross-national perspectives.* Norwood, NJ: Ablex.

Hanson, R. F., & Spratt, E. G. (2000). Reactive attachment disorder: What we know about the disorder and implications for treatment. *Child Maltreatment, 5*(2), 137–145.

Hardin, E. E., Leong, F. T. L., & Osipow, S. H. (2001). Cultural relativity in the conceptualization of career maturity. *Journal of Vocational Behavior, 58*(1), 36–52.

Harding, D. J. (2003). Counterfactual models of neighborhood effects: The effect of neighborhood poverty on dropping out and teenage pregnancy. *American Journal of Sociology, 109*(3), 676–719.

Harel, J., & Scher, A. (2003). Insufficient responsiveness in ambivalent mother-infant relationships: Contextual and affective aspects. *Infant Behavior and Development, 26*(3), 371–383.

Harlow, H. F., & Harlow, M. K. (1966). Learning to love. *American Scientist, 54,* 244–272.

Harlow, H. F., Harlow, M. K., & Suomi, S. J. (1971). From thought to therapy: Lessons from a primate laboratory. *American Scientist, 59,* 538–549.

Harris, D. L., Brown, E., Marriott, C., Whittall, S., & Harmer, S. (1991). Monsters, ghosts, and witches: Testing the limits of the fantasy-reality distinction in young children. *British Journal of Developmental Psychology, 9,* 105–123.

Harris, D. V. (1991). Exercise and fitness during adolescence. In R. M. Lerner, A. C. Petersen, & J. Brooks-Gunn (Eds.), *Encyclopedia of adolescence.* New York: Garland.

Harris, G. (2004, September 14). FDA links drugs to being suicidal. Available at http://www.nytimes.com

Harris, J. (1990). *Early language development.* New York: Routledge.

Harris, J. G., Tulsky, D. S., & Schultheis, M. T. (2003). Assessment of the non-native English speaker: Assimilating history and research findings to guide clinical practice. In D. S. Tulsky et al. (Eds.), *Clinical interpretation of the WAIS-III and WMS-III* (pp. 343–390). San Diego: Academic Press.

Hart, D., Burock, D., London, B., & Atkins, R. (2003). Prosocial tendencies, antisocial behavior, and moral development. In A. Slater & G. Bremner (Eds.), *An introduction to developmental psychology* (pp. 334–356). Malden, MA: Blackwell.

Hart, S., Boylan, L. M., Carroll, S., Musick, Y., & Lampe, R. M. (2003). Breast-fed one-week-olds demonstrate superior neurobehavioral organization. *Journal of Pediatric Psychology, 28*(8), 529–534.

Harter, S. (1987). The determinants and mediational role of global self-worth in children. In N. Eisenberg (Ed.), *Contemporary topics in developmental psychology.* New York: Wiley.

Harter, S. (1988). *The self-perception profile for adolescents.* Unpublished manual, University of Denver.

Harter, S. (1990a). Issues in the assessment of the self-concept of children and adolescents. In A. LaGreca (Ed.), *Through the eyes of a child.* Boston: Allyn & Bacon.

Harter, S. (1990b). Processes underlying adolescent self-concept formation. In R. Montemayor, G. R. Adams, T. P. Gullotta (Eds.), *From childhood to adolescence: A transitional period?* Newbury Park, CA: Sage.

Harter, S. (1990c). Self and identity development. In S. S. Feldman & G. R. Elliott (Eds.), *At the threshold: The developing adolescent.* Cambridge, MA: Harvard University Press.

Harter, S. (1999). *The construction of the self.* New York: Guilford.

Harter, S., & Monsour, A. (1992). Developmental analysis of conflict caused by opposing attributes in the adolescent self-portrait. *Developmental Psychology, 28,* 251–260.

Harter, S., & Pike, R. (1984). The pictorial scale of perceived competence and social acceptance for young children. *Child Development, 55,* 1969–1982.

Harter, S., Waters, P. L., Whitesall, N. R., & Kastelic, D. (1998). Level of voice among female and male high school students: Relational context, support and gender orientation. *Developmental Psychology, 34*(5), 892–901

Hartup, W. W. (1983). The peer system. In P. H. Mussen (Ed.), *Handbook of child psychology, v. 4, Socialization, personality, and social development.* New York: Wiley.

Hartup, W. W. (1992a). Conflict and friendship relations. In C. U. Shantz & W. W. Hartup (Eds.), *Conflict in child and adolescent development.* Cambridge, MA: Cambridge University Press.

Hartup, W. W. (1992b). Friendships and their developmental significance. In H. McGurk (Ed.), *Childhood social development.* Hove, United Kingdom: Erlbaum.

Hartup, W. W. (1993). Adolescents and their friends. In B. Laursen (Ed.), *New directions in child development. no. 60, Close friendships in adolescence.* San Francisco: Jossey-Bass.

Harvey, E. (1999). Short-term and long-term effects of early parental employment on children of the National Longitudinal Survey of Youth. *Developmental Psychology, 35*(2), 445–459.

Hashimoto, N. (1991). Memory development in early childhood: Encoding process in a spatial task. *Journal of Genetic Psychology, 152,* 101–117.

Haskins, R. (1989). Beyond metaphor: The efficacy of early childhood education. *American Psychologist, 44,* 274–282.

Haslam, C., & Draper, E. S. (2001). A qualitative study of smoking during pregnancy. *Psychology, Health, and Medicine, 6*(1), 95–99.

Hasselhorn, M. (1992). Task dependency and the role of typicality and metamemory in the development of an organizational strategy. *Child Development, 63,* 202–214.

Hastings, P. D., Zahn-Waxler, C., Robinson, J., Usher, B., & Bridges, D. (2000). The development of concern for others in children with behavior problems. *Developmental Psychology, 36*(5), 531–546.

Hatch, M. C., Shu, X. O., McLean, D. E., Levin, B., Begg, M., Reuss, L., & Susser, M. (1993).Maternal exercise during pregnancy, physical fitness, and fetal growth. *American Journal of Epidemiology, 137*(10), 1105–1114.

Haugaard, J. J. (2000). The challenge of defining child sexual abuse. *American Psychologist, 55*(9), 1036–1039.

Hauser, P., et al. (1993). Attention deficit-hyperactivity disorder in people with generalized resistance to thyroid hormone. New *England Journal of Medicine, 328,* 997–1001.

Hay, D. F., Caplan, M., Castle, J., & Stimson, C. A. (1991). Does sharing become increasingly "rational" in the second year of life? *Developmental Psychology, 27,* 987–993.

Hay, D. F., & Murray, P. (1982). Giving and requesting: Social facilitation of infants' offers to adults. *Infant Behavior and Development, 5,* 301–310.

Hay, D. F., Payne, A., & Chadwick, A. (2004). Peer relations in childhood. *Journal of Child Psychology and Psychiatry. 45*(1), 84–108.

Hayne, H., & Fagen, J. W. (Eds.) (2003). *Progress in infancy research,* v. 3. Mahwah, NJ: Lawrence Erlbaum Associates.

Health Canada (2000). Perinatal health indicators for Canada: A resource manual. Ottawa: Minister of Public Works and Government Services Canada. Available at http://www.phac-aspc.gc.ca/rhs-ssg/phic-ispc/pdf/indperie.pdf

Health Canada (2001). It takes a community: Framework for the First Nations and Inuit fetal alcohol syndrome and fetal alcohol effects syndrome initiative. Available at http://www.hc-sc.gc.ca/fnih-spni/alt_formats/fnihb-dgspni/pdf/pubs/preg-gros/2001_takes-prend-commun_e.pdf

Health Canada (2002). Canada's Food Guide to Healthy Eating Focus on Preschoolers—Background for Educators and Communicators. Ottawa, ON: Health Canada.

Health Canada (2003). Canadian guidelines for sexual health education. Ottawa, ON: Population and Public Health Branch, Health Canada.

Health Canada (2004). *Exclusive breastfeeding duration: 2004 Health Canada recommendation.* Ottawa: Minister of Public Works and Government Services.

Health Canada (2004b). Trends in the health of Canadian Youth. Available at http://www.phac-aspc.gc.ca/dca-dea/7–18yrs-ans/index_e.html

Health Canada (2005a). Healthy living. Available at http://www.hc-sc.gc.ca/hl-vs/tobac-tabac/body-corps/preg-gros/index_e.html

Health Canada (2005b). Changing fertility patterns: Trends and implications. Available at http://www.hc-sc.gc.ca/sr-sr/alt_formats/iacb-dgiac/pdf/pubs/hpr-rps/bull/2005–10-chang-fertilit/2005–10-chang-fertilit_e.pdf

Health Canada (2005c). Acting on what we know: Preventing youth suicide in First Nations. Available at http://www.hc-sc.gc.ca/fnih-spni/pubs/suicide/prev_youth-jeunes/section1_e.html

Health Canada (2007a). *Eating well with Canada's food guide: A resource for educators and communicators.* Ottawa, ON: Health Canada.

Health Canada (2007b). The sensible guide to a healthy pregnancy. Available at http://www.healthypregnancy.gc.ca

Healthy Active Living Committee, Canadian Paediatric Society (2002). Healthy active living for children and youth. *Paediatric Child Health, 7*(5), 339–345.

Hayward, C. (Ed.) (2003). *Gender differences at puberty.* New York: Cambridge University Press.

Hebert, T. P. (2000). Gifted males pursuing careers in elementary education: Factors that influence a belief in self. *Journal for the Education of the Gifted, 24*(1), 7–45.

Hechtman, L. (1991). Developmental, neuro-biological, and psychosocial aspects of hyperactivity, impulsivity, and inattention. In M. Lewis (Ed.), *Child and adolescent psychiatry: A comprehensive textbook.* Baltimore: Williams & Wilkins.

Heilman, K. M., Nadeau, S. E., & Beversdorf, D. O. (2003). Creative innovation: Possible brain mechanisms. *Neurocase, 9*(5), 369–379.

Heim, C., et al. (2000). Pituitary-adrenal and autonomic responses to stress in women after sexual and physical abuse in child-hood. *Journal of the American Medical Association, 284,* 592–597.

Helms, J. E. (1992, September). Why is there no study of cultural equivalence in stan-dardized cognitive ability testing? *American Psychologist, 47,* 1083–1101.

Hendin, H., Maltsberger, J. T., Lipschitz, A., Pollinger H., & Kyle, J. (2001). Recog-nizing and responding to a suicide crisis. *Suicide and Life-Threatening Behavior, 31*(2), 115–128.

Henker, B., & Whalen, C. K. (1989). Hyper-activity and attention deficits. *American Psychologist, 44,* 216–223.

Henry, D., et al. (2000). Normative influences on aggression in urban elementary school classrooms. *American Journal of Community Psychology, 28*(1) 59–81.

Hensch, T. K. (2003). Controlling the critical period. *Neuroscience Research, 47*(1), 17–22.

Hepper, P. G., Shahidullah, S., & White, R. (1990, October 4). Origins of fetal handed-ness. *Nature, 347,* 431.

Hergenhahn, B. R. (2005). *An introduction to the history of psychology* (5th ed.). Belmont, CA: Wadsworth.

Herman, A. I., Philbeck, J. W., Vasilopoulos, N. L., & Depetrillo, P. B. (2003). Serotonin transporter promoter polymorphism and differences in alcohol consumption behav-iour in a college student population. *Alcohol and Alcoholism, 38*(5), 446–449.

Herr, E. L. (2001). Career development and its practice: A historical perspective. *Career Development Quarterly, 49*(3), 196–211.

Hershberger, S. L., & D'Augelli, A. R. (2000). Issues in counseling lesbian, gay, and bisexual adolescents. In R. M. Perez, K. A. DeBord, & K. J. Bieschke (Eds.), *Handbook of counseling and psychotherapy with lesbian, gay, and bisexual clients* (pp. 225–247). Washington, DC: American Psychological Association.

Hertenstein, M. J., & Campos, J. J. (2004). The retention effects of an adult's emotional dis-plays on infant behavior. *Child Development, 75*(2), 595–613.

Hespos, S. J., & Baillargeon, R. (2001a). Infants' knowledge about occlusion and con-tainment events: A surprising discrepancy. *Psychological Science, 121*(2), 141–147.

Hespos, S. J., & Baillargeon, R. (2001b). Rea-soning about containment events in very young infants. *Cognition, 78*(3), 207–245.

Hetherington, E. M. (1987). Family relations six years after divorce. In K. Pasley & M. Ihinger-Tallman (Eds.), *Remarriage and stepparenting: Current theory and research.* New York: Guilford.

Hetherington, E. M. (1989). Coping with family transition: Winners, losers, and sur-vivors. *Child Development, 60,* 1–14.

Hetherington, E. M., & Clingempeel, W. G. (1992). Coping with marital transitions. *Monographs of the Society for Research in Child Development, 57*(2–3, ser. 227).

Hetherington, E. M., Stanley-Hagan, M., & Anderson, E. R. (1989). Marital transitions: A child's perspective. *American Psychologist, 44,* 303–312.

Hickling, A. K., & Wellman, H. M. (2001). The emergence of children's causal explana-tions and theories: Evidence from everyday conversation. *Developmental Psychology, 37*(5), 668–683.

Hickman, G. P., Bartholomae, S., & McKenry, P. C. (2000). Influence of parenting style on the adjustment and academic achievement of traditional college freshmen. *Journal of College Student Development, 41*(1), 41–54.

Higley, J. D., Lande, J. S., & Suomi, S. J. (1989). Day care and the promotion of emo-tional development: Lessons from a monkey laboratory. In J. S. Lande, S. Scarr, & N. Gunzenhauser (Eds.), *Caring for children: Challenge to America.* Hillsdale, NJ: Erlbaum.

Hinde, R. A., & Stevenson-Hinde, J. (1988) Interpersonal relationships and child devel-opment. *Annual Progress in Child Psychiatry & Child Development,* 5–26.

Hindley, C. B., Filliozat, A. M., Klackenberg, G., Nicolet-Neister, D., & Sand, E. A. (1966). Differences in age of walking for five European longitudinal samples. *Human Biology, 38,* 364–379.

Hindmarsh, G. J., O'Callaghan, M. J., Mohay, H. A., & Rogers, Y. M. (2000). Gender dif-ferences in cognitive abilities at 2 years in ELBW infants. *Early Human Development, 60*(2), 115–122.

Hinojosa, T., Sheu, C., & Michel, G. F. (2003). Infant hand-use preferences for grasping objects contributes to the develop-ment of a hand-use preference for manipu-lating objects. *Developmental Psychobiology, 43*(4), 328–334.

Hirsh-Pasek, K. (1991). Pressure or challenge in preschool? How academic environments affect children? In L. Rescorla, M. C. Hyson, & K. Hirsh-Pasek (Eds.), *New directions in child development, no. 53, Academic instruction in early childhood: Challenge or pressure?* San Francisco: Jossey-Bass.

Hirsh-Pasek, K., Hyson, M. C., & Rescorla, L. (1990). Academic environments in preschool: Do they pressure or challenge young children. *Early Education and Development, 1,* 401–423.

Hodges, J., & Tizard, B. (1989). Social and family relationships of ex-institutional ado-lescents. *Journal of Child Psychology and Psychiatry, 30,* 77–97.

Hoegh, D. G., & Bourgeois, M. J. (2002). Prelude and postlude to the self: Correlates of achieved identity. *Youth and Society, 33*(4), 573–594.

Hoff-Ginsberg, E. (1998). The relation of birth order and socioeconomic status to children's language experience and language development. *Applied Psycholinguistics, 19*(4), 603–629.

Hoffman, L. W., & Youngblade, L. M. (1998). Maternal employment, morale, and parenting style: Social class comparisons. *Journal of Applied Developmental Psychology, 19*(3), 389–413.

Hoglund, C. L., & Bell, T. S. (1991, August). Longitudinal study of self-esteem in chil-dren from 7–11 years. Paper presented at the meeting of the American Psychological Association, San Francisco.

Holland, A. L. (2004). Plasticity and develop-ment. *Brain and Language, 88*(2), 254–255.

Holland, J. J. (2000, July 25). Groups link media to child violence. Available at http://www.ap.org

Holland, J. L. (1996). Exploring careers with a typology. *American Psychologist, 51,* 397–406.

Holland, J. L. (1997). *Making vocational choices: A theory of vocational personalities and work environments* (3rd ed.). Odessa, FL: Psychological Assessment Resources.

Holliday, R. E. (2003). Reducing misinfor-mation effects in children with cognitive interviews: Dissociating recollection and familiarity. *Child Development, 74*(3), 728–751.

Holloway, J. H. (2004). *Part-time work and stu-dent achievement.* Alexandria VA: Association for Supervision and Curriculum Develop-ment. Available at http://www.ascd.org/publications/ed_lead/200104/holloway.html

Holmes-Farley, S. R. (1998, September 16). Who should decide the sex of a baby? *New York Times,* p. A28.

Holobow, N., Genesee, F., & Lambert, W. (1991). The effectiveness of a foreign lan-guage immersion program for children from different ethnic and social class back-grounds: Report 2. *Applied Psycholinguistics, 12,* 179–198.

Holsen, I., Kraft, P., & Roysamb, E. (2001). The relationship between body image and depressed mood in adolescence: A 5-year longitudinal panel study. *Journal of Health Psychology, 6*(6), 613–627.

Honein, M. A., Paulozzi, L. J., Mathews, T. J., Erickson, J. D., & Wong, L. C. (2001).

Impact of folic acid fortification of the U.S. food supply on the occurrence of neural tube defects. *Journal of the American Medical Association, 285*(23), 2981–2986.

Honzik, M. P., Macfarlane, J. W., & Allen, L. (1948). The stability of mental test performance between two and eighteen years. *Journal of Experimental Education, 17*, 309–324.

Hopkins, B., & Westra, T. (1988). Maternal handling and motor development: An intracultural study. *Genetic, Social, and General Psychology Monographs, 14*, 377–420.

Hopkins, W. D., Dahl, J. F., & Pilcher, D. (2001). Genetic influence on the expression of hand preferences in chimpanzees (*Pan troglodytes*): Evidence in support of the right-shift theory and developmental instability. *Psychological Science, 12*(4), 299–303.

Hopkins-Golightly, T., Raz, S., & Sander, C. J. (2003). Influence of slight to moderate risk for birth hypoxia on acquisition of cognitive and language function in the preterm infant: A cross-sectional comparison with preterm-birth controls. *Neuropsychology, 17*(1), 3–13.

Howe, N., Petrakos, H., & Rinaldi, C. M. (1998). "All the sheeps are dead. He murdered them": Sibling pretense, negotiation, internal state language, and relationship quality. *Child Development, 69*(1), 182–191.

Howe, N., Petrakos, H., Rinaldi, C. M., & LeFebvre, R. (2005). "This Is a Bad Dog, You Know...": Constructing shared meanings during sibling pretend play. *Child Development, 76*(4), 783–794.

Howe, N., Rinaldi, C. M., Jennings, M., & Petrakos, H. (2002). "No! The lambs can stay out because they got cozies"; Constructive and destructive sibling conflict, pretend play, and social understanding. *Child Development, 73*, 1460–1473.

Howes, C. (1987). Social competence with peers in young children: Developmental sequences. *Developmental Review, 7*, 252–272.

Howes, C. (1988). Peer interaction of young children. *Monographs of the Society for Research in Child Development, 53*(1, ser. 217).

Howes, C., & Matheson, C. C. (1992a). Contextual constraints on the concordance of mother-child and teacher-child relationships. In R. C. Pianta (Ed.), *New directions for child development, no. 57, Beyond the parent: The role of other adults in children's lives*. San Francisco, Jossey-Bass.

Howes, C., & Matheson, C. C. (1992b). Sequences in the development of competent play with peers: Social and social pretend play. *Developmental Psychology, 28*, 961–974.

Hoy, E. A., & McClure, B. G. (2000). Preschool experience: A facilitator of very low birthweight infants' development? *Infant Mental Health Journal, 21*(6), 481–494.

Hu, F. B., et al. (2000). Physical activity and risk of stroke in women. *Journal of the American Medical Association, 283*, 2961–2967.

Huber, J., Darling, S., Park, K., & Soliman, K. F. A. (2001). Altered responsiveness to stress and NMDA following prenatal exposure to cocaine. *Physiology and Behavior, 72*(1–2), 181–188.

Hudson, J. A. (1990). The emergence of autobiographical memory in mother-child conversation. In R. Fivush & J. A. Hudson (Eds.), *Knowing and remembering in young children*. Cambridge: Cambridge University Press.

Hudziak, J. J. (2001). Latent class analysis of ADHD and comorbid symptoms in a population sample of adolescent female twins. *Journal of Child Psychology and Psychiatry and Allied Disciplines, 42*(7), 933–942.

Huijbregts, S. C. J., et al. (2003). Motor function under lower and higher controlled processing demands in early and continuously treated phenylketonuria. *Neuropsychology, 17*(3), 369–379.

Human Resources Development Canada (2004). Advancing the inclusion of persons with disabilities. Available at http://www.hrsdc.gc .ca/en/hip/odi/documents/ advancingInclusion04/aipd04.pdf

Humphreys, L. G. (1992). Commentary: What both critics and users of ability tests need to know. *Psychological Science, 3*, 271–274.

Hunter, S. C., & Boyle, J. M. E. (2004). Appraisal and coping strategy use in victims of school bullying. *British Journal of Educational Psychology, 74*(1), 83–107.

Huntington, L., Hans, S. L., & Zeskind, P. S. (1990). The relations among cry characteristics, demographic variables, and developmental test scores in infants prenatally exposed to methadone. *Infant Behavior and Development, 13*, 535–538.

Huston, A. C., et al. (1992). *Big world, small screen: The role of television in American society*. Lincoln: University of Nebraska Press.

Hutchison, S. J., et al. (1998). In-utero and neonatal exposure to secondhand smoke causes vascular dysfunction in newborn rats. *Journal of the American College of Cardiology, 32*(5), 1463–1467.

Hutton, U. M. Z., & Towse, J. N. (2001). Short-term memory and working memory as indices of children's cognitive skills. *Memory, 9*(4–6), 383–394.

Hyde, J. S., Fennema, E., & Lamon, S. J. (1990). Gender differences in mathematics performance: A meta-analysis. *Psychological Bulletin, 107*, 139–155.

Hyde, J. S., Krajnik, M., & Skuldt-Niederberger, K. (1991). Androgyny across the life span: A replication and longitudinal follow-up. *Developmental Psychology, 27*, 516–519.

Hymel, S., Schonert-Reichl, K. A., & Miller, L. D. (2006). Reading, 'riting, 'rithmetic and relationships: Considering the social side of education. *Exceptionality Education Canada, 16*(2/3), 149–192.

Hynd, G. W., & Hooper, S. R. (1992). *Neurological basis of childhood psychopathology*. Newbury Park, CA: Sage.

Hynes, M., Sheik, M., Wilson, H. G., & Spiegel, P. (2002). Reproductive health indicators and outcomes among refugee and internally displaced persons in postemergency phase camps. *Journal of the American Medical Association, 288*, 595–603.

Hyson, M. C. (1991). Building the hothouse: How mothers construct academic environments. In L. Rescorla, M. C. Hyson, & K. Hirsh-Pasek (Eds.), *New directions in child development, no. 53, Academic instruction in early childhood: Challenge or pressure?* New York: Jossey-Bass.

Ihle, W., Esser, G., Schmidt, M. H., & Blanz, B. (2000). Praevalenz, Komorbiditaet und Geschlechtsunterschiede psychischer Stoerungen vom Grundschul-bis ins fruehe Erwachsenenalter. *Zeitschrift für Klinische Psychologie und Psychotherapie: Forschung und Praxis, 29*(4), 263–275.

IJzendoorn, M. H. van, & Hubbard, F. O. A. (2000). Are infant crying and maternal responsiveness during the first year related to infant-mother attachment at 15 months? *Attachment and Human Development, 2*(3), 371–391.

IJzendoorn, M. H. van, & Kroonenberg, P. M. (1988). Cross-cultural patterns of attachment: A meta-analysis of the Strange Situation. *Child Development, 59*, 147–156.

IJzendoorn, M. H. van, Moran, G., Belsky, J., Pederson, D., Bakermans-Kranenburg, M. J., & Kneppers, K. (2000). The similarity of siblings' attachments to their mother. *Child Development, 71*(4), 1086–1098.

IJzendoorn, M. H. van, Sagi, A., & Lambermon, M. W. E. (1992). The multiple caretaker paradox: Data from Holland and Israel. In R. C. Pianta (Ed.), *New directions for child development, no. 57, Beyond the parent: The role of other adults in children's lives*. San Francisco: Jossey-Bass.

Ike, N. (2000). Current thinking on XYY syndrome. *Psychiatric Annals, 30*(2), 91–95.

Inhelder, B., & Piaget, J. (1959). *The early growth of logic in the child: Classification and seriation*. New York: Harper & Row.

Insel, T. R. (2000). Toward a neurobiology of attachment. *Review of General Psychology, 4*(2), 176–185.

Insel, T. R., O'Brien, D. J., & Leckman, J. F. (1999). Oxytocin, vasopressin, and autism: Is there a connection? *Biological Psychiatry, 45*(2), 145–157.

International Human Genome Sequencing Consortium (2001). Initial sequencing and analysis of the human genome. *Nature, 409*, 860–921.

Ishikawa, S., Oota, R., & Sakano, Y. (2003). The relationship between anxiety disorders tendencies and subjective school maladjustment in childhood. *Japanese Journal of Counseling Science, 36*(3), 264–271.

Isik, U., Oezek, E., Bilgen, H., & Cebeci, D. (2000). Comparison of oral glucose and sucrose solutions on pain response in neonates. *Journal of Pain, 1*(4), 275–278.

Isley, S., O'Neil, R., & Parke, R. D. (1996). The relation of parental affect and control behaviors to children's classroom acceptance: A concurrent and predictive analysis. *Early Education and Development, 7*, 7–23.

Iverson, J. M., Capirci, O., Longobardi, E., &

Caselli, M. C. (1999). Gesturing in mother-child interactions. *Cognitive Development, 14*(1), 57–75.

Izard, C. E. (1983). *Maximally discriminative facial movement scoring system.* Newark, DE: University of Delaware Instructional Resources Center.

Izard, C. E. (1991). *The psychology of emotions.* New York: Plenum.

Izard, C. E. (1992). Basic emotions, relations among emotions, and emotion-cognition relations. *Psychological Review, 99,* 561–565.

Izard, C. E., Hembree, E. A., & Huebner, R. R. (1987a). Infants' emotion expressions to acute pain: Developmental change and stability of individual differences. *Developmental Psychology, 23,* 105–113.

Izard, C. E., & Malatesta, C. Z. (1987b). Perspectives on emotional development. I. Differential emotions theory of early emotional development. In J. D. Osofsky (Ed.), *Handbook of infant development* (2nd ed.). New York: Wiley.

Jacklin, C. N. (1989). Female and male: Issues of gender. *American Psychologist, 44,* 127–133.

Jacklin, C. N., & McBride-Chang, C. (1991). The effects of feminist scholarship on developmental psychology. *Psychology of Women Quarterly, 15,* 549–556.

Jacklin, C. N., Wilcox, K. T., & Maccoby, E. E. (1988). Neonatal sex-steroid hormones and cognitive abilities at six years. *Developmental Psychobiology, 21,* 567–574.

Jackson, A. P. (2000). Maternal self-efficacy and children's influence on stress and parenting among single black mothers in poverty. *Journal of Family Issues, 21*(1), 3–16.

Jackson, L. A. (1992). *Physical appearance and gender: Sociobiological and sociocultural perspectives.* Albany, NY: SUNY Press.

Jacobi, C., Hayward, C., de Zwaan, M., Kraemer, H. C., & Agras, W. St. (2004). Coming to terms with risk factors for eating disorders: Application of risk terminology and suggestions for a general taxonomy. *Psychological Bulletin, 130*(1), 19–65.

Jacobson, J. L., Jacobson, S. W., Padgett, R. J., Brumitt, G. A., & Billings, R. L. (1992). Effects of prenatal PCB exposure on cognitive processing efficiency and sustained attention. *Developmental Psychology, 28,* 297–306.

Jacobson, S. W., & Frye, K. F. (1991). Effect of maternal social support on attachment: Experimental evidence. *Child Development, 62,* 572–582.

Jamieson, S., & Marshall, W. L. (2000). Attachment styles and violence in child molesters. *Journal of Sexual Aggression, 5*(2), 88–98.

Jang, K. L., Livesley, W. J., Taylor, S., Stein, M. B., & Moon, E. C. (2004). Heritability of individual depressive symptoms. *Journal of Affective Disorders, 80*(2–3), 125–133.

Jarvis, B. (1993, May 3). Against the great divide. *Newsweek,* p. 14.

Jarvis, M. J. (2004). ABC of smoking cessation: Why people smoke. *British Medical Journal, 328*(7434), 277–279.

Javo, C., Ronning, J. A., & Heyerdahl, S. (2004). Child-rearing in an indigenous Sami population in Norway: A cross-cultural comparison of parental attitudes and expectations. *Scandinavian Journal of Psychology, 45*(1), 67–78.

Jayakody, R., & Kalil, A. (2000). Social fathering in low-income African American families with preschool children. Unpublished manuscript, referenced in R. L. Coley (2001), (In)visible men: Emerging research on low-income, unmarried, and minority fathers. *American Psychologist, 56*(9), 743–753.

Jeng, S.-F., Yau, K.-I. T., Liao, H.-F., Chen, L.-C., & Chen, P.-S. (2000). Prognostic factors for walking attainment in very low-birthweight preterm infants. *Early Human Development, 59*(3), 159–173.

Jennings, K. D., & Dietz, L. J. (2003). Mastery motivation and goal persistence in young children. In M. H. Bornstein et al. (Eds.), *Well-being: Positive development across the life course* (pp. 295–309). Mahwah, NJ: Lawrence Erlbaum Associates.

Jensen, J. K., & Neff, D. L. (1993). Development of basic auditory discrimination in preschool children. *Psychological Science, 4,* 104–107.

Jensen, L. A. (1998). Moral divisions within countries between orthodoxy and progressivism: India and the United States. *Journal for the Scientific Study of Religion, 37*(1), 90–107.

Jensen, L. A., Arnett, J. J., Feldman, S. S., & Cauffman, E. (2004). The right to do wrong: Lying to parents among adolescents and emerging adults. *Journal of Youth and Adolescence, 33*(2), 101–112.

Jimerson, S. R., Egeland, B., Sroufe, L. A., & Carlson, B. (2000). A prospective longitudinal study of high school dropouts: Examining multiple predictors across development. *Journal of School Psychology, 38*(6), 525–549.

Joe, S., & Marcus, S. C. (2003). Datapoints: Trends by race and gender in suicide attempts among U.S. adolescents, 1991–2001. *Psychiatric Services, 54*(4), 454.

Johns, A. (2001). Psychiatric effects of cannabis. *British Journal of Psychiatry, 178,* 116–122.

Johnson, C. M. (1991). Infant and toddler sleep: A telephone survey of parents in one community. *Developmental and Behavioral Pediatrics, 12,* 108–114.

Johnson, H. D. (2004). Gender, grade, and relationship differences in emotional closeness within adolescent friendships. *Adolescence, 39,* 243–255.

Johnson, M. H., Dziurawiec, S., Bartrip, J., & Morton, J. (1992). The effects of movement of internal features on infants' preferences for face-like stimuli. *Infant Behavior and Development, 15,* 129–136.

Johnson, W. (2000). Work preparation and labor market behavior among urban, poor, nonresident fathers. In S. Danziger & A. C. Lin (Eds.), *Coping with poverty: The social contexts of neighborhood, work, and family in the African American community.* Ann Arbor: University of Michigan Press.

Johnson, W., Emde, R. N., Pannabecker, B., Stenberg, C., & Davis, M. (1982). Maternal perception of infant emotion from birth to 18 months. *Infant Behavior and Development, 5,* 313–322.

Johnson, W., McGue, M., Krueger, R. F., & Bouchard, T. J., Jr. (2004). Marriage and personality: A genetic analysis. *Journal of Personality and Social Psychology, 86*(2), 285–294.

Johnston, L. D., O'Malley, P. M., & Bachman, J. G. (2001). *Monitoring the Future national survey results on drug use, 1975–2000, v. I, Secondary school students* (NIH Publication 01–4924). Bethesda, MD: National Institute on Drug Abuse.

Johnston, L. D., O'Malley, P. M., Bachman, J. G., & Schulenberg, J. E. (2004). *Monitoring the Future national results on adolescent drug use: Overview of key findings, 2003.* Bethesda, MD: U.S. Department of Health and Human Services, National Institute on Drug Abuse, Table 7.

Jones, D. C., Swift, D. J., & Johnson, M. A. (1988). Nondeliberate memory for a novel event among preschoolers. *Developmental Psychology, 24,* 641–645.

Jones, M. C. (1924). Elimination of children's fears. *Journal of Experimental Psychology, 7,* 381–390.

Jones, T. A., Klintsova, A. Y., Kilman, V. L., Sirevaag, A. M., & Greenough, W. T. (1997). Induction of multiple synapses by experience in the visual cortex of adult rats. *Neurobiology of Learning and Memory, 68*(1), 13–20.

Joos, S. K., Pollitt, K. E., Mueller, W. H., & Albright, D. L. (1983). The Bacon Chow study: Maternal nutritional supplementation and infant behavioral development. *Child Development, 54,* 669–676.

Josefsson, A. M., et al. (2000). Viral load of human papilloma virus 16 as a determinant for development of cervical carcinoma in situ: A nested case-control study. *Lancet, 355,* 2189–2193.

Joseph, H. B., Reznik, I., & Mester, R. (2003). Suicidal behavior of adolescent girls: Profile and meaning. *Israel Journal of Psychiatry and Related Sciences, 40*(3), 209–219.

Joshi, R. M. (2003). Misconceptions about the assessment and diagnosis of reading disability. *Reading Psychology, 24*(3–4), 247–266.

Junger, M., Stroebe, W., & Laan, A. M. van der (2001). Delinquency, health behaviour, and health. *British Journal of Health Psychology, 6*(2), 103–120.

Kaemingk, K. L., & Halverson, P. T. (2000). Spatial memory following prenatal alcohol exposure: More than a material specific memory deficit. *Child Neuropsychology, 6*(2), 115–128.

Kagan, J. (1992). Yesterday's premises, tomorrow's promises. *Developmental Psychology, 28,* 990–997.

Kagan, J., & Klein, R. E. (1973). Cross-cultural perspectives on early development. *American Psychologist, 28,* 947–961.

Kagan, L. J., MacLeod, A. K., & Pote, H. L. (2004). Accessibility of causal explanations for future positive and negative events in adolescents with anxiety and depression. *Clinical Psychology and Psychotherapy, 11*(3), 177–186.

Kahlbaugh, P., & Haviland, J. M. (1991). Formal operational thinking and identity. In R. M. Lerner, A. C. Petersen, & J. Brooks-Gunn (Eds.), *Encyclopedia of adolescence.* New York: Garland.

Kahn, P. H. (1992). Children's obligatory and discretionary moral judgments. *Child Development, 63,* 416–430.

Kail, R. (1990). *The development of memory in children* (3rd ed.). New York: W. H. Freeman.

Kaiser Family Foundation, Holt, T., Greene, L., & Davis, J. (2003). *National Survey of Adolescents and Young Adults: Sexual health knowledge, attitudes, and experiences.* Menlo Park, CA: Henry J. Kaiser Family Foundation.

Kalb, C. (2004, January 26). Girl or boy? Now you can choose, but should you? *Newsweek.*

Kaltiala-Heino, R., Marttunen, M., Rantanen, P., & Rimpel‰, M. (2003). Early puberty is associated with mental health problems in middle adolescence. *Social Science and Medicine, 57*(6), 1055–1064.

Kaltiala-Heino, R., Rimpelae, M., Rissanen, A., & Rantanen, P. (2001). Early puberty and early sexual activity are associated with bulimic-type eating pathology in middle adolescence. *Journal of Adolescent Health, 28*(4), 346–352.

Kamii, C., Lewis, B. A., & Kirkland, L. (2001). Manipulatives: When are they useful? *Journal of Mathematical Behaviour, 20,* 21–31.

Kaminer, Y. (2001). Adolescent substance abuse treatment: Where do we go from here? *Psychiatric Services, 52*(2), 147–149.

Karapetsas, A., & Kantas, A. (1991). Visuo-motor organization in the child: A neuropsychological approach. *Perceptual and Motor Skills, 72,* 211–217.

Karavasilis, L., Doyle, A. B., & Markiewicz, D. (2003). Associations between parenting style and attachment to mother in middle childhood and adolescence. *International Journal of Behavioral Development, 27*(2), 153–164.

Karwautz, A., et al. (2001). Individual-specific risk factors for anorexia nervosa: A pilot study using a discordant sister-pair design. *Psychological Medicine, 31*(2), 317–329.

Katz, P. A., & Walsh, P. V. (1991). Modification of children's gender-stereotyped behavior. *Child Development, 62,* 338–351.

Kaufman, A. S., Flanagan, D. P., Alfonso, V. C., & Mascolo, J. T. (2006). Wechsler Intelligence Scale for Children, Fourth Edition (WISC-IV). *Journal of Psychoeducational Assessment, 24,* 278–295.

Kaufman, J., & Zigler, E. (1992). The prevention of child maltreatment: Programming, research, and policy. In D. J. Willis, E. W. Holden, & M. Rosenberg (Eds.), *Prevention of child maltreatment: Developmental and ecological perspectives.* New York: Wiley.

Kaufmann, D., et al. (2000). The relationship between parenting style and children's

adjustment: The parents' perspective. *Journal of Child and Family Studies, 9*(2), 231–245.

Kaye, W. H., et al. (2004). Genetic analysis of bulimia nervosa: Methods and sample description. *International Journal of Eating Disorders, 35*(4), 556–570.

Kazdin, A. E. (2000). Treatments for aggressive and antisocial children. *Child and Adolescent Psychiatric Clinics of North America, 9*(4), 841–858.

Kazdin, A. E., & Wassell, G. (2000). Therapeutic changes in children, parents, and families resulting from treatment of children with conduct problems. *Journal of the American Academy of Child and Adolescent Psychiatry, 39*(4), 414–420.

Kazui, M., Endo, T., Tanaka, A., Sakagami, H., & Suganuma, M. (2000). Intergenerational transmission of attachment: Japanese mother-child dyads. Japanese *Journal of Educational Psychology, 48*(3), 323–332.

Kearney, C. A., & Silverman, W. K. (1990). A preliminary analysis of a functional model of assessment and treatment for school refusal behavior. *Behavior Modification, 14,* 340–366.

Keating, G. M., McClellan, K., & Jarvis, B. (2001). Methylphenidate (OROS(R) formulation). *CNS Drugs, 15*(6), 495–500.

Keddie, A. (2004). Research with young children: The use of an affinity group approach to explore the social dynamics of peer culture. *British Journal of Sociology of Education, 25*(1), 35–51.

Keenan, P. A., & Soleymani, R. M. (2001). Gonadal steroids and cognition. In R. E. Tarter et al. (Eds.), *Medical neuropsychology: Clinical issues in neuropsychology* (2nd ed.) (pp. 181–197). Dordrecht, Netherlands: Kluwer Academic.

Kellman, P. J., & von Hofsten, C. (1992). The world of the moving infant: Perception of motion, stability, and space. In C. Rovee-Collier & L. P. Lipsitt (Eds.), *Advances in infancy research* (v. 7). Norwood, NJ: Ablex.

Kellogg, R. (1959). *What children scribble and why.* Oxford: National Press.

Kellogg, R. (1970). Understanding children's art. In P. Cramer (Ed.), *Readings in developmental psychology today.* Del Mar, CA: CRM.

Kelly, J. B. (2000). Children's adjustment in conflicted marriage and divorce: A decade review of research. *Journal of the American Academy of Child and Adolescent Psychiatry, 39*(8), 963–973.

Kelly, K. M., Jones, W. H., & Adams, J. M. (2002). Using the Imaginary Audience Scale as a measure of social anxiety in young adults. *Educational and Psychological Measurement, 62*(5), 896–914.

Kendler, K. S., et al. (2000a). Illicit psychoactive substance use, heavy use, abuse, and dependence in a U.S. population-based sample of male twins. *Archives of General Psychiatry, 57,* 261–269.

Kendler, K. S., Myers, J. M., & Neale, M. C. (2000b). A multidimensional twin study of mental health in women. *American Journal*

of Psychiatry, 157, 506–513.

Kennell, J. H., & McGrath, S. (1993, March). Perinatal effects of labor support. Paper presented at the meeting of the Society for Research in Child Development, New Orleans, LA.

Kershner, J. R., & Ledger, G. (1985). Effect of sex, intelligence, and style of thinking on creativity: A comparison of gifted and average IQ children. *Journal of Personality and Social Psychology, 48,* 1033–1040.

Kessen, W., Leutzendoff, A. M., & Stoutsenberger, K. (1967). Age, food deprivation, non-nutritive sucking and movement in the human newborn. *Journal of Comparative and Physiological Psychology, 63,* 82–86.

Key, A., Lacey, J. H., & Nussey, S. (2001). Do starvation diets lead to irreversible lung changes? *European Eating Disorders Review, 9*(5), 348–353.

Kiang, L., Yip, T., Gonzales-Backen, M., Witkow, & Fuligni, A. J. (2006). Ethnic identity and the daily psychological well-being of adolescents from Mexican and Chinese backgrounds. *Child Development, 77*(5), 1338–1350.

Kilgore, K., Snyder, J., & Lentz, C. (2000). The contribution of parental discipline, parental monitoring, and school risk to early-onset conduct problems in African American boys and girls. *Developmental Psychology, 36*(6), 835–845.

Kilpatrick, D. G., et al. (2000). Risk factors for adolescent substance abuse and dependence: Data from a national sample. *Journal of Consulting and Clinical Psychology, 68,* 19–30.

Kim, B. S. K., & Omizo, M. M. (2003). Asian cultural values, attitudes toward seeking professional psychological help, and willingness to see a counselor. *Counseling Psychologist, 31*(3), 343–361.

Kimura, D., & Hampson, E. (1992). Neural and hormonal mechanisms mediating sex differences in cognition. In P. A. Vernon (Ed.), *Biological approaches to the study of human intelligence.* Norwood, NJ: Ablex.

Kindlon, D., & Thompson, M. (2002). Thorns among roses: The struggle of young boys in early education. In *The Jossey-Bass reader on gender in education* (pp. 151–181). San Francisco, CA: Jossey-Bass.

King, L. A., Scollon, C. K., Ramsey, C., & Williams, T. (2000). Stories of life transition: Subjective well-being and ego development in parents of children with Down syndrome. *Journal of Research in Personality, 34*(4), 509–536.

King, R. (2000). Interview comments in L. Frazier (2000, July 16), The new face of HIV is young, black. *Washington Post,* p. C01.

King, S., & Laplante, D. (2005). The effects of parental maternal stress on children's cognitive development: Project Ice Storm. *Stress: The International Journal on the Biology of Stress, 8,* 35–45.

Kinsbourne, M. (2003). The corpus callosum

equilibrates the cerebral hemispheres. In E. Zaidel & M. Iacoboni (Eds.), *The parallel brain: The cognitive neuroscience of the corpus callosum* (pp. 271–281). Cambridge, MA: MIT Press

Kinsey, A. C., Pomeroy, W. B., & Martin, C. E. (1948). *Sexual behavior in the human male.* Philadelphia: W. B. Saunders.

Kinsey, A. C., Pomeroy, W. B., Martin, C. E., & Gebhard, P. H. (1953). *Sexual behavior in the human female.* Philadelphia: W. B. Saunders.

Kirby, J. R., Parrila, R. K., & Pfeiffer, S. L. (2003). Naming speed and phonological awarness as predictors of reading development. *Journal of Educational Psychology, 95*(3), 453–464.

Kirchler, E., Pombeni, M. L., & Palmonari, A. (1991). Sweet sixteen ... Adolescents' problems and the peer group as source of support. *European Journal of Psychology of Education, 6,* 393–410.

Kirkcaldy, B. D., Shephard, R. J., & Siefen, R. G. (2002). The relationship between physical activity and self-image and problem behaviour among adolescents. *Social Psychiatry and Psychiatric Epidemiology, 37*(11), 544–550.

Kirsh, S. J., Crnic, K. A., & Greenberg, M. T. (1995). Relations between parent-child affect and synchrony and cognitive outcome at 5 years of age. *Personal Relationships, 2*(3) 187–198.

Kjelsås, E., Bjornstrom, C., & Götestam, K. G. (2004). Prevalence of eating disorders in female and male adolescents (14–15 years). *Eating Behaviors, 5*(1), 13–25.

Klassen, R. (2002). The changing landscape of learning disabilities in Canada. *School Psychology International, 23*(2), 199–219.

Klaus, M., & Kennell, J. (1976). *Maternal-infant bonding.* St. Louis: C. V. Mosby.

Klaus, M. H., & Kennell, J. H. (1978). Parent-to-infant attachment. In J. H. Stevens Jr. & M. Mathews (Eds.), *Mother/child, father/child relationships.* Washington, DC: National Association for the Education of Young Children.

Klebanoff, M. A., Levine, R. J., DerSimonian, R., Clemens, J. D., & Wilkins, D. G. (1999). Maternal serum paraxanthine, a caffeine metabolite, and the risk of spontaneous abortion. *The New England Journal of Medicine, 341*(22), 1639–1644.

Klein, P. J., & Meltzoff, A. N. (1999). Long-term memory, forgetting and deferred imitation in 12-month-old infants. *Developmental Science, 2*(1), 102–113.

Klimes-Dougan, B. (1993, March). The emergence of negotiation. Paper presented at the meeting of the Society for Research in Child Development, New Orleans, LA.

Klingberg, T., Vaidya, C. J., Gabrieli, J. D. E., Moseley, M. E., & Hedehus, M. (1999). Myelination and organization of the frontal white matter in children: A diffusion tensor MRI study. *Neuroreport: For Rapid Communication of Neuroscience Research,* *10*(13), 2817–2821.

Klintsova, A. Y., & Greenough, W. T. (1999). Synaptic plasticity in cortical systems. *Current Opinion in Neurobiology, 9*(2), 203–208.

Klorman, R., Brumaghim, J. T., Fitzpatrick, P. A., Borgstedt, A. D., & Strauss, J. (1994). Clinical and cognitive effects of methylphenidate on children with attention deficit disorder as a function of aggression/oppositionality and age. *Journal of Abnormal Psychology, 103,* 206–221.

Knighton, T., & Bussire, P. (2006). *Education outcomes at age 19 associated with reading ability at age 15.* Ottawa, ON: Statistics Canada.

Knox, P. L., Fagley, N. S., & Miller, P. M. (2004). Care and justice moral orientation among African American college students. *Journal of Adult Development, 11*(1), 41–45.

Kobayashi-Winata, H., & Power, T. G. (1989). Childrearing and compliance: Japanese and American families in Houston. *Journal of Cross-Cultural Psychology, 20,* 333–356.

Kochanska, G. (2001). Emotional development in children with different attachment histories: The first three years. *Child Development, 72*(2), 474–490.

Kochanska, G., Coy, K. C., & Murray, K. T. (2001). The development of self-regulation in the first four years of life. *Child Development, 72*(4), 1091–1111.

Kogan, M. D., et al. (2000). Trends in twin birth outcomes and prenatal care utilization in the United States, 1981–1997. *Journal of the American Medical Association, 284*(3), 335–341.

Kohl, C. (2004). Postpartum psychoses: Closer to schizophrenia or the affective spectrum? *Current Opinion in Psychiatry, 17*(2), 87–90.

Kohlberg, L. (1963). Moral development and identification. In H. W., Stevenson (Ed.), *Child psychology: 62nd yearbook of the National Society for the Study of Education.* Chicago: University of Chicago Press.

Kohlberg, L. (1966). Cognitive stages and preschool education. *Human Development, 9,* 5–17.

Kohlberg, L. (1969). Stage and sequence: The cognitive-developmental approach to socialization. In D. A. Goslin (Ed.), *Handbook of socialization theory and research.* Chicago: Rand McNally.

Kohlberg, L. (1981). *The meaning and measurement of moral development.* Worcester, MA: Clark University Press.

Kohlberg, L. (1985). *The psychology of moral development.* San Francisco: Harper & Row.

Kohlberg, L., & Kramer, R. (1969). Continuities and discontinuities in childhood and adult moral development. *Human Development, 12,* 93–120.

Kohyama, J., Shiiki, T., Ohinata-Sugimoto, J., & Hasegawa, T. (2002). Potentially harmful sleep habits of 3-year-old children in Japan. *Journal of Developmental and Behavioral Pediatrics, 23*(2), 67–70.

Kolata, G. (1992, June 21). More children are employed, often perilously. *New York Times,* pp. 1, 22.

Kolata, G. (1998, September 9). Researchers report success in method to pick baby's sex. Available at http://www.nytimes.com

Kolb, B., Gibb, R., & Gorny, G. (2001). Cortical plasticity and the development of behavior after early frontal cortical injury. *Developmental Neuropsychology, 18*(3), 423–444.

Konner, M. J. (1977). Infancy among the Kalahari San. In P. H. Leiderman, S. R. Tulkin, & A. Rosenfeld (Eds.), *Culture and infancy: Variations in the human experience.* New York: Academic Press.

Kopp, C. B. (1989). Regulation of distress and negative emotions: A developmental view. *Developmental Psychology, 25,* 343–354.

Kopp, C. B. (1992, Spring). Emotional distress and control in young children. In N. Eisenberg & R. A. Fabes (Eds.), *New directions for child development, no. 55, Emotion and its regulation in early development.* San Francisco: Jossey-Bass.

Korf, B. R. (2003). Essentials of medical genomics. *New England Journal of Medicine, 349,* 409–410.

Koriat, A., Goldsmith, M., Schneider, W., & Nakash-Dura, M. (2001). The credibility of children's testimony: Can children control the accuracy of their memory reports? *Journal of Experimental Child Psychology, 79*(4), 405–437.

Korszun, A., et al. (2004). Familiality of symptom dimensions in depression. *Archives of General Psychiatry, 61*(5), 468–474.

Krackow, E., & Lynn, S. J. (2003). Is there touch in the game of Twister? The effects of innocuous touch and suggestive questions on children's eyewitness memory. *Law and Human Behavior, 27*(6), 589–604.

Kramer, M. S., et al., for the PROBIT Study Group (2001). Promotion of Breastfeeding Intervention Trial (PROBIT): A randomized trial in the Republic of Belarus. *Journal of the American Medical Association, 285,* 413–420.

Kramer, T., & Garralda, M. E. (2000). Child and adolescent mental health problems in primary care. *Advances in Psychiatric Treatment, 6,* 287–294.

Krappmann, L., Oswald, H., Weiss, K., & Uhlendorff, H. (1993, March). *Peer relationships of children in middle childhood.* Paper presented at the meeting of the Society for Research in Child Development, New Orleans, LA.

Kreitler, S., & Kreitler, H. (1989). Horizontal decalage: A problem and its solution. *Cognitive Development, 4,* 89–119.

Krippner, S., & McIntyre, T. (Eds.) (2003). *The psychological impact of war trauma on civilians: An international perspective.* Westport, CT: Praeger Publishers/Greenwood Publishing.

Kroger, J. (2003). Identity development during adolescence. In G. R. Adams & M. D. Berzonsky (Ed.), *Blackwell handbook of adolescence* (pp. 205–226). Malden, MA: Blackwell.

Kuczaj, S. A., II (1982). On the nature of syntactic development. In S. A. Kuczaj II (Ed.), *Language development, v. 1, Syntax and semantics.* Hillsdale, NJ: Erlbaum.

Kuczmarski, R. J., et al. (2000, December 4). *CDC growth charts: United States. Advance Data from Vital and Health Statistics, no. 314.* Hyattsville, MD: National Center for Health Statistics.

Kuczynski, L., & Kochanska, G. (1990). Development of children's noncompliance strategies from toddlerhood to age 5. *Developmental Psychology, 26,* 398–408.

Kuhl, P. K., Andruski, J. E., Chistovich, I, A., Chistovich, L. A., et al. (1997). Cross-language analysis of phonetic units in language addressed to infants. *Science, 277*(5,326), 684–686.

Kumar, B., & Wandel, M. (2006). Nutritional challenges among immigrant children and youth in Norwat. In L. D. Adams & A. Kirova (Eds.), *Global migration and education: Schools, children, and families* (pp. 67–81). Mahwah, NJ: Lawrence Erlbaum.

Kupersmidt, J. B., Bryant, D., & Willoughby, M. T. (2000). Prevalence of aggressive behaviors among preschoolers in Head Start and community child care programs. *Behavioral Disorders, 26*(1), 42–52.

Kutner, L. (1993, May 6). No no no no lima beans: Picky eaters may just be responding to biology. *New York Times,* p. B5.

Kwok, H. W. M. (2003). Psychopharmacology in autism spectrum disorders. *Current Opinion in Psychiatry, 16*(5), 529–534.

Lachance, J. A., & Mazzocco, M. M. M. (2006). A longitudinal analysis of sex difference in math and spatial skills in primary school age children. *Learning and Individual Differences, 16,* 195–216.

Laflamme, D., Pomerleau, A., & Malcuit, G. (2002). A comparison of fathers' and mothers' involvement in childcare and stimulation behaviors during free-play with their infants at 9 and 15 months. *Sex Roles, 47*(11–12), 507–518.

LaFromboise, T., Coleman, H. L., & Gerton, J. (1993). Psychological impact of biculturalism: Evidence and theory. Psychological Bulletin, 114(3), 395–412.

Lai, T. J., Guo, Y. I., Guo, N.-W., & Hsu, C. C. (2001). Effect of prenatal exposure to polychlorinated biphenyls on cognitive development in children: A longitudinal study in Taiwan. British Journal of Psychiatry, 178(Suppl. 40), S49-S52.

Lalumière, M. L., Blanchard, R., & Zucker, K. J. (2000). Sexual orientation and handedness in men and women: A meta-analysis. *Psychological Bulletin, 126*(4), 575–592.

Lam, T. H., Shi, H. J., Ho, L. M., Stewart, S. M., & Fan, S. (2002). Timing of pubertal maturation and heterosexual behavior among Hong Kong Chinese adolescents. *Archives of Sexual Behavior, 31*(4), 359–366.

Lamaze, F. (1981). *Painless childbirth.* New York: Simon & Schuster.

Lamb, M. E. (1996). *The role of the father in child development* (3rd ed.). New York: Wiley.

Lamb, M. E., Ketterlinus, R. D., & Fracasso, M. P. (1992). Parent-child relationships. In M. H. Bornstein & M. E. Lamb (Eds.), *Developmental psychology: An advanced textbook* (3rd ed.). Hillsdale, NJ: Lawrence Erlbaum.

Lamb, M. E., Sternberg, K. J., & Ketterlinus, R. D. (1992a). Child care in the United States: The modern era. In M. E. Lamb, K. J. Sternberg, C. Hwang, & A. G. Broberg (Eds.), *Child care in context.* Hillsdale, NJ: Erlbaum.

Lamb, M. E., Sternberg, K. J., & Prodromidis, M. (1992b). Nonmaternal care and the security of infant-mother attachment: A reanalysis of the data. *Infant Behavior and Development, 15,* 71–83.

Lambert, W. E., Genesee, F., Holobow, N., & Chartrand, L. (1991). *Bilingual education for majority English-speaking children.* Montreal: McGill University.

Lamborn, S. D., Mounts, N. S., Steinberg, L., & Dornbusch, S. M. (1991). Patterns of competence and adjustment among adolescents from authoritative, authoritarian, indulgent, and neglectful families. *Child Development, 62,* 1049–1065.

Lampl, M., Veldhuis, J. D., & Johnson, M. L. (1992). Saltation and stasis: A model of human growth. *Science, 258,* 801–803.

Landau, B. S. M. (2004). *The art of classroom management: Building equitable learning communities* (2nd ed.). Upper Saddle River, NJ: Prentice Hall.

Landau, S., & Milich, R. (1990). Assessment of children's social status and peer relations. In A. M. LaGreca (Ed.), *Through the eyes of a child.* Boston: Allyn and Bacon.

Landesman, S. (1990). Institutionalization revisited: Expanding views on early and cumulative life experiences. In M. Lewis & S. M. Miller (Eds.), *Handbook of developmental psychopathology.* New York: Plenum.

Lane, S. D., & Cherek, D. R. (2001). Risk taking by adolescents with maladaptive behavior histories. *Experimental and Clinical Psychopharmacology, 9*(1), 74–82.

Langbehn, D. R., & Cadoret, R. J. (2001). The adult antisocial syndrome with and without antecedent conduct disorder: Comparisons from an adoption study. *Comprehensive Psychiatry, 42*(4), 272–282.

Lange, G., & Pierce, S. H. (1992). Memory-strategy learning and maintenance in preschool children. *Developmental Psychology, 28,* 453–462.

Langlois, J. H., et al. (2000). Maxims or myths of beauty? A meta-analytic and theoretical review. *Psychological Bulletin, 126*(3), 390–423.

Lanza, S. T., & Collins, L. M. (2002). Pubertal timing and the onset of substance use in females during early adolescence. *Prevention Science, 3*(1), 69–82.

Laplante, D. P., Barr, R. G., Brunet, A., Galbaud du Fort, G., Meaney, M. J., Saucier, J. F., Zelazo, P. R., & King, S. (2004). Stress during pregnancy affects intellectual and linguistic functioning in human toddlers. *Pediatric Research, 56*(3), 400–410.

Largo, R. H., et al. (2001). Neuromotor development from 5 to 18 years. Part 1: Timed performance. *Developmental Medicine and Child Neurology, 43*(7), 436–443.

Larson, L. M., Rottinghaus, P. J., & Borgen, F. H. (2002). Meta-analyses of Big Six interests and Big Five personality factors. *Journal of Vocational Behavior, 61*(2), 217–239.

Larson, R., & Richards, M. H. (1991). Daily companionship in late childhood and early adolescence: Changing developmental contexts. *Child Development, 62,* 284–300.

Larsson, I., & Svedin, C. (2002). Experiences in childhood: Young adults' recollections. *Archives of Sexual Behavior, 31*(3), 263–273.

Laszlo, J. I. (1990). Child perceptive-motor development: Normal and abnormal development of skilled behavior. In C. A. Hauert (Ed.), *Developmental psychology: Cognitive, perceptive-motor and neuropsychological perspectives.* Amsterdam: North-Holland.

Laub, J. H., & Vaillant, G. E. (2000). Delinquency and mortality: A 50-year follow-up study of 1,000 delinquent and nondelinquent boys. *American Journal of Psychiatry, 157*(1), 96–102.

Laufer, A., & Harel, Y. (2003). Correlation between school perception and pupil involvement in bullying, physical fights, and weapon carrying. *Megamot, 42*(3), 437–459.

Laumann, E. O., Gagnon, J. H., Michael, R. T., & Michaels, S. (1994). *The social organization of sexuality.* Chicago: University of Chicago Press.

Laurendeau, M., & Pinard, A. (1970). *The development of the concept of space in the child.* New York: International Universities Press.

Laursen, B. (1993). Conflict management among close peers. In B. Laursen (Ed.), *New directions in child development, no. 60, Close friendships in adolescence.* San Francisco: Jossey-Bass.

Law, J. (2000). The politics of breastfeeding: Assessing risk, dividing labor. *Signs, 25*(2), 407–450.

Lawrence, J. M., et al. (2003). Design and evaluation of interventions promoting periconceptional multivitamin use. *American Journal of Preventive Medicine, 25*(1), 17–24.

Lawrence, R. A. (2001). Breastfeeding in Belarus. *Journal of the American Medical Association, 285*(4), 463–464.

Lawton, C. A., & Morrin, K. A. (1999). Gender differences in pointing accuracy in computer-simulated 3D mazes. *Sex Roles, 40*(1–2), 73–92.

Leahey, E., & Guo, G. (2001). Gender differences in mathematical trajectories. *Social*

Forces, 80(2), 713–732.

Leahey, E., & Guo, G. (2001). Gender difference in mathematical trajectories. *Social Forces, 80*(2), 713–732.

Leaper, C. (2002). Parenting girls and boys. In M. H. Bornstein (Ed.), *Handbook of parenting, v. 1, Children and parenting* (2nd ed.) (pp. 189–225). Mahwah, NJ: Lawrence Erlbaum Associates.

Learning Disabilities Association of Canada (2002). Official definition of learning disabilities. Available at http://www.ldac-taac .ca/Defined/defined_new-e.asp

Lecanuet, J. P., Graniere-Deferre, C., Jacquet, A.-Y., & DeCasper, A. J. (2000). Fetal discrimination of low-pitched musical notes. *Developmental Psychobiology, 36*(1), 29–39.

Lee, D. T. S., et al. (2001). A psychiatric epidemiological study of postpartum Chinese women. *American Journal of Psychiatry, 158*(2), 220–226.

Lee, V. E., & Burkam, D. T. (2003). Dropping out of high school: The role of school organization and structure. *American Educational Research Journal, 40*(2), 353–393.

Leinwand, D. (2000, August 24). 20% say they used drugs with their mom or dad, among reasons: Boomer culture and misguided attempts to bond. Available at http://www.usatoday.com

Lenneberg, E. H. (1967). *Biological foundations of language.* New York: Wiley.

Lenneberg, E. H. (1967). *Biological foundations of language.* New York: Wiley.

Leon, M. R. (2000). Effects of caffeine on cognitive, psychomotor, and affective performance of children with attention-deficit/hyperactivity disorder. *Journal of Attention Disorders, 4*(1) 27–47.

Leonard, S. P., & Archer, J. (1989). A naturalistic investigation of gender constancy in three- to four-year-old children. *British Journal of Developmental Psychology, 7,* 341–346.

Lepola, J., Vaurus, M., & Maeki, H. (2000). Gender differences in the development of academic self-concept of attainment from the 2nd to the 6th grade: Relations with achievement and perceived motivational orientation. *Psychology: The Journal of the Hellenic Psychological Society, 7*(3), 290–308.

Lerner, G. (1993). *The creation of feminist consciousness.* New York: Oxford University Press.

"Less sex, more protection, fewer pregnancies" (2004, March 7). *New York Times,* p. 36N.

Lester, B. M., Boukydis, C. F. Z., Garcia-Coll, C. T., Hole, W., & Peucker, M. (1992). Infantile colic: Acoustic cry characteristics, maternal perception of cry, and temperament. *Infant Behavior and Development, 15,* 15–26.

Letourneau, E. J., Schoenwald, S. K., & Sheidow, A. J. (2004). Children and adolescents with sexual behavior problems. *Child Maltreatment: Journal of the American Professional Society on the Abuse of Children, 9*(1), 49–61.

Letourneau, N., et al. (2001). Supporting parents: Can intervention improve

parent-child relationships? *Journal of Family Nursing, 7*(2), 159–187.

Letourneau, N. L., Duffet-Leger, L., Stewart, M., Hegadoren, K., Dennis, C. L., Rinaldi, C., & Stoppard, J. (in press). Canadian mothers' perceived support needs during PPD. *Journal of Obstetric, Gynecolgic and Neonatal Nursing.*

Leung, C., McBride-Chang, C., & Lai, B. (2004). Relations among maternal parenting style, academic competence, and life satisfaction in Chinese early adolescents. *Journal of Early Adolescence, 24*(2), 113–143.

Leung, P. W. L., & Poon, M. W. L. (2001). Dysfunctional schemas and cognitive distortions in psychopathology: A test of the specificity hypothesis. *Journal of Child Psychology and Psychiatry and Allied Disciplines, 42*(6), 755–765.

Leve, L. D., Winebarger, A. A., Fagot, B. I., Reid, J. B., & Goldsmith, H. H. (1998). Environmental and genetic variance in children's observed and reported maladaptive behavior. *Child Development, 69*(5), 1286–1298.

Leventhal, T., & Brooks-Gunn, J. (2004). A randomized study of neighborhood effects on low-income children's educational outcomes. *Developmental Psychology, 40*(4), 488–507.

Leventhal, T., Graber, J. A., & Brooks-Gunn, J. (2001). Adolescent transitions to young adulthood: Antecedents, correlates, and consequences of adolescent employment. *Journal of Research on Adolescence, 11*(3), 297–323.

Lever, N., et al. (2004). A drop-out prevention program for high-risk inner-city youth. *Behavior Modification, 28*(4), 513–527.

Levitt, M. J., Weber, R. A., Clark, M. C., & McDonnell, P. (1985). Reciprocity of exchange in toddler sharing behavior. *Developmental Psychology, 21,* 122–123.

Levy, G. D., Sadovsky, A. L., & Troseth, G. L. (2000). Aspects of young children's perceptions of gender-typed occupations. *Sex Roles, 42*(11–12), 993–1006.

Lewinsohn, P. M., Brown, R. A., Seeley, J. R., & Ramsey, S. E. (2000a). Psychological correlates of cigarette smoking abstinence, experimentation, persistence, and frequency during adolescence. *Nicotine and Tobacco Research, 2*(2), 121–131.

Lewinsohn, P. M., Rohde, P., Seeley, J. R., Klein, D. N., & Gotlib, I. H. (2000b). Natural course of adolescent major depressive disorder in a community sample: Predictors of recurrence in young adults. *American Journal of Psychiatry, 157,* 1584–1591.

Lewis, C., & Osborne, A. (1990). Three-year-olds' problems with false belief: Conceptual deficit or linguistic artifact? *Child Development, 61,* 1514–1519.

Lewis, H. L. (2003). Differences in ego identity among college students across age, ethnicity, and gender. *Identity, 3*(2), 159–189.

Lewis, M. (1990). Social knowledge and social

development. *Merrill-Palmer Quarterly, 36,* 93–116.

Lewis, M. (1991). Ways of knowing: Objective self-awareness or consciousness. *Developmental Review, 11,* 231–243.

Lewis, M., Alessandri, S. M., & Sullivan, M. W. (1992). Differences in shame and pride as a function of children's gender and task difficulty. *Child Development, 63,* 630–638.

Lewis, M., & Brooks-Gunn, J. (1979). *Social cognition and the acquisition of self.* New York: Plenum.

Lewis, M., & Feiring, C. (1989). Early predictors of childhood friendship. In T. J. Berndt & G. W. Ladd (Eds.), *Peer relationships in child development.* New York: Wiley.

Lewis, M., Worobey, J., Ramsay, D. S., & McCormack, M. K. (1992). Prenatal exposure to heavy metals: Effect on childhood cognitive skills and health status. *Pediatrics, 89,* 1010–1015.

Li, G., Baker, S. P., Smialek, J. E., & Soderstrom, C. A. (2001). Use of alcohol as a risk factor for bicycling injury. *Journal of the American Medical Association, 284,* 893–896.

Lickliter, R. (2001). The dynamics of language development: From perception to comprehension. *Developmental Science, 4*(1), 21–23.

Lidow, M. S., & Song, Z. (2001). Effect of cocaine on cell proliferation in the cerebral wall of monkey fetuses. *Cerebral Cortex, 11*(6), 545–551.

Liebert, R. M., & Fischel, J. E. (1990). The elimination disorders: Enuresis and encopresis. In M. Lewis & S. M. Miller (Eds.), *Handbook of developmental pathology.* New York: Plenum.

Linares, L. O., et al. (2001). A mediational model for the impact of exposure to community violence on early child behavior problems. *Child Development, 72*(2), 639–652.

Lindel, B. U., & Laessle, R. G. (2002). Stress-related determinants of eating behavior in overweight children. *Zeitschrift für Gesundheitspsychologie, 10*(1), 8–14.

Lindgren, M., et al. (2002). Dyslexia and AD/HD among Swedish prison inmates. *Journal of Scandinavian Studies in Criminology and Crime Prevention, 3*(1), 84–95.

Lipsitt, L. P. (1990). Learning process in the human newborn. In A. Diamond (Ed.), *The development and neutral bases of higher cognitive functions.* New York: New York Academy of Sciences.

Lipsitt, L. P. (2003). Crib death: A biobehavioral phenomenon? *Current Directions in Psychological Science, 12*(5), 164–170.

Little, A. H., Lipsitt, L. P., & Rovee-Collier, C. (1984). Classical conditioning and retention of the infants' eyelid response: Effects of age and interstimulus interval. *Journal of Experimental Child Psychology, 37,* 512–524.

Liu, X., et al. (2000a). Behavioral and emotional problems in Chinese children of divorced parents. *Journal of the American Academy of Child and Adolescent Psychiatry, 39*(7), 896–903.

Liu, X., Sun, Z., Uchiyama, M., Li, Y., & Okawa, M. (2000b). Attaining nocturnal urinary control, nocturnal enuresis, and behavioral problems in Chinese children aged 6 through 16 years. *Journal of the American Academy of Child and Adolescent Psychiatry, 39*(12), 1557–1564.

Liu, Y., Curtis, J. T., & Wang, Z. (2001). Vasopressin in the lateral septum regulates pair bond formation in male prairie voles (Microtus ochrogaster). *Behavioral Neuroscience, 115*(4), 910–919.

Lo, J. C. (2003). Patients' attitudes vs. physicians' determination: Implications for cesarean sections. *Social Science and Medicine, 57*(1), 91–96.

Lock, J., & Le Grange, D. (2001). Can family based treatment of anorexia nervosa be manualized? *Journal of Psychotherapy Practice and Research, 10*(4), 253–261.

Loeber, R., Wei, E., Stouthamer-Loeber, M., Huizanga, D., & Thornberry, T. P. (1999). Behavioral antecedents to serious and violent offending: Joint analyses from the Denver Youth Survey, Pittsburgh Youth Study, and the Rochester Youth Development Study. *Studies on Crime and Crime Prevention, 8*(2), 245–263.

Lollis, S., & Kuczynski, L. (1997). Beyond one hand clapping: Seeing bidirectionality in parent-child relations. *Journal of Social and Personal Relationships, 14*(4), 441–461.

Loovis, E. M., & Butterfield, S. A. (2000). Influence of age, sex, and balance on mature skipping by children in grades K-8. *Perceptual and Motor Skills, 90*(3), 974–978.

Lorenz, K. (1962). *King Solomon's ring.* London: Methuen.

Lorenz, K. (1981). *The foundations of ethology.* New York: Springer-Verlag.

Lotspeich, L., et al. (2004). Investigation of neuroanatomical differences between autism and Asperger syndrome. *Archives of General Psychiatry, 61*(3), 291–298.

Lovaas, O. I. (1977). *The autistic child: Language development through behavior modification.* New York: Halstead Press.

Lovaas, O. I., Smith, T., & McEachin, J. J. (1989). Clarifying comments on the young autism study: Reply to Schapler, Short, and Mesibov. *Journal of Consulting and Clinical Psychology, 57,* 165–167.

Love, J. M., Logue, M. E., Trudeau, J. V., & Thayer, K. (1992). *Transitions to kindergarten in American schools.* Portsmouth, NH: RMC Research Corp.

Lowrey, G. H. (1986). *Growth and development of children.* Chicago: Year Book Medical Publishers.

Lowry, R., Galuska, D. A., Fulton, J. E., Wechsler, H., & Kann, L. (2002). Weight management goals and practices among U.S. high school students: Associations with physical activity, diet, and smoking. *Journal of Adolescent Health, 31*(2), 133–144.

Lubell, K. M., Swahn, M. H., Crosby, A. E., & Kegler, S. R. (2004). Methods of suicide among persons aged 10–19 years: United States, 1992–2001. MMWR, 53, 471–473.

Available at http://www.cdc.gov/mmwr/PDF/wk/mm5322.pdf

Lubinski, D. (2004). Introduction to the Special Section on Cognitive Abilities: 100 Years After Spearman's (1904) "General Intelligence,' Objectively Determined and Measured." *Journal of Personality and Social Psychology, 86*(1), 96–111.

Lubinski, D., & Benbow, C. P. (2000). States of excellence. *American Psychologist, 55,* 137–150.

Lucariello, J., & Nelson, K. (1985). Slotfiller categories as memory organizers for young children. *Developmental Psychology, 21,* 272–282.

Lucas, A. R. (1991). Eating disorders. In M. Lewis (Ed.), *Child and adolescent psychiatry: A comprehensive textbook* (pp. 573–583). Baltimore: Williams & Wilkins.

Luciana, M. (2003). Cognitive development in children born preterm: Implications for theories of brain plasticity following early injury. *Development and Psychopathology, 15*(4), 1017–1047.

Ludman, E. J., et al. (2000). Stress, depressive symptoms, and smoking cessation among pregnant women. *Health Psychology, 19*(1), 21–27.

Lukas, W. D., & Campbell, B. C. (2000). Evolutionary and ecological aspects of early brain malnutrition in humans. *Human Nature, 11*(1), 1–26.

Lukashevich, I. P., Machinskaya, R. I., & Shklovskii, V. M. (2002). Role of the right- and left-hemispheric structures in speech and memory formation in children. *Human Physiology, 28*(6), 682–686.

The Lung Association (2006). Facts about smoking. Available at http://www.lung.ca/protect-protegez/tobacco-tabagisme/facts-faits/index_e.php

Luo, Y., Baillargeon, R., Brueckner, L., & Munakata, Y. (2003). Reasoning about a hidden object after a delay: Evidence for robust representations in 5-month-old infants. *Cognition, 88*(3), B23-B32.

Lupart, J. L., Cannon E., & Telfer, J. A. (2004). Gender differences in adolescent academic achievement, interests, values and life-role expectations. *High Ability Studies, 15,* 25–42.

Luster, T., & Dubow, E. (1992). Home environment and maternal intelligence as predictors of verbal intelligence: A comparison of preschool and school-age children. Merrill-Palmer Quarterly, 38, 151–173.

Lykken, D. T., & Csikszentmihalyi, M. (2001). Happiness: Stuck with what you've got? *Psychologist, 14*(9), 470–472.

Lykken, D. T., McGue, M., Tellegen, A., & Bouchard, T. J., Jr. (1992). Emergenesis: Genetic traits that may not run in families. *American Psychologist, 47,* 1565–1577.

Lynam, D. R., et al. (2000). The interaction between impulsivity and neighborhood context on offending: The effects of impulsivity are stronger in poorer neighborhoods. *Journal of Abnormal Psychology, 109*(4), 563–574.

Lyon, G. R., Shaywitz, S. E., & Shaywitz, B. A. (2003). A definition of dyslexia. *Annals of Dyslexia, 53,* 1–14.

Lyons-Ruth, K., Alpern, L., & Repacholi, B. (1993). Disorganized infant attachment classification and maternal psychosocial problems as predictors of hostile-aggressive behavior in the preschool classroom. *Child Development, 64,* 572–585.

Lyons-Ruth, K., Connell, D. B., Grunebaum, H. U., & Botein, S. (1990). Infants at social risk: Maternal depression and family support services as mediators of infant development and security of attachment. *Child Development, 61,* 85–98.

Lytle, D. E. (Ed.) (2003). *Play and educational theory and practice.* Westport, CT: Praeger Publishers/Greenwood Publishing.

Maccoby, E. E. (1984). Middle childhood in the context of the family. In A. Collins (Ed.), *Development during the middle years: The years from six to twelve.* Washington, DC: National Academy of Sciences Press.

Maccoby, E. E. (1990a). *Gender and relationships: A developmental account. American Psychologist, 45,* 513–520.

Maccoby, E. E. (1990b). The role of gender identity and gender constancy in sex-differentiated development. In D. Schrader (Ed.), *New directions for child development, no. 47, The legacy of Lawrence Kohlberg.* San Francisco: Jossey-Bass.

Maccoby, E. E. (1991). Gender and relationships: A reprise. *American Psychologist, 46,* 538–539.

Maccoby, E. E. (1998). *The two sexes: Growing up apart, coming together.* Cambridge, MA: Harvard University Press.

Maccoby, E. E. (2000). Perspectives on gender development. *International Journal of Behavioral Development, 24*(4), 398–406.

Maccoby, E. E. (2002). Parenting effects: Issues and controversies. In J. G. Borkowski et al. (Eds.), *Parenting and the child's world: Influences on academic, intellectual, and social-emotional development* (pp. 35–46). Mahwah, NJ: Lawrence Erlbaum Associates.

Maccoby, E. E., & Feldman, S. (1972). Mother-attachment and stranger reactions in the third year of life. *Monographs of the Society for Research in Child Development, 37*(1, ser. 146).

Maccoby, E. E., & Jacklin, C. N. (1974). *The psychology of sex differences.* Stanford, CA: Stanford University Press.

MacDonald, M. G. (1999). Suicide-intervention trainees' perceptions of awareness for warning signs of suicide. *Psychological Reports, 85*(3, pt. 2 [spec. issue]), 1195–1198.

Macfarlane, A. (1975). Olfaction in the development of social preferences in the human neonate. In M. A. Hofer (Ed.), *Parent-infant interaction.* Amsterdam: Elsevier.

Macfarlane, A. (1977). *The psychology of childbirth.* Cambridge, MA: Harvard University Press.

Macfarlane, A., Harris, P., & Barnes, I. (1976). Central and peripheral vision in early infancy. *Journal of Experimental Child*

Psychology, 21, 532–538.

MacKay, A. P., Berg, C. J., & Atrash, H. K. (2001). Pregnancy-related mortality from preeclampsia and eclampsia. *Obstetrics and Gynecology, 97*(4), 533–538.

Mackic-Magyar, J., & McCracken, J. (2004). Review of autism spectrum disorders: A research review for practitioners. *Journal of Child and Adolescent Psychopharmacology, 14*(1), 17–18.

Mackner, L. M., Black, M. M., & Starr, R. H., Jr. (2003). Cognitive development of children in poverty with failure to thrive: A prospective study through age 6. *Journal of Child Psychology and Psychiatry and Allied Disciplines, 44*(5), 743–751.

Maclean, K. (2003). The impact of institutionalization on child development. *Development and Psychopathology, 15,* 853–884.

MacMillan, H. L., Fleming, J. E., Trocmé, N., Boyle, M. H., Wong, M., Racine, Y. A., Beardslee, W. R., & Offord, D. R. (1997). Prevalence of child physical and sexual abuse in the community: Results from the Ontario Health Supplement. *JAMA 278*(2), 131–135.

Madden, N. A., Slavin, R. E., Karweit, N. L., Dolan, L., & Wasik, B. A. (1991, April). Success for all. *Phi Delta Kappan,* pp. 593–599.

Madon, S., et al. (2001). Am I as you see me or do you see me as I am? Self-fulfilling prophecies and self-verification. *Personality and Social Psychology Bulletin, 27*(9), 1,214–1,224.

Madson, L., & Trafimow, D. (2001). Gender comparisons in the private, collective, and allocentric selves. *Journal of Social Psychology, 141*(4), 551–559.

Maejima, K., & Oguchi, T. (2001). The effect of marital discord on children's self-esteem, emotionality, and aggression. *Japanese Journal of Family Psychology, 15*(1), 45–56.

Maffeis, C., Talamini, G., & Tato, L. (1998). Influence of diet, physical activity and parents' obesity on children's adiposity: A four-year longitudinal study. *International Journal of Obesity and Related Metabolic Disorders, 22*(8), 758–764.

Magill-Evans, J., & Harrison, M. J. (2001). Parent-child interactions, parenting stress, and developmental outcomes at 4 years. *Children's Health Care, 30*(2), 135–150.

Magnuson, K. A., Meyers, M. K., Ruhm, C. J., & Waldfogel, J. (2004). Inequality in preschool education and school readiness. *American Educational Research Journal, 41*(1), 115–157.

Magnusson, C. (2001). Adolescent girls' sexual attitudes and opposite-sex relation in 1970 and in 1996. *Journal of Adolescent Health, 28*(3), 242–252.

Mahler, M. S., Pine, F., & Bergman, A. (1975). *The psychological birth of the human infant: Symbiosis and individuation.* New York: Basic Books.

Mahoney, M. C., & James, D. M. (2000). Predictors of anticipated breastfeeding in an urban, low-income setting. *Journal of*

Family Practice, 49(6), 529–533.

Main, M., & Cassidy, J. (1988). Categories of responses to reunion with the parent at age 6: Predictable from infant attachment classifications and stable over a 1-month period. *Developmental Psychology, 24,* 415–426.

Main, M., & Hesse, E. (1990). Parents' unresolved traumatic experiences related to infant disorganized attachment status: Is frightened and/or frightening parental behavior the linking mechanism? In M. T. Greenberg, D. Cicchetti, & E. M. Cummings (Eds.), *Attachment in the preschool years.* Chicago: University of Chicago Press.

Maine, S., Shute, R., & Martin, G. (2001). Educating parents about youth suicide: Knowledge, response to suicidal statements, attitudes, and intention to help. *Suicide and Life-Threatening Behavior, 31*(3), 320–332.

Malina, R. M., & Bouchard, C. (1991). *Growth, maturation, and physical activity.* Champaign, IL: Human Kinetics Academic.

Malinosky-Rummell, R., & Hansen, D. H. (1993). Long-term consequences of childhood physical abuse. *Psychological Bulletin, 114,* 68–79.

Malone, P. S., et al. (2004). Divorce and child behavior problems: Applying latent change score models to life event data. *Structural Equation Modeling, 11*(3), 401–423.

Maluccio, A. N., & Ainsworth, F. (2003). Drug use by parents: A challenge for family reunification practice. *Children and Youth Services Review, 25*(7), 511–533.

Mandler, J. M. (1990). Recall and its verbal expression. In R. Fivush & J. A. Hudson (Eds.), *Knowing and remembering in young children.* Cambridge: Cambridge University Press.

Mangelsdorf, S. C. (1992). Developmental changes in infant-stranger interaction. *Infant Behavior and Development, 15,* 191–208.

Mangelsdorf, S. C., Gunnar, M., Kestenbaum, R., Lang, S., & Andreas, D. (1990). Infant proneness-to-distress temperament, maternal personality, and mother-infant attachment: Associations and goodness of fit. *Child Development, 61,* 820–831.

Mangelsdorf, S. C., McHale, J. L., Goldstein, L. H., & Lehn, L. (2000). Infant attachment: Contributions of infant temperament and maternal characteristics. *Infant Behavior and Development, 23*(2), 175–196.

Mannucci, P. M., & Tuddenham, E. G. D. (2001). Medical progress: The hemophilias: From royal genes to gene therapy. *New England Journal of Medicine, 344,* 1773–1779.

Marcia, J. E. (1991). Identity and self-development. In R. M. Lerner, A. C. Petersen, & J. Brooks-Gunn (Eds.), *Encyclopedia of adolescence.* New York: Garland.

Marcia, J. E., Waterman, A. S., Matteson, D. R., Archer, S. L., & Orlofsky, J. L. (1993). *Ego identity: A handbook for psychosocial research.* New York: Springer-Verlag.

Marcovitch, S., Zelazo, P. D., & Schmuckler, M. A. (2002). The effect of the number of

A trials on performance on the A-not-B task. *Infancy, 3*(4), 519–529.

Marean, G. C., Werner, L. A., & Kuhl, P. K. (1992). Vowel categorization by very young infants. *Developmental Psychology, 28,* 396–405.

Markovitz, H., & Vachon, R. (1990). Conditional reasoning, representation, and level of abstraction. *Developmental Psychology, 26,* 942–951.

Markus, H., & Kitayama, S. (1991). Culture and the self. *Psychological Review, 98*(2), 224–253.

Marsh, H. W., Craven, R. G., & Debus, R. (1991). Self-concepts of young children 5 to 8 years of age: Measurement and multidimensional structure. *Journal of Educational Psychology, 83,* 377–392.

Marshall, K. (2003). Benefiting from extended parental leave. *Perspectives on Labour and Income, 15,* 15–21.

Marsiglio, W. (2004). When stepfathers claim stepchildren: A conceptual analysis. *Journal of Marriage and Family, 66*(1), 22–39.

Martin, C. L., & Ruble, D. (2004). Children's search for gender cues: Cognitive perspectives on gender development. *Current Directions in Psychological Science, 13*(2), 67–70.

Martin, C. L., Ruble, D. N., & Szkrybalo, J. (2002). Cognitive theories of early gender development. *Psychological Bulletin, 128*(6), 903–933.

Martínez, I., Musitu, G., Garcia, J. F., & Camino, L. (2003). A cross-cultural analysis of the effects of family socialization on self-concept: Spain and Brazil. *Psicologia Educação Cultura, 7*(2), 239–259.

Masataka, N. (1998). Perception of motherese in Japanese sign language by 6-month-old hearing infants. *Developmental Psychology, 34*(2), 241–246.

Masi, G., et al. (2004). Generalized anxiety disorder in referred children and adolescents. *Journal of the American Academy of Child and Adolescent Psychiatry. 43*(6), 752–760.

Masi, G., Mucci, M., & Millepiedi, S. (2001). Separation anxiety disorder in children and adolescents: Epidemiology, diagnosis, and management. *CNS Drugs, 15*(2), 93–104.

Masten, A. S. (2001). Ordinary magic: Resilience processes in development. *American Psychologist, 56*(3), 227–238.

Maternity Center Association. (2004, April). *What every pregnant woman needs to know about cesarean section.* New York: MCA.

Matlin, M. (1999). *The psychology of women* (4th ed.). Fort Worth: Harcourt Brace.

Matthews, J. (1990). Drawing and individual development. In R. M. Thomas (Ed.), *The encyclopedia of human development and education: Theory, research, and studies.* Oxford: Pergamon.

Mau, W. C., & Lynn, R. (2000). Gender difference in homework, and test scores in mathematics, reading and science at tenth and twelfth grade. *Psychology, Evolution, & Gender, 2.2,* 119–125.

Maundeni, T. (2000). The consequences of parental separation and divorce for the economic, social and emotional circumstances of children in Botswana. *Childhood: A Global Journal of Child Research, 7*(2), 213–223.

Maurer, D. M., Lewis, T. L., Brent, H. P., & Levin, A. V. (1999). Rapid improvement in the acuity of infants after visual input. *Science, 286*(5437), 108–110.

Maurer, D. M., & Maurer, C. E. (1976, October). Newborn babies see better than you think. *Psychology Today*, pp. 85–88.

Maxson, S. C. (1998). Homologous genes, aggression, and animal models. *Developmental Neuropsychology, 14*(1), 143–156.

Mayes, L. C., & Zigler, E. (1992). An observational study of the affective concomitants of mastery in infants. *Journal of Child Psychology and Psychiatry, 33,* 659–667.

McBride, C. K., Paikoff, R. L., & Holmbeck, G. N. (2003). Individual and familial influences on the onset of sexual intercourse among urban African American adolescents. *Journal of Consulting and Clinical Psychology, 71*(1), 159–167.

McCabe, M. P., & Ricciardelli, L. A. (2001). Parent, peer, and media influences on body image and strategies to both increase and decrease body size among adolescent boys and girls. *Adolescence, 36*(142), 225–240.

McCain, M., & Mustard, J. F. (1999). The early years study: Final report. Toronto, ON: Ontario Children's Secretariat.

McCall, R. B., Applebaum, M. I., & Hogarty, P. S. (1973). Developmental changes in mental performance. *Monographs of the Society for Research in Child Development, 38*(3, ser. 150).

McCartney, K., Harris, M. J., & Bernjeri, F. (1990). Growing up and growing apart: A developmental meta-analysis of twin studies. *Psychological Bulletin, 107,* 226–237.

McCartney, K., Owen, M. T., Booth, C. L., Clarke-Stewart, K. A., & Vandell, D. L. (2004). Testing a maternal attachment model of behavior problems in early childhood. *Journal of Child Psychology and Psychiatry, 45*(4), 765–778.

McClellan, J. M., & Werry, J. S. (2003). Evidence-based treatments in child and adolescent psychiatry: An inventory. *Journal of the American Academy of Child and Adolescent Psychiatry, 42*(12), 1388–1400.

McConaughy, S. H., & Ritter, D. R. (2002). Best practices in multidimensional assessment of emotional or behavioural disorders. In A. Thomas & F. Grimes (Eds.), *Best practices in school psychology IV: v. 2,* (pp. 1303–1317). Washington, DC: NASP.

McCourt, K., et al. (1999). Authoritarianism revisited: Genetic and environmental influences examined in twins reared apart and together. *Personality and Individual Differences, 27*(5), 985–1014.

McCrae, R. R., et al. (2000). Nature over nurture: Temperament, personality, and life span development. *Journal of Personality and Social Psychology, 78*(1), 173–186.

McCune, L. (1993). The development of play as the development of consciousness. In M. H. Bornstein & A. W. O'Reilly (Eds.), *New directions for child development*, no. 59, *The role of play in the development of thought.* San Francisco: Jossey-Bass.

McDevitt, T. M., & Ormrod, J. E. (2002). *Child development and education.* Upper Saddle River, NJ: Prentice-Hall.

McDonnell, J., Wilcox, B., & Hardman, M. L. (1991). *Secondary programs for students with developmental disabilities.* Boston: Allyn & Bacon.

McDonough, L. (2002). Basic-level nouns: First learned but misunderstood. *Journal of Child Language, 29*(2), 357–377.

McEachin, J. J., Smith, T., & Lovaas, O. I. (1993). Long-term outcome for children with autism who received early intensive behavioral treatment. *Journal of Mental Retardation, 97,* 359–372.

McEwan, M. H., Dihoff, R. E., & Brosvic, G. M. (1991). Early infant crawling experience is reflected in later motor skill development. *Perceptual and Motor Skills, 72,* 75–79.

McGlaughlin, A., & Grayson, A. (2001). Crying in the first year of Infancy: Patterns and prevalence. *Journal of Reproductive and Infant Psychology, 19*(1), 47–59.

McGrath, M. L., Mellon, M. W., & Murphy, L. (2000). Empirically supported treatments in pediatric psychology: Constipation and encopresis. Journal of *Pediatric Psychology, 25*(4), 225–254.

McGuffin, P., Riley, B., & Plomin, R. (2001). Toward behavioral genomics. *Science, 291*(5,507), 1232–1249.

McGuinness, D. (1990). Behavioral tempo in preschool boys and girls. *Learning and Individual Differences, 2,* 315–325.

McGuire, M. T., Wing, R. R., Klem, M. L., Lang, W., & Hill, J. O. (1999). What predicts weight regain in a group of successful weight losers? *Journal of Consulting and Clinical Psychology, 67*(2), 177–185.

McGuire, S., Manke, B., Saudino, K. J., Reiss, D., Hetherington, E. M., & Plomin, R. (1999). Perceived competence and self-worth during adolescence: A longitudinal behavioral genetic study. *Child Development, 70*(6), 1283–1296.

McIlvane, W. J., & Dube, W. V. (2003). Stimulus control topography coherence theory: Foundations and extensions. *Behavior Analyst, 26*(2), 195–213.

McKay, A. (2004). Oral sex among teenagers: Research, discourse, and education. *The Canadian Journal of Human Sexuality,* 201–203.

McKay, A. (2004). Sexual health education in the schools: Questions and answers. *The Canadian Journal of Human Sexuality, 13*(3/4), 129–142.

McKay, A., Pietrusiak, M. A., & Holowaty, P. (1998). Parents' opinions and attitudes toward sexuality education in the schools. *The Canadian Journal of Human Sexuality,* 6, 29–28.

McLaren, L. (2002). Interview comments in "Wealthy women most troubled by poor body image" (2002, February 11), Reuters online.

McManus, C. (2003). Right hand, left hand: The origins of asymmetry in brains, bodies, atoms and cultures. *Cortex, 39*(2), 348–350.

McManus, I. C., et al. (1988). The development of handedness in children. *British Journal of Developmental Psychology, 6,* 257–273.

Meador, K. S. (1992). Emerging rainbows: A review of the literature on creativity in preschoolers. *Journal for the Education of the Gifted, 15,* 163–181.

Meaney, K. S., Dornier, L. A., & Owens, M. S. (2002). Sex-role stereotyping for selected sport and physical activities across age groups. *Perceptual and Motor Skills, 94*(3), 743–749.

Mednick, B. R., Baker, R. L., & Carothers, L. E. (1990). Patterns of family instability and crime: The association of timing of the family's disruption with subsequent adolescent and young adult criminality. *Journal of Youth and Adolescence, 19,* 201–220.

Mednick, S. A., Moffitt, T. E., & Stack, S. (1987). *The causes of crime: New biological approaches.* Cambridge: Cambridge University Press.

Meijer, J., & Elshout, J. J. (2001). The predictive and discriminant validity of the zone of proximal development. *British Journal of Educational Psychology, 71*(1), 93–113.

Meldrum, M, L. (2003). A capsule history of pain management. *Journal of the American Medical Association, 290,* 2470–2475.

Meltzoff, A. N. (1988). Infant imitation and memory: Nine-month-olds in immediate and deferred tests. *Child Development, 59,* 217–225.

Meltzoff, A. N. (1997). Interview comments in B. Azar (1997), New theory on development could usurp Piagetian beliefs, *APA Monitor, 28*(6), 9.

Meltzoff, A. N. (2002). Imitation as a mechanism of social cognition: Origins of empathy, theory of mind, and the representation of action. In U. Goswami (Ed.), *Blackwell handbook of childhood cognitive development.* Malden, MA: Blackwell.

Meltzoff A. N., & Moore M. K. (1977). Imitation of facial and manual gestures by human neonates. *Science, 198,* 75–78.

Meltzoff, A. N., & Moore, M. K. (1998). Object representation, identity, and the paradox of early permanence: Steps toward a new framework. *Infant Behavior and Development, 21*(2), 201–235.

Meltzoff, A. N., & Prinz, W. (Eds.) (2002). *The imitative mind: Development, evolution, and brain bases.* New York: Cambridge University Press.

Mendez, L. M. R. (2000). Gender roles and achievement-related choices: A comparison of early adolescent girls in gifted and general education programs. *Journal for the Education of the Gifted, 24*(2), 149–169.

Mennella, J. A. (2001). Regulation of milk intake after exposure to alcohol in mothers' milk. *Alcoholism: Clinical and Experimental Research, 25*(4), 590–593.

Mennella, J. A., & Garcia, P. L. (2000). Children's hedonic response to the smell of alcohol: Effects of parental drinking habits. *Alcoholism: Clinical and Experimental Research, 24*(8), 1167–1171.

Merewood, A. (1991, April). Sperm under siege: More than we ever guessed, having a healthy baby may depend on dad. *Health,* pp. 53–57, 76–77.

Merrell, K. W., & Walker, H. M. (2004). Deconstructing a definition: Social maladjustment versus emotional disturbance and moving the EBD field forward. *Psychology in the Schools, 41*(8), 899–910.

Merrill, L. L., Crouch, J. L., Thomsen, C. J., & Guimond, J. M. (2004). Risk for intimate partner violence and child physical abuse: Psychosocial characteristics of multi-risk male and female Navy recruits. Child Maltreatment: *Journal of the American Professional Society on the Abuse of Children, 9*(1), 18–29.

Merriman, W. E., & Schuster, J. M. (1991). Young children's disambiguation of object name reference. *Child Development, 62,* 1288–1301.

Meschke, L. L., Zweig, J. M., Barber, B. L., & Eccles, J. S. (2000). Demographic, biological, psychological, and social predictors of the timing of first intercourse. *Journal of Research on Adolescence, 10*(3), 315–338.

Mesman, J., Bongers, I. L., & Koot, H. M. (2001). Preschool developmental pathways to preadolescent internalizing and externalizing problems. *Journal of Child Psychology and Psychiatry and Allied Disciplines, 42*(5), 679–689.

Meyer, S., & Shore, C. (2001). Children's understanding of dreams as mental states. *Dreaming, 11*(4), 179–194.

Meyer, S. L., Murphy, C. M., Cascardi, M., & Birns, B. (1991). Gender and relationships: Beyond the peer group. *American Psychologist, 46,* 537.

Meyer, T. (1997). Americans are getting fatter: The National Health and Nutrition Examination Survey. Associated Press.

Michael, E. D. (1990). Physical development and fitness. In R. M. Thomas (Ed.), *The encyclopedia of human development and education: Theory, research, and studies.* Oxford: Pergamon.

Michel, C. (1989). Radiation embryology. *Experientia, 45,* 69–77.

Miklos, E. A., Brahler, C. J., Baer, J. T., & Dolan, P. (2004). Dietary deficiencies and excesses: A sample of African American mothers and daughters eligible for nutrition assistance programs. *Family and Community Health, 27*(2), 123–129.

Mikulincer, M., & Shaver, P. R. (2001). Attachment theory and intergroup bias: Evidence that priming the secure base schema attenuates negative reactions to out-groups. *Journal of Personality and Social Psychology,*

81(1), 97–115.

Millar, W. S. (1972). A study of operant conditioning under delayed reinforcement in early infancy. *Monographs of the Society for Research in Child Development, 37*(2, ser. 147).

Millar, W. S. (1990). Span of integration for delayed-reward contingency learning in 6- to 8-month-old infants. In A. Diamond (Ed.), *The development and neural bases of higher cognitive functions.* New York: New York Academy of Sciences.

Miller, A. L., Wyman, S. E., Huppert, J. D., Glassman, S. L., & Rathus, J. H. (2000). Analysis of behavioral skills utilized by suicidal adolescents receiving dialectical behavior therapy. *Cognitive and Behavioral Practice, 7*(2), 183–187.

Miller, G. A. (1956). The magical number seven, plus or minus two: Some limits on our capacity to process information. *Psychological Review, 63,* 81–97.

Miller, J. G. (1994). Cultural diversity in the morality of caring: Individually-oriented versus duty-based interpersonal moral codes. *Cross-Cultural Research, 28,* 3–39.

Miller, J. G., & Bersoff, D. M. (1992). Culture and moral judgment: How are conflicts between justice and interpersonal responsibilities resolved? *Journal of Personality and Social Psychology, 62,* 541–554.

Miller, L., & Budd, J. (1999). The development of occupational sex-role stereotypes, occupational preferences and academic subject preferences in children at ages 8, 12, and 16. *Educational Psychology, 19*(1), 17–35.

Miller, S. M., Birnbaum, A., & Durbin, D. (1990a). Etiologic perspectives on depression in childhood. In M. Lewis & S. M. Miller (Eds.), *Handbook of developmental psychopathology.* New York: Plenum.

Miller, S. M., Boyer, B. A., & Rodoletz, M. (1990b). Anxiety in children: Nature and development. In M. Lewis & S. M. Miller (Eds.), *Handbook of developmental psychopathology.* New York: Plenum.

Mills, R. S. L., & Rubin, K. H. (1990). Parental beliefs about problematic social behaviors in early childhood. *Child Development, 61,* 138–152.

Minister of Industry (2006). *Child care in Canada.* Ottawa, ON: Statistics Canada.

Minister of Public Works and Government Services Canada (2005). *Canadian incidence study of reported child abuse and neglect, 2003: Major findings.* Ottawa, ON: Author.

Miranda, A., & Presentacion, M. J. (2000). Efectos de un tratamiento cognitivo-conductual en ninos con trastorno por deficit de atencion con hiperactividad, agresivos y no agresivos: Cambio clinicamente significativo. *Infancia y Aprendizaje, 92,* 51–70.

Mirmiran, M. (1995). The function of fetal/neonatal rapid eye movement sleep. *Behavioural Brain Research, 69*(1–2), 13–22.

Mischo, C. (2004). Fördert Gruppendiskussion die Perspektiven-Koordination? *Zeitschrift für Entwicklungspsychologie und*

Pädagogische Psychologie, 36(1), 30–37.

Mitchell, K. J., Finkelhor, D., & Wolak, J. (2001). Risk factors for and impact of online sexual solicitation of youth. *Journal of the American Medical Association, 285*(23), 3011–3014.

Moeller, F. G., et al. (2001). Psychiatric aspects of impulsivity. *American Journal of Psychiatry, 158*(11), 1783–1793.

Mokdad, A. H., et al. (2000). The continuing epidemic of obesity in the United States. *Journal of the American Medical Association, 284*(13), 1195–1200.

Molfese, D. L., Burger-Judisch, L. M., & Hans, L. L. (1991). Consonant discrimination by newborn infants: Electrophysiological differences. *Developmental Neuropsychology, 7,* 177–195.

Molfese, V. J., DiLalla, L. F., & Bunce, D. (1997). Prediction of the intelligence test scores of 3- to 8-year-old children by home environment, socioeconomic status, and biomedical risks. *Merrill-Palmer Quarterly, 43*(2), 219–234.

Molinari, L., & Corsaro, W. A. (2000). Le relazioni amicali nella scuola dell'infanzia e nella scuola elementare: Uno studio longitudinale. *Eta Evolutiva, 67,* 40–51.

Moliterno, D. J., et al. (1994). Coronary-artery vasoconstriction induced by cocaine, cigarette smoking, or both. *New England Journal of Medicine, 330,* 454–459.

Moller, L. C., Hymel, S., & Rubin, K. H. (1992). Sex typing in play and popularity in middle childhood. *Sex Roles, 26,* 331–353.

Money, J. (1987). Sin, sickness, or status? Homosexual gender identity and psychoneuroendocrinology. *American Psychologist, 42,* 384–399.

Mont, L. (2003). Reversibility of cardiac abnormalities in adolescents with anorexia nervosa after weight recovery. *Journal of the American Academy of Child and Adolescent Psychiatry, 42*(7), 808–813.

Montemayor, R., & Eisen, M. (1977). The development of self-conceptions from childhood to adolescence. *Developmental Psychology, 13,* 314–319.

Montemayor, R., & Flannery, D. J. (1991). Parent-adolescent relations in middle and late adolescence. In R. M. Lerner, A. C. Petersen, & J. Brooks-Gunn (Eds.), *Encyclopedia of adolescence.* New York: Garland.

Moore, C., Pure, K., & Furrow, O. (1990). Children's understanding of the model expression of speaker certainty and uncertainty and its relation to the development of a representational theory of mind. *Child Development, 61,* 722–730.

Moore, L. L., et al. (1991). Influence of parents' physical activity levels on activity levels of young children. *Journal of Pediatrics, 118,* 215–219.

Morales, J. (2003). Sex and sexuality among New York's Puerto Rican youth. *Journal of HIV/AIDS Prevention and Education for Adolescents and Children, 5*(3–4), 165–167.

Morelli, G. A., Oppenheim, D., Rogoff, B., & Goldsmith, D. (1992). Cultural variation in infants' sleeping arrangements: Questions of independence. *Developmental Psychology, 28,* 604–613.

Moreno, M., Trigo, J. M., Escuredo, L., Rodriguez de Fonseca, F., & Navarro, M. (2003). Perinatal exposure to Delta-sup-9-tetrahydrocannabinol increases presynaptic dopamine D-sub-2 receptor sensitivity: A behavioral study in rats. *Pharmacology, Biochemistry and Behavior, 75*(3), 565–575.

Morley, J. E., & Perry, H. M., III (2003). Androgens and women at the menopause and beyond. *Journals of Gerontology, Series A: Biological Sciences and Medical Sciences, 58A*(5), 409–416.

Moro, C., & Rodriguez, C. (2000). La creation des representations chez l'enfant au travers des processus de semiosis. *Enfance, 52*(3), 287–294.

Morrell, J., & Steele, H. (2003). The role of attachment security, temperament, maternal perception, and care-giving behavior in persistent infant sleeping problems. *Infant Mental Health Journal, 24*(5), 447–468.

Morrison, D. R., & Coiro, M. J. (1999). Parental conflict and marital disruption: Do children benefit when high-conflict marriages are dissolved? *Journal of Marriage and the Family, 61*(3), 626–637.

Morrison, E. S., Starks, K., Hyndman, C., & Ronzio, N. (1980). *Growing up sexual.* New York: Van Nostrand Reinhold.

Morrongiello, B. A., & Clifton, R. K. (1984). Effects of sound frequency on behavioral and cardiac orienting in newborn and 5-month-old infants. *Journal of Experimental Child Psychology, 38,* 429–446.

Morrongiello, R. A., Fenwick, K. D., & Chance, G. (1990). Sound localization acuity in very young infants: An observer-based testing procedure. *Developmental Psychology, 26,* 75–84.

Mortimer, J. T., & Johnson, M. K. (1998). Adolescents' part-time work and educational achievement. In K. Borman & B. Schneider (Eds.), *The adolescent years: Social influences and educational challenges—Ninety-seventh yearbook of the National Society for the Study of Education, Part I* (pp. 183–206). Chicago: National Society for the Study of Education.

Morton, J., & Johnson, M. H. (1991). CONSPEC and CONLERN: A two-process theory of infant face recognition. *Psychological Review, 98,* 164–181.

Moses, L. J., Baldwin, D. A., Rosicky, J. G., & Tidball, G. (2001). Evidence for referential understanding in the emotions domain at twelve and eighteen months. *Child Development, 72*(3), 718–735.

Moses, L. J., & Flavell, J. H. (1990). Inferring false beliefs from actions and reactions. *Child Development, 61,* 929–945.

Mosholder, A. D. (2004). Cited in G. Harris (2004, September 24), Warning called likely on drug risk for suicide, available at http://www.nytimes.com

Mueller, E., & Tingley, E. (1990). The bear's picnic: Children's representations of themselves and their families. In I. Bretherton &

M. W. Watson (Eds.), *New directions for child development, no. 48, Children's perspectives on the family.* San Francisco: Jossey-Bass.

Mueller, N., & Hulk, A. (2001). Cross-linguistic influence in bilingual language acquisition: Italian and French as recipient languages. *Bilingualism: Language and Cognition, 4*(1), 1–21.

Mueller, R., Pierce, K., Ambrose, J. B., Allen, G., & Courchesne, E. (2001). Atypical patterns of cerebral motor activation in autism: A functional magnetic resonance study. *Biological Psychiatry, 49*(8), 665–676.

Mueller, U., Overton, W. F., & Reene, K. (2001). Development of conditional reasoning: A longitudinal study. *Journal of Cognition and Development, 2*(1), 27–49.

Mueller, U., Sokol, B., & Overton, W. F. (1999). Developmental sequences in class reasoning and propositional reasoning. *Journal of Experimental Child Psychology, 74*(2), 69–106.

Muir, D. W., & Hains, S. M. J. (1993). Infant sensitivity to perturbations in adult facial, vocal, tactile, and contingent stimulation during face-to-face interactions. In B. de Boysson-Bardies, S. de Schonen, P. W. Jusczyk, P. F. MacNeilage, & J. Morton (Eds.), *Changes in speech and face processing in infancy: A glimpse at developmental mechanisms of cognition.* Dordrecht, The Netherlands: Kluwer Academic.

Muir, G. D. (2000). Early ontogeny of locomotor behaviour: A comparison between altricial and precocial animals. *Brain Research Bulletin, 53*(5), 719–726.

Mullen, B. (2004). Sticks and stones can break my bones, but Ethnophaulisms can alter the portrayal of immigrants to children. *Personality and Social Psychology Bulletin, 30*(2), 250–260.

Multiple Births Canada (2007). Available at http://www.multiplebirthscanada.org

Mumford, M. D. (2003). Where have we been, where are we going? Taking stock in creativity research. *Creativity Research Journal, 15*(2–3), 107–120.

Munarriz, R., et al. (2002). Androgen replacement therapy with dehydroepiandrosterone for androgen insufficiency and female sexual dysfunction: Androgen and questionnaire results. *Journal of Sex and Marital Therapy, 28*(Suppl. 1), 165–173.

Munroe, R. H., Shimmin, H. S., & Munroe, R. L. (1984). Gender role understanding and sex role preference in four cultures. *Developmental Psychology, 20,* 673–682.

Muntner, P., He, J., Cutler, J. A., Wildman, R. P., & Whelton, P. K. (2004). Trends in blood pressure among children and adolescents. *Journal of the American Medical Association, 291,* 2107–2113.

Murphy, L. B. (1983). Issues in the development of emotion in infancy. In R. Plutchik & H. Kellerman (Eds.), *Emotion: Theory, research, and experimentation.* New York: Academic Press.

Murphy, T. K., Bengtson, M. A., Tan, J. Y., Carbonell, E., & Levin, G. M. (2000).

Selective serotonin reuptake inhibitors in the treatment of paediatric anxiety disorders: A review. *International Clinical Psychopharmacology, 15*(Suppl. 2), S47-S63.

Murphy, V., & Hicks-Stewart, K. (1991). Learning disabilities and attention deficit-hyperactivity disorder: An interactional perspective. *Journal of Learning Disabilities, 24,* 386–388.

Murray, B. (1998). Survey reveals concerns of today's girls. *APA Monitor, 29*(10).

Murry, V. M., Bynum, M. S., Brody, G. H., Willert, A., & Stephens, D. (2001). African American single mothers and children in context: A review of studies on risk and resilience. *Clinical Child and Family Psychology Review, 4*(2), 133–155.

Must, A., Jacques, P. F., Dallal, G. E., Bajema, C. J., & Dietz, W. (1992). Long-term morbidity and mortality of overweight adolescents. *New England Journal of Medicine, 327,* 1350–1354.

Nadeau, L., et al. (2003). Extremely premature and very low birthweight infants: A double hazard population? *Social Development, 12*(2), 235–248.

Nagin, D. S., & Tremblay, R. E. (2001). Parental and early childhood predictors of persistent physical aggression in boys from kindergarten to high school. *Archives of General Psychiatry, 58*(4), 389–394.

Nair, H., & Murray, A. D. (2005). Predictors of attachment security in preschool children from intact and divorced families. *The Journal of Genetic Psychology, 166,* 245–263.

Nakkula, M. J., & Nikitopoulos, C. E. (2001). Negotiation training and interpersonal development: An exploratory study of early adolescents in Argentina. *Adolescence, 36*(141), 1–20.

Nansel, T. R., Haynie, D. L., & Simons-Morton, B. G. (2003). The association of bullying and victimization with middle school adjustment. *Journal of Applied School Psychology, 19*(2), 45–61.

Narvaez, D., Getz, I., Rest, J. R., & Thoma, S. J. (1999). Individual moral judgment and cultural ideologies. *Developmental Psychology, 35*(2), 478–488.

Nation, J. R., & Gleaves, D. H. (2001). Low-level lead exposure and intelligence in children. *Archives of Clinical Neuropsychology, 16*(4), 375–388.

National Campaign to Prevent Teen Pregnancy (2003, September 30). Teens say parents most influence their sexual decisions: New polling data and "Tips for Parents" released. Available at http://www.teenpregnancy.org/about/announcements/pr/2003/release9_30_03.asp

National Center for Biotechnology Information (NCBI) (2000, March 30). SRY: Sex determination. National Institute of Health. Available at http://www.ncbi.nlm.nih.gov/disease/SRY.html

National Center for Children in Poverty (2004). Low-income children in the United States (2004). Available at http://cpmcnet.columbia.edu/dept/nccp/

National Center on Educational Restructuring

Inclusion (1995). *National study on inclusion: Overview and summary report, 2,* 1–8.

National Center for Education Statistics (2002, January 16). *Common core of data: Local Education Agency Universe Survey.* Washington, DC: Office of Educational Research and Improvement, U.S. Department of Education. Available at http://nces.ed.gov

National Center for Health Statistics (2002, January 8). Suicide statistics by age, race, and sex. Atlanta, GA: Centers for Disease Control and Prevention. Available at http://www.cdc.gov/nchs/fastats/suicide.htm

National Center for Health Statistics (2003, September 5). *Pregnancy success rates.* Atlanta, GA: Department of Health and Human Services, Centers for Disease Control and Prevention. Available at http://www.cdc.gov/reproductivehealth/ART99/PDF's/art99_3.pdf

National Center for Health Statistics (2004). *America's children in brief, 2004.* Available at http://childstats.gov/americaschildren

National Center for Health Statistics & National Center for Chronic Disease Prevention and Health Promotion (2000). Available at http://www.cdc.gov .growthcharts

National Center for Injury Prevention and Control (2004a). Ten leading causes of death, United States: All races, both sexes. Atlanta, GA: National Center for Health Statistics (NCHS) Vital Statistics System, Office of Statistics and Programming, Centers for Disease Control and Prevention. Available at http://webapp.cdc.gov/cgi-bin/broker.exe

National Center for Injury Prevention and Control (2004a). Ten leading causes of death, United States: All races, both sexes. Atlanta, GA: National Center for Health Statistics (NCHS) Vital Statistics System, Office of Statistics and Programming, Centers for Disease Control and Prevention. Available at http://webapp.cdc.gov/cgi-bin/broker.exe

National Center for Injury Prevention and Control (2004b). Web-Based Injury Statistics Query and Reporting System (WISQARS). Atlanta, GA: Centers for Disease Control and Prevention. Available at http://www.cdc .gov/ncipc/wisqars

National Clearinghouse on Family Violence (2006). *Child maltreatment in Canada: Overview paper.* Prepared by S. Jack, C.Munn, C. Cheng, & H. MacMillan. Ottawa: Public Health Agency of Canada.

National High Blood Pressure Education Program Working Group on High Blood Pressure in Children and Adolescents (2004). The fourth report on the diagnosis, evaluation, and treatment of high blood pressure in children and adolescents. *Pediatrics, 114*(2), 555–576.

National Institutes of Health (2002). Available at http://cerhr.niehs.nih.gov/genpub/topics/vitamin_a-ccae.html

National Library of Medicine (1997, August 28). Thalidomide: Potential benefits and risks. Available at http://www.nlm.nih.gov/pubs/cbm/thalidomide.html

National Research Council (1993). *Understanding and preventing violence.* Washington, DC: National Academy Press.

National Sleep Foundation (2004, March). 2004 Sleep in America poll. Washington, DC: National Sleep Foundation. Available at http://www.sleepfoundation.org

Natsopoulos, D., Kiosseoglou, G., & Xeromeritou, A. (1992). Handedness and spatial ability in children: Further support for Geschwind's hypothesis of "pathology of superiority" and for Annett's theory of intelligence. *Genetic, Social, and General Psychology Monographs, 118*(1) 103–126.

Nauta, M. M., & Kokaly, M. L. (2001). Assessing role model influences on students' academic and vocational decisions. *Journal of Career Assessment, 9(1),* 81–99.

Navarro, J. F., & Maldonado, E. (2002). Acute and subchronic effects of MDMA ("ecstasy") on anxiety in male mice tested in the elevated plus-maze. *Progress in Neuro-Psychopharmacology and Biological Psychiatry, 26*(6), 1151–1154.

Nawaz, H., & Katz, D. (2001). American College of Preventive Medicine practice policy statement: Weight management counseling of overweight adults. *American Journal of Preventive Medicine, 21*(1), 73–78.

Nazzi, T., & Gopnik, A. (2000). A shift in children's use of perceptual and causal cues to categorization. *Developmental Science, 3*(4), 389–396.

Nduati, R., et al. (2000). Effect of breast-feeding and formula feeding on transmission of HIV-1. *Journal of the American Medical Association, 283,* 1167–1174.

Needleman, H. L., & Bellinger, D. (2001). Studies of lead exposure and the developing central nervous system. *Archives of Clinical Neuropsychology, 16*(4), 359–374.

Needlman, R. (2000). What you can do about bed-wetting. America Online, AOL Parenting. Available at http://www.aol.com

Needlman, R. (2001). Understanding encopresis (fecal soiling). America Online, AOL Parenting. Available at http://www.aol.com

Neisser, U. (1997). Interview comments in S. Sleek (1997), Can "emotional intelligence" be taught in today's schools? *APA Monitor, 28*(6), 25.

Neisser, U., et al. (1996). Intelligence: Knowns and unknowns. *American Psychologist, 51,* 77–101.

Nelson, C. A., & Luciana, M. (Eds.) (2001). *Handbook of developmental cognitive neuroscience.* Cambridge, MA: MIT Press.

Nelson, C. A., & Ludemann, P. M. (1989). Past, current, and future trends in infant face perception research. *Canadian Journal of Psychology, 43,* 183–198.

Nelson, K. (1973). Structure and strategy in learning to talk. *Monographs for the Society for Research in Child Development, 38*(1–2, ser. 149).

Nelson, K. (1981). Individual differences in language development: Implications for development of language. *Developmental Psychology, 17,* 170–187.

Nelson, K. (1982). The syntagmatics and paradigmatics of conceptual development. In S. A. Kuczaj II (Ed.), *Language development, v. 2, Language, thought, and culture.* Hillsdale, NJ: Erlbaum.

Nelson, K. (1990). Remembering, forgetting, and childhood amnesia. In R. Fivush & J. A. Hudson (Eds.), *Knowing and remembering in young children.* Cambridge: Cambridge University Press.

Nelson, K. (1993). Events, narratives, memory: What develops? In C. A. Nelson (Ed.), *Minnesota symposia on child psychology, v. 26, Memory and affect in development.* Hillsdale, NJ: Erlbaum.

Nelson, K., & Fivush, R. (2004). The emergence of autobiographical memory: A social cultural developmental theory. *Psychological Review, 111*(2), 486–511.

Neville, B., & Parke, R. D. (1991). Adolescent fathers. In R. M. Lerner, A. C. Petersen, & J. Brooks-Gunn (Eds.), *Encyclopedia of adolescence.* New York: Garland.

Newburn-Cook, C. V., et al. (2002). Where and to what extent is prevention of low birth weight possible? *Western Journal of Nursing Research, 24*(8), 887–904.

Newcomb, A. F., Bukowski, W. M., & Pattee, L. (1993). Children's peer relations: A meta-analytic review of popular, rejected, neglected controversial, and average sociometric status. *Psychological Bulletin, 113,* 99–128.

Newcombe, N., & Dubas, J. S. (1992). A longitudinal study of predictors of spatial ability in adolescent females. *Child Development, 63,* 37–46.

Newport, D. J., Heim, C., Bonsall, R., Miller, A. H., & Nemeroff, C. B. (2004). Pituitary-adrenal responses to standard and low-dose dexamethasone suppression tests in adult survivors of child abuse. *Biological Psychiatry, 55*(1), 10–20.

Newport, E. L. (1992, June). Critical periods and creolization: Effects of maturational state and input on the acquisition of language. Paper presented at the meeting of American Psychological Society, San Diego, CA.

Nicely, P., Tamis-LeMonda, C. S., & Bornstein, M. H. (1999). Mothers' attuned responses to infant affect expressivity promote earlier achievement of language milestones. *Infant Behavior and Development, 22*(4), 557–568.

Nichols, S., et al. (2004). Mechanisms of verbal memory impairment in four neurodevelopmental disorders. *Brain and Language, 88*(2), 180–189.

Nichols, S., & Stich, S. (2000). A cognitive theory of pretense. *Cognition, 74*(2), 115–147.

Nicolson, R. I., Fawcett, A. J., & Dean, P. (2001). Dyslexia, development, and the cerebellum. *Trends in Neurosciences, 24*(9), 515–516.

Niedbala, B., & Tsang, R. (1993). The small for gestational age infant. In S. W. Ekvall (Ed.), *Pediatric nutrition in chronic diseases and developmental disorders: Prevention, assessment, and treatment.* New York: Oxford.

Nielsen, M., & Dissanayake, C. (2000). An investigation of pretend play, mental state terms, and false belief understanding: In search of a metarepresentational link. *British Journal of Developmental Psychology, 18*(4), 609–624.

Nielsen, S., & Palmer, B. (2003). Diagnosing eating disorders: AN, BN, and the others. *Acta Psychiatrica Scandinavica, 108*(3), 161–162.

Nielsen, S. J., & Popkin, B. M. (2003). Patterns and trends in food portion sizes, 1977–1998. *Journal of the American Medical Association, 289*(4), 450–453.

Nigg, J. T. (2001). Is ADHD a disinhibitory disorder? *Psychological Bulletin, 127*(5), 571–598.

Nigg, J. T., Goldsmith, H. H., & Sachek, J. (2004). Temperament and attention deficit hyperactivity disorder: The development of a multiple pathway model. *Journal of Clinical Child and Adolescent Psychology, 33*(1), 42–53.

Nijhuis-van der Sanden, R. W. G., Smits-Engelsman, B. C. M., & Eling, P. A. T. M. (2000). Motor performance in girls with Turner syndrome. *Developmental Medicine and Child Neurology, 42*(10), 685–690.

Noguchi P. (2003). Risks and benefits of gene therapy. *New England Journal of Medicine, 348*, 193–194.

Noll, J. G., Trickett, P. K., & Putnam, F. W. (2000). Social network constellation and sexuality of sexually abused and comparison girls in childhood and adolescence. Child Maltreatment: *Journal of the American Professional Society on the Abuse of Children, 5*(4), 323–337.

Noll, R. B., et al. (2001). Neuropsychological functioning of youths with sickle cell disease: Comparison with non-chronically ill peers. *Journal of Pediatric Psychology, 26*(2), 69–78.

Noller, P., & Callan, V. J. (1990). Adolescents' perceptions of the nature of their communication with parents. *Journal of Youth and Adolescence, 19*, 349–362.

Norlander, T., Erixon, A., & Archer, T. (2000). Psychological androgyny and creativity: Dynamics of gender-role and personality trait. *Social Behavior and Personality, 28*(5), 423–435.

Norwitz, E. R., Robinson, J. N., & Challis, J. R. G. (1999). The control of labor. *New England Journal of Medicine, 341*(9), 660–666.

Nucci, L. P. (2002). The development of moral reasoning. In U. Goswami (Ed.), *Blackwell handbook of childhood cognitive development* (pp. 303–325). Malden, MA: Blackwell.

Nurnberger, J. I., Jr., et al. (2001). Evidence for a locus on chromosome 1 that influences vulnerability to alcoholism and affective disorder. *American Journal of Psychiatry, 158*, 718–724.

Oates, C., Blades, M., & Gunter, B. (2002). Children and television advertising: When do they understand persuasive intent? *Journal of Consumer Behaviour, 1*(3), 238–245.

O'Boyle, M. W., & Benbow, C. P. (1990). Handedness and its relationship to ability and talent. In S. Coren (Ed.), *Left-handedness: Behavior implications and anomalies.* Amsterdam: North-Holland.

O'Brien, L. T., & Crandall, C. S. (2003). Stereotype threat and arousal: Effects on women's math performance. *Personality and Social Psychology Bulletin, 29*(6), 782–789.

O'Connor, J., Fitzgerald, M., & Hoey, H. (2000). The relationship between karyotype and cognitive functioning in Turner syndrome. *Irish Journal of Psychological Medicine, 17*(3), 82–85.

O'Connor, T. G., Caspi, A., DeFries, J. C., & Plomin, R. (2000). Are associations between parental divorce and children's adjustment genetically mediated? An adoption study. *Developmental Psychology, 36*(4), 429–437.

O'Dell, K. M. C., & Kaiser, K. (1997). Sexual behaviour: Secrets and flies. *Current Biology, 7*(6), R345-R347.

O'Donnell, L., et al. (2003). Long-term influence of sexual norms and attitudes on timing of sexual initiation among urban minority youth. *Journal of School Health, 23*(2), 68–75.

Oettinger, G. (1999). Does high school employment affect high school academic performance? *Industrial and Labor Relations Review, 53*(1), 136–151.

Ogrodniczuk, J. S., & Piper, W. E. (2003). Preventing postnatal depression: A review of research findings. *Harvard Review of Psychiatry, 11*(6), 291–307.

Ogura, T. (1991). A longitudinal study of the relationship between early language development and play development. *Journal of Child Language, 18*, 273–294.

Ohnishi, T., et al. (2000). Abnormal regional cerebral blood flow in childhood autism. *Brain, 123*(9), 1838–1844.

Okamoto, Y., Sugano, Y., & Negayama, K. (2003). Mother-fetus interaction from the viewpoint of the pregnant woman's diaries about fetal movements. *Japanese Journal of Developmental Psychology, 14*(1), 64–76.

Okazaki, S., & Sue, S. (2000). Implications of test revisions for assessment with Asian Americans. *Psychological Assessment, 12*(3), 272–280.

Ollendick, T. H., Hagopian, L. P., & Huntzinger, R. M. (1991). Cognitive-behavior therapy with nighttime fearful children. *Journal of Behavioral Therapy and Experimental Psychiatry, 22*, 113–121.

Ollendick, T. H., & King, N. J. (1991). Origins of childhood fears: An evaluation of Rachman's theory of teen-acquisition. *Behavior Research and Therapy, 29*, 117–123.

Ollendick, T. H., King, N. J., & Frary, R. B. (1989). Fears in children and adolescents: Reliability and generalizability across gender, age, and nationality. *Behavior Research and Therapy, 27*, 19–26.

Ollendick, T. H., Yule, W., & Ollier, K. (1991). Fears in British children and their relationship to manifest anxiety and depression.

Journal of Child Psychology and Psychiatry, 32, 321–331.

Oller, D. K. (1995). Development of vocalizations in infancy. In H. Winitz (Ed.), *Human communication and its disorders, a review, v. 4.* Parkton, MD: York Press.

Oller, D. K. (2000). *The emergence of the speech capacity.* Mahwah, NJ: Lawrence Erlbaum Associates.

Olson, M. J. (2003). Counselor understanding of Native American spiritual loss. *Counseling and Values, 47*(2), 109–117.

Olson, S. L., Bates, J. E., Sandy, J. M., & Lanthier, R. (2000). Early developmental precursors of externalizing behavior in middle childhood and adolescence. *Journal of Abnormal Child Psychology, 28*(2), 119–133.

Olson, S. L., Kashiwagi, K., & Crystal, D. (2001). Concepts of adaptive and maladaptive child behavior: A comparison of U.S. and Japanese mothers of preschool-age children. *Journal of Cross-Cultural Psychology, 32*(1), 43–57.

Oman, R. F., et al. (2002). An adolescent age group approach to examining youth risk behaviors. *American Journal of Health Promotion, 16*(3), 167–176.

Omer, H., & Elitzur, A. C. (2001). What would you say to the person on the roof? A suicide prevention text. *Suicide and Life-Threatening Behavior, 31*(2), 129–139.

O'Neill, D. K., & Chong, S. C. F. (2001). Preschool children's difficulty understanding the types of information obtained through the five senses. *Child Development, 72*(3), 803–815.

O'Neill, D. K., & Gopnik, A. (1991). Young children's ability to identify the sources of their beliefs. *Developmental Psychology, 27*, 390–397.

Oniszczenko, W., Wlodzimierz, Z. B., Strelau, J., Riemann, R., Angleitner, A., & Spinath, F. M. (2003). Genetic and environmental determinants of temperament: A comparative study based on Polish and German samples. *European Journal of Personality, 17*(3), 207–220.

O'Reilly, D., & Dillenburger, K. (2000). The development of a high-intensity parent training program for the treatment of moderate to severe child conduct problems. *Research on Social Work Practice, 10*(6), 759–786.

Ornoy, A. (2002). The effects of alcohol and illicit drugs on the human embryo and fetus. *Israel Journal of Psychiatry and Related Sciences, 39*(2), 120–132.

Osborne, J. W. (2001). Testing stereotype threat: Does anxiety explain race and sex differences in achievement? *Contemporary Educational Psychology, 26*(3), 291–310.

Ostatnikova, D., et al. (2002). Biological aspects of intellectual giftedness. *Studia Psychologica, 44*(1), 3–13.

Oster, H., Hegley, D., & Nagel, L. (1992). Adult judgments and fine-grained analysis of infant facial expressions: Testing the validity of a priori coding formulas. *Developmental Psychology, 28*, 1115–1131.

O'Sullivan, L. F., Meyer-Bahlburg, H. F. L., & Watkins, B. X. (2000). Social cognitions associated with pubertal development in a sample of urban, low-income, African-American and Latina girls and mothers. *Journal of Adolescent Health, 27*(4), 227–235.

Owens, R. E. (1990). Development of communication, language, and speech. In G. Shames & E. Wiig (Eds.), *Human communication disorders* (3rd ed.). Columbus, OH: Merrill.

Oyserman, D., Radin, N., & Benn, R. (1993). Dynamics in a three-generational family: Teens, grandparents, and babies. *Developmental Psychology, 29*, 564–572.

Page, K. (1999, May 16). The graduate. *Washington Post Magazine, 152*, 18, 20.

Paikoff, R. L., & Brooks-Gunn, J. (1991). Interventions to prevent pregnancy. In R. M. Lerner, A. C. Petersen, & J. Brooks-Gunn (Eds.), *Encyclopedia of adolescence.* New York: Garland.

Paikoff, R. L., & Collins, A. C. (1991). Editors' notes: Shared views in the family during adolescence. In R. L. Paikoff (Ed.), *New directions for child development, no. 51, Shared views in the family during adolescence.* San Francisco: Jossey-Bass.

Palda, V. A., Guise, J., Wathen, C. N., & the Canadian Task Force on Preventive Health Care (2004). Interventions to promote breast-feeding: Applying the evidence in clinical practice. *Canadian Medical Association Journal, 170*(6), 976–978.

Palmer, E. J., & Hollin, C. R. (2000). The interrelations of socio-moral-reasoning, perceptions of own parenting, and attributions of intent with self-reported delinquency. *Legal and Criminological Psychology, 5*(pt. 2), 201–218.

Palmer, E. J., & Hollin, C. R. (2001). Socio-moral reasoning, perceptions of parenting and self-reported delinquency in adolescents. *Applied Cognitive Psychology, 15*(1), 85–100.

Palmer, E. L. (2003). Realities and challenges in the rapidly changing televisual media landscape. In E. L. Palmer & B. M. Young (Eds.), *The faces of televisual media: Teaching, violence, selling to children* (2nd ed.) (pp. 361–377). Mahwah, NJ: Lawrence Erlbaum Associates.

Papousek, M., Papousek, H., & Symmes, D. (1991). The meanings of melodies in motherese in tone and stress languages. *Infant Behavior and Development, 14*, 415–440.

Papousek, M., & von Hofacker, N. (1998). Persistent crying in early infancy: A nontrivial condition of risk for the developing mother-infant relationship. *Child: Care, Health and Development, 24*(5), 395–424.

Parents Canada. *The new baby and child care encyclopaedia, 14*(2). Toronto, ON: Parents Canada.

Paris, S. G., & Winograd, P. (1990). How metacognition can promote academic learning and instruction. In B. F. Jones & L. Idol (Eds.), *Dimensions of thinking and cognitive instruction.* Hillsdale, NJ: Erlbaum.

Park, K. A., Lay, K., & Ramsay, L. (1993). Individual differences and developmental changes in preschoolers' friendships. *Developmental Psychology, 29*, 264–270.

Parke, R. D. (1996). *Fatherhood.* Cambridge, MA: Harvard University Press.

Parke, R. D. (2002). Fathers and families. In M. H. Bornstein (Ed.), *Handbook of parenting: Vol. 3: Being and becoming a parent (2nd ed.)*, pp. 27–73. Mahwah, NJ: Lawrence Erlbaum Associates Publishers.

Parke, R. D., & Slaby, R. G. (1983). The development of aggression. In P. H. Mussen (Ed.), *Handbook of child psychology, v. 4, Socialization, personality and social development.* New York: Wiley.

Parker, J. G., & Gottman, J. M. (1989). Social and emotional development in a rational context. In T. J. Berndt & G. W. Ladd (Eds.), *Peer relationships in child development.* New York: Wiley.

Parker, J. G., & Herrera, C. (1996). Interpersonal processes in friendship: A comparison of abused and nonabused children's experience. *Developmental Psychology, 32*, 1025–1038.

Parker, K. J., & Lee, T. M. (2001). Central vasopressin administration regulates the onset of facultative paternal behavior in Microtus pennsylvanicus (meadow voles). *Hormones and Behavior, 39*(4), 285–294.

Parks, P., & Bradley, R. (1991). The interaction of home environment features and their relation to infant competence. *Infant Mental Health Journal, 12*, 3–16.

Parrott, A. (Ed.) (2003). Cognitive deficits and cognitive normality in recreational cannabis and ecstasy/MDMA users. *Human Psychopharmacology: Clinical and Experimental, 18*(2), 89–90.

Parsons, J. T., Halkitis, P. N., Bimbi, D., & Borkowski, T. (2000). Perceptions of the benefits and costs associated with condom use and unprotected sex among late adolescent college students. *Journal of Adolescence, 23*(4), 377–391.

Parsons, T. D., et al. (2004). Sex differences in mental rotation and spatial rotation in a virtual environment. *Neuropsychologia, 42*(4), 555–562.

Parten, M. B. (1932). Social participation among preschool children. *Journal of Abnormal and Social Psychology, 27*, 243–269.

Pascual-Leone, J. (2000). Reflections on working memory: Are the two models complementary? *Journal of Experimental Child Psychology, 77*(2), 138–154.

Passell, P. (1992, August 9). Twins study shows school is a sound investment. *New York Times*, p. A14.

Patenaude, J., Niyonsenga, T., & Fafard, D. (2003). Changes in students' moral development during medical school: A cohort study. *Canadian Medical Association Journal, 168*(7), 840–844.

Patterson, C. J. (1992). Children of lesbian and gay parents. *Child Development, 63*(5), 1025–1042.

Patterson, C. J. (2000). Family relationships of lesbians and gay men. *Journal of Marriage and the Family, 62*(4), 1052–1069.

Patterson, C. J. (2003). Children of lesbian and gay parents. In L. D. Garnets & D. C. Kimmel (Eds.), *Psychological perspectives on lesbian, gay, and bisexual experiences* (2nd ed.) (pp. 497–548). New York: Columbia University Press.

Patterson, C. J. (2002). Lesbian and gay parenthood. In M. H. Bornstein (Ed.), *Handbook of parenting, Vol. 3* (2nd ed.), pp. 317–338. Mahwah, NJ: LEA.

Patterson, C. J. (2006). Children of lesbian and gay parents. *Current Direction in Psychological Science, 15*, 241–244.

Patterson, G. R. (1982). *Coercive family processes.* Eugene, OR: Castilia Press.

Patterson, G. R. (1995). Coercion: A basis for early age of onset for arrest. In J. McCord (Ed.), *Coercion and punishment in long-term perspective* (pp. 81–105). New York: Cambridge University Press.

Patterson, G. R., & Fisher, P. A. (2002). Recent developments in our understanding of parenting: Bidirectional effects, causal models, and the search for parsimony. In H. M. Bornstein (Ed.), *Handbook of Parenting, v. 3* (2nd ed.), pp 59–88. Mahwah, NJ: LEA.

Patterson, J. L. (2000). Observed and reported expressive vocabulary and word combinations in bilingual toddlers. *Journal of Speech, Language, and Hearing Research, 43*(1), 121–128.

Patterson, O. (1998). *Rituals of blood: Consequences of slavery in two American centuries.* Washington, DC: Civitas Counterpoint.

Patterson, S. J., Sochting, I., & Marcia, J. E. (1992). The inner space and beyond: Women and identity. In G. R. Adams, T. P. Gullotta, & R. Montemayor (Eds.), *Adolescent identity formation.* Newbury Park, CA: Sage.

Paulhus, D. L., Trapnell, P. D., & Chen, D. (1999). Birth order effects on personality and achievement within families. *Psychological Science, 10*(6), 482–488.

Pauli-Pott, U., Mertesacker, B., & Beckmann, D. (2003). Ein Fragebogen zur Erfassung des fruhkindlichen Temperaments im Elternurteil. *Zeitschrift für Kinderund Jugendpsychiatrie und Psychotherapie, 31*(2), 99–110.

Paus, T., Zijdenbos, A., Worsley, K., Collins, D. L., Blumenthal, J., Giedd, J. N., Rapoport, J. L., Evans, A. C. (1999). Structural maturation of neural pathways in children and adolescents: In vivo study. *Science, 283*(5,409), 1908–1911.

Pear, R. (1993, August 16). U.S. to guarantee free immunization for poor children. *New York Times*, pp. A1, A9.

Pellegrini, A. D. (1990). Elementary school children's playground behavior: Implications for children's social-cognitive development. *Children's Environments Quarterly, 7*, 8–16.

Pellegrini, A. D., & Perlmutter, J. C. (1988, January). Rough-and-tumble play on the elementary school playground. *Young Children*, pp. 14–17.

Pemberton, E. F. (1990). Systematic errors in children's drawings. *Cognitive Development, 5*, 395–404.

Pena, E., Bedore, L. M., & Rappazzo, C. (2003). Comparison of Spanish, English, and bilingual children's performance across semantic tasks. *Language, Speech, and*

Hearing Services in Schools, 34(1), 5–16.

Penner, S. G. (1987). Parental responses to grammatical and ungrammatical child utterances. *Child Development, 58,* 376–384.

Peplau, L. A. (2003). Human sexuality: How do men and women differ? *Current Directions in Psychological Science, 12*(2), 37–40.

Pepler, D. J., & Craig, W. M. (2000). *Making a difference in bullying* (Report #60). Toronto, ON: York University, LaMarsh Institute. Retrieved December 5, 2006, from http://www.arts.yorku.ca/lamarsh/pdf/Making_a_Difference_in_Bullying.pdf

Pereira, B., MendonÁa, D., Neto, C., Valente, L., & Smith, P. K. (2004). Bullying in Portuguese schools. *School Psychology International, 25*(2), 241–254.

Perkins-Dock, R. E. (2001). Family interventions with incarcerated youth: A review of the literature. *International Journal of Offender Therapy and Comparative Criminology, 45*(5), 606–625.

Perry, D. G., Perry, L. C., & Boldizar, J. P. (1990). Learning of aggression. In M. Lewis & S. M. Miller (Eds.), *Handbook of developmental psychopathology.* New York: Plenum.

Perry, E. K., et al. (2001). Cholinergic activity in autism: Abnormalities in the cerebral cortex and basal forebrain. *American Journal of Psychiatry, 158*(7), 1058–1066.

Persson, A., & Musher-Eizenman, D. R. (2003). The impact of a prejudice-prevention television program on young children's ideas about race. *Early Childhood Research Quarterly, 18*(4), 530–546.

Peskin, J. (1992, January). Ruse and representations: On children's ability to conceal information. *Developmental Psychology, 28,* 84–89.

Peterson, C. C. (2001). Influence of siblings' perspectives on theory of mind. *Cognitive Development, 15*(4), 435–455.

Petittio, L. A., & Marentette, P. F. (1991). Babbling in the manual mode: Evidence for the ontogeny of language. *Science, 251,* 1493–1496.

Phalet, K., & Schoenpflug, U. (2001). Intergenerational transmission of collectivism and achievement values in two acculturation contexts: The case of Turkish families in Germany and Turkish and Moroccan families in the Netherlands. *Journal of Cross-Cultural Psychology, 32*(2), 186–201.

Phillips, A. S., & Phillips, C. R. (2000). Birth-order differences in self-attributions for achievement. *Journal of Individual Psychology, 56*(4), 474–480.

Phinney, J. S. (1989). Stages of ethnic identity in minority group adolescents. *Journal of Early Adolescence, 9,* 34–49.

Phinney, J. S. (1992). The multigroup ethnic identity measure: A new scale for use with adolescents and young adults with diverse groups. *Journal of Adolescent Research, 12,* 156–176.

Phinney, J. S. (2000). Identity formation across cultures: The interaction of personal, societal, and historical change. *Human Development, 43*(1), 27–31.

Phinney, J. S., & Alipuria, L. (1990). Ethnic identity in older adolescents from four ethnic groups. *Journal of Adolescence, 13,* 171–183.

Phinney, J. S., & Chavira, P. (1992). Ethnic identity and self-esteem: An exploratory longitudinal study. *Journal of Adolescence, 15,* 1–11.

Phinney, J. S., DuPont, S., Espinosa, C., Onwughalu, M., Revill, J., & Sanders, K. (1992, March). Group identity among minority adolescents: Ethnic, American, or bicultural? Paper presented at the meeting of the Society for Research on Adolescence, Washington, DC.

Phinney, J. S., & Nakayama, S. (1991, April). Parental influence on ethnic identity formation in minority adolescents. Paper presented at the meeting of the Society for Research in Child Development, Seattle.

Phinney, J. S., Ong, A., & Madden, T. (2000). Cultural values and intergenerational value discrepancies in immigrant and nonimmigrant families. *Child Development, 71*(2), 528–539.

Phinney, J. S., & Rosenthal, D. A. (1992). Ethnic identity in adolescence: Process, context, and outcome. In G. R. Adams, T. P. Gullotta, & R. Montemayor (Eds.), *Adolescent identity formation.* Newbury Park, CA: Sage.

Phinney, J. S., & Tarver, S. (1988). Ethnic identity search and commitment in black and white eight graders. *Journal of Early Adolescence, 8,* 265–277.

Phipps, M. G., Blume, J. D., & DeMonner, S. M. (2002). Young maternal age associated with increased risk of postneonatal death. *Obstetrics and Gynecology, 100,* 481–486.

Piaget, J. (1932). *The moral judgment of the child.* London: Kegan Paul.

Piaget, J. (1962). *Play, dreams, and imitation in childhood.* New York: Norton. (Originally published in 1946).

Piaget, J. (1963). *The origins of intelligence in children.* New York: Norton. (Originally published in 1936).

Piaget, J. (1967). In D. Elkind (Ed.), *Six psychological studies.* New York: Random House. (Originally published in 1964).

Piaget, J. (1972). Intellectual evolution from adolescence to adulthood. *Human Development, 15,* 1–12.

Piaget, J. (1976). *The grasp of consciousness: Action and concept in the young child.* Cambridge, MA: Harvard University Press.

Piaget, J., & Inhelder, B. (1969). *Psychology of the child.* New York: Basic Books.

Piaget, J., & Smith, L. (Trans.) (2000). Commentary on Vygotsky's criticisms of language and thought of the child and judgment and reasoning in the child. *New Ideas in Psychology, 18*(2–3), 241–259.

Pickering, S. J. (2001). The development of visuo-spatial working memory. *Memory, 9*(4–6), 423–432.

Pickles, A., et al. (2000). Variable expression of the autism broader phenotype: Findings from extended pedigrees. *Journal of Child Psychology and Psychiatry and Allied Disciplines, 41*(4), 491–502.

Pillard, R. C., & Weinrich, J. D. (1986). Evidence of familial nature of male homosexuality. *Archives of Sexual Behavior, 43,* 808–812.

Pine, D. S., et al. (2001). Fluvoxamine for the treatment of anxiety disorders in children and adolescents. *New England Journal of Medicine, 344*(17), 1279–1285.

Pine, K. J., & Nash, A. (2002). Dear Santa: The effects of television advertising on young children. *International Journal of Behavioral Development, 26*(6), 529–539.

Pinhas-Hamiel, O., & Zeitler, P. (2000). "Who is the wise man? The one who foresees consequences": Childhood obesity, new associated comorbidity, and prevention. *Preventive Medicine: An International Journal Devoted to Practice and Theory, 31*(6), 702–705.

Pinker, S. (1994). *The language instinct.* New York: William Morrow.

Piven, J. (1999). Genetic liability for autism: The behavioural expression in relatives. *International Review of Psychiatry, 11*(4), 299–308.

Plomin, R. (2000). Behavioural genetics in the 21st century. *International Journal of Behavioral Development, 24*(1), 30–34.

Plomin, R. (2001a). Genetic factors contributing to learning and language delays and disabilities. *Child and Adolescent Psychiatric Clinics of North America, 10*(2), 259–277.

Plomin, R. (2001b). Genetics and behaviour. *Psychologist, 14*(3), 134–139.

Plomin, R. (Ed.) (2002). *Behavioral genetics in the postgenomic era.* Washington, DC: American Psychological Association.

Plomin, R., & McGuffin, P. (2003). Psychopathology in the postgenomic era. *Annual Review of Psychology, 54,* 205–228.

Plomin, R., Owen, M. J., & McGuffin, P. (1994). The genetic basis of complex human behaviors. *Science, 264,* 1733–1739.

Plomin, R., & Walker, S. O. (2003). Genetics and educational psychology. *British Journal of Educational Psychology, 73*(1), 3–14.

Pollack, W. (2002). Real boys: The truths behind the myths. In *The Jossey-Bass reader on gender in education* (pp. 88–100). San Francisco, CA: Jossey-Bass.

Pollock, B., Prior, H., & Güntürkün, O. (2000). Development of object permanence in food-storing magpies (Pica pica). *Journal of Comparative Psychology, 114*(2), 148–157.

Pombeni, M. L., Kirchler, E., & Palmonari, A. (1990). Identification with peers as a strategy to muddle through the troubles of the adolescent years. *Journal of Adolescence, 13,* 351–369.

Pomerantz, E. M., Frey, K., Greulich, F., & Ruble, D. N. (1993, March). Explaining the decrease in perceived competence: Grade and gender differences in perceptions of ability as stable. Paper presented at the meeting of the Society for Research in Child Development. New Orleans, LA.

Ponnappa, B. C., & Rubin, E. (2000). Modeling alcohol's effects on organs in animal models. *Alcohol Research and Health, 24*(2), 93–104.

Pope, H. G., Kouri, E. M., & Hudson, J. I. (2000). Effects of supraphysiologic doses of testosterone on mood and aggression in normal men: A randomized controlled trial. *Archives of General Psychiatry, 57,* 133–140.

Porter, R. H., Makin, J. W., Davis, L. B., & Christensen, K. M. (1992). Breast-fed infants respond to olfactory cues from their own mother and unfamiliar lactating females. *Infant Behavior and Development, 15,* 85–93.

Power, T. G., Gershenhorn, S., & Stafford, D. (1990). Maternal perceptions of infant difficulties: The influence of maternal attitudes and attributions. *Infant Behavior and Development, 13,* 421–437.

Power, T. G., Kobayashi-Winata, H., & Kelley, M. L. (1992). Childrearing patterns in Japan and the United States: A cluster analytic study. *International Journal of Behavioral Development, 15,* 185–205.

Powlishta, K. K., Sen, M. G., Serbin, L. A., Poulin-Dubois, D., & Eichstedt, J. A. (2001). From infancy through middle childhood: The role of cognitive and social factors in becoming gendered. In R. K. Unger (Ed.), *Handbook of the psychology of women and gender* (pp. 116–132). New York: Wiley.

Pratt, C., & Bryant, P. (1990). Young children understand that looking leads to knowing (so long as they are looking into a single barrel). *Child Development, 61,* 973–982.

Prenatal Diagnosis and Medical Genetics Program, Mount Sinai Hospital (2001). Publications, news & information for our community. *Your Health Report, Fall 2001.*

Press, A. (1992, August 10). Old too soon, wise too late? *Newsweek,* pp. 22–25.

Principe, G. F., & Ceci, S. J. (2002). "I saw it with my own ears": The effects of peer conversations on preschoolers' reports of nonexperienced events. *Journal of Experimental Child Psychology, 83*(1), 1–25.

Prior, S. M., & Welling, K. A. (2001). "Read in your head": A Vygotskian analysis of the transition from oral to silent reading. *Reading Psychology, 22*(1), 1–15.

Proctor, M. H., et al. (2003). Television viewing and change in body fat from preschool to early adolescence: The Framingham Children's Study. *International Journal of Obesity and Related Metabolic Disorders, 27*(7), 827–833.

Provence, S., & Lipton, R. C. (1962). *Infants in institutions.* New York: International Universities Press.

Pryce, C. R., Bettschen, D., Bahr, N. I., & Feldon, J. (2001). Comparison of the effects of infant handling, isolation, and nonhandling on acoustic startle, prepulse inhibition, locomotion, and HPA activity in the adult rat. *Behavioral Neuroscience, 115*(1), 71–83.

Public Health Agency of Canada (2000). Leading causes of death and hospitalization in Canada. Available at http://www.phac-aspc.gc.ca/publicat/lcd-pcd97/mrt_mf_e.html#no

Public Health Agency of Canada (2002). Health, illness, and medication. Available at http://www.phac-aspc.gc.ca/dca-dea/publications/hbsc_06_e.html

Public Health Agency of Canada (2004). Canadian sexually transmitted infections surveillance report. *CCDR, 33SI,* 1–69.

Public Health Agency of Canada (2006a). *HIV and AIDS in Canada: Surveillance Report to December 31, 2005.* Author.

Public Health Agency of Canada (2006b). Canadian immunization guide. Available at http://www.phac-aspc.gc.ca/publicat/cig-gci/index.html

Public Health Agency of Canada (2006c). *Quick reference: Canadian guidelines on sexually transmitted infections.* Author.

Pugh, K. R., Mencl, W. E., Shaywitz, B. A., Shaywitz, S. E., Fulbright, R. K., Constable, R. T., Skudlarski, P., Marchione, K. E., Jenner, A. R., Fletcher, J. M., Liberman, A. M., Shankweiler, D. P., Katz, L., Lacadie, C., & Gore, J. C. (2000). The angular gyrus in developmental dyslexia: Task-specific differences in functional connectivity within posterior cortex. *Psychological Science, 11*(1), 51–56.

Purvis, A. (1990, November 26). The sins of the fathers. *Time,* pp. 90, 92.

Putallaz, M., Costanzo, P. R., Grimes, C. L., & Sherman, D. M. (1998). Intergenerational continuities and their influences on children's social development. *Social Development, 7*(3), 389–427.

Quatman, T., & Watson, C. M. (2001). Gender differences in adolescent self-esteem: An exploration of domains. *Journal of Genetic Psychology, 162*(1), 93–117.

Quintana, S. M. (1998). Children's developmental understanding of ethnicity and race. *Applied and Preventive Psychology, 7*(1), 27–45.

Quirk, K. J., Keith, T. Z., & Quirk, J. T. (2001). Employment during high school and student achievement: Longitudinal analysis of national data. *Journal of Educational Research, 95*(1), 4–10.

Rabasca, L. (2000). Pre-empting racism. *Monitor on Psychology, 31*(11), 60.

Rabinowitz, F. M., Howe, M. L., & Saunders, K. (2002). Age, memory load, and individual differences in working memory as determinants of class-inclusion reasoning. *Journal of Experimental Child Psychology, 81*(2), 157–193.

Rahman, Q., & Wilson, G. D. (2003). Born gay? The psychobiology of human sexual orientation. Personality and Individual Differences, 34(8), 1337–1382.

Rakic, P. (1991). Plasticity of cortical development. In S. E. Brauth, W. S. Hall, & R. J. Dooling (Eds.), *Plasticity of development.* Cambridge, MA: MIT Press.

Rakison, D. H., & Oakes, L. M. (Eds.) (2003). *Early category and concept development: Making sense of the blooming, buzzing confusion.* London: Oxford University Press.

Ramey, C. T., Campbell, F. A., & Ramey, S. L. (1999). Early intervention: Successful pathways to improving intellectual development. *Developmental Neuropsychology, 16*(3) 385–392.

Ramey, C. T., et al. (1992). Infant health and development program for low birth weight, premature infants: Program elements, family participation, and child intelligence. *Pediatrics, 89,* 454–465.

Ramsey, J. L., Langlois, J. H., Hoss, R. A., Rubenstein, A. J., & Griffin, A. M. (2004). Origins of a stereotype: Categorization of facial attractiveness by 6-month-old infants. *Developmental Science, 7*(2), 201–211.

Randel, B., Stevenson, H. W., & Witruk, E. (2000). Attitudes, beliefs, and mathematics achievement of German and Japanese high school students. *International Journal of Behavioral Development, 24*(2), 190–198.

Rapin, I. (1997). Autism. *New England Journal of Medicine, 337,* 97–104.

Raschka, L. B. (2000). Paternal age and schizophrenia in dizygotic twins. *British Journal of Psychiatry, 176,* 400–401.

Rathus, S. A., Nevid, J. S., & Fichner-Rathus, L. (2005). *Human sexuality in a world of diversity* (6th ed.). Boston: Allyn & Bacon.

Raudenbush, S. W. (1984). Magnitude of teacher expectancy effects on pupil IQ as a function of credibility of expectancy induction: A synthesis from 18 experiments. *Journal of Experimental Psychology, 76,* 85–97.

Ravaldi, C., et al. (2003). Eating disorders and body image disturbances among ballet dancers, gymnasium users, and body builders. *Psychopathology, 36*(5), 247–254.

Raz, S., et al. (1998). The effects of perinatal hypoxic risk on developmental outcome in early and middle childhood: A twin study. *Neuropsychology, 12*(3), 459–467.

Rebar, R. W., & DeCherney, A. H. (2004). Assisted reproductive technology in the United States. *New England Journal of Medicine, 350*(16), 1603–1604.

Reebye, P. N., Ross, S. E., Jamieson, K., & Clark, J. M. (no date). A literature review of child-parent/caregiver attachment theory and cross-cultural practices influencing attachment. Available at http://www.attachmentacrosscultures.org/research/index.html#100

Reef, S., Zimmerman-Swain, L., & Coronado, V. (2004). *Disease description: Rubella is a viral illness caused by a togavirus of the genus* Rubivirus. Available at http://www.cdc.gov/nip/diseases/rubella/default.htm

Reid, M., Ramey, S. L., & Burchinal, M. (1990). Dialogues with children about their families. In I. Bretherton & M. Watson (Eds.), *New directions for child development,* no. 48, *Children's perspectives on their families.* San Francisco: Jossey-Bass.

Reiger, K. (2000). Reconceiving citizenship: The challenge of mothers as political activists. *Feminist Theory, 1*(3), 309–327.

Reinecke, M. A., & DuBois, D. L. (2001). Socioenvironmental and cognitive risk and resources: Relations to mood and suicidality among inpatient adolescents. *Journal of Cognitive Psychotherapy, 15*(3), 195–222.

Reinisch, J. M., Ziemba-Davis, M., & Sanders, S. A. (1991). Hormonal contributions to sexually dimorphic behavioral development in humans. *Psychoneuroendocrinology, 16*(1–3), 213–278.

Reis, O., & Youniss, J. (2004). Patterns in identity change and development in relationships with mothers and friends. *Journal of Adolescent Research, 19*(1), 31–44.

Reisman, J. E. (1987). Touch, motion, and proprioception. In P. Salapatek & L. Cohen (Eds.), *Handbook of infant perception, v. 1, From sensation to perception.* Orlando, FL: Academic Press.

Rempel, L. A., & Rempel, J. K. (2004). Partner influence on health behavior decision-making: Increasing breastfeeding duration. *Journal of Social and Personal Relationships, 21*(1), 92–111.

Renninger, K. A. (1990). Children's play interests, representation, and activity. In R. Fivush & J. A. Hudson (Eds.), *Knowing and remembering in young children.* Cambridge: Cambridge University Press.

Rescorla, L. (1991a). Early academics: Introduction to the debate. In L. Rescorla, M. C. Hyson, & K. Hirsh-Pasek (Eds.), *New directions in child development, no. 53, Academic instruction in early childhood: Challenge or pressure?* San Francisco: Jossey-Bass.

Rescorla, L. (1991b). Parent and teacher attitudes about early academics. In L. Rescorla, M. C. Hyson, & K. Hirsh-Pasek (Eds.), *New directions in child development, no. 53, Academic instruction in early childhood: Challenge or pressure?* San Francisco: Jossey-Bass.

Rest, J. R. (1983). Morality. In P. H. Mussen (Ed.), *Handbook of child psychology, v. 3, Cognitive development.* New York: Wiley.

Reynolds, A. G. (1991). The cognitive consequences of bilingualism. In A. G. Reynolds (Ed.), *Bilingualism, multiculturalism, and second language learning.* Hillsdale, NJ: Erlbaum.

Reynolds, A. J. (1993, March). Effects of a preschool plus follow-on intervention program for children at risk. Paper presented at the meeting of the Society for Research in Child Development, New Orleans, LA.

Reznick, J. S., & Goldfield, B. A. (1992). Rapid change in lexical development in comprehension and production. *Developmental Psychology, 28,* 406–413.

Rezvani, A. H., & Levin, E. D. (2001). Cognitive effects of nicotine. *Biological Psychiatry, 49*(3), 258–267.

Rheingold, H. L., Gewirtz, J. L., & Ross, H. W. (1959). Social conditioning of vocalizations in the infant. *Journal of Comparative and Physiological Psychology, 52,* 68–73.

Rice, M. L. (1989). Children's language acquisition. *American Psychologist, 44,* 149–156.

Rice, M. L., Huston, A. C., Truglio, R., & Wright, J. (1990). Words from "Sesame Street": Learning vocabulary while viewing. *Developmental Psychology, 26,* 421–428.

Richards, H. C., Bear, G. G., Stewart, A. L., & Norman, A. D. (1992). Moral reasoning and classroom conduct: Evidence of a curvilinear relationship. *Merrill-Palmer Quarterly, 38,* 176–190.

Richards, T. W., & Nelson, V. L. (1938). Studies in mental development. 2. Analyses of abilities tested at six months by the Gesell schedule. *Journal of Genetic Psychology, 52,* 327–331.

Richardson, B. A., John-Stewart, G. C., Hughes, J. P., Nduati, R., Mbori-Ngacha, D., Overbaugh, J., & Kreiss, J. K. (2003). Breast-milk infectivity in human immunodeficiency virus type 1-infected mothers. *Journal of Infectious Diseases, 187*(5), 736–740.

Richardson, G. A., Ryan, C., Willford, J., Day, N. L., & Goldschmidt, L. (2002). Prenatal alcohol and marijuana exposure: Effects on neuropsychological outcomes at 10 years. *Neurotoxicology and Teratology, 24*(3), 311–320.

Richardson, H., Franco, E., Pintos, J., Bergeron, J., Arella, M., & Tellier, P. (2000). Determinants of low-risk and high-risk cervical human papillomavirus infections in Montreal University students. *Sexually Transmitted Diseases, 27*(2), 79–86.

Richburg, M., & Fletcher, T. (2002). Emotional intelligence: Directing a child's emotional education. *Child Study Journal, 32*(1), 31–38.

Richter, S., & Barbara, H. (2003). Bullying behavior: Current issues, research, and interventions. *Journal of Developmental and Behavioral Pediatrics, 24*(5), 382–383.

Rieser, J., Yonas, A., & Wikner, K. (1976). Radial localization of odors by human newborns. *Child Development, 47*(3), 856–859.

Rinaldi, C. M. (2002). Social conflict abilities of children identified as sociable, aggressive, and isolated: Developmental implications for children at-risk for impaired peer relations. *Developmental Disabilities Bulletin 30*(1), 77–94.

Rinaldi, C. M., Gates, M., & Urichuk, L. (2007, August). Mothers' and fathers' parenting styles and links to toddler behavior. Poster presented at the Annual Meeting of the American Psychological Association, San Francisco, CA.

Rinaldi, C. M., & Heath, N. L. (2006). An examination of the conflict resolution strategies and goals of children with depressive symptoms. *Emotional & Behavioural Difficulties, 11*(3), 187–204.

Rinaldi, C. M., & Howe, N. (1998). Siblings' reports of conflict and the quality of their relationships. *Merrill-Palmer Quarterly, 44,* 404–422.

Rinaldi, C. M., & Howe, N. (2003). Perceptions of constructive and destructive conflict within the family. *Infant and Child Development, 12,* 441–459.

Ritter, C., Hobfoll, S. E., Lavin, J., Cameron, R. P., & Hulsizer, M. R. (2000). Stress, psychosocial resources, and depressive symptomatology during pregnancy in low-income, inner-city women. *Health Psychology, 19*(6) 576–585.

Ritvo, E. R., Freeman, B. J., Mason-Brothers, A., Mo, A., & Ritvo, A. M. (1985). Concordance for the syndrome of autism in 40 pairs of afflicted twins. *American Journal of Psychiatry, 142,* 74–77.

Rizzolatti, G., Fadiga, L., Fogassi, L., & Gallese, V. (2002). From mirror neurons to imitation: Facts and speculations. In A. N. Meltzoff & W. Prinz (Eds.), *The imitative mind: Development, evolution, and brain bases.* New York: Cambridge University Press.

Roberts, A., et al. (2000). Perceived family and peer transactions and self-esteem among urban early adolescents. *Journal of Early Adolescence, 20*(1), 68–92.

Roberts, L. C., & Blanton, P. W. (2001). "I always knew mom and dad loved me best": Experiences of only children. *Journal of Individual Psychology, 57*(2), 125–140.

Roberts, R. E., Attkisson, C. C., & Rosenblatt, A. (1998). Prevalence of psychopathology among children and adolescents. *American Journal of Psychiatry, 155,* 715–725.

Roberts, R. N., Wasik, B. H., Casto, G., & Ramey, C. T. (1991). Family support in the home: Programs, policy, and social change. *American Psychologist, 46,* 131–137.

Robinson, J. N., Norwitz, E. R., Cohen, A. P., & Lieberman, E. (2000). Predictors of episiotomy use at first spontaneous vaginal delivery. *Obstetrics and Gynecology, 96*(2), 214–218.

Robinson, J. R., Drotar, D., & Boutry, M. (2001). Problem-solving abilities among mothers of infants with failure to thrive. *Journal of Pediatric Psychology, 26*(1), 21–32.

Robles de Medina, P. G., Visser, G. H. A., Huizink, A. C., Buitelaar, J. K., & Mulder, E. J. H. (2003). Fetal behaviour does not differ between boys and girls. *Early Human Development, 73*(1–2), 17–26.

Rockett, H. R. H., Berkey, C. S., Field, A. E., & Colditz, G. A. (2001). Cross-sectional measurement of nutrient intake among adolescents in 1996. *Preventive Medicine: An International Journal Devoted to Practice and Theory, 33*(1), 27–37.

Rodriguez, A., Bohlin, G., & Lindmark, G. (2000). Psychosocial predictors of smoking and exercise during pregnancy. *Journal of Reproductive and Infant Psychology, 18*(3), 203–223.

Rodriguez, C. (2000). Culturally sensitive psychological assessment. In I. A. Canino & J. Spurlocj (Eds.), *Culturally diverse children and adolescents: Assessment, diagnosis, and treatment.* New York: Guilford.

Roebers, C. M., Moga, N., & Schneider, W. (2001). The role of accuracy motivation on children's and adults' event recall. *Journal of Experimental Child Psychology, 78*(4), 313–329.

Roebers, C. M., & Schneider, W. (2002). Stability and consistency of children's event recall. *Cognitive Development, 17*(1), 1085–1103.

Roffwarg, H. P., Muzio, J. N., & Dement, W. C. (1966). Ontogenetic development of the human sleep-dream cycle. *Science, 152,* 604–619.

Rogers, K. N. (2004). A theoretical review of risk and protective factors related to postdivorce adjustment in young children. *Journal of Divorce and Remarriage, 40*(3–4), 135–147.

Rogoff, B., & Mistry, J. (1990). The social and functional context of children's remembering. In R. Fivush & J. A. Hudson (Eds.), *Knowing and remembering in young children.* Cambridge: Cambridge University Press.

Rogoff, B. (2003). *The cultural nature of human development.* New York: Oxford University Press.

Rogowski, J. A., et al. (2004). Indirect vs. direct hospital quality indicators for very low-birth-weight infants. *Journal of the American Medical Association, 291,* 202–209.

Rohde, P., Clarke, G. N., Lewinsohn, P. M., Seeley, J. R., & Kaufman, N. K. (2001). Impact of comorbidity on a cognitive-behavioral group treatment for adolescent depression. *Journal of the American Academy of Child and Adolescent Psychiatry, 40*(7), 795–802.

Romans, S. E., Gendall, K. A., Martin, J. L., & Mullen, P. E. (2001). Child sexual abuse and later disordered eating: A New Zealand epidemiological study. *International Journal of Eating Disorders, 29*(4), 380–392.

Roncesvalles, M. N. C., Woollacott, M. H., & Jensen, J. L. (2001). Development of lower extremity kinetics for balance control in infants and young children. *Journal of Motor Behavior, 33*(2), 180–192.

Rose, A. J., & Asher, S. R. (1999). Children's goals and strategies in response to conflicts within a friendship. *Developmental Psychology, 35*(1), 69–79.

Rose, A. J., Swenson, L. P., & Carlson, W. (2004). Friendships of aggressive youth: Considering the influences of being disliked and of being perceived as popular. *Journal of Experimental Child Psychology, 88*(1), 25–45.

Rose, S. A., & Blank, M. (1974). The potency of context in children's cognition: An illustration through conservation. *Child Development, 45,* 499–502.

Rose, S. A., Feldman, J. F., & Jankowski, J. J. (2001). Visual short-term memory in the first year of life: Capacity and recency effects. *Developmental Psychology, 37*(4), 539–549.

Rose, S. A., Feldman, J. F., & Jankowski, J. J. (2004). Infant visual recognition memory. *Developmental Review, 24*(1), 74–100.

Rose, S. A., Feldman, J. F., & Wallace, I. F. (1992). Infant information processing in relation to six-year cognitive outcomes. *Child Development, 63,* 1126–1141.

Rose, S. A., & Orlian, E. K. (1991). Asymmetries in infant cross-model transfer. *Child Development, 62,* 706–718.

Rosen, H. J., Ojemann, J. G., Ollinger, J. M., & Petersen, S. E. (2000). Comparison of brain activation during word retrieval done silently and aloud using fMRI. *Brain and Cognition, 42*(2), 201–217.

Rosen, K., & Rothbaum, F. (1993). Quality of parental caregiving and security of attachment. *Developmental Psychology, 29,* 358–367.

Rosenbaum, D. E. (2000, May 16). On left-handedness, its causes, and costs. *New York Times,* pp. F1, F6.

Rosenkoetter, L. I., Rosenkoetter, S. E., Ozretich, R. A., & Acock, A. C. (2004). Mitigating the harmful effects of violent television. *Journal of Applied Developmental Psychology, 25*(1), 25–47.

Rosenstein, D., & Oster, H. (1988). Differential facial responses to four basic tastes. *Child Development, 59,* 1555–1568.

Rosenthal, R., & Jacobson, L. (1968). *Pygmalion in the classroom.* New York: Holt, Rinehart & Winston.

Ross, G., Kagan, J., Zelazo, P., & Kotelchuck, M. (1975). Separation protest in infants in home and laboratory. *Developmental Psychology, 11,* 256–257.

Ross, J. L., Roeltgen, D., Feuillan, P., Kushner, H., & Cutler, G. B. (2000a). Use of estrogen in young girls with Turner syndrome: Effects on memory. *Neurology, 54*(1), 164–170.

Ross, J. L., Zinn, A., & McCauley, E. (2000b). Neurodevelopmental and psychosocial aspects of Turner syndrome. *Mental Retardation and Developmental Disabilities Research Reviews, 6*(2), 135–141.

Rotenberg, K. J., et al. (2004). Cross-sectional and longitudinal relations among peer-reported trustworthiness, social relationships, and psychological adjustment in children and early adolescents from the United Kingdom and Canada. *Journal of Experimental Child Psychology, 88*(1), 46–67.

Rotermann, M. (2005). Sex, condoms and STDs among young people. *Health Reports, 16*(3), 39–45.

Rothbart, M. K., & Ahadi, S. A. (1994). Temperament and the development of personality. *Journal of Abnormal Psychology, 103,* 55–66.

Rothbart, M. K., Ellis, L. K., & Posner, M. I. (2004). Temperament and self-regulation. In R. F. Baumeister & K. D. Vohs (Eds.), *Handbook of self-regulation: Research, theory, and applications.* New York: Guilford Press.

Rothrauff, T., Middlemiss, W., & Jacobson, L. (2004). Comparison of American and Austrian infants' and toddlers' sleep habits: A retrospective, exploratory study. *North American Journal of Psychology, 6*(1), 125–144.

Rottinghaus, P. J., Betz, N. E., & Borgen, F. H. (2003). Validity of parallel measures of vocational interests and confidence. *Journal of Career Assessment, 11*(4), 355–378.

Rovee-Collier, C. (1993). The capacity for long-term memory in infancy. *Current Directions in Psychological Science, 2,* 130–135.

Rovee-Collier, C., & Shyi, G. (1992). A functional and cognitive analysis of infant long-term retention. In M. L. Howe, C. J. Brainerd, & V. F. Reyna (Eds.), *Development of long-term retention.* New York: Springer-Verlag.

Rowe, D. C., Rodgers, J. L., & Meseck-Bushey, S. (1992). Sibling delinquency and the family environment: Shared and unshared influences. *Child Development, 63,* 59–67.

Rowen, B. (1973). *The children we see.* New York: Holt, Rinehart & Winston.

Rowland, C. F., & Pine, J. M. (2000). Subject-auxiliary inversion errors and wh- question acquisition: "What children do know?" *Journal of Child Language, 27*(1), 157–181.

Rubin, K. H. (1982). Nonsocial play in preschoolers: Necessary evil. *Child Development, 53,* 651–657.

Rubin, K. H., & Coplan, R. J. (1992). Peer relationships in childhood. In M. H. Bornstein & M. E. Lamb (Eds.), *Developmental psychology: An advanced textbook* (3rd ed.). Hillsdale, NJ: Erlbaum.

Rubinstein, S., & Caballero, B. (2000). Is Miss America an undernourished role model? *Journal of the American Medical Association, 283*(12), 1569.

Rudolph, K. D., Lambert, S. F., Clark, A. G., & Kurlakowsky, K. D. (2001). Negotiating the transition to middle school: The role of self-regulatory processes. *Child Development, 72*(3), 929–946.

Rudy, D., & Grusec, J. E. (2001). Correlates of authoritarian parenting in individualist and collectivist cultures and implications for understanding the transmission of values. *Journal of Cross-Cultural Psychology, 32*(2), 202–212.

Ruffman, T., Olson, D. R., Ash, T., & Keenan, T. (1993). The ABCs of deception: Do young children understand deception in the same way as adults? *Developmental Psychology, 29,* 74–87.

Ruffman, T., Perner, J., & Parkin, L. (1999). How parenting style affects false belief understanding. *Social Development, 8*(3), 395–411.

Ruiz, F., & Tanaka, K. (2001). The ijime phenomenon and Japan: Overarching considerations for cross-cultural studies. *Psychologia: An International Journal of Psychology in the Orient, 44*(2), 128–138.

Runyon, M. K., & Kenny, M. C. (2002). Relationship of attributional style, depression, and posttrauma distress among children who suffered physical or sexual abuse. *Child Maltreatment: Journal of the American Professional Society on the Abuse of Children, 7*(3), 254–264.

Rushton, J. P., Skuy, M., & Fridjhon, P. (2003). Performance on Raven's Advanced Progressive Matrices by African, East Indian, and White engineering students in South Africa. *Intelligence, 31*(2), 123–137.

Russell, G., & Russell, A. (1987). Mother-child and father-child relationships in middle childhood. *Child Development, 58,* 1573–1585.

Rutter, M. (1981). *Maternal deprivation reassessed* (2nd ed.). Middlesex, England: Penguin Books.

Rutter, M., Colvert, E., Kreppner, J., Beckett, C., Castle, J., Groothues, C., Hawkins, A., O'Connor, T. G., Stevens, S. E., & Sonuga-Barke, E. J. S. (2007). Early adolescent outcomes for institutionally deprived and non-deprived adoptees. I: Disinhibited attachment. *Journal of Child Psychology and Psychiatry, 48,* 17–30.

Rymer, R. (1993). *Genie: An abused child's flight from silence.* New York: HarperCollins.

Saab, H. (2004). *Young people in Canada: Their health and well-being.* Ottawa, ON: Health Canada, 51–68.

Saariluoma, P. (2001). Chess and content-oriented psychology of thinking. *Psicologica, 22*(1), 143–164.

Saarni, C., Mumme, D. L., & Campos, J. J. (1998). Emotional development: Action, communication, and understanding. In W. Damon (Editor-in-Chief) & N. Eisenberg (Vol. Ed.), *Handbook of child psychology: v. 3. Social, emotional, and personality development* (5th ed.). New York: Wiley.

Sabattini, L., & Leaper, C. (2004). The relation between mothers' and fathers' parenting styles and their division of labor in the home: Young adults' retrospective reports. *Sex Roles, 50*(3–4), 217–225.

Sachs, S. (2001, August 15). Clinics' pitch to Indian Èmigrès: It's a boy. *New York Times,* pp. A1, B6.

Sadker, M., & Sadker, D. (1994). *Failing at fairness: How America's schools cheat girls.* New York: Scribners.

Sadker, M., & Sadker, D. (2002). The miseducation of boys. In *The Jossey-Bass reader on gender in education* (pp. 182–203). San Francisco, CA: Jossey-Bass.

Safe Kids Canada (2005). Playground safety. Available at http://www.sickkids.ca/SKCForParents/section.asp?s=Safety+Information+by+Topic&sID=10774&ss=Playground+Safety&ssID=11333#

Sagi, A., Koren-Karie, N., Gini, M., Ziv, Y., & Joels, T. (2002). Shedding further light on the effects of various types and quality of early child care on infant-mother attachment relationship: The Haifa Study of Early Child Care. *Child Development, 73*(4), 1166–1186.

Sagi, A., IJzendoorn, M. H.van, & Koren-Karie, N. (1991). Primary appraisal of the Strange Situation: A cross-cultural analysis of preseparation episodes. *Developmental Psychology, 27,* 587–596.

Sagrestano, L. M., McCormick, S. H., Paikoff, R. L., & Holmbeck, G. N. (1999). Pubertal development and parent-child conflict in low-income, urban, African American adolescents. *Journal of Research on Adolescence 9*(1), 85–107.

Saito, S., & Miyake, A. (2004). On the nature of forgetting and the processing-storage relationship in reading span performance. *Journal of Memory and Language, 50*(4), 425–443.

Salapatek, P. (1975). Pattern perception in early infancy. In L. B. Cohen & P. Salapatek (Eds.), *Infant perception: From sensation to cognition.* New York: Academic Press.

Sales, J. M., Fivush, R., & Peterson, C. (2003). Parental reminiscing about positive and negative events. *Journal of Cognition and Development, 4*(2), 185–209.

Salovey, P., Stroud, L. R., Woolery, A., & Epel, E. S. (2002). Perceived emotional intelligence, stress reactivity, and symptom reports: Further explorations using the trait meta-mood scale. *Psychology and Health, 17*(5), 611–627.

Salzarulo, P., & Fagioli, I. (1995). Sleep for development or development for waking? Some speculations from a human perspective. *Behavioural Brain Research, 69*(1–2), 23–27.

Sampaio, D., et al. (2000). Representacoes sociais do suicidio em estudantes do ensino secundario. *Analise Psicologica, 18*(2), 139–155.

Sandler, I. (2001). Quality and ecology of adversity as common mechanisms of risk and resilience. *American Journal of Community Psychology, 29*(1), 19–61.

Santelli, J. S., et al. (2003). Reproductive health in school-based health centers: Findings from the 1998–99 census of school-based health centers. *Journal of Adolescent Health, 32*(6), 443–451.

Santelli, J. S., et al. (2004). Initiation of sexual intercourse among middle school adolescents: The influence of psychosocial factors. *Journal of Adolescent Health, 34*(3), 200–208.

Santelli, J. S., Lindberg, J. D., Abma, J., McNeely, C. S., & Resnick, M. (2000). Adolescent sexual behavior: Estimates and trends from four nationally representative surveys. *Family Planning Perspectives, 32*(4), 156–165, 194.

Santinello, M., & Vieno, A. (2002). The influence of economic and social support on preadolescents' disorders. *Bollettino di Psicologia Applicata, 238,* 33–42.

Santonastaso, P., Friederici, S., & Favaro, A. (2001). Sertraline in the treatment of restricting anorexia nervosa: An open controlled trial. *Journal of Child and Adolescent Psychopharmacology, 11*(2), 143–150.

Santos, D. C. C., Gabbard, C., & Goncalves, V. M. G. (2000). Motor development during the first 6 months: The case of Brazilian infants. *Infant and Child Development, 9*(3), 161–166.

Santos, M. A., & Lopes, J. A. L. (2003). Popularity, friendship, and self-concept. *Psicologia: Teoria, Investigaçã e Prática. 8*(2), 233–252.

Saroglou, V., & Galand, P. (2004). Identities, values, and religion: A study among Muslim, other immigrant, and native Belgian young adults after the 9/11 attacks. *Identity, 4*(2), 97–132.

Saudino, K. J., & Eaton, W. O. (1993, March). Genetic influences on activity level. II. An analysis of continuity and change from infancy to early childhood. Paper presented at the meeting of the Society for Research in Child Development, New Orleans, LA.

Save the Children (2004a). State of the world's mothers 2003. Accessed May 4 from http://www.savethechildren.org/mothers/report_2003/index.asp

Save the Children (2004b). State of the world's mothers 2004. Accessed June 2004 from http://www.savethechildren.org/mothers/report_2004/index.asp

Savin-Williams, R. C., & Berndt, T. (1990). Friendship and peer relations. In S. S. Feldman & G. R. Elliott (Eds.), *At the threshold: The developing adolescent.* Cambridge, MA: Harvard University Press.

Savin-Williams, R. C., & Diamond, L. M. (2000). Sexual identity trajectories among sexual-minority youths: Gender comparisons. *Archives of Sexual Behavior, 29*(6), 607–627.

Saywitz, K. J., Mannarino, A. P., Berliner, L., & Cohen, J. A. (2000). Treatment for sexually abused children and adolescents. *American Psychologist, 55*(9), 1040–1049.

Scarr, S. (1993, March). IQ correlations among members of transracial adoptive families. Paper presented at the meeting of the Society for Research in Child Development, New Orleans, LA.

Scarr, S. (1998). American child care today. *American Psychologist, 53*(2), 95–108.

Scarr, S., & Weinberg, R. A. (1976). IQ test performance of black children adopted by white families. *American Psychologist, 31,* 726–739.

Scarr, S., & Weinburg, R. A. (1977). Intellectual similarities within families of both adopted and biological children. *Intelligence, 1,* 170–191.

Schaffer, H. R. (Ed.) (1971). *The origins of human social relations.* New York: Academic Press.

Schaffer, H. R., & Emerson, P. E. (1964). The development of social attachments in infancy. *Monographs of the Society for Research in Child Development, 29*(94).

Schatz, J., Brown, R. T., Pascual, J. M., Hsu, L., & DeBaun, M. R. (2001). Poor school and cognitive functioning with silent cerebral infarcts and sickle cell disease. *Neurology, 56*(8), 1109–1111.

Schemo, D. J. (2000, October 4). Survey finds parents favor more detailed sex education. *New York Times,* pp. A1, A27.

Scheres, A., & Castellanos, F. X. (2003). Assessment and treatment of childhood problems, 2nd ed.: A clinician's guide. *Psychological Medicine, 33*(8), 1487–1488.

Schiedel, D. G., & Marcia, J. E. (1985). Ego identity, intimacy, sex-role orientation, and gender. *Developmental Psychology, 21,* 149–160.

Schlegel, A. (1998). The social criteria of adulthood. Human Development, 41(5–6), 323–_325.

Schmidtgall, K., King, A., Zarski, J. J., & Cooper, J. E. (2000). The effects of parental conflict on later child development. *Journal of Divorce and Remarriage, 33*(1–2), 149–157.

Schmitt, B. D. (1991). *Your child's health.* New York: Bantam.

Schmitt, D. P. (2003). Universal sex differences in the desire for sexual variety: Tests from 52 nations, 6 continents, and 13 islands. *Journal of Personality and Social Psychology, 85*(1), 85–104.

Schneider, W., & Pressley, M. (1989). *Memory development between 2 and 20.* New York: Springer-Verlag.

Schneider-Rosen, K., & Cicchetti, D. (1991). Early self-knowledge and emotional development: Visual self-recognition and affective reactions to mirror self-images in maltreated and non-maltreated toddlers. *Developmental Psychology, 27,* 471–478.

Shneidman, E. S. (1998). Perspectives on suicidology: Further reflections on suicide and psychache. *Suicide and Life-Threatening Behavior, 28*(3), 245–250.

Schraf, M., & Hertz-Lazarowitz, R. (2003). Social networks in the school context: Effects of culture and gender. *Journal of Social and Personal Relationships, 20*(6), 843–858.

Schreck, K. A., Mulick, J. A., & Smith, A. F. (2004). Sleep problems as possible predictors of intensified symptoms of autism. *Research in Developmental Disabilities, 25*(1), 57–66.

Schredl, M. (2001). Night terrors in children: Prevalence and influencing factors. *Sleep and Hypnosis, 3*(2), 68–72.

Schuetze, P., & Zeskind, P. S. (2001). Relations between women's depressive symptoms and perceptions of infant distress signals varying in pitch. *Infancy, 2*(4), 483–499.

Schuetze, P., Zeskind, P. S., & Eiden, R. D. (2003). The perceptions of infant distress signals varying in pitch by cocaine-using mothers. *Infancy, 4*(1), 65–83.

Schultz, D., & Shaw, D. S. (2003). Boys' maladaptive social information processing, family emotional climate, and pathways to early conduct problems. *Social Development, 12*(3), 440–460.

Schultz, S. R. (1990). Nutrition and human development. In R. M. Thomas (Ed.), *The encyclopedia of human development and education: Theory, research, and studies.* Oxford: Pergamon.

Schwartz, I. M. (1999). Sexual activity prior to coital interaction: A comparison between males and females. *Archives of Sexual Behavior, 28*(1), 63–69.

Schwartz, S. J. (2001). The evolution of Eriksonian and neo-Eriksonian identity theory and research: A review and integration. *Identity, 1*(1), 7–58.

Schwartz, T. H., Haglund, M. M., Lettich, E., & Ojemann, G. A. (2000). Asymmetry of neuronal activity during extracellular microelectrode recording from left and right human temporal lobe neocortex during rhyming and line-matching. *Journal of Cognitive Neuroscience, 12*(5), 803–812.

Schweinhart, L. J., & Weikart, D. P. (Eds.) (1993). *Significant benefits: The High/Scope Perry Preschool Study through age 27.* Ypsilanti, MI: High/Scope Press.

Sciarra, J. J., et al. (2000). *Gynecology and obstetrics.* Philadelphia: Lippincott Williams & Wilkins.

Seefeldt, V., Ewing, M., & Walk, S. (1991). An overview of youth sports programs in the United States. Washington, DC: Carnegie Council on Adolescent Development.

Segal, H. G., DeMeis, D. K., Wood, G. A., & Smith, H. L. (2001). Assessing future possible selves by gender and socioeconomic status using the Anticipated Life History measure. *Journal of Personality, 69*(1) 57–87.

Selman, R. L. (1976). Social-cognitive understanding. In T. Lickona (Ed.), *Moral development and behavior: Theory, research, and social issues.* New York: Holt, Rinehart & Winston.

Selman, R. (1980). *The growth of interpersonal understanding: Developmental and clinical analysis.* New York: Academic Press.

Selman, R. L. (1989). Fostering intimacy and autonomy. In W. Damon (Ed.), *Child development today and tomorrow.* San Francisco: Jossey-Bass.

Selman, R. L., & Schultz, L. H. (1989). Children's strategies for interpersonal negotiation with peers: An interpretive/empirical approach to the study of social development. In T. J. Berndt & G. W. Ladd (Eds.), *Peer relationships in child development.* New York: Wiley.

Sepkoski, C. M., et al. (1993, March). Predicting developmental delay from cry analysis in preterm infants. Paper presented at the meeting of the Society for Research in Child Development, New Orleans, LA.

Sepkoski, C. M., Lester, B. M., & Brazelton, T. B. (1994). Berry neonatal effects of maternal epidurals. *Developmental Medicine and Child Neurology, 36*(4), 375–376.

Sepkoski, C. M., Lester, B. M., Ostheimer, G. W., & Brazelton, T. B. (1992). The effects of maternal epidural anesthesia on neonatal behavior during the first month. *Developmental Medicine and Child Neurology, 34*(12), 1072–1080.

Serbin, L. A., Poulin-Dubois, D., Colburne, K. A., Sen, M. G., & Eichstedt, J. A. (2001). Gender stereotyping in infancy: Visual preferences for and knowledge of gender-stereotyped toys in the second year. *International Journal of Behavioral Development, 25*(1), 7–15.

Serbin, L. A., Powlishta, K. K., & Gulko, J. (1993). The development of sex typing in middle childhood. *Monographs for the Society for Research in Child Development, 58*, 1–74.

Serbin, L. A., & Sprafkin, C. (1986). The salience of gender and the process of sex typing in three- to seven-year-old children. *Child Development, 57*, 1188–1199.

Seymour, S. C. (1999). *Women, family, and child care in India.* Cambridge, UK: Cambridge University Press.

Shaffery, J. P., et al. (1998). REM sleep deprivation in monocularly occluded kittens reduces the size of cells in LGN monocular segment. *Sleep: Journal of Sleep Research and Sleep Medicine, 21*(8), 837–845.

Shahinfar, A., Kupersmidt, J. B., & Matza, L. S. (2001). The relation between exposure to violence and social information processing among incarcerated adolescents. *Journal of Abnormal Psychology, 110*(1), 136–141.

Sharon, T., & DeLoache, J. S. (2003). The role of perseveration in children's symbolic understanding and skill. *Developmental Science, 6*(3), 289–296.

Shaw, G. M., Velie, E. M., & Schaffer, D. (1996). Risk of neural tube defect-affected pregnancies among obese women. *Journal of the American Medical Association, 275*, 1093–1096.

Shaw, J., Claridge, G., & Clark, K. (2001). Schizotypy and the shift from dextrality: A study of handedness in a large nonclinical sample. *Schizophrenia Research, 50*(3), 181–189.

Shaywitz, B. A., et al. (1995). Sex differences in the functional organization of the brain for language. *Nature, 373*, 607–609.

Shaywitz, S. E. (1998). Dyslexia. *New England Journal of Medicine, 338*, 307–312.

Shaywitz, S. E., & Shaywitz, B. A. (2003). Neurobiological indices of dyslexia. In H. L. Swanson et al. (Eds.), *Handbook of learning disabilities* (pp. 514–531). New York: Guilford Press.

Shea, S., Stein, A. D., Basch, C. E., Contento, I. R., & Zybert, P. (1992). Variability and self-regulation of energy intake in young children in their everyday environment. *Pediatrics, 90*, 542–546.

Shenal, B. V., & Harrison, D. W. (2003). Investigation of the laterality of hostility, cardiovascular regulation, and auditory recognition. *International Journal of Neuroscience, 113*(2), 205–222.

Shenassa, E. D., et al. (2003). Intergenerational transmission of tobacco use and dependence: A transdisciplinary perspective. *Nicotine and Tobacco Research, 5*(Suppl. 1), S55-S69.

Shields, A., & Cicchetti, D. (2001a). Parental maltreatment and emotion dysregulation as risk factors for bullying and victimization in middle childhood. *Journal of Clinical Child Psychology, 30*(3), 349–363.

Shields, A., Ryan, R. M., & Cicchetti, D. (2001b). Narrative representations of caregivers and emotion dysregulation as predictors of maltreated children's rejection by peers. *Developmental Psychology, 37*(3), 321–337.

Shields, M. (2006, August) Overweight and obesity among children and youth. *Health Reports, 17*(3), 27–42. Ottawa, ON: Statistics Canada.

Shin, H. B., & Bruno, R. (2003, October). *Language use and English speaking ability: 2000.* Washington, DC: U.S. Bureau of the Census.

Shirk, S., Burwell, R., & Harter, S. (2003). Strategies to modify low self-esteem in adolescents. In M. A. Reinecke et al. (Eds.), *Cognitive therapy with children and adolescents: A casebook for clinical practice* (2nd ed.) (pp. 189–213). New York: Guilford Press.

Shonk, S. M., & Cicchetti, D. (2001). Maltreatment, competency deficits, and risk for academic and behavioral maladjustment. *Developmental Psychology, 37*(1), 3–17.

Shorter-Gooden, K. (1992, February). Identity development in African-American female adolescents. Paper presented at the meeting of the Association of Women in Psychology, Long Beach, CA.

Shortt, A. L., Barrett, P. M., & Fox, T. L. (2001). Evaluating the FRIENDS Program: A cognitive-behavioral group treatment for anxious children and their parents. *Journal of Clinical Child Psychology, 30*(4), 525–535.

Shott, S. R. (2000). Down syndrome: Common pediatric ear, nose, and throat problems. *Down Syndrome Quarterly, 5*(2), 1–6.

Shu, M., Jia, S., & Zhang, F. (2001). Clinical features and brain image of children with autism. *Chinese Mental Health Journal, 15*(1), 39–41.

Shuster, S. M., & Sassaman, C. (1997). Genetic interaction between male mating strategy and sex ratio in a marine isopod. *Nature, 388*(6640), 373–377.

Shute, B., & Wheldall, K. (1999). Fundamental frequency and temporal modifications in the speech of British fathers to their children. *Educational Psychology, 19*(2), 221–233.

Shute, B., & Wheldall, K. (2001). How do grandmothers speak to their grandchildren? Fundamental frequency and temporal modifications in the speech of British grandmothers to their grandchildren. *Educational Psychology, 21*(4), 493–503.

Shweder, R. A., Goodnow, J., Hatano, G., LeVine, R. A., Markus, H., & Miller, P. (1998). The cultural psychology of development: One mind, many mentalities. In W. Damon & R. M. Lerner (Eds.), *Handbook of child psychology: Volume 1: Theoretical models of human development* (5th ed.). (pp. 865–937). Hoboken, NJ: John Wiley & Sons, Inc.

Shweder, R, A., Much, N. C., Mahapatra, M., Park, L. (1997). The "big three" of morality (autonomy, community, divinity) and the "big three" explanations of suffering. In A. M. Brandt & P. Rozin (Eds.), *Morality and health,* (pp. 119–169). Florence, KY: Taylor & Frances/Routledge.

SIDS Network (2001, May 14). Available at http://www.sids-network.org

SIECAN (2005). *Sexual health education in the schools: Questions & answers.* Ottawa, ON: Canadian Federation for Sexual Health.

Siegal, M. (2003). Cognitive development. In A. Slater & G. Bremmer (Eds.), *An introduction to developmental psychology* (pp. 189–210). Malden, MA: Blackwell.

Siegel, L. J. (2004). *Criminology: Theories, patterns, and typologies,* 8th ed. Belmont, CA: Wadsworth.

Siegel, L. S. (1992). Infant motor, cognitive, and language behaviors as predictors of achievement at school age. In C. Rovee-Collier & L. P. Lipsitt (Eds.), *Advances in infancy research,* v. 7. Norwood, NJ: Ablex.

Siegel, L. S. (1993). The development of reading. In H. W. Reese (Ed.), Advances in child development and behavior, v. 24. Orlando, FL: Academic Press.

Siegler, R. S., & Alibali, M. W. (2005). *Children's thinking* (4th ed.). Upper Saddle River, NJ: Prentice Hall.

Siegler, R. S., Liebert, D. E., & Liebert, R. M. (1973). Inhelder and Piaget's pendulum problem: Teaching pre-adolescents to act as scientists. *Developmental Psychology, 9,* 97–101.

Signorella, M. L., & Frieze, I. H. (1989). Gender schemas in college students. *Psychology: A Journal of Human Behavior, 26,* 16–23.

Signorello, L. B., et al. (2001). Caffeine metabolism and the risk of spontaneous abortion of normal karyotype fetuses. *Obstetrics and Gynecology, 98,* 1059–1066.

Silverberg, S. B., Tennenbaum, D. L., & Jacob, T. (1992). Adolescence and family interaction. In V. B. VanHasselt and M. Hersen (Eds.), *Handbook of social development.* New York: Plenum.

Simion, F., Cassia, V. M., Turati, C., & Valenza, E. (2001). The origins of face perception: Specific versus nonspecific mechanisms. *Infant and Child Development, 10*(1–2), 59–65.

Simmons, D. C., Fuchs, D., & Fuchs, L. S. (1991). Instructional and curricular requisites of mainstreamed students with learning disabilities. *Journal of Learning Disabilities, 24,* 354–360.

Simmons, R. G., & Blyth, D. A. (1987). *Moving into adolescence: The impact of pubertal change and school context.* Hawthorne, NY: Aldine deGruyter.

Simonson, B. M., & Glenn, S. (2001). The effects of suggestions on ratings of attention deficit hyperactivity disorder. *Psychology and Education: An Interdisciplinary Journal, 38*(2), 42–47.

Simonton, D. K. (2000). Creativity: Cognitive, personal, developmental, and social aspects. *American Psychologist, 55,* 151–158.

Simpson, J. L. (2000, June 1). *Invasive diagnostic procedures for prenatal genetic diagnosis.* Journal Watch Women's Health. Available at http://womens-health.jwatch.org

Singer, D. G., & Singer, J. L. (Eds.) (2001). *Handbook of children and the media.* Newbury Park, CA: Sage.

Singer, L. T., Arendt, R., Minnes, S., Farkas, K., & Salvator, A. (2000). Neurobehavioral outcomes of cocaine-exposed infants. *Neurotoxicology and Teratology, 22*(5), 653–666.

Singh, G. K., & Yu, S. M. (1995). Cited in R. Pear (1995, July 10), Infant mortality rate drops but racial disparity grows, *New York Times,* p. B9.

Singh, K. (1998). Part-time employment in high school and its effect on academic achievement. *Journal of Educational Research, 91*(3), 131–139.

Singh, K., & Ozturk, M. (2000). Effect of part-time work on high school mathematics and science course taking. *Journal of Educational Research, 91*(2), 67–74.

Skeels, H. M. (1966). Adult status of children with contrasting early life experiences: A follow-up study. *Monographs of the Society for Research in Child Development, 31*(3, ser. 105).

Skinner, B. F. (1957). *Verbal behavior.* New York: Appleton.

Skinner, B. F. (1983). *A matter of consequences.* New York: Knopf.

Skoczenski, A. M. (2002). Limitations on visual sensitivity during infancy: Contrast sensitivity, vernier acuity, and orientation processing. In J. W. Fagen & H. Hayne (Eds.), *Progress in infancy research,* v. 2. Mahwah, NJ: Lawrence Erlbaum Associates.

Skogman, K., Alsén, M., & Öjehagen, A. (2004). Sex differences in risk factors for suicide after attempted suicide: A follow-up study of 1,052 suicide attempters. *Social Psychiatry and Psychiatric Epidemiology, 39*(2), 113–120.

Slater, A. (2000). Visual perception in the young infant: Early organization and rapid learning. In D. Muir & A. Slater (Eds.), *Infant development: The essential readings.* Malden, MA: Blackwell.

Slater, A., Mattock, A., & Brown, E. (1990). Size constancy at birth: Newborn infants' responses to retinal and real size. *Journal of Experimental Child Psychology, 49,* 314–322.

Slijper, F. M. E. (1984). Androgens and **gender role** behaviours in girls with congenital adrenal hyperplasia (CAH). *Progress in Brain Research, 61,* 417–422.

Slobin, D. I. (2001). Form/function relations: How do children find out what they are? In M. Tomasello & E. Bates (Eds.), *Language development: The essential readings.* Malden, MA: Blackwell.

Small, M. Y. (1990). *Cognitive development.* San Diego: Harcourt Brace Jovanovich.

Smetana, J. G. (1990). Morality and conduct disorders. In M. Lewis & S. M. Miller (Eds.), *Handbook of developmental psychopathology.* New York: Plenum.

Smetana, J. G., Daddis, C., & Chuang, S. S. (2003). "Clean your room!" A longitudinal investigation of adolescent-parent conflict and conflict resolution in middle-class African American families. *Journal of Adolescent Research, 18*(6), 631–650.

Smith, B. A., Fillion, T. J., & Blass, E. M. (1990). Orally mediated sources of calming in 1- to 3-day-old human infants. *Developmental Psychology, 26,* 731–737.

Smith, K. E., et al. (1999). Is severity of respiratory disease associated with differences in neurodevelopmental patterns in preterm infants? *Developmental Neuropsychology, 16*(1) 59–77.

Smith, L., Yonekura, M. L., Berman, N., Kuo, J., & Berkowitz, C. (2003). Effects of prenatal methamphetamine exposure on fetal growth and drug withdrawal symptoms in infants born at term. *Developmental and Behavioral Pediatrics, 24,* 17–23.

Smith, P. K. (1979). The ontogeny of fear in children. In W. Sluckin (Ed.), *Fears in animals and man.* London: Van Nostrand Reinhold.

Smith, T. E. C., Polloway, E. A., Patton, J. E., Dowdy, C. A., & Heart, N. L. (2001). *Teaching students with special needs in inclusive settings* (Canadian ed.). Toronto, ON: Allyn and Bacon.

Smith, W. J., & Foster, W. F. (1996). *Equal educational opportunities for students with disabilities.* Montreal, QC: McGill University, Office of Research on Educational Policy.

Smoll, F. L., & Schultz, R. W. (1990). Quantifying gender differences in physical performance: A developmental perspective. *Developmental Psychology, 26,* 360–369.

Smyke, A. T., Dumitrescu, A., & Zennah, C. H. (2002). Attachment disturbances in young children. I: The continuum of caretaking casualty. *Journal of the American Academy of Child and Adolescent Psychiatry, 41,* 972–982.

Snarey, J. R. (1994). Cross-cultural universality of social-moral development: A critical review of Kohlbergian research. In B. Puka (Ed.), *New research in moral development* (pp. 268–298). New York: Garland.

Snarey, J. R., & Bell, D. (2003). Distinguishing structural and functional models of human development. *Identity, 3*(3), 221–230.

Snow, M. E., Jacklin, C. M., & Maccoby, E. E. (1983). Sex-of-child differences in father-child interaction at one year of age. *Child Development, 49,* 227–232.

Snowden, P. E., & Gorton, R. A. (2002). *School leadership and administration* (6th ed.). New York: McGraw-Hill.

Snyderman, M., & Rothman, S. (1990). *The IQ controversy.* New Brunswick, NJ: Transaction.

Sodian, B., Taylor, C., Harris, P. L., & Perner, J. (1991). Early deception and the child's theory of mind: False trails and genuine markers. *Child Development, 62,* 468–483.

Solomon, C. G., Willett, W. C., Carey, V. J., Rich-Edwards, J., Hunter, D. J., Colditz, G. A., Stampfer, M. J., Speizer, F. E., Spiegelman, D., & Manson, J. E. (1997). A prospective study of pregravid determinants of gestational diabetes mellitus. *Journal of the American Medical Association, 278*(13), 1078–1083.

Sommer, I. E. C., Ramsey, N. F., Mandl, R. C. W., & Kahn, R. S. (2002). Language lateralization in monozygotic twin pairs concordant and discordant for handedness. *Brain, 125*(12), 2710–2718.

Sontag, L. W. (1966). Implications of fetal behavior and environment for adult personality. *Annals of the New York Academy of Science, 134,* 782–786.

Sontag, L. W., & Richards, T. W. (1938). Studies in fetal behavior: Fetal heart rate as a behavioral indicator. *Child Development Monographs, 3*(4).

Sorce, J. F., Emde, R. N., Campos, J. J., & Klinnert, M. D. (1985). Maternal emotional signaling: Its effect on the visual cliff behavior of 1-year-olds. *Developmental Psychology, 21,* 195–200.

Souza, I., Serra, M. A., Mattos, P., & Franco, V. A. (2001). Comorbidade em criancas e adolescentes com transtorno do deficit de atencao: Resultados preliminares. *Arquivos de Neuro-Psiquiatria, 59*(2), 401–406.

Spangler, G. (1990). Mother, child, and situational correlates of toddler's social competence. *Infant Behavior and Development, 13,* 405–419.

Spehr, M., et al. (2003). Identification of a testicular odorant receptor mediating human sperm chemotaxis. *Science, 299*(5,615), 2054–2058.

Spelke, E. S., & Owsley, C. (1979). Intermodal exploration and knowledge in infancy. *Infant Behavior and Development, 2,* 13–27.

Spencer, M. B., Dornbusch, S. M., & Mont-Reynaud, R. (1990). Challenges in studying minority youth. In S. S. Feldman & G. R. Elliott (Eds.), *At the threshold: The developing adolescent.* Cambridge, MA: Harvard University Press.

Spencer, M. S., Icard, L. D., Harachi, T. W., Catalano, R. F., & Oxford, M. (2000). Ethnic identity among monoracial and multiracial early adolescents. *Journal of Early Adolescence, 20*(4), 365–387.

Spencer, T. J., et al. (2001). Impact of tic disorders on ADHD outcome across the life cycle: Findings from a large group of adults with and without ADHD. *American Journal of Psychiatry, 158*(4), 611–617.

Speranza, M., et al. (2001). Obsessive compulsive disorders in eating disorders. *Eating Behaviors, 2*(3), 193–207.

Spieker, S. J., Nelson, D. C., Petras, A., Jolley, S. N., & Barnard, K. E. (2003). Joint influence of child care and infant attachment security for cognitive and language outcomes of low-income toddlers. *Infant Behavior and Development, 26*(3), 326–344.

Spitz, R. A. (1965). *The first year of life: A psychoanalytic study of normal and deviant object relations.* New York: International Universities Press.

Spivack, G., Marcus, J., & Swift, M. (1986). Early classroom behaviors and later misconduct. *Developmental Psychology, 22,* 124–131.

Sroufe, L. A. (1979). Socioemotional development. In J. Osofsky (Ed.), *Handbook of infant development.* New York: Wiley.

Sroufe, L. A. (1998). Cited in S. Blakeslee (1998, August 4), Re-evaluating significance of baby's bond with mother, *New York Times,* pp. F1, F2.

Sroufe, L. A., Bennett, C., Englund, M., Urban, J., & Shulman, S. (1993). The significance of gender boundaries in preadolescence: Contemporary correlates and antecedents of boundary violation and maintenance. *Child Development, 64,* 455–466.

Sroufe, L. A., Waters, E., & Matas, L. (1974). Contextual determinants of infant affectional response. In M. Lewis & L. Rosenblum (Eds.), *The origins of fear.* New York: Wiley.

Stagnitti, K., Unsworth, C., & Rodger, S. (2000). Development of an assessment to identify play behaviours that discriminate between the play of typical preschoolers and preschoolers with pre-academic problems. *Canadian Journal of Occupational Therapy, 67*(5), 291–303.

Stahmer, A. C., Ingersoll, B., & Koegel, R. L. (2004). Inclusive programming for toddlers autism spectrum disorders: Outcomes from the Children's Toddler School. *Journal of Positive Behavior Interventions, 6*(2), 67–82.

Stampfer, M. J., Hu, F. B., Manson, J. E., Rimm, E. B., & Willett, W. C. (2000). Primary prevention of coronary heart disease in women through diet and lifestyle. *New England Journal of Medicine, 343*(1), 16–22.

Stams, G. J. M., Juffer, F., & IJzendoorn, M. H. van (2002). Maternal sensitivity, infant attachment, and temperament in early childhood predict adjustment in middle childhood: The case of adopted children and their biologically unrelated parents. *Developmental Psychology, 38*(5), 806–821.

Stanley, C., Murray, L., & Stein, A. (2004). The effect of postnatal depression on mother-infant interaction, infant response to the still-face perturbation, and performance on an instrumental learning task. *Development and Psychopathology, 16*(1), 1–18.

Stanwood, G. D., et al. (2001a). Prenatal cocaine exposure as a risk factor for later developmental outcomes. *Journal of the American Medical Association, 286*(1), 45–47.

Stanwood, G. D., Washington, R. A., & Levitt, P. (2001b). Identification of a sensitive period of prenatal cocaine exposure that alters the development of the anterior cingulate cortex. *Cerebral Cortex, 11*(5), 430–440.

Statistics Canada (2000a). Parent and child factors associated with youth obesity. Available at http://www.statcan.ca/Daily/English/031103/d031103a.htm

Statistics Canada (2000b). Program for international student assessment (PISA). Available at http://www.statcan.ca/english/freepub/81–004-XIE/200406/imm.htm

Statistics Canada (2001). Canada Census 2001. Ottawa, ON: Statistics Canada.

Statistics Canada (2003). Breastfeeding practices, females aged 15 to 55 who had a baby in the previous five years, Canada, provinces, territories and peer groups, 2003. *Canadian Community Health Survey.*

Statistics Canada (2005). Canadian social trends, Winter 2005. Available at http://www.statcan.ca.login.ezproxy.library.ualberta.ca/english/freepub/11–008-XIE/0020411–008-XIE.pdf

Statistics Canada (2006). Television viewing. The Daily (March 31, 2006). Available at http://www.statcan.ca/Daily/English/060331/d060331b.htm

Statistics Canada (2007a). Births and birth rate, by province and territory. Available at http://www40.statcan.ca/l01/cst01/demo04b.htm

Statistics Canada (2007). *CANSIM: Labour force survey.* Ottawa, ON: Statistics Canada.

Steele, C. M., & Aronson, J. (2000). Stereotype threat and the intellectual test performance of African Americans. In C. Stangor (Ed.), *Stereotypes and prejudice: Essential readings* (pp. 369–389). New York: Psychology Press.

Steele, M., Hodges, J., Kaniuk, J., Hillman, S., & Henderson, K. (2003). Attachment representations and adoption: Associations between maternal states of mind and emotion narratives in previously maltreated children. *Journal of Child Psychotherapy, 29*(2), 187–205.

Stein, M. T., Kennell, J. H., & Fulcher, A. (2003). Benefits of a doula present at the birth of a child. *Journal of Developmental and Behavioral Pediatrics, 24*(3), 195–198.

Stein, R. I., et al. (2001). Treatment of eating disorders in women. *Counseling Psychologist, 29*(5), 695–732.

Steinberg, L. (1996). *Beyond the classroom: Why school reform has failed and what parents need to do.* New York: Simon & Schuster.

Steinberg, L., Brown, B. B., & Dornbusch, S. M. (1996). Ethnicity and adolescent achievement. *American Educator, 20*(2), 28–35.

Steiner, J. E. (1979). Facial expressions in response to taste and smell discrimination. In H. W. Reese & L. P. Lipsitt (Eds.), *Advances in child development and behavior,* v. 13. New York: Academic Press.

Steinhausen, H., Willms, J., Metzke, C. W., & Spohr, H. (2003). Behavioural phenotype in foetal alcohol syndrome and foetal alcohol effects. *Developmental Medicine and Child Neurology, 45*(3), 179–182.

Stemberger, J. P. (2004). Phonological priming and irregular past. *Journal of Memory and Language, 50*(1), 82–95.

Steptoe, A., et al. (2004). Drinking and driving in university students: An international study of 23 countries. *Psychology and Health, 19*(4), 527–540.

Stern, M., & Karraker, K. H. (1989). Sex stereotyping of infants: A review of gender labeling studies. *Sex Roles, 20,* 501–521.

Sternberg, R. J. (2000). In search of the zipperump-a-zoo. *Psychologist, 13*(5), 250–255.

Sternberg, R. J. (2001). What is the common thread of creativity? *American Psychologist, 56*(4), 360–362.

Sternberg, R. J. (2003). WICS as a model of giftedness. *High Ability Studies, 14*(2), 109–137.

Sternberg, R. J., & Grigorenko, E. L. (2006). Cultural intelligence and successful intelligence. *Group & Organization Management, 31*(1), 27–39.

Sternberg, R. J., Grigorenko, E. L., & Kidd, K. K. (2005). Intelligence, race, and genetics. *American Psychologist, 60*(1), 46–59.

Sternberg, R. J., Lautrey, J., & Lubart, T. I. (2003). *Models of intelligence: International perspectives.* Washington, DC: American Psychological Association.

Sternberg, R. J., & Lubart, T. I. (1995). *Defying the crowd: Cultivating creativity in a culture of conformity.* New York: Free Press.

Sternberg, R. J., & Lubart, T. I. (1996). Investing in creativity. *American Psychologist, 51,* 677–688.

Sternberg, R. J., & Williams, W. M. (1997). Does the Graduate Record Examination predict meaningful success in the graduate training of psychologists? *American Psychologist, 52,* 630–641.

Stevenson, H. W., Chen, C., & Lee, S. (1993). Mathematics achievement of Chinese, Japanese, and American children: Ten years later. *Science, 259,* 53–58.

Stevenson, J. (1992). Evidence for a genetic etiology in hyperactivity in children. *Behavior Genetics, 22,* 337–344.

Steward, D. K. (2001). Behavioral characteristics of infants with nonorganic failure to thrive during a play interaction. *American Journal of Maternal/Child Nursing, 26*(2), 79–85.

Stewart-Knox, B., Gardiner, K., & Wright, M. (2003). What is the problem with breastfeeding? A qualitative analysis of infant feeding perceptions. *Journal of Human Nutrition and Dietetics, 16*(4), 265–273.

Stice, E., Akutagawa, D., Gaggar, A., & Agras, W. S. (2000). Negative affect moderates the relation between dieting and binge eating. *International Journal of Eating Disorders, 27*(2), 218–229.

Stice, E., & Bearman, S. K. (2001). Body-image and eating disturbances prospectively predict increases in depressive symptoms in adolescent girls: A growth curve analysis. *Developmental Psychology, 37*(5), 597–607.

Stice, E., Hayward, C., Cameron, R. P., Killen, J. D., & Taylor, C. B. (2000). Body-image and eating disturbances predict onset of depression among female adolescents: A longitudinal study. *Journal of Abnormal Psychology, 109*(3), 438–444.

Stice, E., Presnell, K., & Bearman, S. K. (2001). Relation of early menarche to depression, eating disorders, substance abuse, and comorbid psychopathology among adolescent girls. *Developmental Psychology, 37*(5), 608–619.

Stiles, J. (2001). Neural plasticity and cognitive development. *Developmental Neuropsychology, 18*(2), 237–272.

Stipek, D. J., & Gralinski, J. H. (1991). Gender differences in children's achievement-related beliefs and emotional responses to success and failure in mathematics. *Journal of Educational Psychology, 83,* 361–371.

Stipek, D. J., Gralinski, J. H., & Kopp, C. B. (1990). Self-concept development in the toddler years. *Developmental Psychology, 26,* 972–977.

Stipek, D., Recchia, S., & McClintic, S. (1992). Self-evaluation in young children. *Monographs of the Society for Research in Child Development, 57*(1, ser. 226).

Stockhammer, T. F., Salzinger, S., Feldman, R. S., Mojica, E., & Primavera, L. H. (2001). Assessment of the effect of physical child abuse within an ecological framework: Measurement issues. *Journal of Community Psychology, 29*(3) 319–344.

Stockman, I. J., & Vaughn-Cooke, F. (1992). Lexical elaboration in children's locative action expression. *Child Development, 63,* 1104–1125.

Stoel-Gammon, C. (2002). Intervocalic consonants in the speech of typically developing children: Emergence and early use. *Clinical Linguistics and Phonetics, 16*(3), 155–168.

Stone, J. R., & Mortimer, J. T. (1998). The effect of adolescent employment on vocational development: Public and educational policy implications. *Journal of Vocational Behavior, 53,* 184–214.

Stores, G., & Wiggs, L. (Eds.) (2001). *Sleep disturbance in children and adolescents with disorders of development: Its significance and management.* New York: Cambridge University Press.

Storfer, M. D. (1990). *Intelligence and giftedness: The contributions of heredity and early environment.* San Francisco: Jossey-Bass.

Strasburger, V. C. (2001). Children and TV advertising: Nowhere to run, nowhere to hide. *Journal of Developmental and Behavioral Pediatrics, 22*(3), 185–187.

Straus, M. A. (1991). Discipline and deviance: Physical punishment of children and violence and other crime in adulthood. *Social Problems, 38,* 133–154.

Straus, M. A. (1995). Cited in C. Collins (1995, May 11), Spanking is becoming the new don't, *New York Times,* p. C8.

Straus, M. A. (2000). Corporal punishment and primary prevention of physical abuse. *Child Abuse and Neglect, 24*(9), 1109–1114.

Straus, M. A., & Gelles, R. J. (1990). Societal change and change in family violence from 1975 to 1985 as revealed by two national surveys. In M. A. Straus & R. J. Gelles (Eds.), *Physical violence in American families.* New Brunswick, NJ: Transaction.

Straus, M. A., & Smith, C. (1990). Family patterns and child abuse. In M. A. Straus & R. J. Gelles (Eds.), *Physical violence in American families.* New Brunswick, NJ: Transaction.

Straus, M. A., & Stewart, J. H. (1999). Corporal punishment by American parents: National data on prevalence, chronicity, severity, and duration, in relation to child and family characteristics. *Clinical Child and Family Psychology Review, 2*(2), 55–70.

Strayer, F. F. (1990). The social ecology of toddler play groups and the origins of gender discrimination. In F. F. Strayer (Ed.), *Social interaction and behavioral development during early childhood.* Montreal: La Maison D'Ethologie de Montreal.

Strayer, J., & Roberts, W. (2004). Children's anger, emotional expressiveness, and empathy: Relations with parents' empathy, emotional expressiveness, and parenting practices. *Social Development, 13*(2), 229–254.

Streitmatter, J. L. (1988). Ethnicity as a mediating variable of early adolescent identity development. *Journal of Adolescence, 11,* 335–346.

Streri, A. (2002). Hand preference in 4-month-old infants: Global or local processing of objects in the haptic mode. *Current Psychology Letters: Behaviour, Brain and Cognition, 7,* 39–50.

Striegel-Moore, R. H., & Cachelin, F. M. (2001). Etiology of eating disorders in women. *Counseling Psychologist, 29*(5), 635–661.

Striegel-Moore, R. H., et al. (2003). Eating disorders in White and Black women. *American Journal of Psychiatry, 160*(7), 1326–1331

Stright, A. D., Neitzel, C., Sears, K. G., & Hoke-Sinex, L. (2001). Instruction begins in the home: Relations between parental instruction and children's self-regulation in the classroom. *Journal of Educational Psychology, 93*(3), 456–466.

Strock, M. (2004). Autism spectrum disorders (pervasive developmental disorders). NIH Publication NIH-04-5511. Bethesda, MD: National Institute of Mental Health, National Institutes of Health, U.S. Department of Health and Human Services. Available at http://www.nimh.nih.gov/publicat/autism.cfm

Strohner, H., & Nelson, K. E. (1974). The young child's development of sentence comprehension: Influence of event probability, nonverbal context, syntactic form, and strategies. *Child Development, 45,* 567–576.

Strough, J., Berg, C. A., & Meegan, S. P. (2001). Friendship and gender differences in task and social interpretations of peer collaborative problem solving. *Social Development, 10*(1), 1–22.

Strutt, G. F., Anderson, D. R., & Well, A. D. (1975). A developmental study of the effects of irrelevant information on speeded classification. *Journal of Experimental Child Psychology, 20,* 127–135.

Stucky-Ropp, R. C., & DiLorenzo, T. M. (1992, August). Determinants of exercise in children. Paper presented at the meeting of the American Psychological Association, Washington, DC.

Stunkard, A. J., Harris, J. R., Pedersen, N. I., & McClearn, G. E. (1990). The body-mass index of twins who have been reared apart. *New England Journal of Medicine, 322,* 1483–1487.

Subbotsky, E. (2004). Magical thinking in judgments of causation. Can anomalous phenomena affect ontological causal beliefs in children and adults. *British Journal of Developmental Psychology, 22,* 123–152.

Sue, S., & Okazaki, S. (1990). Asian-American educational achievements. *American Psychologist, 45,* 913–920.

Suemer, N., & Guengoer, D. (1999). Cocuk yetistirme stillerinin baglanma stilleri, benlik degerlendirmeleri ve yakin iliskiler uezerindeki etkisi. *Turk Psikoloji Dergisi, 14*(44), 35–58.

Sullivan, A. (2000, April 2). The He hormone. *New York Times Magazine,* pp. 46–51ff.

Sullivan, B. A., & Hansen, J. C. (2004). Mapping associations between interests and personality: Toward a conceptual understanding of individual differences in vocational behavior. *Journal of Counseling Psychology, 51*(3), 287–298.

Sullivan, J. M. (2000). Cellular and molecular mechanisms underlying learning and memory impairments produced by cannabinoids. *Learning and Memory, 7*(3), 132–139.

Sullivan, P. F., Neale, M. C., & Kendler, K. S. (2000). Genetic epidemiology of major depression: Review and meta-analysis. *American Journal of Psychiatry, 157,* 1552–1562.

Sullivan, S. A., & Birch, L. L. (1990). Pass the sugar, pass the salt: Experience dictates preference. *Developmental Psychology, 26,* 546–551.

Sun, Y. (2001). Family environment and adolescents' well-being before and after parents' marital disruption: A longitudinal analysis. *Journal of Marriage and Family, 63*(3), 697–713.

Suomi, S. J., Harlow, H. F., & McKinney, W. T. (1972). Monkey psychiatrists. *American Journal of Psychiatry, 128,* 927–932.

Super, C. M. (1981). Behavioral development in infancy. In R. H. Monroe, R. L. Monroe, & B. B. Whiting (Eds.), *Handbook of cross-cultural human development* (pp. 181–270). New York: Garland.

Susman, E. J., Dorn, D. L., & Schiefelbein, V. L. (2003). Puberty, sexuality, and health. In R.

M. Lerner (Eds.), *Handbook of psychology: Developmental psychology* (v. 6 pp. 295–324). New York: Wiley.

Suzuki, L. A., & Valencia, R. R. (1997). Race-ethnicity and measured intelligence: Educational implications. *American Psychologist, 52,* 1103–1114.

Swearer, S. M., & Cary, P. T. (2003). Perceptions and attitudes toward bullying in middle school youth: A developmental examination across the bully/victim continuum. *Journal of Applied School Psychology, 19*(2), 63–79.

Swinford, S. P., DeMaris, A., Cernkovich, S. A., & Giordano, P. C. (2000). Harsh physical discipline in childhood and violence in later romantic involvements: The mediating role of problem behaviors. *Journal of Marriage and the Family, 62*(2), 508–519.

Taffe, M. A., et al. (2002). Cognitive performance of MDMA-treated rhesus monkeys: Sensitivity to serotonergic challenge. *Neuropsychopharmacology, 27*(6), 993–1005.

Takahashi, K. (1990). Are the key assumptions of the "Strange Situation" procedure universal? A view from Japanese research. *Human Development, 33,* 23–30.

Takahashi, M., & Sugiyama, M. (2003). Improvement and prevention of misbehavior in a junior high school student: An analysis of behavioral contingency and change of stimulus function in a social setting. *Japanese Journal of Counseling Science, 36*(2), 165–174.

Tallandini, M. A., & Valentini, P. (1991). Symbolic prototypes in children's drawings of schools. *Journal of Genetic Psychology, 152,* 179–190.

Tamis-LeMonda, C. S., & Bornstein, M. H. (1991). Individual variation, correspondence, stability, and change in mother and toddler play. *Infant Behavior and Development, 14,* 143–162.

Tamis-LeMonda, C. S., & Bornstein, M. H. (2002). Maternal responsiveness and early language acquisition. In R. V. Kail & H. W. Reese (Eds.), *Advances in child development and behavior,* v. 29. San Diego: Academic Press.

Tamis-LeMonda, C. S., Bornstein, M. H., & Baumwell, L. (2001). Maternal responsiveness and children's achievement of language milestones. *Child Development, 72*(3), 748–767.

Tamis-LeMonda, C. S., Bornstein, M. H., Cyphers, L., Toda, S., & Ogino, M. (1992). Language and play at one year: A comparison of toddlers and mothers in the United States and Japan. *International Journal of Behavioral Development, 15,* 19–42.

Tan, G. (1999). Perceptions of multiculturalism and intent to stay in school among Mexican American students. *Journal of Research and Development in Education, 33*(1), 1–14.

Tang, C. S., Yeung, D. Y., & Lee, A. M. (2003). Psychosocial correlates of emotional responses to menarche among Chinese

adolescent girls. *Journal of Adolescent Health, 33*(3), 193–201.

Tanner, J. M. (1989). *Fetus into man: Physical growth from conception to maturity.* Cambridge, MA: Harvard University Press.

Tanner, J. M. (1991a). Adolescent growth spurt, I. In R. M. Lerner, A. C. Petersen, & J. Brooks-Gunn (Eds.), *Encyclopedia of adolescence.* New York: Garland.

Tanner, J. M. (1991b). Secular trend in age of menarche. In R. M. Lerner, A. C. Petersen, & J. Brooks-Gunn (Eds.), *Encyclopedia of adolescence.* New York: Garland.

Tasker, F. (2005). Lesbian mothers, gay fathers, and their children: A review. *Developmental and Behavioral Pediatrics, 26,* 224–240.

Tassi, F., Schneider, B. H., & Richard, J. F. (2001). Competitive behavior at school in relation to social competence and incompetence in middle childhood. *Revue Internationale de Psychologie Sociale, 14*(2), 165–184.

Taylor, H., & Leitman, R. (Eds.) (2003, April 29). Barriers to the diagnosis and treatment of attention deficit hyperactivity disorder (ADHD) among African American and Hispanic children: The Harris Poll. *Health Care News,* p. 2. Available at http://www.harrisinteractive.com/news/newsletters/healthnews/HI_HealthCareNews2003Vol3_Iss07.pdf

Taylor, H. G., Klein, N., Minich, N. M., & Hack, M. (2000). Middle-school-age outcomes in children with very low birthweight. *Child Development, 71*(6), 1495–1511.

Taylor, H. G., Minich, N. M., Klein, N., & Hack, M. (2004). Longitudinal outcomes of very low birth weight: Neuropsychological findings. *Journal of the International Neuropsychological Society, 10*(2), 149–163.

Taylor, M. (1999). *Imaginary companions and the children who create them.* London: Oxford University Press.

Taylor, M., & Hort, B. (1990). Can children be trained in making the distinction between appearances and reality? *Cognitive Development, 5,* 89–99.

Taylor, S. E., et al. (2000). Biobehavioral responses to stress in females: Tend-and-befriend, not fight-or-flight. *Psychological Review, 107*(3), 411–429.

Taylor-Tolbert, N. S., et al. (2000). Exercise reduces blood pressure in heavy older hypertensive men. *American Journal of Hypertension, 13,* 44–51.

Teller, D. Y., & Lindsey, D. T. (1993). Motion nulling techniques and infant color vision. In C. E. Granrud (Ed.), *Visual perception and cognition in infancy.* Hillsdale, NJ: Erlbaum.

Templer, D. I. (2006). Is the evidence on ethnicity and intelligence conclusive? *American Psychologist, 61*(2), 176–177.

Terry, D. (2000, July 16). *Getting under my skin.* Available at http://www.nytimes.com

Thal, D., & Bates, E. (1990). Continuity and variation in early language development. In J. Colombo & J. Fagen (Eds.), *Individual differences in infancy: Reliability, stability, and prediction.* Hillsdale, NJ: Erlbaum.

Theimer, C. E., Killen, M., & Stangor, C. (2001). Young children's evaluations of exclusion in gender-stereotypic peer contexts. *Developmental Psychology, 37*(1), 18–27.

Thelen, E. (2000). Motor development as foundation and future of developmental psychology. *International Journal of Behavioral Development, 24*(4), 385–397.

Thingujam, N. S. (2002). Emotional intelligence: What is the evidence? *Psychological Studies, 47*(1–3), 54–69.

Thomas, A., & Chess, S. (1989). Temperament and personality. In G. A. Kohnstamm, J. E. Bates, & M. K. Rothbart (Eds.), *Temperament in childhood.* Chichester, England: Wiley.

Thomas, D. E., Townsend, T. G., & Belgrave, F. Z. (2003). The influence of cultural and racial identification on the psychosocial adjustment of inner-city African American children in school. *American Journal of Community Psychology, 32*(3–4), 217–228.

Thomas, J. R., & French, K. E. (1985). Gender differences across age in motor performance: A meta-analysis. *Psychological Bulletin, 98,* 260–282.

Thompson, A. M., Baxter-Jones, A. D. G., Mirwald, R. L., & Bailey, D. A. (2003). Comparison of physical activity in male and female children: Does maturation matter? *Medicine and Science in Sports and Exercise, 35*(10), 1684–1690.

Thompson, O. M., et al. (2004). Food purchased away from home as a predictor of change in BMI z-score among girls. *International Journal of Obesity and Related Metabolic Disorders, 28*(2), 282–289.

Thompson, R. A. (1991). Attachment theory and research. In M. Lewis (Ed.), *Child and adolescent psychiatry: A comprehensive textbook.* Baltimore: Williams & Wilkins.

Thompson, R. A., Easterbrooks, M. A., & Padilla-Walker, L. M. (2003). Social and emotional development in infancy. In R. M. Lerner et al. (Eds.), *Handbook of psychology: Developmental psychology.* New York: Wiley.

Thompson, R. A., Lamb, M. E., & Estes, D. (1982). Stability of infant-mother attachment and its relationship to changing life circumstances in an unselected middle-class sample. *Child Development, 53,* 144–148.

Thompson, R. A., & Limber, S. P. (1990). "Social anxiety" in infancy: Stranger and separation reactions. In H. Leitenberg (Ed.), *Handbook of social and evaluation anxiety.* New York: Plenum.

Thompson, V. J., et al. (2003). Influences on diet and physical activity among middle-class African-American 8- to 10-year old girls at risk of becoming obese. *Journal of Nutrition Education and Behavior, 35*(3), 115–123.

Thomson, M. E., & Kramer, M. S. (1984). Methodologic standards for controlled clinical trials of early contact and maternal-infant behavior. *Pediatrics, 73,* 294–300.

Thurstone, L. L. (1938). Primary mental abilities. *Psychometric Monographs, 1.*

Thyssen, S. (2003). Child culture, play, and child development. *Early Child Development and Care, 173*(6), 589–612.

Tideman, E. (2000). Longitudinal follow-up of children born preterm: Cognitive development at age 19. *Early Human Development, 58*(2), 81–90.

Tiedemann, J. (2000). Parents' gender stereotypes and teachers' beliefs as predictors of children's concept of their mathematical ability in elementary school. *Journal of Educational Psychology, 92*(1), 144–151.

Tigner, R. B., & Tigner, S. S. (2000). Triarchic theories of intelligence: Aristotle and Sternberg. *History of Psychology, 3*(2), 168–176.

Timler, G. R., & Olswang, L. B. (2001). Variable structure/variable performance: Parent and teacher perspectives on a school-age child with FAS. *Journal of Positive Behavior Interventions, 3*(1), 48–56.

Tiwary, C., & Holguin, A. H. (1992). Prevalence of obesity among children of military dependents at two major medical centers. *American Journal of Public Health, 82,* 354–357.

Tizabi, Y., et al. (2000). Prenatal nicotine exposure: Effects on locomotor activity and central[-sup-1-sup-2-sup-5I]alpha-BT binding in rats. *Pharmacology, Biochemistry and Behavior, 66*(3) 495–500.

Tobbell, J. (2003). Students' experiences of the transition from primary to secondary school. *Educational and Child Psychology, 20*(4), 4–14.

Tomasello, M., Brooks, P. J., & Stern, E. (1998). Learning to produce passive utterances through discourse. *First Language, 18*(53), 223–237.

Tong, S., Caddy, D., & Short, R. V. (1997). Use of dizygotic to monozygotic twinning ratio as a measure of fertility. *The Lancet, 349,* 843–845.

Towse, J. (2003). Lifespan development of human memory. *Quarterly Journal of Experimental Psychology: Human Experimental Psychology, 56A*(7), 1244–1246.

Towse, J. N., Hitch, G. J., & Hutton, U. (2002). On the nature of the relationship between processing activity and item retention in children. *Journal of Experimental Child Psychology, 82*(2), 156–184.

Transport Canada (2001). Keep Kids Safe; Care Time 1-2-3-4. Available at http://www.sickkids.ca/SKCForParents/section.asp?s=Safety+Information+by+Topic&sID=10774&ss=Playground+Safety&ssID=11333

Trehub, S. E., Trainor, L. J., & Unyk, A. M. (1993). Music and speech processing in the first year of life. In H. W. Reese (Ed.), *Advances in child development and behavior,* v. 24. San Diego: Academic Press.

Treuth, M. S., Butte, N. F., Adolph, A. L., & Puyau, M. R. (2004). A longitudinal study of fitness and activity in girls predisposed to obesity. *Medicine and Science in Sports and Exercise, 36*(2), 198–204.

Trevarthen, C. (2003). Conversations with a two-month-old. In J. Raphael-Leff (Ed.), *Parent-infant psychodynamics: Wild things, mirrors, and ghosts.* London: Whurr.

Triandis, H. C. (1990). Cross-cultural studies of individualism and collectivism. In J. J. Berman (Ed.), *Nebraska Symposium on Motivation, 1989: Cross-cultural perspectives.* Lincoln: University of Nebraska Press.

Triandis, H. C. (1994). *Culture and social behavior.* New York: McGraw-Hill.

Triandis, H. C. (1995). *Individualism and collectivism.* Boulder, CO: Westview Press.

Trice, A. D. (2000). Italian, Bulgarian, and U.S. children's perceptions of gender-appropriateness of occupations. *Journal of Social Psychology, 140*(5), 661–663.

Trocmé, N., Fallon, B., MacLaurin, B., Daciuk, J., Felstiner, C., Black, T., Tonmyr, L., Blackstock, C., Barter, K., Turcotte, D., & Cloutier, R. (2005). *Canadian incidence study of reported child abuse and neglect, 2003: Major findings.* Ottawa, ON: Minister of Public Works and Government Services Canada.

Trost, S. G., Sirard, J. R., Dowda, M., Pfeiffer, K. A., & Pate, R. R. (2003). Physical activity in overweight and nonoverweight preschool children. *International Journal of Obesity and Related Metabolic Disorders, 27*(7), 834–839.

Troxel, W. M., & Matthews, K. A. (2004). What are the costs of marital conflict and dissolution to children's physical health? *Clinical Child and Family Psychology Review, 7*(1), 29–57.

Truesdell, L. A., & Abramson, T. (1992). Academic behavior and grades of mainstreamed students with mild disabilities. *Exceptional Children, 58,* 392–398.

Tsuneishi, S., & Casaer, P. (2000). Effects of preterm extrauterine visual experience on the development of the human visual system: A flash VEP study. *Developmental Medicine and Child Neurology, 42*(10), 663–668.

Turkheimer, E. (1991). Individual and group differences in adoption studies of IQ. *Psychological Bulletin, 110,* 392–405.

Turnbull, M., Hart, D., & Lapkin, S. (2003). Grade 6 French immersion students performance on large scale reading, writing, and mathematics tests: Building explanations. *Alberta Journal of Educational Research, 49,* 6–23.

Ulloa, E. C., & Ulibarri, M. D. (2004). Man and wife in America: A history. *Archives of Sexual Behavior, 33*(3), 313–315.

Umaña-Taylor, A. J., Yazedjian, A., & Bámaca-Gómez, M. (2004). Developing the ethnic identity scale using Eriksonian and social identity perspectives. *Identity, 4*(1), 9–38.

United Nations Special Session on AIDS (2001, June 25–27). *Preventing HIV/AIDS among young people.* New York: United Nations.

United Nations Statistics Division (2004, March). UNESCO: World and Regional Trends, Table 8. Available at http://millenniumindicators.un.org/unsd/mi/mi_worldregn.asp

U.S. Bureau of the Census (2002). Number, timing, and duration of marriages and divorces: 1996. Available at http://www.census.gov/prod/2002pubs/p70-80.pdf

U.S. Bureau of the Census (2004). *Statistical abstract of the United States* (124th ed.). Washington, DC: U.S. Government Printing Office.

U.S. Department of Agriculture (2000). Dietary guidelines for Americans (5th ed.). Available at http://www.nal.usda.gov/fnic/dga

U.S. Department of Energy Office of Science (2007). Gene therapy. Available at http://www.ornl.gov/sci/techresources/Human_Genome/medicine/genetherapy.shtml

U.S. Department of Health and Human Services (2004). Child abuse and neglect fatalities: Statistics and interventions—Child maltreatment 2002. Available at http://nccanch.acf.hhs.gov/pubs/factsheets/fatality.cfm

U.S. Department of Health and Human Services, National Center for Health Statistics (2001). *Vital statistics mortality data, underlying cause death, 1998.* Hyattsville, MD: U.S. Department of Health and Human Services, Centers for Disease Control and Prevention, National Center for Health Statistics.

U.S. Department of Labor, Bureau of Labor Statistics (2004). *Teachers: Adult literacy and remedial and self-enrichment education.* Available at http://www.bls.gov/oco/ocos064.htm

Valas, H. (2001). Learned helplessness and psychological adjustment: Effects of age, gender, and academic achievement. *Scandinavian Journal of Educational Research, 45*(1), 71–90.

Valleroy, L. A., et al. (2000). HIV prevalence and associated risks in young men who have sex with men. *Journal of the American Medical Association, 284*(2), 198–204.

Van Ausdale, D., & Feagin, J. R. (2001). *The first R: How children learn race and racism.* New York: Rowman & Littlefield.

Van Brunschot, M., Zarbatany, L., & Strang, K. (1993, March). Ecological contributions to gender differences in intimacy among peers. Paper presented at the meeting of the Society for Research in Child Development, New Orleans, LA.

van IJzendoorn, M. H., & Hubbard, F. O. A. (2000). Are infant crying and maternal responsiveness during the first year related to infant-mother attachment at 15 months? *Attachment and Human Development, 2*(3), 371–391.

van IJzendoorn, M. H., & Kroonenberg, P. M. (1988). Cross-cultural patterns of attachment: A meta-analysis of the Strange Situation. *Child Development, 59,* 147–156.

van IJzendoorn, M. H., Moran, G., Belsky, J., Pederson, D., Bakermans-Kranenburg, M. J., & Kneppers, K. (2000). The similarity of siblings' attachments to their mother. *Child Development, 71*(4), 1086–1098.

van IJzendoorn, M. H., Sagi, A., & Lambermon, M. W. E. (1992). The multiple caretaker paradox: Data from Holland and Israel. In R. C. Pianta (Ed.), *New directions for child development, no. 57, Beyond the parent: The role of other adults in children's lives.* San Francisco: Jossey-Bass.

Vandenbergh, J. G. (1993). Cited in N. Angier (1993, August 24), Female gerbil born with males is found to be begetter of sons, *New York Times,* p. C4.

Vander Ven, T. M., Cullen, F. T., Carrozza, M. A., & Wright, J. P. (2001). Home alone: The impact of maternal employment on delinquency. *Social Problems, 48*(2), 236–257.

Vander Wal, J. S., & Thelen, M. H. (2000). Eating and body image concerns among obese and average-weight children. *Addictive Behaviors, 25*(5), 775–778.

van Erp, T. G. M., et al. (2002). Contributions of genetic risk and fetal hypoxia to hippocampal volume in patients with schizophrenia or schizoaffective disorder, their unaffected siblings, and healthy unrelated volunteers. *American Journal of Psychiatry, 159*(9), 1514–1520.

Vartanian, L. R. (2001). Adolescents' reactions to hypothetical peer group conversations: Evidence for an imaginary audience. *Adolescence, 36*(142), 347–380.

Vartanian, L. R., Giant, C. L., & Passino, R. M. (2001). "Ally McBeal vs. Arnold Schwarzenegger": Comparing mass media, interpersonal feedback, and gender as predictors of satisfaction with body thinness and muscularity. *Social Behavior and Personality, 29*(7), 711–723.

Vartanian, O., Martindale, C., & Kwiatkowski, J. (2003). Creativity and inductive reasoning: The relationship between divergent thinking and performance on Wason's 2-4-6 task. *Quarterly Journal of Experimental Psychology: Human Experimental Psychology, 56A*(4), 641–655.

Velez de la Calle, J. F., et al. (2001). Male infertility risk factors in a French military population. *Human Reproduction, 16,* 481–486.

Vellutino, F. R. (2001). Further analysis of the relationship between reading achievement and intelligence. *Journal of Learning Disabilities, 34*(4), 306–310.

Vellutino, F. R., Fletcher, J. M., Snowling, M. J., & Scanlon, D. M. (2004). Specific reading disability (dyslexia): What have we learned in the past four decades? *Journal of Child Psychology and Psychiatry, 45*(1), 2–40.

Velting, D. M., Rathus, J. H., & Miller, A. L. (2000). MACI personality scale profiles of depressed adolescent suicide attempters: A pilot study. *Journal of Clinical Psychology, 56*(10), 1381–1385.

Vermeiren, R., Bogaerts, J., Ruchkin, V., Deboutte, D., & Schwab-Stone, M. (2004). Subtypes of self-esteem and self-concept in adolescent violent and property offenders. *Journal of Child Psychology and Psychiatry, 45*(2), 405–411.

Vilain, E. (2000). Genetics of sexual development. *Annual Review of Sex Research, 11,* 1–25.

Villani, S. (2001). Impact of media on children and adolescents: A 10-year review of the research. *Journal of the American Academy of Child and Adolescent Psychiatry, 40*(4), 392–401.

Vissandjée, B. (2001). The consequences of cultural diversity. *The Canadian Women's Health Network, 4*(2), 3–4.

Vissandjée, B., Carignan, P., & Bourdeau-Marchand, M. (1999). Les nouvelles immigrantes et la santé. *L'infirmière canadienne, 95*(4), 35–41.

Visscher, W. A., Feder, M., Burns, A. M., Brady, T. M., & Bray, R. M. (2003). The impact of smoking and other substance use by urban women on the birthweight of their infants. *Substance Use and Misuse, 38*(8), 1063–1093.

Visser, J. (2002). Inclusion for students with emotional and behaviour difficulties. *Journal of International Special Needs Education, 5,* 5–9.

Vitousek, K., & Manke, F. (1994). Personality variables and disorders in anorexia nervosa and bulimia nervosa. *Journal of Abnormal Psychology, 103,* 137–147.

Vogel, D. A., Lake, M. A., Evans, S., & Karraker, K. H. (1991). Children's and adult's sex-stereotyped perceptions of infants. *Sex Roles, 24,* 605–616.

Voisin, D. R. (2003). Victims of community violence and HIV sexual risk behaviors among African American adolescent males. *Journal of HIV/AIDS Prevention and Education for Adolescents and Children, 5*(3–4), 87–110.

Volkmar, F. R. (2001). Pharmacological interventions in autism: Theoretical and practical issues. *Journal of Clinical Child Psychology, 30*(1), 80–87.

Volkow, N. D., et al. (2001a). Association of dopamine transporter reduction with psychomotor impairment in methamphetamine abusers. *American Journal of Psychiatry, 158,* 377–382.

Volkow, N. D., et al. (2001b). Higher cortical and lower subcortical metabolism in detoxified methamphetamine abusers. *American Journal of Psychiatry, 158,* 383–389.

Volling, B. L. (2001). Early attachment relationships as predictors of preschool children's emotion regulation with a distressed sibling. *Early Education and Development, 12*(2), 185–207.

Volling, B. L. (2003). Sibling relationships. In M. H. Bornstein et al. (Eds.), *Well-being: Positive development across the life course* (pp. 205–220). Mahwah, NJ: Lawrence Erlbaum Associates.

Volling, B. L., McElwain, N. L., Notaro, P. C., & Herrera, C. (2002). Parents' emotional availability and infant emotional competence: Predictors of parent-infant attachment and emerging self-regulation. *Journal of Family Psychology, 16,* 447–465.

Volterra, M. C., Caselli, O., Capirci, E., & Pizzuto, E. (2004). Gesture and the emergence and development of language. In M. Tomasello & D. I. Slobin (Eds.), *Beyond nature-nurture.* Mahwah, NJ. Lawrence Erlbaum.

Vorhees, C. V., & Mollnow, E. (1987). Behavioral teratogenesis long-term influences on behavior from early exposure to environmental agents. In J. D. Osofsky (Ed.), *Handbook of infant development* (2nd ed.). New York: Wiley.

Voyer, D., Nolan, C., & Voyer, S. (2000). The relation between experience and spatial performance in men and women. *Sex Roles, 43*(11–12), 891–915.

Vurpillot, E. (1968). The development of scanning strategies and their relation to visual differentiation. *Journal of Experimental Child Psychology, 6,* 632–650.

Vygotsky, L. S. (1962). *Thought and language,* Cambridge, MA: MIT Press.

Vygotsky, L. (1978). *Mind in society: The development of higher psychological processes.* Cambridge, MA: Harvard University Press.

Vygotsky, L. S, Rieber, R. W., Carton, A. S. (1987). *The collected works of L. S. Vygotsky, v. 1: Problems of general psychology.* New York: Plenum Press.

Wadden, T. A., Brownell, K. D., & Foster, G. D. (2002). Obesity: Responding to the global epidemic. *Journal of Consulting and Clinical Psychology, 70*(3), 510–525.

Wadden, T. A., & Stunkard, A. J. (Eds.) (2002). *Handbook of obesity treatment.* New York: Guilford Press.

Wade, T. D., Bulik, C. M., Neale, M., & Kendler, K. S. (2000). Anorexia nervosa and major depression: Shared genetic and environmental risk factors. *American Journal of Psychiatry, 157,* 469–471.

Wade, T. D., & Kendler, K. S. (2001). Parent, child, and social correlates of parental discipline style: A retrospective, multi-informant investigation with female twins. *Social Psychiatry and Psychiatric Epidemiology, 36*(4), 177–185.

Wadsworth, K. W., & McLoyd, V. C. (1993, March). The impact of mother-adolescent self-esteem: Effects of social support. Paper presented at the meeting of the Society for Research in Child Development, New Orleans, LA.

Wagner, K. D., & Ambrosini, P. J. (2001). Childhood depression: Pharmacological therapy/treatment (pharmacotherapy of childhood depression). *Journal of Clinical Child Psychology, 30*(1), 88–97.

Wahl, K. H., & Blackhurst, A. (2000). Factors affecting the occupational and educational aspirations of children and adolescents. *Professional School Counseling, 3*(5), 367–374.

Wahler, R. G., Herring, M., & Edwards, M. (2001). Coregulation of balance between children's prosocial approaches and acts of compliance: A pathway to mother-child cooperation? *Journal of Clinical Child Psychology, 30*(4), 473–478.

Walkup, J. T., et al. (2001). Fluvoxamine for the treatment of anxiety disorders in children and adolescents. *New England Journal of Medicine, 344*(17), 1279–1285.

Walkup, J. T., et al. (2003). Searching for moderators and mediators of pharmacological treatment effects in children and adolescents with anxiety disorders. *Journal of the American Academy of Child and Adolescent Psychiatry, 42*(1), 13–21.

Walter, J. L., & LaFreniere, P. J. (2000). A naturalistic study of affective expression, social competence, and sociometric status in preschoolers. *Early Education and Development, 11*(1), 109–122.

Walther, F. J., Ouden, A. L. den, & Verloove-Vanhorick, S. P. (2000). Looking back in time: Outcome of a national cohort of very preterm infants born in The Netherlands in 1983. *Early Human Development, 59*(3), 175–191.

Wang, C. (2002). Emotional intelligence, general self-efficacy, and coping style of juvenile delinquents. *Chinese Mental Health Journal, 16*(8), 565–567.

Wang, C., & He, Z. (2002). The relationship between parental rearing styles and general self-efficacy and emotional intelligence in high school students. *Chinese Mental Health Journal, 16*(11), 781–782, 785.

Wang, Q., Leichtman, M. D., & White, S. H. (1998). Childhood memory and self-description in young Chinese adults: The impact of growing up an only child. *Cognition, 69*(1), 73–103.

Wang, X., et al. (2002). Maternal cigarette smoking, metabolic gene polymorphism, and infant birth weight. *Journal of the American Medical Association, 287,* 195–202.

Ward, C. A. (2000). Models and measurements of psychological androgyny: A cross-cultural extension of theory and research. *Sex Roles, 43*(7–8), 529–552.

Ward, M. J., Lee, S. S., & Lipper, E. G. (2000). Failure-to-thrive is associated with disorganized infant-mother attachment and unresolved maternal attachment. *Infant Mental Health Journal, 21*(6), 428–442.

Warren, W. K., & King, A. J. (1994). *Development and evaluation of an AIDS/STD/sexuality program for grade 9 students.* Kingston, ON: Social Program Evaluation Group, Queen's University.

Wasserman, G. A., et al. (2000). Yugoslavia Prospective Lead Study: Contributions of prenatal and postnatal lead exposure to early intelligence. *Neurotoxicology and Teratology, 22*(6), 811–818.

Waterman, A. S. (1985). Identity in the context of adolescent psychology. In A. S. Waterman (Ed.), *Identity in adolescence: Processes and contents.* San Francisco: Jossey-Bass.

Waterman, A. S. (1999). Issues of identity formation revisited: United States and The Netherlands. *Developmental Review, 19*(4), 462–479.

Watson, J. B. (1924). Behaviorism. New York: Norton.

Watson, J. D., & Crick, F. H. C. (1958). Molecular structure of nucleic acids: A structure for deoxyribose nucleic acid. *Nature, 171,* 737–738.

Watson, T. L., Bowers, W. A., & Andersen, A. E. (2000). Involuntary treatment of eating disorders. *American Journal of Psychiatry, 157,* 1806–1810.

Watt, H. M. G., & Bornholt, L. J. (2000). Social categories and student perceptions in high school mathematics. *Journal of Applied Social Psychology, 30*(7), 1492–1503.

Waxman, S. R. (2002). Early word-learning and conceptual development: Everything had a name, and each name gave birth to a new thought. In U. Goswami (Ed.), *Blackwell handbook of childhood cognitive development* (pp. 102–126). Malden, MA: Blackwell.

Waxman, S. R. (2003). Links between object categorization and naming: Origins and emergence in human infants. In D. H. Rakison & L. M. Oakes (Eds.), *Early category and concept development: Making sense of the blooming, buzzing confusion* (pp. 213–241). London: Oxford University Press.

Waxman, S. R., & Senghas, A. (1992). Relations among word meaning in early lexical development. *Developmental Psychology, 28,* 862–873.

Weaver, A. D., Byers, E. S., Sears, H. A., Cohen, J. N., & Randall, H. (2002). Sexual health education at school and at home: Attitudes and experiences of New Brunswick parents. *The Canadian Journal of Human Sexuality, 11,* 19–31.

Weber, J. (1994). *Special education in Canadian schools.* Thornhill, ON: Highland Press.

Weber Cullen, K., et al. (2001). Child-reported family and peer influences on fruit, juice, and vegetable consumption: Reliability and validity of measures. *Health Education Research, 16*(2), 187–200.

Webster-Stratton, C., Reid, M. J., & Hammond, M. (2001a). Preventing conduct problems, promoting social competence: A parent and teacher training partnership in Head Start. *Journal of Clinical Child Psychology, 30*(3), 283–302.

Webster-Stratton, C., Reid, J., & Hammond, M. (2001b). Social skills and problem-solving training for children with early-onset conduct problems: Who benefits? *Journal of Child Psychology and Psychiatry and Allied Disciplines, 42*(7), 943–952.

Wechsler, D. (1975). Intelligence defined and undefined: A relativistic appraisal. *American Psychologist, 30,* 135–139.

Wechsler, D. (2003). *Wechsler intelligence scale for children* (4th ed.) (WISC-IV). San Antonio, TX: The Psychological Corporation.

Weichold, K., Silbereisen, R. K., & Schmitt-Rodermund, E. (2003). Short-term and long-term consequences of early versus late physical maturation in adolescents. In C. Hayward (Ed.), *Gender differences at puberty* (pp. 241–276). New York: Cambridge University Press.

Weinberg, R. A. (2004). The infant and the family in the twenty-first century. *Journal of the American Academy of Child and Adolescent Psychiatry, 43*(1), 115–116.

Weiner, T. S., & Adolph, K. E. (1993, March). Toddler's perception of slant vs. slope height for descending slopes. Paper presented at the meeting of the Society for Research in Child Development, New Orleans, LA.

Weissberg, J. A., & Paris, S. G. (1986). Young children's remembering in different contexts: A reinterpretation of Istomine's study. *Child Development, 57*, 1123–1129.

Weller, E. B., & Weller, R. A. (1991). Mood disorders. In M. Lewis (Ed.), *Child and adolescent psychiatry: A comprehensive textbook.* Baltimore: Williams & Wilkins.

Wellman, H. M. (2002). Understanding the psychological world: Developing a theory of mind. In U. Goswami (Ed.), *Blackwell handbook of childhood cognitive development* (pp. 167–187). Malden, MA: Blackwell.

Wellman, H. M., Cross, D., & Bartsch, K. (1986). Infant search and object permanence: A meta-analysis of the A-not-B error. *Monographs of the Society for Research in Child Development, 5*(3, ser. 214).

Wellman, H. M., Cross, D., & Watson, J. (2001). Meta-analysis of theory-of-mind development: The truth about false belief. *Child Development, 72*(3), 655–684.

Wellman, H. M., & Liu, D. (2004). Scaling of theory-of-mind tasks. *Child Development, 75*(2), 523–541.

Welton, C. & Rinaldi, C. M. (2007, May). Impact of self-efficacy on students' goals and study strategies. Poster presented at the annual meeting of the Canadian Society for the Study of Education, Canadian Association of Educational Psychology, Saskatoon, SK.

Wenar, C. (1990). Childhood fears and phobias. In M. Lewis & S. M. Miller (Eds.), *Handbook of developmental psychopathology.* New York: Plenum.

Wentworth, N., Benson, J. B., & Haith, M. M. (2000). The development of infants' reaches for stationary and moving targets. *Child Development, 71*(3), 576–601.

Wentz, E., et al. (2003). Bone density 11 years after anorexia nervosa onset in a controlled study of 39 cases. *International Journal of Eating Disorders, 34*(3), 314–318.

Wentzel, K. R., Barry, C. M., & Caldwell, K. A. (2004). Friendships in middle school: Influences on motivation and school adjustment. *Journal of Educational Psychology, 96*(2), 195–203.

Weppelman, T. L., Bostow, A., Schiffer, R., Elbert-Perez, E., & Newman, R. S. (2003). Children's use of the prosodic characteristics of infant-directed speech. *Language and Communication, 23*(1), 63–80.

Werker, J. F. (1989). Becoming a native listener. *American Scientist, 77*, 54–59.

Werker, J. F., & Desjardins, R. N. (2001). Listening to speech in the 1st year of life. In M. Tomasello & E. Bates (Eds.), *Language development: The essential readings.* Malden, MA: Blackwell.

Werner, E. E. (1988). A cross-cultural perspective on infancy. *Journal of Cross-Cultural Psychology, 19*, 96–113.

Werner, E. E. (1990). Protective factors and individual resilience. In S. J. Meisels & J. P. Shonkoff (Eds.), *Handbook of early childhood intervention.* Cambridge: Cambridge University Press.

Werner, L. A., & Gillenwater, J. M. (1990). Pure-tone sensitivity of 2- to 5-week-old infants. *Infant Behavior and Development, 13*, 355–375.

Werry, J. S. (1991). Brain and behavior. In M. Lewis (Ed.), *Child and adolescent psychiatry: A comprehensive textbook.* Baltimore: Williams & Wilkins.

Whalen, C. K. (2001). ADHD treatment in the 21st Century: Pushing the envelope. *Journal of Clinical Child Psychology, 30*(1), 136–140.

Whalen, C. K., & Henker, B. (1997). Stimulant pharmacotherapy for attention-deficit/hyperactivity disorders: An analysis of progress, problems, and prospects. In S. Fisher & R. P. Greenberg (Eds.), *From placebo to panacea: Putting psychiatric drugs to the test* (pp. 323–356). New York: Wiley.

Whitall, J. (1991). The developmental effect of concurrent cognitive and locomotor skills: Time-sharing from a dynamical perspective. *Journal of Experimental Child Psychology, 51*, 245–266.

White, C. B., Bushnell, N., & Regnemer, J. L. (1978). Moral development in Bahamian school children: A three-year examination of Kohlberg's stages of moral development. *Developmental Psychology, 14*, 58–65.

White, J. W., & Smith, P. H. (2004). Sexual assault perpetration and reperpetration: From adolescence to young adulthood. *Criminal Justice and Behavior, 31*(2), 182–202.

Whitehead, J. R., & Corbin, C. B. (1991). Effects of fitness test type, teacher, and gender on exercise intrinsic motivation and physical self-worth. *Journal of School Health, 61*, 11–16.

Whitehurst, G. J. (1982). Language development. In B. B. Wolman (Ed.), *Handbook of developmental psychology.* Englewood Cliffs, NJ: Prentice-Hall.

Whitehurst, G. J., & Valdez-Menchaca, M. C. (1988). What is the role of reinforcement in early language acquisition? *Child Development, 59*, 430–440.

Whiteside-Mansell, L., Bradley, R. H., Tresch Owen, M., Randolph, S. M., & Cauce, A. M. (2003). Parenting and children's behavior at 36 months: Equivalence between African American and European American mother-child dyads. *Parenting: Science and Practice, 3*(3), 197–234.

Whiting, B. B., & Edwards, C. P. (1988). *Children of different worlds.* Cambridge, MA: Harvard University Press.

Widaman, J. F., MacMillan, D. L., Hemsley, R. E., Little, T. D., & Balow, I. H. (1992). Differences in adolescents' self-concept as a function of academic level, ethnicity, and

gender. *American Journal on Mental Retardation, 96*, 387–404.

Wiesner, M., & Ittel, A. (2002). Relations of pubertal timing and depressive symptoms to substance use in early adolescence. *Journal of Early Adolescence, 22*(1), 5–23.

Wilder, A. A., & Williams, J. P. (2001). Students with severe learning disabilities can learn higher order comprehension skills. *Journal of Educational Psychology, 93*(2), 268–278.

Wilkinson, K. M., Ross, E., & Diamond, A. (2003). Fast mapping of multiple words: Insights into when "the information provided" does and does not equal "the information perceived." *Journal of Applied Developmental Psychology, 24*(6), 739–762.

Williams, K., Haywood, K. I., & Painter, M. (1996). Environmental versus biological influences on gender differences in the overarm throw for force: The dominant and nondominant arm throws. *Women in Sport and Physical Activity Journal, 5*, 29–48.

Williams, J. M., & Currie, C. (2000). Self-esteem and physical development in early adolescence: Pubertal timing and body image. *Journal of Early Adolescence, 20*(2), 129–149.

Williams, M. S. (2004). The psychology of eating. *Psychology and Health, 19*(4), 541–542.

Williams, R. L. (1974, May). Scientific racism and IQ: The silent mugging of the black community. *Psychology Today*, p. 32.

Williams, T. L., & Gleaves, D. H. (2003). Childhood sexual abuse, body image, and disordered eating: A structural modeling analysis. *Journal of Trauma and Dissociation, 4*(4), 91–108.

Willinger, M., Ko, C.-W., Hoffman, H. J., Kessler, R. C., & Corwin, M. J. (2000). Factors associated with caregivers' choice of infant sleep position, 1994–1998: The national infant sleep position study. *JAMA, 283*, 2135–2142.

Wilson, C., Nettelbeck, T., Turnbull, C., & Young, R. (1992). IT, IQ, and age: A comparison of developmental functions. *British Journal of Developmental Psychology, 10*, 179–188.

Wilson, P. (2004). A preliminary investigation of an early intervention program: Examining the intervention effectiveness of the Bracken Concept Development Program and the Bracken Basic Concept Scale-Revised with Head Start students. *Psychology in the Schools, 41*(3), 301–311.

Windell, J. (1991). *Discipline: A sourcebook of 50 failsafe techniques for parents.* Indialantic, FL: Collier Books.

Winer, G. A. (1980). Class-inclusion reasoning in children: A review of the empirical literature. *Child Development, 51*, 309–328.

Wink, J., & Putney, L. (2002). *A vision of Vygotsky.* Boston, MA: Allyn & Bacon.

Winner, E. (1989). Development in the visual arts. In W. Damon (Ed.), *Child development today and tomorrow.* San Francisco: Jossey-Bass.

Winner, E. (2000). The origins and ends of gift-edness. *American Psychologist, 55,* 159–169.

Winzelberg, A. J., et al. (2000). Effectiveness of an Internet-based program for reducing risk factors for eating disorders. *Journal of Consulting and Clinical Psychology, 68,* 346–350.

Wolchik, S. A., et al. (2000). An experimental evaluation of theory-based mother and mother-child programs for children of divorce. *Journal of Consulting and Clinical Psychology, 68*(5), 843–856.

Wolf, A., & Lozoff, B. (1989). Object attachment, thumbsucking, and the passage to sleep. *Journal of the American Academy of Child and Adolescent Psychiatry, 28,* 287–292.

Wolfner, G. D., & Gelles, R. J. (1993). A profile of violence toward children: A national study. *Child Abuse and Neglect, 17*(2), 197–212.

Woolley, J. D., Phelps, K. E., Davis, D. L., Mandell, D. L. (1999). Where theories of mind meet magic: The development of children's beliefs about wishing. *Child Development, 70,* 571–587.

Wolfner, G. D., & Gelles, R. J. (1993). A profile of violence toward children: A national study. *Child Abuse and Neglect, 17*(2), 197–212.

Wong, S., et al. (2004). Osteoporosis in Chinese patients with anorexia nervosa. *International Journal of Eating Disorders, 36*(1), 104–108.

Wood, N. S., et al. (2000). Neurologic and developmental disability after extremely preterm birth. *New England Journal of Medicine, 343*(6), 378–384.

Woods, S. C., Schwartz, M. W., Baskin, D. G., & Seeley, R. J. (2000). Food intake and the regulation of body weight. *Annual Review of Psychology, 51,* 255–277.

Woolfolk-Hoy, A. (2004). *Educational psychology* (9th ed.). Boston: Allyn & Bacon.

Worell, J., & Johnson, D. (2001). Therapy with women: Feminist frameworks. In R. Unger (Ed.). *Handbook of the psychology of women and gender* (pp. 317–329). New York: Wiley.

World Health Organization (1992). *The ICD-10 classification of mental and behavioral disorders: Clinical description and diagnostic guidelines.* Geneva: Author.

World Health Organization (2003a). *Training in the management of severe malnutrition.* Geneva: World Health Organization Department of Nutrition for Health and Development. Available at http://www.who.int/nut/documents/manage_severe_malnutrition_training_fly_eng.pdf

World Health Organization (2003b). *Global strategy for infant and young child feeding.* Available at http://www.who.int/nut/documents/gs_infant_feeding_text_eng.pdf

World Health Organization (2004, March 3). *Alleviating protein-energy malnutrition.* Available at http://www.who.int/nut/pem.htm

Wright, C., & Birks, E. (2000). Risk factors for failure to thrive: A population-based survey.

Child: Care, Health, and Development, 26(1), 5–16.

Wright, D. W., & Young, R. (1998). The effects of family structure and maternal employment on the development of gender-related attitudes among men and women. *Journal of Family Issues, 19*(3), 300–314.

Wright, S. C., Taylor, D. M., & Ruggiero, K. M. (1996). Examining the potential for academic achievement among Inuit children: Comparisons on the Raven Coloured Progressive Matrices. *Journal of Cross-Cultural Psychology, 27*(6), 733–753

Wu, J., et al. (1999). Serotonin and learned helplessness: A regional study of 5-HT-sub(1A), 5-HT-sub(2A) receptors and the serotonin transport site in rat brain. *Journal of Psychiatric Research, 33*(1), 17–22.

Wu, P., et al. (2001). Factors associated with use of mental health services for depression by children and adolescents. *Psychiatric Services, 52*(2), 189–195.

Wulff, K., & Siegmund, R. (2001). Circadian and ultradian time patterns in human behaviour. Part 1: Activity monitoring of families from prepartum to postpartum. *Biological Rhythm Research, 31*(5), 581–602.

Wynn, K. (1992, August 27). Addition and subtraction by human infants. *Nature, 358,* 749–750.

Yamada, H., et al. (2000). A milestone for normal development of the infantile brain detected by functional MRI. *Neurology, 55*(2), 218–223.

Yamazaki, J. N., & Schull, W. J. (1990). Perinatal loss and neurological abnormalities among children of the atomic bomb. *Journal of the American Medical Association, 264,* 605–609.

Yang, O. S. (2000). Guiding children's verbal plan and evaluation during free play: An application of Vygotsky's genetic epistemology to the early childhood classroom. *Early Childhood Education Journal, 28*(1), 3–10.

Yarrow, L. J., & Goodwin, M. S. (1973). The immediate impact of separation: Reactions of infants to a change in mother figures. In L. J. Stone, H. T. Smith, & L. B. Murphy (Eds.), *The competent infant: Research and commentary.* New York: Basic Books.

Yarrow, L. J., Goodwin, M. S., Manheimer, H., & Milowe, I. D. (1971, March). Infant experiences and cognitive and personality development at ten years. Paper presented at the meeting of the American Orthopsychiatric Association, Washington, DC.

Yatham, L. N., et al. (2000). Brain serotonin2 receptors in major depression: A positron emission tomography study. *Archives of General Psychiatry, 57,* 850–858.

Yokota, F., & Thompson, K. M. (2000). Violence in G-rated animated films. *Journal of the American Medical Association, 283,* 2716–2720.

Youniss, J., & Haynie, D. L. (1992). Friendship in adolescence. *Developmental and Behavioral Pediatrics, 13,* 59–66.

Yu, S. M., Huang, Z. J., Schwalberg, R. H., Overpeck, M., & Kogan, M. D. (2003). Acculturation and the health and well-being of U.S. immigrant adolescents. *Journal of Adolescent Health, 33*(6), 479–488.

Zahn-Waxler, C., Radke-Yarrow, M., & Wagner, E. (1992). Development of concern for others. *Developmental Psychology, 28,* 126–136.

Zajonc, R. B. (2001). The family dynamics of intellectual development. *American Psychologist, 56*(6/7), 490–496.

Zajonc, R. B., & Mullally, P. R. (1997). Birth order: Reconciling conflicting effects. *American Psychologist, 52*(7), 685–699.

Zametkin, A. J., Nordahl, T. E., Gross, M., King, A. C., Semple, W. E., Rumsey, J., Hamburger, S., & Cohen, R. M. (1990). Cerebral glucose metabolism in adults with hyperactivity of childhood onset. *New England Journal of Medicine, 323,* 1361–1366.

Zan, B., & Hildebrandt, C. (2003). First graders' interpersonal understanding during cooperative and competitive games. *Early Education and Development, 14*(4), 397–410.

Zarbatany, L., McDougall, P., & Hymel, S. (2000). Gender-differentiated experience in the peer culture: Links to intimacy in preadolescence. *Social Development, 9*(1), 62–79.

Zaslow, M. J., Rabinovich, B. A., & Suwalsky, J. T. D. (1991). From maternal employment to child outcomes: Pre-existing group differences and moderating variables. In S. V. Lerner & N. L. Galambos (Eds.), *Employed mothers and their children.* New York: Garland.

Zeanah, C., & Boros, N. (2000). Disturbances and disorders of attachment in early childhood. In C. Zeanah (Ed.), *Handbook of infant mental health* (2nd ed.). New York: Guilford Press.

Zelazo, P. R. (1998). McGraw and the development of unaided walking. *Developmental Review, 18*(4), 449–471.

Zevenbergen, A. A., & Ferraro, F. R. (2001). Assessment and treatment of fetal alcohol syndrome in children and adolescents. *Journal of Developmental and Physical Disabilities, 13*(2), 123–136.

Zhang, W., & Lin, C. (1999). The development of children's social perspective-taking and its relation to their peer interaction. *Acta Psychologica Sinica, 31*(4), 418–427.

Zheng, S., & Colombo, J. (1989). Sibling configuration and gender differences in preschool social participation. *Journal of Genetic Psychology, 150,* 45–50.

Zhou, Z., Bray, M. A., Kehle, T. J., & Xin, T. (2001). Similarity of deleterious effects of divorce on Chinese and American children. *School Psychology International, 22*(3), 357–363.

Zigler, E. (1999). Head Start is not child care. *American Psychologist, 54*(2), 192.

Zigler, E., Abelson, W. D., Trickett, P. K., & Seitz, V. (1982). Is an intervention program necessary in order to improve economically disadvantaged children's IQ scores? *Child Development, 53,* 340–348.

Zigler, E., & Seitz, V. (1982). Social policy and intelligence. In R. Sternberg (Ed.), *Handbook of human intelligence.* New York: Cambridge University Press.

Zigler, E., & Styfco, S. J. (2001). Extended childhood intervention prepares children for school and beyond. *Journal of the American Medical Association, 285*(18), 2378–2380.

Zigler, E. Taussig, C., & Black, K. (1992, August). Early childhood intervention: A promising preventive for juvenile delinquency. *American Psychologist, 47,* 997–1006.

Zilberstein, K. (2006). Clarifying core characteristics of attachment disorders: A review of current research and theory. *American Journal of Orthopsychiatry, 76*(1), 55–64.

Zimmerman, B. J. (2000). Self-efficacy: An essential motive to learn. *Contemporary Educational Psychology, 25*(1), 82–91.

Zimmermann, P., Maier, M. A., Winter, M., & Grossmann, K. E. (2001). Attachment and adolescents' emotion regulation during a joint problem-solving task with a friend. *International Journal of Behavioral Development, 25*(4), 331–343.

Ziv, M., & Frye, D. (2003). The relation between desire and false belief in children's theory of mind: No satisfaction? *Developmental Psychology, 39*(5), 859–876.

Zweigenhaft, R. L., & Von Ammon, J. (2000). Birth order and civil disobedience: A test of Sulloway's "born to rebel" hypothesis. *Journal of Social Psychology, 140*(5), 624–627.

Credits

This page constitutes an extension of the copyright page. We have made every effort to trace the ownership of all copyrighted material and to secure permission from copyright holders. In the event of any question arising as to the use of any material, we will be pleased to make the necessary corrections in future printings. Thanks are due to the following authors, publishers, and agents for permission to use the material indicated.

Chapter 1. 29: "One Canadian in five could be a visible minority in 2017", adapted from Statistics Canada publication *Canadian Social Trends*, Catalogue 11–008, Winter 2005, No. 79, page 19.

Chapter 2. 57: Courtesy of Mount Sinai Hospital, Toronto. **71:** "Canadian birthrates by provinces and territories", adapted from Statistics Canada website www40.statcan.ca/101/cst01/demo04a.htm **75:** "Canadian International Adoption Statistics: Adoptions by Country (2003, 2004, 2005)" from *Facts and Figures 2005 Datafiles, Citizenship and Immigration Canada*. Reproduced with the permission of the Minister of Public Works and Government Services Canada, 2007. **77:** Copyright © 2001 by the New York Times Co. Reprinted with permission.

Chapter 4. 131: "Rate of Preterm Birth, Canada (excluding Ontario), 1991–2000", Source: Based on Statistics Canada, *Canadian Vital Statistics System, 1991–2000* (unlinked live birth files).

Chapter 5. 163: National Center for Health Statistics. U.S. Department of Health and Human Services. **164:** National Center for Health Statistics. U.S. Department of Health and Human Services.

Chapter 6. 229: FOR BETTER OR FOR WORSE © 1991 Lynn Johnston Productions. Dist. by Universal Press Syndicate. Reprinted with permission. All rights reserved.

Chapter 7. 241: *A Literature Review of Child-Parent/Caregiver Attachment Theory and Cross-Cultural Practices Influencing Attachment*, Diagram 1: The Interaction between Relationship Building, Parenting Practices, and Socio-Cultural Influences, http://www.attachmentacrosscultures.org/research/. Reproduced with the permission of the Minister of Public Works and Government Services Canada, 2007. **259:** Martha B. Bronson, *Self-Regulation in Early Childhood: Nature and Nurture*, The Guilford Press, 2000. Reprinted by permission of The Guilford Press.

Chapter 8. 294: top left, Source: *Eating Well with Canada's Food Guide*, Health Canada. Reproduced with the permission of the Minister of Public Works and Government Services Canada, 2007; bottom, Source: *Eating Well with Canada's Food Guide*: Educators & Communicators, Health Canada. Reproduced with the permission of the Minister of Public Works and Government Services Canada, 2007. **295:** © WM Hoest Enterprises, Inc. King Features Syndicate. **297:** From *Are We Doing Enough? A Status Report on Canadian Public Policy and Child and Youth Health*. Reprinted by permission of Canadian Paediatric Society. **298:** Source: *Canadian Immunization Guide*, Health Canada, 2006. Reproduced with the permission of the Minister of Public Works and Government Services Canada, 2007. **299:** Source: *Canadian Immunization Guide*, Health Canada, 2006. Reproduced with the permission of the Minister of Public Works and Government Services Canada, 2007. **301:** Source: *Leading Causes of Death and Hospitalization in Canada*, Health Canada. Reproduced with the permission of the Minister of Public Works and Government Services Canada, 2007. **302:** From *Are We Doing Enough? A Status Report on Canadian Public Policy and Child and Youth Health*. Reprinted by permission of Canadian Paediatric Society. **303:** Courtesy of Parents Canada Magazine.

Chapter 9. 333: "Percentage of students in English-language school systems who are currently enrolled in French immersion programs", adapted from Statistics Canada publication *Canadian Social Trends*, Catalogue No. 11–008, Autumn 2004.

Chapter 10. 364: Patterson, G.R. & Fisher, P. A. (2002). Recent developments in our understanding of parenting: Bidirectional effects, causal model#s, and the search for parsimony. In H. M. Bornstein (ed.), *Handbook of Parenting* Vol 3 (2nd ed), pp 59–88. Mahwah New Jersey: LEA **376:** © 1993 Tribune Media Services, Inc. Used by permission.

Chapter 11. 405: National Center for Health Statistics. U.S. Department of Health and Human Services. **406:** National Center for Health Statistics. U.S. Department of Health and Human Services. **408:** "Percentage of overweight or obese, by age group, household population aged 2 to 17, Canada excluding territories, 1978/79 and 2004", adapted from Statistics Canada publication *Health Report*, 82–003, Volume 17, Number 3, Release Date: August 2006, page 29; "Percentage of overweight or obese, by sex, household population aged 2 to 17, Canada excluding territories, 1978/79 and 2004", adapted from Statistics Canada publication *Health Report*, 82–003, Volume 17, Number 3, Release Date: August 2006, page 29. **409:** Source: *Physical Activity Chart*, Health Canada, 2002. Reproduced with the permission of the Minister of Public Works and

Government Services Canada, 2007. **415:** Reproduced with permission from Alberta Education, Guide to Education: ECS to Grade 12 (Edmonton, AB: Alberta Education, September 2006), pp. 44–45. **424:** Courtesy of Learning Disabilities Association of Canada (LDAC).

Chapter 12. 471: "Figure 1: High school completion status at age 19, by average PISA reading score at age 15", from Statistics Canada publication *Educational Outcomes at Age 19 Associated with Reading Ability at Age 15*, Catalogue 81–595–MIE, No. 43, 2006.

Chapter 13. 493: Friendly, M., Beach, J., Ferns, C., & Muriano, M. (2007). Table 7: Workforce participation of mothers by age of youngest child -2005 (rounded estimates). *Early Childhood Education and Care in Canada*, 2006. Toronto: Childcare Resource and Research Unit. **499:** Friendly, M., Beach, J., Ferns, C., & Muriano, M. (2007). Table 9: Selected characteristics of kindergarten programs by province/territory-2006. *Early Childhood Education and Care in Canada*, 2006. Toronto: Childcare Resource and Research Unit. **503:** www.bullying.org "Where you are not alone!

Chapter 14. 525: National Center for Health Statistics. U.S. Department of Health and Human Services. **526:** National Center for Health Statistics. U.S. Department of Health and Human Services. **529:** From The Kinsey Institute New Report on Sex, 1990, p. 272–273. Reprinted by permission of The Kinsey Institute for Research in Sex, Gender and Reproduction, Inc. **532:** From The Kinsey Institute New Report on Sex, 1990, p. 264–265. Reprinted by permission of The Kinsey Institute for Research in Sex, Gender and Reproduction, Inc.

Chapter 15. 582: "High school drop-outs as a percentage of all 20–24 year olds, Canada and provinces, average of 1990–1991 to 1992–1993 and 2002–2003 to 2004–2005 school years", adapted from Statistics Canada publication *Provincial Drop Out Rates: Trends and Consequences*, Catalogue 81–004, http://www.statcan.ca/english/freepub/81-004-XIE/2005004/ drop.htm **583:** "How does Canada compare to other countries?", adapted from Statistics Canada publication *Provincial Drop Out Rates: Trends and Consequences*, Catalogue 81-004, http://www.statcan.ca/english/freepub/81-004-XIE/2005004/drop.htm **589:** "Female high school students with a paid job spend more time on education than those without a job", adapted from Statistics Canada publication *Canadian Social Trends*, Catalogue 11–008, Spring 2003, p. 24.

Chapter 16. 610: Source: www.sexualityandu.ca administered by the Society of Obstetricians & Gynaecologists of Canada (www.sexualityandu.ca/media-room/fact-sheets-1.aspx, 2008) **615:** Copyright © 2004 by the New York Times Co. Reprinted with permission. **616:** top, "Rates of pregnancies by age group: Canada, 1984, 1989, 1994", adapted from Statistics Canada publication *Health Report*, 82–003, Volume 9, Number 3, 1997; bottom, Source: *Progress of Nations Report*, Health Canada, 1998. Reproduced with the permission of the Minister of Public Works and Government Services Canada, 2007. **624:** Source: *Acting on What We Know: Preventing Youth Suicide in First Nations*, Health Canada. Reproduced with the permission of the Minister of Public Works and Government Services Canada, 2007.

PHOTO CREDITS

This page constitutes an extension of the copyright page. We have made every effort to trace the ownership of all copyrighted material and to secure permission from copyright holders. In the event of any question arising as to the use of any material, we will be pleased to make the necessary corrections in future printings. Thanks are due to the following authors, publishers, and agents for permission to use the material indicated.

Chapter Opener 1. 2: © Getty Images
Chapter Opener 2. 50: © iStockphoto.com/Radmila Gajic
Chapter Opener 3. 82: © Merrill Dyck/Shutterstock, Inc.
Chapter Opener 4. 116: © Don Mason/CORBIS
Chapter Opener 5. 158: © 2002 Jeff Sherman/FPG/Getty Images
Chapter Opener 6. 198: © Rubberball/Getty Images
Chapter Opener 7. 234: © Patricia Doyle/Getty Images
Chapter Opener 8. 280: © Ariel Skelley/BLEND
Chapter Opener 9. 314: © Matka Wariatka/Shutterstock, Inc.
Chapter Opener 10. 356: © Tom Prettyman/PhotoEdit
Chapter Opener 11. 402: © David Young-Wolff/PhotoEdit
Chapter Opener 12. 432: © Paul Chesley/Getty Images
Chapter Opener 13. 478: © Larry Williams and Associates/CORBIS
Chapter Opener 14. 520: © David Stoecklein/CORBIS
Chapter Opener 15. 564: © Bob Daemmrich/The Image Works
Chapter Opener 16. 594: © Ryan McVay/Getty Images

Chapter 1. 4: © Digital Vision/Getty Images **7:** center right, © Bettmann/CORBIS **7:** top left, © Erich Lessing/Art Resource, NY **8:** © PhotoDisc/Getty Images **10:** © Bettmann/CORBIS **11:** Courtesy of Renate Horney. **12:** Harvard University Archives, call # HUP Erikson, Erik (2) **15:** The Ferdinand Hamburger

Name Index

Subject Index

Aboriginal children and youth
  Head Start, 345–346
  IQ scores and, 465
  suicide, 624
  teenage pregnancies, 615
abstinence
  sexual, 541, 542, 617
  syndrome, 551, 552, 553–554, 555, 556
abuse. *See* child abuse and neglect
accidents, 301–303
accommodation, 20, 21, 200, 202
achieved ethnic identity, 600
achievement
  identity, 599
  intelligence vs., 451
acne, 527
active-passive controversy, 34–35
adaptation, in cognitive-developmental theory, 20, 21
addictions. *See* substance dependence
adipose tissue, 408
adolescence. *See also* formal operations stage;
  juvenile delinquency; pregnancy: teenage;
  puberty and alcohol, 544, 550, 551–552, 557
  body image, 534–535, 545, 547
  career development, 585–588
  dating, 607–608
  deaths, 544
  early vs. late physical maturation, 531–534
  egocentrism, 570–571
  emerging adulthood, 625–627
  employment, 585–590
  genital stage and, 11, 522–523
  growth, 523–527
  health, 543–558
  identity development, 596–601, 626
  moral development, 576–580
  nutrition, 524, 527, 544–545
  peer relationships, 605–609
  relationships with parents, 604–605
  risk factors, 537
  risk taking, 543–544
  in school, 580–585
  self-concept, 601–604
  sexual activity, 536–543
  sexual behaviour, 613–619
  substance abuse, 537, 550–558
  suicide, 622–625
  weight, 544–545
adoption, 69, 75, 250
adrenaline, 110
adulthood
  adolescence and, 625–627
  definition, 626
  emerging, 625–627
  juvenile delinquency and, 620
AFP. *See* alpha-fetoprotein (AFP) assay
African American children
  early-maturing girls, 534
  IQ scores and, 460, 465
  self-esteem, 602
afterbirth, 91
aggression, 378–383
  biological factors, 379
  cognitive factors, 380

conduct disorders and, 507
daycare and, 272, 274
evolutionary theory and, 379
media influences on, 381–383
and peer relationships, 495
social learning and, 380
theories of, 379–383
AIDS. *See* HIV/AIDS
alcohol. *See also* substance abuse and dependence
  in adolescence, 544, 550, 551–552, 557
  and breast feeding, 170, 190
  MZ twins and, 68
  and prenatal development, 104–105
alleles, 55
alpha-fetoprotein (AFP) assay, 66
altruism. *See* prosocial behaviour
ambivalent/resistant attachment, 237
American Academy of Pediatrics, 169
American Association on Mental
  Retardation, 463
American College of Obstetricians and
  Gynecologists, 100
American Infertility Association, 57
American Pregnancy Association, 101
American Psychiatric Association, 135, 251, 420, 550
American Psychological Association, 380
American Sign Language (ASL), 229
amniocentesis, 64–65
amniotic fluid, 90, 118
amniotic sac, 85, 90, 96, 118
amphetamines, 552–553, 555
amplitude, of sound, 144
anal stage, 11, 12
androgens, 89, 90, 269, 528, 573
androgyny, psychological, 395–396
anencephaly, 59
anesthesia, 123
angular gyrus, 426
animals
  and attachment, 236, 245–246
  experiments using, 41
  and sex differences in children, 269
  social deprivation, 248–249
animism, 319
anorexia nervosa, 545–547
anoxia, 128–129
anterior cingulate cortex (ACC), 103
antibiotics, 101
antidepressant medication, 514, 550
anxiety, childhood, 510–515. *See also*
  separation anxiety disorder (SAD)
Apgar scale, 138
aphasia, 227
apnea, 152
appearance-reality distinction, 337
arms, development of, 87
artificial insemination, 52, 73–74
artificialism, 319
Asian American/Canadian children
  IQ scores, 465
  self-esteem, 602
assimilation, cognitive, 20, 21, 200, 202
Assisted Human Reproduction Act (Bill C-13), 77–78

attachment, 236–244
  ambivalent/resistant, 237
  avoidant, 237
  behavioural view, 244, 247
  cognitive view, 244, 247
  conditioning and, 244
  contact comfort and, 245, 247
  critical periods and, 246
  cross-cultural patterns, 238–239, 242
  daycare and, 271
  disinherited, 251
  emotional development and, 260
  establishment of, 239–242
  ethological view, 245–246, 247
  failure, 248–257, 254
  fathers and, 240–242
  indiscriminate, 242–243, 251
  initial-preattachment phase, 243
  nature vs. nurture in, 244–248
  psychoanalytic theory and, 244, 247
  psychosocial development theory and, 244
  as reciprocal relationship, 243
  secure vs. insecure, 237–240
  sibling patterns, 240
  social deprivation and, 248–252
  stability, 242
  stages, 242–243
  support services and, 240
  theories, 244–248
attachment-in-the-making phase, 243
attention-deficit/hyperactivity disorder
  (AD/HD), 419–422
  and learning disabilities, 425
attributional style, 509
auditory-visual information, integration of,
  470–471. *See also* hearing
authoritativeness, 361–362
autism, 68
autonomous morality, 440–441
autonomy, 264
  shame and doubt stage vs., 12
autosomes, 54
avoidant attachment, 237
axon, 171

babbling, 217, 224
Babinski reflex, 141
baby talk. *See* Motherese
barbiturates, 552
Basic Behavioural Science Task Force, 28
Bayley Scales of Infant Development (BSID),
  103, 107, 212–213
bed-wetting, 14, 308–309
behaviour. *See also* attention-deficit/hyperactivity
  disorder (AD/HD); juvenile delinquency
  aggressive, 378–383
  daycare and, 272
  disorders, 506–507
  divorce and, 492
  goal-directed, 202–203
  instrumental, 393
  modification, 14, 15, 19
  moral reasoning and, 579–580
  parenting styles and, 363–364
  problems, 272, 274, 492